Psychological Evaluations for the Courts

The Guilford Law and Behavior Series
Alan Meisel, Loren H. Roth, and Elizabeth Loftus, *Editors*

PSYCHOLOGICAL EVALUATIONS FOR THE COURTS
A Handbook for Mental Health Professionals and Lawyers

Gary B. Melton, John Petrila, Norman G. Poythress,
and Christopher Slobogin

INFORMED CONSENT
A Study of Decisionmaking in Psychiatry

Charles W. Lidz, Alan Meisel, Eviatar Zerubavel, Mary Carter,
Regina M. Sestak, and Loren H. Roth

Psychological Evaluations for the Courts

A HANDBOOK FOR MENTAL HEALTH PROFESSIONALS
AND LAWYERS

GARY B. MELTON
JOHN PETRILA
NORMAN G. POYTHRESS
CHRISTOPHER SLOBOGIN

Foreword by Richard J. Bonnie, Loren H. Roth, and John Monahan

The Guilford Press
New York   *London*

© 1987 The Guilford Press
A Division of Guilford Publications, Inc.
200 Park Avenue South, New York, N.Y. 10003

Printed in the United States of America

Last digit is print number: 9   8   7   6   5   4   3   2

Library of Congress Cataloging-in-Publication Data
Psychological evaluations for the courts.

  (The Guilford law and behavior series)
  Includes bibliographies and index.
  1. Psychology, Forensic.   2. Forensic psychiatry—
United States.   3. Psychologists—Legal status, laws,
etc.—United States.   4. Psychiatrists—Legal status,
laws, etc.—United States.   I. Melton, Gary B.
II. Series.
KF8922.P77   1987   347.73'66   86-26992
ISBN 0-89862-276-X   347.30766

Foreword

Mental health professionals play a pervasive role in the legal process. Criminal responsibility, involuntary hospitalization, guardianship, competency to make significant decisions, child custody disputes, and assessment of mental disability or psychic trauma are only a few of the entries on the list of legal issues typically involving clinical participation. Unfortunately, the reliance on clinical opinion in most of these contexts has exposed both the legal system and the mental health disciplines to persistent criticism.

Much of this criticism is justified. Mental health professionals are not prepared by the ordinary course of professional education and training to perform evaluations or formulate opinions on the range of issues relevant to legal decisionmaking. Moreover, the law often invites clinical participation without clarifying the purpose of clinical inquiry or the assumptions upon which it should be predicated. The experts are typically puzzled by the constraints of the adversary process and are frequently insensitive to the limits of their own expertise. All too often, legal reliance on expert opinion obscures underlying questions of morality or social policy that those who make and administer the law have failed to recognize or resolve.

It has been argued that the role of mental health professionals in the legal process should be severely circumscribed, both to assure that moral questions are no longer cast as scientific ones, and to take account of the inadequate scientific foundation of much mental health "knowledge." The authors of this *Handbook* take a less sweeping and ultimately more defensible position. They believe that the just disposition of many legal disputes requires informed clinical assistance and, accordingly, that the proper remedy for acknowledged ills is to improve the quality of mental health participation, not to eliminate it.

Gary Melton, John Petrila, Norman Poythress, and Christopher Slobogin are uniquely situated by experience and training to contribute to the effort to improve the quality of mental health participation in the legal process. Their *Handbook* is not an elementary "how to do it" manual for the timorous clinician. Instead, it is a sophisticated and comprehensive effort to inform the potential expert about the many contexts of forensic assessment and to help the clinician understand the purposes, scope, and limits of his or her expertise. A particularly important contribution lies in the authors' effort to summarize the research literature bearing on the administration of pertinent legal doctrines. The book will also be valuable to lawyers because it clarifies the special substantive dimensions of areas of the law involving mental health participation and describes the features of clinical opinion that are, and are not, likely to be useful.

This book will be a valued addition to the bookshelves of practitioners and scholars at the interface of law and mental health. By helping to bridge the gap in interdisciplinary communica-

tion, the authors have made a singular contribution to the field.

Richard J. Bonnie, LL.B.
Loren H. Roth, M.D., M.P.H.
John Monahan, Ph.D.

Preface

General Remarks

This book is aimed at two groups: mental health professionals who are involved in performing psychological evaluations for the courts, and lawyers and judges who request such evaluations. Its purpose is to provide these groups with a comprehensive guide to the issues the legal system has most commonly asked clinicians to address.

The contexts examined in this book are thus quite diverse. They include insanity and competency determinations; sentencing and civil commitment proceedings; probate and guardianship hearings; personal injury, worker's compensation, and Social Security claims; juvenile delinquency and status offense adjudications; and custody and neglect disputes. In each of these areas, we first summarize the relevant legal rules and their jurisprudential underpinnings. We then try to analyze the law's approach *critically*—both to increase the mental health professional's understanding of the issues, and to enhance the lawyer's ability to argue for change. Additionally, unlike many works on "forensics," we incorporate or refer to research on each topic—from studies concerning the reliability of clinical opinions and specific evaluation techniques, through actuarial data on those subject to evaluation, to empirical assessments of the manner

in which the legal process actually works. Finally, we offer suggestions about evaluation procedures and ways of communicating information to the courts. These recommendations are not offered solely for the benefit of the clinician; they should also help demystify the clinical process for the lawyer.

The collective experience culminating in this book is wide-ranging. Two of the authors are lawyers with specialized educational backgrounds in mental health law. The other two are doctorate-level psychologists—one a university professor with a special research interest in children, the other a practicing clinician who has conducted several studies of the forensic process. Each of us has trained both mental health professionals and legal practitioners in mental health law. Each of us has also observed or performed scores of psychological evaluations for the courts. The idea for this book grew out of a training program in Virginia, which involved two of us in establishing a statewide community outpatient evaluation system.*

While the diversity in our backgrounds has led to differing areas of specialization, we have reached some common conclusions about psy-

---

* *See* G. MELTON, L. WEITHORN, & C. SLOBOGIN, COMMUNITY MENTAL HEALTH CENTERS AND THE COURTS: AN EVALUATION OF COMMUNITY-BASED FORENSIC SERVICES (1985).

chological evaluations for the courts. These themes permeate the book and are worth stating here at the outset.

First, we obviously believe that there is a place for mental health professionals in the legal system. To put this somewhat differently, we feel that in most contexts the potential contributions of mental health professionals outweigh the prejudice and systemic inefficiency that may result from their use. Contrary to the assertions of an increasing number of writers, clinicians do have specialized knowledge that can assist judges and juries in arriving at better-informed decisions.

On the other hand, it is apparent that mental health professionals are frequently misused, overused, and, on occasion, underused by the legal system, depending upon the specific issue. At times the law appears interested only in obtaining a conclusory "expert imprimatur," which hides the moral (and uncomfortable) nature of the decision being made [see § 7.10(e) on dangerousness assessments]. At other times, the legal system demands data and inferences from a clinician, but in situations in which lay testimony and common sense are all that are required [see § 13.01(b) on custody determinations]. And at still other times, the courts completely disregard valid scientific findings, apparently out of fear that the factfinder will pay too much attention to them [see § 14.05(a) on judicial acceptance of actuarial evidence].

One of the primary reasons we wrote this book was to try to sort through this often contradictory approach to clinical expertise and to provide some rough guidelines for its use in the legal areas we cover. Put in general terms, we urge throughout this volume, first of all, that lawyers and judges look carefully at the foundations of clinical opinions and that mental health professionals not overstep the bounds of their existing knowledge. More specifically, we admit a strong preference for research-based testimony, although we would not bar evidence founded on theoretical constructs or "educated intuition" in most contexts. Second, we believe that mental health professionals have an obligation to make clear the uncertainty of their offerings, whether research-based or theory-based, and

that lawyers should not attempt to deny or gloss over the probabilistic nature of clinical decision-making. Perhaps most importantly (and most controversially from the practitioner's point of view), we feel strongly that mental health professionals should neither be permitted nor cajoled to give so-called "ultimate" legal opinions, even when they make it clear that the opinions are nonscientific. All of these stipulations stem from our belief that if mental health professionals are to assist the legal system, they and the lawyers who seek their aid must tread a delicate balance between co-opting the legal decisionmaker and condoning legal results uninformed by credible information concerning human behavior.

Assuming that mental health professionals can contribute constructively in the legal process, the task becomes one of maximizing their usefulness. First and foremost, this requires making clinicians (and lawyers) aware of the legal framework in which they will participate, and making lawyers (and clinicians) at least cognizant of basic forensic evaluation procedures. Most of the chapters in this book are devoted to this enterprise. It also requires, in our opinion, that forensic evaluations be tailored to the specific legal problems at hand. At several points in this volume, we stress that lawyers should not request, and that clinicians should not perform, global evaluations aimed at discovering "what's wrong" with clients. Nor should either distort legal issues to fit clinical constructs. Competency evaluations, for instance, primarily require an assessment of the clients' current functioning, not categorization by diagnosis, regurgitation of family and social histories, or intricate psychodynamic formulations.

Adopting these precautions will go far toward achieving full exploitation of expertise. But we believe that if mental health professionals are to be as useful to the courts as they possibly can be, conceptual as well as practical steps need to be taken. First, it is important for members of both professions to develop a better understanding of the paradigmatic differences between them. Second, it is crucial that both groups become sensitive to the ethical and legal dilemmas raised when a court asks a member of the "helping" profession to assess the mental condition of a person whose interests may be harmed by the results of the evaluation. Although these issues are most directly addressed in Chapters 1 and 3, respectively, they too are interwoven throughout the entire book.

A final pervasive theme of this volume has to do with the forensic clinician's "job description." It has become commonplace to characterize the mental health professional involved in the legal system as a "hired gun." Assuming, as we feel confident in assuming, that most professionals honestly believe in their testimony, it is still true that the adversary process tends to define differences sharply. This should not mean, however, that the clinician must be pigeonholed as the mere puppet of the attorney who happens to have retained him or her. At several points in this book, we recommend that the best way to conceptualize the clinician's role is as an exercise in consultation and dissemination of information. That is, the mental health professional is often utilized most efficiently in advising various members of the legal system—judges, lawyers, jail personnel, or parole officers—about the behavioral idiosyncrasies of the individual in question. Certainly, this may involve testimony in an adversarial setting. But this testimony should above all be informative; moreover, there are other less dramatic ways in which the clinician as evaluator can aid the legal system *prior* to adjudication. In this book, we try to identify some of these nontraditional uses of clinical expertise.

The Content of the Book

With these general themes in mind, the specific subject areas covered in the book can be briefly described in context. The book is divided into five parts: Part I, "General Considerations"; Part II, "The Criminal Process"; Part III, "Non-criminal Adjudications"; Part IV, "Children and Families"; and Part V, "Communicating with the Courts."

Part I contains three chapters examining topics of overarching consequence to the book. Chapter 1, "Law and the Mental Health Profes-

sions: An Uneasy Alliance," sets the conceptual stage for the rest of the book by addressing two central questions, both briefly alluded to above. The first of these is itself composed of two queries: What are the theoretical differences between the legal and mental health professions, and what, if any, are the implications of these differences for clinical participation in the legal system? Perhaps members of the two professions are so far apart in their basic worldviews that understanding one another on any more than a superficial level is a hopeless task. Perhaps their assumptions about what motivates behavior, the concept of "knowledge," or the process of discovering "truth" (to name a few points of contention) are so divergent that the law, if it is to maintain its integrity, must either change its basic tenets or refrain from relying on mental health professionals at all.

The second question addressed in Chapter 1 assumes that paradigmatic differences can be resolved short of taking either of these two drastic steps, but is nonetheless also fundamental: Is the type of information a mental health professional is able to provide of any use to the legal system, or are clinical offerings so flimsy that the courts are better off seeking evidence from more traditional sources? That is, are mental health professionals really "experts" who can assist factfinders on the issues raised by the law? As noted above, we think the answer to this question is a qualified yes.

Chapter 2, "An Overview of the Legal System: Sources of Law, the Court System, and the Adjudicative Process," is on a decidedly different level than Chapter 1, but, like that chapter, its objective is to provide a backdrop for subsequent parts to this book. It is essentially a primer on the "infrastructure" of the law—where the law comes from, the procedures governing its application, and the points at which it seeks clinical testimony. It has been our experience that concepts considered part of the lawyer's daily armamentarium sometimes befuddle mental health professionals, thereby reducing their effectiveness as *forensic* clinicians. Chapter 2 provides answers to a number of basic questions: For example, what does it mean to say that a law is "constitutional"? Is there a difference between a state and a federal court? What are the stages of the criminal process, and how do they differ from the stages of a "civil" proceeding? These questions should illuminate the legal arena for the clinician and thus should facilitate interdisciplinary cooperation. The chapter should also help the mental health professional put the legal discussions in the following chapters in context.

The final chapter in Part I, "Constitutional, Common-Law, and Ethical Contours of the Evaluation Process: The Mental Health Professional as Double Agent," serves as a transition to the succeeding portions of this book dealing with specific evaluation issues. It examines the complex, interwoven legal and ethical principles that control the *process* of evaluation, ranging from the Fifth Amendment's privilege against self-incrimination to the *"Tarasoff* duty" and the confidentiality rule. From the clinician's point of view, each of these principles aims at answering a single question, "Who is the client?" Unfortunately, the answers they suggest often conflict. Although Chapter 3 attempts to reconcile the various legal and collegial pressures on the clinician, it is probably impossible to do so entirely satisfactorily, at least in the abstract. The primary goal of the chapter, therefore, is to concisely identify these pressures so that judges, lawyers, and mental health professionals will be sensitive to them in individual cases.

The next three parts of the book deal with "substantive" evaluation areas. Any treatment of forensic issues that attempts to be comprehensive must describe basic legal rules and procedures and must recognize fundamental clinical realities. But we have also tried to add fresh material from the legal, empirical, and clinical archives and to mix in our own insights when we think we have something to offer. In the brief descriptions of Parts II, III, and IV that follow, these latter aspects of the book are emphasized. The table of contents should be consulted to obtain a more complete overview of each chapter's scope.

Part II is devoted to psychological evaluations performed for the criminal justice system. Of course, since well before the trial of John Hinckley, Jr., the classic example of the mental health professions' involvement in this system has been

expert testimony about "insanity." But responsibility assessments are only one small aspect of current clinical participation in the criminal process.

Chapter 4, "Competency to Stand Trial," discusses an issue that demands the services of more mental health professionals each year than all other types of criminal evaluations combined. As a way of combating the abuses associated with the huge and easily manipulated system that fitness determinations have spawned, the chapter emphasizes the narrow focus of the competency evaluation and points out the opportunities clinicians have for consulting with the legal profession about alternative pretrial dispositions. It also examines critically the various psychometric instruments designed to aid in assessing competency.

Chapter 5, entitled "Other Competencies in the Criminal Process," deals with even less frequently acknowledged areas of clinical input in the criminal justice system. Specifically, it covers competency to confess, competency to plead guilty, competency to refuse an insanity defense, competency to be executed, and competency to waive one's right to an attorney—subjects not normally addressed in forensic volumes. It also discusses competency to testify, which is an issue that arises in the civil as well as the criminal context. Of particular note is the chapter's attempt to provide some framework for assessing "voluntariness"—a problematic concept for both lawyers and clinicians, but one that is nevertheless extremely relevant in any situation involving the waiver of rights.

Chapter 6, "Mental State at the Time of the Offense," confronts perhaps the core issue of the criminal law: the scope of one's responsibility for one's actions. Because the insanity defense still triggers the mental health professions' most visible forensic endeavor, the legal portion of this chapter is largely a discussion of that doctrine's historical development, its component parts, and the popular myths that surround it. But this part of the chapter also investigates other doctrines relevant to the responsibility inquiry, such as the defenses of automatism, diminished capacity, and intoxication, and the new verdict of guilty but mentally ill. In the research and clinical sections, we try to be particularly sensitive to the issue of what, if anything, a mental health professional has to offer in these areas. To that end, we investigate studies concerning various novel "syndromes" popularly accorded exculpatory significance; examine research on recently developed techniques for assessing mental impairment; look at the usefulness of "psychodynamic," as opposed to "behavioral," formulations; and offer our own recommendations for conducting a "reconstructive" evaluation of mental state at the time of the offense.

The final chapter in Part II, "Sentencing," considers the area of the criminal law that has long been thought to be a special preserve of the mental health professions. Chapter 7 describes the rise of the "rehabilitative ideal," which led to this notion; the advent of "determinate" sentencing; and the research suggesting that clinical opinion generally has minimal impact under either system. It then discusses the extent to which clinicians *can* offer useful information, focusing on the three "clinical" issues that most often arise in this context—amenability to treatment, culpability, and dangerousness. We pay particular attention to the last of these areas, since much has been said about the "inability" of clinicians to predict violence proneness. In this chapter, we closely examine the research on the topic and address its evidentiary and ethical implications.

The three chapters in Part III of this book leave the criminal arena and deal with contexts that have traditionally been described as "civil" in character. As Chapter 8, "Civil Commitment," makes clear, however, the term is an egregious misnomer when applied to commitment. The deprivation of liberty associated with involuntary hospitalization, combined with the extensive empirical findings indicating the failure of efforts to "legalize" the commitment process and other data suggesting the ineffectiveness of hospital care, lead us to the conclusion that clinicial participation in this area should be steeped in caution. Recognizing that professionals must work within the commitment system despite its defects, we criticize the Supreme Court's recent decisions relaxing strictures on the process; recommend an adversarial role for the attorney; and supply clinicians with current

data on the predictability of short-term dangerousness to self and others. The chapter also deals with the commitment of "special" populations—minors, the mentally retarded, prisoners, and insanity acquittees.

Chapters 9 and 10 look at areas that are more accurately deemed "civil" in nature. Chapter 9, entitled "Civil Competencies," discusses a number of contexts involving assessments of current functioning: competency to handle one's financial and personal affairs (i.e., guardianship); competency to consent to treatment (experimental or otherwise); competency to make a will; and "competency to work" as defined by Social Security regulations governing disability benefits. As in Chapters 4 and 5 on criminal competencies, this chapter stresses the focused nature of the capacity assessment and the consultative role available to the clinician.

Chapter 10, "Compensation for Mental Injuries," describes the two primary systems for reimbursing the individual injured through the "fault" of another: worker's compensation and tort law. Both systems compensate "mental injury," but both have great difficulty designating the circumstances under which such compensation should occur. This chapter exposes the conceptual gap between the legal and clinical professions on the key compensation issue of "causation," and offers some hints as to how mental health professionals should approach it.

Part IV is the final "substantive" section of the book, devoted entirely to the subject of children's involvement in the legal process—a topic that has received considerable legal and empirical attention in recent years. Its three chapters, entitled "Juvenile Delinquency," "Abuse and Neglect," and "Child Custody in Divorce," are all organized around a triad of themes. First, clinicians know very little about the treatability of children and the dynamics of family systems. Second, because of this ignorance, they should view their evaluative role primarily as one of providing information about these issues, not judging what the information means (unless sound research of the type recapitulated in these chapters suggest a valid interpretation of it). Third, this investigative data should come not only from the child and the family, but from a wide range of other sources as well; that is, the evaluation should be *ecological* in nature.

Following the parts dealing with specific evaluation issues, Part V caps off the book by delving into the important task of communicating the results of an evaluation to the legal system. Chapter 14, which provides suggestions to mental health professionals and lawyers about "Consultation, Report Writing, and Expert Testimony," is the principal chapter in this part. But because reports are often the primary way in which many mental health professionals and lawyers communicate, we also include Chapter 15, containing sample evaluation reports on several of the issues covered in this book. This chapter serves two different purposes. First, it provides examples of the type of reports we think should be presented to the courts (although no doubt they can be improved upon substantially). Second, the reports, and the commentary that accompanies each of them, provide concrete illustration of the abstract legal and clinical points made in earlier chapters.

The final chapter in the book, Chapter 16, contains two glossaries—one of legal terms, the other of clinical and research terms. These glossaries define many of the "jargon words" used in this book, as well as other words that might pose obstacles to communication between the lawyer and the clinician.

Some Comments on the Book's Structure

We have already said that this book is geared toward both the mental health professional and the lawyer. Some chapters, especially Chapters 2 and 15, tend to be slanted more toward the former than the latter. But, as noted at the beginning of this preface, all of the chapters on the substantive evaluation issues follow a simple format designed to benefit both types of professionals: They begin with analysis of the law; then examine the research, if any, on the subject; and end with a discussion of the proper method for performing an evaluation in the area.

While the legal sections are written with the layperson in mind, lawyers should find them useful because they try to canvass the relevant legal positions, often include state-by-state reviews of the law, and provide citations to leading cases, statutory material, and secondary resources. Our hope is that this depth of coverage will also help clinicians better appreciate the policies that find expression in "the law."

The research and clinical sections stress precepts unique to forensic practice. While it is obvious that, without basic knowledge about human behavior and psychopathology, one cannot hope to be a skilled forensic clinician, we felt that the most efficient approach to take in this volume would be to assume such knowledge rather than rehearse it. This approach should not frighten the legally trained reader away, however. As already suggested, the research and clinical sections can provide lawyers with insights into the clinical process, as well as with means of measuring the quality of any evaluations or reports they request. Thus, we recommend that lawyers as well as clinicians read both the legal and clinical sections.

Each chapter is divided into numbered sections and lettered and numbered subsections—an organizational device that is perhaps somewhat "bureaucratic," but that we think makes the contents of the chapters more accessible, provides ease of cross-referencing, and facilitates updating (through future supplements). If the practitioner is interested in discovering the relevant law or research on a particular topic, a quick look at the table of contents should generally suffice, although referring to the index may be helpful as well.

The reader interested in exploring further the topics covered in the book should find it useful to consult the bibliography at the end of each chapter. These bibliographies are not meant to be comprehensive. Rather, they represent a compilation of some of the books and articles in each subject area that are noteworthy for their conceptual contributions and their thoroughness. We have also included leading cases. The reader who seeks still further information can find many other sources in the notes to each chapter (collected at the back of the book).

A word about the terminology used in this book is in order. As should already be clear, we use the word "clinician" interchangeably with "mental health professional" to designate any professional in the mental health system, including social workers and psychiatric nurses as well as psychiatrists and psychologists. As we indicate in Chapter 1, many of the distinctions among these groups that are imposed by the law and guild concerns are meaningless in forensic practice.

We hope this book will improve the contributions mental health professionals make to the legal system. We also encourage criticisms and comments about its content so that this improvement can continue.

Gary B. Melton
John Petrila
Norman G. Poythress
Christopher Slobogin

Contents

Psychological Evaluations for the Courts

PART I

General Considerations

1.02. Some Preliminary Problems in Law and Mental Health

Some of the perceived "clashes" between law and psychiatry/psychology are, in fact, fundamental conceptual differences. They are discussed in the next section. Here we tackle some of the nonphilosophical reasons for tension between the two disciplines.

(a) Bridging Gaps in Training

Discussions of what's "wrong" in the relationship between law and the mental health professions have tended to focus on relatively superficial problems of communication. Typically, there is a suggestion that the core problem is that lawyers and mental health professionals do not "speak the same language." Hence, lawyers may be awed when a mental health professional appears to be able to sweep away the complexities of the human mind with profundities about "diffuse ego boundaries," and mental health professionals may complain that the sorts of questions that lawyers ask force them to compartmentalize their observations in foreign and untenable ways. If the tension between law and mental health is the result of semantic difficulties, then it should be erasable through facilitation of communication between the two professional groups. Thus, problems should be remediable through some combination of cross-disciplinary training and transformation of legal tests into language and concepts commonly used by mental health professionals.

Such a view strikes us as naive. We do not mean to minimize the need for training. Indeed, this book is oriented toward facilitation of an understanding of the kinds of questions that the law poses for mental health professionals. We, like others, have been troubled by "expert" mental health professionals who testify on a particular legal issue without any understanding of the nature of the issue they are purporting to address. We are also troubled when legal authorities claim ignorance of "medical" problems in the law and effectively avoid hard decisions by demanding

conclusory opinions from mental health professionals. Both examples are indicative of inappropriate avoidance of "confusion by the facts." Clearly, both legal and mental health professionals whose practice takes them into interdisciplinary matters have an ethical obligation to learn enough to be able to function competently in such a context.

Such training will not eliminate interdisciplinary problems, however. Simply inculcating a common understanding of key terms will not eradicate the philosophical problems inherent in interdisciplinary endeavors. A well-known example of this fact was the failure of the District of Columbia Circuit's experiment in the 1950s with the *"Durham* rule" or "product test" of insanity.[7] Concerned with the lack of meaningfulness of much psychiatric testimony in insanity cases, the District of Columbia Circuit Court of Appeals thought that the problem would be alleviated if the test language were reformed to make it congruent with the jargon of the mental health professions. Accordingly, rather than force mental health professionals to compartmentalize the mind into specific faculties (as the historic *M'Naghten* test, described in § 6.02, appears to demand), the *Durham* test asked mental health professionals to determine whether the criminal act was the "product of mental disease or defect." Essentially, the question was simply one of whether the legally relevant behavior was caused by the defendant's mental illness, a concept assumed to be well within the repertoire of mental health professionals. Overlooking the fact that the concept of mental illness itself may be untenable,[8] it should have come as no surprise that *Durham* was destined to fail.[9] As discussed later in this chapter, there was no coherent conceptual basis for determining which behaviors were produced by "free choice" and which behaviors were the product of mental illness. The question makes little sense in a deterministic paradigm. Simply medicalizing the terms of the insanity test would not, and did not, eliminate the much more fundamental philosophical differences between the law and the behavioral sciences. Similarly, these differences will not be eliminated, although they may be unmasked, by acquisition of

CHAPTER ONE

Law and the Mental Health Professions: An Uneasy Alliance

1.01. The Context for Law and Behavioral Science

In recent years interest in law and behavioral science, and especially in forensic mental health, has mushroomed. A number of specialized professional organizations in both psychiatry and psychology have been established: the American Academy of Psychiatry and Law (AAPL); the American Psychology–Law Society (Division 41) of the American Psychological Association; the American Board of Forensic Psychiatry; and the American Board of Forensic Psychology, among others. There has also been a rapid increase in courses in psychology and law [1] and in scholarship in the area.[2] And, in collaboration with professional groups in the behavioral sciences, the American Bar Association (ABA) recently undertook a massive project to draft standards for mental health input into the criminal justice system.[3]

Although these developments are significant, the relationship between law and behavioral science can hardly be described as unambivalent. For example, describing himself as a "disappointed lover," Judge David Bazelon recently chastised psychologists for overreaching in opinion formation and providing judgments of both policy and case matters that have ventured beyond scientific expertise into the province of those societally delegated to make moral judgments.[4] Similarly, within the field itself, there has been debate about the utility of mental health professionals' opinions as experts[5] and the value of behavioral science research generally in the legal system.[6] Most obviously, the *Hinckley* case (and before it, the Patricia Hearst and Dan White trials) has reignited public outcry about "buying" mental health experts in order to escape criminal punishment. Partly as a result, there has been a move in numerous states and the federal government to curb the involvement of mental health professionals by restricting or eliminating those legal doctrines, such as the insanity defense, that typically bring them to the courtroom.

The purposes of this chapter are to analyze the sources of the current ambivalence about the interaction between law and mental health, and to address generally the limits of expertise possessed by mental health professionals. In the discussion of these questions, we make some initial inquiry into the problems of defining who is an expert and for what purpose—questions that recur throughout this volume.

3

a working knowledge of key concepts in the law (for mental health professionals) or the behavioral sciences (for lawyers).

(b)   Bridging Attitudinal Differences

Just as it is naive to believe that problems in the interaction between law and mental health will be eliminated through training programs, so too is it simplistic to view these conflicts as mere reflections of attitudinal differences. Those who emphasize the significance of these differences tend to perceive lawyers as concerned primarily with the sanctity of legal principles in the abstract and, accordingly, with the vigorous advocacy of civil liberties for mentally disordered persons without regard to their needs. Conversely, mental health professionals are perceived as paternalistic and prone "to try to help" regardless of the cost to liberty, with the result that they advocate hospitalization and treatment whether the context is civil commitment, and criminal trial, or sentencing. Such perceptions lead to the conclusion that conflicts between the law and the mental health professions would be largely eliminated if some middle ground of attitudes toward the mentally disordered were reached; the issues then are simply ones of consciousness-raising.

Undoubtedly, there are substantial differences in the socialization of the professions. However, we believe that differences between libertarian and paternalist attitudes are overemphasized as a source of disciplinary conflict. First, the attitudinal differences among the mental health professions themselves may be as great as, or perhaps even greater than, those between lawyers and mental health professionals generally.[10] Thus, the American Psychiatric Association has commonly advocated less deference to patients' wishes and less legalistic procedures in decision-making about treatment than the American Psychological Association and the American Orthopsychiatric Association.[11] Second, research suggests that lawyers tend to be paternalists themselves when they are actually confronted with people who have been labeled as mentally dis-

ordered. Poythress, for example, was unable to train lawyers to adopt a more adversary stance when representing respondents in civil commitment actions.[12] Although the lawyers were taught the inadequacies of testimony by mental health professionals (e.g., problems of reliability and validity of diagnosis), they persisted in avoiding careful cross-examination of expert witnesses in commitment proceedings because of a belief that it was in the best interests of their clients to be hospitalized and deprived of liberty.

(c)   The State of the Art

A more significant source of trouble between law and the mental health profession, although still one that is practical rather than philosophical, is the paucity of scientific data concerning human behavior. Even if both language and assumptions can be matched sufficiently to allow relatively easy translation of knowledge from the behavioral sciences into legal concepts, there is often little legally relevant knowledge to apply. Moreover, if there is a relevant body of psychological knowledge, the conclusions that can be drawn from it may not be sufficiently reliable to warrant their use in legal decisionmaking.

The state-of-the-art problems may be divided into three types. First, there are general problems of uncertainty in the behavioral sciences. That is, there may be a question of whether there is sufficient rigor in the behavioral sciences to warrant the admissibility of opinions based on these disciplines or, if admitted, to warrant placing much weight on them. For example, although there has been substantial improvement in the technology of clinical diagnosis, even gross diagnoses are far from certain.[13] As discussed in detail in § 7.10, predictions of "dangerousness" are another well-known example of the ambiguities present in the current state of the art. Generally, in considering the certainty attached to behavioral science opinions, it is important to distinguish between *scientific* opinions about processes of human behavior (e.g., evidence from experiments about precipitants of aggression) and *clinical* opinions about psychological functioning of particular individuals (e.g., formulation of the causes of aggression committed by a particular individual at a particular time). In the former instance, the weight placed on opinions will be limited by the level of explanation achieved,[14] the degree of control for extraneous sources of variance in the relevant studies,[15] and the degree of generalizability in the findings of the relevant studies to situations outside the laboratory.[16] Clinical opinions, although often more art and intuition than science,[17] also should be derived from general, scientifically verifiable principles of behavior, and their rigor can often be determined through studies (many of which are described in this book) of their reliability[18] and validity.[19]

Irrespective of general uncertainties in the behavioral sciences, a second type of state-of-the-art problem stems from gaps in the current state of knowledge with respect to questions asked by the law. For example, there is a substantial literature on the effects of divorce on children. However, as discussed in Chapter 13, little of that research is directly applicable to questions pertaining to dispositions of child custody disputes, either in individual cases or as a matter of policy. Similarly, while there are numerous studies of efficacy of training of mentally retarded persons in self-help and social skills, there is virtually no research on training moderately and severely retarded persons in use of contraceptives, avoidance of sexual abuse, and maintenance of menstrual hygiene—all skills that are relevant to determinations of whether a person should be involuntarily sterilized.[20] Thus, while the *general* state of knowledge with respect both to divorce and to training of mentally retarded persons may be rather advanced, the literature may be virtually barren with respect to *specific* legally relevant questions.

A third state-of-the-art problem arises when questions asked by the law are inherently unanswerable. Sometimes the differences between possible dispositions are sufficiently subtle that it is extremely unlikely that behavioral science would ever advance to a point where their effects would be distinguishable. To give an extreme example, one of us was once asked to evaluate a child in a divorce dispute in order to assess the relative impact of spending one week a year versus two weeks a year with his mother.

Alternatively, sometimes the standards themselves (contrasted with their application in specific cases) present questions that on their face appear unanswerable. For example, a leading case on sterilization of mentally retarded persons (*In re Hayes*[21]) requires, among other things, that before a retarded person can be sterilized, the judge must find that there are unlikely to be scientific breakthroughs in the foreseeable future that will ameliorate the individual's disability (and therefore render him or her able to consent or refuse consent competently to sterilization) or that will make available a reversible form of sterilization. Thus, the *Hayes* test requires the proof of a negative; the judge must make a finding that a scientific breakthrough will not occur.

1.03.   *Paradigm Conflicts*

Limitations in the knowledge base of the behavioral sciences obviously pose a major problem in application to legal problems. As we shall see, some scholars have argued that the knowledge base is *so* limited that mental health professionals should not be allowed to testify as experts. Although we do not go quite so far, we do acknowledge major gaps in knowledge about legally relevant behavior and still more problems in application of what is known generally about behavior to individual cases. As discussed in the preceding section, some of these problems are state-of-the-art problems. Other problems are philosophical: For example, even assuming much less uncertainty than is present in our current state of knowledge about the behavior of certain groups, how, if at all, might these group data be applied to individual cases? Does justice demand that legal decisionmakers essentially ignore social scientists' probability statements and rely exclusively on individualized assessments? This section is devoted to such differences in paradigm: How is interaction between lawyers and mental health professionals likely to be affected by differing ways of approaching and conceptualizing problems? Do the differences in the philosophies of law and science imply inherent conflict?

(a)   Free Will versus Determinism

Perhaps the most obvious philosophical difference between the law and the behavioral sciences is that the former is predicated on an assumption of free will, while the sciences are generally solidly deterministic. Indeed, the behavioral sciences are generally directed toward an explanation or prediction of the factors determining behavior. On the other hand, the law holds individuals responsible for their conduct, unless the behavior appears to be the product of a will overborne by external pressure or internal compulsion, or of a mind so irrational as to raise questions about the individual's capacity to function in the community of independent moral actors.[22]

In the present context, the significance of these differing underlying assumptions about motivation and freedom is that there is no basis in any of the prevailing models of abnormal behavior to differentiate "caused" or "overborne" behavior from behavior that is the product of free and rational choice. In a provocative analysis of the use of voluntariness in determining the validity of confessions, Grano recognized this point:

> [E]ven assuming a person's will can be overborne without rendering the person unconscious, the tools do not exist to tell us whether the breaking point has been reached. If we reject, as we must, a literal notion of overborne wills, our only alternative is to shift from the empirical inquiry regarding what happened to a professedly normative inquiry regarding the degree of mental freedom necessary to produce a "voluntary" confession.[23]

A cursory review of major models of abnormal behavior underscores the incompatibility of their basic assumptions with legal decisionmaking. The most marked example of such incompatibility is the behaviorist model, which conceptualizes behavior as the product of the individual's history of rewards and punishments, in combination with the specific contingencies of reward and punishment present in a given situation.[24] Because *all* behavior is thought to be so determined, there is no basis in behaviorist thinking for identifying "voluntary" behavior. Even models of abnormal behavior that su-

perficially are more compatible with legal assumptions about the origins of conduct on closer examination fail to fit. Psychoanalytic theories of behavior provide individual, intrapsychic explanations of conduct. Because they may "explain" the underlying motivations of people, they may appear to provide a measure of which behavior was in fact compelled. The problem with such application is that psychoanalytic psychology is *generally* deterministic. As reflected in Freud's paper "Psychopathology of Everyday Life,"[25] psychoanalysis posits that much behavior that may be partially the result of rational decisions or conscious choices (e.g., embezzling money in order to pay one's bills) may also be "overdetermined" by unconscious motives (e.g., a desire to be punished). In the example given, most people would view the thief as criminally responsible and in control of his or her behavior; there is no basis in psychoanalytic theory for making such a determination, however. Even if one makes a distinction, as do later psychoanalytic theorists,[26] between behavior that is motivated initially by conflict-laden experiences (and therefore "driven") and behavior that is "conflict-free,"[27] such a distinction does not provide a tenable basis for identifying compelled versus free behavior. In a strong criticism of such a position, May, an eminent existential theorist, pointed out that a concept of "autonomy of the ego" (the rational, "executive" part of the psyche) "becomes something akin to Descartes' theory that the pineal gland, the organ at the base of the brain between body and head, was the place where the soul was located."[28] If the personality as a whole is not free, it is hard to conceptualize a *part* of the personality as autonomous outside its totality.

Unlike members of the two schools of thought discussed thus far, humanistic/existential theorists (e.g., Viktor Frankl, Abraham Maslow, Rollo May, Carl Rogers) have generally started from a fundamental premise that human behavior is the result of free choice. In this instance, however, the problem is that the psychological model is *too* undeterministic to match legal assumptions. Existentialists generally hold that, even in the most dire circumstances, people ultimately have choices.

A final model of abnormal behavior, which more closely matches legal assumptions about the causation of behavior, is a true (organic) medical model.[29] To use a common textbook example, suppose that a man standing near the edge of a cliff has an epileptic seizure. As he falls to the ground, he bumps a bystander and knocks that person off the cliff. The epileptic's behavior was clearly not the product of voluntary, conscious choice. To punish him for a symptom of his disease would offend most people's sense of justice.[30] Analogously, if legally relevant behavior could be shown to result directly from a disease process, that behavior would also be excused. This principle is embedded in the language of insanity standards, which generally require that a threshold of "mental disease or defect" is crossed.

Rarely, however, is there such a direct relationship between organic condition and behavior. For example, with respect to severe mental disorders for which there appears to be a genetic basis,[31] the relationship is generally one in which genetic factors account for only a portion of the variance. Commonly, genetic background is thought merely to *predispose* the individual to psychopathology, such that the psychopathology is activated only when the individual has experienced a pathogenic, stressful environment.[32] Moreover, neither the specific anatomical or biochemical abnormality that is inherited nor the specific mechanism of genetic transmission is likely to be known.

Even with wholly organic explanations for behavior, we inevitably uncover a tension between determinism and free will. Lest an untenable dualism remain, we are left with an assumption that *all* behavior is controlled by the nervous system. There is no apparent philosophical basis for distinguishing between behavior resulting from a central nervous system lesion and behavior resulting from a "normal" system, as it is shaped by genetic composition in interaction with life experiences.

In short, if the clinician is theoretically consistent, the paradigm within which mental health professionals (of whatever theoretical orientation) work would appear to be in inherent con-

flict with legal worldviews. Although some would disagree,[33] the philosophical assumptions that govern these disciplines seem to a large extent mutually exclusive. These conflicts are of substantial significance as a matter of policy in attempting to apply the behavioral sciences or clinical opinions to legal problems.

However, the individual expert need not be paralyzed by this dilemma. Indeed, there is at least a partial solution: Mental health professionals should be neither permitted nor cajoled to give opinions on the ultimate legal issue (i.e., the conclusion that the factfinder must ultimately draw—e.g., was the act voluntary?). Although we recognize the resulting practical problems [see § 14.05], we feel that clinicians should resist drawing causal conclusions with respect to voluntariness or responsibility when the concept does not make sense within a scientific paradigm.[34] Rather, the relevant findings should be presented so that the factfinder (i.e., the judge or the jury) may fit them into the legal framework and may make whatever moral–legal judgments follow. For example, as discussed in more detail in § 1.04, in assessing the "voluntariness" of an act, the clinician might assist the factfinder by describing the types of choices confronting a person of particular characteristics in a specific situation. However, whether the behavior was "involuntary"—whether the choice was so hard as to represent an "overbearing" context—should be left to the factfinder.

(b)   The Nature of a Fact

Assuming for argument's sake that the clash in assumptions about causal relations need not be a major obstacle in the interaction between law and mental health, there still remain fundamental but more subtle and probably more problematic epistemological issues. Specifically, major disciplinary differences exist in both the conceptualization of a fact and the process of "finding" facts. The definition and process issues are closely linked, in that whether the law and the behavioral sciences recognize particular information as a relevant "fact" depends upon whether the respective truthfinding process has been followed. However, for clarity of analysis, we separate the process of finding facts from the question of whether a fact exists, and deal with the latter problem first.

Perhaps the most basic problem rests in differing conceptions about the role of probability assessments. Although the sciences are inherently probabilistic in their understanding of truth, the law demands at least the appearance of certainty, perhaps because of the magnitude and irrevocability of decisions that must be reached in law. As Haney has noted, "there is a peculiar transformation that probabilistic statements undergo in the law. The legal concept of 'burden of proof,' for example, is explicitly probabilistic in nature. But once the burden has been met, the decision becomes absolute—a defendant is either completely guilty or not." [35]

To give an example of this difference in conceptualization of facts, suppose that a construction company is charged with negligence after a bridge that it built collapses. Specifically, the company is alleged to have used steel rods that were too small for the construction needs. A civil engineer is asked, as an expert, to measure the rods and to determine the length that the rods should have been in order to provide a safe structure. The engineer might take several measurements of the rods and conclude that the probability is greater than .95 that the true length of the rods was between 1.35 meters and 1.37 meters, when measured at 75°F. The engineer then might note the probability of contraction to a given length at the lowest temperature observed in the particular locality. Still another probability judgment might be made as to the likelihood of an even lower temperature's occurring in the future. On the other hand, from a legal perspective, either the rod was too small, or it was not. Although the tolerable risk of error is acknowledged in the standard of proof applied (e.g., preponderance of the evidence), the conclusion of fact is made in all-or-none fashion.

While this difference may seem rather trivial at first glance, its import is actually quite substantial. There is a danger that, because of the law's preference for certainty, experts will

overreify their observations and reach beyond legitimate interpretations of the data in order both to appear "expert" and to provide usable opinions. Similarly, legal decisionmakers may discard testimony properly given in terms of probabilities as "speculative," and may defer instead to experts whose judgments are expressed in concrete opinions of what did or will happen. The result is a less properly informed court. The risk of distorting the factfinding process is particularly great in the behavioral sciences, given that single variables rarely account for more than 25% of the variance in a particular phenomenon and that the reliability and validity of observations by mental health professionals are far from perfect.

Part of the problem is simply intellectual dishonesty, however well intended. In the desire to be helpful, experts may permit themselves to be seduced into giving opinions that are more certain than the state of knowledge warrants. In our view, experts are ethically obligated to describe the uncertainty in their conclusions, even though such honesty may result in the courts' reducing the weight accorded the testimony, even unduly so. [36]

The problem is not simply one of professional ethics, or even of overzealousness by attorneys in their attempt to elicit strongly favorable opinions from experts. An additional concern is that the style of decisionmaking necessary for clinical practice (as opposed to scientific research) often may not be conducive to the truthfinding process. Although researchers customarily report their findings in terms of probability statements, practitioners often must make judgments that are of an all-or-none character. Because of the need to develop and implement treatment plans, clinicians must make decisions as to what the problem is and as to how best to treat it. Moreover, because of placebo effects, the efficacy of treatment may be enhanced as a function of the display of confidence by clinicians in the treatment they are administering. In short, even if mental health professionals are fully cognizant of the weaknesses in the scientific basis of their work, they are probably advised to behave as if there were near-certainty in their formulations and the efficacy of their treatment. The problem in the present context is that if this style of presentation is carried into the reporting of forensic evaluations, the legal factfinder may be misled as to the certainty of the conclusions.

Unfortunately, this style of presentation—especially when it is *idiographic* in nature (i.e., case-centered rather than based on group data)—is preferred by the courts over testimony by researchers. Although we do not wish to denigrate careful clinical testimony, we also find it unfortunate if, as they sometimes do, the courts reject the testimony of scholars whose work sheds light on the behavioral phenomenon in question. This rejection is especially serious if the topic is one on which academic psychologists are more likely to be expert, such as eyewitness testimony.[37] In any case, the general point is that clinicians involved in the legal process should be careful to think like scientists in order to give an accurate picture of the probabilistic nature of their facts, even if this stance heightens the discomfort of both the clinician and the court.

This general admonition is appropriate even in jurisdictions that attempt to transform probabilistic judgments into certain facts by application of a standard of "reasonable medical (psychological, scientific) certainty" when deciding the admissibility of expert testimony. As Martin has pointed out, professionals are likely to have idiosyncratic subjective judgments of "reasonable certainty"[38]; moreover, uncertain opinions may still be relevant and of assistance to the trier of fact, provided that the conclusions have *some* probative value and are not unduly prejudicial. Most importantly, the standard of reasonable certainty may in fact result in prejudicial opinions, because the fact that the opinions *are* probabilistic is masked by the certainty standard. Experts should leave to the judge the question of whether the opinions are *so* uncertain as to be helpful.[39]

Assuming that the probabilistic nature of the opinions is acknowledged, another problem arises. The scientific data base for the behavioral sciences upon which all researchers and many clinicians rely is generally *nomothetic:* that is, principles of behavior are derived from comparisons of *groups* differing on a particular dimension. Given

that, in psychology, a particular variable will almost never perfectly account for the variance in another variable, the problem is one of how to apply psychological findings based on group data to individual cases. Although this problem is not one for the experts themselves, it is a major conceptual obstacle for legal factfinders and may result in rejection of the experts' opinions.

Some case examples may indicate the significance of the philosophical dilemmas that are presented when the problem arises of applying nomothetic data to the resolution of individual cases.

Case 1.[40] The defendant's 14-year-old daughter accused him of raping her. Two months later (and on two subsequent occasions), she wrote statements recanting her accusation; she said that she had lied so she could get "out on her own." However, at trial, she returned to her original story. Experts testified that such inconsistency is common among victims of incest.

Case 2.[41] The defendant was charged with third-degree murder of his three-month-old son. An expert on child abuse testified that the pattern of injuries was consistent with "battered child syndrome." He testified further that abusing parents tend to have been abused as children themselves and that they also are prone to a number of negative personality characteristics (e.g., short temper, social isolation). The state then called two witnesses from the defendant's past (his caseworker as a youth; an employee of a therapeutic school that he had attended). The caseworker testified that the defendant had been abused; both testified that the defendant had many of the personality traits identified by the first expert. Other witnesses provided additional testimony suggesting that the defendant possessed characteristics identified by the expert as consistent with those common to battering parents.

Case 3.[42] The defendant was stopped by Drug Enforcement Administration (DEA) agents after she disembarked from an airplane at the Detroit Metropolitan Airport. The DEA agents' suspicions were aroused because the defendant's behavior fit a "drug courier profile": (1) the plane on which she arrived had originated in a "source city" (Los Angeles, thought to be the origin of much of the heroin brought to Detroit); (2) she was the last person to leave the plane; (3) she appeared to be nervous and watchful; (4) she did not claim any luggage; (5) she changed airlines for her flight from Detroit. On questioning, the defendant appeared nervous, and it became known that her ticket had been purchased under an assumed name. A search revealed heroin hidden in her undergarments. The defendant contested the search on the ground that the agents had no reasonable basis for suspecting that she was involved in criminal activity and stopping her for an investigation. Testimony at trial indicated that during the first 18 months of the surveillance based on behavioral profiles, agents had searched 141 persons in 96 encounters and had found illicit substances in 77 instances.

Case 4. An offender in Michigan is denied parole because he is a "very high" assaultive risk. Of parolees whose behavior fits this category, 40% are rearrested and returned to prison for a violent crime while on parole. The offender protests that he has been placed in the very-high-risk group because of a juvenile arrest for an offense of which he was never convicted. Moreover, he asserts that he has "reformed" and that he should be considered to be among the 60% of very-high-risk offenders who will not be recidivists.

These four cases starkly pose the question of whether attention to probability data in the legal system is legitimate. The cases represent four different temporal problems (respectively, whether a crime occurred; the identity of a past legal actor; the identity of a present legal actor; the identity of a future legal actor). Is the issue of whether to consider this type of probability evidence merely a function of its reliability and explanatory power, or is there something inherently unfair about determinations of past, present, or future guilt on the partial basis of group data? Suppose that the data make explicit that a powerful variable in identifying probable offenders is race. What level of predictive power, if any, would justify searching blacks disproportionately often or keeping them in prison disproportionately longer?

A thorough consideration of these issues has been presented in an influential article by Tribe,[43] who concludes that, for the most part,[44] the law should bar evidence expressed in mathematical probabilities. Tribe has raised a number of objections to "precision" in the consideration of evidence:

1. Probability estimates are themselves inherently probabilistic, in that the validity of the probability itself must be considered. For example, a juror's assessment of the probability of finding a brown-eyed, brown-haired male in a bank in a small town in Finland must take into account the probability of the initial eyewitness's account of the Finnish bank robber and the probability of the validity of the reported statistics. Consequently, the presentation of a single statistic or even a string of statistics may be deceptive. Moreover, the juror's consideration of the statistics may be complicated by their interdependence. For example, brown eyes and brown hair are correlated; so one cannot do a simple Bayesian computation[45] to learn the probability of their joint occurrence.

2. The presumption of innocence may be effectively negated by permitting consideration of the probability that a person with X characteristic is guilty.[46] For instance, direct consideration at trial of such probabilities will necessarily force the factfinder to include in the calculus the probability of guilt that is associated merely with having been brought to trial. Presumably, this initial probability is likely to be greater than zero, despite legal assumptions to the contrary.

3. Soft variables will be dwarfed by more easily quantifiable ones.[47] To return to our example of the Finnish bank robber, the attention to the defendant's physical characteristics might divert attention from the probability that he has been framed.

4. The "quantification of sacrifice" (i.e., the recognition of the risk of a wrongful conviction) is intrinsically immoral.[48] There is something intuitively unjust in telling a defendant that the jury is willing to tolerate X risk of error in convicting him.

5. Reliance on statistical evidence dehumanizes the trial process by diminishing jurors' ritualized intuitive expression of community values.[49] Rather than clarify the jury's role in expressing the will of the community, statistical evidence will obscure this role and make the legal process seem alien to the public.

Although Tribe has articulated important issues, we are more persuaded by Saks and Kidd's critique[50] of his article. First, Tribe's analysis relies in part on unverified psychological assumptions (e.g., jurors will be overinfluenced by quantified evidence; jurors feel subjectively certain in their judgments when they reach a verdict based on a standard of "beyond a reasonable doubt").[51] Second, research on intuitive information processing suggests that jurors will make errors of analysis in their consideration of implicit probabilities unless the actual probabilities are brought to their attention.[52] Third, as Tribe himself acknowledges,[53] all evidence is ultimately probabilistic, regardless of whether it is quantified. Simply pretending that it is not, and ignoring the clearest, most specific evidence, do not lead to morally superior decisionmaking.

Ultimately, of course, there is a judgment of legal policy to be made in the determination of when, if at all, probability evidence should be considered. Nonetheless, scientific integrity and the desire for informed decisionmaking demand that mental health professionals present their opinions as clearly and as specifically as possible, with due attention to the uncertainty of the conclusions and the observations themselves. At the same time, however, experts should be aware that their departure from all-or-none concepts of facts is likely to create a tension with respect to their position in the legal system.

(c)   The Process of Factfinding

Still another source of potential stress in the relationship between the law and the mental health professions lies in the nature of the process of inquiry on which the disciplines rely. It is commonplace for mental health professionals to express discomfort with the adversary process employed in Anglo-American law. Part of this discomfort probably stems from the differing social purposes of the law and the behavioral sciences. The behavioral sciences (even more so, the mental health professions specifically) are dedicated to the development and application of knowledge designed to promote positive interpersonal relations—in a sense, to *prevent* or at least to dampen social conflict. Although the ultimate social function of law in resolving disputes is compatible with the ends served by the behavioral sciences, the law accomplishes this function by *sharpening* conflict so as to ensure that issues in dispute are carefully posed and that they are resolved fairly in accordance with societal values. In view of these differing functions, it would be unsurprising to find disciplinary differ-

ences in the comfort experienced when dealing with conflict generally and adversariness in particular.

Although procedural differences may stimulate interdisciplinary problems, this problem may be more exaggerated in significance than others we have discussed. It can be largely resolved by remembering that the purpose of forensic evaluation differs qualitatively from the purpose of other forms of observation and study in the behavioral sciences or the mental health professions. Although mental health professionals may correctly complain that the adversary system distorts their conclusions by stimulating the presentation of only the evidence that is favorable to one or the other side, it should be remembered that the legal process is designed not just to uncover *truth,* but to render *justice.*[54] Due process demands that each side have the opportunity to put forward whatever evidence best makes its case. This is not to say that the law should or does ignore reality, only to indicate that the goal of truthfinding in law is subordinate to the pursuit of justice—a synthesis of two antithetical views. Hence, so long as they maintain intellectual integrity and recognize the limits of their observations and expertise, mental health professionals should be undisturbed if they are "used" by one side in the dispute.[55]

A similar source of tension comes when experts find that their observations are "pigeonholed" into concepts that seem to strip the data of their richness. Thus, one often observes a lawyer straining to have an expert curtail an intricate explanation about the subject's relations with the victim and urging the expert to "stick to the point"—the point being, perhaps, whether the defendant "planned" the attack on the victim. Similarly, clinicians may feel constrained by certain legal rulings, such as the inability to talk about prior criminal offenses. Concern about these practices again arises from a misunderstanding of purpose. The law is fundamentally conservative. As legal scholar Paul Freund noted, "no Nobel Prize is awarded for the most revolutionary judicial decision of the year."[56] The reliance on precedents and rules of law ensures the maintenance of the social fabric and the even-handed and predictable administration of justice. For instance, the evidentiary rule barring evidence of past crimes rests on the conclusion, stemming from centuries of trial experience, that otherwise the factfinder may convict a person for what he or she did in the past, rather than deliberate on the current charge. Thus, although at times examination of the evidence within a narrow historical framework may seem to pull attention away from the best interests of the parties, such narrowness of concern ensures that specific points of dispute will be resolved justly.

There is a problem, however, when jurists become so focused on normative analysis and historic legal values that they carry precedent beyond its logical bounds. Sometimes, in their zeal to protect legal values, judges seem to derive an "is" from an "ought"—that is, to assume that the world in fact operates in the way that they think it should. Such blinders to the real world promote unfair decisionmaking. For example, limits placed by the United States Supreme Court on minors' autonomy and privacy have frequently been ostensibly based on empirically unsupportable assumptions about adolescents' competency and family life (e.g., that children under 18 are not competent to make treatment decisions).[57] It is unjust and intellectually dishonest to base the deprivation of liberty on invalid assumptions. If a decision is in fact based on particular values, those values should be clearly expressed. Thus, in terms of the example given, if the Supreme Court wishes to support a particular view of family autonomy, it should make clear its preference for that policy.[58] On the other hand, if there really are empirical assumptions underlying the analysis, whether of case facts or of legislative facts,[59] the parties should be able to expect that a persuasive display of evidence on point will turn the case.

The range of evidence that may be relevant obviously may include the opinions of behavioral scientists and mental health professionals. As discussed in the following section, we support the liberal presentation of behavioral science and mental health evidence where relevant in order to ensure that the parties are able to bring forward empirical evidence on empirical assumptions.

1.04. Should Mental Health Professionals Be Considered Experts?

Our expression of bias toward liberal use of behavioral science expertise leads us to what may be the core problem in contemporary forensic mental health: Should mental health professionals be recognized as experts by the law, and, if so, for what purposes? For the convenience of non-legally-trained readers, the relevant Federal Rules of Evidence, which also have been adopted by many state jurisdictions, are listed in Table 1-1.

The first point to note is that, whereas laypersons are generally limited in their testimony to descriptions of direct observations,[60] experts may testify as to opinions based upon their specialized knowledge, provided that the expertise of the witness will assist the trier of fact in determination of a relevant issue.[61] In considering the import of this rule, it should be recognized that there are several levels of opinion that might be rendered; it is conceivable that some, but not all, levels of expert opinion would assist the trier of fact. For example, in consideration of whether a defendant meets the *M'Naghten* test of insanity [see § 6.02], there are minimally the following levels of inference, all of which represent increments in opinion formation:

1. Application of meaning (perception) to a behavioral image (e.g., "He was wringing his hands").
2. Perception of general mental state (e.g., "He appeared anxious").
3. "Formulation" of the perception of general mental state to fit into theoretical constructs or the research literature and/or to synthesize observations (e.g., "His anxiety during the interview was consistent with a general obsession with pleasing others").
4. Diagnosis (e.g., "His behavior on interview and reported history are consistent with a generalized anxiety disorder").
5. Relationship of formulation or diagnosis to legally relevant behavior (e.g., "At the time of the offense, his anxiety was so overwhelming that he failed to consider the consequences of his behavior").

Table 1-1
Federal Rules of Evidence, Article 7: Opinions and Expert Testimony

Rule 701.
OPINION TESTIMONY BY LAY WITNESSES

If the witness is not testifying as an expert, his testimony in the form of opinions or inferences is limited to those opinions or inferences which are (a) rationally based on the perception of the witness and (b) helpful to a clear understanding of his testimony or the determination of a fact in issue.

Rule 702.
TESTIMONY BY EXPERTS

If scientific, technical, or other specialized knowledge will assist the trier of fact to understand the evidence or to determine a fact in issue, a witness qualified as an expert by knowledge, skill, experience, training, or education, may testify thereto in the form of an opinion or otherwise.

Rule 703.
BASIS OF OPINION TESTIMONY BY EXPERTS

The facts or data in the particular case upon which an expert bases an opinion or inference may be those perceived by or made known to him at or before the hearing. If of a type reasonably relied upon by experts in the particular field in forming opinions or inferences upon the subject, the facts or data need not be admissible in evidence.

Rule 704.
OPINION ON ULTIMATE ISSUE

Testimony in the form of an opinion or inference otherwise admissible is not objectionable because it embraces an ultimate issue to be decided by the trier of fact.

Rule 705.
DISCLOSURE OF FACTS OR DATA UNDERLYING EXPERT OPINION

The expert may testify in terms of opinion or inference and give his reasons therefor without prior disclosure of the underlying facts or data, unless the judge requires otherwise. The expert may in any event be required to disclose the underlying facts or data on cross-examination.

6. Elements of the ultimate legal issue (e.g., "Although he was too anxious at the time of the offense to *reflect* upon the consequences of his behavior, he was *aware* of the nature and consequences of his acts").
7. Ultimate legal issue (e.g., "He was sane at the time of the offense").

In considering the question of which, if any, levels of inference mental health professionals should be permitted to reach in their testimony, on one point there is near-unanimity among scholarly commentators.[62] Despite the fact that such opinions are commonly sought and unfortunately are commonly given, often without foundation, *mental health professionals should refrain from giving opinions as to ultimate legal issues.* Questions as to criminal responsibility, committability, and so forth are legal and moral judgments outside the expertise of mental health professionals *qua* mental health professionals. Moreover, as we have already seen, the constructs about which an opinion might be sought (e.g., voluntariness) are often inconsistent with the model of behavior on which the expert's observations are based. Experts should avoid giving ultimate-issue opinions even when the constructs appear familiar, however. For example, the types of behavior that constitute a "mental disorder" as a matter of law may be substantially different from the range of behaviors subsumed under that concept in the expert's mind. Similarly, opinions as to "dangerousness" require the drawing of legal lines as to how high the probability of particular kinds of behavior must be to warrant state intervention. Indeed, the definition of "dangerous" behavior itself involves legal judgments. When experts give such opinions, they usurp the role of the factfinder and may mislead the factfinder by suggesting that the opinions are based on specialized knowledge specific to the profession. Note that while Federal Rule 704 allows opinions on ultimate issues by experts, Rule 702 prohibits *any* opinion not based on specialized knowledge.[63]

We realize that a clear prohibition against any ultimate-issue opinion (levels 6 and 7 in the list above) may sometimes appear to be an artificial constraint, provided that any opinions are admissible. It is often difficult to discuss competency to stand trial [see Chapter 4], for example, without directly discussing the defendant's ability to assist counsel—one of the elements of the competency standard. However, the question of how much and what kinds of assistance the defendant must give are purely legal issues. Consequently, even in this instance, the clinician should give observations relevant to the functions involved in competency and should leave the ultimate determination to the factfinder.

The question is harder as to whether opinions based on intermediate levels of inference (2 through 5 in the list above) should also be barred. The most articulate proponent of exclusion is Morse, who has argued that only two types of testimony by mental health professionals (when testifying in that capacity) should be permitted.[64] First, Morse would permit presentation of "hard actuarial data," where relevant and available. Second, because mental health professionals usually have much more experience with "crazy" persons than do laypersons, and thus are likely to be better observers of the kinds of behavior that may be legally relevant, he would allow them to present their observations of behavior. For example, Morse believes that mental health professionals are likely to be more skilled than laypersons in asking the right questions to elicit information about hallucinations, suicidal plans, and so forth, and should thus be able to describe the answers to those questions. On the other hand, Morse would not allow opinions as to the meaning of the behavior; he would bar formulations and diagnoses as well as conclusions on ultimate issues. Therefore, the role of mental health professionals would be that of specially trained fact witnesses.

Morse has summarized his objections to most expert testimony by mental health professionals on the following grounds:

> [F]irst, professionals have considerably less to contribute than is commonly supposed; second, for legal purposes, lay persons are quite competent to make judgments concerning mental disorder; third, all mental health law cases involve *primarily* moral and social issues and decisions, not scientific ones; fourth, overreliance on experts promotes the mistaken

and responsibility-abdicating view that these hard moral questions (i.e., whether and in what way to treat mentally ill persons differently) are scientific ones; and fifth, professionals should recognize this difference and refrain from drawing social and moral conclusions about which they are not expert.[65]

We have already indicated our agreement with Morse as to his third, fourth, and fifth points. We are also in agreement, for the most part, with his second point: Whether a person appears sufficiently "crazy" to warrant special legal treatment is an intuitive social and moral judgment. Diagnosis, for example, is largely irrelevant to mental health law questions.[66] Similarly, whether a mental disorder *caused* (or, for predictive questions, will cause) particular behavior is, as we have seen, a question that is incompatible with mental health professionals' models of behavior.

Where we part company with Morse is with respect to his first point.[67] We agree strongly that the wisdom of mental health professionals has been overvalued and that experts have often exceeded the bounds of special knowledge. However, in our view, Morse underestimates the degree to which mental health professionals can assist the factfinder in making legal judgments, *provided* that professionals both know and acknowledge the limits of their expertise, including, where relevant, the lack of a hard scientific data base. As Bonnie and Slobogin have pointed out, the law's approach to the admissibility of expert opinions is incremental: The main consideration, as formulated in Federal Rule 702, is whether it will *assist* the factfinder (not whether it is or should be dispositive). Stated somewhat more precisely, the question is whether the probative value of the evidence outweighs its tendency to be inefficient, misleading, or prejudicial.[68] Rather than completely exclude opinions that offer marginal assistance, the modern trend in evidence law, as Morse acknowledges,[69] is to admit the testimony and to assign the weight given it proportionately.

Nonetheless, Morse argues that the mental health professions' scientific basis is so limited as to warrant an exception to the general rule of liberal admission of expert testimony.[70] We recognize the well-known,[71] although at times exaggerated,[72] vagaries of mental health assessment and prediction. The literature with respect to specific forensic questions is reviewed throughout this volume. But while we share Morse's uneasiness about the state of the art in mental health assessment and his preference for testimony based on valid, quantified research, we would still permit mental health professionals to offer other opinions short of the ultimate issue.

There are two reasons for our approval of liberal admission of mental health professionals' opinions. First, by way of precedent, expert opinion is commonly admitted in situations where the opinions are no less speculative and probably more prejudicial than those commonly offered by mental health professionals. The opinions of experts employed by forensic science laboratories, which are rarely challenged, are based on mistaken identifications as much as 70% of the time.[73] Moreover, psychiatric diagnosis is as reliable as numerous other areas of health science diagnosis.[74]

Second, even if it is assumed for the sake of argument that speculative opinions from other disciplines have been admitted erroneously, we still would contend that justice would be served by the liberal admission of mental health professionals' opinions. Mental health professionals *do* have access to a body of specialized knowledge (i.e., knowledge commonly unshared by the lay public) that may assist legal factfinders in making informed judgments. Melton, Weithorn, and Slobogin administered a test of knowledge about clinical syndromes commonly observed in criminal and juvenile forensic practice and the research relevant to those syndromes to samples of mental health professionals and trial judges.[75] Mental health professionals' performance was generally superior to that of judges; among mental health professionals specialized in forensic practice, the differences were especially marked.

Even where the research basis of opinions is weak, there may be instances where the underlying knowledge is sufficiently great to warrant the admission of the opinions.[76] For example, in contrast to Morse,[77] we favor admission of psychological formulations (levels 3 and 4 in the typology of inference set out above), although

we acknowledge, as Morse persuasively shows, that the scientific basis of psychodynamic formulations particularly is often inadequate for their verification. Such opinions are clearly outside the bounds of precise "science." However, they are also neither folklore nor homespun wisdom. The argument here is analogous to Morse's approval of mental health professionals as trained observers of "crazy" behavior. Mental health professionals are trained and experienced in generating explanations of abnormal behavior. Even if these formulations are at times mere "stories,"[78] their narration may provide plausible explanations of a defendant's behavior that would otherwise be unavailable to the trier of fact. If these possible explanations are delivered with appropriate caution,[79] they may well assist the factfinder in reaching a judgment.

Admittedly, these conclusions may provide more assistance in some contexts than in others. They seem particularly germane when the clinical testimony is offered by an individual to rebut allegations made by the state designed to deprive the individual of his or her liberty (as in criminal and civil commitment proceedings). In such situations, it would be unjust to deprive a defendant of the option of bringing appropriately framed evidence before the factfinder. However, we are less sanguine about how helpful professional testimony is when the expert is presented by the state and the defense does not present an opposing expert, particularly when the subject addressed is fraught with uncertainty, as in cases involving the prediction of violence [see § 7.10]. Under such circumstances, the possibility that the factfinder will be unduly influenced by the state's lone clinician is great, given that the natural assumption is already that any individual who is being "tried" must be in court for a reason. The so-called "probative value" of the evidence, which is low, may easily be outweighed by the possibility of prejudice.

This evidentiary problem, which has been discussed at length elsewhere,[80] should not deter the lawyer from seeking clinical evaluations of individual clients, nor should it deter mental health professionals from performing such evaluations. It is up to legislatures and courts to decide the appropriate approach to the problem. But, to us, the possibility of undue influence—which is particularly acute in commitment hearings and death sentence proceedings, where the individual does not control the introduction of clinical testimony—is a major caveat to the general conclusion that such testimony can assist the factfinder.

In summary, although the range of opinions with which mental health professionals provide the courts should be narrowed to exclude opinions of a purely moral or legal nature, the door should be left open to professional opinions, including formulations of legally relevant behavior, that might assist (as opposed to overwhelm) the trier of fact. At the same time, mental health professionals should be careful to indicate the level of scientific validity or certainty attached to their opinions.[81]

1.05. Which Mental Health Professionals Should Be Considered Experts?

Assuming that mental health professionals' opinions should be admissible in at least some instances, the question arises as to *which* mental health professionals should be considered experts by the courts. Traditionally, this question has been answered by examining educational credentials, particularly with respect to discipline. In general, physicians have been considered experts in mental health matters, often without regard to psychiatric training. In recent years, courts have also admitted testimony by clinical psychologists, although some jurisdictions require psychologists to meet special experiential or training requirements before they can be acknowledged as experts, and fewer than half of the jurisdictions permit civil commitment orders to be filed by psychologists.[82] Psychiatric social workers are often considered experts in juvenile and domestic relations matters and sometimes at sentencing in criminal cases, but are generally not permitted to offer opinions as to a defendant's competency to stand trial or mental state at the time of the offense.[83]

These general guidelines have evolved more

from the internecine conflicts among the mental health guilds and the law's comfort with a medical model than from any systematic attempt to identify which mental health professionals possess sufficient specialized knowledge to assist the trier of fact on particular forensic issues. A recent survey of psychiatrists and psychologists indicated the depth of interdisciplinary antipathy.[84] Members of both professions were asked to evaluate their relative competence in 11 tasks performed by mental health professionals, including assessment, treatment, program administration, and expert testimony. Psychiatrists viewed themselves as more competent on eight of the tasks (including testimony), equally competent on two of the tasks, and less competent only with respect to administration of psychological tests. In contrast, psychologists perceived themselves as superior to psychiatrists on nine of the tasks, equal with respect to testimony, and inferior only with respect to the management of medication. In the face of such marked differences in perception of expertise, any comparison of disciplinary differences in knowledge and skills is likely to be fraught with controversy. Although reliance on objective indicators of expertise (e.g., form of training) clearly is the easiest method of determining qualifications as an expert, it is not the best.

Our own preference is for establishment of qualifications that are both broader and narrower than those commonly used; these should focus not only on educational attainments, but also on experience in the relevant area and on the evaluation procedures used. This preference is based on an assumption that the law should use a functional approach to evaluation of qualifications, as in fact is suggested in Rule 702 (which uses a criterion of probable assistance to the trier of fact).[85] The prevailing standard as to qualifications should be broader, in that the available research gives no basis for the historic preference for medically trained experts. The level of knowledge about forensic practice is not predictable by discipline, either among general clinicians or among clinicians with special forensic training.[86] As we point out in Chapter 4, for example, there is no basis for excluding social workers from competency evaluations; indeed, trained laypersons reach conclusions similar to those of mental health professionals. On the other hand, the standard as to qualifications should be narrower, in that training as a mental health professional by itself is insufficient to guarantee a specialized knowledge of forensic mental health. For example, to the extent that there are observed disciplinary differences, they suggest some bias against medically trained experts in many types of forensic assessments. Petrella and Poythress found that psychologists and social workers tended to do more thorough forensic evaluations and more comprehensive and more relevant forensic reports than their psychiatric colleagues.[87] There may be some specific topics on which medically trained clinicians are more likely to be expert, but even on these topics there is not likely to be exclusive expertise. For example, psychiatrists by training are more likely than other mental health professionals to have specialized knowledge about the effects of psychotropic medication; however, some psychologists specialized in psychopharmacology may be more expert on such matters than the average psychiatrist. Conversely, although psychologists are more likely to be knowledgeable about research methods, some psychiatrists active in research are likely to be more expert on research design than the average psychologist.

In short, the various mental health professions should be perceived as equally qualified as experts with respect to *general* training in legally relevant assessment,[88] but attention should be given to the specific spheres of specialized knowledge that the expert may offer. For example, clinicians without detailed knowledge of the available research on predictions of violent behavior should not be rendering opinions as to dangerousness. Mental health professionals should not perform evaluations of competency to stand trial without knowledge of the standard. Even more generally, clinicians without sensitivity to the special ethical and legal problems raised by forensic evaluation itself [see Chapter 3] should avoid responsibility for forensic work. The knowledge level and evaluation procedures appropriate for a given type of testimony should become apparent as one examines the relevant portions of this book.

Even the cursory examination of necessary knowledge and skills in the preceding paragraph suggests that forensic practice requires knowledge and skills more specialized than those developed in general training as a mental health professional, regardless of one's disciplinary pedigree. Melton, Weithorn, and Slobogin found that the knowledge base of forensic clinicians about legal issues, empirical research, and clinical theory commonly encountered in forensic practice was substantially greater than that of community mental health professionals engaged in general practice.[89] Such a finding should be unsurprising. Simply put, mental health professionals are unlikely to encounter rapists and murderers in either their training or their practice; similarly, the information about legal issues, research, and clinical practice presented in this volume still is not a staple of training in any of the mental health professions.

Each of us is a present or former director of a forensic training program; we are convinced of the efficacy of specialized, interdisciplinary training for mental health professionals who seek to offer assistance to the legal system. Such training should be useful in knowing as much what cannot be said about a given phenomenon as well as what can be said. Thus, we applaud the development of both academic courses[90] and internship experiences[91] designed to provide such training. The recently constituted American Board of Forensic Psychiatry and American Board of Forensic Psychology, although motivated at least in part by guild interests,[92] may also facilitate the development and recognition of a specialty in forensic mental health. Moreover, although this discussion has been focused on the training of mental health professionals, development of a specialized branch of the bar sensitive to the limits and contributions of mental health expertise on various legal issues may also be useful in matching behavioral science knowledge and legal needs within the bounds of the current state of the art.

1.06. *Conclusions*

In titling this chapter "an uneasy alliance" between the law and the mental health professions, we have called attention both to the conflicts in perspective—some of them inherent—between lawyers and clinicians, and to the points of alliance. The reader will recognize this ambivalent theme throughout this volume. On the one hand, there are paradigmatic disciplinary differences in conceptualizing and finding facts, and the state of the art in the mental health professions renders a level of certainty far lower than the law would like in many instances. On the other hand, there is a corpus of knowledge in the behavioral sciences that, if available to legal decisionmakers, would result in more informed judgments on many issues. Our primary admonition to mental health professionals and to lawyers who would consult them is that both aspects of this theme should be kept in mind. Mental health professionals who exaggerate the state of knowledge (either their own as individuals or that of the field as a whole), or who ignore problems in translating the behavioral sciences into legal findings, do the law no service. At the same time, lawyers who ignore the behavioral sciences or, conversely, who swallow whole the conclusions of mental health professionals fail to exercise proper diligence in generating the facts necessary for the pursuit of justice. We hope that readers from both perspectives will find this volume useful in developing an interdisciplinary alliance wherever doing so would improve the quality of legal decisionmaking. Less globally, this volume is intended to demystify the arcane aspects both of the courts and of the mental health system.

BIBLIOGRAPHY

D. BARNES, STATISTICS AS PROOF: FUNDAMENTALS OF QUANTITATIVE EVIDENCE (1983). (An overview of statistics for lawyers.)

Bonnie & Slobogin, *The Role of Mental Health Professionals in the Criminal Process: The Case for Informed Speculation,* 66 VA. L. REV. 427 (1980).

T. GRISSO, EVALUATING COMPETENCIES: FORENSIC ASSESSMENTS AND INSTRUMENTS (1986). (Critiques of structured forensic assessment instruments.)

Haney, *Psychology and Legal Change: On the Limits of a Factual Jurisprudence,* 4 LAW & HUM. BEHAV. 147 (1980).

J. MONAHAN & L. WALKER, SOCIAL SCIENCE IN LAW: CASES, MATERIALS AND PROBLEMS (1985).

M. MOORE, LAW AND PSYCHIATRY: RETHINKING THE RELATIONSHIP (1984).

Morse, *Crazy Behavior, Morals, and Science: An Analysis of Mental Health Law,* 51 S. CAL. L. REV. 527 (1978).

Morse, *Failed Explanations and Criminal Responsibility: Experts and the Unconscious,* 68 VA. L. REV. 971 (1982).

Saks & Kidd, *Human Information Processing and Adjudication: Trial by Heuristics,* 15 LAW SOC'Y REV. 123 (1980–81).

Tribe, *Trial by Mathematics: Precision and Ritual in the Legal Process,* 84 HARV. L. REV. 1329 (1971).

CHAPTER TWO

An Overview of the Legal System: Sources of Law, the Court System, and the Adjudicative Process

2.01. Introduction

The forensic specialist works in a world defined largely, if not exclusively, by "the law." Through administrative licensing agencies, legal rules governing malpractice and confidentiality [see § 3.04], and constitutional principles limiting evaluation procedures [see §§ 3.02, 3.03], the law regulates forensic practice. Judges, attorneys, probation officers, and clerks initiate forensic referrals, and sheriffs and other law enforcement officers transport the client to and from hospital and jail. And, of course, legal factfinders—judges and juries—are the ultimate arbiters of those cases evaluated by the forensic specialist.

Most importantly, at least from the perspective of this book, the law establishes the guidelines that define the scope of forensic evaluation. Chapters 3 through 13 describe this substantive law in detail. But before undertaking an investigation of these legal rules, it is important to understand from whence they come, and when and by whom they are applied. The "law" is not derived from a single, readily accessible or static source. Nor is it *always* implemented by a judge or jury. To function competently, the forensic specialist must have a basic knowledge of the sources of law, the institutions that shape it, the various points in the legal process at which it can be applied (especially those points at which

"mental health law" is applied), and the types of individuals who apply it. This chapter is devoted to an acquisition of that basic knowledge. Much of its content will probably be familiar to the lawyer; it is aimed primarily at the clinician with no legal training.

2.02. Sources of Law

Tradition has it that the legislature "makes" the law, while the executive branch enforces the law and the judicial branch interprets the law. In actuality, each of these governmental institutions produces legal rules. Moreover, they are not the only sources of law; in particular, constitutional provisions can often affect legal analysis. Added to all this is the fact that the federal and state systems each have their own constitutions, and their own legislative, executive, and judicial arms, each of which develops legal principles. Before discussing the various ways in which law is manufactured, a word must be said about this latter aspect of our form of government.

(a) Federal–State Relations

The United States is a "federation" of states. This means that while each state has retained its own government and its own system of laws, the states have collectively ceded certain powers to the central government. The United States Constitution is the document that sets out the various powers held by the federal government on the one hand and the state governments on the other. For instance, it reserves the power to regulate interstate commerce and provide for the national defense exclusively to the federal government. On the other hand, the Tenth Amendment to the Constitution reserves to the states those "powers not delegated to the United States by the Constitution, nor prohibited by it to the States."

Although the federal government's authority under these constitutional provisions was originally narrowly construed, it is now clear that Congress may pass laws affecting any activity that can conceivably be said to involve the "public welfare" (assuming that federal funds are part of the statutory package) or "interstate commerce." Thus, under its public welfare authority, the federal government has been able to affect dramatically the provision of health care in this country; it has set institutional and staffing standards under which Medicare and Medicaid monies will be made available to state facilities,[1] has attempted to stimulate the growth of community mental health services through the Community Mental Health Centers Act,[2] and has significantly advanced the habilitation opportunities of the developmentally disabled through the Education for All Handicapped Children Act.[3] Relying on its authority to regulate interstate commerce, it has passed a number of laws only tangentially related to business activity, including civil rights legislation.

Nevertheless, with two possible exceptions, federal law will usually have relatively little direct impact on clinicians in their *evaluative* capacity. The first exception is in the area of federal criminal law. Federal crimes fall into four major categories: (1) interstate crimes (e.g., mail fraud, robberies of federally insured banks, abduction across state lines, and, most prominently, narcotics violations involving international or interstate transactions); (2) offenses in which the victim was a federal official (e.g., the President); (3) violations of civil rights laws; and (4) offenses

involving or committed on federal property. The second area in which federal law governs forensic practice is in disability determinations for Social Security benefits, discussed in Chapter 9.

In practice, then, the states retain primary authority over most substantive areas with which forensic evaluators are concerned. Most criminal law, domestic, or "family" law, juvenile law, civil commitment law, and "tort" law (which includes "personal injury," malpractice, and confidentiality rules) stem from state sources of law.

There are some instances when federal and state laws overlap. In the criminal area, they can coexist. For instance, an armed robbery of a federally insured bank in Missouri could be punishable under Missouri's armed robbery statute and federal law as well. Since the state and federal governments are seen as separate "sovereigns," both may prosecute for the same robbery without fear of violating the double jeopardy clause of the Constitution. In the noncriminal area, on the other hand, certain federal enactments are said to *preempt* the substantive area with which they deal, to the exclusion of state law. The preemption doctrine is designed to promote a unified approach to "federal" problems. As a result, a federal law that deals with a preempted issue will supersede all state laws on the subject. For example, the Department of Health and Human Services regulations governing confidentiality in substance abuse treatment programs have been found to preempt the area; state statutes in conflict with these regulations are thus inapplicable.[4]

With these points about federal–state relations in mind, we can now turn to an investigation of how the various sources of law at the federal and state levels operate.

(b)   Constitutions

The United States has a "constitutional" form of government, meaning that the United States Constitution is the ultimate authority in the country. The rules found in all other forms of law must be consistent with it; in other words, they must be "constitutional." The provisions of the United States Constitution that affect forensic practice most significantly are the Fifth, Sixth, and Fourteenth Amendments to the Constitution. The Fifth Amendment establishes the so-called "privilege against self-incrimination" and the Sixth Amendment provides each criminal accused with the "right to counsel"; the implications of these concepts for forensic evaluation are discussed in Chapter 3. The Fourteenth Amendment guarantees that no state shall deprive any citizen of the United States of life, liberty, or property without "due process of law" and that no state shall deny an individual "equal protection" of the laws. The due process and equal protection clauses have had a significant impact on a wide range of forensic issues, including the criteria and procedures for civil and criminal commitments [see Chapter 8], the admissibility of clinical testimony in criminal trials on issues other than insanity [see § 6.03(b)], and the procedures to be followed in capital sentencing cases [see § 7.06(b)].

Within the parameters set by the United States Constitution, the federal and state branches of government may devise legal rules. The state branches are further limited in their actions by the constitutions of the particular states, although in practice the provisions of most state constitutions are similar to those in the federal constitution.

(c)   Statutes and Regulations

As noted earlier, the federal government and the various state governments parallel one another. Each has a legislative branch (Congress at the federal level; "general assemblies," "houses of delegates," etc., at the state level), an executive branch (the President and the federal departments in the federal system; the governor and state agencies in the state system), and a judicial branch. This section looks at the type of law produced by the first two branches.

The laws that legislatures pass are called "statutes" and are codified, or collected, into codes, which are organized by subject. In the federal system, for instance, Title 18 is the section of the United States Code that deals with federal crimes. State codes may also be organized

according to titles, or by chapters, sections, or some other nomenclature, but each represents the product of the state legislature's deliberations.

As might well be imagined, legislatures often find themselves unable to treat by statute all situations or circumstances which they want to address. Accordingly, they have increasingly delegated rulemaking authority to government agencies, which are units of the executive branch. In the federal system, for instance, in establishing "conditions of participation" that facilities must meet under Medicare and Medicaid statutes, Congress merely drafted general standards and left it up to the Department of Health and Human Services to decide, within the ambit of those standards, the precise conditions that must be met. Similarly, a state legislature might direct its Department of Mental Health to devise guidelines for the provision of forensic evaluation services. This administrative law, usually promulgated in the form of "regulations" and also found in "codes," has become so complex in some areas that legislatures have required several of the executive's agencies to set up their own "judicial" bodies to adjudicate disputes arising under the regulations. Alleged violations of regulations must first be considered by these administrative hearing boards before they are considered by a court.

(d)   The Judiciary

Despite the advent of administrative hearing boards, the primary interpretive institution within both the federal and state systems remains the judicial system. The interpretation performed by courts takes place through deliberation on individual cases that raise an issue concerning a particular legal principle. The holding and reasoning of the courts in these cases are recorded in *Reports* or *Reporters,* which are organized according to the type and level of court. Thus, for instance, for the federal court system, *United States Reports* and the *Supreme Court Reporters* contain opinions of the United States Supreme Court; the *Federal Reporters* contain the decisions of the federal circuit courts of appeals; and the *Federal Supplement* contains opinions of the federal district courts (the next section describes the various levels of courts in more detail).

The United States Supreme Court has conferred upon itself and the lower federal courts the authority to review all federal enactments to determine their constitutionality, their meaning, and, in the case of regulations, whether they exceed the delegation made by Congress.[5] The federal courts also have the authority to consider the validity, under the United States Constitution, of any *state* constitutional, statutory, or regulatory provision[6] (although the state courts are the ultimate arbiter of the *meaning* of state law).

Of particular significance here is the fact that the review and explication functions of the courts imbue them with frequent opportunities to "make" law. Thus, for instance, federal and state courts construing the constitutionality of state civil commitment statutes have not only found state provisions unconstitutional, but have also indicated what they felt were permissible criteria and procedures for commitment [see Chapter 8]. Some commentators have argued that such instances are examples of inappropriate "legislating" by the courts, but in fact they occur with increasing frequency.

A second situation in which the courts make law is when the textual sources of law (e.g., constitutions and statutes) are silent on a particular issue. In performing their interpretive function, courts will first look at the plain words of any relevant constitutional provision, statute, or regulation, and then review the legislative history of a given law, including statements made by the law's sponsors, or during committee or public hearing sessions. But if neither of these sources are helpful, or if no relevant law exists, then the courts themselves must devise principles to govern the case before them. The principles articulated by courts when they create law are collectively known as "common law," or judge-made law.

In areas of civil law, such as tort law, many of the guiding legal principles are found in reported judicial decisions rather than statutes or regulations. In the criminal area, on the other hand, common-law pronouncements are rare, because virtually all crimes are now defined by statute. However, some defenses to crimes are not statutorily defined. For instance, until recently Congress had not passed a statute setting forth a test of insanity for federal criminal cases; the federal courts thus adopted their own "common-law" standards for insanity [see § 6.02(b)]. Moreover, in both the civil and criminal areas, even when statutes do apply, they may use terms that have been developed in common law (such as "malice aforethought") and that are left undefined in the statute. In such cases, the courts rely on the common-law tradition for interpretive aid.

As should be apparent from this last statement, the common law—unlike statutory and regulatory law, which often create rules out of whole cloth—usually develops according to the principle of *stare decisis,* which holds that present controversies should be decided according to past cases, or "precedents." This doctrine tends to make judge-made law conservative in nature, but it has the advantage of avoiding abrupt and perhaps ill-reasoned changes; it also serves to provide notice to those who come before the courts of the general principles that will govern resolution of their cases.

In sum, there are several sources of law: the United States Constitution; state constitutions; statutes passed by legislatures; regulations promulgated by agencies; and interpretive and common law handed down by the courts. There are other sources of law as well: "Executive orders" issued by the President's office are one example. Clinicians in their evaluative capacity, however, will be concerned with the types of federal and state law described above.

2.03. The Court System

Just as the federal and state governments have parallel branches of government, they have roughly parallel judicial structures. Both the federal and state judiciaries have two types of courts: "trial courts" and "appellate courts." The primary functions of the trial court are to ascertain the facts of the case before it and then to apply "the law" to those facts. The facts are gleaned through an "adversarial" process, which, as described in § 1.03(c), envisions an impartial "trier of fact" (either a judge or a jury) considering evidence chosen by the parties to the dispute (to be distinguished from an "inquisitorial" process, found in some European countries, which combines the investigative and decisionmaking roles). In most instances, the trial court's decision may be appealed to an appellate court, which determines whether the correct legal principles were applied by the trial court. No "trial" takes place at the appellate level; rather, the court bases its decision on the record developed by the trial court, the briefs (written memoranda of law) submitted by opposing counsel, and, occasionally, oral argument by counsel.

Beyond this basic structure, the federal and state judicial systems tend to diverge.

(a)   The Federal Court System

In the federal system, the "district court" serves as the trial court. Each state is divided into one or more districts over which a district court judge presides. The district courts have jurisdiction over many types of cases, but the primary authority is over cases arising under federal law. Thus, any claim that a federal or state statute or practice is unconstitutional under the United States Constitution may be brought in federal court. So, too, may any claim for an entitlement under federal law (e.g., welfare benefits). All defendants charged with federal offenses are also tried in federal court.

There are two levels of appellate courts in the federal system: the Circuit Courts of Appeals and the United States Supreme Court. The country is divided into 12 circuits, each including several states (except the District of Columbia Circuit); the judges on the circuit courts of appeal hear appeals from the district courts within their circuit. A decision by a particular court of appeals determines the law only for that particular circuit.

The United States Supreme Court, comprised of nine Justices, is the highest court in the country. Its decisions regarding the United States Constitution and federal and state enactments apply nationwide and are final—that is, unappealable. Its jurisdiction is primarily appellate, although it has original trial jurisdiction over some types of cases, such as controversies between a state and the United States and between a state and citizens of another state.[7] The Court is required to take certain types of cases on appeal, including cases in which a district court declares a federal statute unconstitutional and in which a circuit court declares a state statute unconstitutional.[8] For the most part, however, the Court may exercise its discretion in deciding which cases to consider; otherwise, it would be overwhelmed. The primary mechanism for petitioning the Court to hear one's case is called a "writ of certiorari." The Court denies or grants certiorari on a particular case, depending upon its legal and systemic significance. For instance, the Court often "grants cert" in cases that provide an opportunity to resolve a conflict between courts of appeal or those in which a state supreme court has interpreted a federal constitutional or statutory provision in a questionable manner. Many of the mental health law cases decided in the 1970s and early 1980s (e.g., *O'Connor v. Donaldson*,[9] *Addington v. Texas*,[10] *Jones v. United States*,[11] and *Mills v. Rogers*[12]) were certiorari cases.

(b)   State Judicial Systems

Most states have at least two levels of "general-jurisdiction trial courts"—one that tries civil matters involving small sums of money and minor crimes, and another that handles major civil and criminal trials. With a few exceptions (most importantly, federal criminal cases), a state court with general jurisdiction may hear cases involving federal as well as state law. Additionally, most states have "special-jurisdiction courts" for designated subject areas, such as civil commitment, domestic relations, juvenile matters, and probate. Many of the special jurisdiction courts and the lower-level general-jurisdiction courts are relatively informal: The proceedings are not transcribed as a matter of routine, the rules of evidence may not apply, and witnesses may not be required to testify under oath. Litigation over the level of formality which should adhere in

Figure 2-1. *The relationship between federal and state courts. [From W. LOH, SOCIAL RESEARCH IN THE JUDICIAL PROCESS 33 (1984). Reprinted by permission.]*

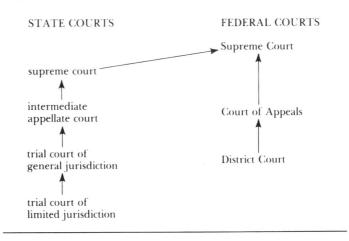

these types of courts has achieved mixed results [see, e.g., § 8.05].

Like the federal system, most states also have two appellate levels—an intermediate appeals court and a supreme court—although some states have only the latter. The state supreme court is the ultimate authority on the interpretation of state law; even the United States Supreme Court must respect the state court's decision with respect to its own law, unless it is in conflict with the United States Constitution or a federal enactment that has preempted the area.

Figure 2-1 illustrates in simplified form the relationship between the federal court system and the typical state court system.

2.04. The Adjudicative Process

There are four major types of judicial proceedings: criminal, civil, administrative, and what this chapter calls "quasi-criminal." Each process aims at different objectives, has different rules of evidence and procedure, and involves different types of personnel. The forensic clinician should be aware of the principal differences among these proceedings in order to understand the context in which clinical input is sought.

(a) The Criminal Process

A criminal prosecution occurs when the government (federal or state) charges an individual with the commission of an act that is forbidden by statute and punishable either by imprisonment or a fine. Conviction of and punishment for a criminal offense have traditionally been viewed as the most severe actions society can take against one of its members. Accordingly, the criminal process is the most highly formalized of any adjudicatory proceeding, at least in felony cases. The prosecution must prove each element of the crime charged "beyond a reasonable doubt" (a level of certainty that can reasonably be quantified at above 90%).[13] The defendant is afforded the right to counsel, not only at trial but at any "critical" stage before trial, including lineup identifications and custodial interrogations.[14] To prevent "star chamber proceedings," the defendant is entitled to a public jury trial, the right to compel witnesses to testify in his or her behalf, and the right to cross-examine the prosecution's witnesses.[15]

There are two generic types of offenses: "misdemeanors" and "felonies." A misdemeanor is usually defined as an offense punishable by imprisonment up to one year, a fine, or both. The place of imprisonment, if it occurs, is usually the local jail rather than a state prison. Felons, on the other hand, are incarcerated in the state prison system, for terms ranging from a few months up to life—depending, of course, upon the crime. Roughly 25 states also authorize the death penalty [see § 7.06].

(1)   The Stages of a Criminal Prosecution

A criminal prosecution is a highly structured event, established by statute, court rule, or long tradition. Although the details vary from jurisdiction to jurisdiction, the following typology is representative:

1. Detention. The state has authority to detain an individual on a criminal charge if there is "probable cause" (a degree of certainty perhaps roughly equivalent to 40–50%) to believe that the individual has committed the crime charged. Information constituting probable cause can come from direct police observation, reports from informants, or complaints by ordinary citizens. Once sufficient grounds exist for believing there is probable cause to arrest an individual, the police may either seek an arrest warrant from a judge or magistrate (a judicial officer who presides over pretrial hearings) or, if there is no time to seek a warrant, or some other extenuating circumstance exists, they may make a warrantless arrest. In rare cases (e.g., those involving political corruption), an arrest may be made pursuant to a grand jury indictment or to an "information" from the prosecutor, both indicating that, after a formal investigation, grounds exist for detaining the named individual. As will be noted later, however, the indictment or information usually follows, rather than precedes, arrest.

2. Booking. Immediately after arrest the defendant is taken to the station house, where appropriate paperwork is completed, and, if necessary, fingerprinting and photographing take place.

3. The initial hearing. The United States Supreme Court has held that, as soon as possible after arrest (e.g., 48 to 72 hours), the government must afford the accused a hearing to determine whether there is probable cause to detain him or her, unless the arrest is based on a warrant or an indictment (since, in the latter instances, a judicial determination of probable cause has already been made).[16] Those charged with misdemeanors may be tried at this time. Those charged with felonies will usually have counsel appointed if they cannot afford one and will either have their bail set or be released on their own recognizance.

4. Defensive motions and discovery. Once the defendant has obtained counsel, several events may occur, depending upon the nature of the case and the competence of counsel. First, defense counsel may try to "discover" the prosecution's case, which he or she can do by making a motion to the court asking for specific information (e.g., confessions by the defendant) in the prosecution's files. The drawback to this maneuver is that many states follow a reciprocity principle with respect to discovery: With the exception of incriminating statements by the defendant, the prosecutor may obtain data in the defense file once the defense ask for data in its file. Thus, for instance, some states permit the prosecution to discover the results of the defendant's clinical evaluations once the defendant makes a discovery motion [a rule that is criticized in § 3.02(b)]. The defense attorney may also make a "motion to suppress" (or render inadmissible) certain evidence. For instance, the attorney may try to argue that a confession the defendant made to the police was invalidly obtained; the issue is addressed at a "suppression hearing."

5. The *prima facie* showing. At some point following the initial hearing, it is incumbent upon the prosecution to formally "make its case" in front of a judicial body—either a judge, a magistrate, or a grand jury. This stage is designed to ensure that the prosecutor has a *"prima facie* case" (i.e., sufficient evidence against the defendant to justify going forward with the criminal prosecution). In order to meet this burden, the prosecutor will often present the results of lineup identifications, police interrogations, searches of the defendant's home or the crime scene, and any discovery that he or she is able to make of information that the defense counsel has in his or her possession. In many states, this presentation is made to a magistrate or judge at a preliminary hearing, at which the defendant and coun-

sel are present. Most states east of the Mississippi,[17] as well as the federal courts, require an indictment by a grand jury in addition; here the public and the defendant are barred from the proceedings.

6. The arraignment. Although the term "arraignment" is sometimes used to refer to the initial hearing (step 3), technically it is the stage at which the accused pleads, which may not occur until well after that hearing (and in fact often occurs just before trial). In most states, there are four possible pleas: "guilty," "not guilty," *"nolo contendere"* (by which the defendant indicates he or she will not contest the state's charges), and "not guilty by reason of insanity." Most jurisdictions permit a defendant to plead not guilty and not guilty by reason of insanity simultaneously (on the theory that the defendant should not be barred from asserting other defenses—e.g., self-defense—just because he or she claims insanity). If one or both of the latter pleas are entered, the case is usually set for trial. If the plea is guilty, the judge must ascertain whether it was voluntarily, intelligently, and knowingly made[18]; if so, the defendant is sentenced, either at arraignment (in misdemeanor cases) or at a later proceeding (step 8).

Most guilty pleas are the result of "plea bargaining," which involves an agreement between the defendant (through his or her attorney) and the prosecutor providing that if the defendant pleads guilty to a specified charge, the prosecutor will recommend to the judge that the plea be accepted. In order to encourage such pleas, the prosecutor will often reduce the charges, drop one or more charges, or pledge to recommend a lenient sentence to the judge. Since over 90% of all criminal cases are disposed of through a bargained plea,[19] this relatively hidden procedure is an extremely significant aspect of the criminal process.

7. Trial. If the defendant chooses to go to trial, and does not waive his or her right to a jury, a jury is selected through *"voir dire."* This process permits each side to exclude individuals from the jury using a limited number of "peremptory challenges" (which require no stated reason) and an unlimited number of "for-cause challenges" (which must be justified). Most states require 12-member juries in felony cases, al-though six-member juries are becoming more common. Once a jury is properly impaneled, the trial begins. After opening arguments, the state presents its evidence, through submission of exhibits and direct examination of witnesses. The defendant may challenge this evidence through cross-examination and, in the court's discretion, rebuttal witnesses. The defendant then puts on his or her evidence, which the state may contest. If insanity is an issue, some states permit a "bifurcated trial," with the insanity evidence introduced at the second stage [see § 6.02(b)]. After closing arguments, the judge provides the jury, if there is one, with instructions on the law it is to apply to the facts of the case. In a case in which insanity is raised as a defense, for instance, the jury will be told the jurisdiction's test for insanity. After instructions are given, the jury retires until it can produce a verdict, which usually must be unanimous (although the Supreme Court has held that 11–1, 10–2, and 9–3 decisions are not unconstitutional).[20] If the jury is "hung" (i.e., cannot reach a proper verdict), a new trial is held.

8. Disposition: sentencing and commitment. A few states permit the jury to sentence the defendant once it finds him or her guilty. However, most states leave the sentencing decision up to the judge, who will often request a "presentence report" from the probation officer and will occasionally hold a sentencing hearing before announcing the penalty. The latter hearing is usually much more informal than a trial [see § 7.03(c)], although again both sides are given the opportunity to present evidence. The sentencing authority may impose any sentence within the statutory range and may also impose probation, with conditions. An individual acquitted by reason of insanity, on the other hand, is usually required to undergo a short commitment for evaluation purposes and is then subjected to a hearing that results in prolonged commitment if he or she is found to be mentally disordered and dangerous [§ 8.13(c)].

9. Appeal. After conviction and sentencing, a defendant has the option of appealing the trial court's decision. An appeal must be taken within a certain period of time, and must be based on factual issues (e.g., insufficient evidence to convict) or legal ones (e.g., the defendant's confes-

sion was obtained in violation of the Fifth Amendment) that have been objected to before or during trial. The prosecution may not appeal an acquittal (under the double-jeopardy clause of the United States Constitution), although in a few states it may appeal a sentence.

10. Collateral attack. Once appeal routes are exhausted, it is still possible for both the offender and the insanity acquittee to attack their confinement "collaterally" through a writ of "habeas corpus" (or, in some states, a write of "coram nobis"). The gist of these writs is an allegation that the state is illegally detaining the person. Although the scope of habeas corpus has been narrowed in recent years, it does enable the prisoner or acquitee to make certain claims regarding the fairness and adequacy of the trial or plea bargain that resulted in incarceration.

11. Dispositional review. Most offenders and insanity acquittees are not released via appeal or collateral attack. Instead, most are released through state-initiated review of their status. Although some states have abolished parole in favor of "fixed" sentences [see § 7.04], in most states the convicted offender who has served a minimum period of time is entitled to have a parole board determine his or her eligibility for early release, based on the individual's criminal record, behavior in prison, and perceived tendency to recidivate. Similarly, in most states the insanity acquitee is entitled to periodic reviews of his or her mental state and dangerousness either by a probate court or by a board of mental health professionals.

12. Post sentence treatment hearings. Many states transfer prisoners needing psychiatric care to secure mental hospitals until they no longer need inpatient treatment; others seek such treatment for prisoners under the new "guilty but mentally ill" statutes [§ 6.02(c)]. A recent United States Supreme Court decision requires that, before an involuntary transfer from prison to a hospital takes place, some type of hearing be held.[21]

*(2)   Clinical Input: Issues, Points of Entry,
and Contacts*

During the above-described process, myriad issues arise that may call for clinical expertise. Due

process requires that before an accused pleads guilty or undergoes trial, he or she must be competent to do so. The clinician may be asked to evaluate the accused's "competency to plead guilty" [see §§ 5.03, 5.04] at virtually any point prior to arraignment; an assessment of the defendant's "competency to stand trial" [see Chapter 4] could be called for at any time up *through* the conclusion of trial. Occasionally, the evaluator may even be asked to address these issues retrospectively if, for instance, the competency issues are raised via a writ of *habeas corpus.*

If the defendant confesses, the clinician may be requested to determine whether, at the time of the incriminating statement, the defendant was "competent to confess" [see § 5.02], and may be asked to explain his or her findings at a suppression hearing. If the defendant wants to proceed *pro se* at either arraignment or trial, or both, the clinician may be asked to evaluate the defendant's "competency to waive an attorney" [see § 5.05]. A final competency issue that the clinician may address is whether the defendant (or, more likely, one of the trial witnesses) is "competent to testify" [see § 5.06]. All of these evaluations are likely to be ordered at some time between the initial hearing and the trial.

Both the defense and the prosecution may also want an evaluation of the defendant's "mental state at the time of the offense" [see Chapter 6]. Most states require the defendant to give the state formal notice of an intent to raise an insanity defense at least ten days before trial, so the defense will usually ask the clinician to evaluate the defendant's sanity well before this time. The prosecution, on the other hand, arguably does not need its own evaluation or any information on this issue until after the defendant raises it [see § 3.02(b)]. Nonetheless, in practice, the prosecution often requests an evaluation before notice occurs. Occasionally, the defense may actually encourage such action; the available data indicate that a large percentage of insanity acquittals are the result of quasi-plea bargaining [see Chapter 6, note 24], which may occur well before notice by the defendant is required.

If the defendant is convicted, either the state or the defendant may want a presentence evaluation of the defendant focusing on his or her "dangerousness," "treatability," mental state at the time of the offense, or "culpability" or other issues. Frequently, such evaluations will take place before the determination of guilt or innocence, either because, as is the case with capital sentencing procedures in most states, the sentencing hearing immediately follows trial, or because both sides want to reach a bargain and the defendant's treatability is an issue that will influence the ultimate plea and recommended sentence. Another issue that may require clinical expertise at or after sentencing is competency to be sentenced or executed [see § 5.07].

Finally, in the context of parole board decisionmaking and release hearings for insanity acquittees, the clinician may be asked to evaluate the defendant's mental state and dangerousness; in the context of prison transfers, treatability may be an issue.

The mental health professional should also be aware of the different actors involved in the criminal process. The prosecutor is perhaps the most powerful, at least during the pretrial stages, since he or she is the official responsible for deciding what charges to bring against the defendant; indeed, the prosecutor has the authority to dismiss the charges entirely even if the victim wants them pressed. Moreover, the prosecutor's discretion during the plea bargaining process to reduce charges and fashion a disposition is enormous.

The defense attorney is also obviously of extreme importance, since without this individual the process would probably not be adversarial in any real sense. Because most defendants are indigent, few defense attorneys are retained. Most are either court-appointed attorneys or public defenders. Both types of defense attorneys are paid by the state, the former on a per-case basis, the latter by salary. Increasingly, states are moving toward public defender offices as the method for providing legal services to indigent defendants; while public defenders may represent *only* criminal defendants, court-appointed attorneys are often marginally involved in criminal practice, and may resent having to take time out from the rest of their caseload.

Other actors in the system have already been briefly described. Judges make rulings of law and instruct the jury at trial as to the proper law to

apply. Magistrates issue warrants and preside over preliminary hearings. Probation officers prepare presentence reports and supervise offenders put on probation. Court clerks issue the judge's orders and organize the court docket. The sheriff and jail personnel provide security and transportation. All of these individuals are important to the evaluator because of their control over various aspects of the criminal process. Moreover, each can provide useful information about the person being evaluated. Serious forensic practitioners need to establish a credible relationship with each of them if evaluations are to reflect a comprehensive assessment of the client, and if reports and testimony are to receive the full attention they deserve.

(b)   Civil/Administrative Proceedings

Unlike a criminal adjudication, a truly civil proceeding involves a dispute between private parties. The government merely provides the forum for resolving the dispute. A simple civil suit might involve a claim by one party (the "plaintiff") that the other party (the "defendant") negligently operated his or her automobile and caused injury to the plaintiff. Or the plaintiff may claim that the defendant breached a contract. A slightly different type of civil suit involves custody over children during a divorce proceeding[22]; here the goal is not money damages but possession of the children. The common thread among these cases is that all involve disputes between citizens rather than between a citizen and the state.

Because a civil proceeding of this type does not result in a loss of liberty and is viewed as a conflict between parties with roughly equivalent resources, the degree of certainty required to reach a decision is much lower than in the criminal process. Although the plaintiff has the burden of proof, he or she can meet it merely by a "preponderance of the evidence," meaning a showing that the plaintiff's version of the facts is more likely than the defendant's.

Nor are the stages of civil adjudication as highly ritualized as those in the criminal context. Under the federal rules of civil procedure, which many states have also adopted in whole or in part, a civil suit is commenced by filing a "complaint," to which the defendant responds with an "answer." No further steps are required until trial.

Typically, of course, both sides make numerous "pretrial motions." The most frequent are those designed to "discover" the other side's case. The scope of discovery has expanded in the past several decades in order to avoid surprise at trial. A number of mechanisms are available to facilitate this process, including "depositions" (during which witnesses are questioned and their testimony transcribed); "interrogatories" (sets of written questions that are answered in writing); requests to produce documents and other tangible evidence; mental and physical examinations; and requests to admit facts relevant to the case.

Of particular importance here are motions to obtain a mental examination and motions to discover the content and basis of opinions held by a party's experts. Under the rules applicable in federal court, a party can obtain a mental examination only of another party to the case or a person in that party's "custody or control"; for privacy reasons, examinations of nonparties cannot usually be obtained. Moreover, before a mental examination of a party can be obtained, the court must be convinced that his or her mental condition is "in controversy" and that there is "good cause" for the evaluation. The rules also place obstacles in the way of the party seeking to discover the gist of what opposing experts will say. The moving party must first file interrogatories specifying the requested information. Only if the moving party can convince the judge that the answers to these interrogatories are insufficient may further discovery take place. Usually, this second stage of discovery will involve a deposition, during which the expert is, in effect, cross-examined with his or her attorney present. The transcript of this deposition may be used at trial to impeach the expert's testimony. Although objections to questions asked during deposition may be made, they are usually merely noted for the record; the expert must generally answer all questions put to him or her, even if the answers will not later be admissible at trial. The most relevant exception to this rule is when the ques-

tions ask for privileged information or information that the expert's attorney can convince the court is entitled to protection for confidentiality reasons.[23] As § 3.04 makes clear, in most jurisdictions neither objection affords much protection.

Very frequently, once discovery is complete, the parties will settle rather than go to trial. Although "settlement" is analogous to plea bargaining, the terms of the settlement agreement need not be approved by, or even divulged to, the judge.

If settlement is not reached, *voir dire* of the jury venire is conducted and the trial begins. The civil adjudication, like the criminal trial, is adversarial in nature. The plaintiff's evidence is presented first and his or her witnesses subjected to cross-examination; the defendant's case follows. Again, to illustrate the differing stakes involved, in many states the civil jury need only produce a majority verdict in order for one party to prevail (in the federal courts, a unanimous verdict is required unless the parties stipulate otherwise before trial[24]).

The psychological issues that arise in civil cases will depend, of course, on the substantive nature of the case. In the typical personal injury, or "tort," case, the plaintiff may claim that the defendant's negligence caused not only physical harm, but mental pain and suffering as well, and may request an evaluation gauging the nature and extent of this pain and suffering [see Chapter 10]. In custody disputes, the issues will be whether one or either of the parents is fit to care for the child and, in a larger sense, what is in the best interests of the child [see Chapters 12 and 13]. As in the criminal context, there are also several competency issues that may arise in a civil adjudication, all discussed in Chapter 9. In probate cases, the clinician may be asked to evaluate whether the deceased was competent to make a will at the time it was executed; in guardianship cases, he or she may have to assess whether the proposed ward is competent to make personal or business decisions; in treatment cases, the issue is whether the proposed patient is competent to make a treatment decision; and, in contract cases, a question may arise as to whether a party to the agreement was competent to enter into a contractual relationship. As in criminal cases, there may also be a need to determine whether a particular witness is competent to testify [see § 5.06].

Virtually all administrative hearings in front of executive adjudicative bodies are also deemed "civil" in nature. However, in these cases the government is a party and is often acting to confer property on or take it away from a citizen (e.g., licensing, social security determinations). Therefore, the standard of proof used in these proceedings is usually the "clear and convincing" standard, which falls between the "beyond a reasonable doubt" rule used in criminal cases and the "preponderance of the evidence" standard used in the typical civil case. Otherwise, the procedures in administrative hearings are similar to those in purely civil disputes.

Probably the most common psychological issue in administrative adjudication is the level of mental disability suffered by an applicant for government benefits in the form of Social Security [see § 9.06] or worker's compensation [see § 10.02]. As legislatures begin conferring authority on administrative bodies to hear issues, such as the right to refuse treatment,[25] traditionally heard in the courts, greater clinical participation in administrative hearings can be expected.

(c) Quasi-Criminal Proceedings: Civil Commitment and Juvenile Delinquency

There exist entirely discrete types of cases that have traditionally been labeled "civil" in nature, but that, because they potentially involve a significant deprivation of liberty, are best characterized as "quasi-criminal." The two types of quasi-criminal cases discussed in this book are "civil commitment" and "juvenile delinquency" cases. "Civil commitment" is the process by which the state institutionalizes those found to be mentally disordered and either dangerous or in need of care. Juvenile courts provide a mechanism separate from the adult criminal justice system for trying allegedly antisocial juveniles. Traditionally, both civil commitment and the juvenile

courts were seen as means of providing state resources to relatively helpless groups within society; their objective was not punishment, but rehabilitation. But in the last two decades, the courts have determined that the primary result under both systems is a "deprivation of liberty" that often does little to help and may actually harm those involved.

As a result of this shift in perspective, significant changes have occurred in both areas, described in detail in Chapters 8 (on civil commitment) and 11 (on juvenile delinquency). For present purposes, only a few recent developments need be noted. In the civil commitment context, the United States Supreme Court has held unconstitutional state statutes that permit commitment by the civil "preponderance of the evidence" standard; instead, it has required the higher "clear and convincing evidence" test to be met.[26] Lower federal courts and some state courts have also held that formal evidentiary rules and the rights to subpoena and cross-examine witnesses apply in commitment hearings.[27] In the juvenile context, the United States Supreme Court has, in effect, equated juvenile delinquency proceedings with adult criminal trials. With a few exceptions (e.g., the right to jury trial),[28] every right afforded adult criminal defendants must also be afforded juveniles charged with committing a crime, including the right to require proof beyond a reasonable doubt that the crime was committed.[29] It would be naive to conclude that the "therapeutic ideal" no longer exerts a strong influence on the civil commitment and delinquency adjudicatory systems; in practice, the new procedural requirements have often been disregarded. Nonetheless, with a few exceptions, those subjected to these types of proceedings are theoretically entitled to the same type of adversarial proceeding that adult criminal defendants are.

As described in detail in Chapter 8, the issues that will confront the clinician performing civil commitment evaluations focus on the need to hospitalize the individual in question. State statutes vary, but usually require a finding that the individual is mentally ill plus either dangerous to others, dangerous to himself or herself, or in need of care or treatment before involuntary commitment may occur. The clinician may also be asked to evaluate the individual's competency to make treatment decisions.

Juvenile delinquency proceedings, as Chapter 11 makes clear, may require a number of different decisions that can be informed through clinical expertise. Just as in the criminal process, issues of competency to stand trial and waive certain rights may arise, as well as the question of whether the juvenile was insane at the time of the offense. On the other hand, unique to the juvenile system is the determination of whether certain children (usually between 15 and 18 years of age) are "amenable to treatment" within the juvenile system; if not, there may be a transfer of the juvenile to adult court jurisdiction, a procedure also known as "waiver" of juvenile court jurisdiction. Finally, the child who remains in the juvenile court system and is convicted will as a matter of course be evaluated, often by a mental health professional, to determine the best disposition. This presentence evaluation is much more wide-ranging than the analogous adult assessment; most states provide several types of rehabilitative services for children, all of which must be considered by the evaluator.

It should be remembered that both civil commitment and juvenile courts are special-jurisdiction courts, with separate personnel and facilities. Many states do not appropriate funds for a prosecutor in either civil commitment or juvenile cases. In the former context, very often the committing judge or the examining clinician fills that role; in the latter area, many states confer prosecutorial discretion on the juvenile probation officer.

2.05. Conclusion: The Interplay among Systems

Lest the impression be created that the criminal, civil, and quasi-criminal systems described above operate entirely independently of one another, it may be helpful to conclude this chapter with a hypothetical situation that illustrates the extent to which they can overlap. The reader may also wish to refer to Figure 2-2, which depicts in a schematic fashion many of these connections.

Assume that a quarrel erupts between a husband and wife, which climaxes in the husband's beating the wife as well as the couple's child. Of course, the woman may decide not to report the event to anyone in authority. Or she may contact the local police, triggering the criminal process. Finally, if she thinks her husband may have mental problems, she may attempt to seek professional intervention, possibly triggering the civil commitment process. If the police are called in, they may decide to book the husband for assault and battery, take him to a hospital for mental evaluation, or do nothing. Whatever their decision, the prosecutor, assuming that he or she hears of the case, may decide to handle the case quite differently. Moreover, in many states, an offense against a child is tried in juvenile court; if charges are pressed, the whole matter may end up there and the husband's fitness as a parent may become an issue. Simultaneously, the wife may decide to sue the husband for divorce, custody of the child, and damages on the assault and battery; all three claims are heard in civil court, but the first two may be tried in juvenile court (or "family" or "domestic relations" court), and the latter in a court of general jurisdiction.

This hypothetical illustrates two different points. First, whether a case enters the criminal, civil, or quasi-criminal system depends, in many instances, on the preferences of the victim, the predilections of the police and the prosecutor, and the relevant state law. Especially in situations where mental disorder is an issue, the room for discretion and flexibility is quite large. "Criminal" cases may be "diverted" to civil commitment or juvenile court jurisdiction, or to private psychiatric care. Or they may result in hospitalization following a finding of incompetency to stand trial or an insanity finding. If conviction occurs, psychiatric care may take place in prison or after a transfer from prison to a mental hospital.

A second point to be garnered from this brief hypothetical situation is the importance of finding out the context of an evaluation. A mental health professional who is asked to evaluate an individual needs to know who is asking for the evaluation, what court will use the evaluation results, and, most crucially, precisely what is to

Figure 2-2. *The mental health process. [From THE MENTAL HEALTH PROCESS (F. Miller, R. Dawson, G. Dix, & R. Parnas eds., 2d ed. 1976). Reprinted by permission of Foundation Press, Mineola, N.Y.]*

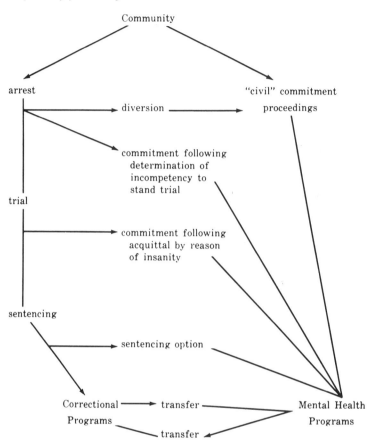

be evaluated. For example, the husband of the hypothetical victim could be evaluated on the following issues, depending upon which "process" has been triggered and the stage to which it has progressed: (1) his competency to plead guilty, stand trial, or waive an attorney; (2) his sanity at the time of the offense; (3) his "intent" to hit his wife (relevant to the civil assault and battery claim as well as the criminal charge); (4) the extent to which he is presently mentally ill and either dangerous to himself or others; (5) his fitness as a parent; and (6) his "treatability" for sentencing purposes. And this list does not exhaust the possibilities.

Ideally, a court order or the party making the referral will clarify these contextual issues. If no clarification is forthcoming, the professional must find out personally. Otherwise, the evaluation may yield results that are useless to the legal system. This theme is one sounded throughout this volume.

BIBLIOGRAPHY

R. BROUSSEAU, CIVIL PROCEDURE: A FUNCTIONAL APPROACH, ch. 1 (1982).

R. ROSS, AMERICAN NATIONAL GOVERNMENT: AN INTRODUCTION TO POLITICAL INSTITUTIONS (1972).

C. WHITEBREAD & C. SLOBOGIN, CRIMINAL PROCEDURE: AN ANALYSIS OF CONSTITUTIONAL CASES AND CONCEPTS, ch. 1 (2d ed. 1986).

CHAPTER THREE

Constitutional, Common-Law, and Ethical Contours of the Evaluation Process: The Mental Health Professional as Double Agent

3.01. Introduction

Suppose that you are ordered to evaluate the competency of a criminal defendant—a man who has never met with an attorney; who has no idea why he is seeing you; and who proceeds to tell you that he has committed a murder, that his brother was also involved in the crime, and that he'd like to kill the victim's sister as well. Although it is unlikely that all of this would happen in one case, the individual aspects of this hypothetical situation are not uncommon. Should you refuse to evaluate the defendant, despite the court order, until he has had an attorney appointed for him? What should you tell him about the nature of the evaluation? Should you interrupt him immediately and tell him he has a "right to remain silent"?

The defendant has incriminated himself and his brother, and has stated a desire to harm another. Should any of this information be disclosed? If so, when should it be disclosed—immediately, after an attorney has been appointed, or at some later point in time? And to whom—the judge, the prosecutor, the defense attorney (once appointed), or someone else? Would you be liable to the defendant for breach of confidentiality if you told *anyone* about the defendant's revelations? Could you be held liable

if you did *not* disclose these revelations, and harm to a third party (e.g., the victim's sister) resulted?

Suppose instead that you are the lawyer appointed (somewhat tardily) to represent the defendant described above. What steps should you take to protect your new client? Can you "muzzle" the clinician? If you want to assert an insanity defense, can you prevent the clinician from disclosing what he or she knows, or participate in any further evaluation he or she conducts?

The mental health professional who performs evaluations for the courts and the lawyer who represents those evaluated must be aware of several constitutional, common-law, and ethical principles that have a direct bearing on the conduct of forensic evaluations. The first two sections of this chapter discuss when an "accused" who is being evaluated has a Fifth Amendment right to remain silent during the evaluation or to prevent state use of its results, and the ramifications of the Sixth Amendment's right to counsel for forensic assessment. The chapter then addresses the evaluator's common-law and statutory duties not only toward the person being evaluated, but also toward the court and society at large; the focus is on privilege and confidentiality rules, the somewhat opposed *"Tarasoff* duty" to take preventive measures when a defendant being evaluated appears dangerous, and the doctrines of informed consent and negligent misdiagnosis. Finally, this chapter examines several issues that are closely related to many of these legal doctrines but that stem from the mental health professions' own attempts to regulate their evaluation practices.

In discussing the often controversial issues covered in this chapter, we take the view that, whenever possible, legal and ethical principles should be formulated to facilitate the interchange between the evaluator and the person being evaluated. Unfortunately, the conflicting and complex demands made on the evaluator by these principles make it impossible to develop an entirely consistent approach to many problems that arise in the evaluation process. The aim of this chapter, therefore, is to provide answers when they seem clear, and to present the available alternatives when, as is frequently the case, the answers seem less than obvious.

3.02. The Fifth Amendment and the Right to Remain Silent

The principle behind the Fifth Amendment's privilege against "self-incrimination" is that one accused of a crime should not be forced to provide evidence against oneself; the state should be required to prove its case on its own, without bringing its formidable power to bear on the accused. Thus, as presently construed by the United States Supreme Court, the Amendment prohibits the state from using at a criminal trial any (1) "testimonial' statement (2) of an "incriminating" nature (3) that it "compelled" from the defendant being tried.[1]

The requirement of "testimonial evidence" comes from a long line of cases distinguishing between "testimonial" or "communicative" evidence on the one hand, and "noncommunicative" or "physical" evidence on the other. The latter type of evidence does not fall within the scope of Fifth Amendment protection. To hold otherwise, pointed out Justice Holmes in *Holt v. United States,* "would forbid a jury to look at a prisoner and compare his features with a pho-

tograph in proof."[2] Using similar reasoning, the Supreme Court has held that the state may require a defendant to submit to a blood test, give a voice exemplar, stand in a lineup, and try on articles of clothing, even if these actions assist the state in securing a conviction.[3]

A few lower courts have held that clinical evaluations do not implicate the Fifth Amendment, because the defendant's disclosures during such evaluations are not relied upon for their content but rather serve merely to identify mental traits of the accused, much as a fingerprint measures certain physical characteristics. But by far the majority of courts agree with the D.C. Court of Appeals that "the words of the accused are critically important in determining his mental condition."[4] The Supreme Court itself appears to agree with this conclusion. In *Estelle v. Smith*[5]—the sole case in which the Court has considered the application of the Fifth and Sixth Amendments to psychological evaluations, and therefore one that is referred to frequently throughout this and the following section—it cited approvingly a statement from the American Psychiatric Association's amicus brief that "absent a defendant's willingness to cooperate as to the verbal content of his communications . . . a psychiatric examination . . . would be meaningless."[6]

It appears settled, then, that the disclosures typically made during a clinical evaluation are testimonial rather than "noncommunicative." When particular disclosures by the defendant are "incriminating" and when they may be compelled from the defendant and used at trial have been more controversial topics. To a great extent, the answers to these questions depend upon the type of evaluation at issue and the purpose for which the results of the evaluation will be used.

(a)   Competency Evaluations

As Chapter 2 indicates, there are several different types of legal competencies that can arise in the criminal process: competency to stand trial, competency to plead guilty, competency to waive certain rights, and so forth. With a few exceptions, a competency evaluation involves an assessment of the defendant's present mental state, rather than his or her mental state at the time of the offense. Thus, at first glance, it may seem unlikely that anything "incriminating" will be revealed during such assessments.

As Chapters 4 and 5 make clear, however, any comprehensive competency evaluation of a defendant, regardless of the specific competency in question, *can* involve delving into incriminating matters. In an evaluation of competency to stand trial, for example, the clinician may inquire into the defendant's memory of the offense in order to ascertain whether the individual can adequately assist an attorney in his or her defense. Similarly, an examination of competency to plead guilty will probably involve asking questions about the offense in order to determine the extent to which the defendant understands the implications of a guilty plea.

Even without such direct questions, the defendant could easily divulge information during a competency evaluation that could prove "incriminating," in light of the broad scope given that term: The Supreme Court has held that any disclosure by the defendant is potentially self-incriminating if it might "furnish a link in the chain of evidence needed to prosecute."[7] Thus not only outright "confessions," but statements that provide investigative leads (e.g., "I threw the gun in the bushes" or "My wife saw me do it"), implicate the Fifth Amendment.

There is a good possibility, then, that incriminating evidence will be produced during a competency evaluation. Yet virtually every state permits the prosecution to compel the defendant to undergo a competency evaluation upon showing that the defendant's competency is in question. The central justification for permitting this state coercion is that the state's interest in protecting the integrity of the criminal process by ensuring that the defendant understands what he or she is doing overrides the defendant's Fifth Amendment interest in remaining silent. In many jurisdictions, a second justification, at least in the context of competency *to stand trial,* is that statutory provisions prohibit the use of the evaluation results at trial.[8] In these states, disclosures made during an evaluation of competency to stand trial may be used by the prosecution only to determine the defendant's competency, not guilt; *incrimination* of defendants through their own words is thereby avoided. When there are no such statutory limitations (e.g., in the context of competency to plead guilty or confess), defense attorneys can accomplish the same result by inserting language in the court order to the effect that use of the results of the evaluation at trial is prohibited.

Even with statutory or court-ordered protection, there remains the possibility that the competency evaluation report will contain disclosures by the defendant that could provide leads to incriminating evidence, even though the statements themselves cannot be used at trial. In such a case, when the prosecution will receive the competency report, the mental health professional has two options: (1) to retain the incriminating information in the report and leave it to the court to decide whether the prosecution's trial evidence is in fact the fruit of the defendant's evaluation statements, or (2) to refrain from including in the prosecution's report any possibly incriminating disclosures by the defendant. Admittedly, the latter approach may require deletion of some probative information. But the alternative—the inclusion of potentially incriminating information, which usually will be only tangentially relevant to the competency issue—may lead to difficult-to-detect prosecutorial abuse of the evaluation process.[9] Thus, for example, Virginia provides by statute that "no statement of the defendant relating to the time period of the alleged offense shall be included in the [competency] report."[10] (Note that statements by others—e.g., witnesses and police—are not *self*-incriminating and thus do not receive Fifth Amendment protection.)

These rules should apply even when it is the defendant who wants the assessment. One could argue that in such a case the defendant is not being forced to give up the right to remain silent. But the Supreme Court has made it clear that an accused may not be penalized for exercising the right.[11] Here the accused would be penalized because remaining silent prevents him or her from obtaining an evaluation of competency. Those states that bar the use of competency evaluation results on the issue of guilt[12] do not distinguish between defense- and prosecution-requested evaluations, thereby implicitly recognizing this point. This approach has the added benefit of encouraging the defendant to be communicative during the competency evaluation.

(b) Evaluations of Mental State at the Time of the Offense

It should be obvious that the various legal doctrines addressing an accused's mental state at the time of the offense [see Chapter 6] require the forensic evaluator to ask questions of the accused that could easily lead to incriminating disclosures. A comprehensive evaluation on issues of insanity, automatism, or diminished capacity necessitates detailed inquiry into the defendant's thoughts and actions during the time period of the crime. For this reason, most courts that have addressed the issue do not permit the state to compel an evaluation of the defendant before he or she has formally indicated a desire to assert one of these defenses.[13] On the other hand, by far the majority of courts impose sanctions on the defendant who refuses to cooperate with a state-requested evaluator, once notice of intent to raise a defense has been given.[14] In *Estelle v. Smith,* the Supreme Court implicitly condoned this practice, on the ground that to permit the defendant to assert the right to remain silent after giving notice "may deprive the state of the only effective means it has of controverting his proof on an issue that he interjected into the case."[15]

In the event the defendant does refuse to cooperate with the state in the postnotice context, most courts prohibit the defendant from presenting expert evidence. A second, less frequently utilized sanction is permitting the defendant's expert to take the stand, but allowing the prosecutor to inform the jury that the defendant will not talk to the state's expert.[16]

A difficult issue, which has yet to be resolved, is when the defendant deserves such sanctions. Outright refusal to talk might normally be considered noncooperation. But often the truly disordered defendant will be hostile to the evalua-

tor for irrational reasons having nothing to do with the constitutional right to remain silent. As one court put it: "The fact, amply demonstrated over the years, is that a failure of a defendant . . . to cooperate most often reflects an even greater degree of insanity rather than less."[17] The court attempting to decide whether sanctions should be imposed on the recalcitrant defendant needs to consult the evaluating clinician as well as the defense attorney, in order to determine both the extent of the defendant's resistance and whether his or her attorney condones it.

As in the competency context, the Fifth Amendment not only dictates when the prosecution can compel a mental state at the time of the offense evaluation; it also places restrictions on when the state can use its results. The modern trend, similar to that in the competency context, is to limit trial use of disclosures made during such an evaluation to the issue being evaluated. To this effect, the Model Penal Code formulation, which has been adopted in several states, reads: "A statement made by a person subjected to a psychiatric examination or treatment . . . shall not be admissible in evidence against him in any criminal proceeding on any issue other than that of his mental condition."[18]

The newly adopted Federal Rule of Criminal Procedure concerning this issue provides even more comprehensive protection:

> No statement made by the defendant in the course of any [psychiatric] examination . . . , whether the examination be with or without the consent of the defendant, no testimony by the expert based upon such statement, and no other fruits of the statement shall be admitted in evidence against the defendant in any criminal proceeding except on an issue respecting mental condition on which the defendant has introduced testimony.[19]

Thus, the Federal Rules not only prohibit direct use of the defendant's evaluation statements on issues other than those he or she has raised, but also forbid use of the defendant's disclosures for investigative purposes. In several other jurisdictions, similar Fifth Amendment protection has been extended to the defendant through judicial decision.[20] Where statutory or judicial provisions do not exist, the defense attorney can request the court to provide such protection via court order.

Even this protection may not be enough. To prohibit "fruits" of the defendant's statements from being admitted at trial, one must be able to discover when the state's evidence is in fact such a fruit—a task that, as pointed out earlier, may often be impossible. Therefore, the best method of reducing the potential for prosecutorial and police abuse of the evaluation process is to restrict state access to the results as much as possible. When the clinician is *retained* by the defendant, this objective is easily achieved: Virtually every court that has considered the matter has held that the retained professional is an "agent" of the attorney, and that the results of such an evaluation are therefore protected by the "attorney–client privilege" until the defense "waives" the privilege by putting the defendant's mental state at the time of the offense at issue.[21] Unfortunately, the dictates of the attorney–client privilege and the Constitution have not generally been recognized in those cases where a state-employed clinician performs an assessment requested by an *indigent* defendant. Typically, the report of the clinician employed by the state is sent to all parties, whether or not notice of a defense has been given. Yet, if the indigent defendant has requested the evaluation, he or she should be able to rely upon the same protection (whether based on Fifth Amendment or privilege principles) as one who can afford a private clinician. Thus, we recommend that *whenever* a mental state at the time of the offense evaluation is defense-requested, and the law or court order does not otherwise specify, the full evaluation report should *not* be sent to the prosecution or the court unless and until the defendant affirmatively indicates a defense will be asserted; or unless the court so orders. Only at that point does the prosecution need to know the content of the defendant's statements. Up to that point, delivering the report to the prosecution is unnecessary, provides the state with too great a temptation to use the information therein for investigative purposes even if it is barred from using it directly at trial, and tends to discourage full disclosure by the defendant who knows the clinician is a conduit to the prosecutor.

Thus, for example, in Virginia it is provided by statute that, prior to notice of a mental state defense, the prosecution is to receive only a summary of the clinical report, from which all statements by the defendant about the time period of the alleged offense have been deleted.[22] After notice is given, the prosecution can obtain the full report, as well as its own evaluation, if it wants one.[23] An innovative proposal having much the same effect has been put forward by the American Bar Association (ABA) in its Criminal Justice Mental Health Standards. Under standard 7-3.4, the prosecutor may compel the defendant to undergo an evaluation within 48 hours of the defendant's own evaluation, but the results of the prosecution's evaluation are sealed until formal notice of an intent to raise a defense based on mental abnormality is given by the defendant. (The results of the defendant's own evaluation are, of course, protected by the attorney–client privilege.) This device honors the defendant's Fifth Amendment interest, but also gives the prosecution access to evaluation results "as fresh" as those obtained by the defendant's expert.

The whole issue of pretrial disclosure of evaluation results is complicated by "reciprocal discovery" provisions in many states (usually incorporated in the state's rules of criminal procedure), allowing the prosecution to "discover" the reports and statements of the defense's experts once the defense asks for information from the prosecution, even if the defense request precedes the defendant's decision to raise a defense.[24] To the extent that such discovery rules require prenotice disclosure of defense evaluation results, they would seem to be in violation both of the Fifth Amendment and of the attorney–client privilege.

A final point with respect to the application of the Fifth Amendment in this context has to do with the courts' treatment of testimony derived from an evaluation of mental state at the time of the offense. If and when the state's expert takes the stand and testifies, he or she will probably reveal incriminating information disclosed by the defendant, even if the testimony is limited to a discussion of the defendant's mental condition. Clinical testimony about the defendant's sanity, for instance, will usually reveal admissions by the defendant with respect to the act associated with the crime in question. But preventing disclosure of this information would probably seriously undermine the credibility of the testimony.

This problem has been dealt with in two ways. At one time, several states provided for mandatory "bifurcation" of the trial process, with the first stage focusing on the "guilt" of the defendant and the second stage, if necessary, reserved for trying the sanity of the defendant found to have committed the offense charged. In this way, the potentially incriminating testimony of the clinician was reserved until after the defendant was found "guilty." Unfortunately, there are many practical problems with bifurcation[25]; moreover, most state courts that have addressed the issue have declared that prohibiting admission of clinical testimony at the initial stage of the process is unconstitutional, because it denies the defendant the opportunity to introduce all relevant testimony in his or her defense.[26] Thus, under constitutionally correct procedures, the bifurcated trial does not always avoid the incrimination problem and will often produce duplicative proceedings. For these reasons, all but three of the nine states that adopted a mandatory bifurcation procedure have since abandoned it.[27] However, several states still permit bifurcation on the defendant's request, if the court agrees.[28]

A second approach to the problem of trial incrimination, followed by most states, is to hold a unitary trial but to caution the jury to consider the clinician's testimony only on the issue of mental condition, and not on other issues, which the jury must decide.[29] Obviously, a mere instruction will not prevent misapplication of the clinician's testimony by the jury. However, provided that the other protections discussed in this chapter are available, a unitary trial is not likely to create much actual prejudice to the defendant's Fifth Amendment interest. Moreover, the defendant will often have an expert of his own describing the offense in detail, and the prosecution will usually have evidence independent of the clinical evidence sufficient to prove that the defendant committed the act associated with the crime. Perhaps the best approach, endorsed by the ABA in standard 7-6.7 is to hold a unitary trial with a precautionary instruction under most circumstances, but to allow bifurcation if the court considers it appropriate (as in situations where the defendant is presenting clinical testimony only on the insanity issue and also has a colorable nonclinical defense, such as self-defense, which might be prejudiced by the clinical testimony if heard at the same proceeding).

(c)   Sentencing Evaluations

The few courts that have addressed the issue have all declared that the Fifth Amendment does not apply to the typical sentencing evaluation.[30] Initially, this result seems logical, since if the defendant is being considered for sentencing, he or she presumably has been convicted and thus can no longer be "incriminated." Yet in reality, presentence evaluations often take place before trial and thus can provide still another source of investigative leads. Additionally, the postconviction sentencing process itself can result in a type of "incrimination." In the typical first-degree murder case, for instance, the judge has the authority to impose a sentence ranging from a few years to life. Arguably, the defendant should not be forced by the state to reveal information that may tend to increase the sentence in such a case.

The Supreme Court has obliquely accepted this line of argument in the unique context of capital sentencing. In *Estelle v. Smith,* the Court found that when the defendant's statements to a clinician who later testifies for the state expose the defendant to the "ultimate penalty of death," there is "no basis to distinguish between the guilt and penalty phases of a capital murder trial so far as the protection of the Fifth Amendment privilege is concerned."[31] After *Estelle,* it appears that, procedurally, the capital sentencing evaluation should be treated like an evaluation of mental state at the time of the offense. That is, until the defendant indicates a desire to use a clinician at the capital sentencing hearing, the state should not be able to obtain its own clinical evaluation on capital sentencing issues. After such notice is given, on the other hand, the prosecution should be entitled to obtain its own assessment as well as the results of the defendant's evaluation.

It is important to note, however, that *Estelle* is limited to *capital* sentencing. The Court was careful to point out that its decision in *Estelle* did "not hold that the same Fifth Amendment concerns are necessarily presented by all types of interviews and examinations that might be ordered or relied upon to inform a sentencing determination."[32] Thus, while the mental health professional or lawyer may want to seek court-ordered restrictions on the state's access to and use of noncapital presentence evaluation results, there is no constitutional foundation for such restrictions.

(d) Juvenile Delinquency and Commitment Proceedings

Technically, the Fifth Amendment only prohibits use of incriminating statements at *criminal* trials. But as § 2.04(c) points out, modern courts have consistently characterized juvenile delinquency proceedings and civil commitment as "quasi-criminal" in nature, given the "massive deprivation" of liberty that may result from a finding that a person should be punished as a delinquent or institutionalized in a mental hospital. The Supreme Court has held, in *In re Gault,*[33] that the Fifth Amendment applies in juvenile delinquency proceedings. Presumably, the same constitutional rules that govern adult evaluations should also apply to these proceedings.

The judiciary's approach to civil commitment has been more cautious. Some courts have applied the Fifth Amendment to civil commitment proceedings and evaluations,[34] on the ground that a defendant's disclosures during a commitment hearing or a prehearing assessment are "incriminating" (even though they may not constitute admission of a crime) if they could lead to involuntary hospitalization, and that they are "compelled" if the individual is not told of the right to remain silent. Most courts, however, have concluded that while a civil commitment hearing is analogous to the criminal process in many

ways, it is not a criminal trial and should not be encumbered with all of the procedures afforded the criminal defendant.[35] The trend, then, is to avoid applying the Fifth Amendment to the civil commitment process, a trend the Supreme Court seems willing to encourage.

Indeed, in *Allen v. Illinois*[36] the Court held, 5–4, that commitment under a "sexually dangerous offender" statute is not a "criminal" proceeding for purposes of the Fifth Amendment, at least when the statute permits the prosecution to seek commitment *in lieu of* criminal conviction for a sexual offense. (Some states provide for special commitment of the "sexually dangerous" *after* conviction [see § 7.05(b)].) Thus, the state may compel an individual to undergo a psychiatric evaluation of his or her dangerousness, so long as the results are used only as a basis for seeking commitment under such a statute; similarly, the individual may not exclude compelled statements from such commitment proceedings. The Court's justification for this holding was that the primary purpose of the Illinois statute in question was treatment, not punishment. Thus, there is no danger of "incrimination" at this type of commitment proceeding unless the consequences of such a proceeding turn out to be identical to those faced by a felon. Allen (who, had he been convicted of the offense that triggered the statute, would have received at most a year's imprisonment and a $500 fine) had been confined for five years in the psychiatric unit of the state's maximum security prison under authority of the Illinois Sexual Offender Act. Yet because he made no showing that the state had failed to afford him treatment different in kind from that afforded felons, he was not entitled to Fifth Amendment protection.

Allen is important because it firmly repudiates the suggestion in *Gault* that the Fifth Amendment should apply whenever the proceeding in question may lead to loss of liberty. Rather, the sole question for Fifth Amendment purposes is whether the primary purpose of the proceeding in question is treatment or punishment. One could certainly argue that the type of commitment at issue in *Allen* more resembled punishment than treatment, particularly since under these types of statutes confinement is indeterminate and release is conditioned on a finding that the individual is no longer dangerous; the primary purpose of such statutes would seem to be incapacitation bordering on retribution, not treatment. Moreover, as Justice Stevens pointed out in his dissenting opinion in *Allen,* the Illinois statutory framework is decidedly criminal in flavor: Commitment is triggered by a criminal offense, is initiated by the state prosecutor, requires the criminal standard of proof, and results in confinement in prison. But after the Court's holding in *Allen,* it seems clear that not only sexually dangerous offender proceedings of the type at issue in *Allen* but also civil commitment proceedings and post-insanity-acquittal hearings will be considered "civil" for Fifth Amendment purposes.

(e)   Other Civil Proceedings

It is possible that incriminating information will be revealed during evaluations that are more properly labeled "civil" in nature. Since several states render child neglect a criminal offense, for instance, it is possible that incriminating statements may be made during a child custody evaluation. Generally, such incriminating information is admissible at a subsequent criminal trial if it is not protected by the attorney–client privilege (i.e., if the evaluation is conducted at the behest of the state). It is up to the individual's attorney to assure that the client "takes the Fifth" during such evaluations when asked questions that might reveal incriminating information. If the privilege is not asserted, it is very likely that the disclosures will be admissible in any criminal proceeding initiated against the individual. If, on the other hand, the privilege is asserted, the client may not be held in contempt; otherwise, the Fifth Amendment would be meaningless.

(f)   The *"Miranda* Warnings"

In *Estelle v. Smith,* the Supreme Court held that when the defendant "neither initiates [a] psychiatric evaluation nor attempts to introduce any psychiatric evidence" at a subsequent capital sentencing proceeding, statements made by the defendant during the evaluation are inadmissible at the capital sentencing proceeding unless the defendant has first been given warnings to this effect: "You have the right to remain silent, and anything you say may be used against you." *Estelle* has caused considerable confusion among mental health professionals; on a first reading, the decision seems to require that every forensic evaluation be preceded by *"Miranda* warnings" (so-called because the above-described litany is taken from the Supreme Court's famous decision in *Miranda v. Arizona*). In the typical case, however, such warnings are not required; indeed, they would be inaccurate. As noted earlier, the defendant has no right to remain silent during a competency evaluation, a postnotice state-requested evaluation of mental state at the time of the offense or capital sentencing issues, or a noncapital sentencing evaluation. And if his or her evaluation disclosures are protected by the attorney–client privilege [see § 3.02(b)], the defendant has no *reason* to remain silent. Only when, as in *Estelle* itself, the defense attorney has no idea the evaluation is taking place and has no intention of presenting psychiatric evidence in support of the client's case does the clinician need to tell the defendant, "You may refuse to talk, and anything you say may be used against you."

Whether persons subjected to civil commitment evaluations must be warned of the right to remain silent depends, of course, on whether such a right has been found to exist by the relevant tribunal. If individuals are entitled to such a right, they should be told they possess it; otherwise their Fifth Amendment guarantee is likely to be meaningless. The fact that such warnings might inhibit disclosure is legally irrelevant, although perhaps clinically unfortunate. Courts consistently refuse to abate the Fifth Amendment right in the criminal context merely on the ground that its implementation might complicate the states' efforts to secure a conviction.

Although the law may not require that "warnings" be given prior to most forensic evaluations, the mental health professions' own ethical guidelines may necessitate a short preevaluation discussion with the subject, describing the content of the evaluation and its possible uses.

This topic is dealt with at greater length in § 3.05(b).

3.03. The Sixth Amendment and the Right to Counsel

The Sixth Amendment promises the criminal defendant the "assistance of counsel for his defense." The Supreme Court has held that the amendment actually guarantees two different rights: (1) the right to presence of counsel and (2) the right to effective assistance of counsel. Both rights have implications for the conduct of forensic evaluations.

(a) Counsel's Presence during the Evaluation

Over the past two decades, the Supreme Court has decided a number of cases granting the criminal defendant a constitutional right to counsel not only at the trial itself, but also at several so-called "critical" stages of the criminal process that precede trial. Thus, for instance, the defendant has the right to have counsel present at a postindictment lineup, at a preliminary hearing to determine whether there is probable cause to prosecute, and at arraignment.[37] A minority of courts have equated the pretrial clinical evaluation with these stages of the criminal process and have held that the Sixth Amendment guarantee applies to forensic assessments.[38] Most courts, however, have held that the defendant does not have a right to counsel's presence during the actual evaluation.[39] In *Estelle v. Smith,* the Supreme Court intimated that it agreed with this latter approach. While the court *did* establish that the state must inform the defendant's attorney about any evaluation that it plans to conduct (so a decision can be made as to whether to advise the defendant to cooperate with the state), it also cited with approval a lower court's opinion that the attorney's actual presence during the psychiatric interview "could contribute little and might seriously disrupt the examination."[40]

A cogent argument can be made that the Su-

preme Court's caution on this issue is unfounded. The leading Court case on the right to counsel is *United States v. Wade,*[41] which held that a criminal defendant has the right to counsel during postindictment identification lineups. The Court appeared to rely primarily on two justifications for its ruling. First, an attorney should be present because the identification made at the lineup might substantially prejudice the defendant's interests. Secondly, reconstructing at trial what actually occurred during the lineup identification might be difficult if counsel did not observe it. The Court noted, for instance, that "neither witnesses nor line-up participants are apt to be alert for conditions prejudicial to the suspect," and that "[i]mproper influences may go undetected by a suspect, guilty or not, who experiences the emotional tension which we might expect in one being confronted with potential accusers."[42] The court also pointed out that "any protestations by the suspect of the fairness of the line-up at trial are likely to be in vain; the jury's choice is between the accused's unsupported version and that of the police officers present."[43]

The analogy to the clinical evaluation process should be apparent. The results of state-requested competency, insanity, and sentencing evaluations can have a substantially adverse impact on the defendant's case. A defendant with mental problems is unlikely to be able to reconstruct accurately for the attorney what occurred during such an evaluation, nor is such a person's testimony alone likely to fare well against the testimony of a mental health professional.

The facts of *United States v. Byers*[44] illustrate the vagaries of reconstructing the clinical evaluation and why counsel must be personally cognizant of the relationship between the evaluator and the defendant. Charged with the murder of his lover of 15 years, Byers raised an insanity defense based on the results of a clinical evaluation performed at St. Elizabeths Hospital in Washington, D.C. The defendant then was evaluated by government-appointed clinicians at a federal hospital in Springfield, Missouri. Dr. Kunev, one of the psychiatrists who evaluated Byers at Springfield over an eight-week period, testified for the government at trial. In supporting his opinion that Byers was sane at the time of the offense, Kunev stated that while initially Byers had said he did not know why he committed the murder, when "pressed" he had indicated that at one point his wife suggested that he might have been under a "spell." Apparently inferring that Byers had leaped on this suggestion as a possible way of avoiding criminal conviction, Kunev testified that Byers was probably fabricating the paranoid delusions he claimed to have had at the time of the offense. The jury found Byers sane and guilty.

According to the trial judge, Kunev's recitation of Byer's conversation with his wife was "devastating" to the defendant. The prosecutor called this testimony the "critical thing" in the case. Yet Kunev had not included this information in his report, nor had he mentioned it to the defense attorney prior to trial.

As Judge Bazelon noted in his dissent to the court's *per curiam* decision affirming the admissibility of Kunev's testimony:

> We have no record of the defendant's exact words, we know hardly anything about their context and nothing about the intention behind them. Accordingly, we have no basis upon which we can decide whether the government's exploitation of this ambiguous statement violates "our sense of fair play" which must temper the tactics of the government "in its contest with the individual."[45]

Judge Bazelon also noted other "significant factual issues" that were not in the record, including the nature of Dr. Kunev's interviewing technique and whether his "repeated inquiries had a coercive impact upon the defendant."[46]

Byers amply demonstrates why defense counsel should be able to discover verbatim what transpires during a state-requested evaluation. But even if one accepts the premise that the Sixth Amendment prohibits the state from denying the defense attorney access to the details of the assessment, it can be argued that the attorney's physical presence is not necessary to protect the defendant's constitutional rights. It has been suggested, for instance, that a videotape or audiotape of the evaluation would afford the attorney with a sufficient record of the relevant events,

at the same time that it avoids the possible disruptive impact occasioned by the attorney's presence.[47]

Admittedly, when the attendance of the defendant's attorney would be inimical to the *efficiency* of the evaluation (as could have been the case in *Byers,* where the evaluation took place far from the trial court and over a long period of time), taping or written records may prove to be the only possible solution. But in those cases where attorney access is practicable, we suggest that defense counsel be permitted to observe the evaluation process. Even a videotape will not accurately transmit all the possible contextual variables at work during an evaluation. And the fear that the attorney's presence will prove disruptive does not justify denying the attorney the opportunity to witness these variables personally. As the Supreme Court itself stated in *Wade,* "to refuse to recognize the right to counsel for fear that counsel will obstruct the course of justice is contrary to the basic assumptions upon which this Court has operated in Sixth Amendment cases."[48] Moreover, it is not a foregone conclusion that the attorney will have a negative impact on the evaluation process. As noted in § 3.02, in the typical evaluation the defendant does not have the right to remain silent, and the attorney risks sanctions against the client if he or she advises the client not to cooperate or prevents the client from cooperating. Indeed, given the fact that the relationship between the state's clinician and the defendant may be somewhat strained to begin with, the attorney's presence is unlikely to harm, and may even contribute to, development of an evaluation dialogue.

Given the *possibility* of disruption by the attorney, however, it is likely that most courts confronted with this issue will, at most, permit the defense attorney to tape the clinician's evaluation—an option that is consistent with *Estelle's* reasoning. An alternative is to have the defendant's own expert observe the evaluation in place of the attorney. Even if the actual presence of an attorney is not constitutionally required, it seems clear that one of these "substitute" procedures is constitutionally mandated in those cases where the defendant requests it. It should also be kept in mind that, regardless of constitutional demands, practical considerations connected with certain types of evaluations may warrant the presence of an attorney. In particular, when one of the issues to be assessed is the relationship between the attorney and a client, as in evaluations of competency to stand trial, it may make good sense to allow the attorney to participate in the assessment.[49]

(b)　Presenting an Effective Defense

Two issues involving the defendant's right to effective assistance of counsel are briefly mentioned here. The first is the indigent defendant's right to an independent state-funded evaluation. The second is the nonindigent defendant's right to prevent the prosecution from using experts the defendant has decided not to call.

(1)　The Right to an Independent Evaluation

Although virtually every state provides the indigent defendant with free evaluation services at state institutions, only a few provide funds on a systematic basis for the indigent who wishes to consult a *private* forensic specialist. It has been argued that the failure to provide such funds makes it impossible for the defendant's attorney to represent his or her client adequately, since the client must depend upon state-employed clinicians. It is also contended that making indigents rely on state clinicians violates notions of equal protection, since wealthier defendants can choose from as many clinicians as their resources permit.[50] Yet these arguments usually fail, partially because courts make the dubious assumption that state evaluations are "impartial," and partially because of the staggering costs that would be associated with an independant evaluation program (although this latter argument is seldom explicitly made by the courts.)

Thus, for instance, in *Ake v. Oklahoma*, the Supreme Court held that indigent defendants are guaranteed psychiatric assistance under the Sixth Amendment when raising an insanity defense or mitigating circumstances at capital sentencing, but also decided that the indigent individual does not

have the right to a clinician of his or her own choosing. Rather, it is up to the states to decide how to implement the right to such assistance.[51] It is doubtful many states will feel compelled by *Ake* to provide funds for private, as opposed to state employee, clinical assistance. Moreover, *Ake* specifically held that an indigent is entitled to only *one* state-funded evaluation.

One compromise solution is to decentralize state evaluation capacity so that clinicians with different backgrounds are involved. In several states, for instance, community mental health professionals, as well as state hospital personnel, are available to provide evaluations, thereby offering the indigent defendant a greater variety of clinicians from which to choose.[52]

(2)　The Edney Problem

A quite different problem arises when the *nonindigent* defendant consults more than one expert, decides to raise a psychiatric defense using only some of the experts, and the prosecution then subpoenas the remaining expert or experts. In *United States ex. rel. Edney v. Smith,*[53] the court held that the state should have access to the experts the defendant has decided not to use, once the issue of mental state at the time of the offense is properly raised. Otherwise, the *Edney* court stated, the defendant would "be permitted to suppress any unfavorable psychiatric witness whom he had retained in the first instance, under the guise of the attorney–client privilege, while he endeavors to shop around for a friendly expert, and take unfriendly experts off the market."[54] Several courts have followed the *Edney* rationale.

A slightly smaller number of courts follow *United States v. Alvarez,*[55] which held that the defendant's right to effective assistance of counsel is curtailed when the state is permitted to use experts the defendant has discarded. According to the *Alvarez* court, the "attorney must be free to make an informed judgment with respect to the best course for the defense without the inhibition of creating a potential government witness."[56]

Since the state is entitled to its own evaluation once the defendant gives notice of an intent to raise a psychiatric defense, the prosecution will rarely be severely hampered by the *Alvarez* rule. Yet if the defense attorney is able to gag experts merely by consulting them, however briefly, the prosecution could be denied access to valuable, and arguably much fresher, data if the *Edney* approach is not followed. Deciding which rule is best in a particular case may depend largely on the number of experts available in the particular community and on whether the defense attorney has acted in good faith when consulting with the various experts. But it is clear that the *Edney* rule has more of an inhibiting effect on open disclosure during the evaluation.

3.04. Common-Law and Statutory Duties of the Evaluator

This section discusses the nonconstitutional legal principles governing the conduct of forensic evaluations. In particular, it focuses on the types of acts or omissions for which the evaluator may be legally liable. As will be seen, the evaluator (as opposed to the therapist) has little to be concerned about in this regard.

(a) Confidentiality and the Court-Ordered Evaluation: General Observations

In the typical *therapeutic* relationship, in which the mental health professional and another individual enter into an arrangement designed to provide therapy for the latter, the law encourages confidentiality. A clinician who divulges information about a patient to unauthorized parties without the patient's consent is liable for any resulting damage to that patient's reputation and privacy interests.[57] Additionally, under limited circumstances[58] the patient, through assertion of a "privilege," can prevent the therapist from testifying about the patient at trial or from obeying a records subpoena. Many states recognize only a physician–patient or psychiatrist–patient privilege, although an increasing number have also established psychotherapist–patient,

psychologist–patient, and social worker–patient privileges.[59] As with the attorney–client privilege discussed in § 3.02, these privileges are designed to encourage discussion between the professional and the person seeking the professional's services by protecting against unwarranted disclosures to third parties.

In the purely *evaluative* relationship, however, confidentiality is close to nonexistent. The clinician–patient privileges do not apply when the clinician–"patient" relationship is the creature of the court, as in the case with court-ordered evaluations. And, as noted in § 3.02, even the attorney–client privilege applies only when the clinician is an agent of the defendant's attorney. In short, the law takes the position that the evaluator's client is the party that requests the evaluation, not the defendant. Generally, therefore, the evaluator must include in the report and testimony any information about the defendant that is relevant to the questions specified by the requesting party, subject to constitutional limitations on self-incrimination [see § 3.02]. This is true despite the fact that court files (which often contain clinical reports and trial transcripts) are usually matters of public record; most states protect against public disclosure only in the case of presentence reports.[60] Such openness may seem anathema to the mental health professional trained to honor the patient's privacy, and may run afoul of central ethical precepts [see § 3.05]. But it stems from the conviction, rooted in the First Amendment, that the public and press have the right to know about and monitor the judicial process—a concept that has been re-emphasized by the United States Supreme Court in several recent decisions.[61].

Thus, so long as the evaluator's disclosures do not stray beyond the terms of the court order and are made in good faith, it is extremely unlikely that he or she could be found liable for breach of privacy or damage to reputation. In fact, at least one court has held, in a slightly different context, that an evaluator is absolutely immune from a claim that an evaluation report defames the subject of the report if the report was requested by the prosecution for purposes of litigation pending against the subject.[62] Of course, such rules should not lead evaluators to neglect their ethical duty toward anyone whom they see professionally. As discussed more fully in § 3.05, because of the public nature of their product, evaluators should not gratuitously include material of only marginal relevance in their reports.

However, under limited circumstances having to do with protection of the public, the law may *require* the evaluator to provide information beyond that requested by the court order. The clearest situation of this sort is when a statute commands the mental health professional to report certain types of discoveries to the proper authorities. Virtually every state, for instance, provides that specified professionals (including clinicians) who observe or suspect child abuse must notify the appropriate agency, even if the information is obtained through a confidential relationship.[63] Similarly, some states have statutes that require clinicians to contact the authorities if patients tell them of plans to commit a crime.[64]

(b) The *"Tarasoff* Duty*"*

A separate legal development, in the courts rather than the legislatures, has created the possibility of significant monetary liability for the clinician who concludes, or should have concluded, that the person evaluated is dangerous. In the famous case of *Tarasoff v. Regents of the University of California,*[65] the Supreme Court of California imposed a duty upon therapists to take preventive measures whenever it would appear to a reasonable and competent therapist that a patient is likely to harm another person in the near future. Applying this rule to the facts in *Tarasoff,* the court found that the two therapists involved could be sued by the family of a woman who was killed by one of their patients, on the ground that they had failed either to inform the victim that the patient had threatened to harm her or to take other measures to protect the victim.

Only a handful of states explicitly follow *Tarasoff,*[66] and only one court has applied its reasoning to evaluations.[67] A few states have expressed reservations about recognizing a *Tarasoff* duty in *any* clinical context.[68] Thus, in many jurisdictions, whether *Tarasoff* applies is open to question.

If *Tarasoff* does apply to therapists, the argument that it does not apply to evaluators is weak. Under the common law, a person does not normally have a legal obligation to help another unless he or she stands in a "special relationship" to that person. The *Tarasoff* court found that the therapist has such a special relationship not only with any patients whom he or she may be treating, but also toward the potential victims of such patients. The court was willing to extend the special-relationship rationale to a third party, despite confidentiality concerns, in part because the therapist's involvement with the party's potential assailant is "significant," and in part because, according to the court, the therapist possesses expertise in predicting who may be violent. The evaluator does not have as much contact with the subject of an evaluation as a therapist does with a patient; on the other hand, the evaluative relationship is hardly a casual one, given the length of time necessary for a comprehensive evaluation and the intimacy that may develop during such an assessment. And although there is currently some question over whether any mental health professional is adept at predicting dangerousness [see § 7.10], to the extent that such expertise does exist, there is little reason to distinguish between a therapist and an evaluator in this regard. Moreover, it is arguable that, given the minimal degree of confidentiality associated with evaluations, there is even less reason to refrain from disclosure than there is in the therapeutic context.

If *Tarasoff* is applied to evaluations, what type of obligation does it impose on the evaluator? First, the court that decided *Tarasoff* later held that no duty exists unless the potential victim is specifically identified; threats directed at groups or "types" of individuals are too amorphous to trigger any legal obligation on the part of the clinician.[69] Second, contrary to popular perception, *Tarasoff* did not create an automatic "duty to warn" the potential victim if and when the victim is identified. The court recognized several alternatives to a warning, including notification of the police and commitment of the individual—in short, any steps reasonably necessary under the circumstances. Unlike the typical pa-tient in therapy, a person being evaluated is usu-ally already in custody. Therefore, if such a per-son is suspected of future violence, the clinician's *Tarasoff* duty may be met merely by notifying the court or the custodial agency of this suspicion. If the individual is not in custody, on the other hand, other measures, including commitment, should be considered in addition to notification of the court. Standard 7-3.2(b) of the ABA's Criminal Justice Mental Health Standards sug-gests that when the evaluation is initiated by the defense attorney, the attorney should be notified of any imminent risk to self or others posed by the defendant, and that if the evaluation is initi-ated by the court or prosecution, both the court and the defense attorney should be notified.

There is evidence to suggest that *Tarasoff* has inhibited the therapeutic process and that apply-ing its rule to either the therapeutic or evalua-tive context does more harm than good.[70] On the other hand, the American Psychiatric Asso-ciation has indicated it may be proper to hold a psychiatrist liable for "flagrantly negligent" fail-ures to protect others from harm.[71] It is impos-sible to predict at this early date what those states outside of those that have already considered the issue will decide with respect to either therapy or evaluations. In states where the law is indefi-nite, professional evaluators are probably best advised to act as if they were in a *Tarasoff* juris-diction, remembering that disclosure should oc-cur only when there are sufficient indications of dangerousness to lead a competent clinician rea-sonably to conclude the individual will act out violently toward a specific person, and that only the information that is necessary to prevent the foreseen dangerous act should be divulged.

(c)　The Nonprotection Afforded by Clinician–Patient Privileges

A final situation that might raise a confidentiality issue is when the evaluator is (or was) also the therapist of the person being evaluated. In this hybrid context, which is not uncommon, the evaluator may feel particularly concerned about the competing duties of confidentiality and obe-dience to the court. As might be expected, the

law gives precedence to the latter duty. A pa-tient may claim that a privileged relationship ex-ists between the therapist/evaluator and the pa-tient, and may attempt to prevent disclosure of at least the information that was obtained during the therapeutic encounter. However, there are several exceptions to the clinician–patient priv-ilege. In civil cases, most jurisdictions hold that patients waive the privilege whenever they have initiated litigation or raised a defense that might involve the issue of their mental status (although some states abrogate the privilege only if the benefit to be gained by the disclosure outweighs its negative effects).[72] In criminal cases, the priv-ilege is even less useful. A small number of states follow the balancing approach just described; most, however, simply state the privilege is not avail-able. Thus, in the typical case, the therapist or the therapist *cum* evaluator can usually be re-quired to reveal what has been learned about the individual through therapy. The only recourse in the face of a subpoena for records or testimony is to argue that the adverse effects of disclosure outweigh the benefits or that the material sought is irrelevant to the pending litigation.

As should be obvious from the discussion above, common law and statutory principles, unlike constitutional dictates, may tend to dis-courage communication between the clinician and the subject. The problem is exacerbated if the clinician feels ethically compelled to "warn" the person being evaluated of the potential for dis-closure to third parties—an issue taken up in § 3.05.

(d)　Informed Consent and Negligent Misdiagnosis

Although it is extremely unlikely, the evaluator may be sued for damages on a number of other claims arising out of civil tort law. The two most probable such claims, and the only two to be discussed here, are informed consent and negli-gent misdiagnosis.

(1)　The Informed Consent Doctrine

If a doctor treats a competent individual in a nonemergency situation without obtaining that person's consent, then the doctor is liable for battery and any damages resulting from the treatment. In order both to define what constitutes a valid consent and to encourage consensual treatment, courts developed the doctrine of "informed consent." Recently, the doctrine has become relatively sophisticated. As discussed in detail in § 11.02(a), it requires, in the *treatment* context, that the clinician provide the patient with as much information about the proposed treatment technique as is therapeutically possible; that the consent not be "coerced"; and that the individual from whom consent is sought be competent or have a guardian protecting his or her interests.[73]

The relevance of the doctrine to the *evaluation* process is minimal in the typical case, since the evaluation is court-ordered and will proceed whether the subject wants it or not; in fact, as noted earlier, in criminal cases the defendant may risk sanctions upon a refusal to cooperate. However, if the evaluator decides to use evaluation techniques other than the usual verbal or written question-and-answer modes, the doctrine may come into play. For example, before administering sodium amytal to an individual [see § 6.05(a)(3)], the subject should be told of the possible dangers of the drug, and the clinician should make sure that any consent obtained is given intelligently and voluntarily. Otherwise, the clinician might be held liable for any harm caused by the procedure, even if it is performed in a competent manner.

(2)   Negligent Misdiagnosis

Generally, a mental health professional is not liable for negligent misdiagnosis unless the failure to diagnose correctly a patient results in the administration of the wrong treatment and subsequent harm. The standard for deciding what is negligent usually focuses on customary practices of those who practice locally.[74] It is conceivable, although unlikely, that a person who was found "incompetent," "insane," or "dangerous" (or "competent," "sane," or "not dangerous") on the basis of a professional's testimony might sue the professional on the ground that the clinician's opinion was arrived at negligently and that it caused harm. However, it is probable that, as

discussed in § 3.04(a), absent a showing of bad faith, clinicians would be given immunity from such a suit if their information or opinions were the result of a court order. Several states grant clinicians who testify at commitment hearings absolute immunity from claims based on their hearing testimony.[75]

3.05.   Ethical Considerations in the Evaluation Process

(a)   Introduction

In addition to the legal principles of which the forensic examiner must be aware, a variety of ethical principles are implicated in evaluations for the courts. In some instances the ethical concerns parallel those issues raised by the legal principles discussed above; in others, the ethical considerations impose additional constraints on the examiner. Because of the complexity of the issues raised in forensic evaluations, the various practical, ethical, and legal considerations are not always "in sync," and forensic examiners may find themselves faced with contradictory, conflicting, and seemingly irreconcilable demands on their behavior in the process of conducting evaluations. This section deals primarily with the ethical issues that are implicated in conducting the forensic evaluation. Additional ethical issues arise for mental health professionals in their roles as expert witnesses; these are discussed in Chapter 14.

Presently, there is no uniform set of professional or ethical standards that all mental health professionals are obliged to follow. The governing bodies of the various mental health disciplines—medicine, nursing, psychology, and social work—have independently established ethical guidelines for their respective members. This section discusses several primary ethical concerns that arguably apply across disciplines; it does not attempt an analysis comparing and contrasting the ethical codes of the various professions, and thus avoids digressions to address minute differences between disciplines. Primary resource material for this section includes principles,[76] standards,[77] and recommendations promulgated by the American Psychological Association. Through discussion and example, our objective is to raise the consciousness of examiners regarding ethical issues that arise in the context of forensic evaluations, and to encourage ethical evaluation practices.

(b) The Caregivers' Dilemma: Who Is the Client?

Both by training and by the socializing forces within mental health practice, clinicians are predisposed to be helpers. The focus of evaluation and treatment is typically on the individual, and the objective is on the individual's personal psychological growth or well-being. Alleviation of anxiety, depression, or other subjective symptoms of psychological distress, and the extrication from or improved skills for coping with stressful situations, are among the primary therapeutic concerns of the caregiving professional. It could be argued that members of the helping professions have an ethical obligation to orient their evaluation procedures toward outcomes that foster the psychological growth and well-being of the individuals being examined.

For clinicians strongly committed to this perspective, participation in forensic evaluations may pose a dilemma. In child custody proceedings, for example, the dilemma may lie in providing data and recommendations that potentially enhance the well-being of one or more family members at the cost of increased psychological discomfort for others. In guardianship proceedings, the clinician's assessment may indicate that a conservator be appointed to protect an elderly person's accumulated material resources, possibly at the expense of that individual's sense of autonomy, competence, or self-worth. In capital sentencing proceedings, a clinician's findings regarding the offender's potential for future violent behavior may be pivotal in the jury's decision to invoke the death penalty. Due to the complexity of issues raised in forensic evaluations and to the conflicting interests of the social institutions and the individuals involved, it may be the exception, rather than the rule, that a mental health professional can undertake a fo-

rensic evaluation and feel confident that he or she will be able to adhere faithfully to the "helping ethic."

One solution is for mental health professionals to decline to perform forensic evaluations. They can limit their practice to those diagnostic and therapeutic endeavors designed to identify and relieve psychological disturbance in clients. Alternatively, clinicians may choose to perform only certain types of evaluations. Obviously, they should refuse to perform forensic evaluations for which they lack adequate training.[78] More problematically, they may also refuse to conduct assessments if they consider the intended application of the evaluation data to be an immoral one (e.g., applying assessments of dangerousness to death penalty considerations).

Another solution to the caregivers' dilemma has been proposed by Diamond and Louisell,[79] who suggest that mental health professionals perform evaluations only for the defense. The results of these assessments are protected by the attorney–client privilege, which can be invoked to prevent disclosure of findings inconsistent with the legal disposition sought by the individual.

Problems with this proposal are readily identified. First, the proposal does not coincide with the state of the law. As pointed out in § 3.02(a), institutional policy or statutory requirements may, and usually do, make the results of an evaluation performed in the hospital available to both parties, even when the evaluation is requested by the defendant. And, as noted in § 3.03(b), jurisdictions following *Edney* may still require the defense-retained expert to testify, even when the expert's findings would not support the disposition being sought by the individual who was evaluated. Second, the proposal is an attempt to impose on society ideals and values held in the community of helping professionals. The legal system, in its struggle to develop procedures for conflict resolution that balance the needs of both society and the individual, has determined that both parties in a legal action should have access to expertise from the medical or behavioral sciences in certain instances. For mental health professionals to subvert the rules by universally denying their services to one party would be tantamount to usurping the responsibility of lawmakers to determine how those conflicting interests should best be served. The proposal is an example of what Shah has referred to, in another context, as "ethnocentric zeal," which "seems to demand that the entire society should accept the values and ideologies of psychotherapists."[80]

The most significant problem with the therapeutic perspective, and with Diamond and Louisell's proposal to maintain it, is that it fosters an inaccurate conceptualization of the clinician's role in the legal process through an inappropriate narrowing of focus on the individual as *the* client.

The task force of the American Psychological Association commissioned to study the role of psychology in the criminal justice system found this question—"Who is the client?"—to be of overriding significance.[81] In making recommendations regarding ethical behavior, the first issue addressed by the task force was "questions of loyalty." Following the task force's analysis, it appears to us that a resolution to the caregivers' dilemma stems from the realization that there are numerous situations in which the mental health professional legitimately serves more than one client; the problem then becomes one of recognizing the various legitimate claims on the professional's findings and on establishing priorities. Evaluations for civil and criminal courts are instances in which the clinician's loyalties may be legitimately divided between the judicial system and the individual, and the primary goal of assessment is not to assure the individual's optimal psychological adjustment or well-being, but to assist the courts in making fully informed dispositional decisions.

To state it differently, there is no conflict with the helping ethic in situations where there is no explicit or assumed understanding that the examiner–individual relationship is primarily a therapeutic one. Thus, the first priority for the forensic examiner is one of clarifying, for each party having a claim on his or her professional services, the nature of the relationship to each of the other parties. A second but obviously related ethical issue is the confidentiality of information obtained in the evaluation process; in most instances, the issue of divided loyalties reduces to one of sharing information with various third parties. In dealing with these two primary ethical concerns, however, a variety of others are implicated, including freedom of choice in being evaluated; invasion of privacy; a general ethical mandate to "avoid any action that will violate or diminish the legal or civil rights of clients or of others who may be affected by their actions";[82] and the issue of special competence. These issues are discussed below.

(1)   Clarifying Relationships

When the forensic evaluation is arranged or requested by a third party—which is what is done most of the time, either by an attorney or by the court—the mental health professional has an obligation to clarify for all parties his or her various loyalties and obligations.[83] The party who often knows the least about the contours of the evaluation is the individual to be examined. This is particularly true in cases where the court has ordered an evaluation on the motion of the state or on its own motion. Thus, the mental health professional must be particularly alert to the individual's perception of the evaluation.

It is advisable to begin evaluations by asking persons what their expectations regarding the purpose of an evaluation are and whether or not they have discussed the evaluation with their attorneys. While laws governing state-requested evaluations may make provisions for notice to individuals and their attorneys, in practice this ideal may not be met. In some jurisdictions, individuals may be committed to a state hospital for an evaluation before an attorney has been retained or appointed, or without the opportunity for consultation with counsel. The individuals may have been misled about the real purpose of the commitment by jailors, transport officers, or others, who may inform them that they are going to the hospital for some form of treatment. Others may bring no externally imposed expectations to the evaluation, but they may misperceive clinicians' responsibilities due to stereotypic notions of doctors' or other clinicians' as health services providers who are trusted to have the individuals' best interest as their primary concern.

Thus, the examiner should accept the responsibility to fully inform the person of the purpose and nature of the evaluation procedure.[84] This responsibility must be exercised in all evaluation situations, whether or not the *Miranda* warnings [discussed in § 3.02(f)] apply. Meeting the "fully informed" principle may require, among other things, an explicit statement of the various legal questions to be addressed in the evaluation (e.g., competency to stand trial, presentence evaluation, etc.); identification of all third parties to whom a report will be sent; a discussion of the circumstances in which testimony in court might be required; and a discussion of the implications of possible findings for the individual in terms of future exercise of rights and freedoms. [See the warnings described at the end of § 3.05(b)(2).]

Also implicated here, we feel, is the individual's right to counsel. If the individual has not had an opportunity to confer with counsel about the evaluation, then that should be arranged. If no counsel has been retained or appointed, the mental health professional should go through proper channels to notify the court and defer the evaluation until the opportunity for legal consultation can be arranged. This ethical duty would appear consonant with the Supreme Court's decision in *Estelle v. Smith,* discussed in § 3.03(a).

(2) Confidentiality

A major issue for mental health professionals involved in forensic evaluations is the question of confidentiality.[85] In their traditional role as health services providers, clinicians consider confidentiality to be the paramount issue—so much so that they are reluctant to disclose information obtained from a client even when there are explicit legal[86] or countervailing ethical mandates[87] to do so. But, for reasons that should be obvious by now, such an attitude is not realistic in the forensic context.

There are actually two distinguishable, but related, concerns associated with the issue of confidentiality. One concern is the impact that exceptions to confidentiality may have on the evaluation itself. In therapy, confidentiality is the cornerstone of trust in the relationship. For the

therapist to gain the client's trust and facilitate disclosure of the intimate secrets, fears, fantasies, and experiences that reveal the nature of the problem and provide the substance for a healing interaction, the privacy of such revelations must be assured—some say at all costs.[88] Absent strong assurances of privacy, the client may resist taking the risks of self-disclosure that may be integral to progress in therapy.[89]

Though forensic evaluations are not primarily therapeutic interactions, they are still situations that call for a mental health professional to come to some understanding of the personality and functioning of the individual. A variety of forensic evaluations may involve inquiry into sensitive material that the individual would not ordinarily reveal to a relative stranger. As noted in § 3.02(b), the fact that the information may be further disclosed to specific third parties or discussed in the open forum of a public court may discourage an individual from discussing his or her case openly with the forensic examiner.

The decision to disclose personal material that might later become public is one best made by the individual after being advised by the attorney of the legal implications for both disclosing and witholding information. As noted in § 3.02, risks for disclosure vary, depending on (1) which side has requested the evaluation; (2) the type of evaluation requested; and, in certain criminal contexts, (3) whether the evaluation takes place before or after notice of an intent to use clinical testimony is given. The mental health professional can best facilitate understanding of these risks by ensuring that the individual is informed of these alternatives and has an opportunity to confer with counsel. In a case seen by one of us, the defendant was referred for an evaluation of mental state at the time of the offense after he shot and killed his wife and then shot himself. When informed that the evaluation results might be presented in court at trial if the insanity defense were raised, the defendant elected not to discuss the case with the examiner to avoid what he anticipated would be public humiliation for himself, his children, and the memory of his wife. A preliminary report was submitted, indicating that no substantive findings could be offered and advising that the defendant have further consultation with his attorney to reconsider the desirability of a defense based on mental state. Several weeks later, the defendant returned and the evaluation was completed.

The more difficult cases are those in which the individual gives only partial cooperation, leaving the examiner with a suspicion that the picture is an incomplete one. Often, a forensic evaluation must be completed within time constraints imposed by the court, and the examiner will not have the opportunity to develop a relationship with the individual that might permit secret information to be revealed. The examiner may feel that no report, or only a very qualified report, can be submitted. In fact, either of these is preferable to eliciting more complete information through false promises of confidentiality.

A second concern related to confidentiality is that the information revealed might be used to effect an outcome not desired by the individual. Whether, and to what degree, any assurances of confidentiality can be offered to protect self-incrimination considerations will depend on the applicability of the attorney–client privilege, if any, and the rules of evidence governing testimony by defense-retained witnesses. Mental health professionals retained by the defense in jurisdictions that follow *Alvarez* [see § 3.03(a)] may be able to offer fairly strong assurances of confidentiality; the findings of the evaluation will be made available to the individual's attorney, but to no one else without the individual's consent. In jurisdictions following *Edney* [see § 3.03(a)], such assurances should not be made.

For mental health professionals obligated to report their findings to the court or to the state, assurances of full confidentiality may not ethically be offered. These clinicians should identify all parties to whom reports will be sent and any parties having the power of subpoena to gain access to the full clinical record. If clinicians are aware that it is common practice in the jurisdiction for certain reports to become part of the public record (e.g., competency evaluations) or to be forwarded to other agencies or institutions (e.g., presentence reports), they should advise individuals of this.

As noted in § 3.02, statutes may limit the substance of initial reports to the prosecution; in these jurisdictions, a degree of confidentiality is obtained until the defense places the individual's mental condition at issue in the proceedings. Although such statutes do restrict the use of a person's disclosures, they do not guarantee absolute confidentiality. We take the position that examiners appointed by the state or the court should inform individuals that nothing is entirely confidential. On the other hand, preinterview notifications are not intended to discourage an individual's participation, particularly where protections for confidentiality or Fifth Amendment concerns exist. The following sample notification statements are suggested for use prior to competency and insanity evaluations in jurisdictions that provide the type of Fifth and Sixth Amendment protection we have advocated earlier in this chapter.

COMPETENCY EVALUATION: I will be asking you questions concerning your relationship with your attorney and your understanding of the legal process. Any information you reveal will be disclosed to your attorney, the court, and the prosecutor, either through a written report or my testimony, or both. It may be used by the judge to determine whether you are able to stand trial or plead to your charges. However, it cannot be used to secure a conviction against you during trial or during plea bargaining. You also have the right to have your attorney present during this evaluation. If you refuse to cooperate during this evaluation, or your attorney prevents you from cooperating, the court may hold you in contempt, which could result in further confinement.

EVALUATION OF MENTAL STATE AT THE TIME OF THE OFFENSE: I will be asking you questions concerning your present mental state and certain aspects of your past life, in particular the time period of the alleged offense. [Choose option 1, 2, or 3. (1) Defense-employed evaluator in *Alvarez* jurisdiction: Any information you reveal will be disclosed only to your attorney unless you and your attorney decide to use me as an expert witness to support an insanity defense or a similar defense. In that case, the information will form the basis for a report sent to the court and the prosecution, and if your case goes to trial, it will form the basis for any testimony I give as well. (2) Defense-employed evaluator in *Edney* jurisdiction: Any information you reveal will be disclosed only to your attorney unless you and your attorney decide to raise an insanity defense or a similar defense. In that case, the information may form the basis for a report sent to the court and the prosecution, and, if your case goes to trial, it will form the basis for any testimony I give as well. If you and your attorney decide not to use me to support your case, I may be called by the prosecution to testify against you. (3) State-employed evaluator: Any information you reveal will form the basis for a report sent to your attorney, the court and the prosecution, and, if your case goes to trial, it will form the basis for any testimony I give as well.]

What you say during this evaluation, and what is included in my report and testimony, can only be used to address the issue of your mental state at the time of the offense. The prosecution may not use me or information you give me merely to prove you committed the act you are charged with.

[The state-employed evaluator should then add:] You have the right to have your attorney present during this evaluation. If you do not cooperate during this evaluation, or your attorney prevents you from cooperating, the court may decide to prohibit you from asserting an insanity defense.

In jurisdictions that follow *Tarasoff,* forensic examiners should also consider giving an explicit admonition that evidence of dangerousness toward others may lead to commitment or warnings to those specifically threatened (if the individual is not otherwise in custody) or may have to be disclosed to appropriate authorities (if the individual is in jail at the time of the evaluation). Of course, to the extent that any of the warnings suggested above need to be further explicated, the clinician should do so.

Although warnings in the contexts of competency and insanity evaluations may be the most complex and most important, the clinician should develop similar prefatory remarks for any type of evaluation, whether it be related to sentencing, civil commitment, or custody. Only in this way can the ethical obligations to clarify relationships and the boundaries of confidentiality be met.

(3)   Freedom of Choice to Participate

Mental health professionals have an ethical mandate to acknowledge that individuals have a "freedom of choice with regard to participation" in any assessment procedures.[90] There are two ways in which this assumed freedom of choice may be restricted in forensic evaluations. First, the law may provide for specific sanctions for nonparticipation; for example, as discussed in § 3.02(b), most states have provisions for barring the use of the insanity defense by defendants who fail to cooperate with state appointed examiners. Parenthetically, there may be *de facto* informal sanctions as well for individuals committed to state hospital facilities for evaluation but who refuse to participate. For instance, the courts (or, worse, the clinicians) may decide to let an individual remain in the hospital for an extended period to "think about it," in effect punishing the person for his or her refusal.

Second, freedom of choice to participate may be a moot issue in some situations. For example, an individual referred for evaluation regarding civil commitment on the grounds of mental illness and dangerousness may lawfully be detained on a psychiatric unit, pursuant to an order of protective custody pending evaluation by a mental health professional [see § 8.05(a)]. During such detention, the individual may be observed by nurses and psychiatric aides to voice clearly delusional beliefs and to be combative with staff, thereby providing sufficient behavioral evidence for the clinician's report even if no formal assessment is agreed to. Similarly, during the brief period of explaining to a criminal defendant the purpose of a pretrial competency evaluation, the defendant may appear guarded, may voice presecutory delusions involving his or her attorney as a central figure, and may provide evidence of other mental disturbance sufficient to indicate a compromised ability to reasonably assist counsel.

The ethically proper course of action when the individual refuses to cooperate is not clear. If, as in the examples above, an evaluation of some sort can be completed and a report generated from the informal data, the question remains: Should the clinician offer a report of the findings? Clinicians who take a strong stance favoring the individual's right to nonparticipation may view the submission of a report based on informal observation and third-party data as unethical. At an emotional level, such a position is easier to maintain with clients who appear relatively undisturbed than it is in cases where individuals are babbling incoherently or engaging in self-injurious behavior. Others may feel that there is no ethical dilemma in submitting a report or testifying in cases where informal observation and third-party data provide adequate and potentially useful information to the attorney or to the court.

When the individual has been informed of the purpose and nature of the evaluation and has declined to participate, we recommend the following course of action, which overlaps partially with recommendations already made. First, advise the person of any known sanctions that may be imposed as a result of a refusal (e.g., a prohibition of the insanity defense). Second, arrange for the individual to talk with his or her attorney for further explanations or guidance. Third, advise the individual whether or not a report may be sent anyway and of the implications of the refusal for the completeness or validity of the report. Fourth, take precautions against the use of undue pressure of "scare tactics" to coerce the individual's participation (e.g., threats by any staff members that "You're going to stay in seclusion until you talk to the doctor!"). If a report is ultimately sent, the fact of the individual's noncooperation should be clearly stated, and any inferences drawn by the clinician from the refusal or reasons for the refusal should be indicated. Appropriate qualifications regarding the completeness or validity of the findings should also be included.

(4)　Invasion of Privacy

Whether a referral is for a voluntary or involuntary evaluation, orders for forensic evaluation do not constitute a *carte blanche* license for examiners to do with individuals what they will. Clinicians have an ethical responsibility to "avoid undue invasion of privacy."[91] In respecting the individuals' right to privacy, forensic clinicians must be careful to avoid two types of intrusions: (1) seeking or obtaining clinical information not relevant to the referral question, and (2) addressing forensic issues not raised in the referral order. Where forensic evaluations are conducted

on an inpatient basis at a psychiatric hospital, mental health professionals must also be alert to the efforts of overzealous staff who attempt to make available to the examiner information that the persons being evaluated might not voluntarily disclose.

The first problem is pertinent to the clinician's choice of evaluation procedures and techniques. As noted in § 3.05(b)(2), there are many situations in which a clinician may have to delve into personal, secret, and sensitive material with an individual. However, there are some forensic referral questions that are appropriately addressed in a more straightforward manner. The assessment of competency to stand trial [see Chapter 4] is a good example. The dual focus in a competency assessment is the defendant's ability to understand the nature and object of courtroom proceedings (e.g., that he or she is on trial; that his or her liberty is in jeopardy; that the proceeding is adversarial and that certain parties have explicit roles and responsibilities; etc.) and the defendant's ability to assist counsel in a reasonable manner (e.g., to answer questions with relevant, coherent responses; to choose among alternative courses of action; etc.). In the majority of referrals, the competency assessment can be completed in a relatively short period of time (one to two hours), using a structured interview or assessment procedure designed expressly for competency evaluations. One may question whether a "deep" psychological evaluation is appropriate in such cases. Clinicians who find themselves performing extensive batteries of tests or conducting in-depth, psychodynamically oriented interviews routinely might well explore their motivations for doing so, particularly if the referral question is one that can be addressed more directly.

By judiciously selecting evaluation procedures and techniques, clinicians can fulfill their professional obligation to assist individuals in limiting disclosures only to that information required in order to answer the referral question.[92] There are situations, however, in which some censorship of information may be advisable even when it *is* relevant. This occurs most commonly in evaluations of criminal offenders who reveal information protected by the Fifth Amendment [see § 3.02]. One situation not discussed earlier involves defendants who, in the course of the clinical interview, admit their involvement in other, as yet unsolved, crimes. While such information may be relevant to establishing a clinical diagnosis (e.g., antisocial personality) or in making an appraisal of, for example, violent tendencies, we recommend—in view of both privacy and Fifth Amendment considerations—that clinicians exercise caution in their manner of documentation and disclosure to avoid becoming unwitting agents of the prosecution in establishing new charges against the individual. Rather than detailed descriptions of previous assaults, global statements such as "The defendant reported being involved in three prior fights in which weapons were used" may suffice for the needs of the present evaluation and will avoid unnecessary betrayal of the client by the examiner.

The second aspect of invasion of privacy involves applying the evaluation findings or inferences to legal issues other than those about which the individual was informed. This was the problem in *Estelle v. Smith,* in which clinical information was obtained ostensibly for a competency determination prior to a capital murder trial, but was later introduced at the sentencing phase. Clinicians may violate the individual's right to privacy by soliciting cooperation in addressing one question and then applying the findings to a different one. (This ethical issue overlaps with the issue of confidentiality, with the obligation to "fully inform," with the respect for "freedom of choice to participate," and with Fifth Amendment concerns.)

In particular, mental health professionals employed in state facilities may experience administrative pressure to violate this ethical consideration. In one case, an individual was committed by the court for an evaluation of competency to stand trial. A comprehensive interdisciplinary evaluation was completed, in accordance with hospital policy; it included a psychiatric mental status examination, ratings by a psychologist using the Competency to Stand Trial Assessment Instrument, and a social history study. Furthermore, extensive information about the defendant's behavior at the time of the offense was

available in the form of the police investigation report, which included statements of several eyewitnesses. After the competency evaluation was completed, the defendant was discharged from the hospital and transported back to the county jail, which was located quite some distance from the hospital. At a later date, the prosecutor requested an amended report to include the clinical staff's opinion ragarding mental state at the time of the offense. Considering the imminent court date, the significant expense of recommitting the patient, and the fact that most of the required information was already available, the hospital administrator directed the evaluation team to prepare an amended report as requested by the prosecutor. This directive led to a major confrontation with the clinical staff, who refused to submit a report because the defendant had not been advised of this possible use of the clinical data at the time of the evaluation.[93]

Clinicians may avoid problems of this type by seeking confirmation, early in the referral procedure, of all forensic issues to be addressed [see § 14.02(a)]. The court or the attorneys may intend that the evaluation address other questions or provide general clinical information beyond what would be obtained by adhering literally to the order. In such cases, amended orders can be obtained, or the examiner may provide a much broader "notification of rights" to the individual to insure that all intended uses of the data are explained. Where the individual has not been informed of a particular use for the evaluation findings, however, it would appear to be a clear breach of ethics to submit amended reports, as in the example above.

Finally, in inpatient evaluation settings, mental health professionals must be alert to invasions of privacy by overzealous staff members who might inappropriately seize personal items of an individual—letters or other written documents, for example—and secure them for the clinicians to review in completing the evaluation. Consistent with privacy considerations and respect for the individual's right to volunteer or withhold information of a personal nature, personal items should be returned to the patient and should not be examined or used by the forensic examiner without first obtaining the patient's permission to do so.

(5) Broader Ethical Considerations

Forensic examiners may also be bound by a broader ethical requirement to "avoid any action that will violate or diminish the legal or civil rights of clients or of others who may be affected by their actions."[94] This is the most difficult ethical mandate for mental health professionals to honor, because it is so sweeping and so vague. Zealous adherence would require that the clinicians be both fully trained in the law, in order to know the full range of legal rights that could potentially be violated, and clairvoyant, in order to perceive the impact of their actions on all others who may be affected. Most forensic clinicians will be neither fully trained lawyers nor clairvoyant, but this principle does imply an obligation to become minimally educated in the nuances of law and legal procedure, for potential violations may be subtle and not readily recognized by conscientious clinicians without such training.

It is impossible to list for the reader the myriad of possible ethical problems that may fall under this broad principle. The following examples, however, provide a sampling of the problems that may be encountered.

Case 1. The facts of the case and the results of the clinical evaluation are consistent in revealing the defendant to have been clearly psychotic at the time of his alleged offense, and there is a strong basis for inferring that the symptoms contributed to the occurrence of the crime. However, there is a differential diagnostic question regarding the etiology of the psychosis: The defendant may have experienced a brief schizophrenic episode, which would permit a finding of "insane"; or his condition may have been drug-induced, and the prevailing statutes explicitly prohibit a finding of insanity if the disturbed mental condition is secondary to drug or alcohol intoxication.

The clinician interviews an individual named by the defendant as his drug supplier, a person who can potentially verify the frequency and quantity of drug usage during the relevant time period. This person, however, is reluctant to answer any questions unless he is given absolute assurances of confidentiality. Can the examiner assure confidentiality to the source? If the examiner refuses to keep the source's identity confidential, he will refuse to answer questions,

and the differential diagnosis may go unresolved. If the examiner guarantees confidentiality and receives important information, the examiner's testimony may be challenged or excluded if he or she fails to provide the full basis for the findings or fails to identify the source for cross-examination. If the examiner reveals the source's identity, then that person may be subjected to increased scrutiny by the police as a drug user–dealer.

Case 2. The clinician examines both parents in a child custody dispute. The father reveals a strong homosexual orientation and his intention to be open and uninhibited in the gay lifestyle in the presence of the child, even though the jurisdiction outlaws open homosexual conduct. The examiner's report supports custody by the mother, based in part on the father's voiced intention to display behavior that is considered against the law.

Should the examiner discuss this basis in her report or in testimony in open court? If she does not, then the court may not be fully informed in reaching its understanding of her findings and recommendations. If the examiner does report the father's sexual orientation, the father may suffer criminal sanctions. There may also be other consequences for the father in terms of sanctions imposed by employers, landlords, or others who do not approve of homosexuality. Can the examiner exert any appreciable control over the potential long-range impact of her revelation of the father's sexual orientation?

Case 3. A defendant is committed for an inpatient evaluation regarding competency to stand trial and mental state at the time of a capital murder. The patient appears floridly psychotic and regressed, with delusional speech, apparent hallucinations, and smearing of feces. The clinician receives a letter from the county jail; included is a photocopy of a handwritten letter signed by the defendant. The letter reads as follows:

Dear Daddy:

How is everything going? I am writing to let you know that I am going to play crazy so that I can get out of jail, but I don't have much time. What I want you to do is go along with my act, so come up here as soon as possible and play like you think they are feeding me something in my food, and please tell the Chief that something is going to have to be done about my condition. And if everything works out, they will send me to the hospital for a year or two and after then I will be free. All the guys locked up with me are going along with my act. Dear Daddy, I might be facing the electric chair and I don't want to die because I have a capital murder case.

Daddy, but for real I am fine, just fine, just go along with my act. But don't say much, just act real worried about me to the Chief. Daddy, once more— I am not going to know anyone, not even you. And Daddy, please pray to the Lord that this works.

How should the clinician treat this letter, which may have been obtained illegally?[95] Should he ignore it (can he truly ignore it)? Suppose the staff was previously convinced that the defendant was truly psychotic: How does the clinician treat this letter in reporting to the court that the defendant is now considered a malingerer? If the court determines that the letter was improperly obtained and may not be used as a basis for opinions about the offender's mental state, can the clinician ethically testify based on the staff's previous, but apparently erroneous, judgment about the defendant's mental state?

Case 4. A patient is referred to a state facility for a pretrial evaluation. The district attorney provides a copy of the complete police investigation report to assist the staff in reconstructing the defendant's probable mental state at the time of the offense—with the express understanding that the report not be made available to the defense.

The defense attorney visits the hospital and talks with the staff about the ongoing evaluation. A staff member alludes to her inferences drawn from material in the police report, and the attorney asks to see any and all documents relied upon by the staff in their evaluation of his client.

How does the clinician respond to this request? Is the district attorney's information protected as privileged information? Is it protected by rules governing discovery? Does the defense attorney have a right to see this material at this time? (From a practical standpoint, will the district attorney *ever* cooperate again if this material is revealed to the defense?)

Case 5. The clinician is asked to perform an evaluation of competency to stand trial for a 39-year-old male with a three-page rap sheet listing prior offenses ranging from property crimes to violent offenses. The defendant married a passive, naive, and dependent woman three months prior to his most recent arrest. The current charge is attempted murder of a police officer; the defendant was shot in the head during a shoot-out at the time of the arrest. Since brain surgery, the defendant has been claiming total retroactive amnesia, as well as transient confusion and disorientation. His wife has earlier reported that he appeared very regressed during recuperation, having to relearn self-care habits (use of toilet, dressing, feeding). Based on the defendant's self-report and the wife's confirmation of his disabled condition, several prior examiners have recommended the defendant as incompetent for trial.

During the present evaluation, the defendant reveals that his wife has filed for divorce. Suspicious that the defendant may have been malingering, the clinician contacts the wife for confirmation of her earlier observations and statements about her husband's behavior during convalescence. The wife is vague about confirming or denying her previous reports; she speaks cautiously and inquires whether her husband might ever learn of her answers to the examiner's questions. The clinician confirms that he may have to make reference to their conversation in disclosing the basis for his ultimate findings. The wife blurts out, "I did what I thought was the right thing to do at the time," but she refused to provide substantive responses to inquiries about her husband's behavior. When pressed, she confesses that the defendant has made threats toward her and her children if she does not "play along with his story."

The clinician concludes that the defendant has been feigning. Should he refer to the conversation with the wife in his report or in testimony? Should the clinician shield the wife from possible retaliation by her husband (or by his friends) by keeping secret the fact of their conversation, or does he have an overriding ethical obligation to explain the full basis for his findings? If he decides to disclose the information obtained from the wife, what actions, if any, should he take to see that the wife is protected?

As these examples illustrate, the forensic examiner may often be caught between conflicting ethical considerations. The obligation to "tell the whole truth" may conflict with the need to shield a confidential informant (Case 1) or a person whose safety may be jeopardized by his or her revelations (Case 5). Information having great significance for the validity of a clinical appraisal may have been illegally obtained or may be inadmissible in court (Case 3). Clinical information made public in court testimony may lead to further civil and legal complications over which the examiner may have little or no control (Case 2). Divided loyalties mean conflicting claims on the clinician's sources of information, with legal rules governing admissibility, discovery, and privilege, as well as ethical considerations of confidentiality, clashing together (Case 4).

As a general principle, the clinician should not be deterred from collecting as much information as possible and from reporting as much of that information as is relevant to the issue being addressed. But, as the examples above illustrate, values other than relevance can upset implementation of this simple rule. Moreover, relevance itself is a flexible concept. Prior unreported crimes are very relevant to a prediction of dangerousness [see § 7.10], but can probably be left out of an insanity report and are immaterial to most competency evaluations. How important is the Father's homosexuality in the custody determination in Case 2?

Not all situations involving conflicting ethical–legal issues can be brought to an ideal resolution. Mental health professionals are obligated to do what they can to resolve these conflicting situations, and there are some resources that can be called upon for assistance. Clinicians may request advisory legal opinions from the attorney general's office regarding the priority of conflicting legal principles (as in Cases 3 and 4). They may refer ethical quandaries (as in Cases 1 and 5) to the ethics committee of the appropriate state or national professional organization for advice. Preliminary hearings can make clear what types of evidence (like that involved in Case 3) may be relied upon in court. Once in court, a clinician may appeal to the judge's discretionary power to clear the courtroom if material considered particularly sensitive, private, or damaging is to be discussed (as in Cases 1, 2, and 5). Discussion of difficult cases with colleagues may reveal new ways of thinking about a problem or help in setting priorities.

Where situations of ethical–legal conflict exist, clinicians must ultimately establish some priorities in order to select a course of action. Though few, if any, immutable principles can be derived to guide clinicians through the ethical and legal mazes they may encounter, we believe that the following general guidelines are reasonable ones that may help in establishing priorities. First, the physical welfare of the individual being examined must be given overriding consideration. Whatever rights or privileges the person may be entitled to exercise or pursue, they all assume the integrity of the person's physical well-being. There is room within both the legal guidelines and the ethical requirements for forensic examiners to attend to personal health and safety concerns, regardless of how their own allegiances are divided. Similarly, when an examiner discovers that the client may cause serious harm to others, legal and ethical considerations dictate that the clinician first look to the safety of third parties at risk.[96] Thus, the clinician should consult with the referral source or other appropriate agencies regarding the proper action whenever the subject of the evaluation appears imminently dangerous to others or suicidal.

When health or physical welfare considerations are not at issue, then perhaps the phase of the legal proceeding itself can best help the examiner establish priorities. Given the importance of the Fifth Amendment and the elaborate legal structure that protects Fifth Amendment rights, the examiner might consider the primary client to be the individual being examined *until* that person's state of mind officially becomes the subject of court inquiry. As implied in § 3.02, even forensic examiners retained by the state ought to protect individuals from self-incrimination, by submitting only broad, general reports prior to the defense attorney's actually placing the person's mental state into question. Beyond that point, the forensic clinician's primary obligation is to the trier of fact, to whom must be communicated as clearly and objectively as possible the clinical findings that may be relevant to the legal issue at hand, fending off the efforts of both parties to slant, bias, or misrepresent the findings to fit their own needs.

(c) A Summary: Competence in Forensic Practice

We have stressed in Chapter 1 that mental health professionals need special training to be competent forensic practitioners. It is not necessary that such clinicians be lawyers, nor is it particularly desirable. However, the present discussion reiterates the earlier point about specialized training: Forensic examiners need to be sensitive to a variety of legal principles and procedures, as well as to their own code of professional ethics, and to possible conflicts that arise in conducting and reporting forensic evaluations. This chapter's subtitle—"The Mental Health Professional as Double Agent"—alludes to the abandonment of the traditional therapist's role and the assumption of divided loyalties. Forensic examiners who conduct evaluations without careful consideration of the legal and ethical implications of their actions may truly become "double agents" in the worst sense of the term: They may offer, and then betray, the confidence of their clients.

Table 3-1 outlines a series of steps that clinicians may follow to help ensure that proper attention is paid to important legal and ethical is-

Table 3-1
Steps to Ensure Ethical Evaluation Procedures

Stage of Evaluation	*Relevant Text*
I. Preevaluation	
A. Obtain any necessary clarification of ambiguous or overly general referral orders.	§ 3.05(b)(1); § 14.02(a)
B. In obtaining necessary third-party information, decline to review information *known* to have been illegally obtained that may jeopardize the admissibility of the evaluation report.	§ 3.05(b)(5)
II. During clinical evaluation	
A. Notify the person of all legal issues to be addressed in the evaluation.	§ 3.05(b)(1)
B. In those few situations in which a legal right to remain silent pertains, inform the person using *Miranda* language.	§ 3.02 [especially (f)]
C. If necessary, notify defense attorney of evaluation and the referral source.	§ 3.03(a); § 3.05(b)(2)
D. Advise the person of limited confidentiality associated with the particular evaluation issue(s).	§ 3.04; § 3.05 (b)(2)
1. Identify persons or agencies to whom reports may be sent.	
2. Identify possible legal proceedings in which testimony might be given.	
3. Advise the person of other known uses of the clinical report (e.g., presentence report routinely sent on to the Department of Corrections Parole Board).	
4. (Optional) Administer explicit *Tarasoff* warnings.	
E. Clarify your own role as that of evaluator; dispel any preconceived notions the person may have that you are there in a therapeutic capacity.	§ 3.05(b)(1)
F. Request the person's participation in the evaluation and advise him or her of any known sanctions if participation is declined.	§ 3.05(b)(3)
G. Respect privacy interests and Fifth Amendment concerns in the evaluation.	§ 3.05(b)(3),(5)
1. Keep clinical inquiry within the boundaries of the referral question.	
2. Do not gratuitously address legal or clinical issues not contained in the referral order.	
3. Assist the person in limiting disclosure of information not relevant to the present evaluation.	
III. Postevaluation	
A. Let *relevance* be the guide in determining the content and degree of detail in written reports and in testimony.	§ 3.05(b)(2),(5); § 14.03(b)(2)
1. Avoid detail that might unnecessarily embarrass the person or result in jeopardizing other rights.	
2. Refrain from moral–legal conclusions that are properly the responsibility of the factfinder to draw.	§ 1.04; § 14.05
B. In *Tarasoff* situations, notify the referral source (attorney, court) of the existing threat.	§ 3.04(b); § 3.05(b)(2)

sues discussed in this chapter and in other portions of the text. This outline is offered as a guide that may help clinicians to avoid some of the conflict situations that have been discussed; however, they should also be familiar with the caveats and countervailing considerations that apply at each step, and to this end citations to relevant portions of the text are also provided.

BIBLIOGRAPHY

American Psychological Association, *Ethical Principles of Psychologists,* 36 AM. PSYCHOLOGIST 633 (1981).

Estelle v. Smith, 451 U.S. 454 (1981).

Meister, Miranda *on the Couch: An Approach to Problems of Self-Incrimination, Right to Counsel and* Miranda *Warnings in Pre-Trial Psychiatric Examinations of Criminal Defendants,* 11 COLUM. J.L. SOC. PROBS. 403 (1975).

Merton, *Confidentiality and the "Dangerous" Patient: Implications of* Tarasoff *for Psychiatrists and Lawyers,* 31 EMORY L. J. 263 (1982).

Slobogin, Estelle v. Smith: *The Constitutional Contours of the Forensic Evaluation,* 31 EMORY L.J. 71 (1982).

WHO IS THE CLIENT? (J. Monahan ed. 1980).

PART II

The Criminal Process

CHAPTER FOUR

Competency to Stand Trial

4.01. *Introduction*

The "competency" paradigm permeates the law. An individual must be "competent" to enter a contract; otherwise, that contract may be void. A will written by an individual lacking the "competency" to write it may not be admitted to probate. An individual must be "competent" to consent to medical treatment. And, as discussed in this chapter, the state may not subject an "incompetent" individual to trial on criminal charges. In each of these situations, the law seeks to implement a basic premise: that only the acts of a rational individual are to be given recognition by society. In doing so, the law attempts to reaffirm the integrity of the individual and of society generally.

We devote an entire chapter to competency to stand trial because it is by far the most frequently adjudicated competency issue. Other contexts in which competency is an issue in the criminal process are the subject of Chapter 5, while Chapter 9 discusses competency issues arising in civil litigation. In this chapter, we discuss the source of the legal requirement that the individual be competent to stand trial; the current definition of competency to stand trial; the manner in which the issue arises and the myriad

reasons, often unrelated to the defendant's competency, that result in its being raised; the theoretical and actual decisionmakers on the issue; and the consequences of an adjudication of incompetency. The chapter also considers the implications of the competency doctrine for the amnesic defendant and the restoration of competency through medication. Although empirical studies are referred to throughout the chapter when appropriate, a separate research section focuses on those studies most relevant to the competency evaluation—specifically, those describing the characteristics of defendants found incompetent, and those examining the reliability and validity of competency evaluations generally and of the various competency-gauging instruments in particular. The chapter concludes with a discussion of the clinical evaluation of competency to stand trial.

4.02. *The Legal Standard*

This section examines the historical basis for the competency test, its modern formulation, and the attempts made to break down its component parts into functional criteria.

(a) Historic Antecedents

The requirement that an individual must be competent in order to undergo the criminal process originated in the common law, and has been traced at least to the 17th century.[1] The English system of criminal justice incorporated, as does the American system today, a requirement that the defendant plead to the charge prior to trial. Some commentators believe that the concept of "competency" first arose as a reaction by the English courts to defendants who, rather than making the required plea, stood mute. The court in such a case then sought to ascertain whether the defendant was "mute of malice" or "mute by visitation of God." If the individual fell into the first category, the court sought to force a plea by use of a process in which increasingly heavier weights were placed upon the individual's chest. If the individual fell in the latter category, he or she was spared this ordeal. The category "mute by visitation from God" initially included the literally deaf and mute, but over time was expanded to include the "lunatic."[2]

While the requirement that the defendant be competent may have developed as a practical response to a practical problem, it also seems to have its roots in a more general concern that it was simply unfair to subject certain types of individuals to trial. Thus, Blackstone observed that a defendant who before arraignment for an offense "becomes mad, he ought not to be arraigned for it; because he is not able to plead to it with that advice and caution that he ought. And if, after he has pleaded, the prisoner becomes mad, he shall not be tried: for how can he make his defense?"[3] As judicial decisions began formalizing the competency doctrine, the idea that it was unfair to try an individual who lacked the ability to defend himself was maintained. For example, in *Frith's Case,* the court found that trial must be postponed until the defendant "by collecting together his intellects, and having them entire, he shall be able so to model his defense and to ward off the punishment of the law."[4]

American courts, which relied heavily upon English common law both substantively and procedurally,[5] also utilized the competency doctrine. In 1835, for instance, the man who attempted to assassinate President Andrew Jackson was declared unfit to stand trial.[6] In 1899, a federal court of appeals gave the doctrine constitutional status, observing that "it is fundamental that an insane person can neither plead to an arraignment, be subjected to a trial, or, after trial, receive judgment, or, after judgment, undergo punishment; . . . to the same effect are all the common-law authorities . . . It is not 'due process of law' to subject an insane person to trial upon an indictment involving liberty or life."[7] Over the years, the doctrine has retained this constitutional status, with the United States Supreme Court only recently finding the principle that an incompetent defendant may not be tried "fundamental to an adversary system of justice."[8]

As competency law has developed, the underlying value at stake has remained constant: The doctrine is necessary to preserve the essential fairness of the criminal justice system. As one commentator has observed, the defendant must be competent so that (1) the trial or plea hearing will arrive at accurate results ("one who cannot comprehend the proceedings may not appreciate what information is relevant to the proof of his innocence"); (2) the criminal process will be dignified ("the adversary form of the criminal proceeding necessarily rests on the assumption that defendant will be a conscious and intelligent participant; the trial of a defendant who cannot fulfill this expectation appears inappropriate and irrational"); and (3) the imposition of any punishment will be morally justified ("in part there is the notion that the state is justified in imposing sanctions only where there is a possibility that the person convicted will realize the moral reprehensibility of his conduct").[9]

Probably the most important basis for the competency rule is the second one listed above. Ideally, the criminal process should provide a trial between adversaries as evenly matched as possible. It was in recognition of the fact that this was often not the case that the Supreme Court handed down its well-known criminal law decisions of the 1960s, which guaranteed defendants the rights to be represented by counsel, to confront their accusers, and to present witnesses on their own behalf. However, this entire process posits a defendant able to *participate* in his or her own defense. Without the competency doctrine, the rights afforded would be useless for at least some individuals, and the process itself would be a sham.

(b) Current Formulation of the Competency Test

The United States Supreme Court, in the case of *Dusky v. United States*,[10] established the modern legal definition of competency to stand trial. The Court held that "the test must be whether he [the defendant] has sufficient present ability to consult with his attorney with a reasonable degree of rational understanding and a rational as well as factual understanding of proceedings against him."[11] Since this test sets forth the constitutional standard for determining competency, it is the basis today of all state statutes.[12] While the Court did not amplify the meaning of this language, the test enunciated suggests that competency to stand trial has several core elements.

First, competency assesses the defendant's *present* ability to consult with counsel and to understand the proceedings. It therefore differs fundamentally from the test for criminal responsibility, which is a *retrospective* inquiry focusing on the defendant's state of mind at the time of the offense.

Second, the test focuses on the defendant's *capacity,* not willingness, to relate to the attorney and understand the proceedings. The defendant who refuses to talk to the attorney even though capable of doing so is making a rational choice knowing the consequences. Unless the lack of motivation is based on irrational factors, thereby calling into question one's capacity to assist in one's defense, it is not ground for an incompetency finding.

Third, the requirement that the defendant possess a "reasonable" degree of understanding suggests that the test as applied to a particular case is a flexible one. "Perfect" or complete understanding on the part of the defendant will not be required—in fact, most observers agree that the threshold for a finding of competency is not particularly high.[13]

Fourth, the emphasis on the presence or absence of "rational" and "factual" understanding suggests an emphasis on cognitive functioning. It is important to note that the test equates neither mental illness nor the defendant's need for treatment with lack of competency. Indeed, the presence of mental illness is relevant only insofar as that illness affects one's "rational understanding" as one consults with counsel and undergoes criminal trial. Thus, the mere fact that a defendant is psychotic does not mean that he or she is incompetent to stand trial; only if the illness impairs the defendant's ability to participate in the defense is the legal test met.

There have been a number of efforts by the courts, by legislative draftsmen, and by clinicians to add content to the rather sparsely worded standard enunciated by the Supreme Court. These efforts typically focus on two generic issues: the defendant's capacity to *understand* the criminal process, including the role of the participants in that process; and the defendant's ability to *function* in that process, primarily through consulting with counsel in the preparation of a defense. For example, one federal court concluded that a defendant will be found competent if the following hold true:

1. The defendant has "the mental capacity to appreciate his presence in relation to time, place, and things."
2. The defendant has "sufficient elementary mental processes to apprehend (i.e., to seize and grasp with what mind he has) that he is in a court of justice, charged with a criminal offense."
3. The defendant understands that there is a judge on the bench.
4. The defendant "understands that a prosecutor is present who will try to convict him of a criminal charge."
5. The defendant "understands that a lawyer will undertake to defend him against that charge."
6. The defendant understands that "he is expected to tell his lawyer the circumstances, to the best of his mental ability (whether colored or not by mental aberration) the facts

surrounding him at the time and place where the law violation is alleged to have been committed."

7. The defendant understands that there will be a jury present to determine guilt or innocence.

8. The defendant "has memory sufficient to relate those things in his own personal manner."[14]

Items 1–5 and item 7 of this list test the defendant's basic understanding of the criminal process and the participants in that process. Items 6 and 8 examine the defendant's ability to function in that context, primarily through communication to counsel of remembered facts (note, however, that amnesia is not generally considered a bar to a finding of competency [see § 4.05(a)]).

As this list makes evident, a great deal of sophistication about criminal process is not required. Rather, the defendant need possess only the most rudimentary understanding. On the other hand, evaluating the defendant's capacity to communicate meaningfully with counsel is more problematic, both because it is a more subjective inquiry and because any problems in the relationship may not necessarily result from the defendant's deficiencies but from problems in the counsel–client relationship. Relevant in this regard is a recent Supreme Court decision, which held that the Constitution does not *guarantee* a "meaningful relationship" between a defendant and his or her attorney, primarily because such a guarantee is impossible.[15] Although this decision was in the context of claims that counsel's assistance was ineffective, it suggests that the Court will not require a particularly high quality of communication between attorney and client.

Most state statutes simply adopt or provide variations on the test announced in *Dusky*. For instance, the Michigan statute[16] directs that "the court shall determine the capacity of one to assist in his own defense by his ability to perform in the preparation of his defense." The New Jersey statute, on the other hand, is very explicit.[17] It is nearly identical to the judicially articulated test noted above. The standard proposed by the American Bar Association (ABA) uses the *Dusky*

language to define competency,[18] but the commentary to the standard stresses that evaluation of the issue should focus on the defendant's skills relative to trial rather than the defendant's general mental condition.[19]

Table 4-1
List of Items Relevant to Competency to Stand Trial

Competency to Stand Trial may involve the ability of a defendant:

1. To understand his current legal situation.
2. To understand the charges against him.
3. To understand the facts relevant to his case.
4. To understand the legal issues and procedures in his case.
5. To understand legal defenses available in his behalf.
6. To understand the dispositions, pleas, and penalties possible.
7. To appraise the likely outcomes.
8. To appraise the roles of defense counsel, the prosecuting attorney, the judge, the jury, the witnesses, and the defendant.
9. To identify the locate witnesses.
10. To relate to defense counsel.
11. To trust and to communicate relevantly with his counsel.
12. To comprehend instructions and advice.
13. To make decisions after receiving advice.
14. To maintain a collaborative relationship with his attorney and to help plan legal strategy.
15. To follow testimony for contradictions or errors.
16. To testify relevantly and be cross-examined if necessary.
17. To challenge prosecution witnesses.
18. To tolerate stress at the trial and while awaiting trial.
19. To refrain from irrational and unmanageable behavior during the trial.
20. To disclose pertinent facts surrounding the alleged offense.
21. To protect himself and to utilize the legal safeguards available to him.

Note. From GROUP FOR THE ADVANCEMENT OF PSYCHIATRY, MISUSE OF PSYCHIATRY IN THE CRIMINAL COURTS: COMPETENCY TO STAND TRIAL 896–97 (1974). Reprinted by permission of Group for the Advancement of Psychiatry.

In addition to the efforts of judges and legislators, clinicians have developed a number of checklists and tests designed to assist the clinician in the actual evaluation of competency. For instance, the Group for the Advancement of Psychiatry, composed primarily of psychiatrists, has derived a 21-item list from existing test instruments [see Table 4-1]. It has cautioned, however, that the list is meant only to identify areas of inquiry and should not leave the impression that "enormous legal sophistication is required of both psychiatrist and defendant."[20] Other instruments developed for use by clinicians are discussed in § 4.06(b). Central to all of these tests is an emphasis on examining specific dysfunction related to the defendant's understanding or ability to understand the legal process and the roles of the participants to that process, as well as to the capacity to exercise certain skills in the preparation of his defense.

In sum, it is important to remember that competency to stand trial is concerned with *present* levels of functioning; that a finding of mental illness or need for treatment is not analogous to, or necessarily even relevant to, a finding of incompetency to stand trial; and that the legal test, while sketchy, is concerned with the level of the defendant's cognitive functioning and its impact upon his or her ability, as opposed to willingness to understand and participate meaningfully in the criminal process.

4.03.　Procedural Issues

The issue of the defendant's competency to stand trial may be raised at any point in the criminal process. While it is raised most typically prior to trial, the defendant's competency may become an issue during trial if a question arises as to the individual's ability to participate in the proceedings.

(a)　Who May Raise the Issue?

The defense attorney most frequently raises the issue of competency.[21] However, in most juris-

dictions, the issue may be raised on motion either by prosecution or defense, or by the court *sua sponte* (on its own motion).

There has been much debate over the propriety of prosecution-initiated examinations. There is a concern that such examinations may occur without the knowledge of defense counsel, or even prior to appointment of counsel for the defendant, thereby prejudicing the constitutional right of the defendant to counsel and the right to avoid self-incrimination [see § 3.02(a)]. As a result, the American Psychiatric Association has instructed its members that they have an ethical obligation not to perform a competency examination prior to the appointment of defense counsel, and that the examiner should ascertain that defense counsel is aware that the examination is being conducted.[22] The ABA standards provide similar protection.[23] This suggests, as discussed in § 3.05(b)(1), that the clinician asked to evaluate competency should ascertain immediately whether the defendant has counsel; if not, the examiner should indicate to the referral source that the examination must be deferred until counsel is obtained.

(b)　The Standard for Raising the Issue

The United States Supreme Court has ruled that the trial court must order an inquiry into competency if a "bonafide doubt" exists as to the defendant's competency.[24] The Court has made clear that in making its decision the trial court must take into account and weigh any factor suggestive of mental illness. For example, in *Drope v. Missouri,* where the defendant's wife testified concerning his "strange behavior" and where the defendant on the second day of trial shot himself in an attempted suicide, the Court ruled that a competency exam should have been ordered and suggested that the threshold for obtaining evaluation on the issue of competency is not very high:

> [E]vidence of defendant's irrational behavior, his demeanor at trial, and any prior medical opinion on competence to stand trial are all relevant in determining whether further inquiry is required, *but even one of these factors*

standing alone may, in some circumstances, be sufficient. There are, of course, no fixed or immutable signs which invariably indicate the need for further inquiry to determine fitness to proceed; the question is often a difficult one in which a wide range of manifestations and subtle nuances are implicated. That they are difficult to evaluate is suggested by the varying opinions trained psychiatrists can entertain on the same facts."[25] (emphasis added)

In practice, a court will rarely refuse a request for a competency examination, if for no other reason than that a refusal may result in reversal of a conviction upon appeal, on the ground that the defendant's constitutional right to due process has been violated. Legal–ethical considerations also exert pressure, upon defense counsel in particular, to raise the issue. For example, the ABA has concluded:

> Defense counsel should move for evaluation of the defendant's competence to stand trial whenever the defense counsel has a good faith doubt as to the defendant's competence. If the client objects to such a motion being made, counsel may move for evaluation over the client's objection.[26]

The commentary to this proposed standard recognizes that a counsel may be reluctant to request an examination for a number of reasons. For example, particularly with a minor offense, the length of commitment for treatment of an incompetent defendant may exceed the potential sentence for the offense if trial proceeds. The commentary concludes nonetheless that defense counsel's "obligation to the court" requires the issue to be raised.[27] The proposed standard reemphasizes a point previously made: Preventing trial of an incompetent defendant is sufficiently important in the criminal law that the system, and those who shape the system, tend to resolve marginal cases by calling for inquiry into the defendant's competency.

(c) Reasons Evaluation Is Sought

Unfortunately, the low threshold for seeking competency evaluations, while justifiable and even necessary from a constitutional perspective, has encouraged misuse of the system. Data on attorney's rationales for referral suggest that the evaluation is often precipitated by concerns that are in some sense illegitimate.

One prominent reason for evaluation is simply attorney ignorance. Rosenberg and McGarry found that only 10 of 28 trial attorneys they interviewed had any knowledge at all of the legal standards for incompetency.[28] Similarly, attorneys (and clinicians) may frequently confuse incompetency with mental disorder per se or with insanity, and may request evaluation of the former when in fact they want an evaluation on the latter issues.[29]

Even when there is no such conceptual confusion, competency evaluation referrals are sometimes used to obtain information relevant to a defense based on the defendant's mental state at the time of the offense or to a dispositional plan. For example, in a questionnaire study of defense attorneys who had referred their clients to Dorothea Dix Hospital in North Carolina for an evaluation of competency to stand trial,[30] almost half indicated that they were actually seeking an opinion as to the defendant's criminal responsibility. They also indicated that they hoped to obtain information relating to disposition. Why do attorneys who understand the law misuse it in this way? In fairness, some states have no procedures for obtaining evaluation of an indigent defendant's mental state at the time of the offense or treatment needs. In other states, however, the procedures for obtaining such evaluations do exist; they appear to be neglected because they are more cumbersome than those associated with obtaining an evaluation of competency to stand trial.

Of more concern than these abuses is evidence suggesting that incompetency referrals are used as a ruse to force treatment of bizarre persons who do not meet dangerousness requirements for civil commitment.[31] Stone has suggested that, when police learn the strictures of "imminent dangerousness" in the context of civil commitment, they are more likely to rely on the criminal justice system to force entry of "crazy" people "disturbing the peace" into the mental health system.[32] When a defendant acts bizarrely or presents management problems in jail, he or she is most readily placed in the mental health system through a request for an evaluation of competency, particularly since the court itself or the prosecution may raise the question. Thus, the sheriff can call the prosecutor or the judge and—with a court order, perfunctorily obtained—can have the defendant transferred from the jail to the mental health system, ostensibly for an evaluation of competency. This circumvents the need to establish that the defendant meets civil commitment standards through a procedure affording due process rights [see Chapter 8]. Such a shortcut through system boundaries is spurious not only because of the insult to defendants' rights.[33] It may also fail on pragmatic grounds. Forensic units may lack clear authority to provide involuntary treatment to defendants admitted for evaluation.[34] Moreover, hospitals may—and should—limit their intervention to the scope of orders for admission. Consequently, defendants should be returned to the jail quickly, immediately after competency is evaluated.

Finally, and perhaps most objectionably, competency referrals may be for purely strategic reasons unrelated to *any* concern with defendants' mental status. Perhaps foremost among these purposes is simply delay. In a case where the alleged offense has created public uproar, defense counsel may succeed in bringing about the defendant's removal from the community until public emotions have calmed by having him or her hospitalized for a competency evaluation. Similarly, if the evidence is weak but the public sentiment for prosecution is strong, prosecutors may have the defendant "put away" for a period through a competency evaluation. The result may be pretrial detention without the opportunity for bail.

The abuses for stategic purposes unrelated to mental status extend beyond delay. In particular, prosecutors may use competency evaluations as a means of discovery. Even if the defendant's statements during a competency evaluation are inadmissible at trial on the issue guilt, they may provide the prosecution with leads in its investigation if information from the evaluation is available to all parties [see § 3.02(a)]. Regardless of whether this is the primary intention, prose-cutors may use competency evaluations effectively to interrogate and investigate defendants in derogation of Fifth and Sixth Amendment protections.

Interestingly, in a survey of North Carolina judges, Roesch and Golding found that judges suspect abuses of the competency referral process, especially by defense attorneys who misunderstand the concept or who merely seek delay.[35] Nonetheless, the majority of judges reported that they routinely grant motions for competency evaluations without requiring evidence that there is cause to raise the issue.

As this brief discussion makes clear, the competency issue may be raised for a variety of reasons unrelated to concern over defendants' competency. Clinicians must be sensitive to the dynamics of the criminal process and the varying impulses that result in referrals. Otherwise, they may become unwitting participants in strategic ploys by one side or the other having nothing to do with competency—the ostensible reason for the referral, and the only issue with which clinicians should be concerned. At the same time, lawyers must assure that their uses of the competency referral conform with its purposes; failure to do so, while perhaps attaining short-term strategic goals such as delay, may result in harm to clients (e.g., through unnecessary confinement in a mental health facility).

(d) The Competency Examination: Situs and Length

After the court grants the motion for an examination into the defendant's competency, regardless of the real reason the examination is sought, one or more clinicians will examine the defendant.

Traditionally, competency examinations were performed by psychiatrists in "remotely located state institutions far from . . . family and community ties"[36] where the defendants were hospitalized for lengthy periods of time, often lasting from one to three months.[37] However, as it became evident that a competency evaluation could be performed adequately in a much shorter period of time and in an outpatient rather than an inpatient setting,[38] states began moving tentatively toward decentralizing their forensic services systems, at least to the point of encouraging if not requiring that competency examinations be performed locally and on an outpatient basis.[39] In addition, states have increasingly authorized psychologists and social workers to perform competency examinations,[40] a development that has facilitated the decentralization of forensic systems by expanding locally available forensic resources.

Defendants' constitutional rights to a speedy trial[41] and to nonexcessive bail[42] also have influenced decisions to rely on outpatient exams conducted by clinicians geographically proximate to the referring court. Since courts are under increased pressure to dispose of cases expeditiously, they may begin to favor outpatient examinations performed locally, which return the defendants to court for trial much more quickly than inpatient examinations conducted to remote facilities. At the present time, however, unnecessary hospitalization persists [see § 4.06(a)].

(e)   The Adjudication of Competency

The determination of the individual's competency is a legal, not a clinical, decision. The clinician simply offers an opinion; the court decides. As one commentary has observed, "[M]edical opinion about the defendant's condition should be only one of the factors relevant to the determination [of competency]. A defendant's abilities must be measured against the specific demands trial will make upon him and psychiatrists have little familiarity with either trial procedure or the complexities of a particular indictment."[43] The courts have emphasized this point. One federal court of appeals noted that "[t]he chief value of an expert's testimony in this field, as in all other fields, rests upon the material from which his opinion is fashioned and the reasoning by which he progresses from his material to his conclusion. . . . The conclusions, the inferences, from the facts, are for the trier of the facts."[44]

Unfortunately, many courts appear to abdicate their role as decisionmaker too readily. State statutes typically call for a court hearing on the issue of competency, but in reality hearings are often not held and defendants are frequently adjudicated incompetent after the parties stipulate to the results of the clinical evaluation.[45] Thus, 59% of North Carolina judges reported that they typically did not hold a formal hearing to assess the evidence as to a defendant's competency; rather, they relied on the clinicians' reported conclusions.[46] Even if a hearing is held, it is likely to be perfunctory. Studies showing judge–clinician agreement to be greater than 90% have been reported in numerous jurisdictions.[47] In fact, the clearest conclusion that can be reached about the nature of the class of incompetent defendants is that its composition is almost entirely dependent upon clinical opinions. That is, whomever examining mental health professionals characterize as incompetent is likely ultimately to be found incompetent.

These data suggest that clinicians should attempt to avoid offering legal conclusions about competency, or, if the court orders otherwise, to couch their conclusions in cautious terms. Moreover, they should include in their reports and testimonies descriptive details about defendants' functioning that will enable the court to reach its own opinions on the issue [see, e.g., the Mills and Premington reports, § 15.02]. At a minimum, clinicians should explain what underlies their diagnoses, in an effort to avoid the undue reliance courts place on diagnoses in reaching what are ostensibly legal conclusions.

4.04. Disposition of the Incompetent Defendant

The response of the legal system to the defendant found incompetent has been sharply criticized. This section examines the typical disposition of the person found incompetent and possible ways of improving the situation.

(a)   The Legal Standard

If the court finds the defendant competent, the criminal process resumes. However, if the defendant is adjudicated incompetent, criminal proceedings are suspended. In some cases, particularly if the defendant is charged with a non-serious offense, the charges may be dropped (or, in the alternative, *nolle prossed*) at that point, in exchange for the defendant seeking treatment as a civil patient. However, if the criminal proceeding is not short-circuited through an arrangement of this type, the defendant is often committed to the public mental health system for treatment.

The stated purpose of such treatment is to restore the individual to competency so that trial may resume. However, until the early 1970s, commitment of an individual as incompetent often resulted in long-term confinement, sometimes for life, in a state maximum security unit.[48] These individuals were literally forgotten by the court system, despite the fact that they were neither tried nor convicted of a crime. In 1972, however, the United States Supreme Court decided *Jackson v. Indiana*.[49] In *Jackson,* the Court confronted the case of a deaf–mute who was found incompetent to stand trial, and who, because of his underlying mental condition, was unlikely ever to be restored to competency. The Court found that Jackson's disposition—indefinite if not lifelong commitment to a mental health facility—violated constitutional equal protection and due process guarantees. The Court held that

> A person charged by a State with a criminal offense who is committed solely on account of his incapacity to proceed to trial cannot be held more than a reasonable period of time necessary to determine whether there is a substantial probability that he will attain the capacity in the foreseeable future. If it is determined that this is not the case, then the State must either institute the customary civil commitment proceedings that would be required to commit indefinitely another citizen or release the defendant.[50]

This decision means that after a "reasonable period of time," the state may retain an incompetent defendant in a hospital only if it finds the individual mentally ill and dangerous to self or others, using the standards and procedures provided for in its civil commitment laws. However, like most of the Court's decisions in this area,

the *Jackson* opinion offers only a general guideline. The Court did not define what is a "reasonable period of time" to determine whether an individual can be restored to competency, nor did the Court define what constitutes a "substantial probability" that competency would be restored. Stone has suggested that in the vast majority of cases six months is sufficient to determine whether the defendant can be restored to competency,[51] a period of time with which others have tended to agree.[52] It should be observed that there is nothing particularly magical about this figure; it simply represents a judgment that competency is restored most frequently through medication, "and that positive responses to medication will occur relatively quickly, if they are to occur at all."[53]

As a result of the *Jackson* decision, many states have revamped their statutes, limiting the length of time that an individual may be confined as incompetent to stand trial. However, not all jurisdictions have acted. Roesch and Golding, for example, found in 1979 that 19 states and the District of Columbia allowed the automatic commitment of incompetent defendants. They also found that once admitted, either under mandatory or discretionary commitment, incompetent defendants could be held indefinitely in 24 states and the District of Columbia. Thus, nearly half of the country's jurisdictions had not responded statutorily to the Supreme Court's stipulation in *Jackson* that defendants not be held for more than a reasonable period of time necessary to determine whether competency will be regained.[54]

(b)   Inappropriate Hospitalization

Even in those states that place a reasonable limit on the length of time a defendant found incompetent can be hospitalized to restore competency, other problems remain. First, it appears that just as those subject to competency evaluation are often unnecessarily hospitalized, those found incompetent as a result of those evaluations may also be needlessly confined. This occurs in large part because many jurisdictions continue to authorize automatic commitment of an individual found incompetent, without first requiring a finding that inpatient hospitalization is necessary. In addition, as Steadman has found,

> Overall, for most incompetent defendants, particularly for those who are not indicted, mental hospitals are simply an alternative place to do time. This is particularly true for the unindicted defendants because so few are subsequently convicted. Just over half of the indicted defendants are eventually convicted. Many do get and serve additional prison time, but many others are given "time-served" sentences in recognition of the length of time they were hospitalized. The detention times of these incompetent defendants make a much stronger case for the use of this diversion as an easy way for the state to detain defendants in very secure facilities without the ordeal of prosecution . . . Certainly . . . it appears that the length of time most of these defendants are off the street is quite similar to what would have resulted had they remained in jail.[55]

One proposal to eliminate the problem of inappropriate hospitalization comes from the ABA, which proposes that inpatient hospitalization of an incompetent defendant be permitted only if the court determines by clear and convincing evidence that

1. there is substantial probability that defendant's incompetence will respond to treatment or habilitation and defendant will attain or maintain competence in the reasonably foreseeable future;
2. treatment or rehabilitation appropriate for the defendant to attain or maintain competence is available in a residential facility; and
3. no appropriate treatment or habilitation alternative is available less restrictive than that requiring involuntary hospitalization.[56]

The ABA also recommends that periodic redeterminations of the defendant's competency occur at intervals not to exceed 90 days.[57] These proposals have much merit, particularly in keeping the attention of the courts, counsel, and those charged with treatment focused upon the issues of competency and the necessity of hospitalization.

(c) The Nondisposition of Criminal Charges

A second problem remaining after *Jackson* is the fact that many of those adjudicated incompetent may not have their criminal charges resolved for significant periods of time, if at all. In *Jackson,* the Supreme Court withheld judgment on the question of when, if ever, the state had to dismiss criminal charges against an individual who was unlikely to be restored to competency. As a result, criminal charges in some cases may remain pending for years while the system waits for the defendants to return to competency. If they are restored, they can be tried on the charges. If the individuals remain incompetent, on the other hand, they could easily continue to be hospitalized as a *result* of the charges. Although under *Jackson* the defendants presumably will eventually be converted to civil status,[58] the fact that the criminal charges have not been dropped may result in their being hospitalized in a secure unit, or in continued extensions of their commitment by hospital staff unwilling to risk the release of criminal defendants.[59]

(d) A Possible Solution: Trying the Incompetent Defendant

This situation and the problem of inappropriate hospitalization generally arise from a dilemma described by Roesch and Golding:

> [I]f [the state] tries and punishes the defendant despite his lack of competency to stand trial, he has been denied due process; if it commits him until he is competent to stand trial, which if he is permanently incompetent, he will never be, he has in effect been punished without trial; and if it finds him incompetent to stand trial yet is not allowed to commit him, he may as a practical matter have been given carte blanche to commit other crimes.[60]

Another commentator has observed that protection of the defendant's constitutional right to due process, which precludes a trial if he or she is not competent, may paradoxically result in the defendant being deprived of other, perhaps equally valuable rights. Unlike the competent defendant, the defendant found incompetent to stand trial may never have his day in court. Potentially lost are the rights to jury trial, to confront opposing witnesses, to call witnesses for the defense, to testify, and to have guilt determined beyond a reasonable doubt. Quixotically, the very insistence by the court on protecting the defendant's due process rights may deprive the defendant of due process of law.[61]

An idea for breaking this logjam, which may be finding growing acceptance, is that of trying the incompetent individual. For example, Burt and Morris[62] would allow a six-month commitment of an incompetent individual. At the expiration of that period, the state either would have to dismiss the charges, with continuing hospitalization available only through civil commitment, or would have to proceed to trial on guilt or innocence. In the latter instance, the state would be required to assist the defendant in a number of ways designed to compensate for the difficulties the defendant would have as a result of a disability. For example, they would require that (1) the prosecution provide the defense with full pretrial discovery; (2) the prosecution meet the "beyond a reasonable doubt" standard in *all* phases of the proceeding (including, for instance, when contesting a defendant's motion for a directed verdict of acquittal, which is normally dismissed once the prosecution meets a much lesser burden of proof); (3) a corroborating eyewitness establish some or all elements of the alleged offense; (4) special instructions be given the jury; and (5) procedural rules governing postconviction relief be made less stringent when new evidence is discovered that was unavailable at trial because of the defendant's incompetence.[63]

In seeking a practical solution to the problem posed by the "permanent incompetent," the drafters of the ABA standards originally devised three alternative approaches, all of which stopped short of Burt and Morris's proposal permitting conviction of the incompetent defendant.[64] Although the ABA has officially adopted the third

of these three alternatives, it is useful to examine the various ways in which the problem could be approached.

The first approach simply establishes a time limit, within which the court must hold a hearing to determine whether the defendant is, in fact, permanently incompetent. The hearing must be held either when the treating professional reports permanent incompetency, or at the expiration of the maximum time of sentence for the crime charged, or five years from the date of adjudication of incompetence, whichever comes first.[65] If found to be permanently incompetent, the defendant could be confined only through involuntary civil commitment. This proposal, limited though it may be, has the advantage of establishing a specific limit upon the state's authority to confine an individual as incompetent to stand trial.

The second alternative distinguishes between minor offenses and felonies involving the causation or threat of serious bodily harm. If the defendant is not charged with a felony involving bodily harm, and is judged permanently incompetent, the charges would be dismissed at the expiration of the maximum time of sentence for the crime charged, or 12 to 18 months from the date of adjudication of incompetence, whichever occurs first.[66] The defendant charged with a felony causing or threatening bodily harm could obtain a hearing on guilt or innocence upon adjudication of permanent incompetence, or at any time after the expiration of either 12 or 18 months[67] from the initial adjudication of incompetence. The hearing would be conducted like a criminal trial. It would be adversarial in nature, rules of evidence would apply, as would all constitutional guarantees for the defendant, and there would be a right to a jury determination.[68] If the defendant is found not guilty, a judgment of acquittal would be entered disposing of the criminal charges. Further confinement would be possible only through civil commitment. The individual found "guilty" would remain in incompetent status, and the criminal charges would remain pending. As the commentary points out, prosecutors are generally opposed to this "innocent only" trial, since a finding of guilt would not constitute conviction, and, assuming a later return to competence, a trial on guilt or innocence would be necessary.[69] The alternative does, however, have the merit of at least allowing for disposition of serious charges if the defendant is found not guilty, as well as requiring the dismissal of nonserious charges.

The third alternative, the one officially adopted by the ABA, is much the same as the second, but differs in one critical respect. If, at the "factual guilt" hearing, the prosecutor has proved beyond a reasonable doubt that the defendant has committed the offense charged, the defendant may be subject to special-commitment proceedings.[70] This alternative would not allow punishment of the defendant through incarceration in prison—a disposition that appears to be constitutionally prohibited—but would recognize the societal "right to greater scrutiny of the defendant from perspectives of treatment, incapacitation and security, and release, while also permitting the defendant to obtain a judgment of acquittal in those instances where the prosecution cannot prove guilt."[71] While the standards on special commitment are not specific in terms of the locus of such confinement,[72] the drafters would apparently, at a minimum, allow for use of secure facilities and lengthier periods of confinement than would be allowed for the civilly committed; in other words, the commitment would be analogous to the type of detention typically reserved for insanity acquittees [see § 8.10(c)].

Given the interest of the ABA, and a growing recognition that the *Jackson* decision provided only incomplete relief to dispositional problems faced by incompetent defendants, it appears likely that legislatures will begin considering one of the forementioned approaches to these problems. In the interim, clinicians need to acquaint themselves with the consequences of adjudications of incompetency in their own jurisdictions. As this discussion has suggested, the consequences for defendants extend far beyond temporary suspension of trial, and may include lengthy hospitalization and an indefinite period of time in which defendants are charged with but are not tried for a criminal offense.

4.05. Special Problems: The Amnesic Defendant; Restoration of Competency through Medication

Resolution of the question of competency in an individual case may prove difficult because of problems that the legal definition of competency does not address. There are two issues that the clinician is likely to confront with some regularity. The first is that of the defendant who claims, and perhaps suffers from, amnesia for the period during which the criminal offense was committed. The second is that of the defendant who can be found competent only through the use of medication. Each is addressed briefly below.

(a) The Amnesic Defendant

At first glance, the defendant who has amnesia for the criminal act would appear to be incompetent, on the ground that such a person cannot possibly consult with counsel to prepare a defense for an act he or she cannot remember. As a general rule, however, there is no bar to finding competent a defendant who claims amnesia for the period in which he or she allegedly engaged in criminal behavior.[73] This principle appears to be predicated primarily upon judicial distrust of the authenticity of such claims.[74] For example, one court, in rejecting a claim that a defendant's amnesia should bar his trial, expressed concern over the ease with which amnesia could be feigned, and observed that a defendant, while entitled to a fair trial, is not entitled to a perfect trial.[75]

However, while the courts have been unanimous in rejecting the invitation to equate amnesia per se with incompetency, they have had more difficulty in establishing guidelines to aid courts and clinicians in determining whether an amnesic defendant is competent. Perhaps the most comprehensive attempt to construct a functional test is found in the case of *Wilson v. United States*.[76] In *Wilson*, the defendant, charged with assault and robbery, had fractured his skull while being chased by police, had no memory of the incidents with which he was charged, and was deemed unlikely ever to regain his memory. The federal court of appeals found that amnesia per se did not bar prosecution, but issued the following guidelines to assist the trial court in determining whether the defendant was competent:

1. The extent to which the amnesia affected the defendant's ability to consult with and assist his lawyer.
2. The extent to which the amnesia affected the defendant's ability to testify in his own behalf.
3. The extent to which the evidence could be extrinsically reconstructed in view of the defendant's amnesia. Such evidence would include evidence relating to the crime itself as well as any reasonably possible alibi.
4. The extent to which the government assisted the defendant and his counsel in that reconstruction.
5. The strength of the prosecution's case. The court observed that "most important here will be whether the Government's case is such as to negate all reasonable hypotheses of innocence. If there is any substantial possibility that the accused could, but for his amnesia, establish an alibi or other defense, it should be presumed that he would have been able to do so."
6. Any other facts and circumstances that would indicate whether or not the defendant had a fair trial.[77]

The *Wilson* case also gave the prosecution the burden of assisting the defense in the reconstruction of its case. This approach, which basically calls for pretrial discovery broader than that ordinarily permitted in criminal cases, is similar to the approaches suggested for dealing with the permanently incompetent defendant discussed above: In each case, normally inflexible rules would be relaxed in the interest of accommodating both state and individual interests in fair resolution of the criminal case. A similar approach was taken in *United States v. Stubblefield*,[78] in which the court emphasized the obligation of the prosecution to assist the defense not only in reconstructing the events surrounding the offense, but in constructing any reasonably possible alibi or other defense as well.

In evaluating competency in these circumstances, the clinician must first attempt to determine whether the amnesia is genuine. If it is, the "usual" competency evaluation may nonetheless proceed, since the quality of the communication between counsel and client, as well as the defendant's understanding of the criminal process, may well be unimpeded by the amnesia for the events in question. In addition, the defendant may be able to participate in the defense by evaluating other evidence depicting his or her conduct at the time of the offense. Despite the undeniable difficulties amnesia may present, the defendant's performance in the other functional areas judged in assessing competency may well be deemed sufficient for the defendant to be found legally competent.

(b) Drug-Induced Competency

The most common method of restoring incompetent defendants to competency is the use of psychotropic medication.[79] This should not be surprising when one considers the generally low threshold for being found competent[80] and the fact that most of those who have been found competent have been diagnosed as psychotic.[81] Yet some courts have refused to find medicated defendants competent, apparently under a miscomprehension that medication will distort defendants' thought processes; the result of this rule, of course, is to prevent trial of a defendant for whom medication is the sole vehicle for restoration. Fortunately, the trend is to recognize drug-induced competency.[82]

The use of medications to restore competency raises other issues as well. One is the effect that the artificially induced and presumably calmer, more organized demeanor the defendant presents may have on the potential success of any defense to the charges, particularly in the use of the insanity defense. Some commentators have noted that one reason the insanity defense is seldom successful before a jury is that the defendant at trial presents a normal or at least "noncrazy" picture, thereby making more difficult the task of proving that same defendant "crazy."[83] In response, some have urged that the parties should be able to obtain a jury instruction explaining the effects of the medication.[84] The New Hampshire Supreme Court has permitted another procedure as well. In *State v. Hayes*,[85] it indicated that defendants should be allowed to appear at trial without medication, provided that they are medicated and competent when they make the decision to appear at trial unmedicated, thereby insuring a valid waiver of their right to be tried while competent. In those cases where such a procedure is appropriate, the period between the time that defendants are taken off medication and trial must equal the period between their last medication before the offense and the offense itself.

Unlike New Hampshire, most jurisdictions have not resolved the legal right of incompetent defendants to refuse medication that would render them competent. The issue is not precisely identical to the issue of whether an individual has a right to refuse medication for treatment purposes: It is at least arguable that the state has more of an interest in bringing a defendant to trial than it does in forcing a nonconsenting patient to undergo treatment. Moreover, a defendant found incompetent to stand trial may also be incompetent to exercise a right to refuse treatment. Given the unsettled nature of the law on right to refuse treatment generally,[86] the clinician confronted with a nonconsenting patient who has been adjudicated incompetent to stand trial is advised to seek the guidance of legal counsel or administrative officials as to the appropriate course to follow in the particular jurisdiction.

4.06. *Research Relating to Clinical Evaluations of Competency*

As a result of several book-length research reports,[87] a substantial literature has developed in recent years about the nature of the competency evaluation. This literature has examined several specific topics, which are discussed here in turn: the frequency with which the question of incompetency is raised and with which a finding of incompetency is made; the characteristics of defendants found incompetent; and the reliability and validity of competency evaluations generally and of several structured evaluation formats that have been developed.

(a) Frequency of Competency Evaluations and Findings

As noted at the beginning of this chapter, in terms simply of number of cases, competency is by far the most significant criminal issue in forensic mental health. In terms of defendants actually found incompetent, restoration of competency is the most frequent reason for commitment to state forensic hospitals.[88] In 1978 there were 6,420 such commitments nationally.[89] When admissions for *evaluation* of competency are added, the figures become much larger. Roesch and Golding reviewed ten studies of the frequency of competency evaluations and of findings of incompetency.[90] Averaging the findings across studies, they suggested that only about 30% of defendants referred for competency evaluations are actually found incompetent. Using this percentage, competency evaluations in 1978 might well have numbered over 20,000.

It is important to note, however, that the percentage found incompetent varies widely across jurisdictions (1.2% to 77.0%) and within jurisdictions across time. The variance appears to result from the fact that in many jurisdictions only one or two hospitals perform forensic evaluations. Consequently, when there is a change of staff in these facilities, there can be a striking change also in the proportion of defendants found incompetent. The higher figures seem to result when clinicians confuse incompetency to stand trial with psychosis, or when incompetency is used essentially as a dispositional device for defendants believed to be in need of treatment. When there is a change toward more rigorous (i.e., more valid) evaluation standards and procedures, the percentage actually found incompetent is typically less than 10%.

Whether the proportion of those found incompetent is 10% or 30% of evaluated defendants, it is clear that many defendants are referred—and typically hospitalized—for evaluation needlessly. That is, the question of incompetency is raised much more frequently than it is answered in the affirmative. This fact has provided incentive to develop the screening instruments and outpatient evaluation systems described in later sections of this chapter, since substantial costs to both the defendant (e.g., *de facto* imprisonment without bail) and the state (e.g., economic costs of professional time and inpatient care) may be incurred during the course of a competency evaluation.

(b) Characteristics of Incompetent Defendants

The most extensive study of defendants actually found to be incompetent was undertaken by Steadman,[91] who followed for three years 539 males charged with felonies and found incompetent between September 1971 and August 1972. Steadman summarized the demographic characteristics of the incompetent defendants as representative of "marginal individuals with much less than average education and few useful job skills. Most have few community ties, either through employment or family. An unusually high proportion have never married."[92] The study group was also noted to have had much difficulty with substance abuse; 48% had a record of heavy drug use, and 38% had a record of alcohol abuse.[93] Unfortunately, however, Steadman did not compare the study group with a control defendant population. Thus, although it is clear that the incompetent defendants were "marginal" relative to the general population, it is unknown whether they differed appreciably from the competent defendant population.

There are two ways, though, in which Steadman's sample clearly was atypical of most defendant populations. First, the incompetent defendants usually had a long history of shuttling between the criminal justice and mental health systems.[94] No less than 81% of the sample had been previously hospitalized in psychiatric facilities. Among those previously hospitalized, the median length of time in the hospital was almost

two and a half years. More than two-thirds of the study group had been previously arrested. Indeed, 24% had three or more prior mental hospitalizations and three or more prior arrests.

Second, the incompetent defendants were more likely than general defendant populations to be charged with serious offenses.[95] Whereas only .8% of felony arrests in New York were for murder, 15.2% of Steadman's sample faced a murder charge. Charges for arson were similarly disproportionate: .5% versus 7.1%. The most frequent charges facing the incompetent groups were not so serious, however: assault (16.3%), robbery (20.0%), and burglary (20.0%). The high proportion of violent offenses facing the incompetent group was probably reflective of the seriousness of charges facing the overall group of defendants referred for competency evaluations,[96] although Roesch and Golding did find incompetent defendants in North Carolina to be somewhat more likely to be accused of violent crimes (77% vs. 67%) than defendants referred but found competent.[97] The probable explanation for these numbers: Where charges are relatively minor, defense attorneys are likely to try to achieve a community diversion from the criminal process or a plea bargain for probation, rather than to proceed toward trial. In such an instance, a defendant is likely to suffer greater loss of liberty if the competency issue is raised than if it is not.

One other distinguishing variable is diagnosis, although that variable was not examined by Steadman. In Roesch and Golding's study of defendants referred for evaluation of competency, 87% of the incompetent defendants were diagnosed as psychotic or, less frequently, mentally retarded, but only 15% of those found competent obtained such a diagnosis.[98]

(c) The General Quality of Competency Evaluations

Of most direct utility to forensic clinicians is research on the process of forensic evaluation itself. How much confidence can be placed in the opinions derived from evaluations of competency to stand trial? That is, how reliable and valid are such opinions? What level of expertise in the mental health professions is required before adequate reliability and validity can be achieved? How intensive or broad does the evaluation need to be to achieve adequate reliability and validity? Do packaged evaluation formats facilitate competency evaluations?

To summarize the answers to these questions before discussing them in turn, it is noted that competency evaluations are typically "easy" evaluations. In the majority of cases, as suggested by the research reviewed thus far, there is no real question of the defendant's competency, at least to someone who understands the concept. Also, as noted in § 4.02, the evaluation is *functional* and *present-oriented*. There is no need to speculate about the defendant's state of mind at some point in the past, and little need to predict the defendant's conduct in the future. Indeed, there is no need even to reach a diagnosis of the defendant's condition at present. Rather, the only relevant questions are the defendant's ability to assist counsel and to understand the nature of the legal proceedings. Thus, high reliability and validity of evaluation can be expected as long as the evaluation is focused on those skills, as they are presently manifested. Moreover, such quality can be expected insofar as the examiners, regardless of disciplinary background, understand the criteria for competency.

The available research indicates that competency evaluations are typically highly reliable and *potentially* highly valid. Exemplary of the research on reliability is Poythress and Stock's examination of interclinician agreement on a series of 44 cases at the Center for Forensic Psychiatry in Michigan.[99] Pairs of clinical psychologists interviewed defendants and then reached opinions without consultation within pairs. There was 100% agreement as to the ultimate opinion on competency. Similarly high reliability has been reported by several other investigators.[100] Interestingly, Golding, Roesch, and Schreiber[101] and Roesch and Golding[102] found that high reliability was maintained even when the evaluators were not mental health professionals, if they were given a structure for the interviews and an explanation of the concept of competency to stand trial.

Roesch and Golding reported 90% agreement between trained laypersons (members of the local Association for Mental Health) and hospital-based forensic clinicians.[103] Golding, Roesch, and Schreiber observed 97% agreement between lawyers and clinicians on global assessments of competency to stand trial, although there were varying emphases in their opinion formation.[104] (Lawyers attended more to "crazy" thinking, while clinicians placed greater weight on communication skills and recall ability.) In short, reliability tends to be high, without regard to the disciplinary background of the examiners. However, it should be noted that all of the studies cited used samples of examiners who had been trained together, and all of the studies except that of Poythress and Stock[105] involved use of a structured interview format. Consequently, it is possible that "real-world" reliability is substantially lower than in the reported studies, especially if reliability is compared across evaluation centers. It is clear, though, that examiners with a common framework for assessment can easily attain high reliability in competency evaluations, and that this level of reliability is not dependent upon a particular disciplinary background.

The data with respect to the validity of competency evaluations are less clear. In view of the fact that judges seldom challenge clinicians' opinions as to a defendant's competency, there is no independent criterion available in the legal system against which to compare clinicians' opinions. Therefore, researchers have examined the validity of competency opinions less directly through study of the kinds of variables that predict ultimate opinion,[106] comparison with "blue-ribbon" experts' judgments,[107] and experts' analyses of report quality.[108]

Taken in sum, these studies suggest that examiners trained in the nature of the competency construct typically achieve high validity. However, there is also evidence that untrained clinicians may frequently, and erroneously, directly translate diagnoses of psychosis and mental retardation into a finding of incompetency.[109] There is some suggestion, though, that the modal competence of forensic examiners on this point may be changing,[110] particularly where efforts are made to ensure that examining clinicians understand the legal contours of competency and the relevant empirical research.[111]

It should also be noted that, where the clinicians in a given center share a misunderstanding of the relationship between psychosis and incompetency, there may still be respectably high reliability, although low validity. First, gross distinctions between psychosis and the absence thereof tend themselves to be reasonably reliable, particularly when tight diagnostic criteria are used.[112] Second, most defendants will still be held to be competent, whether under a functional decision rule or (erroneously) a diagnostic decision rule. The disagreements would come over the subset of psychotic and mentally retarded defendants who meet criteria for competency to stand trial.

Not only are evaluations of competency to stand trial usually highly reliable and potentially highly valid, but these levels of psychometric rigor can be achieved in a brief interview.[113] Nonetheless, the typical practice is still to hospitalize the defendant for about a month at a cost to the state of thousands of dollars and to the defendant of loss of liberty and stigma resulting from hospitalization. It is clear that there is no sacrifice in quality of evaluation when trained community-based clinicians are used, and there may even be an improvement in quality.[114] Community clinics are more likely than hospitals to have easy access to important sources of information (e.g., the defense attorney), and they are less likely to be staffed by foreign-born, foreign-trained physicians who may have difficulty communicating with the client.[115]

(d)   Reliability and Validity of Interview Formats

In part as an attempt to facilitate community-based evaluations, a number of structured interview and questionnaire formats have been developed. In view of the large proportion of defendants who are ultimately found competent, it would be useful to have means of screening out defendants who are clearly competent. Such an instrument might even be administered by the defense attorney or court personnel.[116] It could substantially reduce costs associated with evaluations that are essentially frivolous. Moreover, given the relatively clear range of functions associated with competency to stand trial, structured interview formats would be likely to facilitate clinicians' focus on these functions rather than on extraneous clinical concerns (e.g., diagnosis). The result would probably be increases in efficiency and validity of assessment.

(1)   Competency Screening Test

Initial efforts toward such structured evaluation formats arose in a project conducted in Massachusetts by McGarry, Lipsitt, and their colleagues at the Harvard Laboratory of Community Psychiatry, in conjunction with Bridgewater State Hospital.[117] The McGarry group developed a sentence-completion test, the Competency Screening Test (CST), to be used in screening defendants for competency,[118] and a semistructured interview, the Competency Assessment Instrument (CAI),[119] to be used for evaluation of those defendants who fail such a screening [see § 4.06(d)(2)].

Since its use is widespread, a relatively extensive examination of the CST is appropriate. The CST consists of 22 sentence stems, each scored on a scale of 0–2. Representative items include: "When I go to court the lawyer will . . ."; "If the jury finds me guilty, I . . ."; "When they say a man is innocent until proven guilty, I . . ."; "What concerns Fred most about his lawyer . . .". Lipsitt, Lelos, and McGarry have established a cutoff score of 20. That is, defendants who score below 20 would be screened in for further evaluation.

The CST has been criticized primarily for a bias toward a positive view of the legal system.[120] For example, in response to the stem "Jack felt that the judge . . . ," "was fair" is a 2-point (competent) answer, but "was unjust" is a 0-point (incompetent) answer. Similarly, a response of "is tardiness" is a 0-point answer to "What concerns Fred most about his lawyer. . . ." Presumably, Lipsitt, Lelos, and McGarry are attempting to differentiate defendants based on their understanding of the way the system is supposed to work. In so doing, however, they have biased the scoring such that defendants will score low if they have a negative opinion of the legal system, even if their awareness of it is impeccable. It has been our experience that defendants who are "false positives" on the CST (i.e., who score below the cutoff score but whom interviews reveal to be competent) tend to be either cynical about the system (perhaps correctly in some instances) or simply depressed and expecting (again often accurately) an unfavorable disposition of their cases.

As might be expected, given the bias described in the preceding paragraph, "misses" on the CST tend to be false positives. Of course, errors should be in that direction on a screening instrument. More harm results from prematurely labeling defendant as competent and subjecting them to a trial they may not understand than from subjecting defendants who actually are ultimately found to be competent to a more thorough evaluation. At the same time, though, the false-positive rate should be sufficiently low that the instrument is efficient as a screening device and prevents unnecessary full evaluations, especially if they are to take place in the hospital. Obviously, if few are screened out, then the instrument has minimal utility and may even have negative effects if it unduly biases clinicians performing the full evaluation.

A review of studies of the CST's validity suggests that the false-positive rate is undesirably high (14.3% to 28.6%), but probably not so high as to render the instrument clinically useless as a screening measure [see Table 4-2]. Confidence in the instrument's utility as a screening instrument must be somewhat attenuated, however, because of data from two samples studied by Roesch and Golding.[121] In one study [Study 3b in Table 4-2], the total error rate was, in fact, more than 50%. In a second study [Study 3a in Table 4-2], two of five incompetent defendants were false *negatives*. While the criterion variable used in both studies was Dorothea Dix Hospital psychiatrists' conclusions—conclusions that, as noted earlier, were found to be heavily and presumably invalidly influenced by diagnosis[122]—in

view of the general tenor of these studies and the distorted base rate in the original validation study by Lipsitt and colleagues (only the most disturbed defendants at Bridgewater were included), caution must be exercised in using the CST as a screening instrument in the community.

The interrater reliability of the CST is also not well established. Lipsitt's group reported "interrater reliability (between bachelor's-level raters) using standard Z scores" as .93.[123] The details of the procedure were not given, but scores were probably standardized around each rater's individual mean and variation. If so, as Roesch and Golding have pointed out,[124] the reliability coefficient would be spuriously high, because variance attributable to rater scoring biases (i.e., whether the scorer's tendency is to be "tough" or "easy") would be masked. Randolph, Hicks, and Mason did report a similar range of interrater reliability ($r = .86–.98$),[125] but accurate scoring apparently required eight to ten hours of training and practice—more than is probably realistic if the CST is in fact to be used as a screening instrument.

One of us (Melton) has collected data on the CST in an informal study; these suggest that reliability of the CST is problematic, without further clarification of scoring rules. Twenty-seven community mental health clinicians were asked to score three CST protocols as part of their training in forensic assessment. Item-by-item agreement ranged from 36% to 100%, with mean agreement of only 73.3%. This finding should not be overinterpreted. The participants were inexperienced in the use of the CST, and the scoring was presented as a training exercise. As a result, items about which the participants were unsure were sometimes left blank, therefore deflating the level of agreement. Nonetheless, the data raise a question about the reliability of the CST when used as a general screening device by persons without substantial training in its use, and when supplementary scoring rules (beyond those in the CST manual) have not been agreed upon.

Two types of vagueness in the scoring manual seemed especially to stimulate low reliability in Melton's study. First, the scoring rules for some

Table 4-2
Predictive Validity of the Competency Screening Test (CST)

Study 1: Lipsitt, Lelos, & McGarry (1971)			Study 3b: Roesch & Golding (1980)		
	Staff Recommendation			Staff Recommendation	
CST Score	Competent	Incompetent	CST Score	Competent	Incompetent
> 20	17	3 (7.0%)	> 20	5	5 (23.8%)
< 20	7 (16.3%)	16	< 20	6 (28.6%)	5

Note. $n = 43$ most disturbed males at Bridgewater (Massachusetts) State Hospital. Data from Lipsitt, Lelos, & McGarry, *Competency for Trial: A Screening Instrument,* 128 AM. J. PSYCHIATRY 105 (1971).

Note. $n = 21$ defendants at Dorothea Dix Hospital (North Carolina). Data from R. ROESCH & S. GOLDING (see Study 3a) at 63.

Study 2: Shatin & Brodsky (1979)			Study 4: Randolph, Hicks, & Mason (1981)	
	Staff Recommendation		Staff Recommendation	Mean CST Score
CST Score	Competent	Incompetent	Competent	29
> 20	9	1 (4.8%)	Incompetent	19.9
< 20	3 (14.3%)	8		

Note. $n = 21$ females at Elmhurst (New York) Hospital Forensic Services. Data from Shatin & Brodsky, 46 MT. SINAI J. MED. (1979).

Note. $n = 25$ male defendants at Chester (Illinois) Mental Health Center. Data from Randolph, Hicks, & Mason, *The Competency Screening Test: A Replication and Extension,* 8 CRIM. JUST. BEHAV. 471 (1981). Mann–Whitney $U = 47$, $p < .02$. Data as to hit rate were apparently reported inaccurately, in that percentages exceed 100% (i.e., false positives, 47%; false negatives, 0%; hits, 72%). Cell frequencies were not reported.

Study 3a: Roesch & Golding (1980)			Study 5: Nottingham & Mattson (1981)		
	Staff Recommendation			Staff Recommendation	
CST Score	Competent	Incompetent	CST Score	Competent	Incompetent
> 20	101	2 (1.6%)	> 20	37	0 (0.0%)
< 20	22 (28.6%)	3	< 20	9 (18.0%)	4

Note. $n = 128$ defendants at Dorothea Dix Hospital (North Carolina). Data from R. ROESCH & S. GOLDING, COMPETENCY TO STAND TRIAL 63, 181–83 (1980).

Note. $n = 50$ male defendants at Southwestern (Virginia) State Hospital. Data from Nottingham & Mattson, *A Validation Study of the Competency Screening Test,* 5 LAW HUM. BEHAV. 329 (1981). CST sentence stems were presented orally.

items are presented largely in terms of the affective response to the item, with the result that scoring of concrete or affectively neutral responses is unclear. For example, scoring for responses to "The lawyer told Bill that . . ." is based largely on the expressed attitude toward the lawyer (score 2: "includes obtaining and/or accepting advice or guidance"; score 0: "includes regarding lawyer as accusing or judgmental"). Participants found it difficult to score responses that might reflect an awareness of the legal situation but that did not bear directly on the defendant's relationship with the attorney—for example, "he will go home"; "to meet her in the courtroom at 10 o'clock"; "that he was instant till proving gulte" (sic). Second, the scoring manual requires fuzzy value judgments as to what degree of affective involvement by the defendant is adaptive. Thus, in response to "While listening to the witnesses testify against me, I . . .", "would listen carefully" is a 2-point response, but "listened" is worth only 1 point. Similarly, in response to "When I think of being sent to prison, I . . .", "get very depressed" is worth 2 points, but "go into a deep depression" is given only 1 point. "Feel uneasy" is a 1-point response, while "get scared" is an example of a 2-point answer.

These points of vagueness appear related to the validity problem described earlier, in that they emanate from questionable assumptions about how competent defendants should feel about their involvement in the criminal justice system. It is probable that further refinement of the scoring system to de-emphasize the significance of these attitudes would substantially improve the psychometric soundness of the CST. Both improved predictive validity (i.e., fewer false positives) and improved interrater reliability would probably result.

Despite the problems with the CST described above, the relatively high rate of "screen-outs" (i.e., true negatives) on the CST and its ease of administration suggest that it does bear promise as a screening instrument. Until there is further development and evaluation of the scoring system, however, it should be treated as an experimental measure and used only with great caution in clinical decisionmaking. It is unwise at this point to use a CST score as the primary basis of a decision as to whether a defendant's competency should be further explored.

(2) Competency Assessment Instrument

For full-fledged evaluations of competency to stand trial, the McGarry group developed the CAI.[126] The CAI is a semistructured interview that is scored with 5-point Likert ratings

(1 = "total incapacity" to 5 = "no incapacity") on 13 functions (e.g., "appraisal of available legal defenses"; "planning of legal strategy, including guilty pleas to lesser charges where pertinent"; "capacity to testify relevantly").

Although the CAI manual emphasizes that the weight to be given particular functions is a matter for the court to decide, it suggests that "a majority or a substantial accumulation" of scores of 3 or less may be cause for inpatient observation.[127] This suggestion may imply a higher threshold for competency to stand trial than is in fact present in the minds of most judges, especially since some of the functions assessed (e.g., "capacity to disclose to attorney available pertinent facts surrounding the offense including the defendant's movement, timing, mental state, actions at the time of the offense"; "capacity to testify relevantly") may bear little weight in judges' ultimate determinations of competency. Whether the CAI scoring system is helpful is essentially unknown, however. No predictive validity studies have been undertaken using it, and the only reliability studies[128] have involved comparisons of ratings of small samples of defendants, with inconsistent results.[129]

The CAI is probably most useful as an interview-structuring device, and it has been substantially utilized in that manner.[130] The CAI manual[131] includes a large number of sample interview questions and case examples that may be useful to clinicians learning to perform competency evaluations.

(3) Interdisciplinary Fitness Interview

Probably the most tightly conceptualized of the structured competency assessment guides is the Interdisciplinary Fitness Interview (IFI) developed by Golding and Roesch[132] and evaluated by Golding, Roesch, and Schreiber.[133] The IFI is a semistructured interview format that includes ratings from 0 ("no or minimal incapacity") to 2 ("substantial incapacity") on a variety of dimensions of specific legal functioning; psychopathology, and general impressions of competency [see Table 4-3]. The raters also record on a scale of 0–2 the weight given each particular dimension in the formation of an opinion about the

Table 4-3
Interdisciplinary Fitness Interview (IFI) Items

Section A: Legal Items
1. Capacity to appreciate the nature of the alleged crime, and to disclose pertinent facts, events and motives.
2. Quality of relationship with one's current attorney.
3. Quality of relationship with attorneys in general.
4. Anticipated courtroom demeanor and trial conduct.
5. Appreciating the consequences of various legal options.

Section B: Psychopathological Items
6. Primary disturbance of thought.
7. Primary disturbance of communication.
8. Secondary disturbance of communication.
9. Delusional processes.
10. Hallucinations.
11. Unmanageable or disturbing behavior.
12. Affective disturbances.
13. Disturbances of consciousness/orientation.
14. Disturbances of memory/amnesia.
15. Severe mental retardation.
16. General impairment of judgment/insight.

Section C: Overall Evaluation
1. Overall fitness judgment.
2. Rating of confidence in judgment.
3. Comment on basis for decision about defendant.
4. Other factors taken into account in reaching decisions.

Note. From Golding, Roesch, & Schreiber, *Assessment and Conceptualization of Competency to Stand Trial: Preliminary Data on the Interdisciplinary Fitness Interview,* LAW & HUM. BEHAV. (in press). Reprinted by permission.

defendant's overall competency to stand trial. Golding and Roesch intend the IFI to be administered jointly by a mental health professional and an attorney.

Golding and Roesch have justified the second scale (Influence on Decision) on the assumption that the significance of a given dimension will vary with the particular facts of a defendant's case. Thus, if a defendant's testimony is considered necessary for a proper defense, then his or her ability to maintain appropriate courtroom demeanor would be more important than in a case where testimony by the defendant is not basic to the defense case. Similarly, rigid rejection of plea bargaining for irrational reasons would be insignificant if plea bargaining is not a real option.

Although there is an intuitive appeal to such a notion, the idea that the functional standard for competency to stand trial is related to the complexity of the case is deceptively simple. The requirement for defendants being tried while competent is based not just on the minimization of error as a result of inadequate confrontation of prosecution witnesses. As noted in § 4.01, it is also grounded in a moral belief that it is unjust to subject defendants to criminal penalties when they are not fully cognizant of the reasons for such punishment or when they have not had a real opportunity to present their defense, to have their say. Therefore, the law may require defendants to be capable of full participation in a case even if defense strategy may not require it.

The judgment of which theory is correct is of course a legal one, and the dilemma is illustrative of the foibles of clinicians' providing conclusory, ultimate-issue opinions, even on a "simple" question like competency to stand trial. It is presumptuous for clinicians to decide which factors are important in competency to stand trial on a particular charge. However, the second scale on the IFI at least makes these judgments explicit, so that the hearing judge can evaluate the calculus used in the opinion.

In the one study available on the IFI,[134] interviewer pairs of one clinician and one attorney used the IFI to evaluate 77 defendants in Massachusetts. On final judgments of competency, the interviewers agreed in 75 of the cases (97%). In those cases, 58 defendants were found to be competent and 17 to be incompetent. In terms of item-by-item agreement, interrater reliability was greatest for the legal items most directly related to competency, but there was also respectable agreement between attorneys and clinicians on psychopathology items, especially with respect to delusional processes. Indeed, overall, the reliability was higher for the psychopathology than the legal items. The relative lack of cross-disciplinary agreement on the legal nuances unrelated directly to competency suggests the utility of adding lawyers' input on a routine basis. This implication is reinforced by the different judgments of the lawyers and the mental health professionals in considering the relevance of specific personality disturbances. Although one cannot say which is the more "correct" decision style, it would be unsurprising to find lawyers more attuned to personality disturbances that clearly interfere with attorney–client relationships and to find clinicians more sensitive to subtle signs of mental disorder.

Regardless, the preliminary data on the IFI suggest that it is a time-efficient interview format (about 45 minutes per interview) that produces rich observations with high reliability. Golding, Roesch, and Schreiber acknowledge, though, that there has been insufficient research on the IFI thus far to characterize it as more than an experimental instrument.[135] Particularly given the fact that the IFI is distinguished from other formats (notably the CAI) by the addition of ratings explicitly describing the nature of personality dysfunctions, future research might usefully explore further the relationships between specific behavior disturbances and specific legal functions, both as a general matter and in terms of assessment biases.

(e) Summary

The research on competency to stand trial leads to several conclusions. Referrals for evaluation are frequent and grossly overused. Most defendants evaluated are ultimately found competent; those who are not tend to have had extensive psychiatric and criminal histories. Although the practice in most jurisdictions is to perform the evaluations over a period of weeks in forensic hospitals, brief outpatient assessments are highly reliable, are potentially highly valid, and can be performed by evaluators without doctoral-level training (indeed, without any mental health training at all) if the evaluators are trained in the nature of the behavioral functions subsumed in competency to stand trial. Several structured evaluation formats have been developed that may

be useful in ensuring that assessments are germane to the legal criteria. However, each of these instruments has unproven psychometric rigor and might be considered to be an experimental measure.

4.07. Guidelines for Evaluation

(a) The Social Context of Evaluation

In view of both the nature of the competency construct itself and the research suggesting that relatively few defendants are actually found incompetent, clinicians should approach the competency evaluation as a problem in *consultation*. Although the legal paradigm demands a case-by-case determination of competency as if it rested within the individual,[136] competency might more properly be viewed as a transactional construct lying somewhere between the attorney and the client. After all, one prong of the competency standard is directly concerned with the *relationship* between the attorney and the client, and the other prong is partially dependent upon the success of the attorney's efforts to educate the defendant about the nature of the proceedings. The clinician asked to perform a competency evaluation should be alert, therefore, to assistance that might be rendered to the defense attorney in preparing the client for the defense. The cliche that "there are no incompetent defendants, only incompetent attorneys," overstates the case. Nonetheless, it is true that the typical lawyer receives little, if any, formal clinical training in counseling disturbed clients. Consequently, referral of a defendant who may be "strange" or "difficult" but who clearly passes the threshold for competency may reflect the attorney's frustration or discomfort in working with a disturbed client. To the extent that this is a general problem, careful consultation may decrease future unnecessary referrals. Indeed, attorneys themselves might profitably initiate such consultation when deciding whether to seek an evaluation. Still more basically, where attorneys do not understand the standard for competency, the

Figure 4-1.   *Referral form.*

Defendant: _____ DOB: _____

Attorney: _____

Charges for which defendant is standing trial:

Describe the specific offenses with which defendant is charged (alleged act, time, place):

Describe the *specific* behavior of the defendant which leads you to believe that he/she may be incompetent to stand trial or was suffering from significant mental abnormality at the time of the offense:

Have you observed this behavior yourself? If not, who are the sources of these observations?

---

forensic clinician may help to clarify the nature of the construct, again with the probable result of decreasing unnecessary referrals.

Moreover, as Golding and Roesch have noted,[137] it is probable that certain kinds of attorneys have more success in counseling clients of particular characteristics, just as therapist and client characteristics interact. Where there seems to be a mismatch between attorney and client, the clinician may be able to offer suggestions as to ways of getting the relationship "unstuck." Also, careful reporting of the evaluation data should give a sense of the specific points about which the defendant needs further education or counseling [see, e.g., Mills report, § 15.02].

The consultation process should not be conceptualized as limited to a unidirectional intervention in the attorney–client relationship, however. The clinician also needs to *obtain* information from the attorney in order to be able to perform the evaluation well, especially if the referral is not frivolous. To be able to evaluate the defendant's understanding of the charges and potential penalties, the clinician obviously needs to know what they are. Also, it is not uncommon to have referrals before the attorney has met with the client at any length. Points of misunderstanding by the defendant after 20 hours

of counseling by the attorney have a very different meaning than do similar points of misunderstanding or ignorance after a five-minute meeting at a preliminary hearing. The clinician needs to know how much interaction there has been between attorney and client and what the quality of that interaction has been. We strongly recommend that clinicians routinely seek such information from attorneys representing defendants referred for competency evaluations (and, conversely, that referring attorneys routinely provide it). The form shown in Figure 4-1 may be helpful in that regard.

(b)   Evaluation Content

The available research clearly indicates that competency evaluations can almost always be performed with a brief outpatient interview. Clinicians performing such evaluations should be careful to focus the inquiry on assessment of the functions related to competency to stand trial. In so doing, there may be some initial resistance from some judges and others in the legal system who believe incompetency to be a diagnosable psychiatric condition. Hence, based on their experience, they may expect the clinician to con-

Table 4-4
Knowledge of Information Significance

Question Number	Responses	Trial Judges (n = 52)	Forensic Clinicians (n = 27)	General Clinicians (n = 134)
30[1]	A	9 (17.3%)	27 (100%)	35 (26.1%)
	B	2 (3.8%)	0	1 (0.7%)
	C	8 (15.4%)	0	22 (16.4%)
	D	33 (63.5%)	0	76 (56.7%)
47[2]	A	7 (13.5%)	26 (96.3%)	34 (25.4%)
	B	21 (40.4%)	0	42 (31.3%)
	C	0	0	2 (1.5%)
	D	22 (42.3%)	1 (3.7%)	53 (39.6%)
	Blank	2 (3.8%)	0	3

Note. For details of the study from which these data are drawn, *see* G. MELTON, L. WEITHORN, & C. SLOBOGIN, COMMUNITY MENTAL HEALTH CENTERS AND THE COURTS: AN EVALUATION OF COMMUNITY-BASED FORENSIC SERVICES (1985).

1. Question 30:   For which type of evaluation is it usually *least* important to obtain family history of the client?
   (A) Competency evaluation
   (B) A pre-sentence evaluation
   (C) An evaluation of mental state at the time of the offense
   (D) Family history is essential in all of the above types of evaluations
2. Question 47:   What item of information below is least likely to be needed for an evaluation of competency to stand trial?
   (A) Projective test results
   (B) A copy of the indictment
   (C) A mental status examination
   (D) What the defense attorney has told his client about the legal process

duct what they believe are the rudiments of a psychiatric evaluation (e.g., thorough history taking, psychological testing, inpatient observation).

Consider, for example, the responses to an item about information useful in competency assessments on a test of knowledge about forensic assessment [see Table 4-4].[138] It is noteworthy that judges tend to perceive family history to be a necessary part of the evaluation, although such information is likely to be tangential to assessment of an understanding of the legal process and ability to assist in one's defense. Although we do not wish to minimize the significance of such misconceptions in interactions between the courts and the mental health system, it has been our experience that resistance can be reduced if efforts are made to involve key figures in the legal system in the development of the system for evaluations, and if feedback is requested periodically.[139] Once judges and attorneys receive reports containing information that is germane to the inquiry, they typically are pleased at having the foundation for opinions well developed and made explicit. Again, clinicians—and attorneys—are well advised to consider the evaluation of competency to stand trial as a two-way consultation problem.

(1)   Interview Format

In exploring defendants' competency to stand trial, clinicians may find it helpful to refer to the packaged evaluation formats available. As noted previously, the manuals for both the CAI and the IFI contain guidelines for interview content, including specific questions that may reveal pertinent information. Table 4-5 shows the outline used for competency interviews at the Forensic

Table 4-5
Competency Interview Format

A. Mental status
  1. Reality testing; orientation as to time, place, and person
  2. Capacity for relationships; ability to establish and maintain a relationship with counsel; trust of attorney
  3. Ability to conceptualize behavioral alternatives and consequences and to plan a course of action; social judgment
  4. Mannerisms, odd behavior—likely to be considered disruptive by judge or jury
  5. Adequacy of ego defenses; deterioration of ego functioning under stress
  6. Suggestibility
B. Awareness and comprehension of courtroom procedures
  1. Role of defense attorney:
     Who is he (she)?
     What is he (she) supposed to do? What is his (her) job?
     Understanding of attorney–client privilege: Does attorney have to report client's conversations?
     Magical expectations about the attorney
  2. Role of prosecuting attorney
  3. Role of judge
  4. Role of jury
  5. Expectations about witnesses:
     Who are they likely to be?
     What are they likely to say?
     Awareness of process of testimony: Who asks questions?
     Understanding of cross-examination: What would client do if a witness told a lie about him (her)?
  6. Understanding of pleas
     What do "guilty" and "innocent" mean?
     What are the consequences of each of these pleas?
     Understanding plea bargaining
  7. Understanding the "right to remain silent"
     Dictionary definition
     Application: If a judge asks client a question, does client have to answer it?
     Awareness of client that he (she) will be cross-examined if he (she) chooses to testify
  8. Awareness of appropriate courtroom behavior
C. Awareness and comprehension of the charges
  1. Knowledge of the charges
  2. Comprehension of the charges
  3. Knowledge of the specific act charged
  4. Knowledge of potential and likely penalties; understanding of probation
  5. Appreciation of the strength of the prosecutor's case
  6. Knowledge and appreciation of available defenses

Psychiatry Clinic at the University of Virginia.

Each of these interview formats is "semi-structured," and clinicians should avoid following a rigid, test-like series of questions. In particular, poorly educated defendants sometimes perceive the list of factual questions about the legal system as a "schoolmarmish" test (as in some sense it is), and are accordingly reluctant to answer fully lest their ignorance be uncovered. Also, such defendants may be unable to give dictionary definitions of terms, even though they have a basic understanding of the underlying concepts. For example, a defendant may be unable to tell in the abstract what the prosecutor does, but discussion of the courtroom situation in terms of a particular case may reveal a good understanding of the adversary system. Defendants re-

ferred for competency evaluations will typically have court experience (from previous arrests or pretrial hearings on the current charges, or both). Conversation about these experiences (e.g., "Tell me who was there and what they did/were supposed to do") often reveals a substantially more sophisticated understanding of the legal process than does direct questioning about relevant concepts. Alternatively, discussion of hypothetical cases may provide insight into the defendant's understanding of, and approach to, the legal process.

In beginning the interview, it is important to ascertain the defendant's understanding of the purpose of the evaluation, to clarify the purpose where necessary, and to give information about the limits of confidentiality [see § 3.02, 3.05(b)].

By this time, the interviewer should also have received information from the defense attorney about the reason for referral. This combination of information from the attorney and impressions from the defendant as to reasons for referral is likely to suggest directions for the interview. For example, as a general rule, extensive history taking is unnecessary for a competency evaluation. However, if the reason for referral is that the defendant has previously decompensated under the stress of a trial, learning more both about that particular event and about the defendant's coping in analogous situations would be important.

It is also sometimes helpful to ask defendants to fill out the CST while they are waiting for the evaluation to begin. Although this is not exactly the way in which the CST is intended to be used, we have found the CST to be useful as a quasi-projective instrument (rather than a psychometric screening instrument) suggesting points that particularly bear examination. With its here-and-now focus on matters that are likely to be salient and immediately accessible to the client, the CST frequently gives an indication of issues in the client's relationship with the legal system and his or her general personality functioning.

Beyond the CST, administration of psychological tests is unlikely to be a cost-efficient means of gathering information. Because the nature of the cognitive defect in incompetency is rather specific, generalized measures of intelligence or personality are unlikely to pertain directly to questions of competency. However, in cases in which the client appears incompetent or marginally competent on the bases of interview data, cognitive testing may sometimes be useful for one of the following purposes: (1) corroboration of degree of mental retardation or other generalized impairment of ego functioning; or (2) assessment of ability to consider alternatives and process information in a structured situation. Even these purposes may often be more efficiently and perhaps more validly met, though, by examination of agency records and discussions about the defendant's typical behavior with relatives, employers, and others who know the suspect well.

(2)   Mental Status

The clinician performing competency evaluations will generally want to obtain a picture of the client's overall present mental status. A *formal* mental status examination (e.g., proverbs, digit spans) will usually not be necessary, although it may sometimes be useful to determine the seriousness of a particular deficit or to confirm its existence. At the risk of belaboring a point made throughout this chapter, it should be remembered that these general personality and cognitive functions should be related specifically to the kinds of skills and traits necessary for competency. For example, delusions per se are insufficient to render a defendant incompetent. On the other hand, delusions of certain content may be highly relevant. A belief that one's attorney is part of a conspiracy to poison one's mind would be likely to interfere substantially with the attorney–client relationship, and a delusion that one is immune from punishment as a result of a supernatural power would also be likely to interfere with the client's understanding of the proceedings and motivation to assist in the defense. Similarly, general incapacity to establish or sustain relationships should be explored to learn whether it would render the attorney–client relationship unworkable.

In reviewing the client's mental status, the clinician can generally limit the inquiry to *present* mental status. Behavioral observations can be simply organized and reported. However, there are some predictive elements potentially involved. Opinions are likely to be sought as to how particular deficits will or might affect the defendant's behavior at trial. Most notably, there may be a question of the defendant's deteriorating while under the stress of trial. If the defendant's ego defenses are sufficiently brittle that such decompensation is possible or even probable, the clinician should so note in the report. However, the clinician should not worry too much about making such probability estimates. As noted in § 4.03, the competency question can be raised at any time. Hence, if a currently marginally competent defendant does decompensate at trial, a referral can be made for an evaluation of the defendant's competency at that time. In general, clinicians should be primarily concerned with present competency. They may be helpful to attorneys, though, in providing sufficient support to marginally competent defendants to help them make it though a very stressful time.

(3) Understanding of the Legal Situation

Given the nature of the competency construct, the clinician will, of course, need to interview the client concerning his or her understanding of the purpose of a trial, of the roles of the various participants in the trial process, and of the process of a trial itself (e.g., the nature of examination and cross-examination of witnesses) [see Table 4-5]. It is also necessary to ascertain the client's understanding of the specific charges involved and their possible penalties, as well as the available options (e.g., judge or jury trial; plea bargaining; range of defenses). Particularly given the possibility of plea bargaining or of self-incriminating guilty pleas, it is also important that the client demonstrate an understanding of the pleas available and their probable consequences. Finally, the clinician should, of course, learn the defendant's perceptions and expectations of his or her attorney. In that regard, it is useful to have the defendant describe previous interactions, including both their quantity and quality (as already noted, these responses may be compared with the attorney's referral information).

Information about the client's understanding of the legal situation can usually be obtained most efficaciously in a nonconfrontative conversational interview. While abstract definitions of concepts (e.g., "What is the judge's job?") should be obtained, it is also important to find out whether the defendant has a concrete understanding of the relevant concepts and principles and can apply them to the case. For example, knowing that one does not have to answer questions in interrogation or at trial is more important as a practical matter than being able to give a definition of "the right to remain silent." Thus, as noted earlier, abstract questions should be followed up with questions about application in

hypothetical situations or in situations previously encountered by the defendant.

(4) Amnesia

One of the most troublesome problems in evaluating competency is the weight to be given reported amnesia. As noted in § 4.05(a), amnesia per se is not a bar to competency. The competency standard emphasizes *present* ability to communicate with the attorney and to understand the proceedings. Also, there is often sufficient extrinsic evidence available to obviate the need for the defendant's version. Indeed, general memory problems are more likely to be probative on the issue of competency to stand trial than is amnesia for the specific time of the offense, because the former may interfere with the defendant's ability to follow a trial and communicate with his or her attorney about it.

Nonetheless, because amnesia for the time of the offense is sometimes relevant to a competency determination, the clinician should report the defendant's claims in that regard and allow the court to determine whether it is relevant. In doing so, the clinician should be alert to Fifth Amendment issues [see § 3.02(a)]. We recommend that if the report is to go to all parties, it should state simply, "The defendant claims to be unable to remember/to have difficulty describing the time period of the alleged offense as a result of a memory deficit"; it should not report specific statements by the defendant about the offense, although statements by the defendant as to what others (e.g., the police) say he or she did are quite germane to the defendant's understanding of the charges and should be reported. It may also be useful to report information about the probable source of the amnesia and whether it is remediable, as these determinations will be relevant to the defendant's restorability if the defendant is found to be incompetent partially on the basis of amnesia.

(5) Treatment and Restorability

Although the purpose of a competency evaluation is not to determine the nature of a client's treatment needs, the clinician should feel free to make written or oral statements in that regard if sufficient information is gathered during the competency interview to make such judgments and (1) emergency treatment needs are identified, and/or (2) the basis for referral initially was behavior management problems. For example, in one case seen by us [see the Mills report, § 15.02], referral was precipitated in part by the defendant's attorney's observing his depression. Thus, while appropriately focusing the interview on competency issues as requested in the court order, the evaluating clinicians also noted suggestions that the defendant was actively considering self-destructive behavior and recommended immediate psychotherapeutic intervention.

Moreover, where the defendant appears to be incompetent or marginally competent, statements should be made to the court as to the probability of the defendant's achieving a higher level of competency under various treatment regimens; the length of time that would constitute a reasonable treatment trial; and the level of confidence with which such conclusions are made. If the treatment can be administered on an outpatient basis, such information should also be given. If there is no substantial probability of the defendant's achieving a higher level of competency, then attempts at restoration (especially those involving hospitalization in maximum security forensic units) constitute a needless deprivation of liberty.

4.08. Conclusion: The Need for Policy Consultation

A final point is that attorneys and forensic clinicians can be helpful in educating the community, including legislators, about the system of competency evaluations and problems associated with it. Although public outcry is likely to be attached to alleged abuses of the insanity defense, abuses of competency evaluations and of commitments for restoration of competency are far more common and far more costly in the aggregate. Similarly, if attorneys and clinicians often confuse incompetency and insanity, the error is much more common in the general public. Whether directly through public lectures or interviews or indirectly through education of community leaders and the news media, attorneys and forensic clinicians might perform a useful service in teaching the distinctions between these concepts and the legal and moral underpinnings of the competency question. Such education and consultation might ultimately prevent some of the abuses of the system (e.g., *de facto* incarceration of "incompetent" defendants who have been arrested on the basis of weak evidence). It might also persuade policymakers to reduce some of the wasteful practices (e.g., routine hospitalization) commonly associated with the forensic mental health system.

BIBLIOGRAPHY

Burt & Morris, *A Proposal for the Abolition of Incompetency Plea,* 40 U. CHI. L. REV. 66 (1972).

CRIMINAL JUSTICE MENTAL HEALTH STANDARDS, part IV (1984).

Drope v. Missouri, 420 U.S. 162 (1975).

Dusky v. United States. 362 U.S. 402 (1960).

Jackson v. Indiana, 406 U.S. 715 (1972).

LABORATORY OF COMMUNITY PSYCHIATRY, COMPETENCY TO STAND TRIAL AND MENTAL ILLNESS (1974).

G. MELTON, L. WEITHORN, & C. SLOBOGIN, COMMUNITY MENTAL HEALTH CENTERS AND THE COURTS: AN EVALUATION OF COMMUNITY-BASED FORENSIC SERVICES (1985).

Steadman & Hartstone, *Defendants Incompetent to Stand Trial,* in MENTALLY DISORDERED OFFENDERS: PERSPECTIVES FROM LAW AND SOCIAL SCIENCE (J. Monahan & H. Steadman eds. 1983).

A. STONE, MENTAL HEALTH AND LAW: A SYSTEM IN TRANSITION, ch. 12 (1975).

Winick, *Incompetency to Stand Trial: Developments in the law,* in MENTALLY DISORDERED OFFENDERS: PERSPECTIVES FROM LAW AND SOCIAL SCIENCES (J. Monahan & H. Steadman eds. 1983).

CHAPTER FIVE

Other Competencies in the Criminal Process

5.01. Introduction

Competency to stand trial is not the only specific legal competency that the mental health professional may be asked to evaluate. Human dignity demands respect for individual autonomy unless there are compelling reasons to infringe upon that autonomy.[1] In such a framework, the state can validly invoke its *parens patriae* (literally, "state as parent") power[2] only if the individual is incompetent to make the *specific* decision or to perform the specific act.

As we have discussed in Chapter 4, the most common error that clinicians make in assessing competency to stand trial is assuming that diagnoses of general impairment (e.g., mental retardation, psychosis) translate into incompetency in performance of the specific functions involved in competency to stand trial. Generally speaking, this concern applies in evaluation of other legal competencies, which also involve competency to perform specific functions.[3] Some of these questions of competency involve civil issues and are discussed in Chapter 9. In the present chapter, guidelines are discussed for evaluations of specific competencies arising in the criminal process (other than competency to stand trial): competency to confess; competency to plead guilty; competency to refuse an insanity defense; competency to waive the right to an attorney; competency to testify[4]; and competency to be sentenced and executed.

5.02. Competency to Confess

Unlike most competency issues (which are likely to involve questions of *present* mental functioning), a defendant's competency to confess is likely to be raised only after the fact. Typically, the defense will claim that, at the time the defendant made a self-incriminating statement, the individual was incompetent to waive his or her rights under the Fifth and Sixth Amendments, and the statement should therefore be suppressed. The clinician will usually be asked then to form an opinion about the defendant's state of mind at the time the statement was made. This inquiry is complicated by the fact that the condition that is alleged to have created incompetence often has disappeared or at least has been alleviated by the time of the evaluation. Perhaps most commonly, defendants claim to have been under the influence of drugs and alcohol at the time that they were interrogated. At other times, defendants assert that, as a result of immaturity or mental disability, they did not understand their

rights during interrogation, although this problem has since been remediated through education and counseling by their defense attorneys.
[Cf. Mills, Bates reports in §§ 15.05, 15.06.]

(a)   The Law of Confessions[5]

Evaluation of a defendant's competency to confess is complicated not only by the fact that it
usually involves post hoc speculation. The question of admissibility of confessions is fraught with
competing values. On the one hand is the desire
for fairness in police interrogation and for procedures to ensure that the statements obtained
are reliable; on the other, confessions are generally considered to be highly probative evidence, which many believe to be necessary for
effective prosecution of criminals and protection
of the public safety.[6] Although a thorough discussion of the psychological issues implicated by
the law of confessions is beyond the scope of this
book, a brief review of the evolution of standards for assessing the admissibility of confessions may illuminate the limits and the complexity of clinical evaluation of a defendant's
competency to confess.[7]

The Supreme Court's concern with the constitutional limits of police interrogations began
with Brown v. Mississippi[8] in 1936. In Brown, the
Court vacated the convictions of three black defendants whose signatures on confessions to
murder had been extorted through physical torture—hanging and severe beatings—by police.
The Court held that the defendants' Fourteenth
Amendments rights to due process were violated. In Brown and nearly 40 cases thereafter,[9]
the Court examined the validity of confessions
on the basis of whether the totality of circumstances combined in such a way as to deprive
the defendants of their will to resist police coercion.[10] Then, for a brief period, the Court shifted
its focus in confession cases to whether the Sixth
Amendment right to counsel was violated by
failure to provide counsel during interrogation.[11]
Not until Miranda v. Arizona[12] did the Court firmly
adopt the Fifth Amendment's "privilege against
self-incrimination" as the prime basis for evaluation of confessions.

Besides the doctrinal shift, Miranda is of course

important for the adoption of per se rules for
invalidating confessions. Unless defendants, while
subjected to custodial interrogation, are given the
famous warnings mandated by Miranda, any
statements they make are inadmissible.[13] After
being read their rights, defendants may waive
these rights, but only if the waiver is knowing,
intelligent, and voluntary.[14] Moreover, interrogation must cease if a defendant says that he or
she does not want to talk or invokes the right to
counsel "in any manner and at any stage in the
process."[15]

The per se rules in Miranda were designed to
provide defendants with a measure of protection
against sophisticated psychological ploys of police interrogators[16] without the necessity of dis-
cerning the facts of an essentially "secret
inquisition"[17] and subjecting them to the hoary
rules of the law of voluntariness.[18] While the
Supreme Court has undercut Miranda in the past
decade,[19] it has shown little inclination to overrule it altogether.[20] Nonetheless, analysis of voluntariness remains a key element in confession
cases. Voluntariness is still at issue in determining the validity of a defendant's waiver of the
right to remain silent, even when Miranda warnings are properly given.[21] Moreover, the Burger
Court has construed statements taken in violation of Miranda to be admissible to impeach defendants' testimony, provided that they were
voluntarily given.[22] The Court has also held that
the improper admission of statements taken in
violation of Miranda may be harmless error, provided that the confession was voluntary.[23] Finally, Miranda does not apply outside "custodial
interrogation"; thus, the Court has held that investigative interviews in the home, or in public
after a stop for a traffic arrest, or even at the
station house may not implicate Miranda in situations that are not the functional equivalent of
arrest.[24]

This partial return to due process voluntariness analysis is complicated by the Court's willingness to consider questions of subtle, psychological coercion.[25] While there may be little question
of the offensiveness of physical abuse as a tactic
in eliciting confessions,[26] such moral consensus
clearly does not apply in analyses of the appropriateness of police exerting "a tug on the suspect to confess."[27] When police casually men-

tion to a suspect known to have fundamentalist religious beliefs that falling snow may prevent a child murder victim's Christian burial, is such a statement an unduly coercive elicitation of information concerning where the body is hidden? The Supreme Court has implied that the answer to this question is yes.[28] Is there any less coercion when police state in the presence of a murder suspect that it would be a shame if children at a school for the handicapped find the gun used in the murder and hurt themselves? In *Rhode Island v. Innis,*[29] the court held that no coercion existed under this set of facts.

Part of the confusion displayed by the Court emanates from a mix of philosophical paradigms regarding the nature of choice [see § 1.03(a)]. In short, there is a rather incoherent mix of free will (how "hard" did the police make the defendant's choice?) with determinism (was the defendant psychologically incapable of resisting?), such that the analysis of facts in individual situations like those described above remains often unpredictable.[30]

This philosophical confusion is exacerbated by conflicts in attitudes toward police interrogation. On the one hand there is a desire to receive and admit confessions from guilty defendants, when these statements are elicited under circumstances that do not precipitate false confessions. Accordingly, there is a need for effective police interrogation. On the other hand, there is a concern that police procedures not be *too* effective. Confessions—even if reliable—are seen as unfairly obtained if they were elicited in a situation in which the defendant's will was overborne. Moreover, there is concern that some police tactics are unfair regardless of their impact on individuals. Thus, there is ambivalence about the desirability of effective interrogation ploys.

One answer may be to go beyond *Miranda* and establish new per se rules that explicitly indicate which interrogation tactics are believed to elicit confessions unfairly. Thus, White has suggested rules banning the admission of incriminating statements obtained when police underplay the seriousness of the charges, announce that the suspect is known to be guilty, or assume a nonadversary stance (e.g., indicate that their purpose is to help the defendant.)[31]

A final point about the law of confessions is that unless there is some connection between police tactics and the confession, due process and *Miranda* are not implicated because there is no *governmental* coercion. In *Colorado v. Connelly,*[32] the defendant flew from Boston to Denver to confess to Denver police about a murder committed several months earlier in Colorado. Despite *Miranda* warnings and repeated reminders that he did not need to talk, Connelly insisted on giving police self-incriminating details of the murder. The police observed no signs of mental illness at that time. However, in trying to exclude Connelly's admissions at a subsequent hearing, the defense presented the testimony of a psychiatrist stating that although Connelly understood his right to remain silent, he had been "compelled" to confess by so-called "command delusions" from God. The Supreme Court held that neither voluntariness analysis nor *Miranda* required the exclusion of the admissions in this case, even assuming such delusions existed, because there was no police conduct "causally related to the confession." While Connelly's illness may have rendered his statements unreliable, this was a matter to be decided under state evidentiary law.[33] After *Connelly,* then, statements not "caused" by the police (a term, it should be noted, as amorphous as the voluntariness concept itself) will be admissible regardless of the defendant's mental state, so long as they are considered admissible under state law and so long as the defendant was not so *cognitively* impaired that the right to remain silent was not understood.

(b)   Evaluation Issues

The scope of the questions that the mental health professional is to consider when performing an evaluation of competency to confess is at least superficially clear. Was the defendant's behavior "knowing" (i.e., did the defendant understand that he or she was waiving rights)? Was it "intelligent" (i.e., was the waiver of rights the product of a rational reasoning process?)? Most problematically, was it "voluntary" (i.e., was the situation in its totality—and in its interaction with the defendant's state of mind—so coercive that the defendant's will was overborne?)?

However, as is perhaps apparent from the

preceding discussion of law, it is unlikely that clinical opinion will be considered very probative.[34] The inquiry is likely to focus instead on whether police "followed the book" (e.g., whether they properly read *Miranda* warnings; whether they refrained from unduly threatening behavior) and on whether the defendant "seemed OK" at the time of the interrogation. In both instances, courts are likely to rely primarily on the testimony of eyewitnesses, who are most likely to be the police themselves, or audiotapes and videotapes when they are available. Thus, defendants' claims that their statements were involuntary because they were too fatigued and/or too intoxicated to be able to withstand police pressure or to know what they were doing are unlikely to stand unless there is corroborating evidence to that effect.

Similarly, barring gross mental disorder or obvious mental retardation, claims that defendants did not understand what rights they were waiving are unlikely to prevail if the defendants responded affirmatively to the yes–no questions asked at the time interrogation began (e.g., whether they understood the warnings read to them; whether they wished to make a statement), especially if such defendants have had previous court experience. Yet, several studies have indicated that the *Miranda* warnings have failed to change suspects' behavior in interrogation and that defendants frequently do not fully comprehend the warnings.[35] In the best-designed research of this sort, Grisso found juveniles' understanding of *Miranda* warnings to be particularly likely to be deficient; however, results of interviews with the adult comparison groups showed that many adults from lower socioeconomic strata also lacked adequate comprehension of *Miranda* rights. For both juveniles and adults, previous court experience was not a predictor of understanding of the *Miranda* warnings. It is thus suggested that repeated exposure to the *Miranda* warnings (at least within the emotionally charged setting of interrogation) does little to remediate the ignorance and misunderstanding of *Miranda* rights.[36]

Despite such evidence, and despite the state's burden to prove that defendants' waivers of their Fifth and Sixth Amendment rights were competently made, there will most commonly need to be clear evidence of police misbehavior or gross mental disability of a defendant before a confession will be suppressed. Nonetheless, in cases where the question is raised, clinicians should first question the defendants about the meaning of the *Miranda* warnings (both definitions and applications) to obtain a sense of their present understanding. Then the clinicians should learn step by step from the defendants what they recall about the interrogation. What did they think they were doing when they signed the waivers? What choices did they think they had? Thus, evaluation of the "knowing" and "intelligent" prongs of the competency standard is relatively straightforward. In addition to reporting defendants' present and claimed past level of understanding of their rights, clinicians may also help the court to evaluate this information by reporting norms of comprehension of rights for persons of similar age, socioeconomic status, and court experience, especially if a defendant claims misunderstanding but does not appear grossly disordered [see, e.g., Grisso's work[37] and Bates report, § 15.02].

Evaluation of "voluntariness" is more speculative and far-ranging. A step-by-step retrospective interview about the interrogation will still be necessary, but other information may also be needed. If, for example, there is a question about a defendant's being especially suggestible, the clinician will want to find out more about the defendant's response to authority figures in other situations. Similarly, if a defendant claims to have been intoxicated at the time of interrogation, information will be needed about the individual's previous drug and alcohol history in order to evaluate this report of his or her mental state at that time. Police reports and other eyewitness accounts of the defendant's behavior are also sometimes helpful, as are transcripts or tapes of the confession itself.

In view of the fuzziness of the concept in the law and the illogic of the concept in a deterministic paradigm, clinicians should not couch their report in terms of "voluntariness."[38] Rather, the clinician should report on those aspects of the defendant's functioning that might make him or her especially vulnerable to influence by the police. Where systematic data are available as to the effectiveness of a given interrogation technique with people of similar characteristics, such research should also be noted.[39]

After *Connelly,* the mere presence of a severe mental dysfunction will not support a constitutional claim that a confession was involuntarily made—some proof that police took advantage of the defendant's condition is required. Thus, whenever the defense theory is that a confession was unduly coerced, clinicians should be careful to report from available sources the extent of police interaction with the defendant so that the "causal connection" issue can be addressed intelligently.

5.03. *Competency to Plead Guilty*

Analogous to competency to confess is the question of competency to plead guilty. In the former instance, the issue is whether the defendant knowingly, intelligently, and voluntarily waived Fifth and Sixth Amendment rights. Similarly, competency to plead guilty subsumes competency to waive the privilege against self-incrimination, the right to a jury trial, and the right to confront one's accusers,[40] in that a plea of guilty results in conviction without a trial. It also requires an understanding of the elements of and the penalties associated with the offense to which the defendant is pleading guilty.[41]

In view of the fact that specific constitutional rights are effectively waived by a plea of guilty, the Supreme Court has held that the judge must affirmatively establish on the record the defendant's competency to plead (i.e., to waive these rights.)[42] However, in the majority of jurisdictions the standard for competency to plead guilty is the same as competency to stand trial.[43] Such a standard obfuscates the specific points that the defendant must understand.

A more appropriate standard was suggested by Judge Hufstedler in her dissent in *Schoeller v. Dunbar*[44] and subsequently by the Ninth Circuit[45] and D.C. Circuit[46] Courts of Appeals:

> The standards measuring a defendant's competency to stand trial are not necessarily iden-

tical to his competency to enter a plea of guilty. To the extent that they differ, the standards of competency to plead guilty are higher than those of competency to stand trial. A defendant is not competent to plead guilty if mental illness has substantially impaired his ability to make a reasoned choice among the alternatives presented to him and to understand the consequences of his plea.[47]

The mental health professional performing an evaluation of competency to plead guilty is thus well advised to treat the question in terms of the defendant's reasons for the plea, understanding of the *specific* rights being waived, and understanding of the charge being admitted. Although the court may ultimately treat some of the information as extraneous, the court should have available to it information about considerations that on their face appear particularly germane to competency to plead guilty, as well as more general information about the defendant's competency to stand trial [see, e.g., the Bates report, § 15.03].

Finally, the same problems noted in the preceding section about "voluntariness" of confessions apply in assessments of "voluntariness" of guilty pleas. The vast majority of criminal convictions arise in plea bargains, not as the result of trials.[48] Guilty pleas typically result in less aversive consequences than are risked by going to trial. Are such avoidance responses voluntary? The issue is starkly reflected in a case of a defendant who pleaded guilty to first-degree murder in exchange for a life sentence because he was "paralyzed with fear of the death penalty" he might receive at trial and consequently unable to weigh alternatives rationally.[49] Obviously, less dramatic examples happen daily in which a defendant who may have some defenses available chooses to accept a plea bargain in order to avoid risk of more severe consequences. Are such instances also involuntary? Suppose also that a defendant places trust in the attorney, to the extent of immediately accepting the attorney's suggestion to plea-bargain. Is such a plea voluntary? As noted in the preceding section, there is no *scientific* basis for differentiating these cases on the basis of voluntariness. The mental health professional should report a defendant's reasoning about the decision and any external pressures to accept a bargain, and should leave to the judge determination of whether the choice was so hard as to render the plea involuntary.

5.04.   Competency to Refuse an Insanity Defense

A relatively uncommon variant of competency is competency to refuse a plea of not guilty by reason of insanity. The basic legal issue is whether the court may impose such a defense on a defendant who was possibly insane at the time of the offense. Taking the issue one step further, does the court in fact have a *duty* to impose such a defense *sua sponte* [50] when it believes that the evidence points toward an acquittal by reason of insanity?

The appellate courts that have considered the questions of the judiciary's authority and duty to impose an insanity defense on mentally disabled defendants have been divided in their approach to the issue. [51] One line of cases emphasizes the social cost of permitting a waiver of an insanity defense and, therefore, upholds judges' authority to raise the insanity defense *sua sponte*. Illustrative of this point of view is *Whalem v. United States.* [52] In *Whalem*, the Circuit Court of Appeals for the District of Columbia appeared to establish a duty of trial judges to impose an insanity defense when the defense would be likely to succeed:

> One of the major foundations for the structure of the criminal law is the concept of responsibility, and the law is clear that one whose acts would otherwise be criminal has committed no crime at all if because of incapacity due to age or mental condition he is not responsible for those acts. . . .
>
> In the courtroom confrontations between the individual and society the trial judge must uphold this structural foundation by refusing to allow the conviction of an obviously mentally irresponsible defendant, and when there is sufficient question as to a defendant's mental responsibility at the time of the crime, that issue must become part of the case. Just as the judge must insist that the *corpus delecti* be proved before a defendant who has confessed may be convicted, so too must the judge forestall the conviction of one who in the eyes of the law

is not mentally responsible for his otherwise criminal acts. [53]

The *Whalem* formulation thus emphasizes society's interests in avoiding the conviction of a morally blameless person. Although it permits judges in their discretion to take the *defendant's* interests into account as well, [54] these interests would not be dispositive.

In a second line of cases, led by *Frendak v. United States,* [55] the defendant's decision with respect to raising the insanity defense is to be followed so long as the defendant is competent to make the decision. Pointing to the United States Supreme Court's post-*Whalem* decisions in *North Carolina v. Alford* [56] (a competent defendant is permitted to plead guilty even when denying guilt) and *Faretta v. California* [57] (establishing the right to represent oneself), the District of Columbia Court of Appeals concluded in *Frendak* that "respect for a defendant's freedom as a person mandates that he or she be permitted to make fundamental decisions about the course of the proceedings." [58] The court noted several reasons why a defendant might choose to refuse an insanity defense: (1) an insanity acquittal may result in a longer period of confinement than would conviction; (2) the defendant may believe that better treatment will be received in prison than in a mental hospital; (3) the defendant may wish to avoid the stigma associated with mental disorder; (4) commitment to the mental health system may result in collateral loss of legal rights (e.g., the ability to obtain a driver's license); (5) the defendant may view the crime as a political or religious act, which an insanity defense would negate. [59] The court was persuaded—properly, in our view—that, because the defendant must bear the consequences of any decision, these reasons are more compelling than the *Whalem* purpose of upholding a societal concept of justice. [60] Accordingly, *Frendak* limits the inquiry about whether a defendant may refuse an insanity defense to an investigation of the defendant's competency to waive the defense. [61]

Obviously, the nature of the inquiry concerning a defendant's ability to refuse an insanity defense will vary with the jurisdiction's approach to the problem. Clinicians asked to perform evaluations on this point should be careful, therefore, to identify the specific issues that the court or the referring attorney wishes addressed. In jurisdictions emphasizing societal interests, the scope of the evaluation may be akin to a typical evaluation of mental state at the time of the offense. The issue in such an instance is simply whether the weight of the evidence points toward a viable insanity defense, although the defendant's reasoning process in rejecting the defense may be considered relevant. On the other hand, in a jurisdiction emphasizing the defendant's interests in a *Frendak*-style analysis, the nature of the evaluation will be similar to that of competency to plead guilty. The clinician will need to explore the defendant's understanding of alternative pleas and their consequences, and the perceived probability of success of various defenses in the defendant's case.

In jurisdictions following *Frendak,* it will also be important to determine the defendant's reasoning in rejecting an insanity defense. In that regard, the scope of the evaluation may extend more broadly than is typical in an evaluation of competency to plead guilty. In particular, the clinician may need to determine whether the defendant's refusal to pursue an insanity defense is related to denial of the severity of his or her mental disorder.[62] In such a case, it will be necessary to perform a more general examination of present mental status and perhaps mental state at the time of the offense—at least at a screening level [see § 6.05(a)]—in order to assess the rationality of a defendant's claim that an insanity defense should be rejected because "there is nothing wrong" with him or her. Whether the level of denial (or lack of understanding of the alternative pleas and defenses) is sufficiently severe to warrant a finding of incompetency to refuse an insanity defense is, of course, a matter for the judge to decide.

5.05. *Competency to Waive the Right to Counsel*

The decision that is probably most likely to have an adverse effect on a defendant's ability to achieve a fair trial is the waiver of the right to counsel. By making such a decision, the defendant is de-prived of a legally trained advocate of the defendant's interests. Waiver is seldom, is ever, likely to be in a defendant's best interests.

Nonetheless, in *Faretta v. California,*[63] the United States Supreme Court held that the Sixth Amendment guarantees criminal defendants a right to self-representation. Writing for the majority, Justice Stewart emphasized that procedural rights of due process belong to the accused, not his or her counsel:

> It [the Sixth Amendment] speaks of the "assistance" of counsel, and an assistant, however expert, is still an assistant. The language and spirit of the Sixth Amendment contemplate that counsel, like the other defense tools guaranteed by the Amendment, shall be an aid to a willing defendant—not an organ of the State interposed between an unwilling defendant and his right to defend himself personally. To thrust counsel upon the accused, against his considered wish, thus violates the logic of the Amendment. In such a case, counsel is not an assistant but a master; and the right to make a defense is stripped of the personal character upon which the Amendment insists.[64]

The Court noted further that, while the defendant may ultimately be acting to his or her detriment in deciding to proceed *pro se,* the value of free choice is worthy of constitutional protection even in criminal proceedings.[65]

The right to self-representation is not absolute, however. The defendant proceeding *pro se* may not disrupt the dignity of the courtroom.[66] Moreover, in view of the benefits which the defendant loses through waiver of the right to counsel, justice requires that the waiver be competently made.[67] Accordingly, the judge should warn the defendant of the dangers of self-representation and conduct an inquiry to ensure that the defendant has made a knowing and intelligent choice.[68]

The precise standard to be used in judging a defendant's competency to waive the right to counsel is unclear in *Faretta.* What *is* clear is what the standard is *not:* technical legal knowledge.[69] The Supreme Court found the trial judge's quiz of Faretta on the exceptions to the hearsay rule and the rules for challenges of potential jurors to be irrelevant to the competency issue. Rather, the question is whether the defendant is approaching the waiver decision "with eyes open"—

that is, whether the defendant is "literate, competent, and understanding, and . . . voluntarily exercising his informed free will." [70]

Obviously, however, some legal knowledge is necessary to appreciate the dangers of self-representation.[71] Presumably the level of knowledge required is higher than for competency to stand trial; defending oneself necessitates greater awareness of the legal process than merely assisting in one's defense. The mental health professional asked to perform an evaluation of a defendant's competency to waive the right to counsel should proceed as in an evaluation of competency to stand trial, with special emphasis on the functions that legal counsel performs. The question of whether a defendant knows enough to be able to decide competently to proceed *pro se* should then be left to the judge. In this regard, it should be noted that even if the judge decides the defendant can make this decision, the judge has the authority to appoint standby counsel to advise the defendant.[72]

While the elements of "knowing" are vague, "intelligent' and "voluntary" are still more problematic, and the latter prongs of the test are likely to be the foci of evaluation. In the rare instances in which a defendant is referred for evaluation, the referral is likely to be based on a question of the defendant's soundness of judgment, rather than his or her understanding of the risks of self-representation. The decision may have been based on a defeatist attitude[73] or, perhaps most commonly, at least questionably paranoid ideation (e.g., a desire to put forward a defense based on a theory that extraterrestrial forces were in control of one's behavior). In the absence of a clear standard, identifying whether such reasoning abrogates a defendant's right to self-representation is especially difficult when *any* invocation of the right is likely to be ill-advised. In view of this lack of clarity, our usual injunction to refrain from ultimate issue conclusions is particularly pertinent.

5.06.   *Competency to Testify* [74]

The competencies discussed in the preceding sections have been concerned only with the de-

fendant. "Competency to testify" refers, of course, to a prospective *witness's* capacity to give testimony.[75] Taking into account that the vagaries of perception and memory may distort the testimony of any witness,[76] the courts have been concerned with excluding testimony that may be so unreliable as to mislead the factfinder. Of particular concern is the reliability of testimony by individuals whose memory and reality testing may be substantially impaired by reason of developmental immaturity or mental disorder. Thus, in a criminal trial, the question of competency to testify is most likely to arise if the victim of the alleged offense is a child, mentally retarded, or psychotic.

This review focuses on children, although the legal standards to be discussed apply to all three groups. The developmental literature is useful in understanding the likely effects of cognitive immaturity for both children and mentally retarded adults. Where the prospective witness is a severely mentally disordered person, an individual assessment will need to be made of the severity of impairment in cognitive functioning.

(a)   The Law on Children's Competency to Testify

There is generally a rebuttable presumption that children are incompetent to testify, although the age at which the presumption is set varies across jurisdictions from seven to ten.[77] Through the presumption, the law is recognizing that children may be less likely than adults to give reliable testimony, but that children below the designated age should not be per se incompetent to testify. Rather, the competency of child witnesses of any age must be established on a case-by-case determination of whether the child's testimony will enhance justice.[78]

This principle has been established in Anglo-American law since the 18th century.[79] The traditional view is reflected in the United States Supreme Court's 1895 decision in *Wheeler v. United States*.[80] In that case, the Court held that the five-year-old son of a murder victim was properly qualified as a witness:

> That the boy was not by reason of his youth, as a matter of law, absolutely disqualified as a

witness, is clear. While no one would think of calling as a witness an infant only two or three years old, there is no precise age which determines the question of competency. This depends on the capacity and intelligence of the child, his appreciation of the difference between truth and falsehood, as well as of his duty to tell the former. The decision of this question rests primarily with the trial judge, who sees the proposed witness, notices his manner, his apparent possession or lack of intelligence, and may resort to any examination which will tend to disclose his capacity and intelligence as well as his understanding of the obligation of an oath.[81]

As *Wheeler* suggests, in determining a child's competency to testify, the courts have tended to place primary emphasis on the child's ability to differentiate truth from falsehood, to comprehend the duty to tell the truth, and to understand the consequences of not fulfilling this duty.[82] This inquiry has often followed a line of questions on *voir dire* directed toward ascertaining a child's religious and moral beliefs.[83] The child need not, however, understand the legal and religious nature of an oath.[84] Rather, it is sufficient that the child have a general understanding of the moral obligation to tell the truth.

While necessary, adherence to the truth is not sufficient to establish competency. There is also a necessity that the witness have cognitive skills adequate to comprehend the event witnessed and to communicate memories of the event in response to questions at trial.[85] Thus, competency to testify implies some measure of competency at the time of the event witnessed as well as at the time of the trial.[86] The child must be able to organize the experience cognitively and to differentiate it from other thoughts and fantasies.[87] Furthermore, the child must be able to maintain these skills under psychological stress and under pressure, real or perceived, from adult authority figures to shape his or her responses in a particular way. Thus, level of suggestibility is an important factor.[88] Particular kinds of testimony may require further specific competencies. Most notably, testimony by a child on sexual abuse may require verification of the child's comprehension of the meaning of sexual terms and behavior.[89]

The implication of the discussion thus far is

that assessment of a child's competency to testify may require a rather extensive and formal assessment of the child's cognitive, moral, and emotional capacities on *voir dire*. Given that time will be consumed in any event and that there is no litmus test for competence, Wigmore has recommended abolition of the requirement that a child's competency be established before being allowed to testify.[90] Wigmore would have the trier of fact simply evaluate a child's testimony in context, just as any witness's testimony must be examined for its credibility:

> A rational view of the peculiarities of child-nature, and of the daily course of justice in our courts, must lead to the conclusion that the effort to measure a priori the degrees of trustworthiness in children's statements, and to distinguish the point at which they cease to be totally incredible and acquire some degree of credibility, is futile and unprofitable. . . . Recognizing on the one hand the childish disposition to weave romances and to treat imagination for verity, and on the other the rooted ingenuousness of children and their tendency to speak straightforwardly what is in their minds, it must be concluded that the sensible way is to put the child upon the stand and let the story come out for what it may be worth.[91]

Wigmore's view has not been adopted by any American jurisdiction. Consequently, it is useful to examine psychological research that may be helpful to courts faced with assessing the value of children's testimony.

(b) Psychological Research

(1) Memory

There has been little research directly related to children's behavior on tasks such as courtroom testimony. The most germane study compared children's and adults' performance on eyewitness tasks by Marin, Holmes, Guth, and Kovac.[92] In that study, students aged 5 to 22 were placed in a situation in which a confederate of the experimenter interrupted a session to complain angrily about the experimenter's using a room supposedly already scheduled. Subjects were questioned about the incident after a brief interval (10–30 minutes) and after two weeks. Memory was assessed using free recall, objective questions (including one leading question), and photo identification. Older subjects were superior only on the free-narrative task. Older subjects produced much more material on free recall (mean number of descriptive statements: kindergarten and first grade, 1.42; third and fourth grades, 3.75; seventh and eighth grades, 6.50; college students, 8.25). However, the youngest subjects were significantly more likely to recall correctly those items that they did produce (only 3% incorrect). The investigators suggested that the results supported the use even of young children as witnesses in court, particularly given that the objective-questions task most closely paralleled the trial situation:

> This additional finding [of accuracy on free recall] lends . . . further support to the conclusion that even very young children can be credible eyewitnesses, particularly when combined with the other findings that children are as capable as adults of answering direct objective questions and are no more easily swayed into incorrect answers by leading questions. It appears that children are no more likely than are adults to fabricate incorrect responses, and that when their testimony is elicited through the use of appropriate cues, it is no less credible than that of adults.[93]

Marin, Holmes, Guth, and Kovac's findings are consistent with earlier laboratory studies suggesting that children as young as age four or five perform as well as adults on recognition-memory tasks,[94] but that there are marked developmental trends in free-recall ability. The latter trends appear related to developmental differences in retrieval strategy. That is, young children require direct cues, such as specific, direct questions, to stimulate recall.[95]

In sum, the available data suggest that, given simple, supportive questions, even young children generally have sufficient memory skills to respond to the recall demands of testimony. However, two qualifiers must be added to this conclusion. First, although some studies used lengthy recall intervals,[96] available research has not tested possible developmental differences in recall over periods of months, as is a common demand in the legal system. Second, available

studies have not involved recall under stress or in situations of great personal involvement.

(2) Cognitive Development

Even if children have sufficient recall ability to testify, such testimony would be of dubious value if the memories were based on erroneous impressions. Consequently, a child's ability to conceptualize complex events and to order them in space and time are of importance. It is a truism of Piagetian theory that "preoperational"[97] children, often up to age seven, are unable to "decenter" from the most obvious attribute of a stimulus so that they can make use of all of the relevant information. To cite a classic example, young children who observe a clay string rolled into a ball and then rolled back into a string believe that there is more clay present when it is in a ball, which looks more massive. This inability to deal with multiple stimulus characteristics and relationships may affect a child's ability to recite facts accurately.

For example, young children have difficulty in understanding time independent of distance and speed, and may have difficulty in describing the chronology of events. Piaget observed three stages in development of concepts of time.[98] In the first stage, common among four- and five-year-olds, time is defined in terms of spatial stopping points of objects. The object that stops further ahead is perceived as having traveled faster, longer, and further. In the second stage, the child begins to consider other factors, such as starting points. In the third stage, achieved by age seven or eight, the child masters the concept of time. Later investigations have indicated that acquisition of the concept of time distinguished from speed and distance typically comes even later than Piaget thought, perhaps near age ten on the average.[99]

However, some recent critics of Piagetian theory have suggested that, on many tasks, preschoolers may be less egocentric and illogical in their thinking than Piaget believed.[100] Borke[101] has found that children three to four years old have the capacity to take the perspective of another,[102] provided that the specific task is a simple one and involves little use of language.[103] Siegel has argued that the classical finding of young children's inability to pass "conversation" tasks (e.g., the ball-of-clay example cited at the beginning of this section) is often a manifestation of linguistic deficits.[104] That is, young children may not understand the words "more," "bigger," and the like, but they may be able to demonstrate understanding of the concepts nonverbally. Furthermore, there is considerable evidence that preschoolers can be trained in conservation skills,[105] contrary to the Piagetian hypothesis that the necessary cognitive structures would not be expected to have developed adequately. In some instances, apparent failures on Piagetian tasks may also be the result of recency effects (with the most recently presented material remembered best)[106] and organizational difficulties in recall rather than failures in conceptualization.[107]

Although these studies have considerable significance in understanding the nature of child development generally, they do not moot the point here that young children are likely to have difficulty in conceptualizing complex events and possibly therefore in describing them reliably.[108] Borke, for example, interpreted previous findings of egocentrism on perspective-taking tasks as resulting from "children's inability to perform on tasks which were cognitively too difficult for them, rather than any inherently egocentric orientation on the part of young children."[109] Borke also noted that the cognitive changes in middle childhood do result in significant transformations in the child's capacity for empathy and reciprocal social interaction. Furthermore, while the work of Brainerd, Siegel, Trabasso, and others indicates that children's capacities may be greater than frequently assumed,[110] there is also little evidence that these abilities will be demonstrated without special training or assessment. Consequently, given the realities of the courtroom situation, cognitive–developmental factors remain a problem for evaluating children's testimony.[111]

Nonetheless, young children's immaturity of conceptualization may have less import for the reliability of their testimony than appears at first glance. First, the question at hand is whether children's testimony is so unreliable that jurors would be unduly influenced by it. Thus, the question is one of jurors' behavior as well as children's competency. Specifically, in the present context, can jurors accurately perceive what the objective reality was from an account of the subjective reality of a child? If so, the child's cognitive immaturity would be of less significance.

Second, children's lack of ability to comprehend a situation fully may not be so severe as to render them incapable of the level of observation required by the law. For example, understanding of sexuality and reproduction requires an understanding of physical causality and social identity. An accurate concept of the origin of babies is not reached typically until about age 12.[112] On the other hand, there is evidence that by age four most children are quite aware of sex differences and willing to speak freely about them.[113] Thus, in cases of sexual abuse, children can be expected to give an accurate description of what happened, provided that questions are direct and in language familiar to a child. Children *will* appear incompetent, however, if the examiner uses technical vocabulary rather than slang or dolls or drawings. Monge, Dusek, and Lawless[114] found that even ninth graders are often unfamiliar with "proper" terms for sexual anatomy and physiology:

> [O]nly 38.4% of the students knew the meaning of the word *menstruation;* 13.1% knew the definition of *scrotum;* 14.1% knew what *coitus* means; 30.3% knew that *Fallopian tubes* were part of the female reproductive system, and 54.5% knew that *seminal vesicles* were part of the male reproductive system; the meaning of *menopause* was known by 27.5% of the students.[115]

(3) Moral Development

If in fact children can relate their experiences adequately, then the principal concern is whether they will do so truthfully. While the courts have been particularly concerned with this problem in assessing competency to testify, the concern here seems misplaced. There is in fact little correlation between age and honesty.[116] Indeed, police experience with child victims confirms the research experience in other settings. From 1969 to 1974, Michigan police referred to a polygraph

examiner 147 children whose veracity about allegations of sexual abuse was questioned. Only
one child was judged to be lying.[117]

Where there *is* a developmental trend, though,
is in the reasons that children give to justify behavior. As children grow older, they become more
sociocentric and oriented toward respect for
persons.[118] Several points are noteworthy in this
context.

First, the law is less interested in witnesses'
attitude toward the truth and conceptualization
of the truth than in their behavior. Justice will
be served if witnesses tell the truth, regardless
of their reasons for doing so. Therefore, such
inquiry probably is superfluous.[119]

Second, even if there is some reason to ascertain a child's conceptualization of duty to tell the
truth, the yes–no and definition questions common used on *voir dire* are inadequate measures.
One of the philosophical underpinnings of current cognitive–developmental theories of moral
development is that a given behavior may be
motivated by vastly different levels of moral reasoning.[120] Similarly, asking a child to tell the
meaning of "truth," "oath," or "God" probably
tells more about the child's intellectual development than about his or her propensity to tell
the truth.[121]

Third, understanding of the oath is probably
unimportant. Indeed, it probably has little effect
on adult behavior. To the extent to which the
oath does have an effect, it would be on a primitive level of moral development common among
young children: reification of rules[122] and avoidance of punishment.[123]

Where immature moral development may be
a factor is in suggestibility. Young children tend
to perceive rules as "morally absolute," un-
changeable, and bestowed by authority.[124]
Therefore, they may confuse the suggestions of
an adult authority figure with the truth. This
hypothesis is considered next.

(4)   Suggestibility

One of the problems that has been noted generally in eyewitness testimony is witnesses' frequent vulnerability to suggestion by opposing attorneys in leading questions.[125] That is, even in

average adults, suggestibility is a real problem in
credibility and competence of witnesses. Given
the greater suggestibility that is frequently assumed to occur in children,[126] children's testimony might be *so* unreliable that in those instances the courts would not want to take the
risk of unreliability that inheres in any testimony. In addition to the cognitive–developmental factors described in the preceding section, it
might be expected on the basis of simple learning theory that children's behavior would be
shaped by their perceptions of adults' expectations for their testimony (and hence the kind of
testimony that will be rewarded or punished),
particularly given young children's essentially
dependent status.

In Marin, Holmes, Guth, and Kovac's investigation,[127] young children were no less affected
by a leading question than were adults. This
finding needs to be further investigated, however. There was only one leading question used
in Marin's group's study, and the interviewer
probably had less authority in the eyes of a child
than would an attorney asking what seem to be
threatening, challenging questions in the imposing setting of a courtroom.

There is some experimental evidence for developmental changes in suggestibility, although
the changes are complex ones. In one frequently
cited study involving conformity to suggestions
by peers,[128] it was found that task difficulty in-
teracted with age in the degree of conformity to
peer judgments. Children in second, fifth, and
eighth grades were asked to determine which of
two drawings shown briefly by a slide projector
contained more dots. In the most difficult condition, both drawings contained 15 dots. In a
medium-difficulty condition, one drawing contained 15 dots and the other 16. In the third,
easiest condition, one drawing contained 15 and
the other 17. Before giving their answer, the
children heard two other children respond.
Hoving, Hamm, and Galvin found increasing
conformity by age on the most difficult task. In
the medium-difficulty condition, there was increasing conformity from second to fifth grade
but decreasing conformity from fifth to eighth
grade. Conformity decreased by age in the least
ambiguous situation. Thus, in relatively straight-

forward situations, older children and early ad-olescents were willing to withstand peer pres-sure and make independent judgments. On the other hand, in situations requiring careful judg-ment, young children were actually less vulner-able to suggestion than were older ones, who presumably wanted some verification of an un-certain judgment. This result is consistent with Marin's group's finding that young children were particularly unlikely to fabricate or distort mem-ories in response to direct questions.[129]

Perhaps more directly germane to the legal situation is research on adult influence on chil-dren. Again, though, there is no simple relation-ship between age and conformity. In research involving first, fourth, seventh, and tenth grad-ers, Allen and Newtson observed adult influence on children's judgments to decrease sharply from first to fourth grade and then to increase slightly in tenth grade.[130] This result was consistent across several forms of judgments: "visual" (judgment of length of line), "opinion" (e.g., "kittens make good pets"), and "delay of gratification" (e.g., "I would rather have 50¢ today than $1 tomor-row"). Such a finding is consistent with the moral development and legal socialization literature in terms of young children's inflated perception of the power of authority.[131] There is the obvious related problem of coaching or of the threat (real or perceived) of punishment for unfavorable tes-timony when parents or other adults important to children are involved in legal action.

Most directly to the point, Fodor found that children who yielded to the suggestions of an adult interviewer tended to score lower on as-sessments of level of moral judgment (according to Kohlberg's criteria) than children who re-sisted such suggestions.[132] Given the prevalence of low-level moral judgment among young chil-dren,[133] there is some confirmation of the cog-nitive–developmental prediction of high vulner-ability to adult influence among young children.

It should also be noted that young children's need for cues to stimulate recollection may ex-acerbate the problem of suggestibility in testi-mony.[134] Even if (as the Marin group's data sug-gest) children are no more swayed by leading questions than adults, that they are exposed to more of them means that their testimony may

be less credible.[135] In short, while more research is needed, there is some reason to be concerned about the suggestibility of young children (per-haps up to age seven). This might be evaluated on *voir dire* through the use of leading questions on matters not related to the case.

(5)   Conclusions

While there are some gaps in the relevant liter-ature, the available research in sum suggests that liberal use of children's testimony is well founded, to the extent that the primary consideration is a child's competency to testify.[136] Memory ap-pears to be no more of a problem than in adult eyewitnesses when recollection is stimulated with direct questions. Children are also no more prone to lying than adults. Data on suggestibility are less clear, but seem to indicate fewer age differ-ences than might be suspected—a finding that needs to be further investigated. Young chil-dren's ability to conceptualize complex events is more problematic, although it is possible that, with skillful examination, jurors can follow chil-dren's line of inference sufficiently to evaluate their testimony. That hypothesis is worthy of in-vestigation, particularly given that the task of weighing children's competency is currently strictly the province of the judge.

The conclusions described here could be made more confidently if they were based on chil-dren's functioning outside the laboratory. Only Marin's group's investigation involved a court-room-like task.[137] Even that investigation in-volved interrogation under low stress. There are obvious ethical problems in inducing such stress. As an alternative, recall, conceptual skills, and the like might be evaluated in situations of nat-urally occurring stress, such as hospitalization. Experimentation might also be attempted in simulations of trials in courtrooms or simulated courtrooms.

Research is also needed on children's percep-tion of the trial setting. No such data are avail-able for young children.[138] In the present con-text, such research would help to define the psychological demands of courtroom environ-ments and possible effects on children's compe-tency to testify. Such research might also be useful in preparing children for testimony, both to enhance the quality and probative value of their testimony and to reduce the stress that the legal process may induce in child witnesses.

(c) Guidelines for Evaluation

The clinician asked to perform an evaluation of a child's competency to testify may be most helpful in presenting the relevant research in order to correct any misconceptions about typical behavior of children at a given age. In that sense, the clinician—or research psychologist—may provide assistance in evaluating the testimony in a manner similar to that of a psychologist giving expert testimony on eyewitness testimony generally.[139]

In terms of the evaluation itself, the content is obviously far-ranging. Perhaps the best tactic is simply to engage the child in conversation and to observe the child's ability to relate stories of events in his or her life. It may also be helpful to obtain perceptions of the child's typical behavior in this regard from teachers, parents, and others who know the child well.

Probably the most problematic aspect of the evaluation is assessing whether the memory of the prospective witness for the crime is a "true" memory or one that is the product of suggestion. The difficulty is that by the time the question of the child's competency is raised, the potential witness is likely to have been asked about the alleged offense numerous times. If it was perceived as a traumatic event or if a family member is the defendant, the child may even have been in psychotherapy, and therefore may have received interpretations of the event as well as simply discussing it at length. Moreover, where the event in question was one previously outside the child's experience or one that he or she had not previously identified as deviant, the child may be dependent upon adults to provide meaning to the experience.[140] Hence, the "memory" may be suggested inadvertently as an adult helps the child to make sense of the experience.

Although it may not be possible to determine the origins of the child's memories with certainty, some clues may be obtained by interviewing the child and adults who have talked with him or her. It will be useful to determine as precisely as possible when and with whom the child has talked, and the content and process of these discussions. If depositions have already been taken, they should be reviewed and compared with the interview notes.

These general guidelines also apply when the prospective witness is psychotic or mentally retarded. In each instance, an assessment should be made of the witness's (1) understanding of the obligation to tell the truth, (2) reliability of memory, (3) ability to perceive reality accurately, and (4) vulnerability to suggestion. Also, in each case, the clinician may be able to provide assistance as a consultant to the attorney seeking—or challenging—the prospective witness's testimony. In the former instance, the clinician may be helpful in preparing the witness for testimony both by desensitizing the witness to the courtroom and providing the attorney with advice on ways of interviewing the witness. As a consultant to the challenging attorney, the clinician may point out factors likely to affect the reliability of the witness's testimony and ways of highlighting these factors on *voir dire*.

5.07. *Competency to Be Sentenced and Executed*

The prohibition against sentencing and executing those adjudged incompetent to understand what is being done to them has its origins in the common law.[141] Most states have since codified the rule that an incompetent individual may not be sentenced to prison or executed.[142] The reasons advanced for this stance are several: (1) an incompetent individual cannot assist counsel in challenging the sentence imposed; (2) it is inhumane to imprison or execute such a person; (3) neither the deterrence nor retributive rationales of punishment are served by punishing an "insane" person [see § 6.02].

As these rationales suggest, there are actually two stages at which competency may be relevant after conviction. The first is at the sentencing proceeding itself. The second is while punishment is being carried out. This section examines both stages.

(a) Competency at the Sentencing Proceeding

The most common standard utilized at this stage parallels the competency to stand trial standard [see § 4.02(b)]. In *Saddler v. United States,*[143] for instance, the Second Circuit held that sentencing must be postponed if the judge has "reasonable grounds to believe that the defendant may not have a level of awareness sufficient to understand the nature of the proceeding or to exercise his right of allocution." The right of allocution—which exists in the federal courts and most state courts but is not constitutionally required—provides the defendant with an opportunity to speak in his or her behalf and offer information in mitigation of punishment prior to its imposition.[144] The Ninth Circuit, per *Chavez v. United States,*[145] even more closely follows the competency to stand trial test by requiring that, to be sentenced, the offender must understand the nature of the proceedings and be able to "participate intelligently to the extent that participation is called for."

As applied, the competency to be sentenced standard is probably easier to meet than the competency to stand trial test. First, although the defendant does have a right to counsel,[146] the sentencing proceeding is much more informal than trial and concern over accuracy much reduced [see § 7.03(c)]. Thus, the defendant's ability to consult with counsel or understand the proceedings is not perceived to be as crucial as in the trial context. Second, as a corollary of this fact, the right to allocution is often honored in the breach; again, therefore, unless the defendant's disability makes allocution impossible and allocution is considered important in the particular case, a finding of incompetency is unlikely.[147] As one court has pointed out, unlike other contexts where competency is considered significant, the defendant at sentencing has no *constitutional* rights to waive.[148]

If a bona fide doubt as to competency is raised, many states require an evaluation by experts and a hearing to determine if the standard is met.[149] If the individual is found incompetent, he or she is usually committed to a hospital for treatment until the proper authorities believe competency to be regained. Thus, hospitalization takes the place of imprisonment. In some states, time spent in the hospital does not count against time to be served under sentence.[150]

The American Bar Association (ABA) Criminal Justice Mental Health Standards take a different approach. The ABA proposes that, at least in non-capital cases, a provisional sentence be imposed despite incompetency, so long as the judge indicates on the record the extent to which the incompetency affected the sentencing proceeding.[151] The test to determine whether such incompetency exists is a paraphrase of the *Dusky* standard [see § 4.02(b)].[152] The fact that the defendant cannot exercise the right to allocution is not considered important, given the other safeguards at sentencing designed to elicit information about the defendant, including the presentence report, submissions by defense counsel, and the sentencing hearing itself. However, after imposition of sentence, the ABA standards would permit the defendant who has regained competency to present any evidence in mitigation.[153]

(b) Competency during Punishment

Virtually every state provides some mechanism for treating prison inmates who are "incompetent to serve sentence." In the typical sentencing context, the determination as to whether an individual is incompetent in this sense is in reality merely a decision as to whether the person is so mentally disturbed that transfer from prison to a mental health or mental retardation facility is necessary. Because this matter has more to do with commitment for treatment than with competency to understand or waive rights, it is considered in Chapter 8 [see § 8.10(b) (2)].

The principal issue covered here is the proper approach to deciding whether a person who has received the death penalty may be executed. For reasons suggested above, no state allows the execution of one deemed incompetent. In Florida, for instance, it must be shown that the defendant understands the nature and effect of the death penalty and why it is to be imposed before execution may take place.[154] The ABA's provisional standard on the issue, combining the rule for competency to be sentenced to death with that for competency to be executed, defines incompetence in death penalty cases as an inability on the part of the defendant to "understand the nature of the proceedings against him, what he was tried for, the purpose of the punishment, or the nature of the punishment [in addition to the inability to] recognize or understand any fact which might exist which would make his punishment unjust or unlawful, or . . . to convey such information to counsel or to the court."[155]

In *Ford v. Wainwright*,[156] the Supreme Court held, 7–2, that the Eighth Amendment (banning cruel and unusual punishment) prohibits the execution of an "insane" person, thereby constitutionalizing the centuries-old common law rule. The Court did not formulate a definition of competency to be executed, since the issue was not raised. In a concurring opinion, however, Justice Powell suggested that the Eighth Amendment "forbids the execution only of those who are unaware of the punishment they are about to suffer and why they are to suffer it." He also felt that the state could properly presume the prisoner's competency at the time sentence is to be carried out and that it could require "a substantial threshold showing of insanity merely to trigger the hearing process." Whether the Court will adopt these suggestions remains to be seen.

More controversially, five members of the Court found Florida's procedure for making the competency determination unconstitutional, on three grounds: (1) it provided no opportunity for the prisoner or his or her counsel to be heard; (2) it did not permit challenge of the state-employed mental health professionals' findings on the competency issue; (3) it left the final decision as to competency to the executive, rather than the judicial, branch. It is important to note that the Court did not explicitly establish a right to counsel at competency proceedings, nor did it require that the prisoner have a formal opportunity to cross-examine opposing experts or be provided funds for an independent expert. While Justice Marshall, who wrote the Court's opinion,

suggested that Florida might want to create a competency procedure similar to that used in the competency to stand trial or civil commitment contexts, several members of the Court cautioned against requiring, as a constitutional ruling, a full-blown "sanity trial."

The ABA's provisional standards recommend that the indigent prisoner be entitled to an independent evaluation of competency, that the prisoner be represented by counsel at the competency hearing, and that the burden be on the prisoner to show incompetence by a preponderance of the evidence standard (thus, in effect, establishing a presumption of competence).[157] With respect to its provision for expert assistance, the ABA explains its adoption of the adversarial model rather than the inquisitorial one traditionally relied upon in the competency to stand trial context on the ground that the adversarial positions are more clearly established in the capital sentencing situation.

(c)   Evaluation Issues

The principal focus of a competency evaluation in the sentencing context will be the individual's cognitive functioning, specifically whether the individual has the capacity to understand in a general way the penalty that could or will be imposed and the reason for its imposition. If competency at the sentencing *proceeding* is at issue, a second issue is whether the defendant can communicate relevant facts in mitigation to the attorney [see generally, Chapter 7 for factors relevant in mitigation]. Although the problematic voluntariness concept will normally not be a major issue in such evaluations, it also may arise. For instance, in *Gilmore v. Utah*,[158] the defendant waived his right to appeal his death sentence. The Supreme Court held that he could do so, so long as the waiver was "knowing and intelligent." Implicit in this ruling is a requirement that neither the state nor another third party somehow coerced the waiver.[159]

At least one court has imposed certain conditions on the competency evaluation in the death penalty situation. In *Hays v. Murphy*,[160] the Tenth Circuit required that evaluations be performed somewhere other than on death row and be "the type of extended close observation in a proper setting which is generally recognized as essential for all psychiatric and psychological evaluations." Although the court's concern for thoroughness is understandable, given the stakes involved, it is not necessarily the case that an evaluation of this type, focused on a very specific competency, requires "extended" observation. From a clinical standpoint, at least, the evaluation in this situation is one of the least complex discussed in this volume.

On the other hand, there are of course sensitive ethical issues associated with performing an evaluation which could contribute to a judicial finding that the subject should be executed. As discussed in § 3.05(b), the mental health professional should determine, *before* conducting such an evaluation, whether his or her personal beliefs permit participation in such an enterprise and allow a modicum of objectivity. In thinking about this issue, the professional should remember that the legal standard does *not* contemplate a general assessment of treatability or an attempt to diagnose, but rather calls for a straightforward determination of the ability to understand the consequences of execution and why execution has been ordered.

BIBLIOGRAPHY

Faretta v. California, 422 U.S. 806 (1975). (Competency to waive attorney.)

Frendak v. United States, 408 A.2d 364 (D.C. 1975). (Competency to waive insanity defense.)

Goodman, ed., *The Child Witness,* 40(2) J. Soc. Issues (1984). (Special issue.)

Grano, *Voluntariness, Free Will, and the Law of Confessions,* 65 Va. L. Rev. 581 (1979).

T. Grisso, Juveniles' Waiver of Rights: Legal and Psychological Competence (1981).

Kamisar, Brewer v. Williams, Massiah, *and* Miranda: *What is Interrogation? When Does It Matter?,* 67 Geo. L. Rev. 1 (1978).

Melton, *Sexually Abused Children and the Legal System: Some Policy Recommendations,* Am. J. Fam. Therapy (in press). (Discussion of psychological and legal issues concerning child victims and witnesses.)

Miranda v. Arizona, 384 U.S. 436 (1966). (Competency to confess.)

North Carolina v. Alford, 400 U.S. 25 (1970). (Competency to plead guilty.)

Ward, *Competency for Execution: Problems in Law and Psychiatry,* 14 Fla. St. Univ. L. Rev. 35 (1986).

White, *Police Trickery in Inducing Confessions,* 127 U. Pa. L. Rev. 581 (1979).

C. Whitebread & C. Slobogin, Criminal Procedure: An Analysis of Constitutional Cases and Concepts, chs. 16, 26 (2d ed. 1986).

CHAPTER SIX

Mental State at the Time of the Offense

6.01. Introduction

This chapter discusses a number of defenses that can be raised by the criminal defendant at the guilt determination phase of the criminal process. Specifically, it addresses the insanity defense, the automatism defense, the so-called "diminished capacity" concept, defenses associated with use of psychoactive substances, and the "guilty but mentally ill" plea. These doctrines all have one common attribute: When they are invoked, they require an investigation of the defendant's "mental state at the time of the offense" (MSO)—a reconstruction of the defendant's thought processes and behavior before and during the alleged crime. While there are other doctrines in criminal law that necessitate a similar assessment,[1] those named above are most likely to bring lawyers to the clinician's door. Of course, not all states recognize each of these defenses; moreover, each comes in various guises. This chapter attempts to outline for each defense the majority approach and the most significant competing approaches. It also attempts to provide some guidance regarding the clinical syndromes most likely to form the bases for these defenses.

6.02. The Insanity Defense

The bulk of this chapter focuses on the insanity defense, because it is the most commonly invoked doctrine relating to MSO. The premise of the defense is as follows: Most criminal offenders choose to commit crime for rational reasons and of their own "free will," and are therefore deserving of punishment; some mentally disturbed offenders, however, are so irrational in their behavior, or so unable to control it—that is, so unlike "us"—that we feel uncomfortable imposing criminal liability on them. To put it another way, these individuals are not properly punishable as criminals because the principal grounds for such punishment—retribution and deterrence—are not applicable to them. Society should not feel vengeful toward persons who, at the time of the offense, "did not know what they were doing" or "could not help themselves"; such individuals should be treated with compassion, not branded as criminals. Nor can society hope either to deter such persons from committing other crimes or to deter others like them from crime, since "crazy" people are oblivious to the constraints of the real world. Such people may need treatment, and perhaps restraint, but these two objectives are most properly met through hospitalization, not imprisonment.

The defense of insanity is probably the most controversial issue in all of criminal law. Thousands of pages have been written debating the value of a defense that excuses one for one's antisocial actions. Some have argued that the theoretical assumptions underlying the defense are unfounded—that very few, if any, individuals are actually totally nondeterrable or undeserving of punishment.[2] From a practical viewpoint, it has been contended that treatment of dangerous mentally ill persons can be better accomplished through alternative methods,[3] that the terms used to define "insanity" are unconscionably yet inevitably vague,[4] and that mental health professionals are unable to provide meaningful testimony on the issue.[5] Other commentators, the clear majority, have just as vigorously rejected the abolitionist stance.[6] They see the defense as the sole vehicle society possesses for publicly debating the meaning of "criminal responsibility"—for examining the assumption, basic to the criminal law and our notions of personhood generally, that by far the majority of those who commit crime could have acted otherwise. To proponents of the defense, those criminal defendants who are afflicted by severe mental disorder at the time of the offense—and who are therefore intuitively, if not demonstrably, less able to control or appreciate their behavior—must be afforded the opportunity to argue their lack of blameworthiness, or the moral integrity of the law will suffer.

(a)   Common Misperceptions about the Defense

While the academic battle has raged, the public has increasingly expressed its dissatisfaction with the defense.[7] Popular opinion about the insanity plea appears to be based largely on impressions gained from the extensive media coverage that inevitably accompanies insanity trials such as that of John Hinckley. In one sense, this publicity may be desirable; it tends to encourage public examination of the moral premises underlying the criminal justice system. But it also appears

to have given the public a somewhat distorted view of the nature of the defense. For example, many appear to believe (1) that a large number of defendants use the defense, and (2) that most are successful (in part because defendants and their expert witnesses are able to deceive gullible juries). It also seems to be commonly assumed that (3) those acquitted by reason of insanity are released upon acquittal or shortly thereafter, even though (4) they are extremely dangerous. These perceptions, if accurate, would understandably lead to antipathy toward the defense. Yet, based on available data, they appear to be unsupportable.

(1)   How Often Is the Plea of Insanity Made?

A study conducted in Wyoming between 1970 and 1972 indicated that the "average" community resident in that state believed the insanity defense was raised in 43% of all criminal cases in Wyoming during those years.[8] In fact, fewer than half of 1% (.47%) of all criminal defendants arrested in Wyoming during the time period of the study raised the plea.[9] In Michigan, data collected in the early 1970s suggest that the defense is raised in only 1 out of every 1,000 cases in that state involving serious offenses such as homicide, assault, and burglary.[10] A similar finding was made in St. Louis for the year 1982.[11] In New York it has been estimated that, between 1965 and 1978, 1 out of every 600–700 serious cases involved an insanity plea.[12] A 1977 study of criminal cases in Richmond, Virginia, over a year's time found that the plea was raised in less than .5% of all felony cases during that period.[13] Finally, of the 32,000 adult offenders represented by the Public Defenders' Office in New Jersey in 1982, only 52 insanity pleas were entered.[14] Older studies show similar results.[15] Thus, available data appear to counter effectively the belief that the plea is an everyday occurrence in the criminal courts.

(2)   How Often Is the Plea Successful?

Data on the success rate of the insanity defense are less uniform, but they suggest that the defense frequently fails. The Wyoming study cited above found that while the "average" citizen in that state thought the defense was successful 38% of the time, in reality only one person (or .99%) of the 102 who pleased insanity during the period of the study was acquitted.[16] Wyoming may not be representative, however. In Hawaii, between the years 1969 and 1976, approximately 19% of those who pleaded insanity were acquitted[17]; in Erie County, New York, roughly 25% of those who pleaded insanity were successful[18]; and in New Jersey the analogous figure for 1982 was 30%.[19] Obviously, the success of the defense varies from jurisdiction to jurisdiction. But Steadman, Pantle, and Pasewark have estimated that, nationally, the defense prevails one out of every four times it is raised.[20] As a general statement, it is probably not inaccurate to say that when the defense is challenged, it fails more often than it succeeds.

It can also be said that the absolute number of individuals found not guilty by reason of insanity (NGRI) is very low. In the five state jurisdictions where recent data are available, the number of NGRI verdicts ranged between 1 and 259 cases per year, representing an average well below 1% of all felony arrests in those states.[21] Nationwide statistics indicate that only 8.1% (or 1,625) of the 19,171 admissions to mental hospitals in the United States during 1978 were defendants found NGRI,[22] representing fewer than .3% of all felony cases for that year.[23]

Finally, and perhaps most importantly, it appears that well over 70% of these insanity acquittals resulted from a plea-bargaining or quasi-plea-bargaining arrangement rather than a full-fledged trial.[24] In these cases, the prosecution *agreed* that the defendants were so "crazy" they should be hospitalized rather than convicted and imprisoned. Thus, the number of cases in which there is any potential for the defendant to somehow "fool" a trial jury is extremely small to begin with. Even if there is some abuse of the defense in such trials [see, e.g., § 6.04(a)], it would seem that the total number of "valid" acquittals far outweighs the number of "invalid" ones. This point is substantiated by evidence that most insanity acquittees (60–90%) continue to be diagnosed as "psychotic after acquittal."[25]

(3)   What Happens to Those Found NGRI?

A commonly held and not illogical assumption about defendants found NGRI is that they are treated like the typical acquitted defendant and permitted to "walk" after acquittal. In reality, this disposition is the exception. One commentator who surveyed the laws of the 50 states in 1981 concluded that "[a]n acquittal by reason of insanity is rarely a ticket to freedom."[26] Many states require automatic commitment of those acquitted on insanity grounds, usually for a minimum averaging 60 days. Those states that do not have automatic commitment permit confinement for an initial period of up to a year upon relatively meager evidence of mental illness, dangerousness, or both. As § 8.10(c) discusses in more detail, the statutory criteria for releasing persons found NGRI after this initial detention period (which typically focus on the individuals' mental illness and potential for endangering others) are more restrictive—either on their face or "as applied"—than similar criteria used in the civil commitment process. Moreover, the release of NGRI individuals is usually dependent on judicial approval, in contrast to the typical discharge from civil commitment, which only requires the hospital director's authorization.[27] Finally, most states place no limit on the length of time NGRI individuals may spend in confinement, so long as they continue to meet the commitment criteria.[28] These facts substantiate the contention of Professors Katz and Goldstein that the insanity defense is as much a method for restraining persons seen as "crazy" and "dangerous" as it is a means of airing the moral issues discussed earlier.[29]

How long does the typical NGRI individual spend in the mental institution? Data on this subject are available from at least three states. The most comprehensive information comes from Pasewark, Pantle, and Steadman's study of New York.[30] Of the 178 persons found NGRI between 1965 and 1976 in that state, 40% were still hospitalized in 1978. The average length of stay for these individuals by the end of the study period in 1978 was three and a half years. Of those who had been released without supervision during this period, the average length of stay was about 15 months. Pasework, Pantle, and Steadman also found that those charged with more severe crimes spent more time in the hospital (e.g., a 1,102-day average for those charged with rape vs. a 398-day average for those charged with assault).

In Michigan, a state that significantly relaxed its release criteria in 1975, the average confinement for those released after that date was only nine and a half months. However, 25% of those acquitted were still confined five years after passage of the liberal release provisions.[31]

A study of persons found NGRI in Illinois, conducted in 1979,[32] suggests that both the New York and Michigan data may be somewhat misleading. The Illinois study found the average stay in the hospital for those acquittees who were released to be 17.1 months. But it also found that 71% of all NGRI individuals had previously been found incompetent to stand trial, and that the average length of institutionalization between the finding of incompetency and the NGRI finding was 38.4 months. Since there is nothing to indicate that the Illinois experience is unique, these data suggest that the bare postinsanity acquittal figures for New York and Michigan may have seriously underestimated the total duration of confinement for many of those ultimately found NGRI.

An interesting perspective on the confinement issue is provided by four studies that compared length of hospitalization for persons found NGRI to length of imprisonment for felons who were matched with the NGRI individuals according to the nature of the crime charged and demographic variables. The two studies of this nature conducted in New York found no appreciable differential in confinement duration when the NGRI individuals were hospitalized in a facility operated by the Department of Corrections, and a ten-month differential (with NGRI individuals being released earlier) after jurisdiction over the NGRI cases had been transferred to the Department of Mental Health.[33] A third study, conducted in Connecticut—a state that limits hospitalization of persons found NGRI to the maximum prison term prescribed for the offense—found that NGRI individuals were released an average of 19 months earlier than the felons with which they were paired.[34] On the

other hand, a fourth study, from New Jersey, indicated that insanity acquittees were confined about twice as long as the average convicted felon.[35] None of these studies took into account pretrial detention for either the NGRI individuals or the felons.

Assuming that the pretrial detention periods were similar for all groups, the second New York study and the Connecticut study do indicate that in some jurisdictions persons found NGRI spend a significantly shorter time in confinement than do felons. But this differential is obviously not the case everywhere, as the New Jersey research indicates. More importantly, it does not by itself signify that there is a problem with either the insanity defense or the disposition of insanity acquittees. Only if NGRI individuals *need* to be confined for longer periods of time would these data merit such a conclusion. This point anticipates the fourth and final perception of the insanity defense that will be discussed here.

(4)   How Dangerous Are Those Found NGRI?

An interesting study conducted in New York asked 417 randomly selected citizens to name offenders they believed to be "criminally insane."[36] Of those offenders named by more than one of those interviewed, none could be classified as either insane, incompetent to stand trial, or prisoners who had become mentally ill. In fact, all had been *convicted* of murder, kidnapping, or bombings. The term "insanity" seems to attach itself to notorious individuals, whether or not they actually plead the defense and are successful with it.

There are no studies examining the "dangerousness" of persons found NGRI at the time of acquittal, since, as indicated earlier, these individuals are almost always automatically institutionalized and subjected to treatment. However, there are three studies comparing the recidivism rates of NGRI individuals who have been released after hospitalization with released felons charged with similar offenses. Two of the studies indicated that NGRI individuals as a group were slightly less likely to have recidivating members than felons as a group (although of those who did recidivate, those found NGRI repeated more often than the felons),[37] and the third study showed the recidivism rates between the two groups to be about even.[38] As with research comparing the recidivism rates of those who are civilly committed to those of the general population,[39] these studies tentatively suggest that the most accurate predictor of violence is the number and nature of prior offenses, not mental illness. They also suggest that the treatment provided to those found NGRI is not particularly effective at removing criminal tendencies. What they do not support is the contention that typical released insanity acquittees are "abnormally" dangerous or that such persons should be confined longer than felons because they are more likely to recidivate than their convicted counterparts.

More data need to be collected on all of these issues. But the available research suggests that support for abolishing the defense is misguided inasmuch as it is based on the belief that the insanity defense is frequently raised and usually successful, or on the impression that the insanity acquittee is a dangerous "monster" who is let loose once acquitted or at the whim of unmonitored hospital staff. It should also be noted that the last two subjects discussed—the duration of confinement for persons found NGRI and their potential dangerousness—have more to do with the correct *disposition* of the NGRI cases than with the insanity defense itself. The defense, and what is done with those who successfully assert it, are two separate issues. The latter subject is discussed in more detail in § 8.09(c).

Over time, the defense of insanity has shown remarkable resiliency. Despite recent intense public hostility toward the doctrine and the introduction of scores of bills proposing its elimination, only three states have abolished it as of this writing.[40] For better or for worse, the lawyer and the mental health professional must continue to grapple with both the evolution and the scope of the defense.

(b) The History of the Defense

The idea of a defense to criminal responsibility based on mental disability goes back as far as the ancient Greek and Hebrew civilizations.[41] English case law, which heavily influenced early American courts, has long recognized the concept. At least as early as 1300, records show that English kings were pardoning murderers because their crimes were committed "while suffering from madness."[42] Over the next several centuries, many different formulations of the defense emerged. Sir Edward Coke, a famous legal scholar of the late 16th and early 17th century, felt that "idiots" and "madmen" who "wholly loseth their memory and understanding" should be found insane.[43] Sir Matthew Hale, Chief Justice of the King's Bench in the 17th century, concluded in his private papers that the "best measure" for determining insanity was whether the accused had "as great understanding as ordinarily a child of fourteen hath."[44] In 1723 Justice Tracy held that in order to be found insane "a man must be totally deprived of his understanding and memory so as not to know what he is doing, no more than an infant, brute or a wild beast."[45] At about the same time, other English courts were excusing those who lacked the capacity to distinguish "good from evil" or "right from wrong."[46]

It was this latter approach that, in slightly modified form, became the so-called *"M'Naghten* test" of insanity. In response to controversy surrounding the insanity acquittal of Daniel M'Naghten for killing the private secretary of Prime Minister Robert Peel, the House of Lords announced the following rule: "To establish a defense on the ground of insanity, it must be clearly proved that, at the time of the committing of the act, the party accused was laboring under such a defect of reason, from disease of the mind, as not to know the nature and quality of the act he was doing; or, if he did know it, that he did not know he was doing what was wrong."[47] This formulation, announced in 1843, became the accepted rule in both England and the United States.

Criticism of the test was immediate, especially from the medical community. Indeed, five years before the House of Lords' pronouncement, Sir Issac Ray, a noted American physician, had argued that the "insane mind" is often "perfectly rational, and displays the exercise of a sound and well-balanced mind."[48] Thus, according to Ray, a defense based on mental illness that focuses merely on cognitive impairment is incomplete; the defendant's ability to control his or her acts must also be considered.[49] Although directed at the law as it existed in 1838, Ray's comments applied with equal force to the *M'Naghten* test, which varied only slightly from its predecessors.

A second criticism of the rule was its rigidity. Even if one accepts the premise that cognitive dysfunction is the only appropriate focus of the insanity defense, the *M'Naghten* rule, it was claimed, did not fairly pose the question; a literal interpretation of the *M'Naghten* test would seldom, if ever, lead to exculpation. In the words of one psychiatrist, "[if the test language were taken seriously,] it would excuse only those totally deteriorated, drooling hopeless psychotics of long-standing, and congenital idiots."[50]

In the United States, the legal response to the first criticism came in the form of a supplementary test for insanity, which eventually came to be called the "irresistible impulse" rule. One of the first courts to adopt the rule described it as follows:

> [The defendant is not] legally responsible if the two following conditions concur: (1) If, by reason of the duress of . . . mental disease he had so far lost the power to choose between the right and wrong, and to avoid doing the act in question, as that his free agency was at the time destroyed; (2) and if, at the same time, the alleged crime was so connected with such mental disease, in the relation of cause and effect, as to have been the product of it solely.[51]

The adoption of the test was usually justified on the ground that those offenders who could not control their behavior at the time of the offense were not deterrable by criminal sanctions; therefore, no legitimate moral or policy purpose was served by convicting them.[52]

The "irresistible impulse" test met resistance from several fronts. Many in the legal community believed that impulsivity could easily be feigned, and feared that the test would lead to numerous invalid insanity acquittals.[53] From the medical side came the criticism that a separate "control" test furthered the mistaken impression that the human psyche is compartmentalized into cognitive and volitional components.[54] And, like *M'Naghten,* the test was seen as too

rigid, excusing only those who were totally unable to prevent their unlawful behavior.[55]

In 1954, partly in response to the latter two contentions and the criticisms of *M'Naghten,* the federal District of Columbia Court of Appeals adopted the "product test" for insanity—a rule originally devised by the New Hampshire Supreme Court in 1870,[56] but one that had received little notice until this time. As set forth in *Durham v. United States,*[57] the test stated simply that "an accused is not criminally responsible if his unlawful act was the product of mental disease or defect." Judge Bazelon, the author of the *Durham* opinion, hoped the rule would encourage mental health professionals to explain all aspects of a defendant's personality and functioning by removing legal strictures on such professionals' testimony.

In time, however, this lack of guidance became a problem in itself. The product test asked essentially two questions: (1) Did mental disease or defect exist at the time of the offense? (2) Was the offense the product of this disease or defect? The *Durham* court failed to define either "mental disease" or "product." Trial courts had particular difficulty dealing with the meaning of the former term, since it was no longer modified by functional criteria, as it had been in earlier tests.[58] The problem surfaced dramatically in 1957 when staff members at St. Elizabeths Hospital, which provides the District of Columbia courts with most of their experts on the insanity issue, suddenly voted to incorporate the personality disorders, including the so-called "sociopathic personality," within the definition of "mental disease" for purposes of the insanity defense.[59] Since many criminal offenders have some type of personality disorder, this well-known weekend change in hospital policy had a major impact on the courts. Not surprisingly, the insanity acquittal rate in the District of Columbia rose precipitously in the following years.[60]

In the 1962 decision of *MacDonald v. United States,*[61] the District of Columbia Court of Appeals finally conceded that trial courts required some guidelines in implementing the product test, and declared that henceforth "the jury should be told that a mental disease or defect includes any abnormal condition of the mind which substantially affects mental or emotional processes and substantially impairs behavior controls."[62] With the judicial gloss added by *MacDonald,* the difference between the product test and a test combining *M'Naghten* and the "irresistible impulse" rule was reduced substantially. Even so, definitional problems persisted, and *Durham* was finally overruled in 1972.[63] The only state besides New Hampshire to adopt the test later abandoned it as well.[64]

In place of the product test, the District of Columbia Court of Appeals adopted still another version of the insanity test, which, ironically, was first proposed a year after the *Durham* decision. This test, drafted by the American Law Institute (ALI), was an attempt to deal with most of the problems associated with previous tests by avoiding the "all-or-nothing" language of the *M'Naghten* and "irresistible impulse" formulations, while retaining some specific guidelines for the jury. The rule reads as follows: "A person is not responsible for criminal conduct if at the time of such conduct as a result of mental disease or defect he lacks substantial capacity either to appreciate the criminality [wrongfulness] of his conduct or to conform his conduct to the requirements of the law."[65] This language combines the notions underlying both the *M'Naghten* and irresistible impulse formulations, but makes it clear that a defendant's cognitive or volitional impairment at the time of the offense need only be "substantial," rather than total, in order to merit an insanity defense.

The ALI's proposal also included a second paragraph, which, according to its drafters, was designed specifically "to exclude from the concept of 'mental disease or defect' the case of so called 'psychopathic personality.'"[66] It states: "As used in this Article, the terms mental disease or defect do not include an abnormality manifested only by repeated criminal or otherwise anti-social conduct."[67] Interestingly, this proposal was published two years before the St. Elizabeths incident.

The ALI test proved to be a popular one: Over the next two decades, a majority of the country's jurisdictions adopted the first paragraph, and many of these also adopted the second. Nonetheless, the ALI test came under attack by a new

wave of critics, who felt that it and all of the tests that preceded it relied too heavily on the so-called "medical model."[68] In 1979, the Rhode Island Supreme Court held that a person should be found insane if [he] is so substantially impaired that he cannot justly be held responsible."[69] This test did away with the "mental disease or defect" requirement, as well as any specific requirement of functional impairment. It gave the factfinder virtually limitless discretion to decide what types of "impairment" merit excusing one for one's behavior.

The "justly responsible" formulation has not received widespread acceptance. Only Rhode Island has adopted it. A more popular (and the most recent) trend in insanity jurisprudence has been to attack the volitional prong of the defense. In the early 1980s, both the American Bar Association (ABA) and the American Psychiatric Association recommended the elimination of the so-called "control" inquiry, although they continued to support the "appreciation" prong of the ALI's test, thereby indicating an unwillingness to return to the original *M'Naghten* formulation.[70] The ABA's test reads as follows: "[A] person is not responsible for criminal conduct if, at the time of such conduct, and as a result of mental disease or defect, that person was unable to appreciate the wrongfulness of such conduct." Echoing past criticism, both the ABA and the American Psychiatric Association reasoned that if mistakes do occur in the administration of the insanity defense, they are most likely to result from utilizing a volitional test.[71] As the commentary to the ABA's standard states: "Clinicians can be more precise and arrive at more reliable conclusions about a person's awareness, perceptions and understanding of an event, than about the "causes" of his behavior. . . . The control tests are more likely to involve the professional in this latter type of assessment, increasing the possibility of opinions steeped in uncertainty."[72]

In 1984, the United States Congress adopted an insanity test that essentially tracked the ABA proposal (although, contrary to that proposal, which placed the burden of disproving insanity on the prosecution, the federal statute places the burden of proving insanity on the defendant by clear and convincing evidence) [see § 6.02(c)(5)].[73]

Thus, as of 1985, the federal courts used the ABA truncation of the ALI test. The full ALI test was being used in close to half of the states (Alabama, Arkansas, Connecticut, Hawaii, Illinois, Indiana, Kentucky, Maine, Maryland, Massachusetts, Michigan, Missouri, Ohio, Oregon, Tennessee, Texas, Vermont, West Virginia, Wisconsin, Wyoming, and the District of Columbia). Some variation of *M'Naghten* was the exclusive test of insanity in a little over one-third of the states (Alaska, Arizona, California, Florida, Iowa, Kansas, Louisiana, Minnesota, Mississippi, Nebraska, Nevada, New Jersey, New York, North Carolina, North Dakota, Oklahoma, Pennsylvania, South Carolina, South Dakota, and Washington). Five states added the "irresistible impulse" standard to some version of the cognitive test (Colorado, Delaware, Georgia, New Mexico, and Virginia). New Hampshire continued to use the "product" test; Rhode Island relied on the "justly responsible" formulation; and three states, Idaho, Montana, and Utah, had abolished the defense, although expert testimony is still admissible on *mens rea* [see § 6.03].[74]

(c)   A Closer Look at the Insanity Defense

With the exception of the "justly responsible" test, each of the tests described above incorporates the notion that in order to be excused on the basis of insanity, the defendant must have been suffering from a "mental disease or defect." Additionally, each test requires that this mental disease or defect "cause" some type of dysfunction at the time of the offense. Finally, except for the original *Durham* rule, each test indicates in more specific terms the type of dysfunction that must occur in order to justify a finding of insanity. (Under *Durham,* the offense itself is sufficient evidence of dysfunction.)

This section focuses on these three components of the tests in more detail. It also looks at the issues of burden and standard of proof; even though traditionally viewed as a procedural matter, a jurisdiction's rules concerning how much evidence each party must produce in order to prevail can have a significant substantive impact.

The following discussion attempts to delineate the major legal trends in each area discussed. However, as is true in other legal contexts described in this book, whether an individual meets particular legally defined criteria, such as those associated with insanity, is ultimately a legal–moral question to be decided by the judge or jury on a case-by-case basis. Reference to past cases or medical–psychological concepts cannot provide a definitive answer in a given case because of the inevitable ambiguity of legal terminology. The observations below are offered merely as guideposts to the clinician performing evaluations or testifying for the courts and to the lawyer making tactical decisions.

(1)   Mental Disease or Defect

From its inception, the insanity defense has been available only to those individuals who are seen as "lunatics" or "idiots," or, to use more modern terminology, those who suffer from mental illness or mental retardation. It has been argued that since environmental and sociological factors, such as poverty and cultural "proclivities," can have as significant an impact on an individual's functioning as psychological ones, they too should have exculpatory effect.[75] But the law has continued to adhere to the so-called "medical model" of insanity. This tenacity seems to be due partly to a desire to restrict the scope of a defense that can lead to acquittal, and partly to the belief that "exogenous" factors such as one's environment are more subject to an individual's control, and therefore less deserving of consideration for purposes of assessing criminal responsibility.[76] In any event, with the exception of Rhode Island's formulation, every currently accepted test for insanity establishes "mental disease or defect" as a threshold consideration. The term "mental disease" has usually been equated with "mental illness," while the term "mental defect" is usually thought to be synonymous with "mental retardation," although some courts have indicated that "defect" refers to any condition that is incapable of improving.[77]

It has been suggested that this threshold adds nothing to the test for insanity beyond the above-described preference for endogenous causes. For instance, one well-known criminal law text has stated, "[I]t would seem that any mental abnormality, be it psychosis, neurosis, organic brain disorder, or congenital intellectual deficiency . . . will suffice *if* it has caused the consequences described in the second part of the test."[78] In other words, any mental disability that causes significant cognitive or volitional impairment will meet the threshold.

This statement is probably true to the extent that it implies that courts and juries pay more attention to the degree of impairment than to the specific mental disability suffered by the defendant. But it can also be misleading. In historical fact, most successful insanity defenses are based on the presence of one of two mental conditions: psychosis or mental retardation.[79] As noted earlier, virtually all studies of the subject indicate that the majority (60–90%) of defendants acquitted by reason of insanity are diagnosed as psychotic.[80] To judges, lawyers, and juries, these individuals are more sick than evil, and do not deserve criminal punishment. Moreover, some offenders who may be able to meet the second "functional" part of the tests are clearly not the types of individuals the law wishes to excuse. For example, sociopaths (or, using modern nomenclature, "antisocial personalities") are individuals who may very well be unable to "appreciate" the quality or wrongfulness of a criminal act because of their lack of moral inhibition; yet they are not generally considered legally insane, as the earlier discussion of the ALI test illustrates. Similarly, most courts would probably not consider any condition listed in the third edition of the *Diagnostic and Statistical Manual of Mental Disorders* (DSM-III) a "mental disease or defect" for purposes of the insanity test merely because defendants can show that such a condition substantially impaired their capacity to appreciate the criminality of or to control their acts.

The actual number of written opinions attempting to grapple with the definition of "mental disease or defect" for purposes of the insanity defense is extremely small. But those decisions that do exist define the concept narrowly. Some courts have emphasized that *mild* symptomatology will not support a defense, presumably even if the individual is psychotic.[81] A few have expressed some distaste for "temporary insanity"—pleas based on nonpsychotic disorders such as "dissociative states," which appear to take hold of the defendant at the time of the offense, but at no other time.[82] Finally, alcohol- or drug-induced "insanity" is rarely a successful claim, especially when the dysfunction is caused by short-term or one-time use of the psychoactive substance.[83] Usually, only in cases involving "settled insanity" from prolonged alcohol or drug abuse (resulting in significant organic damage) are the courts willing to recognize an insanity defense [see § 6.03(c)].

In light of this history and their view of the appropriate scope of the defense, both the American Psychiatric Association and the ABA have proposed definitions of mental disease and mental defect that would adopt a narrow threshold.[84] The American Psychiatric Association's definition reads: "[T]he terms mental disease and mental retardation include only those severely abnormal mental conditions that grossly and demonstrably impair a person's perception or understanding of reality and that are not attributable primarily to the voluntary ingestion of alcohol or other psychoactive substances."[85]

It must also be pointed out, however, that equating "mental disease or defect" with psychosis and retardation would be too simplistic a summary of the law, especially as it has developed in modern times. More and more frequently, individuals who are neither psychotic nor retarded have been found insane. In Connecticut during 1970 to 1972, for instance, 40% of those acquitted by reason of insanity were classified as having personality disorders.[86] Similar data, described in § 6.04, have been reported in other states. Obviously, the concept of "mental disease or defect" is given a relatively elastic definition (or, more likely, no definition at all) in some jurisdictions.

Figure 6-1 is a chart that attempts to relate various DSM-III diagnoses to the requirements of the insanity defense (as well as the defenses of automatism and diminished capacity). Prepared for use in Virginia, it is provided as an interpretation of how one jurisdiction approaches the issue of mental disease or defect; it is not meant to be a definitive statement of the

Figure 6-1. *Legally relevant clinical syndromes (based on Virginia law—see footnotes).*

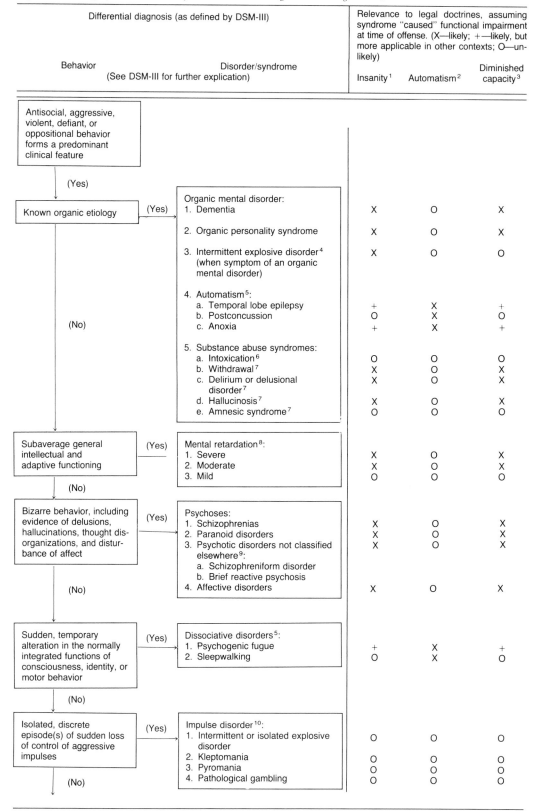

Differential diagnosis (as defined by DSM-III)		Relevance to legal doctrines, assuming syndrome "caused" functional impairment at time of offense. (X—likely; +—likely, but more applicable in other contexts; O—unlikely)		
Behavior	Disorder/syndrome (See DSM-III for further explication)	Insanity[1]	Automatism[2]	Diminished capacity[3]
Antisocial, aggressive, violent, defiant, or oppositional behavior forms a predominant clinical feature				
(Yes)				
Known organic etiology → (Yes)	Organic mental disorder: 1. Dementia	X	O	X
	2. Organic personality syndrome	X	O	X
	3. Intermittent explosive disorder[4] (when symptom of an organic mental disorder)	X	O	O
	4. Automatism[5]: a. Temporal lobe epilepsy	+	X	+
(No)	b. Postconcussion	O	X	O
	c. Anoxia	+	X	+
	5. Substance abuse syndromes: a. Intoxication[6]	O	O	O
	b. Withdrawal[7]	X	O	X
	c. Delirium or delusional disorder[7]	X	O	X
	d. Hallucinosis[7]	X	O	X
	e. Amnesic syndrome[7]	O	O	O
Subaverage general intellectual and adaptive functioning → (Yes)	Mental retardation[8]: 1. Severe	X	O	X
	2. Moderate	X	O	X
	3. Mild	O	O	O
(No)				
Bizarre behavior, including evidence of delusions, hallucinations, thought disorganizations, and disturbance of affect → (Yes)	Psychoses: 1. Schizophrenias	X	O	X
	2. Paranoid disorders	X	O	X
	3. Psychotic disorders not classified elsewhere[9]: a. Schizophreniform disorder b. Brief reactive psychosis	X	O	X
(No)	4. Affective disorders	X	O	X
Sudden, temporary alteration in the normally integrated functions of consciousness, identity, or motor behavior → (Yes)	Dissociative disorders[5]: 1. Psychogenic fugue	+	X	+
	2. Sleepwalking	O	X	O
(No)				
Isolated, discrete episode(s) of sudden loss of control of aggressive impulses → (Yes)	Impulse disorder[10]: 1. Intermittent or isolated explosive disorder	O	O	O
	2. Kleptomania	O	O	O
	3. Pyromania	O	O	O
(No)	4. Pathological gambling	O	O	O

Continued

Figure 6-1. Continued

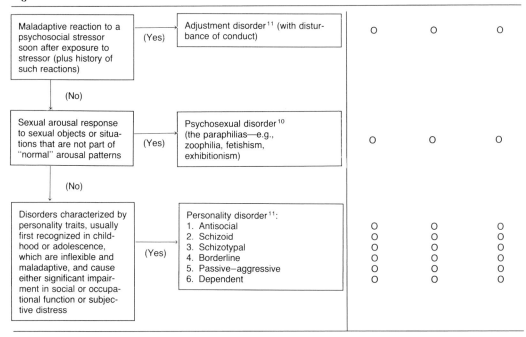

1. Virginia recognizes the *M'Naghten* test, supplemented by the so-called "irresistible impulse" test. *See, e.g.,* Dejarnette v. Comm., 75 Va. 867 (1881); Thompson v. Comm., 193 Va. 704, 70 S.E. 2d 284 (1952).

2. Greenfield v. Comm., 214 Va. 710, 204 S.E. 2d 414, 417 (1974) stated, "Where not self-induced, unconsciousness is a complete defense to a criminal homicide."

3. In Dejarnette v. Comm., 75 Va. 867 (1881), the Virginia Supreme Court declared, *in dicta,* that evidence of mental abnormality not amounting to insanity would be admissible on the issue of specific intent to commit murder; however, at the time this figure was prepared, there was no Virginia law directly endorsing or rejecting the defense of diminished capacity. In 1985, however, the defense was rejected. *See* Stamper v. Comm., 324 S.E. 2d 682 (Va. 1985).

4. This disorder is unlikely to affect cognitive functioning.

5. These conditions result in impairment of one's conscious control of one's motor coordination, and therefore are more properly analyzed under the automatism doctrine.

6. Under Virginia law, voluntary intoxication is relevant only to negate homicidal premeditation; involuntary intoxication resulting in lack of *mens rea* results in acquittal. *See* Greenfield v. Comm., 214 Va. 710, 204 S.E. 2d 414, 417 (1974).

7. Virginia law appears to recognize alcohol or drug-induced insanity when there is evidence of prolonged psychoactive substance use and psychotic symptoms at the time of the offense. *See* Johnson v. Comm., 135 Va. 524, 115 S.E. 673 (1923); Wood v. Zahradnick, 429 F. Supp. 107 (E.D. Va. 1977), *aff'd,* 578 F.2d 980 (4th Cir. 1978), Boswell v. Comm., 61 Va. 860 (1871). Unconsciousness due to voluntary alcohol use is not a defense. Chittum v. Comm., 211 Va. 12 (1970).

8. Retardation or feeblemindedness may form the basis for an insanity defense under Virginia law. Graham v. Gathright, 345 F. Supp. 749 (E.D. Va. 1965). However, rarely will mild retardation result in cognitive impairment sufficient to support a legal defense.

9. Clinicians should be careful in distinguishing between these psychotic conditions and bizarre criminal acts produced by stress that are not accompanied by the DSM-III criteria for psychosis.

10. Several Virginia Supreme Court cases have stated that if there is any indication of planning preceding the criminal act, the defendant cannot be found to have surrendered to an irresistible impulse. Thompson v. Comm., 193 Va. 704, 717, 70 S.E. 2d 284, 292; Rollins v. Comm., 207 Va. 580, 151 S.E. 2d 625. In Snider v. Smith, 187 F. Supp. 299 (E.D. Va. 1960), the court denied an insanity instruction in a case involving a sex offender "with an irresistible sex urge which he [was], at times, unable to control," both because no "mental disease or defect" was shown to have existed and because there were indications of advance planning. With disorders such as kleptomania and pyromania, the afflicted individual is able to control impulses to the extent necessary to elude detection and thus, under the restrictive Virginia legal framework, would not qualify for an insanity defense under the irresistible impulse prong. In short, the Virginia courts have been extremely reluctant to uphold a defense based on allegations of impulse dyscontrol.

11. In none of these disorders is the defendant's cognitive or volitional control severely impaired to the extent seemingly required by Virginia law. *See* cases cited above and Davis v. Comm., 214 Va. 681, 294 S.E. 2d 272 (1974); Thurman v. Comm., 107 Va. 912, 60 S.E. 99 (1908). The borderline personality does exhibit substantial dyscontrol at times; if, at the time of the offense, the symptoms reach psychotic proportions, the defendant would probably meet the criteria for brief reactive psychosis.

law nationally, which, as the discussion above makes clear, is extremely vague. But it should give the clinician some idea of the clusters of behavior that may be legally relevant in the insanity context.

(2) Causation

Every test of insanity requires that the mental disease or defect "cause" either the offense itself (*Durham*) or a dysfunction that in turn impairs the individual's appreciation or control of the acts constituting the offense (*M'Naghten,* "irresistible impulse," ALI, ABA/American Psychiatric Association). To put it simply, there must be a link between the mental disease or defect and the crime.

One might assume that proving the defendant was suffering from a legally relevant disability at the time of the offense would be sufficient to meet this element of the defense. But, in fact, the few courts that have addressed this issue (in particular, the District of Columbia Court of Appeals during the *Durham* era) have held that if the disorder did not affect the defendant's actions at the time in question, it is irrelevant. It is not presumed that one's illness causes all of one's acts; as the District of Columbia Court put it, it must be shown that "but for" the disorder, the criminal act would not have occurred.[87]

As a rule, courts make no distinction between "conscious" and "unconscious" causes of behavior. For instance, courts usually permit testimony based on psychodynamic or psychoanalytic theories, which often assume that a person's actions are the result of factors not consciously perceived by the individual. In his recent book, Moore has argued that, even assuming such evidence is sufficiently reliable to meet the test for expert testimony, it is usually irrelevant to the issue of criminal responsibility.[88] Arguing from a linguistic–philosophical perspective, Moore contends that the language of "responsibility" refers to persons acting for reasons. The language of "causation," on the other hand, refers to events occurring because of antecedent events. According to Moore, the latter concept is totally distinct from the former. To conclude otherwise would lead to the untenable position that no one

is responsible for one's actions, because all behavior can be said to be "caused" by factors other than an individual's desires and beliefs—factors such as physiological processes or the environment, or, most relevant here, the "unconscious." To put Moore's thesis another way, even if one assumes that a person's behavior is "caused" by unconscious beliefs, the environment, or some other factor, that person is nonetheless "responsible" for his or her behavior if he or she engaged in it for conscious reasons that were "rational" (i.e., intelligible and relatively consistent with one another). Moore's argument reinforces the contentions summarized in § 1.03(a): namely, that the determinism of the behavioral sciences is inappropriate in the criminal context because it threatens the central premise of the criminal law—that people are generally responsible for their behavior. His reasoning suggests that, in insanity cases, testimony describing unconscious motivation should be excluded in all but a few instances.[89]

Despite the cogency of Moore's argument, the law's penchant for seeking explanations of human behavior is likely to lead to continued reliance on any competent evidence offered by mental health professionals. Even if one attempts to focus on a defendant's conscious thought processes, the deterministic influence will be hard to dispel. Assume, for example, that a schizophrenic woman states that she shoplifted from a grocery store because she needed the food, and that it was discovered that she in fact had no money with which to buy such food. Assume also, however, that the manner in which she states her reason for the theft is somewhat loose and flippant, as if she were kidding the interviewer. Under these circumstances, the woman's explanation of why she shoplifted cannot be take at face value. At the least, the factfinder will want to know why the defendant gave the explanation she did and whether the explanation is in fact "credible." To answer these questions, it will be hard to a void speculation about this woman's personality, perhaps based in part on hypotheses about her "psychodynamics."

Nonetheless, in light of Moore's conclusions, it would seem advisable for mental health professionals to focus primarily on the rationality of defendants' conscious reasoning when evaluating whether their mental disease or defect "caused" the criminal behavior at issue; only if this approach does not seem to provide a person's true reasons for acting (i.e., reasons that are intelligible and internally consistent), should a clinician rely upon other data.

(3) Cognitive Impairment

The *M'Naghten* test, the first prong of the ALI test, and the ABA/American Psychiatric Association formulation permit a defense of insanity only if a mental disease or defect causes cognitive impairment at the time of the offense. The *M'Naghten* test actually permits exculpation on either of two grounds: (1) when the defendant did not know the nature and quality of the criminal act, or (2) when the defendant did not know that the act was wrong. Presumably, an accused who does not meet the first test will not meet the second. The ALI/ABA/American Psychiatric Association formulation, on the other hand, focuses on the single standard of whether the defendant substantially lacked the ability to appreciate the "criminality" (or, as an alternative term, the "wrongfulness") of the act.

Looking solely at the language of the two tests, it is clear that *M'Naghten* is the more restrictive of the two. Yet, according to Professor Goldstein, few courts interpret *M'Naghten* literally.[90] His study of evidence presented and instructions given in jurisdictions that use the *M'Naghten* rule indicates that each component of the test is usually construed liberally, when defined at all. Thus, the word "know" is usually given broad construction to encompass defendants' ability to "understand" or "appreciate" the nature and consequences of their actions. The phrase "nature and quality of the act" is either eliminated altogether from the jury's instructions or, in Professor Goldstein's words, is "treated as [if it added] nothing to the requirement that the accused know his act was wrong."[91] And while the meaning for the word "wrong" has been interpreted restrictively by some courts, which hold that defendants are sane under *M'Naghten* if they knew their offenses were prohibited by law, other courts take the position that "wrong" should be read to mean "morally wrong."[92] Thus, to use Professor Goldstein's example, according to these courts, a man who thinks God ordered him to kill an individual would be found insane even if he knew it was legally wrong to take another's life.

The *M'Naghten* case itself provides an illustration of the degree of "stretch" in the language of the test. Daniel M'Naghten shot Edward Drummond, private secretary to Prime Minister Peel, apparently under the mistaken impression that Drummond was the Prime Minister. The defense attorneys introduced evidence tending to show that M'Naghten felt persecuted by a "system" that followed him, allowed him no peace of mind, and was out to kill him; the defense also claimed that M'Naghten thought the person he shot was part of this "system." However, there is little doubt that M'Naghten knew the nature and quality of his act in the literal sense: He knew he was firing a pistol, knew he was shooting a human being, and had every intention of killing that human being. It also appears that he knew in the abstract that it was unlawful to shoot another.[93] Yet he was acquitted under instructions that were very similar to the rules subsequently pronounced by the House of Lords.[94]

Given the flexibility of the *M'Naghten* rules as applied by most jurisdictions, it is arguable that the ALI/ABA/American Psychiatric Association reform of the cognitive prong was unnecessary. What little evidence exists is inconclusive with respect to whether the ALI test leads to more pleas of insanity and more successful defenses.[95] But the literal language of the ALI test, unlike the *M'Naghten* terminology, leaves no doubt that this standard for assessing insanity is not a rigid one. It has already been noted that the test does not require total absence of memory or understanding of the offense. As the drafters of the test stated, whether an offender possessed substantial capacity is all "that candid witnesses, called on to infer the nature of the situation at a time that they did not observe, can ever confidently say, even when they know that the disorder was extreme."[96] In the same liberal spirit, use of the word "appreciate" is designed to permit testimony about the defendants' emotional and affective attitude toward their offenses as well as their perceptions and memory of the crimes.[97] Finally, the ALI test provides two optional approaches to the "wrongness" issue. If the word "criminality" is adopted, the test is meant to apply only to those who did not appreciate that their act was legally wrong because of mental disorder. If the word "wrongfulness" is adopted, individuals who know that their acts were illegal, but whose mental disorder nonetheless led them to feel morally justified in committing these acts, may be excused by reason of insanity.[98] Although "criminality" is thus more restrictive than "wrongfulness," it is important to remember that the word "appreciate" acts to broaden the wrongfulness inquiry under either option, especially as compared to a literal interpretation of *M'Naghten*.

Whatever the applicable test, the type of evidence submitted is not likely to vary, since the basic issue—degree of cognitive impairment—is the same. Later in this chapter, we suggest some specific areas that can be investigated in this regard [see § 6.06(a)].

(4) Volitional Impairment

The "irresistible impulse" test and the second prong of the ALI test excuse individuals whose mental disease or defect cause a loss of control over their actions at the time of their offenses. Similar to the experience with the cognitive tests, it appears that the more restrictive terminology of the "irresistible impulse" test has not led to less testimony on the impulsivity issue than is offered in ALI jurisdictions,[99] despite the popular characterization of the former standard as the "policeman at the elbow" test, under which offenders will be found insane only if they could have committed their offenses in the presence of an officer.[100] But it is also clear that, whether the traditional test or the ALI version is employed, the legal community is not as receptive toward the "control" tests as it is toward the *M'Naghten* rule and the first prong of the ALI test. As of 1983, only 23 states use one of the two control formulations,[101] and several states have specifically rejected it.[102] As related earlier, critics of the control tests claim that there is no objective basis for distinguishing between the

impulse that was irresistible and the impulse not resisted, and therefore, that a test calling for such a distinction is subject to gross abuse.

It should also be remembered that, as with the cognitive tests, a defendant seeking acquittal on grounds of lack of control must meet the threshold requirement of mental disease or defect. As one court has put it, the irresistible impulse "is to be distinguished from mere passion or overwhelming emotion not growing out of, and connected with, a disease of the mind. Frenzy arising solely from the passion of anger and jealousy, regardless of how furious, is not insanity."[103]

As noted earlier, both the American Psychiatric Association and the ABA have recommended that the volitional prong of the insanity test be dropped.[104] Both groups deny that by so doing they are barring evidence of volitional impairment; it is suggested that if the cognitive prong of the ALI test is retained and the word "appreciate" is interpreted broadly, most cases involving a serious lack of control will still result in an insanity acquittal because they will also involve cognitive, affective impairment. Whether this assumption is merited or not, this approach obviously de-emphasizes inquiry into volitional dysfunction.

Despite these developments, it remains a fact that some offenders are acquitted by reason of irresistible impulse or because of a lack of substantial capacity to conform their conduct to the requirements of the law. While appellate courts have interpreted the control tests somewhat restrictively, juries still seem willing to acquit on lack of control grounds, even when there is some evidence of planning. Later in this chapter, we attempt to pinpoint the factors that seem most relevant to the impulsivity inquiry [see § 6.06(a)].

(5) Burden of Proof and Standard of Proof

In most cases, neither side will be able to present evidence that is overwhelmingly convincing to the factfinder. The law has developed the "burden of proof" and "standard of proof" concepts to deal with this probability. If the party with the burden of proof does not meet the standard of proof established by law, then that party loses.

Arguably, the outcome of an insanity case could depend as much on a jurisdiction's approach to these proof issues as on its substantive test of insanity.

There are two major competing approaches to proof issues in the insanity context. One-third of the states require the prosecution to prove sanity "beyond a reasonable doubt" (which computes to perhaps a 90–95% degree of certainty). If the factfinder is not convinced beyond a reasonable doubt that the defendant was sane at the time of the offense, the prosecution loses. Most of the remaining states, on the other hand, place the burden of proof on the defendant to show by a "preponderance of the evidence" (or with a 51% degree of certainty) that he or she was insane at the time of the offense. If the defendant's evidence does not meet this standard, the prosecution wins.[105] Arizona and the federal courts require the defendant to prove insanity by "clear and convincing" evidence (or with approximately a 75% degree of certainty).[106]

The courts that follow the first approach base their stance primarily on the theory that sanity is an element of every crime, just as some type of unlawful act is an element of every crime.[107] Since the prosecution must prove beyond a reasonable doubt that the act associated with a given crime was in fact committed by the defendant, it must also prove beyond a reasonable doubt that the defendant was sane at that time. Courts and legislatures that have adopted the second approach do not consider sanity a formal element of every crime or disregard the elements analysis entirely; their principal concern is that the "beyond a reasonable doubt" standard of proof might unfairly hinder the prosecution in cases involving the ambiguous matters raised by an insanity plea.[108] In fact, the data that exist do not suggest any consistent relationship between burden of proof and the acquittal rate.[109]

Interestingly, the ABA proposes that while the burden of proof should be on the prosecution under its test, if the ALI cognitive–volitional test is retained, the burden should be on the defendant.[110] The ABA drafters feel that the prosecution should normally bear the burden of proving sanity beyond a reasonable doubt, but that the difficulty in proving lack of impulsivity should

permit shifting the burden to the defendant when the control test is relied upon.

A final proof issue deserving of mention is the so-called "presumption of sanity." This evidentiary doctrine, which exists in all jurisdictions, permits the factfinder to presume that the defendant was sane at the time of the offense, unless the defendant is able to produce enough evidence to overcome the presumption. Most state courts hold that a "scintilla" of evidence satisfactorily rebuts this presumption[111]; offering experts' or lay witnesses' testimony tending to show insanity is usually sufficient. If no such evidence is forthcoming, however, the presumption requires a finding for the prosecution.

6.03.　*Exculpatory and Mitigating Doctrines Other than Insanity*

Except for strict liability offenses, which are not relevant to the topic of this chapter, every crime is comprised of at least two elements: (1) the physical conduct associated with the crime (known as the *"actus reus"*); and (2) the mental state, or level of intent, associated with the crime (known as the *"mens rea"*). To convict an individual of a particular crime, the state must prove beyond a reasonable doubt that the defendant committed the *actus reus* with the requisite *mens rea* for that crime. Whether conviction also requires proof of a third element—sanity—has been discussed in the preceding subsection and is not re-examined here.

The law requires an act as a predicate for criminal liability because "evil thoughts" alone, however repugnant morally, have never been considered sufficient to justify the imposition of criminal sanctions. It has developed the *mens rea* requirement because proof that an individual has committed a given act is not viewed as a sufficient measure by itself of criminal culpability. All would agree, for example, that the killing of another is reprehensible. But should the driver who accidentally runs into a child, the husband who kills his wife's paramour, and the "cold-blooded" murderer all be punished equally? Determining the individual's *mens rea* at the time of the offense provides a mechanism for deciding how much retribution is justifiable in such cases.

Most of the legal doctrines to be discussed in the following subsections have developed out of the law's attempt to define the *actus reus* and *mens rea* concepts.

(a)   The Automatism Defense

The *actus reus* contemplates a voluntary physical act. For instance, if *A* pushes *B*'s arm into *C, B* cannot be convicted of assault even though *B*'s arm committed the actual touching, because *B*'s act was not voluntary. It could also be said that *B* did not intend to commit the assault, and thus did not have the *mens rea* for the crime. But a distinction is usually made between an act over which there is no conscious control and a conscious action with unintended consequences. The assault above is an example of the first type of act and has traditionally been analyzed under the voluntariness requirement of the *actus reus.* An example of the latter situation would be if *B* meant to tap *C,* but instead killed *C; B*'s act would be voluntary, but *B* would not have the *mens rea* for murder.

The automatism (or "unconsciousness") defense recognizes that some criminal acts may be committed "involuntarily," even though no third party (like *A* in the example above) is involved. The classic example of the "automaton" is the person who commits an offense while sleepwalking; courts have held that such an individual does not have conscious control of his or her physical actions and therefore acts involuntarily.[112] Other situations in which the defense might be implicated arise when a crime occurs during a state of unconsciousness induced by concussion following a head injury; by shock created by bullet wounds; or by metabolic disorders such as anoxia, hypoglycemia, or the involuntary ingestion of alcohol or drugs.[113] As discussed in more detail below, events caused by epilepsy and dissociation are probably best placed in this category as well. Figure 6-1 attempts to relate diagnoses found in DSM-III to the automatism doctrine. Although these relations are tentative,

the figure should prove helpful in fixing the universe of possible conditions that are legally relevant in this area.

Several courts have limited the automatism defense by holding that a person claiming to have been affected by one of the above-named conditions at the time of the offense cannot prevail with the defense if the disability has been experienced on previous occasions and steps reasonably could have been taken to prevent the criminal occurrence.[114] Thus, if a man knows he is subject to epileptic seizures, loses control of a car because of a seizure, and kills someone in the process, he may not be able to take advantage of the defense.

Conceptually, the automatism defense differs from the insanity defense in three ways. First, insane persons, unlike "automatons," are generally conscious of their acts but either do not understand the true nature of the acts or cannot stop themselves from performing them. Second, while there is some dispute over whether sanity is an element that must be proven for each offense, the prosecution clearly bears the burden of establishing the *actus reus* and thus bears the burden of negating an automatism claim beyond a reasonable doubt. Finally, to prevail, a person alleging insanity must be found to have a mental disease or defect; there is no such requirement when automatism is involved.

Partly because the "automaton" is not perceived to be as "sick" as the insane person, and partly because cases raising the issue of legal unconsciousness are rare, there are no special-commitment statutes analogous to those used in the insanity context governing those who are acquitted on automatism grounds. But occasionally, of course, a person suffering from a condition that causes involuntary behavior in the legal sense may be both in need of treatment and quite dangerous. Thus, many courts confronted with an automatism defense have glossed over the theoretical distinctions between insanity and automatism in order to insure the commitment of violent offenders. For example, most commentators agree that an epileptic seizure is best characterized as an involuntary act rather than an "irresistible impulse," because the seizure is not triggered by the individual's conscious, or even unconscious, processes.[115] Yet courts in Britain, where the law of automatism is well developed, have rejected automatism defenses based on epilepsy and instead have permitted only claims of insanity, on the explicit ground that to do otherwise would result in immediate release of dangerous individuals.[116] Rather than distorting the insanity doctrine in such a fashion, it would make more sense to subject those acquitted on automatism grounds to commitment provisions similar to those applicable in the insanity context.

The automatism defense is infrequent in the United States, probably because the American defense bar is relatively unaware of the defense's advantages. Cases involving dissociation provide an illustration of this point. Conduct committed by a person who is in a dissociative or fugue state is probably best described as activity that, although purposive in nature, is no longer subject to the conscious constraints of the superego or conscience,[117] and is therefore "involuntary" or "automatic." Yet American defendants claiming to have experienced dissociation at the time of the offense usually rely upon the insanity defense rather than the automatism doctrine. Moreover, they are usually convicted; as discussed in § 6.03(c), courts and juries tend to reject an insanity defense based on a dissociative incident because of their dislike for the notion of temporary insanity.[118] Since (1) there is, as yet, no analogous hostility toward "temporary automatism"; (2) the prosecution bears the burden of disproving an automatism claim; and (3) the dispositional consequences of an automatism verdict are unlikely to be more onerous than, and will probably be preferable to, those resulting from an insanity finding, the failure to assert automatism is more likely to be the result of ignorance than the result of an intelligent assessment of its potential success.

Of course, if the automatism defense were to become more popular in the United States, it would probably come to be interpreted as restrictively as the insanity defense, and the necessary special-commitment statutes would probably be passed. At present, however, the defense remains an attractive plea for defendants who lacked conscious awareness of their conduct at the time of their offenses.

(b) Clinical Testimony Relevant to *Mens Rea* (Diminished Capacity)

As noted in the beginning of this discussion, the principal device the law uses to grade culpability is mental state. A person who deliberately plans a crime is more culpable than one who accidentally commits one. Under the common law, courts developed literally scores of *"mens rea"* terms to describe various levels of culpability. Unfortunately, these terms—"willful and wanton," "with a depraved heart," and so on—were more colorful than descriptive. Over the years, two generic categories were created to help categorize these diverse mental states, although they were only partially successful in doing so. "Specific intent" was meant to designate the *mens rea* for those crimes that require a *further intention* beyond that identified with the physical act connected with the offense (e.g., "premeditated" murder, "aggravated" assault, assault "with intent to rape"). One had the *mens rea* for "general intent," on the other hand, if one was merely conscious or should have been conscious of one's physical actions at the time of the offense (e.g., the intent for manslaughter, assault, rape).

Because neither the original *mens rea* terms nor the concepts of specific and general intent were necessarily self-defining, modern statutory codes have attempted to be more precise on issues relating to mental state. Most influential in this regard has been the ALI's Model Penal Code formulation, which attempts to simplify the *mens rea* inquiry by specifying a total of four *mens rea* components. In descending order of culpability, they are (1) "purpose," when the criminal conduct is the offender's conscious object; (2) "knowledge," when the offender is aware of the circumstances that make the conduct criminal; (3) "recklessness," when the offender "consciously disregards a substantial and unjustifiable risk" that the conduct will produce a given result; and (4) "negligence," when the offender "should be aware of a substantial and unjustifiable risk" that the conduct will produce a given result.[119] The first two mental states focus on subjective mental state, "negligence" is objectively defined, and "recklessness" falls somewhere in between. Although the common-law terms are so amorphous that equating them with Model Penal Code mental states is a somewhat risky venture, it is probably fair to say that "specific intent" most closely coincides with "purpose" and "knowledge," while "general intent" can be analogized with "recklessness" and "negligence."

As will become clear below, distinguishing between subjective mental states (purpose, knowledge, and specific intent) and objectively defined mental states (negligence, general intent) is important in understanding the courts' approach to clinical input on *mens rea*. It is also important to recognize that the *mens rea* inquiry described above is quite distinct from the insanity inquiry. While it may be true that persons who meet the *M'Naghten* test may also be incapable of forming the requisite intent for an offense, it is theoretically and practically possible for persons to have the appropriate *mens rea* and yet still to have been insane. Their reasons for committing acts may be so "crazy" that no jury would be willing to hold them criminally responsible, even though their knowledge of what they were doing was relatively unimpaired. To use the *M'Naghten* case as an example once again, Daniel M'Naghten probably met the *mens rea* requirements for the crime charged (i.e., knowingly shooting at another with the purpose of killing him), but he was nonetheless found insane.

Out of this distinction has developed the so-called "diminished capacity" concept. In its broadest sense, this "doctrine"[120] permits the accused to introduce clinical testimony focusing directly on the *mens rea* for the crime charged, without having to assert an insanity defense. For example, in a murder case, clinical evidence relevant to whether the defendant purposely or knowingly committed the killing would be admissible. If the charge is assault with intent to rape, mental health professionals would be permitted to address whether the defendant acted with the purpose of committing rape at the time of the offense. When the *mens rea* for the crime charged is negated by the clinical testimony, the defendant is acquitted only of that charge. The prosecutor is still entitled to try convicting the accused of a lesser included offense involving a lesser *mens rea*. Thus, in the first example, conviction might still be sought on a manslaughter charge (requiring a reckless or negligent *mens rea*). Of course, the defendant might be able to show the absence of *mens rea* for these lesser included offenses as well, in which case complete acquittal may result.

Evidence of "diminished capacity" should be distinguished from evidence of "diminished or partial responsibility," which mitigates the penalty imposed on a person whose mental disorder causes cognitive or volitional impairment but produces neither insanity nor an inability to form the *mens rea* for the offense. The doctrine of diminished responsibility has never enjoyed theoretical support in the courts except at sentencing and, in a few states, in first-degree murder and death penalty cases.[121] Given the difficulty of implementing such a concept at the trial stage (how does one sensibly define "partial responsibility" for the jury, and what crime is the partially responsible defendant guilty of?), it will probably remain dormant.[122]

The doctrine of diminished capacity, on the other hand, has found increasing acceptance. While 14 states have held that clinical testimony on any issue other than insanity is inadmissible (generally on the ground that such testimony is too speculative),[123] the clear trend is toward admitting clinical testimony on *mens rea*.[124] Indeed, several courts have found it unconstitutional to hold otherwise. Some of these courts merely state that principles of fairness and due process require that defendants be permitted to introduce any competent relevant evidence, including psychiatric testimony, in their defense.[125] It could also be argued that since the prosecution is entitled to an inference that accused persons intend the natural consequences of their acts, denying defendants the opportunity to present competent clinical evidence when such evidence is the only means of overcoming the inference would in effect permit the prosecution to convict the defendants when there is a reasonable doubt as to their guilt.[126]

Although an increasing number of states are thus permitting clinical testimony on *mens rea,* many are doing so grudgingly. There are three types of limitations on such evidence. First, in order to prevent clinicians from testifying on the "ultimate issue" of whether defendants in fact possessed the requisite *mens rea* at the time of their offenses, many courts permit clinicians to testify only as to the "capacity" of the defendants to form the *mens rea* (thus one reason for the name "diminished capacity").[127] Second, courts may require proof that some severe "mental disease or defect," analogous to that required in the insanity context, caused the lack of capacity.[128] Finally, most states restrict the admissibility of clinical evidence to certain types of crimes.

This third limitation on *mens rea* evidence is itself of two types. One approach, apparently followed by 8 of the 28 states that recognize the doctrine of diminished capacity in some form, permits clinical testimony only in cases where defendants are charged with some type of intentional homicide.[129] A second approach, taken by most other states that allow clinical testimony on *mens rea,* admits clinical testimony for any crime involving "specific intent" (in "common-law" jurisdictions), or any crime for which intent is subjectively defined in terms of "purposefulness" or "knowledge" (in "Model Penal Code" jurisdictions), but does not admit such evidence for crimes involving "general intent" (in "common-law" states) or crimes for which intent is defined in terms of "recklessness" or "negligence" (in "Model Penal Code" states).[130]

The "capacity" and "severe mental abnormality" limitations on *mens rea* testimony represent an attempt by the courts to ensure that any opinions proferred by mental health professionals on *mens rea* are in fact clinical in nature. They are also motivated by a fear that without such restrictions every case will turn into a psychiatric one, since there is always something "expert" to be said about the psychological processes of criminals. Limiting *mens rea* evidence to certain types of crimes is directed toward another concern: that some mentally ill defendants (including those who ordinarily would have pleaded insantiy and thus been committed) will otherwise be able to use clinical evidence to elude confinement completely.[131] The public is protected in states limiting testimony on *mens rea* to homicide cases, because a defendant who has killed another can almost always be convicted of at least

negligent homicide (involuntary manslaughter), no matter how mentally ill; the *mens rea* for that crime is objectively defined in terms of what a reasonable person would do, making clinical evidence of the defendant's subjective state of mind irrelevant. Similarly, in those states where the defense is available only for crimes involving specific intent, the mentally ill defendant can usually be convicted of some lesser included offense involving general intent.

The limitations on *mens rea* evidence thus grew from practical concerns. However, none of these limitations are conceptually justified. If, as many courts have held, due process prohibits barring competent evidence on *mens rea,* the sole requirement for clinical testimony relevant to that subject should be whether it is admissible as expert opinion [see § 1.04]. If a clinician's opinion is based on specialized knowledge and can assist the trier of fact in reaching a conclusion on the issue, it should be admissible whether it is phrased in terms of capacity or actual intent, whether it is based on a finding of significant mental abnormality or mere "quirkiness," and regardless of the offense charged.[132] Admittedly, deciding when a particular opinion is in fact based on "specialized knowledge" may be difficult in certain cases. But this problem is alleviated somewhat by the narrow confines of the *mens rea* concept. Mere proof of "craziness" is insufficient for purposes of negating *mens rea;* it must be shown that because of mental aberration the defendant was actually unable to formulate the requisite intent. If *A,* a schizophrenic, intends to kill *B, A* has the *mens rea* for some type of intentional homicide; only if *A*'s illness negates intent—for example, *A* thinks that *B* is a tree or that the gun is a toy— would *A* be able to benefit from a "diminished capacity" defense. Evidence of volitional impairment is also completely irrelevant to the *mens rea* issue [see Figure 6-1].

The fear that the public will be endangered unless the doctrine is limited in scope is also exaggerated. Since most mentally ill defendants are conscious of their actions, they will often be guilty of some crime involving general intent, objectively defined, even without the restriction limiting clinical evidence to offenses involving specific intent. And, as noted in the discussion of automatism, there is no obstacle to adopting special-commitment statutes for the dangerously mentally ill who somehow do escape conviction altogether.

A description of a recent case may help illustrate why clinical testimony about *mens rea* should generally be admissible. In *Bright v. United States,*[133] the defendant was charged with possession of stolen checks—a crime requiring proof that the accused knew the checks were stolen. The defendant in the case received six checks under circumstances that would have suggested to most people that they were stolen. However, the defendant offered testimony by a psychiatrist suggesting that she had in fact not known they were stolen. According to the psychiatrist, the defendant had a "passive–dependent" personality and possessed a "childlike character structure," which led her to trust implicitly those close to her; since the person who gave her the checks was a good friend of her boyfriend and told her the checks were legitimate, she did not think the checks had been stolen. One may question whether the clinician's testimony was based on specialized knowledge. But his testimony, if accepted as competent, was clearly relevant to the issue of whether the defendant knew the checks were stolen, even though it was neither phrased in terms of capacity, nor based on a finding of severe mental illness. To exclude it would have permitted conviction of a person who may not have been guilty of the crime as defined by the legislature.

In some jurisdictions, the testimony in *Bright* could also have been admitted on the ground that it helped define the defendant's "character." Unfortunately, an increasing number of courts are permitting clinical testimony, whether or not based on an identifiable mental disease, when introduced as evidence to show whether a person with particular character traits could have committed the crime in question. This development is an outgrowth of the traditional rule that opinion evidence of a "pertinent" trait of an accused's character is admissible if proffered for the purpose of proving that the accused acted in conformity with that trait.[134] In *O'Kon v. Roland,*[135] for instance, the court permitted psychiatric testimony that the defendant, charged with

murder, was a passive person and unlikely to commit a violent act.

The problem with evidence of "character" is that, as *O'Kon* demonstrates, it tends to resemble a mere assessment of whether the defendant is "good" or "bad," rather than an opinion as to the defendant's MSO, as in *Bright*. While some courts have decided that such evidence is relevant, testimony about general character traits is much broader in scope than insanity, automatism, or *mens rea* testimony, and thus more subject to abuse. Clinicians should be particularly cautious about offering such opinions. Assessments that individuals are or are not "violence-prone" are notoriously unreliable [see § 7.10]; clinicians should make sure that "character evaluations" are based on specialized knowledge and not on a bare appraisal of the defendants' credibility. Otherwise, every criminal case may indeed become merely a forum for "diagnosing" the defendant.

(c)   Defenses Based on Intoxication

Just as mental illness and mental retardation may lead to exculpation for a criminal offense, intoxication—either by alcohol or by narcotic drugs—may form the basis for a defense to crime. Although the intoxication defenses are often viewed as distinct from the defenses already discussed in this chapter, they are in fact subcategories of the doctrines of insanity, automatism, and diminished capacity.

Because intoxication, unlike mental illness or mental retardation, is usually the product of a defendant's own actions, the law is cautious about giving it mitigating effect. In some states, evidence of so-called "voluntary" intoxication is considered relevant only on the issue of whether a defendant charged with first-degree murder premeditated the crime. Most states also permit such evidence if offered to prove that a defendant did not possess the *mens rea* for a crime involving specific intent.[136] But, unless there is evidence that a defendant is suffering from some underlying mental abnormality, the mere fact that he or she was voluntarily intoxicated will not justify a finding of automatism or of insanity, even if the defendant can show that the alcohol or drugs caused him or her to be "unconscious" or unaware of the nature or wrongfulness of the act at the time of the offense.[137]

Courts are more lenient in cases involving "involuntary" intoxication. Such intoxication occurs when a defendant is tricked into ingesting drugs or alcohol, or otherwise unknowingly takes the substance.[138] Also conceivably falling in this category are cases of "pathological intoxication," where a defendant knows what has been taken but where the substance produces an atypical and excessive reaction that the defendant could not have foreseen.[139] If involuntary intoxication makes it impossible for the defendant to form the *mens rea* for the crime, or renders the defendant's criminal act "automatic," courts will generally require acquittal of the crime charged[140]; the limitations imposed on evidence of intoxication that is "voluntary" do not apply in such a situation, given the accused's underlying innocence with respect to the initial ingestion of the substance.

A final type of intoxication, which may be seen as either voluntary or involuntary, is that resulting from chronic use of psychoactive substances. Some courts have held that alcoholic or drug addicts are impelled to drink or use drugs, and that any use of such substances is thus "involuntary" in nature.[141] If this is true, then chronic users of psychoactive substances who can show that, due to intoxication, they did not commit the *actus reus* or have the *mens rea* for the crimes charged will be acquitted of those crimes. Most courts, however, have been reluctant to interpret ingestion by addicts as involuntary, with the result that these cases are most often analyzed as situations involving voluntary intoxication.[142]

Chronic alcohol or drug users may nonetheless be able to prove that they have a mental disease or defect that caused significant cognitive or volitional impairment at the time of their offenses, and that they were thus insane. As pointed out in the discussion of the insanity defense, if there is evidence of "settled insanity" due to substance abuse, the "mental disease or defect" requirement of the insanity defense may be met. For instance, some courts have indicated that an accused suffering from delirium tremens may be able to obtain acquittal on insanity grounds.[143] Of course, to be found insane, addicts must also produce evidence relevant to the functional parts of the applicable insanity test.

(d) The "Guilty But Mentally Ill" Plea

Since 1976, at least 12 states have passed statutes authorizing the factfinder to return a verdict of "guilty but mentally ill" (GBMI).[144] Although there are many different versions of the GBMI concept, most proposals work basically as follows: A defendant who pleads NGRI may be found not guilty, guilty, insane, or, in the alternative, GBMI at the time of the offense. If the jury makes the last-mentioned finding, the defendant may be sentenced to any term appropriate for the offense, with the opportunity for treatment in a mental hospital during that period. Thus, jurors in insanity cases are given three sets of instructions with respect to the ultimate verdict they may reach: One explains under what circumstances a defendant may be found guilty of the crime charged; one describes the state's test for insanity; and one informs the jury when a defendant who is guilty beyond a reasonable doubt but not insane may be found GBMI. The defintion of mental illness found in the last of these instructions varies from state to state, but usually borrows heavily from the definition of mental illness in the state's civil commitment statute. In Michigan, for instance, the definition is taken directly from the mental health code and states that mental illness is "[a] substantial disorder of thought or mood which significantly impairs judgment, behavior, capacity to recognize reality, or ability to cope with the ordinary demands of life."[145]

Proponents of GBMI statutes hope to reduce insanity acquittals and to provide greater protection to the public by offering jurors a compromise verdict, which insures prolonged incarceration of the dangerously mentally at the same time it provides treatment for the sick. Yet it is not clear that the verdict is any better at accomplishing these goals than the traditional system. Research suggests that the verdict may actually increase insanity acquittals by encouraging defendants to raise the plea in the hopes of at least obtaining a GBMI verdict.[146] And a person found GBMI must be considered for parole, just like any other convicted offender. Once the minimum period of confinement necessary to establish eligibility for parole has passed, the primary criterion governing the release of the person found GBMI is the same as that ruling the release of the person found NGRI—namely, dangerousness. As a result, the duration of a given individual's confinement should be roughly similar under either the traditional system or one that employs the GBMI verdict.

Even if one assumes that the GBMI verdict does reduce insanity acquittals and result in longer confinement, it is deficient for two other reasons. First, the verdict creates a significant potential for jury confusion and abuse, given the similarity between its definition of mental illness and the definition of insanity (compare, for instance, the definition of mental illness under Michigan's GBMI statute with the language of the ALI rule, which is the test for insanity in Michigan). Jurors who see little difference between the competing terminologies may choose the GBMI verdict solely because it (supposedly) results in longer confinement. A person with a valid insanity defense may therefore be convicted instead. Unfortunately, there is probably no way to define mental illness so as to avoid this result and still meaningfully distinguish between noninsane but mentally ill offenders and "normal" offenders.

Most importantly, the GBMI verdict is deficient because it is not a proper "verdict" at all. It is neither a device for assessing criminal responsibility, as is the insanity defense, nor a method of grading culpability, as is the doctrine of diminished capacity. Rather, it is a dispositional mechanism transferred to the guilt determination phase of the criminal process. The hybrid nature of the verdict is made apparent by the fact that, under the GBMI scheme, the jury's determination of mental illness at the time of the offense is relevant only to whether the accused requires treatment at the time of trial—a finding that is best made and acted upon at sentencing, when information about various dispositional alternatives can be obtained and proper experts

can be consulted. Even if the jury can somehow accurately identify who needs treatment, virtually every state already provides for the hospitalization of prisoners requiring inpatient care.[147]

Nonetheless, the GBMI idea seems to be attracting interest in the wake of the Hinckley trial and the subsequent dissatisfaction with the defense. At the present time, several other states are considering adopting some version of the GBMI verdict.[148]

6.04. Research

In § 6.02(a), we have touched on some research questions related to the systemic impact of the insanity defense—the frequency with which it is raised and is successful, what happens to those found NGRI, and their tendency to recidivate. In this section, we review research relevant to the types of mental disorder that may be involved in an MSO defense, including a closer look at psychiatric diagnosis and legal insanity, unusual syndromes and novel defenses, and studies of the reliability and validity of mental health professionals' opinions on insanity. We also review the Rogers Criminal Responsibility Assessment Scales, a series of scales designed to measure, with some degree of scientific validity, the concept of legal insanity.

(a) Diagnosis and Insanity: Some Questionable Subgroups

Figure 6-1 [in § 6.02(c)] provides a tentative linkage between currently accepted diagnostic categories and various MSO defenses. This figure is based on an analysis of the law in one state (Virginia), rather than on an investigation of the types of diagnoses most often associated with those defendants benefiting from an MSO defense. The research that has been conducted on this latter issue is limited primarily to the insanity defense. The GBMI plea is relatively new; consequently, little is known about it (although preliminary reports indicate that most of those found GBMI are diagnosed as having a personality disorder

Table 6-1
Characteristics of Four NGRI Samples

Variables	Michigan 1967–72	Michigan 1975–79	New York 1971–76	New York 1976–78
Sex				
Male	87	85	87	87
Female	13	15	13	13
Race				
White	68	54	65	60
Black	32	45	27	*
Other	0	1	8	*
Type of offense				
Murder	71	48	59	48
Other assault	16	27	24	22
Other crimes	13	25	17	30
Prior psychiatric hospitalization	46	66	42	42
Incompetent for trial for NGRI offense	40	45	*	*
Prior criminal record	26	33	44	*
Diagnosis				
Psychosis	68	73	67	*
Organic brain syndrome	4	0	2	*
Neurosis	0	1	3	*
Personality disorder	25	22	11	*
Mentally retarded	0	1	2	*
Other/deferred/no diagnosis	3	3	15	*

Note. All figures are percentages. * = Data not available.

and probably come from the "guilty" group rather than the "NGRI" group.[149] The automatism defense is extremely rare; thus, there are few aggregate data to be gathered and analyzed. Defenses of diminished capacity or intoxication, even when successful, do not create a discrete population of offenders; rather, these defendants are convicted of a lesser included offense and subjected to normal sentencing. Only the insanity defense has spurred extensive research, though one recent reviewer found the literature woefully deficient.[150]

Table 6-1 displays various characteristics of individuals found NGRI from two studies based on Michigan samples and two studies based on New York samples.[151] The "typical" NGRI patient is a white male who, as likely as not, has a record of prior psychiatric hospitalization, and who has been acquitted of an assaultive crime

(most likely murder).[152] Though whites are more often acquitted NGRI than are blacks, blacks are overrepresented in the NGRI population when population base rates are considered.

Of interest for the present discussion is the breakdown by psychiatric diagnosis at the bottom of Table 6-1. As noted earlier, the majority of insanity acquittees are diagnosed as suffering from a major psychiatric disorder, usually psychosis. This, along with the relatively low success rate for the insanity defense, provides some comfort to skeptics who view the defense as a scam allowing criminals to "get away with murder."[153] However, note the substantial minority of NGRI acquittees diagnosed as having a personality disorder. Given the prevalent view in the mental health community that personality disorders are not "mental illness," and legislative efforts to exclude personality disorders (e.g., antisocial personality) from the legal definition of "mental disease or defect," these figures suggest that a small number of insanity acquittals may be inappropriate.[154]

Clinical examiners at forensic hospitals rarely support an insanity defense based on a diagnosis of personality disorder.[155] Therefore, the characteristics and disposition of this subgroup of NGRI acquittees are of particular interest. Howard and Clark[156] gathered data on four groups of patients ($n = 20$ per group) who had been referred from various courts in Michigan for pretrial examination. Of interest to this discussion are the 20 defendants recommended and acquitted NGRI (NGRI/NGRI) and the 20 defendants recommended as criminally responsible but adjudicated NGRI (CR/NGRI). Howard and Clark were particularly interested in characteristics that distinguished the CR/NGRI group.

The NGRI/NGRI and CR/NGRI groups did not differ significantly in terms of frequency of prior hospitalization or type of offense charged, nor did they differ in the frequency of a pretrial finding of incompetent to stand trial (eight and seven cases, respectively). Diagnosis was significantly different across groups, however: The NGRI/NGRI group included 19 persons diagnosed as psychotic and 1 diagnosed as having a personality disorder; the CR/NGRI group included 4 defendants diagnosed as psychotic and 10 as having personality disorders. More interesting was the finding that the members of the CR/NGRI group adjudicated incompetent to stand trial were initially diagnosed as psychosis with malingering suspected, and during hospitalization were confirmed as malingerers and returned to court with a diagnosis of personality disorder.

Howard and Clark also developed a reliable method for rating the "rationality" of the various offenses charged. Offenses could be grossly classified as "Rational," "Intermediate," or "Irrational." Predictably, the NGRI/NGRI group had committed crimes classified as predominately Irrational (75%) or Intermediate (25%). The CR/NGRI group committed offenses from all three classifications, but mostly Intermediate offenses (65%) in which the offender's motive, while not bizarre, was not obvious. The CR/NGRI group was also distinguished by a more extensive arrest history (13 vs. 6), more frequent reports of in-

toxication at the time of the alleged crime (9 vs. 3), and a greater propensity for claimed amnesia (7 vs. 1) than the NGRI/NGRI group.

These data suggest that a subgroup of NGRI acquittees who suffer primarily from relatively mild psychiatric disturbance (i.e., personality disorder) are capable of complicating their pretrial examinations through the presentation of questionable symptoms (initial diagnosis of psychosis) and claims of amnesia that make it difficult for clinicians to reconstruct the prior MSO. These individuals have an apparent criminal lifestyle (increased report of drug and/or alcohol abuse, prior arrest record), but a history of psychiatric hospitalizations that lends some credence to their claims, later judged to be suspect, of major psychiatric disturbance. With supportive psychiatric testimony (which for the Michigan group, came from privately retained clinicians), they are able to obtain an NGRI acquittal.

Do such individuals "beat the rap?" It is probable that, in Michigan at least, some of them do. In Michigan, all defendants acquitted NGRI are sent to the Center for Forensic Psychiatry for a 60-day diagnostic commitment to determine whether they are subsequently committable as mentally ill and dangerous to themselves or to others. This is the same facility that conducts the pretrial examination. Criss and Racine[157] reported differential rates for release from the 60-day commitment, depending on whether the Center's pretrial examiner had recommended the defendant as CR or NGRI. Patients of the NGRI/NGRI category were released from the 60-day commitment without involuntary hospitalization 43% of the time; this figure escalated to 72.3% for patients of the CR/NGRI category. Of course, some of the acquittees in the latter group may have been individuals with personality disorders who suffered a "break" at the time of the offense.

Pasewark, Pantle, and Steadman have tentatively identified other subgroups of NGRI acquittees who, in retrospect, might not have been so adjudicated under a more strict application of the insanity test.[158] These suspect groups include (1) some women committing infanticide, (2) law enforcement officials, and (3) a group of defendants for whom the judge or jury "felt sorry" but whom they could not otherwise exonerate.

Among the women committing infanticide were some who presented no psychotic symptoms at the time of the offense and who had no history of psychiatric hospitalization. Pasewark and his colleagues speculated that some of these mothers were basically inadequate individuals whose children were convenient and available targets for anger and hostility. The NGRI acquittal of such individuals reflects society's general belief that no mother who kills her own infant could be "normal," regardless of psychiatric assessment.

Widely publicized cases provide illustrations of the latter two groups. Robert Torsney was a New York City police officer who shot and killed an unarmed boy for no apparent reason; there was no struggle, and the boy was unarmed. The examining psychiatrist diagnosed a rare form of epilepsy—automatism of Penfield—which resulted in a "dissociative psychotic state" and a psychomotor seizure.[159] This rare disorder also caused Torsney to "hallucinate" a gun in the boy's hand. This diagnosis was made in spite of the facts that Torsney had no history of epilepsy or any other mental disorder, and that his electroencephalogram (EEG) was normal! He was acquitted NGRI and was released within the year when staff could find no signs of mental illness.

Francine Hughes killed her ex-husband[160] after enduring repeated physical abuse over a number of years, including the day of the crime. As her ex-husband slept, Hughes poured gasoline in his bedroom and then set the room on fire. She then drove to the police station to report the incident. In a case involving conflicting psychiatric and psychological testimony, Hughes was acquitted NGRI. Following the acquittal, she was re-examined and determined to be not committable as mentally ill and a danger to herself or to others, and she was released back into the community.

(b) Unusual Syndromes and Novel Defenses

As noted in § 6.02, most MSO defenses proceed on the basis of symptoms and behaviors associated with fairly mainstream psychiatric disorders. But there are also a number of relatively unusual syndromes that may be asserted as the basis for alleged criminal behavior. While it is statistically rare for MSO defenses to be advanced on the basis of these unusual syndromes, and rare for such efforts to succeed, it may be useful to the clinician to consider briefly the potential applicability and limits associated with some of these disorders.

(1) Seizure Disorder

Occasionally defendants will assert an MSO defense, particularly in cases involving assaultive crimes, on the theory that the assaults were triggered by abnormal electrical patterns in their brains. The clinical condition most often diagnosed in such cases is psychomotor or temporal lobe epilepsy,[161] though recently the episodic dyscontrol syndrome has also been advanced as a clinical condition underlying uncontrolled (or uncontrollable) aggression.[162]

The literature on which these defense theories are based consists primarily of studies exploring the effects of electrical stimulation or ablation of brain sites.[163] These studies have led to the hypothesis that there are one or more "aggression centers" in the temporal lobe or limbic system structures—primarily the amygdala. This literature, along with the frequent occurrence of abnormal EEG tracings in individuals who have seizures, gives rise to the notion that sustained aggressive behavior by these individuals may be exclusively (or at least primarily) the product of randomly occurring, abnormal brain waves over which the individuals have no control. Since they cannot control the behavior, they cannot be held accountable or responsible.

Despite the easy logic of this argument, and a number of judicial decisions excusing epileptics, there is little empirical evidence to justify accounting for legally relevant violent behavior on the basis of abnormal electrical activity in the brain. Valenstein's[164] critical review of the brain–behavior literature reveals methodological weaknesses in prior studies and unwarranted inferences by investigators who have fostered the hypothesis of a relatively circumscribed "aggression center" in the amygdala.[165] Further, studies by epileptologists cast considerable doubt on the proposition that aggressiveness in seizure patients is primarily related to or a function of the abnormal electrical activity in the brain.[166]

Research has shown that the kinds of aggressive behavior observed during the seizure proper—the "ictus" or "ictal period"—is extremely unlikely to result in legally relevant violent behavior. Blumer[167] reported that during seizures, epileptics typically present an expressionless stare and are passive, displaying stereotypic behavior but not relating to the environment around them. The ictal phase typically lasts from a few seconds to one and a half minutes. Aggressive behavior during a seizure is likely to be "the unintended consequence of nonpurposeful movements such as swinging the arms wildly or kicking."[168] Attacks by patients during the seizure episode are likely to occur spontaneously, without provocation or evidence of planning; complex, sustained sequences of assaultive behavior are extremely unlikely. A study sponsored by the American Epilepsy Foundation involving an international panel of 18 epileptologists noted the "extreme rarity of directed aggression during seizures and the near impossibility of committing murder or manslaughter during random and unsustained automatisms."[169]

Conversely, the kinds of aggressive behaviors (e.g., directed violence toward others) likely to have legal significance are more likely to occur during the period *between* seizures (the "interictal period") and are *not* likely to be accompanied by symptoms of disturbed consciousness or mental state of an exculpating nature. Devinsky and Bear have noted:

> [P]atients with temporal lobe epilepsy may display disparate forms of aggressive behavior and . . . the more frequent, clinically important, and mechanistically significant aggressive behaviors do not occur during the ictal period. . . . Most of the aggressive acts follow a provocation, although it may seem a trivial one to others. The aggressive act may be planned out in clear consciousness over a significant period of time . . . The patient characteristically recalls and acknowledges his behavior and may experience sincere remorse concerning the consequences.[170]

Blumer has also commented on the modicum of control that is maintained during many such outbursts[171] and the fact that the violent episodes can "usually be avoided by a considerate, patient, and gentle approach."[172]

The phase of a seizure episode during which sustained violent behavior may occur in the context of an altered mental state is the "postictal period," that part of the interictal period that follows immediately after the ictus and that typically lasts from several minutes to an hour. During this period, the individual is confused but is interactive with the environment. Amnesia for this period is common and may extend beyond the confusional stage, covering periods of coherent responding and appropriate behavior. However, violent behavior during this phase is also extremely rare, and to guard against unwarranted attributions of violence to an epileptic state, clinicians should consider the criteria suggested by Walker:

1. Confirm that the individual was previously subject to bona fide epileptic attacks.
2. Confirm that the spontaneous attacks of the individual are similar to the one which allegedly occurred at the time of the crime.
3. Confirm that the loss of awareness alleged to have been present is commensurate with the types of epileptic attack the individual had.
4. Confirm that the degree of assumed unconsciousness is consistent with that reported from previous attacks.
5. Confirm that EEG findings are compatible with the type of disorder assumed to be present; repeated normal EEG's should be construed as decreasing to a one-to-twenty chance the possibility of epilepsy.
6. Confirm that the circumstances of the crime are compatible with the assumption of lack of awareness at the time—obvious motives are absent, the crime appears senseless, the mutilation was unnecessarily violent and extensive, there was no evidence of premeditation, and the offender did not attempt to escape.[173]

Where these criteria are not met, the clinician may still offer descriptive testimony regarding the characteristic moodiness and irritability of temporal lobe patients,[174] though the degree to which such information can be developed for mitigating or exculpatory purposes is questionable, given that most incidents of violence by epileptics occur during the interictal period and are associated with provocation, planning, and otherwise undisturbed cognitive functioning.[175] Clinicians must be wary of overselling laboratory findings, such as an abnormal EEG obtained quite some time after the alleged crime occurred. Attempts to infer the presence of insanity or automatism on the basis of belated laboratory findings betray a mistaken emphasis on psychophysiological measures; it is the associated psychological conditions—thoughts, feelings, motivational states—that constitute the proper focus of these determinations.

(2) Hypoglycemic Syndrome

Another defense theory occasionally encountered in court (e.g., in Dan White's "Twinkie defense" murder trial in San Francisco) is lack of criminal responsibility due to mental aberrations secondary to hypoglycemia. Unlike other organs of the body, the brain obtains its energy solely from the combustion of carbohydrates. The brain itself has such small carbohydrate stores that it is "uniquely dependent on a constant supply through the blood stream."[176] When the blood sugar level drops substantially, the brain has no alternative energy source. "Its metabolism must naturally slow down and cerebral function will suffer . . . the cerebral hemisphere and parts of the cerebellum metabolize at the highest rate and therefore are the first to suffer."[177] Lyle states the potential consequences most dramatically: "At the lower levels of blood sugar, humans are effectively decerebrated and are capable of nearly anything they have ever thought of or seen out of others in fiction or elsewhere."[178]

Lyle reviews an extensive literature, including numerous case studies of psychological disturbance associated with low blood sugar. Individuals may vary in terms of their symptom presentations, though one investigator described the attacks as "episodic and repetitive." He continued, "although the tempo and severity of attacks may vary, the same patient will most often ex-

perience the same symptom complex . . . Recognition of the episodic nature of the patient's symptoms is of diagnostic significance."[179] Other features of the hypoglycemic episode include amnesia for the episode, as well as a transitory nature (recovery quickly follows the ingestion of appropriate nutrients).[180] Finally, since blood sugar levels may be related to the recency of ingestion of carbohydrates, there may be a tendency for episodes to occur early in the morning, late at night, or before mealtimes. Alcohol ingestion, particularly after fasting, can exacerbate the condition by further lowering blood sugar level.

The coincidence of criminal behavior with hypoglycemic states is unknown, but the descriptions of crimes committed by hypoglycemics reveal features that may be important in determining when, and to what degree, to attribute the offense to low blood sugar levels. The crimes committed by hypoglycemics are characterized as showing poor motivation and no planning; the behaviors are atypical for these individuals, and they are amnesic following the episode. These features, along with the characteristics summarized above—episodic and repetitive "attacks"; intraindividual consistency; transient symptomatology; and possible relationship to eating schedule, fasting, and/or alcohol ingestion—suggest that Walker's guidelines for attributing crime to seizure states could be applied, with minor modification, to the investigation of crimes allegedly committed in a hypoglycemic condition. Along with glucose tolerance or other appropriate laboratory tests, the examiner should look for a documented history of prior episodes with symptoms similar to those displayed at the time of the alleged crime, and for a crime scenario bereft of obvious motive, lack of evidence of planning or preparation, lack of escape attempt, and so forth.

As with positive EEG findings in the case of epilepsy, the clinician should be careful not to overstate the importance of laboratory evidence of hypoglycemia obtained several weeks after the alleged crime. Lyle's review (particularly of the work of Wilder) documents that the degree of mental abnormality varies from mild to severe according to blood sugar level, and it is the degree of mental disturbance, not the mere presence of a metabolic etiological component, that is dispositive in an MSO defense.

(3) Dissociative States

Among those psychiatric conditions having potential legal relevance in reconstructive defenses, none are more perplexing or poorly understood than those falling under the heading of "dissociative states." The essential feature of dissociative disorders is "a sudden, temporary alteration in the normally integrative functions of consciousness, identity, or motor behavior."[181] These disorders subsume the variants of dual or multiple personality, including psychogenic fugue states, in which the individual wanders off for what can be a substantial period of time and assumes an identity and personality that is fully integrated but wholly different from his or her original or usual personality. Total or partial amnesia is often present in fugue states or in multiple-personality cases (i.e., where one personality is unaware of the existence of another). These conditions are often sufficiently chronic or recurring in nature that they may be seen in the clinical presentation of the individual, or third-party confirmation of the existence and behavior of the "other" personality may be obtained. More problematic for the forensic examiner are the brief, transient episodes of depersonalization or dissociation for which often little evidence other than the individual's subjective recall, or claim of amnesia, exists. As noted in § 6.02(c)(1), the courts rarely grant mitigating effect to such claims.

During dissociative episodes, individuals are capable of complex sequences of behavior that are purposeful and goal-directed. The quality of the consciousness of such individuals, however, may vary considerably. Individuals suffering from a temporary alteration of identity, such as multiple personalities, may be fully alert and cognizant of what is transpiring around them, with good reality testing save for the alternate identity they have adopted. Others may experience serious disruption in their processing of information, such that their usual associations to incoming stimuli are disrupted and their behavior takes on a mechanical quality. Individuals reporting depersonalization episodes describe their

experiences as if they were "in a dream state," or as if they were third-person observers, watching themselves act. Though the individuals are obviously the persons acting, their experience of the acts is that these are not in their control—that is, disruptions in the executive and organizing functions of thought are reported. In some cases, perceptual aberrations such as "tunnel vision" have also been reported.

Dissociative disorder is statistically quite rare, at least as a primary diagnosis,[182] and is clinically more common in individuals who are emotionally immature, self-centered, and dependent.[183] This premorbid personality type may be one diagnostic clue the clinician may use in judging the validity of a claimed dissociative experience. According to psychodynamic theory, dissociative phenomena serve a primary function of reducing anxiety; thus, the clinician might be more inclined to consider as valid reports of dissociative symptoms by individuals whose lives are interpersonally conflicted, and to be more suspicious of such claims from individuals who are anxiety-free and unconcerned with the evaluative judgments of others. Akhtar and Brenner,[184] however, provide examples of a wide variety of other primary psychiatric diagnoses with which some symptoms of dissociation may be associated. Add to these the frequent spurious claims of criminal defendants that they "blacked out" at the time of the offense, and one can appreciate the diagnostic difficulty that arises when claims of dissociation are made.

As will be discussed in § 6.05(d), the use of hypnosis or narcoanalysis may be of value when psychogenic amnesia is suspected. A careful drug and alcohol history may be helpful in judging the presence of chemical induced altered states at the time of the offense, which may be pertinent to certain MSO defenses (e.g., intoxication defense or diminished capacity). Gathering and reporting third-party data describing any past "blackouts" and the defendant's behavior immediately prior to and during the period of the offense will be of considerable assistance. However, clinicians should remember that philosophical and moral judgments about responsibility are out of their realm. For example, consider a crime that was committed by an individual with two distinct and distinguishable personalities (e.g., a person with a fugue state or a case of multiple personality). The clinician may describe clinically and (possibly) measure psychometrically or with other laboratory devices relevant behavior of the two personalities; it remains, however, for the trier of fact to determine whether *either* personality was sufficiently disturbed, or whether the mere fact of having more than one personality is a sufficient ground to mitigate guilt.

(4)   Genetic Aberrations: The XYY Syndrome

The existence of a chromosomal abnormality involving an extra male sex chromosome—XYY—has been discussed in the literature for nearly a quarter of a century.[185] Associated with this unusual genotype has been a syndrome of physical and behavioral markers, including tallness, lower intelligence, and a tendency toward aggressive or violent behavior. The legal implications of a link between genetic endowment and crime, however, were apparently grossly exaggerated at one time, as Craft's review noted:

> Initial studies tended to concentrate on institutionalized populations for ease of access, and showed . . . sex chromosome abnormalities to be relatively common in prisons and hospitals treating criminals. These early surveys . . . suggested that XYY men tended to be over 180 centimetres tall, and to be more determined, aggressive and sexually active than their peers. Thus, courts as far apart as Melbourne and Lyons were assured, according to Kessler, that "every cell in (the defendant's) brain is abnormal," resulting in verdicts of legal insanity.[186]

In our review of court decisions, and in our experience with the legal system in the United States, it is quite rare for an MSO defense to be advanced on the basis of the XYY chromosomal abnormality. However, for those who might consider, or encounter, such a defense theory in court, a brief summary from some recent reviews may be instructive.

Epidemiological studies confirm that the XYY genotype does appear more frequently in mental or penal groups than in newborn or adult normals. Studies reviewed by Jarvik, Klodin, and Matsuyama[187] indicated incidence estimates in the normal/newborn populations to be 13–20 per 1,000, or .13–.20%. In comparison, samples from mental institutions revealed population incidence estimates of .7% (5.3 times greater), and samples from penal institutions revealed an incidence of 1.9% (approximately 15 times greater). Somewhat different figures were reported in a review by Walzer, Gerald, and Shah,[188] but the relatively higher estimates for mental and penal populations were affirmed: .001% in newborns or the adult populations; approximately 3 times that in studies from mental settings, 4 times that in penal settings, and 20 times that in mental–penal settings.

Reservations regarding the accuracy or importance of such figures are widespread. Craft[189] criticized the methodology of epidemiological studies and the purported relationship between the XYY genotype and aggressive behavior, noting (1) that different laboratories had used different criteria for determining the presence of the genotype, deriving markedly different incidence rates and thus suggesting experimenter bias; and (2) that "aggressive tendencies" had been poorly defined in many studies, resulting in unreliable or invalid dependent measures. Walzer and colleagues also noted the inadequacies in classifying human aggressive behaviors and concluded, "[W]e cannot state definitely whether there is an increase in aggressive behavior associated with this genotype."[190] Jarvik's group concluded:

> Whatever incidence may eventually be determined, it is safe to predict that persons with an extra Y chromosome will constitute but an insignificant proportion of the perpetrators of violent crime . . . Being genetic, such a relationship cannot depend exclusively on external factors, although undoubtedly home environment, early upbringing, and a host of sociocultural factors have either reinforcing or inhibiting effects.[191]

Craft cited the findings from European twin studies comparing the coincidence of XYY genotype with criminality in either monozygotic (MZ) or dizygotic (DZ) twin paris, and concluded: "It seems that similarity of upbringing is more associated with criminality than genetic endowment, for in the most recent twin register studies the differences between MZ (23%) and DZ (18%) are statistically not significant."[192]

In summary, the current reviews of the XYY genotype suggest that these individuals may, at worst, be weakly disposed toward criminal activity. A host of environmental factors are implicated in the development of criminal activities by them. No reliable cluster of psychological characteristics has been identified with this genotype, leading some researchers to question whether there is a bona fide syndrome associated with this chromosomal aberration.[193]

(5)　Alcohol and Narcotics Addiction

Of the syndromes discussed in this section, addiction is by far the most likely to surface at a criminal trial, either under the rubric of "irresistible impulse" or as support for an argument that the defendant's criminal act (whether it involved obtaining the addicting substance or money with which to buy it) was involuntary. Research on the nature of addiction is relevant to these issues.

After a comprehensive review of studies conducted prior to 1974,[194] Fingarette and Hasse concluded the following with respect to the alcoholic:

> Possibly partly due to some abnormal physical condition, the chronic alcoholic is one who for any of a variety of other reasons, often rooted in his past or current patterns of life, has increasingly used drinking as a way of adapting to his life-problems. He has reached the point where the personal and social consequences of his drinking and the life that goes with it would require him to act in a way which, though usually genuinely practicable, would now be so very distressing and so very difficult, both physically and mentally, that he is unlikely to act that way entirely on his own initiative. He may do so with the aid of special encouragement, professional guidance, and/or coercive influences.[195]

From this they concluded that "the threat of the criminal sanction may be a factor in controlling such drinking as is likely to lead to criminal offenses,"[196] and that, for legal purposes, alcoholics thus do not suffer from "loss of control," but rather have some volition. They also admitted, however, that "the alcoholic is one who faces a choice that is (increasingly) more difficult than for most people."[197]

Similarly, with narcotic addicts, Fingarette and Hasse pointed to several studies[198] suggesting that the craving for drugs such as heroin and morphine is not overpowering. They noted that "only a small fraction of the many millions of patients who receive morphine ever attempt to take the drug again, and only an exceedingly small proportion of addicts owe their dependence to medically initiated narcotic use."[199] They also pointed to a study of 13,240 Army enlisted men returning from Vietnam in 1971, which found that although almost half had tried heroin or opium while in Vietnam, only about 20% had developed signs of physical or psychological dependence, and of those, only 5% experienced such signs at any time after their return to the United States.[200] Finally, Fingarette and Hasse noted that "cold turkey" withdrawal from narcotics "is apparently never fatal; its effects are temporary, continuing at worst for no more than several days."[201]

The available evidence indicates that the longer a person uses alcohol or drugs to produce an intoxicated state, the harder it is to stop and the more likely it is that the addict will engage in behavior that will bring about intoxication. In evaluating addicted individuals, the mental health professional should attempt to ascertain facts that cast light on the difficulty the addicts experience in choosing between satisfying their craving (through criminal action) and suffering the consequences of not being able to ingest the sought-after substance. Information from the studies alluded to above may also be useful to the fact-finder. As always, the clinician should decline from stating whether the choice was so hard as to mitigate responsibility.

(6)　Other Novel Defenses

Other novel defenses have been raised in selected cases; some of these have achieved considerable notoriety through extended media coverage (e.g., the "television intoxication" defense

of Ronnie Zamora,[202] the Vietnam post-traumatic stress syndrome,[203] and the "brainwashing" defense of Patricia Hearst[204]). Premenstrual
syndrome,[205] unusual plasma androgen levels,[206]
and coercive hypnosis[207] are also among the
diverse subjects in the current literature that might
be creatively argued as "causes" of criminal activity in support of an MSO defense. An attorney
might argue that the physiological changes associated with the menstrual cycle, which correlate with alterations in mood, reduce the capacity of female offenders to conform their conduct
to the requirements of law; similarly, "raging
hormones" might be offered as an explanation
for illegal sexual behavior by individuals whose
androgen levels exceed the physiological norm;
and Hollywood, at least, has been willing to sell
to the public the notion that an individual under
hypnosis gives up his or her free will to the hyp-
notist and can be coerced through suggestion to
the most heinous of offenses. The possibilities
are seemingly endless, bounded only by the creativity of the attorney and the availability of data
or theory from the social sciences that may be
brought to bear on some aspect of criminal behavior.

In the context of understanding criminal behavior, there may be few, if any, data on some
such topics, and alleged theoretical bases for the
phenomena may be conflicting. We would not
advise mental health professionals against any use
of social science data or theory in MSO cases
simply on the basis that such defenses are "usually" not presented. However, where data and
theory are weak, missing, or poorly understood,
testimony should be ventured with considerable
caution, if at all. Factors that may be contributory or weakly predisposing should be explained
for what they are, and poorly understood relationships, such as that between viewing television and actual criminal behavior, should not
be elevated to the status of syndromes, as with
"television intoxication." The more unfamiliar or
poorly understood the phenomenon, the more
restrained clinicians should be in their advocacy
of its potential relevance.

It is also of relevance here that to the extent
the law does or should adopt Moore's conceptualization of responsibility—that is, that the fact

that behavior is "caused" by a particular physiological mechanism or a peculiar situation is irrelevant unless it also renders the person's reasoning process unintelligible [see § 6.03(c)(2)]—
many of these "defenses" should not be recognized. For example, unless a Vietnam veteran actively hallucinates during commission of a crime,
his mental functioning is likely to be rational.
The fact that the war (or poverty or television)
caused or helped cause the crime does not, according to Moore, absolve him, although it may
explain his actions.

(c) Reliability and Validity of MSO Opinions

Though mental health professionals have long been
involved in insanity defense cases, there has been
relatively little systematic research in the area of
reliability and validity of clinical judgments in
insanity defense cases. The absence of good, well-
publicized research has resulted in public perception on this issue being shaped almost exclusively by a few, highly publicized cases in which
opposing expert witnesses have offered inconsistent or contradictory testimony. One caustic ob-
server has noted, "For every Ph.D there is an
equal and opposite Ph.D."[208]

Throughout this volume, we have argued that
there has been a misplaced emphasis on the ultimate-issue opinions and conclusions reached by
mental health professionals. Nevertheless, it has
been common for psychiatrists and psychologists
to venture such opinions, and the discrete legal
categories into which such opinions fall ("sane"
vs. "insane") lend themselves quite readily to the
analyses necessary for reliability and validity estimates. Inasmuch as that is the nature of the
existing literature, we briefly review studies or
reliability (interrater agreement) and validity
(agreement with external criterion) of clinicians'
opinions in insanity defense cases.

(1) Reliability Studies

To date, there have been six studies of interrater
agreement in insanity evaluations. Stock and
Poythress[209] examined the reliability of insanity

opinions formulated by 12 Ph.D. psychologists at Michigan's Center for Forensic Psychiatry. A total of 33 criminal defendants were examined. In each case, a pair of psychologists simultaneously interviewed the defendant and then provided the investigators their opinions regarding insanity without conferring with each other. Each member of the pair had equal access to relevant third-party information, such as police reports or prior medical records. The pairs of psychologists agreed in 97% of the cases; 29 were agreed to be sane, 3 were agreed to be insane, and the examiners disagreed on 1 case.

Fukunaga, Pasewark, Hawkins, and Gudeman[210] obtained a similar reliability estimate in a study of 355 cases in Hawaii. Each defendant had been examined by two psychiatrists; the examiners were in agreement about sanity at the time of the crime in 92% of the cases. In their study, however, there was no precaution taken against different examiners' conferring with one another prior to forming their opinions. Thus, the rate of agreement may have been inflated, due to examiners' "ironing out" their differences.

Raifman[211] reported reliability estimates for psychiatrists who performed insanity evaluations in Arizona. A total of four psychiatrists were involved in the study, though only two were involved in any one case. Though both psychiatrists were technically appointed by the court, one was selected from a list provided by the prosecutor, the other from a list provided by the defense. A total of 214 criminal defendants were examined independently by each member of the psychiatrist pairs. Raifman reported overall agreement of 64%, with considerable variation among the different pairs.

Recently Rogers and his colleagues, in three separate studies, have reported interrater agreement between experienced clinicians (either psychologists or psychiatrists) in insanity evaluations in which the examiners used the Rogers Criminal Responsibility Assessment Scales (RCRAS),[212] a series of explicit rating scales designed to measure a number of essential variables pertinent to legal insanity [see § 6.04 (d)]. In the first study,[213] a correlation coefficient of .82 was obtained between opinions offered by different examiners in each of 25 cases.[214] In a second study,[215] another 25 cases were evaluated by two experienced forensic clinicians; high reliability was achieved, as indicated by a kappa coefficient (which corrects for chance agreement) of .93.[216] Finally, in a third study,[217] Rogers and colleagues reported perfect agreement between examiners who completed 30 insanity evaluations—kappa = 1.00.

These studies differed in a number of important ways, which renders comparability among them or generalization of findings quite limited. First, the studies used examiners of different professional disciplines—psychiatrists (Raifman) versus psychologists (Stock and Poythress) versus both psychiatrists and psychologists (Rogers and colleagues). Second, the examiners may have differed in terms of forensic training—a factor that may influence the quality of examination performance.[218] The psychologists in the Stock and Poythress study had received several months of supervised training in performing insanity evaluations; the specific training of the clinicians in the other studies is not known. Third, there may have been differences attributable to different examination settings—clinician's private office (Raifman) versus hospital setting (Stock and Poythress). Different legal tests were also applied—ALI (Stock & Poythress) versus *M'Naghten* (Raifman). Finally, the examiners may have differed in terms of allegiances—court-appointed (Stock & Poythress) versus allegiance to a particular party (Raifman). The ease with which important methodological differences can be identified serves to highlight the difficulty doing research in this area.

No broad conclusions can be drawn concerning the reliability of mental health professionals' opinions on the insanity question. The higher reliability figures reported by Stock and Poythress and by Rogers and colleagues suggest that the reliability of insanity opinions may be quite respectable under certain conditions—namely, among clinicians with forensic training, working in a hospital or clinic setting where shared and similar concepts and approaches may be developed, with no *a priori* allegiance to either party. The substantially lower figure reported by Raifman paints the darker side of the picture and leaves open to question (and, we hope, further empirical study) which factor or factors contribute to low agreement between examiners.

To our knowledge, there are no published reliability studies involving clinicians' judgments on MSO defenses other than insanity. Interrater agreement for issues such as GBMI, diminished capacity, or automatism would be expected to be somewhat lower than for insanity opinions, as these issues may be raised in the context of mental conditions that are typically less "black and white" than those required for consideration of an insanity acquittal.

From our perspective, which discourages forensic examiners from addressing ultimate-issue opinions [see § 1.04], the more interesting research question would be the reliability of clinicians' judgments, theoretical formulations, and inferences that stop short of the ultimate legal issue. We are unaware of studies addressing the reliability of clinical judgments of these types in a legal context. Studies conducted in clinical settings have not been encouraging. Staller and Geertsma[219] reported a study of the clinical judgments of 27 psychiatrists who were faculty members at a major medical school. These clinicians viewed a 30-minute videotaped interview of a patient and then rated the applicability, on a scale from 0 to 5, of each of 565 descriptive statements that the investigators had prepared. The mean correlation coefficient over all pairs of clinicians was .37. The investigators had hoped to use the procedure to develop a device for assessing students' clinical skills; instead, they concluded:

> [E]xperts with the highest credentials did not agree on a sufficient number of the 565 items given them to make up an examination . . . instead of reporting here on a new device for assessing clinical skill in psychiatry, we are presenting these sobering findings on the failure of psychiatric experts to agree in their clinical judgments.[220]

Morse's review of the literature addressing the reliability of psychodynamic formulations led to a similar conclusion: "The very few studies of the reliability of dynamic formulations that exist are mostly impressionistic and suggest that these formulations are unreliable."[221]

Clearly, more than a few "impressionistic" studies need to be conducted; in the interim, theory-based formulations should be prefaced with appropriate qualifiers and caveats regarding scientific robustness. We can only speculate at this point that, give the abstract and flexible nature of personality theory constructs, it is unlikely that examiner agreement would approach the levels presently obtained in assigning criminal defendants to discrete (albeit moral rather than psychological) categories of "sane" versus "insane."

(2)   Validity Studies

While studies of the reliability of clinicians' MSO opinions are rare, good validity studies are almost nonexistent. An ongoing difficulty is the problem of defining an adequate criterion for a "correct" judgment. Because of this problem, investigators have compromised on the criterion measure and have utilized court decision as the criterion. This is a "contaminated" measure, since the clinical opinion(s) to be validated are usually part of the evidence from which the criterion is developed. This creates the possibility of inflated validity estimates if the court decisions have been unduly influenced by the psychiatric or psychological evidence. As noted in § 6.02, some jurisdictions report that most insanity findings do not result from a truly adversarial inquiry, but through a quasi-plea bargain arrangement in which the prosecution agrees that the defendant was insane.[222]

Where cases are brought to trial and the bases for the insanity defense are explored, court decision may be the best criterion currently available. Bonnie and Slobogin have argued that there is a natural skepticism in judges and jurors who serve in criminal cases, and that this skepticism serves as a legitimate check against undue weight being assigned to mental health expert opinions.[223] Some empirical findings support the existence of this natural skepticism.[224] Unfortunately, the studies reporting concordance between examiner opinion and court decision do not always indicate whether the trial proceeding was adversarial. Thus, the concordance or "validity" studies must be viewed with caution.

To date, we have found four studies reporting

concordance figures between examiner opinion and court finding. Daniel and Harris[225] reported the results of pretrial examinations of female criminal defendants ($n = 66$) conducted at a large state hospital in Missouri from 1974 to 1979. Twenty-five (37.9%) were recommended NGRI; the court returned an NGRI verdict in 22 of these cases (88%).

Fukunaga and colleagues[226] reported an overall agreement rate of 93% in their study of 315 cases in Hawaii; the court disagreed with 11 of the clinicians' 105 insanity findings and 10 of the clinicians' 210 sanity conclusions. But this validity estimate is probably inflated, due to the method of sampling cases for analysis. The investigators excluded, among others, 44 cases in which the examining psychiatrist did not state a definite opinion. While it is to the psychiatrists' credit if they refused to offer an opinion when none could be formed, this probably biased the sample from a research perspective by excluding the more difficult cases.

Poythress[227] gathered data on 139 cases tried in Michigan. In each case, a Ph.D. clinical psychologist from Michigan's Center for Forensic Psychiatry had completed an insanity evaluation. Each case involved testimony in court, usually with opposing testimony by a psychiatrist from the private sector. The overall agreement rate was 93% (3 of the 41 defendants recommended insane by clinicians were found sane by the courts, and 6 of the 98 defendants recommended sane by the clinicians were found insane by the courts). Here there was little chance of inflation due to "rubber stamping," since the proceedings were, in most cases, adversarial and involved opposing expert testimony.

A fourth concordance study was published by Rogers, Cavanaugh, Seman, and Harris.[228] Forensic psychiatrists and psychologists in Illinois and Ohio used the RCRAS to derive opinions regarding legal insanity for 139 consecutive referrals. At the time of the data analysis, 104 cases had been resolved by court verdict of either guilty or insane. There was agreement in 93 of the 104 cases, or 88%. Of the 11 variances, 3 were false positives, 8 false negatives. Since the study consisted of consecutive referrals, it is likely that a number of the cases proceeded to trial without

raising the insanity defense; not every pretrial evaluation leads to an actual insanity defense in court. Therefore, some of the agreement on "sane" cases may have occurred by default, not as the result of court review.

While the concordance rates reported are all fairly respectable, the methodological problems already mentioned make it difficult to place much confidence in them as true validity estimates. Further compounding the problem is the fact that in all these studies the examiners were employed at state or private facilities, performing evaluations for the courts without allegiance to either party in litigation. The parties calling these clinicians probably portrayed them in court as "neutral" while characterizing private-sector clinicians as "hired guns." The judges or jurors may have been influenced to view the "neutral" examiners as less biased or more trustworthy, and their verdicts may have been based on trust rather than on a critical, independent assessment of the evidence.[229]

Like the reliability studies, these concordance studies have important methodological differences that limit their comparability and the generalization of their findings. Inasmuch as legal judgments regarding responsibility are social and moral determinations, "validity" research of the type described here is of limited value and interest without a further showing that clinicians are superior to laypersons in determining when the discretionary legal standard has been met.[230] Such a showing would require an independent criterion against which to compare the moral judgments of clinicians and laypersons, and the mere existence of such a criterion might further obviate the need for moral speculations by the clinician.

(d) Formal Assessment of Insanity: The RCRAS

In the preceding section, we have mentioned the RCRAS, a series of explicit scales designed to measure essential variables pertinent to legal insanity. These scales are available for general use in the forensic community[231] and represent the first serious attempt by mental health professionals to formalize the clinical inquiry and de-cisionmaking processes on the issue of legal insanity.

It is apparent from the RCRAS test manual that Rogers is concerned with the lack of scientific respectability associated with clinicians' judgments and testimony on the issue of insanity. In the overview of the scales, he has noted:

> Mental health professionals testify with "a reasonable degree of medical or scientific certainty" regarding the sanity of patient–defendants whom they evaluate. The scientific basis of such judgments remains practically unresearched. This absence of empirical data, compounded with problems of perceived financial self-interest, has led authors addressing this issue to conclude that psychiatric testimony lacks the requisite scientific precision for rendering expert opinions regarding sanity.

Later on the same page, Rogers indicates:

> The purpose of the RCRAS is to provide a systematic and empirically based approach to evaluations of criminal responsibility . . . The RCRAS is designed to *quantify* essential psychological and situational variables at the time of the crime and to implement criterion based decision models for criminal responsibility. This allows the clinician to *quantify* the impairment at the time of the crime, to conceptualize this impairment with respect to the appropriate legal standards and to render an expert opinion with respect to that standard.[232] (emphasis added)

It is clear that the RCRAS is intended to correct deficiencies in the scientific rigor of insanity evaluations and opinions. The rating scales purport to allow the clinician to quantify and conceptualize such aspects of human behavior as (1) the relative severity, for *legal* purposes, of disordered behavior; and (2) the relative contribution, for *legal* purposes, of symptoms of disordered mental states to the criminal behavior itself. The mechanism by which this transformation is accomplished is the translation of an insanity standard (the ALI test) into a "testable psychological construct":

> The psychological construct for legal insanity developed in the RCRAS validation research

paradigm is the presence, at the time of the crime, of (1) a severe mental disorder which results in (2) a substantial impairment of the individual's cognitive and/or behavioral control . . . The first element of the construct, the mental disorder, is operationalized as a major psychiatric disorder (which parallels the ALI "mental disease or defect"). With regards to the second element, cognitive control (ALI, "ability to appreciate") is defined as the individual's awareness, knowledge, and comprehension of the criminal act while it was occurring. Further, behavioral control (ALI, "ability to conform conduct") is defined as the deliberateness and self-control that the individual was able to exert over the criminal behavior. In this way, the ALI standard of insanity is transformed into a testable psychological construct entailing the mental disorder and its potential impact on the commission of the crime.[233]

Rogers proposes to demonstrate empirically the validity of the psychological construct for legal insanity through testing a series of derived hypotheses. Defendants evaluated as insane using the RCRAS should demonstrate (1) a relative absence of malingering, and (2) more severe psychopathology associated with major mental disorder, as well as (3) greater loss of cognitive and/or behavioral control than their criminally responsible counterparts.[234] Rogers and his colleagues have conducted a number of studies exploring these hypotheses;[235] these studies are discussed briefly, following a description of the scales themselves.

The individual scales that comprise the RCRAS are 25 in number. The clinician's ratings on these 25 scales are assimilated and translated into six summary "Psycholegal Criteria," which are plugged into a decision tree that produces the clinical opinion—sane, insane, or no opinion. The 25 basic scales address a number of different factors that clinicians ought to consider in conducting an MSO evaluation, including the reliability of the defendant's narrative and possible malingering (#1 and #2), possible organic conditions (#4), mental retardation (#5) and the possible presence of symptoms of functional disturbance such as anxiety (#9), hallucinations (#12), and thought or language disturbance (#15, #17).

The six summary "Psycholegal Criteria" address the presence of malingering (A1); the presence of organicity (A2); the presence of major psychiatric disorder (A3); loss of cognitive controls ("lacked the ability to comprehend the criminality of his behavior") (A4); loss of behavioral control ("was unable to change, monitor, or control his criminal behavior") (A5); and a judgment (A6) of whether the assessed loss of control (A4, A5) was a direct result of the organic (A2) or psychiatric (A3) disturbance. Regarding these six crucial judgments, the RCRAS test manual states:

> Based on the standard of medical and scientific certainty, each decision model requires that individual psychological criterion be met with either a definite "yes" or a definite "no". Judgments as "more likely than not" (i.e., preponderance) or based on personal unvalidated judgments are excluded from the decision models.[236]

A casual reading of the RCRAS test manual and of the research published thus far by Rogers and his colleagues instills a sense of optimism that a degree of scientific rigor and precision is possible in insanity evaluations; interrater reliability is good, and concordance between opinions based on RCRAS ratings and court verdict is respectable [see § 6.04(c)]. As has already been noted, clinicians are promised that they can "quantify the impairment at the time of the crime"[237] and deliver opinions based on a "testable psychological construct entailing the mental disorder and its potential impact on the commission of the crime."[238]

A closer look, however, suggests that the RCRAS promises much more than it delivers. An inspection of the individual scales uncovers numerous, and familiar, problems for the clinician. Each of the individual scales calls for the examiner to assign a number from 0 to 5 (or in some cases to 6) to reflect the relative severity of the factor being rated; it is presumably this assignment of numbers that constitutes the RCRAS's ability to "quantify" the impairment at the time of the crime. However, these are all *ordinal* ratings. Only in a few instances are the

scale points anchored to objective or normative measures of behavior; for example, Scale #6, "Mental retardation," anchors the higher scale points to definite "mild" (3), "moderate" (4), "severe" (5), or "profound" (6) retardation as supported by scores on recognized intelligence tests. More typically, the numbers reflect a continuum or gradient of severity for recording the examiner's global judgment. For example, Scale #9 purports to measure "Anxiety present at the time of the alleged crime" and includes anchor statements such as "(2) Slight. Felt apprehensive for a few minutes; (3) Mild. Felt a little anxious . . . ; (4) Moderate. Was fairly anxious . . ."; and so on.

Other scales "quantify" the relationship, if any, between a symptom or diagnostic condition and the criminal act. For example, Scale #5 addresses "Relationship of brain damage to the commission of the alleged crime." To assign a score of 5 on this scale, the examiner must find that "the patient lacked intentionality, could not comprehend the criminality of what he was doing, or lacked control over his behavior." It is no surprise that the manual provides no instructions on how to *measure* intentionality, comprehension of criminality, or self-control. Simply assigning ordinal numbers to a continuum of conclusions of this type does not disguise the fact that these are the same philosophical and commonsensical judgments that mental health professionals have previously been criticized for passing off as scientific appraisal based on "reasonable certainty."[239] We are unconvinced that simply assigning ordinal numbers to a continuum of global judgments constitutes quantification or measurement, in the scientific sense, of the behaviors about which the judgments are made.

Problems of these types are pervasive throughout the individual rating scales. The questionable value of ordinal numbers as true quantifiers becomes even more dubious when the clinician proceeds to the important summary decisions, A1 through A6 (the "Psycholegal Criteria"). The clinician must review and consider the ordinal ratings assigned to a subset of the basic 25 scales in reaching each of these six summary decisions. For example, summary decision A4—"Definite loss of cognitive controls"—requires a review of basic ratings assigned to scales #15 ("Patient's level of verbal coherence at the time of the alleged crime . . ."), #17 ("Evidence of formal thought disorder"), #18 ("Planning and preparation for the alleged crime"), and #19 ("Awareness of criminality during the commission of the alleged crime . . ."). However, in reviewing the numerical ratings (e.g., 0–5) assigned to each of the basic scales, the clinician is not required by the test manual to treat them in any arithmetical way (e.g., by adding them together). Rather, a global or commonsensical (or intuitive) judgment about "loss of cognitive control" is all that is called for. It is therefore the case that the basic judgments involved in the RCRAS are not based on truly quantitative or empirical measurement, but on logical and/or intuitive attributions.

The analysis above notwithstanding, the published research to date claims to validate the psychological construct of legal insanity described in the RCRAS manual. The hypotheses noted earlier—(1) less malingering in insane defendants, (2) greater pathology in insane defendants, and (3) greater loss of control in insane defendants—have been supported in Rogers' research.[240] However, these studies all contain a serious methodological flaw, which renders the results of dubious value. This flaw is that there has been no independent criterion for classifying subjects as "sane" or "insane." Rather, the classification "sane" or "insane" has been derived from the RCRAS decision tree itself. By virtue of the internal logic of the scales, this conclusion *must* have been reached in a manner that "confirms" the hypotheses to be tested. If the clinician assigns low ratings to scales that address malingering (hypothesis 1), high ratings to scales that address psychopathology (hypothesis 2), and high ratings to scales that address loss of control (hypothesis 3), a psycholegal finding of "insane" is virtually assured; conversely, if the opposite pattern of ratings is assigned (high malingering, low pathology, low loss of control), the clinician would be hard pressed to develop a psycholegal finding other than "sane" without violating the

logic of the scales. The "findings" of the studies on the three hypotheses are thus tautological, trivial in the absence of an uncontaminated criterion for the sane–insane classification.

The RCRAS is not without merit. Rogers has identified and presented in an organized fashion many of the factors that an examiner must consider in an insanity evaluation. Malingering; amnesia; degree and type of pathology present; third-party information about the defendant's behavior at the crime—all are important factors that must be considered. The RCRAS may help clinicians to organize their interviews or their thoughts about the data gathered in investigations. The weaknesses of the RCRAS include its misplaced emphasis on addressing ultimate-issue questions; its claims to quantify in areas of judgment that are actually logical and/or intuitive in nature; and the manual's claims to scientific rigor, which assures that RCRAS-based opinions have "reasonable medical and scientific certainty." The major risk involved in its use at this time is that clinicians or courts may, in light of the unsubstantiated claims in the manual, attribute undeserved scientific status to judgments that remain, ordinal ratings notwithstanding, logical and commonsensical in nature.

6.05. MSO Investigation

This section discusses the data-gathering process involved in a clinical evaluation of MSO. The next section discusses the manner in which the results of the evaluation may be formulated. The substance of the two sections is summarized in § 6.07.

The clinical evaluation of MSO is one of the more difficult forensic evaluations. As with other forensic evaluations, the clinician attempts to determine whether and how the individual's mental condition may be related to legally relevant behavior. But this effort is made difficult by virtue of the retrospective focus of the examination; many traditional clinical evaluation procedures may be limited in their applicability, and the examiner must also be concerned with the

possible impact of events that occur in the intervening time period between the alleged crime
and the examination. Further, weighing or describing the relative contribution of mental factors requires some consideration of the evidence
for alternative motives, causes, or explanations,
which may also be difficult, given the occasional
unavailability of desired third-party information
and the incentives for the defendant to be un-
cooperative or dishonest in his or her presentation.

We thus use the term "investigation" intentionally. MSO examinations differ significantly
from traditional clinical evaluations. It is customary in the clinical setting to consider the
clinical interview and testing results to represent
a microcosm of the client's functioning outside
the clinic; third-party information, such as prior
treatment records or family input, may be requested, but rarely is it elevated to the level of
importance that is accorded the client's own
presentation. In complex MSO cases, however,
forensic examiners may function more as investigative reporters[241] than as traditional clinicians, and they may spend as much effort outside the interview room gathering and reviewing
third-party information as they spend inside with
the defendants in these cases. At the same time,
sessions with these defendants are likely to be
much more confrontive than is typical of therapy.

The reason for this difference between forensic and therapeutic assessments is simple. As noted
by Bonnie and Slobogin,

> Few forensic clients would seek assistance were
> they not involved in the criminal justice sys-
> tem; most are cajoled into participating by their
> lawyers, or forced to do so by the prosecution
> or the court. . . . The significance of this
> problem is heightened by the fact that the fo-
> rensic clinician, to a much greater extent than
> the therapist, must try to ascertain whether
> the subject's story is fabricated, unconsciously
> distorted, or honestly reported.[242]

Since the credibility of these defendants is such
a key issue, clinicians must do everything within
their power to test it (and to inform factfinders

why, after such investigations; they choose to
believe or disbelieve the defendants). Under such
circumstances, neglecting third-party information would be foolish. At the same time, the defendants themselves must be carefully examined.

This section discusses the collection of third-
party information, and then recommends the
proper approach to examining defendants themselves. But before looking at either of these topics, which have to do with what we call the
"comprehensive" MSO investigation, it is
worthwhile to consider the feasibility of a brief
screening evaluation as a preliminary approach.

(a) Preliminary Screening for MSO Defense

That a brief screening evaluation should be useful is suggested by the relatively high percentage
of defendants evaluated who are not diagnosed
as seriously disturbed,[243] the infrequency with
which the insanity defense is raised,[244] and the
reported high percentage of "obvious" cases
among those which are successful.[245]

A study by Slobogin, Melton, and Showalter[246]
demonstrated the feasibility of a brief screening
procedure. These investigators developed a brief
mental status examination (MSE) consisting of
three phases: questions about the alleged offense, questions about the defendant's general
psychohistory, and an examination of present
mental state. Twenty-four mental health professionals were instructed in the use of the MSE
and then worked in pairs to conduct brief
screening evaluations of criminal defendants (n-
36). Each team had available a limited amount of
third-party data, including a description of the
charges and, in some cases, a preliminary hearing
transcript. Trainees were asked to conclude
whether or not significant abnormality may have
affected the defendants' actions at the time of
the offense, but were asked to err on the positive
side so as to avoid prematurely screening out a
defendant with a possible legal defense.

The criterion judgment regarding mental state
at the time of the offense was that of an interdisciplinary team at a state hospital, which

Table 6-2
Concordance of Hospital Staff MSO Examination Opinion and Screening Examiners' Opinions

MSO Screening Opinion	Hospital Staff Opinion	
	Potential Legal Defense	No Legal Defense
Might have significant abnormality	10 (27.7%)	10 (27.7%)
No significant abnormality	0 (0%)	16 (44.4%)

Note. From Slobogin, Melton, & Showalter, *The Feasibility of a Brief Evaluation of Mental State at the Time of the Offense,* 8 LAW & HUM. BEHAV. 305 (1984).

conducted comprehensive inpatient MSO examinations on each of the 36 defendants. The cross-tabulation of trainees' recommendations and hospital staff findings is shown in Table 6-2. These data suggest that a brief screening interview is a feasible way to readily identify cases in which no MSO defense is present. The trainees successfully screened out 44% of the referrals and had zero false negatives. Moreover, though clinicians in this study were not asked to do so, the brief screening evaluation can occasionally detect the obviously insane individual for which a more comprehensive evaluation is not needed. It might be particularly useful for the clinician performing outpatient evaluations at the initial stages of the criminal process.

(b) Comprehensive MSO Investigation Procedures

When a screening procedure fails to resolve the possibility of an available MSO defense, the clinician should conduct a comprehensive inquiry utilizing information from a wide variety of sources. As suggested above, this inquiry can be divided into the collection of third-party information and deriving information from the defendant.

(1) Third-Party Information

As Morse has stated, "In determining whether a defendant is crazy, there is simply no substitute for the fullest possible account from all sources of the defendant's behavior at the time of the alleged crime."[247] Third-party information is essential in the MSO evaluation. Which third-party information to pursue, and how best to pursue it, will depend upon the complexity of the evaluation.

Table 6-3 identifies several potential sources of third-party information. Information regard-

Table 6-3
Sources of Third-Party Information

1. Information re: evaluation itself
   a. Referral source
   b. Referral questions
   c. Why evaluation is requested (i.e., what behavior triggered the evaluation?)
   d. Who is report going to?
   e. When is report to be used?
2. Offense-related information
   a. From attorney's notes
   b. From witnesses, victim(s)
   c. From confession, preliminary hearing transcript, etc.
   d. Autopsy reports
   e. Newspaper accounts
3. Developmental/historical information
   a. Personal data (traumatic life events, unusual habits or fears, places lived)
   b. Early childhood illnesses (if organic deficit suspected)
   c. Family history (especially if young and/or still living with family)
   d. Marital history (especially in spousal homicide cases)
   e. Educational, employment, and military history
   f. Social relationships
   g. Psychosexual history (especially if sex offense)
   h. Medical and psychiatric records
4. "Signs of trouble"
   a. Juvenile and criminal court records
   b. Probation reports
5. Statistical information (i.e., studies of the behavior of individuals with the defendant's characteristics)

ing the referral itself, which should come through the initial consultation with the referral source, is crucial in defining the scope of the evaluation and ethical obligations [see § 3.05]. Information describing aspects of the crime scenario, usually available from police and the attorneys, is essential for purposes of comparison with the defendant's narrative and for developing leads for further investigation. Developmental and historical information can usually be obtained from the defendant and the pertinent records; the degree and amount of corroboration sought from friends or family of the defendant is discretionary with the examiner. Of course, the more corroboration, the more confidence in one's opinion; moreover, it clearly looks better in court if such corroboration has been sought. Often, records of prior hospitalization and treatment are available at the time of the evaluation, having already been requested by the attorney; otherwise, the examiner may have to get signed release forms from the defendant and wait until the information arrives to integrate it with the other data. Prior court records are usually more easily obtained, although juvenile records are sometimes "expunged" after a fixed time and therefore unavailable. Statistical information is of course very relevant but unfortunately extremely rare.

The most essential third-party data are those pertaining to the crime scenario. This is usually obtained from the police file, and from it the clinician can often get good descriptive accounts of the defendant's behavior, or circumstantial and material evidence that has implications regarding the planning and execution of the crime. In particularly difficult cases, examiners may want to conduct their own interviews with complainants, witnesses, or codefendants, or with others who may help to reconstruct defendants' MSO. While we encourage such thorough investigation when needed, we recommend that clinicians go through the proper legal channels to establish personal contact with others who may be witnesses in a trial. If retained by the defense, clinicians should notify defense counsel of their desire to interview potential prosecution witnesses; if retained by the state or if court-appointed, they should go through the prosecutor's office to gain access to these witnesses. This

will avoid any unnecessary allegations of "witness tampering" and will legitimize contact with these sources.

Caution must be exercised with certain kinds of information obtained from the police. If the police file contains information that is not legally admissible at trial, then a clinician's report, testimony, and findings may be challenged if he or she was exposed to the inadmissible data. This may pose a difficulty for the clinician, since it may not be known at the early stages of prosecution that certain evidence is inadmissible. We do not suggest that mental health professionals get in the habit of "playing lawyer" by trying to guess whether or not various items of evidence are, or will be, admissible [see § 3.05(b)(5)]. We do suggest, however, that clinicians *initially* refuse to review and consider any third-party information that is known to be inadmissible. After completing their usual investigations, clinicians can determine their clinical formulations of cases, and their confidence level in these formulations, and *then* they can decide whether to review the evidence known to be inadmissible. In this way, they can assure the court that they have developed clinical formulations that have not been contaminated by exposure to the inadmissible evidence.

Caution must also be exercised in reviewing statements or confessions by defendants whose intelligence is low or who may be suffering from mental disorder; the police's method of obtaining and recording such defendants' statements may significantly influence the validity (in the clinical sense) of the information gathered [see § 5.02(a)]. Examiners should be particularly careful with handwritten confessions; often these statements are written in the first person ("I, John Doe, on the evening of November 4, did break and enter . . .") and then signed by defendants. The actual writing in such a case is often that of the police investigator who has elicited the story from the defendant and summarized it in his or her own words for the defendant to sign. Consciously or unconsciously, the officer screens out potentially important diagnostic information, such as language reflective of formal though disturbance; this leaves the confession a "cleaned-up" sample of the defendant's speech and thought at the time of the confession. A verbatim transcript is preferred, though even this may not insure a good accounting of the defendant's behavior at the time. Officers will often ask "yes" or "no" questions, sometimes leading defendants to admit to certain facts about a case. Given the tendency of retarded persons to acquiesce and say "yes" to persons in authority,[248] a transcript of a confession by a person of low intelligence that consists primarily of "yes" responses and no free narrative is of questionable value.

The forensic examiner should also strongly consider obtaining prior hospital records in any MSO evaluation. These records may contain a wealth of descriptive information regarding the frequency and duration of symptoms, response to medication or other intervention, and prior displays of legally relevant behavior. Records may also be helpful in resolving a diagnostic question or in assessing possible malingering. From a purely cosmetic point of view, attorneys on both sides will expect the examiner to have obtained all available records, and testimony in court will generally go better if the examiner has done so.

The actual value of prior records diminishes in proportion to the length of time between the hospitalization or treatment and the alleged crime—at least insofar as the records are used to enhance the picture of a defendant's functioning at that particular point. Records are likely to be crucial if the crime was committed while the patient was in the hospital, was on a "home visit," or had recently been discharged or was on outpatient treatment status. If the professional contact was several months or years prior to the offense, the records will clearly be of less value.

Records of treatment following arrest may also be important. These may include records of formal hospitalization or consultative treatment at the jail. Jail records may be particularly important if an examiner suspects that a defendant's mental condition has changed significantly since the arrest.

Finally, often invaluable are records of prior criminal activity. Such records may suggest patterns of behavior, or types of triggering events, that can help the clinician gain insight into reasons for the individual's current criminal act.

(2) Phases of the Defendant Interview

Presently there is no standard interview procedure for use in MSO evaluations that is widely used. We offer, however, an interviewing outline that may assist forensic clinicians in organizing their clinical examinations. The first phase consists of introduction, orientation, and rapport building. The examiner introduces whoever may be participating in the interview. The purpose of the interview is then explained, as well as limitations on confidentiality (e.g., the possibility of a report to the court or the prosecution, or the possibility of testimony [see Chapter 3]); the examiner also explains any special equipment in use, such as a one-way mirror, recording devices, and the like. The defendant is asked to state his or her perception of the purpose and potential uses of the evaluation, and is also invited to ask questions where uncertainties exist.

The second phase involves the examiner's obtaining a developmental and sociocultural history from the defendant. At this stage many of the questions are relatively innocuous, and the interchange helps to establish rapport between the defendant and the examiner, as well as to give the examiner a feel for how the individual functions in society. A third phase involves an assessment of present mental status, including current or recent symptoms of thought, mood, perception, or behavioral disturbance. Such information is suggestive of past mental state, although, of course, it cannot be assumed that the defendant's status has remained constant.

At the fourth phase the examiner finally zeroes in on the crime itself, inquiring about the defendant's recall of thoughts, feelings, and behavior at the time of the alleged crime. Information is also sought regarding situational variables (e.g., intoxicants, actions of others) that may have contributed to the criminal act. Table 6-4 identifies specific areas of concentration at this point of the interview. At the end of this stage, the examiner should have developed a preliminary judgment about the degree and type of disturbance present at the time of the offense, and at the time of the interview itself.

If other professionals are participating in the MSO examination, the fifth phase involves con-

Table 6-4
Offense-Related Information from the Defendant

1. Defendant's present "general" response to offense—for example,
   a. Cognitive perception of offense
   b. Emotional response
2. Detailed account of offense
   a. Evidence of intrapsychic stressors—for example,
      1. Delusions
      2. Hallucinations
   b. Evidence of external stressors—for example,
      1. Provoking events
      2. Fear or panic stimulants
   c. Evidence of altered state of consciousness—for example,
      1. Alcohol-induced
      2. Drug-induced
   d. Claimed amnesia
      1. Partial
      2. Complete
3. Events leading up to offense
   a. Evidence of major changes in environment—for example,
      1. Change in job status
      2. Change in family status
   b. Relationship with victim
   c. Preparation for offense
4. Postoffense response
   a. Behavior following act
   b. Emotional response to act
   c. Attempts to explain or justify act

ferring with these others and comparing impressions. If third-party data have been gathered, comparison of the defendant's narrative with the crime scenario based on third-party information may give leads to further inquiries by the examiner. At the sixth phase, if required, the examiner reviews with the client any areas of inconsistent or contradictory information, and explores any potentially important areas that the defendant was initially reluctant to discuss.

(3)   The "Tone" of the Interview: Handling Malingering and Amnesia

The examiner's interviewing style and tone may vary, depending on the phase of the interview,

the attitude or mental state of the defendant, or the consistency of the information received. If the client is depressed, guarded, or of low intelligence, the examiner may have to be more active throughout the interview; with clients who are cooperative and verbal, the examiner may be fairly low-key while obtaining general or historical information. At the fourth phase—reconstruction of MSO—the examiner will be most active, soliciting details involving actions, feelings, perceptions, reactions, and memories of the alleged criminal act. The examiner may ask for repeated narratives from the defendant, looking for inconsistencies across versions or internal inconsistencies in a version. The examiner's tone may vary significantly as well: It may be receptive and supportive or skeptical and confrontive, depending on how the defendant's honesty and candor are perceived. The examiner may also have to use interviewing "tricks" or seek corroboration from external sources if malingering is suspected.

Malingering is sometimes difficult to detect. Theoretical and empirical models suggest that malingerers are more likely than reliable, defensive, or confused subjects to recount symptoms of extreme severity, "over-report" symptoms, describe symptoms that are inconsistent with clinical impressions, endorse highly specified symptoms, and exhibit a "heightened" memory of psychological problems.[249] Thus, within the context of the interview, an examiner may seek the defendant's endorsement of bogus symptoms if he or she suspects that the defendant's endorsement of potentially real symptoms is not valid. The examiner may ask with straight face and apparent interest about unusual thoughts or experiences that are strange-sounding but that are simply fabrications (e.g., "When you experience these dizzy spells, do you also experience an itching behind one or both of your knees?"). Psychological testing may also be employed, though the clinician must be cautious about overinterpreting conventional indices of "fake bad" response sets.[250]

Malingering may also be established by conferring with third parties. One defendant who was referred for an MSO evaluation sat with his head in his hands, running his fingers through his hair as if anxious and distraught, ignoring the examiner's questions but occasionally muttering audible phrases such as "I can't take it . . . something is snapping inside." The examiner conferred with jail personnel, who reported that the defendant was usually active and good-natured; that he got along well with guards and inmates; that he frequently volunteered for "lineups"; and that, when transported to court four days earlier for a related civil action, he had been an active and appropriate participant. In another case, a defendant claimed the belief that he was being held in an army hospital in Korea and that the date was 1981; he expressed surprise and suspicion when the clinician informed him that he was in a state psychiatric hospital in the summer of 1983. The defendant indicated that his wife lived with his mother and requested to call her to confirm the date and place of his present incarceration. When the examiner offered to let him use the phone, he declined, stating "I'll have to wait until after 4:00 P.M.— that's when she gets off work." The examiner then called the defendant's mother, who confirmed that the wife would be home after 4:00 P.M.; she also indicated that the wife had obtained her present job in November 1982, and that she had not previously worked. How, then, could the defendant know what time his wife would be home from work if he genuinely believed the year to be 1981? The examiner confronted the defendant, and the malingering was confessed.

Perhaps the most common bogus presentation by criminal defendants during pretrial evaluations is amnesia. Some studies indicate that as many as 60% of defendants involved in violent crime report amnesia symptoms.[251] However, it also appears that many of these claims are simulated.[252] A number of defendants claim amnesia simply as a means of not confessing their involvement in an offense; some even believe that amnesia alone affords them a defense. Clinicians should take care to explain to all defendants, with help from the client's attorney if necessary, that amnesia is not a defense, and patient questioning should be used to facilitate remembering. Leading questions, such as "Do you remember *X*?," are to be avoided, as defendants may simply wait

until some potentially exculpating or mitigating issue is suggested, at which time "It's starting to come back to me now" responses can be expected.

In summary, the examiner's tone and style of interviewing in an MSO evaluation may vary, depending on a number of factors. Most significantly, the examination process may call for the clinician to be active and directive, confrontative and accusatory—not completely accepting and supportive, as in a therapeutic session.

(4)   Special Interview Techniques: Hypnosis and Narcoanalysis

As mentioned above, it is not uncommon for criminal defendants to claim partial or total amnesia for their behavior at the time of the alleged crime. The techniques discussed above may help the evaluator decide whether the claim of amnesia is fabricated. Additionally, Schacter suggests that defendants claiming amnesia be asked whether they feel they could remember the incident with sufficient prodding. His research suggests that simulators are more likely to deny a "feeling-of-knowing" than those who truly cannot remember.[253]

In a case in which the defendant professes amnesia and there appears to be a legitimate clinical basis for it, an interview of the defendant under the influence of hypnosis or a general anesthetic should be considered [see, e.g., the Wertz report, § 15.04]. Before considering hypnosis or narcoanalysis, however, the clinician should be satisfied that the type of amnesia present is potentially recoverable through these techniques, ensure that the parties understand their limitations, and become cognizant of any legal strictures on their use.

With respect to the first issue, amnesias can be classified as either "registration amnesia" or "recall amnesia." With registration amnesia, the memories sought to be recovered were never permanently stored because some incident (e.g., a blow to the head) or some agent (e.g., certain drugs, such as hypnotic sedative compounds[254] or certain psychedelics[255]) interfered with the encoding process. As such, the individual has no record of prior events waiting to be called up;

the memory traces were never laid down, and recovery using special interviewing techniques is thus (theoretically) impossible. Where the problem is one of recall, hypnosis or narcoanalysis may be able to facilitate retrieval of the forgotten material. In these cases, the original memories were registered but access to them has been disrupted, often because (according to Freud) the memories are too psychologically painful to be admitted into consciousness and therefore have been repressed.[256] Theoretically, hypnosis and narcoanalysis are procedures that bypass the individual's psychological defenses and allow repressed material to surface, allowing access to thoughts, feelings, and memories that are not accessible during normal consciousness.

Assuming hypnosis or narcoanalysis is indicated, the clinician should next explain in advance of the procedure the nature of any memories that might be recovered. Contrary to what many laypersons seem to believe, memories are not photographic recordings. What a person remembers may be influenced by a great number of factors, both situational and personal, and there is no assurance that a person's recovered memories will be either complete, or accurate by some objective standard. An individual's own needs, beliefs, prejudices, attitudes, and other personal factors may influence the events attended to or his or her interpretation of them. Apart from whatever "real" memories may be activated by these special procedures, there is the problem of the demand characteristics of the situation itself. Defendants will have been briefed in advance about the procedure and the expectations of them during the procedure. The demands of the situation may lead defendants to report as personal memories variations of one or more accounts of their behavior that have been previously provided by others, or they may develop "memories" by patching together clues from the examiner's questions (leading or otherwise). Finally, there is still the possibility of malingering. Experimental studies have shown that subjects may persist in presenting a previously rehearsed and untruthful story,[257] or they may prevaricate while in the altered state.[258] The clinician should also warn all parties that there is no guarantee of success with these procedures; some clients may

prove not susceptible to the hypnotic or chemical induction, and in some cases, memory will not be enhanced even where an altered state is induced.

In summary, all parties should be warned in advance that hypnosis and narcoanalysis have no demonstrated value as "truth serums" and that no particular claims about the "honesty" or objective validity of the subject's report can be made. They are simply procedures that may result in a verbal description where there previously was none; they are procedures that potentially allow defendants to give their accounts of their behavior at the time of alleged crimes. As they would do with the scenarios provided by any other defendants, forensic examiners should compare these defendants' accounts with the other information available and should seek corroborating information where possible. Where the behavior or memories recalled are entirely subjective and not subject to verification (e.g., "Just as I was strangling her, her face looked like my mother's face!"), no assertion of the truth or validity of the information should be offered.

Legal issues that must be considered when contemplating the use of these procedures include the doctrine of informed consent [see § 3.04(d)(1)], the defendant's Fifth Amendment right against self-incrimination [see § 3.02], and the general rules concerning admissibility of expert testimony [see § 14.04(d)]. Under the informed consent doctrine, a clinician must ensure that a defendant's consent to the procedure is knowing and voluntary. And both Fifth Amendment and evidentiary considerations may place clinicians in an ethically awkward position. Though their testimony may be based in part on the information gathered by these special techniques, and the opinions and inferences drawn may be admissible, defendants' statements themselves may not be admissible.[259] Thus, clinicians may have to offer summary findings or conclusions while being asked to secrete at least part of the data base upon which they rest. Packer[260] reviewed the status of hypnosis and narcoanalysis in legal settings and reported that a clinician's *entire* testimony may be barred if the court finds that the procedure does not meet the criteria of being "sufficiently established to have gained general

acceptance in the particular field to which it belongs."[261] To avoid unnecessary steps, the legal
status of the procedures themselves might best
be explored in court prior to proceeding with
them.

(5)   Psychological Testing (and Other Laboratory Procedures)

In the minds of many practitioners in the criminal justice system, psychological testing is an integral part of any insanity evaluation. Cameron's
comments are representative of this expectation:

> Clinical psychologists generally utilize a stan-
> dardized, self-report personality inventory in
> conjunction with one or two other tests usu-
> ally of the projective type; however, any relia-
> ble psychological evaluation of a defendant
> should consist of an extensive battery of tests,
> both of the self-report personality inventory
> nature and projective techniques.[262]

This expectation is, of course, not just the product of fantasies by professionals in the criminal
justice system, but a reflection on the observed
practice of psychologists in legal proceedings for
many years. Test results and interpretations have
been offered with some regularity as a basis for
conclusions and opinions regarding a defendant's
MSO or propensity for specific criminal action.

Despite what has become common practice,
we suggest a much more limited role for psychological testing in the MSO examination. The assessment of MSO does not routinely require *any*
formal psychological testing. Psychological tests
provide information about *current* functioning,
whereas an MSO examination seeks to reconstruct the defendant's *prior* mental state. While
it may be argued that some aspects of personality and behavior may be relatively stable over
time (e.g., intelligence), many conditions of interest in the MSO examination may be expected
to change naturally over time (e.g., the cyclical
nature of some disorders; spontaneous remission; reactions to situational factors or to medication; etc.). Further, tests tap a general level of
functioning, while the behaviors of interest in
the MSO evaluation are relatively specific (e.g.,
thoughts or feelings about the particular victim

or situation). The longer the interval between
the offense and the administration of the tests,
the less representative any current appraisal is
likely to be of the previous mental state. Not
surprisingly, the professional literature is barren
in terms of sound empirical studies demonstrating that psychological test data are useful as a
means of establishing a link between particular
diagnostic conditions and legally relevant behavior in individual cases, or are useful for assigning
individuals to discrete legal categories (e.g., sane
vs. insane).[263]

This analysis applies to other laboratory procedures as well. As Kubie[264] noted in his analysis
of the Jack Ruby case, knowing that a defendant
may produce an abnormal EEG in the laboratory
gives no particular assurance that seizure activity
was present at some particular remote point in
time [see also the discussion in § 6.04(b)]. At
best, such tests can suggest what a person's behavior *may* have been like, though they provide
no certain information about the specific thoughts,
feelings, motives, or behaviors that may have
constituted the reconstructed mental state.

These criticisms notwithstanding, there are
potential though limited uses for psychological
tests. Their possible contribution in the assessment of malingering has been mentioned.[265] Tests
may also be a source of normative data. The examiner may make reference to a defendant's scores
as compared to known populations—for example, "The defendant's full scale IQ score on the
Wechsler Adult Intelligence Scale (WAIS) places
him at the X percentile for persons his age. Persons at this level of functioning typically display
behaviors *A, B,* and *C.*" Or, "This defendant's
Minnesota Multiphasic Personality Inventory
(MMPI) protocol is similar to those of adult psychiatric patients diagnosed as paranoid schizophrenic. Common symptoms of this disorder include *E, F,* and *G.*" Test data may be used to
confirm the presence of a particular disorder at
the time of the examination and to *suggest,* but
not to ascertain, that a particular condition may
have existed at the time of an offense. For example, a young woman provided a convincing
narrative describing what appeared clinically to
have been a dissociative episode at the time of
an offense. The MMPI was administered and was

considered valid; the protocol was a 1–3 code type with the "conversion V," a protocol suggesting hysterical personality, with which dissociative experiences are frequently associated. Finally, projective tests may be used as part of the inference base for examiners who develop theory-based formulations of criminal behavior using the psychodynamic model.

In summary, we suggest that laboratory tests of present state, particularly psychological tests, have much less relevance to the MSO evaluation than has previously been claimed. We regard these procedures as adjunct or supplementary to interview and investigative procedures, and we urge forensic examiners to admit candidly the limited use of these techniques for reconstructing the MSO. Expert witnesses should be prepared to concede the modest reliability and validity of many tests for diagnostic and predictive purposes, and to make other appropriate qualifications as needed to ensure that the trier of fact is not misled regarding the power or precision of these techniques.

6.06. The Relationship between Clinical Findings and Criminal Behavior: Formulating an Opinion

As a result of the investigation and reconstruction of a defendant's MSO, the clinician may have a wealth of information that is potentially useful to the judge and jury. How best should he or she assimilate and present the findings?

A typology of inferences has been developed and discussed in some detail in § 1.04. As we have stressed throughout this volume, mental health professionals should avoid inference levels 6 and 7, which require a social and moral judgment or a legal interpretation that is not within the realm of mental health expertise. As the data permit, however, inferences at other levels are defensible within the broad range of applications of mental health or social sciences knowledge. As we suggested in § 6.02(c)(2), the most relevant inferences will be those based on the defendant's conscious reasons for committing the offense (which may be ascertained from the

defendant or inferred from other information). However, there may be cases where a person's unconscious "reasons" appear to explain the person's behavior best. The following two subsections look at both types of formulations.

(a)   Behavioral Formulations

In deciding how far toward inference levels 6 and 7 they should venture, the primary guideline for clinicians is, as usual, whether they have specialized knowledge (or a specialized skill that can produce otherwise inaccessible knowledge) that will help factfinders. In reporting on defendants' conscious reasons for acting, forensic examiners, at a minimum, can usually offer extensive descriptive information (levels 1 and 2) based on their own observations and those of their investigative sources. Where a pattern of behavior over time (e.g., through the social history study) or a complex of behaviors recognizable as a clinical syndrome is observed, observations may be synthesized into constructs or diagnoses (levels 3 and 4); with appropriate caution, examiners may elaborate to include other behaviors often associated with the syndrome or diagnosis—type and degree of cognitive impairment, perceptual disturbances, range and control of emotional expression, and so on.

The importance of diagnosis (level 4) in MSO evaluations has been both overstated and understated. Its importance has been overstated by those mental health professionals who have fashioned crude diagnostic decision rules for formulating their opinions on legal insanity.[266] As the discussion in § 6.02 and the empirical data relating insanity findings to diagnosis illustrate, psychosis does not equal insanity. The other extreme position is that of Morse,[267] who argues that not only are diagnoses *not* dispositive in legal cases, they are essentially irrelevant. Diagnoses are abstractions that tell the trier of fact nothing about a defendant's specific clinically relevant behavior, and they are not translatable (at least not by mental health witnesses) into legal terms such as "mental disease or defect."

Our position is closer to that of Morse. We are in essential agreement that diagnostic labels are of little use to the trier of fact, particularly if unexplained. Morse's position somewhat understates the importance of diagnosis, however. Determining which diagnoses are present in MSO evaluations may serve important functions for forensic examiners, if not for factfinders. If clinicians endeavor to keep their formulations and opinions globally in line with the values of the legal system, then the use of a chart such as Figure 6-1 [in § 6.02(c)(1)] may be one way for them to calibrate their sights; while they should always be alert for idiosyncrasies of particular cases, they may use a listing of legally relevant diagnoses to help keep any speculative tendencies they may have in check. Further, some statutes or case law may dictate or limit the applicability of specific diagnoses to certain mental state defenses (e.g., drug or alcohol intoxication may be explicitly excluded as a basis for legal insanity). In order to consult intelligently with counsel, clinicians should know whether the clinically relevant behaviors they observe or infer are attributable to diagnoses explicitly addressed in the controlling laws.

Clinicians' knowledge of different disorders may also be of help to factfinders in determining whether "mental disease or defect" is or was present in defendants. While clinicians should not attempt a direct translation of clinical diagnoses into legal concepts, they may provide information about disorders that allows judges or juries to assess the "fit" between specific diagnoses and the disease concept generally. Disorders such as schizophrenia or major affective disorder—which appear to have an etiological component in the biological substrata, remit in response to medication, have a predictable course if left untreated, and can be "chemically induced"[268]—fit the disease concept better than do disorders that have none of these features. Furthermore, clinical research on legally relevant behavior, such as the incidence of violence in different diagnostic groups, may be of interest to factfinders; in order to make such information relevant to a particular case, the diagnosis of the defendant must be mentioned.[269]

In summary, determination of a psychiatric diagnosis where applicable is of some, but limited, value in the MSO investigation. Diagnostic labels *alone* have no value for the trier of fact in making dispositional judgments; a more concrete level of analysis of a defendant's behavior is required for such decisions. Contemplation of diagnosis does provide a convenient opportunity for a clinician to consider the probable legal relevance of the findings, and it may serve as a focus for discussion and planning during consultation with counsel. The formulation of a diagnosis also facilitates the discussion of etiological and prognostic issues,[270] as well as the introduction of research findings associated with specific diagnoses.

Where clinically significant behavior is determined to have been present at the time of an offense, the clinician may proceed to inference level 5—the relationship of the clinically relevant behavior to the alleged criminal act. At this point, the clinician's focus is on the specific symptoms determined to be present and their impact on the mental processes ordinarily considered to mediate instrumental behavior. The clinician may indicate how certain symptoms reflect impairment in judgment, concentration, focus of attention, interpersonal functioning, or other aspects of experience reasonably related to the relevant legal mental state.

Within the context of the insanity defense, evidence of either cognitive impairment or volitional impairment is pertinent [see § 6.02]. Cognitive impairment may be reflected in a variety of ways, but most typically through perceptual distortions (e.g., hallucinations), deviant thought content (e.g., delusions or idiosyncratic interpretations of ordinary events), or disruptions in the thought process (e.g., confused thoughts, disorganized thoughts, illogical thoughts). Volitional impairment is most obviously reflected in states in which cognitive control mechanisms appear to be functionally disengaged, as in dissociative or depersonalization episodes and confusional states following head trauma or epileptic seizure (the postictal phase), or when controls are compromised (as in kleptomania or pyromania).

Many of these same symptoms, especially those relating to cognition, may be even more relevant in the context of MSO defenses other than insanity. Persons whose conscious control was impaired (as in dissociative states) may be argued to have been acting "automatically" [see § 6.03(a)], and persons with significant symptoms of thought or mood disturbance may be argued to lack the capacity to premeditate, to have "malice", or to possess other mental elements required for conviction [see § 6.03(b)]. Except where the application of a defense requires a threshold finding of a major psychiatric disorder or specifically limits the applicability of certain diagnostic conditions, forensic examiners should not be overly concerned with which particular MSO theory is being pursued in a given case. They should take care to avoid testifying in the language of the legal test (e.g., "lacked substantial capacity . . .") or making assertions about legally defined mental states that cannot be directly assessed (e.g., intent, malice).[271] In relating their clinical formulations, they can keep their statements at a descriptive level and leave it to the attorneys to argue the points of legal application. Rather than offering opinion testimony that paraphrases the legal test or incorporates legally defined mental elements, we suggest that clinicians follow Morse's recommendation that clinicians explain the ways in which clinical symptoms made it difficult for defendants to act in the legally prescribed manner.[272] The following cases give illustrations of possible formulations relating symptoms of psychopathology to legally relevant behavior.

Case 1: Delusional Beliefs. A defendant charged with unlawfully driving away a bus was diagnosed as a paranoid schizophrenic, with symptoms including delusions of grandeur at the time of the offense. The clinical formulation included the following:

> Mr. Doe knew that he needed to return to his home city. While he indicated to me that he knew that the Greyhound bus did not literally belong to him, he stated that he felt entitled to take it. Mr. Doe described the strong belief, which was of course erroneous, that he was an important law enforcement official—specifically, the FBI Director. It should be noted that records from several prior psychiatric hospitalizations describe similar exaggerated and erroneous beliefs of this type by Mr. Doe in the past. Thus it appears feasible that his delusional belief may have contributed to his unlawfully taking the bus, as he reported reasoning that he had the discretionary authority to commandeer public transportation vehicles in the execution of his official duties. It appears that Mr. Doe may have had some difficulty distinguishing between his legitimate authority, and

the authority he imagined himself to have as a result of his illness.

Case 2: Mental Retardation. A mildly retarded young man was charged with third-degree sexual misconduct after approaching a woman outside the lion's cage at the city zoo and grabbing her from behind, briefly fondling her breasts before running away. The clinical formulation included the following:

> Mr. Roe is a mildly retarded young man who functions, intellectually, in the lower 1–2% of the population of persons his age. During psychological testing he was presented with hypothetical social situations involving two or more people and asked to describe what might be going on between them. In most instances his responses were brief, were poorly articulated, and reflected a poor understanding of how social relationships are developed and appropriately maintained. This is consistent with the information provided by family members, who indicated that Mr. Roe does not know how to approach other people or make friends; significantly, he is described as shy and uncomfortable around women, having had no dating or courting experience to speak of.
>
> When asked to describe what happened at the zoo, Mr. Roe provided a factual account which, consistent with what I have already described regarding his limited social skills, reflects his naiveté in these matters. He reported that he had seen his cousin and girlfriend "hugging" on each other as they walked through the zoo with him, and he noted, "It didn't seem like she minded it at all." He also indicated that during recess at school, "The boys chase the girls around the playground and grab them. They usually just laugh and giggle. . . . I figured she [the victim] would too."
>
> In summary, Mr. Roe is a mildly retarded individual who has extremely poor social skills and very minimal ability to discern appropriate behavior in social contexts, particularly where relationships with women are involved. His intellectual and social impairment appears to make it difficult for him to distinguish between, for example, what is appropriate conduct with classmates on the school playground, and what would be appropriate contact with a stranger in a public place. This difficulty appears to have contributed to the present offense.

Case 3: Dissociation. A young man was charged with second-degree murder. The victim was a woman who had been his date on the evening in question; she had died as a result of extensive internal bleeding and ruptured internal organs secondary to a severe vaginal assault. The defendant was amnesic for the incident. The examiner located another woman, the defendant's usual girlfriend, who described a similar but substantially less serious assault on her approximately a week before the crime. She reported,

While we were making love, he suddenly changed. It was like he was a different person—like he wasn't really there. He looked off to the side, his eyes were half closed and he had this strange look on his face. He kept saying, "You've wanted this for all these years . . . now you're going to get it." And then he shoved his whole hand in me. I don't know who he thought I was, because I've only known him a few months. It didn't matter, because he was off in another world. I yelled and told him to stop, that it hurt, but it was like he didn't even hear me. No response, no recognition, no nothing. Then suddenly he quit, he just changed back into himself. He didn't even know what had happened.

In the clinical formulation, the examiner relied heavily on this witness's account of the assault, offering that the present offense could feasibly have occurred during a similar episode. The examiner suggested that the defendant "may have experienced a brief dissociative episode during which he was unaware of or unresponsive to others in his presence or his impact on them. This impairment in his ability to receive and critically process information, including feedback about his own behavior, would have made it difficult for him to modulate his actions."

These examples illustrate how clinicians might provide descriptive accounts and logical links between symptoms associated with conventional psychiatric disturbance and alleged criminal behavior. Similar accounts could be developed to explain the possible impact of hallucinations, the effects of drugs and/or alcohol, or other symptom patterns determined to have been present at the time of an offense [see, e.g., the Wertz report, § 15.04].

(b)   Psychodynamic Formulations

The law has historically been concerned *primarily* with individuals' conscious reasons and motives for their criminal behavior. If an analysis of the individuals' conscious reasons and means for controlling their behavior yields a clear understanding and explanation of their offenses, the primary needs of the law are satisfied. The characterization of a defendant's behavior at the time of the offense, as validly perceived, is accepted at face value—that is, the behavior is not interpreted; it is held to mean what it appeared to mean. If the defendant appeared to be crazy, re-

sponsibility is said to have been diminished; if the defendant appeared not to be crazy, he or she is held responsible. The legal constructs of "mental disease" and "mental defect," discussed above, provide the mechanisms by which responsibility is said to have been diminished.

Psychodynamic formulations[273] are most often applied (and applicable) in cases where the usual constructs (mental disease and mental defect) do not appear to apply, yet the defendants' behavior nevertheless seems illogical or inscrutable. Psychodynamic formulations provide an *interpretation* of the defendants' behavior by providing insight into unconscious motives for their actions, usually said to originate in their psychosexual development, that were not obvious upon inspecting their behavior as it appeared. Since the defendants could not know about, and therefore could not control, motivations that are by definition unconscious, their responsibility for their actions is held to have been diminished. Thus, psychodynamic formulations are usually offered as the basis for an insanity defense (Was there true "appreciation" of the act? Was there difficulty in "conforming to the requirements of the law?").[274]

The case of F.N. illustrates the potential usefulness of psychodynamic explanations in a legal setting.

Case 4.   F.N. was a divorced white male in his mid-20s. One evening he went to the apartment of a woman whom he had known only as an acquaintance of his ex-wife. She recognized him and allowed him to enter the apartment, whereupon he commenced a lengthy and brutal sexual assault involving verbal and physical sadistic acts, including the forcing of various foreign objects into the victim's anal cavity. The case appeared on the surface to be a straightforward rape; the defendant did not have a documented history of any major psychiatric disorder, and from the victim's account he very clearly knew what he was doing at the time of the offense. Certain peculiarities in his behavior, however, as described by the victim, suggested a psychodynamic explanation for the crime. She described him as speaking throughout the ordeal in an unusual voice, and on several occasions he stated to her rhetorically, "How do you like getting it from a big stud Mexican?" Since the defendant was Caucasian, the comment made no sense. The comment, plus the severity of the attack, suggested that the defendant was symbolically acting out hatred that was intended for someone else.

When the defendant was interviewed by the forensic examiner, he recalled little of the assault. Exploring the defendant's psychohistory, however, revealed some startling information. He recalled how his mother had physically coddled and caressed him well into late adolescence, and he intimated that he might have had intimate sexual contact with her at the age of 18. Long after they were living apart, she would continue to call him on the phone and describe in graphic detail her latest sexual encounters. One such occasion that stuck particularly firmly in his memory was his mother's account of her escapades with a "big stud Mexican." In this case, given the victim's account of his strange behavior and the psychohistory, along with the defendant's amnesia for the assault, a psychodynamic explanation based on repressed anger toward a seducing mother was developed and provided a feasible explanation (although not necessarily a legal excuse) for the crime—one that might otherwise have been unavailable to the fact-finder.

Theory-based formulations have a strong intuitive appeal and provide feasible explanations for unusual defendant behavior in cases where organic-model formulations and commonsensical inferences fail to provide a complete accounting of the available data. In the case described above, F.N.'s behavior could be construed as simply a sadistic rape, though such an accounting would not explain his altered voice quality and repeated (and peculiar) reference to "getting it from a big stud Mexican." Other cases, such as sexually motivated burglaries,[275] invite a theoretical explanation where the ordinary and preferred models of comprehension leave unanswered questions.

In spite of their intuitive appeal and apparent usefulness, the application of psychodynamic formulations to criminal behavior carries considerable risks.[276] One problem is that psychodynamic explanations can be generated to explain virtually every human behavior—criminal or noncriminal, normal or "crazy." The same theoretical constructs and explanatory devices that seem to make sense of unusual behavior also apply to behaviors we would consider perfectly ordinary. Without some threshold question (such as the need to prove substantial mental disorder) to govern when such formulations are to be applied, virtually every criminal case—including those in which obvious criminal motives appear

conscious and controlling—is susceptible to psychodynamic theorizing. Because the theory relies on unconscious factors to explain defendants' behavior, and therefore to reduce the perceived impact their conscious processes had on their criminal acts, the formulations are always exculpatory in nature; psychodynamic theory is exclusively a theory for defendants.

Apart from the fact that psychodynamic theory "overexplains," there are also problems of unreliability of formulations and the sometimes speculative (and potentially invalid) nature of the explanations derived. The reliability of theory-based formulations has yet to be demonstrated. The main constructs and explanatory devices are so abstract and flexible that two practitioners from the same school might offer strikingly different formulations, and, given the "armchair" nature in which such formulations are seemingly derived, neither might be valid by external criteria.[277]

A case study reported by Ayllon, Haughton, and Hughes[278] clearly demonstrated the potential foibles of psychodynamic interpretations of behavior. A chronic schizophrenic was observed compulsively carrying a broom with her around the hospital ward. Two board-certified psychiatrists observed her through a one-way mirror. Both confirmed this odd behavior as a symptom of disturbed behavior; their interpretations were as follows:

Dr. X: "The broom represents to this patient some essential perceptual element in her field of consciousness . . . it is certainly a stereotyped form of behavior such as is commonly seen in rather regressed schizophrenics and is rather analogous to the way small children or infants refuse to be parted from some favorite toy, piece of rag, etc."

Dr. Y: "Her constant and compulsive pacing, holding a broom in the manner she does, could be seen as a ritualistic procedure, a magical action . . . Her broom would be then (1) a child that gives her love and she gives him in return her devotion, (2) a phallic symbol, (3) the sceptre of an omnipotent queen . . . this is a magical procedure in which the patient carries out her wishes expressed in a way that is far beyond our solid, rational and conventional way of thinking and acting."[279]

With apparent ease, the two psychiatrists generated at least four possible symbolic meanings for the peculiar behavior. Apart from the fact that the two did not agree in the symbolic meaning of the target behavior, none of their psychodynamic insights appeared to have the slightest validity in light of the additional information provided by the authors. In actual fact, the broom-carrying behavior had been acquired and maintained in response to a carefully controlled schedule of reinforcements using cigarettes. The behavior was just as easily extinguished by altering the contingency schedule according to learning theory principles; the "symptom" was a learned behavior and nothing more.

This example illustrates another problem in the use of theory-based formulations to explain criminal behavior. Theories with widely differing assumptions and constructs may be applied to explain the very same phenomenon. The choice of a particular dynamic theory, or of a dynamic explanation over a learning theory explanation, may be more a function of the values and training of the practitioner than of the data in the case in hand.[280] Lest the reader think too much is being made of a single example involving simply broom-carrying behavior, consider the following case that confronted one of us (Poythress).

Case 5.   A white male, married, in his early 20s, was charged with attempted rape, The defendant concealed himself in the rear of a van parked at a busy shopping center. By his own statement, he had noticed an attractive woman driving alone in the van and had followed her in his own car. When she parked and got out to go shopping, he hid in the back of the van. When she returned to the van she noticed a movement in the rear-view mirror and screamed. The defendant was flushed from his hiding place; as he ran forward, they struggled briefly before he escaped and fled on foot. He was apprehended a short time later in a nearby wooded area.

A surface analysis of this offense suggested a straightforward sexual assault case. In the clinical interview, however, the defendant admitted sheepishly that he frequently hid in the rear of automobiles (usually station wagons) or vans driven by single women whom he initially followed in his car. He reported having done this for several years; with obvious embarrassment, he admitted feeling sexually excited while hiding, wondering whether he would be discovered. This aspect of the case easily lent itself to a psycho-

dynamic interpretation (or several of them), based on retarded psychosexual development, regressed behavior, and the like. However, further exploration of the defendant's sexual history invited an equally plausible explanation based on learning theory. The defendant recalled that at approximately age 12 he had experienced his first waking ejaculation. He was playing 'Army" with some friends and was hiding in the back seat of an old, abandoned car. He recalled feeling quite excited as he heard his friends walking by outside as they looked for him. As he pressed himself further down on the seat of the car, he became aware that in doing so he was creating considerable friction between his penis (inside his trousers) and the car seat. He continued rubbing himself against the seat in this manner, increasing his sexual arousal to the point of orgasm, all the while continuing to experience the excitement of hiding in close proximity to his friends. He later returned to the same location and reexperienced sexual gratification as he fantasized that others were looking for him.

How might a forensic examiner have responded in this case? Should a potentially exculpating explanation, based on psychodynamic interpretations of the defendant's unusual behavior, have been advanced? Should an explanation based on learning principles (sexual gratification as reinforcement for learned behavior) have been advanced? Or, in the absence of any symptoms of major disorder, should the examiner have just let the defendant's behavior speak for itself?

These are the quandaries that confront the forensic clinician who contemplates offering theory-based explanations for criminal behavior. Given the problems associated with such formulations, we restate our recommendation [see § 6.02(c)(2)] that non-organic-model formulations be advanced only when an analysis of a defendant's conscious reasons and motivations for a criminal act, including the possible effects of major psychiatric disorders, fails to provide a satisfactory understanding of the crime scenario. The clinician should be prepared to identify the specific features of the case that invite or compel further analysis. He or she should weigh the applicability of various alternative theories, and should willingly concede that theory-based formulations other than the one chosen may offer other feasible explanations. The clinician should be candid about the reasons for selecting the particular theory chosen, and should be prepared to discuss the research, if any, on reliabil-

Figure 6-2.   *The MSO evaluation.*

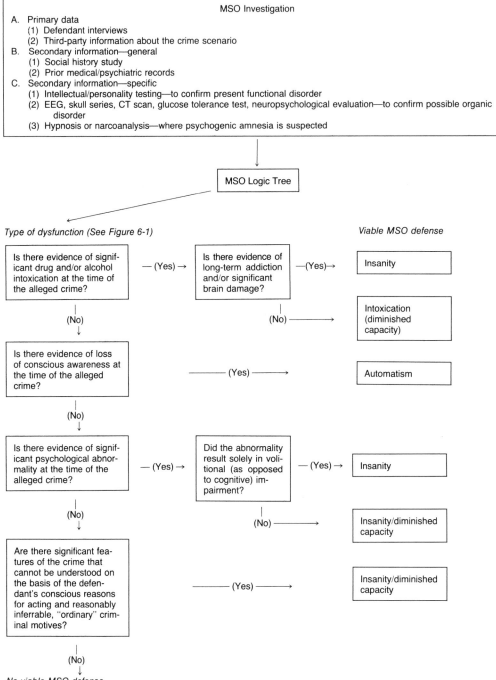

ity and validity of formulations based in that theory. As with formulations and explanations based on the medical–behavioral model, theory-based formulations should not embrace the ultimate legal issue.

6.07.   *Conclusion*

As a way of synthesizing the various points made concerning the clinical evaluation of MSO, Figure 6-2 is offered. Note that once the MSO investigation is completed, the clinician can focus on four different types of dysfunction (in the left-hand column of the "Logic Tree") in determining whether the defendant's MSO was legally relevant. As pointed out earlier, the actual MSO defense the defendant presents is not a concern of the clinician's; the figure lists the defense or defenses most probably related to each type of dysfunction, merely to tie together the points made in the first half of this chapter.

BIBLIOGRAPHY

Arenella, *The Diminished Capacity and Diminished Responsibility Defenses: Two Children of a Doomed Marriage,* 77 COLUM. L. REV. 827 (1977).

Becker, Durham *Revisited: Psychiatry and the Problem of Crime,* in PSYCHIATRISTS IN THE LEGAL PROCESS: DIAGNOSIS AND DEBATE (R. Bonnie ed. 1977).

Bonnie & Slobogin, *The Role of Mental Health Professionals in the Criminal Process: The Case for Informed Speculation,* 66 VA. L. REV. 427 (1980).

CRIMINAL JUSTICE MENTAL HEALTH STANDARDS, part VI (1984).

Durham v. United States, 214 F.2d 862 (D.C. Cir. 1954).

A. GOLDSTEIN, THE INSANITY DEFENSE (1967).

H. HART, PUNISHMENT AND RESPONSIBILITY (1968). (See particularly pp. 90–112 on unconsciousness.)

M'Naghten's Case, 10 Cl. F.200, 8 Eng. Rep. 718 (H.L. 1943).

M. MOORE, LAW AND PSYCHIATRY AND LAW: RETHINKING THE RELATIONSHIP (1984). (See particularly chs. 6 and 10.)

N. MORRIS, MADNESS AND THE CRIMINAL LAW (1982).

Morse, *Failed Explanations and Criminal Responsibility: Experts and the Unconscious,* 68 VA. L. REV. 971 (1982).

Pasewark, *Insanity Plea: A Review of the Research Literature,* 9 J. PSYCHIATRY & L. 357 (1981).

Rogers, *Toward an Empirical Model of Malingering and Deception,* 2 BEHAV. SCI. & LAW 93 (1984).

Schacter, *Amnesia and Crime: How Much Do We Really Know?* 41 AM. PSYCHOLOGIST 236 (1986).

Slobogin, *A Rational Approach to Responsibility: A Review of Michael Moore's* LAW AND PSYCHIATRY: RETHINKING THE RELATIONSHIP, 83 MICH. L. REV. 820 (1985).

Slobogin, *The Guilty But Mentally Ill Verdict: An Idea Whose Time Should Not Have Come,* 53 GEO. WASH. L. REV. 494 (1985).

United States v. Brawner, 471 F.2d 969 (D.C. Cir. 1972).

CHAPTER SEVEN

Sentencing

7.01. *Introduction*

"Sentencing" is the dispositional phase of the criminal process for those found guilty of a criminal offense. Other dispositional mechanisms available to the criminal justice system (competency adjudications, findings of insanity) resolve the criminal proceedings without a finding of guilt. Sentencing is reserved for those adjudicated guilty.[1]

Sentencing practices in Anglo-American law have been motivated by one or more of the following goals: the deterrence of crime; incapacitation of the offender; vindication of the social order; and rehabilitation of the offender.[2]

"Deterrence" as a sentencing goal seeks to prevent crime. "General" deterrence imposes sanctions in order to discourage others from committing the proscribed offense. "Special" or "specific" deterrence imposes sanctions to discourage offenders from repeating their offenses. Deterrence assumes that if a sanction is made unpleasant enough, individuals will refrain from committing an offense in order to avoid the sanction.

"Incapacitation" means simply that the sanction renders the offender physically incapable of committing an offense. Forms of incapacitation in the past have been geared specifically toward the offense (e.g., castration of a sex offender). They also include the death penalty and incarceration. In the future, they may include chemical restraints in lieu of prison.

"Vindication of the social order" is more commonly known as "retribution." It is based primarily on two premises, both concerned with maintaining societal balance and stability. The first assumes a societal need to punish transgressors. The second assumes that punishment of violators of the social norm is necessary to preserve the norm itself.

Sentencing based on "rehabilitation" of offenders assumes that offenders can be "cured" of their criminal tendencies through individualized rehabilitation programs. This model focuses attention on offenders rather than offenses.

Obviously, of the four goals described above, the last is most closely related to the clinical endeavor. Other forensic inquiries, such as determinations of competency or insanity, are narrowly focused on mental states at a particular point in time and are only tangentially related to treatment concerns. Clinical input at sentencing, on the other hand, has traditionally been sought as a means of directly addressing an offender's potential for rehabilitation, and the related inquiry as to whether the offender, with or without treatment, will offend again. Although this latter task has expanded into the arguably non-clinical assessment of "dangerousness," and other issues, such as "offender culpability," have been added to the questions clinicians are asked to address, sentencing under the rehabilitation model remains the legal domain that is least alien to traditional clinical practice.

Thus, it is not surprising to find that to the extent that rehabilitation has been an important sentencing objective, the law has invited clinical participation at the dispositional stage.[3] In the United States, the rehabilitative model has been part of sentencing since at least the latter part of the 19th century, and only in recent years has it been challenged in any significant way. As a result, mental health professionals have been heavily involved in the sentencing process for some time, although their actual influence on sentencing determinations is open to dispute [see § 7.07].

The perceived "match" between clinical expertise and the rehabilitative goal of the criminal justice system has led not only to increased clinical participation in ordinary sentencing,[4] but to the creation of special dispositional statutes that seek to identify certain types of offenders—for example, "sex offenders" or "youthful offenders"—who are presumably amenable to treatment and cure by the clinical professions. Offenders falling into these categories are sentenced under special sentencing provisions designed to maximize clinical involvement in their cases. These statutes became prevalent when psychiatry was at its zenith in the respect it commanded from the criminal justice system.

Since the mid-1970s, however, this familiar rehabilitative model of sentencing has been shaken to its core. Its twin premises—that a system of punishments could be molded to rehabilitate offenders, and that professional predictions of future behavior could be reliably and validly made so that the criminal justice system would "know" when the offender was rehabilitated—have been challenged both by commentators and by some courts.[5] While the United States Supreme Court has continued to authorize the use of clinical predictions of dangerousness at sentencing,[6] these challenges have proved influential. As a result, beginning in 1976, a growing number of states have de-emphasized the rehabilitative goal and turned to sentencing models based primarily on

retribution and deterrence. Legislatures have reduced the discretion of courts and parole boards, and have directed them to adhere to more specific sentencing guidelines. The forward-looking rehabilitative model, which asks whether individuals can be rehabilitated and whether they will offend again, has been replaced by myriad variations of the backward-looking "just desserts" model, which focuses on defendants' culpability as exhibited by such objective factors as the offense committed and prior record.

Some have predicted that the changes now taking place in sentencing will result in greatly decreased clinical participation in the sentencing phase.[7] We do not share this conclusion, in large part because statutory changes designed to reduce discretion at sentencing have uniformly failed to eliminate considerations of individual traits—the situation in which clinicians are most likely to be called upon. But since sentencing *has* been affected by recent reforms, knowledge of the major issues in the debate over sentencing and the role of the clinician under alternative sentencing schemes is important for clinicians and lawyers who will participate in the process.

Thus, this chapter begins with a brief overview of the history of sentencing and the societal goals that have informed sentencing. It then discusses the rehabilitative (or therapeutic) model of sentencing, including its purposes; the premises upon which it is constructed; a description of the roles exercised by the various participants (the legislature, the prosecutor, the court, the parole board); and the procedure under such a model. Next, the shift in some jurisdictions to a "determinate" model of sentencing is described, including the purposes of the model; the manner in which determinate sentencing may change the roles of the various participants in sentencing; procedures; and the anticipated utility of clinical expertise in jurisdictions relying on the determinate approach.

The chapter then discusses "special" sentencing statutes, including those for repeat or habitual offenders, sex offenders, youthful offenders, and those addicted to narcotics. This is followed by a discussion of capital sentencing, including the governing principles articulated by the United States Supreme Court, from 1972 through the early 1980s, as well as observations concerning the propriety and utility of clinical expertise at capital sentencing.

Finally, the chapter then turns to a discussion of the three issues that clinicians are most likely to confront during the sentencing phase: treatment needs assessment, culpability determination, and predictions of dangerousness. In each of these areas, relevant research and appropriate clinical evaluation techniques are examined.

7.02. A Brief History of Sentencing

In 1978 there were 307,384 individuals imprisoned in the United States, the highest number in United States history.[8] These individuals were distributed between federal (29,803 inmates) and state (277,581 inmates) prisons.[9] There were also more than 158,000 individuals in local jails.[10] The vast majority (96%) of those serving time in federal and state prisons had been sentenced to more than one year's imprisonment; in contrast, only 60% of those in local jails had been convicted of a crime, most frequently a misdemeanor, and many (40%) were still awaiting trial.[11] The United States utilizes imprisonment at a higher rate per capita with longer prison terms than any other Western country.[12]

This extensive reliance on imprisonment as a means of punishment has not always been the norm. Rather, Anglo-American law has varied punishments as societal goals for sentencing have changed from retribution and deterrence to rehabilitation and back again.

In England, early common law made death the penalty for all offenses except petty larceny and mayhem.[13] Imprisonment was not used as a dispositional device. As has proven true whenever the death penalty is available, mechanisms developed that made its imposition discretionary in certain cases. Two of the most common devices were "transportation" (i.e., the defendant was literally transported from the country to one of the colonies) and "benefit of clergy" (i.e., the individual was tried by an ecclesiastical court, which did not have the authority to impose the death sentence).[14]

This system was largely retributive in nature. It assumed behavior to result from free will, and

held that individuals were both morally and legally responsible for their actions.[15] Thus, they deserved the punishment they received. To a much lesser extent, it was also based on a theory of general deterrence, which assumes that rational people will refrain from committing an offense if the penalty exacted is sufficiently severe.

In colonial America, disposition of criminals was also based primarily upon retribution and general deterrence.[16] Incarceration was seldom relied upon in this period, though corporal punishment was used frequently, as were banishment of the offender from the community, and fines and restitution for economic crimes.[17] Penalties were prescribed specifically for offenses, and so the sentencing judge had little if any discretion.[18]

The pre-Civil War period, beginning in approximately 1790, saw the eventual abolition of corporal punishment and the introduction of incarceration as a method of punishment.[19] The legislature continued to fix sentences for particular offenses, and the penalty continued to be a function of the severity of the crime rather than the personal characteristics or attributes of the offender. Over time, however, this period also witnessed the emergence of another goal for sentencing—that of the moral reformation of the offender. Criminality came to be explained as "a function of defective moral training, a byproduct of rapid urbanization and industrialization. The proposed solution was programs of moral training . . ."[20]

After the Civil War, a sentencing policy based upon moral training evolved finally into the rehabilitative model with the emergence of "positivism," which promised that the causes of crime could be identified and cured.[21] This body of thought found expression in 1870 in the enunciation of a Declaration of Principles by the National Prison Congress. The premise of this new philosophy of sentencing was that crime is

a moral disease, of which punishment is the remedy. The efficiency of the remedy is a question of social therapeutics, a question of the fitness and the measure of the dose . . . [P]unishment is directed not to the crime but the criminal . . . The supreme aim of the prison discipline is the reformation of criminals, not the infliction of vindictive suffering.[22] (emphasis added)

The Congress also recommended adoption of indeterminate sentences (i.e., sentences indefinite in length when imposed) in order to allow reformation to occur on an individual basis, unhampered by artificial time constraints. The ultimate length of a sentence would be determined by the success of the rehabilitation effort.

This movement enjoyed wide popularity; it resulted in revision of sentencing laws to provide for a maximum length of imprisonment, leaving to the managers of the reformatory the exact length of each sentence. By 1922, 37 states had enacted indeterminate sentencing statutes, and 7 others had parole systems functionally similar to the indeterminate sentence.[23] The United States Supreme Court, in 1948, noted the primacy of the rehabilitative model when it described the

> prevalent modern philosophy of penology that the punishment should fit the offender and not merely the crime [cite omitted]. The belief no longer prevails that every offense in a like legal category calls for an identical punishment without regard to the past life and particular habits of a particular offender . . . Retribution is no longer the dominant objective of the criminal law. Reformation and rehabilitation of offenders have become important goals of criminal jurisprudence.[24]

The rehabilitation model was radical in construct, for, as the Supreme Court noted, it focused neither on the crime involved (the retribution model) nor on the effect that the prescribed punishment would have on others (the deterrence model), but instead on the attributes possessed by the individual offender. It was forward-looking: The idea was to "cure" offenders so that they would not offend again. As Dershowitz points out, this resulted in an infusion of psychiatric terminology and methodology into the prison system (an individual was "classified," the functional equivalent of diagnosis; treatment plans were established: and the inmate's progress was closely monitored.)[25] It also led to the advent in prisons of an array of clinicians and administrative personnel (parole boards) who would decide when an offender had been rehabilitated, thereby resulting in release from prison.

As noted in the introduction, since the mid-1970s, the rehabilitation model has been attacked and, in some jurisdictions, abandoned as the primary goal of sentencing. In its place has come determinate sentencing, which emphasizes fixed retribution for the offense committed, regardless of the defendant's rehabilitative potential. However, the rehabilitative ideal retains much force and continues to be a primary goal of the sentencing laws of the majority of jurisdictions. It therefore deserves detailed discussion before proceeding to an examination of determinate sentencing.

7.03. The Rehabilitative Model: Indeterminate Sentencing

(a) Goals and Premises

As noted above, the rehabilitative model of sentencing has as its principal goal the reform or "cure" of offenders. Thus it holds that offenders should be sanctioned based on their individual characteristics, particularly their rehabilitative potential. Sentencing under this model

> is premised on the assumption that a sentencing judge, armed with an intimate knowledge of the offender's character and background and aided by scientific and clinical evaluations, can determine an appropriate sentence and treatment program that will rehabilitate the offender. Under this model, the sentencing judge seeks to define the offender's exact personality and social situations, and then prescribes an "individualized" sentence and treatment program. Because rehabilitation is the primary concern, the sentencing judge theoretically is less concerned with deterring future crime or achieving retribution for society.[26]

The core element of the rehabilitative model is the indeterminate sentence. A sentence is "indeterminate" in two ways: First, the court has wide leeway in imposing a sentence; and second, the actual length of a sentence is not decided until well into the term of imprisonment, when the parole board determines when release shall actually occur.[27] Because sentences are indeterminate, and because the rehabilitative model depends upon individualized assessments of each offender, sentencing schemes based on this model are marked by three things: The decisionmakers enjoy enormous discretion; the sentencing process focuses on gathering as much information about the defendant as possible; and the actual process of sentencing is informal, designed to facilitate the gathering of information and the exercise of discretion. Each of these elements is discussed in more detail below.

(b) Decisionmakers and the Importance of Discretion

There are four principal decisionmakers in the sentencing process: the legislature, the prosecutor, the court, and the parole board.

(1) The Legislature

In nearly all jurisdictions, the legislature establishes the statutory scheme for sentencing.[28] It does this first by defining what constitutes a criminal offense, and then by fixing the penalties for each offense, or, more commonly, each category of offense. The two generic categories of offenses are felonies and misdemeanors. The distinction between the two typically is drawn in terms of the maximum sentence available for the offense and the place the term is to be served: Misdemeanors are generally punishable by incarceration in jail of no more than a year, while the available penalty for a felony includes the possibility of incarceration in prison for more than a year. The legislature also commonly establishes different classes of felonies and misdemeanors, with the range of penalties possible upon conviction depending upon the class in which the legislature places a particular offense.

For example, in New York there are five major classes of felonies. A "Class A-I" felony is the most severe, and is punishable by a maximum sentence of life imprisonment. The legislature has also established minimum sentences for each class. For example, a Class A-I felony such as first-degree homicide carries a minimum period of imprisonment that must be at least 15 years but not more than 25 years. Therefore, when the court imposes sentence, it will sentence the de-

fendant to a sentence ranging from a minimum of 15 years to 25 years to a maximum sentence of life imprisonment.

Unless the death penalty is involved, appellate courts have indicated that the sentence established for an offense is a matter of legislative prerogative, which will not be disturbed except in those extremely rare instances constituting "cruel and unusual punishment" under the Eighth Amendment.[29]

(2) The Prosecutor

The prosecutor exerts tremendous influence over the sanction imposed in a given case. He or she does this in two ways: through charging the alleged offender, and through plea bargaining.

The decision to charge an individual with a criminal offense is wholly discretionary, as is the decision concerning what offense to charge. The prosecutor's discretion in charging is enhanced by the fact that the same conduct may constitute several offenses, each falling within a different offense category and therefore carrying different potential penalties. For example, if a man assaults and chokes his spouse, the conduct may result in one of several charges. In New York, these include attempted murder, a Class A-II felony punishable by a maximum of life imprisonment; assault in the first degree, a Class C felony punishable by a maximum of 15 years' imprisonment; assault in the third degree, a Class A misdemeanor, punishable by no more than one year's imprisonment; or menacing, a Class B misdemeanor punishable by no more than three months' imprisonment. The decision which, if any, to charge is the prosecutor's.

The prosecutor enjoys similar discretion in resolving cases through plea bargaining, a process that resolves over 90% of all criminal cases short of trial, and usually heavily influences the sentence ultimately given.[30] There are two types of plea bargaining.[31] With the first, known as "charge bargaining," the defendant pleads guilty or *nolo contendere* (i.e., "no contest," a functional equivalent of a guilty plea) to one charge, while the prosecutor in return agrees to dismiss or reduce other charges. In the second, called "sentence bargaining," the defendant pleads guilty to the original charge in exchange for the prosecutor's recommendation of a reduced sentence. In both cases, the court must approve the agreement, but this is usually *pro forma.*

(3)   The Court

The court imposes sentence in the vast majority of jurisdictions, though the jury has sentencing authority in several states,[32] and jury sentencing is the preferred method of sentencing in capital cases [see § 7.06]. The court, like the prosecutor, has broad discretion. The court simply must fix sentence within the range set by the legislature; if that is done, the appellate courts as a rule will refuse to disturb the sentence.[33]

In shaping the sentence to individual characteristics, the court has a wide variety of options.

1. The court may incarcerate the individual for any term of years within the range established by the legislature.
2. The court may suspend all or part of the sentence.
3. In conjunction with a suspended sentence, the court may require that certain conditions be met in order to avoid reimposition of sentence; these "probation" conditions can include attendance in treatment programs, "work-release," and restrictions on travel.[34]
4. In lieu of sentence, the court may order the payment of a fine to the court or restitution to the victim, or the court may order forfeiture of property, such as contraband or that used in criminal activity. It may also order the offender to engage in work that benefits the community.

Additionally, a defendant convicted of more than one offense may be sentenced for each offense. In such a case, the court also has the discretion to impose consecutive or concurrent sentences. If the sentences are consecutive, one begins upon completion of the other. If the sentences are concurrent, they run simultaneously.

(4)   The Parole Board

The parole board is an independent administrative body with the authority to determine the

actual length of an individual's imprisonment. It is a body essential to the operation of an indeterminate sentencing scheme. In determining that an individual may be paroled from prison, the board theoretically is deciding that the individual is sufficiently rehabilitated to warrant supervised return to the community. The Supreme Court has described parole in the following manner:

> During the past 60 years, the practice of releasing prisoners on parole before the end of their sentences has become an integral part of the penological system . . . Rather than being an *ad hoc* exercise of clemency, parole is an established variation on imprisonment of convicted criminals. Its purpose is to help individuals reintegrate into society as constructive individuals as soon as they are able, without being confined for the full term of the sentence imposed. It also serves to alleviate the costs to society of keeping an individual in prison. The essence of parole is release from prison, before the completion of sentence, on the condition that the prisoner abide by certain rules during the balance of the sentence.[35]

The legislature typically determines when an individual becomes *eligible* for parole by creating presumptive eligibility after the inmate serves a certain proportion (e.g., one-third) of the sentence received. At that point, the parole board holds a hearing on the inmate's suitability for parole—a determination usually based on the seriousness of the inmate's crime, previous offenses, and behavior in prison. The hearing is informal and subject to few procedural constraints.[36] Like the court's sentencing decision, the board's decision on the merits of parole is virtually unreviewable. When parole is granted, it is generally accompanied by a set of conditions, similar to those imposed on probationers, that the parolee must meet. For example, parolees may be forbidden to use alcohol or drugs, or to associate or correspond with certain individuals; parolees may also need to seek permission from their parole officers before traveling, changing employment, or operating a motor vehicle. In addition, they are required to report on a regular basis to their parole officers.

If a parolee violates a condition of parole, he or she faces possible revocation of paroled status and reimprisonment. The Supreme Court has ruled that a parolee is entitled to certain procedural rights before parole may be revoked, including (1) a "probable cause" finding, with notice to the parolee that parole has been violated; and (2) a revocation hearing, where the parolee is entitled to written notice, the disclosure of adverse evidence, an opportunity to be heard in person and to present witnesses, an opportunity to confront and cross-examine adverse witnesses (unless the hearing officer finds "good cause" not to allow this), a neutral and detached hearing officer (who need not be a judge or a lawyer), and a written statement giving the decision and the reasons for it.[37]

The discretionary authority of the parole board, like that of the sentencing judge, has come under attack from the advocates of determinate sentencing. However, in those jurisdictions retaining indeterminate sentencing, the parole board continues to play a pivotal role in determining the actual length of an individual sentence.

(c) The Sentencing Process

(1) Procedural Informality as the Norm

The Supreme Court has decided several cases concerning sentencing practices. After reviewing the Court's decisions, Dix concluded that the cases "provide no consistent pattern except perhaps to demonstrate sympathy for the state's interest in preserving flexible and minimally restricted sentencing procedures."[38] Although some states do provide for more formal process, typically under certain special sentencing statutes [see § 7.05] or as part of a move to determinate sentencing,[39] the Supreme Court does not require procedural stringency in "normal" sentencing.

The decisionmaking process in sentencing is informal in character for three reasons. First, the success of individualized sentencing is premised upon the ability of the judge to "know" the defendant. The Supreme Court has found that "highly relevant . . . if not essential . . . to [the judge's] selection of an appropriate sentence is the possession of the fullest information possible concerning the defendant's life and characteristics."[40] Because obtaining information about the defendant is deemed so important, courts have resisted arguments that the legal protections available to the defendant at trial—such as the Fifth Amendment's privilege against self-incrimination, or the hearsay rules—should apply to sentencing. There is a perception that formalizing the process would diminish the court's ability to obtain and use information about the defendant. According to the Supreme Court, "modern concepts of individualizing punishment have made it all the more necessary that the sentencing judge not be denied an opportunity to obtain pertinent information by a requirement of rigid adherence to restrictive rules of evidence properly applicable to trial."[41]

A second reason why the sentencing process is informal is parallel to the principle originally governing civil commitment proceedings and juvenile proceedings—an assumption that the state is acting in the individual's interest in constructing a plan for rehabilitation. Therefore, adherence to strict principles of due process, which are applied when the interests of state and individual are in conflict, is unnecessary.

Third, the informality is based in part on the assumption that society has "earned" the right to punish the individual, once convicted. The due process protections associated with trial are in place to reduce error in determining guilt to a permissible level. Once guilt is determined, the defendant, because of his or her convicted status, in some measure forfeits the right to strict due process protections when society determines the consequences of the criminal conduct.

(2) The Process Examined

In those jurisdictions where the jury sentences, the jury will either return a sentence with the verdict, or, if the statute calls for a bifurcated proceeding, return its verdict first and then consider sentence.

If the court is going to sentence, it may first order preparation of a presentence report. In federal court, similiar to most state jurisdictions, the court must order preparation of a report unless the defendant with the court's permission waives a presentence investigation and report, or the court finds that the record before it already contains sufficient information to enable the court to properly exercise its sentencing discretion.[42] The presentence report is prepared by a probation officer, following a standardized format composed of five core categories[43]: the offense, including the official version and the defendant's version, information about any codefendants, and statements of witnesses and victims; prior record, including juvenile adjudications; personal and family data, including the defendant's educational and employment background, financial condition, and physical and mental health; an evaluation section, which consists of alternative sentencing plans and data; and a recommendation for sentencing.[44]

The report is submitted to the court, which typically holds a conference with the probation officer.[45] The sentence hearing is then held. The defendant has a right to counsel at the hearing,[46] but other rights associated with trial (e.g., adherence to the rules of evidence and a right to cross-examine adverse witnesses) are not constitutionally mandated. Because hearsay evidence is admitted (and the presentence report relies heavily on such evidence), the ability of the defendant to obtain a copy of the report is critical. However, the extent to which disclosure is mandated is still debated, and it is less than total in even the most disclosure-oriented jurisdictions [see § 7.07(a)]. In reaching a sentencing decision, the court may consider any information, whether or not it has been presented in the presentence report or adduced by the defense. The only general exception to this principle is that the court cannot rely upon "misinformation of constitutional magnitude."[47] In articulating this exception, the Supreme Court barred the use by a sentencing judge of two prior convictions that were later found to be constitutionally invalid (because obtained when the defendant did not have counsel). This exception is limited, however; for example, the Court has allowed a sentencing judge to take into account a defendant's prior refusal to cooperate with a government investigation into other individuals,[48] as well as a belief that the defendant testified falsely at trial.[49]

At the conclusion of this informal process

(again noting an exception for capital penalty cases) the court imposes sentence.

7.04. Determinate Sentencing

A determinate sentencing scheme is premised upon the philosophy that "those whose criminal actions are equally reprehensible deserve like amounts of punishment."[50] Advocates of determinate sentencing posit several critical differences between it and the rehabilitative model. First, rehabilitation of the offender is not a primary goal of sentencing. Rather, retribution—that is, exacting from the offender "just desserts" for the offense—predominates.[51] Second, the "just deserts" model depends on the notion of proportionality: It requires that the severity of the sentence be proportionate to the gravity of the defendant's criminal conduct, whereas the indeterminate model focuses not on the defendant's conduct, but prospectively on his or her rehabilitative potential. Most importantly, the determinate model seeks to diminish discretion at sentencing. It does so by setting presumptive sentences that the court must impose, absent certain legislatively created aggravating or mitigating circumstances, and by allowing enhanced opportunities for appellate review of the sentencing court's decision. Such schemes also either reduce the parole board's authority to fix the ultimate length of sentence or, most commonly, eliminate the parole board altogether.

Despite these changes, we are persuaded that there is a continued, if somewhat modified, role for the clinician in a determinate scheme. Before discussing this role, we briefly describe the motivations behind the "just desserts" movement and look more closely at the basic tenets of determinate sentencing and how it works.

(a) Reasons behind the Shift to Determinate Sentencing

Some commentators believe that the perceived failure of the clinical professions has contributed to dissatisfaction with the rehabilitative model.

VonHirsch, for example, points out that the stage was set for rejection of the rehabilitation model by studies showing, first, that rehabilitation was simply not occurring,[52] and second, that clinicians could not reliably predict future dangerousness.[53] Monahan and Ruggiero have stated, "The move throughout the United States toward reducing judicial and parole board discretion in setting sentence is in large part an attempt to empty the basket of what is perceived to be its psychological and psychiatric refuse."[54] Others believe that clinicians have assumed an inappropriate role in the rehabilitative model. Hogarth, for example, asserts that the model leads clinicians into "the business of attempting to control people," and concludes that "It can be demonstrated that the rehabilitative ideal has led to neither humane nor effective sentencing decisions. Rather, it has led to massive disparity in the name of individualization, and longer sentences in the name of treatment."[55]

But the perceived failings of the clinical professions are only partly to blame for the move away from the rehabilitative model and indeterminate sentencing. First, as discussed more fully in § 7.07, it is clear that the primary reason for sentencing disparity is not clinical information per se, but the differing philosophies (e.g., retribution orientation rather than rehabilitation orientation) among sentencing judges themselves. Secondly, much of the criticism of the model has been ideological in nature and has had very little to do with the proper role of mental health professionals as witnesses or treaters. From the Left has come the complaint that indeterminate sentencing has "legitimated the expansion of powers used in practice to discriminate against disadvantaged groups and to achieve covert organizational goals (such as alleviating court backlogs and repressing political opposition),"[56] while those on the Right have favored determinate sentencing primarily as a means of ensuring more certain punishment. Others have wondered whether the rehabilitative model has not actually been countertherapeutic:

> The principal practical effect of an emphasis on "cure" has been to encourage convicts to

view their time in prison as an exercise in theatre. They "volunteer" for group therapy and other rehabilitative programs, say the right things about the help that they have received, and even find Christ and become guinea pigs for medical experimentation in hypocritical efforts to curry favor with parole boards. In addition, it has become increasingly apparent that the very indeterminancy of indeterminate sentences is a form of psychological torture.[57]

Such broad disenchantment with existing models made some change in sentencing statutes inevitable, regardless of the success of the mental health professions. Nonetheless, a widespread perception that clinicians have failed in a central role or have assumed an inappropriate role has fueled the trend toward determinate sentencing, just as similar perceptions of clinical shortcomings and abuses have been responsible for changes in civil commitment laws [see Chapter 8]. While the point is obvious, it is worth stating: Perceptions of clinical competence, derived largely from the legal system's experience with clinicians, play an important part not only in defining the impact clinical expertise may have in a given case, but also the legal context, as defined by statute and case law, in which clinicians will work.

(b) How Determinate Sentencing Schemes Work

Determinate sentencing models have gained increasing popularity since Maine enacted the first statute in 1976. By the early 1980s, at least 20 states were engaged in enacting major revisions of their sentencing laws, most based on some variation of a determinate sentencing model.[58]

As with the rehabilitative model, the nature of determinate sentencing can best be illustrated through an examination of the roles of the chief participants (the legislature, the prosecutor, the court, and the parole board).

(1) The Legislature

In indeterminate sentencing, the legislature sets wide ranges of possible sentences for categories of offenses, from which the sentencing judge chooses a sentence. Determinate sentencing attempts to reduce discretion, which can be accomplished in several ways. For instance, the authority for establishing sentence guidelines may be given to a sentencing commission. In 1982, at least three states (Washington, Pennsylvania, and Minnesota) had such commissions.[59] A sentencing commission sets sentencing guidelines by developing an actuarial-like table of penalties, using as criteria the severity of the offense and a prediction factor based primarily on prior criminal record.[60] The table establishes a recommended sentence, which becomes the "tariff" for that particular category of offense. The ma-

trix established by the Minnesota commission is set out in Figure 7-1.

If the legislature retains the authority to establish sentencing guidelines, it may attempt to reduce discretion in sentencing in one of the following ways. First, it may use presumptive sentencing, whereby the legislature establishes three possible terms for each offense.[61] The middle term is the presumptive one, which will become the sentence unless the court specifically finds the existence of statutorily created aggravated circumstances (in which case the higher sentence will be given) or mitigating circumstances (in which case the lower sentence will be assessed). For example, the legislature might establish five

Figure 7-1. *Minnesota Sentencing Matrix: Sentencing by severity of offense and criminal history. [From Tonry,* Real Offense Sentencing: The Model Sentencing and Correction Act, *72 J. CRIM. L. & CRIMINOLOGY 1550, 1558 (1981). Reprinted by permission.]*

		CRIMINAL HISTORY SCORE						
SEVERITY LEVELS OF CONVICTION OFFENSE		0	1	2	3	4	5	6 or more
Unauthorized Use of Motor Vehicle Possession of Marijuana	I	12*	12*	12*	15	18	21	24
Theft-related Crimes ($150-$2500) Sale of Marijuana	II	12*	12*	14	17	20	23	27 25-29
Theft Crimes ($150-$2500)	III	12*	13	16	19	22 21-23	27 25-29	32 30-34
Burglary - Felony Intent Receiving Stolen Goods ($150-$2500)	IV	12*	15	18	21	25 24-26	32 30-34	41 37-45
Simple Robbery	V	18	23	27	30 29-31	38 36-40	46 43-49	54 50-58
Assault, 2nd Degree	VI	21	26	30	34 33-35	44 42-46	54 50-58	65 60-70
Aggravated Robbery	VII	24 23-25	32 30-34	41 38-44	49 45-53	65 60-70	81 75-87	97 90-104
Assault, 1st Degree Criminal Sexual Conduct, 1st Degree	VIII	43 41-45	54 50-58	65 60-70	76 71-81	95 89-101	113 106-120	132 124-140
Murder, 3rd Degree	IX	97 94-100	119 116-122	127 124-130	149 143-155	176 168-184	205 195-215	230 218-242
Murder, 2nd Degree	X	116 111-121	140 133-147	162 153-171	203 192-214	243 231-255	284 270-298	324 309-339

1st Degree Murder is excluded from the guidelines by law and continues to have a mandatory life sentence.

*   one year and one day

Source: Minnesota Sentencing Guidelines Commission, Report to the Legislature 14 (1980)

years' imprisonment as the presumptive term for armed robbery, four years as the term to be imposed if the defendant can demonstrate the existence of a legislatively created mitigating circumstance (e.g., age, mental disturbance), and six years as the term if the prosecution can show the existence of a legislatively created circumstance that allows the "normal" penalty to be enhanced (e.g., multiple counts, prior convictions). Therefore, all defendants convicted of armed robbery in such a jurisdiction would normally receive a five-year term. Individual differences in sentencing would depend upon proof of mitigating or aggravating circumstances.

A second approach is the definite sentence, whereby the legislature sets a range of sentences, and the court imposes a sentence within that range.[62] However, unlike an indeterminate sentence, a "definite sentence" is fixed, so the defendant knows the time to be served when the sentence is imposed. Moreover, the court in these jurisdictions is usually directed to consider only specific factors in choosing a sentence.[63]

Thus, all determinate sentencing schemes are more specific than the typical statute in a rehabilitative sentencing model; rather than setting a very wide range of punishments, the legislature provides explicit alternative terms. However, as discussed in more detail below [see §7.04(c)], the use of aggravating and mitigating factors continues to evidence legislative recognition that it is appropriate to differentiate among offenders on the basis of at least some individual characteristics.

(2)   The Prosecutor

The determinate sentencing statutes enacted to date do not appreciably curb prosecutorial discretion. While some local jurisdictions and one state have attempted to reduce or eliminate plea bargaining, the impact upon sentencing has been limited.[64] At least one commentator has predicted that determinate sentencing statutes will not achieve their objectives until the prosecutor's power to formulate charges and to bargain for guilty pleas is checked.[65]

(3)   The Court

Judicial discretion is reduced (though, as made clear above, not eliminated) in a determinate sentencing scheme. First, the court generally must impose a specific sentence, and has less discretion in choosing the actual term imposed. Second, the statutes typically require the court to state in writing the reasons for any deviation from the legislated norm, and make such sentences more readily appealable. In addition, since rehabilitation is no longer the primary goal, and since the statutes list aggravating and mitigating circumstances, a court in a determinate sentencing jurisdiction must narrow its focus—looking not at the "total" offender, as it is encouraged to do in indeterminate sentencing, but only at offender traits matching the characteristics that the sentencing commission or legislature deems relevant.

(4)   The Parole Board

The parole board loses most of its discretion in a determinate sentencing scheme. In fact, it is often abolished,[66] or its authority is drastically diminished,[67] since it exists to determine when the offender serving an indeterminate sentence is sufficiently rehabilitated to leave prison. The board is a creature of the rehabilitative model; as that model is abandoned, the board loses its primary reason for existence.

(c)   Process in a Determinate Sentencing Scheme

The provisions described above are designed to curb judicial discretion at sentencing. But they also lead to a more formal process, for three reasons. First, a judicial finding that an aggravating or mitigating circumstance exists is a finding of fact that may lead to an enhanced or reduced penalty. The traditional response of the legal system when a decisionmaker must determine the existence of a fact, particularly with consequences for individual liberty, is to formalize the process by adopting an adversarial proceeding in which each party presents evidence and has the right of cross-examination.

Second, in determinate sentencing, when assessing whether the sentencing court acted properly, the appellate court will need to examine the reasons for the court's action. The reasons will be a product of the facts of the case—facts that, it will be argued, should have been developed through an adversary process preserved on a written record.

A movement toward a more formalized process also may be hastened by the abandonment of the rehabilitative ideal and the substitution of a more punitive sentencing philosophy. Weissman has argued that "the relaxed practices associated with rehabilitative sentencing cannot be reconciled with a sentencing model that does not emphasize values of individualization and treatment"[68]; he believes that as sentencing moves from an "inquisitorial" to an "accusatorial" model, it must inevitably become more formal in order to protect adequately individual interests.[69]

Such a transformation would not be without precedent. An analogous situation developed in both civil commitment and juvenile law. As the courts rejected the notion that the state's interest was fundamentally benevolent in these contexts and defined the primary area of concern as the individual's liberty interests, more safeguards were applied at the point of decisionmaking. Whether the sentencing process becomes as formal may depend on the willingness of the judiciary to accept an argument that convicted individuals have liberty interests in sentencing analogous to those of juveniles and potential patients.

(d) Preliminary Assessments of Determinate Sentencing Statutes

A few studies have addressed the impact of determinate sentencing statutes, with mixed results. A study in Minnesota found the statute in that state has met *some* goals.[70] First, there has been a change in the composition of the population sentenced to prison, with the percentage of those convicted of more serious offenses increasing in proportion to those convicted of property offenses.[71] According to the author of

the study, this reflects a changed focus from the offender to the seriousness of the offense—a change that is a stated goal of determinate sentencing. Second, more severe sanctions have been imposed for more severe offenses, so the concept of proportionality has not been offended.[72]

At the same time, the study revealed continued sentencing disparities across judicial districts.[73] Sentencing has been more uniform for Caucasians than for members of minority groups, and the use of aggravating factors has been significantly more prevalent in the cases of minority-group members than in those of Caucasians.[74] Also, though the guidelines prohibit consideration of employment status at sentencing, such status has continued to affect disposition significantly, with the unemployed being imprisoned five times as frequently as the employed.[75] Finally, evidence of prosecutorial manipulation of charging and plea bargaining has been observed.[76]

Similar findings come from an analysis of the Indiana statute.[77] This study found that the statute fails to curb prosecutorial or judicial discretion, and permits penalties that are so harsh that it may affect the willingness of parties to utilize them. As a result, the probable outcome of the statute, according to the researchers, will be creation of a low-visibility process for arranging sentences: The statute "combines such wide discretion with untenably heavy penalties that actual decisionmaking will exist informally through judges, prosecutors, and correctional officers, and through manipulation of prosecutorial charges and evaluation of inmate behavior through credit time."[78] The authors conclude that "our closing comments may well be summarized as a question: why did they bother with it?"[79]

Research has also indicated a lack of consistent adherence to the goals of determinate sentencing. A comparative analysis[80] of the first determinate sentencing statutes (Maine, California, Illinois, and Indiana) has revealed "vast differences" in the following:

- Constraints on judicial discretion to choose or reject incarceration.
- The delimitation of judicial discretion generally at sentencing.

- The specificity of aggravating and mitigating factors.
- The use of "good time" to reduce the length of incarceration.
- The range of possible penalties for a given offense.
- The degree to which determinate sentencing as practiced in the particular jurisdiction resembles indeterminate sentencing.

The analysis concludes that "it would appear that the speed with which sentencing revisions are being endorsed may well hinder reasoned analysis of the need for reform, the nature of desired reform, and the outcome of reform once implemented."[81]

While assessment of the impact of these statutes awaits further empirical analysis, it is clear that the concept of determinate sentencing is not without its problems. Assuming, however, that the concept continues to be attractive to state legislatures, the important question for our purposes is its impact on clinical participation at sentencing.

(e) Is There a Role for the Clinician in Determinate Sentencing?

The law has long relied upon and utilized clinical opinion in assessing culpability and in measuring the "worthiness" of imposing punishment. Even under determinate sentencing, it is unlikely that the criminal law will abandon this tradition of allowing a defendant an opportunity to present distinguishing individual characteristics that provide mitigation to the offense. As Monahan and Ruggiero have asserted,

> [T]o the extent predictions by psychiatrists and psychologists of future criminal behavior are eliminated from the sentencing process, these disciplines will assume a correspondingly larger role as experts on "culpability" during the trial itself, at sentencing, or in post trial "diversionary" commitments imposed in lieu of imprisonment.[82]

In fact, most determinate sentencing statutes invite clinical participation—primarily through the use of mitigating circumstances, proof of which may result in a reduced sentence. For example, the Minnesota guidelines include the following as mitigating circumstances:

> (1) the offender played a minor or *passive* role in the crime or participated under circumstances of coercion or *duress.*
> (2) The offender, because of physical or *mental impairment,* lacked *substantial capacity* for judgment when the offense was committed . . .
> (3) Other substantial grounds exist which tend to excuse or *mitigate the offender's culpability,* although not amounting to a defense.[83] (emphasis added)

In other states, such as Florida, mitigating factors are unspecified but judges continue to rely on "psychiatric reasons" for setting sentences below the presumptive level. Thus, even in jurisidictions where the court is bound to reduce the presumptive sentence by the same amount for everyone proving a mitigating circumstance because the legislature has created a uniform "mitigated" sentence for those who qualify for it, the *potential* for clinical opinion in a defendant's effort to show mitigation appears to be little affected.

7.05. *Special Sentencing Provisions*

Most jurisdictions have devised special sentencing statutes for discrete populations. These statutes reflect a legislative determination that certain populations are sufficiently different from the mass of criminal defendants to warrant the use of specialized procedures. The populations most frequently singled out for special sentencing are repeat offenders; those who have committed or may commit sexual offenses; youthful offenders; and certain types of drug users.

(a) Repeat Offender Statutes: Mandatory Sentencing

Nearly all jurisdictions have statutes allowing and in many cases mandating increased sentencing for those convicted repeatedly of felonies.[84] These statutes, usually called "repeat" or "habitual" offender statutes, typically prescribe enhanced sentencing upon conviction of a third or fourth felony. For example, Indiana law defines a habitual offender in the following way:

> A person is an habitual offender if the jury (if the hearing is by jury), or the court (if the hearing is to the court alone), finds that the state has proved beyond a reasonable doubt that the person had accumulated two (2) prior unrelated felony convictions.[85]

A person found to be a habitual offender receives an increased sentence for the conviction which triggered the habitual offender finding. For example, the Indiana law provides for imposition of an additional 30-year term of imprisonment above the usual penalty for the offense.[86]

These statutes assume that "the effect of imprisonment on street crime is a direct function of the rate at which incarcerated offenders would have committed crimes if they were not confined."[87] However, they have been criticized for falling most heavily upon petty criminals and older offenders who may be approaching the end of their criminal careers.[88]

Despite the harshness of the penalties available under these statutes, they have survived constitutional scrutiny. In the case of *Rummel v. Estelle*,[89] the Supreme Court upheld a Texas habitual offender statute that set a sentence of mandatory life imprisonment for a person convicted of a third felony. The case involved a defendant convicted of using a credit card to fraudulently obtain $80 worth of goods. He had previously been convicted of forging a check for $28.36, and of obtaining $120.75 by false pretenses. Sentenced to life imprisonment for the third conviction, he challenged his sentence on the ground that it violated the Eighth Amendment prohibition against cruel and unusual punishment. The Court rejected the challenge, finding that it was for the legislature to determine when an individual could be found to warrant such sentencing. The Court has thus placed its imprimature on virtually unlimited legislative discretion in sentencing repeat offenders.[90] It later held, in *Solem v. Helm*,[91] that the imposition of a life sentence for a sixth check-writing crime was unconstitutional where, unlike the situation in *Rummel*, there was no possibility of parole. However, the Court in *Solem* vigorously reaffirmed the general principle that habitual offender statutes are constitutional and that individual sentences will be overturned only in extreme circumstances.

Because habitual offender statutes are not rehabilitative, and are designed to segregate certain offenders from society for long periods of time in order to incapacitate them, clinical involvement at the formal sentencing process is likely to be minimal—particularly because the statutes operate primarily on the basis of accumulated convictions, an objective measure. Nonetheless, the enhanced penalties make it probable that defense counsel will seek clinical opinion in order to introduce ameliorative factors that might influence the prosecutor in deciding whether to invoke the habitual offender statute. A desire to avoid such statutes may also result in referral on the issue of criminal responsibility: Hospitalization, even for a long term, may appear desirable in contrast to a mandatory term of imprisonment lasting several decades.

(b) Sexual Offender Statutes

A decreasing but still significant number of states have special dispositional provisions for individuals charged with multiple "sexual offenses," who are designated as "sexual psychopaths," "mentally disordered sex offenders" (MDSOs), or by some similar rubric.[92] These statutes have two primary goals: the protection of society by sequestering sexual offenders so long as they remain a danger to others; and the rehabilitation of such individuals through treatment.[93] These twin concerns, involving prediction and treatment, invite clinical participation as forthrightly as any area of criminal law. In fact, these statutes "were meant to be harbingers of a future in which all criminals would be 'treated' under similar provisions."[94]

The offenses that these statutes attempt to reach typically involve sexual acts of a threatening or violent nature or those involving minors. There are two types of proceedings for determining whether an individual meets statutory criteria. The first type determines whether there should be special commitment as a "sexual psychopath" *after* conviction of an offense falling within the statute.[95] Such proceedings require more formal procedural protections than are required ordinarily at sentencing. The Supreme Court has ruled in *Specht v. Patterson,*[96] that a finding that an individual was a "sexual offender" constitutes a new finding of fact of serious consequence to the defendant, and that the defendant therefore is entitled to an adversary proceeding on the issue.

The second type of proceeding takes place after a charge for a sex offense has been filed but *before* conviction occurs.[97] A proceeding of this type is labeled "civil" in nature. "While *Specht* probably requires notice, a right to hearing, and a right to counsel under such statutes,[98] the Supreme Court has also indicated that the Fifth Amendment's privilege against self-incrimination does not apply at such proceedings.[99]

Regardless of approach, the statutes share several attributes:

- Commission of a sexual offense is required.
- The conduct generally must involve force or aggression, or involve minors.
- The conduct must be repetitive. Unlike repeat offender statutes, however, actual demonstration of specific past offenses is not always required, and the idea of repetition may be satisfied by a prediction of future conduct.
- The offender has a mental illness, though the term as used is broad enough to include many types of character disorders.
- The individual, once labeled, is to be treated, though a finding on the question of whether in fact the offender is treatable is typically not required.
- Commitment is indeterminate, based on the individual's continued "need for treatment."[100]

Since the 1970s, these statutes have been stongly attacked. The Group for the Advancement of Psychiatry (GAP) concluded that "first and foremost, sex psychopath and sexual offender statutes can best be described as approaches that have failed,"[101] and called for repeal of all sexual psychopath statutes. The proposed standards of the American Bar Association (ABA) call for repeal as well.[102] These recommendations are based upon a conclusion that the assumptions underlying sexual offender legislation are unsupportable.

For example, according to GAP's report, the categorization process projected by sexual psychopath statutes lacks clinical validity. The assumption that a "hybrid amalgam of law and psychiatry can validly label a person a 'sex psychopath' or 'sex offender' and then treat him is rejected as analogous to creating special categories of 'burglary offender' statutes or 'white collar' offender statutes."[103]

GAP also concluded that while the statutes promise therapy, they in fact serve primarily to reassure the community of its own safety.[104] They thus may compromise clinicians in two ways. First, clinicians may be asked to make "generalizations about sex offenders not grounded in empirical data from the individual case which often do more harm to the individual and society than no statements at all."[105] Second, the absence of meaningful treatment programs for the condition diagnosed raises an ethical as well as practical dilemma for clinicians: "[P]erhaps the worst thing a psychiatrist can do is tailor his opinion to whatever compromised versions of treatment are currently being offered, thus putting himself in the role of sanctioning treatments in which he does not believe."[106] GAP also noted the invalidity of predictions about sexual dangerousness.

There is evidence that these criticisms have had an impact, and that these statutes have lost favor in many jurisdictions.[107] However, where they continue to exist, the clinician called upon to perform such an examination should be aware that they rest upon assumptions of dubious validity, thus raising ethical and practical questions for the clinician that may demand nonparticipation [see § 7.08 (a)].

(c) Youthful Offenders

Special sentencing procedures also exist for "youthful" offenders, a category of offenders defined by age. This category falls between "juveniles," who are usually tried in juvenile court, and adult offenders, who are generally subject to the "normal" sentencing procedures described earlier in this chapter. This section describes briefly the Federal Youth Correction Act (YCA),[108] the prototype of similar state statutes.

Congress passed the YCA in 1950. Its passage arose from perceptions that youths committed a disproportionate amount of crime and that the penitentiary system had failed as applied to youths.[109] The YCA was rehabilitative in intent,[110] and was designed to "cure" young offenders while this might still be possible.

The YCA defines a "youthful offender" as a "person under the age of twenty two years at the time of conviction."[111] An individual between the ages of 22 and up to but not including 26 at the time of conviction may also be sentenced under the YCA if the court finds there are "reasonable grounds" to believe that the defendant will benefit from treatment. The court is to make this decision after considering the previous record of the defendant as to delinquency or criminal experience; the defendant's social background, capabilities, and mental and physical health; and other pertinent factors.[112]

If an individual meets the age requirements, the court must sentence him or her as a youthful offender, absent an explicit finding that the individual would not derive benefit from treatment.[113] The court may sentence a youthful offender for an indeterminate period generally not to exceed six years, with confinement not to exceed four years.[114] The "treatment" provided is defined in the YCA as "corrective and preventive guidance and training designed to protect the public by correcting the antisocial tendencies of youth offenders."[115] This reflects concern not only with the offender's rehabilitation, but with community protection.

The parole commission sets the actual length of sentence, as it does with adult offenders.[116] If the youthful offender is unconditionally discharged prior to the expiration of the maximum sentence imposed, the conviction is automatically "set aside," and the individual is given a certificate to that effect.[117]

The YCA and its progeny are pristine examples of the rehabilitative model of sentencing. They combine clearly articulated rehabilitative intent, indeterminate sentencing for "treat-

ment," and a presumption that the defendant qualifies for such a disposition. Given this orientation, such statutes present myriad opportunities for clinical participation, from assessing defendants' eligibility for inclusion to design of a rehabilitative plan to govern the terms of disposition.

At the same time, the lawyer and the clinician should be aware that such laws have been fairly criticized for a number of important failings. For example, Ritz has concluded that those charged with minor offenses receive disproportionately harsh sentences under the YCA.[118] This results from the fact that the statute authorizes sentence of up to six years for even the most minor offense. The provision for setting aside a YCA conviction in certain situations is "overrated," in part because the YCA does not require, nor by its terms expressly authorize, the sealing of a youth's criminal records.[119] Finally, Ritz concludes that the court can and does manipulate the provision requiring a finding that the defendant will not benefit from treatment before refusing to apply the YCA, depending upon technically irrelevant factors such as perceived dangerousness.[120]

As these criticisms demonstrate, the fact that a proceeding on its face is primarily rehabilitative does not mean that it should be uncritically embraced by the clinician as the most desirable dispositional alternative in a given case. The reality is that in a particular case a statute or process may work in a fashion antithetical to individual interests. This suggests, as is observed continually throughout this book, the need for the clinician to obtain comprehensive information about the case *and* its context (including the possible implications of the legal proceeding giving rise to the referral), and to avoid the ultimate issue of disposition.

(d) Drug-Dependent Offenders

The final category of special sentencing statutes considered here is that for drug-dependent offenders. Application of these statutes turns on the issue of an offender's addiction. The statutory goals of rehabilitation and community protection[121] are implemented primarily through diversion of the offender for an indeterminate period of time for treatment of the addiction. The federal law[122] again illustrates the most important statutory features.

The court may order the postconviction examination of any "eligible offender" who it believes is an "addict."[123] "Eligible offenders" include anyone convicted of *any* offense against the United States, except those convicted of a crime of violence or of importing or selling narcotics, and certain categories of prior offenders.

The examination and subsequent court determination are to decide whether an offender is an "addict." An "addict" is defined as "any individual who habitually uses any narcotic drug as defined in section 102(16) of the Controlled Substance Act so as to endanger the public morals, health, safety, or welfare, or who is or has been so far addicted to the use of such narcotic drugs as to have lost the power of self-control with reference to his addiction."[124] If the court finds that the offender is an addict, and is likely to be rehabilitated through treatment, the individual is committed for treatment for an indefinite period not to exceed ten years. The individual must be treated for at least six months before becoming eligible for conditional release. After this, the determination as to the offender's status rests with the parole commission.

The statute broadly defines "treatment" to include institutional care; community-based care; medical, educational, social, psychological, and vocational services; corrective and preventive guidance and training; and other rehabilitative services designed to protect the public and benefit the addict by eliminating his or her dependence.

As with the YCA, the opportunities for clinical participation under this act are not only evident but explicit in the statutory goals, definitions, and procedures. The cautionary concerns expressed with reference to the YCA also apply here: The lawyer and the clinician should not automatically assume that disposition under this statute is necessarily in the best interests of the client. Familiarity with the facts of the given case, and with the implications of the legal proceeding in which the defendant is involved, is a prerequisite to the informed clinical evaluation.

7.06. Capital Sentencing

Clinical opinion will be preferred or sought in most capital cases. The impulse to collect all available information about the defendant, which drives all sentencing procedures, is strongest when the penalty may be death. At the same time, because of the ultimate nature of the death penalty, a number of issues that often lurk underneath the surface of "normal" sentencing (e.g., qualitative problems with many forensic reports, and certain ethical problems) emerge in sharp focus.

This section describes the substantive and procedural criteria that the United States Supreme Court has found acceptable at sentencing when the death penalty may be imposed. The ethical problems that clinicians must confront when participating in such a process are discussed in § 7.10(f).

(a) Substantive Criteria

In a long series of decisions, beginning in 1972 with *Furman vs. Georgia,*[125] the United States Supreme Court has shaped the constitutionally permissible substantive and procedural criteria for imposition of the death penalty. In *Furman,* the Court found the Texas and Georgia statutes unconstitutional because they were applied in an arbitrary and irrational manner. Each of the nine Justices wrote a separate opinion, making it fruitless to describe the "Court's opinion." However, Justice Brennan perhaps best articulated a theme running through the opinions of the five Justices who voted to invalidate the statutes:

> [W]hen a country of over 200 million people inflicts an unusually severe punishment no more than 50 times a year, the inference is strong that the punishment is not being regularly and fairly applied. To dispel it would indeed require a clear showing of nonarbitrary infliction

. . . [otherwise] it smacks of little more than a lottery system.[126]

Justice Douglas described the populations arbitrarily singled out for those rare occasions when death was imposed: "It is the poor, the sick, the ignorant, the powerless and the hated that are executed."[127]

Since 1972, the Court has attempted to make imposition of the death penalty less arbitrary. It has started with the premise that the death penalty is unique in the criminal justice system:

> The penalty of death is qualitatively different from a sentence of imprisonment, however long. Death, in its finality, differs more from life imprisonment than a 100 year prison term differs from one of only a year or two.[128]

The court has emphasized that the substantive criteria for determining the appropriateness of the death penalty must give the judge or jury the opportunity to consider the individual offender's characteristics. Thus, it has banned mandatory death sentences for certain types of offenses,[129] and upheld those statutes listing aggravating and mitigating circumstances for the decisionmaker to consider in imposing sentences.[130] The court has also made clear that the decisionmaker must be allowed to consider *all* relevant mitigating evidence about the defendant. In *Lockett v. Ohio*, it struck down an Ohio law that "did not permit the sentencing judge to consider as mitigating factors, (the defendant's) character, prior record, age, lack of specific intent to cause death, and her relatively minor part in the crime."[131] The Court reiterated an earlier observation that "in capital cases the fundamental respect for humanity underlying the Eighth Amendment . . . requires consideration of the character and record of the individual offender and the circumstances of the particular offense as a constitutionally indispensable part of the process of inflicting the penalty of death."[132]

As a result, the typical capital sentencing statute sets out a list of both aggravating *and* mitigating factors. The prosecution must prove the existence of at least one of the aggravating factors before the death penalty may be imposed. In most states, this proof must be beyond a reasonable doubt, although in some states the statute is silent on this point.[133] None of the capital sentencing statutes tells the factfinder how to balance aggravating and mitigating circumstances. Presumably, the jury is permitted to treat an offender with only one aggravating trait and six mitigating traits in the same way as an offender who meets two aggravating factors and is unable to produce any evidence in mitigation. Thus, although some potential for discrimination has been removed, considerable leeway for discretion still exists.

The specific aggravating and mitigating factors vary among jurisdictions. However, most are phrased in terms that seem to invite clinical participation. For example, roughly half the states provide that facts in mitigation may include proof that

(ii) . . . the defendant was under the influence of extreme mental or emotional distress or . . .

(iv) . . . the capacity of the defendant to appreciate the criminality of his conduct or to conform his conduct to the requirements of law was significantly impaired . . .[134]

Similarly, often included among the *aggravating* factors the decisionmaker may consider is future dangerousness. For example, Virginia provides that the death sentence may not be imposed unless the state proves either that the offense had certain characteristics (e.g., was "outrageously or wantonly vile") or that "there is a probability . . . that he would commit criminal acts of violence that would constitute a continuing serious threat to society."[135]

Despite the difficulty of predicting violent behavior, the Supreme Court has upheld the constitutional validity of statutes mandating an affirmative prediction of future dangerousness as a prerequisite for imposing death.[136] It has also explicitly found that the Constitution does not bar clinical testimony on the subject. To the American Psychiatric Association's argument that long-term predictions of dangerousness are so unreliable that they should be proscribed at capital sentencing, the Court, in *Barefoot v. Estelle*, glibly responded: "The suggestion that no psychiatrist's testimony may be presented with regard to dangerousness is somewhat like asking us to disinvent the wheel."[137] More is said about *Barefoot* in § 7.10.

(b) Procedural Criteria

In contrast to normal sentencing, the process when death is the potential sentence is much more formalized and provides the defendant with many of the procedural protections normally associated with trial. As Justice Blackmun has observed:

> In ensuring that the death penalty is not meted out arbitrarily or capriciously, the Court's principal concern has been more with the procedure by which the State imposes the death penalty than with the substantive factors the state lays before the jury as a basis for imposing death, once it has been determined that the defendant falls within the category of persons eligible for the death penalty.[138]

In large part, this concern with process reflects a need for increased reliability in the information utilized at death penalty proceedings, a need stemming from the "ultimate" nature of the penalty. The typical death penalty statute provides the following procedural protections[139]:

- The determination of guilt or innocence and sentencing is bifurcated—that is, occurs at two separate proceedings.
- The defendant must have access to all information to be relied upon by the decision-maker, and if certain information is withheld, it must be made available in the record for appeal.[140]
- The reasons for the sentence must be stated in writing.
- Automatic appellate review by the state's highest court is available.
- Rules of evidence usually apply, though their application is not constitutionally compelled.[141]

Additionally, in practice, any obstacles to obtaining expert assistance are normally relaxed in capital cases. Indeed, in *Ake v. Oklahoma*,[142] the Supreme Court held that the capital defendant is *entitled* to psychiatric assistance when dangerousness is an issue in capital sentencing (although it also limited this assistance to *one* clinician).

7.07. Factors Influencing Sentencing and Their Implications for the Mental Health Professional

The foregoing analysis reveals that mental health professionals may provide input on a variety of issues relevant to sentencing. Though different sentencing philosophies emphasize different roles for the clinician, in actual practice there is room under various sentencing schemes for clinical input. Whether, and under what circumstances, this input might be pivotal at sentencing is difficult to say, since sentencing may be influenced by a variety of considerations other than clinical factors. Before examining the various roles a clinician might take at sentencing, we review briefly some of the nonclinical influences on the sentences assigned by judges and juries.

(a) Presentence Reports

The probation officer's presentence report described in § 7.03(c) (2) is generally conceded to be the most influential factor in those cases where it is prepared.[143] Judges are more likely to pay attention to it than to any other piece of evidence introduced at sentencing. The clinician and the lawyer should be aware of the central role occupied by the presentence report, if for no other reason than to check any assumption that the clinical report prepared for sentencing is the sole or even the primary source of information available to the court.

It is also important to note that the presentence report plays a critical role in the life of the offender after sentencing. For example, in the federal system, the Bureau of Prisons uses the report in assigning the individual to a particular institution; in assigning him or her to a particular level of security within the institution; in preparation of the "classification" study, which is the plan designed to meet the offender's particular needs; in determining the conditions of the inmate's existence (e.g., visitation rights, work-study release, transfer to another institution) and making decisions on granting or withholding good-time credits; and in assisting the parole commission in determining the appropriateness of granting parole.[144]

Because of the importance attached to the presentence report both during and after sentencing, its accuracy is a paramount concern. However, more than one study has concluded that there are "numerous instances of serious inaccuracies in presentence reports."[145] Despite this, mandatory disclosure of the presentence report to the defendant traditionally has not been required. Only in recent years has a trend developed toward disclosure to the defense to provide an opportunity for correcting erroneous information. A paradigmatic example is rule 32 of the Federal Rules of Criminal Procedure. Effective in 1974, the rule provides that before imposing sentence, the court upon request shall permit the defendant or counsel to read the presentence report, exclusive of any sentence recommendation.[146] Disclosure is not complete, however. In addition to excising the sentence recommendation, the court may limit disclosure if in the court's opinion "the report contains diagnostic opinion which might seriously disrupt a program of rehabilitation, sources of information obtained upon a promise of confidentiality, or any other information which, if disclosed, might result in harm."[147] The court is to summarize deleted information and provide the summary to the defendant; the defendant may comment upon both the report and the summary of deleted information, and may introduce information relating to any alleged factual inaccuracy in the presentence report.[148]

The rule represents an attempt to balance the court's interest in obtaining and relying upon *all* information about the defendant, and the defendant's interest in having sentencing based upon accurate information. A study of the impact of this rule concluded that disclosure, despite fears

to the contrary, had not had a negative impact on the sentencing process.[149] However, the manner in which some courts utilized the exceptions to disclosure had potentially troubling consequences for the expressed aim of the rule, which is to improve the accuracy of the presentence report. For instance, some courts withheld disclosure of law enforcement information under the rubric of "diagnostic information."[150] Since this information is notoriously unreliable, and may have a significant impact on sentencing, these courts were undercutting the purpose of disclosure.

To the extent that the clinician can gain access to the presentence report, it may provide useful information. Clearly, its impact on sentencing will be substantial.

(b) Judicial Philosophy

A second important factor influencing sentencing, perhaps obviously, is the judge's own predilections. One study, which examined on a national level sentencing in the federal courts, focused specifically on the disparity among judges in sentencing for similarly situated offenders; it concluded that "more variance in sentences is explained by differences among individual judges than by any other single factor."[151]

Similarly, in her discussion of factors that contribute to sentencing disparity, Diamond[152] identified varying judicial goals in sentencing as an important factor. Some judges seem more attuned to retributive considerations, while others are prone to seek dispositions that further rehabilitative ends. Cases in which individual philosophies among judges play the most important role are probably those in which conflicting information (e.g., both aggravating and mitigating) is present.

(c) Other Nonclinical Factors

A variety of other factors have been shown to be related to sentencing decisions.[153] In one study, it was revealed that offenders who were found guilty by a jury received harsher sentences than offenders found guilty through plea bargaining[154]; the implication was that the defendants were being penalized for exercising their constitutional right to a trial by jury. Another study identified factors associated with the administration of the criminal justice system that affected sentencing decisions: Individuals who did not gain pretrial freedom through bail and those who had appointed as opposed to retained counsel were subject to more severe sentences.[155] Not surprisingly, factors related to characteristics of the offender also play a role in sentencing. In the same study, it was shown that more severe sentences resulted in cases involving the use of threat of physical harm, and a record of prior felony convictions (but not misdemeanor convictions) was also significant. Among demographic variables considered (age, marital status, educational level, race, etc.), gender was the most important variable, with women receiving less severe sentences.[156]

(d) The Impact of Clinical Recommendations

Despite the widespread use of clinicians at sentencing, and the law's traditional acceptance of mental disorder as a mitigating factor at disposition, the impact of clinical opinion may be insignificant in many cases—either in the sense that the judge pays no attention to it, or in the sense that the judge merely uses it to justify "scientifically" a decision he or she has already made.

Several studies have reported concordance rates between psychiatrists' presentence recommendations and the courts' sentences. Studies from other countries reviewed by Campbell[157] revealed high concordance rates—93% in Tasmania, 77–95% in England. Rates of agreement varied, however, with the specific type of disposition recommended: 17% when the recommendation was for discharge from court custody, 77% when probation was recommended, and 91% when incarceration was advised.[158] Smith[159] reported overall significant agreement

in his study of North Carolina sentencing practices, where the court concurred with 87% of the recommendations for probation and with 70% of the recommendations for treatment.

Moderately high concordance rates have thus been reported. However, it would be erroneous to read this literature as indicating that psychiatric recommendations are overly influential. Campbell[160] has noted that agreement estimates may be high in part because in some cases the disposition is "obvious," and in others because the courts and the clinicians may use common criteria in their decisionmaking. It has also been speculated that the courts' agreement with psychiatric recommendations may vary as a function of the seriousness of the offense charged. Dershowitz[161] has noted that the high concordance rates reported by Smith and others occurred in settings where court referral of less serious offenders was common. In studies where more serious offenders were referred, as in Bohmer's study of sex offenders in Philadelphia, agreement rates were substantially lower.[162]

One reason for the lack of influence attributable to clinical input in many types of cases is the relatively significant impact of the other types of input previously discussed. For example, Bohmer found that recommendations contained in presentence reports received considerably more attention than psychiatric reports, which had a "low rate of acceptance" by the courts.[163] A second reason is that many judges may be inclined to view mental health professionals as "bleeding hearts" who too often find pathology as an excuse for criminal behavior and are unrealistic about the true rehabilitative potential in a given case. A third reason—and one that mental health professionals may be prone to forget—is that even under an indeterminate sentencing scheme, rehabilitation is only one of many factors the judge must consider. In particular, retributive, incapacitative, and deterrence concerns may become paramount, especially as the seriousness of the crime escalates.

Whereas the data regarding ordinary sentencing suggest that clinical opinion has little sustained effect on judicial sentencing policy, research looking at clinical input in special-track sentencing suggests the opposite. The most systematic studies have focused on the influence of psychiatric classifications of "defective delinquent" and "mentally disordered sex offender" (MDSO). Studies conducted when the Maryland "defective delinquent" statute was in force revealed 82% and 91% concordance between the Patuxent Institution staff's recommendations for commitment and the courts' dispositions in two separate ten-year samples.[164] A study in California involving offenders evaluated for MDSO status resulted in a similar finding: 91% of the court's placements were consistent with the clinicians' recommendations.[165]

While these studies suggest that clinicians held considerable power in the disposition of these cases, the investigators in California discovered that both the clinicians' classifications (MDSO/not MDSO) and the judge's dispositions were highly influenced by a single variable—prior convictions for sexual offenses.[166] The information in the psychiatrists' reports thus added little discriminating power to the judge's decisions. The clinicians' judgments were highly predictable from information that is readily available to the layperson and that requires no particular clinical skill or acuity either to gather or to interpret [see § 7.10(b)]. As others have contended, psychiatric involvement in these kinds of decisions may serve primarily to pacify the public and policymakers by providing a humanistic facade to what is primarily a social control function.[167]

(e) The Role of the Mental Health Professional at Sentencing

Despite this rather grim assessment of clinical participation at sentencing, mental health professionals do have a role to play at this stage of the criminal process, although one that is perhaps more restricted than the role envisioned by those who most avidly support the rehabilitative model. In our view, the mental health professional can best serve the sentencing process by carefully developing material about the individual that helps explain the way in which the offender differs from stereotypical notions the court might have about those convicted of a particular offense. That is, the clinician should try, in those cases where it is appropriate, to answer the judicial question: "How is this offender different from any of the hundreds of others I've seen?"

The content of the answer to this overarching question will be defined by the type of sentencing scheme (indeterminate or determinate) that exists in the clinician's jurisdiction and the specific areas the referral source wants the clinician to address. One or more of the following assessments will usually be involved: (1) the offender's need for treatment (relevant under indeterminate sentencing); (2) information bearing on the offender's personal culpability (relevant under determinate and indeterminate sentencing); and (3) future dangerousness (relevant under indeterminate sentencing). While these three issues can be conceptually distinguished, they may overlap in practice. For example, information bearing on an offender's need for treatment (e.g., drug addiction) may be integrated into an explanatory theme for the criminal actions (e.g., the offender's "addiction" made him or her do it), and may also be brought to bear on the issue of violence potential (drug abuse is positively related to recidivism). One of the first tasks for the clinician will be to determine which issue is to be the focus of the clinical inquiry.

The next three sections focus in turn on each of these issues. We give greatest emphasis to the issue of clinical involvement in the determination of future dangerousness. The issue of assessment of offenders' needs requires relatively little coverage, in light of the significant overlap with those concerns common in ordinary clinical practice; similarly, much of what can be said about presentence evaluations on culpability overlaps both conceptually and practically with the clinical portions of Chapter 6. Offender dangerousness, however, is a topic that pervades most present sentencing schemes and is the most difficult for clinicians to appropriately address. Clinical involvement in dangerousness prediction is extremely controversial, particularly in capital sentencing—so much so that the need for special ethical guidelines has been identified.

7.08.　The Assessment of Treatment Needs

Arguably, the most appropriate role for the mental health professional in presentencing is in the assessment of the offender's need for treatment. This role is the most consistent with the clinician's training and technical expertise in the identification of psychopathology and in the development of treatment planning. But before this topic can be addressed in a straightforward manner, it is important to highlight the appropriate scope of a needs assessment.

(a)　Defining "Need for Treatment"

As is true in every other context discussed in this book, the clinician's job in assessing treatment needs is to provide the data, not the ultimate decision. Thus, while a clinician may feel that an offender "needs" treatment, in the sense that it will improve the individual's mental condition or behavioral skills, the clinician should not go further and conclude that the offender "needs," in the sense of "requires," a particular disposition.[168] To illustrate this concept, it is useful to look at four possible roles identified by Bartholomew that clinicians can play in assessing treatment needs:

- The certification of "psychotics and defectives" for placement in special facilities (i.e., hospitals or training centers).
- Identifying other offenders less disturbed but still appropriate for mental health intervention, and advising the court of the circumstances under which suitable treatment might be provided.
- Advising the court of treatments available in corrections and of the length of sentence necessary to complete treatment in that setting.
- The determination of "the appropriate sanction for the particular individual."[169]

The first three roles focus on the identification of deficits at different levels of functioning and identifying treatment availabilities; the fourth, however, focuses on the final dispositive action, which involves the contemplation of contrasting moral goals of sentencing and of current social and political pressures beyond the responsibility and clinical expertise of the clinician.

From our perspective, clinicians should limit their role in needs assessment to identifying deficits and describing treatment availabilities. Within their ability to prognosticate, clinicians might advise the court of what is likely to happen if the treatment is provided or not—for example, whether a person with limited vocational skills is likely to continue to function at the current level if vocational rehabilitation is not provided; or whether a decompensating psychotic is likely to become severely dysfunctional if psychiatric treatment is not provided. The clinician, however, should resist judgments that an offender's problem areas *require* a particular disposition, for that responsibility lies with the court [see, e.g., Sanders report, § 15.05].

(b)　Characteristics of Offenders Evaluated for Treatment

Dix[170] has noted that the most seriously disordered offenders should have been diverted before sentencing—either through civil commitment, through adjudication as incompetent to proceed, or through acquittal by reason of insanity. Thus, as a group, presentence referrals should usually not exhibit serious mental illness.

Nevertheless, offenders referred for presentence examination are likely to display some level of impaired functioning. Offenders are not selected randomly for presentence psychiatric workups; rather, a referral is likely to stem from a judge's or attorney's perception that there is "something wrong" or "different" about an offender. In our experience, the types of offenders most often referred for treatment evaluation, in descending order of frequency, are as follows:

- Youthful adult offenders "at a crossroad."
- Persons charged with offenses (not necessarily serious) that are intuitively associated with psychological aberration (e.g., exhibitionism, fire

setting, conduct associated with drug or alcohol use).

- Persons charged with serious crimes who do not have a significant history of prior criminality (i.e., their crime is "ego-dystonic").
- Persons with an obvious serious mental disorder.

The available research indicates that psychiatric recommendations for treatment do result in a substantial number of cases. Caravello, Ginnetti, Ford, and Lawall reviewed studies reporting frequency of treatment recommendations ranging from "more than half the cases" to as many as 90%.[171]

(c) Conducting the Treatment Evaluation

The preceding subsections have set out the scope of the clinician's role in assessing treatment needs and the types of offenders for whom clinical assistance is most likely to be requested. Together, they suggest certain typical areas of inquiry. The National Institute of Corrections has provided an extensive breakdown of these areas; its list includes the assessment of the following:

- Serious psychological abnormality (e.g., acute functional disturbance).
- Drug/alcohol abuse or addiction.
- Deficits in intelligence and/or adaptive behavior.
- Academic training.
- Vocational skills.
- Interpersonal/social skills.[172]

In investigating these areas, clinicians should be able to make use of their usual array of structured and unstructured interviews, objective and projective psychological tests, laboratory testing procedures, or the collateral input of various consultants (e.g., educational or vocational counselors) in determining areas of potential treatment [see in this regard § 11.05, discussing treatment evaluations of children]. One source that clinicians may find particularly useful is the recent manual on the assessment of offenders'

needs, developed by Clements and his colleagues for the National Institute of Corrections.[173] For each of the areas of needs assessment listed above, this manual identifies formal psychological tests and/or structured questionnaires that have been developed to assist in evaluation of offenders. While the manual is aimed primarily at clinicians working within corrections, a number of the needs assessment concerns are the same for clinicians who see clients prior to sentencing; thus this manual may serve as an excellent tool for this purpose.

We recommend, as the manual does, that clinicians stick to instruments that produce diagnostic information relating to conventional diagnostic categories, such as those in DSM-III. In recent years, a number of offender classification systems have been developed that produce categories or types unrelated to conventional treatment classifications. One such classification system currently enjoying considerable attention in the research literature is Megargee and Bohn's system, based on the Minnesota Multiphasic Personality Inventory (MMPI).[174] While these typologies have shown some promise in the "treatment" of corrections inmates in the broader sense (i.e., security classification and management within the prison environment), they have not been extensively tested and validated for the diagnosis and treatment planning of recognized psychiatric and psychological disorders. Thus, while it might be very appropriate to use the MMPI in a presentence evaluation, we advise that in interpreting its results the clinician rely on normative data, developed on offender populations where available, that relate to *conventional* diagnostic categories.

In the course of assessing the presence or absence of specific deficits and the offender's general treatability, it may help to keep in mind the types of "data" courts especially focus on in evaluating the treatment recommendations in clinical reports. In our experience, the information that the courts find most relevant fall into five categories:

- The offender's motivation. (Does the offender express remorse about the act and express a desire to be treated?)

- Family/environmental situation. (Would it be beneficial or harmful to the offender and his or her associates if the offender returned to it?)
- Past treatment attempts. (If there have been successes, can they be repeated? If not, is there a treatment modality that has not been tried with this offender, and that has demonstrated—preferably empirically—its efficacy?)
- Past offense record. (Is there a pattern that treatment might affect?)
- Need for external control. (Can treatment safely take place in an unsecure environment?)

Obviously, some of these issues, especially the last two, are related to dangerousness assessments—the subject of § 7.10. As developed in that section, "treatability" and "dangerousness" are two sides of the same coin to many courts.

(d)   Formulating the Treatment Recommendation

As the above comment makes clear, the court may have a different focus on need for treatment than the traditional clinical concerns of simply alleviating suffering or improving level of functioning. The court may ask for opinions regarding the impact of treatment, if successful, on whatever criminal tendencies a person may be deemed to have. If the possibility of treatment under conditions of minimum or no security is contemplated, a clinician may be asked to comment on the risk involved in such a placement. Issues connected with responding to these collateral inquiries are covered later in this chapter. Even in the straightforward needs assessment, however, there are particular problem areas to keep in mind in formulating a recommendation. These include treatment bias, unrealistic recommendations, "forced" treatment, and limiting the scope of recommendations.

(1)   Treatment Bias

Because of their training in the medical model, psychiatrists, and to a lesser degree other mental health professionals, are inclined to see problem behavior as stemming primarily from personal pathology. Thus, they may be inclined to see every referral as a treatment case. Campbell has reported that "Prominent forensic psychiatrists almost uniformly express the view that presentence reports ought to advocate lenient, individualized treatment."[175] Clinicians may underestimate the role of learning factors or social/environmental conditions in the offender's illegal behavior, and may be inclined to suggest treatment oriented dispositions in cases in which negative reinforcement (e.g., fine, incarceration) might be more appropriate. Thus, clinicians need to guard against overdiagnosing and against the psychiatrization of criminal behavior.[176]

(2)   Unrealistic Recommendations

Also mentioned in the literature is the problem of recommending treatment that either is not available, or is available at a facility that has no input into the treatment and may be under no obligation to accept the offender as a client.[177] The problem of recommending nonexistent treatment may be the greatest when evaluations are conducted by staff members at a remote state hospital who are not familiar with the treatment programs actually available. Bartholomew[178] has recommended that presentence evaluations be conducted by clinicians who will ultimately provide any treatment that the offenders are ordered to undergo. This would appear to offer a solution, though upon reflection it is actually quite unrealistic. Careful diagnosis and treatment planning will frequently lead clinicians to advise treatments that they themselves are unable to provide. For example, a psychologist may identify a chronic schizophrenic who will need a maintainence dosage of medication or possibly consideration for placement in a day treatment program, neither of which the psychologist could provide through a private practice. Similarly, a dynamically oriented psychiatrist might diagnose a social skills deficit best remedied by group therapy, which is not offered in his or her practice, or the need for long-term drug rehabilitation, which is ideally offered in a residential setting.

Given the importance of matching clients'

problems with specific treatment approaches for those problems, the most reasonable approach would be for clinicians to extend their investigative efforts to include inquiries in the state or region regarding available treatment programs. They may also be able to use defendants' attorneys in this regard; even if clinicians do not know of the available treatment programs statewide, they can describe clients' diagnoses to their attorneys, who can then use their own resources to seek out possible placements.

Connected to the tendency to make unrealistic recommendations is the failure to provide sound information to the court as to what "works." Here, however, the fault is usually not with the evaluator, since very little empirical data analyzing particular types of programs exist. Although Martinson's survey of prison treatment modalities prior to 1967[179] has been construed to stand for the proposition that "nothing works,"[180] in fact few of the studies he reviewed were based on sound theoretical premises, used valid criterion variables, or even ensured the treatment being evaluated was actually effectively implemented.[181] Even today, few studies meeting these criteria exist.[182] To the extent such information is available, however, it should be reviewed by the clinician and provided the court, lest unrealistic assumptions concerning program efficacy or inefficacy be made.

(3) "Forced Treatment

The clinician should also be sensitive to potential problems that arise if their recommendation links the duration of a sentence to the offender's participation in a treatment program. Clients who know that leniency may be gained by participating in a treatment program may exaggerate their true problems or interest in treatment in order to gain a less punitive disposition. Once in treatment, shamming is encouraged; participation is motivated by the ulterior goal of obtaining a favorable recommendation for early release.[183] Moreover, because the treating clinician is required to report progress (or other aspects of treatment), the usual guarantees of confidentiality considered of paramount importance to successful therapy may be abrogated, thus threatening the therapist–client relationship with the

individual who truly wants to be treated. Therefore, where feasible, the clinician should recommend that dispositions that address the offender's need for treatment not entangle the degree of participation or success in therapy with the criteria for termination of sentence.

(4) Limiting the Scope of Recommendations

As noted in § 7.08(a), diagnosing a problem that might be the appropriate focus for a treatment intervention is not the same as determining that treatment for the problem should be ordered. The proper role for the mental health professional in presentence evaluations is not to tell the court whether or where to place the offender in treatment, but to identify problems and potential treatment alternatives that the court may consider along with the other goals and influences on the final disposition.

Consistent with this posture, we advise against direct recommendations for disposition or placement, such as "This patient should be sent to place X to receive treatment Y." Rather, we recommend that clinicians provide the court with a series of "If . . . , then . . ." statements that provide the court with alternatives, depending on what dispositional action is taken. For example, "If the court is inclined to a disposition such as probation, then Mr. Doe's inadequate social skills may be the focus of treatment through group therapy at the Westside Mental Health Center. If the decision is to place Mr. Doe in the state prison, then his limited social skills are not likely to improve, as the clinical staff members at the prison inform me that they presently have no active therapy that focuses on social skills training." The court can then decide whether to afford Mr. Doe that opportunity for group therapy in light of competing concerns, such as retribution or the need for preventive detention.

7.09. Assessments of Offenders' Culpability

Offenders' culpability is an issue considered in most determinate sentencing schemes, in all indeterminate sentencing jurisdictions, and in capital sentencing deliberations. From the defendants' perspective, clinicians may contribute to the culpability assessment in any of three ways. A clinician's most conventional role would be to make the judge or jury aware of situational factors that contributed to the occurrence of the crime; enhanced awareness of situational factors may lead the fact finder to perceive the crime as less a function of the offender's free choice. A second way in which the clinician may affect the culpability assessment would be to make the judge or jury aware of factors that emphasize the offender's suffering, thus arousing sympathy for the victim. Finally, the clinician may serve in a consultative capacity to assist the defense in overcoming the retributivist "set" in sentencing hearings. These three roles are discussed here in turn.

(a) Mitigation through Understanding: Modifying the Court's Perceptions of the Offender's "Choice"

"The jury and judge must be made to understand what caused a crime, particularly in homicides . . . It is the role of psychiatry and related professions to provide that understanding so a rational approach to a penalty can be taken." [184] In order to set punishment, the sentencing judge or jury must determine the seriousness of the crime committed. This requires that they consider both the harm done and the culpability of the offender. Assessments of the harm factor have been shown to be reliable: People can agree, for example, when contemplating different crimes in the abstract, that armed robbery is more serious than shoplifting but less serious than murder. The same is not true, however, of judgments in the area of personal culpability; "attributions of culpability or blame are highly influenced by factors having little relevance to notions of justice." [185] This is because, as Bonnie has noted in discussing the culpability issue in the context of capital sentencing, the law is seeking to make the difficult moral distinction between "a person who has chosen evil" and "the person whose homicidal behavior arose from significant impairment in his normal psychological controls." [186]

The clinical explanations for "how" or "why" a crime occurred that are offered at sentencing are similar to those described in Chapter 6, which discusses mental state defenses. However, to be admissible at the sentencing stage, explanatory formulations do not have to be so compelling as to constitute a possible defense. At sentencing, the door is open to a wider range of clinical input and explanatory formulations than is true at trial. For example, as the capital sentencing provisions quoted in § 7.07(a) illustrate, there is generally no requirement that the examiner be constrained by a threshold finding of mental disease or defect.[187] The possible influence of (1) chronological youth, (2) psychological immaturity, (3) unstable family background, (4) lack of adequate role models, (5) physical or neurological impairment, (6) the influence of chemical intoxicants, (7) stress due to situational factors, or (8) psychodynamic factors might all be woven into a clinical formulation that permits the judge or jury to attribute the crime, in part, to influences other than the offender's free choice.

However, the clinician's responsibility in this capacity is limited to the development of the explanatory formulations. Whether, and to what degree, leniency should be accorded an offender should be left to the attorney to argue and to the judge or jury to decide.

(b) Mitigation through Sympathy

In some instances, mitigation occurs, whether intended or not, simply by identifying factors that might arouse the judge's or jury's sympathy without integrating them into an explanatory theme. Kalven and Zeisel noted that extraneous suffering by the offender sometimes influenced jury decisions.[188] Similarly, a study by Cooke and Pogany[189] illustrated that having a history of psychiatric problems might serve to mitigate punishment. A group of 130 defendants who had been referred to the Center for Forensic Psychiatry in Michigan for pretrial competency evaluations were subsequently sentenced to prison. The sentences given to this group were compared with those given to a control group of offenders who had not been referred for pretrial evaluation. No significant differences between the

overall severity of sentences was found. However, when the referral group was partitioned as
a function of the results of the psychiatric evaluation, it was found that relatively shorter sentences had been given to offenders who had either
(1) been diagnosed as schizophrenic, or (2) been
found incompetent for trial. Though no presentence report relating mental state to culpability
issues had been issued, the sentencing courts apparently gave consideration to the offenders'
psychiatric histories.

However, mitigation efforts that revolve around
sympathy arousal may be less successful as the
severity of the crime increases. This relationship
has been demonstrated in laboratory research
using simulated sentencing exercises. Austin[190]
varied the amount of extraneous offender suffering (none, moderate, excessive) in each of three
cases involving increasingly more harm done (i.e.,
victim suffering)—purse snatching, purse
snatching plus assault, or rape. Undergraduate
students acting as jurors were asked to impose
the most appropriate sentence, given the circumstances of each case. Results indicated that
for the minor offense of shoplifting, sentences
decreased as a function of offender suffering. With
crimes of moderate or high severity, potentially
mitigating information that the offender had suffered moderate physical injuries had no sentence
reducing impact; only when the offender's suffering was excessive did this information mitigate the sentence.

Austin interpreted these findings to suggest
that jurors will sentence according to "just deserts" principles for offenses of low severity, but
that the application of these principles will be
modified by other considerations (i.e., retribution) for offenses that are more severe:

> As crimes grow in seriousness decision makers
> become more retributivist in their motives. The
> quantitative difference in crimes may be large
> enough to create a qualitative distinction so
> that retribution supercedes deserts as the guid-
> ing goal. Retribution . . . is probably more easily
> aroused for particularly heinous acts . . .[191]

Austin's findings are consistent with Dix's[192]
finding that potentially mitigating information
offered in capital sentencing hearings in Ohio

was generally ineffective in efforts to persuade
sentencing juries to forego the death penalty and
instead impose a sentence of life in prison. Dix
speculated that the ineffectiveness may have been
due to the expert witnesses' failure to relate the
mitigating information to the offenses by using
an explanatory theme.[193]

Mitigating information submitted purely to
arouse sympathy thus appears to have little impact on serious cases. It should also be pointed
out that in most determinate sentencing jurisdictions, such mitigating information may well
be considered inadmissible because it is not directly tied to the offense, as required by statute.

(c)   Consultation to Minimize the Retributivist "Set" in Sentencing Hearings

For attorneys seeking to mitigate their clients'
sentences, retributivist tendencies in the court
may constitute the major hurdle. One of the factors that may influence retribution is the court's
perception of what the victim(s) of a crime would
consider a "just" sentence. This information
usually comes before the court via the presentence report that is prepared by the pa-
role/probation department. As noted in § 7.03(c)
(2), this report usually includes a victim impact
statement, including the investigating officer's
summary of the victim's stated desires regarding
sentencing. Moreover, states' attorneys will often
argue for severe punishment in part to vindicate
the victim's sense of justice.

Henderson and Gitchoff[194] have suggested that
this information may induce a retributivist "set."
They reported techniques developed in their
practice, which include the use of mental health
consultation to potentially nullify this "set." First,
they noted that the way in which probation officers interview the victims may influence the
responses they receive. Officers typically asked,
"What do you think the punishment should be?,"
without providing the victims with a menu of
possible sentences or other information about
sentencing (e.g., the cost of incarceration). When
these investigators approached the victims and
described the various sentencing options avail-

able, they found that the victims were often quite willing to vacate positions of retribution and select viable alternatives. They also noted that victims seemed to "mellow" with time and were more amenable to less severe punishment when the presentence interviews were conducted a longer period after the trial.

Henderson and Gitchoff's study suggests two possible roles for the mental health professional. First, they have suggested that the defense use a mental health expert in presentencing—one whose duties include interviewing the victim and obtaining a victim impact statement independent of that obtained by the probation department. Though this would appear at first blush to be an unconventional use of the clinician at sentencing, the investigative model we have suggested for use in reconstructive defenses [see Chapter 6] provides for clinician–victim contact if appropriate legal procedures are followed; a similar investigative effort might be necessary in developing mitigating information [see § 7.09 (a)], which would provide an opportunity for the clinician to inquire about the victim's desires regarding sentencing. Second, even if the clinician does not gather an independent victim impact statement, he or she may be able to testify regarding the influence of the probation officer's style of questioning on the answers obtained from the victim, thus enlightening the court about the influence of methodology on the probation report's portrayal of the victim's desires.[195]

(d) Evaluating Culpability

The clinical evaluation at presentencing that focuses on possible mitigating factors at the time of the crime should be, in large part, similar to the investigative inquiry involved in reconstructive defenses [see Chapter 6]. Many of the same tools and techniques, including close attention to a variety of third-party information, may be helpful in this evaluation.

In jurisdictions that have statutes explicitly identifying mitigating factors to be considered, clinicians should also familiarize themselves with the statutes and consider the implications of the wording of the particular factors for their inves-

tigative inquiries. For example, the Alabama Code governing sentencing in capital cases includes this mitigating factor: "The defendant acted under extreme duress or under the substantial domination of another person."[196] Depending on the facts of the case, clinical inquiry into the issue of the "domination of another person" might entail interviewing accomplices to the crime and developing some judgments as to the relative strengths of the various personalities involved and the dependencies among them.

As noted above the clinical investigation at presentencing is not constrained by threshold tests such as the presence of mental disease or defect. The door is open to a wider range of descriptive and theoretical formulations, such as those discussed in § 6.06. Any information that helps the judge or jury understand limitations in the development of an offender's psychological controls, or that identifies factors that may have undermined the offender's controls, may be of use in their determination of the individual's culpability. As elsewhere, clinicians should be candid about reliability and validity with respect to their data and inferences, and should be clear in advising the court of the theoretical nature of their formulations. They should also avoid the moral conclusions regarding whether the developmental deficits, environmental stresses, or functional pathology assessed are of sufficient magnitude to meet the discretionary legal test.

7.10. *Mental Health Involvement in Violence Prediction*

> The idea that as a society we now send people to prison for punishment is as much a pretense as the idea that we sent them to prison twenty years ago primarily for rehabilitation. The bush we are beating around . . . is the desire to confine people whom we perceive as a danger so that public protection is served.[197]

Regardless of the theoretical bases underlying different sentencing structures, most make room for consideration by the sentencing judge or jury of information regarding the offender's potential

for future violence. The forward-looking indeterminate scheme—including special-track provisions, such as those for the "defective deli-
quent" or the "MDSO"—explicitly considers
violence potential as part of the problem to be
treated and reduced; the offender's release is often
contingent on the judgment of a parole board or
a judge, usually following the opinion of a psychiatrist that the individual's potential for violence has been reduced to an acceptable minimum. While the backward-looking "just desserts"
model is much less accommodating to considerations of future violence, Professor Monahan
has illustrated how predictive deterrence could
become a legitimate consideration in fixing the
specific punishment within the range permitted in
"modified desserts" sentencing schemes.[198] And
in jurisdictions having capital sentencing, the judge
or jury may be required to consider evidence on
future dangerousness in deciding whether to invoke the death penalty.[199]

Mental health professionals' testimony—often
in the form of predictive opinions—is frequently
sought as evidence on dangerousness. With years
of confinement, or possibly the offender's life,
hanging in the balance, there is no other area of
the law in which expert testimony may exert so
significant an impact. Unfortunately, there may
be no other issue that clinicians are so inadequate in assessing. Indeed, many have questioned
whether mental health professionals' predictions
of violent behavior are sufficiently accurate to
meet acceptable scientific or legal standards.

This section discusses much of the literature
on the assessment and prediction of dangerous
behavior. We first review a number of factors
that contribute to erroneous predictions, and then
look at some accounts of the processes clinicians
have used to predict dangerousness in different
contexts. Next, we review empirical studies of
violence prediction and focus on the type and
magnitude of error associated with psychiatric
predictions of violence. We then briefly address
the controversy surrounding clinical versus statistical prediction, and we close with a consideration of the implications of the empirical studies for presentence reports and testimony on
dangerousness.

(a) Factors Associated with Overpredictions of Violence

One of the most consistent findings in the literature on violence prediction is the tendency for
mental health professionals to overpredict violence. Anticipating the thrust of empirical studies to be reviewed below, we note Rubin's conclusion from over a decade ago: "Even in the
most careful, painstaking, laborious and lengthy
clincial approach to the prediction of dangerousness, false positives may be at a minimum of 60%
to 70%."[200] Numerous authors have addressed
the problem of overprediction and have identified factors that contribute to it. Among the factors identified are political influences, illusory
correlations, low base rates for violence, cultural
differences, and conceptual/contextural problems.[201]

(1) Political Influences

"Political influences" refers to the fact that there
may be different consequences for the predictor,
depending on whether the offender actually
commits another violent act or not. If the clinician predicts that the person will not be dangerous and no subsequent violent act occurs, there
are no unpleasant repercussions for the clinician;
however, if the client is released on the basis of
the clinician's prediction and subsequently commits a violent act, the clinician can expect extensive negative publicity in media coverage of the
violent crime, as well as possible legal action for
negligent release [but see § 3.04(d)(2)].[202] Of
course, the risk of such negative consequences
can be avoided by "finding" that the person is
potentially violent, since such opinions usually
lead to preventive detention.[203] Considerations
such as these may influence examining clinicians
to view a greater number of persons as potentially violent.

(2) Illusory Correlations

An illusory correlation occurs when a relationship between two variables is believed to exist,

although it is empirically demonstrated that no such relationship exists (or not to the degree believed). Clinicians may base their opinions about potential dangerousness on the presence or absence of variables that are not truly related to violence proneness. In the civil commitment context, it is not uncommon for psychiatrists to assert that prospective patients are potentially dangerous because they are mentally ill—an opinion that may proceed from a common but erroneous belief that violence and mental disorder are generally correlated.[204] Illusory correlations exist in the clincial lore and are maintained by selective attention to and recall of individual cases in which the relationship is confirmed.

(3)   Low Base Rates for Violence

Part of the problem of erroneous positive predictions of violence is appropriately attributed to the low frequency of occurrence of violent acts. When the truly violent population is quite small compared to the nonviolent population, then even predictor variables having high validity (i.e., low percentage of errors) will generate large numbers of false positives. A brief example illustrates this phenomenon.

Assume that in a population of 1,000 subjects, 15% ($n = 150$) will commit a violent act and 85% ($n = 850$) will not. Assume also that the clinician has a screening test that accurately classifies 90% of each group. In screening this population, the clinician will identify 135 (150 × .90) truly violent individuals, and 85 (850 × .10) false positives—persons predicted to be violent who in fact will not be. Thus, the clinician will be in error 39% (85 divided by 135 + 85) of the time when he or she predicts a person to be violent. As the incidence of violence gets smaller or the validity of the predictor test gets lower, the error rate increases. The same example using a test that is 75% valid results in an error rate of 65%. Because we do not have tests with demonstrated high validity, and the actual incidence of violence is relatively low, our accuracy in assessing future dangerousness is limited.

(4)   Cultural Differences

Levinson and Ramsay[205] note that cultural differences between the examining clinician and the person whose violence potential is to be assessed may contribute to errors in clinical judgment. Clinicians are typically white male psychiatrists from middle- to high-income families, while the offender population is composed predominantly of low-income, low-socioeconomic-status males. Resentment over cultural or racial differences may inhibit rapport between the examiner and the client; even where rapport is established and the client talks freely, the client's experiences may be foreign to the clinician and their relevance for violence potential understood poorly, if at all.

(5)   Conceptual/Contextual Problems

A significant conceptual problem is that mental health professionals have traditionally looked for explanations of violence in the personal pathology of the individual; dangerousness is conceived of as a trait. This conceptual stance tends to limit the nature and scope of their inquiry into violence proneness. Contemporary scholars note the inappropriateness of the trait formulation of dangerousness[206] and emphasize the importance of social and situational variables in understanding violence when it occurs. Recognizing the importance of situational and interaction factors, critics of the trait approach discourage categorical predictions of individuals as "dangerous" or "not dangerous," and encourage appraisals of violence potential that result in probability statements regarding which individuals are more or less likely to act aggressively, toward what kinds of victims, and under what circumstances.

Despite this modern thinking, mental health practitioners are inclined toward dispositional explanations for violent behavior; they typically focus on clinical signs, symptoms, or diagnostic labels as predictors.[207] This practice may be in part the result of training in and commitment to the medical model. It is also fostered, however, by the context in which evaluations of dangerousness typically occur. Clinicians see the individuals in hospital settings that are often far removed from the social environment in which the persons typically function. There is only limited access to others in the individuals' social communities, and this further discourages clinicians from going beyond the usual hospital assessment techniques of interview and psychological testing, despite (or in ignorance of) the fact that such techniques have poor predictive validity in the area of violence prediction.[208] Thus, clinicians' commitment to an outdated conceptualization of dangerousness as a personality trait and the contextual disadvantages of seeing the person in the hospital setting combine to encourage overpredictions of dangerousness.

(b)   Clinicians' Processes for Generating Long-Term Predictions of Violence

Given the number and diversity of the factors that may contribute to inaccurate predictions of dangerous behavior, it may come as no surprise that studies of clinicians' processes for generating such predictions reveal that assessment techniques are unsystematic, inconsistent, and unscientific.

Pfohl[209] studied the decisionmaking processes of 12 teams of mental health professionals at the Lima State Hospital in Ohio. These teams were charged with the responsibility of reviewing the cases of all clients involuntarily committed to determine whether they were still dangerous. He noted that the various teams periodically used differing and idiosyncratic criteria, including (1) a client's past record, (2) the client's ability to express insight into past deeds of violence, (3) the client's dreams and fantasies, (4) the results of psychological tests or signs of "repressed anger." One team reportedly considered "how they would 'feel having this man as (their) next door neighbor.'"[210] Pfohl also found that the ultimate impression of a patient's dangerousness was the outgrowth of compromise and negotiation among various team members, many of whom yielded to the most influential team member, usually the psychiatrist. The written report, however, was couched in technical and diagnostic language that kept hidden the compromise nature of the finding.

Steadman and his colleagues[211] conducted extensive studies of the determinations of dangerousness of 257 incompetent criminal defendants examined by psychiatrists in New York. Though a variety of factors were offered as the basis for predictions of future violence,[212] statistical analysis revealed that a single factor was given overriding significance in the clinicians' assessments: "Psychiatrists seem to be making recommendations as to dangerousness based almost exclusively on the defendants' charges, with little additional discrimination evident."[213] Cocozza and Steadman[214] noted that the current criminal charge was also the criterion used by judges in deciding whether to adopt the psychiatrists' recommendation. These studies provide another instance of mental health professionals' developing "expert opinions" primarily on the basis of information that is a matter of public record and that requires no special skill or expertise either to gather or to interpret.[215]

A final anecdotal incident worth noting is the psychiatric testimony in *Estelle v. Smith,* a Texas death penalty case.[216] On the basis of a single "mental status examination," the examining psychiatrist concluded that Smith was a "very severe sociopath"[217] who, if given the opportunity to do so, "is going to go ahead and commit other similar or same criminal acts given the opportunity to do so."[218] These conclusions apparently followed from the single clinical impression that the offender "lacked remorse," which is neither necessary nor sufficient to establish a sociopathic personality diagnosis in any conventional nosology. Given that Smith had not actually killed the victim in the case at hand (an accomplice had), given the absence of any prior documented history of violent behavior (Smith's prior record consisted of a single conviction for possession of marijuana), and given the obviously flimsy basis for the conclusions offered before the sentencing court, Dix concluded that the psychiatrist was operating "at the brink of quackery,"[219] a conclusion with which it is difficult to muster much disagreement.[220]

The abuse of psychiatric opinions on the issue of future dangerousness has led to several proposals for legal and/or ethical limitations on mental health involvement in this area.[221] While the thrust of these proposals varies, most agree that clinicians testifying about long-term dangerousness should be familiar with the research on violence predictions. The next section reviews empirical studies on violence prediction.

(c) Clinical Predictions of Dangerousness and the Problem of False Positives

Since 1970, there have been a large number of studies investigating mental health professionals' predictions of dangerous behavior, involving subjects from a variety of populations. Table 7-1 summarizes the essential findings from a number of prediction studies. The table is divided according to the populations of persons about whom the predictions were made. These studies differ in ways that render them not directly comparable with one another. Collectively, however, they are sufficiently methodologically sound to reflect the state of the art in long-term predictions of dangerousness. Though we briefly discuss each of the studies, the reader is encouraged to review the original studies.

(1)   Studies of Department of Corrections Parolees

Three large-scale studies on the prediction of violence were undertaken by the California Department of Corrections.[222] While these studies attempted to develop violence prediction scales, psychiatric and/or psychological data were also included as part of the predictive battery.

In the first study, potential scale items included such factors as length of imprisonment, type of offense, and history of opiate use. A follow-up study of offender behavior while on parole revealed that the scale was accurate in only 14% of the cases predicted to be violent; 86% of those predicted to be violent while on parole in fact were not.

A second study involved a careful review of each offender's case history, as well as psychiatric reports on each offender. Offenders were assigned to categories based on their potential for violence. A total of 1,630 parolees were keyed as "potentially aggressive." During a one-year fol-

low-up, however, only 5 were actually involved in a violent crime, yielding a false-positive rate of 99.7%.

A third study involved an attempt to predict violent crime by wards of the California Youth Authority. Prior history of violence, general background information, results from a psychological test battery, and psychiatric diagnoses were among the primary sources of information subsequently used in a multivariate analysis to predict violent behavior during a 15-month follow-up period. As in the prior studies, the overwhelming majority of subjects predicted to be violent in fact were not violent—93.8%.

(2)   Studies of Maximum Security Forensic Patients

A series of studies by Steadman and his colleagues examined the careers of "criminally insane" offenders detained in New York's maximum security hospitals who were subsequently transferred to less secure civil hospitals or released into the community as a result of *Baxstrom v. Herold*,[223] a Supreme Court decision mandating the review and release from prison of offenders who had served their sentences. A typical finding of those studies was that reported by Steadman and Cocozza[224] subsequent to a three-and-a-half-year follow-up of 98 males who had been released into the community. A total of 20 men were arrested, though only 7 were arrested for violent offenses; 7 other former patients were rehospitalized for assaultive behavior. Thus, 14 of the 98 former patients, all of whom had presumably been considered dangerous, were actually violent recidivists; the remaining 84, or 85%, were false positives.

A court decision similar in effect to the *Baxstrom* case[225] resulted in an extensive study by Thornberry and Jacoby[226] of former maximum security forensic patients who were released into Pennsylvania communities. Using rearrest or rehospitalization for violent behavior as a criterion, these investigators found that only 14.5% of the sample engaged in violent behavior during a four-year follow-up. For the remaining 85.5% of the sample, the positive predictions of dangerousness were erroneous.

In Texas, Mullen and Reinehr[227] gathered

Table 7-1
Summary of Violence Prediction Studies

Study	Criterion Behavior	False Positives	Follow-Up
Studies of Department of Corrections Parolees			
Wenk, Robison, & Smith[1]			
Study 1	Documented act of violence	86%	?
Study 2	Crime involving violence	99.7%	1 year
Study 3	Documented violent act	93.8%	15 months
Studies of Maximum Security Forensic Patients			
Steadman & Cocozza[2]	Rearrest or rehospitalized for an assaultive act	85%	$3\frac{1}{2}$ years
Thornberry & Jacoby[3]	Arrest or rehospitalization for a violent act	85.5%	4 years
Mullen & Reinehr[4]	Arrest for violent crime	89%	1–2 years
Studies of Special-Track Offenders (Dangerous Sex Offenders, Defective Delinquents)			
Kozol, Boucher, & Garofalo[5]	Committing a serious assaultive act	65%	5 years
Rappeport[6]	Rearrest for *any* offense, violent or nonviolent	19–61%	?
Sidley[7]	Commission of an "aggravated" crime	67–81%	?
Studies of Pretrial Offenders (Incompetent to Stand Trial)			
Steadman & Cocozza[8]	Assaultive behavior while in the hospital	44%	?
	Assaultive behavior in community (arrest or rehospitalization for assaultive crime)	84%	?
Cocozza & Steadman[9]	Rearrest for violent offense	86%	3 years
Sepejak, Menzies, Webster, & Jensen[10]	Criminal charges; behavior precipitating hospitalization; behavior in hospital and prison	44%	2 years
Studies of Community Residents Evaluated for Dangerousness			
Levinson & Ramsay[11]	Threats or actions that endangered the well-being of others	47%	1 year
	Acts that endangered the well-being of others	71%	1 year

1. Data from Wenk, Robison, & Smith, *Can Violence Be Predicted?*, 18 CRIME & DELINQ. 393 (1972).
2. Data from Steadman & Cocozza, *The Prediction of Dangerousness—Baxstrom: A Case Study*, in THE ROLE OF THE FORENSIC PSYCHOLOGIST (G. Cooke ed. 1980).
3. Data from T. THORNBERRY & J. JACOBY, THE CRIMINALLY INSANE: A FOLLOW-UP OF MENTALLY ILL OFFENDERS (1979).
4. Data from Mullen & Reinehr, *Predicting Dangerousness of Maximum Security Forensic Patients*, 10 J. PSYCHIATRY & L. 223 (1982).

follow-up data on 165 maximum security forensic patients who had been in the community for an average period of just under two years. Sixty-one of these patients had previously been designated as "dangerous" by clinical staff at the hospital. Of these 61, only 7 had been rearrested for a violent crime during the follow-up period. The remaining 89% were false positives.

(3) Studies of Special-Track Offenders

Slightly lower false-positive rates have been reported in studies of special-track offenders. Kozol, Boucher, and Garofalo[228] reported the results of a five-year follow-up of male offenders, most of whom had previously committed sex crimes, who had been discharged from the Massachusetts Center for the Diagnosis and Treatment of Dangerous Persons. Comprehensive evaluations were completed on each offender, resulting in a recommendation to the court for either commitment or release. In the five-year follow-up period, 34.7% of those predicted to be dangerous who had been released had committed a serious assaultive act. The false-positive rate was 65.3%.

Rappeport[229] reported recidivism rates for three groups of offenders diagnosed as "defective delinquents" by the clinical staff at Maryland's Patuxent Institution but subsequently released by the court before the clincial staff viewed them as clinically suitable for release. Of those who received no treatment prior to release, 81% were recidivists, yielding a false-positive rate of 19%. Of those released after partial treatment ("half treated"), 46% were recidivists, yielding a false-positive rate of 54%. Of those released

against medical advice after partial treatment plus conditional release experience ("⅔ treated"), 39% were recidivists, yielding a false-positive rate of 61%. Rappeport's figures probably underestimate the false-positive rates for violence predictions, however, since both violent and nonviolent crimes were considered in classifying former patients as recidivists.

In an article that appeared in the same journal as Rappeport's paper, Sidley[230] also discussed studies of offenders who were diagnosed as "defective deliquents" at Patuxent, but who were not committed for treatment and who subsequently committed "aggravated" crimes. He reported a recidivism rate of 33% for aggravated crimes in an untreated group, which yields a false-positive rate of 67%. For offenders who received partial treatment and were subsequently released by the court, only 19% were found to have committed aggravated crimes, yielding a false-positive rate of 81%.

(4) Studies of Pretrial Offenders

Steadman and Cocozza[231] examined the accuracy of predictions of future violence by psychiatrists who had examined 257 male offenders determined to be incompetent to stand trial. The patients' behavior was documented both while they were in the hospital and upon their release into the community. Of the 154 persons predicted to be assaultive, only 68 (44%) were observed to be assaultive in the hospital (a 56% false-positive rate), and only 14% were rearrested for violent crime after release (an 86% false-positive rate).[232] Of course, the latter figure is somewhat difficult to interpret, given the con-

---

5. Data from Kozol, Boucher, & Garafalo, *The Diagnosis and Treatment of Dangerousness,* 18 CRIME & DELINQ. 371 (1972).

6. Data from Rappeport, *Enforced Treatment: Is It Treatment?,* 2 BULL. AM. ACAD. PSYCHIATRY & L. 148 (1974).

7. Data from Sidley, *The Evaluation of Prison Treatment and Preventive Detention Programs: Some Problems Faced by the Patuxent Institution,* 2 BULL. AM. ACAD. PSYCHIATRY & L. 73 (1974).

8. Data from Steadman & Cocozza, *Psychiatry, Dangerousness and the Repetitively Violent Offender,* 69 J. CRIM. L. & CRIMINOLOGY 226 (1978).

9. Data from Cocozza & Steadman, *Prediction in Psychiatry: An Example of Misplaced Confidence in Experts,* 25 SOC. PROB. 266 (1978).

10. Data from Sepejak, Menzies, Webster, & Jensen, *Clinical Prediction of Dangerousness: Two-Year Follow-Up of 408 PreTrial Forensic Cases,* 11 BULL. AM. ACAD. PSYCHIATRY & L. 171 (1983).

11. Data from Levinson & Ramsay, *Dangerousness, Stress, and Mental Health Evaluations,* 20 J. HEALTH SOC. BEHAV. 178 (1979).

founding effect of treatment received in the hospital.

A Canadian study involving 364 defendants evaluated prior to trial obtained a relatively good false-positive rate of 44%.[233] The predictions were made by an interdisciplinary team of clinicians (psychiatrist, psychologist, social worker, nurse, and correctional officer), which used a 4-point dangerousness scale ("no," "low," "medium," and "high"). The criterion was an overall dangerousness rating made by three master's-level students in criminology, using an 11-point scale designed to synthesize the data concerning the defendants' antisocial acts during the two years subsequent to the prediction.

(5) Studies of Community Residents Evaluated for Dangerousness

Levinson and Ramsay[234] conducted a one-year follow-up of community residents who had been evaluated regarding their potential for violence. Two separate criteria for dangerousness—one broad and one narrow—were used. The broad criterion was evidence of either threats or actions that might endanger the well-being of others; the narrow definition was limited strictly to overt acts. Using the broad criterion, the examiners achieved a false-positive rate of 47%; 9 of 17 subjects (53%) actually met the criterion. When the narrower definition was used, only 5 of 17, or 29%, were actually found to have committed aggressive acts. The false-positive rate was 71%.

(6) Discussion

Monahan's[235] review of substantially this same body of research concluded that long-range predictions of violent behavior are accurate in no more than one of three cases. A few observations on this conclusion, which has been widely cited, are in order. First, some critics have argued that false-positive rates in these studies may have been exaggerated due to the underreporting of crimes—suggesting, in other words, that some of the false positives had been violent but had not been caught at it. Monahan's analysis of collateral studies on this issue concluded

that the one-third of the individuals who are predicted as violent and are arrested for a violent crime are in fact the same people who commit *most* of the unreported and unsolved violent acts. It is not that the false positives are really true positives in disguise but rather that the true positives are "truer" (i.e., more violent) than we imagined.[236] (emphasis added)

Nonetheless, as Monahan's use of the word "most" indicates, at least some of the false positives in these studies were incorrectly classified.

Other criticisms of the research include the charge that in some of the studies—in particular, Steadman and Cocozza's *Baxstrom* study and Thornberry and Jacoby's work—it is not clear that any *clinical* prediction of dangerousness was made (instead, the prediction was inferred from the fact that the patients remained institutionalized, perhaps due to administrative inertia).[237] It has also been pointed out that in those studies where clinical predictions *were* the basis for treating the research sample as "dangerous," the clinicians' definition of that term could have been much broader than the researchers' (e.g., any threatening behavior vs. actual assaultive behavior), especially since the relevant statutes provided no clear guidelines.[238] Similarly, in most of the studies, the clinicians' predictions were naturally focused on dangerousness in the community. Yet, for obvious reasons, the individuals they designated as "dangerous" were institutionalized immediately and subjected to treatment, making the predictor variable (any "dangerous" behavior in the community, assuming immediate release) different from the criterion variable (assaultive behavior in the institution or in the community after treatment).[239]

Perhaps with some of these criticisms in mind, Monahan has recently stated:

> There may indeed be a ceiling on the level of accuracy that can ever be expected of clinical prediction of violent behavior. That ceiling, however, may be closer to 50% than to 5% among some groups of clinical interest. And a growing number of people are choosing to light small but valid research candles rather than continue to curse the empirical darkness.[240]

Even recognizing methodological problems with the research, however, an optimistic appraisal leads one to the conclusion that, *at best,* the accuracy rate of clinical predictions of long-term dangerousness behavior falls below 50%. Given these rather dismal findings, it is difficult to condone clinicians' practice of offering categorical long-term predictions, and indeed we counsel against such practices [see § 7.10(e)].

This is not to argue that clinical evaluations of violence potential have no validity. In some of the studies reviewed above, other measures of clinical acuity reveal that clinicians' assessments of dangerousness have some discriminating power. In the Mullen and Reinehr study,[241] for example, only 37% of the follow-up sample had been predicted to be violent, but 47% of the violent crimes detected were accounted for by this group. Similarly, in the study of dangerous sex offenders by Kozol and colleagues,[242] only 11% of the follow-up sample was regarded as dangerous, but 35% of the subsequent offenders came from this group. Nevertheless, the large number of false positives is difficult to ignore in decisionmaking contexts such as criminal courts, where predictions must be made on an individual basis.

An alternative that must be considered is the use of statistical predictors that, in a variety of other contexts, have been shown to be superior to clinical predictions.[243] If the problem of substantial false positives can be eliminated by using actuarial techniques, then there may be a legitimate basis for categorical predictions such as "dangerous" or "not dangerous."

(d) Actuarial Predictions of Dangerousness

An alternative to the unsystematic and subjective predictions generated by clinical intuition would be predictions generated from statistical procedures, in which the specific variables weighed would be known and the manner in which they were combined to generate the prediction would be explicitly stated.[244] To develop actuarial predictors, it is necessary to identify two samples of subjects from the population whose violence potential is to be predicted. Researchers can then measure the first sample (derivation sample) on a large number of variables (clinical, behavioral,

demographic, etc.) thought *a priori* to have some relevance to the prediction of dangerousness. The derivation sample can then be followed for some designated period to see which subjects actually behave violently. When the derivation sample has been partitioned into "dangerous" and "nondangerous" subgroups, a statistical procedure such as discriminant function can be applied to the variables previously measured to determine which ones are most useful in distinguishing the two subgroups. The original number of predictors can be substantially reduced by eliminating those that have little or no discriminating power. Finally, an equation can be developed to indicate how the remaining variables should be weighed and combined to yield a prediction. The equation can then be applied to the second sample (cross-validation) to estimate the true discriminating power of the equation.[245]

It may be helpful to contrast the differences between clinical and actuarial prediction. Whereas actuarial prediction explicitly identifies the criteria used and the weights assigned to each, clinical predictions of dangerousness have been faulted because the process for generating the prediction may be difficult to ferret out. Clinicians may indicate that they attend to a large number of variables, but the manner in which their contemplation gives rise to a classification of "dangerous" or "not dangerous" is unknown. The clinical reasoning may also be put forth in a fashion that is difficult to penetrate by cross-examination or other means; lawyers may find the obfuscation of labels and jargon too much to cope with.[246]

Two primary shortcomings of actuarial prediction have to do with its inability to consider case-specific information and the practical problem of getting judges or jurors to understand and use it. With respect to the first, once the specific predictors in an actuarial technique are set, all other information is irrelevant. Thus, an offender who may have been rendered "not dangerous" by misfortune, such as paralysis, may still be classified as "dangerous" by an actuarial procedure—equations tend to be inflexible. With respect to the second criticism, research has shown that persons in decisionmaking positions who receive both clinical case material and statistical information tend to prefer the former and to ignore the latter, even though the latter information may be highly relevant.[247] The possibility of the misuse of statistics is also a concern that has led some to propose special procedures for the admission of this type of evidence.[248]

For the purposes of this discussion, we are most interested at this point in the possible reduction of false-positive predictions through the use of actuarial techniques. Empirical studies on this point include those reported by Wenk, Robison, and Smith [see the top of Table 7–1]. These studies were undertaken in an effort to aid in parole decisionmaking. Although clinical variables were measured (e.g., diagnosis, psychological test outcomes), attempts were made to develop objective scales for classifying convicts at different levels of risk. As previously discussed, false positives in these studies were substantial.

In their study of the *Baxstrom* patients, Steadman and Cocozza[249] developed the Legal Dangerousness Scale (LDS), an actuarial device that assigns to each individual a numerical score on four variables: (1) presence or absence of a juvenile record, (2) number of previous incarcerations, (3) history of conviction for violent crime, and (4) type of current offense. Refinements in the use of the scale led to the addition of an age

factor. Use of the LDS with *Baxstrom* patients resulted in a false-positive rate of approximately 66%, a modest improvement over the 85% associated with psychiatric predictions.

Subsequent applications of the LDS with other offender populations revealed a familiar problem in the area of prediction—generalizability. Thornberry and Jacoby[250] applied the LDS to the maximum security forensic patients followed in their study, with disappointing results. They obtained 80% false positives using the LDS, a meager improvement over the 85.5% associated with clinical predictions. Steadman and Cocozza[251] applied the age-adjusted LDS to a sample of pretrial defendants judged incompetent for trial, again with disappointing results. False positives with the LDS were at 78%, again a slim improvement over the 84% rate associated with psychiatrists' predictions in the same sample.

Because of the differences between the *Baxstrom* population (older maximum security patients' institutionalized on the average for 14 years) and the population of incompetent defendants (younger, arrested only 11 weeks earlier), Steadman and Cocozza[252] developed new actuarial predictors of violence for the latter group, using a discriminant function routine to select from 53 variables those that maximally discriminated the

Table 7-2

Validity of Clinical versus Statistical Predictions of Dangerousness: Summary of Comparative Data from Steadman and Cocozza

| | % Classified Correctly | | | | | | % False Positives | |
| | Clinical | | | Actuarial | | | | |
Criterion Behavior	V	NV	Total	V	NV	Total	Clinical	Actuarial
Assaultive in the hospital	51	61	55	54	67	63	49	46
Assaultive in the community leading to rearrest or rehospitalization	21	87	59	29	90	70	79	70
Assaultive in the community leading to arrest for violent crime	14	84	43	31	92	75	87	69

Note. Data from Steadman & Cocozza, *The Dangerousness Standard and Psychiatry: A Cross National Issue in the Social Control of the Mentally Ill,* 63 SOCIOLOGY & SOC. RESEARCH 649 (1979). V = patients who were violent by the criterion; NV = patients who were not violent by the criterion.

violent from the nonviolent. The criterion groups were defined in three separate ways, and separate discriminant analyses were run for each partitioning. The first analysis distinguished patients who were assaultive versus not assaultive in the hospital setting; the second analysis distinguished patients who had been in any way assaultive in the community (leading to either arrest or rehospitalization); the third analysis distinguished assaultive versus nonassaultive patients in the community *only* on the basis of arrest for violent crime. Table 7-2 summarizes the results of these three analyses.

The results indicate that for all three analyses, statistical prediction was more accurate than clinical predictions of violence by psychiatrists. In particular, where the criterion was assaultiveness in the community resulting in rearrest for violent crime—arguably, the criterion in which a sentencing judge would be most interested—the improvement was the most substantial.

Though modest improvements in predictive accuracy have been demonstrated using actuarial techniques, the studies to date can be regarded as, at best, only encouraging. In populations having a very low base rate for violence, as in those studied by Wenk and colleagues, actuarial procedures may offer no particular advantage. Where modest improvement has been shown in one application, the gains may not persist when the predictive procedure is applied to a new sample. Even the more encouraging studies[253] may overestimate the advantage to be gained with statistical techniques, due to failure to apply the new method to a cross-validation sample.[254] Finally, even accepting the reduced error rates that have been obtained with derivation samples, the error in violence prediction remains so high that there will probably still be two incorrect designations of persons as "dangerous" for each correct one.

(e)   Implications of the Research for Reports and Testimony on Dangerousness

It is current practice among many mental health professionals involved in sentencing (and other

proceedings where long-term dangerousness may be an issue) to offer opinions to the effect that a given individual is or is not "dangerous" or is or is not "likely to be dangerous." Should mental health professionals offer such testimony, in view of the empirical research? A brief review of the legal requirements for the admissibility of expert testimony suggests that they should not.

There are two factors for primary consideration in the admissibility of opinion testimony [see § 1.04]. One is that the proposed witness has special knowledge beyond the ken of laypersons,[255] and the other is that the admission of such opinions will incrementally assist the factfinder in reaching a correct decision.[256]

Predictions of dangerousness based on actuarial procedures may be able to meet the criteria of special knowledge and incremental validity. Testimony that explains how predictor variables are identified, measured, tested, and combined takes the witness into areas beyond the ken of laypersons (e.g., explanations of test construction, item analysis, or multivariate procedures). Moreover, testimony based on actuarial data will not give the factfinder vague probability statements, but will precisely identify the likelihood of recidivism.

The literature reviewed above on *clinical* predictions of dangerousness, on the other hand, raises doubts that either the specialized knowledge or incremental assistance criteria could be met, at least if the predictions are made in the manner described in the studies cited earlier. The research reveals that mental health assessments of dangerousness are typically completed in an unsystematic and unscientific manner. Final opinions, though couched in clinical jargon and technical-sounding language, are often the result of compromise between team members and thus reflect an underlying democratic, but not necessarily scientific, procedure. Predictions of dangerousness also rely heavily on information readily available to the layperson, information that requires no particular expertise either to collect or to interpret. Thus, most "clinical" predictions do not appear to be based on the requisite special knowledge.

Even if one concludes, as we do, that there is a body of knowledge upon which clinicians *could* rely in assessing dangerousness (see the following subsection), it is clear that there is no specialized clinical knowledge that permits *categorical,* or even *relative,* conclusions about dangerousness. The most the clinical literature suggests is that there are certain factors that enhance or diminish the likelihood of violent behavior. Thus, the clinician should only be permitted to make statements such as "Factor X increases the likelihood of violent acts" or "Factor Y decreases the likelihood of assaultive behavior." Conclusions that someone is "dangerous" or even "more likely than not dangerous," in the absence of valid actuarial data, are inappropriate.

Opinion testimony in the form of categorical or relative predictions of dangerousness will also have difficulty meeting the test of incremental assistance. A review of the false-positive figures in Tables 7-1 and 7-2 reveals that under the *best* of circumstances, the expert's prediction will be wrong two times out of three. Even correcting for methodological problems in the studies, the error rate is over 50%. Are opinions with this magnitude of error likely to be of assistance to judges or lay jurors?

The Levinson and Ramsay[257] study listed in Table 7-1 is the only research reviewed in which the predictions of dangerousness were made by examiners who were essentially laypersons. The examiners in this study were employees at an emergency mental health service agency in a large metropolitan area and carried the title "Mental Health Associate" (MHA). The MHAs had all completed bachelor's degrees, and some had worked toward advanced degrees. None, however, could be considered the equivalent of a psychiatrist, nor is it likely that an MHA would have been allowed to give opinion testimony in court.[258] Yet it is evident from a review of the false-positive rates listed for various studies that the MHAs false-positive rate of 71% is competitive with the best rates achieved using either clinical or statistical prediction techniques. Discounting the Rappeport study, which used an inappropriate criterion for violence recidivism, only the study by Kozol, Boucher, and Garofalo resulted in a clearly lower rate of false positives for predictions of violence in the community. This finding suggests that in most instances, expert opinions in the form of unqualified predictions would not contribute appreciably to the accuracy of opinions that laypersons themselves would develop.

However, it should also be pointed out that a mental health professional may be able to identify certain violence-enhancing or violence-inhibiting factors that a judge or juror (as opposed to someone used to evaluating offenders) would not identify. Thus, while conclusory clinical opinions may be of no aid to the courts, it is inaccurate to say that clinicians *cannot* assist the factfinder in making dangerousness assessments.

A final evidentiary argument, advanced by Slobogin,[259] suggests that even if clinical prediction testimony does qualify as expert opinion, there are certain circumstances in which it will unduly mislead the factfinder. Specifically, when the state produces testimony unopposed by a defense expert, the factfinder will find it hard to resist a conclusion that the offender is dangerous, regardless of any "lay" testimony presented by the offender. Slobogin suggests that if clinical prediction testimony is to be admitted at all, it should only be permitted after the offender has decided to rely on such testimony.

Though this analysis, and others before it,[260] suggest that evidentiary rules might be used to exclude or limit clinical prediction testimony, the legal system has shown extreme reluctance to develop its own restraints. Most relevant here are rulings by the Supreme Court in death penalty litigation. The Court has affirmed the constitutionality of the capital sentencing criterion that "there is a probability that the defendant would commit criminal acts of violence that would constitute a continuing threat to society."[261] Similarly, as noted in § 7.06, in response to the American Psychiatric Association's concession that long-term predictions of dangerousness were so unreliable that they should be prohibited at capital sentencing, the Court responded flippantly that "[t]he suggestion that no psychiatrist's testimony may be presented with regard to dangerousness is somewhat like asking us to disinvent the wheel."[262] Professor Dix has summarized the Supreme Court's and lower courts' attitudes as reflecting "a total and unobscured abdication by both state and federal courts of the responsibility for assuring that imposition of the death penalty based on predictive testimony by mental health professionals bear some relationship to accuracy, reliability, or rationality."[263]

Though the courts seem comfortable with an "anything goes" attitude in prediction testimony, mental health professionals need not share the feeling. Awareness of the underlying research and sensitivity to issues of reliability and validity are ethically mandated for forensic clinicians. In view of this research, clinicians may decide that they cannot ethically offer prediction testimony. If, on the other hand, such testimony is offered, we feel certain practices should be followed in evaluating dangerousness and testifying about it.

(f) The Assessment of Long-Term Dangerousness

From our review of the literature on the long-term prediction of dangerous behavior, we have concluded that mental health professionals should not offer unqualified and categorical predictions in individual cases. Given, however, that the courts will continue to seek clinical input in assessing offenders' future dangerousness, this section addresses the nature of the inquiry regarding violence assessment and ethically acceptable forms in which information related to dangerousness might be communicated.

(1) Assessing Violence Potential

If a clinician is going to make statements about an individual's violence potential, he or she may do so either by describing the risk factors associated with a particular class of individuals whose violence potential is known and to which the subject belongs, or by conducting a careful inquiry into the personal and situational factors that have contributed to the individual's violent behavior in the past, in an effort to identify those conditions under which the likelihood of a future aggressive act is increased.

The first type of inquiry described is essentially an actuarial one, though the final outcome is not a categorical prediction of "dangerous" or

Table 7-3
Factors Associated with Violence Recidivism

Factor	Association with Violence
Prior arrest for violent crime	Probability of future violence increases with each prior criminal act. Various studies indicate that recidivism risk exceeds 50% for persons with more than five prior offenses.
Current age	Strong association between youth and criminal activity.
Age at first serious offense	Violence potential greater for offenders who were juveniles when the first serious offense occurred. Chronic juvenile offenders at greatest risk.
Sex	Males at significantly higher risk than females.
Race	Blacks at higher risk than other races.
Socioeconomic status and employment stability	Lower status and job instability associated with higher incidence of crime.
Opiate or alcohol abuse	Abusers at higher risk than nonabusers.
Family environment	Stable, supportive family environment associated with relatively lower risk.
Peer environment	Higher risk associated with "bad company."
Availability of victims	Higher risk if offender's prior violence has been toward a broad range of victims, or if there is history of multiple assaults on narrow class of victims (e.g., wife, girlfriends) who remain available.
Availability of alcohol or weapons	Risk increases with heavy drinking and ready access to weapons.

Note. Adapted from J. MONAHAN, PREDICTING VIOLENT BEHAVIOR: AN ASSESSMENT OF CLINICAL TECHNIQUES (1981).

"not dangerous," but a statement of relative risk. Some factors that have a correlation with violence recidivism are indicated in Table 7-3.[264] There is presently no equation that permits the clinician to systematically integrate all of these factors in a reliable manner, and Monahan[265] warns that some factors may be of little predictive value depending on the presence or absence of others. Prior history for violent crime should perhaps be given greater consideration than other variables; other variables, such as race, may mean little if anything in the absence of prior history.

It is also worth mentioning that some factors thought by many to be highly associated with violence are not. The illusory correlation between mental illness and violence has been mentioned,[266] and the strength of the association between sociopathy and criminal recidivism also bears careful reconsideration. Inconsistencies in the way the terms "sociopath" or "psychopath" have been defined both clinically[267] and in research[268] make it difficult to establish what relationship—or how strong a relationship—that diagnostic category may have with violence potential. We would also reiterate at this point the lack of any valid relationship between psychological test results and positive predictions of violence.[269]

By referring to the factors in Table 7-3, the clinician may be able to generate some useful information for the court's consideration. Where a clinician is familiar with particular studies showing the strength of the association between a particular factor and risk for future violence, he or she may choose to present those statistical data. For example, a clinician in New York might refer to a study such as Steadman and Cocozza,[270] which provides relative risk rates for previously incompetent offenders, depending on their history of prior arrests for violent crime: 7% of those with no prior offenses or one prior offense were rearrested for violent crime, as opposed to 20% of those with two to five priors and 64% of those with six or more priors. The court can then weigh these risk levels and other data presented to determine whether some legally relevant level of risk has been reached.

While relative risk data may be of some use to the court, the clinician's presentation is likely to be richer and more informative if descriptive information and explanatory themes developed from a careful investigation of the offender's prior violent episodes are included. The primary clinical technique in this kind of inquiry into dangerousness is the reconstructive interview, in which the clinician tries to discover both the personal and situational factors that have contributed to the offender's prior acts of violence. This may entail interviewing not only the offender, but also current or prior victims, or witnesses to the offender's violent acts who can report on their occurrence. The clinician may be able to uncover particular personal dynamics (e.g., a male offender responds aggressively to challenges to his masculinity) or situational variables (e.g., an offender is violent only when associating with certain other individuals) that may make some difference in the court's perception of the person's violence potential or need for preventive detention. This clinical information may also help to confirm or disconfirm inferred relationships among other variables related to violence potential. For instance, if it is discovered that an offender is addicted to heroin and purchases it with money obtained by selling stolen items, the offender may be at increased risk of violence, because of the possibility of a home owner's arriving home unexpectedly and finding the offender burglarizing the house.

(2) Ethical Considerations in Reporting Violence Potential

As noted in § 7.10(e), the courts have thus far been unresponsive to suggestions that clinical testimony on dangerousness prediction be excluded or modified due to the gross inaccuracy of such predictions. It appears that the courts, both in the sentencing context and in other areas, will continue to accept, encourage, or even require clinical input on the issue of dangerousness. Given this state of affairs, Dix has described the options for continuing to participate in proceedings involving the assessment of offenders' dangerousness:

> Mental health professionals have two choices. They can continue to participate in such proceedings knowing that the adversary system will

not function as intended, thereby securing un-critical—and potentially inaccurate—acceptance of the opinions of individual members of the profession. Or they can, in recognition of the apparent fact that any limitations upon such testimony must be self-imposed, formulate their own standards for professionally-acceptable testimony as to the dangerousness of a person.[271]

Given the weight often accorded clinicians' testimony about dangerousness, and the extreme consequences for the offender in certain contexts (felony sentencing, capital sentencing) in which mental health professionals might participate, the latter course of action seems the clear choice. We therefore recommend the following guidelines for clinicians in reporting the results of their assessments of violence potential:

1. Mental health professionals should offer no long-range clinical predictions of dangerousness behavior couched in absolute terms (e.g., "In my opinion, he will commit future acts of violence"). Nor, unless there is valid actuarial data indicating the precise probability of recidivism, should the professional couch testimony in relative terms (e.g., "In my opinion, this person is likely to be dangerous"). Rather, the clinician should only refer to violence-enhancing or violence-inducing factors (e.g., "This man reacts violently to threats to his masculinity," or "This person does not appear to engage in violent behavior when under medication").[272]

2. To deter the judge or jury from giving undue weight to clinical testimony about violence potential, clinicians should volunteer prefatory comments, both in written reports and in oral testimony, regarding the poor validity (i.e., no better than one in three) of clinicians' positive predictions of dangerousness.

3. Clinicians should minimize reference to diagnostic labels in reports addressing dangerousness. (Diagnoses themselves have no demonstrable utility in violence prediction, and their meaning is highly susceptible to being augmented by the judge or juror with negative connotations based on stereotypic definitions—particularly where the diagnosis is schizophrenia or some variety of sociopathic/psychopathic/antisocial personality.)

4. Consonant with recommendation 1, to the degree permitted by the available clinical and actuarial data, clinicians should identify the circumstances in which the person is more or less likely to behave aggressively, and should identify the class of victims at greater risk. The clinician should also identify circumstances that may inhibit violence by the individual.

If these rules are followed, the clinical opinion may in fact be helpful to the factfinder and not unduly prejudicial.

BIBLIOGRAPHY

Barefoot v. Estelle, 463 U.S. 880 (1983).

A. CAMPBELL, THE LAW OF SENTENCING (1978).

Cavender & Mushenko, *The Adoption and Implementation of Determinate-Based Sentencing Policies: A Critical Perspective,* GEO. L. REV. 425 (1983).

Dershowitz, *The Role of Psychiatry in the Sentencing Process,* 1 INT'L J.L. & PSYCHIATRY 63 (1978).

Dix, *The Death Penalty, "Dangerousness," Psychiatric Testimony and Professional Ethics,* 5 AM. J. CRIM. L. 151 (1977).

Konecni, Mulcahy, & Ebbesen, *Prison or Mental Hospital: Factors Affecting the Processing of Persons Suspected of Being "Mentally Disordered Sex Offenders,"* in NEW DIRECTIONS IN PSYCHOLEGAL RESEARCH (P. Lipsitt & B. Sales eds. 1980).

Lockett v. Ohio, 438 U.S. 586 (1978).

J. MONAHAN, PREDICTING VIOLENT BEHAVIOR: AN ASSESSMENT OF CLINICAL TECHNIQUES (1981).

Monahan, *The Prediction of Violent Behavior: Developments in Psychology and Law,* in PSYCHOLOGY AND THE LAW (Volume 2 of the American Psychological Association's Master Lecture Series, J. Schreirer & B. Hammonds eds. 1983).

Monahan & Ruggiero, *Psychological and Psychiatric Aspects of Determinate Criminal Sentencing,* 3 INT'L J.L. PSYCHIATRY 143 (1980).

NATIONAL INSTITUTE OF CORRECTIONS, OFFENDER NEEDS ASSESSMENT: MODELS AND APPROACHES (1984).

Slobogin, *Dangerousness and Expertise,* 133 U. PA. L. REV. 97 (1984).

United States v. Grayson, 438 U.S. 586 (1978).

A. VONHIRSCH, DOING JUSTICE (1976).

D. WEXLER, CRIMINAL COMMITMENTS AND DANGEROUS MENTAL PATIENTS: LEGAL ISSUES OF CONFINEMENT, TREATMENT, AND RELEASE (1976).

PART III

Noncriminal Adjudications

CHAPTER EIGHT

Civil Commitment

8.01. Introduction

The term "civil commitment" refers to the state-sanctioned, involuntary hospitalization of mentally disordered individuals who are thought to need treatment, care or incapacitation because of self-harming or antisocial tendencies. Like the criminal justice system, the civil commitment process authorizes institutionalization of an individual because of behavior deemed unacceptable to the community. However, there are major differences between the two systems, including differences in the jurisprudential basis for the state's intervention, the definition of behavior that may trigger that intervention, the process by which the state accomplishes intervention, and the duration of the intervention.

The jurisprudential basis of criminal law is the so-called "police power," which authorizes the state to protect the community and to "ensure domestic tranquility."[1] While the criminal justice system may seek to rehabilitate offenders, it serves other purposes that are at least as important, such as retribution and deterrence [see § 7.01]. In contrast, civil commitment has traditionally been justified under the state's *parens patriae* authority to act as the "general guardian of all infants, idiots and lunatics."[2] The grounds for intervention have been focused on the needs

of the *individual,* not society. Today, as a result of legal challenges making dangerousness an explicit criterion, the jurisprudential basis for commitment is an uneasy mixture of the police and *parens patriae* powers; however, this mixture still emphasizes treatment rather than punishment.

Similarly, although the behavior that precipitates intervention may be the same in either system, it is described differently. An act is not criminal unless the legislature has specifically defined it as such, in enough detail that the individual can fairly be said to have sufficient "notice" that the behavior is outlawed by society.[3] With civil commitment, on the other hand, the terms describing the grounds for intervention—"mental disorder," "need for treatment," "dangerousness"—have eluded precise definition. It is probably inevitable that the predicate for commitment will be amorphous, at least relative to the criminal law. While the criminal system may be triggered only in response to an event that has already occurred because it is premised on *punishment*, commitment is designed to prevent a future occurrence. Thus, it is probably impossible, and may in any event be counterproductive, to specify with the degree of detail required under the criminal law the type of behavior that will lead to commitment.

The criminal and civil processes also differ.

As described in § 2.04(c), the criminal process, because it may result in incarceration, affords a panoply of procedural protections, including the right to counsel, to cross-examination, and to an open hearing. Perhaps most importantly, from a symbolic standpoint at least, the state is forced to bear the burden of proving its case by proof "beyond a reasonable doubt." As the Supreme Court has noted, use of this highest standard of proof "manifests our concern that the risk of error to the individual must be minimized even at the risk that some who are guilty might go free."[4] In contrast, the civil commitment process, though "legalized" in the last decade, is still lax procedurally [see § 8.05(c)] and demands proof only by the lesser standard of "clear and convincing evidence,"[5] reflecting the notion that society is not as troubled by false commitment as it is by false conviction.

Finally, the duration of intervention varies in each system. In the criminal process, the length of sentence is fixed by the legislature, guided by retributive notions (as well as, perhaps, by rehabilitative, deterrence, and incapacitative concerns). While convicted offenders may be somewhat uncertain as to when they will be released, the scope of their sentence is established by law and may not be altered.[6] With civil commitment, on the other hand, most jurisdictions impose no limits on the cumulative length of stay, so long as the individual continues to meet the statutory basis for commitment. The length of each discrete commitment is usually limited (e.g., an individual may be committed for a period of time not to exceed six months), but neither the legislature nor any other authority poses limits on the number of recommitments, and hence on the total length of time the individual may spend hospitalized.

On the basis of these differences, the criminal system has been called an example of the "sanction model" of state intervention, and the civil commitment process an example of the "control model."[7] The precise ways in which civil commitment controls behavior, rather than punishes it, are spelled out in Stone's summary of what he calls the four social goals to which commitment is responsive[8]: (1) By hospitalizing the mentally disordered, it provides care and treat-

ment for those requiring it; (2) by removing the individual to a protective environment, it prevents allegedly irresponsible people from harming themselves; (3) by removing the individual from the community, it protects society from the anticipated dangerous acts of the person; and (4) by placing the individual in an environment providing basic needs in a setting isolated from the general community, it relieves society and the family from accommodating those who are bothersome through perhaps not dangerous.

The conflicted nature of the control model is evident from this enumeration. Commitment may be viewed as benevolent in intent because it effectuates the provision of treatment. But it also has protective functions generally associated with the criminal law. Moreover, it arguably serves a political function by making possible the removal from society those considered nuisances or troublesome.

Thus, while the need for a criminal justice system is generally accepted, questions over the underlying legitimacy of civil commitment persist. Some commentators, most prominently Szasz,[9] question whether the state should ever be permitted to confine an individual involuntarily except through the sanction model. Others, like Morse,[10] believe that clinical decisionmaking is so flawed, and the tendency of the legal system to rely on clinical opinion is so pervasive, that the deprivation of individual liberty represented by the institution of commitment is completely unjustified. Still others, while conceding the propriety of intervention as a general principle, question its application to the facts of a given case.

Partly driven by these types of concerns, and also influenced by the generic civil rights movement of the time, a series of lawsuits beginning in the early 1970s sought to change drastically the institution of civil commitment. The suits were of three types: those challenging the substantive and procedural criteria of state commitment laws[11]; those attacking institutional conditions (e.g., "right to treatment" and "least restrictive alternative" suits)[12]; and those addressing the administration of treatment (e.g., cases asserting a right to refuse treatment).[13] Although, as described above, this litigation did not erase the differences between commitment and the criminal system, it did have a significant impact on the law of commitment.

The legal segment of this chapter describes the impulses that spawned the first type of litigation, its legal antecedents, and the current trend toward dismantling some of its accomplishments. To a lesser extent, this chapter also looks at the second type of litigation. The third species of suit is examined in § 9.03(b).

The chapter then examines the research concerning the impact of recent changes in commitment law (concluding that it has not been as significant as one might hope), as well as studies looking at the "benefits" of hospitalization. Next, it recommends the proper role for both attorneys and mental health professionals who participate in commitment. Finally, it discusses the nature and process of commitment evaluations.

8.02.   The Jurisprudential Basis for Commitment

As noted above, the law's conceptualization of the justification for involuntary hospitalization has changed over time. This section begins with a brief history of the institution of commitment, and then examines its traditional underpinnings and the changes that have occurred in the past two decades.

(a)   A Brief Historical Overview

Ancient civilizations dealt with the problems of the mentally disordered by means of familiar-sounding methods. According to Brakel and Rock, Greek philosophers recommended that the mentally disabled be cared for in a comfortable, sanitary, well-lighted place.[14] The Romans appointed a "curator" (guardian) to safeguard the property of the mentally disabled, and debated the legal effect of decisions made by the ward during lucid moments.[15]

During the Middle Ages, medical definitions of mental disorder were supplanted by theories of possession by demons, and exorcism and forms of torture become primary antidotes.[16] Nonetheless, there was no drastic change in the *law's* approach to mental disorder, except for a more refined effort to differentiate between the mentally retarded and the mentally ill. In England, the *De Praerogativa Regis* (literally, the "Prerogative of the King") was enacted between 1255 and 1290. It divided the mentally disabled into two classes, "idiots" and "lunatics."[17] The King took custody of the lands of an idiot defined as a person who "hath no understanding from his nativity," and could retain any profits from the land.[18] In contrast, the King merely served as guardian of the lands of a lunatic, defined as "a person who hath had understanding, but . . . hath lost the use of his reason"; any profits from such guardianships were not retained by the crown, but were applied to the maintenance of the mentally disordered persons and their households.[19] Over time, procedures developed whereby a jury determined whether an individual was an idiot or a lunatic. While the former were often confined in public houses, the latter were usually committed to the care of friends or relatives who received an allowance for the cost of care; the management of an individual's estate was placed with the incompetent's heir or nearest relative in order to prevent its depletion.[20]

In colonial America, the indigent mentally disordered often formed bands, wandering the countryside.[21] Only occasionally did a community arrange for the sustenance of these individuals, utilizing a guardian or custodian. More typically, they were the subject of ridicule, harassment, and in some cases whipping from a society that equated a failure to work with immorality.[22] The first American hospital for the exclusive care of the mentally disordered was not established until 1773, in Williamsburg, Virginia; the second came in 1824 in Lexington, Kentucky. These "asylums" were designed initially for the primary purpose of confining the violent mentally disordered.[23] The evidence suggests that there were more procedural safeguards available to individuals deprived of the right to manage their property than there were to the persons placed in such institutions.[24] For nearly a century, the latter intervention often could be secured based on the request of a friend or relative to the staff of the institution.[25]

In the latter half of the 19th century, reform efforts led by individuals who had been confined on flimsy authority[26] and by those concerned with the lack of adequate facilities for the mentally disordered[27] stimulated cosmetic changes in commitment laws, some reformation of existing facilities, and the construction of new ones. Perhaps in part because of these new facilities, the census in public mental hospitals grew virtually unimpeded for nearly a century.

Then, beginning in the 1950s, the hospital population began dropping drastically. Between 1955 and 1975, the confined population appears to have slipped from approximately 560,000 to under 200,000, a 65% decrease.[28]

Several events may explain this sudden change. First, the mid-1950s saw the first use of psychotropic medication on a wide scale, seemingly making possible the stabilization and return to the community of thousands of formerly overtly psychotic patients.[29] Second, in 1963 President Kennedy called for the development of community services for the mentally disabled, and the subsequent passage of the Community Mental Health Centers Act promised the development of a capacity to treat individuals on an outpatient basis in the community.[30] Finally, beginning in the early 1970s the legal profession began examining the institution of commitment in earnest—a subject to which we now turn.

(b) The Legal Authority for Commitment: The Traditional View

As noted earlier, the *parens patriae* power, rooted in English law, enabled the King to act as "general guardian of incapacitated classes, including infants and the mentally disordered."[31] When the state acts as *parens patriae,* the theoretical impulse for its action is benevolent.[32] The state's police power, on the other hand, enables it to act as protector of the community—to make law and regulations for the protection of public health, safety, welfare, and morals. When a state action is meant to vindicate a societal interest rather than to further the interest of an individual, it constitutes an exercise of the police power.[33]

Until the debates of the 1960s and 1970s, courts viewed civil commitment as an exercise of *parens patriae* power. For example, the Iowa Supreme Court characterized commitment as fundamentally and acceptably paternalistic in nature:

> It must be kept in mind that Appellant is not charged with a crime and is not so incarcerated. He is being restrained of his liberty in that he is not free to come and go at will *but such restraint is not in the way of punishment, but for his own protection and welfare* as well as for the benefit of society.[34] (emphasis added)

The court went on to conclude that the liberty interest infringed by civil commitment was "not such liberty as is within the meaning of the constitutional provision that 'no person shall be deprived of life, liberty or property without due process of law.'"[35] Since liberty in the constitutional sense was not being deprived, little if any "process" was "due." Wexler has summarized the traditional response of the judiciary to challenges to civil commitment law as follows:

> Where the state's aim is not to punish but to assist by providing therapy, there is no need for an adversary process because *all* parties have the best interest of the deviant at heart. And, the argument continues, the criminal law safeguards have no place in a therapeutic proceeding, for they serve only to "criminalize" the process and further stigmatize the subject, and they are simply unnecessary impediments to achieving the central goal, which is to help the deviant actor.[36]

Courts and legislators, assuming that mental illness was an identifiable entity like other illnesses, and that the medical profession was best equipped to determine whether an individual was ill, premised civil commitment statutes upon the medical model of mental illness, and identified physicians rather than judges as the primary decisionmakers at commitment. For example, in 1970, 31 states provided for hospitalization of an individual based simply on the certification of

one or more physicians that the individual suffered from mental illness.[37]

Even in jurisdictions where the judiciary was
the principal decisionmaker, courts routinely deferred to medical opinion. For example, the
American Bar Foundation study of hospitalization and discharge concluded:

> The judicial commitment procedure thus
> amounts to administrative monitoring, often
> cursory, or a medically oriented process upon
> which jural apparatus has been grafted . . .
> the court becomes essentially ministerial . . .
> The medical treatment questions are deter-
> mined by medical testimony from examiners
> whose opinions are rarely at variance and are
> rarely disputed.[38]

While commitment laws and process were medically oriented, in the view of organized psychiatry there was still too *much* legal involvement:

> [F]rom a medical point of view, the worst fea-
> tures of commitment law . . . include these:
> Insistence that the patient appear personally in
> court . . . the acceptance of a lay judgment as
> to the degree of illness . . . the use of archaic
> legal terminology such as "insane," "of un-
> sound mind," "idiot," "feebleminded," etc., all
> of them conveying a legal, rather than a med-
> ical, meaning . . .[39]

It was this attitude that became the focus for
challenge in the courts.

(c)   The Reform Movement

Challenges to civil commitment statutes in the
1970s represented the juxtaposition of three related strands of thought. The first questioned the
validity of the medical model itself and its corollary assumption that commitment was properly a medical decision made for benevolent reasons; the second questioned whether the
consequences of commitment were in fact humane; and the third asked whether the criteria
for commitment and the process by which commitment occurred were inherently flawed. The
underlying premise that unified these challenges
was a belief that civil commitment had consequences for the committed individual at least as
serious as those faced by a convicted criminal.

(1)   Challenges to the Medical Model

Civil commitment is premised upon a belief that
"mental illness" is definable and treatable. The
frontal assault on this concept, and on the credibility of the psychiatric profession generally, was
critical in providing a conceptual basis for the
reformation movement. Reformists characterized the term "mental illness" as nothing more
than a label the state used to legitimize the segregation of individuals who were unacceptable
to the majority of citizens. The acts of diagnosis
and commitment were characterized by "Szasz-
ians" as political acts of a decidedly negative type.[40]
The decision to commit was cast not as a medical decision by which an incapacitated individual
obtained needed treatment, but as a deprivation
of constitutionally protected individual liberty.

The attack on the validity of mental illness
was accompanied by an attack on its high priests,
the psychiatric profession. A variety of studies
questioned the validity and reliability of psychiatric diagnosis,[41] and a consensus developed that
psychiatrists were unable to predict dangerousness with any greater degree of accuracy than a
layperson.[42]

This challenge resulted in a fundamental redefinition by the courts of the values at stake in
commitment. The redefinition was bolstered by
the United States Supreme Court, which in the
1972 decision of *Humphrey v. Cady* helped reverse
a century of judicial characterization of commitment as a medical decision by concluding that
commitment involved a "massive curtailment of
liberty."[43] In the same term, the Court seemed,
in *Jackson v. Indiana*,[44] to invite challenges to
commitment laws, commenting that given the
number of persons affected by commitment in
its various forms, "it is perhaps remarkable that
the substantive constitutional limitations on this
power have not been more frequently liti-
gated."[45]

The lower courts were quick to recognize the
challenges to the credibility of psychiatric decisionmaking. In the leading lower-court decision,

Lessard v. Schmidt, the court quoted a law review article to this effect:

> "Obviously, the definition of mental illness is left largely to the user and is dependent upon the norms of adjustment that he employs. Usually the use of the phrase 'mental illness' effectively masks the actual norms being applied. And, because of the unavoidably ambiguous generalities in which the American Psychiatric Association describes its diagnostic categories, the diagnostician has the ability to shoehorn into the mentally diseased class almost any person he wishes, for whatever reason, to put there."[46]

Another court, expressing concern over the broad latitude given psychiatrists by statutes relying on the vaguely defined concept of "mental illness" as a basis for commitment, concluded that the courts were "blindly relying on the conclusion drawn by the examining psychiatrist."[47] Creation of stricter statutory terms was thought necessary to avoid commitment decisions "dependent upon the examining psychiatrist's *personal conception* of normal social behavior."[48]

(2)   Challenges to the Consequences of Commitment

A second prong of the reform movement challenged the conditions to which a person committed civilly was subjected. These included both the physical setting of the facilities in which the committed person purportedly was treated, and the loss of other civil rights that often ensued automatically as a result of commitment.

The committed patient was and still usually is the responsibility of the public mental health system. A major facet of the reform movement was exposing the failures of the system through litigation as well as through journalistic "muckraking." One group, recapitulating the challenges to civil commitment laws, observed:

> The loss of physical freedom resulting from civil commitment is, for all practical purposes, little different from that which results from a prison sentence. Depending upon the quality of the hospital, a person committed may be subject to overcrowding, unsanitary conditions, poor nutrition and even to brutality at the hands of attendants or other hospital residents. Com-

mitment also infringes grossly upon privacy, and committed patients may be subjected to compulsory medication, electroconvulsive therapy and other potentially hazardous and intrusive procedures . . ."[49]

Even leading psychiatrists confirmed that "the megainstitutions presided over by the mental health professions are an acknowledged disaster."[50] "Right to treatment" litigation epitomized by the seminal case of *Wyatt v. Stickney,* which ordered sweeping reforms in Alabama's mental health facilities, epitomized the view that the state could not be assumed to be acting benevolently when it commits an individual.[51]

Critics also pointed to the collateral consequences of commitment. The most significant was (and is) the "stigma" attaching to the individual labeled "mentally ill" and committed to an institution. The label "mental illness" was said to have replaced such terms as "lunacy," "insanity," and "pauper lunatic," which carried with them notions of "alienation, [and] banishment from society into asylums located away in the country."[52] The conclusion that commitment stigmatized its subject fueled the argument that the act of diagnosis itself was an inherently destructive act.[53] A second collateral consequence of commitment was (and is) an increased risk of institutional dependency, which undercut the individual's ability to deal with the world outside the institution.[54] Finally, commitment often resulted in the loss of important civil rights, including the right to enter into a contract, the right to vote, the right to marry and to bear children, the right to obtain a driver's license, and the right to serve on juries.

These arguments elicited a sympathetic judicial response. The West Virginia Supreme Court of Appeals, considering a challenge to that state's commitment laws, found that "in determining whether there is any justification under the doctrine of *parens patriae* for deviation from established due process standards, it is appropriate for this court to consider that the State of West Virginia offers to those unfortunates who are incarcerated in mental institutions Dickensian squalor of unconscionable magnitudes."[55] The federal court that decided the seminal case of *Lessard v. Schmidt,*[56] noting the low number of physicians available in Wisconsin's public mental health facilities, observed that "perhaps the most serious possible effect of a decision to commit an individual lies in the statistics which indicate that an individual committed to a mental institution has a much greater chance of dying than if he were left at large."[57] It summarized its findings by observing:

> It is obvious that the commitment adjudication carries with it an enormous and devastating impact on an individual's civil rights. In some respects, such as the limitation on holding a driver's license, *the civil deprivations which follow civil commitment are more serious than the deprivations which accompany a criminal conviction.*[58] (emphasis added)

The conclusion that commitment was largely deleterious to the individual shook the *parens patriae* basis of commitment to the core. The District of Columbia Federal Court of Appeals held that "without some form of treatment the state justification for acting as *parens patriae* becomes a nullity,"[59] and the West Virginia Supreme Court concluded that "the ancient doctrine of *parens patriae* is in full retreat on all fronts except in those very narrow areas where the state can demonstrate, as a matter of fact, that its care and custody is superior to any available alternative."[60]

(3)   Challenges to the Process of and Criteria for Commitment

Those hoping to *abolish* commitment relied on the foregoing contentions: that mental illness is a bankrupt term easily manipulated to effectuate political acts and that the "treatment" provided those so confined was more likely detrimental than beneficial. On the realistic assumption that the commitment system would continue to exist, *reformers* used these two arguments as the basis for seeking to replace the medically dominated and informal judicial process by which commitment occurred with legalized procedure designed to minimize error in decisionmaking and criteria designed to narrow the scope of intervention.[61] The argument was that the state may constitutionally deprive individuals of liberty only after affording them "due process of law."

On the procedural front, plaintiffs turned naturally to the criminal justice system for their model, because it represented the ultimate use and refinement of the constitutional "due process" model of decisionmaking. The Supreme Court provided impetus for this approach with its 1967 decision *In re Gault,*[62] imposing the adult criminal model on a juvenile court system that until that time had been grounded on the same therapeutic, *parens patriae* principle underlying civil commitment. To the critics of the medical model of decisionmaking, adoption of the criminal procedure approach, including the right to counsel, to confront one's "accusers," and to notice, would not only improve the accuracy of commitment decisions, but would also alter the basic nature of the inquiry conducted at commitment. Dershowitz,[63] for example, argued that if the commitment decision is perceived as primarily medical in nature, medical control of the inquiry is inevitable, because the pertinent questions will be posed in medical terms (e.g., does a *physician* believe that the individual is in *need of treatment?).* Assumptions about the validity and reliability of medical decisionmaking and the therapeutic intent underlying the state's intervention will go unchallenged. However, when loss of liberty is seen as the chief consequence of commitment, *courts* will become the decisionmakers of choice, and the inquiry will ideally involve more formalized scrutiny of the state's interests in restricting the individual's liberty.

The critics argued, furthermore, that the Constitution required changes not simply in the procedural trappings of civil commitment, but also in its substantive criteria. If clinical decisionmaking was inherently flawed because of its inexact nature and because of the vague criteria for commitment, then something more than clinical opinion on treatability was required. Again borrowing from the criminal law, the idea grew that the individual must be shown to have committed an "overt act" unacceptable to society (the equivalent of the *actus reus* in the criminal law) before commitment can occur.[64] More fundamentally, the mere existence of mental illness and need for treatment was no longer deemed sufficient to commit an individual. Following the analogy with criminal law, plaintiffs argued that the state's *parens patriae* power should be strictly curtailed, and that commitment should be viewed primarily as an exercise of the police power. Thus, some argued that it should be permitted only when the individual was found dangerous to others. Others would permit commitments on "dangerousness to self" grounds as well, but strictly defined to exclude nonsuicidal behavior.

The judiciary accepted many of these arguments. The courts ordered state legislatures to reform civil commitment statutes to incorporate a more legalistic process for commitment and more specific substantive criteria.[65] These statutes, largely products of the 1970s, are discussed in § 8.03 below. But first, to complete the historical picture, we trace the legal developments of the late 1970s. They appear to signal a retreat from the reform movement's efforts to equate civil commitment with the criminal model, and may well augur a new generation of statutes.

(d)   Supreme Court Retrenchment

As the 1970s drew to a close, the medical model of commitment stood largely discredited, and the "legalistic" model held sway. However, while the lower courts were almost unanimous in their view of civil commitment, the United States Supreme Court, primarily through the opinions of Chief Justice Burger, encouraged the emergence of a less "legalistic" approach to commitment issues. In a series of cases, the Court reasserted the legitimacy of the state's *parens patriae* authority and, more importantly, began rehabilitating the medical/administrative model as a constitutionally permissible method of decisionmaking.

In doing this, the Court did not retreat from its earlier statement that commitment involved a "massive curtailment of liberty." In *O'Connor v. Donaldson*,[66] involving the lengthy coerced confinement of an individual who had repeatedly sought his freedom, the court defined the issue as a "single, relatively simple, but nonetheless important question concerning every man's constitutional right to liberty."[67] The Court ruled that "the State cannot constitutionally confine without more a non-dangerous individual who is capable of surviving safely in freedom by himself

or with the help of willing and responsible family members or friends."[68]

Although the meaning of this rather conservative and ambiguous holding has been much debated,[69] it did emphasize the Court's belief that the civil commitment process must answer to the Constitution. On the other hand, the majority opinion is studiously vague with respect to the precise limitations imposed by constitutional precepts and thus did not endorse explicitly any of the libertarian reforms adopted by the lower courts. And Chief Justice Burger, in a much less ambiguously worded concurring opinion, put forward a generous view of the *parens patriae* power and the permissible consequences of its use which suggested a skeptical attitude toward these reforms. The Chief Justice acknowledged that involuntary commitment constituted a deprivation of liberty, which the state could not accomplish without due process of law.[70] But he rejected the contention, accepted by the lower court in *Donaldson*,[71] that the state could confine those who were not physically dangerous only if it provided treatment for them. Instead, he noted, "custodial confinement" was a long-recognized and legitimate purpose of commitment.[72] He concluded:

> [T]he idea that states may not confine the mentally ill except for the purpose of providing them with treatment is of very recent origin, and there is no historical basis for imposing such a limitation on state power . . . [in addition to the police power] the states are vested with the historic *parens patriae* power . . . The classic example of this role is when a state undertakes to act as "the general guardian of all infants, idiots, and lunatics."[73]

The Chief Justice wrote for a unanimous Court in its next major mental health decision on civil commitment, *Addington v. Texas*.[74] The Court held that the Constitution required use of a "clear and convincing" standard of proof at a commitment hearing—a level of certainty falling between the "beyond a reasonable doubt" standard the Court required in juvenile delinquency cases and in criminal cases,[75] and the "preponderance of the evidence" standard typically used in civil proceedings [see § 2.04].

In so holding, the Supreme Court moved some distance from lower courts' pronouncements on the subject of involuntary commitment. While acknowledging that commitment involved a constitutionally significant loss of liberty, and noting that "stigma" could have a "very significant impact on the individual,"[76] the Court reiterated that the state had authority to commit both under its police power and under its *parens patriae* power. The Court also characterized the exercise of this power in decidedly less negative terms than had the lower courts, and said explicitly that commitment and the criminal process were dissimilar: "In civil commitment state power is not exercised in a punitive sense. Unlike the delinquency proceeding . . . . *a civil commitment proceeding can in no sense be equated to a criminal prosecution*"[77] (emphasis added).

The opinion also planted the seeds for a characterization of the commitment *process* that differed significantly from the views of the courts that had earlier considered the issue. The Supreme Court asserted that "whether the individual is mentally ill and dangerous to himself or others and is in need of confined therapy turns on the *meaning* of the facts *which must be interpreted by expert psychiatrists and psychologists*"[78] (emphasis added). Other courts had assumed that it was for the judiciary to draw the necessary conclusions from the facts; *Addington* intimated that the Chief Justice and a majority of the Court did not accept that view.

The *Addington* opinion did emphasize the "lack of certainty and fallibility of psychiatric diagnosis."[79] But it did so only to support its rejection of the reasonable doubt standard. It stated that because the art of psychiatry was insufficiently precise, the state could not meet the burden imposed by the criminal standard and therefore only need meet the less stringent "clear and convincing evidence" test. But Chief Justice Burger did not evidence any further willingness to question the pre-eminence of clinical expertise. In fact, as the Chief Justice soon demonstrated, he could find many strengths in psychiatry when it served the jurisprudence he was attempting to develop in the field of mental health law.

The Supreme Court took its most dramatic step in the rehabilitation of the medical model of commitment in *Parham v. J.R.*, another opinion authored by Chief Justice Burger.[80] The *Parham* case presented a challenge to Georgia's vol-

untary commitment procedures for children under the age of 18. Under these procedures, a facility superintendent could admit a child temporarily for observation and diagnosis, upon receipt of an application for hospitalization signed by a parent or guardian. If observation revealed that the child suffered from mental illness and was suitable for treatment in the hospital, the superintendent could admit the child "for such period and under such conditions as may be authorized by law."[81] The superintendent also had what the Court described as an "affirmative duty" to release a child who had recovered from mental illness or who had improved sufficiently to render hospitalization no longer desirable.[82]

This statutory scheme had few of the elements that lower courts had found necessary to satisfy due process. It depended wholly on the judgment of the admitting parent or guardian (the latter including the state acting as custodian) and the facility medical staff. No attorney was provided for the child, nor was there any requirement of a finding of "dangerousness." The lower federal court had found the statute unconstitutional because it failed to protect children's due process rights.[83] But the Supreme Court reinstated the statutory scheme.

The Court began by stating that, in determining whether the admission procedures were constitutional, it had to consider the child's interest in not being committed (an interest in this case "inextricably linked with the parents' interest in and obligation for the welfare and health of the child"), the state's interest in the procedures it had adopted for the commitment and treatment of children, and how well the scheme protected against arbitrary commitment decisions.[84] The Court agreed that the child had a substantial and constitutionally protected liberty interest in not being confined unnecessarily. However, the Court rejected the notion that the "stigma" resulting from being adjudicated criminal, delinquent, or mentally ill and dangerous attached in the case before it: The state, acting through its voluntary procedures, "does not 'label' the child; it provides a diagnosis and treatment that medical specialists conclude the child requires."[85]

The opinion also rejected the argument that the child's interests were of such magnitude and the likelihood of parental abuse so great that a formal adversary hearing had to be provided prior to commitment. The Court noted the law's traditional concept of the family "as a unit with broad parental authority over minor children."[86] That authority should be presumed to be exercised appropriately, since the law has long "recognized that natural bonds of affection lead parents to act in the best interests of their child."[87] The exercise of that authority should not be subject to a formal, adversary hearing, because "the fact that a child may balk at hospitalization or complain about a parental refusal to provide cosmetic surgery does not diminish the parents' authority to decide what is best for the child."[88] Other courts had depicted commitment as a negative experience, far removed from the realm of "normal" or usual medical decisions; to the Chief Justice, on the other hand, the decision to hospitalize a child was like a tonsillectomy, appendectomy, or other medical procedure.[89] Other courts viewed an adversary proceeding as a necessary way of guarding against unnecessary or inappropriate commitments; the Chief Justice, assuming the necessity of hospitalization, concluded that "the *parens patriae* interest in helping parents care for the mental health of their children cannot be fulfilled if the parents are unwilling to take advantage of the opportunities because the admission process is too onerous, too embarrassing, or too contentious."[90]

As this last statement suggests, the Court also emphasized its adherence to the medical decisionmaking model hinted at in *Addington.* The Court acknowledged that the risk of error inherent in parental decisionmaking was sufficiently great to require an inquiry by a "neutral factfinder," who would probe the child's background using all available sources.[91] However, a judge would not be required, since the decision to hospitalize was a *medical* decision, and " 'neither judges nor administrative hearing officers are better qualified than psychiatrists to render psychiatric judgments.' "[92] Lower courts had consistently characterized the decision to commit or not to commit as a *legal* decision informed by medical evidence. However, the Court thought the issue to be "essentially medical in character . . . Even after a hearing, the nonspecialist decisionmaker must make a medical–psychiatric decision."[93] The Court also concluded that de-

spite "the fallibility of medical and psychiatric diagnosis," shifting the locus of decision making from a "trained specialist" to an "untrained judge" would not remedy those shortcomings.[94]

The implication of these remarks is quite clear. To the Court, psychiatric decisionmaking is sufficiently refined to label the issues involved as medical rather than legal in nature, and deserves the type of deference generally reserved for judicial decisionmaking when constitutionally protected values are at stake. The fact that *Parham* involved the commitment of children should not obscure the fact that the decision represents a distinct departure from the tone of earlier lower-court decisions. Indeed, one could argue that those who seek to commit adults have the adults' best interest at heart as well (since the would-be committers are often family members or clinicians). Arguably, the underlying rationale of the majority opinion in *Parham* would apply as well to general-commitment statues.

These cases, plus a number of other Court decisions in the area of mental health,[95] have laid the groundwork for a new round in the debate over the legalization of the commitment process and the amount of deference that courts should properly pay to clinical decisionmakers. There is clear evidence that these decisions have had an impact on at least some lower courts,[96] despite criticism both within the Court[97] and from commentators.[98] It may be concluded, at a minimum, that it is highly unlikely that either the substantive or procedural criteria for civil commitment will be further legalized in the near future. It also may be predicted that administrative and clinical forms of decisionmaking in other areas (e.g., issues of consent to treatment) will be given wider latitude than had become the norm in the 1970s.

8.03. Substantive Criteria for Commitment

While the constitutional challenges to state commitment laws did not result in the abolition of commitment, they did effect significant statutory change, which to date has been largely unaffected by the Supreme Court's retrenchment. A description of each state's commitment laws is impossible; however, certain key elements are incorporated in each and are discussed in this section and the next section. This section discusses the substantive criteria that define the universe of those who may be committed. The next section [§ 8.04] discusses the procedurial rules that must be followed in determining whether the substantive criteria are met.

(a) An Overview

While state statutes vary in defining each substantive criterion, certain requirements are relatively uniform. First, the starting point in all statutes is the existence of mental disorder. Second, in defining mental disorder, many jurisdictions inject what is in effect another substantive criterion by requiring that the disorder result in lack of capacity to recognize the need for treatment. Third, each statute also requires a finding that the individual is or may be dangerous to self or others as a result of the mental disorder. This emphasis on dangerousness is the clearest legacy of the reform movement.

Fourth, most statutes allow commitment on the ground that the mental disorder renders the individual unable to care for self. This latter criterion may be a part of the definition of danger to self, or it may stand as a separate justification for commitment. A few states also insist that there be a "need for treatment," although permitting commitment on this ground alone would probably be unconstitutional under *Donaldson*.

Finally, many statutes require consideration of the place of treatment at the time of commitment. This criterion, generally called the "least restrictive alternative" or "least restrictive environment," seeks to limit hospitalization to those cases in which no alternative (or less restrictive) locus for treatment exists.

The content of each of these criteria is considered briefly below.

(b) Mental Disorder

The first criterion for commitment is the existence of mental disorder. Many statutory defi-

nitions of "mental disorder" or "mental illness" are still vague, despite the efforts of the reform movement. One of the most specific definitions is as follows:

> "Mental illness" means a substantial disorder of thought, mood, perception, orientation or memory, any of which grossly impairs judgment, behavior, capacity to recognize reality, or ability to meet the ordinary demands of life, but shall not include mental retardation.[99]

This definition gives notice that the "disorder" must be serious ("substantial") with significant consequences ("grossly impairs"). It recognizes different types of disorder ("thought, mood, perception") and impairment (of "judgment, behavior, capacity to recognize reality"). It is much more specific than this tautological example from the Texas statute: A "mentally ill person means a person whose mental health is substantially impaired."[100] Yet both definitions, representing the spectrum of specificity in state statutes, are vague. All statutes depend ultimately on clinicians to provide content for the definitions.

The statutes are more successful when they exclude, as most do, certain conditions from the definition of mental illness. In most jurisdictions, mental illness does *not* include mental retardation, alcohol or substance abuse, or epilepsy. Individuals with these conditions are institutionalized under separate provisions. Those dealing with the mentally retarded are described in § 8.10(d).

(c) Capacity to Make Treatment Decisions

A number of influential commentators, including Roth[101] and Stone,[102] have argued that individuals should not be subject to commitment unless they lack the capacity to make an informed decision concerning their need for and desire to obtain treatment. The determination of incapacity, in the view of these observers, should constitute the threshold inquiry in a commitment proceeding. [See § 8.03(i) for further discussion of Roth's and Stone's views.]

At the time of this writing, nearly one-quarter

of the states use this criterion in their commitment laws.[103] The criterion is either part of the statutory definition of a mentally ill person (and therefore is a required finding in all commitments), or is incorporated in one of the criteria (e.g., dangerousness) that may result in commitment.

It is probable that the importance of competency to make treatment decisions as a threshold point of inquiry at commitment will grow. A number of courts have recognized a constitutional right to refuse treatment for at least some patients in some circumstances [see § 9.03]. These courts usually hold that what divides those non-consenting patients who may be treated from those able to exercise the right to refuse treatment is the capacity to consent to treatment. Thus, at a minimum, the issue of capacity will have to be confronted prior to the administration of treatment. Over time, those states that have not done so will probably move toward statutes that make explicit an inquiry into capacity at the time of commitment, in order to facilitate treatment of nonconsenting individuals immediately after their commitment.

A second reason why capacity issues should assume importance in involuntary commitment is the increased preference for *voluntary* hospitalization. All state statutes authorize "voluntary" or noncoerced admissions to mental health facilities. These statutes typically require that the individual must have the capacity to determine his or her need for treatment and to understand the consequences of being admitted to a mental health facility. That is, the decision to be a voluntary patient is theoretically an informed decision. Moreover, under the literal mandate of many of these statutes, *all* indivudals subjected to commitment should be evaluated to determine whether they have the capacity to make the treatment decision themselves and, if so, whether they reject treatment, before voluntary institutionalization proceedings may commence.[104]

Unfortunately, these provisions are often honored in the breach. Commentators have expressed doubt that the admitting facility actually determines whether an individual has the capacity to make the admission decision; they suggest

that many "voluntary" patients are in fact patients who either are subtly coerced into accepting the label or in fact are unable to understand its implications.[105] The latter is true particularly with populations for whom the "voluntary" label seems clearly fictitious—for example, minors admitted by parents or guardians, and the mentally retarded, who are most often admitted by another party.[106]

(d) Danger to Others

All states allow the commitment of individuals who present a danger to others. Given the Supreme Court's statements in *Donaldson* and *Addington*, dangerousness has firm support as a commitment criterion. The concept is usually expressed by use of either the word "dangerous" or the term "likelihood of serious harm." Schwitzgebel has noted the increased use of the word "dangerous" in commitment statutes (four jurisdictions used the word explicitly in 1974; in 1981 his survey showed an increase to 20 jurisdictions).[107]

Like definitions of "mental disorder," statutory definitions of "dangerousness" to others are generally vague, though most attempt to qualify the "danger" that must be presented by requiring that it be "substantial." At one end of the definitional spectrum are statutes like Alaska's (mentally ill "and likely to injure himself or others"[108]). At the other end are laws that seek to refine this criterion by requiring evidence of a recent overt act before dangerousness may be found. For example, Pennsylvania requires proof that the person poses a "clear and present danger" to self or others as shown by conduct that has occurred "within the past 30 days."[109] Additionally, some statutes limit the range of predicted conduct to which civil commitment applies (e.g., Arkansas defines only the "homicidal" individual as dangerous to others, with "homicidal" meaning "pos[ing] a significant risk of physical harm to others as manifested by recent overt behavior evidencing homicidal or other assaultive tendencies toward others."[110]. Between these two extremes, "dangerousness" is defined simply as a "substantial risk that [the patient] will harm himself or others."[111] In most juris-dictions, despite the efforts of the reform move-ment, overt conduct is not a prerequisite to a finding of dangerousness.

It should be noted that almost all statutes concern themselves exclusively with physical harm. The Hawaii Code at one point allowed any harm to property to suffice as a ground for commitment. However, a federal court of ap-peals found this criterion unconstitutionally broad.[112] Additionally, a few states allow com-mitment based on a prediction that emotional harm to others will be caused by the individual's actions.[113]

Professor Brooks has helpfully conceptualized the analysis of dangerousness to others as focus-ing on four variables: (1) the severity of the harm predicted; (2) the probability that the predicted harm will occur; (3) the frequency with which the harm might occur; and (4) how soon the harm will occur.[114] Assuming that the data rel-evant to these variables are available, the fact-finder should assess their relative impact in de-ciding whether confinement should result. For instance, one might be more willing to confine a person who is predicted to have a 20% chance of committing a homicide within the next few weeks than a person who is predicted to have a 50% chance of hurling occasional epithets at passers-by.

(e) Danger to Self

Each statute also allows commitment of an in-dividual presenting a danger to self. The defini-tion of "danger to self" tends to mirror the def-inition of "danger to others." Thus, statutes providing little or no content in defining "dan-ger to others" provide little or no content in defining "danger to self." Compare, for example, Alaska's statute ("likely to injure himself or others"[115]) to Pennsylvania's (suicidal act within 30 days or an act of mutilation required to dem-onstrate danger to self; violent act within 30 days to demonstrate danger to others[116]).

Every state statute appears to contemplate commitment for suicidal behavior. Additionally, as the next section discusses in more detail, those states that do not have an "inability to care" criterion define "dangerousness to self" as en-compassing nonsuicidal conduct that nonethe-less could cause serious harm to the person.

(f) Grave Disability/Inability to Care for Self

As noted earlier in this chapter, the underlying premise of the reform movement was the belief that, because the consequences of commitment were as damaging to the individual as criminal conviction, the substantive and procedural cri-teria for commitment should approximate as nearly as possible those used in criminal law. This reform movement was egalitarian and antipater-nalistic in spirit. Attempts to commit an individ-ual because of a supposed inability to meet the needs of daily living, or solely because of a need for treatment, were viewed as primary examples of the paternalistic use of state authority.

However, the United States Supreme Court, in *O'Connor v. Donaldson*,[117] suggested the contin-ued vitality of the state's authority to confine the gravely disabled, as well as hinting at the limits on that authority. The Court observed that the state could not hospitalize someone simply to improve his or her living conditions.[118] At the same time, the Court noted that "the State may arguably confine a person to save him from harm . . . ."[119]

Approximately three-quarters of the states use a variation of "grave disability" or "inability to meet basic needs" as an alternative criterion for commitment.[120] No state explicitly prohibits commitment on this ground, so it is likely that the criterion exists *de facto* in most other juris-dictions, presumably as evidence that the indi-vidual presents a danger to self. The definitions, as usual, vary among the states. Some simply al-low commitment of the "gravely disabled,"[121] defined as a person who by reason of mental illness "is unable to maintain himself in his nor-mal life situation without external support."[122] Other jurisdictions delineate the "needs" that the individual must be found incapable of meeting; the five usually listed are food, clothing, shelter, medical care, and the ability to secure personal safety.[123] A third variant, proposed by the American Psychiatric Association, would permit commitment if the person "will if not treated suffer or continue to suffer severe and abnormal mental, emotional or physical distress, and this distress is associated with significant impairment of judgment, reason, or behavior causing a substantial deterioration of his previous ability to function on his own."[124] The important point is that this criterion, however phrased, is designed to address a different situation from that presented by the actively suicidal individual.

The grave problems associated with the move toward deinstitutionalization[125] and the call in some quarters for reinstitutionalizing the homeless mentally ill[126] probably guarantee the continued vitality of this criterion, in large part because of an apparent public perception that there are too many mentally disordered persons in the community. Yet commitment under this standard raises difficult issues because of the fine line it seems to require drawing between an individual living an impoverished existence and an individual living an existence impoverished because of mental disorder. This criterion raises most starkly issues of state power, individual autonomy, and the multiplicity of causes for any specific living situation.

(g) Need for Treatment

The majority of states also include as part of their commitment laws the concept that the individual to be committed needs treatment.[127] The definition is frequently incorporated into the definition of mental illness. For example, Colorado defines a "mentally ill person" as "a person who is of such mental condition that he is in need of medical supervision, treatment, care or restraint."[128] It may also be included as part of another criterion—for example, that of "grave disability."

The fact that an individual "needs treatment" from a clinical point of view, standing alone, probably does not provide sufficient legal justification for involuntary commitment. Rather, according to *O'Connor v. Donaldson,* "something more," in the form of one of the behavioral criteria described above, seems to be required. The continued presence of the concept of the "need for treatment" has been described as a "vestigial structure,"[129] and its relative lack of importance in demonstrating the legal case for commitment is another example of the focus on dangerousness that runs throughout civil commitment law.

(h) The Least Restrictive Alternative

The last substantive criterion to be considered is the requirement that the state intervention resulting from commitment take place in the "least restrictive manner." The legal basis for this doctrine is the constitutional requirement, developed in cases involving the First Amendment,[130] that the state may restrict the exercise of fundamental liberties only to the extent necessary to effectuate the state's interest. Since the fundamental interest of individual liberty is infringed by civil commitment, it is argued that the state may authorize commitment only to the extent necessary to effectuate its interests in providing treatment and protecting the individual or community. Under this scheme, the state hospital is posited as the most restrictive environment, with community-based services and outpatient care seen as less restrictive.

The doctrine was first applied to the commitment process in *Lake v. Cameron,*[131] a case decided by the Circuit Court of Appeals for the District of Columbia. The court, relying on statutory rather than constitutional grounds,[132] found that the state and the court had an affirmative duty to explore alternatives to hospitalization before committing Lake to an institution. The court noted that "though she cannot be given such care as only the wealthy can afford, an earnest effort should be made to review and exhaust available resources of the community in order to provide care reasonably suited to her needs."[133]

The doctrine later attained constitutional status in a number of cases.[134] At least two-thirds of the states have incorporated the requirement into their commitment laws, either explicitly or implicitly.[135] As with the other criteria discussed, statutory guidelines are not particularly precise and may consist only of the requirement that the treatment occur in "the least restrictive environment." The goal of the doctrine, which seeks to assure that hospitalization is used only as a last resort, is laudable. However, as Hoffman and Foust have pointed out,[136] the doctrine has not developed sufficiently to resolve satisfactorily several critical issues.

First, the doctrine is preoccupied with physical setting. It presumes that hospitals are the most restrictive environment, with settings becoming less restrictive as one moves into community and "less hospital-like" facilities. This superficial analysis fails to take into account the restrictive nature of the treatment modality itself, regardless of the locus of treatment; most importantly, it fails to recognize that certain physically restrictive treatments might be more efficacious and might therefore result in an overall reduction in the duration of state intervention.

Second, it is not always clear who is responsible for the search for alternatives (the judge, the individual, or the state), or what the extent of that responsibility is. Even where the responsible party is identified, one study found that the responsibility was often ignored.[137]

Third, what if alternative resources simply do not exist? Is the inquiry limited to a search of available resources, or must it consider the most appropriate resource for the individual living in an ideal world? Several courts have found that the doctrine requires the development of community-based resources.[138] However, other courts have rejected this argument, and the Supreme Court has expressed some distaste for the idea even when it is incorporated into federal legislation.[139] In so doing, the Court may have drastically weakened the constitutional validity of the doctrine.[140]

(i)　A Note on the Stone and Roth Proposals

In recent years, a number of new models for commitment laws have been proposed.[141] Those advanced by Professors Stone[142] and Roth[143] are worth noting, because they propose explicitly to revitalize the *parens patriae* model as the primary basis for commitment. Although they thus run counter to the reform movement that occurred in the 1970s and that is reflected in the emphasis on dangerousness in all of today's statutes, these proposals are discussed briefly here because, given the Supreme Court's retrenchment in mental health litigation, these or similar models may receive renewed consideration in the future.

The two models are similar in intent and in form. Each is intended to focus clinical attention and resources upon the treatment of illness rather than upon the patient's dangerousness. Each also seeks to limit the use of civil commitment only to the most seriously ill, and each attempts to assure that treatment will be made available to the patient. Each is in response to what the authors view as the central failing of the due process model: By committing competent patients who are able to refuse proffered treatment, "the risk is that the mental hospital will again become custodial, which would ensure the patient's civil rights while failing to restore health."[144] The main features of these proposals are the following:

1. The individual must be reliably diagnosed as suffering from severe mental illness.[145]
2. In the absence of treatment, the prognosis for the individual is major distress.
3. The individual is incompetent—that is, the illness substantially impairs the person's ability to understand or communicate about the possibility of treatment.[146]
4. Treatment is available.
5. The risk–benefit ratio of treatment is such that a reasonable person would consent to it.[147]

If these conditions are met, as determined at a hearing at which the person has full procedural rights, then a brief period (six weeks in Roth's proposal[148]) of treatment may occur. Because the patient has been found to lack capacity on the issue of treatment, a substitute decisionmaker is permitted to give or withhold informed consent to the proffered treatment.[149]

Roth would also allow limited use of commitment on dangerousness grounds,[150] while Stone would relegate the control of dangerousness to the criminal justice system.[151] However, the point of each proposal is to restore *parens patriae* as the primary source of civil commitment. Stone calls this the "Thank You Theory of Civil Commitment": "[I]t asks the psychiatrist to focus his inquiry on illness and treatment, and it asks the law to guarantee treatment before it intervenes in the name of *parens patriae.*"[152] The proposals have been criticized on both theoretical and practical grounds,[153] and they have not been incorporated in any revised state statute. However, their existence demonstrates the continued vitality of the argument over the use, bases, and substantive criteria for civil commitment.

8.04. *Procedural Due Process*

The movement to reform civil commitment laws sought to "legalize" the commitment process. Because deprivation of liberty was at issue, the argument went, judges rather than clinicians should serve as primary decisionmakers, and the proposed patient should have procedural protections approaching those afforded a criminal defendant. The newly legalized process, combined with stricter and better defined substantive criteria, would theoretically improve the accuracy of the decisions made at commitment, eliminating inappropriate confinement.

The commitment process has in fact been legalized on paper, although perhaps not in practice [see § 8.05(c)]. Even those jurisdictions retaining the most medically oriented statutes grant a wide range of procedural rights. State commitment laws do not differ greatly today in the procedural protection given patients or the substantive criteria governing commitment decisions; the primary difference appears to be *when* the judicial model for decisionmaking supplants the clinical. The following subsections contrast four representative statutes, which fall along a continuum from medically oriented (New York) to relatively legalistic (Washington and California) to primarily legalistic (Virginia).

(a) Emergency Admissions

Each state allows for emergency admissions, designed in even the most legalistic states to allow admission of a seriously disordered and imminently dangerous individual with a minimum of process. Any procedural protections that are afforded the individual attach only after hospitalization has occurred. This posture is justified by the need to intervene immediately to prevent harm to the individual or others.

In California[154] and Washington,[155] either a police officer or a clinician may authorize emergency admission of an individual. In New York,[156] the decision is made by a clinician at a facility or by the county director of mental health. By contrast, a judge or magistrate makes the emergency detention decision in Virginia,[157] although it is not necessary that he or she actually see the patient.

In none of these states is the patient afforded a hearing, granted the right to contest the action at a formal proceeding, or afforded counsel prior to hospitalization. Nor does the petitioner for emergency admission have to meet a high level of proof in establishing committability; no standard of proof is established in New York, Washington, or Virginia,[158] and California requires only that the decisionmaker state that "probable cause"[159] exists to believe that the person is mentally disordered and, as a result, gravely disabled or a danger to self or others.

This initial admission, unencumbered by procedural requirements, is usually sharply circumscribed (48 hours in Virginia[160]; 72 hours in California[161] and Washington[162]). However, in New York, the individual may be detained up to 15 days if a second physician has examined the person within 48 hours of admission and finds that the individual is mentally ill and dangerous to self or others.[163] This provision is tempered somewhat by a provision that the patient may request a judicial hearing at any time; if one is requested, it must be held within five days of the request.[164]

In addition to circumscribing the duration of the emergency admission, each state requires that the detained individual be given prompt notice of rights, including notice of the potential duration of the confinement, of when the right to counsel becomes available, and of when the patient becomes entitled to a hearing. In Virginia, these rights are told to the individual by a judge at a "probable cause" hearing held within 48 hours of detention[165]; in Washington they are given either by the person taking the patient into custody or the faciliity at which the patient is detained[166]; and in New York[167] and California[168] the detaining facility provides the necessary notice. Counsel is theoretically made available immediately after notice except in California, where the right becomes available only if the individual is held longer than 72 hours.[169] In New York, patients automatically have the benefit of the Mental Health Information Service, a legal advocacy organization located on facility grounds.

The primary difference among emergency admission provisions does not lie in the criteria for admission, or in the procedural rights afforded the patient. Rather, the main difference is one of time, with New York allowing an "emergency" to remain legally unmonitored up to 15 days—a much longer period than permitted by the other jurisdictions.

(b) Long-Term Retention

In contrast to emergency admissions, which are designed to effectuate the state interest in confinement of acutely ill and presently dangerous persons, long-term retention requires judicial approval after the case for continued confinement is presented in an adversarial, "legalized" proceeding.

(1) The Commitment Hearing

There are few significant differences in the procedural protections granted the individual before and at the commitment hearing. In each jurisdiction, the patient is entitled to the following rights before or during the hearing to determine long-term commitability:

1. Written notice of the fact that the patient faces a commitment proceeding, his or her

rights therein, and with the possible exception of New York,[170] the underlying reasons for the proposed commitment.
2. A right to counsel, and to have counsel appointed if necessary.[171]
3. The right to call witnesses and to cross-examine witnesses.
4. The right to request a jury trial, though in Virginia and New York this right does not attach unless the patient appeals the initial determination.[172]
5. The right to have a judge rather than a clinician make the ultimate decision.
6. The right to have the state prove its case by clear and convincing evidence.[173]

The states may differ on issues such as the admissibility of hearsay evidence [see § 14.04(e)],[174] the applicability of the privilege against self-incrimination [see § 3.02(d) & § 8.08(b)],[175] the right of the individual to an independent clinician to assist in the preparation of a "defense" [see § 3.03],[176] and the confidentiality of the commitment proceeding. But the core procedural rights are fairly standarized throughout the country, whether the statute is "legalistic" or "medical" in general orientation. To a great extent, the criminal model has been adopted.

(2) When Due Process Becomes Due

The procedural differences most revealing of the balance drawn by each particular jurisdiction in weighing individual and state interests involve the time at which the more formal adversary proceedings must occur and the duration of the resulting confinement. The relevant statutory provisions of the four sample states are set out below for comparison purposes.

In Virginia, a judicial hearing must occur within 48 hours of the initial detention.[177] If the court determines that the individual meets the commitment criteria, it may commit the person for a period of up to 180 days, at which time another full judicial hearing is required.[178]

Washington requires a "probable cause" judicial hearing within 72 hours of the initial detention; if the facility can show by a preponderance of the evidence that the individual meets the criteria, he or she may be detained for 14 days.[179] Before hospitalization can extend beyond 14 days, the individual is entitled to a full judicial hearing and a jury trial.[180] If committed after a full hearing, the patient may be hospitalized for no more than 90 days, with subsequent confinement of 180 days possible after another hearing.[181]

In California, an individual may be confined for more than 72 hours only if "certification" occurs[182]—a process that requires two clinicians to file a written certificate with the court describing the basis for continued hospitalization of the patient.[183] Within seven days of certification, a certification review hearing, presided over by a clinician, must be held. If certification is approved, commitment may last no more than 14 days from the date the individual was hospitalized.[184] If further care is required at the expiration of the 14 days, it may be obtained either through a second 14-day certification (for an "imminently suicidal" person),[185] "conservatorship" (guardianship) proceedings (if the person is gravely disabled),[186] or a full judicial hearing (for all others). Detention pursuant to the latter provision may last 180 days and may be renewed after a judicial hearing.

New York's scheme is quite different from the three just described. Confinement extending to 60 days may occur, based on a certification by two physicians that the individual meets commitment standards.[187] Some effort is made to assure that hospitalization is, in fact, appropriate: A third physician, at the institution, must examine the patient and also consider alternatives to hospitalization.[188] A patient may also request a judicial hearing after admission. But no hearing is *required* until the expiration of the 60 days.[189]

(3)   Summary

Even the most legalistic statutes allow a certain amount of clinical discretion, primarily in an emergency. And even the most medically oriented statutes provide procedural protection to a patient at the commitment hearing. As with

the substantive criteria for commitment, statutory procedural protections attempt to accommodate both the state's and the individual's interests. The balance struck, however, does make a difference. For example, New York's scheme, which does not require a judicial hearing for two months, may vitiate the effect of procedural protections in checking unwarranted commitment, simply because of the delay after confinement in making the protections available. In contrast, Virginia's law, which requires a full hearing within 48 hours of the initial detention, may allow insufficient time for a complete clinical evaluation prior to hearing. Given insufficient data, the system may react by deciding close or undeveloped cases in favor of commitment.

The balances struck by the Washington and California statutes seem more desirable. The California law in particular—which establishes clinical gate-keeping, an informal "probable cause" hearing conducted administratively before a 14-day confinement can occur, and a judicial hearing before longer detention—seems particularly suited to accommodate both individual and state interests. It also closely tracks the model for the commitment of children proposed by Justice Brennan in his concurring and dissenting opinion in the *Parham* case.[190] While its use of substantive criteria may be controverisal (e.g., suicidal patients are not subject to long-term detention), the manner in which it utilizes *procedural* protections may well serve as a model for other jurisdictions.

8.05.   Research on the Effects of Commitment Laws and Commitment

Although reforms of commitment laws toward a more legalistic model were rampant in the 1960s and 1970s, it is important to acknowledge that these changes in the law were uniformly moderate ones. No state abandoned civil commitment. Moreover, as noted in the preceding section, "medical" and "legalistic" statutes are typically more alike than they are different, with the major difference being in the point in the process at which judicial review is involved.

Moreover, even the most legalistic statutes have generally failed to result in a more lawful approach to civil commitment. This conclusion is based on an examination of data regarding the frequency of hospitalization, the manner in which the new standards are applied, and the lack of adherence to procedural rules. When these are combined with other data suggesting the general ineffectiveness of hospitalization as a treatment modality, one is led to the further conclusion that mental health professionals must be extremely cautious when participating in the commitment process as it exists at present.

(a) Frequency of Commitment

As noted in § 8.02(a), there has been a striking decrease in the number of people hospitalized in state facilities in the past two decades. However, while legal incentives, the advent of new treatment techniques, and changing ideology in the mental health professions may have contributed to this decrease,[191] changes in civil commitment laws do not appear to have had much of an impact.[192] In the best-designed study on this point, Luckey and Berman[193] examined the effects of the Nebraska Mental Health Commitment Act.[194] Although the Nebraska law has some unusual provisions,[195] it is a particularly comprehensive legalistic statute. Using an interrupted time-series design,[196] Luckey and Berman found that the statute had had an immediate but transitory effect on the number of commitments. Within 18 months after passage of the law, the total number of commitments had returned to the preform level, given admission trends prior to enactment of the law. Indeed, much of the initial observed decrease may have been the result simply of the time required to put the new commitment system into place. Corroborative of this interpretation is the fact that the decrease was largely specific to rural counties, where the necessary professionals were in short supply.

Further evidence of the fact that changes in the law have not been primarily responsible for changes in commitment practices is provided by the fact that the frequency of institutionalizations, as opposed to the number hospitalized at

a given time, actually increased between 1955 and 1975.[197] In view of mental health professionals' tendency to err on the side of overdiagnosis and overprediction ("false positives"),[198] one could assume that rigorous testing of their testimony in commitment proceedings would produce a drop in the number of commitments. That such a drop has not occurred indicates that the tighter standards and procedures required by the revised commitment statutes have not been applied in practice. Studies of commitment hearings themselves, to which we now turn, confirm this interpretation.

(b) Standards

In general, clinicians' opinions as to committability or need for treatment are dispositive, regardless of the legal standard to be applied. Studies indicate an agreement rate between clinicians' conclusions and factfinders' decisions of between 90% and 100%.[199] This evidence suggests, although it does not prove, a failure to adhere to the supposedly narrower substantive criteria imposed by commitment reform.

More direct evidence on the elastic interpretation of the standards comes from studies indicating that the "overt act" requirements are often ignored or interpreted so broadly as to provide no real standard at all. For example, in a survey of participants in Iowa's civil commitment system,[200] 47% of attorneys and 71% of referees (judges) included "potential psychological harm" in the concept of dangerousness to others. Presumably, then, a person might be committed on the ground that his or her behavior is foreseeably upsetting to family members. Still more problematically, 40% of the attorneys and 30% of the referees in Iowa defined dangerousness to include "impudent" sexual behavior.[201]

It is not merely the elements of "mentally ill" and "dangerous" that may be ignored or distorted. Several studies show that need for hospitalization is often assumed without critical application of the "least restrictive alternative" concept.[202] There is also evidence that movement to a pure *parens patriae* model would not substantially increase the size of the population subject to commitment.[203] The rigorous safe-guards against erroneous or unnecessary depri-vation of liberty created by recent legislation, far from "criminalizing" commitment,[204] appear to be neglected because of a misconceptualization of the civil commitment decision as medical or psychological rather than legal.[205]

(c) Procedures

As a practical matter, this errant conceptualiza-tion is played out in a neglect of form as well as substance. Adversary procedures are especially well suited to enhancement of perceived jus-tice.[206] Such procedures theoretically underlie commitment statutes, regardless of model, at least at the hearing stage. However, there is substan-tial empirical evidence that informal, inquisito-rial procedures are pervasive in civil commit-ment proceedings, no matter what the statutes say.[207]

Consider the following data, both self-report and observational, from the Iowa study cited previously.[208] Three-fourths of referees and clerks of court admitted that commitment hearings were usually not conducted in an adversary manner. Defense attorneys were found to request an in-dependent mental health evaluation (available by right under the statute) in fewer than 1% of cases, and they rarely called more than two witnesses (often none). The majority failed to put the re-spondents on the stand. One attorney even rea-soned that to do so would risk the defendants' persuading the referee that they were not men-tally ill! Consistent with their lack of active par-ticipation in the hearings, the attorneys uni-formly spent less than two hours in preparation of these cases.

For their part, the referees encouraged pas-sivity on the part of defense attorneys. Some ref-erees expressly discouraged cross-examination of witnesses; if questions were to be asked, the ref-erees themselves would ask them. The result was that commitment hearings were little more than a stamp of approval for the attending physician's opinion. In fact, a change in treatment plan from that which the hospital physician had recom-mended was observed to occur in fewer than 1%

of cases. Referees and attorneys generally agreed that clinicians should decide whether the ele-ments of the standard for civil commitment had been met, and, if so, what the conditions of treatment should be. This finding is echoed in several other studies, which have also found that attorneys rarely act in an adversarial manner during commitment hearings and indeed often assist the state in its task of proving committa-bility.[209]

(d) Why the Laws Have Failed: Pressures for Hospitalization

Deference to mental health professionals seems to emanate from an intuition commonly held by both lawyers and clinicians that crazy people are sick and belong in the hospital. This view has persisted even amidst calls for medical cost con-tainment; it is reflected in a continuing *de facto* policy of hospital-based care for mentally disor-dered persons. Moreover, the bias toward hos-pitalization is remarkably resistant to change. Poythress[210] trained mental health lawyers in cross-examining mental health professionals, but he found that the attorneys did not apply their new knowledge in commitment hearings. Their reluctance stemmed most often from their con-viction that their clients belonged in the hospi-tal. When the attorneys did begin to act as ad-versaries, judges typically made clear that such advocacy would be to no avail if it controverted the experts' opinions.

As the high incidence of hospitalization itself demonstrates, mental health professionals are also prone to reject challenges to civil commitment of persons who "clinical intuition" says should be institutionalized. Zwerling, Conte, Plutchik, and Karasu[211] offered a dramatic example of this principle. As director of a major urban teaching hospital, Zwerling established a "No-Commit-ment Week." During that week, no commit-ments were to be made unless *absolutely* neces-sary. This judgment required corroboration by supervising clinicians. The result of the experi-ment was that the commitment rate did not change at all. Each clinician thought that each case was the extraordinary one in which commitment was absolutely morally and clinically required.

Of course, legally suspect civil commitment is not simply the result of the conventional wisdom that doctors know best about crazy people and that crazy people belong in the hospital. Despite the discomfort that many clinicians have about civil commitment,[212] commitment is usually the politically safest course of action for clinicians and judges when a serious question of involuntary hospitalization is raised. No one hears about the persons who did not commit suicide or did not assault someone else. On the other hand, false negatives may have disastrous consequences for the patients themselves or their victims, public criticism of the professionals involved, and perhaps feelings of personal guilt. Families may push to have their disturbed relatives "put away," and clinicians are likely to choose the most intrusive treatments for the most serious disorders.[213]

(e) The Questionable Benefit of Civil Commitment

Despite these substantial pressures toward involuntary hospitalization, there are serious questions as to its desirability in most cases.[214] We have already noted the substantial risk of overcommitment, resulting in the egregious wrong of unjustified deprivation of liberty.[215] This wrong is multiplied by the institutional dependency and stigma that are generally acknowledged to accompany a history of psychiatric hospitalization.[216]

Even if it is assumed, though, that the commitment is valid, it does not follow that hospitalization is the treatment of choice. Kiesler reviewed all of the existing experimental comparisons of hospitalization and alternate care.[217] The ten studies made use of a multiplicity of interventions and outcome measures, but came to consistent conclusions:

> It seems quite clear from these studies that for the vast majority of patients now being assigned to inpatient units in mental institutions, care of at least equal impact could be otherwise provided. There is not an instance in this array of studies in which hospitalization had any positive impact on the average patient care investigated in the study. In almost every case, the alternative care had more positive outcomes. There were significant and powerful effects on such life-related variables as employment, school attendance, and the like. There were significant and important effects on the probability of subsequent readmission. Not only did the patients in the alternative care not undergo the initial hospitalization but they were less likely to undergo hospitalization later, as well. There is clear evidence here for the causal sequence in the finding alluded to earlier that the best predictor of hospitalization is prior hospitalization. These data across these 10 studies suggest quite clearly that hospitalization of mental patients is self-perpetuating.[218]

Moreover, in no study was alternative care found to be more expensive than hospitalization.[219]

Although Kiesler has been careful to point out that the available research does not prove that no one should be hospitalized,[220] he has made a persuasive case for a strong presumption against hospitalization. Only in very rare cases will hospitalization be the least restrictive alternative for provision of treatment.

To take the argument a step further, even if it is assumed that hospitalization is indicated, it is unlikely that necessary treatment will be accorded in the state hospitals to which civilly committed patients are often sent. For many years, conditions of care in many state hospitals have been nothing short of scandalous.[221] Moreover, even if state legislatures were willing, as they often have not been,[222] to provide sufficient funding for humane care, it is not clear that the quality of professional staff would improve substantially.[223] Certainly, at present, the qualifications of state hospital professionals are often marginal at best.[224]

Of course, even if one accepts that hospitalization generally does not have positive effects for patients (especially relative to alternative forms of treatment), one could argue it has some marginal utility for society, because it results in confinement of the dangerous. But justifying commitment solely on this ground violates the *parens patriae* notion. Moreover, it does not appear to be supportable on empirical grounds. Not only is it difficult to predict who will be dangerous [see § 8.08(d)], but it has been shown that mental illness is not substantially correlated with violent behavior.[225] As Morse has argued, it may be that overall social utility would be enhanced if resources currently used for civil commitment purposes were diverted to provide services to those who seek treatment on a voluntary basis.[226]

(f) Discussion: The Need for Caution

When taken together with the literature on decisionmaking in civil commitment proceedings, research on the iatrogenic effects of hospitalization leads to a conclusion that mental health professionals should exercise extraordinary care in evaluating persons for possible civil commitment.[227] In the current state of things, clinicians' opinions are likely to be dispositive, and the risk of harm resulting from these opinions (when the recommendation is for hospitalization) is enormous. At least, it can be said with confidence that in the vast majority of cases hospitalization is not likely to be the least restrictive alternative. In view of the great deference apt to be accorded their views in civil commitment proceedings, clinicians bear a special ethical obligation to ensure that factfinders are aware of possible alternatives to involuntary hospitalization and their relative efficacy.[228]

We do not intend to suggest by our review of how the civil commitment system typically works that legal reforms have had no effect at all. Particularly in states using a legalistic model of commitment, civil commitment reforms may have contributed to the enormous drop in the average length of stay in state hospitals[229] and to an increased appreciation of patients' human rights.[230] Moreover, the rampant reliance on hospitalization of severely disordered persons may have as much to do with financial disincentives[231] as with loose application of civil commitment laws.

There is also at least anecdotal evidence that civil commitment laws can work as intended when legal authorities take their obligations seriously.[232] Although such an orderly, responsible approach may require careful engineering of the civil commitment system as a whole,[233] it is clearly

the appropriate goal, and most of the remainder of this chapter focuses on how the system should operate. At the same time, though, it is important for lawyers and clinicians to go into commitment proceedings with eyes fully open to both how the process is likely to work and what state hospitals realistically may offer.

8.06. The Attorney's Role

Perhaps the most important participant in civil commitment is the respondent's attorney. Whether the procedure is meaningful is likely to turn largely on whether the attorney assumes an adversary stance. Without vigorous advocacy for the client, there is almost no point in having a hearing at all. Indeed, the civil commitment reforms rested on an assumption that the state should be required to *prove* that the respondent is committable.[234] Deprivation of liberty, even with benevolent or at least benign intent, is not a trivial matter, and the evidence supportive of such a disposition should be thoroughly tested for its reliability and probative value. In essence, justice demands that the respondent is able to put the best possible case forward and that state power does not go unchecked. Moreover, as a practical matter, the research evidence is clear that civil commitment procedures and standards will be just so many words unless attorneys behave adversarily.[235]

Nonetheless, we recognize the difficulties inherent in adopting such a stance. As already noted, many lawyers do not appreciate the legal–moral aspects of civil commitment, and they may be mystified by clinical phenomena presented to them. On the other hand, when attorneys are neither naive nor lackadaisical, they may nonetheless find judicial resistance to their doing their job.

Perhaps most problematically, the mental health attorney has no clear ethical mandate. It is cardinal in American jurisprudence that attorneys are "zealous advocates" of their clients' wishes.[236] Although this canon of professional responsibility may at times be a legal fiction,[237] it nonetheless provides a clear guide for lawyers in conceptualizing their role in most circumstances. Such clarity evaporates in mental health law, however. Does the lawyer zealously advocate the wishes of a client who seems to behave irrationally? What are the client's interests? The American Bar Association's (ABA's) Model Code of Professional Responsibility does not endorse a pure adversarial stance. It recognizes that "the responsibilities of a lawyer may vary according to the . . . mental conditions of a client. . . . Any mental or physical condition of a client that renders him incapable of making a considered judgment on his own behalf casts additional responsibilities upon his lawyer. . . . If a client under disability has no legal representative [a guardian], his lawyer may be compelled in court proceedings to make decisions on behalf of the client."[238]

However, the Model Code still retains a preference, albeit ambivalent, for an advocate's rather than a guardian's stance by the lawyer:

> If the client is capable of understanding the matter in question or of contributing to the advancement of his interests, regardless of whether he is legally disqualified from performing certain acts, the lawyer should obtain from him all possible aid. If the disability of a client and the lack of a legal representative compel the lawyer to make decisions for his client, the lawyer should consider all circumstances then prevailing and act with care to safeguard and advance the interests of his client.[239]

In general, the attorney should advocate the client's wishes. When the client is unable to express a preference, or expresses *clearly* irrational wishes, the attorney should pursue the least restrictive alternative rather than what is perceived to be the client's best interests. The attorney's role is not to act as a guardian or an *amicus* (an attorney for the court) would. Although some authorities have argued that attorneys for allegedly mentally disordered persons should act as paternalists,[240] these authorities have ignored the reality that the civil commitment system *requires* an advocate for the respondent if it is to work at all.[241] They have also unrealistically minimized the risk of harm resulting from involuntary hospitalization.

We do not mean to imply that an attorney must necessarily pursue "getting the client off" with single-minded zeal (unless a competent client so directs). As with most legal issues, much of the work of an effective mental health lawyer will be in investigation and bargaining.[242] The unfortunate reality is that in most civil commitment cases the judge will be unwilling to permit the respondent to go free without any treatment or supervision. Consequently, attorneys should investigate and challenge the validity of the facts underlying commitment petitions, but they should not stop with scrutiny of the evidence. They should also be prepared to suggest and argue for alternative, less restrictive dispositions.

Wexler has provided a terse summary of minimal work required for effective representation by counsel prior to the hearing:

> The attorney should make a thorough study of the facts of the case, which should include court records, hospital records, and information available from social agencies. Communication with the patient is, in the ordinary case, a must. The family and friends of the patient should also be contacted to ascertain the true facts behind the petition. It is essential that the attorney have a full understanding of the events preceding the filing of the petition. An investigation of the financial condition of the patient and his family—including their hospitalization insurance—is necessary to determine if certain alternatives to hospitalization should be explored. Finally, the attorney should explore the treatment and custodial resources of the community, should understand the various services offered by social agencies, and should know the avenues by which these resources can be applied to meet the needs of the client as alternatives to involuntary commitment.[243]

Admittedly, these tasks will entail a considerable amount of time and effort on the part of the attorney. If time is needed, the attorney can ask for a continuance (assuming that the client will agree to the delay). A vigorous pretrial effort will not only assure a well-prepared case, but may also result in a "settlement," obviating the need for a hearing.

If a hearing is held, advocacy should also be vigorous.[244] Cross-examining a psychiatrist may be difficult for one who is not trained in mental health, but not more so than in the criminal or tort context. And, as is *not* the case in these other situations, the attorney may be unencumbered by the objections of opposing counsel. Additionally, relatively simple questions designed to force the doctor into revealing why the subject is believed to be mentally ill or dangerous can have a surprising effect on the course of the hearing. In justifying the opinion, the doctor will have to divulge whether his or her conclusions are based on hearsay, and to what degree they reflect a "gut reaction" to a given situation as opposed to a scientifically verifiable fact. Asking the expert to examine a list of outpatient facilities and explain why each is not a feasible treatment alternative may also prove beneficial.

Pursuing the case after the hearing—either through an appeal or, if the court orders outpatient treatment, through monitoring the client's compliance—is a further important element of advocacy. When the judge and doctor know there is a good possibility that their decision will be reviewed by a higher court, they may devote more effort to meeting their obligations under the commitment statute. Follow-up of the client by the attorney is necessary to ensure that treatment is received and that a second commitment petition is avoided.

A more detailed analysis of the commitment attorney's obligations can be found elsewhere.[245] What is needed is a means of alerting the legal community to these obligations. A forceful approach to the problem is through legislation. The state of Arizona, for example, has provided that counsel for a defendant in a commitment hearing must perform certain duties or be subject to a citation for contempt of court.[246] Legislation could also raise the fee of the commitment attorney and allow him or her to obtain funds for independent psychiatric evaluations and other expenses.

Effective counsel *can* assure that commitment hearings are fairer, simply by assuring that the evidentiary bases for and against commitment are adequately developed. It is our belief that, by so doing, counsel can change the tendency of judges to rely solely on the conclusory opinions of expert clinicians. If counsel is acting effectively, then the evidence will necessarily consist of more than

conclusions phrased in clinical jargon. To reiterate, the role of counsel is fundamental to assuring that the "legalized" model of commitment process accomplishes the goals for which it was adopted.

8.07. The Clinician's Role

A general injunction to mental health professionals throughout this volume is to monitor, and to take care to avoid exceeding, the limits of their expertise. In particular, clinicians must be careful to refrain from invading the province of factfinders, and lawyers and judges must not delegate their responsibilities to the clinicians. Nowhere is this theme more pertinent than in civil commitment. Because of the great deference usually given to clinicians' opinions in civil commitment, the calculus of the proper admissibility of such opinions is likely to be altered substantially. As noted in § 1.04, the moderate probative value of mental health professionals' speculations is apt to be outweighed by their high prejudicial value in commitment proceedings. Attorneys should make the proper evidentiary objections, but mental health professionals themselves bear much of the responsibility for staying within the boundaries of their expertise. Clinicians should resist giving ultimate-issue opinions. Whether a respondent is so crazy and dangerous as to merit deprivation of liberty is a legal–moral decision, not a medical or psychological one. More specifically, the decision as to whether a respondent is "dangerous" subsumes a series of conclusions of law: the threshold probability of dangerous behavior; the range of behaviors that are "dangerous"; the period of time to be covered by the prediction; and the necessary level of validity for the prediction.

Rather than making such conclusions, mental health professionals should describe respondents' behavior, their treatment needs, and alternatives for meeting these needs. When actuarial data relevant to the predictive questions are available, these should also be described. If the court insists on testimony about dangerousness, clinicians should only offer information about violence-enhancing and violence-reducing factors [see § 7.10(f) and the Smith report, § 15.06)]. Regardless of the nature of the evidence being presented, it is incumbent upon clinicians to make clear the uncertainties of their opinion [see § 1.04], especially in view of the weight likely to be given to those opinions.

Mental health professionals may also serve as consultants to attorneys for respondents in exploring alternatives to commitment and examining the reliability of evidence supporting commitment. Indeed, the effectiveness of legal aid programs in civil commitment cases would probably be enhanced by having clinicians on their staffs to assume such a consulting role.[247] Where such "in house" professional consultation is not provided, procedures should allow attorneys for indigent respondents to select independent mental health professionals to examine their clients and to assist in identifying possible alternative forms of treatment.[248] We strongly recommend this because, in view of the enormous social costs imposed upon respondents by civil commitment, fairness dictates that the respondents should be able to develop the strongest case they can make. The assistance of an independent expert may be very important in developing lines of defense against commitment (e.g., possible less restrictive alternatives). Perhaps most importantly, a "second opinion" might reduce the probability of an erroneous commitment resulting from the low reliability of clinical opinions and the usual unquestioning acceptance of a lone expert's opinion. Justice might well be served by a "battle of the experts" in commitment cases. Certainly, without access to independent experts and incentives for their use, commitment cases are unlikely ever to become truly adversary.

8.08. The Commitment Evaluation

(a) Mental Illness and Need for Treatment

To a large extent, the content of an evaluation for civil commitment is similar to that of a "regular" clinical evaluation. That is, a clinician must determine, as a threshold question, whether a respondent has a significant mental disorder, and, if so, how it might be treated. In making such judgments, clinicians will probably find their usual armamentarium of diagnostic techniques appropriate. Even the second-order questions (e.g., dangerousness to self) may be ones that clinicians would typically ask themselves when examining persons believed to be seriously disordered. Perhaps the key distinction between a regular evaluation for development of a traditional treatment plan and an evaluation of mental disorder for civil commitment arises from the fact that the latter involves *involuntary* treatment. There are special obligations for care and certainty in the invasion of liberty. Hence, the *content* of commitment evaluations may be typical, but the *attitude* of clinicians should not be. As recommended above, in performing evaluations of individuals for possible civil commitment, clinicians should note the points of uncertainty in their evaluations, the possible alternatives for treatment (including no treatment), and the probable levels of efficacy of each.

(b) Dangerousness to Self

There are a number of steps in the evaluation of suicidal potential that are standard in the mental health professions. Typically, depressed clients are asked whether they have suicidal motives, plans, and means (e.g., presence of a weapon or lethal doses of medicine). The adequacy of defences—both internal (e.g., availability of rationalization) and external (e.g., whether someone is present as a monitor and a support)—is examined, along with any history (remote or recent) of self-destructive behavior. The history may be interpreted in purely clinical terms (e.g., patterns of precipitants) or in conjunction with actuarial data. Such standard approaches are both intuitively and theoretically sound.

However, it should be noted that mental health professionals' track record in prediction of suicide is very poor. Pokorny, the leading investigator of the subject, recently reached the "inescapable" conclusion that "we do not possess any item of information or any combination of items that permit us to identify to a useful degree the particular persons who will commit suicide, in spite of the fact that we do have scores of items available, each of which is significantly related to suicide."[249] On the basis of discriminant analyses of data derived from five-year follow-ups of 4,800 first admissions to a Veterans Administration psychiatric unit, Pokorny found that, in order to identify one-half of the 63 actual suicides, one-fourth of the total sample (i.e., 1,200) would have to be falsely identified![250] It would seem unjust to commit falsely 98 of each 100 persons predicted to be suicidal. Even if it is just, it is certainly impractical, as Pokorny himself noted: "[I]t is simply not feasible to maintain one fourth of psychiatric inpatients on 'suicidal precautions' indefinitely."[251]

In fairness, it should be noted that Pokorny's data directly indicate only that even when objective clinical measures as well as demographic variables are considered, actuarial data cannot be combined to make long-term predictions of suicidal behavior without grossly unacceptable numbers of false positives. The validity of diagnosis of a "suicide crisis" may be substantially better.[252] Nonetheless, Pokorny's findings should give clinicians and judges considerable pause in weighing the probability of a respondent's engaging in life-threatening behavior.

(c) Grave Disability or Inability to Care for Self

A logical extension of the criterion of dangerousness to self is inability to care for self. Inability to provide for one's own basic needs is ultimately no less dangerous than active self-destructive behavior. As noted in § 8.03 (f), some statutes actually combine these factors into one prong of the civil commitment standard[253]; others provide a special prong of the standard and sometimes special procedures for civil commitment based on "grave disability."[254] It is in consideration of this prong that evaluations for commitment may deviate most from standard clinical assessments. In order to determine respondents' inability to care for themselves, it is important to identify the particular survival skills

that they do or do not have, as well as any means of protecting themselves that might be less restrictive than hospitalization. There have been some recent attempts to develop standardized techniques for assessment of competency to live safely in the community.[255] We discuss these measures in the context of our examination of evaluations for general guardianship [see § 9.02]. In substance if not in procedure, the question of the propriety of general guardianship is often virtually identical to the problem of whether an individual merits civil commitment because of grave disability.[256]

(d) Dangerousness to Others

It has become a truism of the mental health professions and the mental health bar that clinicians are unable to predict violent behavior.[257] But the research bases for this conclusion, described in § 7.10, consist almost exclusively of studies of *long-term* predictions. Thus, although the findings are sufficiently robust to suggest extreme caution in prediction of dangerousness to others in civil commitment, the research is also insufficiently apposite to suggest that such prediction is a "doomed" enterprise.[258] Intuitively, it seems reasonable to assume that short-term prediction can better long-term prediction because of the greater foreseeability of contextual variables that might influence violence-proneness.

Monahan, the leading contributor to this literature, has suggested that the "second generation" of research of predictions of violent behavior should include the following:

> [F]irst, studies that vary the methods of prediction to focus on actuarial techniques, including those that incorporate clinical information in statistical tables and those that provide statistical tables to clinicians as an additional source on which to base clinical judgments; second, studies that vary the factors used in making predictive decisions to include situational items such as characteristics of the family environment, the work environment, and the peer group environment in which the individual is to function; and, third, studies that vary the populations upon which predictive

technology is brought to bear, to include short-term predictions made in the community.[259]

There is some preliminary evidence that the approach Monahan has suggested may result in improved validity of predictions. One recent study found young male paranoid schizophrenics admitted on an emergency basis to be especially prone to violence in the hospital, regardless of whether they had committed an overt violent act prior to admission.[260]. However, that conclusion must be tempered by acknowledgment of serious methodological problems with the study.[261] In a better-designed study of short-term predictions of violent behavior, Werner, Rose, Yesavage, and Seeman found that psychiatrists' predictions were not significantly correlated with the actual assaultiveness of patients in the hospital.[262] However, they also noted that this predictive invalidity appeared to be related to the psychiatrists' attending to the "illusory correlation"[263] between hostility and propensity to violence.[264] Thus, the *potential* validity of judgments about short-term dangerousness may be greater if other variables are actually predictive. As it turned out, two admission variables generally not considered by the psychiatrists *did* significantly correlate ($r = .56$) with actual violence: emotional withdrawal (weighted negatively) and hallucinatory behavior.[265] Presumably, attention to these new actuarial data and to other tables derived from similar studies, rather than clinical intuition alone, would heighten the validity of prediction.

Nonetheless, the point must not be lost that the psychiatrists' opinions were in fact highly invalid in Werner and colleagues' study, even with respect to short-term predictions of violence. It is premature to assert that predictions of dangerousness in civil commitment are more valid than such predictions in other legal contexts (e.g., sentencing). Moreover, there is evidence that many mental health professionals will resist applying research that contradicts their intuitions or "gut feelings" about respondents' dangerousness.[266] Beigel and colleagues found that informing psychiatrists about the statutory definition of dangerousness in a state with an overt act requirement actually *decreased* the interrater reliability of

their assessments, possibly because some of the psychiatrists persisted in using their intuitive criteria, no matter what the statute required.[267]

Moreover, there is not much research available yet of the sophisticated sort that Monahan has recommended. *Ecologically* based predictions, in which both the situation and the person are considered, have yet to be empirically tested.

Table 8-1

Monahan's Recommended Approach to the Assessment of Violence Potential

---

1. Is it a prediction of violent behavior that is being requested?
2. Am I professionally competent to offer an estimate of the probability of future violence?
3. Are any issues of personal or professional ethics involved in this case?
4. Given my answers to the above questions, is this case an appropriate one in which to offer a prediction?
5. What events precipitated the question of the person's potential for violence being raised, and in what context did these events take place?
6. What are the person's relevant demographic characteristics?
7. What is the person's history of violent behavior?
8. What is the base rate of violent behavior among individuals of this person's background?
9. What are the sources of stress in the person's current environment?
10. What cognitive and affective factors indicate that the person may be predisposed to cope with stress in a violent manner?
11. What cognitive and effective factors indicate that the person may be predisposed to cope with stress in a nonviolent manner?
12. How similar are the contexts in which the person has used violent coping mechanisms in the past to the contexts in which the person likely will function in the future?
13. In particular, who are the likely victims of the person's violent behavior, and how available are they?
14. What means does the person possess to commit violence?

Note. From J. MONAHAN, THE CLINICAL PREDICTION OF VIOLENT BEHAVIOR (1981). Reprinted by permission of the National Institute of Mental Health.

Theoretically, such predictions would be expected to be the most valid; as already emphasized, however, great caution should be exercised in reporting such results.

For the present, we advise clinicians to use the approach developed by Monahan in his important book *The Clinical Prediction of Violent Behavior*.[268] In many ways, the evaluation that Monahan suggests [see Table 8-1] parallels the standard clinical inquiry in prediction of suicidal behavior. That is, the clinician should identify whether the respondent has homicidal motives, plans, or means. Are there particular situations that, by history, provoke the respondent to violent behavior, and are these situations likely to recur in the immediate future? At the same time, what restraints on such behavior exist? Does the respondent have skills in dampening hostile affect? Are there friends or relatives available to monitor the respondent's behavior and provide external supports [see the Smith report, § 15.06]?

In deriving his guide for clinical prediction of violent behavior, Monahan appears to have relied heavily upon the work of Novaco on cognitive-behavior modification of inappropriate responses to anger.[269] Novaco's theory examines the individual's cognitive *expectations* and *appraisals* of provocation and the resulting physiological arousal. By systematically examining the respondent's anger-intensifying cognitions, the situations in which these cognitions occur, and the responses (both cognitive and behavioral) that the individual has available for coping with them, the clinician may obtain a fairly sophisticated and specific picture of the likelihood of violence by the respondent, particularly when base-rate information is also considered.

8.09. The Process of the Evaluation

(a) The Right to Silence

Regardless of the specific content of the commitment evaluation, we have suggested that the *process* of civil commitment is, or should be, adversary. This assumption raises the question of whether the respondent should be compelled to submit to an evaluation—in effect, to give "incriminating testimony." As noted in § 3.02(d), the majority view, now firmly supported by the Supreme Court, is that the Fifth Amendment is not applicable to civil commitment. Usually, however, this holding has been based on a conclusory statement that the Fifth Amendment is applicable only to criminal proceedings.[270] This pat conclusion is belied both by cases applying the Fifth Amendment in noncriminal proceedings[271] and by a more thoughtful analysis of the purpose of the privilege against self-incrimination. In a truly adversary system, the state should not be permitted to use "legal process to force from the lips of the accused the evidence necessary" to deprive him or her of liberty.[272]

Nonetheless, even if the Fifth Amendment is not applicable to civil commitment, there are both ethical and strategic issues to be considered in determining whether a respondent should be compelled to speak to a mental health professional. First, the clinician is ethically obligated to inform the respondent of the purpose of the evaluation and limits on confidentiality [see § 3.05]. By its nature, such a requirement is based on a tenet that the privacy of the individual should not be invaded without the individual's permission. In a situation such as emergency detention for possible civil commitment, where the individual is in fact compelled to appear if not to talk, the clinician should also make clear any sanctions present in that jurisdiction for noncooperation [see §§ 3.02, 3.05].[273]

Under some circumstances, counsel for the respondent may find it wise to advise the client not to talk to the examining mental health professional. Particularly in jurisdictions with "overt act" requirements, the defense might want to force the state to develop the evidence from witnesses and other sources to indicate that the respondent does in fact deserve civil commitment. Moreover, given the tendency of mental health professionals to overdiagnose,[274] withholding of "testimony" may be in the client's best interest, lest his or her statements be interpreted with a *de facto* presumption of mental illness. However, the attorney considering such a tactic should be aware that, especially in jurisdictions where no right to silence applies, silence itself may be perceived as indicative of pathological interpersonal relations. Also, when the client has been detained for observation, it is practically impossible to maintain silence over the course of the evaluation.

(b) The Right to Assistance of Counsel

Although the presence of counsel for the respondent is required during the commitment hearing itself,[275] in some jurisdictions it will be late in the process before counsel is assigned.[276] This fact makes it especially important for mental health professionals to inform respondents about what is happening or potentially happening; their rights during the process[277]; and the means of obtaining counsel if it is desired. Even if not legally required,[278] it would also be advisable to tape the clinical interviews so as to provide the attorney eventually appointed with a basis for competent cross-examination of the examining mental health professionals [see § 3.03(a)].

(c) The Context of Civil Commitment Evaluations

Clinicians must also be aware of their double-agent status [see Chapter 3], which is starkly raised in civil commitment. Especially in the case of *parens patriae* commitments, the clinician may perceive what he or she is doing to be *for* the respondent, as part of treatment planning. Indeed, the clinician may have an ongoing therapeutic relationship with the respondent. At the same time, though, it is important for the clinician to remain mindful of the fact that he or she is also an agent of the state, potentially instrumental in the deprivation of the respondent's liberty; accordingly, there is a need to keep some distance from the situation. As we have repeatedly noted in this chapter, the stance of *caution* should be maintained to a substantially greater degree in a commitment evaluation that it would be in a normal therapeutic relationship.

Mental health professionals involved in "prescreening" for civil commitment, a statutorily required step in some jurisdictions,[279] should also be mindful of their role as gatekeepers and should remain cognizant of community resources. "Prescreeners" may be crucial actors in ensuring continuity of care.[280] If a respondent is in fact committed, the prescreener should ensure that necessary background information is transmitted to the receiving hospital and that steps are taken for initiation of liaison with community clinics for eventual aftercare.

Finally, clinicians doing commitment evaluations should remember that they are often seeing respondents under especially strained circumstances. It may be, for example, that an irate family member has summoned the police after a domestic squabble. Then the police have forcibly brought the respondent to the emergency room. Thus, the situation is almost guaranteed to elicit disturbed behavior. Care should be taken to try to identify and reduce such stress-induced sequelae of the evaluation itself. Such thoughtfulness is necessary for maintaining the reliability and validity of assessments, as well as for providing humane care.

8.10. Special Commitment Settings and Populations

Although the discussion thus far has broad applicability to evaluations for civil commitment, it is important to recognize that there are some special circumstances in which the prevailing standards, procedures, or both may differ from ordinary civil commitment. We briefly examine four such circumstances: when the respondent is a minor; when the respondent is a jail or prison inmate; when the respondent has been acquitted of a crime by reason of insanity; and when the respondent is mentally retarded. Although *civil* commitment may not be involved when the respondent is a jail or prison inmate or one who has been acquitted of a crime by reason of insanity, we have included them here because the nature of the inquiry is usually similar to that in civil commitment, and because there is substantial interplay among the standards and procedures for civil and criminal commitment.[281]

(a) Minors

At several points in this chapter, we have mentioned the Supreme Court's decision in *Parham v. J.R.,*[282] addressing the constitutional requirements for due process when parents or guardians seek to "volunteer" their children or wards for admission to mental hospitals. In brief, the Court held that the only process due children in such situations was review of the child's need for hospital treatment by the admitting physician, acting as a "neutral factfinder." It is important to recognize, however, that many states in fact require more procedural protections than the constitutional minimum for minors facing commitment.[283] Therefore, lawyers and mental health professionals involved in hospitalization of minors should take care to determine the law in their own jurisdictions.

In determining that nonadversary, administrative procedures would adequately protect minors' constitutional interests, the Supreme Court relied on rather idyllic assumptions about the biological families of mentally disordered children (as well as the "families" provided by state social workers), state hospitals, and administrative procedures.[284] The questionable nature of these assumptions has been discussed elsewhere in detail.[285] Suffice it to say that the modal resident of state hospital facilities for minors is a troubled and troubling, but not crazy,[286] adolescent[287] who is a ward of the state[288] and simply has nowhere else to go.

Much of what we have already said about the roles of lawyers and mental health professionals in civil commitment of adults applies also to civil commitment of minors, but perhaps with even more force. The populations of residential facilities in mental health, juvenile justice, social service, and special educational systems are to a large extent interchangeable.[289] There is no research establishing the efficacy of hospital-based treatment of minors,[290] especially the conduct-disordered youngsters who are often sent to psychiatric facilities in lieu of juvenile correctional institutions.[291] For many of these youths, an approach that is more "educational" than "medical" may be the treatment of choice [see § 11.06]. Although hospitals are not per se the most re-

strictive or intrusive settings for treatment,[292] special care should be taken to ensure that minors are not being "dumped" into a hospital because it is the easiest—not necessarily the best or the least restrictive—thing to do with them[293] or simply because they have no advocates to watch out for them.[294] The "investigative" role of lawyers and clinicians in civil commitment thus assumes special importance in cases of minors.[295]

(b) Jail and Prison Inmates

(1) Inmates Convicted of a Crime

The stigma and intrusions upon privacy involved in mental hospitalization are sufficiently great that the Supreme Court held in *Vitek v. Jones*[296] that prisoners are entitled to an administrative hearing to determine the need for a transfer to a psychiatric facility before they can be so transferred. They are entitled to the services of a "qualified and independent" advocate, but not necessarily a licensed attorney, to assist them in the hearing.[297] *Vitek* thus recognizes residual liberty interests of prisoners in avoiding involuntary mental health treatment, but it suggests that those interests can be protected with less procedural rigor than required in civil commitment and with a mere showing of a need for treatment.[298]

Some commentators have suggested that the Court did not go far enough in *Vitek*. They argue that equal protection and due process demand that standards and procedures used in mental health commitment of prisoners should be largely indistinguishable from those used in civil commitment.[299] The ABA's Criminal Justice Mental Health Standards appear largely to endorse this view. The Standards provide for judicial commitment proceedings, with the prisoner having a right to legal counsel.[300] However, only the threshold prong of most civil commitment statutes (i.e., that the prisoner is "seriously mentally ill") need be met for transfer.[301]

The Standards also recognize that a problem which may actually be more prevalent is the difficulty in obtaining treatment for an inmate who wants and needs it.[302] Such treatment is probably required on both moral and constitutional grounds.[303] The Standards provide for administrative procedures and, if these are unsuccessful, for judicial proceedings to effect a transfer for an inmate in need of psychological treatment that cannot be obtained in the correctional facility.[304]

It is noteworthy that the inquiry for assessment purposes is similar, regardless of whether the proposed transfer is involuntary or voluntary. The clinician should determine whether the inmate has a bona fide mental disorder, what his or her needs for treatment are, and whether those needs can be met within the prison. The last element of this inquiry indicates the need for clinicians performing transfer evaluations to be aware of the services available within the correctional system (which are often woefully inadequate[305]) and the particular stresses and demands of prison life.[306] There is some controversy as to whether *any* effective treatment can be accomplished in prisons, given the conflicts that frequently arise between treatment and security goals.[307] Regardless, however, it should be recognized that the facilities receiving mentally disordered inmates may be little better.

It is not clear how broadly even the limited requirements of *Vitek* apply. For example, is a hearing necessary before transfer to a "hospital" run by the department of corrections, or to a psychiatric wing of a regular prison?[308] What is clear is that *Vitek* is not being applied at all in many jurisdictions,[309] in part because prison transfers remain a largely hidden process. Indeed, it is probably true that less is known about the evaluation and treatment of prisoners than any other aspect of the forensic mental health system.[310]

(2)   Inmates Awaiting Trial

If persons sentenced to prison still have an interest in avoiding involuntary mental health treatment, then surely persons who are in jail awaiting trial have an interest analogous to that of respondents who are living in freedom. Too frequently, jail management problems are dealt with by sending prisoners to the state hospital for competency evaluations when there is no real question about their competency to stand trial.

As we have noted in § 4.03(c), in such instances the proper procedure would be to seek civil commitment, rather than to apply a ruse that is more convenient to carry out. This recommendation is based not only on protection of the respondent's civil rights. It is also based on the practical reality that the purpose of obtaining treatment may be frustrated by use of the mechanism for competency evaluations. The receiving facility may promptly return the clearly competent, albeit disturbed, defendant, and it may lack authority to treat the defendant.

Regardless, the clinician asked to evaluate a defendant in jail for possible treatment should view the assessment as a consultation in the strict sense. What might be done to stabilize the individual through the crisis engendered by arrest and incarceration? In that regard, it should be noted that mental health professionals and jail staff—unlike clinicians and prison administrators—typically have compatible goals.[311] Typically, mental health interventions in jail will be directed toward stabilization of the defendant, which has the effect then of helping the jail to run more smoothly.

(c)   Insanity Acquittees

After a person is acquitted by reason of insanity, he or she is usually committed automatically to a forensic unit for evaluation, typically for 30 to 60 days. At the end of this period, a court must decide whether the acquittee is mentally ill and dangerous. If commitment occurs, the acquittee is confined anywhere from six months to two years after the original commitment until the next release hearing.[312]

In participating in these "criminal commitments," the clinician is asked to assess whether the acquittee is any longer mentally ill (e.g., "restored to reason") and/or dangerous.[313] Although these questions are similar, if not identical, to those posed in civil commitment, it is important to note that both standards and procedures for criminal commitment often differ significantly from those in civil commitment. For example, the state must prove by clear and convincing evidence that a civil respondent meets the commitment standard,[314] but the burden of proof may be shifted to the defendant in postacquittal commitment.[315] Moreover, one study found that the standards, though identical, were more broadly applied to insanity acquittees than in the civil commitment context.[316] Further, the release decision was often made by a different process and in a different forum (e.g., by the judge who heard the insanity trial rather than by a hospital administrator).[317]

These differences are based on two assumptions: that defendants acquitted by reason of insanity are unusually dangerous (because they have committed a violent act, though not a technical crime), and that they are mentally ill (because of the insanity plea).[318] However, these assumptions may often be faulty. As to the first, the crime of which the defendant was accused may have been minor[319]; if so, that offense might not even qualify as the overt dangerous act necessary for civil commitment in many jurisdictions. Moreover, even a serious crime (for instance, murder of one's spouse) does not mean that the individual is likely to commit a similar act. As to the assumption regarding "continuing" mental illness, in jurisdictions where an insanity acquittal can be based on a reasonable doubt as to sanity, mental disorder may not be proven to the requisite degree necessary even for civil commitment.[320] Also, it is quite possible that an acquittee's mental condition may have improved markedly since the offense, either spontaneously or because of treatment.

Nonetheless, in *Jones v. United States,*[321] the Supreme Court recently reaffirmed both of these assumptions about acquittees as a basis for differentiating between criminal and civil commitment. It held that *any* criminal act by a defendant "certainly indicates dangerousness"[322]—even if, as in *Jones,* the act was attempted shoplifting of a jacket! The Court also maintained that "it comports with common sense to conclude that someone whose mental illness was sufficient to lead him to commit a criminal act is likely to remain ill and in need of treatment."[323]

As a result of these assumptions, the Court held that defendants may be constitutionally required to remain in confinement until they can prove that they no longer merit commitment,

even though the maximum possible sentence for the offense of which a defendant was charged may have long since passed.[324] It also sanctioned the automatic posttrial evaluative commitment described above.

Although it is likely that evaluation for commitment of acquittees will take place in a different setting (e.g., a forensic hospital) from that of the civil commitment evaluation, and with different standards and different procedures, the scope of the evaluation itself is likely to be similar. We turn once again, though, to our plea for caution. The *Jones* definition of "dangerous" behavior starkly exemplifies the need for clinicians to avoid conclusions as to ultimate legal issues. Although insanity acquittees as a group are not particularly prone to subsequent violent or criminal behavior, especially when compared to felons,[325] the legal meaning of a standard may indeed depart from a clinician's understanding of the language.

(d) The Mentally Retarded

Most states have enacted separate statutory provisions for commitment of the mentally retarded which, on the whole, provide less procedural protection than commitment statutes for the mentally ill and are less explicit with respect to commitment criteria (often merely requiring a finding of mental retardation and need for treatment or habilitation).[326] In part, this is the result of historical accident. As noted in § 8.01(a), the law's approach to the mentally retarded, premised on the irreversibility of their condition, was less solicitous of their property and person than was the case with the mentally ill. Additionally, there may have been an underlying assumption that the mentally retarded require less legal protection because they are more easily identifiable than the mentally ill and thus are less likely to be committed arbitrarily.

In reality, however, there is no reason for treating the mentally ill and the mentally retarded differently as far as the legal structure for commitment is concerned. The line between "mental retardation" and "normal" intellectual and adaptive functioning is as difficult to discern as that between "mental illness" and "mental health." Institutionalization is as much a deprivation of liberty for the mentally retarded as it is for the mentally ill, and should only occur after appropriate due process has taken place. If dangerousness to self or others and grave disability are considered the proper criteria for commitment of the mentally ill, the same should be true of the mentally retarded. Those individuals who are not dangerous and can subsist on their own with or without the help of support in the community should not be committable on the grounds of mental retardation alone. Given the relatively stable nature of their condition, particular attention should be paid in cases involving the mentally retarded to the least restrictive alternative criterion and to periodic review provisions. Otherwise, hospitalization of such individuals could amount to confinement for life.[327]

Modern statutes, while still segregating the commitment provisions concerning the mentally retarded and the mentally ill, recognize these realities. In Florida, for instance, mental retardation is defined as "significant subaverage general intellectual functioning [meaning two standard deviations from the mean score on a standardized intelligence test specified by the mental health department] existing concurrently with deficits in adaptive behavior and manifested during the period from conception to age 18,"[328] thus signaling that IQ alone is not ground for meeting the disability threshold. Commitment may occur only if retardation, so defined, causes a propensity for violence toward others or a lack of sufficient capacity to give informed consent to treatment and a lack of basic survival and self-care skills that could lead to a "real and present threat of substantial harm to the person" if close supervision is not maintained.[329] Placement in a residential setting must be the least restrictive and most appropriate setting to meet the person's needs.[330] These criteria must be proven by clear and convincing evidence at a fully adversarial proceeding.[331] Even this relatively sophisticated statute, however, fails to require, when commitment is on "danger to other" grounds, a recent act or threat and a prediction of *imminent* harm to others, provisions that are present in

the statute governing commitment of the mentally ill.[332] Moreover, discharge reviews are not automatic, but depend upon the initiaton of the retarded person, his or her guardian, or the hospital,[333] a framework that facilitates neglect.

In the criminal commitment context, the mentally retarded have traditionally received even less explicit attention than they have in connection with civil commitment. Indeed, many state statutes fail to include provisions for commitment of the mentally retarded who have been acquitted by reason of insanity (although the courts, when confronted with this fact, construe the term "mentally ill" in these provisions to encompass the mentally retarded).[334] More importantly, given the permanence of their condition, the mentally retarded who are committed after an insanity acquittal are particularly disadvantaged in those states that permit continued confinement on the basis of *either* mental disability or dangerousness and that do not provide for *automatic* periodic review.[335] Provisions such as those recommended by the American Bar Association, permitting continued detention only upon a finding of mental disability *and* dangerousness and establishing periodic review,[336] are necessary to ensure that the mentally retarded, whether in the civil or criminal system, are not warehoused or forgotten after commitment.

8.11.   Summary

The evidence as to the effectiveness of hospitalization, relative to less restrictive alternatives, is generally not very promising. Similarly, predictions of dangerousness, even in the short term, are highly suspect. Nonetheless, even under legalistic statutes, clinicians may find their opinions almost automatically dispositive. There is a need for clinicians to exercise great caution in their opinions and for attorneys to assume the adversary stance that the law presumes. Members of both professional groups might work together to investigate alternative dispositions for respondents in commitment proceedings. Such a collaborative relationship is in fact compatible even with an adversary system, given that much of the work should be investigation and negotiation.

BIBLIOGRAPHY

Addington v. Texas, 441 U.S. 418 (1978).

Churgin, *The Transfer of Inmates to Mental Health Facilities: Developments in the Law,* in MENTALLY DISORDERED OFFENDERS: PERSPECTIVES FROM LAW AND SOCIAL SCIENCES (J. Monahan & H. Steadman eds. 1983).

CIVIL COMMITMENT AND SOCIAL POLICY: AN EVALUATION OF THE MASSACHUSETTS MENTAL HEALTH REFORM ACT OF 1970 (1981).

CRIMINAL JUSTICE MENTAL HEALTH STANDARDS, part VII (1984). (Commitment of insanity acquittees.)

Developments in the Law: Civil Commitment of the Mentally Ill, 87 HARV. L. REV. 1190 (1974).

Donaldson v. O'Connor, 422 U.S. 563 (1975).

Ennis & Litwack, *Psychiatry and the Presumption of Expertise: Flipping Coins in the Courtroom,* 62 CALIF. L. REV. 693 (1974).

Hermann, *Automatic Commitment and Release of Insanity Acquittees: Constitutional Dimensions,* 14 RUTGERS L.J. 667 (1983).

Hoffman & Foust, *Least Restrictive Treatment of the Mentally Ill: A Doctrine in Search of Its Senses,* 14 SAN DIEGO L. REV. 1100 (1977).

Kiesler, *Mental Hospitals and Alternative Care: Noninstitutionalization as Potential Public Policy for Mental Patients,* 37 AM. PSYCHOLOGIST 349 (1982).

Lessard v. Schmidt, 349 F. Supp. 1078 (E.D. Wis. 1972).

Melton, *Family and Mental Hospital as Myths: Civil Commitment of Minors,* in CHILDREN, MENTAL HEALTH, AND THE LAW (N.D. Reppucci, L. Weithorn, E. Mulvey, and J. Monahan eds. 1984).

J. MONAHAN, THE CLINICAL PREDICTION OF VIOLENT BEHAVIOR (1981).

Morse, *A Preference for Liberty: The Case against Involuntary Commitment of the Mentally Disordered,* 70 CALIF. L. REV. 54 (1982).

Parham v. J.R., 442 U.S. 584 (1979).

Project Release v. Prevost, 722 F.2d 960 (2d Cir. 1983).

Roth, *A Commitment Law for Patients, Doctors, and Lawyers,* 136 AM. J. PSYCHIATRY 1121 (1979).

A. STONE, MENTAL HEALTH AND THE LAW: A SYSTEM IN TRANSITION (1975).

D. WEXLER, MENTAL HEALTH LAW: MAJOR ISSUES, chs. 2 and 3 (1981).

CHAPTER NINE

Civil Competencies

9.01. Introduction

In Chapters 4 and 5, we considered the range of competencies that come into question when a criminal defendant may be mentally disordered. A theme throughout those chapters is that mental disability does not, in and of itself, imply incompetency in *all* areas of functioning. Instead, mental health professionals and jurists should attend to whether there are specific *functional* incapacities that render a person incapable of making a particular kind of decision or performing a particular kind of task. Thus, as noted in the introduction to Chapter 5, respect for individual autonomy demands that individuals be allowed to make those decisions of which they are capable, even if they have a severe mental disorder. This principle is even more starkly raised in the civil context. For example, do civilly committed persons retain control over their property? Do they have a residual right to privacy, such that they can decline intrusive treatments? If a mentally retarded person is unable to conceptualize large sums of money, but does know what money is and can perform simple calculations, should that person not be able to decide how to spend his or her money, perhaps up to a limit? These questions are considered in this chapter in the context of evaluations for guardianship, compe-

tency to consent to treatment and research, and testamentary capacity (competency to make a will).

The underlying rationale for the competency rules alluded to above is that mentally disabled persons *as persons* have the right to self-determination, in the absence of compelling reasons to the contrary. Beside this fundamental interest in the preservation of autonomy and privacy in the face of potential governmental intrusion, mentally disabled persons also have special *entitlements,* usually statutorily based, to protection and provision of resources to meet their basic needs if they are "incompetent" to meet them on their own. In the mid-1970s, the federal government created substantial fiscal incentives for states to meet at least some of these needs.[1] In addition, the federal government itself provides basic financial support to disabled people, specifically those who because of disability cannot work or would have trouble doing so.[2] Mental health professionals may be called upon to evaluate whether an individual meets the threshold level of disability for eligibility for these entitlement programs and what level of need the individual has. Although we do not review all of the specific contexts in which these questions arise,[3] the final section of the chapter discusses the nature of evaluations for disability under the Social Security program, the largest such entitlement program in the country

9.02.   Guardianship

(a)   Forms of Guardianship

"Guardianship" is the delegation, by the state, of authority over an individual's person or estate to another party. It is probably the most ancient aspect of mental health law. In both Roman and English common law, the sovereign possessed the power and duty to guard the estate of incompetent persons.[4] This power, which emanated from the state's interest in the preservation of its wealth, is the historic basis of the *parens patriae* power, which has since been applied broadly—and perhaps illogically[5]—to the regulation by the state of many other aspects of decisionmaking by children and mentally disabled people.

Today guardianship reflects this historical development. In some jurisdictions, there are separate provisions for appointment of a guardian of one's person (e.g., with authority over health care decisions) and a guardian of one's estate (e.g., with authority over the making of contracts to sell one's property).[6] The latter type of guardian of often called a *conservator* or *committee,* although this nomenclature is not consistent across jurisdictions.[7]

In addition to, or instead of this distinction, some jurisdictions also distinguish between *general (plenary)* and *specific* guardianship.[8] As the name implies, in the latter form of guardianship, the guardian's powers are restricted to particular types of decisions. Thus, with respect to guardianship of the person, the guardian may have authority only to make a specific treatment decision (e.g., consent to a specific course of treatment that has been proposed) or "nonroutine" treatment decisions (e.g., consent to any major surgery); the disabled person would remain free to make other health care decisions. Similarly, a disabled person under limited guardianship of the estate might be able to make decisions about the property, except with respect to a particularly compli-

cated business deal that has been proposed, or any purchase over $100. On the other hand, under general guardianship, the guardian has total control of the individual's person, estate, or both.[9] Obviously, limited guardianship schemes are more respectful of disabled persons' autonomy. However, a limited guardianship need not be very circumscribed. For example, a guardian might be appointed for the specific purpose of consent to psychiatric hospitalization after an individual has been found to be incompetent to make that decision. The guardian could then "voluntarily" commit the individual.

Beyond these distinctions about the *scope* of guardianship, it is also important to recognize disparate *bases* of guardianship. In most instances, individuals are found, on the basis of particularized evidence, to lack specific or general capacities. They are actually (or *de facto*) incompetent and in need of a guardian to make decisions for them. On the other hand, some people are *presumed* to require a guardian. Regardless of their *de facto* level of competency, they are incompetent in law *(de jure).* For example, even though older minors are often as competent as adults to make decisions of various types,[10] they are *de jure* incompetent for most purposes and, as a result, lack legal authority to act on their own behalf.[11] Even in those instances in which the law permits some minors to make decisions independently,[12] they generally are presumed incompetent until they are able to rebut this presumption.[13] Because there is such a strong legal presumption of minors' incompetency, there usually is no need to adjudicate their need for guardianship. In most cases, there also is no need to determine who the guardian will be.[14] Children are generally subject to the wishes of their "natural" guardians—their parents—who are presumed, in the absence of strong evidence to the contrary, to act in their best interests.[15]

Civilly committed adults may also find themselves presumed incompetent to make many decisions. Civil commitment sometimes carries collateral loss of rights to marry,[16] possess a driver's license,[17] refuse intrusive treatments,[18] manage one's property,[19] and so forth. In such instances, there often is no need to appoint a guardian, in that state statutes provide authority to particular officials to make decisions on behalf of the committed person.[20] Moreover, in some states, determination of general guardianship and civil commitment are coextensive. For example, in California, commitment as a "gravely disabled" person takes place through a conservatorship proceeding.[21]

Three separate issues arise in the guardianship context: determining whether someone needs a guardian; deciding, if a guardian is necessary, who that person shall be; and determining, once a guardian is appointed, what he or she should do. These issues are discussed below.

(b) Determining the Need for Guardianship

(1) Legal Requirements

Proceedings to determine whether a guardian will be appointed occur only in those cases where a person is not presumed incompetent because of age or other status (e.g., civilly committed); that is, a guardian is necessary only when there is some question as to whether the individual is *de facto* incompetent. These proceedings typically lack procedural rigor. Indeed, one commentator has asserted that "informality is the hallmark of incompetency proceedings."[22] In most jurisdictions, any interested person can petition to have someone declared incompetent and subject to guardianship.[23] Often there is no requirement of specific allegations in the petition, and notice to the respondent is limited to the fact that a hearing will be held.[24] At the hearing itself, the respondent often has no right to counsel[25] or trial by jury,[26] and, in some jurisdictions, the respondent is rarely present.[27] If counsel is appointed, he or she is often designated a *guardian ad litem* who is free to act in what he or she believes to be the respondent's best interests.[28] Moreover, if found to be in need of a guardian, incompetent persons usually bear the burden of raising the issue at a latter time if they believe they are no longer in need of a guardian.[29] At the later hearing, such individuals are placed in the ironic position of persuading the court that circumstances have changed and that they are

now competent, although they have had no opportunity to manage their own affairs.

This procedural laxity is commonly matched by ambiguity of standards. For general guardianship, most state statutes simply require findings of a threshold status (e.g., mental illness, idiocy, senility) and incapacity "to care for oneself or one's estate."[30] As Alexander has noted, this vague standard leaves the door wide open for essentially arbitrary judicial decisions:

> The ambiguous standards of the substantive law in guardianship proceedings preclude effective application of procedural due process analysis to guardianship proceedings. In particular, the standard of what is an appropriate ability to manage property is unclear. Are persons who manage to meet the challenges of daily life with assistance from friends and families incompetent because they could not do it alone? Are they incompetent when they make decisions preventing the dissipation of their property but are noticeably less effective than those who managed it before? Are they incompetent if their property management skills are marginal, irrespective of their prior abilities? What does the word "properly" mean in the statutes relating to property management? Do persons whose survival is not in question manage "improperly" if they fail to live up to standards the trial court finds appropriate? How does the court decide on an appropriate standard?
>
> The statutory standards seem to allow definitions of functional ability ranging from simple improvidence in occasional transactions to incapacity to provide for food or medical care for extended periods of time. Since one can almost always find property managers who can improve on a particular owner's management, it is unclear when it becomes appropriate to impose such a manager on an unwilling recipient.[31]

As we shall see in § 9.03 even standards for specific competencies are little better defined. Rarely are the elements of a specific competency spelled out in either statutory or common law.

As might be expected, given these ambiguities, there is considerable variation in the application of guardianship statutes. On the one hand, courts are sometimes prone to enter orders for guardianships on the basis of medical opinion alone or on the basis of what appears to the court to be the "reasonable" or "rational" course of action individuals should take (and whether they have taken, or plan to take, that action). For example, the Nebraska Supreme Court recently upheld appointment of a conservator for an elderly woman, where the evidence showed that she had used most of the estate left by her husband (indeed, she had only $19.18 left in her checking account); that she had given much of it away; and that she had made some foolish real estate deals.[32] Apparently no evidence was taken as to her actual capacity to manage her property. Two members of the court entered an impassioned dissent:

> The fact that one has made bad investments or is inclined to give one's property away is not sufficient to justify the appointment of a conservator over the objections of the one for whom the conservator is being sought. Were it otherwise, a number of us would have conservators appointed for us. Often all that persons of advanced age have left is their dignity and the ability to dispose of their property as they may choose. We should not take that right away so quickly, absent evidence of mental incapacity.[33]

On the other hand, some courts have required considerable evidence of incompetency before entering an order for guardianship. For example, an Illinois appellate court recently affirmed a decision by the trial court denying appointment of a guardian for a man with progressive brain disease and several serious physical conditions.[34] In his own testimony, the respondent discussed management of a triplex he owned and his Social Security allotment, but he also said that he invented the snowmobile, that he once had a pet black widow spider, and that he could produce fire by pointing his finger. The respondent's testimony about his financial dealings was enough evidence of competency to convince both the trial court and the appellate court that there was no need to present further evidence as to his incompetency. Similarly, a California appellate court recently overturned a conservatorship for a schizophrenic man who lived in his sister's backyard much of the time and who was described as dirty, disheveled, and incontinent.[35] The court held that it was reversible error for

the trial judge to fail to admit evidence and to instruct the jury on the availability of assistance by others in meeting the respondent's basic needs.

(2) Clinical Evaluation

In the absence of clear standards, clinicians are advised to be as thorough as possible in documenting what an allegedly incompetent person can and cannot do. As already noted, the assessment should be focused on the range of *functions* that the respondent can perform, not the nature of any mental disorder per se. Such detailed evaluation will be especially useful in jurisdictions in which limited guardianship is an option. Clinicians should also attend to whether weaknesses in the individual's performance are, or might be, alleviated by assistance from others.

Despite the ancient basis of guardianship and the frequency with which the issue arises, little attention has been given to the reliability and validity of guardianship evaluations, or even to formats for such assessments. One procedure for which there are promising preliminary data is the Community Competency Scale (CCS), developed by a group of researchers at St. Louis University.[36] Although the psychometric properties of the CCS are not yet well established,[37] it is a well-conceptualized instruments[38] that relies on behavior samples of "real-life" survival skills. There are 16 subscales: Judgment; Emergencies; Acquire Money; Compensate for Incapacities; Manage Money; Communication; Care of Medical Needs; Adequate Memory; Satisfactory Living Arrangements; Proper Diet; Mobility; Sensation; Personal Hygiene; Maintain Household; Utilize Transportation; Verbal–Math Skills. The "apparatus" for the CCS is indicative of its relationship to the kinds of tasks involved in basic independent living: telephone, blank checks, telephone book, envelope, and play money.

In the absence of a well-established format for evaluation of general incompetency, one strategy would be to have the person review a typical day and how everyday tasks (e.g., food preparation, payment of monthly bills) are accomplished. As suggested by the CCS items, actual performance of some of these tasks may be requested during the interview. A home visit may also be useful to observe the individual's adaptation in that setting.

When complex estates are not involved, the scope of evaluation for guardianship of the estate may differ little from evaluation for guardianship of the person.[39] In these cases, everyday use of money will be highly correlated to general success in independent living. For individuals with larger and more complex estates, competency in handling property per se will need to be discussed in detail. Among the areas that should be probed when evaluating such persons are their knowledge of the nature and purpose of money, the extent of their wealth, the alternatives for disposing of the estate, their skills in everyday management (e.g., balancing of accounts, payment of bills), their plans for disposing of their estates, and the reasons underlying these plans. Where there are gaps in knowledge, the clinician should attempt to discern whether these are the result of inexperience or lack of education, rather than incapacity. A comprehensive social history should also be taken, both for corroboration of impressions from individual assessment and for determination of the resources for assistance that may be available [see the Dyer report, § 15.07].

(c)   Determining Who Shall Be the Guardian

Mental health professionals will generally have little involvement in assessment of the proper guardian to be appointed, once the need for a guardian is established. There are several kinds of parties who may be appointed (ranging from family members to government agencies to sheriffs),[40] but the preference for one sort of guardian or another is likely to be a matter of policy or law. There are pros and cons for each type of guardian, but it is worth noting that family members may have conflicts of interest, especially when the ultimate distribution of the respondent's estate is at issue, the management of family-owned businesses is involved, or the respondent's values are deemed improper by the rest of the family.[41] Clinicians are most likely to

become involved at the decisionmaking phase[42] when the conflicts are made manifest. Consider, for example, a situation in which a mentally retarded adult's parents are divorcing. In that instance, analogous to a custody battle, each parent may claim to be the potential guardian who would be most likely to meet the child's best interests. Another choice-of-guardian situation in which clinical assessment might be sought (albeit rarely) would be when there is a special attempt to match an incompetent person with a guardian who would be especially attuned to the person's needs and able to communicate easily.

(d)   Determining What the Guardian Shall Do

Once a guardian is appointed, there are essentially two models for guiding decisionmaking. In one model, the guardian acts according to an objective test: What action will most effectively serve the ward's best interests? In the alternative model, exemplified by a series of cases in Massachusetts and New Jersey,[43] the guardian is instructed to rely upon a subjective substituted judgment—that is, to act as he or she thinks the ward would have acted, if the ward were competent. Although it is easy to construct hypothetical cases in which the decision made by the guardian should differ, depending upon which of the two models is used,[44] the subjective test usually becomes a *de facto* best-interests test.[45] Because the specific situation in which the guardian is required to act may be a novel one for the ward, there is often no basis on which to hypothesize what the ward would have done if competent, except what the guardian believes is the best course of action after objectively weighing the merits. Indeed, when the ward is incompetent because of mental retardation, he or she may never have been competent.[46]

Thus, if the decision to be made by the guardian involves treatment of the ward, and a mental health professional is asked to provide information to assist in the decision, the evaluation will typically be a traditional treatment-oriented assessment, focused on the ward's best interests. Given the individual's needs, what are the treatment plans available, their probable efficacy, and their probable side effects? To put it another way, enough information needs to be generated for the guardian to give informed consent, a topic addressed in more detail below.

9.03. Competency to Consent to Treatment

(a) Requirements for Informed Consent

One of the most controversial areas of potential proxy decisionmaking is in regard to treatment of persons whose competency is in doubt. The doctrine of informed consent is designed to address this issue. A relatively recent development in tort law,[47] the doctrine may impose liability on clinicians for battery[48] or negligence[49] for treating patients whose consent is invalid [see § 3.04(a)]. It has two primary purposes: "(1) to promote individual autonomy and (2) to encourage rational decisionmaking."[50] As Katz has eloquently shown,[51] the interest in protection of autonomy in treatment decisions is not simply a reflection of a value placed on liberty or free agency for its own sake (which is not to imply that such a value is in any way trivial). Protection of autonomy also serves to "humanize" the clinician–patient relationship and to restore the balance in authority between the clinician and the patient, upon whose body or mind the proposed treatment would intrude. Theoretically, the requirement of informed consent serves to ensure that the patient is respected as a person— that he or she is not simply patronized, taken for granted, or treated as a dependent child or simply an object of treatment ("a case") by medical professionals.[52]

In determining whether a consent is valid, there are essentially three elements: disclosure, competency, and voluntariness.[53] Although there is consensus about these elements, the tests to be used in determining their presence are far less settled.

(1) Disclosure

In regard to disclosure, there have been two streams of thought. The first, which went essentially unchallenged until 1972,[54] examines the adequacy of disclosure from the point of view of the clinician—whether a reasonable clinician would disclose particular information under the same circumstances.[55] The second line of analysis attends to the adequacy of disclosure from the patient's perspective—whether the patient is given sufficient information to make a reasonable decision.[56] Courts adopting the second line of analysis have divided in whether they espouse an objective test[57] (i.e., whether the patient is given the information that a reasonable person would need to make an informed judgment) or, less commonly, a subjective test[58] (i.e., whether the patient is given the information that an individual would need to make an informed judgment). Under each of these tests, the elements of disclosure are commonly the same—the nature of the recommended treatment procedure and its risks and benefits[59]—although the evaluation of the adequacy of disclosure obviously varies across tests.

Recently there has been some retrenchment toward a malpractice standard of disclosure (i.e., viewing disclosure from a clinician's perspective).[60] Katz has concluded with chagrin that the law of informed consent remains a "fairy tale."[61] Courts, concerned with patients' ability to deal with uncertainty and the awesome decisions that sometimes arise in health and mental health,[62] have sanctioned limited disclosure, usually a mere recital of treatment risks. In Katz's view, this tendency renders "the objective of giving patients a greater voice in medical decisionmaking well-nigh unattainable. For such disclosures do little to expand opportunities for meaningful consent, particularly in surrender-prone medical settings, in which a proposed treatment is zealously advocated despite its risks."[63] For truly informed consent, Katz argues, not only must clinicians be empathetic with patients' needs for respect and information, but they must be willing to share authority and to engage in a dialogue. Simply put, informed consent is a process, and it cannot be a one-way process if the goals of the informed consent doctrine are to be met.

(2) Competency

As noted in § 9.02, some classes of persons (e.g., children) are presumed to be incompetent. They are per se incapable of validly consenting to most forms of treatment. However, among classes in which persons are presumed to be competent (as most adults are), or in which there is a rebuttable presumption of incompetency,[64] a need for evaluation may arise if a question of an individual's competency to consent is raised. There are several contexts in which such a question is likely to be given attention. First, and perhaps most commonly, a person of uncertain competency may *refuse* the treatment prescribed. (There is likely to be substantially less question of competency to consent if the individual does in fact consent to the treatment.) Second, if an individual of uncertain competency is to undergo a major medical procedure, a physician may seek consultation to ensure that the patient can give informed consent, less tort action be brought later for treatment without consent.[65] In that instance, evaluation is realistically more oriented toward protection of the physician from liability than toward respect for the patient's autonomy. Third, evaluation may be sought in those instances in which a patient who is *de jure* incompetent for most purposes may, if *de facto* competent in a particular context, give informed consent in that limited, legally sanctioned context (e.g., sterilization).[66] Again, evaluation may be motivated as much by defensive practice as by concern about the limits of the patient's competent exercise of self-determination.[67]

Regardless of how the issue arises, the elements of competency to consent to treatment are rarely elaborated in law. The clinician is left, then, to a logical analysis of the scope of the evaluation. In that regard, Roth, Meisel, and Lidz have made a useful initial contribution to such a conceptualization.[68] They have identified four types of competency tests: expression of a preference; understanding; reasonable decisionmaking process; reasonable outcome.

The simplest of these standards, and the one most respectful of individual autonomy, is expression of a preference. As long as the patient can indicate a decision, that decision is considered to have been competently made. Generally, determination of competency under this standard is straightforward: The patient says yes (competent), no (competent), or nothing (incompetent). There are times, however, when it is not so clear. Patients may be very ambivalent and may waver in their preferences. Consider, for example, a man who is brought to a psychiatric emergency room and, after disclosure of risks and benefits, is advised to take an injection of antipsychotic medication. He says "no" but holds out his arm. Should his clear verbal expression of a preference be accepted when his nonverbal behavior implies a different decision? Acceptance of *any* preference creates the possibility, of course, that mentally disordered individuals may be permitted to make decisions without even knowing what they are doing, and that they may be especially likely, therefore, to make choices that are potentially harmful to themselves.

The standard of understanding is intended to reduce this risk. Generally, it is aimed at ensuring that individuals have a reasonable knowledge of the major information disclosed. But there is of course a possibility that the legal threshold for understanding will be set so high that most laypersons could not pass it. In such cases, individuals whose competency is brought into question will be held to a higher standard than most persons before they are permitted to exercise self-determination. Understanding is also sometimes transformed into "appreciation," which takes into account the affective meaning to the individual of the information disclosed.[69] In that regard, a particularly thorny problem is presented by those persons who understand the nature, risks, and benefits of a procedure, but who deny that they have a mental disorder and thus may not appreciate the need for treatment.[70]

When the focus of the test shifts from understanding to the process of decisionmaking, there is a requirement that patients not only understand the major information that has been disclosed to them about treatments, but that they weigh the information rationally. According to one variant of this test, attention would be given to the cognitive process itself. That is, does the patient consider each aspect of the information and logically perform a calculation of the expected value of each possible alternative? The major problem with this standard is that it assumes a quality of reasoning that most people rarely exercise in treatment decisions.[71] Another variant, which is especially important because of its central place in Stone's model of civil commitment [see § 8.03(i)],[72] is a determination of incompetency whenever a decision to refuse treatment is "irrational and is based on or related to the diagnosed illness."[73] This determination is not as easy as it may sound. Suppose, for example, that a patient declines a phenothiazine[74] because "it makes my mouth dry [a real side effect], and the doctor doesn't want me to tell the truth about the FBI." As mentioned in regard to the appreciation standard, denial may also be a problem. If individuals who appear floridly delusional but who also have a good understanding of a treatment refuse the treatment because they think that they are not in need of treatment, can their reason for refusing be said to be a product of their disorder?

The final type of test—reasonable outcome—is the least respectful of personal autonomy. Under that standard, a person is judged competent to consent if his or her decision, irrespective of its foundation, is the choice that a reasonable person would have made. It is unsurprising to find that most clinicians believe that reasonable people would accept the treatment recommended.[75] Thus, despite its being an "objective" test, assessment of competency under the standard of reasonable outcome is especially vulnerable to the evaluator's values. The test does not leave room for preferences that are idiosyncratic, even if they are "knowing" and "intelligent."

(3)   Voluntariness

As we have noted in other contexts [see §§ 1.03(a) and 5.02], the assessment of voluntariness is especially problematic because the concept does not fit within the paradigm in which most mental health professionals work. The law's use of the concept in the determination of the validity of consent to treatment has also lacked consistency and coherence. Specifically, some courts have worried that institutionalized patients' consent to particularly intrusive kinds of treatment may be rendered involuntary by the condition of institutionalization.[76] There is probably some merit in this argument, but only if it is more broadly applied. Obviously, institutionalized persons are in an especially powerless position,[77] but there is no reason to believe that this dependency would make consent to one form of treatment less voluntary than consent to others.[78]

Separation of competency and voluntariness may also not be conceptually sound. It is easy to imagine a person who has a thorough understanding of the pros and cons of a treatment and who has the capacity to reason quite logically, but who makes a decision under duress. In clinical situations, though, there is rarely such a clear distinction between competency and voluntariness. The same immaturity in social and moral development that may make some children and mentally retarded persons incapable of perceiving rights as applicable to themselves (a cognitive deficit relevant to competency) may also render them especially vulnerable to influence by authorities (a volitional deficit relevant to voluntariness).[79] Similarly, competency itself is an *interactive* construct; the quality of one's reasoning is likely to be affected by the degree of support and strain in the social context.[80]

(b)   The Right to Refuse Psychoactive Medication

(1)   Constitutional Basis

Beyond the general legal requirements for consent to treatment, a special body of law has developed as to whether mental patients may refuse psychoactive medication. Although styled as a right to refuse treatment, the cases have generally been focused on the right to refuse major tranquilizers (phenothiazines) primarily used in the treatment of schizophrenia,[81] and the holdings are often specific to that form of treatment.[82] In general, courts that have considered the question have found at least an abstract constitutional right to refuse medication,[83] and most states recognize such a right.[84] Nonetheless, the matter remains unsettled[85] and is the subject of intense controversy. The issue has divided the mental health professions,[86] and it has sometimes attracted rather vitriolic commentary.[87]

The constitutional basis of the right to refuse medication has not been well explicated. The most expansive constitutional construction of the issue was rendered by the federal district court in *Rogers v. Okin (Rogers I)*,[88] a case that has been considered by several levels of the judiciary.[89] The district court,[90] and later the First Circuit Court of Appeals,[91] found a right to refuse based on the constitutional right to privacy.[92] This analysis seemed to have two aspects: (1) Decisionmaking about psychoactive medication is an "intimate" matter,[93] and (2) the potential for harmful side effects of phenothiazines (which are numerous)[94] raises the question of significant bodily intrusion.[95] Although the circuit court declined to reach the issue,[96] the district court also located the right to refuse in the First Amendment.[97] The district court described psychoactive medication as "mind-altering" and potentially interfering with the "right to produce a thought" by causing "involuntary mind control."[98] The court added that "the fact that mind control takes place in a mental institution in the form of medically sound treatment of mental disease is not, itself, an extraordinary circumstance warranting an unsanctioned intrusion on the integrity of a human being."[99]

To the extent that the courts are constructing a "privacy of the mind" rationale for the right to refuse, separate from the general right to bodily privacy and restricted to the phenothiazines, conceptual problems arise. It is certainly arguable that *any* medication, not just the phenothiazines, affects the mind. If one takes medication for a physical condition that has the effect of making one feel better (or, as a side effect, feel groggy), it is undeniable that one's mental state has been altered. Indeed, *psychological* (as opposed to organic) treatments have the same objective. Moreover, if direct effects on the logic of one's thinking are the factor implicating privacy of mind, then some powerful psychoactive medications (e.g., lithium carbonate[100]) that primarily affect mood would be excluded from the right to refuse.[101]

The First Amendment argument is equally problematic. The district court's logic in regard to the "right of communication" or the "right to produce a thought"[102] may in fact be turned around. Arguably, phenothiazines *enhance* schizophrenics' capacity to produce and communicate ideas. A plausible argument might in fact be made that there is a First Amendment-based duty to medicate an individual whose capacity to communicate is seriously impaired as a result of psychosis.

In short, the most persuasive constitutional basis for a right to refuse medication lies in the general interest in preservation of bodily integrity, as explicated in earlier privacy cases.[103] Arguably, this interest in maintenance of control over one's body intensifies as the potential adverse consequences become more profound. In that regard, the sometimes frightening and irreversible effects of phenothiazines[104] raise such risks that the significance of an individual's preferences should be given great weight. The choice may be a difficult one (risking side effects or being incapacitated as a result of mental disorder), but respect for personal autonomy demands that, in most circumstances, individuals' decisions be honored, even if a particular preference (i.e., accepting treatment) appears to be the "reasonable" decision in the eyes of clinicians or others.

(2) Scope of the Right to Refuse

Although the constitutional basis of the right to refuse psychoactive medication is not well developed, there is relatively little controversy over the existence of *some* right to refuse treatment.[105] The center of the controversy concerns instead (1) the breadth of situations in which state interests are sufficiently compelling to overcome the individual's right to refuse, and (2) the rigor of procedures used to determine whether patients meet this standard. To a large extent, this debate is analogous to the ongoing dispute over the appropriate scheme to be used in civil commitment [see Chapter 8]. That is, most persons interested in the issue are willing to acknowledge that patients have at least some interest in avoiding involuntary treatment, but most are also willing to acknowledge some circumstances in which involuntary treatment is justified. The differences that exist seem to turn to a large extent on whether the issue is conceptualized as a *medical* or a *legal* question. Those who take the medical perspective tend to emphasize the potential harm of a lack of treatment, to perceive refusals of treatment as a product of mental illness, and to advocate deference to clinical judgment. Others, however, emphasize the significance of intrusion upon individual autonomy and privacy—interests that they believe to be as applicable to mentally disordered persons as to other persons. Advocates of the latter perspective understand the question of whether treatment should be administered involuntarily to be a legal–moral issue that should be decided by a judge or jury.

Illustrative of the former view is the opinion for the Third Circuit Court of Appeals in *Rennie v. Klein*,[106] which involved a test of New Jersey's regulations for forcible administration of psychoactive medication. The court upheld involuntary treatment of any civilly committed patient "whenever, in the exercise of professional judgment, such an action is deemed necessary to prevent the patient from endangering himself or others."[107] The New Jersey procedure does provide for administrative review of the professional judgment by successively higher levels of physicians.[108] But one commentator has acerbically described the right to refuse medication in New Jersey as being nothing more than a right to create administrative delay.[109]

The legal model is reflected in the Massachusetts Supreme Judicial Court's opinion in *Rogers IV*.[110] Relying on Massachusetts common law, the court expressly rejected a medical decisionmaking model. Except in emergencies,[111] the court forbade forcible medication of patients unless they have been judicially certified to be incompetent to make treatment decisions. Even in those instances, because of the remaining "value of human dignity,"[112] patients may not be forcibly medicated unless a jury determines that the patient, if competent, would have consented to medication. In making this decision, the jury must rely on a subjective substituted judgment [see § 9.02(d)].[113] The court noted that this judgment of what the patient would have chosen requires no medical expertise (although it does require full medical disclosure of information about the proposed treatment).[114] The court explicitly rejected even the contention that doctors can be trusted to protect patients' interests.[115]

In summary, both the Third Circuit Court and the Massachusetts Supreme Court acknowledged a right to refuse medication and some circumstances under which medication may not be refused. However, they characterized the nature of the decision to be made—and, therefore, the nature and degree of the procedural protection required—quite differently. As a practical matter, it is questionable whether the *Rennie* rule adds any protection of patients' privacy at all.[116]

(c)   Research on Informed Consent

(1)   Disclosure

The most general thing that can be said about disclosure in health and mental health settings is that there is rarely adherence to the spirit of informed consent.[117] Consent forms are often lengthy,[118] written in vocabulary beyond the comprehension of many or even most patients,[119] and presented as a mere formality.[120] Information about alternative treatments is often omitted; patients may be given the option to refuse treatment, but not to decide which treatment will be administered.[121] Negative information (e.g., the risks of tardive dyskinesia; severe or stigmatizing diagnosis) also is often omitted,[122] whether as a clinician's avoidance of bad news, fear of admitting weaknesses,[123] or a conscious invocation of "therapeutic privilege."[124] In regard to the last reason, there is virtually no empirical proof of the harm that is purported to arise from disclosure of risk information to patients in either medical or mental health units.[125]

(2) Competency

Naturalistic studies of patients' competency to consent have typically been rendered uninterpretable by failure to document the information that was disclosed.[126] Thus, it is unclear whether substantial gaps in relevant knowledge, which are often reported in studies of both medical and psychiatric patients,[127] are the result of lack of disclosure or incompetency. Those studies conducted in mental health settings have yielded inconsistent results. Roth and colleagues found that, after administration of a two-part consent form (i.e., presentation of information and then questions about it) and an interview, about three-fourths of patients demonstrated a competent understanding of electroconvulsive treatment.[128] Nonpsychotic patients of high occupational status and high educational level were most likely to appear competent. Soskis found that, relative to medical patients, schizophrenics tended to have a good understanding of the side effects and risks of their medication.[129] However, they tended not to understand the relationship between the medication and their disorder. In some contradiction to Soskis's findings, Munetz and colleagues were able to teach only 3 of 13 patients with tardive dyskinesia that their movement disorder was related to their medication.[130]

There is a more extensive research literature on *developmental* factors in competency to consent to treatment, although it primarily (but not exclusively) involves nonclinical samples.[131] In general, the available studies indicate that, by age 14, minors are typically as competent as adults in making treatment decisions.[132] Moreover, if a "reasonable outcome" standard is used, even elementary-school-age children appear as competent as adults, as least for routine health care decisions.[133]

(3) Voluntariness

The available research raises substantial doubt as to whether most consent in health and mental health care settings is truly voluntary ("voluntary" is used in this context to mean behavior that *appears* to be the product of free choice rather

than the result of overbearing third-party influence). As already noted, medical professionals typically treat consent requirements in a *pro forma* fashion. They seldom make an effort to involve a patient in a truly collaborative relationship, and they often cajole agreement to accept a particular treatment.[134] (It is noteworthy in that regard that obviously nonconsensual treatment is common on general medical wards as well as psychiatric wards.[135]) These situational constraints on patients' freedom of choice are frequently exacerbated by the "white-coat phenomenon"—the naive trust and acceptance of authority that patients sometimes place in their doctors.[136] Although the occasionally observed psychological attempts to salvage freedom may make patients' compliance with medical regimens less than doctors desire,[137] direct refusal of "doctor's orders" is rare.

(d) Evaluation of Competency to Consent to Treatment

When competency to consent to a *particular* proposed treatment is at issue, the task is to determine whether the elements of informed consent are present. It is important to find out first (usually by talking with the patient's physician or social worker) what the patient has been told about the treatment. If during the interview it becomes apparent that the patient has misunderstandings or points of ignorance about the treatment, it is usually a good idea to try to teach the relevant information to him or her to ensure that these problems are not simply the result of inadequate disclosure. In order to carry out this sort of interview, the clinician obviously needs to have at least a basic knowledge of the treatment. Unless there is reason to believe that the physician (or other treating professional) is intimidating to the patient, it is sometimes useful to have the physician present for at least part of the interview to answer questions that the patient may have and to try to clear up misunderstandings.

In general, the clinician will want to learn the patient's understanding of the nature and purpose of the treatment; its risks and benefits; and the nature, risks, and benefits of alternative treatments. Under the "reasonable process" test of competency, it will also be important to determine the patient's reasons for consenting or refusing consent. This information may also be relevant to determination of voluntariness of consent.

The clinician may also be able to rely on basic social psychology to identify situational factors arguably affecting the "voluntariness" of consent. For example, according to Saks's study of procedures for children's consent to organ and tissue transplants,[138] consent was typically obtained to a succession of procedures (e.g., blood samples to test donor compatibility; counseling) before consent was finally sought for the transplant. By that time, there had been so many affirmative steps consented to that the probability of consent to the transplant was increased significantly.[139]

With respect to the issue of competency to consent to treatment as a more general matter, presenting hypothetical treatment decisions and then probing as described above can be a useful strategy. In that regard, some vignettes have been developed for research purposes, with reasonably uncomplicated scoring systems that are potentially adaptable for clinical evaluation.[140]

There may be additional evaluation questions when the issue is whether psychoactive medication should be administered involuntarily. Besides competency to make treatment decisions, there may be questions of the degree to which other circumstances (e.g., imminent dangerousness or deterioration, combined with probable efficacy of medication) are present that may justify involuntary medication. In jurisdictions using a medical model, clinicians may find themselves doing civil-commitment-style, short-term predictive assessments [see § 8.09], but without much guidance as to the calculus to be used. For example, in what was almost a "nonopinion" as to the standard to be used, the First Circuit Court of Appeals in *Rogers II* held that the Constitution requires only that clinicians do an idiosyncratic "*ad hoc* balancing" of "the varying interests of particular patients in refusing antipsychotic medication against the equally varying interests

of patients—and the state—in preventing violence," with "neither . . . allowed necessarily to override the other in a blanket fashion."[141]

(e) Toward a Collaborative Model

Regardless of the standard to be used for determining competency, it is important not to lose sight of the purposes of requiring informed consent. These purposes remain viable even when the patient is not fully competent to consent to treatment. As Stone is fond of pointing out, the pure contractual model of health care may be naive today, given the intrusion of insurance companies and other third parties into that relationship.[142] Nonetheless, the spirit of a voluntary collaboration is fully consistent with respect for persons and should be followed insofar as possible.[143] Even if some measure of proxy decisionmaking is required, patients should be permitted to participate in treatment planning. Weithorn has described well some models for such shared responsibility.[144] Although competent patients should be permitted self-determination, with the practitioner acting as counselor but not as parent,[145] some participation in decisionmaking by even incompetent patients is ethically mandated[146] whenever possible and facilitative of successful treatment.[147]

9.04. Competency to Consent to Research

(a) Legal Requirements

The regulation of research using human participants is primarily subject to rules promulgated by the Department of Health and Human Services[148] and adopted by most other federal agencies.[149] These regulations, described in more detail below, provide for administrative review of procedures for human research by local institutional review boards (IRBs).

The rarity of "malresearch" litigation[150] should not be taken to indicate triviality. Although most human research, especially in the social and behavioral sciences, is innocuous, it still presents serious ethical problems. The "usual" problems in mental health law concerning whether mentally disordered persons are owed self-determination or protection are heightened because such research is rarely intended for the participants' direct benefit. Thus, the Nuremburg Code prohibits any research using persons who are not in a position to give valid informed consent, regardless of how experimental the research is.[151] It is also important to note that some human research, especially in biomedical areas, *does* necessarily present significant—albeit often unknown—risk to the participants, while at the same time holding the prospect of significant benefit to the society.[152]

Drawing from discussions of these issues by a national commission,[153] federal regulations represent an attempt to strike a balance between the conflicting interests by providing special requirements for research involving participants of uncertain competency.[154] A key threshold question under the regulations is whether the research involves more than "minimal risk," which "means that the risks of harm anticipated in the proposed research are not greater, considering probability and magnitude, than those ordinarily encountered in daily life or during the performance of routine physical or psychological examinations or tests."[155]

In general, the regulations require that researchers inform potential participants of the nature and purpose of the research, its risks and benefits, alternative treatments (in treatment-oriented research), the limits of confidentiality,[156] compensation and treatment for any injuries (in research involving more than minimal risk), whom to contact with questions, the choice of participating, and the freedom to withdraw at any time.[157] The requirement of full disclosure may be waived by the IRB when the research cannot be undertaken without deception or withholding of information,[158] there is no more than minimal risk, and the participants will be fully informed during "debriefing."[159]

Special regulations pertain to groups who may not be expected to give consent competently or voluntarily. Research on prisoners, for example, is forbidden (because of the potential for coer-

cion) unless the research is directly related to the special aspects of criminal behavior or incarceration[160] and there are no rewards for participation that would unduly influence decisions whether to participate.[161]

Research on children generally requires the *assent* of the children themselves and the *permission* of their parents.[162] Additional review is required when the research involves more than minimal risk[163] or the potential paticipants are wards of the state.[164] The requirement of parental consent may be waived by the IRB if it is found that parental involvement will harm, or at least not protect, the potential child participants (e.g., neglected or abused children).[165]

The Department of Health and Human Services has never implemented proposed regulations for research involving the "institutionalized mentally infirm."[166] These would have paralleled the regulations for children, with requirements for assent to minimal-risk research, increased supervision, and various forms of substituted consent in risky research. Critics of the proposed regulations regarded them as insufficiently respectful of patients' autonomy.[167] Presumably, in the absence of special regulations, research involving mental patients would follow the general regulations on human research. If so, such research requires the informed consent of the patients themselves or their legal representatives (e.g., a guardian). IRBs would, of course, remain free to require more protection than do the regulations themselves.

(b) Research

Empirical studies on consent to research is sparse. It is probable that much of the literature on consent to treatment (e.g., comprehensibility of forms) is generalizable to consent to research, especially when it is treatment-oriented research.[168] However, some aspects of research are unique and deserve exploration. First, the concept of research itself is important to comprehend, and there is no work on development of the concept. It is known that participants in experimental treatment studies often do not understand that they are part of a research project[169]; this is perhaps understandable, because their perception is primarily the provision of *treatment* to which they have consented.

Second, the nature of a rational risk assessment for consent to research is inherently different from that for consent to treatment. For the latter, the provision of actuarial tables concerning treatment success or their equivalent is at least theoreticially possible, although patients may find it difficult to apply such base-rate information to their own cases.[170] On the other hand, the risks in research are generally unknown. The best that can be done is to generalize from analogous situations and to speculate on the basis of theory. For example, the first humans to be administered an experimental drug can be told the effects the drug has had in animal studies and the theories about the drug's action, but the precise risks cannot be known until the research has been performed.

Third, the motivations for consent to research are presumably different from those for consent to treatment. It is conceivable that the desire to be altruistic or to receive compensation might dwarf other factors in the calculus of whether to participate.

Nonetheless, it should be noted that the few studies that have been conducted of elementary-school-age children's[171] and mental patients'[172] competence to consent to research have suggested that their capacity to attend to the basic purposes of research and their reasons for participating (or refusing to participate) may approximate the capacity and reasons of normal adults, on the average. At least for minimal-risk research, there appears to be little reason not to honor these groups' preferences.

(c) Evaluation

The evaluation of competency to consent to research will mirror the evaluation of competency to consent to treatment, to a large extent. The clinician should be careful, however, to evaluate the elements of informed consent that are specific to research (e.g., the nature of research; freedom to withdraw; when relevant, the lack of

benefit to the participants). To determine understanding of the nature of research, use of hypothetical situations derived from the few studies of competency to consent to research[173] may be a good strategy.

9.05. *Testamentary Capacity*

Another type of competency that the clinician may be asked to evaluate is whether an individual is (or, more commonly, was) competent at the time of executing a will. This type of "competency," like those referred to throughout this chapter, does not refer to the individual's general competency, but rather the capacity to meet the legal threshold required to perform a particular act—in this case, the writing of a will. If the individual (the "testator") is judged to have lacked competency (referred to in this context as "testamentary capacity") at the time of the writing of the will, the will is not "admitted to probate" (judged legally valid), and its provisions have no effect. In such cases, distribution of the estate will proceed under the terms of any valid will that exists or, in the absence of a will, under the rules of "intestate succession," which favor the immediate family.

(a) Legal Requirements

The requirement that testators must be competent is most often expressed by the simple admonition that they be "of sound mind."[174] The courts have interpreted this to require the following:

1. Testators must know at the time of making their wills that they are making their wills.
2. They must know the nature and extent of their property.
3. They must know the "natural objects of [their] bounty."
4. They must know the manner in which the wills they are making distribute their property.[175]

In determining whether testamentary capacity exists under these standards, the law is not interested in "perfect" capacity or knowledge. As with many competencies, only a low threshold of functioning is required: "Capacity" in this context means testators' ability to understand in a general way the nature and extent of their property, their relation to those who may naturally claim to benefit from the property they leave, and the practical effect of their wills.[176] For example, testators need not know every detail concerning their property. Similarly, more forgetfulness is not equivalent to a lack of capacity: If a testator has forgotten about a cousin who lives 3,000 miles away and, as a result, has not included that cousin as a beneficiary, the will is not automatically invalidated.

Most relevant for present purposes, the simple existence of mental illness is not equivalent to testamentary incapacity. A mentally ill person may make a valid will, as may an individual addicted to narcotics or alcohol.[177] The question is the individual's state of mind at the time of making the will; if the will has been executed during a "lucid interval," it will be deemed valid.[178] Similarly, prejudices against a particular individual, no matter how ill-founded, are not the same as a lack of capacity, nor is a belief on the part of a testator that another party has been attempting to injure him or her. The issue is not the existence of such beliefs, but their cause; the court, and clinicians called upon to assist it, must distinguish between beliefs that might be mistaken and actual delusions. The latter will not be found to exist unless the testator's belief "has no basis in reason, cannot be dispelled by reason and can be accounted for only as the product of mental disorder . . ."[179]

As the reader may have surmised from the foregoing, the competency requirement creates a tension between the desire to allow individuals control over their property and a tendency to question abnormal distribution patterns. Suppose a man leaves his property to an animal shelter rather than to his family. The competency paradigm allows the family members to question this bequest, and may lead to invalidation of the will. A valid question, raised by Szasz,[180] among others, is why such challenges should be allowed; even if the man is psychotic, he has expressed a desire through the will that arguably should be honored to the same extent a bequest based on "reasonable" mistake should be. But, as in other areas, of the law [see § 6.02(c)(2)], the medical model has provided the dividing line. Correcting for all "mistakes" would violate libertarian notions; allowing "irrational" ones would insult those same notions. The difficulty, of course, is separating the rational from the irrational bequests. Again, as always, the clinician is well advised to avoid any attempt to perform this separation.

(b) Clinical Evaluation of Testamentary Capacity

One obvious difference between the evaluation of testamentary capacity and the assessment of other capacities is that in most instances the subject of the evaluation is dead. This assures that in the vast majority of cases "the best evidence of capacity—the testator himself,"[181] will be unavailable to the clinician.

In at least some cases, however, the testator will be available. A few states, for example, have adopted antemortem probate statutes, which allow a will to be probated prior to the testator's death,[182] and attorneys in other jurisdictions may advise their clients to seek an evaluation of capacity at the time of execution of the will in an attempt to reduce the possibility of a contest later.

The areas of inquiry will be similar, whether or not a testator is alive. The primary difference will be in the source of information—obviously, the testator will be the primary source if alive. In such cases, we recommend videotaping the evaluation, since the tape may be persuasive in demonstrating the reasons for clinical conclusions on the subject's mental state and functioning. If the testator is not alive, the information will have to be obtained from friends, acquaintances, family, available medical records, and any other source that might shed light on the testator at the time of making the will.

As a general rule, clinicians should remember that the question of testamentary capacity is best conceptualized as a functional one, focusing on the testator at the time the will was made. Thus, they may want to structure their evaluation and report to conform with the legal elements of the capacity test.

(1) Testator Knowledge that Will Is Being Made

When testators are available for interview, they should be asked about their conception of a will, what it is intended to do, and why they are preparing theirs at this time. The last piece of information is important in part because it may provide a key to any delusional system that might exist (e.g., "I'm writing a will because the television tells me my death is near") and in part because it will enable clinicians to ascertain that individuals are, in fact, aware that they are preparing their wills. In some cases, the question may also be useful in determining whether individuals are writing wills of their own volition, rather than as the result of coercion from others. Virtually every jurisdiction invalidates an otherwise valid will that is the result of "undue influence" by a third party.[183]

If the testator is not alive, the fact that a will exists may often be considered sufficient to demonstrate he or she had a basic understanding of what a will does, as long as the will purports to distribute the testator's property. Spaulding suggests that the question of whether a testator knew he or she was making a will should be left to the commonsense of the factfinder,[184] and in the case of a retrospective inquiry into capacity, we concur that an expert generally will have little to offer on this prong of the test.

(2) Testator Knowledge of Nature and Extent of Property

If the testator is alive, questions designed to elicit information about his or her property holdings are appropriate. These might include questions on occupation, salary, living accommodations, personal possessions, intangibles (e.g., bank accounts or notes), and any other possessions. Questioning should be open-ended, and designed to let subjects describe their property in their own words. Again, clinicians are interested in this material primarily to determine whether subjects can make realistic assessments of their possessions, or whether such assessments are wholly at odds with the facts. To make this assessment, clinicians obviously need to obtain corroborative information about the estates in question.

If the testator is dead, the determination as to knowledge of the nature and extent of the property will be determined by the factfinder, relying on objective evidence found in the will: Does the disposition made by the testator match the estate, or does the will attempt to bequeath items that the testator does not possess? For example, if a will states that "I give the $1 million in my State Bank account to the Society for the Preservation of Prince Philip's Ponies," and neither the bank account, the $1 million, nor the society exists, the factfinder may fairly weigh the testator's capacity from this provision in the will. Accordingly, clinical opinion on the issue of whether testators knew the nature and extent of their property may often be unnecessary.

(3) Testator Knowledge of Natural Objects of Bounty

Spaulding has pointed out that clinicians will probably be most helpful in this area of inquiry, because they can ascertain testators' actual values and preferences, thus inhibiting application of an objective "reasonable person" test that might not reflect a testator's intent.[185] If testators are alive, they should be asked to identify family, friends, and those who might have played a major role in their lives, and then ask about relations with them, so as to assist the factfinder in answering the following sorts of questions: Is a particular relationship a loving one? If not, why not? Does a testator believe that the other party is "out to get" him or her? If so, what is the basis of the belief? The clinician should remember that prejudice or hostility held by a testator against another, no matter how (to the clinician) unreasonable, does not automatically render the testator incapable.

This part of the inquiry obviously will be much more difficult when testators are dead. In many cases, disputes over a will's validity will have arisen because one or more individuals who believe themselves the "natural object" of the testator's "bounty" will have been excluded. In such cases, clinicians will have to attempt to reconstruct the testator's relationships with these significant others by relying on extrinsic sources—including, quite probably, the individuals embroiled in contesting the wills. Therefore, clinicians must take particular care to corroborate the information relied upon, and to keep in mind that information may be suspect because of the source.

(4)   Testator Knowledge of the Effect of Manner in Which Property Is Disposed

If the testator is alive, clinicians should ask questions about the general consequences of the property disposition made. For example, if a woman intends to leave her only daughter a few dollars a month out of a considerably greater fortune, does the testator know the likely impact on the daughter's life? Does she believe that a greater sum is unnecessary because the daughter has independent means of her own? If so, is that true, or is the daughter in fact living an impoverished existence that will be unchanged by the disposition? If the latter situation obtains, is the testator's belief a product of delusion, personal pique, or simply mistake?

If the testator is dead, inquiry into his or her understanding of the dispositions made is problematic. In a case such as the one described, a question as to capacity would probably be raised because the disposition is "unnatural." As when the testator is alive, the focus of clinical inquiry would then be on any material that would reveal why the testator made the disposition. The difficulty lies, of course, in finding and assessing the material. As before, the role of the clinician is not to evaluate the wisdom of the choices made by the testator, but rather to discover the factors leading to those choices.

(c)   Conclusion

Clinical opinion as testamentary capacity has often been denigrated and ignored [186]; Bromberg attributes this to a suspicion that clinicians testifying for a particular side, like others involved in a will contest, have an "undiluted interest in the money involved." [187] A second reason that clinical testimony may have negligible impact is that it is often superfluous. As should be clear from this discussion, the inquiry into testamentary capacity is largely a commonsense one. In some cases, clinicians may be able to provide useful information to the probate court. Senility, psychosis, or mental retardation may have some impact on capacity, and clinicians—through physical and neurological examinations, intelligence tests, and interviews if the testator is alive, and through careful information collection if the testator is dead—may be able to cast light on the extent of these conditions and the thought processes they engendered. But in many cases, clinicians will simply have nothing to add to the bare facts. In such cases, there is no point in their testifying at all. It is important to remember that here, as in every context discussed in this book, opinion testimony is permissible only when it will add incrementally to what factfinders could find out for themselves. This admonition is stressed here because of the real pressures that can come to bear in probate contests where considerable money is involved, and thus, to put it bluntly, where greed can become an overriding motivation in those contesting the wills.

9.06.   *Social Security Determinations: "Competency" to Work*

Since the 1930s, the federal government has funded "income maintenance" programs for persons who, because of physical or mental disability, are unable to engage in substantial gainful employment. These programs are not based on tort principles, which, as described in the next chapter, seek to compensate individuals for disabilities suffered as a result of another's intentional or negligent conduct. Rather, they are intended simply as a means of providing sufficient income to allow disabled individuals to "maintain" themselves at a minimum level. The theory underlying these benefits is that society should provide for the basic needs of those too disabled to work.

The two programs to be focused on here are Social Security Disability Insurance (SSDI)[188] and Supplemental Security Income (SSI).[189] Together, they comprise the bulk of the federal government's effort to aid those who are incompetent to work. Since the procedural and substantive criteria for eligibility are substantially the same under both SSDI and SSI provisions, we do not distinguish here between the two programs, except to note at the outset that the former is an insurance program that requires applicants to prove they have worked for a given number of "quarters," while the latter is a welfare program designed to supplement the income of those who have few other resources. The regulations governing the determination of whether an individual is sufficiently impaired to qualify for benefits under either program are extremely complex and detailed. Furthermore, they change frequently. The attempt here is merely to familiarize the reader with the basic guidelines for such determinations. The reader should check the relevant regulations to ensure access to the most recent version.

(a) Procedural Apparatus

(1) Responsibility for Making Determinations

The determination of disability rests initially with a state agency, acting on behalf of the Secretary of Health and Human Services.[190] The state may decline this function if it desires.[191] Whether or not the state chooses to perform the function, the ultimate authority for determining whether disability exists is retained by the federal government, acting through the Secretary of Health and Human Services. Thus, the Secretary may determine that an individual is not disabled, even though the state agency has reached a contrary conclusion.[192]

(2) Adjudication Procedures

Whether an individual is disabled is an administrative rather than a judicial determination [see § 2.04(b)]. The proceedings are informal in nature.

A claimant initiates a determination by applying for benefits. This is done most commonly by filling out a claim form at the local Social Security office or state office performing determinations on behalf of the federal government. This form asks for work and medical history, requests the identity of any doctors consulted, and requires the claimant to describe the basis for the belief that he or she is disabled.[193] There is no hearing at this point, and the claimant is advised by letter of the outcome of the claim.

If benefits are denied, the claimant may seek reconsideration of the decision by the program administrators. If the claim is denied again, the claimant may request a hearing before an administrative law judge. The conduct of the hearing is almost wholly within the control of the law judge.[194] Rules of evidence do not apply, and the hearing officer may consider written as well as oral submissions. Two sources of information are particularly important. One is a "vocational expert," who may help the judge determine whether there is a job in the "national economy" (see below) that fits the claimant's skills. Secondly, the government will often require the claimant to undergo a medical examination at government expense (called a consultative examination, or "CE").[195] After considering this evidence, the law judge must render a decision in writing, and include findings of fact and conclusions of law. Administrative appeal is available, and ultimately the regulations provide for judicial appeal.[196]

It is evident from this brief description that establishing disability requires negotiating a many-tiered administrative structure. Given that most applicants will suffer from some impairment (whether or not it turns out to be severe enough to show disability), and given that many claimants have been recently hospitalized for psychiatric disorders, many disabled individuals have difficulty achieving hearings on their claims.

(b) Substantive Criteria

Assuming that the other technical requirements for Social Security benefits are met, the relevant federal statutes provide that individuals are eligible for such benefits if they can show

> an inability to engage in substantial gainful activity by reason of any medically determinable mental or physical impairment which can be expected to result in death or which has lasted or can be expected to last for a continuous period of not less than twelve months.[197]

The mental or physical impairment is disabling if it is of

> such severity that the applicant is not only unable to do his previous work but cannot, considering his age, education and work experience, engage in any other kind of substantial gainful work which exists in the national economy regardless of whether such work exists in the immediate area in which he lives, or whether such a specific job vacancy exists for him, or whether he would be hired if he applied for work.[198]

In interpreting these statutory requirements, the Social Security Administration (SSA) has developed a multistage process for determining eligibility, summarized in Figure 9-1.[199] First, the law judge is to ascertain whether an individual is engaged in "substantial gainful activity," which is defined as work for pay or profit that meets earning levels and activity levels set by guides within the regulations. If the individual is not so gainfully employed, the judge may then proceed to determine whether the person has a severe impairment that results in a significant limitation on the person's physical or mental abilities to perform basic work activities. According to the regulations, this impairment "must be established by medical evidence consisting of signs, symptoms, and laboratory findings."[200]

If there is such an impairment, it can result in eligibility on "medical grounds alone" if it

Figure 9-1.   *Logic tree: Competency to work.*

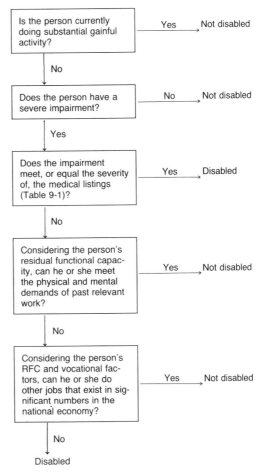

"meets or equals" a specified physical or mental disability. The *mental* impairments so specified fall into eight categories of disorders: organic mental disorders; schizophrenic, paranoid, and other psychotic disorders; affective disorders; mental retardation; anxiety-related disorders; somatoform disorders (i.e., those indicated by "physical symptoms for which there are no demonstrable organic findings or known physiological mechanisms"); personality disorders; and substance addiction disorders. In Table 9-1 can be found the regulations' definition of the first three categories. In each of these categories, the law judge must find that symptoms from both "A" (clinical signs) and "B" (functional impair-

Table 9-1
Mental Impairments Resulting in Disability Finding on "Medical Grounds Alone"

12.02 *Organic Mental Disorders* (Psychological or behavioral abnormalities associated with a dysfunction of the brain. History and physical examination or laboratory tests demonstrate the presence of a specific organic factor judged to be etiologically related to the abnormal mental state and loss of previously acquired functional abilities.)

The required level of severity for these disorders is met when the requirements in both A and B are satisfied.

A. Demonstration of a loss of specific cognitive abilities or affective changes and the medically documented persistence of at least one of the following:

1. Disorientation to time and place; or

2. Memory impairment, either short-term (inability to learn new information), intermediate, or long-term (inability to remember information that was known sometime in the past); or

3. Perceptual or thinking disturbances (e.g., hallucinations, delusions); or

4. Change in personality; or

5. Disturbance in mood; or

6. Emotional lability (e.g., explosive temper outbursts, sudden crying, etc.) and impairment in impulse control; or

7. Dementia involving loss of measured intellectual ability of at least 15 IQ points from premorbid levels or overall impairment index clearly within the severely impaired range on the Luria–Nebraska or Halstead–Reitan; and

B. Resulting in at least two of the following:

1. Marked restriction of activities of daily living; or

2. Marked difficulties in maintaining social functioning; or

3. Deficiencies of concentration and persistence resulting in frequent failure to complete tasks (in work settings or elsewhere); or

4. Repeated episodes of deterioration or decompensation in work or work-like situations which cause the individual to withdraw from that situation and/or to experience exacerbation of signs and symptoms.

12.03 *Schizophrenic, Paranoid, and Other Psychotic Disorders* (Characterized by the onset of psychotic features with deterioration from a previous level of functioning.)

The required level of severity for these disorders is met when the requirements in both A and B are satisfied, or when the requirements in C are satisfied.

A. Medically documented persistence, either continuous or intermittent, of one or more of the following:

1. Delusions or hallucinations; or

2. Catatonic or other grossly disorganized behavior; or

3. Incoherence, loosening of associations, illogical thinking, or poverty of content of speech if associated with one of the following:

a. Blunt affect; or

b. Flat affect; or,

c. Inappropriate affect; or

4. Emotional withdrawal and/or isolation; and

B. Resulting in at least two of the following:

1. Marked restriction of activities of daily living; or

2. Marked difficulties in the maintaining social functioning; or

3. Deficiencies of concentration and persistence resulting in frequent failure to complete tasks (in work settings or elsewhere); or

4. Repeated episodes of deterioration or decompensation in work or work-like situations which cause the individual to withdraw from that situation and/or to experience exacerbation of signs and symptoms; or

C. Medically documented history of one or more episodes of acute symptoms, signs and functional limitations described in A and B of this listing, although these symptoms or signs are currently attenuated by medication or psychosocial support, and one of the following:

1. Repeated deterioration with increased mental demands requiring substantial increases in mental health services and withdrawal from the stressful environment; or

2. Documented current history of two or more years of inability to function outside of a highly supportive living situation.

12.04 *Affective Disorders* (Characterized by a disturbance of mood, accompanied by a full or partial manic or depressive syndrome. Mood refers to a prolonged emotion that colors the whole psychic life; it generally involves either depression or elation.)

The required level of severity for these disorders is met when the requirements in both A and B are satisfied.

A. Medically documented persistence, either continuing or intermittent, of one of the following:

1. Depressive syndrome characterized by at least four of the following:
   a. Anhedonia; or
   b. Appetite disturbance with change in weight; or
   c. Sleep disturbance; or
   d. Psychomotor agitation or retardation; or
   e. Decreased energy; or
   f. Feelings of guilt or worthlessness; or
   g. Difficulty concentrating or thinking; or
   h. Thoughts of suicide; or
2. Manic syndrome characterized by at least three of the following:
   a. Hyperactivity; or
   b. Pressure of speech; or
   c. Flight of ideas; or
   d. Inflated self-esteem; or
   e. Decreased need for sleep; or
   f. Easy distractibility; or

   g. Involvement in activities that have a high probability of painful consequences which are not recognized; or
3. Bipolar syndrome with episodic periods manifested by the full symptomatic picture of either or both manic and depressive syndromes; and
B. Resulting in at least two of the following:
   1. Marked restriction of activities of daily living; or
   2. Marked difficulties in maintaining social functioning; or
   3. Deficiencies of concentration and persistence resulting in frequent failure to complete tasks (in work settings or elsewhere); or
   4. Repeated episodes of deterioration or decompensation in work or work-like situations which cause the individual to withdraw from that situation and/or to experience exacerbation of signs and symptoms.

Note. From 20 C.F.R. § 404.112 subpt. P, app. 1 (1985).

ment), or their equivalent, are present before benefits will be extended.

If the impairments of individuals seeking benefits do not meet or equal one of the listed physical or mental "medical" disabilities, they may still be able to receive benefits if they can show they are unable to perform gainful employment for other reasons. To use the jargon created by the regulations, this involves consideration of their "residual functional capacity" (RFC). The determination as to whether RFC exists involves, first, determining the extent to which the persons can still perform work they have performed in the past. But even if they show they cannot perform the type of work they have previously performed, they may be denied eligibility if they are able to perform any *other* job that "exists in the national economy"—that is, one that exists in significant numbers either in the region where the claimant lives or in several other regions of the country.[201] A finding of disability under this "general work ability" criterion is not permitted merely because an individual cannot *obtain* a job (a situation that is covered by unemployment compensation laws). Rather, disability for Social Security purposes exists only when the individual's impairment has destroyed the *capacity* to hold such a job.[202]

As can be seen from the foregoing, the statute and regulations are relatively strict in defining what types of disability merit benefits. In recent years, the interpretation of these regulations has been particularly niggardly. In early 1980, the SSA adopted a policy that, in essence, established that individuals whose mental impairment did not meet or equal the disabilities in the medical listings retained sufficient residual functional capacity to perform at least unskilled work. Therefore, if a person did not meet the "medical grounds alone" criterion, he or she was ineligible for benefits. In *Mental Health Association v. Heckler,*[203] a federal court held this policy to be "arbitrary, capricious, irrational, and an abuse of discretion." The court held that consideration of RFC was necessary in order to determine whether the individual possessed the capacity to engage in substantial gainful work. Even after this holding, however, the Government Accounting Office (GAO), in testimony in front of the United States Senate, criticized the SSA for being "overly restrictive" in its interpretation of the medical listings.[204] It also found there to be "inadequate development and consideration of a person's residual functional capacity and vocational characteristics" and "inadequate development and use of existing medical evidence, resulting in an overreliance and misuse of consultative examinations."[205]

These observations are of relevance to the clinician in two ways. First, they point up the need to marshal all evidence relevant to occupational disability. Second, they illustrate, once again, that legal determinations are subject to political vagaries and should not be considered primarily medical or psychological in nature.

(c) The Clinical Evaluation of Occupational Incompetency

The clinical examination and report are critical to determinations of disability under the Social Security regulations; indeed, without appropriate clinical evidence, the determination cannot be made. As noted earlier, the regulations require that impairment be proven through "medical evidence." Moreover, the consultative evaluation, which is commonplace when a hearing is held, requires a clinician. Although we focus here on mental impairment, it should be remembered that physical impairment, which is evaluated in much the same way, is just as relevant to disability determinations.

The SSA's regulations break down the clinical evaluation of mental impairment into three stages. The first deals with whether the individual being evaluated has an impairment that "meets or equals" the types of listings found in Table 9-1; the second examines residual functional capacity with respect to past work; and the third assesses the individual's general work ability. From a clinical point of view, all three inquiries aim at the same notion—the degree to which mental impairment curtails one's capacity to work. Indeed, the regulations themselves recognize that the central question throughout is whether the impairment significantly limits the person's ability to perform the following basic work activities:

—physical functions such as walking, standing, sitting, lifting, pushing, pulling, reaching, carrying, or handling;
—capacities for seeing, hearing, and speaking;
—understanding, carrying out, and remembering simple instructions;
—use of judgement;

—responding appropriately to supervision, coworkers, and usual work situations;
—dealing with changes in a routine work setting.[206]

We recommend that professionals performing disability evaluations focus on these criteria. However, clinicians should be aware of the SSA's multitiered approach, since they may be asked to address each tier in turn in reports or in testimony. Moreover, as indicated below, the SSA has developed forms that may *require* evaluators to follow certain rules.

(1) Medical Grounds Alone

In order to "facilitate uniform and accurate application of the listings at all levels of administrative review," the SSA has developed a "Psychiatric Review Technique Form" (PRTF), which must be used in evaluating whether an individual has a mental impairment that meets or equals the medical listings illustrated by Table 9-1.[207] The PRTF is divided into three sections: medical summary (indicating the severity of the disability and the category or categories into which the individual may fit); a checklist designed to help the evaluator assess the presence or absence of each of the disorders; and a checklist designed to assist the evaluator in judging the severity of functional impairment caused by the disorder. Figure 9-2 displays the two checklists for the category of organic mental disorder.

While this rating system is a commendable attempt to standardize the evaluation of disability, it could easily shift the focus of the disability determination from consideration of an individual's symptoms to the conclusory findings found on the checklists. According to the GAO's testimony mentioned earlier, use of a previous version of these checklists led to reliance on the *conclusions* reached with respect to degree of limitation (e.g., "marked" as opposed to "moderate"), rather than on the facts underlying this judgment.[208] To counteract this tendency, the clinician should take full advantage of the PRTF's provision for a "narrative summary" of findings, focused, as the regulations provide, on the effect of an individual's disorder on daily activities (both

Figure 9-2. *Psychiatric Review Technique Form (PRTF) checklists for rating organic mental disorders.*

12.02 Organic Mental Disorders

A. *Documentation of Factors that Evidence the Disorder*

☐ No evidence of a sign or symptom CLUSTER or SYNDROME which appropriately fits with this diagnostic category. (Some features appearing below may be present in the case but they are presumed to belong in another disorder and are rated in that category.)

☐ Psychological or behavioral abnormalities associated with a dysfunction of the brain . . . . as evidenced by at least one of the following:

Present–Absent–Insufficient Evidence

1. ☐ ☐ ☐ Disorientation to time and place
2. ☐ ☐ ☐ Memory Impairment
3. ☐ ☐ ☐ Perceptual or thinking disturbances
4. ☐ ☐ ☐ Change in personality
5. ☐ ☐ ☐ Disturbance in mood
6. ☐ ☐ ☐ Emotional lability and impairment in impulse control
7. ☐ ☐ ☐ Dementia involving loss of measured intellectual ability of at least 15 IQ points from premorbid levels or overall impairment index clearly within the severely impaired range on the Luria–Nebraska or Halstead–Reitan
8. ☐ ☐ ☐ Other _____

B. *Rating of Impairment Severity*

Functional Limitation	Degree of Limitation					
1. Restriction of activities of daily living	None ☐	Slight ☐	Mild ☐	Moderate ☐	Marked* ☐	Insufficient evidence ☐
2. Difficulties in maintaining social functioning	None ☐	Slight ☐	Mild ☐	Moderate ☐	Marked* ☐	Insufficient evidence ☐
3. Deficiencies of concentration and persistence resulting in failure to complete tasks	Never ☐	Seldom ☐	Occas. ☐	Often ☐	Frequent* ☐	Insufficient evidence ☐
4. Episodes of deterioration or decompensation in work or work-like situations which cause the individual to withdraw from that situation and/or experience exacerbation of signs and symptoms	Never ☐	Once ☐	Twice ☐		Repeated* (three or more) ☐	Insufficient evidence ☐

*Degree of limitation required by the listings

---

social and occupational), range of interests, ability to take care of personal needs, and ability to relate to others.[209]

(2) Residual Functional Capacity

The regulations identify several similar areas of investigation when assessing a person's RFC. In assessing the extent to which mental impairment will prevent the individual from performing what he or she used to do, the examiner is to evaluate the person's ability to understand, remember, and carry out instructions; respond appropriately to supervision, coworkers, and work pressures; deal with the public; and maintain concentration and attention.[210] As with the "medical grounds" inquiry, the SSA has prepared a form for this stage of the examination; however, this form does not rely on a rating scale, but merely asks for determinations as to whether the individual is "limited" or "unlimited" in each category.[211]

(3) General Work Ability

If a disability decision cannot be made on medical considerations alone, and the person cannot do past work, the final inquiry is whether he or she can do *any* work in the national economy. According to the regulations, the relevant types of information at this stage are age, education, and previous work experience.[212] The younger, better educated, and more skilled an individual is, the less likely it is that disability will be found. Again, the SSA provides a form to assist the judge in this inquiry.[213]

(4) General Considerations

Although the phases described above appear discrete, SSA regulations and instructions also stipulate that the examiner follow several basic procedures in performing or reporting on *any* phase of the evaluation. First, a mental status examination is a prerequisite to a determination of psychiatric disability. Although the exact parameters of this requirement are not clear, the SSA has observed that the absence of such an examination is the most common error in cases reversed on review.[214] Second, the regulations explicitly state that diagnosis alone is insufficient as a basis for a finding of impairment. Behavioral observations must be reported as well.[215] Third, according to the SSA, "in psychiatric claims, perhaps more so than in any other [area], a detailed longitudinal history is needed."[216] Thus, the clinician should evaluate and describe the length and history of the impairment, points of exacerbation and remission, any history of hospitalization and/or outpatient treatment, and modalities of treatment used in the past. Fourth, the severity of the impairment must be addressed. As noted earlier, the statute itself requires that the impairment must reasonably be expected to result in death or be shown to have lasted or be expected to last at least 12 months in order for the claimant to qualify. Finally, the clinician should consider the claimant's treata-

bility, which in this context means the extent to which treatment will restore the person's capacity to work. According to the regulations, a claimant will receive benefits only if he or she follows treatment prescribed by a doctor,[217] so the treatment recommendation made by the examiner may have a significant impact on the eligibility determination.

(d) Conclusion

As should be apparent from the foregoing, the evaluation of competency to work under the Social Security laws is highly structured by regulations. Nonetheless, the basic tenets we have emphasized throughout this book can still be followed. As the regulations themselves provide, clinicians should avoid reliance on diagnosis. They should also refuse to address the ultimate issue (i.e., whether individuals are unable to engage in "substantial gainful activity" due to "severe" mental impairment). To the extent possible, clinicians should attempt to alert judges to the facts about the individuals' ability to perform basic work activities, and should de-emphasize conclusory "ratings." With these points in mind, clinicians should be able to assist the legal system in arriving at just conclusions in disability cases.

BIBLIOGRAPHY

Appelbaum & Roth, *Competency to Consent to Research: A Psychiatric Overview*, 39 ARCH. GEN. PSYCHIATRY 951 (1982).

Callahan & Longmire, *Psychiatric Patients' Right to Refuse Psychotropic Medication: A National Survey*, 7 MENTAL DISABILITY L. REP. 494 (1983).

CHILDREN'S COMPETENCE TO CONSENT (G. Melton, G. Koocher, & M. Saks eds. 1983).

20 C.F.R § 404.1501 *et seq.* (1985).

Hodgson, *Guardianship of Mentally Retarded Persons: Three Approaches to a Long Neglected Problem*, 37 ALB. L. REV. 407 (1973).

C. LIDZ, A. MEISEL, E. ZERUBAVEL, M. CARTER, R. SESTAK, & L. ROTH, INFORMED CONSENT: A STUDY OF DECISIONMAKING IN PSYCHIATRY (1984).

J. KATZ, THE SILENT WORLD OF DOCTOR AND PATIENT (1984).

Massad & Sales, *Guardianships: An Acceptable Alternative to Institutionalization?*, 24 AM. BEHAV. SCIENTIST 755 (1981).

Melton & Scott, *Evaluation of Mentally Retarded Persons for Sterilization: Contributions and Limits of Psychological Consultation*, 15 PROF. PSYCHOLOGY: RESEARCH PRAC. 34 (1984).

Mental Health Ass'n v. Heckler, 720 F.2d 965 (8th Cir. 1983).

Munetz, Roth, & Cornes, *Tardive Dyskinesia and Informed Consent: Myths and Realities*, 10 BULL. AM. ACAD. PSYCHIATRY L. 77 (1982).

B. SALES, D.M. POWELL, & R. VAN DUIZEND, DISABLED PERSONS AND THE LAW: STATE LEGISLATIVE ISSUES (1982).

Spaulding, *Testamentary Competency: Reconciling Doctrine with the Role of the Expert Witness*, 9 LAW & HUM. BEHAV. 113 (1985).

CHAPTER TEN

Compensation for Mental Injuries

10.01. Introduction

Society has long been concerned with compensating those injured by the action or inaction of others. Of course, the criminal law in a sense "compensates" the victim of a crime by exacting vengeance. But criminal prosecution primarily serves society as a whole. The individual victim instead seeks compensation through "tort" law, the law of civil "wrongs," which provides monetary damages for injuries suffered. The same act can trigger both systems. An assault, for example, may be punished by the state in a criminal act, and may lead to damages for the victim in a tort action. In the first instance the state will be the "complainant," while in the second it merely provides the forum for a dispute between private parties [see § 2.04].

The separation between the criminal law and civil compensation law was not always so distinct. Initially, efforts to adjudicate disputes peacefully and to compensate the injured party arose from a search for alternatives to the warfare that traditionally occurred when the honor of one clan was affronted by another.[1] The system that developed in Anglo-Saxon times ranked individuals in terms of relative worth and assigned a tariff, known as the *"wer,"* establishing the official money worth of each person.[2] When a clan caused injury to a member of another clan, the *wer* was offered in compensation, and was distributed in prescribed allowances to the paternal and maternal kin of the injured party.[3] Over time, however, penalties also became due the King when the transgression disturbed the King's peace; this payment became known as the *"wite."*[4] Eventually, the functions of appeasement of the family and atonement for the breach of the King's peace became separate: The latter emerged as the criminal law, and the former became the law of "torts."[5]

As tort law developed, it came to incorporate a broad universe of harms. Today, the American Law Institute's Restatement (Second) of the Law of Torts defines the word "tortious" as

> appropriate to describe not only an act which is intended to cause an invasion of an interest legally protected against intentional invasion, or conduct which is negligent as creating an unreasonable risk of invasion of such an interest, but also conduct which is carried on at the risk that the actor shall be subject to liability for harm caused thereby, although no such harm is intended and the harm cannot be prevented by any precautions or care which is practicable to require.[6]

As this comment makes clear, tortious conduct may result from intentional conduct, from negligent conduct, or in some instances from conduct in which the actor's motivation is not at issue and for which strict liability is imposed. It should also be noted that in determining the compensability of an injury, the law not only considers the actor's conduct, but may consider that of the injured party as well. For example, if the injured party has consented explicitly or implicitly to the invasion of the protected interest (i.e., has "assumed the risk"), or has been negligent as well, damages may not be assessed at all, or at least may be apportioned according to the relative "fault" of the parties.[7] Finally, it should be noted what does *not* constitute a tort. It is not an action for breach of contract.[8] It is not a crime, nor is it necessarily accompanied by evil intent or motive.[9] Conversely, a moral wrong does not always constitute tortious conduct, if the actor's conduct is "within the rules."[10] Thus, for instance, failure to save a drowning child is not considered a tort in some jurisdictions, because there is no affirmative duty to endanger oneself in such situations.

Because of the complex, fault-oriented nature of the present tort system, other streamlined systems of compensation have developed over the years. The most extensive such system is worker's compensation. Designed to provide monetary relief to injured workers in order to compensate them for the loss or impairment of their wage-earning power,[11] "worker's comp" developed largely from a sense that employees, who traditionally had to rely on tort doctrine to gain compensation for work-related injuries, were being grossly undercompensated in large part because of the defenses available to employers in an action of tort.[12] Worker's compensation, unlike most torts, ignores the potential fault or negligence of the injured party, and instead provides compensation for all injuries arising out of employment.

The clinician may be asked to provide evaluations under either system of compensation, since each system compensates "mental injuries."[13] In each, the law may call upon clinical expertise to assess the impact of a particular work-related injury or tortious conduct on an individual's mental status and prognosis for recovery.

This chapter discusses both torts and work-

er's compensation. Because it is the context in which clinicians are most likely to be involved, the worker's compensation system is described first in this chapter. We then examine compensability for mental injury under tort law. In the latter area, we focus particularly on the tort of infliction of emotional distress, since it most clearly raises the issue of "mental suffering." Differences between the worker's compensation and tort systems are noted throughout. We conclude with a discussion of the clinical evaluation in these situations, since the evaluation itself will be approximately the same in either type of case.

10.02.   Worker's Compensation Law

(a)   Purposes

Before the development of worker's compensation law, an employee injured at work could only be compensated through tort law. The employer had available several defenses that made it difficult for an employee to gain compensation: contributory negligence on the part of the employee; the defense that the employee had assumed the risk of injury by taking the job; and, under the "fellow-servant" rule, the defense that the worker's injuries resulted from the negligence of another worker.[14] These defenses effectively barred many workers or their families from recovering any compensation for the workers' deaths or injuries and subsequent loss of employment. An Illinois study at the turn of the century found that of 614 death cases, 214 families had received no compensation, and 111 cases were in pending litigation. In New York City in 1908, there had been no compensation in 42.3% of those accidents in which disposition was known.[15] This state of affairs has been described as "a complete failure [, which], in most serious cases, left the worker's family destitute."[16]

The worker's compensation system was designed to change this situation. The system represents a compromise by both employers and employees of rights possessed in tort law. Employers, through insuring their employees, "[bear] the initial cost of injuries that result from employment related risks and [waive] the immunity [they] might otherwise enjoy if [they] were not at fault."[17] Employees, for their part, waive their common-law right to sue in tort when their injuries result from a risk related to employment. The employees also give up the potentially unlimited compensation available in a tort case (assuming the requisite proof of tortious conduct and damages) for a legislatively or administratively fixed but more certain compensation.

This compromise also reflects the fact that traditional systems of compensation, dependent on the fixing of fault, may be virtually unworkable:

> [I]n the highly organized and hazardous industries of modern times the causes of injury are often so obscure and complex that in a large proportion of cases it is impossible by any method correctly to ascertain the facts necessary to form an accurate judgment, and . . . in a still larger proportion the expense and delay required for such ascertainment amount in effect to a defeat of justice.[18]

(b) Substantive Criteria for Compensation under Worker's Compensation Laws

Today, all states and the federal government have worker's compensation laws,[19] and approximately 80% of all civilian employees are covered.[20] While the laws may vary in certain respects, they contain certain salient features that comprise the substantive criteria for compensation. Typically the worker, or in the case of death, the beneficiary,[21] must demonstrate (1) an injury or disability, (2) arising out of or in the course of employment, (3) which is "accidental," as that term has come to be used in worker's compensation laws. If this showing is made, the worker receives a compensation award that is fixed by a schedule (based upon the type and duration of the disability and the worker's preinjury salary), and is generally paid in a specified amount at regular intervals over a definite period. In addition, the disabled worker will receive payment for medical care, surgery, nursing, and burial services.[22] The compensation, unlike that available in tort law, is not designed to "make the person whole" or to compensate for sequelae associated with the injury, such as emotional distress. Rather, worker's compensation is designed to give workers sufficient compensation to enable them, using any remaining wage-earning ability, to exist without burdening others for their livelihood.

We turn now to an examination of the three criteria for compensation.

(1) Injury or Disability

The first substantive criterion for compensation, and therefore a limitation on compensability, is the requirement that the worker show that he or she has suffered an injury or disability. In contrast to tort law, not every injury is compensable. The only injuries compensated are those producing disability and thereby presumably affecting earning power.[23]

Because of this limitation, certain types of injuries, in the absence of legislative authorization, have been held noncompensable under worker's compensation. Examples include facial disfigurement, loss of sexual potency, and pain and suffering.[24] Under a tort theory, each is compensable and may result in large monetary awards. However, because they are judged to have nothing to do with earning power, they are technically not compensable under worker's compensation. Despite this substantive limitation, the types of injuries and disabilities found compensable are legion and encompass nearly every other type of disability imaginable.[25] Moreover, a "backdoor" route may exist to compensation even for those conditions excepted. As mental injury increasingly becomes compensable under worker's compensation laws [see § 10.02(d)], workers may be able to obtain damages for disabling mental trauma resulting from previously noncompensable conditions.

(2) Injury Arising Out of and in the Course of Employment

The employee, having established the existence of a compensable injury, must also demonstrate that it was "arising out of and in the course of employment." The criterion is generally considered to contain two separate ideas. The first, "arising out of" employment, is the more complex. It involves the question of a causal relationship between the employment and the injury[26]—that is, of whether the disability resulted from a risk faced by the employee as a condition of employment. In the past, courts required a showing that the injury suffered resulted from an increased risk that the worker, as distinct from the general public, faced as a result of employment.[27] This was modified in many jurisdictions to allow a showing that the risk was actually a risk of employment, whether or not it was common to the public.[28] Today, a growing number of courts are adopting the "positional-risk" test. Under this test, an injury is compensable if it occurred because the conditions or obligations of the employment placed the claimant in the position where the injury occurred.[29] The effect of these modification has been to make more types of injuries compensable. For example, the last theory mentioned allows compensation "in cases of stray bullets, raving lunatics, and other situations in which the only connection of the employment with the injury is that its obligations placed the employee in the particular place at the particular time. . . ."[30]

There is not as much conceptual difficulty with the second requirement—that the injury arise "in the course of employment." If the injury occurred within the period of employment, at the place of employment, or where the employee might reasonably be expected to be while fulfilling duties associated with employment, this prong of the test is satisfied.[31] But what if an injury appears to occur while an individual is working, but it is also discovered that he or she has a preexisting disability [see, e.g., the Cates report, § 15.08]? As a general rule, employers are said to take employees as they find them, and a history of either physical or mental problems or a preexisting sensitivity to them will not in itself result in a denial of compensation.[32] The question in such a case is whether an injury, arising out of and in the course of employment, has accelerated or aggravated the existing disease or infirmity.[33] Examples of "acceleration" are cases involving various kinds of heart failure due to

exertion, excitement that results in the failure of an already weak heart, or the "lighting up" of tuberculosis because of exposure.[34] "Aggravation" of a disease is demonstrated by cancer cases in which the employee's work ruptures or spreads the malignancy.[35] More is said on this topic in the discussion on compensation for mental injury.

(3)   Injury Arising "by Accident"

The requirement that the injury be "accidental" may focus either on the cause of the injury or the effect of the injury on the worker's discharge of assigned duties. The cause of the injury must usually be "accidental"—that is, an unanticipated event that occurs at the work site. However, "nonaccidents," in a lay sense, may also be compensable. For example, if a worker who is routinely expected to lift heavy objects in the course of employment one day collapses during the course of these exertions, the result of the job performance is unexpected, and therefore the injury is compensable.[36] In short, in most instances, either an event that accidentally causes injury or an accidental result of normal job performance will satisfy the test.

While "usual exertion" with an unexpected result generally suffices for compensability, courts have been reluctant to apply this principle when heart disease is involved. Rather, a number of courts have required "unusual exertion" before awarding compensation.[37] This represents a policy limitation on compensability because of a concern over difficulties in proving that heart deaths actually arise out of employment.[38] It is noted here because it is similar to limits courts have placed on recovery for mental injuries, again because of concern over difficulties in proving etiology and causation.

(c)   Procedures for Determining Worker's Compensation Claims

One of the primary goals of worker's compensation is the expeditious adjustment of claims for compensation.[39] Therefore, nearly all jurisdictions provide for summary and generally informal proceedings before an administrative agency, as well as for appeal in the courts. The process for resolving claims typically includes the following elements.

(1) Notice

The worker must give notice of the injury to the employer, and, in some jurisdictions, to the worker's compensation board. The notice must provide the name and address of the employee; the time, place, and circumstances of the accident; and the nature and extent of the injury.[40]

(2) Medical Examination of the Employee

The employee may be required to submit to a medical or physical examination to determine whether there is an injury and, if so, its extent.[41] If the employer has requested the examination, the patient–physician privilege is considered inapplicable as to the content of that evaluation.[42]

(3) The Proceeding for Adjustment and Compensation

The statutes generally provide an opportunity for the parties to reach a voluntary settlement on the claim. If a settlement cannot be reached, adjudication of the claim occurs.

The adjudicative proceedings are generally administrative in nature. The proceeding is initiated when the claimant files a claim, and the employer is given notice of the filing. While technical rules of pleading are not followed, the claim must set forth facts adequate to establish the case for compensation.[43]

The actual adjudication is informal in character. The case is typically tried before a hearing officer (who may be called a "commissioner"). The parties may or may not be represented by counsel.[44] The rules of evidence do not apply, and so hearsay may be admitted.[45] The claimant has the burden of making out a case for recovery. The standard of proof, which courts have described in various ways, is equivalent to the preponderance of the evidence test, which means that the claimant must show that "in a more-probable-than-not sense" the employment caused the injury.[46] Expert testimony is allowed at the hearing, though the expert may and should be barred from testifying on the "ultimate issue" as to the percentage of loss of earning power suffered by the claimant.[47]

The hearing officer determines questions of both law and fact, and is often required to make express findings of fact. The hearing officer determines whether an injury has occurred, its extent, and its compensability. These findings, and any award, unless reversed on appeal, are conclusive as to the parties' interests in the case. As noted earlier, worker's compensation was designed to supplant use of tort law in the adjudication of work-related injuries, and so the employee cannot take the case to court under a tort theory in the hopes of supplementing the compensation award.

(d) The Compensability of Mental Injury under Worker's Compensation Laws

We can now look at the specific issue of how mental injury is compensated under worker's compensation laws. One commentator has noted that worker's compensation cases involve mental disorders of "almost every conceivable kind of neurotic, psychotic, depressive, or hysterical symptom, functional overlay, or personality disorder."[48] But while the array of mental injuries for which compensation is *sought* is nearly endless, many jurisdictions exclude mental disorder from compensation in certain types of cases.

A systemic reluctance to compensate mental injury stems from a number of concerns. Courts[49] that have refused to allow compensation have generally done so on the grounds that mental disorders could not be said to have been caused by an "accident" as required by the compensation statutes, or that mental disorder could not constitute an "injury" within the statutory meaning. But, at bottom, the findings that mental injury did not meet statutory requirements seem to reflect inherent distrust of such claims, fear of malingering,[50] and concern over the problem of objectively linking employment with mental injuries whose etiology was unknown.[51]

The initial reluctance to accept claims of mental injury mirrors the experience in the tort field, where the courts have been slow to accept mental injury as a legitimate claim unless it was the result of another, independently litigable tort [see § 10.03 (b)]. However, in both systems, the reluctance has gradually given way in favor of expanded coverage, at least in part because of an increased willingness to accept diagnosis and prognosis as legitimate skills. Today, there are three types of mental injury that are compensable in varying degrees: physical trauma causing mental injury; mental stimulus causing physical injury; and mental stimulus causing nervous injury.[52]

(1)   Physical Trauma Causing Mental Injury

In a situation in which a physical stimulus or trauma either causes a mental injury or causes a physical injury resulting in a mental disorder, it is the general rule that the mental injury is compensable.[53] In such cases, the courts have little difficulty with the causation issue (that is, the linking of employment with the injury); the usual reasoning is that "the existence of an objective, traumatic, work connected physical impact or injury provides an intuitive guarantee that the mental disorder is genuine and that the employment genuinely caused it."[54] While such an analysis may overstate the case in clinical terms (e.g., by ignoring the multiple causative factors that may underlay the now discernible mental disorder [see § 10.04]), the reliance by the legal system upon the presence of physical impact to relieve doubts about the genuineness of a claimed mental injury is not confined to worker's compensation. As will be seen, it is also the case in torts law.

There are myriad physical situations that have given rise to compensable mental injury. The following provide some idea of the variety: emotional trauma caused by rape at gunpoint; mental injury resulting from a pulled muscle sustained while swinging a sledgehammer; a "posttraumatic neurosis' resulting from an employee's fall from a scaffold; a ''conversion reaction" caused when a 20-pound steel weight struck

an employee; a neurosis that developed without any discernible physical cause, but that arose after several work-related accidents; a mental disorder resulting nine years after a work-related amputation of an arm; traumatic neurosis that developed from the loss of an employee's eye, suffered while removing the cap of a fire extinguisher; and a "fear complex" that prevented an employee from working after suffering severe finger fractures and lacerations from operation of a power press.[55]

(2)   Mental Stimulus Causing Physical Injury

When the worker suffers physical injury as a result of a mental stimulus, the injury is compensable.[56] This is true whether the mental stimulus is sudden (e.g., extreme fright resulting in physical consequences) or more protracted. For example, if the individual suffers a long period of emotional strain that culminates in heart failure, the consequence of that strain constitutes an injury and is compensable. Courts have also upheld awards for a claims adjuster who as a result of exhaustion suffered angina pectoris; a negotiator who after 65 days of work-related tension suffered a stroke and paralysis; an insurance administrator who had a cerebral thrombosis as a result of job pressures; an employee who suffered a heart attack after becoming emotionally upset over office clerical errors; and an employee who suffered a stroke while arguing over the amount of his paycheck.[57]

(3)   Mental Stimulus Causing Mental Injury

The most difficult of these categories is the last, in which a claimant seeks compensation for a mental injury caused by a mental stimulus. Courts initially resisted compensating injuries that fell into this category because there was no "physical" evidence (i.e., a definable event or observable bodily changes, which in the view of the law vouchsafed the genuineness of the injury). However, that traditional view has changed—in part because, according to Joseph, medical science "has discredited the judicial belief that the presence of 'some shred of the 'physical' assured the genuineness of the injury and the causal relation" with employment.[58] Today a "distinct majority" of jurisdictions find such injuries compensable.[59]

There are two types of situations that fall into this category. One involves a sudden stimulus (e.g., fright or shock); the other involves a lengthier, more gradual period of stress.[60] Some states limit compensation to the former—a limitation much like the traditional "physical" limitation formerly imposed by courts uncertain of the genuineness of certain injuries. In those jurisdictions that allow compensation for mental injuries arising from gradual stress, the courts typically impose a requirement that the stimulus complained of "exceeds in intensity the emotional strain and tension normally encountered by employees on a daily basis."[61] In other words, the stress or strain the employee undergoes that culminates in the mental injury cannot simply be the routine stress associated with the job. This distinction, like the others noted throughout this section, represents a choice to limit coverage as a matter of policy. One court, upholding the denial of a claim for compensation for mental injury resulting from "a tremendous amount of pressures and tensions," put the matter most succinctly when it observed that the concept of a compensable injury "still does not embrace every stress or strain of daily living or every undesirable experience" presented by employment.[62]

(4)   Pre-existing Mental Disorder

It should be remembered that the mere fact that a claimant had a mental disorder prior to the transaction at work that allegedly caused the mental injury does not automatically render a claim for mental injuries noncompensable. The question is whether the employment "aggravated" or "accelerated" the course or severity of the pre-existing disorder. If this inquiry is answered affirmatively, the employee may receive compensation.[63] Note, however, that the presence of a pre-existing disorder will make proof of a casual connection between the employment and the mental injury more difficult, given the somewhat ephemeral quality of the concepts of "acceleration" and "aggravation."

(e)   Summary

What started out as a relatively narrowly conceived compensation system has expanded considerably over the past decade. Mental health professionals are certainly partly responsible for the expansion, since they have been willing to testify about mental injury. In §§ 10.04 and 10.05, we examine the proper scope of that testimony. But first we look at the tort system's approach to compensating mental injury.

10.03.   The Tort of Emotional Distress

As noted earlier in this chapter, "tort law" is a system of law designed to allow adjudication of private wrongs, so that a party injured by the actions or omissions of another may be compensated for damages suffered. Like the worker's compensation system, it is designed to provide monetary compensation for certain types of injuries. However, tort law differs from worker's compensation in several critical respects:

1. Worker's compensation in nearly all jurisdictions depends upon administrative decision-making. Tort law relies on judicial proceedings.
2. The guidelines for compensability under worker's compensation are statutorily created by the legislature. Tort law is developed by the courts, based on doctrines enunciated by the courts.
3. Worker's compensation seeks to provide monetary compensation for the impairment in earning capacity suffered by the worker; while certain associated costs (medical care, nursing care, etc.) may be compensated as well, the basic award is limited by a fixed schedule. In addition, worker's compensation does not fix a price for pain and suffering. In contrast, tort law seeks to compensate all damages resulting from the tortious conduct, including physical damage as well as more ephemeral categories like "pain and suffering." Tort damages are therefore theoretically limitless,

and are set by the jury, subject only to review by the presiding judge for reasonableness in light of the facts.

(a) Substantive Criteria for Torts

There are many separate torts. Examples include assault, battery, false imprisonment, defamation, libel, slander, invasion of privacy, and malicious prosecution. While the definitional criteria differ for individual torts, there are certain core concepts that define generally whether an actionable wrong has been committed. These have usually been said to consist of (1) the existence of a duty owed the plaintiff by the defendant; (2) the violation of that duty by the defendant; and (3) an injury "proximately caused" by the violation, which is (4) of the type that is recognized as compensable.[64]

(1) Duty

Prosser has defined the first prong of a tort as "an obligation, to which the law will give recognition and effect, to conform to a particular standard of conduct toward another."[65] He acknowledges the vague quality of the concept, concluding that "no better statement can be made, that the courts will find a duty where, in general, reasonable men would recognize it and agree that it exists."[66]

"Duty" is probably best understood by considering certain principles governing relationships between individuals. For example, an individual has a "duty" to refrain from going uninvited on the property of another; if the individual nevertheless does so, he or she may have violated that duty and may be subject to damages for the tort of trespass. A physician has a "duty" to treat patients according to accepted professional standards; a failure to perform this duty may result in a claim for damages based on the tort of malpractice. An individual has a "duty" to avoid engaging in uninvited physical contact with another individual; to strike the other person violates the duty and may make the actor liable for the torts of assault and battery. Duties may be created by the legislature, by the courts,

by a jury ruling in a case where neither legislative or judicial guidelines exist, or by the general understandings of everyday existence.

(2) Violation of the Duty

An individual may violate a duty either by act or by omission. An example of the latter type of violation is when a clinician fails to warn a third party of possible danger from the clinician's patient, as occurred in *Tarasoff v. Board of Regents,*[67] discussed in § 3.04 (b).

As noted in the introduction to this chapter, violation of a duty may be intentional, negligent, or, in some cases, neither. An example of an intentional tort is the "intentional infliction of emotional distress," to be discussed below. A second is assault and battery. The central issue in intentional tort cases is whether the actor intended the result of the act, not the act itself.[68]

"Negligence" does not describe a state of mind, but rather is defined as "conduct which falls below the standard of care established by law for the protection of others against unreasonable risk of harm."[69] The standard against which the actor's conduct is measured is commonly known as the "reasonable man" standard. In other words, the question is "Would a reasonable man have acted as did the defendant in similar circumstances?"[70] If the jury finds that a reasonable man would not have acted as did the defendant, the defendant will be found negligent. It is this type of standard that governs in malpractice cases.

Finally, certain conduct brings liability whenever it causes injury, regardless of whether it was intentional or reasonable. "Product liability" is an example of this strict liability concept. For instance, a manufacturer of pharmaceuticals may be held liable merely on proof that it manufactured defective drugs and that the defect caused injuries. Strict liability represents a policy judgment that certain entities owe a heightened duty to society, as well as a practical judgment that proof of actual intent or negligence would often be difficult.

It should be clear from this brief discussion that distinguishing between duty on the one hand and its violation on the other is somewhat artificial. Both concepts aim at defining the type of conduct that we as a society view to be wrong, if it causes foreseeable injury.

(3) Proximate Cause

Whether conduct is intentional, negligent, or of the type relevant to strict liability torts, it will not lead to liability unless it legally or "proximately" caused the injury. The concept of "proximate cause" is elusive. The traditional method of determining whether one event is the proximate cause of another is asking whether one could "reasonably foresee" that the former would lead to the latter. The concept has also been defined as "the conduct or thing, which, in the ordinary unbroken sequence of events, without a new factor intervening, produces injury, and but for which that injury would not have occurred."[71] Thus, for example, a driver's hitting a child while speeding may not be the proximate cause of a child's injury, if the child was shoved into the driver's path at the last minute by a third party. Slovenko calls proximate cause "legal cause, a pragmatic view, and not . . . the 'first cause' of philosophy or 'field theory' of science . . . As one judge put it . . . 'What we do mean by the word proximate is that because of convenience, public policy, or a rough sense of justice, the law arbitrarily declines to trace a series of events beyond a certain point.' "[72] The concept has also been characterized as "the near issue, not the remote one,"[73] and "the straw that broke the camel's back."[74]

In other words, tort law, like worker's compensation law, is prone to conceptualize causation as a series of events, with the most recent event or events being the only legally relevant one(s). The problems that this approach to causation produces for the clinician are discussed in § 10.04.

(4) Compensable Damages

Not every harm or injury proximately caused by violation of a duty is compensable. "Damages" or "injury" as used in the tort context means that there has been "an invasion of a legally protected interest."[75] In other words, even though the individual may feel harmed, that harm is not compensable unless the law defines it as sufficiently important or worthy of protection to hold the person causing the harm liable. For example, as discussed in more detail below, some jurisdictions do not provide compensation for emotional distress: Harm may have occurred, but it is not compensable because of a policy decision that broadening the scope of liability to include "bruised feelings" would make the conduct of daily life intolerable.

(5) Summary

These are the basic elements comprising tortious conduct. It should be remembered that they are not defined precisely, and that their application to the facts of a given case will depend not on a mechanically applied test but on the jury's evaluation of the case, weighed through the collective and individual experience of its members.

(b) Mental Injury and Tort Law

It has been claimed that "in every case of personal injury, there will be some accompanying mental damage."[76] The question, however, is whether the law will compensate that damage.

Traditionally, compensation was denied for mental injury (referred to variously as "psychic trauma," "emotional distress," or "emotional harm") unless it resulted from another, independently recognized tort.[77] For example, if an individual was slandered and suffered emotional distress as a result, the harm was compensable. However, it was compensable because it was a consequence of a tort, that of slander. If an individual could not trace a mental injury to the tortious conduct of another, compensation was not possible. The law was reluctant to recognize an independent basis for compensating such injuries, for a number of reasons. There was a fear of false claims; a concern that it would be too difficult to quantify and prove emotional injury; a belief that emotional injury was "too removed" from the claimed source of an injury; and, finally, a fear that compensation would "open the floodgates" to litigation.[78] Those jurisdictions that did allow recovery generally insisted that there be a physical impact upon the injured party as well[79]; as we have seen, a physical predicate was traditionally required in worker's compensation as well.

However, the law of many jurisdictions has moved away from this traditional view. The trend of the law "has been to give accelerated, increasing and extensive protection to feelings and emotions and to enlarge and redress reparation for psychic injuries."[80] The most concrete illustration of this trend is the recognition in the past several decades of the independent torts of intentional infliction of emotional distress and negligent infliction of emotional distress. While our discussion here is limited to these torts, the elements identified below are likely to be the focus of any tort case where mental injury is alleged.

(1)   The Tort of Intentional Infliction of Emotional Distress

Recognition that an individual could engage in tortious conduct by attempting to cause emotional harm to another first came in 1948, in the Restatement of Torts. The tort "provides that liability may be imposed where a wrongdoer's extreme and outrageous conduct, intended to inflict severe emotional distress in another, in fact proximately causes that result."[81] Today, at least 38 jurisdiction recognize the tort.[82]

In order to prove a case, the plaintiff must show the following elements:

1. the defendant acted intentionally or recklessly;
2. the conduct was "extreme and outrageous";
3. the conduct caused the plaintiff's emotional distress; and
4. the emotional distress was severe.[83]

Under the first prong, the defendant must have intended not only to perform the act, but to produce emotional distress.[84] The traditional tort notion of foreseeability comes into play here: The defendant may be liable if he or she knew or should have known that emotional distress would ensue. The defendant has acted recklessly when he or she has acted in deliberate disregard of a high degree of probability that emotional distress will follow.[85] If the defendant knows that the plaintiff is particularly susceptible to emotional distress, the requisite intent may be inferred.[86]

The second requirement recognizes that not all conduct resulting in distress is tortious. An evaluation of whether the conduct at issue meets this requirement turns on the circumstances of the particular case. The test is sometimes posed as whether the defendant's conduct has been such as to greatly offend the community's sense of decency.[87] A wide variety of conduct has been labeled "extreme and outrageous" in past cases.[88] Thus, for example, although the courts have ben reluctant to impose liability for harm caused by an individual's words—in part because of concern for the constitutional right of free speech[89]— there are exceptions. Abusive language in certain circumstances may give rise to liability,[90] and a majority of jurisdictions hold radical or religious epithets actionable if they result in emotional harm.[91] In addition, innkeepers, common carriers, and others in a business relationship with an individual may be subjected to liability for insulting or abusive language.[92]

The third requirement is the familar one that the conduct must have been the "proximate cause" of the injury; this has been discussed previously. Finally, the fourth requirement for this tort bars compensation unless the injury is severe. In attempting to provide content to this concept, one authority suggests that the distress must be so severe that no reasonable person could be expected to endure it:

> Complete emotional tranquility is seldom attainable in this world, and some degree of transient and trivial emotional distress is a part of the price of living among people. The law intervenes only where the distress inflicted is so severe that no reasonable man could be expected to endure it. The intensity and duration of the distress are factors to be considered in determining its severity.[93]

The distress compensated may be fright, grief, humiliation or shame, embarrassment, anger, chagrin, or disappointment,[94] but only if it is demonstrated by substantial evidence and is severe.

(2)   The Tort of Negligent Infliction of
Emotional Distress

The courts have been particularly reluctant to impose liability where mental injury was caused by the mere negligence of another party. However, a handful of jurisdictions today recognize a tort of negligent infliction of mental or emotional distress.[95]

The elements of this tort are the traditional ones necessary to establish an action for negligence: that is, a duty on the part of the defendant to protect the plaintiff from injury; a violation of that duty; and injury to the plaintiff, for which the defendant's failure to adhere to his or her duty was the proximate cause.[96]

The tort is relevant most frequently in two types of situations: bystander recovery cases, and product liability cases. The former is illustrated by the following example: If a mother sees her child struck and killed by a negligently driven automobile, and suffers emotional distress as a result, she may be able to recover under the tort of negligent infliction of emotional distress, even though she was a bystander to the central action. There are limitations on the compensability of bystanders, however. For example, California requires that the plaintiff/bystander and the victim be related.[97] In addition, the distress must be severe, and there may be a requirement that it be manifested by objective symptomatology (e.g., vomiting, loss of sleep, or nervousness).[98] Courts have also devised a series of tests designed to limit coverage to plaintiffs who were at the scene of the defendants' conduct. These rules, which have nuances not relevant here, have been gradually liberalized in those jurisdictions recognizing this tort, consistent with the overall expansion of compensability for mental injury.[99]

Courts have also shown increased willingness to compensate individuals who suffer emotional distress as a result of manufacturers' negligence. For example, a mother was compensated for emotional distress suffered as a result of seeing her son gag and choke on foreign material contained in baby food.[100] In another case,[101] a family was compensated for the death of their children, who had been thrown from their car after being struck by another car. The automobile manufacturer could be sued for damages on a theory of negligent infliction of emotional distress caused by the incident because its defective manufacture of the rear door latch resulted in the children being thrown from the car.[102]

(c)   The Predisposed Plaintiff

As in worker's compensation cases, there may be evidence that the plaintiff was predisposed to the resultant mental injury. The rule applied in torts cases is the same as that found in worker's compensation cases. A plaintiff's preexisting condition or susceptibility does not *per se* bar compensation. However, if the emotional distress that the plaintiff claims would have resulted without the defendant's intervening act, then the defendant should prevail.[103] The subtle nature of this inquiry is discussed below.

10.04.   Causation in Mental Injury Cases: A Paradigm Clash?

Although the terminology may be different or more flexibly applied under the former system, both worker's compensation and tort law refuse to hold a defendant liable unless he, she, or it "proximately caused" the victim's injury. As noted above, for practical reasons, the concept of proximate cause connotes "recent" cause, "the straw that broke the camel's back." Several commentators have recognized that the "fit" between this legal definition of causation and the behavioral sciences' view of the concept is not precise, especially in mental injury cases. As Blinder states, for instance, "Speaking medically, the true cause of the . . . illness lies within [the claimant's] personality structure—who he was at the time of the injury rather than what happened to him. This deviant personality was no less immediate—no less proximate as it were—than the physical injury (leading to the injury)."[104] Sheeley puts the matter slightly differently:

> The syllogism, "The patient has no pain and he was working before the industrial incident; he

now has pain and is not working: ergo, the industrial incident produced the psychiatric disorder or at least aggravated it," may be false. The danger of such conceptual error is magnified by the patient's characteristically denying evidence of a pre-existing disorder and by his exaggerating current symptoms that he ascribes to the industrial incident and that may themselves be suggested by the very psychiatric procedure itself.[105]

Marcus, in critiquing judicial efforts to apply clinical concepts in worker's compensation cases, concludes that judicial reasoning is often "both logically and psychiatrically fallacious."[106] He asserts that the issue of causation is "exceedingly complex," but is in large part a "chicken or the egg" question that "cannot be determined with any degree of 'reasonable medical probability.'"[107] Because of judicial failure to subject clinical opinion on the issue to rigorous scrutiny, however, its resolution has become "primarily the function of the subjective value judgments of the examining psychiatrist."[108]

In short, the concept of proximate cause may not make sense in a deterministic paradigm [see § 1.03 (a)]. In addressing the causation issue, therefore, the clinician should merely indicate whether the legally relevant incident (the employment injury, or the negligent act by the defendant) played a role in the claimant's current mental injury; pronouncements to the effect that the work-related event is the sole or primary cause of the claimant's state should be avoided. This approach not only better reflects the clinical view of causation and the extent of clinical knowledge; it also prevents the legal decision-maker from abdicating responsibility for analyzing the causation issue and for translating expert evidence into data that meshes with the applicable legal construct.

10.05. The Clinical Evaluation of Mental Injury

The evaluation of mental injury is similar in worker's compensation and in tort cases. Each type of evaluation requires, at the outset, an un-

derstanding of the context of the evaluation, extensive information gathering, and a determination of whether mental injury has in fact occurred. If mental injury is found, the evaluation also requires assessing whether it has any connection with the "defendant" (the employer in worker's compensation cases, the alleged tortfeasor in tort cases). This investigation will inevitably involve the corollary question of whether there are any pre-existing disorders. Finally, assuming that there is an injury and that it is connected with the defendant, the impact of the mental injury on the individual's ability to function at the time of the evaluation and in the foreseeable future must be examined. These facets of the evaluation are discussed below.

(a) The Context of the Evaluation

Clinicians preparing to perform evaluations in worker's compensation and tort cases must first examine themselves as to any possible bias regarding the propriety of compensating mental injury. Davidson has observed that a psychiatrist who "does much medical–legal work soon acquires a personal philosophy with respect to psychoneuroses following injury. He believes either, (a) that most of these patients are motivated primarily by greed; or (b) that they have a genuine illness in which the money-motivation factor is of minor importance."[109] Before conducting an evaluation, a clinician should attempt to assess whether either of these descriptions fit and the effect they may have on the evaluation; if the effect would be substantial, the clinician should withdraw.

It should also be recognized that a clinician's posture relative to a case may affect the attitude of the claimant. Davidson has observed:

> In a sense, the opposing doctors are examining different patients. The plaintiff-selected physician starts off with a good rapport. He is the helping doctor. The claimant trusts him—but sees the defense physician as the enemy. The first physician gets the picture of sincere, trusting, and friendly soul. The defense examiner sees a surly and suspicious one. These differences obviously affect the examination tech-

nique, as well as the credibility of the history and subjective symptoms.[110]

A related point is that participation in the legal process may exacerbate certain personal traits of the claimant. Bromberg notes that "emotional tensions stimulated by the legal process tend to support a suspicion of exaggeration, malingering, or excess interest in remuneration."[111] The clinician will have to sort out these myriad "causative" factors in forming a picture of the individual—a task discussed more fully below.

(b)   What Types of Information Are Relevant?

An evaluation in a mental injury case has been likened to mental status at the time of the offense,[112] another retrospective inquiry fraught with difficulty [see § 6.05]. Yet the mental injury evaluation in some respects is even more difficult: Not only is a retrospective construction of the claimant's mental functioning necessary (in order to determine the extent, if any, to which past events "caused" the injury), but a prospective inquiry is also required. In worker's compensation cases, this latter inquiry involves assessing the effect the injury will have on the claimant's wage-earning capacity. In tort law, it is the effect on the claimant's continued ability to function as the "person he or she was" prior to the defendant's tortious conduct.

Because the issues are so broad, these evaluations require the clinician to come to know and to explain the claimant's life much more thoroughly than do most of the evaluations discussed elsewhere in this book. A complete history must be gathered, with emphasis not only on the events surrounding the alleged injury, but also on the period before, extending into the past as far as the clinician deems relevant in understanding why the injury may have occurred. Since the issue of the claimant's predisposition to mental injury or possible preexistence of the mental injury is certain to be raised, particular attention must be paid to the gathering of clinical and medical histories; of any evidence of behavioral or emotional disorder that did not reach the stage of

formal clinical intervention; and of any other social history that might shed light on the claimant's condition. If the evaluation is being performed for a worker's compensation case, the clinician must also obtain in as much detail as possible a descripton of the claimant's employment, place of work, conditions of employment, and all other work-related information.

Psychological testing, particularly the personality inventories, may be more relevant here than in other forensic areas, especially if their results can be compared to tests taken before the legally relevant event [see § 10.05 (d)]. It will also be important to investigate the extent of physical injury, if any, using neurological testing if necessary. The "total person" of the claimant will be considered when the claim for damages is adjudicated, and a clinical picture given without reference to other possible explanations for and consequences of the claimed injury will not only be less useful than it might be to the legal system, but may expose the clinician to personal embarrassment. A clinician who testifies only as to the emotional effects of trauma, while failing to address its effects upon physical functioning, "is asking to have his or her testimony impeached."[113]

With the types of information that are relevant in mind, we can not turn to how it should be evaluated.

(c)   Does Mental Injury Exist?

The law requires that there be some objective indicia of mental injury in order for compensation to occur. There are several typical "conditions" that the clinician should look for in determining whether injury exists and what its significance may be.

(1)   Traumatic Neurosis

The constellation of effects most frequently reported in worker's compensation or emotional distress cases is usually termed "traumatic neurosis," although it has been called by a variety of other names as well.[114] The concept posits a reaction to some "trauma," but beyond this no clear definition seems to exist. Perhaps partly because of the lack of definitional clarity, the "concept of a nervous reaction of some kind after trauma remains suspect in many quarters."[115]

However, despite the skepticism of many about the validity of claims of psychological impairment secondary to trauma, there are many research reports from diverse quarters to confirm this phenomenon. Symptoms of posttraumatic stress disorder have been documented in released prisoners of war,[116] concentration camp survivors,[117] victims of stressful crimes,[118] and victims and observers of natural disasters.[119] Thus the clinician has ample research to turn to in response to general suspicions about the diagnosis of traumatic neurosis.

As noted above, the real problem is the lack of careful and systematic documentation of the symptom constellations that have been reported in many studies. Most of the studies have been anecdotal case reports of individuals or groups experiencing trauma,[120] and rarely have investigators concerned themselves with the presence of pre-existing symptoms or the need for a group of control subjects in documenting the psychological responses that characterize the disorder. One author has admitted, "The traumatic neurosis can take many forms, including all of the known psychiatric illnesses."[121] The contemporary diagnostic criteria for posttraumatic stress disorder (i.e., those set forth in the third edition of the *Diagnostic and Statistical Manual of Mental Disorders,* or DSM-III) require the presence of a "recognizable stressor that would evoke significant symptoms of distress in almost everyone."[122] This definition would make the diagnosis more difficult to establish in situations where the claimed stressor is, for example, a tedious job that gradually affects the individual over time,[123] even if the behavioral or subjective symptoms of distress are similar to those observed in situations of more acute trauma. To our knowledge, there are no specific tests or inventories for assessing either DSM-III's posttraumatic stress disorder or a broader variant of it. However, Wilkinson[124] has developed a checklist for use with disaster victims, based on the traumatic neurosis literature and on current DSM-III criteria. We present a more generalized version of that checklist here; it may serve as a convenient inventory for the clinician conducting an examination regarding stress-related disturbance.

• Repeated recollections of the incident
• Sadness
• Fatigue
• Recurrent feelings, usually anxiety and depression
• Sleep disturbance
• Loss of appetite
• Loss of enthusiasm
• Ease of startle
• Difficulty concentrating
• Guilt
• Avoidance of situations that cause recollection of the incident
• Reminders of the incident leading to worse feelings
• Inability to feel deeply about anything
• Anger
• Loss of interest (in general activities)
• Feelings of detachment
• Memory difficulties
• Psychosomatic complaints
• Diminished sexual interest

All of these symptoms need not be present; the existence of one or more may be compensable if the requisite "causation" element is met and if wage-earning capacity is affected (worker's compensation) or the jury finds that damages should be awarded (torts). The legal system seems both accustomed to and curious about the "traumatic neurosis." Despite its amorphous nature, it is reported that "more lawyers and physicians attend programs on the legal aspects of traumatic neurosis than on the subject of sex."[125]

(2) Other Conditions

Although "traumatic neurosis" is the most commonly observed mental injury, other "disorders" may crop up as well. One example is "post-physical-injury trauma."[126] This involves a change in the injured person's "body image," or self-perception in the aftermath of physical injury.[127] This phenomenon is particularly prevalent (at least in the eyes of plaintiffs' lawyers) in cases where the person has suffered disfigurement or trauma to the head and spinal chord.[128]

Other compensable conditions the clinician may encounter include grief or sorrow.[129] This will be true particularly in cases involving death, where the survivors may claim damages for "sorrow, mental anguish and solace which may include society, companionship, comfort, guidance, kindly offices, and advice of the decedent."[130]

In addition, the claimant may present evidence of the symptoms and sequelae of concussion and postconcussion syndrome,[131] various neurotic reactions to spinal injuries,[132] and (on occasion) psychosis following trauma,[133] as well as posttraumatic epilepsy[134] and deficits in intellectual functioning.[135] Finally, given the broad nature of the compensability of mental injury and the fact that the constellation of symptoms for which the claimant seeks relief need not fit into formal diagnostic nomenclature, the clinician may be asked to evaluate the existence or impact upon the client of a host of vaguely defined "symptoms," such as irritability and headache. These may not readily lend themselves to diagnostic labels, but compensation may nonetheless be sought.

(3) Malingering

Probably most if not all of the above-described conditions can be "faked" or exaggerated.It is almost guaranteed that a clinician performing a mental injury evaluation will be asked whether the claimant is malingering. Bromberg defines "malingering" as "an assumed state which feigns illness but may be built on an historical event preceding it, i.e., an actual injury."[136] In his view, it is synonymous with "simulation," which he defines as "an assumed state of pain and disability, an imitation of illness without any etiological or organic basis."[137] The clinician may also confront "exaggeration," which is defined as a "magnification of pain and disability"; "overevaluation," an "individual reaction to pain which may appear feigned but is not"; "functional overlay," an "emotional superimposition on the original symptoms of an injury or illness"; and

"hysteria"—"i.e., conversion hysteria . . . a physical representation of an emotional conflict."[138]

None of these reactions is automatically noncompensable. However, the label that is ultimately attached to the individual, and the response of the decisionmaker to the explanation of the label (i.e., a jury is less likely to respond sympathetically to someone labeled a malingerer), will have an impact on whether an award is made and, if so, its amount.

For this reason, the clinician should merely describe the etiology of the alleged injury, carefully backing up each inference with behavioral observations, and let the factfinder decide whether it merits compensation. Some techniques for detecting malingering have been discussed elsewhere [see § 6.05 (6)(3)]. In this specific context, probably the best single device is corroboration through third-party information of the symptoms reported by the plaintiff.

(d) Connecting the Mental Injury to the Legally Relevant Event

Of course, the mere fact of mental injury will not lead to liability. The defendant must have proximately caused the injury. The conceptual problems attending this issue have been discussed in § 10.04. Here we attempt to provide some techniques that will help in assessing and reporting this difficult aspect of mental injury cases.

To begin with, the clinician should be familiar with the literature on the relationship between life events and subsequent psychological adjustment; numerous studies have demonstrated a positive relationship between life change and psychological adjustment/psychiatric illness,[139] and several structured questionnaires have been developed to assess the frequency and/or impact of life changes. The most comprehensive questionnaire is the PERI Life Events Scale,[140] which contains 102 items inquiring about change in 11 different areas: School, Work, Love and Marriage, Having Children, Family, Residence,Crime and Legal Matters, Finances, Social Activities, Health, and Miscellaneous. A life change questionnaire is potentially useful in helping to de-termine the presence of factors that predate the accident/incident that is the focus of inquiry, and that may have contributed to psychological dis-tress or decompensation in the client. The clini-cian can specify a particular time frame (e.g., six weeks, six months) prior to the acci-dent/incident and have the individual (or a close friend or family member) complete the life events survey regarding changes that occurred during that period. Areas of change noted provide the clinician with substantive areas for further in-quiry regarding the individual's adjustment and reactions to the prior changes. In this manner, the clinician can try to establish some "baseline" data regarding the client's prior adjustment against which to compare the posttrauma presenta-tion.[141]

The creative examiner may also make use of other, unobtrusive measures of preaccident ad-justment (e.g., change in job performance rat-ings; change in absenteeism record; change in attendance at church, clubs, social activities) in developing a data base from which to infer preincident adjustment [see, e.g., Cates report, § 15.08]. As noted earlier, preaccident and post-accident psychological testing also could be par-ticularly useful. The more objectively and sys-tematically the clinician can document the preaccident-to-postaccident change, the more complete and compelling will be the clinical for-mulation regarding the relative contributions of various factors that may have contributed to the client's distress.

Once this and other data have been accumu-lated, the clinician may find useful the following analytic structure proposed by Ebaugh and Ben-jamin, designed to help sort out alternative con-clusions on causation:

1. The trauma (or event or accident) was the sole cause of the psychoneurosis (or mental injury). This would be the case when there were neither manifest or latent signs of mental disorder before the trauma; when the mental injury, in the clinician's best opinion, would not have occurred now or later, had there been no trauma. These cri-teria can be met only in head injury cases, and not in many of them.
2. The trauma was a major precipitating fac-

tor. For example, this would be the case in head injuries where the emotional disorder was present in latent or potential form, but where it is reasonable to suppose that, but for the accident, the symptoms would not have occurred at this time.
3. The trauma was an aggravating factor. In these cases, some emotional disorder was clinically manifest prior to the trauma, but the cause of the condition was materially affected by the injury.
4. The trauma was a minor factor. In these cases, the emotional disorder was well-de-veloped before the trauma, but the psycho-logic or mechanical effects of the claimed precipitating event contributed somewhat to the intensity of the present symptoms.
5. The trauma is unrelated to the emotional disorder.[142]

Whether the clinician adopts this or another analytical structure for considering the causation issue, it is important to remember, as argued in § 10.04, that the factfinder decides where, if anywhere, along this type of spectrum "proxi-mate cause" has occurred. The clinician's job is to report the data and distinguish between spec-ulation and behavioral observation.

(e)   The Effects of Mental Injury on the Claimant

If a mental injury has been "caused" by employ-ment conditions or the tortfeasor's actions, the decisionmaker must then examine the extent of the injury and determine whether it is "severe." Thus, it is incumbent upon the clinician to ex-amine this issue as well.

In worker's compensation cases, the question is the impact of the injury upon the claimant's wage-earning capacity, considering his or her background, training, and employment prior to the injury. This will require the clinician to focus upon types of impairment similar to those rele-vant in Social Security determinations of the sort described in § 9.05 (to which the reader is re-ferred). For example, if the claimant now has difficulty coping with stress, but formerly held a job involving little stress, does the disability af-fect the claimant's capacity to return to the same job, and if so, in what fashion? Or will it simply affect non-work-related areas of life, in which case it is of little relevance to the worker's compensation inquiry?

In tort law, the clinician may consider issues of broader impact, since all injury is potentially compensable (assuming that the other substantive criteria for imposition of tort liability are met). But the clinician must still focus on ways in which the individual is "diminished" from the person he or she was prior to the trauma or accident. For example, the mere presence of increased irritability, depression, or constant headache will probably be insufficient to convince a jury that an award should be made, unless it is convinced that such problems substantially alter the individual's life from what it had been previously. The clinician's data can assist in this comparison, but, of course, the question as to whether the injury is "severe" enough for compensation purposes is for the factfinder to decide.

(f) Prognosis

The clinician not only must gather information relevant to whether the mental injury is severe at the present time, but must attempt to predict its likely impact in the future and whether treatment might alleviate its debilitating effects. In tort cases, and, to a lesser extent, worker's compensation cases, this information is extremely relevant to the *amount* of damages the plaintiff will receive, assuming that liability is found. This kind of prognosis is similar to those clinicians often make in traditional practice.

However, one issue is problematic—the possibility of "secondary gain," or "the unconscious 'fringe benefits' often consequent to disability." Blinder states:

> Though not causative (in that secondary gain arises as an issue following injury), such secondary gain factors as financial compensation, the solicitude of others, freedom from responsibility and/or restitution for real or imagined past exploitation may greatly prolong convalescence and prevent recovery.[143]

Another author concludes that "one of the peculiar aspects of 'treatment' and 'compensation'

is that both these supposedly reparative procedures can themselves further complicate the problems they address."[144] The clinician may feel the need to appraise the factfinder of this possibility, in appropriate cases. Whether it is deserving of compensation is up to the factfinder.

(g) Writing Reports and Giving Testimony

Detailed guidelines for writing reports and testifying are found in Chapter 14 of this book. But as a way of summing up the various aspects of the clinical evaluation of mental injury, two important general points about these topics are made here.

First, the clinician should avoid reliance on diagnosis as explicative of anything. The inquiry in worker's compensation and tort cases seeks ultimately to explain why a particular individual reacted in a particular way to a particular event or series of events. A diagnostic label may provide an organizing principle for the constellation of symptoms demonstrated by the claimant; however, it does little more than that. The clinician must provide explanatory material, and must explain not only how the claimant has been affected but why. If a diagnosis is given, its relative lack of importance to the questions posed by the legal system should be noted explicitly, or implicitly through a more detailed narrative in which the clinician provides the substantive bases for the opinion. It should be noted in this regard that, in the worker's compensation area, the appellate courts in California are reversing compensation awards that are based primarily on conclusory labels rather than upon more detailed data.[145]

Second, it bears repeating that the clinician must be sensitive to the causation issue. He or she should note the presence of any pre-existing condition or predisposition, and explain why it may or may not be relevant to the claimant's current condition. The influence of the trauma or event upon which the legal system is focusing must also be explained from the clinical perspective and not from that of the ultimate issue: It is insufficient to simply note that it "caused" (or "did not cause") the claimant's current condition. Most of all, the clinician must attempt to make clear that he or she is describing causation from a clinical point of view, and that, from that perspective, multiple causation is the rule rather than the exception. The clinician can certainly weigh the event focused upon by the law, much in the manner that Ebaugh and Benjamin suggest. However, for clarity, if nothing else, the clinician must indicate the differences between clinical and legal causation.

10.06.   Conclusion

The conceptual and practical difficulties involved in worker's compensation and tort cases are legion. Because of the amorphous nature of the concepts involved, plaintiffs' attorneys, making use of clinical testimony, have vastly expanded the scope of compensable injury. Some have found this state of affairs reprehensible. Blinder summarizes it thus:

There is probably never a physical injury without some measurable psychic trauma or functional overlay. The past 30 years, and particularly the last decade, however, have seen the exploitation of this truism in worker's compensation and personal injury litigation coupled with ever broader interpretations of the concepts of proximate cause, predisposition, work-connection, and secondary gain, resulting in a staggering number of physically fit, mentally competent individuals forever being relieved of responsibility for earning a living—on psychiatric grounds. The medicolegal system as it is presently construed not only drains

away funds necessary for the sustenance of those truly disabled but may foster or even increase disability where one otherwise would not have occurred . . . resulting in intolerable financial burdens for compensation funds, employers and carriers alike, substantially higher costs to the consumer, and ultimately, loss of coverage.[146]

This view is not universally shared, of course, and some have applauded the dramatic expansion of worker's compensation and tort recovery for mental injury.[147] But to the extent that it is a reaction to legal decisionmakers' accepting on face value conclusory statements by mental health professionals about causation and degree of impairment, we are in agreement with it. The clinician should be a disseminator of information, not of benefits.

BIBLIOGRAPHY

Annot., 97 A.L.R. 3d 181 (1980).

Blinder, The Abuse of Psychiatric Disability Determinations, 1979 MED. TRIAL TECH. Q. 84 (1979).

J. DOOLEY, MODERN TORT LAW: LIABILITY AND LITIGATION (rev. ed. by Lindahl 1982).

Joseph, The Causation Issue in Workers' Compensation Mental Disability Cases: An Analysis, Solutions, and a Perspective, 36 VAND. L. REV. 263 (1983).

Lambert, Tort Liability for Psychic Injuries: Overview and Update, 37 ATLA. L.J. 1 (1978).

LARSON'S WORKMEN'S COMPENSATION LAW (rev. ed. by M. Bender 1982).

Marcus, Causation in Psychiatry: Realities and Speculations, 1983 MED. TRIAL TECH. Q. 424 (1983).

J. O'CONNELL & R. HENDERSON, TORT LAW: NO-FAULT AND BEYOND (1975).

PART IV

Children
and
Families

CHAPTER ELEVEN

Juvenile Delinquency

11.01.   *Introduction*

Perhaps nowhere in the legal system is there as much deference to mental health professionals as in the juvenile court. Indeed, the child mental health and social service professions have grown up with the juvenile court to a large extent.[1] Although this symbiosis has been under attack in the last two decades, it persists and shows no sign of disappearing.[2] In view of the special role of mental health professionals in the juvenile process, it is particularly important for child clinicians and juvenile attorneys to have an appreciation of the situations in which clinical opinions are likely to be significant in juvenile court, as well as of the limits of expertise on these questions.

11.02.   *The Rise and Fall of the "Therapeutic" Juvenile Court*

(a)   Juvenile Justice in the Common Law

The juvenile court is a relatively recent jurisprudential invention. Indeed, the first juvenile code (in Illinois) did not appear until 1899. Prior to that time, juveniles' indiscretions were considered within the general body of criminal law. There was, however, an assumption that immaturity might reduce or even exculpate the blameworthiness of errant youth. Specifically, in the common law, infancy[3] was an absolute defense against criminal charges until age 7; for children aged 7 to 14, the presumption of capacity to form criminal intent was rebuttable by a showing of immaturity.[4]

Two points are noteworthy about the common-law heritage. First, the age at which children were held fully responsible for adhering to adult standards of conduct was quite young in comparison with current social and moral standards. Second, when charges were brought against children and youths, the action was indeed *against* them. The question was whether the juveniles had engaged in conduct deserving of criminal punishment, not whether the state might assist the youths in their socialization.

(b)   The Social and Legal Segregation of Youth

The prevailing ethos with respect to both of these points began to change late in the 19th century. First, the industrial age brought with it both a need for a prolonged period of personal development to permit adaptation to the demands of the workplace and a need to socialize the immigrant class lured by visions of corporate opulence in the New World. These social needs led to the "invention" of adolescence and the postponement of adult responsibilities.[5] For the first time, there was clear demarcation of youth as a special time of life, an identifiable stage of development.

Second, with the invention of adolescence came demands for age-grading of responsibilities and increasing segregation of youth from the adult world.[6] This policy trend was endorsed by the leading social reformers and scholars in the nascent social sciences. For example, starting from the premise that ontogeny (the development of the individual) recapitulates phylogeny (the development of the species), G. Stanley Hall, the father of developmental psychology, conceptualized adolescence as an evolutionary way station between primitive savagery and civilization.[7] In the view of Hall and his contemporaries, special legal and social structures for youth were necessary to ensure their socialization as rational contributors to the common weal. Less elegantly, "child saving" became the rubric for protecting middle-class, small-town youth from the threats that the lifestyle of working-class immigrants allegedly posed to the American way.[8] Age-graded institutions were thus perceived as highly compatible with the interests of *both* the state and the juvenile. Paternalistic social structures for youths would protect society from the persistence of an immature class ill-suited to American industrial life and would assist in their acculturation; it would also "save" youths from both the "lower" elements of the culture and their own baser instincts.

(c) The Invention of the Juvenile Court

Around the turn of the century, a number of age-graded legal structures were developed in response to these beliefs; one of these structures was the juvenile court.[9] These legal reforms all were founded on a philosophical assumption that the interests of the state and the juvenile were coextensive. In the juvenile court, unlike the criminal court, the state as *parens patriae*[10] would act *on behalf of* youths and provide them with the treatment needed to ensure that they overcame their youthful indiscretions and adopted civilized mores.

The overriding *raison d'être* of the juvenile court was, therefore, rehabilitation. Because it did not subject youths to punishment, there was no need for formal protections of due process. Indeed, there was nothing adversary about the proceeding (the state, after all, was acting *for* the juvenile), and the trappings of criminal procedure and formal rules of evidence might interfere with the "therapy" that the court would initiate.

Several additional features followed from this philosophy. To avoid stigma (and resulting self-fulfilling prophecies of criminal behavior), and to promote the beneficent appearance of the juvenile court, proceedings would be closed, and records would be sealed. The proceeding would be "civil," and terminology derived from civil procedure would be used.[11] Because the focus was on rehabilitation rather than retribution, the disposition would fit the offender and not the offense. A remorseful, troubled juvenile murderer might be treated by a social worker in freedom, while another, more streetwise youth might be incarcerated for several years for engaging in behavior that was neither clearly defined nor illegal for an adult (e.g., "incorrigibility"). And as this latter example illustrates, because the aim was reform of errant youth, a whole new category of offenses based on "status"—for example, incorrigibility, unruliness, and truancy, today all lumped together under the rubric "children [or persons] in need of supervision" (CHINS)—was invented to provide the courts with the authority to implement this reform.

Perhaps most important, the key actors in the juvenile court would be social workers, mental health professionals, and probation officers. There was, after all, very little law and even less need for lawyers. Indeed, many of the juvenile court *judges* were untrained legally.[12] From intake to release, the key questions were need for, and amenability to, treatment, and the experts on these questions were clinicians and caseworkers, not lawyers.

(d)   The Fall of the Rehabilitative Ideal

In the view of the reformers, the juvenile court was the paragon of legal realism,[13] the ideal marriage of "science"[14] and law for the social good. Even as late as 1950, Dean Roscoe Pound, an illustrious proponent of "sociological jurisprudence,"[15] lauded the juvenile court as "the greatest step forward in Anglo-American jurisprudence since the Magna Charta."[16]

In fact, however, there was very little science in the juvenile court. Although clinicians were invited to diagnose the psychopathology of wayward youth, to design dispositions, and in effect to adjudicate cases, there was little attention to the assumptions of social fact[17] that were fundamental to the court's work. The malleability of youth, the incompetency (and, therefore, lack of responsibility) of youth, the desirability of informal proceedings for juveniles, and the rehabilitative potential of the court were all taken for granted rather than empirically tested.

Gradually, however, it became clear that juvenile court had failed to match its promise. As Justice Fortas wrote in the majority opinion in *Kent v. United States* in 1966, "[T]here may be grounds for concerns that the child [brought before juvenile court] gets the worst of both worlds: that he gets neither the protections accorded to adults nor the solicitous care and regenerative treatment postulated for children."[18] The criticism was even more strident a year later in Justice Fortas's opinion for the Court in *In re Gault,*[19] doubtless the most important case in juvenile law specifically and children's rights generally. In *Gault,* Justice Fortas described juvenile courts as "kangaroo court[s]"[20] characterized by arbitrariness,[21] ineffectiveness,[22] and the appearance of injustice.[23]

The *Gault* case had two major effects. First, it made clear for the first time that children are "persons" within the meaning of the Constitution; in the words of the Court, "neither the Fourteenth Amendment nor the Bill of Rights is for adults alone."[24] These dicta opened the door to a whole series of questions about the limits of constitutional rights for minors and their competence in exercising these rights.[25] Second, *Gault* "legalized" the juvenile court. by establishing that

juveniles were owed at least those elements of the due process essential to fundamental fairness (e.g., the rights to counsel, to written and timely notice of the charges, and to the privilege against self-incrimination).[26] The Court made clear that a tradeoff between fair procedures and the provision of "treatment" or custody[27] would no longer be tolerated.

It is indisputable that *Gault* has had a profound effect on the juvenile court system. Lawyers and law-trained judges in juvenile courts are now commonplace, and in many jurisdictions juvenile courts have the same trappings and most of the same procedures as criminal courts.

At the same time, though, it is noteworthy that ambivalence—less charitably, false hope—about the juvenile court has persisted since *Gault.* The *Gault* Court itself seemed to suggest that the failures of the juvenile court were, to a large extent, the result of inadequate resources rather than inherent flaws.[28] Four years after *Gault,* the Supreme Court clearly enunciated that belief in denying juveniles the right to a jury trial:

> The juvenile concept held high promise. We are reluctant to say that, despite disappointments of grave dimensions, it still does not hold promise, and we are particularly reluctant to say . . . that the system cannot accomplish its rehabilitation goals. So much depends on the availability of resources, on the interest and commitment of the public, on willingness to learn, and on understanding as to cause and effect and cure. In this field, as in so many others, one perhaps learns best by doing. We are reluctant to disallow the States to experiment further and to seek in new and different ways the elusive answers to the problems of the young, and we feel that we would be impeding that experimentation by imposing the jury trial. . . .
>
> If the formalities of the criminal adjudicative process are to be superimposed upon the juvenile court system, there is little need for its separate existence. Perhaps that ultimate disillusionment will come one day, but for the moment we are disinclined to give impetus to it.[29]

Consistent with this ambivalence, some juvenile courts still are not "*Gault* courts" in that they are loath to permit full adversariness and strict application of the rules of evidence.[30]

Analogously, as discussed below, there is a continuing controversy about the proper role of defense attorneys in juvenile court.[31] In short, there is a persistent debate about how to reconcile the promise of the juvenile court as a therapeutic instrument with requirements for due process.

11.03.   The New Juvenile Court

(a)   The Juvenile Justice Standards

The most influential scholarship in this debate was produced by the Juvenile Justice Standards Project, a mammoth interdisciplinary undertaking sponsored by the Institute of Judicial Administration and the American Bar Association (ABA). The Standards Project produced 23 volumes of standards and commentary on various topics of juvenile court administration, procedure, and substance. Most of these volumes have been adopted as official ABA policy.[32]

The Standards are important not simply because of their official status and the stature of the panels that composed them. They are also significant as the model for the new, post-*Gault* juvenile court. Indeed, the Standards go well beyond *Gault,* based on a desire to diminish discretion and on a rejection of the assumption that juvenile courts are primarily agencies for treatment. Procedurally, they emphasize the appearance and reality of fairness through adherence to the sorts of procedures that have been linked in the Constitution and the common law with due process (including the right to public jury trial).[33] Although a full summary of the substantive provisions of the Standards is beyond the scope of this discussion,[34] several of the most significant (and most controversial) provisions should be mentioned. The Standards would replace offender-based dispositions with determinate sentences proportionate to the offenses in question (the "just desserts" approach, discussed in § 7.04). On the theory that the juvenile justice system is usually more debilitative than rehabilitative, there would be a presumption at intake in favor of referrals to community agencies in lieu of filing charges, and postadjudicative dispositions would

be to the least restrictive alternatives. Status offenses would be "decriminalized" and removed from the jurisdiction of the juvenile court.[35] In short, in addition to a rejection of rehabilitation as a feasible and fair primary basis for a primary basis for a justice system, the Standards provide for the "five D's": due process, desserts, diversion, and deinstitutionalization, and decriminalization.

(b)   How New Is the New Juvenile Court?

Clearly, the Supreme Court's activism in the late 1960s in dismantling the broad discretion in the juvenile court has been taken several steps further in legislation. The major recent casebook on children and the law concludes, for example, that "in the period from 1970 to the present, nearly every state has radically revised its juvenile code—usually to provide more exacting and precise guidelines for the exercise of discretion by juvenile judges, especially in delinquency cases."[36] Analogously, federal legislation has placed strong disincentives on the states for maintenance of expansive juvenile court jurisdiction and restrictive dispositions.[37] These "radical" reforms have doubtless been stimulated in part by the growing disenchantment among liberals with the lack of efficacy in treatment by the juvenile justice system, and with the potential for arbitrary intrusion into the lives of juveniles and their families. At the same time, there has been growing disenchantment among conservatives with juvenile justice, which is perceived as coddling juveniles who are in fact real threats to public safety.[38] Thus, proposals have come as much from the right as from the left for limiting the jurisdiction of juvenile courts to the "deserving"[39] and paying due attention to retribution and incapacitation in construction of dispositions for juveniles.

It is a mistake, however, to see the new juvenile court as very different from the old juvenile court. We have already noted the persistent ambivalence about the promise of the juvenile court. No state has come even close to adoption of the entire code recommended in the Juvenile Justice Standards, despite the fact that they bear, for the most part, the official imprimatur of the ABA. Offender-based dispositions are still the rule, except for the most serious offenses by the oldest juveniles.[40]

The Juvenile Justice Standards themselves also reflect substantial ambivalence about the juvenile court. Despite having rejected the philosophical justification for the juvenile court, the Standards Project remarkably avoided addressing the desirability of the court's continued existence.[41] Similarly, despite having obliterated the *quid pro quo* theory (i.e., the theory that fewer protections are permissible because treatment is the goal) implied by an explicit rehabilitative purpose, the Standards provide for a right to treatment for incarcerated juveniles.[42] That is, the Standards would result in the release of any juvenile who is desirous of treatment and is not receiving it.[43] The Standards also retain, or even expand, the broad jurisdiction of the juvenile court in many instances. For example, the court would maintain jurisdiction over the parents of delinquent youths, even though the parents have committed no crime.[44] At the same time, the Standards would actually expand the juvenile court into a family court, with jurisdiction over not only delinquency cases, but also abuse/neglect cases, adoptions, divorces, and cases of intrafamilial violence, including spouse abuse.[45]

Perhaps most important, juvenile court judges have proven very resistant to any diminution of their jurisdiction and discretion. Judges Wilfred Nuernberger of the Lincoln, Nebraska, Separate Juvenile Court and Justine Wise Polier of the New York City Family Court dissented from many of the recommendations of the Standards. This dissension by juvenile judges within the Standards Project itself has been consistently repeated on the floor of the ABA convention and in other public debates. For example, the judges have led the opposition to the ABA's adoption of the tentative draft of the Standards on Non-criminal Misbehavior, which would remove status offenders from the court's jurisdiction.[46] The resistance of the judges is, of course, important not only because of their influence in lobbying on matters affecting juvenile law. It is also important in a more subtle, but perhaps also more significant way. If judges are unconvinced of the desirability of substantially reducing their paternalistic discretion, they are likely to reflect this belief on a day-to-day basis in the administration of their courts. Consistent with this hypothesis, juvenile judges are more likely than juvenile attorneys to favor attorneys' assuming a guardian's role in representing their clients.[47] It is likely that this attitude is often translated into discouragement of attorneys' being active advocates (e.g., making vociferous objections to the introduction of questionably reliable or technically inadmissible evidence) in their courts. As a result, both attorneys and clinicians familiar with practice in criminal court still may find the juvenile court a relatively foreign, informal setting.

(c) A Typical Statute

As noted above, no state has adopted the Juvenile Justice Standards in their entirety, although most have adopted some of their provisions or provisions similar in tone. Thus, state juvenile court statutes are an uneasy mixture of the old "therapeutic" approach and the new "criminalized" approach. In order to present some idea of how the states have responded to the Supreme Court's decisions and the Standards, a typical state statute (Virginia's)[48] is described below.

(1) Jurisdiction

There are several types of "jurisdictions" connected with the juvenile court. *"Act"* jurisdiction concerns the types of conduct that trigger juvenile court adjudication. In Virginia, the juvenile court has jurisdiction over cases involving delinquency, CHINS, domestic relations, and civil commitment. Delinquency jurisdiction, which is the primary subject of this chapter, may be exerted over any act that would be a crime if committed by an adult, including traffic offenses. CHINS jurisdiction encompasses habitual truancy, habitual running away, habitual disobedience to reasonable and lawful commands of one's parents, and illegal acts committable only by children (e.g., violation of curfew), *if* these acts present a substantial danger to the child's health, or the child or family is in need of services not presently received and court intervention is necessary to provide them. Domestic relations adjudications, which include neglect, abuse, abandonment, and custody determinations, are discussed in Chapters 12 and 13. Civil commitment jurisdiction allows the juvenile court to hospitalize involuntarily children found to be mentally disordered and dangerous to themselves or others [see § 8.09(a)].

The retention of CHINS jurisdiction illustrates the continued resistance, alluded to above, toward completely criminalizing the juvenile court system. It may be that Virginia and other states that recognize status offenses see them as mechanisms for protecting the child from unpleasant family situations rather than as disciplinary devices. But to the extent that this is the case, CHINS jurisdiction overlaps with domestic relations jurisdiction and is unnecessary.

"Age" jurisdiction determines at what point in a child's life the court loses control over him or her. In Virginia, the juvenile court has authority to adjudicate claims against any child who has not yet reached the age of 18 at the time the act complained of was committed. It has dispositional control over a youth through the age of 20; this means, for instance, that a 17-year-old who is found delinquent may be detained in a juvenile facility until that age. The court also has jurisdiction over adults in abuse, neglect, and CHINS cases.

A final type of jurisdiction possessed by the juvenile court in Virginia as well as most other states is *"transfer"* or *"waiver"* jurisdiction. This gives the court authority to decide whether a child charged with a delinquency offense should be tried in adult court. Transfer is effected if the child is aged 15 or over, the charge is supported by probable cause, the child is "not amenable to treatment in available facilities," the child is not "mentally retarded or criminally insane," and "community interests require that the child be put under legal restraint." If transfer occurs, the juvenile court loses jurisdiction over the child.

(2) Procedure

The stages of a juvenile delinquency or CHINS proceeding parallel those in adult criminal court [see § 2.04(a)(b)(c)], although the terminology used to describe these stages reflects the continuing influence of the desire to avoid equating delinquency with criminality. After arrest (which is called *"apprehension"* in juvenile court), the juvenile has the right to a *"detention hearing"* to determine whether release is appropriate (analogous to the adult's bail hearing). In Virginia, juveniles may be detained if there is no suitable person to whom they can be discharged or if release would endanger the juveniles or the public. A second preliminary hearing *("intake")* is held within a few days (or weeks) and is presided over by a probation officer. The purpose of intake is to determine whether there is probable cause to believe an offense has been committed, and, if so, whether it would nonetheless be in the best interests of the child to be diverted out of the juvenile court system. If diversion is found to be inappropriate, the probation officer files a *"petition,"* and an *"adjudicatory hearing"* (trial) is held, at which a judge determines whether the petition is "true" or "not true." At the hearing, the juvenile is entitled to counsel and all other adult rights, except the right to a jury. If the juvenile is found "not innocent," a *"dispositional hearing"* (sentencing) takes place. The judge usually depends heavily on the probation officer's *"social study"* (presentence) report. Appeal may be taken to a trial court; if so, the trial is *de novo.*

Although the description above depicts the law in one state, it can fairly be said to represent the typical juvenile court statute.

11.04. The Mental Health Professional's Role in Juvenile Court

The following discussion focuses on the clinician's role in juvenile delinquency cases and, to a lesser extent, CHINS cases. Chapters 8, 12, and 13 deal with other clinical issues that may arise in juvenile court.

(a) Criminal Forensic Questions

One result of the substantive changes in juvenile law designed to tie it more closely to precepts of the criminal law is that forensic questions commonly raised in the criminal process [see Chapters 4–6] may now arise in juvenile cases. For example, if the proceedings are truly adversary, then the question of juveniles' ability to assist in their defense is enlivened. Consistent with that logic, several states have amended their statutes to give express authority for preadjudicatory evaluation of competency to stand trial,[49] and the few appellate opinions on the subject have all included a holding that the issue of a defendant's competency is relevant to delinquency proceedings.[50] However, the reported cases have all involved older juveniles, usually where they were at risk for transfer to criminal court.[51] Therefore, the difficult practical questions arising from a finding of incompetency in juvenile court have yet to be confronted. Suppose, for example, that a seven-year-old accused of shoplifting is found to be too immature to understand the nature of the proceedings or to assist counsel in preparing a defense. Is the adjudicatory hearing to be postponed then until the juvenile is, say, 14 and "restored" to competency? If so, what is to be done with the juvenile in the interim?

The case law is divided with respect to whether the insanity defense is applicable in juvenile cases. Those courts holding to the contrary have usually argued that, because the juvenile respondent is not subject to criminal penalties, there is no need for exculpation of mentally disordered juveniles, and that in any event there is already provision for adequate care and treatment under the juvenile code.[52] Such a conclusion flies in the face of the logic underlying *Gault* and its progeny. As Chief Justice Burger wrote for the Supreme Court in *Breed v. Jones,* "it is simply too late in the day to conclude . . . that a juvenile is not put in jeopardy at a proceeding whose object is to determine whether he has committed acts that violate a criminal law and whose potential consequences include both the stigma inherent in such a determination and the deprivation of liberty for many years."[53] If we are to excuse criminal conduct because of insanity, it is hard to understand why the same defense should not also be available to juveniles whose conduct is doubly mitigated by mental disorder and immaturity.

Regardless, however, clinicians are unlikely to be asked to evaluate juveniles with respect to either competency to stand trial or insanity, unless the juvenile may be transferred to an adult court. Defense attorneys are apt to conclude that the results for their juvenile clients found incompetent or insane will be nearly identical to the dispositions to which they would be subject if adjudicated not innocent.

Clinicians are even less likely to encounter a defense of diminished capacity [see § 6.03(b)] in juvenile court. When the disposition is linked to the offender's needs rather than to the offense, there is little strategic advantage to focus the defense on reducing guilt from, for example, first-degree to second-degree murder. Hence, negation of the capacity to premeditate is unlikely to have any significant practical import.

(b)   Amenability to Treatment

In contrast to the infrequency with which they assess either competency to stand trial or mental state at the time of the offense, forensic child clinicians are likely to spend most of their time in juvenile cases in the evaluation of respondents' amenability to treatment. Indeed, it may be fairly stated that amenability to treatment remains the overriding question in the juvenile process. It is typically the key question at every pre- and postadjudicatory stage of the proceeding, and it remains important, although less so, even under the "just deserts" model underlying the Juvenile Justice Standards.[54]

At intake, as noted earlier, a probation officer must decide whether to release the juvenile outright, to release with conditions, or to pursue delinquency proceedings (i.e., to file a "petition"). Some of the issues at this point are analogous to those presented in a criminal preliminary hearing (e.g., legal sufficiency of the complaint). Perhaps the most significant question, though, is usually whether the juvenile is amenable to treatment by a community agency other than the court. Theoretically, this phase of the proceeding is designed to minimize the number of youths who come before the juvenile court. However, there is substantial research evidence

suggesting that the development of special programs for diversion tends actually to "widen the
net" of the youths caught by the juvenile court.[55]
The same youths who would have been adjudicated still are, and juveniles who would have been
released through police, prosecutorial, or court
discretion are coerced into special treatment
programs under the aegis of the court.

Amenability to treatment is also likely to arise
in the context of "dispositional bargaining," the
juvenile equivalent of plea bargaining. Indeed, "for
the attorney who represents accused delinquents, often the most critical issue is devising
an appropriate disposition."[56] As we have noted
in the discussion of diminished capacity, the specific charge of which a juvenile is eventually convicted makes little difference in most jurisdictions, if the juvenile is guilty of *something*. Unlike
the situation in criminal court, a defense attorney has won little if he or she bargains successfully for reduction of an aggravated assault charge
to simple assault in exchange for a juvenile's plea
of not innocent. Therefore, whether at the formal intake conference or in negotiation with the
prosecutor, bargaining in juvenile court is likely
to focus on the intrusiveness of the disposition.
Will the prosecutor accept a relatively unrestric-
tive treatment plan in exchange for a plea of not
innocent? In order to have a strong hand in negotiation, the defense attorney may need a clinical opinion as to the respondent's amenability
to treatment in an alternative other than incarceration. It is likely that clinicians' involvement
(at least indirectly) in preadjudicatory dispositional bargaining is very frequent.[57]

For some juveniles, the next point in the process at which amenability to treatment is at issue
is at the transfer or waiver proceeding. As noted
above, juveniles above a certain age and/or charged
with a serious felony may be transferred (waived)
to criminal court, provided that certain findings
are made. Some of these findings are not within
the expertise of mental health professionals (e.g.,
whether probable cause exists to believe that the
juvenile has committed the felony; whether
transfer would serve the public interest). Commonly, however, transfer hearings focus on general questions of the juvenile's "best interests"
or "amenability to treatment" as a juvenile. As

the Juvenile Justice Standards frame the issue,
the ultimate question is whether the juvenile is
"a proper person to be handled by the juvenile
court." To reach such a conclusion, the court
must find, by clear and convincing evidence,
"[1] the likely inefficiency of the dispositions
available to the juvenile court as demonstrated
by previous dispositions; and [2] the appropriateness of the services and dispositional alternatives available in the criminal justice system
for dealing with the juvenile's problems."[58]

If the juvenile is not transferred and is found
to be delinquent at the adjudicatory hearing,
amenability to treatment arises as an issue at the
dispositional hearing. Because most jurisdictions
still insist upon rehabilitation as the basis for the
juvenile justice system, amenability to treatment
is ostensibly the primary question in determining
the disposition.[59]

Finally, if the juvenile is found not amenable
to treatment in the community (on probation)
and is committed to a juvenile correctional facility or "training school," the period of incarceration will be indeterminate (at least so long as
the individual remains young enough to be subject to juvenile jurisdiction), so that release will
be contingent upon the juvenile's progressing to
a point where he or she is found to be amenable
to treatment in the community.

In short, dispositional issues arise at every phase
of the juvenile process except adjudication.[60] Because amenability to treatment remains the
ubiquitous, practically dispositive issue in juvenile court, clinicians tend to play an important
role in the process.

(c) Consultation

A second major role clinicians can fulfill is as
consultants. We have already implied the potential usefulness of clinicians in assisting attorneys
in the development of treatment plans that may
be used as negotiating chips. Perhaps less obviously, forensic clinicians often may be of more
help to attorneys, at least in "*Gault* courts," in
the process of "lawyering" with juveniles than
with the substance of the case itself. The role of

defense attorneys in juvenile court—not unlike their role in civil commitment [see § 8.10]—is ambiguous and controversial.[61] How much weight should an attorney give to the wishes of a 12-year-old client in "zealously" defending the client's interests? Still more basically, is it really the juvenile who is the client? Should the attorney's primary allegiance be to the juvenile or the juvenile's parents (who may be paying the bill for the attorney's services)? To the extent that a true adversary system applies in juvenile court, the answer is superficially clear: The attorney zealously advocates the wishes of the juvenile respondent. However, there is presumably some point of cognitive and social immaturity in the client, such that even the most adversarial attorney begins to shift into a guardian-like role, in which decisions about defense strategy are made independent of the client's wishes.[62]

Obviously, the less attuned attorneys are to their clients' concerns and the less able the attorneys are to communicate with youths, the more problematic their representation of juveniles becomes. The research literature strongly suggests that such communication is a substantial problem in juvenile cases. Although there is little evidence concerning what actually happens between attorneys and juvenile clients,[63] it is well substantiated that juveniles' understanding of the legal process is substantially less complete and accurate on the average than that of adult defendants.[64] Juveniles are less likely to conceptualize rights as entitlements applicable to their own cases,[65] and they tend—perhaps realistically—to perceive the juvenile court as inquisitory rather than adversary.[66] Consistent with that view, juveniles frequently do not appreciate the meaning of the attorney–client privilege.[67] Moreover, juveniles often have trouble comprehending the vocabulary in *Miranda* warnings and other legal contexts.[68] These misunderstandings are not alleviated by previous experience with the law,[69] contrary to the assumption of many courts.[70] When juveniles' understanding of the process is so likely to be at least partially incorrect, it would certainly be unsurprising to find that attorneys fail to appreciate their clients' concerns fully and that juvenile clients fail to make good use of their attorneys. In such a situation, mental health

professionals who are knowledgeable about children's and adolescents' understanding of the legal system could be very helpful in consulting with attorneys about communication with their clients, and even in acting as "interpreters" or "legal educators" for the juveniles.

Mental health professionals may also be useful adjuncts to attorneys in preparing juveniles for intake hearings and court appearances. For example, the proportion of juvenile delinquents who have diagnosable learning disabilities is known to be very high.[71] It has often been suggested that learning disabilities in some way predispose juveniles to delinquency. Learning-disabled youths, it is said, might be more likely to behave impulsively, or their delinquency might be responsive to frustration resulting from repeated school failure. However, a study conducted by the National Center for State Courts[72] suggests that neither explanation is valid. Learning-disabled youths are in fact no more likely to *commit* delinquent offenses than are other youths, as measured by both self-report and police contacts. The difference comes in the proportion actually *adjudicated* for delinquency. Presumably, the learning-disabled youths appear less amenable to treatment (perhaps realistically), or they are simply not very adept at appearing appropriately remorseful and respectful. In other words, they are not skilled in manipulating the system. In such cases, clinicians acting as consultants might be very helpful to attorneys in preparation of clients for the legal process.

Finally, mental health professionals may take a consultant's role more typical among expert witnesses: evaluation of the evidence of the opposing side. In particular, clinicians may be able to assist in supporting (or rebutting) assessments of amenability to treatment through discussion of the outcome research on various treatments of juveniles with particular characteristics and presentation of the literature on clinical prediction. Similarly, in transfer hearings, the conclusions as to a juvenile's amenability to treatment often turn on findings as to why previous treatments, if any, have failed. Therefore, clinicians may often be very helpful in evaluating the adequacy and appropriateness of previous efforts to rehabilitate the juvenile.

11.05.   The Nature of the Evaluation

(a)   The Process of the Evaluation

If mental health professionals do act as clinical evaluators of juveniles, it is important for them to be cognizant of some special issues in forensic evaluation of juveniles. First, in our experience, although adult defendants often wish to appear "sick" in order to facilitate what they believe will be less aversive dispositions of their cases, adolescents almost never adopt such a stance. Indeed, a far more common problem is that juveniles "clam up," or, alternatively, try to present themselves as streetwise "tough guys," lest clinicians conclude that they are crazy. For many adolescents, including those whose misbehavior is more neurotic or impulsive than characterological, the label of "delinquent" or "troublemaker" is less threatening to their self-esteem than being considered "crazy" or "wierd."[73] Second, juveniles whose understanding of the legal process is inaccurate may be suspicious about the purpose of an evaluation. Third, it must be acknowledged that the consequences for juveniles, particularly those charged with minor offenses, may well be more intrusive—even if necessary or desirable—if they are considered in need of treatment (as opposed to in need of a moral lecture). Thus, juveniles may be *realistically* unmotivated to cooperate with evaluations.

For these reasons, juveniles referred for evaluation typically require more "warming up" than adult defendants, and it is especially important to spend a substantial amount of time going over the purpose of an evaluation and the limits of confidentiality. Although allowance must be made for individual differences, it is usually true that juveniles reveal more when the interviews are low-key and conversational rather than confrontational. Moreover, juveniles are more likely to require "patching up" and reassurance at the end of the interviews, especially when their offenses are masked symptoms of depression[74] and their evaluations touch, therefore, on especially painful and conflict-laden memories. In part because more time usually must be given to establishing rapport and ending evaluations supportively, it is our experience that juvenile assessments often take longer (e.g., require more interviews) than evaluations of adult defendants on comparable questions.

(b)   The Scope of the Evaluation

The greater typical length of juvenile assessments is not simply a matter of clinical technique. It also reflects the greater typical scope of juvenile forensic evaluations. The evaluator may occasionally be asked to focus on competency or insanity issues alone (in which case we refer the reader to Chapters 4, 5, and 6). But as we have discussed earlier in this chapter [see § 11.04(b)], evaluations in juvenile cases are usually focused on amenability to treatment. Thus, the juvenile court evaluator should be particularly aware of the scope of this type of evaluation, which is defined by the legal meaning of treatment, the dispositions available, and the dispositions most likely to work.

(1)   The Meaning of "Treatment"

Amenability to treatment should not be read as "amenability to psychotherapy"; rather, it refers to amenability to treatments available, or even potentially available, in the juvenile court. Because the range of dispositions open to juvenile judges in most jurisdictions is very broad [see § 11.05(b)(2) below], the evaluation of amenability to treatment should also be very broad. As discussed in detail in the next section, a thorough assessment of a juvenile's amenability to treatment should usually include an evaluation not only of personality functioning, but also of cognitive, educational, vocational, and social needs in the context of the various systems (e.g., family, school, neighborhood) of which he or she is a part. As already noted, the assessment may also require evaluation of previous treatment efforts.

A qualifier to this broad conceptualization of "treatment" is that the meaning of "amenability to treatment" may vary, depending on the stage of the proceeding. Mulvey has articulated this point well:

Each different proceeding presents potentially different factors weighing on the amenability judgment, and no single decision equation applies to all hearings where amenability is at issue. In the transfer decision, for example, the consideration of amenability is explicit (usually defined by statute), and must be documented in the judge's written decision. Also, the consequences of a judgment of nonamenability in this hearing is that the juvenile is processed through the adult system. For transfer, the question for the clinical profession is, thus, usually one of whether the youth is treatable at all.[75] In contrast, the diversion and disposition decisions present a much more implicit amenability question, often framed by its interaction with several unstated but influential variables (e.g., concern for public safety and court philosophy). Clinical information in these situations is deemed valuable for matching a juvenile with an appropriate service. The point is that, while pervasive, the amenability determination and the clinical question related to it are far from uniform. Different court proceedings frame the decision differently.[76]

Mulvey's point notwithstanding, however, the clinician asked to assess a juvenile's amenability to treatment should consider *all* of the alternatives: those that are easily available (e.g., a local court diversion program); those that are available but require extraordinary efforts (e.g., fashioning an individualized program from the offerings of several agencies) or expense; and those that might work but are not presently available (i.e., a particular kind of program that is matched to the offender's needs but that is unavailable in the community or the state). It is true that the factfinder—whether a judge or an intake officer—may choose to consider only certain kinds of alternatives at particular points in the proceeding. However, the clinician should recognize that the possibilities for treatment at all stages of the proceeding are very broad, and should permit the factfinder to make the legal judgment of whether the level of effort or expense required for a particular plan of treatment is justifiable. Such a stance is especially appropriate in jurisdictions in which the juvenile court exercises judicial oversight over public agencies (or private agencies receiving public funds) serving youths and their families.[77] The clinician may be very

helpful to the court in the identification of gaps in services to troubled youths. Regardless, the more specificity that is present in the conclusions to a report about the sort of program that would aid a juvenile, the better. The seemingly ubiquitous recommendation for a "structured treatment program" is practically worthless to a court trying to make a transfer or dispositional decision. Clinicians should be similarly straightforward in reporting the *level* of juveniles' amenability to particular treatments and the level of confidence they attach to these opinions.

On the other hand, the probability of success required to warrant a finding of amenability at various stages of the juvenile process is a legal judgment that should be vested with the factfinder. A related qualifier is that the *definition* of success implicit in the judgment of amenability should also be left to the factfinder. It has been our experience that, in the minds of legal authorities, there is usually an implicit clause in the standard: amenability to treatment, *such that the juvenile will be less likely to recidivate*. That is, as is true in the adult context as well [see § 7.08(a)], the court tends to be most interested in treatment as it affects legally relevant behavior, and predictions should be made in that regard if there are data available on which to base a valid prediction. Nonetheless, given the historic child-centered approach of the juvenile court, clinicians should also feel free to make assessments of amenability to treatment in the context of juveniles' treatment needs even if there is no clear connection to the juveniles' offenses [see the case of Tom Young, § 15.09]. The factfinder can then decide whether it is appropriate to consider such treatment options in its findings as to the juveniles' amenability.

(2) Dispositional Alternatives

To reinforce the point about breadth of "treatment" available to the juvenile court, it may be useful to consider in some detail the range of dispositions at the disposal of a creative juvenile court. The juvenile court in Virginia, for example, may (1) order state and municipal agencies to provide services to the juvenile; (2) order the parent(s) of the juvenile to participate in treatment or "be subject to such conditions and limitations as the court may order and as are designed for the rehabilitation of the child"; (3) place the juvenile on probation "under such conditions and limitations as the court may prescribe"; (4) levy a fine; (5) suspend the juvenile's driver's license; (6) transfer custody of the juvenile to an individual, a private agency, or the department of welfare; (7) if the juvenile is at least age ten, commit him to the department of corrections (youth services); or (8) if the juvenile is at least age 15 and unamenable to treatment as a juvenile in available facilities, send him to jail.[78] Other states provide express authority for imposition of a requirement of restitution,[79] community service,[80] full-time employment,[81] or psychiatric hospitalization.[82] Even when there is no explicit authority for creative dispositions, juvenile judges generally have wide-open discretion for establishing special conditions of probation for juveniles and/or their parents, as long as the conditions are believed to be in the juveniles' best interest. Indeed, juvenile judges' authority over probationers may be limited only by a lack of power to order them to go to church![83] And, as in Virginia, judges may even be able to order agencies to provide the treatment plans they construct.[84] In some sense, the juvenile court's dispositional authority is limited only by a judge's imagination and the finite nature of human and economic resources.

Moreover, in the transfer context, even finite resources may not be a permissible consideration in the determination of amenability to treatment. Although the issue is unsettled, unavailability of resources may be a constitutionally indefensible basis for a finding of unamenability to treatment when such a finding subjects a juvenile to possible criminal penalties.[85] The explicit purpose of rehabilitation in many state juvenile codes may create a right to treatment requiring that some rehabilitation effort be made for *all* delinquents.[86]

(3)   What Works

Evaluation of amenability to treatment requires not simply a knowledge of the range of treatments available to the court. A prediction of the outcome of treatment obviously also requires a knowledge of which treatments work, and for whom. The state of the literature is such that we must remind clinicians again to exercise care in monitoring the limits of their expertise in making conclusions concerning amenability to treatment. In a review of the efficacy of rehabilitative programs in both criminal justice and juvenile justice, a task panel of the National Academy of Sciences concluded that, unfortunately, there is no evidence to refute the pessimist's contention that "nothing works."[87] At the same time, however, the panel made it clear that few outcome studies met basic methodological requirements. In particular, the integrity of correctional programs has usually been insufficiently preserved to provide a fair test of their efficacy.[88] In such a context, the pat conclusion that nothing works is not supportable, but neither is it refutable.

A similar situation exists in evaluation of children's mental health services. There is no solid empirical support for the efficacy of child therapy.[89] However, in neither juvenile justice nor child mental health has there been a very sophisticated approach to outcome research and, to a large extent, individual assessment. In adult mental health, psychotherapy outcome studies began to show much more positive results when there began to be attention to a match between client characteristics and type of treatment.[90] The question of "What works?" is too simple; the query should instead be "What works for which children in which ways under which conditions?" Too frequently, juvenile treatment programs have been aimed at delinquents as a class, without attention to individual differences. Such an approach seems at best to minimize the possibility of demonstrating success, because the individuals for whom the program is successful become absorbed in the group data. More likely, the failure to target juveniles with particular needs or styles reflects an inadequate conceptualization of the kind of treatment likely to be effective, and thus a real lack of efficacy. At worst, the group approach to treatment planning threatens harm (e.g., when depressed juveniles are placed in highly confrontational programs). Regardless, the literature on treatment outcome in juvenile justice is unlikely to improve substantially until (1) programs are sufficiently funded, staffed, and administered to guarantee a fair evaluation, and (2) a sufficiently complex research design is used to detect person–treatment interactions.

A few generalizations are suggested by the existing outcome literature, however. For example, individualization of treatment, appropriate resources, and care in evaluation research design are insufficient (although probably necessary) for a successful program. For example, two of the most extensively evaluated residential treatment programs for delinquents (Achievement Place in Kansas and the Robert F. Kennedy Center, a federal facility in West Virginia) involved careful application of operant learning principles to treatment, and both were well-supported demonstration projects. In studies of both programs, juveniles showed impressive in-program gains on a variety of behavioral and educational dimensions.[91] Nonetheless, neither program was found to result in a reduction of postrelease recidivism,[92] apparently because there had been no alteration of the behavioral contingencies maintaining the antisocial behavior that had brought the juveniles to the treatment programs.

The experience of these well-known behavior modification programs suggests that, to be successful in reducing delinquent behavior, the treatment must be based not only on analysis of juveniles' psychological needs. The evaluation, and treatment based on it, should be *ecological* in scope. That is, one has to assess the interaction between juveniles' psychological characteristics and the settings of which they are a part. Ultimately, to be effective, change may be necessary on both sides of the interaction.

Two small programs originated in such a community orientation and had demonstrable success in treating "hard-core" delinquent boys: Massimo and Shore's vocationally oriented psychotherapy[93] and Goldenberg's Residential Youth Center (RYC).[94] Both programs involved substantial follow-up of the youths in the community—in the case of Massimo and Shore, over a 15-year period[95]—and neither has ever been fully replicated or implemented on a large scale. Massimo and Shore's program contained only

10 clients, and Goldenberg's RYC had just 25 residents. Nonetheless, these two programs are important because they are virtually the only delinquency programs in which there was a carefully designed evaluation and posttreatment follow-up.

In that regard, it is interesting that there were a number of aspects of program design common to the two programs[96]:

1. Therapists were available on 24-hour call. Contacts took place several times a week and were not limited to the office.
2. The focus of the therapy was on "real-life" concerns, particularly with development of skills needed in the workplace.
3. The therapists moved outside the traditional neutral role and acted as advocates in the community for "their kids": "In essence, the therapist entered all areas of the adolescent's life. Job finding, court appearances, pleasure trips, driving lessons when appropriate, locating and obtaining a car, arranging for a dentist appointment, going for glasses, shopping for clothes with a first pay check, opening a bank account and other activities require this maximum commitment."[97] Thus, the therapists worked actively to increase the fit between the boys and "the system."
4. Both programs were small, thus increasing the possibility of individual attention and planning.[98]

The two programs demonstrate that it is possible to have an impact on the lives of delinquent youth. However, especially when taken together with those demonstration projects that have failed to have a positive long-term effect, they suggest the need to consider the "whole juvenile" and to take advantage of the full range of options open to the court, in determinination of both amenability to treatment and dispositional plans. At the same time, a note of caution should be reiterated, at least until more research showing postitive outcomes is available. Vocationally oriented psychotherapy of the intensity Massimo and Shore have described will require both money and skill in implementation.[99] Indeed, Shore and Massimo themselves have contended that the program is likely to be ineffective if it is "watered down" from the comprehensive, ecological intervention it was designed to be.[100]

11.06. Specific Areas for Evaluation

Given, then, the range of dispositions available to the juvenile court and the outcome research, what sorts of things should a clinician asked to do an evaluation of amenability to treatment examine? The general answer, which should be obvious by now, is anything relevant to determination of interventions (including interventions outside the mental health system) that would assist in the adaptation of the juvenile to the community. Therefore, if the evaluation is indeed comprehensive, it will often require an interdisciplinary approach, or at least a thorough investigation of a juvenile's behavior in home, school, workplace, and neighborhood. The clinician will need to adopt a broad, ecological perspective for evaluation, and it will also often be helpful to enlist the assistance of the defense attorney or court staff (depending on the stage of the proceeding and the source of the referral) in the gathering of information for the evaluation.

The specific content of the evaluation will obviously vary, depending upon the issues that seem to be presented by the case and upon the orientation and style of the evaluation. However, we present some areas that are common considerations.

(a) Family

(1) Reasons for the Assessment

There are three major reasons for conducting a thorough family evaluation. First, evaluation of the family is often important in formulating the causes of the delinquent behavior, just as such an evaluation is usually helpful or perhaps even necessary in the nonforensic assessment of an adolescent. Such assessment obviously becomes central if the offense itself is familial—for example, if the juvenile is charged with violence

against another family member,[101] if a family member is a prosecuting witness,[102] or if the offense may have been perpetrated by multiple family members. Second, parents and other family members can provide historical information to supplement or corroborate the juvenile's own account. Third, as we have noted in the preceding section, the juvenile court has authority in many jurisdictions to order a family disposition. It also has the power to remove the juvenile from the home. Accordingly, the clinician should be alert to the possibility of treatment of the juvenile through family therapy or parent counseling. The clinician's assessment of the emotional supports available or potentially available in the family may also inform the judge's determination of the juvenile's amenability to treatment while living at home.

(2) Clinical Issues

Generally, there are two themes in the literature about families of aggressive children.[103] First, aggressive children tend to come from families in which there are high levels of hostility and aggression. There are frequently cycles of coercive behavior[104] (e.g., parents are targets as well as instigators of coercive behavior) and high levels of parental rejection[105] and punitiveness, especially physical punitiveness.[106] There is sometimes direct reinforcement of aggression, especially that directed toward people outside the family.[107] Second, aggressiveness in children is related to parental ineffectiveness and family disorganization. Generational role boundaries are commonly blurred,[108] and parents are relatively likely to respond positively to deviant behavior and aversively to appropriate behavior.[109] There are also high levels of parent absence[110] and, when both parents are present, conflict between spouses.[111] Commonly, then, there is a need to restructure the family to provide nonaggressive models and clear, consistent norms for behavior.

These conclusions should not be interpreted, however, to indicate that there is a well-developed technology of change in families of aggressive children. Although some research-based programs exist,[112] most of the literature on family therapy where the presenting problem is aggressive behavior by a child has involved status offenders.[113] Even clinical program reports (in contrast with systematic evaluation studies) are largely unavailable with respect to treatment of families of children who have displayed serious violent behavior.[114] It is unclear in that regard whether the gap is an artifact of the dispositions chosen (e.g., such youths are removed from their homes and incarcerated) or a result of a belief that family therapy is impractical in such families.

(b) Community

The reasons for evaluating the community (as it interacts with the juvenile) parallel the reasons for assessing the family. First, consideration of support systems (or lack thereof) in the community may suggest both reasons for the delinquent behavior and resources for changing it. Neighbors, youth group leaders, and teachers can be valuable informants about the juvenile's behavior. Moreover, as already noted, long-term change in the juvenile's behavior is unlikely to result without there also being change in the community.[115] Some creativity may be necessary in identifying, and making use of, both natural helpers and formal programs that might assist the juvenile and prevent further delinquency. Even if the juvenile is going to be removed from the home or incarcerated, ultimately there must be attention to the preparation of the community for his or her return. There needs to be sufficient assessment of the community to construct such plans. Second, in some jurisdictions, the juvenile court has authority over public agencies.[116] The court may order agencies to provide services that might contribute to the rehabilitation of the juvenile. Therefore, some assessment of the match between the juvenile and the community's resources is useful.

It is known that neighborhood cohesiveness is negatively related to delinquency.[117] Obviously, however, the court's ability to deal with this factor is limited. The limitation is not simply one of the boundaries of technology. It is also a problem of paradigm: It is difficult to change

communities when the disposition is necessarily fashioned around the individual.[118] Nonetheless, there has been some success with juvenile advocacy programs in reducing recidivism.[119] Broad assessment will be necessary to construct such programs.[120]

One issue that is noteworthy in the assessment of community resources is that the use of an "amenability to treatment" standard is likely to result in more restrictive dispositions for juveniles from lower-class communities. We do not mean to imply that poor people are untreatable. Indeed, there is substantial evidence to the contrary, even with traditional verbal therapies.[121] However, it is doubtless true that the resources for significant change—or simply for elaborate, if not necessarily effective, treatment plans—are increasingly less likely to be available as the socioeconomic ladder is descended. At the same time, the level of "drain" on the resources that are available is likely to be higher. Although the inequities of disposition arising from use of the standard of amenability to treatment may not be an immediate concern of forensic evaluators, they should be considered by policymakers in the analysis of the proper bases for punitive interventions.[122]

(c) Academic and Vocational Skills

It is especially important to identify a juvenile's academic and vocational skills, because such skills are what enable a youth to adapt to the environment. That is not to say that improving achievement level will prevent recidivism as a rapist, for example. Obviously, academic and vocational skill levels on their face have little to do with such a crime. On the other hand, it can be said with some confidence that, without sufficient skills, the probability of a juvenile's getting into some kind of trouble is increased substantially. Whether treatment gains will be maintained over time appears to be highly related to the seriousness of academic deficits that remain.[123] As already noted, the programs that have demonstrated some success in treatment delinquency have had a strong educational/vocational component. Analogously, the only adult correctional programs that have shown evidence of effectiveness are those that have combined work and financial support.[124]

Beyond their obvious implications for establishing a niche in the community, vocational/educational skill levels would be expected to be important for several more subtle reasons. First, such skills are important in establishing a sense of self-esteem and active mastery of conflicts.[125] Second, the ability to verbalize conflicts contributes to delay in expression of impulses and probably to less reliance on physical aggression.[126] Third, a carefully designed educational treatment program may increase social skills and accuracy of social perceptions,[127] which may in turn improve interpersonal relationships[128] and the ability to navigate through the juvenile justice system itself.[129] The ability to conceptualize behavioral alternatives and to plan accordingly may be a bridge between cognitive development and personality functioning.

In order to reach conclusions sufficiently refined to base an individualized educational program upon them, it will generally be necessary to perform a formal psychoeducational assessment—one of the few situations in which we believe psychological testing to be an efficient means of gathering data to answer a forensic question. It is important in that regard not to stop with vocational interest scores, grade levels, and IQs, but to develop a full picture of a juvenile's learning style and the interaction of that style with the juvenile's emotional development and behavior.[130] Such a profile will be more useful than global scores in both understanding the juvenile's fit with the environment and developing a specific treatment program.

In most cases, the attorney should see not only that the broad evaluation recommended here is used for assessing the juvenile's amenability to treatment and developing a dispositional plan in juvenile court, but also that it is transmitted directly to the local school system. Under the Education for All Handicapped Children Act,[131] an individualized educational plan (IEP) paves a procedural avenue for ensuring that a juvenile receives appropriate educational treatment, whether he or she remains in the local school system or is institutionalized.[132] Official identification as a pupil with special needs may also

substantially reduce the juvenile's future vulnerability to suspension or expulsion for school misbehavior.[133]

(d) Personality Functioning

It is, of course, in the area of personality functioning that the assessment of a juvenile is most likely to resemble a traditional mental health evaluation. We need not prescribe the format for such an evaluation, but we do wish to offer several notes of caution. First and most important, it should be emphasized that the same behavior may have multiple etiologies. It has been our experience that clinicians often generalize from preconceptions about delinquent behavior without really examining the environmental and intrapsychic determinants of the behavior in a particular juvenile. Even from a psychodynamic perspective, serious delinquent behavior may be the product of group norms (i.e., "sociosyntonic"[134] or "socialized aggressive"[135] behavior), a "pure" character disorder, "overdetermined" neurotic motivation (e.g., when the delinquent behavior is a depressive equivalent[136]), or truly crazy thinking. There may be substantial differences in the mental health treatment of choice, given these various etiologies. Second, the diagnostic system currently in use (the third edition of the *Diagnostic and Statistical Manual of Mental Disorders,* or DSM-III) still does not closely reflect the empirical literature on classification of children's behavior.[137] Third, clinicians need to be attuned to base rates of behavior. In that regard, it is useful to note that mental health professionals tend to ascribe more disturbance to *normal* adolescents than even *clinical* groups of adolescents themselves report.[138] Fourth, at the risk of rekindling the classical debate about the relative validity of clinical and actuarial prediction,[139] we remind clinicians that the best predictor of adolescents' behavior—like adults' behavior—is simply past behavior.[140] Fifth, although we have contended that child therapy has yet to be given a fair test, it must also be acknowledged that conclusions as to juveniles' amenability to psychotherapy have little empirical basis. The need for modesty may be accentuated by the observation that the best-validated "treatment" of violent and antisocial behavior in juveniles is their getting older![141]

11.07. Do the Mental Health and Juvenile Justice Systems Belong Together?

Although this volume is focused primarily on *evaluation* in the legal system, it is appropriate in this chapter to discuss the *initiation* of forensic evaluations. As we have noted in § 8.10(a), the populations of youth in juvenile justice facilities and in mental hospitals are to a large extent interchangeable. Indeed, in many jurisdictions, juvenile courts are the primary referral agents for hospitalization of children and adolescents[142]; the specific route that homeless, difficult youths travel is dependent largely on the ease of entry into one system or the other,[143] and on other criteria that are unrelated to the juveniles' treatment needs or the nature of their behavior disorders.[144] Among violent adolescents, there is usually a career of placement in *both* psychiatric and juvenile justice systems.[145] To a large extent, this checkered life is the result of not knowing what to do with very troubled and troubling youths whom nobody really wants, but of wanting to do *something*—of being unwilling simply to let the juveniles go.

Even in less serious cases, though, there is often such movement back and forth between the mental health and juvenile justice systems. In particular, mental health and social service personnel sometimes use the juvenile court—especially status offense jurisdiction—as a means of obtaining treatment for youths.[146] There may be various motives for this strategy: (1) a juvenile, the juvenile's parents, or both may be refusing treatment; (2) public agencies may be slow to respond for bureaucratic reasons,[147] in the absence of a court order; (3) the court may be perceived as an avenue for integrating services for a multiproblem family.[148]

The practice of invoking juvenile court jurisdiction as a means of obtaining treatment is mistaken, albeit benevolently motivated. Pragmatically, the experience of the juvenile court over the past three-fourths of a century certainly reveals the necessity of reasonable goals for the court. As Mulvey has pointed out,[149] courts are ill-equipped to deal with family problems; the juvenile court is not in fact structured as a crisis intervention or mental health agency. If the need is to make treatment available, it would be more effective and more efficient to focus advocacy upon the systems designed to provide human services, rather than to try to deflect courts from their central purposes.[150] Expansion of juvenile court jurisdiction will not result in a substantial increase of services to children, youths, and families, but it will transform them into *coercive* services,[151] and it will subject them to added stigma from the label of "delinquent."[152]

We concur with Morse and Whitebread that mental health professionals (and legal authorities) should welcome the trend toward an increasingly legalistic model in juvenile law:

> Although the [Juvenile Justice Standards] clearly have shifted from the traditional discretionary, medical model of juvenile justice, it is apparent nonetheless that mental health service providers will continue to play a substantial if considerably more modest role. The opinions of mental health professionals will be sought regularly and they will be asked to provide services in both institutions and community programs. Although informed consent will be required for most mental health services, we suspect that many juveniles will accept such services if their benefits are patiently and clearly explained. Moreover, treatment under such conditions is not only more likely to be successful, it is also more respectful of the juvenile's autonomy and privacy[153] than coerced treatment. Mental health professionals are vitally concerned with respect for the individual and should therefore applaud a model that enhances autonomous, contractual relations between helping professionals and their patients or clients. It is true, of course, that some juveniles who might have been helped by coerced treatment will refuse such treatment. But, again, we suspect that such cases will be few in number and it is a price worth paying in order to develop a freer and more respectful treatment regime. Mental health professionals will lose some power, but they are still charged with performing those services they are trained best to provide—evaluating and treating patients who want and need such services.[154]

BIBLIOGRAPHY

CHILDREN, MENTAL HEALTH, AND THE LAW (N.D. Reppucci, L. Weithorn, E. Mulvey, & J. Monahan eds. 1984).

THE FUTURE OF CHILDHOOD AND JUVENILE JUSTICE (L. Empey ed. 1979).

T. GRISSO, JUVENILES' WAIVER OF RIGHTS: LEGAL AND PSYCHOLOGICAL COMPETENCE (1981).

G. MELTON, CHILD ADVOCACY: PSYCHOLOGICAL ISSUES AND INTERVENTIONS (1983).

Melton, *Developmental Psychology and the Law: The State of the Art,* 22 J. FAM. L. 445 (1984).

Morse & Whitebread, *Mental Health Implications of the Juvenile Justice Standards,* in LEGAL REFORMS AFFECTING CHILD AND YOUTH SERVICES (G. Melton ed. 1982).

J. MURRAY, STATUS OFFENDERS: A SOURCEBOOK (1983).

W. WADLINGTON, C. WHITEBREAD, & S. DAVIS, CHILDREN IN THE LEGAL SYSTEM (1983).

CHAPTER TWELVE

Abuse and Neglect

12.01. The Nature of Abuse and Neglect Proceedings

As discussed in Chapter 11, the separate system of juvenile justice has its roots in *parens patriae* doctrine; it was intended to reflect state interests in the socialization of children. An even more direct reflection of the state's interest and duty in protecting children is found in the invocation of state power on behalf of abused and neglected children, an issue that is usually considered by the same specialized court that has jurisdiction over delinquency cases. State action in cases of child maltreatment represents a direct conflict with family privacy and parental liberty; as such, it is an area of the law in which the complex and sometimes confusing mixtures of interests among child, family, and state is most starkly presented.[1] These philosphical issues, combined with difficulties in clearly and narrowly defining abuse and neglect,[2] have made the question of the proper breadth of state jurisdiction and intervention in cases of child maltreatment a hotly debated one in recent years. The attempt to balance the state's interest in protecting children with the parents' interest in family privacy is especially troublesome because of questions about the state's ability to fulfill its interest. The documented lack of stability in foster care in most jurisdictions frames the balancing of interests in terms of a dreadful dilemma: Are children worse off in the care of abusing and neglecting parents or in that of the state?[3] Although there are no clear answers to this question yet, the fact that it is seriously posed indicates both the depth of the controversy about policies concerning child maltreatment, and substantial skepticism about the ability of the social service and mental health professionals to evaluate possible maltreatment validly and to treat parents and children successfully.

(a) Stages of the Proceeding

The issues described above are raised at each stage of abuse and neglect proceedings, from the identification of "abuse" to the resolution of abuse cases. First, mental health professionals are usually required by law to report any case in which they have reasonable cause to suspect that child abuse or neglect has occurred. Therefore, initial state intervention, in the form of investigation and any emergency action, often takes place on the basis of an assessment by a professional that abuse or neglect has occurred. Although all 50 states have laws on reporting,[4] the statutes have been criticized for disrupting ongoing services by requiring a breach of confidentiality; at the same

time, they increase caseloads of protective services workers to a level that makes it questionable whether any substantial degree of protection is added by the mandated referral.[5] It is
undeniable that laws on reporting have greatly
increased the incidence of reported cases.[6] At
the same time, though, it is unlikely that the law
is applied uniformly, because of some professionals' resistance to reporting,[7] the ambiguity of
what behavior should be reported, and differences among demographic groups in the degree
to which they are subject to scrutiny by mandated reporters.[8]

Once possible child maltreatment has been
investigated, there may be a second stage, in which
a petition is filed by a state attorney or social
worker alleging that the child is in fact abused
or neglected.[9] At the hearing that results, there
is an adjudication of whether the allegation is
valid—that is, whether there is a legally sufficient basis for the state to assume jurisdiction
over the child and family. It is at this phase that
definitional problems and questions of the proper
balance between state and parental authority are
most directly presented.

If the child is found to be abused or neglected, there is a third phase, in which disposition is determined. There are two sorts of dispositional questions that may be posed. The first
concerns temporary or time-limited dispositions. The inquiry in that regard typically follows
a best-interests standard, in which the court has
broad authority to require the parents to meet
conditions designed to improve the quality of
their care of the child (e.g., to attend parent education classes; to obtain vocational training) and
to ensure the safety and welfare of the child (e.g.,
the court may transfer custody to the department of social services). The second kind of dispositional question, typically not raised at the
initial dispositional hearing, concerns permanent
termination of parental rights. Besides consideration of the best interests of the child, termination typically requires specific findings of the
parents' lack of amenability to treatment, and
sometimes requires documentation that the state
has made diligent efforts to remediate the parents' propensity to maltreat the child. If rights

are terminated, the parents become strangers to
the child, from the point of view of the law. The
child becomes available for adoption, and the
parents lose even visitation rights. Both kinds of
questions demand predictions of future parental
behavior and the efficacy of treatment, and both
again present issues concerning the proper reach
of the state and the proper deference to parents.
The latter issue is acutely presented in cases in
which children are in foster care for extended
periods of time, but are unavailable for adoption
or are even returned to parents with whom they
have lived for little, if any, of their lives. Questions of vagueness of standards and validity of
clinical predictions are also raised.

(b)   General Policy Perspectives

As the preceding discussion shows, the general
problem of balancing state and parental interests, and the corollary problem of the proper
level of involvement of mental health professionals, arise at several different points in the process. There is no consensus on these questions,
and indeed different answers may be given for
different stages of the proceedings. For example,
"child savers" have historically preferred to err
on the side of ensuring protection for the child.[10]
They would, therefore, establish low standards
for invoking state jurisdiction, and they would
prefer high levels of intervention once that
threshold is crossed. In its modern version, proponents of this perspective argue that deference
to family privacy is ultimately destructive of
families and is certainly not in the best interests
of children.[11] Indeed, they would prefer community intervention even before serious maltreatment occurs, so as to maximize the probability of effective intervention to prevent harm
to a child.[12] The modern child savers also believe
that, if intervention is to accomplish its goals,
state social workers need broad discretion and
considerable resources so as to fashion and implement a comprehensive plan for rehabilitation
of the family.[13]

A second perspective emphasizes the potential harm, or at least the lack of clear benefit, of state intervention in many cases; the frequently arbitrary grounds for intervention; and the limits of available resources. Advocates of this perspective argue for clearly defined, very limited bases for state intervention, and they state a preference for minimal intrusions upon family privacy once jurisdiction is taken. The leading scholar holding this point of view is Michael Wald,[14] whose arguments heavily influenced the relevant volume of the Juvenile Justice Standards.[15] Unlike most of the volumes of the Standards, the Standards Relating to Abuse and Neglect have yet to become the official policy of the American Bar Association, but they remain important authority for the advocates of limited state intervention in cases of child maltreatment. State intervention under the Standards, discussed in more detail in the following section, is generally limited to situations in which there are findings that a child has suffered, or is at substantial risk of suffering, serious harm, and that intervention is necessary to protect the child from being endangered in the future. If this high standard is crossed, the court is required to choose the disposition that, while protecting the child from the harm justifying intervention, is least invasive of family privacy.

A third perspective is offered by Goldstein, Freud, and Solnit,[16] who would set a very high threshold for state intervention (significantly higher than that of the Standards), but, once that threshold has been crossed, would make it easy to terminate parental rights. Relying on psychoanalytic theory, Goldstein and colleagues argue that the prime considerations in family policy should be preservation of continuity in the child's "psychological parent" and respect for the authority of that parent. They claim that children need the security of a parent who is perceived as omnipotent, and that the state is not equipped to meet the emotional needs of the child. Therefore, they would permit state intervention only under circumstances of the direst and clearest harm to the child, with no prospective inquiry. That is, there must have already been serious harm before abuse jurisdiction can be invoked. The range of circumstances in which Goldstein

and colleagues would permit state jurisdiction include the following:

> *Para. 30.6* A Parent's conviction, or acquittal by reason of insanity of a sexual offense against his child.
> *Para. 30.7* Serious bodily injury inflicted by Parents upon their Child, or an attempt to inflict such injury, or the repeated failure of Parents to prevent their Child from suffering such injury.
> *Para. 30.8* The refusal by Parents to authorize medical care for their Child when
> (a) Medical experts agree that treatment is nonexperimental and appropriate for the Child; *and*
> (b) Denial of that treatment will result in the Child's death; *and*
> (c) The treatment can reasonably be expected to result in a chance for the Child to have normal healthy growth or a life worth living.[17]

If the child is placed in foster care, the foster parents may assume parental rights under this proposal after they have established themselves as "longtime caretakers" (i.e., they have cared continuously for the child for at least one year if the child was placed at less than three years old, or for two years if the child was placed at age three or older).[18] If placement has been pursuant to Paragraph 30.6 or 30.7 above, or if the child was placed when less than six years old, the natural parents would not even have a right to a hearing on the matter.[19]

12.02. Legal Definitions of Child Maltreatment

It is clear, then, that there is no consensus among authorities as to even the overall framework that should guide legal policies on child maltreatment. There is basic disagreement over the proper balance among interests at both the invocation of state authority and the dispositional phase. This philosophical disagreement—in combination with *conceptual* unclarity among mental health professionals about what child maltreatment is [see § 12.03]—has led to often vague standards with respect to "abuse" and "neglect," which are widely divergent across jurisdictions.

(a) Physical Abuse

All jurisdictions provide for state intervention to protect physically abused children. They differ substantially, however, in terms of the degree to which the finding of abuse is based on value judgments as to what behavior is abusive and the nature of the proof required. In view of the ubiquity of corporal punishment as a disciplinary technique in American families,[20] and its relatively greater frequency in particular social groups,[21] there is the possibility of arbitrariness and the probability of unreliability in the application of broad standards.

In recognition of this problem, the Juvenile Justice Standards propose a standard that is much stricter than in most state statutes (although not as limited as Goldstein and colleagues advocate): Intervention is permitted in this context only if "a child has suffered, or there is a substantial risk that a child will imminently suffer, a physical harm, inflicted nonaccidentally upon him/her by his/her parents, which causes, or creates a substantial risk of causing disfigurement, impairment of bodily functioning, or other serious physical injury."[22] The commentary to the standard indicates that its "intent . . . is to prevent injuries such as broken bones, burns, internal injuries, loss of hearing, sight, etc. It is not intended to cover cases of minor bruises or black and blue marks, unless the child was treated in a way that indicates that more serious injury is likely to occur in the future."[23] In making that judgment, the drafters have emphasized that it "does not imply acceptance of corporal punishment as a means of discipline. Rather, it reflects the judgment that even in cases of physical injury, unless the actual or potential injury is serious, the detriment from coercive intervention is likely to be greater than the benefit."[24]

Like the Standards, many state statutes require a finding of "harm" or at least "danger of harm" as a result of intentional infliction of physical injury; the abusive act alone is not enough. In some of these states, the *level* of harm re-

quired is also similar to that of the Standards. Florida, for example, defines physical injury to include "death, permanent or temporary disfigurement, or impairment of any bodily part."[25] However, the Florida statute would also seem to subsume physical abuse resulting in mental injury.[26] There is a similar open-ended quality to some of the statutes that at first glance seem to conceptualize physical abuse in terms of intentional action resulting in serious bodily harm. Wyoming, for example, defines physical injury as "death or *any harm* to a child *including but not limited to* disfigurement, impairment of any bodily organ, skin bruising, bleeding, burns, fracture of any bone, subdural hematoma or substantial malnutrition" (emphasis added).[27]

Most problematic, though are those statutes that expressly call for a value judgment as to the limits of acceptable physical punishment independent of its actual or probable harm. Some states in fact include "excessive corporal punishment" in the definition of abuse[28] or even of neglect.[29] Others define abuse in terms of "cruel or inhumane" parental practices.[30] Courts are divided as to whether such standards are so vague as to be violative of due process.[31] As a practical matter, they are difficult to apply, given both individual and group differences in attitudes toward corporal punishment, as well as psychological research and theory suggesting that any physical punishment has deleterious psychosocial consequences.[32]

(b) Physical Neglect

As in the standard defining abuse, the Juvenile Justice Standards require a finding of serious physical harm before a child can be adjudicated to be neglected. That is, it must be found that "a child has suffered, or . . . there is a substantial risk that the child will imminently suffer, physical harm causing disfigurement, impairment of bodily functioning, or other serious physical injury as a result of conditions created by his/her parents or by the failure of the parents to adequately supervise or protect him/her."[33] The drafters of the standard have made clear that they have avoided state intervention on the basis of "inadequate" parental behavior, which is viewed as both too vague and too likely to result in overintervention.[34] Nonetheless, neglect statutes frequently require only that the state show that the parents have failed to provide "proper supervision."[35] Some states even invoke jurisdiction if there is sufficient "immorality" to make the home unfit.[36]

(c)   Sexual Abuse

The Juvenile Justice Standards would permit coercive intervention in cases of sexual abuse, although there has been ambivalence among the drafters on this point.[37] An alternative standard has been offered requiring a finding of serious harm, on the theory that the intervention may often engender more distress than the sexual abuse itself.[38] Sexual abuse is not defined in the Standards, because of a preference for using the definition of the term found in a state's *penal* code.[39] While several states do define the term in their criminal statutes,[40] many do not, and most of the states that specifically include sexual abuse in their *civil* child abuse statutes[41] do not define it further.[42]

(d)   Emotional Abuse and Neglect

Emotional abuse is the most controversial aspect of abuse/neglect jurisdiction, probably because it is so difficult to define. Although one can imagine cases in which most people would agree that there was emotional abuse (e.g., locking a child in a dark closet for prolonged periods of time), there is no such consensus for most questionable parental practices. It is probably also true that in many, perhaps most, circumstances where there is a consensus that emotional abuse is present, there would be other grounds for invocation of jurisdiction.

Another problem is that establishing the basis for emotional harm presents difficult problems of proof. How does one really know whether a child's maladjustment is the result of parental practices? It is clear in this regard that many children develop appropriately in spite of growing up with parents who are unresponsive or who have what may be mistaken ideas about children's needs [see § 12.05]. Moreover, given the myriad of parental behaviors that may adversely affect child development,[43] do we really want to expand jurisdiction to the range of situations that may be psychologically unhealthy? If not, what *is* to be the decision rule for determining whether an unwise practice is also an abusive practice that warrants state intervention to protect the child?

For these reasons, the Juvenile Justice Standards would permit invocation of state authority in cases of emotional abuse and neglect in only a single narrow situation: when "a child is suffering serious emotional damage [not necessarily as a result of parental actions], evidenced by severe anxiety, depression, or withdrawal, or untoward aggressive behavior toward self or others, *and* the child's parents are not willing to provide treatment for him/her."[44] Those states providing for emotional abuse/neglect tend to use broad definitions of "mental injury" that offer little guidance. Wyoming, for example, permits state intervention when parental action results in "an injury to the psychological capacity or emotional stability of a child as evidenced by an observable or substantial impairment in his ability to function within a normal range of performance and behavior with due regard to his culture."[45]

(e)   Conclusions

There clearly is great diversity in statutory definitions of abuse and neglect. There also is often sufficient vagueness in state statutes to raise constitutional questions.[46] Vague or value-laden definitions unfortunately do often result in arbitrary application. There is solid empirical evidence of gross unreliability in perceptions of child maltreatment, with the groups most likely to be involved in initial investigations (i.e., social workers and the police) being those that tend to have the most expansive concepts of child abuse and neglect.[47] Even within the social work profession, though, there is substantial variation in understanding of the definition of child maltreatment, as a result of differences in the setting in which social workers are employed and in their theoretical orientation.[48] We turn now to examination of these clinical concepts.

12.03. Child Maltreatment as a Clinical Phenomenon

(a) The "Discovery" of Child Abuse

Although the juvenile court has had jurisdiction over poorly supervised children since its inception,[49] the development of a special system of legal regulation and social services for abused and neglected children is a rather recent phenomenon. The major impetus for this development came from an article published in the *Journal of the American Medical Association* in 1962.[50] In that article, Henry Kempe and his colleagues identified the existence of "battered-child syndrome" as a clinical condition. There was a considerable hue and cry thereafter, and all 50 states enacted mandatory reporting laws over a four-year period in the mid-1960s.[51] Federal involvement with the problem of child maltreatment began with the enactment in 1974 of the Child Abuse Prevention and Treatment Act, which authorized the establishment of the National Center on Child Abuse and Neglect (NCCAN).[52] NCCAN has been especially involved with facilitating reporting laws, and it has kept national statistics on the reported incidence of child abuse and neglect. There has been a dramatic increase in reporting—from 8,000 cases in 1968, to 416,000 in 1976, to 700,000 in 1978.[53]

Child maltreatment is certainly not new; indeed, trends across generations have been toward more humane treatment of children and more recognition of children as persons.[54] However, the identification of child maltreatment as a clinical entity *is* new. While we do not wish to minimize the realities of abuse of children, it is important to recognize that child abuse and neglect are *social constructs* that have entered the behavioral sciences only in the past two decades. Thus, the "eye-of-the-beholder" problem is as real for

the social welfare and mental health professions as it is for the law.

(b) Social Science Definitions

Definitions of child maltreatment used by social scientists tend to be substantially broader than those in law, at least in the more carefully drafted statutes. Parke and Collmer advocate a culturally relative definition: "non-accidental physical injury (or injuries) that are the result of acts (or omissions) on the part of parents or guardians that violate the community standards concerning the treatment of children."[55] Also using a culturally relative but still broader definition, the Garbarinos define child maltreatment as including "acts of omission or commission by a parent or guardian that are judged by a mixture of community values and professional expertise to be inappropriate and damaging."[56] They further define emotional abuse to include parental behavior that hampers the development of social competence by penalizing a child for normal exploration and expression of affect, discouraging attachment, lowering self-esteem, or discouraging relationships outside the family.[57] Another well-known researcher, sociologist David Gil, defines physical abuse as "the intentional, nonaccidental use of physical force, or intentional, nonaccidental acts of omission, on the part of a parent or caretaker interacting with a child in his care, aimed at hurting, injuring, or destroying that child."[58] Gil's definition would appear to include all corporal punishment.

The broad and inconsistent definitions used by social scientists are problematic not only because of the difficulty in applying vague definitions. They are troublesome also because of their potential influence on helping professionals, who may apply even broader standards than the law permits. Inconsistent definitions make comparisons across studies difficult, and overly broad definitions render research questionably applicable to legal policy.

Probably of even more consequence than the specific *definitions* used by social scientists are the overall *perspectives* adopted, which tend to shape both standards for intervention and the kinds of interventions employed. In that regard, one can discern psychodynamic, social learning, socio-logical, and ecological approaches, all of which are discussed below.

(c) Psychodynamic Perspective

Probably the most influential view of child mal-treatment is that it is a reflection of psychiatric dysfunction—a "syndrome"—in the parent. From this perspective, in order to understand child abuse, it is most important to identify the per-sonality traits and personal histories of abusers. Similarly, intervention would be primarily indi-vidually based and psychodynamically oriented (e.g., psychotherapy aimed at changing the un-derlying psychological disorder).

The literature expressing the psychodynamic perspective has consisted largely of clinical impressions based on case reports. The more systematic studies have often failed to include appropriate comparison groups, so that the traits that set abusers apart from nonabusing parents of similar demographic characteristics and from other clinical populations cannot be clearly identified.

Psychodynamic researchers have not suc-ceeded in identifying a consistent pattern of traits common among abusers. Gelles found that at least two or more authorities agreed on only 4 of 19 traits reported in the literature.[59] A largely un-critical review by Spinetta and Rigler reached a similar conclusion:

> A review of opinions on parental personality and motivational variables leads to a conglom-erate picture. While the authors generally agree that there is a defect in the abusing parent's personality that allows aggressive impulses to be expressed too freely, disagreement comes in describing the source of the aggressive impulses.[60]

Simply saying that an abusive parent has trouble controlling aggression is, of course, tautological and offers no help in understanding the phe-nomenon. Although still at a descriptive level, the consensus seems to be that the aggressive outbursts of abusive parents are rarely the prod-uct of psychosis.[61] There is generally a belief that abusive parents typically have a personality dis-order,[62] but there is no consensus as to the na-ture of the personality disorder.

One notion is that child maltreatment is one aspect of a more general antisocial behavior pat-tern. Exemplary of this view of child abusers is Wright's excessively glib identification of a "sick but slick" syndrome.[63] In comparing personality test performance of 13 abusive parents with 13 matched nonabusive parents of hospitalized chil-dren, Wright found that the abusers looked healthier than the comparison group on mea-sures that on their face appear to be highly re-lated to psychopathology, but that they also scored high on scales of the Minnesota Multiphasic Per-sonality Test (MMPI) that are empirically related to psychopathy.[64]

Another common theme in the literature (based largely on clinical impressions without comparison groups) is that abusers are immature and dependent.[65] Therefore, it is argued, they depend upon children to meet their own needs and become outraged when they fail to do so. Another aspect of this role reversal is application of adult expectations to children. Such social perceptions would result in punishment for non-volitional behavior (e.g., crying by an infant) or childish behavior that does not conform to adult norms (e.g., rowdiness).

A related theme is that abusive parents have themselves been abused—that child abuse is passed across generations in a seemingly perpet-ual cycle.[66] Within a psychodynamic framework, this sort of early experience would explain the difficulties with nurturance described in the pre-ceding paragraph. However, it is important to note that the evidence for the intergenerational hypothesis is actually rather weak. In Gil's na-tional survey, only 14% of abusive mothers and 7% of abusive fathers reported having them-selves have been abused as children.[67]

(d) Social Learning Perspective

In another psychological view of child abuse, child abuse is understood as a reflection not of intra-psychic character defects, but of skill deficits and learned maladaptive responses. Assuming the existence of an intergenerational phenomenon, social learning theorists would ascribe child abuse in part to parents' having had models who did not modulate the expression of anger appropriately. Accordingly, the tasks are to teach parents to be good behavior modifiers,[68] and, in particular, to help the parents to interrupt cycles of aggression and other coercive behavior within the family.[69]

Social learning theorists also tend to understand child abuse as a result of inappropriate or inadequate cognitive responses by parents. Thus, the parents need to learn a wider range of possible behavioral responses that they might choose,[70] internal statements (i.e., things to say to oneself) to dampen anger,[71] and appropriate expectations for children. This view is compatible with the psychodynamic perspective in the description of the problem (e.g., inappropriate expectations), but not in the understanding of the etiology or the appropriate intervention. Psychodynamically oriented clinicians would tend to use insight-oriented therapy to help the parents understand their frustrated need for nurturance and its effect on their parental behavior. Clinicians with a social learning orientation would work to change the cognitions directly and to teach strategies of self-control.

A caveat that must be issued in terms of both perspectives is that the evidence for inappropriate expectations—at least in terms of expectations for the child—is equivocal. Rosenberg and Reppucci reported data from a study that cast doubt on this hypothesis,[72] although their findings do raise other possible explanations, which are interesting from both psychodynamic and social learning perspectives. In presenting abusive and matched nonabusive parents with vignettes about childrearing, the abusive group actually perceived *more* alternative reasons for their children's behavior (e.g., they more often saw misbehavior as possibly accidental as opposed to purposeful), and there were no group differences in attribution of intentionality. The abusive mothers tended to be much more self-critical, however. Rather than misperceiving the children's behavior, they seemed to experience behavior management problems as threats to their own self-esteem. The more alternatives that they could generate for their children's difficulties, the more responsible—and the more out of control—they felt. Thus, the mothers may have had expectations that were too high for *themselves,* not their children. The abusive mothers also indicated significantly more sources of stress upon them in the past year than did the nonabusive parents. Therefore, there is the suggestion of a lethal combination of high stress, self-reproach (perhaps abusive parents blame themselves not just for childrearing problems, but for other sources of stress as well), and displacement of anger onto children.

(e) Sociological Perspective

In contrast to the psychological perspectives on child abuse, sociologists have tended to conceptualize child maltreatment as a societal problem reflecting institutional pressures and class-related stresses. Accordingly, they would expect little change in the incidence of child abuse without broad social reform aimed at enhancing the social status of children and decreasing the socioeconomic inequities that put some children at risk of abuse.[73] From this point of view, individually oriented interventions "blame the victim"[74] and implicitly sustain the root social causes of child maltreatment.

Sociologists perceive parental child abuse as merely the tip of the iceberg in regard to socially sanctioned violence against children. About 90% of Americans use physical punishment on occasion.[75] This proportion is only slightly higher than the proportion of *psychologists* who use such punishment, according to a Pennsylvania survey,[76] despite the official stand of the American Psychological Association[77] and other professional organizations[78] against corporal punishment.

Perhaps the most dramatic evidence of the frequency of serious violence against children comes from Gelles and Straus's interviews of a large representative national sample of parents.[79] Because it was a self-report study, the resulting figures are almost surely underestimates of the actual incidence.[80] Not surprisingly, minor physical punishment was reported the most frequently, but there were also shocking levels of serious violence. According to parents' reports, 82% of 3- to 9-year-olds, 66% of 10- to 14-year-olds, and 34% of 15- to 17-year-olds had been hit during the year of the survey.[81] Three percent had been kicked, bitten, or punched by their parents during the year; 8% had been so attacked at some point during their lives.[82] Again, by parents' *own* report, 3% of children had been threatened by a parent with a gun or a knife at least once; in the same proportion of cases, a gun or a knife had actually been *used.*[83]

There is also strong evidence for the hypothesis of class-related stress as a factor in child maltreatment. Although child maltreatment is not limited to low-income groups, there appears to be a strong negative correlation with socioeconomic status (SES). In reaching this conclusion, Pelton made three points: (1) Proportions of reports of abuse by SES have not changed, even though the absolute number of reports has changed dramatically with laws on reporting; (2) maltreating families tend to be the poorest of the poor; (3) the severity of injuries is class-related.[84] There is also evidence that, even though they are less subject to scrutiny by public agencies, middle-class parents may be no less vulnerable than low-SES parents to reports of abuse, because of a greater tendency of laypersons in middle-class groups to report child maltreatment.[85] The cumulated evidence seems to indicate, therefore, that class differences in reported child maltreatment are not simply the reflection of reporting biases.

Such a relationship should be unsurprising because of the relationship between stress and child abuse,[86] and between stress and social class. Low-income parents are more likely to have reality-based pressures upon them and less likely to have resources to deal with these pressures. A difficult child (e.g., one who is premature) is a potential source of great frustration on top of a myriad of other stressors.

While there is clearly some validity to the sociological perspective, it is an incomplete view. Most Americans, including most low-SES parents, do not abuse their children. There is a need to understand the social factors *in interaction with* individual differences in psychological traits. Such

a complex perspective is offered by ecological theorists.

(f) Ecological Perspective

Ecological theorists[87] emphasize the fit between the person and the environment. The environment itself is recognized to consist of several levels, each in interaction with the other: (1) the "microsystem," the immediate social context of the child (e.g., the family); (2) the "mesosystem," the connections among microsystems of which the child is a part (e.g., an older sibling's accompanying the child to school); (3) the "exosystem," external influences on the life the child (e.g., the flexibility of the father's place of employment enabling him to set aside time for the family); (4) the "macrosystem," the broad cultural blueprint influencing the structure and processes of lower-level systems (e.g., the overall concept and status of childhood). Thus, while ecological theorists do not deny the effects of individual differences in personality and skills, they look to diverse and complex social factors to determine how those individual differences will be expressed.

For example, the effects of unemployment on a family might be expected to vary with the following factors, among others: (1) the parents' ability to respond to frustration (microsystem); (2) the degree of interaction between the family and social resources (e.g., friendly teachers) that might help to alleviate stress (mesosystem); (3) the availability of help in finding jobs (exosystem); (4) the national economic policy in regard to tolerable levels of unemployment (macrosystem). Therefore, to say that unemployment[88]— or poor impulse control—is the cause of child maltreatment is to oversimplify a complex social phenomenon. Assessment of only one level or aspect of the situation will be shortsighted, and intervention directed at only one level or aspect is unlikely to have substantial effects.

Ecological theorists also recognize that cause–effect relationships are rarely unidirectional, although differentials in power may make effects in one direction stronger than the other. For example, it is obvious that, in most families most of the time, parents have more effect on children than the converse. Parents generally have greater control over reinforcements and greater physical strength, cognitive skills, social experience, and behavioral repertoire.[89] However, it is also clear that the presence of children changes the life of adults, and that the care of some children is much more demanding and stressful than the care of others. Although there are probably other reasons as well,[90] it is likely that part of the explanation for the disproportionately high rate of abuse of infants[91] is their great need for care. Consistent with this hypothesis, premature and handicapped infants, who tend to require the most care of all, are at especially high risk for abuse.[92] Similarly, older abused children may often unwittingly have learned behavior that really "gets to" their parents.[93] We do not mean to suggest, of course, that children should be viewed as responsible for parental abuse. At the same time, however, it is important to recognize that a parent with poor childrearing skills, high stress, and a limited system of social supports might be able to cope adequately with an "easy" child,[94] but not with one who requires special care. Evaluators for disposition and planners of interventions may find that work to increase the social competence of abused children may be an important ingredient in reducing the probability of child maltreatment.

Ecological theorists tend to place primary emphasis, though, on the parents' support system.[95] Parents' social networks of course have direct influence on the development of the child.[96] Of special consequence in this context, though, is the *indirect* role these networks play in supporting and shaping childrearing skills (a feedback function) and in diffusing stress. Probably the most firmly established correlate of child abuse is social isolation. Abusive parents have been found to be less likely than nonabusers to belong to organizations, to have a telephone, to have relationships outside the home, and so forth.[97]

The direction of causality is not clear from these correlations. Socially isolated parents may find themselves excluded from the community, unable to form relationships, or prone to withdraw from the community; or there may be a combination of social explanations (exclusion) and psychological explanations (incompetence or withdrawal). In discussing the psychodynamic perspective, we have mentioned some reasons why abusive parents might have difficulty in adapting to the standards of the community. However, the possibility that there is minimal availability of social supports for abusive parents should also be recognized.

Particularly strong evidence for the latter hypothesis comes from the work of James Garbarino, the leading ecologically oriented scholar on child abuse, and his colleagues. In one study, it was found that economic factors alone accounted for 52% of the variance in the rate of child abuse across communities, but variables related to neighborhood stability were also significant correlates.[98] Examining the latter finding in more detail, Garbarino and Sherman studied two low-income neighborhoods in the same Midwestern city that had dramatically different reported rates of child abuse.[99] The two neighborhoods had identical proportions of low-income families living in them (72%), but child maltreatment was eight times more prevalent in one neighborhood than in the other. Interviews with expert informants (ranging from scout leaders to school principals to letter carriers) gave contrasting pictures of the two neighborhoods as places to live—impressions confirmed by interviews with residents. One-third of the families in the high-risk neighborhood, compared with just 8% of the families in the low-risk neighborhood, reported no interaction with other people in the neighborhood. Only 40% of the children in the high-risk neighborhood, compared with 86% in the low-risk neighborhood, played regularly with children in the neighborhood. Parents in the high-risk neighborhood were much less likely to be available for their children after school, much more likely to have experienced multiple major stressors in the previous year, and likely to have fewer other adults whom they considered to be interested in their children. The general picture of the high-risk neighborhood was of a community in which there were great emotional drains and few social supports to replace the depleted human resources. In such a situation, regardless of the personal inadequacies which parents have, intervention must take into account the need to build the community as a whole if it is to be successful.

(g) Prognosis and Treatment

In view of the multitude of factors involved in child maltreatment and their complexity, it is perhaps unsurprising that the prognosis in cases of child maltreatment is generally poor. The following overview of the literature by a researcher in the federal Administration for Children, Youth, and Families paints a quite gloomy picture:

> The present state of the art can be generalized as follows: Current intervention modes with abusive and neglecting or maltreating parents are not very effective and do not meet even the first criterion, that of ensuring the child's safety. In addition, while we have good evidence that children do not recover from the effects of abuse and neglect without specific intervention, it is very unlikely that the affected children will receive either a medical or a psychiatric evaluation, and only a very small minority receive anything except the obviously needed medical service, or protective foster care, which carries its own risks.[100]

Although this quote emphasizes the problem of inadequacy of resources, it would be a mistake to miss the initial point that we lack even the technology for preventing recidivism in maltreatment, much less that for increasing parental acceptance of children or for enhancing children's development. Even in federally funded demonstration projects, recidivism has occurred among at least one-third of abusive clients (including more than half of the clients whose initial abusive behavior was severe).[101] The best estimate is that about one-third of the clients in demonstration projects have improved during treatment.[102] Such statistics do not necessarily indicate that these programs have not been worthwhile; it may be that significantly fewer parents would have improved without treatment. However, it is clear that nothing approaching a guarantee of safety can be offered to children of abusive parents, even when parents are enrolled in model programs.

Besides the difficulty of the problem, the low success rate of programs for abusive and neglecting parents may be a function of inadequate conceptualization. There simply have not been adequate attempts to match the mode of intervention with the nature of the problem or the specific needs of the client.[103] Only about $2 million of NCCAN's budget goes to research, and few of those grants have been directed toward acquisition of better basic knowledge about child maltreatment.[104] Probably in part as a result of this gap, even the model programs have typically relied on traditional services (e.g., psychodynamically oriented therapy and casework). Rosenburg and Hunt have lamented this lack of innovation:

> Outcome evaluations of the effectiveness of nontraditional services (e.g., parent aides, Parents Anonymous, homemaker services, crisis nurseries, drop-in centers, etc.) for abusive and neglectful families have not been performed. Further, there are not studies that compare the relative effectiveness of traditional and nontraditional interventions, nor the additive effect of a combination of two service types. . . . The paucity of outcome data on nontraditional services is unfortunate, considering their potential for effectiveness with families who may not benefit from more traditional, verbal therapies.[105]

Regardless, though, of whether the low success rate is an inherent reflection of the complexity of child maltreatment or a function of inadequate resources and conceptualization, it is clear that, in the present state of the art, knowledge about intervention in families in which maltreatment has occurred is limited.[106] The safety of children in the home is questionable, even with intervention, but removal from the home carries its own human and economic costs.[107] The unfortunate reality is that the past and present record of state intervention to protect maltreated children is unimpressive at best. While clinicians involved in dispositional assessments should try to construct possible plans for intervention that take into account the diverse social and psychological factors in child maltreatment in a particular case, experts should also be careful to avoid overstating the scientific basis for their conclusions or their confidence in their recommendations.

12.04. Clinicians' Involvement in the Legal Process

(a) Adjudication

As we have noted early in this chapter, mental health professionals may be involved at all stages of legal inquiry in cases of child maltreatment. Indeed, the case may be initiated upon a clinician's report of suspicion that child abuse or neglect has occurred.

The phase of the process in which clinical involvement is least likely is the adjudication— the determination of whether abuse or neglect, as legally defined, has occurred. If an evaluation is sought, it will probably be under a statute requiring a finding of harm as an element of abuse or neglect. In such a case, the clinician will usually be asked to determine whether a "mental injury" has resulted from maltreatment of the child. Thus, the evaluation will be focused on the child's mental status and, if significant disturbance is present, whether it was caused by trauma.

Another possible, and very controversial, use of clinical testimony, is in establishing that abuse has occurred. In one scenario, the expert would be called to testify as to the characteristics of child abusers. There would then be testimony as to the match between these characteristics and the defendant. In a second scenario, the testimony would be directed toward the characteristics of abused children and the match between these characteristics and the alleged victim.

(1) Testimony on the Characteristics of Abusers

Illustrative of the former scenario is the Minnesota case of State v. Loebach,[108] an appeal of the conviction of Robert Loebach for the third-degree murder of his three-month-old son Michael. Although Loebach was a criminal case, the evidentiary issue presented in it is equally applicable to civil adjudication of child abuse. In Loebach, Dr. Robert ten Bensel, an expert on "battered-child syndrome," testified that the pattern of injuries that Michael had sustained was consistent with the syndrome. This testimony presumably fell well within the boundaries of acceptable expert testimony in terms of assisting

the jury to determine whether the death of Michael was the product of nonaccidental injury. However, Dr. ten Bensel also described the psychosocial characteristics of "battering parents": a history of abuse in their own childhoods; role reversal; low empathy; "short fuse" and "low boiling point", high blood pressure; strict authoritarianism; uncommunicativeness; low self- esteem; isolation; and lack of trust. The prosecution then called two caseworkers who had known Loebach since he was a child to testify that he did in fact possess many of those characteristics.

The Minnesota Supreme Court ruled that Dr. ten Bensel's testimony as to the characteristics of "battering parents" and the related testimony by the caseworkers should have been excluded. The court seemed to rely initially on the fact that the evidence was admitted essentially to establish that the defendant's character was such that he was prone to child abuse. Under traditional evidence law, such evidence is not admissible unless the defendant places his or her character at issue, which the defendant in Loebach did not. Ultimately, however, the court's decision did not rest on the bar against gratuitous prosecution use of character evidence.[109] Rather, the holding was said to be "required until further evidence of the scientific accuracy and reliability of syndrome or profile diagnoses can be established."[110]

We have no quarrel with the result in Loebach. The review of the literature in § 12.03(c) indicates that the scientific basis for the battering-parent syndrome is very weak. When used in combination with medical evidence as to the cause of physical injuries, it is likely to be highly prejudicial and misleading.[111] Although the low validity of the syndrome could have been elicited through skillful cross-examination and rebuttal testimony by other experts, it is unlikely that Dr. ten Bensel's testimony on the syndrome could have assisted the jury.

However, the ultimate reliance on possible scientific invalidity may have been a ruse. The court apparently did not review the scientific evidence on the battering-parent syndrome, and it avoided the more basic and harder question of when group data should be used in individual cases [see § 1.03(b)]. Suppose that Dr. ten Bensel had given a scholarly, comprehensive review of the literature in terms comprehensible to a lay jury. Suppose that he had indicated the proportion of abusers possessing each of the characteristics, the proportions in other groups in the population, and the methodological strengths and weaknesses of the literature. This information would be likely to provide the jury with base rates that would assist it in weighing the evidence.

Consider also the fact that child abuse cases, both civil and criminal, often necessarily rely largely on circumstantial evidence. The abuse may take place in the home with children too young to give eyewitness testimony. In such cases, the state's interest in protecting children may be frustrated by a bar on expert testimony on the characteristics of abusers. Especially in a civil case, there is a plausible argument that an exception should be made on this basis to the rule regarding character evidence.[112]

One can counter these arguments by noting that a description of the general characteristics of many child abusers is only tangentially relevant to the question of whether a *particular* defendant abused a child. Moreover, the lack of direct evidence of the defendant's responsibility is usually not fatal in and of itself to the prosecution's case, in that other possibilities can be systematically rebutted. It may also be unfair to require the defendant, in effect, to disprove that he or she is a "battering parent," in the absence of direct evidence of the parent's having abused the child.[113]

In the event, though, that behavioral scientists are called to testify as to the characteristics of abusive parents, they are certainly ethically obligated to indicate the limitations of the literature and the overlap among populations.[114] To prevent misuse of the evidence, they should also make clear to the factfinder the difficulties in drawing inferences about individual events on the basis of group data.

(2) Testimony on the Characteristics of Abused Children

A mental health professional may also be asked to give an opinion as to whether a child has been abused.[115] This sort of testimony is directly anal-

ogous to a forensic physician's opinions as to the cause of a physical injury.[116] *If based on hard data,* this sort of evidence may assist the factfinder to determine whether maltreatment has occurred. In principle, we are not bothered by this kind of testimony if (1) it is not allowed to stand alone without other, more direct evidence; and (2) the expert is limited to the probability evidence, without invading the province of the factfinder in determining whether this particular child was abused, with in the legal meaning of the term. However, it is hard to imagine careful psychological testimony that would be very helpful to the factfinder. Although child maltreatment is certainly not benign in its psychological effects,[117] the behavioral signs are not distinguishable from those seen in other clinical populations.

The issue is especially difficult if the expert's opinion seems to be directed toward the factual issue not only of whether the child as abused, but also *who* was the abuser. Suppose, for example, that a five-year-old girl is noticed by the clinician to be avoidant of discussing her father to a much greater extent than other key adults in her life; to engage in doll play in which the father doll screams at the other dolls and throws the baby dolls across the room; and to be anxious and tearful when the father is physically present. The factual *observations* by the clinician would seem to be clearly relevant and probative, albeit circumstantial. The question of admissibility of *opinions* as to the meaning of the observations is more problematic,[118] although it is conceivable that, at some point, sufficient data would be available as to indicate the frequency with which such a reaction is seen in relationships between abusive parents and their children, as compared with other parent–child relationships. Without the comparison groups, though, any opinions would be misleading. The mental health professional might also be able to assist the factfinder in providing the framework for weighing the evidence (e.g., describing issues in deriving inferences as to the reality of an event on the basis of symbolic interpretations of children's play).

A related, and increasingly common, use of expert testimony is to assist the factfinder in weighing children's testimony. For example, if a child recants an accusation of abusiveness but then makes the accusation again, can it be reasonably assumed that the child was lying initially? This sort of expert testimony might be very helpful to the factfinder in assessing the child's behavior, and there is in fact a rather substantial literature to consider that is probably unknown to most laypersons [cf. § 5.06(b)]. As long as the expert does not directly assess the credibility of the particular child, he or she would be unlikely to invade the province of the factfinder.

A troubling result of admission of expert testimony on the behavior of abused children is that it opens the door to, in effect, placing victims "on trial." Suppose that a child's behavior is *not* typical of maltreated children. Should the defense then be able to call an expert to describe the "typical" abused child; to call fact witnesses to establish that the alleged victim does not conform to this "syndrome;" and then to argue that the child obviously was not abused? We admit to a gut reaction against this practice. However, insofar as there is a scientific basis for the testimony, there is no logical reason to exclude testimony that may assist the factfinder in weighing other evidence, particularly when the additional testimony tends to exonerate the defendant. Regardless, given the lack of a unique set of characteristics of maltreated children and the probable availability of other, case-specific evidence for the prosecution, it is unlikely that such a defense-strategy would often be effective.

(b) Temporary Disposition and Review

Mental health professionals are most likely to be involved in child maltreatment cases at the dispositional phase and at the periodic reviews that are apt to follow.[119] At the initial dispositional hearing, the inquiry is typically a far-ranging assessment of the best interests of the child, analogous to disposition in delinquency cases [cf § 11.05(b)]. The principal questions usually involve means of ensuring the safety and welfare of the child and of rehabilitating the parents. Under some statutory schemes, there may also be specific findings required before a child found to be abused or neglected can be removed from the home.[120] At reviews, the general inquiry is likely to be similar to that at the initial dispo-

sition. However, there will often be additional questions of the degree to which the situation in the parents' home has improved,[121] the adequacy of services rendered thus far by the state,[122] and the adjustment of the child to the interventions under the initial plan [see Jones report, § 15.10].[123]

The major problem for the clinician in providing an evaluation for the court is that the major inquiry, especially at the initial dispositional hearing, is *predictive*. Given the unreliability of assessment of past and present abuse, the problems in evaluating the likelihood of future abuse are obvious. They are compounded by the generally poor record of intervention efforts and the gaps in knowledge about the effects of nontraditional interventions.

Mental health professionals involved in dispositional assessments can perhaps be of most use to the court as *investigators* and *informed speculators* [cf. § 1.04].[124] The former role may be obvious. The clinician is especially apt to be expert in asking the "right questions" so as to identify the precipitants of abuse, the particular needs of the family as a whole and as individuals, and the nature of relationships within the family. The role of speculator in this context may be less obvious, however. In the present state of the literature, mental health professionals can best help the court by speculating as to interventions that might meet the needs of the family. Research and theory on the causes of child maltreatment and the literature on treatment of families may provide some bases for speculation unavailable to the court itself. In providing such observations, however, clinicians should indicate their bases and should identify them as speculations. They should not go beyond the state of the art and the role of the expert to make predictions on whether a child would be safe under various dispositions, although presentation of actuarial data may assist the court in making its own determination as to whether removal of the child from the home is necessary [cf. § 7.10].

(c) Termination of Parental Rights

Although it sometimes arises at the initial dispositional phase,[125] the question of whether parental rights should be terminated will commonly arise, if at all, at a later hearing to review disposition. In some states, the question will automatically arise if the child has been in foster care for a particular period of time, although a more common procedure is to consider the question only if the state moves for termination.[126] Termination itself occurs in a single proceeding in most states, although the proceeding is bifurcated in some jurisdictions.[127] In the bifurcated procedure, there is an initial "factfinding" proceeding to determine whether particular threshold conditions (e.g., parental unfitness) exist. If the threshold questions are answered in the affirmative, there is a second "dispositional" hearing to consider whether termination of parental rights would be in the best interests of the child.

Termination of parental rights may be one of the most difficult decisions a court is required to make.[128] On the one hand, permanent severance of family ties is recognized as an especially grave step, perhaps even more severe than imprisonment.[129] On the other hand, authorities are increasingly mindful of the history of "legal abuse" of children by bouncing them among foster homes because the children are unavailable for adoption. Amidst this profound conflict, there is concern about the high risk of error, in view of both vagueness of standards and unreliability of assessment. This risk is compounded by the fact that mental health and social service evaluations are usually crucial evidence in termination proceedings. The deck is usually stacked against the parents in that regard, in that they will typically have substantially less access to these professionals than the state will have.[130]

In § 12.02, we have noted the common problems of vagueness of standards for abuse and neglect, and of reliance in the standards on individual value judgments as to proper childrearing practices. These problems are often compounded at the termination phase. Although some standards rely on relatively objective determinations of fact (e.g., whether the parents abandoned the child; whether the parents failed to maintain contact with the child or to comply with orders of the court after the child was placed in foster care), even in these instances termination typically is discretionary, based on the judge's

conclusion as to the child's best interests. More troublesome are statutes that permit termination if the parents are found to be "unfit," usually without further explication of the standard. Often these broad, value-laden grounds for termination are accompanied by an express or implicit presumption of unfitness on the part of parents who are mentally ill, mentally retarded, or dependent upon drugs or alcohol. Nebraska, for example, permits termination if "the parents are unfit because of debauchery, habitual use of intoxicating liquor or narcotic drugs, or repeated lewd and lascivious behavior, which conduct is found by the court to be seriously detrimental to the health, morals, or well-being of the juvenile.[131] Termination may also occur if "the parents are unable to discharge parental responsibilities because of mental illness or mental deficiency and there are reasonable grounds to believe that such condition will continue for a prolonged indefinite period."[132]

The model statute recommended by the National Council of Juvenile Court Judges also permits termination based on a broad inquiry leading to a finding that "the parent [is] unfit or that the conduct or condition of the parent is such as to render him/her unable to properly care for the child and that such conduct or condition is unlikely to change in the foreseeable future.[133] The model statute directs the court to consider a number of factors (e.g., parental mental disorder; "excessive use of intoxicating liquors or narcotic or dangerous drugs"; "conduct towards a child of a physically, emotionally or sexually cruel or abusive nature"), but it is given discretion as to the weight accorded these and any other relevant factors.[134] When the child has been in foster care, the court is also required to consider the child's relationship with the foster family and its suitability as a permanent home.[135]

Concern about the risk of error arising from such broad discretion had led to a trend toward more clearly limited inquiry. This limitation takes two forms. One approach is to move the focus somewhat away from the failings of the parents to the adequacy of the services offered, and procedures followed, by the state. It is increasingly common to require a showing of "reasonable"[136] or even "diligent"[137] efforts by the state to rehabilitate the parents.

A second approach, exemplified by the Juvenile Justice Standards, is to rely on relatively narrow and objective standards. The Standards would permit termination at the initial disposition only if the child has been abandoned[138]; or if the child has been previously removed because of maltreatment, then returned to the parent, and now requires removal again; or if another child in the family has been abused and the parent has received treatment thereafter.[139] At the review phase, termination would occur if the child has been in foster care for six months (if placed when under age three), or one year (if placed when over age three) and cannot be returned to the home.[140] However, ultimately even under the Standards, a more psychological (albeit limited) inquiry would take place because of exceptions to automatic termination. Termination would not occur in any of the following circumstances:

A. because of the closeness of the parent–child relationship, it would be detrimental to the child to terminate parental rights;
B. the child is placed with a relative who does not wish to adopt the child;
C. because of the nature of the child's problems, the child is placed in a residential treatment facility, and continuation of parental rights will not prevent finding the child a permanent family placement if the parents cannot resume custody when residential care is no longer needed;
D. the child cannot be placed permanently in a family environment and failure to terminate will not impair the child's opportunity for a permanent placement in a family setting;
E. a child over age ten objects to termination.[141]

If termination is ordered, the court would be directed to consider whether the foster home is suitable and whether "the child has substantial psychological ties to the foster parents."[142] If so, the child would remain in the foster home even if the foster parents are unable or unwilling to adopt the child. Unlike the Juvenile Court Judges' model statute, the Standards do not require consideration of this factor in the termination decision itself, except insofar as it arises in Paragraph D above.

Under the Standards, the involvement of mental health professionals in a termination proceeding would be similar to that in a temporary dispositional assessment, in that the key question would generally be whether the child could be safely returned home. There would be additional special evaluation questions relating to the intensity of the parent–child relationship (Paragraph A) and the adoptability of the child (Paragraphs C and D).

Under the Juvenile Court Judges' model statute and the statutes prevailing in most jurisdictions, the nature of questions likely to be posed to mental health professionals in a termination proceeding is also likely to be very similar to that in any dispositional review. The focus of the inquiry is likely to be slightly different, however, in that the prognosis for successful treatment of the parent is the key question. The mental health professional might also be asked to evaluate the adequacy of efforts to treat the parent and the nature of the child's relationship with the foster parents.

12.05. Mentally Ill, Mentally Retarded, and Substance-Abusing Parents

The various special provisions for termination of the parental rights of mentally disordered parents have been subject to considerable litigation in recent years.[143] There are two broad constitutional challenges to these provisions. First, it is argued that the statutes violate equal protection, because there is no compelling basis for discrimination on the basis of a parent's mental condition. Second, particularly when the statutes do not expressly require a finding that a parent's condition is directly and adversely related to his or her competence as a parent, there is a claim that due process is violated. Relatedly, there may be an argument that provisions for termination of the parental rights of mentally disordered parents are so vague as to violate due process.[144] Nonetheless, in recent cases considering termination of mentally disordered parents' parental rights, appellate courts have almost uniformly upheld the order to terminate.[145]

In the recent reported cases, the state has

generally taken at least some care to relate the parents' disorder to childrearing practices, and the results of the various cases may have been proper. However, the rationality of a lower threshold for termination of the parental rights of mentally disordered persons is questionable. Perhaps contrary to intuition, having a mentally disordered parent—even a very crazy parent— is in fact not very predictive of inadequate adjustment in the child. Although children of disordered parents are at relatively high risk for significant developmental problems, most develop normally.[146] Insofar as children of disordered parents are prone to disorders themselves, there is still a question of whether the developmental risk is a result of parental incompetence.[147] The state would have no interest in termination of parental rights unless a child's welfare would be substantially improved in another home.

(a)   Children of Mentally Ill Parents

It might be expected that the greatest risk would be incurred by children of schizophrenic parents. If parents are behaving in ways that are out of touch with reality and are unable to form relationships, it would be unsurprising to find that their children would suffer from the expereince of unpredictability, deviant social norms in the home (in contrast to school and neighborhood), and emotional distance in the family. In fact, there is now a rather substantial research literature indicating lower social competence, on the average, among children of schizophrenics than among children of normal parents. But their competence is no lower than that of children of parents with other mental disorders (e.g., depression), although one might expect these latter parents to provide a less deviant environment.[148] Of still greater policy significance, the differences between children of schizophrenics and children of normals tend to disappear when appropriate controls are added for social class.[149]

A qualifier to this conclusion is that the studies thus far have focused for the most part on early development, presumably under the hypothesis that a parent's schizophrenic disorder, and the accompanying affective shallowness, would

inhibit the development of an attachment between the parent and the child. However, it may be that the most significant effects occur later in development, when a deviant style of information processing in the family[150] might adversely affect a child's ability to deal with school tasks. On the other hand, the effects of a parent's affective disorder (e.g., major depression) might be most profound in early childhood, when the emotional availability of the parent is perhaps most important and the child learns basic emotional responses.[151]

Nonetheless, it still must be acknowledged that there is little empirical basis for special presumptions toward terminating the parental rights of psychotic parents. It should be remembered in that connection that few abusive and neglecting parents—perhaps 10%—are psychotic.[152]

(b)   Children of Mentally Retarded Parents

There is also weak empirical support for special provisions for terminating the parental rights of mentally retarded persons. It is important to note that most mentally retarded parents are *mildly* retarded and that mildly retarded people are typically capable of holding jobs and living independently under reasonably normal conditions.[153] Moreover, mild mental retardation is heavily related to social class[154]; a heightened review of parental competence of mildly retarded persons is in effect a heightened review of parental competence of lower-class persons. The risk of capriciousness in application of the policy is obvious.

Furthermore, the risks of substantial adverse effects on the children of retarded parents are in fact not that great. Although mildly retarded parents are more likely than nonretarded parents to bear retarded children, most retarded parents' children are not identified as retarded. The risk in such instances is only about 10%,[155] although it rises substantially if both parents are retarded *and* they have already had a retarded child.[156] If the child is mentally retarded, it is likely that he or she will be mildly retarded, and it is highly questionable whether this fact alone warrants state intervention. It is also unclear whether whatever heightened risk there is results from parental incompetence, apart from genetic factors and the effects of poverty.

(c) Children of Alcoholic Parents

There is virtually no literature from which to draw conclusions about the risks incurred by children of alcoholic parents. In a review of the literature in 1978, Jacob, (Favorini, Meisel, and Anderson) uncovered only 16 studies of children of alcoholics, and only one of these studies included appropriate comparison groups.[157] Most of the studies on the effects of alcoholic mothers on their children have looked at toxic effects of drinking during pregnancy, not the adequacy of childrearing.[158] The childrearing outcome literature that does exist gives reason for caution in assuming that alcoholism in a parent is often related to poor socialization of a child. In a comprehensive review of the literature, Vaillant concluded: "Perhaps for every child who becomes alcoholic in response to an alcoholic environment, another eschews alcohol in response to the same environment."[159]

(d) Conclusions

The available social science research gives great reason to question whether special provisions for terminating the parental rights of parents in clinical groups are legally permissible. Regardless, however, neither clinicians nor legal authorities should infer from a diagnosis that a parent is unfit. To guard against such inferences, clinicians should make clear in their reports and testimony that conclusions as to parental difficulties based on the presence of a mental disorder per se are at present scientifically unsupportable.

12.06. The Technique of Abuse/Neglect Evaluations

The most important point to be made about evaluation of child maltreatment prior to dispo-

sition, whether temporary or permanent, is that it should in fact focus on the parent's competence *as a parent* and on the relationship between the parent and the child (and, when relevant, the parent and the foster family). Conclusions as to adequacy as a parent should not be based on general mental status evaluations. In most cases, the child should also be interviewed, and, whenever possible, the child and the parent should be observed together [see § 15.10].

In addition to clinical interviews, there are a number of structured instruments for assessment of parental competence,[160] parental attitudes,[161] and family relationships.[162] These instruments may be very helpful in clinical evaluation, although the fact that most have not been validated for use in abuse/neglect dispositions should make clinicians cautious in interpreting observations drawn from them. There are also several instruments available for assessing "abuse potential," some of which have shown promise in correctly classifying abusive and non-abusive parents.[163] However, as Grisso has concluded, use of the latter instruments in forensic evaluation is premature and may be misleading:

> These measures are intended for use in social service agencies, in order to identify parents who may be in need of special counseling services. What is worrying some of us, though, is the possibility that examiners will begin to use the instruments as evidence of a parent's abusiveness in legal hearings on termination of custody. Now, we know that some of these instruments identify families in which abuse has occurred in the *past,* as well as families that need assistance. The thing to remember is that we have no evidence concerning whether these instruments detect *current* abuse or predict *future* child abuse. Yet this fact can get lost in zealous efforts to protect children, or in difficult legal cases in which objective information for decisionmaking is hard to come by and may be too quickly welcomed or inadequately scrutinized.[164]

A final point is that collecting records of a family's involvement with helping agencies is especially important in dispositional evaluations. At a dispositional review, the degree of improvement in the parents, the adjustment of the child, and the adequacy of services are typically all at issue, and agency records will usually be necessary to address these issues fully. At the initial diposition, knowledge of past treatment and its outcome is helpful in developing recommendations as to possible interventions and reaching conclusions about prognosis. Social service and police reports, in combination with interviews of the parent, may also be useful in identifying possible precipitants of maltreatment—information that is often helpful both for designing interventions and for determining prognosis.

Finally, we return to the cautions arising throughout § 12.03: Know what you don't know! The available research suggests some directions for exploration in clinical evaluation (e.g., adequacy of social supports), but it gives little reason for confidence in making predictions. Clinicians should be correspondingly careful in limiting their opinions in cases of child maltreatment, and lawyers should be equally careful in determining the foundation of these opinions and varying the weight given to them accordingly.

BIBLIOGRAPHY

CHILD SEXUAL ABUSE AND THE LAW (J. Bulkey ed. 1981)

J. GARBARINO & G. GILLIAM, UNDERSTANDING ABUSIVE FAMILIES (1980).

J. GOLDSTEIN, A. FREUD, & A. SOLNIT, BEFORE THE BEST INTERESTS OF THE CHILD (1979).

Rosenberg & Reppucci, *Child Abuse: A Review with Special Focus on an Ecological Approach in Rural Communities,* in RURAL PSYCHOLOGY (A. Childs & G. Melton eds. 1983).

THE SOCIAL CONTEXT OF CHILD ABUSE AND NEGLECT (L. Pelton ed. 1979).

Spinetta & Rigler, *The Child Abusing Parent: A Psychological Review,* 77 PSYCHOLOGICAL BULL. 296 (1972).

Wald, *State Intervention on Behalf of "Neglected Children: A Search for Realistic Standards,* 27 STAN. L. REV. 985 (1975).

Wald, *State Intervention on Behalf of "Neglected" Children: Standards for Removal of Children from their Homes, Monitoring the Status of Children in Foster Care, and Termination of Parental Rights,* 28 STAN. L. REV. 625 (1976).

CHAPTER THIRTEEN

Child Custody in Divorce

13.01. The Scope of Clinicians' Involvement in Custody Disputes

(a) Current Involvement

Disputes about child custody—the determination of who shall retain legal authority over a child when parents divorce—probably represent the legal context in which mental health professionals believe that they have the most to offer the courts. Although no studies have been conducted on this point, it would also be unsurprising to find that clinicians believe that divorce (given its seeming ubiquity in contemporary America[1]) is the problem about which the legal system is most likely to seek their expertise. After all, family dynamics are the stuff of which clinical work is often made,[2] and these dynamics surely are relevant to divorce decrees. It follows, some would argue, that clinicians are, and should be, frequently involved in resolution of custody disputes.

However, it is our contention that both of these assumptions are mistaken. First, at present, mental health professionals are directly involved in only a small fraction of custody cases in most jurisdictions. Most custody decisions— perhaps 90%— are made in bargaining between the divorcing spouses.[3] Even in those instances

in which cases make their way to trial, only a small proportion involve presentation of testimony or a report by a mental health professional. In one national sample of judges who hear such cases, 55% reported that such opinion evidence is presented in fewer than 10% of the custody cases they hear.[4] Only 25% said that such evidence is presented in the majority of contested custody cases in their courts, and none reported receiving such evidence in more than three-fourths of cases.[5] This lack of mental health involvement is perhaps less surprising when it is remembered that in most jurisdictions divorce cases, unlike cases of delinquency and child maltreatment, are not heard in separate juvenile or family courts where there is a strong tradition of mental health or social service involvement.[6]

Second, mental health professionals may have little expertise that is directly relevant to custody disputes. Thus, there are probably substantive as well as structural impediments to mental health involvement. It is noteworthy that almost half of the judges in the study mentioned above reported that clinicians' opinions in custody disputes were useful no more than occasionally— substantially less frequently than for other forensic issues.[7] Some of the considerations most relevant to determination of child's best interests in law (e.g., parental "responsibility" and moral guidance) are ones that are arguably well within the province of the factfinder and about which clinicians have no special expertise.[8] Moreover, there is virtually no scientific basis for provision of opinions about the kinds of questions that the courts must decide in divorce cases when children are involved. Although there has recently been a significant, albeit still very limited, expansion of knowledge about the effects of *divorce* on children [see § 13.03(a)], there has been virtually no research meeting minimal standards of methodological rigor about the effects of various *custody arrangements* on children and families of different characteristics. Even basic descriptive data (e.g., what "joint custody" usually means in reality; how stepfamilies work) are lacking, much less the sort of research from which one can draw casual conclusions. Furthermore, it may be impossible to generate such data at a level that would be very helpful in determination of best interests in individual cases [see § 13.02(f)].

Thus, the state of the literature does not promote confidence as to the validity of opinions about the dispositions that judges may consider in custody cases.[9] Indeed, there is probably no forensic question on which overreaching by mental health professionals has been so common and so egregious. Besides lacking scientific validity, such opinions have often been based on clinical data that are, on their face, irrelevant to the legal questions in dispute. As one distinguished commentator on forensic assessment has noted:

Custody cases involving divorced or divorcing parents rarely involve questions of parental fitness, but rather the choice between two parents, neither of whom are summarily inadequate as caretakers. Mental health professionals do not have reason to be proud of their performance in this area of forensic assessment. Too often we still evaluate the parent but not the child, a practice that makes no sense when the child's own, individual needs are the basis for the legal decision. Too often we continue to rely on assessment instruments and methods that were designed to address *clinical* questions, questions of psychiatric diagnosis, when clinical questions bear only secondarily upon the real issues in many child custody cases. Psychiatric interviews, Rorschachs, and MMPIs might have a role to play in child custody assessments. But these tools were *not* designed

to assess parents' relationships to children, nor to assess parents' childrearing attitudes and capacities, and *these* are often the central questions in child custody cases.[10]

Problems of clinicians' reaching beyond their expertise and data in custody disputes have become sufficiently visible and important that the American Psychological Association's ethics committee devoted two pages of its published summary of sanctions and cases in 1981–83 to such issues.[11] The committee noted that clinicians' involvement in custody disputes often raises questions related to Principle 1f of the Ethical Principles of Psychologists: "As practitioners, psychologists know that they bear a heavy social responsibility because their recommendations and professional actions may alter the lives of others. They are alert to personal, social, organizational, financial, or political situations and pressures that might lead to misuse of their influence."[12] The problem of managing these pressures is discussed later in this chapter [see § 13.04]. For now, however, it is important to note that the most basic ethical issue for clinicians involved in custody disputes may be one of monitoring the limits of competence and avoiding trespass across these limits. Although this issue is not unique in forensic practice to custody evaluation, it is rendered especially acute in that context because of the small body of relevant specialized knowledge and the complex interests and relationships typically involved in custody disputes. Both the superficial relevance of everyday clinical practice to custody disputes and the shifting boundaries and allegiances within families (and the resulting pulls on clinicians) may sometimes seduce mental health professionals into reaching unwarranted opinions.

(b) Some Possible Roles

(1) Evaluator

Although we have begun this discussion by expressing serious reservations about mental health professionals' present and potential involvement in custody disputes, we do not wish to imply that clinicians have no proper role at all. There are probably times when conventional clinical speculation about family dynamics will provide judges with some assistance (albeit limited) in making decisions about child custody. For example, although the opinions reached will probably have less scientific foundation than Professor Morse would require [see § 1.04],[13] clinical impressions as to alliances and conflicts within the family and their bases might present judges with a useful framework for consideration of which child goes where. Similarly, opinions as to present and past intensity of marital conflict and its sources may provide the factfinder with some basis for prediction of the probable success of various conditions of custody and visitation. Certainly, it is conceivable that research will develop that will provide a basis beyond mere speculation for links between pre- and postdivorce behavior.

However, at present, we find ourselves close to Morse's position in regard to the proper roles of clinicians in custody evaluations. That is, as in abuse and neglect cases [§ 12.04(b)], mental health professionals are primarily helpful as *investigators* in custody disputes, particularly if they perform a thorough, wide-ranging evaluation of the type we recommend in § 13.04. Analogous to Morse's observation about clinicians' having more experience than laypersons in interviewing mentally disordered people,[14] clinicians (at least those specialized in child or family practice) are trained in, and used to, talking with children and families under stress and gathering information from diverse sources about the life of the family. Therefore, child and family clinicians are likely to be efficient and effective gatherers of facts for the court, even when they are able to add few opinions based on specialized knowledge of the implications of the facts for custody dispositions.

Unfortunately, given present practice, the courts often do not obtain the significant amount of relevant information clinicians can provide. Although, as we shall see, the standards in most jurisdictions would seem to demand such extensive evidence, current procedures inhibit it. Because only the parents have "standing,"[15] any evidence that is not clearly helpful to the case of one of the divorcing spouses will probably not be presented, even though it might be very probative as to the child's best interests. Even if the court appoints a guardian *ad litem* to represent the child's interests, this development of evidence may not occur, in part because of the ambiguities attached to the role. In § 13.04(a), we suggest ways of overcoming these obstacles to the mental health professional's fulfilling an investigative role.

Mental health professionals (and other behavioral scientists) may also assist the court by pointing out what is not known about psychological factors in the effects of various custody arrangements. This honesty about the limits of knowledge serves dual purposes. It assists the factfinder in determing the degree of confidence to attach to any speculations about the import of psychological factors, and it deters the court from "psychologizing" what are really value preferences. A good example of the potential for such a role came in the Supreme Court's recent consideration of *Palmore v. Sidoti*.[16] The trial court, affirmed by the Florida Circuit Court, had transferred custody of a child from her mother to her father after her mother had married a black man. The lower court relied on psychological assumptions (i.e., the "inevitable" vulnerability to "peer pressures" and "social stigmatization") to justify its decision.[17] Although the Supreme Court ultimately rejected this argument unanimously,[18] evidence as to the *lack* of psychological authority for the Florida courts' assumptions might have served to focus attention from the start on the constitutional values at stake.

(2)   Mediator

Mental health professionals often may be useful as adjuncts to the negotiation process in clarifying points of agreement and disagreement. In performing custody evaluations, we have been struck by the number of times the spouses' disagreements—on which they are expending substantial energy and money—are objectively rather insignificant (e.g., a difference of one or two hours a week in how much time each parent has the children). In an emotionally charged atmosphere, the availability of a third party to mediate the dispute might facilitate settlement.[19]

There are two important caveats to be made

to this general point, however. First, when a clinician is employed as an *evaluator,* he or she should be careful not to slip into the role of *intervener* unless the parties or the court so requests. It is presumptuous of a clinician hired for the purpose of an evaluation to attempt to force a settlement, although the report might help to clarify topics for potential negotiation. Indeed, one or both attorneys might request an evaluation for just such a purpose. There are also potential ethical pitfalls when clinicians begin skirting— or crossing—the bounds of legal practice. Although mental health professionals may be sensitive to the emotional fallout of separation and divorce, they are more often than not ignorant of the property issues at stake. Analogous caveats are obviously applicable to lawyers who begin acting as therapists. Even for those mental health professionals who are also trained as lawyers, there are serious problems of dual practice and dual representation.[20] Also, despite calls of some commentators for mental health professionals to serve as compulsory *arbitrators*[21] in divorce cases, there is no reason to expect them to be especially skilled legal decisionmakers, whatever their prowess as evaluators.

Second, as a more general matter, the move toward compulsory mediation of divorce cases, already required by statute or court rule in some states,[22] is not justified by the data currently available. The conventional wisdom that adversary procedures heighten distress and acrimony is probably illustrative of the logical fallacy of casual inferences drawn from correlational observation; in this context, it may be that the degree to which disputes over custody persist is more closely related to the degree of pre-existing conflict than to the nature of the resolution procedure. The adversary process provides the forum for resolution of the dispute, but it is probably not the cause of the acrimony.[23] Indeed, any exacerbation of the conflict by the legal system that occurs is more likely the effect of *standards* for divorce and custody than of procedure. For example, there is some unsurprising evidence that requirements for establishing fault as a basis for marital dissolution result in greater acrimony between divorcing spouses.[24] In recognition of this fact, every state except South

Dakota has changed its statutes to permit no-fault divorce.[25] Similarly, changes in standards for determination of custody that seem to lower the risk of going to trial or that make custody an all-or-none decision[26] are likely to increase the degree of conflict over custody.[27]

There is in fact basis in social-psychological research and theory for assuming *positive* effects of adversary procedures.[28] Disputants generally feel more satisfaction in both the process itself and the outcome when they have been able to have their say in an adversary forum. Moreover, while mediation sometimes assists parties near settlement by providing an opportunity to save face,[29] it actually heightens conflict and increases the time and expense given to the dispute when there is a high level of pre-existing conflict.[30]

In that regard, despite the euphoria among the advocates of divorce mediation, it is important to note that the few evaluation studies showing positive effects of divorce mediation[31] have all involved couples who *voluntarily* chose mediation. Even at that, it is not clear what the import of these studies is, because of the wide variations in program auspices, program ideology and technique, staff characteristics, issues deemed appropriate for mediation, and the range of parties included (e.g., whether children themselves are included in the mediation). Long-term evaluations are also missing.[32]

Data from the best-designed evaluation study of mediation, conducted by Pearson at the Denver Custody Mediation Project, give particular reason for a "go-slow" policy on requirements for mediation. Although Pearson is a strong advocate of statutory authority for divorce mediation,[33] her data suggest that mediation may be harmful for a significant number of families. At the least, it unnecessarily increases the time and money spent by couples in many cases. About half of the initial sample of referrals of cases of contested custody were deemed inappropriate for mediation.[34] Of the remaining cases, Pearson indicated that about half declined mediation, "much to our surprise."[35] Of the remaining cases, only about half were successfully mediated (i.e., resulted in a settlement without premature termination of the mediation).[36] Those cases in which there was successful mediation tended to be ones in which one spouse (usually the husband) felt that the chances of winning custody at trial were slim.[37] Mediation rarely worked when couples were not on speaking terms or described themselves as unable to cooperate.[38] Moreover, contrary to claims by advocates of mediation, the method of dispute resolution was found on follow-up not to affect "the level, nature, or severity of the problems people commonly experienced with the court order."[39] In fact, couples who mediated were relatively *more* likely to seek to modify custody and visitation orders.[40]

In summary, mediation may assist couples who would reach settlement without it, but it is likely, at best, to delay resolution of high-conflict custody disputes. Therefore, beyond the ethical issues raised by mediation, it is important for lawyers and mental health professionals to try to avoid becoming involved in mediation except when couples desire the intervention of a third party to help them reach a settlement.

13.02. Standards for Resolution of Custody Disputes

Although sensitivity to the procedural issues in divorce is desirable, mental health professionals conducting custody evaluations need, of course, to be especially knowledgeable about the *standards* for determination of custody. The prevailing standard should define the scope of the evaluation. However, as we shall see, the most common standard gives clinicians—and, ultimately, the courts—little guidance.

(a) Historic Preferences

Until recently, there was rarely any real contest for custody of children following divorce. Until well into the 19th century, custody was routinely perceived as a concomitant of the power of the father; children, like wives, were in effect the father's chattels.[41] However, late in the 19th century, the predominant view began to be that the determining factor in a child's custody should be the child's own best interests.[42] With that change in perspective also came a presumption

that children of "tender years" are best served by remaining with their mothers.[43] Thus, although the best-interests standard is theoretically indeterminate,[44] in fact the question of custody was usually settled *a priori* by award of custody to the mother, unless the presumption of "tender years" could be rebutted by a showing of unfitness. When that event occurred, it was often *de facto* punishment for the mother's fault in the divorce (e.g., adultery) rather than a real concern with the mother–child relationship.[45]

The women's movement has ironically resulted in a weakening of the maternal preference. With new social and legal concern for the equality of the sexes, the trend has been toward rejection of the preference for either sex, on the basis of either a judicial theory of equal protection[46] or a clear statutory directive.[47] Although it is important to recognize that the presumption of "tender years" is still given great weight in some jurisdictions,[48] in general the trend is toward determining the best interests of the child by examining the relationship with both parents. Therefore, the room for clinical input has increased substantially in recent years.

(b) The Best-Interests Standard

Most jurisdictions now determine custody on the basis of the best interests of the child. The court is usually given some guidance as to the factors to be included in determining best interests, but the weight to be accorded them is left to judicial discretion. Thus, custody determinations will usually be reversed only if the judge refuses to consider a factor that the appellate court believes is, as a matter of law, a part of "best interests."[49] The calculus is necessarily idiosyncratic. Moreover, except for certain suspect classifications that are constitutionally or statutorily impermissible as bases for custody,[50] courts are free to weigh any factors that they believe are important in any particular case.

This indeterminate approach is illustrated by the model standard incorporated in the Uniform Marriage and Divorce Act, which has been adopted in many states[51]:

The court shall determine custody in accordance with the best interest of the child. The court shall consider all relevant factors including:

(1) the wishes of the child's parent or parents as to his custody;
(2) the wishes of the child as to his custodian;
(3) the interaction and interrelationship of the child with his parent or parents, his siblings, and any other person who may significantly affect the child's best interest;
(4) the child's adjustment to his home, school, and community; and
(5) the mental and physical health of all individuals involved.

The court shall not consider conduct of a proposed custodian that does not affect his relationship to the child.[52]

Just as the implicit elements of the best-interests test are almost infinite (i.e., "all relevant factors"), the desired outcome against which the factors must be weighed is also indeterminate. There is usually no clear guideline, for example, as to whether the best-interests standard is present- or future-oriented. Should the court be concerned with the child's immediate welfare, or the child's well-being 10 or 20 years from now?

More broadly, the best-interests test seems to demand no less than a judicial determination of the desirable traits of a citizen. This principle is graphically illustrated by the often-cited opinion of the Iowa Supreme Court in *Painter v. Bannister*.[53] Custody of seven-year-old Mark Bannister was awarded to the parents of his deceased mother instead of his father, who was described as an agnostic and a "political liberal" living in an unpainted house in northern California.[54] The court concluded that Mr. Bannister would provide Mark with an "unstable, unconventional, arty, Bohemian, and probably intellectually stimulating" home.[55] The grandparents were said to be church-going, "highly respected members of the community" who offered a "stable, dependable, conventional, middle-class middlewest [sic] background."[56] The court "unhesitatingly" believed the Painters' home to be more suitable for a child: "We believe security and stability in the home are more important than intellectual development in the proper development of a child."[57]

Cases rarely offer such dramatically different

potential households, and courts rarely are as forthcoming as to the values upon which they have relied. Nonetheless, the sort of situation presented by *Painter* is common. Custody determinations are easy only in those rare cases in which one and only one parent is obviously unfit, or one and only one parent is attached to the child.[58] More commonly, courts are faced with circumstances in which, whether because of divergent personalities, educations, or social and financial resources, each home is likely to nurture somewhat different traits in the child, but in which the ultimate well-being of the child is unlikely to be substantially different. The case is likely to turn, then, on the judge's own view of the most desirable traits and his or her prediction as to the parent more likely to socialize them. This decision is not necessarily arbitrary; the judge may be guided by a sense of the values of the community. Nonetheless, there is clearly an indeterminancy in the nature of "best interests" themselves, and clinicians performing custody evaluations should try to minimize the degree to which their own values about the "best" outcome shape their opinions. To some extent, however, the lack of statutory guidance makes such subjective influences inevitable; the clinician has little objective basis for determining what to examine in a custody evaluation. Recognizing this point, clinicians should report their assumptions about the factors and outcomes to be considered (as they shape the scope of the evaluation and the opinion resulting from it), as well as the uncertainties of their opinion.

It should also be clear that, despite the objective sound of the best-interests conclusion, it is in fact quite value-laden and unscientific. At least as much as in other legal tests, the ultimate-issue conclusion as to a child's best interests is a moral and legal question that should be preserved for the factfinder. A clinician should *never* reach a conclusion as to the parent who would better meet a child's interests.

(c) Changing Lifestyles and Changing Preferences

The flexibility of custody rules has not only been affected by the decline of gender-based preferences. The determination of custody and collateral issues (e.g., the amount, place, and other conditions of visitation) has been complicated by other changes in the nature and structure of American families.

(1)   Homosexuals' Rights

Perhaps the best-known of these issues is the question of the rights of homosexual parents. The developing rule in the majority of jurisdictions that have considered the question seems to be that homosexuality of a parent is not per se a bar to finding that visitation or even custody by that parent is in the best issue of the child.[59] Indeed, the parent's sexual preferences are irrelevant, except insofar as they affect the parent–child relationship or the child's well-being directly.

Nonetheless, even courts that have adopted such a rule have often been ambivalent about it; parents can be homosexual as long as they are not *too* homosexual. For example, a Virginia trial court[60] upheld joint custody[61] of a nine-year-old girl, when her homosexual father had been found to be "like a rock" who had sustained her during emotional crises. The court's ambivalence was derived from "the real kicker in the case"— that the father lived with his male lover. The court resolved its ambivalence by ordering the father not to share a bedroom with his lover while his daughter was in the house. Similarly, a Missouri appellate court[62] disregarded the testimony of "expert" psychologists (quotation marks are the court's) that a father's open homosexuality had no adverse effect on his 11-year-old son, who was said to be enuretic. The court upheld an order that barred overnight visits with the father, and the court also prohibited the father from taking his son to gay social gatherings and a gay church.

(2)   Grandparents' Rights

Less controversially, there has also been concern about preservation of extended-family supports, as the divorce rate and residential mobility have often fractured these ties. Senior-citizen groups have lobbied for recognition of grandparents' rights to visitation of their grandchildren. All but three states (Nebraska, Wyoming, and Vermont) and the District of Columbia now guarantee such rights,[63] and the United States House of Representatives has unanimously endorsed a resolution calling upon the National Conference of Commissioners on Uniform State Laws to adopt a Model Act on Grandparent Visitation.[64]

Some interesting legal issues have arisen as to whether the grandparents' rights are derived from the parents' rights. For example, if parental rights are terminated, is there collateral termination of grandparental rights?[65] Do grandparents have a right to visitation even if both parents object? An interesting example of the latter issue arose in California, where an appellate court directed married, objecting parents to permit visitation by grandparents, even though there was "continuing coldness and hostility" between the grandparents and the parents; the grandparents had undermined weaning and toilet training; and the grandparents had taken the child to physicians and dentists other than those whom the parents had selected.[66] Engaging in the common practice of literary excesses in family law opinions,[67] a dissenting judge said that his colleagues had made the child "a football in the game of life instead of a player."[68]

(d)   Joint Custody

The contemporary inquiry about child custody is not necessarily wide open. The difficulty in choosing between two fit parents has resulted in a movement toward a preference for joint custody.[69] In 1975, only one state, North Carolina, had a joint-custody law. Spurred by the enactment of a statutory preference in favor of joint custody in California in 1979,[70] today about 30 states have joint-custody statutes.[71] The more recent statutes tend to have stronger presumptions in favor of joint custody.[72]

Technically, "joint custody" refers to shared parental authority in law to make decisions on behalf of children. It does not necessarily include joint physical custody, and it is unclear how frequently such an arrangement in fact exists.[73] However, California has recently amended its law to define joint legal custody in terms of joint physical custody,[74] and it is clear that the proponents of joint custody expect there to be both shared legal authority and shared physical custody.[75]

Among those states with a strong legal preference for joint custody,[76] joint custody must be ordered unless the court finds that such an arrangement would be harmful to the child, presumably even if both parents object.[77] Even among states with weaker presumptions, the preference for parental cooperation is often expressed in a "friendly parent" rule that, if joint custody is not awarded, sole custody should be granted to the parent more likely to facilitate the noncustodial parent's involvement with the child.[78] As Scott and Derdeyn have pointed out, this rule is likely to diminish the probability of courts' hearing evidence suggesting that joint custody will be detrimental.[79] Parents may be reluctant to present evidence of continuing conflict or questionable fitness of the other parent, lest they be viewed as "unfriendly."[80]

(e) Least Detrimental Alternative

Another new rule, suggested by Goldstein, Freud, and Solnit[81] [discussed in more detail in § 12.0l(b)], has not been adopted in state statutes, but it has nonetheless been quite influential in the thinking of many judges, lawyers, and mental health professionals.[82] Although the scientific foundation for their argument is highly dubious,[83] Goldstein and colleagues emphasize what they believe is children's primary need for a seemingly omnipotent, omnipresent attachment figure.[84] Therefore, they advocate vesting total legal authority for a child in the "psychological parent."[85] The psychological parent would not only have physical custody and authority for medical and educational decisionmaking on behalf of the child, but would be able to regulate how much involvement, including visitation, the noncustodial parent is able to have in the life of the child.[86] When both parents are equal psychological parents[87]—a situation that is probably rather common in divorce—the couple would draw straws for custody.[88]

Under the theory that the state is ill-equipped to regulate the lives of children and that, in any event, *any* determination of custody is likely to have an untoward effect on the child,[89] Goldstein and colleagues call their proposed standard the "least detrimental alternative." However, the standard, if adopted, is likely to have substantial undesirable effects. For example, the all-or-nothing custody decision would probably result in more custody fights by parents who wish to avoid the possible loss even of visitation.[90] It also raises the possibility of the custodial parent's using the child as a marble in "visitation roulette" so as to punish or manipulate the noncustodial parent.[91] Because there is a presumption that the parent who has custody is the psychological parent,[92] the standard might also increase the incidence of parental kidnapping.[93] Nonetheless, Goldstein, Freud, and Solnit's treatises represent important authority for foes of joint custody. They may also serve as guideposts for judges in best-interests jurisdictions who seek to find "psychological parents," although it should be noted that multiple psychological parents may be the norm.

(f) The Multiplicity of Issues

A final point with respect to the standards for child custody is that, under every standard except the least detrimental alternative, there are actually numerous issues at stake in custody disputes beyond the award of custody per se. Even in joint custody, the allocation of physical custody may be subject to the discretion of the court, as may be the arrangements for financial support of the children. In more traditional, sole-custody arrangements, there is a seemingly infinite array of possibilities for amount and conditions of visitation. Moreover, the court may make other determinations (e.g., whether Johnny will go to summer camp; if so, who will pay, if they are in dispute. Finally, as Mnookin and Kornhauser have pointed out,[94] money issues may be inextricably intertwined with custody issues in divorce bargaining. For example, a father who values time with his children may not feel the need to fight a property settlement that is generous to his wife and may not resist her having custody, if visitation arrangements are liberal.

The broad range of potential dispositions in

custody disputes, particularly when a best-interests standard is employed, is important in the present context for two reasons. First, the breadth of possible dispositions suggests the need for a wide-ranging evaluation. Second, it creates inherent difficulty in ever generating an adequate research data base to be useful in charting specific dispositions in individual cases. The possibilities are simply too numerous to compare.

13.03.   What Do We Know?

(a)   Effects of Divorce on Children

Knowledge about the effects of divorce on children has increased substantially over the past several years, primarily as a result of data gathered in two longitudinal studies[95]: the Virginia Longitudinal Study of Divorce by Hetherington, Cox, and Cox,[96] and the California Children of Divorce Project by Wallerstein and Kelly.[97] Before discussing what has been learned from these projects, it is useful to indicate their limitations. Hetherington, Cox, and Cox conducted a carefully designed quasi-experimental[98] study of 72 white, middle-class four- and five-year-old children and their divorced parents (maternal custody in all cases) and a matched control group. Thus, although conclusions from the Virginia study can be drawn with some confidence, the population to which they are applicable is limited. The California project had some different limitations. The sample consisted of 60 white, middle-class divorcing families in northern California, including 131 children ranging in age from 3 to 18. The sample was recruited through an offer of counseling; hence, it was essentially a clinical sample, which might be expected to differ from a general sample of divorcing families in coping with marital breakup. There are also significant methodological problems with the California data. Wallerstein and Kelly often have not reported quantified data, and when they have, there have typically been no measures of interrater reliability.

The general findings of these studies have been aptly summarized by Thompson:

[T]hese investigations characterize divorce as a multistage process with multiple influences on family members. During the period immediately following the divorce, the family is in crisis, characterized by emotional turmoil in parents and children and impaired parent–child relationships. Most of these stresses were still evident one year following the divorce, with boys in mother-custody families displaying more acute difficulties in adjusting to divorce than girls. Following this, however, was a period of restabilization for the family and its individual members. Parents achieved greater personal stability and happiness, and this fostered improved interactions with their children. The children themselves also showed signs of growing adjustment to new family conditions, although persisting difficulties remained even at five years, especially for boys. Children's long-term divorce adjustment was a function of both their earlier success at coping and the growing stability and support of the home environment. But even long after the parents had separated, children and their families were still adjusting to the effects of this critical event on their lives. Divorce is, in short, a difficult transition for all concerned, and long-term outcomes vary considerably for parents and children.[99]

The crisis model suggested by the research must be qualified by the findings indicating that high conflict in *intact* families is even more deleterious for children than divorce.[100] Nonetheless, divorce obviously has a negative effect. Both studies indicate that during the first year after the divorce, conflict typically escalates as both parents deal with the depression and anger engendered by the divorce as well as the practical problems resulting from separate households.[101] The crisis for the children is particularly exacerbated if there is very high conflict between their parents.[102] In such cases, children are worse off when their parents remain in contact. In an average, less conflicted divorce, however, postdivorce adjustment (especially for boys) is apparently facilitated by frequent visitation by the father (assuming maternal custody).[103]

It should be remembered, however, that all of these conclusions are based on correlational data, and the causal links are not clear. For example, paternal visitation is presumably more likely to occur if there is cooperation between the spouses. Is the enhanced well-being of children who are frequently visited the result primarily of their access to their fathers or the relative lack of acrimony in their homes? Moreover, the data from the Virginia study and the California project give bases only for speculation as to what the result would be of judicial interventions to increase visitation or to require parental cooperation (e.g., through imposition of joint custody). They provide no direct evidence on this point.

The Virginia and California studies do offer four more reasons to be very cautious in drawing conclusions from custody evaluations. First, it was found that postdivorce relationships were largely unpredictable from predivorce behavior. For example, some fathers who had been largely uninvolved in child care prior to the divorce become "super-dads" afterwards. Others who were intensely attached to their children found the intermittent visitation relationship too painful and withdrew.[104] Second, long-term effects may be very different from those during the first months or even years following the divorce. For example, preschoolers were the age group most traumatized by separation and divorce, but ten years later they were only minimally affected by the experience.[105] Third, at the time of divorce, both parents and children are being seen at a time of acute and sometimes disorganizing stress. The general level of adjustment of parents and children, parent–child relationships, and parental skills are all likely to be atypical of usual functioning. Thus, the inference that can be drawn from behavior samples taken during a custody evaluation are limited. Fourth, although both the Virginia and the California studies were focused on parent–child relations, the glimpses they provided of extrafamilial influences suggest that the factors affecting the success or harm of a custody disposition are quite complex. The warmth of schoolteachers and the level of structure in the school day both affect postdivorce adjustment[106]—especially for children with "difficult" temperaments[107] and presumably for children who must move to a new school or neighborhood (or even shuttle between neighborhoods[108]) as a result of divorce. Similarly, the degree of economic downward mobility engendered by the divorce is likely to affect

the probability of success of various dispositions in supporting children's adjustment.[109]

In short, the available literature on the effects of divorce gives little basis for either policy or individual case dispositions, even for the narrow (white, middle-class, predominantly preschool) population that has been studied thus far. We do not mean to denigrate the available studies. They offer important initial descriptions that may assist clinicians in recognizing, preventing, and alleviating the deleterious effects of divorce. At the same time, though, it is important to recognize that this literature gives little help in decisionmaking about custody. Indeed, if anything, it suggests the pitfalls in making predictions from clinical assessments at the time of divorce.

(b) Father Custody

Given the limited literature available as to the aftermath of divorce under traditional arrangements (i.e., maternal custody with some parental visitation), it is hardly surprising that there is scant authority as to the effects of nontraditional dispositions. Thompson's summary of the available studies of father custody is instructive:

> Unfortunately, the research studies we have to draw upon in this area are scanty and somewhat qualified. First, with only one exception, all of these studies rely upon interviews with single fathers without direct observation of father–child interaction. Their portrayal of family life is thus inherently subjective and, quite likely, positively skewed. Second, the fathers who were interviewed included widowed and abandoned fathers as well as those who were divorced, although the large majority were the latter. Among the divorced group, most fathers received custody by mutual consent of both spouses, but some fought for custody in the courts. Thus the causes of the marital breakup and custody decision were varied, and this undoubtedly had an effect on subsequent family interaction. Third, nearly all of these studies report on single fathers who were interviewed long after making the adjustment to being the sole caregiver. Their descriptions of the transition were thus retrospective rather than direct, and it is sometimes difficult to know how they should be interpreted. Finally, these fa-

thers were contacted through informal, word-of-mouth sources, advertisements or, on occasion, single-parent support groups (such as Parents Without Partners), and thus probably reflect a select, highly motivated, and involved sample. This final concern over unrepresentative sampling may be excused, in part, due to the rarity of single fathers in most Western cultures.[110]

Beyond the methodological issues raised by Thompson, there is an additional question of whether findings derived from these studies of "pioneers" in father custody are informative as to the probable outcomes of father custody when it becomes more commonplace. In particular, father custody has heretofore been observed largely in cases in which there was allegedly maternal unfitness or at least fault for the divorce.[111] Some confidence in ultimate generalizability of the results can be based, though, on the finding (albeit in a single study) that custodial fathers, compared with noncustodial fathers, typically show similar gender-related behavior and have a history of a similar level of child care.[112]

With these several caveats, the evidence from the available studies of father custody as well as of father–child relations in intact families gives no reason for a general gender-based preference.[113] Fathers who become principal caretakers of their children are able to become competent in "maternal" caregiving while maintaining the sort of physical, rough-housing style of relating to children common among men.[114]

(c)   Same-Sex Custody

The only study that has compared observations of maternal-custody, paternal-custody, and two-parent, intact families (20 famiLes per group) indicates that the social development of children aged 6 to 11 proceeds more smoothly when children live with the same-sex parent.[115] Indeed, boys in single-father homes were found to be more socially competent than boys in intact families.[116] A conclusion that children will do better with the parent of the same sex is inappropriate, however, since this study, like most studies to

date, included only *single* parents. A general problem of both the research and the policy debate on various custody arrangements is that the possibility of remarriage is ignored.[117] The lack of a same-sex model would presumably be mitigated in a stepfamily.

In single-parent families, though, same-sex children would be likely to do better, both because of the availability of a model of gender-related behavior and the parent's own experience and comfort with the experience of growing up as a boy (for fathers) or a girl (for mothers). However, there are also important liaisons offered a child by the opposite-sex parent.[118] Moreover, a same-sex-parent preference would require separating brothers from sisters. The conventional wisdom is that, all things being equal, children adjust better when the sibling group remains intact, although there are no studies testing this assumption.

(d)   Joint Custody

There have been two excellent recent reviews of the literature on joint custody.[119] Both have concluded that the existing studies are "egregiously inadequate"[120] and that they provide "little direction for public policy."[121] None of the existing studies have examined the effects of judicially imposed joint custody,[122] and they give "little substantive basis for the hope that joint custody itself will reduce conflict between divorced parents."[123] Indeed, the studies of the effects of divorce raise the possibility that the requirement that couples in high conflict deal with each other on a regular basis (as may be the case when there is joint custody) will actually make life substantially more difficult for the children.[124] Such a conclusion is also consistent with basic social-psychological research that, contrary to what may be common belief, contact *alone* between individuals in high conflict (i.e., forcing them to communicate) rarely ameliorates conflict. Indeed, it may exacerbate it.[125]

One of the more extensive studies of joint custody was conducted by Steinman, who interviewed 24 mothers and fathers and their 32 children in joint custody in northern California.[126] As with the other studies on the topic, there are substantial methodological problems with this study. Notably, no control groups were included, so no firm conclusions can be drawn as to the effects of joint custody, as compared with sole custody. Also, the data were taken primarily from "semistructured clinical interviews" without standardization of the interview protocol or quantification of the interview material. Hence, Steinman's results consist primarily of subjective clinical impressions. Nonetheless, the study is important because the sample consisted of parents who were ideologically committed to joint custody and who indeed had chosen joint custody before the law in California permitted it. Also, Steinman excluded families from the sample if they did not have de facto joint custody— that is, a near 50–50 split in physical custody; shared decisionmaking; and a self-perception that the parents were equally significant to the children. Consistent with their beliefs, the parents had apparently put substantial effort into making joint custody work, and most ex-spouses lived within five miles of each other.

In this context, Steinman's study is important because a significant number of children reported some difficulty with the arrangement. About one-third of the children developed a "hyper-loyalty" to both parents and felt compelled to ensure fairness in relationships with them (e.g., through monitoring time spent with each parent to ensure equality). About one-fourth of the children, especially the preschoolers, expressed anxiety and confusion about the schedules for shifting from one home to another, and some of the school-age children indicated concern about being able to navigate the distance between the parents' houses. The two adolescent girls in the sample expressed some resentment of disruptions in relationships with friends and school-based activities. Even though most of the children had lived in joint custody for several years, most still harbored fantasies that joint custody would result ultimately in reconciliation of the parents. Thus, although the children in Steinman's study generally welcomed access to both parents, there were sufficient problems even in her highly motivated sample to lead her to conclude that "joint custody is not a simple solution. It requires considerable effort on the part of parents and children. Nor is it a solution that all parents or all children will find beneficial."[127]

As Clingempeel and Reppucci have persuasively shown, any real understanding of the desirability of joint custody requires a multivariate approach.[128] There needs to be attention to a multitude of variables and the interactions among them: parental characteristics and relationships; degree of similarity of home environments; child characteristics (e.g., age, gender, temperament); geographic proximity; sociodemographic variables (e.g., social class; ethnic background); school characteristics; informal social supports; presence of stepkin. Such specific variables as flexibility of school transportation arrangements and a child's preference for structure may be very important. At present, however, we lack even basic descriptive data about what joint legal custody typically means in practice or what types of joint-custody arrangements exist. The effects even of obvious variables (e.g., age) have yet to be systematically examined.

It should be noted that Clingempeel and Reppucci's criticisms apply to the custody literature generally. For example, only Wallerstein and Kelly's study has systematically explored the effects of a child's age on his or her reaction to divorce. Moreover, the need for a multivariate, ecological approach is clear in evaluating any of the various custody standards and in attempting to formulate individual dispositions under a best-interests standard.

(e) Special Populations

Clinicians may be especially likely to become involved in those cases in which there is an unusual circumstance that a court is apt to believe is unlikely to be illuminated by commonly shared knowledge of families. In view of the inadequacies of the literature we have discussed, it should come as no surprise that virtually nothing is known about the effects of custody dispositions or even divorce itself in families in such "special" circumstances. Indeed, the special circumstances need not be very unusual to justify such a statement. The existing literature is limited almost exclusively to white, middle-class families.[129]

The small range of evidence that does exist in this area is mixed. For some specific topics (e.g., visitation of parents in prison), the literature is virtually nil.[130] For some clinical populations (e.g., parents with serious mental disorders [see § 12.05]), though, there is at least some research on typical parental behavior and children's outcomes. These studies may be useful in determining the range of parental characteristics that are in fact related to success as a parent.

One special population on which there is some but not much research is homosexual parents. The few studies available suggest that children of homosexual single parents are no more likely to be significantly disturbed than children of heterosexual single parents,[131] and that their sex-role development, as measured by the nature of their play, is likely to be normal.[132] We are aware of no research that has examined the long-term consequences of being reared by a homosexual parent.

(f) Children's Participation in Decisionmaking

As noted in the discussion of the best-interests standard, the Uniform Marriage and Divorce Act considers the child's wishes as a determinant in best-interests analysis, but it does not indicate the weight to be given to the child's preference. Some states have provided statutory guidelines based on age, reasoning ability, or both.[133] Nebraska, for example, requires consideration of a child's wishes if he or she is at an "age of sufficient comprehension, regardless of chronological age, when desires are based on sound reasoning."[134]

Nonetheless, there is little research to guide evaluators or judges in determining a child's competence to participate in decisionmaking about divorce. The one study on this point[135] found that even elementary-school-age children gave adult-like reasons, in response to hypothetical situations, for preferring a particular custody arrangement. The rationality of the responses was

more highly related to the children's general cognitive competence than to their ages. The direct application of these results is limited somewhat by the fact that children whose parents were divorced or divorcing were removed from the sample.

There is no research directly testing the assumption by some commentators that querying children about their preferences is psychologically harmful because of the bind in which it places them.[136] There is, on the other hand, a general literature in social psychology, including developmental social psychology, indicating positive effects of being permitted to have some control over one's fate and of reducing ambiguity about a strange situation through direct discussion of it.[137] There is also no research on the effects of the procedure for involving a child (e.g., whether interviewing takes place in chambers; who does the interviewing).[138]

13.04. The Technique of Custody Evaluations

(a) Auspices: Who Is the Client?

Although in other contexts (e.g., criminal evaluations [see generally Chapter 3]), we have defended the practice of opposing parties' employing experts, we do not recommend this procedure in custody evaluations. First, it is the child's interests, not the parent/parties' interests, that are theoretically paramount; accordingly, some of the usual reasons for protecting the interests of the parties with standing do not so readily apply. That is, there may be substantial reason for the court to seek its own evidence as to the interests of a third party (i.e., the child); this is unusual in an adversary system where justice normally is served by giving each side the chance to put its best case forward. Second, as a practical matter, it is difficult to do a solid custody evaluation without access to both parents. Yet under a pure adversarial approach, the clinician may have no basis for rendering an opinion as to the effects of an award of custody to the parent not employing the clinician. Even if the clinician is asked to address only the effects of custody granted to the employing party, he or she is hampered by not hearing the other parent's side of things, because the family history and family process are likely to be perceived differently by each party. Accordingly, as a general rule, we suggest that clinicians seek to enter custody disputes as an expert for the court or the guardian *ad litem,*[139] although there may be some rare circumstances in which it is sufficient to have access to only one parent.[140]

A clinician who already has an ongoing relationship with one or both of the spouses should be especially careful to avoid giving opinions without adequate foundation. In particular, there is often a temptation when an adult client is involved in a custody dispute to act to protect the client. After all, if the client is heavily invested in being a parent, then an adverse ruling will be likely to take a substantial psychological toll. Even when a clinician is treating both parents, as in marriage counseling, there may be pulls to take sides.[141] One parent may feed information damaging to the other. Obviously, the clinician must take care to keep the roles of therapist and evaluator separate. There are similar issues when a clinician hired as a mediator begins to act like an evaluator. Opinions as to parental competence or parent–child relationships should never be given unless there has been specific focus on these topics. Generally, an interview with the child, or with the parent and child together, or both kinds of interviews will be necessary if there is to be any substantial basis for an opinion on custody issues.

(b)   Application of the Clinician–Patient Privilege

There are other pitfalls in moving from the role of therapist to that of evaluator (even if the clinician does so unwillingly under subpoena). The applicability of psychotherapist privilege[142] in custody cases is unclear and is highly variable across jurisdictions.[143] Can one spouse waive privilege for both when they have been jointly involved in marriage counseling?[144] Can a child assert (or waive) privilege?[145] Or can privilege

be claimed at all in custody disputes?[146] These issues are unsettled, but the therapist should be aware that material from family, child, or marital treatment may not be privileged in a custody case, even in jurisdictions recognizing a psychotherapist privilege and even when at least one person involved in the treatment objects to the admission of evidence based on it. Clinicians involved in marital or family therapy should seek legal advice as to the limits of privilege in their jurisdiction.

(c)   Scope of the Evaluation

In view of both the breadth of the best-interests concept and the multiplicity of factors potentially affecting the outcome of various custody and visitation arrangements, a child custody evaluation can be best summarized as *comprehensive* [see, e.g., the Jensen report, § 15.11]. Parents, stepparents, and children should all be interviewed as to their perceptions of relationships in the family (past, present, and future), their preferences to custody, and any special needs of the children. Because of the significance of interparental conflict in the literature on effects of divorce, special attention should be given to the parents' capacity for cooperation, the nature and intensity of disagreements about the children, and points of possible compromise. As discussed in connection with abuse/neglect evaluations [see § 12.06], structured instruments to assess parent–child relations and parental skills may also be useful.

The evaluation should not stop with interviews of the immediate family. Contact with teachers and extended family can illuminate potential sources of support (or the lack thereof) under various custody arrangements (e.g., switching between parental homes). Sources outside the nuclear family may also give important, relatively objective glimpses of children's responses to arrangements developed during separations and under temporary custody orders. In that regard, the existing and previous custody arrangements can be conceptualized as natural experiments of a sort. The clinician should be sure to elicit information as to the parties' attitudes and behavioral responses to those arrangements.

However, even these directly relevant data may have limited usefulness in predicting children's long-term responses to custody dispositions. The California and Virginia studies have made it clear that these responses shift substantially over time. We return in conclusion, then, to the point we have made throughout this chapter: Careful attention must be paid to the limits of expertise in custody evaluations.

BIBLIOGRAPHY

Clingempeel & Reppucci, *Joint Custody after Divorce: Major Issues and Goals for Research,* 92 PSYCHOLOGICAL BULL. 102 (1982).

Derdeyn, *Child Custody Consultation,* 45 AM. J. ORTHOPSYCHIATRY 791 (1975).

Hetherington, *Divorce: A Child's Perspective,* 34 AM. PSYCHOLOGIST 851 (1979)

Koch & Lowery, *Evaluation of Mediation as an Alternative to Divorce Litigation,* 15 PROF. PSYCHOLOGY: RESEARCH PRAC. 109 (1984).

Melton & Lind, *Procedural Justice in Family Court: Does the Adversary Model Make Sense?,* in LEGAL REFORMS AFFECTING CHILD AND YOUTH SERVICES (G. Melton ed. 1982).

Mnookin & Kornhauser, *Bargaining in the Shadow of the Law: The Case of Divorce,* 88 YALE L.J. 950 (1979).

THE PSYCHOLOGIST AND CHILD CUSTODY DETERMINATION: ROLES, KNOWLEDGE, AND EXPERTISE (L. Weithorn ed. in press).

Scott & Derdeyn, *Rethinking Joint Custody,* 45 OHIO ST. L.J. 455 (1984).

Thompson, *The Father's Case in Child Custody Disputes: The Contributions of Psychological Research,* FATHERHOOD AND FAMILY POLICY (M. Lamb ed. 1983).

J. WALLERSTEIN & J. KELLY, SURVIVING THE BREAKUP: HOW CHILDREN AND PARENTS COPE WITH DIVORCE (1980).

PART V

Communicating with the Courts

CHAPTER FOURTEEN

Consultation, Report Writing, and Expert Testimony

14.01. Introduction

The use of reports and testimony by medical and mental health expert witnesses dates back over a century,[1] and there is every indication of increased use of mental health expertise in future litigation. Some contemporary observers, however, appraise the involvement of mental health professionals in the courtroom with cynicism and doubt. One judge has labeled psychiatry the "ultimate wizardry,"[2] and attorneys often view mental health professionals as "fuzzy apologists for criminals."[3] Both the integrity of expert witnesses[4] and the adequacy of their scientific data base for addressing certain kinds of legal questions[5] have been questioned by legal and lay observers alike. In Chapter 1, we have discussed some of the differences in assumptions, philosophy, and practice that result in inevitable difficulties in the alliance between the law and mental health professionals. Not infrequently, the caustic barbs cast at the mental health professionals individually or collectively are in response to communications by clinicians—usually in the form of "expert" testimony—that fail to respect the legitimate differences between the legal and social science professions. These *mis*communications may result from several factors, including ignorance on the part of clinicians, poor preparation prior to their appearing in court, and the enticement of the role of "expert," which may lead mental health professionals to feel that they must appear authoritative on any subjects that the lawyer may introduce.

In order for communications, both written and oral, to be presented clearly, careful preparation is required. The preceding 13 chapters have been designed to provide the minimal substantive knowledge in specific legal areas to permit well-trained clinicians to bring their professional skills to bear on questions of interest to the law. Substantive knowledge alone, however, is not enough. The information must be organized and presented in such a manner as to be useful to legal consumers (lawyers, judges, jurors), and witnesses must be prepared to endure the sometimes harsh scrutiny that the adversary process demands. Thus, in addition to having substantive knowledge, the forensic clinician needs to develop skills in consultation, forensic report writing, and delivery of oral testimony.

In this chapter, we explore the formal and informal communications between the clinician and agents of the court. The section immediately following deals with initial consultation between the clinician and the lawyer (or court) who retains him or her. The next section gives suggestions for the preparation of written reports. The final two sections deal with various aspects of testimony in court.

14.02. Preliminary Consultation

Ideally, the groundwork for a forensic evaluation, report, or testimony is laid through a series of consultations between the clinician and the attorney (or court) responsible for the referral. The preliminary consultation consists of the initial contact and a subsequent verbal report of evaluation findings.

(a) Initial Contact

The initial contact with the attorney or the court is the most important one. The primary tasks at this stage are clarification of issues and sharing of information.

(1) Clarification of Issues

When the initial referral is made requesting a forensic evaluation, the clinician should verify the legal issues to be addressed. A brief, informal call from a court clerk may be followed by a written court order for evaluation that is unclear. Courts may get in the habit of using dated order forms that are overly restrictive or vague in light of what the referring judge intends; amended orders may need to be requested. When the referral is from a private attorney, a similar clarification should be attempted. Brodsky and Poythress have noted:

> The first task is to insure that the attorney's expectations and the expert's knowledge and plans to testify are congruent. As elementary as it may seem to do so, attorneys do not always tell the mental health professional in clear terms the focus of the examination and testimony to be provided. Attorneys may confuse the different legal issues, or they may mistakenly assume that one examination will suffice for a variety of purposes.[6]

All intended uses of the examiner's report should be determined so that the clinician knows what issues to probe during the examination, and so that a proper notification can be given to the examinee. As discussed in Chapter 3, there may be legal or ethical barriers to the admissibility of clinical information gathered in a forensic evaluation if the proper notification to the individual was not provided. Additionally, referrals to state forensic facilities often have hidden agendas, about which the examiner may remain ignorant without consultation. For example, as discussed in § 4.03(c), an examination of competency to stand trial may actually be requested because (1) the sheriff wants to reduce overcrowding in the jail; (2) the defendant is considered a suicide risk and civil commitment is being sought; (3) the defendant has medical problems for which the county does not wish to pay; or (4) the attorney is using the referral as a tactical delay. Careful clarification of the bases for the referral may save time later in the evaluation process.

The clinician should also clarify for the attorney the limits of his or her knowledge and expertise on the referral questions. Legal professionals may approach mental health professionals with mistaken assumptions about what is possible in a clinical evaluation. The clinician should indicate the limits of assessment or prediction as appropriate [see, e.g., § 7.10] and should discuss the possible range of outcomes from an assessment procedure.

Clinicians should also indicate their posture with respect to testifying on ultimate legal issues. Attorneys will probably expect, based on prior experience, that clinicians will readily offer opinions or conclusions within the full scope permitted by the rules of evidence [see Table 1-1]. Clinicians who intend (as we encourage in § 14.05) to deviate from this traditional posture should so advise lawyers, who can then decide whether to make another referral.

(2) Sharing of Information

At the initial contact, most of the information will be in the attorney's possession. What current behavior or background information has prompted the referral? What legal theory is the attorney trying to pursue through mental health consultation? What prior records have been obtained or requested through the attorney's office? Where is the client residing, and what special arrangements, if any, must be made for the clinical evaluation? What time constraints, if any, exist? Is a written report requested regardless of the outcome, or only if the clinical data are favorable to the attorney's case?

At this stage, the clinician may put the attorney to work requesting or gathering information that will later be needed for the evaluation, but to which the clinician may have restricted access. The attorney, as the legal representative of the client, may gather records of prior hospitalization or treatment, records of performance in school or in employment settings, or information from other institutions where the client has served (e.g., military, correctional). Letters from the attorney to individuals or institutions may include signed release forms granting the clinician access to otherwise confidential information. Clinicians should also suggest potentially useful information available through discovery, subpoena, or private investigation. If there initially appear to be time constraints for the examination, the clinician should suggest that the attorney request a continuance so that a proper evaluation can be completed.

It is also prudent at this point to discuss various practical issues, such as the clinician's availability in light of existing court schedules, and manner of payment. Anecdotal reports from colleagues in private forensic practice lead us to recommend that private clinicians request a moderate retainer fee in advance of the evaluation. Clinicians should also consider offering a sliding-scale fee structure, which permits the less wealthy client access to good forensic evaluation services.

(b) Preliminary Report of Findings

When the assessment has been completed, the examiner should contact the attorney and give an oral summary of the findings. The focus will be on the agreed-upon referral questions, but discussion may lead to alternative uses of the clinical findings if the initial legal strategies are not supported. Following this oral report and discussion, the attorney should decide whether or not a written report is needed. In situations where the referral originated with the court, it is more commonly the practice that a written report is prepared without preliminary oral communication of the findings.

It is not uncommon that the clinical evaluation will result in findings that are useful in strategies other than those originally considered. An evaluation of competency to stand trial [see Chapter 4] may reveal that the individual has a chronic mental impairment that may have affected the capacity to competently waive *Miranda* warnings in giving a confession [see Chapter 5]. A clinician in a divorce/custody case may find that both partners are amenable to a mediated settlement, which would be less costly, both emotionally and financially, than proceeding to an adversary hearing [see § 13.01 (b)(2)]. Where alternative uses of the data appear viable, the clinician should work through the individual(s)' attorneys to insure that the proper notifications and waivers are obtained. If the individual examinee(s) will agree to the alternative uses of the clinical findings, the clinical formulations may then be revised to address the new legal issues.

Clinicians may also be able to give feedback that will assist attorneys in working more effectively with their clients. This is particularly true when clients appear somewhat mentally disordered; attorneys may not be accustomed to working with such individuals and may feel frightened or uncomfortable around them. In appropriate cases, clinicians may offer assurances that the clients are not as aggressive or volatile as the attorneys fear, and they may offer specific recommendations for communicating more effectively with certain kinds of clients. For example, clients with manic symptoms such as elated affect and pressured speech can be extremely difficult to interview, due to rapid speech, poor transitions between topics, and excessive emotionality and movement that may be intimidating. When such symptoms are not extreme, the individuals can often be interviewed more successfully if the attorneys impose structure on the interviews (e.g., ask brief, focused questions) and are not fearful that the clients' outbursts will get "out of control." Similarly, in cases where intellectual impairment is mild, but perhaps not obvious, clinicians can recommend the use of closed questions and simplistic language or the use of metaphor (e.g., "The judge is like a referee or an umpire") to facilitate communication with the client about the case. Clinicians can also offer advice about the appropriate precautionary measures to be taken for recurring disturbances, such as epileptic seizures, and can warn attorneys or the court of the probable extent of trial delay should a seizure occur. Examiners may also comment on interactions between individuals and their social–legal environment (e.g., their relationships to family members, to the court, or to jail personnel) and suggest ways to improve such persons' coping skills while awaiting the resolution of their cases.

Following a preliminary oral report and discussion of evaluation findings, the attorney will determine which legal strategies to pursue and whether a written report and/or testimony will be needed. If there does appear to be a further need for the clinician's involvement, the next task is the preparation of a written report.

14.03.   Report Writing

Virtually all cases taken on referral from a court, and most cases on referral from private attorneys, will result in the preparation of written reports. Reports of forensic evaluations differ in a number of important ways from reports prepared for use in traditional clinical settings. The persons receiving and using the report will not be colleagues from the mental health professions, but legal personnel and laypersons not familiar with the clinical shortcuts in report writing that clinicians often use; thus, jargon should be kept to a minimum. The substance of the report may become public knowledge through being made part of a court record, through word-of-mouth statements of courtroom spectators, or through media coverage of court proceedings. Thus, special care must be taken to minimize any infringement on the privacy rights of persons mentioned in the report. The report and the clinician who writes it may become the subjects of unusually close scrutiny through the adversary proceedings. Therefore, attention to detail and to the accuracy of information is required.

A well-written report may suffice in many cases in which an appearance for court testimony might otherwise be required. A poorly written report may become, in the hands of a skillful lawyer, an instrument used to discredit and embarrass the mental health professional who has written it. Thus, the points made above require expansion and elucidation.

(a)   Functions of a Forensic Report

The written report serves several important functions. It is, first of all, a professional record documenting that an evaluation has taken place. The nature of the evaluation and the extent of professional contacts with the client are documented through a summary of the contacts, investigative methods, and referrals to other professionals. Findings, and limitations in the clinical data, are preserved through the preparation of the report.

The act of creating the report serves a second function: It forces the clinician to impose some organization on his or her data. Data may be gathered from widely diverse sources for integration into a "best" formulation related to complex legal issues. The examiner must weigh and consider the data, looking for a coherent theme that best integrates the various findings, and must develop that theme for the legal consumer. Inconsistencies or contradictions will be noted in the course of organizing the data; these will force the examiner to consider alternatives and will warn of points vulnerable to cross-examination. In organizing data and thoughts for the report, the mental health professional covertly prepares and rehearses the essence of any direct testimony.

In many cases, the written report alone will function to allow disposition or adjudication. A well-written, articulate report may satisfy both parties in litigation, to the degree that stipulations to the written findings and conclusions are entered. Finally, the report may be used as a basis for informal negotiations, as in plea bargaining or out-of-court settlements.

(b)   General Guidelines for Report Writing

Though preparation of the forensic report is a very important issue, a review of the recent psycholegal literature reveals relatively few papers specifically devoted to this topic.[7] This may be due in part to the fact that there are no hard and fast rules for writing forensic reports, and to the fact that substance and organization may vary, depending on the type of referral. However, several general guidelines appear applicable across many contexts and are offered here for consideration by the reader.

(1)   Separate Facts/Observations from Inferences/Conclusions

Factual information and descriptive material based on clinical observations should be presented separately from the theoretical formulations that link the clinical data to the legal referral question. The factual/observational material should be presented first; the inferential or conclusory material should be presented later in the report. This organization allows the clinician to "build" a case, organizing the investigative data in a manner that invites the reader to reason along with the author. If the judge or jury wishes to independently consider and assimilate the examiner's data, this segregation of data from inferences also facilitates their effort.

It is difficult to develop a generic report format suitable for use in all forensic evaluations, because the kinds of evaluations themselves are so different. We have nevertheless attempted to identify certain items of information that we think should be included in most forensic reports, and the following list may be useful in imposing organization on the data.

1. *Date and nature of clinical contacts.* This section would list chronologically the examiner's contacts with the person and describe the na-

ture of the contact (e.g., interview, psychological testing, family observation, etc.).
2. *Data relied upon.* In this section, the clinician would identify sources of information other than the individual who was examined (e.g., third-party interviews; written material such as academic, medical, or employment records; etc.).
3. *Circumstances of the referral.* Here the clinician would identify the referral source, legal issues addressed, and the circumstances leading to the clinical evaluation (e.g., a description of ongoing litigation in custody/divorce or criminal proceedings).
4. *Relevant personal background information.* Historical information about the client relevant to the clinical formulation would be stated here. This section might be extensive in some kinds of cases (e.g., a lengthy history of illness and treatment in a disability case), and extremely brief in others (e.g., an evaluation of competency to stand trial).
5. *Present clinical findings.* This section would summarize the clinician's own observations, test results, and so forth. Observations about present mental functioning, or, where appropriate, statements of diagnosis, would be included here.
6. *Psychological–legal formulation.* In this section, the examiner would draw on information reported in the previous sections and integrate the data, using a logical or theoretical theme to indicate the possible relevance of the clinical material to the legal issue being decided.

Chapter 15 presents model reports based on several different types of forensic evaluations. These reports reflect variations in the use of this general format, based on the type of evaluation conducted. They also illustrate appropriate content for reports addressing particular issues.

It should be noted that some sections of the report may, on occasion, include two or more summaries. Situations that would warrant this include (1) reports based on evaluations by a team (rather than an individual examiner), in which two or more team members have significantly different views about the data or the meaning of the data; and (2) evaluations in which there is conflicting factual information, such that assuming one set of facts leads to one formulation, while assuming a different set of facts leads to a different one. In these situations, the reports should carefully spell out the data and assumptions associated with each of the formulations or opinions presented. Where appropriate, the examiner(s) may also address the level of confidence associated with one formulation or the other. Generally, clinicians should avoid becoming embroiled in the controversy over which of two or more factual situations is the "real" one; they should leave that to the trier of fact to decide.

(2) Stay within the Scope of the Referral Question

As noted in Chapter 3, a referral for forensic evaluation is not a license to do as one will with the client. Clinicians privately retained by counsel may have somewhat greater latitude in their examinations than mental health professionals working for the court, where a court order may specify limits of inquiry. In either case, however, examiners should limit themselves to inquiries legitimately raised by the referral source and should limit the substance of their reports accordingly.

As obvious as this recommendation may seem, mental health professionals occasionally err by either (1) failing to address issues that have been raised in the referral, or (2) offering gratuitous opinions on issues that have not been raised. McGarry's study of competency evaluations in Massachusetts documented the first type of error.[8] Of 130 reports audited, none spoke to the issue of the defendant's competency to stand trial, which was an explicit referral question in the court orders. We have anecdotally observed the second type of error. To provide just one example, a defendant was referred to a psychiatrist for evaluation of his mental state at the time of a crime. The following paraphrase fairly reproduces the examiner's written summary:

> It does not appear that Mr. S. was suffering from any psychosis at the time of the assault. He may have been under the influence of various drugs and alcoholic beverages, which he reported consuming at that time. There is no

clinical basis for an insanity defense here. Mr. S. is one of the most dangerous persons I have ever examined; the only appropriate disposition would be a lengthy prison sentence.

Here the psychiatrist went beyond the referral question and made uninvited statements about disposition and sentencing. With these damning statements appended, it is unlikely that the defendant's attorney would have felt comfortable about submitting the report to the court, even though parts of it (e.g., the defendant's drug history) would have been relevant in weighing culpability.

(3) Avoid Information Overkill

In preparing a written report, the clinician must make some decisions about the volume of information to be included. Any written report will be a distillation of essential material from a larger body of data. There are two schools of thought about this issue of data reduction, and both have their costs and benefits. Individual preferences may dictate which philosophy a clinician will follow.

At one extreme are those who advocate very brief reports. These reports tend to be disproportionately conclusory in nature, with extensive data and justification being excluded by design. The objective is to provide as little ammunition as possible for the cross-examining attorney. At the other extreme are those who encourage lengthy, overly detailed reports. Such reports "cover all bases" and usually leave the clinician an "out" from a tight situation in testimony. The problem with very lengthy reports is that they may not be read, or, if read, may not be understood.[9] The longer reports may include irrelevant detail, redundancies, or excessive equivocations, which may convey to the reader the impression of uncertainty or lack of self-confidence in the examiner.

For the written report to be useful, it should be brief enough that the attorney, judge, or juror is not intimidated by the mere magnitude of the document. However, we feel that *relevance* to the factfinder, and not tactical considerations (such as minimizing information to be scrutinized for cross-examination), should guide the clinician in condensing the data. Extraneous social history data or overly technical accounts of formal testing results, or reference to dated and perhaps marginally relevant records of prior medical or psychiatric involvement, may be excluded (or at least deemphasized). Findings essential to the clinical formulations advanced, including most of the rich descriptive material and the inferences drawn, should be included. Consultation with the attorney may help the clinician determine which, and how much, information needs to be included in the written report. The clinician is obliged to make known all sources of data and to present a balanced account of the evaluation, but the attorney may assist in selecting the anecdotal or historical material that is most important in light of the legal arguments being pursued.

(4)   Minimize Clinical Jargon

In the clinical setting, mental health professionals' reports are replete with clinical jargon. A client who knows his or her own identity and the date and place of the interview is "oriented times three"; a client who tenaciously holds to obviously mistaken beliefs, even in the face of good evidence to the contrary, is said to exhibit "delusional thinking."

As useful as this shorthand may be in the clinical setting, it may be confusing to the legal consumer. Many terms that appear unexplained in written reports will be unclear to the judge or jury member, or lay meanings will be attached to terms that have a quite different meaning in the clinical context (e.g., "paranoid" or "ego"). Petrella and Poythress[10] conducted a study in which legal experts (judges and lawyers) were asked to review reports prepared by experienced forensic clinicians; one of the experts' tasks was to identify words or phrases whose meaning was unclear. The following items of clinical jargon were identified:

1. "delusional ideation"
2. "affect"
3. "neologisms"
4. "loosening of associations"
5. "flight of ideas"
6. "blocking"
7. "his paranoid ideation is non-specific, completely unsystematized"
8. "oriented to time, place, and person"
9. "lability"
10. "loose associations and tangentiality"
11. "flat affect"
12. "grandiosity"
13. "personality deficit"
14. "hysterical amnesia"
15. " 'lack of registration' amnesia"
16. "psychotic mentation"

Though clinical jargon can be problematic, it also has its merits. In addition to serving as a convenient shorthand, it also helps to establish that the clinician is dealing with a special body of knowledge. Psychological terms and constructs may be useful in developing and explaining theoretical formulations of the type that would not be obvious to the trier of fact. However, in order to be used effectively—that is, in a way that they can be understood—the terms must be *explained*. Once explained, the terms also acquire their "shorthand" function for the new audience.

Clinicians should therefore be sensitive to their use of clinical jargon in report writing and should take care to explain such terms when they are first used. The explanations need not be elaborate, but some effort to translate from clinical terms to conventional language should be made. For example, a clinician might use such terms as "delusions" and "hallucinations" in the following manner: "During the clinical interview Mr. Jones voiced several delusional beliefs (i.e., strongly held but bizarre and obviously mistaken beliefs) and reported a history of auditory hallucinations (i.e., hearing imaginary voices)." The sample reports in Chapter 15 offer additional examples of explaining jargon in written reports.

We encourage clinicians to develop their own jargon–conventional-language dictionaries (mental, if not written) to assist them in explaining jargon used in forensic reports. Chapter 16's glossary of clinical and research terms [see § 16.02] may be of some aid in this regard, as well as of assistance to lawyers attempting to decipher "clinicalese."

Reports that explain the meaning of psychological terminology convey the message that the clinician is an expert in a specialized field of study without creating the problems associated with the use of unexplained jargon.[11]

14.04.   Expert Testimony: General Issues

For many mental health professionals, notification that testimony in court is required arouses considerable anxiety. Whether the anxiety is based in personal experience or in the anecdotal tales of colleagues who have been embarrassed by clever attorneys, many clinicians look forward to appearing in court with great trepidation.

There are legitimate causes for clinician's anticipatory anxiety. Nowhere are the differences in training, philosophy, and objectives between lawyers and mental health professionals more clearly on display than in an adversarial proceeding. The clinician as scientist–practitioner is accustomed to the pursuit of truth through dispassionate examination of data; the attorneys on *both* sides are committed primarily to persuasion, and the "truth" as the clinician sees it is but one more piece of information subject to manipulation in service of the greater goal of achieving the desired verdict. As such, clinicians for each side may be selected more on the basis of personality and charisma than on professional expertise; opposing witnesses whose clinical findings do not support the desired verdict become fair game for critical and occasionally vicious cross-examination, which attempts to discredit their findings, their professions, or them as individuals.

In spite of the horror stories that abound concerning witnesses' being destroyed by the clever ploys of attorneys, presenting testimony in court is rarely the traumatic experience that the clinician anticipates. It is the exception rather than the rule that attorneys are truly malicious in their cross-examinations; as often as not, it is lack of preparation by witnesses or their inexperience in detecting or anticipating cross-examination gambits that leads to embarrassing

moments in court. Once an appreciation for the games attorneys play is developed, and strategies are worked out for dealing with common ploys, then the battle of wits can be an enjoyable experience, as well as informative to the factfinder.

This section is intended to prepare clinicians for going to court by describing the various stages of testimony and some of the experiences they can anticipate at each stage. We first discuss substantive issues commonly explored during pretrial conferences, *voir dire,* direct examination, and cross-examination, and suggest ways in which clinicians can prepare for each. The final subsection addresses the issue of impression management.

(a)   Pretrial Conference

Although it may not always be feasible, we recommend that whenever possible the mental health professional and the attorney confer with each other prior to trial.[12] This meeting is often invaluable in planning strategy on direct examination, in anticipating questions during cross-examination, and in generally learning about each other's attitudes toward the case.

The attorney should make clear to the clinician the theory of the case, what the opposing side will try to prove, how the clinician's data should be presented, and, if necessary, the nature of the courtroom process. The clinician should make sure the attorney knows his or her qualifications, describe the evaluation procedure, admit possible weaknesses in his or her own opinion, expose possible weaknesses in the other side's opinion, and rehearse the data base so the attorney will know what types of background information will need to be introduced. The clinician should also critique the attorney's plans for presenting the clinical opinion. For example, through knowledge of social-psychological factors that are important in presentation and persuasion,[13] the clinician may suggest that more important findings or conclusions should be presented very early or very late in the testimony, because of "primacy" and "recency" effects. Without overly rehearsing the specific responses to direct testimony questions (so as to avoid mechanical presentation at trial), some minimal roleplaying may also be helpful at this stage.

In the discussion of the clinician's data base, it may become clear that the witness feels ethically obliged to disclose information that the attorney would prefer to remain undisclosed. The attorney may decide to use avoidance tactics by not eliciting the troublesome information; alternatively, the attorney wish to develop specific questions for direct testimony that allow the clinician to "explain away" the inconsistent data or provide alternative formulations. Such issues should be resolved prior to trial; otherwise, the clinician may find it necessary to withdraw as an expert because he or she cannot explain the data base [see § 14.04(d)].

While the conference will probably focus on direct testimony, it may also be used to identify areas best reiterated on redirect testimony after cross-examination. Some of these will be rescue points—areas in which it is known in advance that concessions will have to be made. Some patch-up work may be in order after a particularly aggressive cross-examination. Additionally, a small number of major points should be identified for the benefit of repetition on redirect testimony, to capitalize on "recency" effects.

Finally, the witness and the attorney should be in agreement with each other on the clinician's posture with respect to ultimate-issue questions. As we discuss more fully in § 14.05, the attorney's inclination will probably be to ask the clinician questions about the clinical formulation that are couched in the explicit language of the statutory test or verdict. These questions will often be prefaced with inquiries about "reasonable medical certainty" or "reasonable scientific certainty." While these terms may have some meaning to the clinician with respect to confidence in the clinical diagnosis or assessment results, the questions will usually be asked in such a way that the desired legal conclusion is cast as having medical or scientific validity. We recommend that the clinician take steps to avoid being misused in this fashion; to ensure that the flow or impact of direct testimony is not disrupted, these issues should be discussed and clarified prior to testimony.

(b) *Voir Dire:* **Qualifying as an Expert**

Voir dire is the first stage of testimony and consists of an examination of a witness by the attorney in order to determine the witness's qualifications to testify. Under the rules of evidence, "lay" witnesses usually may offer only factual observations in testimony; "expert" witnesses, on the other hand, may offer inferences, conclusions, and opinions regarding matters in their fields of expertise. The *voir dire* establishes the extent and limits of the witness's expertise.

The side calling a witness to testify initially leads him or her through a fairly standard series of questions designed to elicit for the judge and jury a history of the witness's education, training, and professional experience. In preparation for testimony, the clinician should meet with the attorney, who can mimic direct examination and discuss the substance of *voir dire* testimony. Brodsky and Poythress[14] suggest the following items for review in preparation for *voir dire:*

- Formal education, including dates and places of degrees awarded, major areas of study, title of thesis or dissertation if appropriate.
- Practical experience, including internship, residency, and professional positions held; type of work (teaching, research, administration, or service provision); and kinds of clients served (adult, adolescent, child; inpatient or outpatient).
- Professional certification or licensure; Board certification, where applicable.
- Membership in professional organizations (e.g., American Psychiatric Association, American Psychology–Law Society).
- Professional publications—books, journal articles.
- Prior court experience as an expert and in what kinds of litigation.

Voir dire questions should be tailored to the particular case at hand—emphasizing, for example, experience or training with children and families in a custody case, or experience with adult offenders in a sentencing hearing.

Following the litany of credentials on direct questioning, the opposing attorney has an opportunity to question the witness further. Predictably, the emphasis will be on the weaker points in the witness's experience and training, such as limited contact with particular populations, lack of training (especially if the witness is a nonphysician), or lack of prior court experience. Less common, but equally appropriate for exploration during *voir dire,* is an inquiry into the evaluation procedure and data relied upon. Admissibility of expert testimony may be challenged if the clinician has used procedure(s) "not generally accepted in the field"[15] or if he or she has relied on data other than those upon which experts in the field "reasonably rely."[16] Another reasonable, but uncommon, tactic is to question the proposed witness regarding familiarity with the published literature on the topic to be covered in the testimony. For example, the attorney might seek exclusion or at least a motion *in limine* (i.e., a motion limiting the scope of testimony) to restrict the clinician's testimony if the issue before the court is the defendant's propensity for future violence and the witness is not knowledgeable regarding the literature on the prediction of dangerousness [see § 7.10].

Following *voir dire,* the attorney calling the witness to testify will make a motion to the judge requesting that the court acknowledge on the record that the clinician is an expert witness. If forthcoming, this designation allows the witness to offer inferences, opinions, and conclusions that go beyond the data. If the clinician is not designated as an expert witness, he or she can still testify on the observations and descriptive data.

Members of the medical profession, particularly psychiatrists, enjoy rather widespread acceptance by most courts as expert witnesses. Non-medically-trained witnesses, including psychologists, social workers, psychiatric nurses, or other mental health personnel, should be prepared to assist attorneys in making a positive case for their acceptance as expert witnesses. In jurisdictions in which forensic practice by nonphysicians is underdeveloped, attorneys and judges may not be familiar with empirical research[17] or case law[18] that supports the use of nonphysician expert witnesses. This issue should be discussed prior to court if the attorney or clinician anticipates opposition to the clinician's testifying as an expert, and the clinician should be prepared to provide the attorney with relevant citations or documents that support expert status. The acknowledgment of any clinician as an expert witness is, within statutory guidelines, at the discretion of the trial judge. Not infrequently, judges will allow clinicians whose credentials have been challenged to testify as experts, instructing the jury that the limits in their training or experience go not to the admissibility, but to the weight of their testimony. Judicial preferences among clinicians of different training may be influenced not only by the clinicians' credentials, but also by the type of litigation involved.[19]

Voir dire testimony is typically not particularly difficult or traumatic for the witness. The issues to be covered are prepared for in advance, and the challenges from opposing counsel are predictable. Witnesses who are comfortable with their professional skills and status can matter-of-factly state for the court what they are and what they are not, and leave it to the attorneys to argue the issue of "expert witness" status. In a number of cases, attorneys on both sides will have reviewed clinicians' credentials prior to court and will jointly stipulate to their expertise. In such cases, judges will routinely acknowledge the clinicians as expert witnesses, and the hearings will proceed to the next stage.

It is worth noting here that mental health professionals will occasionally attempt to bolster their credentials with claims or elaborations that come off as phony. One psychologist who had received his doctorate three years earlier from a nonaccredited program offered that he had worked in the field of psychology for 15 years; for 12 of these years he had worked as a nonprofessional, as a paraprofessional, and as a student, though he implied that he had worked during this period as a professional. When questioned about the nonaccreditation of his doctoral program, instead of modestly conceding the point, he launched into a defensive narrative that doctoral training at nonaccredited programs was widely regarded as superior to that provided at accredited programs. Another form of deceitful testimony is to use approximate answers or half-truths that leave a positive, though erroneous impression. One psychiatrist had attended some classes at Harvard Law School but had not earned a law degree. When asked on *voir dire* about having a law degree, he responded, "Well, I attended Harvard Law School, but I never took the bar exam to practice law." He thus avoided the true concession that he did not have a law degree, and left hanging a possible erroneous impression.

We strongly discourage any such efforts to enhance perceived expertise through fabricated or contrived credentials or half-truths. Mental health professionals have an ethical responsibility to avoid misrepresentation, no matter how cleverly disguised.[20] Judges and jurors will probably see through such contrivances and attribute them to lack of confidence or, worse, to dishonesty in the witness. Trustworthiness is perhaps the most important component of credibility,[21] and to compromise personal or professional integrity is probably the single greatest error a witness can make in court. Clinicians should present themselves as confident and enthusiastic about their professional identities, but they should remain nondefensive and detached during the discussion of whether or not expert status will be granted.

(c) Direct Testimony

Following *voir dire,* the witness undergoes direct examination by the attorney who has called him or her to court. Direct testimony involves describing the evaluation procedures conducted, the data obtained, and the conclusions drawn by the clinician. As discussed above, a pretrial conference can help immeasurably in preparing for this phase of the trial.

It is probably best to structure the body of the testimony like an inverted pyramid—beginning with evaluation techniques and the data those techniques have produced; then proceeding to inferences; and ending with the "peak," the summary conclusion. If tests or laboratory procedures have been used, the clinician should be prepared to discuss their validity and to describe the method of test development. And, as noted throughout this volume, the clinician should not hesitate to describe uncertainty in the process of opinion formation.

As to the style of the testimony, it is probably best to avoid staccato-like questions and answers that come across as rehearsed. The style of speech should include relatively few hesitations, "qualifiers," or "intensifiers."[22] In general, the same suggestions we have made with respect to writing reports—avoiding information overkill, eschewing unexplained jargon, separating facts from inferences—are useful here as well.

An attorney may wish to establish the credibility of a client by seeking to have the witness affirm the honesty and candor of the client. In such situations, a clinician should be careful to avoid taking a strong position on which of two (or more) feasible factual situations is the "true" one. The clinician may, however, allude to third-party information corroborating that obtained from the client, or may offer feasible clinical explanations for contradictions or inconsistencies in the data base. In developing a formulation that relates the clinical data to the legal issue, the clinician may assume hypothetically each of the competing factual situations and report formulations consistent with each. Clinicians should carefully avoid being used as "lie detectors" and should leave it to the trier of fact to determine the most feasible factual situation.

With careful preparation, direct examination is usually the smoothest stage of testimony. The clinician can expect open-ended questions that allow considerable latitude in responding, and the only interruptions will be the succession of questions from the attorney and, infrequently, objections from opposing counsel.

(d) Cross-Examination

Cross-examination follows direct testimony, and it is the stage of testimony that is most trying for the inexperienced witness. Gone is the friendly, understanding expression of the attorney who has led direct testimony; in its place is the scowl or piercing stare of the opposing attorney, whose tone of voice and looks of astonishment convey to the jury the "unbelievable" nature of the clinician's testimony. A variety of verbal and nonverbal ploys are tried in an effort to confuse or discredit the witness, the testimony, or the witness's profession. In place of the logical progression of open-ended questions are narrow, constricting inquiries that emphasize vulnerable points in the clinical findings and attempt to distort the very message the witness is trying to convey.

On *voir dire,* the opposing attorney may attempt to discredit the witness by emphasizing who or what the witness is not. On cross-examination, the attorney will emphasize that whatever the witness did in the evaluation was insufficient, and that whatever he or she did not do was essential. Apart from what the witness did or did not do, the attorney may also emphasize what he or she does not know.

(1) Cross-Examination Gambits and Witness Responses

Cross-examination of the expert witness in mental health has been the subject of considerable writing, and the attorney has numerous sources to call upon in preparing an attack.[23] However, coping responses for a number of common gambits have also been developed, and clinicians may also turn to the professional literature for guidance in preparing for cross-examination.[24] While it is beyond the scope of this chapter to review the full range of cross-examination ploys, this section describes several of the more common ones and indicates appropriate responses by the mental health witness. Readers who anticipate appearing frequently in court as expert witnesses may wish to become more intimately familiar with the literature on cross-examination.

Common cross-examination ploys include the following:

1. "Infallibility complex." To overcome any perception the jury may have of the witness as infallible, the attorney asks a question designed to suggest fallibility. The attorney may ask the witness about the relevance of some very new, or very obscure, research that the witness will probably have not read; this, the attorney hopes, will result in an "I don't know" response.

2. "God only knows" gambit. The attorney may ask questions to which there is no sure, easy,

or precise answer (e.g., "What really causes schizophrenia?").

3. "Yes–no" questioning. The attorney attempts to box the witness in by phrasing questions in such a way as to force a "yes" or "no" answer.

4. "Bought or biased" testimony. The attorney tries to portray the witness as having been bought (e.g., "Doctor, how much are you being paid for your opinion in this case?") or as biased toward one party (e.g., "Doctor, you quite frequently testify for the plaintiff in these malpractice cases, don't you?").

5. "Unreliable examination" gambit. The attorney will question the witness about the uncertainty of his or her findings (e.g., low reliability/validity of individual tests or diagnosis, low accuracy of predictions, etc.).

6. "Subjective opinion" ploy. The attorney will ask whether the witness has personally been involved in systematic research to investigate the reliability and/or validity of his or her own clinical opinions and judgments.

7. "Loaded question" ploy. The attorney will misstate what the witness has said or agreed to in an earlier response, usually by "loading" the prior statement with additional information. For example, if a witness has previously agreed to assertions X, Y, and Z, a later question by the attorney might be, "Doctor, you earlier testified that W, X, Y, and Z were true. Doesn't that mean that . . . ?"

8. "Lawyer as expert" ploy. Here the attorney graciously volunteers to testify for the clinician regarding the clinician's own field (e.g., "Doctor, doesn't a standard psychological evaluation consist of . . . ?"); this sets the clinician up for later questions that depend on the *attorney's* definition of what is "standard."

Through anticipation and careful preparation, the mental health professional can handle most cross-examination ploys without significant difficulty. Some ploys can be handled through good preparation in specific knowledge areas: Familiarity with the reliability and/or validity of tests used, reliability of diagnoses, and accuracy of specific predictions should be part and parcel of the witness's pretrial preparation. Controversial points should be acknowledged and minor or indefensible points should be readily conceded, though not at the expense of a balanced presentation that includes positive support for the witness's position.

When confronted with the "infallibility complex" or "God only knows" gambits, the witness can use an "admit–deny" response. With this response, the witness admits that there is no literal response to the question, but denies ignorance of the subject. Here is an example:

Q: Doctor, do you think that the new research by Smith and Jones might be relevant here?

A: The studies having the most direct bearing on this issue are those by Holmes, Dawson, and Wortman. I don't recall seeing citations to Smith and Jones. If you have the paper, perhaps I could look it over during a recess.

Rather than simply conceding ignorance of the Smith and Jones study (which would be, of course, an acceptable response), the witness answers in such a way as to affirm expertise in the area generally. The final statement—the offer to review the paper during a court recess—shows an openness to new information that may enhance the witness's trustworthiness in the eyes of the jury; it will also force the attorney to withdraw if he or she has simply posed a misleading citation for purposes of confrontation. Here is a similar response to the "God only knows" gambit:

Q: Doctor, what really causes schizophrenia?

A: Research has implicated a number of factors that contribute to schizophrenia. There is some evidence for a genetic contribution, as biological relatives of schizophrenics are at much greater risk for the illness than are persons selected randomly. Pathological family relationships may also contribute. Unfortunately, the state of the science at present does not permit us to determine what has caused schizophrenia in a particular case.

Again, the witness admits ignorance in such a way as to appear well informed.

In response to "yes–no" questioning, the clinician should be assertive and state that a "yes" or "no" response would be inappropriate or misleading. If the attorney presses for a "yes–no" answer, the witness may appeal to the judge ("Your Honor, I believe than an answer of "yes" or "no" without explanation would be misleading"), who will either instruct the witness to answer the question or instruct the attorney to rephrase it. In any event, the other attorney will be alerted to clear up this matter with clarifying questions on redirect examination.

The "bought or biased" ploy is usually easily dispensed with, if the clinician simply states that he or she is being paid for the time spent professionally on the case, not for the particular opinion or formulation developed in the case. Similarly, the witness can in most cases diffuse assertions of bias toward one party in litigation; for example,

Q: Doctor, you quite frequently appear in court as an expert witness for criminal defendants, don't you?

A: Actually, fewer than 40% of my referrals from defense attorneys result in court testimony. It does seem that my practice is more accessible to defense attorneys, however, as your office, Mr. Prosecutor, has asked for my consultation in only a few cases.

The "unreliable examination" gambit can be dealt with in numerous ways. When the attorney questions the accuracy or validity of a finding or an opinion, the witness can simply concede the degree of inaccuracy or unreliability that exists. Simple concessions, if made nondefensively, convey a sense of honesty and candor that the judge or jury will appreciate. Indeed, they are sometimes best made during *direct* examination, so as to avoid the impression that the witness is hiding something. If they *are* made for the first time during cross-examination, concessions can often be used to the witness's advantage, through the "push–pull" response. With this response, the witness doesn't simply concede the point; rather, the concession is exaggerated so that it appears as a point the witness wants to impress on the jury, not one the attorney has forced the witness to make. For example:

Q: Doctor, isn't it true that the validity of the Rorschach test has been seriously questioned by some psychologists?

A: No psychological test, the Rorschach included, is a perfectly valid test. It is important that you [the jury] not place undue weight on any of the particular test results I've described, but consider all of the information as a whole.

Conceding the substantive point about the Rorschach, the witness recaptures this loss in openness and candor by extending the point to other findings as well. Simple concessions and "push–pull" should be used when the substantive concessions being sought are reasonable. When the attorney asks for too much, the appropriate response is to correct him or her:

Q: Doctor, isn't it true that psychiatric diagnosis is generally unreliable? Isn't it true that you psychiatrists rarely agree on when somebody is, or is not, suffering from schizophrenia?

A: No, that is not true. In fact, the reliability of a diagnosis of schizophrenia using DSM-III criteria is quite good. Agreement among trained clinicians may be as high as 80–90%.

The "subjective opinion" ploy attempts to impress upon the jury that the clinician's formulations and opinions are simply "what the witness *thinks*," as opposed to findings having any scientific legitimacy. Innuendoes about the influence of personal values are common. Responses to this ploy should include a brief statement of the scientific underpinnings of the clinician's training and a modest statement of personal and professional integrity, to this effect: "*Because* I am a person with a particular personal set of values, I am careful in the collection and analysis of data to ascertain that my clinical formulations are consistent with known data or widely accepted theory." If in fact the witness's clinical judgments have been the subject of systematic study, the results of such study may be described.

The "loaded question" and "lawyer as expert" ploys primarily require good listening by

the witness. If clinicians are very familiar with their written reports (as they should be) and are careful in their own testimony, then they will be able to pick up on the gratuitous "findings" or concessions that such attorneys may attribute to them when they load their questions. At such points, clinicians should clarify what they do or do not agree to or what they have or have not stated in their reports. Under no circumstances should clinicians take the "lawyer as expert" ploy casually. Leading questions regarding what is "standard," or "acceptable," or "proper" clinical practice or procedure should be scrutinized very carefully. The safest response to such questions is *never* to answer them simply with a "yes." By never simply agreeing with attorneys' definitions of "standard" or "proper" procedure, clinicians will ultimately force the attorneys to ask them to define such terms themselves. Then they are on safe ground, for they can offer such definitions of the terms that are sufficiently broad or appropriately qualified that the procedures they have used meet the definitions. Clinicians should jealously guard their area of expertise and should not give it over to the clever phrases of cross-examining attorneys.

(2)   Hypothetical Questions

Clinicians should also be alerted to the potential use of hypothetical questions by attorneys. Such questions are usually prefaced by a clear signal (e.g., "Doctor, I'm going to ask you a hypothetical question") and consist of a statement of several assumptions, followed by an inquiry as to the clinician's opinion about them. For example:

Q: Doctor, I am going to ask you to assume certain facts, and then I want you to tell the jury what you would conclude about the defendant's mental condition if all of these facts were true. I want you to assume that $W, X, Y,$ and Z are true. Given these facts, what would you conclude about the defendant's mental state at the time of the murder?

The clinicians may answer hypothetical questions of this type, but should be careful in doing so. The attorney will usually have arranged the assumed facts in such a way as to force a conclusion or opinion that supports the theory or verdict being pursued. In doing so, the attorney may (1) exclude factual information that the clinician knows to exist; (2) include factual information of which the clinician is unaware; or (3) include as information to be assumed facts not in evidence in the case. In the third of these instances, the other attorney may successfully object, and the hypothetical question may have to be rephrased. In the first two instances, the clinician may answer the hypothetical question but may wish to qualify the opinion or conclusion, if only to remind the jury that the response is tailored exclusively to the hypothetical question and is not based on his or her entire information base. Thus, the witness might respond to the question above as follows:

A: Assuming only *W, X, Y,* and *Z* is difficult for me, because in my own investigation I found *A* and *B,* as well as *C,* which contradicts *W.* However, if I assume only what you stated and disregard what else I know, a reasonable inference would be *R.*

The clinician might appropriately avoid drawing a conclusion or inference if the information to be assumed is not clear, as in the following response:

A: You've asked me to assume that a neighbor testified that Mr. Doe was acting crazy before the shooting. Without knowing more about what was meant by "crazy" behavior, I don't know what I would make of all this.

It is worth noting that hypothetical conclusions and inferences may be offered not only in response to limited situations constructed by the attorney; they may also be volunteered by the clinician on either direct examination or cross-examination. Situations in which this might be appropriate have been described in § 14.03(b).

(3) "Learned Treatise" Assault

One additional cross-examination tactic worthy of special attention is the "learned treatise" assault. In this approach, the attorney attempts to undermine the clinician's testimony by showing that it is contradicted by findings in the published literature. The attorney may produce copies of published research or clinical commentary, such as journal articles or books, and attempt to establish that these documents are by authorities in the field. Once the credibility of the documents is established, the attorney then reads excerpts (usually carefully selected) that contradict the oral testimony of the clinician on the stand, thus raising questions in the jurors' minds about the credibility of the witness.

Clinicians may employ different tactics to combat this assault.[25] One approach is to deny that the proposed source is authoritative; in some jurisdictions, the rules of evidence governing learned treatises require that the witness acknowledge the authority of the source before it can be used. Another approach is to acknowledge the authority of the source but deny that the source has been relied on in this particular case; again, in some jurisdictions, the rules of evidence require that the document must have been relied upon by the witness before its content can be used to impeach testimony. Both variations of the "refuse to acknowledge" response carry substantial risks: If the witness refuses to acknowledge the authority of the source or admits being ignorant of much of the published research, then he or she may appear to the jury as not up to date or even as dishonest.[26]

An alternative response tactic is for the clinician to accept the proposed document; to criticize the findings where appropriate (e.g., flawed methodology, poor external validity, etc.); and to counter with specific citations that support this position. By anticipating major issues to be debated prior to court, the clinician can review the relevant literature and be prepared to parry the "learned treatise" assault without resorting to avoidance tactics. Poythress[27] has identified some items of literature most likely to be used in the "learned treatise" assault for several common areas of inquiry, as well as some of the rebuttal literature with which the clinician should be familiar. However, the possible issues for debate are extensive and vary considerably from one type of litigation to another. Professional preparation calls for clinicians to be well read on topics about which they will testify. Note that it is always permissible for the witness to ask to see the text from which the lawyer purports to quote, in order to put the quotation in context.

(e)   Objections to Testimony: Hearsay and Other Limitations on Admissibility

During both direct examination and cross-examination, the attorney who is not asking the questions may object to a question that is asked. When an objection is made, the clinician should not answer until the judge rules on the objection. If the objection is "overruled," then testimony may proceed. If the objection is "sustained," then the question should not be answered in open court (although the judge or lawyer may request an answer for the record).

Typical objections made by the clinician's own attorney during cross-examination might include "badgering the witness," "asked and answered" (suggesting that the cross-examiner has already obtained one answer and is now fishing for a better one), and "irrelevant" (suggesting that the cross-examiner is asking for information that is not legally material to the case). Often, objections by experts' own attorneys are strategic moves designed to allow the witnesses to "catch their breath" and think through a good answer.

During direct examination, objections by opposing counsel include those designed to prevent the direct examiner from asking leading questions (e.g., "Is it true that . . . ?") and those attempting to exclude "hearsay" statements. The former objection is often sustained because the direct examiner is supposed to let witnesses speak for themselves rather than put words in their mouths (leading questions are permitted, however, on cross-examination). Rulings on "hearsay" objections are more complicated, especially when a witness is an expert. "Hearsay" is any statement made by a person who is not available for questioning at the time of trial. Statements obtained from the subject's family, the police, or the clinician's own colleagues who have assisted in the evaluation are hearsay unless those who

have made the statements testify in court and are subject to cross-examination.

A hearsay statement is not generally admissible, because its reliability cannot be assessed through cross-examination of the declarant. However, there are several exceptions to the hearsay rule, including "party admissions" (which include statements made by a criminal defendant or party to a civil lawsuit) and statements contained in "routinely kept" records. These exceptions are based in part on the assumption that the hearsay involved is nonetheless reliable, given the circumstances under which it is declared or transcribed, and in part on the perception that there are often no alternative sources for such information. Thus, statements the clinician obtains from parties to the litigation and hospital records are usually admissible under existing exceptions to the hearsay rules. Moreover, in the Federal Rules of Evidence and in the rules of an increasing number of states, an *expert's* opinion may be based on information that is otherwise inadmissible (such as hearsay) if it is of the type "reasonably relied upon" by experts in the same field.[28] Thus, other out-of-court statements may form a legitimate basis for a clinical opinion if they meet the "reasonably relied upon" criteria.

It has been argued that the "reasonable reliance" language should be narrowly construed so as to allow the clinician to report only those hearsay statements with demonstrated validity[29]; according to this view, the jury should not be forced to judge the credibility of an unavailable source, based solely on what the clinician says. There are strong arguments for requiring everyone who is a *significant* source of information to testify in the court, including, for instance, all the members of the evaluation team. However, there may be times when the hearsay data are trivial, or when they are significant but the source is practically unavailable. In any event, clinicians, aided by their lawyers, should be prepared to explain why sources they have relied upon are not available and why they feel comfortable in relying upon them.

If, however, judges do rule against the legitimacy of particular hearsay information, then clinicians must decide whether they can ethically deliver their opinions, knowing that they can no longer explain those opinions using the excluded information. The same type of dilemma will confront clinicians whenever a court rules out the admission of evidence upon which the clinicians rely, be it on Fifth Amendment, relevance, or other grounds.

(f) Impression Management

Up to this point, we have discussed primarily substantive features of expert testimony. Another very important consideration, and one to which many mental health professionals pay insufficient attention, is the image that clinicians convey through their nonverbal behavior. For better or worse, dress, posture, tone of voice, and a variety of other factors inevitably have a considerable impact on the impression jurors form of the witness; perceived expertise is not determined simply by the litany of credentials recited on *voir dire*.

(1) Style of Dress

Clinicians are advised to dress conservatively when going to court. Dress does not have to be expensive, but it should be neat. Blue jeans and a sweater may be fine in the private office for conveying a "low-key" image and making therapy clients feel comfortable, but they are not suitable for the courtroom. The clinician's attire should be selected so as to reinforce the judge's or jurors' stereotype of a professional person; bright or flashy colors, excessive makeup or jewelry, or "mod" attire are not consistent with that image. An unusually short skirt on a female witness, or an open collar and four gold chains around the neck of a male witness, will probably distract courtroom personnel from thinking of the clinician as an expert.

(2) Familiarity with Courtroom Protocol

The courtroom is not the place to appear timid, passive, or unsure. Clinicians should learn in ad-

vance what is expected of them and execute these behaviors in a manner that reflects comfort and familiarity.

The clinician should not wait to be ushered around the courtroom like a lost child. When called to testify, he or she should stride forward confidently, stopping at the witness stand to face the judge or bailiff and be sworn in. In giving testimony, the clinician should take time to think through a question, pause reflectively if necessary, and respond in a clear, even tone. Information should not be volunteered from the witness stand, but should be provided only in response to questions. As noted earlier, when an attorney raises an objection, the clinician should not attempt an answer until the judge has ruled on the admissibility of the question.

(3) Speaking to the Jury

The witness should face the jury (or judge, in a bench trial or hearing) when answering questions. He or she should make good eye contact and maintain a clear, even voice. Dramatics are to be avoided, but the witness should be sufficiently personable and animated to maintain the audience's attention.

This is important at all times, but perhaps most important during cross-examination. Opposing attorneys may attempt to interrupt the channel of nonverbal communication between the witness and the jury in either of two ways. The attorney may approach the witness stand, almost to the point of invading the witness's personal space, becoming a physical obstruction between the witness and the jury. More subtly, the attorney may wander across the room away from the jury box, speaking in such a low voice that the witness must look away from the jury in order to hear the question. The witness will occasionally forget to turn back to face the jury, and the nonverbal communication will have been severed.

In testimony, as in report writing [see § 14.03(b)], the clinician should use language that the jury members can easily understand. A limited amount of clinical jargon may serve to reaffirm the clinician's expertise, but any jargon used should be explained in order to ensure the jurors' comprehension.

(4)   Maintaining Composure

The importance of maintaining composure cannot be overstated. Apart from any substantive concessions made in testimony, the most damaging thing that can happen to a witness is to become angry, defensive, or flustered.

One technique that cross-examining attorneys use to frustrate witnesses is to ask complex, convoluted questions to which no simple response can be given. Rather than becoming frustrated and grasping for an adequate response when none is possible, clinicians should ask that attorneys simplify such questions, thus placing the responsibility on them for clarifying confusing situations of their own creation.

Attorneys may also engage in argumentative or harassing tactics simply to destroy clinicians' demeanor, caring little for substantive points gained or lost. A witness should endeavor to maintain a polite, respectful posture toward a hostile lawyer, even in the face of a personal attack. This may leave the jury with the impression that the lawyer is a "bully." Though the witness should never become flippant in tone, the use of humor can be effective in judiciously selected situations. One colleague reported being badgered about her inability to clinically distinguish between an "irresistible impulse" and an "impulse that was not resisted." Noting (to herself) that the hostile attorney was quite overweight, she drew the analogy of a person on a diet who succumbed to the temptation of a double chocolate sundae—was the temptation irresistible or simply not resisted? The line of questioning abruptly ended.

Attorneys will attempt to induce an apologetic tone when getting witnesses to concede substantive points. Unless a witness is admitting an error, there is no need for an apologetic tone. Limits in the technology, data, or precision of the mental health profession are not a clinician's fault; they are simply the way things are. The clinician may *explain* limitations in his or her knowledge or formulation, but apologies for the

state of the art and science of behavior are uncalled for.

(5)   Conclusion

Mental health professionals who anticipate engaging in forensic work as part of their practice should try to learn and develop skills for effective testifying. One way to do so is simply to go to court and observe expert witnesses testifying in other cases. The opportunity to observe various role models can be a good vicarious experience for clinicians who lack prior experience in testifying in court. Another good learning exercise is to rehearse expert testimony with other colleagues who play the parts of judge and attorneys; critique and feedback from the role-playing experience can be significantly enhanced if the exercise is videotaped. Though impression management should never take priority over clinical acuity, we encourage mental health professionals to develop a calm, friendly, and professional manner for testifying, in order to maximize the chances that their testimony will be carefully attended to.

14.05.   Expert Testimony and the Ultimate Legal Issue

Throughout this volume, we have discouraged mental health professionals from offering opinions or conclusions couched in the language of the ultimate legal issue. Chapter 1 has developed the differences in attitude, philosophy, objectives, investigative methods, and assumptions between the law and the social sciences. An analysis of these differences has led to a reiteration of the position convincingly argued by Morse,[30] Bonnie and Slobogin,[31] and other concerned critics of mental health participation in the legal process: Ultimate legal issues are issues of social and moral policy, and they properly lie outside the province of scientific inquiry. We have subsequently analyzed the various levels of inference that might be utilized by clinicians, and have concluded that inferences drawn should stop short of those that embrace elements of the ultimate legal question.

Our analysis and recommendation notwithstanding, contemporary practices encourage, permit, or require mental health professionals to address ultimate legal issues in their reports and testimony. In that we are encouraging a posture by witnesses that is unconventional by current standards, and one not likely to be well received by the court, it is incumbent upon us to suggest methods of implementation. How important is it, from the court's view, that mental health professionals address ultimate-issue questions? What are the various pressures on mental health professionals to do so? How, in the context of actual testimony, can these pressures be resisted? It is to these questions that we now turn our attention.

(a) Perceived Importance of Mental Health Experts' Opinions on Ultimate Legal Issues

Avoiding the ultimate legal issue in forensic reports or in testimony would be a relatively simple matter, were it not for the fact that attorneys and trial court judges regard ultimate-issue opinions as very important. This fact was borne out in a recent survey of circuit court judges in Michigan, who were asked to express their preferences for and to rate the importance of different aspects of mental health expert testimony.[32] In the survey, eight different aspects of mental health testimony were described. These eight aspects represent the range of issues on which testimony might be given; all but the first two (having to do with actuarial statistical data) have their analogues in the levels of inference described in Chapter 1. Table 14-1 arrays the typology of inferences and the (roughly) parallel aspects of testimony.

The eight aspects of testimony covered in the survey were described to the Michigan judges as follows:

A. Statistical/actuarial data on diagnosis or clinical observation. The clinician may refer to statistical or actuarial data from experimental studies on the subject before the court (e.g., epidemiological data regarding the incidence of a disorder; normative data regarding scores on a test; reliability of diagnosis).

B. Statistical/actuarial data on the relationship between clinical findings and legally relevant behavior. The clinician may refer to such research findings as the relationship between clinical diagnosis and relative probability of suicide; correlational data relating number of prior arrests to criminal recidivism; the relationship between chronological age and memory or susceptibility to leading questions; and the like.

C. Descriptive testimony. The clinician describes the clinical observations and test results of a particular individual who is the subject of the court hearing. The description may include physical appearance, nonverbal behavior, attitudes, affect, memory, mental status, historical data, and so on.

D. Diagnosis. Formal (e.g., from DSM-III) or informal diagnosis (e.g., "competent parent") will be given in many instances. The clinician identifies the clinical data that meet the diagnostic criteria and conveys the message of having observed a recognized clinical syndrome.

E. Theoretical accounts or explanations for legally relevant behavior. The clinician offers an interpretation of the individual's behavior and an explanation for the legally relevant behavior by invoking the constructs of some formal or implicit personality theory. Most commonly, the medical ("mental illness") model is invoked, followed closely in popularity by the psychodynamic theory.

F. Weighing the relative contribution of different motives or explanations for legally relevant behavior. The clinician may voice an opinion on which of several contributory factors or conflicting theoretical explanations appears most applicable in a given case (e.g., "While it is true that Ms. Doe suffered a severe loss of income following her separation from her husband, it is my opinion that her sense of failure as a woman and as a wife and an unconscious feeling of guilt and need to be punished were the primary factors contributing to her shoplifting").

G. Interpreting the legal standard for mental disorder. The clinician may attempt to relate a clinical diagnosis or condition to a legal standard or definition (e.g., "This person has below-average intelligence, though not to the degree that the legal term 'mental defect' would apply").

H. Ultimate legal issue. The testimony of the witness may embrace the ultimate legal issue, often including the specific language of the legal test that the judge or jury is to consider (e.g., "This person is unable to assist his attorney in a reasonable

Table 14-1
Types of Testimony Presented in Court

Typology of Levels of Inference [1]	Aspects of Mental Health Testimony [2]	Judges' Ratings of Probative Value [2]	
		Median Rating	Rank Order
	A. Statistical/actuarial data on diagnosis or clinical observations.	5.25	7
	B. Statistical/actuarial data on the relationship between clinical and legally relevant behavior.	3.20	8
1. Application of meaning (perception) to a behavioral image. 2. Perception of a general mental state.	C. Descriptive testimony.	7.83	1
3. "Formulation" of perceived mental state to fit into theoretical constructs or research literature, and/or to synthesize observations. 4. Diagnosis.	D. Diagnosis.	5.83	5
5. Relationship of "formulation" or diagnosis to the legally relevant behavior.	E. Theoretical accounts or explanations for legally relevant behavior.	6.00	4
	F. Weighing of different motives or explanations for legally relevant behavior.	5.50	6
6. Elements of the ultimate legal issue.	G. Interpreting the legal standard for mental disorder.	6.83	3
7. Ultimate legal issue.	H. Ultimate legal issue.	7.60	2

1. See § 1.04.
2. From N. Poythress, Conflicting Postures for Mental Health Expert Witnesses: Prevailing Attitudes of Trial Court Judges (1981) (unpublished manuscript on file with the Department of Training & Research, Center for Forensic Psychiatry, P.O. Box 2060, Ann Arbor, Mich. 48106).

manner; in my opinion, he is incompetent to stand trial").

In the survey, Poythress asked judges to rate the importance of these eight aspects of testimony. In rating importance, the judges were asked to consider "how essential is each particular aspect of testimony to the judge or jury in reaching a fair and accurate finding in cases involving mental health issues." After each aspect of testimony was described briefly, an example of possible testimony from a hypothetical insanity defense case was given.

Judges' ratings were indicated on a 9-point scale. Scale points were anchored as follows:

- Scale points 7, 8, and 9 should reflect that "you consider the element/item to be *essential* to dispensing justice; judgments by the trier-of-fact would be seriously hampered if this element/component were not included."
- Scale points 4, 5, and 6 should reflect that "you consider the element/item *desirable* for inclusion in expert testimony. Justice could be fairly dispensed without this particular feature having to be present, but its inclusion would perhaps allow for more fully informed decisions."
- Scale points 1, 2, and 3 should reflect that "you consider the element/item either unnecessary, uninformative, or *undesirable* as a feature of expert testimony. Its presence would add

Figure 14-1. *Judicial perceptions of clinical opinions. [From N. Poythress, Conflicting Postures for Mental Health Expert Witnesses: Prevailing Attitudes of Trial Court Judges (1981) (unpublished manuscript on file with the Department of Training & Research, Center for Forensic Psychiatry, P.O. Box 2060, Ann Arbor, Mich. 48106). Used by permission.]*

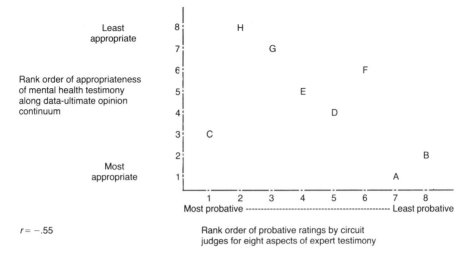

nothing of particular significance for the trier-of-fact, and possibly it might have negative impact by confusing or clouding the issue."

The survey findings clearly support the commonly accepted belief that mental health professionals' opinions on ultimate legal issues are viewed as very important. Table 14-1 lists the median ratings based on the responses of 30 judges; also shown are the relative rankings of probative value for each of the eight aspects of testimony (with B = 8, or least probative; C = 1, or most probative). Both aspects of testimony involving opinions on ultimate legal issues (G and H) were rated by the judges in the "essential" range and were outranked in importance by only one factor, descriptive testimony.

Following the current trend in much of the critical dialogue regarding the appropriate role for mental health experts, we assigned ordinal values of 1 through 8 to each of the eight aspects of testimony listed in Table 14-1; aspects in which the witness stays close to the data are rated as most appropriate (A = 1, B = 2, and so forth), while those aspects that involve the witness addressing issues beyond the realm of clinical inquiry are rated least appropriate (G = 7, H = 8).

These rankings of "appropriateness" of testimony can be compared with the rankings based on the judges' ratings of probative value. These two sets of rankings are plotted in Figure 14-1. The inverse correlation (Spearman rank-order correlation r is = −.55) reflects the judges' preference generally for testimony of a more theoretical or conclusory type and a rejection, ironically, of aspects of testimony arguably based on the hardest scientific data (A and B) social scientists can muster.[33]

It appears clear that judges do not want to struggle alone with the difficult moral issues raised in legal decisionmaking.

(b) Pressures on the Clinician to Address Ultimate Legal Issues

Several factors operate to influence the clinician to offer opinions on the ultimate legal issues. Before offering suggestions for avoiding ultimate legal issues, it may be of some benefit to identify and briefly discuss some of these factors.

One factor that has historically been a problem is the failure of mental health professionals to distinguish properly between clinical and legal conclusions and the nature of each. Clinicians have operated with crude and erroneous diagnostic decision rules (e.g., psychosis = insanity), on occasion expressing exasperation that jurors might disagree with their professional judgments. One psychiatrist's commentary is illustrative: "[I]f a jury found that the accused was not insane, then it was a fact that he was not insane, no matter what any number of medical men might say! What a source of confusion." [34]

Legal statutes or rules of evidence that permit or require the examining clinician to reach a conclusion on the ultimate legal issue are a second influence. Clinicians working at state forensic facilities may have the further pressures of department or facility policies dictating that such opinions be generated. Such policies might be resisted in rare cases, but usually not without creating some subjective concern over job security.

Economic considerations also enter in. Clinicians in private practice whose livelihood may depend on attracting a certain amount of forensic evaluation business may feel that their market value will diminish if they too strenuously resist providing the range of opinions and conclusions that may be easily obtained elsewhere. [35]

A fourth factor may be the relationship between the clinician and the attorney seeking clinical assistance. Brodsky and Poythress have noted:

> Mental health professionals who testify regularly find themselves subjected to pressures to join the attorney in the adversarial process. After all, the attorney who has engaged the experts is the person with whom the personal relationship has been established. A sense of loyalty exists. . . . It is not unusual, therefore, for some experts to find themselves committed to defending "their" attorney's position in a fierce and vigorous manner. [36]

The dynamics of the courtroom may also contribute to seduce the clinician to address questions that are properly beyond his or her expertise. The process of *voir dire* is a public statement of professional expertise by the witness, a statement subsequently endorsed by the trial judge's official proclamation of the witness as an expert on issues before the court. Given the expectations of the expert, it would be incongruent for the witness to demur and state "I have no opinion" at just the point when the issues of greatest concern are raised. Bradley's research [37] suggests that persons who have openly professed expertise will guess rather than admit ignorance in response to questions arguably related to their areas of expertise, even if the questions are virtually impossible to answer. Modesty, it would appear, is not a trait of individuals cast in the role of "expert."

In summary, there are a variety of inducements for the mental health professional to give testimony that embraces the ultimate legal issue. The precedents for doing so have been established by the past practices of psychologists and psychiatrists, who pass the tradition on to their protégés through the processes of socialization and training. Because of competition in the marketplace among the various disciplines, none can unilaterally impose a "gag" rule on its members without risking forfeiture of its share of the business. In spite of a growing number of hortatory appeals from legal academicians, there is little movement in the law toward imposing formal restrictions on these witnesses. [38] The momentum of the traditional practice, therefore, continues.

(c) Resisting the Ultimate-Issue Question

"Since it is not within the professional competence of psychologists to offer conclusions on matters of law, psychologists should resist pressure to offer such conclusions." [39] This recommendation of the American Psychological Association's task force on the role of psychology in the criminal justice system is applicable, we feel, to all mental health professionals and in virtually all litigation. Mental health professionals do have considerable expertise in their own fields of study—for example, in identifying and describing abnormal behavior, providing information about etiology and prognosis, and offering theoretical formulations that provide the factfinder with feasible psychological explanations for complex human behavior. However, they do not have the expertise, nor are they charged with the responsibility, to make legal judgments that involve moral values or policy decisions that involve the weighing of competing social interests. Clinicians may provide useful information about the mental infirmities of an elderly person, but they have no barometer for determining when such infirmities are sufficient to warrant the appointment of a guardian or conservator in light of the individual's interests of self-autonomy. Clinicians may provide diagnostic and prognostic information about a criminal offender at sentencing, but their scientific expertise does not allow them to determine what a proper sentence would be in light of the competing goals of sentencing—retribution, rehabilitation, and deterrence. Conclusions on questions such as these are the responsibility of the judge and jury, and clinicians should resist drawing them.

Careful preparation with attorneys is advised. Refusing to reach ultimate-issue conclusions is likely to run counter to the expectations most attorneys have of mental health professionals. A careful analysis, however, reveals that this posture by a clinician may be used to advantage. The posture we are advocating here requires only that the mental health professional make openly and candidly the same concessions that a good attorney could extract through careful cross-examination. Few knowledgeable clinicians would maintain, under close examination, that they are experts in moral decisionmaking or that such decisions can be made scientifically. While attorneys will typically seek an equal and opposite opinion to counter the "expert" opinion on the ultimate issue offered by the opposition's witness, a denial that any such opinions are within the province of the mental health sciences can be an equally effective rebuttal. Moreover, if one witness tries to defend the indefensible position (that clinicians *are* experts in drawing legal conclusions) but the other witness readily concedes otherwise, an advantage in trust goes to the second witness. If both sides concede the point, then ultimate-issue opinions by both may be discarded without loss, leaving both free to develop their data, observations, and theoretical formulations, and leaving argument and persuasion to the attorneys. Under this arrangement, cross-examination will go more smoothly as well. With no straw figures to knock down, the opposing attorney is more likely to try to use the clinician's data than to discredit either the data or the clinician.

The posture advocated here can be used to advantage whether the clinician is testifying for the first party to introduce mental health testimony, or as a rebuttal witness for the second party. Let's consider a hypothetical civil commitment proceeding, in which the state attempts to prove that the subject should be involuntarily committed. If the clinician is acting as a witness for the state, testimony might proceed as follows:

Attorney: Doctor, is Mr. Doe presently suffering from any mental disorder, and, if so, what symptoms does he display?

Doctor: Mr. Doe is presently diagnosed as suffering from schizophrenia, paranoid type. His primary symptoms include excessive distrust of family members, to the point that he has nailed boards over the doors and windows to his room to keep other from looking in or entering. He also reported excessive fears that his parents are trying to hurt him, to the degree that he no longer eats with other family members for fear of poisoning; he also reported that he sleeps with a knife and loaded gun under his bed.

Attorney: Have there been prior incidents of actual violent behavior?

Doctor: None to my knowledge, though Mr. Doe admitted to prior threats and the intent to protect himself by whatever means necessary.

Attorney: What kind of treatment is needed for this disorder, and in what setting might it be appropriately given?

Doctor: Psychotropic medication with supportive verbal therapy would provide the best chance for remission of symptoms and the restoration of more normal functioning in the family. However, Mr. Doe adamantly denies that he is ill in any way; thus, I doubt that he would take medication or attend therapy sessions voluntarily. Thus, treatment might have to be administered on a locked hospital ward.

Attorney: Doctor, are you saying that Mr. Doe should be committed to the state hospital for treatment?

Doctor: Whether he *should* be committed is a decision the judge must make. It is beyond my skills as a psychiatrist to say that Mr. Doe is mentally ill and dangerous *enough* that his freedom should be restricted and treatment provided involuntarily. If it is the court's decision that he does need involuntary treatment, then I consider the most appropriate treatment setting to be a locked hospital ward.

Alternatively, suppose that our hypothetical clinician has been called by the prospective patient's attorney and has testified that the subject has grudgingly admitted a willingness to go the the community mental health center for outpatient treatment if it will mean avoiding commitment to the state hospital. Assume also that the state's clinician has offered the conclusion that "Mr. Doe is so mentally ill and so dangerous that he should be committed to the hospital for involuntary treatment." Cross-examination of our clinician by the state's attorney might go as follows:

Attorney: Doctor Smith, you seem to be suggesting that Mr. Doe *might* be treatable on an outpatient basis, but you're not sure. Your colleague, Dr. Jones, testified with reasonable medical certainty that Mr. Doe was *too dangerous* to remain at liberty and *required* involuntary treatment on a locked hospital ward. You don't seem very confident in your opinion, Dr. Smith.

Doctor: I have not offered an opinion, counselor. Dr. Jones and I have both described the threats that Mr. Doe has made to family members, but neither he, nor I, nor any other psychiatrist has any way of determining whether those threats are sufficient cause to legally restrict his freedom. That is a decision the judge must make by weighing the risks to Mr. Doe's family against his rights as a free citizen. As to whether or not Mr. Doe will actually follow through with outpatient treatment if it is offered, again, no one can say with certainty. There is no prior history of treatment or medication com-

pliance to draw on, and though he denies that he is ill, he stated that he would go to the health center if necessary in order to avoid being locked up. Dr. Jones has no more scientific basis for saying that Mr. Doe won't keep outpatient appointments than I would have for asserting that he will.

As these examples illustrate, clinicians called by either party in a legal dispute can avoid being dragged into the "battle of the experts" revolving around ultimate-issue opinions by modestly asserting the limits of mental health expertise. In casting the ultimate issue as a moral and legal judgment outside the realm of scientific inquiry they can maintain integrity in testimony and force the trier of fact to focus on the clinical data and formulations that make up the substance of mental health testimony.

In recommending that mental health professionals resist embracing ultimate legal issues in testimony, we should make it clear that this resistance will not be a very pleasant task. Pressure to form ultimate-issue opinions will come from judges who do not want the responsibility for making tough moral decisions alone, and from attorneys who do not see the advantage to the posture we advocate and who are accustomed to using "expert opinions" to sway the jury. Clinicians can expect to be asked questions that paraphrase the ultimate legal test, and judges may give instructions that such questions be answered. Clinicians working in jurisdictions or hospitals where statutes or hospital policy dictate that opinions on legal issues be developed will find additional pressure to testify on these issues.

Recognizing that there may be situations in which clinicians will not be able to resist the pressures to deliver opinions on legal issues, we strongly recommend the following tactics. First, clinicians should try to define exactly what they mean when they use legal language. Thus, for instance, if the word "sane" must be used, clinicians should link it to the appropriate test, and then explain how they understand each component of the test. If, for example, the test is the American Law Institute's formulation for insanity [see § 6.02(b)], a clinician can explain what he or she means by the word "appreciate"; if that word has been defined by case law in the jurisdiction, the clinician can point out how his or her definition of "appreciate" differs, if at all, from the court's. In this way, the clinical nature of the testimony will be driven home to the fact-finder.

Similarly, in any cases in which opinions on legal issues are delivered, clinicians should deny that such opinions are derived from scientific inquiry. They can state in their written reports of findings that their "opinions" are not scientific determinations and that the evidence they have to offer should be considered only advisory.[40] In testimony, clinicians should deny that forthcoming opinions on legal issues are based on "reasonable medical certainty" or "reasonable scientific certainty."[41] Thus, it should be clear that such opinions, if given, will not be offered for more than they really are—judgments based in commonsense and personal moral values. These steps, we believe, will encourage more ethically sound testimony by mental health professionals, and more independent decisionmaking by the trier of fact.

On the question of the ultimate legal issue, the relationship between the law and the mental health sciences invokes the analogy of a couple in psychotherapy who are locked in an overly dependent relationship. The legal system resists dealing with problems of its own by demanding that mental health professionals accept responsibility for them, conferring special status and confirming relevance as inducements. Mental health professionals experience an increasing awareness of the unreasonable demands being made, but are unsure how to break the bond. Though ambivalence is felt by both, it is a relationship with old roots and considerable inertia. Change, when attempted, is slow to take effect and is usually resisted. It is our hope that suggestions in this volume for changes in the relationship will contribute to a weaning that is long overdue.

BIBLIOGRAPHY

Brodsky, *The Mental Health Professional on the Witness Stand: A Survival Guide,* in PSYCHOLOGY IN THE LEGAL PROCESS (B. Sales ed. 1977).

Brodsky & Poythress, *Expertise on the Witness Stand: A Practitioner's Guide,* in PSYCHOLOGY, PSYCHIATRY AND THE LAW: A CLINICAL AND FORENSIC HANDBOOK (C. P. Ewing ed. 1985).

Brodsky & Robey, *On Becoming an Expert Witness: Issues of Orientation and Effectiveness,* 3 PROF. PSYCHOLOGY 173 (1972).

Jenkins v. United States, 307 F.2d 637 (D.C. Cir. 1962).

W. O'BARR, LINGUISTIC EVIDENCE: LANGUAGE, POWER AND STRATEGY IN THE COURTROOM (1982).

Petrella & Poythress, *The Quality of Forensic Evaluations: An Interdisciplinary Study,* 51 J. CONSULTING CLINICAL PSYCHOLOGY 76 (1983).

Poythress, *Coping on the Witness Stand: Learned Responses to "Learned Treatises,"* 11 PROF. PSYCHOLOGY 139 (1980).

Watson, *On the Preparation and Use of Expert Testimony: Some Suggestions in an Ongoing Controversy,* 6 BULL. AM. ACAD. PSYCHIATRY L. 226 (1978).

J. ZISKIN, COPING WITH PSYCHIATRIC AND PSYCHOLOGICAL TESTIMONY (3d ed. 1980).

CHAPTER FIFTEEN

Sample Reports

15.01. Introduction

In Chapter 14 (specifically § 14.03), we set out detailed guidelines for report writing. Here we attempt to flesh out those guidelines, using a number of the substantive areas covered in this book as a subject matter. Thus, this chapter not only should illustrate a number of recurring problems in report writing, but also should provide concrete examples of the types of information we feel should be communicated to the courts.

Before we present the reports, a brief summary of what has been said in this book about reporting results to the courts may be helpful. Above all, a forensic report is a vehicle for transmitting clinical data and opinion to a lay audience. Writing a report requires thought and preparation. Regardless of the legal issue presented, the clinician should develop an outline to make sure that the report will be organized, that it addresses each issue raised by the referral source, and that it informs the reader of the underlying bases for each conclusion reached in the report.

The report writer should strive for clarity and conciseness. Because most readers of a forensic report will not be clinicians, the writer should either avoid clinical jargon or explain it if it is used. The writer should generally avoid giving gratuitous opinions on questions that have not been asked, although there are exceptions to this rule, as the first report in this chapter illustrates. When possible, "facts" or "data" should be separated from "inference" and "opinion." Sources should be attributed.

Finally, the writer should always be sensitive to the limits of his or her expertise. Speculation should be identified. Most importantly, conclusions as to whether a legal test or standard is met should be avoided because of their non-scientific nature.

Of course, all of what has been said above applies to testimony as well. Reports like those in this chapter will usually mirror testimony, though the latter may involve greater or lesser detail, depending upon the efforts of the examining lawyers.

In the reports that follow, which are all taken from actual cases, identifying information has been changed to ensure confidentiality. The reports follow a fairly similar sequential format (subject name, date of birth, and date of referral; data sources for the evaluation and other background information, including identification of the issues presented; relevant personal history; presentation of clinical data; and discussion of the legal issues). But they do not rigidly adhere to any one structure. The clinician will soon develop a report-writing style suited to his or her personal needs; we would only re-emphasize the importance of organization, both to assure that the report is understandable to the nonclinicians who are its primary audience, and to assist the clinician in assuring that all relevant issues have been addressed.

Following each report are editorial comments, pointing out how the report deals with particular issues. We do not offer a report on each of the subjects covered in this book, both because of space considerations and because reports on some subjects (e.g., the various competencies) will be similar in tone even if the specific legal issue addressed varies. We do provide at least one sample report for each chapter from Chapters 4 through 13, however. The subjects covered by the reports are competency to stand trial, competency to plead and confess, mental state at the time of the offense, sentencing under a special-track (sexual offender) statute, short-term dangerousness in the civil commitment context, competency to handle finances, employment-related mental injury, transferability of a juvenile, review of disposition in an abuse case, and visitation rights.

15.02. Competency to Stand Trial [Chapter 4]

(a) Harry Mills Report

NAME: Harry Mills
D.O.B.:   August 6, 1947
DATE INTERVIEWED: November 4, 1980
SUBJECT: Competency to stand trial

SOURCES OF DATA: Interview of defendant by Harry P. Nelson, Ph.D.; interview of defendant's attorney by Dr. Nelson; indictment; police report.

REFERRAL AND BACKGROUND INFORMATION: Mr. Mills was referred to the Clinic by his court-appointed attorney, Mr. Hahnemann, of Luther, Minnesota, for evaluation of his competency to stand trial on a charge of rape. Mr. Hahnemann also indicated concern that Mr. Mills appeared to be ex-

periencing a significant degree of depression, although he has no history of psychiatric problems.

MENTAL STATUS: Mr. Mills communicated effectively throughout his interview and did not hesitate to answer questions. However, his affect (emotional demeanor) was sad, and on several occasions he described suicidal thoughts. In particular, he stated he would commit suicide if sent to jail. (These statements are discussed in more detail below.)

While no formal assessment of Mr. Mills's intellectual ability was conducted, he appeared to be of grossly normal (perhaps low-average) intelligence. He appeared to have no significant problems with either recent or remote memory. However, at several points during the interview, he described himself as "dumb about things." These statements appear to reflect both an accurate assessment of his low fund of general information and his low self-esteem at present.

UNDERSTANDING OF LEGAL SITUATION: Mr. Mills can state the charge against him, describe its elements (he defined it as "nonconsensual intercourse"), and describe the possible sentence he'll receive if convicted. He is able to give a coherent description of the circumstances surrounding the alleged offense. He is able to describe in a basic way the actors in the court process. For instance, he stated that the prosecutor "is the attorney who presents the evidence against me," and that the judge "runs the trial and decides what to do with me." He can describe the process of testimony and cross-examination. He knows that he has a right to remain silent when asked questions by the judge. He describes the jury as a "group of citizens who decide whether you're guilty." When asked to describe "plea bargaining," he stated, "It's when the two attorneys agree on a charge for me."

Mr. Mills understands his attorney is supposed to "represent" him in court and states he has no difficulty conferring with him (a statement that Mr. Hahnemann confirms). Mr. Mills also stated, however, that one of Mr. Hahnemann's jobs is "to decide if I'm guilty or innocent." It might be helpful if Mr. Hahnemann clarified the exact nature of his role to Mr. Mills.

CONCLUSIONS CONCERNING COMPETENCY TO STAND TRIAL: As indicated above, Mr. Mills has no difficulty describing the charges against him, nor does he appear to have significant difficulty communicating in general or with his attorney in particular. He does have some misconceptions about the legal process—specifically about the role of his attorney, which Mr. Hahnemann should be able to clear up. Whether Mr. Mills accepts a plea-bargaining agreement or decides to go to trial may be influenced by his expressed dislike for jail, discussed more fully below.

COMMENTS CONCERNING TREATMENT: During the course of this evaluation, it became obvious that Mr. Mills is suffering from an acute depression. The most notable consideration is his clearly stated suggestion that the notion of self-destruction is not foreign to him and that in fact he has considered killing himself on a number of occasions. Mr. Mills stated that upon his release from an earlier prison sentence, he vowed that he would "never be placed in prison again." Today Mr. Mills reiterated several times that he had made this promise to himself; this suggests that he would at least consider self-destruction as an alternative to serving further time in prison.

The scope of the examination today did not allow for a thorough review of this man's history of covert, if not overt, suicidal ideation and/or intent. It is my recommendation at this time that he seek immediate psychotherapeutic follow-up, specifically for the purpose of establishing an appropriate treatment program for the depression that he currently experiences. In this regard, it should be noted that he is not particularly introspective and finds it difficult to verbalize a number of the strong emotions that he is experiencing. These feelings may only surface through this type of treatment.

Harry P. Nelson, Ph.D.

(b) Discussion

The Mills report is fairly typical of many reports on the issue of competency to stand trial. As is true in most such cases [see § 4.06(a)], there was not much room for doubt as to the defendant's competency, although Mr. Mills was obviously experiencing some mental difficulties.

When competency (criminal or civil) is the issue, the forensic report should be very focused. For example, the writer of the Mills report presented virtually none of the individual's personal history. While historical material may be critical in the evaluation of certain issues (e.g., in sentencing), it has little utility in most evaluations of competency to stand trial.

Note that details of the offense were not given. The writer observed that Mr. Mills could describe the offense, which was relevant to whether he was competent [see § 4.02(b)]. However, the *details* of the offense are usually irrelevant in reporting on competency to stand trial, and, in any event, should not be included due to Fifth Amendment concerns [see § 3.02].

Note also that the writer dealt with each of the functional elements of the competency test in describing Mr. Mills's abilities [see § 4.02(b)]. He observed that Mr. Mills could describe the court process and the roles of the participants, and gave specific examples using the defendant's own words. He then described Mr. Mills's relationship with his attorney, using information from both Mr. Mills and the attorney. Whether these statements in fact indicated sufficient knowledge about the legal process to merit a finding of competency was a question the writer left to the factfinder (although in this case the answer seems to have been clear). In addition, the descriptive details demonstrated clinical awareness of the competency standard, and may have saved the writer a trip to court.

Finally, this case presents three examples of situations in which the clinician appropriately included in the report material somewhat beyond the narrow issue of the person's competence. First, the report writer, in delineating the various elements of competency, noted that Mr. Mills was unclear about the role of his own lawyer, and suggested that a conversation between the two should alleviate this problem. Second, the writer highlighted a clinical concern (Mr. Mills's fear of jail) and its possible impact upon the legal process (i.e., Mr. Mills's fears could influence a plea-bargaining decision). This concern was more directly relevant to Mr. Mills's competency to plead, but also had ramifications for the extent to which Mr. Mills would cooperate with his attorney. Third, the writer strongly suggested further clinical evaluation of and treatment for Mr. Mills's depression. While comments on treatment may not always be appropriate in a competency evaluation, in this case the combination of possible acute depression on the client's part with a strong aversion to jail raised legitimate questions over the issue of harm to self. The oblique reference to Mr. Mills's previous prison term, while "prejudicial," was probably unavoidable if the writer was to give a complete clinical picture of Mr. Mills's suicidal thought patterns.

It is quite possible that Mr. Mills's attorney was more concerned about the treatment issue than about Mr. Mills's competency when he asked for the evaluation. Ideally, in such cases the attorney would communicate this interest via the court order rather than leave its assessment to the discretion of the examiner.

(c)   Warner Premington Report

NAME: Warner Premington
D.O.B.:   November 18, 1922
DATE INTERVIEWED: October 24, 1979
SUBJECT: Competency to stand trial

SOURCES OF DATA: Interview by Samuel Tatum, M.D., and Guy C. Harris, Ph.D.; interview of Mrs. Premington by Drs. Tatum and Harris; Competency Screening Tests; University of Virginia Hospital Chart.

REFERRAL INFORMATION: Mr. Premington was referred to the Forensic Psychiatry Clinic for evaluation of competency to stand trial by his attorney, Mr. Smith of Fairfax, Virginia. Specifically, the Clinic was asked to determine whether Mr. Premington has substantial mental capacity to understand the proceedings against him, whether he has the mental capacity to aid and assist his counsel in his defense, and whether more extensive evaluation and observation are required. The present evaluation concerns Mr. Premington's charges of driving after having been adjudged an habitual offender. These charges result from incidents in Fairfax County on April 25, 1979, and in Loudoun County on May 19, 1979. Also pending is an appeal in Loudoun County General District Court on a related charge of driving under the influence.

Mr. Smith has represented Mr. Premington for a number of years, and he was concerned about a steady deterioration that he has observed in Mr. Premington's ability to understand and orient himself to present events. Particular precipitants of the current evaluation were Mr. Premington's tendency to confuse the Loudoun County charge with the incident in Fairfax County and his disorientation at the time of a preliminary hearing in Loudoun County, according to Mr. Smith.

BACKGROUND INFORMATION: Mr. Premington has a lengthy history of psychiatric problems. He was hospitalized on several occasions for paranoid schizophrenia at the Salem Veterans Administration Hospital after a psychiatric discharge from military service in World War II. He was evaluated here at the Forensic Psychiatry Clinic in December 1970, subsequent to charges of breaking and entering. At that time, he was apparently actively delusional and hallucinating. Of most relevance to the current situation, Mr. Premington suffered rather severe damage to the cortical area of the brain as a result of head trauma incurred in a motorcycle accident in July 1977. Since that time he has had serious memory deficits and, according to his wife, periodic rage reactions. He has been hospitalized for these problems on occasion at the University of Virginia Hospital. He is currently being maintained on Haldol (an antipsychotic medication) 2 mg per day. It is also noteworthy that Mr. Premington has a history of chronic alcohol abuse.

MENTAL STATUS EXAMINATION: Mr. Premington presented as a rather tense, anxious man who appeared somewhat bewildered by the evaluation process. It was immediately apparent that he has some difficulty in recalling life events. He stated that his memory "has really gone downhill" since the accident of July 1977. The problems in recall were somewhat diffuse, but appeared to be more pronounced when he was attempting to relate events in the recent past. On examination, Mr. Premington was able to retain and recall a series of three digits; when four digits were given, his sequential recall deteriorated significantly. He had very inconsistent recall when asked to repeat several series of three and four digits in reverse order. He could, however, recall his own telephone number, but claimed no recall for the telephone numbers of his children (who live in the area). He also stated he cannot remember the extent of his extended family (he is not sure how many grandchildren he has).

Mr. Premington was unable to engage in abstract thinking in the evaluation. This was tested through the presentation of a series of items, one of which does not belong to the set (i.e., "Which one does to belong to the series?—Apple, orange, pear, ice cream cone").

The client was fully oriented to time, person, place (i.e., his awareness of his whereabouts and identity was intact), and to his situation (i.e., being evaluated by physicians), although it cannot be assumed that he understood the actual medical–legal significance of this examination. It is noteworthy also that Mr. Premington had a marked tendency to perseverate. That is, he would make an appropriate verbal response but then would continue to repeat that response in contexts where it no longer made any sense. He was apparently unable to shift his understanding of the situation when the situation had in fact changed. For example, on a sentence completion task (the Competency Screening Test), Mr. Premington repeatedly responded, "I'd tell the truth" when that answer was not relevant to the sentence stems presented. An originally appropriate response was thus repeated in inappropriate contexts. Largely because of this confusion, Mr. Premington scored below the cutoff point for competency on the Competency Screening Test, an instrument that has been found to discriminate validly between defendants later found incompetent to stand trial and those found competent. As a screening instrument, however, the Competency Screening Test slightly overpredicts incompetency, so it should not be relied upon as the sole factor in a determination.

UNDERSTANDING OF THE LEGAL SITUATION: Mr. Premington is aware that he was not supposed to be driving because he did not have a driver's license. He apparently does not understand the reason why his permit was revoked, though. He defined "habitual offender" as "driving the car more than once." He does understand the meaning of "driving under the influence" and its illegality. Mr. Premington was able to give a reasonably cogent description of the circumstances surrounding the offense in Fairfax County. However, when he was asked about other charges, Mr. Premington stated several times that he had no other charges pending. During the second interview, Mr. Premington did recall the Loudoun County offense, although he did not seem to realize that he was still liable for it. At best, he confuses the two events and has a clear awareness only of the Fairfax County charge. He was aware of no current charges of driving under the influence. He also had no memory of any recent court appearances.

Mr. Premington has some limited understanding of the process of a trial. He knows that a judge "gives you time" or "dismisses the case if you're not guilty." He observed that police are often present at the court, but he was unable to describe why. He also had no idea how an attorney might help him. Mr. Premington claimed to have no memory of what had happened in previous trials in which he had been a defendant. He described a jury as "three or four people together saying that you're guilty." On questioning,

Mr. Premington was able to recall a newspaper story he had read in which a jury had found a man not guilty. Nonetheless, he did define "guilty" as meaning that one is "charged with a crime." It was not clear if he understood that one could be charged but actually found not guilty; that is, it was unclear if he really knew what "being charged" means. Mr. Premington does not understand his rights in a trial. He said that the right to remain silent means that one is "not guilty" or "telling the truth." According to Mr. Premington, it means that, if a policeman says it, "he don't believe that you're guilty." He also does not understand the process of confrontation of witnesses. When asked what he would do if a witness lied about him, he reasoned that "I'd just feel bad" and that "I wouldn't do nothing."

CONCLUSIONS CONCERNING COMPETENCY TO STAND TRIAL: Subsequent to head trauma, Mr. Premington has suffered a significant memory loss. In the current context, he confuses the offenses with which he is charged, and it is questionable whether he would be able to keep the events of a trial in sequence in his mind. Because of his tendency to perseverate, it is also questionable whether he would be able to follow the trial as it progresses. Mr. Premington does understand that it was against the law for him to drive, and he remembers the Fairfax County incident reasonably well. While he does understand a trial as possibly resulting in "giving him time," Mr. Premington has numerous misconceptions and gaps in knowledge about the process of a trial. Mr. Premington's ability to engage in abstract thinking is so minimal that he is unable to conceptualize the roles of various participants in the trial. It is not likely that Mr. Premington would be able to give his attorney relevant facts as the trial progresses, because he could not be expected to understand the implications of testimony. He is compliant, though, and he would probably assist his attorney as much as he could, which realistically would be on an extremely limited basis.

CONCLUSIONS CONCERNING TREATMENT: We believe that Mr. Premington's lapses are largely related to brain damage. These lesions are permanent, and, as a result, he cannot be expected to become more competent, even with treatment. In our opinion, he does not require hospitalization at this time. Continued supervision by Mrs. Premington at home with medication would be the "less restrictive alternative" for his care.

Samuel Tatum, M.D.
Guy C. Harris, Ph.D.

(d) Discussion

The Premington report is more complicated than the Mills report, because the issue of Mr. Premington's competency was much more in doubt. Several things about the report are worth noting.

First, in contrast to the situation with Mr. Mills, historical information was very relevant to Mr. Premington's evaluation. The most significant information related to his competency was his history of brain damage, and therefore this had to be reported. Some of this background information was received from the attorney; a form such as that found in Table 4-4 can help focus the attorney (or other informant) on the relevant considerations.

Second, note the cautious manner in which clinical information was offered. For instance, several examples were given of Mr. Premington's problems with memory and abstract thinking. Such examples are less misleading than bald assertions that an individual has a "poor memory." By providing the court with the basis for their clinical judgments, the report writers enhanced the court's ability to judge the validity of their conclusions. Toward the same end, clinical terms (e.g., "perseverate") were explained in lay terms. Note also the explanation of the Competency Screening Test, and the qualification that it tends to overpredict incompetency slightly [see § 4.06(d)(1)].

Third, as in the Mills report, the writers explained Mr. Premington in terms of the specific functional elements of competency. His understanding of court process and of the roles of the various participants was described, and examples were given, primarily from his statements at the interview. While the court might not have credited the information (e.g., the court might have asked whether other individuals—say, Mr. Premington's wife—could corroborate what appeared to be his extremely hazy notion of court process), it would at least have been made aware of the reasons for the clinical opinion.

Fourth, note that while, on balance, the writers appeared to suggest that Mr. Premington was not competent, they avoided the ultimate issue, leaving this judgment to the legal system. This might have frustrated the court and counsel, but competency is a legal issue, not a medical issue and its determination may involve considerations that are not clinical in nature. In this case, for instance, the state needed only to prove that Mr. Premington had a previous driving offense and was "behind the wheel" on this occasion in order to obtain a conviction under the "habitual offender" statute. The court might have decided that Mr. Premington was competent to understand his relatively simple charges and to confer with his attorney about them.

Finally, the report noted the permanency of Mr. Premington's condition. This was relevant because it would affect the issue of restoration of competency, if the court found Mr. Premington incompetent [see §4.04].

15.03. Competency to Plead and Confess [Chapter 5]

(a) Carl Bates Report

NAME: Carl Bates
D.O.B.: March 28, 1927
DATE OF REPORT: June 22, 1984

DATES OF INTERVIEWS: Social history by John Waggoner, M.S.W., on June 6, 1984. Psychiatric evaluation by George Fordham, M.D., on June 13, 1984.

REFERRAL INFORMATION: Mr. Bates is a 57-year-old white male charged with one count of felonious attempted shooting. The charge arose out of an incident that occurred on March 19, 1984, in which Mr. Bates allegedly shot an airplane as it flew over his property. The plane, a crop duster, was hit five times, but no one was injured. Mr. Bates has signed a confession stating that he did shoot at the plane.

Mr. Bates was referred to the Clinic pursuant to an agreement between the Commonwealth's Attorney of Marion County, Charles Daniels, and Mr. Bates's attorney, Sam James of Ocala, Florida. The Clinic was asked to address the following questions:

1. Was Mr. Bates's confession voluntary and intelligent?
2. Is Mr. Bates competent to plead guilty?

The Clinic has available to it the following sources

of information: a summary of the police investigation relating to Mr. Bates's charge, prepared on March 13, 1984, by Trooper G.W. Jones; a summary of a psychiatric report on Mr. Bates from Brisbane Hospital in Pensacola, Florida, prepared by Mr. Lester Oldes, Jr., psychiatrist at the Marion County Family Guidance Center; a copy of Mr. Bates's indictment; and the Clinic's own evaluation, consisting of a two-hour social history interview, a two-and-a-half-hour psychiatric evaluation, and the administration of the Comprehension of *Miranda* Rights and Comprehension of *Miranda* Vocabulary tests.

PERSONAL HISTORY: Mr. Bates has been admitted to a psychiatric facility on only one occasion. In 1968, he was hospitalized at Ocala General Hospital and then transferred to Brisbane Hospital, a mental health institution. Mr. Bates is not sure why he was hospitalized, though he suspects it may have had something to do with his drinking. (He told the Clinic that prior to his hospitalization he would often consume a fifth of whiskey while watching a baseball game on TV.) While the Clinic does not have access to the final report from Brisbane, a summary of the report prepared by Dr. Oldes indicates that the Hospital staff believed Mr. Bates was manifesting "paranoid delusions of a great variety" upon his admission to Brisbane. His condition was diagnosed as "chronic undifferentiated schizophrenia with organic features." Signs of heavy drinking were also noted. Mr. Bates told the Clinic that he received no treatment at Brisbane. He was apparently released after approximately six months.

According to Mr. Bates, his admission to Brisbane marked a time of significant change in his life. He stated that while he had enjoyed an active sex life before his admission, afterward he did not engage in sex at all. He began having trouble sleeping; he said that this was the result of loud pounding noises originating from rooms adjacent to his. Most significantly, it was at this time that Mr. Bates began to believe that government officials were attempting to harass him. He eventually came to believe that the noises were made by these government agents, whom he alternatively characterized as the "Law," the "Metropolitan Police," the "Government," or "Plainclothesmen."

Mr. Bates reported other manifestations of government harassment over the years since 1968. He stated that even though he changed residences several times in the years between 1968 and 1979, the night noises continued. The "Law" allegedly placed bugging devices in his bed and kept him under constant surveillance with cameras and other electronic equipment. Automobiles with Washington, D.C. plates (apparently indicating a connection with the government) would be waiting outside his door to tail him. He said that the government even began making use of his neighbors and family in its attempt to harass him. He reported that while he used to have a close relationship with his family, he no longer trusts them because they have been "turning to the Law."

From Mr. Bates's description, it appears that the government's scheming increased after he moved to his present location in Archer, Florida, which happens to be near a military training center. He claimed that eavesdropping devices were planted all over his house and that government cameras were set up in his elder brother's home across the street. Neighbors' children were supposedly employed by the "Law" to observe his activities. The ploy that most annoyed Mr. Bates was the alleged use of planes and helicopters by the "Law" to conduct surveillance and bombard his home with electronic weapons. According to Mr. Bates, the latter action resulted in damage to his house and the death of one of his dogs.

According to Mr. Bates's confession, he admitted to the shooting incident that led to the current charges. In the confession, he justified his act as an effort on his part to retaliate against the long years of government surveillance and to bring attention to government methods. Though asked at several points during the clinic interview why he thought the government was conducting this campaign against him, he could recite no reason other than the possibility of "some sort of grudge." When confronted with the suggestion that perhaps the cameras and bugging devices did not exist (he admitted to not being able to find them) and that the planes were engaged in legitimate enterprises, he rejected the notion vigorously. He appears to be convinced that the government is "out to get him" and that the plane he shot at was just another indication of this plot.

Since his arrest, Mr. Bates has been living at home. He reported that he has not observed any government-sponsored plane flying over his house, though he believes the cameras are still in place. He stated that he is not concerned about the outcome of the pending proceedings because he has "everything in his hands"; this appears to mean that he has caught the government in the act and it will eventually suffer for it. He believes that his trial and incarceration, if they take place, will be the "match to the gasoline barrel" that will highlight the misdeeds of the "Law" and its officials. He compared himself in this regard to Jack Anderson, the columnist.

Mr. Bates also believes that the "Law" has been behind the delay in having his case heard. He stated that if he is sent to jail he would not be surprised if it was because the judge and the lawyers had been bribed.

MENTAL STATUS: Mr. Bates is a 57-year-old white male with a ruddy complexion who appears to be slightly overweight. He rarely smiled during the interview and assumed a belligerent tone during most of it; however, his irritation was directed toward those he believed to be harassing him and not toward the interviewers. Mr. Bates was oriented to time, place, and person; that is, he knew what time of the year and day it was, where he was, who he was, and who the interviewers were. He did seem somewhat confused as to the purpose of the interview, at one point stating that he felt his evaluation at the Clinic was another attempt at delay by the "Law." He understood, however, that the interview was somehow connected with his pending criminal proceeding.

Mr. Bates exhibited significant signs of delusion when discussing the "Law's" involvement in his life. On other topics he did not exhibit such delusional symptoms; he was able to discuss rationally such subjects as his weight, gardening, different types of guns, and the weather.

Clinically, there is some evidence of incipient organicity (i.e., damage to brain tissue, which often manifests itself through deficits in memory and orientation). Mr. Bates could have done damage to his brain through his heavy drinking in the past. Such damage could also result from deterioration due to the aging process. Mr. Bates's thought content was often tangential (i.e., divergent from the topic under discussion). When confronted with the assertion that some of his statements contradicted reality, he answered with seemingly irrelevant pronouncements. For instance, when it was noted that he had never been able to discover any bugging devices in his home, he responded, "I don't have to find it because I know just what I'm looking for." Clinically, Mr. Bates is estimated to be of average intelligence.

Mr. Bates' affect (his emotional response to the content of the interview) also appeared abnormal. He exhibited little emotion other than anger or irritation throughout most of the interview.

OBSERVATIONS ABOUT MR. BATES'S COMPETENCY TO CONFESS: Mr. Bates could coherently describe the events leading up to his confession, the important aspects of which are corroborated by the police account. Mr. Bates stated that he was arrested by three policemen shortly after the alleged offense and was taken to the station house. He was not asked any questions on the ride to the station, and he did not volunteer any information, other than exclaiming "You'll pay for this" from time to time. After booking, he was given *Miranda* warnings and was asked several questions about the offense; the session took about an hour and took place in a windowless room on the second floor of the police station, with three plainclothes officers and a tape recorder present. About one hour after the questioning ended, he was asked to sign a document purporting to summarize his statements, which he did.

When asked during the interview, Mr. Bates could state with reasonable precision the *Miranda* warnings. However, he did forget the fourth prong of the warnings (i.e., that if the person cannot afford an attorney, one will be appointed for him). He was given two tests developed by Grisso* to examine understanding of *Miranda* rights. He scored 7 on the Comprehension of *Miranda* Rights test, and 10 on the Comprehension of *Miranda* Vocabulary test, both of which represent scores in the upper 60% of the 203 adults evaluated by Grisso using the same tests. Of course, these scores are relevant primarily to Mr. Bates's present understanding of *Miranda,* not his understanding at the time of the arrest.

Mr. Bates stated that he had not felt physically threatened by the police at the time of the confession, nor was he under the influence of drugs or alcohol at that time. As evidenced during his interview, he does not seem particularly suggestible, particularly when an aspect of his delusional system is challenged (see above).

OBSERVATIONS ABOUT MR. BATES'S COMPETENCY TO PLEAD GUILTY: In the state of Florida, to be competent to plead one must be competent to stand trial, plus understand the various rights that are waived through a guilty plea; in addition, the plea must be voluntary.

Thus, competency to plead guilty first requires a capacity to communicate with one's lawyer. Mr. Bates's mental condition, which demonstrates clear evidence of paranoia, distorts his perception of reality. But he is able to communicate verbally with relative ease. He can recite the events leading up to his arrest and what occurred thereafter. While his interpretation of these events is somewhat abnormal, he is able

---

* *See* T. GRISSO, JUVENILES' WAIVER OF RIGHTS: LEGAL AND PSYCHOLOGICAL COMPETENCE (1981).

to describe them in sufficient detail to give an attorney a factual basis upon which to work.

Mr. Bates stated that he does not believe his attorney is part of the plot to harass him, and in fact told the Clinic interviewers that he "trusts" Mr. James. There is a possibility that Mr. Bates could change his opinion of Mr. James as the trial date approaches or after he sees how the trial progresses. However, at present he appears willing to cooperate with his attorney in his own defense.

The other prong of the test of competency to plead guilty is whether the defendant possesses a rational and factual understanding of the proceedings against him. As noted previously, Mr. Bates's perception of the legal process is distorted by his belief that if he is found guilty it will be because the court has been corrupted, and not because he has done something illegal. This belief is not "rational" in the sense that it does not comport with reality (thought it is "rational" if one accepts Mr. Bates's premise that the "Law" is determined to martyr him). The important point here, however, is that Mr. Bates's delusion does not obscure his understanding of the functions of various court personnel, nor does it hinder his grasp of the purpose of trial. He was able to explain adequately what the judge and lawyers are expected to do in and out of the courtroom. For instance, he said that the judge "makes the decision about the case" and lawyers "help him do it, by showing him both sides of the case."

Mr. Bates also was able to demonstrate a minimal understanding of what it means to plead guilty. When asked if he would receive a trial after pleading guilty, Mr. Bates stated "No." When asked what he would plead guilty to, he stated, "Shooting an airplane." As noted previously, he understands that a plea of guilty could potentially result in incarceration, although he did not know the maximum penalty. (As it turns out, no one knows the maximum penalty for "shooting an airplane," since technically it is not a crime in Florida. Mr. Daniels states he will probably eventually charge Mr. Bates with some type of assault.) Whatever the charge, it seems probable that Mr. Bates, on a cognitive level, would understand the implications of pleading guilty to it.

It is noteworthy in this regard that if Mr. Bates did plead guilty, he would still in all likelihood believe that his acts were totally justified and that he is not "guilty" in the moral sense. He would probably admit to shooting the airplane but would never admit that he was "wrong" in doing so.

The Clinic has no opinion as to the voluntariness prong of the guilty plea test, as that will presumably depend upon the circumstances surrounding the occasion of the plea. Our observations with reference to Mr. Bates's suggestibility in a general sense are stated above.

George Fordham, M.D.
John Waggoner, M.S.W.

(b) Discussion

The Bates report is interesting from a number of perspectives. First, it demonstrates a point made in all of the chapters dealing with competency [Chapters 4, 5, and 9]: that psychosis or delusions do not automatically render a person incompetent. A competency evaluation must focus on the individual's understanding of the specific functions considered relevant by the law; even if the person is "out of touch with reality" in a general sense, he or she may still be able to grasp the narrow notions encompassed by the legal test. Here, the data presented in the report suggest that Mr. Bates was competent to stand trial and plead guilty (and that his confession was valid as well), despite his paranoid delusions. Of course, a judge might have decided that Mr. Bates's delusional system, and specifically his refusal to admit any moral wrongdoing, rendered his confession or guilty plea "unknowing"; this argues for avoiding the ultimate issue, as the examiners did.

With respect to the portion of the report concerning competency to confess, it is worth noting the use of Grisso's assessment instruments to gauge present understanding of the *Miranda* litany, and the careful recitation of the events surrounding the confession. Both these aspects of the report, together with the observation about Mr. Bates's suggestibility (or lack thereof), would be relevant to the voluntariness determination required in such cases [see § 5.02(b)].

With respect to the portion of the report concerning competency to plead guilty, it should be pointed out that the writers first set out the legal test and then addressed each aspect of it—including the important issues of whether Mr. Bates' paranoia would affect his relationship with his attorney; the extent to which he would in fact believe he was guilty if and when he pled guilty; and the voluntariness of such a plea. On the last-mentioned issue, as the report noted, a prospective assessment such as the one required here could not be made because the examiners had no knowledge of the circumstances surrounding the plea arrangement.

Because of the complicated nature of Mr. Bates's delusional system and its possible relevance to the competency issues, the report spent more time recounting Mr. Bates's personal history than many competency reports do. Given Mr. Bates's history, and his apparent perception of the offense, it is interesting to speculate whether Mr. Bates should have been found "insane" at the time of the offense. Under the *Durham* rule [see § 6.02(b)], he would probably have been found insane, since the shooting was the "product" of his paranoia. Under the American Law Institute or *M'Naghten* formulations, on the other hand, whether he would have been found insane might have depended upon whether the "appreciation of wrongfulness" notion incorporated in each referred to awareness that the offense was legally wrong or morally wrong [see § 6.02(c)(3)]. Mr. Bates clearly knew his act was wrong in the first sense, but just as clearly believed it was "right" in the second sense. Since, for him, the "Law" was in essence breaking the law by gratuitously attacking his home, killing his pets, and monitoring his every move, he might have been justified in retaliating. On the other hand, if what he believed to be happening had actually been happening, it might still have been wrong (morally as well as legally) to react in the way he did, rather than, for instance, contacting other authorities.

15.04.   Mental State at the Time of the Offense [Chapter 6]

(a)   Ed Wertz Report

NAME: Ed Wertz
D.O.B.:   July 27, 1946
DATE OF REPORT: July 20, 1984

REFERRAL INFORMATION: Mr. Wertz is a 37-year-old, married, white male who is charged with armed robbery. The offense occurred on or about March 3, 1984, when Mr. Wertz allegedly entered the K&K Gun Shop and robbed the owner at gunpoint, leaving the scene with two semiautomatic rifles and ammunition. Mr. Wertz was referred to the clinic by his attorney, Mr. Ed Whitley, who requested an assessment of Mr. Wertz's mental state at the time of the offense.

INTERVIEW   DATES   AND   INFORMATION SOURCES: First interview (two hours) by Sally Patton, Ph.D., on June 19, 1984. Second interview (one hour) and sodium brevital interview (one hour, 15 minutes) performed by Louis Beck, M.D., on July 3, 1984.

Third-party information reviewed by the examiners include: (1) summary of the investigation report describing the crime scenario, prepared by Det. Warren Bond of the Columbia police department; (2) two transcripts of statements given by Mr. Wertz to police officers on March 4 and 5, 1984; (3) photocopies of handwritten statements prepared by each of three witnesses present at the scene of the crime and by the arresting officer.

Professional literature pertinent to the present clinical findings includes the following:

Atkinson, Sparr, Sheff, White, & Fitzsimmons, *Diagnosis of Post-Traumatic Stress Disorder in Vietnam Veterans: Preliminary Findings,* 114 AM. J. PSYCHIATRY 694 (1984).

Hendin, Haas, Singer, Houghton, Schwartz, & Wallen, *The Reliving Experience in Vietnam Veterans with Post-Traumatic Stress Disorder,* 25 COMPREHENSIVE PSYCHIATRY 165 (1984).

D. Spyker, The Acute Toxicity of Ethanol: Dosages and Kinetic Monograms (1984) (manuscript submitted to J.A.M.A.).

Williams, *The Mental Foxhole: The Vietnam Veteran's Search for Meaning,* 53 AM. J. ORTHOPSYCHIATRY 4 (1983).

PERSONAL BACKGROUND: Mr. Wertz was born in Minnesota and lived there until the age of four, at which time his parents separated and he moved to Texas and continued living with his mother. He described both parents as heavy drinkers and reported that at approximately age 12 he ran away from home because "my mom was an alcoholic . . . I was tired of her drinking and the constant parade of men she brought into the house." He was subsequently picked up and placed in a foster care home, where he remained until age 18.

At age 21 he entered the U.S. Army and served a two-year tour of duty in Vietnam. It was considered clinically noteworthy that Mr. Wertz had significant difficulty discussing his Vietnam experiences; with persistent questioning, however, he gave a brief summary of his combat experiences, including one occasion on which he killed approximately 31 North Vietnamese soldiers holed up in a concrete bunker with the use of a .50-caliber machine gun.

In 1972 he married his present wife, Jane (Decker) Wertz. Also at that time he began working at the Columbia City Hospital as a maintenance mechanic, a job that he held continuously until his arrest on the present charge. Mr. Wertz's feelings about his job appear quite mixed. On the one hand he reported, in an almost boastful tone, that when on duty he had the maintenance responsibility for the entire hospital and additional duties as a security person; with respect to the latter duties, he seemed quite concerned that the examiners understand the importance of his role. He repeatedly stressed the value in having a "nonviolent person" responsible for calming agitated patients. On the other hand, he also described considerable anxiety associated with his job, primarily in relation to concerns of how workers on other shifts might perceive him (and his competence) if he passed uncompleted projects to them at the end of his shift. He also admitted feeling chronically dissatisfied with the lack of opportunity for advancement.

Mr. Wertz denied any current use of illicit drugs, though he admitted that he had smoked marijuana while in Vietnam. He reported that he occasionally drinks alcoholic beverages (usually beer) but not to the point of feeling intoxicated.

Mr. Wertz denied any prior contact with the mental health professions. However, he did describe one prior episode of behavior that is regarded as clinically significant. In September of 1983, he was packing his car to leave for a hunting trip. As he was doing so, he began ruminating about the anxiety and dissatisfaction associated with his employment, and he considered that he might be forced to desert his family and "run away" in order to escape the situation. His next memory of the event is waking up at the hunting cabin, initially quite disorganized because he could not recall having driven up there (a drive of over four hours). He reported feeling even more perplexed after inspecting his automobile, which was packed with virtually all of his personal possessions (e.g., tools, clothing); further, he had apparently acquired a powerful rifle (30.06) but had no recollection of having purchased it. Feeling quite upset, he returned home to his family the next day. Jane Wertz remembers her husband telling her about the experience on the day he returned, describing it essentially in the same terms just reported.

There was no indication of prior criminal behavior, either in the police files or in the self-report from Mr. Wertz.

CIRCUMSTANCES OF THE OFFENSE: At the June 19 interview, Mr. Wertz provided the following information regarding the alleged crime. After having worked the midnight shift on his job at the hospital, he arrived home in the morning in time to see his wife off to work and his daughter off to school. He then drove to a nearby store, purchased some beer, and returned home, where he began working in his garage. He reported that he was building a lawn cart for a friend, and his last memory of the morning was of standing in the garage, staring at the blueprints.

His next memory was of "being in the gun shop with a shotgun in my hand . . . I can see John [owner], and I remember pointing the gun at him." He also recalled leaving the gun shop with two automatic rifles and "starting heading west on a dirt road, back toward Winford County." He could recall no other details regarding the robbery, nor could he recall the route he took after "heading west." Mr. Wertz could not recall stopping his jeep, nor could he explain why he stopped where he did. His next memory was of standing in a field, shooting one of the automatic rifles at an abandoned farm building. He recalled that a deputy sheriff approached and asked, "Why are you shooting at that building?" Mr. Wertz recalled feeling very exasperated by the question, for he had no idea why he was standing in the field and firing the weapon. He reported that he readily put the weapon down and agreed to talk with the officer after receiving his *Miranda* warnings. Initially he could not recall the robbery and could not explain how the automatic rifles came to be in his possession. When the officer mentioned a robbery at the K&K Gun Shop, Mr. Wertz's memory was jogged, and he reported to police the sketchy memories summarized above.

Because Mr. Wertz's memory at the time of the first interview was quite sketchy, the examiners elected to conduct a subsequent interview with the defendant under the influence of sodium brevital. Sodium brevital is a general anesthetic that can be administered intravenously to create an altered state of consciousness in the subject. While such chemicals have no proven validity as "truth serums," they may be useful in relaxing the subject's psychological defenses and may permit repressed memories to surface into consciousness. The brevital interview was conducted on July 3, 1984, and Mr. Wertz's memory was somewhat enhanced by this procedure. He recalled working in his garage on the morning in question and stated that his cousin, David, dropped in for a visit. He estimated that he consumed ten beers before leaving home around 11:30 A.M. He reported entering the K&K Gun Shop two times, the first time simply to use the men's room. Before entering the second time, he removed the shotgun from his jeep and loaded it as he walked toward the door. He described feeling "nervous, scared, hurt . . . I wanted to give the butt end of the gun to them . . . so they could stop me from what I was doing." After driving away from the gun shop, he stopped the jeep and loaded the automatic rifles. He then proceeded to a deserted farm and began firing on a concrete outbuilding. He stated that the building reminded him of concrete bunkers he had assaulted in Vietnam, and he recalled having been bothered by ruminations of Vietnam earlier that day.

PRESENT MENTAL STATUS: Mr. Wertz was on bond at the time of the clinical evaluation. He was on time for both appointments and presented as a tall, slender white male who was dressed in casual but neat clothing. He was a cooperative informant who responded to all questions from the staff; he responded without undue delay and discussed positive and negative aspects of his background without becoming guarded or defensive. This, along with the consistency between his account of his behavior and the account distilled from third-party sources, led the staff to view him as a candid respondent. There was no evidence of bizarre or peculiar thought patterns or perceptual distortions (e.g., hearing imaginary voices), nor did Mr. Wertz report having previously experienced such symptoms. His mood was variable and appropriate to the topic of conversation, though he was predominately serious and somber and appeared to have difficulty relaxing. He admitted to some chronic feelings of depression and dissatisfaction associated with his employment situation, and to transient periods of increased anxiety and depression associated with memories of combat experiences in Vietnam. He reported that he tries to cope with these disturbing memories by "not thinking about it." He otherwise presented himself as a conscientious and responsible member of the community, a characterization that appears consistent with the available prior history.

MENTAL STATE AT THE TIME OF THE OF-FENSE: In the opinion of the clinic staff, Mr. Wertz

was suffering from a significant psychological disturbance at the time of the offense. As noted above, this defendant is a Vietnam veteran. He reported extremely stressful events during the war, including witnessing the gruesome deaths of many fellow soldiers who fought next to him in the field. He recalled ambivalent feelings about his role as a soldier, feeling guilt about having killed other human beings, but also feeling anger and hatred sparked by his desire to avenge the deaths of his own comrades. Since his discharge, he has experienced anxiety and depression associated with ruminations about his Vietnam experiences; he reported such ruminations on the day of the offense.

Mr. Wertz's behavior on the day of the crime is, in the staff's opinion, reasonably viewed as a response to the recurring stress associated with painful memories of combat in Vietnam. Delayed responses to wartime stress are well documented in Vietnam veterans (see studies cited). One characteristic stress response is for individuals to "relive" through their own thoughts and fantasies the original stressful episodes, in an apparent effort to bring about more successful (i.e., psychologically acceptable) solutions. Such "reliving" episodes are sometimes referred to as "flashbacks"; during these episodes the individuals' behavior is marked by feelings of detachment or estrangement from the present-day world around them, and they act "as if" they are back in time when the stressful event occurred. One study reported that such reliving episodes occur in as many as 20% of Vietnam veterans suffering from delayed stress response syndrome (Hendin *et al.,* 1984).

Several features of Mr. Wertz's behavior and recollection of March 3, 1984, suggest that he may have been in an altered state of consciousness in which he was reliving Vietnam experiences. Most obvious is the choice of a target for assault with the semiautomatic weapons taken from the gun shop—a concrete building on a deserted farm, which visually reminded him of concrete bunkers he had assaulted during the war. It should also be mentioned that Mr. Wertz admits owning several rifles and handguns, but no semiautomatic weapons such as those he used in the war. Thus, a special purpose in obtaining the semiautomatic weapons is implied. His sketchy memory and reported subjective feelings of ambivalence during the robbery ("I wanted to give them the butt end of the gun . . . so they could stop me . . .") are also consistent with the kind of altered state associated with reliving prior experiences, during which the experience of self-control is diminished. In the opinion of the clinic staff, the absence of evidence of careful planning of the offense, the lack of resistance at the time of arrest, and the absence of other apparent motive for obtaining these particular weapons lends further credence to the psychological explanation described here.

It should be noted further that Mr. Wertz reported consuming as much as ten cans of beer on the morning of the offense. The effect of the alcohol may have been to weaken the elements of self-control he normally uses to control or repress these recurring feelings about his Vietnam experience. The alcohol alone would not have been sufficient to account for his behavior, but may have contributed by lowering Mr. Wertz's usual inhibitions or psychological mechanisms of self-control.

A computer program developed by Dr. Daniel Spyker (see Spyker, 1984) provides data on this issue that might be useful. The program makes use of several variables that the literature considers essential in computing the blood alcohol level of humans and the impact of alcoholic intoxication on their functioning. These variables include the age and weight of the subject, which both relate to the individual's "tolerance" level and to the volume of alcohol distribution within the blood; the quantity of alcohol ingested; and whether or not the subject has recently consumed food (a variable that affects the absorption rate of the alcohol). The program combines information concerning these variables with a constant ("V_{max}" = 230 mg/ml/hr), which expresses the rate at which an "average" male drinker (i.e., one who has developed some tolerance for alcohol but who is not an alcoholic) "eliminates" alcohol from his system over time. The result is a relatively accurate Blood Ethanol Concentration (BEC), expressing the amount of alcohol within the individual's blood stream at the given time. (Under this program, it should be noted, it is assumed that 99% of the alcohol consumed is eventually absorbed by the blood. The program does not account for the possible variances in the "natural" genetic alcohol tolerance level of particular individuals, since this variable is essentially impossible to measure. Nor is the V_{max} figure—the elimination rate—fine-tuned for each individual measured.)

Assuming that Mr. Wertz is telling the truth with respect to his consumption of alcohol, and assuming further that, as he told us, he did not eat before the offense was committed and that the drinking took place approximately three hours before the offense, and factoring in Mr. Wertz's age and weight, the program would produce a BEC in Mr. Wertz at the time of the offense of 139 mg/dl (milligrams per decaliter). "Legal intoxication" in the state of Minnesota is a BEC of 100 mg/dl. In many individuals, "ataxia," or

severely impaired leg and arm coordination, sets in at a BEC of 200 mg/dl.

Sally Patton, Ph.D.
Louis Beck, M.D.

(b) Discussion

The Wertz report is an evaluation of mental state at the time of the offense (MSO) in a case presenting an unusual clinical picture. Several points are worth making.

First, with an MSO exam, it is important for the clinician to note the sources of information used in the evaluation, particularly those describing the offense. This will assist the legal system in assessing the credibility of the description of the offense presented in the report (if the offense is described). Second, much more historical material is presented in an MSO report than in the previous competency reports, particularly that relevant to clinical opinion on the individual's status at the time of the offense. For example, in this report, both Mr. Wertz's Vietnam experience and employment were discussed. His war experiences were directly related by the writers to the clinical formulation of the offense, as were his attitudes toward his job (i.e., his "chronic dissatisfaction" with a lack of advancement opportunities).

Third, the writers described the offense, Mr. Wertz's feelings while committing it, and his later recall of it in some detail. Such a discussion is generally useful in MSO reports, primarily because it enables the legal system to "see" an offense through a clinician's eyes and thereby to better evaluate the clinical opinion offered to explain the individual's behavior at the time of the offense. For example, if the clinician describes the offense in a manner wholly at variance with the eventual determination by the legal system as to how the offense actually occurred, clinical explanations of behavior will become less compelling. Conversely, if the explanation of the offense is generally consistent with the legal system's views (or at least those of one side of the controversy when the facts are seriously disputed), the clinical conclusions may be more persuasive. In this regard, it should be noted that the writers carefully gave reasons why they believed Mr. Wertz to be credible about the offense; this is an issue of paramount importance to an MSO report.

Fourth, the writers sought and relied upon a wide range of data outside of the clinical interview in order to support their opinion. Relevant literature about post-wartime stress was cited; a brevital interview was conducted; and a sophisticated assessment of Mr. Wertz's ability to withstand the impact of the alcohol he said he consumed was made. In each case, the report tried to make clear the extent to which the data were relied upon and the possible problems with their use. For instance, the writers were careful to avoid equating sodium brevital with "truth serum," and they specified the methodological qualifications connected with the computer analysis of Mr. Wertz's BEC at the time of the offense. In cases involving amnesia and alcohol or drug use, such caution is especially important, since these techniques might otherwise assume undue importance for the factfinder.

Finally, note that while the clinical conclusions were given in detail and with an absence of jargon, the report did not give an opinion on the ultimate legal issue of insanity. The report— properly, in our view—left to the legal system the legal significance of the clinical material, which may or may not have established insanity, automatism, diminished capacity, or some other defense [see §§ 6.02, 6.03].

Consonant with our recommendations in § 3.02(b), a report of this type should not be sent to the prosecution prior to notice of an intent to raise a defense of mental abnormality. Instead, unless the court orders otherwise, we recommend that only a short summary containing no incriminating material be sent to the prosecutor prior to such notice.

15.05. Special-Track Sentencing [Chapter 7]

(a) George Sanders Report

The Sanders referral was under a special-track dispositional statute in which the question was

whether the defendant was a "mentally disordered sexual offender." The statutory definition of such a person is "any person who has a mental disorder and who, because of the mental disorder, has been determined to be disposed to repeated commission of sexual offenses (sexual assault or debauching a minor) which are likely to cause substantial injury to the health of others." If an individual is found to meet this statutory standard, the court must then determine where the individual should be confined (either in prison or a hospital), with the decision turning upon the person's treatability within facilities available within the state.

NAME: George Sanders
D.O.B.:   July 5, 1958

REFERRAL AND SOURCES OF INFORMATION: Mr. Sanders was referred by the Hon. John Lamb of Middlesex County District Court for evaluation and possible sentencing as a mentally disordered sex offender (MDSO). (Mr. Sanders recently pled guilty to one count of first-degree sexual assault committed while on escape from a work-release center.) Specifically, evaluation was requested as to whether Mr. Sanders meets the statutory definition of an MDSO, and, if so, if he is treatable and if the appropriate treatment is available in Massachusetts.

Mr. Sanders was previously evaluated by this examiner as to his competency to stand trial, mental state at the time of the offense, and need for treatment. Where material from that evaluation is pertinent to the MDSO questions, it is included herein.

In the current evaluation, Mr. Sanders was interviewed for approximately one and a half hours on June 21, 1982. In addition, the county attorney made available police reports, including accounts of their investigation and interviews of the victim and the defendant.

In the previous evaluation, Mr. Sanders was interviewed on August 3, 7, and 21, 1981 (a total of approximately three and a half hours). Psychological testing was also conducted (i.e., Wechsler Adult Intelligence Scale—Revised [WAIS-R] and Competency Screening Test on August 7, 1981; Thematic Apperception Test, Rorschach, and Draw-a-Person on August 21, 1981). Also available at that time were the following: a statement written by Mr. Sanders on August 6, 1981; the affidavit for the warrant for his arrest; notes from an interview of Mr. Sanders by his attorney (Ronald Jones) on July 27, 1981. Correctional evaluation and treatment records were requested but were unobtainable.

HISTORY: Mr. Sanders is the oldest of three sons of Edward Sanders and Wendy Martin. His parents divorced when Mr. Sanders was about age 12 or 13, and he lived with his mother thereafter. Mr. Sanders's mother married Harry Martin when Mr. Sanders was in high school (about ninth grade). Then they moved from Springfield to Boston. Mr. Sanders's father has also remarried; he now lives in Framingham. Brothers are named Adam, 21, and Carl, 17; Mr. Sanders thinks that they still live at home, but he is not sure.

Mr. Sanders described considerable conflict with his stepfather. He said that they never got along and that they never really talked to each other. When Mr. Sanders tries to call home, Mr. Martin is said to hang up on him. Mr. Martin had refused to allow him to come home after his release. At the time of his escape from the the work-release center (the present offense was committed while he was AWOL), Mr. Sanders was worried that he had no place to go and that, therefore, he would be denied parole. Prior to going to prison, Mr. Sanders had moved out and was living in motels because of conflicts with his stepfather. Mr. Sanders stated that his stepfather may have gone to Hartford at one point for inpatient alcoholism treatment. He could not be sure, however, because Mrs. Martin would not confirm his stepfather's whereabouts at that time. Most recently, Mr. Sanders claimed that he wrote his stepfather's employer earlier this month with an allegation that Mr. Martin had been stealing from the company; this allegation was designed to retaliate against him.

Mr. Sanders seemed not to be able to say very much about his mother, but he insisted that relationships with her had been pleasant until she remarried. Until then, Mr. Sanders said that he felt that he could talk with her about his problems (many of which apparently were school-related). It is not clear, however, that there was much active interaction. Mr. Sanders indicated that "Mom always left me alone when I had problems." He would then go into his room and lock the door. Mrs. Martin did visit him when he was in the work-release center; she has not visited him in prison, however, although she is said to write about one time per month. Mr. Sanders claimed to find female counselors easier to talk to than male counselors; he related this greater ease of interaction to his relationship with his mother.

Mr. Sanders had minimal contact with his natural father after the divorce. Some years thereafter, they did resume occasional contact. Mr. Sanders said that he was the only member of the family who ever spoke to his father. He denied knowing the reason for the divorce or even having any ideas about it.

Relationships between Mr. Sanders and his brothers are also strained. He knows virtually nothing about their current circumstances. He said that he read in the newspaper that Carl had been arrested for assault. Mr. Sanders speculated that the reason his brothers do not talk to him is "because I'm heavyset." In his opinion, both brothers were more favored than he by his parents because they were more successful in school.

Mr. Sanders described himself as having always been "quiet" and isolated. In fact, his greatest wish was and is "to be alone by myself somewhere." He described himself as having been a loner as long as he can remember. For recreation, he eschewed organized sports and instead went fishing by himself. Mr. Sanders reported being overwhelmed by anxiety and becoming tongue-tied when he is in large groups of people or in the center of a group of people. When asked what he needed to change about himself, he could think of only his "fear of people"—a fear that he said he has not divulged to his counselor in the prison mental health unit, where he is currently incarcerated.

Mr. Sanders's general lack of relationships carries over to relationships with women. He reported never having had a real date. In the August 1981 interviews, he said that his only close relationship was with Joan, a woman who was said to have died a few months prior to the escape from the work-release center. However, in the June 1982 interview, he stated that her relatives lied about her "going away" so as to end their relationship. In the more recent interviews, Mr. Sanders blamed Joan for all of his problems, and he said that he would not want another girlfriend because it "would make me depressed." It is important to note that Mr. Sanders never actually met Joan. She was the sister of a fellow inmate, and they corresponded and had phone conversations. Mr. Sanders said that he and Joan had planned to be married. He also thought that his mother liked her, although he was not sure why. Mr. Sanders said that his only other girlfriend was Susan, whom he met while he was in school. Susan was a drinking buddy, but they never dated formally. However, police records of an interview with her suggest that Mr. Sanders had sent her love letters on occasion.

Although he graduated from Southern High, Mr. Sanders's school career apparently consisted almost exclusively of special education classes. Upon graduation, he went to work as a laborer on sewers for the city of Boston. This job lasted about one and a half years. Mr. Sanders quit because of conflicts with his supervisor, who said that he was not a good driver. Thereafter, he worked for about six months as a security guard for Acme Security Company. He was fired from that job for being out of uniform.

While unemployed, Mr. Sanders turned to criminal activity (check forgeries, burglaries) to support himself. The burglaries were all in his neighborhood. For example, he broke into the house of one man who he knew collected coins. Mr. Sanders was apprehended and convicted of two burglaries. On April 6, 1981, he was sentenced to two to four years. At the time of his escape, he had only 75 days remaining in his term. Most of Mr. Sanders's incarceration has been in the prison mental health unit. He spent seven months there during his incarceration for the burglaries, and he is currently on that unit.

Mr. Sanders seemed not to be able to identify why he was on the prison mental health unit for so long, except that "I cracked up." He said that he had asked to go to the state hospital during his previous stay at the mental health unit and that he wished that he could go there now. In his opinion, the counseling there would be better than in the correctional system. Mr. Sanders said that his most recent counselor at the mental health center, Harold Nevins, had indicated that he was ready to leave the mental health unit and enter the medium-security portion of the prison. However, Mr. Sanders said that he had resisted a transfer because he would only stay in his room at the medium-security prison; in the mental health unit, on the other hand, he felt comfortable enough to mix among people a bit. He also said that he has difficulty controlling his temper when he is amid the general inmate population, and that several inmates had assaulted him during his three-month stay at the medium-security prison before his escape. In fact, as he told it, he was sent to the work-release center essentially for protective reasons. Unfortunately, that option may be foreclosed this time, because his offense may result in a tightening of admission into work-release.

Mr. Sanders became introduced to amphetamines while at the work-release center. He said that "some kid gave me two to lose weight." He began using them more frequently to suppress his appetite and to keep from becoming nervous. He claimed that he had in fact taken 24 pills on the day that he was apprehended. Mr. Sanders said that his only drug use prior to going to prison was of marijuana on a couple of occasions. He did admit to drinking binges on the weekends, with occasional consumption of several six-packs of beer.

Except for his stay in the prison mental health unit, Mr. Sanders has had no psychiatric hospitalization. He reported having had an evaluation at a community mental health center in 1979. He said that when he was younger, his mother had taken him to "another place across the street from Boston Garden" (Family Services?). He is uncertain what the reasons were for these evaluations.

As far as Mr. Sanders knows, the only psychiatric history in his family was that his paternal grandfather "went crazy" when he was very old.

ACCOUNT OF THE CURRENT OFFENSE: Mr. Sanders's account of the offense for which he is currently awaiting sentencing matched the victim's report as well as his own confession to the police. He claimed that he did not know that anyone might be in the apartment; he entered in search of food. When someone did come home, he hid in the closet and became increasingly panicky. Mr. Sanders claimed not to remember when he got the idea to assault the woman, or what any of his thoughts or feelings were at the time of the assault itself. He also claimed not to know why he committed the assault. All that he could say is that he took advantage of the situation to "find out what it was like. I thought that I could get away with it." His motivation to "find out what it was like" is consistent with the victim's report that he stated initially that "he just wanted to look." Additionally, in the August 1981 interviews, Mr. Sanders did recall being mad at the victim "for coming home. She wasn't supposed to do that." He said that he was mostly just scared, though. Mr. Sanders claimed in the June 1982 interview that he had given the matter little more thought. Although he related this lack of preoccupation with bravado ("I couldn't care less about that broad"), further questioning suggested that Mr. Sanders avoided thinking about the incident to avoid depression.

OBSERVATIONS: Mr. Sanders is a tall, somewhat obese man. He impresses one almost immediately as being a rather schizoid (withdrawn, isolated) man. Verbal productions were terse, and affect (expression of emotion) was generally flattened. In the August 1981 interviews, Mr. Sanders did seem quite depressed, however. He did express sadness directly at times and in fact became tearful at one point in the first interview. In the June 1982 interview, although his facial expression seemed never to change, there was considerable anger in his voice. He seemed to be attempting to master the situation by being a tough guy (e.g., "I'm not a rapist; I'm a burglar") and to be indicating that he did not care about other people because no one cared about him. In none of the interviews was there evidence of delusions or hallucinations.

IMPRESSIONS FROM INTERVIEWS AND TESTING: Mr. Sanders is of borderline intelligence. His poorest performance on the WAIS-R was on a subtest in which the task is to arrange pictures into order to tell a story. Mr. Sanders seemed generally to miss the point of the picture stories. Although his ideation was not bizarre, he seemed to lack a sense of the course of social relationships.

Indeed, such social ineptitude and isolation from people seem to constitute a persistent theme throughout Mr. Sanders's history and the material presented in the evaluations, in both interviews and psychological testing. For example, Mr. Sanders was unable to find people in a Rorschach stimulus on a card on which they are commonly seen, even after it was suggested that most people perceive people on that card. Similarly, his human figure drawings were distorted and suggested serious isolation from people.

Mr. Sanders seems generally to expect interactions with people to be frustrating and typified by a lack of reward and loss. He may occasionally act impulsively in response to frustration or as a way of dealing with loss (i.e., hurting other people before they hurt him).

Mr. Sanders had difficulty in integrating affect. His defenses (i.e., his ways of dealing with reality) seem to be limited largely to simple withdrawal and denial, and he has difficulty in responding to feelings and conflict. He probably presents some suicidal risk. Mr. Sanders left a suicide note when he escaped, and he claimed that his original reason for escaping was to commit suicide. He said that a combination of not having a girlfriend, being rejected by his parents, facing parole with no place to go, and having taken a number of amphetamines had become too much. Mr. Sanders claimed that he tied weights around himself and that he planned to jump in the lake. He saw a police car, though, and threw the weights away and "just ran." He said in the June 1982 interview that he now wishes that he had jumped into the lake. At the time of the August 1981 evaluation, Mr. Sanders was obviously depressed. He complained of headaches, and he wrote that "I'm dieing [sic] slowly and god is helping me." When asked to clarify, Mr. Sanders said that his medication had been switched to a liquid base because he had been saving pills for the purpose of a suicidal attempt. (According to Mr. Sanders, he is currently taking Atarax 50 mg q.i.d. and Elavil 25 mg b.i.d.) He said at the more recent interview that if his sentence is more than 10 years, he will definitely commit suicide. He said that he

"couldn't care less about anybody," and that if he committed suicide, his mother "would not have to worry about me."

Although there may be slips at times in Mr. Sanders's reality testing (i.e., his ability to differentiate reality from fantasy), and his judgment is poor, he seems generally to be in contact with reality. His range of ideation is constricted, but its quality is not bizarre.

In summary, Mr. Sanders presents generally as a schizoid, inadequate man who has severe difficulty in the formation and continuation of relationships. He is subject to depression, but he has little capacity to integrate affect, and he may present some suicidal risk.

CONCLUSIONS: In response to the specific issues raised by the MDSO statute, the following impressions are offered.

Presence of a Mental Disorder: Although Mr. Sanders is not psychotic, he is seriously disturbed. He is suffering from a schizoid personality disorder, a disorder typified by social isolation and detachment and difficulty in the integration and expression of affect. In addition, he is subject to recurrent depression, and he requires support and monitoring to avoid expression of self-destructive impulses.

Predisposition to Sexual Offense: With respect to the offense for which Mr. Sanders is currently awaiting sentencing, he apparently entered the victim's apartment for the purpose of obtaining food. His motivation for the sexual assault that ultimately occurred is unclear. It is possible that he tried to master the anxiety created by the situation by assuming a power stance vis-à-vis his victim. It is also possible that he simply took advantage of the victim's vulnerability to satisfy his sexual curiosity, and to do so within a context in which he was in control. Regardless of which explanation (or combination of explanations) is true, it is clear that Mr. Sanders has little, if any, appreciation of the impact of the offense upon the victim, and that he has few skills either for development of a normal relationship with a woman or for social expression of hostile feelings.

Whether, if freed, Mr. Sanders would repeat sexual offenses is a difficult question. The validity of mental health professionals' predictions of assaultive behavior is quite low.* However, research suggests that the best predictor of future behavior is simply past behavior. There is no evidence to suggest that Mr. Sanders

* *See generally* J. MONAHAN, THE CLINICAL PREDICTION OF VIOLENT BEHAVIOR (1981).

will experience less anxiety and anger related to women, or that he will react to these emotions in a more adaptive, integrated fashion than he has in the past. However, it should also be noted that he is known to have committed a sexual assault on only one occasion and that on this occasion he did not seek a woman with the idea of assaulting her; rather, as noted above, the assault apparently occurred when he was "surprised" by the victim.

Treatability: Mr. Sanders's chronic problems relate primarily to his severe difficulty in forming and sustaining relationships (described in detail in earlier portions of this report). These difficulties are characterological (i.e., reflective of general personality structure) and consequently resistant to change. Mr. Sanders's limited verbal skills and poor capacity for insight also make traditional (insight-oriented) forms of psychotherapy unlikely to result in substantial change. One approach that might be taken would be to do relatively concrete social skills training (i.e., to have Mr. Sanders practice specific social situations, particularly those involving women)—a common form of treatment that should be available in the state hospital. Even here, however, the range of skills to be addressed is both basic and pervasive. Consequently, any significant change is likely to require arduous, long-term work, although such an approach might give him sufficient concrete skills for at least minimal maintenance of relationships.

With respect to his depression and possible self-destructive behavior, Mr. Sanders requires supportive counseling and monitoring at times of personal crisis. Mr. Sanders appears to depend to a certain extent on the availability of such external supports and controls. Although such counseling is unlikely to result in basic personality change, it does offer some short-term alleviation of distress and management of impulses. It may also be that continued use of an antidepressant is advisable; such a determination should be made through psychiatric consultation, however.

Harriet A. Wilson, Ph.D.

(b)   Discussion

The author of the Sanders report was responding to a specific statutory standard, which narrowed the possible range of the report relative to that of a general sentencing report. As noted in Chapter 7, a "normal" sentencing referral allows the clinician to explore the client's clinical needs more freely than any other type of criminal court evaluation.

Yet even within this somewhat narrower context, the author presented a rather detailed history, particularly concerning Mr. Sanders's social relationships—with men as well as women—and his past violent behavior. This historical material was necessary to establish the foundation for the later clinical conclusions concerning the existence of a "mental disorder," and was also obviously useful in setting the context for the discussion of dangerousness and treatability at the end of the report.

Note also that the writer observed that Mr. Sanders's account of the offenses matched those of the victims, as well as that contained in his confession. This was a useful point for the examiner to make: Her clinical conclusions drew heavily from the manner in which the offense was committed, and an apparent consensus concerning those facts would make it less likely that the foundation of her conclusions would be shaken. If the version was of the offense were dramatically different, it is not inconceivable that the writer would have presented alternative clinical explanations, allowing the fact finder to determine which version of the offense was "true."

In addition, the author broke down the statutory definition governing the referral into its individual components, and discussed each in turn. This is a useful device in such reports, not only for enabling the legal system to better understand the clinical observations, but also for enabling the writer to organize thoughts. At the same time, opinion on the ultimate issue was avoided. Specifically, no statement that Mr. Sanders *required* a certain disposition (e.g., incarceration, behavior modification, outpatient treatment) was made [see § 7.08(a)].

The report also qualified the validity of long-term dangerousness predictions. The court was essentially told that very little can be said on this subject. Thus, no statement as to the likelihood of "dangerousness" was made. Rather, the report only identified situations that tend to enhance or inhibit violence.

Finally, the proposals for treatment were fairly concrete. Discussions of treatability are of little utility to the court system unless they are offered in the context of available resources, or, if resources are presently unavailable, are accompanied by realistic proposals for obtaining the necessary resources.

15.06. *Dangerousness to Others* *[Chapter 8]*

(a) J. Smith Report*

Judge Jane Doe
County Court House

Dear Judge Doe:

This letter reports my evaluation of the likelihood that Mr. J. Smith (Case No. 1234) will inflict serious bodily harm upon another person during the next 2-week period. This evaluation was done in response to the Court's request for information relevant to the issue of whether Mr. Smith's petition for release from the County Medical Center Psychiatric Unit should be granted. Mr. Smith has been involuntarily committed for a 72-hour observation period under Section 5150, and the hospital wishes to continue his commitment for an additional 14 days of intensive treatment. Mr. Smith, through his attorney, contests the allegation that he constitutes a continuing "danger to others."

I interviewed Mr. Smith at the Medical Center for approximately 1 hour on Monday, August 14. I informed him of the purpose of the examination before it began. I also read Mr. Smith's hospital records and the written police report on him. I discussed Mr. Smith's case with the ward staff.

Mr. Smith, is a 20-year-old, never-married, male who appears to be of dull–normal intelligence. He has been intermittently employed as a factory worker since dropping out of high school in the ninth grade several years ago. At the time of his commitment, he had been working on the assembly line at the NT Company for a period of 1 month.

His police record reveals that he has been arrested three times during the past 4 years—once for aggravated assault, once for simple assault, and once for public intoxication. He received a suspended sentence for the first incident, charges were modified to disturbing the peace in the second incident, and he served several days in the County Jail on the final charge. His hospital record reveals no prior hospital-

izations. He admits to several school suspensions for fighting and several barroom altercations that did not result in an arrest.

The police file for the incident precipitating his commitment states that the police responded to a call from a supervisor at the NT Company on Friday, August 11. When they arrived they found Mr. Smith with a crowbar in his hand threatening to kill a Mr. Brown, his foreman. Mr. Brown had barricaded himself into an office. Mr. Smith appeared to the officers to be intoxicated from alcohol or some other substance and his screaming at Mr. Brown was described as "incoherent" and "bizarre." The officers failed to talk him into putting down the metal bar, and, when he broke the window on the door of the office into which Mr. Brown had fled, the police forcibly subdued him and brought him to the Medical Center.

During the interview, Mr. Smith was clearly upset at the incident. He raised his voice frequently and began to pace the room. He stated that Mr. Brown had told him when he was hired that he could progress through the ranks of the company "all the way to the top," if he had the ability and the energy. Now, 1 month later, he was still on the assembly line "going nowhere." He blamed Mr. Brown for his predicament and said that Mr. Brown was deliberately "holding me down" so that his superior talents would go unnoticed and not become a source of competition to Mr. Brown himself. When Mr. Brown criticized Mr. Smith for arriving at work several hours late and appearing in a state of intoxication, Mr. Smith states that he "just saw red" and told the foreman that he could do a better job drunk and in half the time than the foreman could ever do. Mr. Brown thereupon fired Mr. Smith and ordered him out of the plant. At that point, Mr. Smith said that he "went wild" and began chasing Mr. Brown with the iron bar.

During the interview, Mr. Smith repeatedly and with much anger referred to his former foreman as "that ———." He states that Mr. Brown "has not heard the end of this—not by a long shot" and that "nobody makes a fool of me and gets away with it." When asked directly whether he intended to harm Mr. Brown, Mr. Smith was evasive and would only reply "We'll see, we'll see." He intends to confront Mr. Brown at his first opportunity. He denied owning a gun but stated that he had easy access to the gun of a friend. The ward staff confirmed his state of acute agitation.

Based upon the above data, in particular upon his demographic profile, his history of violent behavior including a recent overt act of violence, his currently stressful employment situation, his alcohol-suppressed inhibitions, and his acute and clearly unre-

* From J. MONAHAN, THE CLINICAL PREDICTION OF VIOLENT BEHAVIOR 120–22 (1981). (Reprinted by permission of the National Institute of Mental Health.)

solved hostility toward Mr. Brown, it is my professional opinion that Mr. Smith, if released at this time, is most likely to commit serious bodily harm if permitted contact with Mr. Brown [,particularly if he is in an intoxicated state at the time.]

Martha Questin, M.D.

(b) Discussion

The sole issue addressed in this report was Mr. Smith's dangerousness to others over the two-week period following the evaluation. Note that the interviewer took full advantage of available third-party information, including Mr. Smith's hospital records, the police report, and comments from the staff on Mr. Smith's ward, in order to obtain information on this question. She also carefully elicited Mr. Smith's account of the event that precipitated the original commitment, as well as of past assaultive behavior.

Note further that the relevant demographic characteristics were cited, that the recent violent act was meticulously described, and that other factors that might be violence-enhancing (e.g., the employment situation, alcohol use) were noted. By implication, the elimination of these factors would reduce Mr. Smith's violence potential.

Finally, note that an expression that bodily harm *would* occur or was *likely* to occur was avoided, since a conclusion of this sort is impossible to make with any such precise degree of certainty. However, the report did indicate the constellation of events (e.g., release, alcohol ingestion, and contact with Mr. Brown) most likely to produce a violent act.

15.07. *Competency to Handle Finances [Chapter 9]*

(a) Dorothy Dyer Report

NAME: Dorothy Dyer
D.O.B.   September 3, 1952
DATE OF REPORT: September 4, 1984

CIRCUMSTANCES OF REFERRAL: Dorothy Dyer, a 32-year-old white female, was referred to the Elk County Clinic for evaluation by her attorney, Sally Hudson of the Elk County Legal Aid Society. On March 9, 1974, Ms. Dyer was found incapable of handling business matters due to "retarded physical and mental condition, as a result of congenital deficiency." Richard Perkins, an attorney from Athens, Arizona who had handled her family's legal affairs, was appointed as her guardian at this time. At the present time, Ms Dyer would like to have the guardianship dissolved, because she believes she is able to handle her own financial affairs. As a result, she has procured the counsel of Ms. Hudson in the hope of restoring her legal competency. Ms. Hudson has requested the Clinic to assess Ms. Dyer's present competency as it pertains to the management of her financial affairs.

SOURCES OF INFORMATION: In conducting its evaluation, the Clinic had available to it information from the following sources:

1. Court order appointing Guardian from the Corporation Court of the City of Athens, Arizona, dated March 9, 1974.
2. Medical records from the Elk County General Hospital regarding Ms. Dyer's treatment immediately after birth, dated September 4, 1952 through September 29, 1952.
3. Medical records from the Neuropsychiatry Department at the Elk County General Hospital regarding outpatient speech and play therapy with Ms. Dyer dated December 1, 1958 through June 1, 1959.
4. Medical records from the Neurology Clinic at the Elk County General Hospital regarding an evaluation of Ms. Dyer, dated April 10, 1968.
5. A report of psychological testing of Ms. Dyer, performed at age 12, from the file of the Social Security District Office, Athens.
6. A telephone interview with Mr. Perkins, the Guardian, by Janet Higham, Ph.D., conducted on August 30, 1984.
7. A telephone interview with Sarah Smith, Ms. Dyer's supervisor at the Frost Diner, by Lisa Madding, D.S.W., conducted on August 27, 1984..
8. A telephone interview with Jean Smart, the babysitter for Ms. Dyer's two-year-old son, by Lisa Madding, D.S.W., conducted on August 27, 1984.
9. A telephone interview with Farah James, a Health Department nurse who has treated Ms. Dyer's son, by Lisa Madding, D.S.W., conducted on August 27, 1984.

10. A psychosocial interview by Lisa Madding, D.S.W., with Ms. Dyer, conducted on August 30, 1984.
11. A psychosocial interview by Lisa Madding, D.S.W., with Mr. John Daniels, Ms. Dyer's boyfriend (and father of her child), conducted on August 30, 1984.
12. Psychological testing of Ms. Dyer by Marci Levin, M.S., a clinical psychology resident supervised by Janet Higham, Ph.D., conducted on August 30, 1984.
13. A competency assessment interview of Ms. Dyer by Janet Higham, Ph.D., conducted on August 30, 1984.

PERSONAL/FAMILY BACKGROUND: Ms. Dorothy Dyer was born on September 3, 1952, and has lived all her life in Athens, Arizona. According to Ms. Dyer, she was the youngest of the six children born to the Dyer family. She reported that her father supported the family by working in a garage, while her mother supplemented the family income by doing laundry. She stated that her father died in 1972 and her mother in 1975, and that her grandparents also died around this time—"They all went one after another." Ms. Dyer indicated that she does not get along well with her three brothers and two sisters (the oldest of whom is 53 years of age) because of their chronic use of alcohol. Related to this point, she noted that the guardianship was initially established because her mother was afraid that Ms. Dyer's sister would "use up all my money drinking."

Ms. Dyer explained that she attended school in Athens through the fourth grade. She remarked that she "liked it one time" but quit because "I couldn't talk." (In this respect, she referred to a pronounced speech impediment from which she suffers.) She reported that she had been living with her parents, and following her mother's death moved in to live with a sister. In 1979, she moved out of her sister's home and established her own residence. She described the move as "hard at first," stating that "at first I was lonely, but then I enjoyed myself." She remarked that she wanted her own place "because all my friends got one."

Ms. Dyer stated that she met her first and current boyfriend, John Daniels, in late 1980 at her aunt's home. Mr. Daniels reported in this regard: "We watched each other for a couple of weeks and then decided to go out." The couple began dating steadily at this point; in December 1981, one year later, Ms. Dyer gave birth to a male child, whom she named Larry. Following the birth of the child, she and John began living together and have resided together since

that time. Their relationship has lasted four years, and they both speak of it in positive terms. Ms. Dyer reported that she loves John and hopes to marry him some day but also indicated that she's "not quite ready yet." Mr. Daniels described Ms. Dyer as a "good and understanding person." He explained that they "just took to each other." During the last year, Mr. Daniels was in Nevada for 12 months between April of 1982 and April of 1983. According to Ms. Dyer, he sent her about $250.00 during that time and called on a regular basis. He explained that he was involved in a one-year training program to become a mechanic, but indicated that he had to withdraw from the program when Ms. Dyer asked him to come home.

Larry, their son, is presently two and a half years old. Ms Dyer and Mr. Daniels spoke of him with apparent affection, and both agreed that "he's real smart for a two-year-old." Ms. Dyer explained that he "loves McDonalds" and reported that he even "jogs" with the two of them. She stated that she hopes to have one more child but commented, "I'm going to wait until Larry's a little older. Then, I'm going to stop—two's enough." Farah James, a public health nurse, reported that Ms. Dyer is very regular with her appointments at the Care-Baby Clinic and apparently devotes considerable energy to being a good mother. She stated that Larry is developing normally and suffers from no observable impediments.

Ms. Dyer stated that she works as a dishwasher at the Frost Diner in Athens. She stated that she "likes my job," where she has been working for 10 years. She stated that she works from 7:30 A.M. to 2:30 P.M. daily during the winters and is free to spend the summers at home with her son.

Her supervisor, Sarah Smith, reported that Ms. Dyer is very responsible in her work and gets along well with the other employees. She stated that she follows instructions well and never misses work unless she is taking her son to an appointment.

DETERMINATION OF INCOMPETENCY: On March 9, 1974, Ms. Dyer was deemed incompetent in the Corporation Court of the City of Athens. Donald Siegle, the guardian *ad litem,* reported that as a result of "some congenital deficiency," Ms Dyer is a "person of retarded physical and mental condition." Thus, Ms. Dyer was considered "incapable of handling business affairs." The court order provided no further elaboration regarding the reasons for the ruling of incompetency. At that time, Richard Perkins (an attorney for the Dyer family prior to the death of Ms. Dyer's mother) was appointed guardian of the estate.

BEHAVIORAL OBSERVATIONS: Ms. Dyer was neatly and casually dressed for her sessions at the Elk County Clinic. She made good eye contact and was cooperative throughout the sessions. She seemed well aware of the nature and purpose of the evaluation, and clearly understood the Clinic's role in providing her attorney with information about her need, or lack thereof, for a guardian. She responded to questions directly.

Ms. Dyer has a severe speech impediment, which made it difficult to understand her speech most of the time. She patiently repeated responses to items until she was certain she was understood. She was aware of this deficit and was able to discuss her impairment openly and nondefensively. Similarly, Ms. Dyer worked patiently and conscientiously on difficult test items. Although she was aware that she was unable to respond correctly to many items, she continued patiently and methodically to attempt new items.

Ms. Dyer also appeared to have some gait disturbance; however, she was able to walk without assistance. She reported poor fine motor coordination. Her fingers appeared stiff.

In general, Ms Dyer appeared friendly and well motivated to perform well on tasks. In spite of speech, motor, and intellectual deficits, she was able to relate in an effective way to others.

ASSESSMENT OF INTELLECTUAL FUNCTIONING: In 1964, Ms. Dyer was administered Form 1 of the revised Stanford–Binet intelligence test by a Dr. D.T. Fletcher. At that time, she was 12 years of age and in the fourth grade. Ms. Dyer's mental age was calculated as five years, eight months, giving her an IQ of 47. Dr. Fletcher suggested that she be referred to a class for the trainable mentally retarded.

On August 30, 1984, at the Elk County Clinic, Ms. Dyer was administered the Wechsler Adult Intelligence Scale—Revised (WAIS-R) and the Peabody Individual Achievement Test (PIAT) to identify specific strengths and deficits that characterize her present intellectual and neuropsychological functioning. Neuropsychological assessment involves the evaluation of the behavioral expression of brain dysfunction.

Ms. Dyer is currently functioning in the upper end of the mild mental retardation range of intellectual functioning. Her scores on the Verbal and Performance scales of the WAIS-R did not differ significantly from one another. The Verbal scale includes subtests that focus primarily on skills related to fund of general information, vocabulary, abstract reasoning, social judgment, auditory memory, concentration, attention, and mathematical skills. The Performance scale subtests measure perceptual–motor integration and motor coordination, ability to perceive visual details, ability to solve visual and spatial problems, and sense of the appropriate sequences of social interactions.

Relative to her overall functioning, Ms. Dyer evidenced particular strength in her social judgment skill—the ability to use facts in a pertinent, meaningful, and emotionally relevant manner. Ms. Dyer also performed relatively well on the Block Design subtest. This subtest assesses visual organization skills of analysis (breaking down a pattern) and synthesis (building the pattern up again with blocks). She performed relatively poorly on a subtest (i.e., the Object Assembly subtest) measuring perceptual organization skills. The subtest requires a person to arrange parts into a meaningful whole.

On the PIAT, Ms. Dyer performed relatively well on the subtest measuring spelling ability. Her poorest performance was on a subtest measuring general fund of information. This latter score can be explained in part by her limited schooling. The other subtests measured reading and mathematics skills. Ms. Dyer's achievement scores all fell in the lower elementary grade range.

ASSESSMENT OF ADAPTIVE FUNCTIONING: Ms. Dyer was administered subscales of the American Association of Mental Deficiency (AAMD) Adaptive Behavior Scale. Information provided by Jean Smart, the babysitter for Ms. Dyer's child, and Farah James, a Health Department nurse, as well as information obtained from Ms. Dyer and Clinic staff's observations, were also used to determine the level of Ms. Dyer's adaptive functioning. According to reports from Ms. Smart and Ms. James, Ms. Dyer is able to care adequately for her child. Additionally, Ms. Dyer's supervisor at work, Sarah Smith, reported that Ms. Dyer is capable of functioning well at her job. In general, Ms. Dyer appears capable of self-care skills required in independent functioning. These skills include the ability to eat, clean, and dress herself and maintain an appropriate appearance. Additionally, she indicated that she is able to ride a bus or call a taxi to travel places locally by herself. She reported an awareness of how to use the telephone and find a phone number. She maintains her own phone notebook, and can use a directory in some instances. She stated that she shops for herself and is able to make simple purchases. She also reported knowledge of how to use a bank.

COMPETENCY TO MANAGE HER FINANCIAL AFFAIRS: An assessment of Ms. Dyer's competency to manage her financial affairs was performed. The accuracy of her understanding of her financial assets, and the practicality and soundness of logic underlying her financial planning, were assessed.

Ms. Dyer was asked a series of specific questions about her financial assets. This information regarding her assets was compared with information provided by Mr. Perkins. Mr. Perkins had reported to Ms. Hudson that Ms. Dyer receives her weekly pay checks directly from her employer. However, Supplemental Security Income checks for both herself and her child are sent to Mr. Perkins, who reportedly deposits the money in bank accounts, drawing upon these funds when Ms. Dyer's or the child's expenses are greater than her salary. Additionally, Ms Dyer has a savings account including money left to her by her family, as well as a savings certificate from her father. In total, the various accounts currently total over $7,000. Mr. Perkins stated that he was not certain whether or not Ms. Dyer had been informed as to the specific amount and nature of her assets.

When asked to do so, Ms.Dyer was able to describe her assets only partially. She knew that her salary check was $101 weekly. However, she only knew the approximate amount of her Supplemental Security Income checks and did not know how much money she had in the bank. She was aware of the existence of a large sum of money left to her by her family. She reported that it was her understanding that her father left her enough money in the bank to live the rest of her life. It appears that someone told Ms. Dyer that this was the case, since she was not aware of the specific amount of money.

Ms. Dyer was able to provide a fairly detailed description of her bills and how she pays each bill. For example, she reported that she receives a $101 check at work, which she cashes at work. Groceries cost approximately $30, which she pays in cash. She pays the babysitter $20 in cash each week. She stated that she puts aside the remainder of each week's money to pay the monthly utility bills and other expenses (such as shoes). Although she plans ahead by saving this money, she does not appear to budget systematically specific amounts of money for each expense. Rather, she saves what is left over and pays her bills. If she requires additional funds—for clothing, for instance—she contacts Mr. Perkins, who writes her a check, or arranges payment for such items directly with the merchant. She stated that she obtains a money order at the post office to pay phone and electric

bills. Although she does not write checks, she stated that she knows how to do this. Ms. Dyer demonstrated her ability to work with money during the sessions. She was given coins and bills and could "pay for" hypothetical items. She also would calculate in her head in some instances—how many bills of specific types would be needed to pay for an item costing $30, for example. However, whereas she knew that three $10 bills or a $20 bill and a $10 bill could pay for the item, she was unable to estimate how many $5 bills would equal $30. In contrast, she could count out $30 in $5 bills. This differentiation of skills suggest that whereas Ms. Dyer is able to work with actual money, her ability to work abstractly with monetary concepts is somewhat limited. This appears to be the case when she is asked to consider larger sums of money. She could not *fully* comprehend, for example, the difference between $500 and $5,000. She could only say the latter sum was "bigger" than the former. She did not have a clear idea as to what could be bought (e.g., a car, a house) with the latter sum.

Although Ms. Dyer demonstrated a working knowledge of how to buy items, and could provide a detailed account of her regular daily expenses, she was not able to grasp more complex concepts that would be necessary in the administration of large sums of money. For example, she could not comprehend the difference between a checking and a savings account. When these concepts were explained to her, she did state that if she had control of all of her money, she'd "put it away in a bank."

CONCLUSIONS AND RECOMMENDATIONS: Ms. Dyer demonstrated several strengths and weaknesses related to her ability to manage her financial affairs. She is currently functioning in the upper end of the mild mental retardation level of intelligence. She also has a severe speech impediment. Despite her speech impediment and impaired intellectual functioning, she has adapted well to her environment. She is able to work effectively and care for herself and her child. She is also able to travel within this local environment using the public transit systems. She responsibly manages the money to which she has access, successfully paying her bills and shopping to meet food and clothing needs. She currently sets aside money to pay bills that are due at the end of the month. Clearly, she has learned to adjust to her environment in an adaptive and productive manner. However, her intellectual deficits limit her ability to deal with abstract and symbolic concepts, including monetary concepts. She is most adept when dealing with the concrete physical reality of a situation, rather than theoretical concepts requiring her to plan for the future. She is not able to specify how much money should be set aside each week to ensure a total amount at the end of the month to cover her bills. She cannot perform the arithmetic necessary to handle large sums of money. Although this inability does not currently interfere with her management of money, it would likely pose a problem with transferring larger sums of money, to the extent that this requires "paper transactions" rather than direct use of the money itself. Moreover, her ability to conceptualize the actual value of large sums is limited.

> Janet Higham, Ph.D.
> Clinical and Supervising Psychologist
> Marci Levin, M.S.
> Clinical Psychology Resident

(b)   Discussion

This report was triggered by Ms. Dyer's desire to have her guardianship dissolved. As noted in § 15.02 and 15.03, a competency report must zero in on the specific function the law has made relevant. The writers of this report painstakingly obtained information from Ms. Dyer about her ability to handle various sums of money. She was asked to describe her assets and the bills she paid; was given hypothetical situations requiring her to use money to pay for different items; and was quizzed about other aspects of financial dealings, including banks and checking accounts. Of particular note is the examiners' use of hypothetical situations: What better way to determine if a person will be able to perform a task than to have her perform it in front of an examiner?

The examiners also attempted to gather information relative to Ms. Dyer's general ability to deal with abstract, as well as concrete, notions. Several sources were consulted (her guardian, her employer, her nurse, her boyfriend, and even her babysitter) in an effort to derive useful data on this point. Additionally, performance-oriented psychological tests were administered that focused on organizational and social judgment skills. This kind of information might have been very relevant to the court attempting to determine the extent, if any, to which Ms. Dyer should be given control of her affairs.

On the central question presented by this case—whether Ms. Dyer should be allowed to control the $7,000 managed by her guardian—the examiners suggested that while Ms. Dyer appeared capable of handling small sums of money, larger sums were difficult for her to fathom. Whether this fact should deny her control of the money was a legal–moral issue that the examiners left to the judge. The Dyer report does illustrate, however, that in competency cases (as opposed to most of the other types of cases discussed in this book), the gap between clinical data and the ultimate issue is often miniscule.

15.08.   Worker's Compensation for Mental Injury [Chapter 10]

(a)   Lane Cates Report

NAME: Lane Cates
D.O.B.:   April 1, 1957

REFERRAL INFORMATION: Lane Cates is a 27-year-old, married, white male who was referred for a clinical evaluation regarding possible psychiatric or psychological disturbance secondary to injuries received due to an accident on his job.

CLINICAL CONTACTS AND SOURCES OF INFORMATION: Mr. Cates was interviewed at my office on the following dates: April 11, 1984 (two hours); April 30, 1984 (one-hour interview and administration of the Minnesota Multiphasic Personality Inventory [MMPI]); and May 16, 1984 (one-and-a-half hour joint interview of Mr. Cates and his wife and administration of Life Experiences Survey).

Additional information received included the following: records of hospitalization and treatment associated with the surgical removal of Mr. Cates's right testicle in October 1983; records of attendance and disciplinary actions from Mr. Cates's employer, the Acme Machine Shop, from February 1980 through March 1984; brief interviews with two of Mr. Cates's fellow workers, Mr. Jones and Mr. Smithers.

CIRCUMSTANCES OF THE REFERRAL: Mr. Cates reported that he has worked at the Acme Machine Shop since February of 1980. His duties have included operating various power tools, including a lathe, a table saw, and a grinding machine. He reported that in late September 1983 he was struck in the groin while operating the grinding machine. He developed an abscess, which resulted in the surgical removal of his right testicle on October 4, 1983. He returned to work in December 1983, but was assigned primarily to janitorial and "clean-up" duties. He reported that he continues to experience periodic "nagging" pain in the right groin area and occasional sharp or shooting pain extending to his right pelvic region. A lawsuit against the manufacturer of the machine is pending.

PRESENT CLINICAL FINDINGS: Lane Cates is a slender white male of medium build. He was on time for each of the three interviews I had with him and was accompanied by his wife on each occasion. Mr. Cates has been married for six years and has one child, a daughter two years old. He indicated that he comes from a big family (three brothers and four sisters) and that he and his wife had also planned to have a large family.

In presenting his current problems, Mr. Cates began by stating that "it all happened as a result of my accident" (referring to the groin injury and subsequent surgery). He complained of occasional difficulty in maintaining an erection (corroborated by his wife's statements) and a fear of pain during sexual intercourse; he indicated that since his operation he has been occasionally fearful of having relations with his wife, who has at times responded with anger and frustration. He voiced the fear that his "sexual problems" might lead to further problems in his marriage, and his wife stated that they had talked about going to their minister for counseling. Both Mr. Cates and his wife voiced concerns that they may not be able to have any more children; laboratory findings from tests conducted at Harper Heights Clinic indicated that a February 1984 sperm count from his left testicle was zero.

During the interviews Mr. Cates appeared alert and oriented to his surroundings; he neither complained of physical pain nor displayed pain response behavior. His speech was relevant, organized, and coherent, and there was no interview behavior suggestive of major thought disturbance. Mr. Cates did, however, appear both anxious and depressed. Anxiety was manifest in nervous movements of his hands (e.g., picking at his skin or clothing) and face (e.g., grimaces), and in his frequently averting his eyes from the examiner's, particularly when discussing his groin injury and diminished sexual activity. He also reported feeling fatigued, unhappy, and self-conscious,

particularly around other men at work who know the nature of his injury. Transient sleep disturbance was also noted. His wife corroborated that he had had trouble sleeping for the past several months and that he had become progressively "more nervous-acting."

The results of the MMPI, a self-report objective personality measure, were consistent with the interview impression of mild to moderate depression. The validity scales suggest that Mr. Cates may have mildly exaggerated his current symptomatology, though there is no indication of outright feigning or malingering, and the elevation on the clinical scales measuring anxiety and depression is at a level consistent with interview presentation.

I also interviewed two men who work with Mr. Cates, Mr. Jones and Mr. Smithers. They both stated that Mr. Cates seemed more withdrawn and nervous "lately."

OTHER PSYCHOLOGICALLY IMPORTANT EVENTS: An examination of Mr. Cates's attendance record at the Acme Machine Shop revealed almost perfect attendance (except for approved vacation time off) until July 1983, two months *before* his accident. In July Mr. Cates took four days' sick leave; two additional days of sick leave were taken in August, and three sick days were taken in September *before* his accident. When questioned about this, Mr. Cates responded that his father passed away in July and that "it hit me pretty hard." He indicated that he had been very close to his father when he was younger, but had felt more distant from him in recent years. He had intended to try to "mend the fences between us"; he indicated that his father had always been quietly dissatisfied with Mr. Cates's choice of a wife, and, later, with the way he was raising his child. His father's sudden and unexpected death in July precluded any possibility of restoring their relationship. As a result, Mr. Cates felt guilty about not having made up with his father and was described by Mrs. Cates as "all torn up" following the funeral. The subsequent absences from work in late July, August, and September were a result of continued mourning for his deceased father and "difficulty getting going again" after the father's death.

Partly as a result of this information, I administered the Life Experiences Survey to Mr. Cates and his wife in the course of interviewing them. The inventory surveys the occurrence and perceived impact of potentially stressful life events during a given period of time; Mr. and Mrs. Cates were each asked to complete the survey for the six-month period preceding Mr. Cates's accident at work. Mr. Cates identified the loss of his father as one stressful event, though he tended to minimize its impact on him; the only other stressful events identified by Mr. Cates were receiving a traffic ticket for running a red light and decreased attendance at church.

Mrs. Cates, however, identified several other life changes during that period, including "trouble with in-laws" (Mr. Cates's parents, prior to Mr. Cates's father's death) and changes in social activities for the family generally. Further inquiry into these areas revealed that Mr. Cates had been openly criticized by his father at a family reunion approximately six weeks before the father's death, primarily about the way he was raising his child and his failure to be more financially successful. Mrs. Cates indicated that her husband could never stand up to his father face to face, but later at home ruminated excessively about the confrontation and defended himself to her against his father's accusations. She indicated that he became preoccupied with proving himself to his father and was subsequently distant from her and other family members for a period. It was during this period that he received his traffic ticket for running a red light— an incident that Mrs. Cates described as resulting from her husband's "driving around in a daze . . . like he was lost in a fog." She also reported other incidents—for example, $1,200 damage to the family car; this was never fully explained, though she clearly suspected that Mr. Cates was at fault. During Mrs. Cates's narrative, Mr. Cates was noticeably uncomfortable and appeared embarrassed, though he never mustered up the initiative to defend himself except to assert meekly that the car had been "sideswiped" while parked on the street. Mrs. Cates described her husband as periodically "absent-minded" and possibly accident-prone, though she could recall no other specific events in their recent history to illustrate this impression.

This description was corroborated by Mr. Jones and Mr. Smithers, both of whom described Mr. Cates as "spacey." Mr. Jones elaborated that Mr. Cates had begun to "stare into space" during work hours beginning over a year ago and that on several occasions prior to the accident had forgotten to turn off the machine he was using after he was through with it.

CLINICAL FORMULATION: Lane Cates is a 27-year-old, married, white male who presently reports residual, transient pain secondary to an injury that necessitated the removal of his right testicle, and mild to moderate anxiety and depression of approximately four months' duration. He complains that his sexual relationship with his wife has been unsatisfactory since his surgery, and his wife confirms this. Both appear disappointed at the prospect of not being able to have any more children.

Given the medical evidence available regarding the nature of Mr. Cates's surgery and the subsequent laboratory sperm count, it appears reasonable to infer that Mr. Cates's present anxiety and depression is, in part, an emotional reaction to the effects of his job-related injury. Other factors, however, must be considered in weighing the relationship between Mr. Cates's accident and his emotional state.

Most particularly, assuming that the above reconstruction of events concerning his father is accurate, it appears reasonable to infer that Mr. Cates may have been clinically depressed prior to the accident that led to his subsequent surgery. Having not had the opportunity to examine Mr. Cates at that time, I cannot describe in detail the symptoms associated with the probable grief reaction and depression or comment in any precise way about their possible contribution to his job-related accident. However, it is probable that the loss of his father currently contributes to his depression and loss of self-esteem, though there is no precise way to tease apart the relative impact of this loss and that of the accident on his present emotional state.

Finally, a key facet of Mr. Cates's personality may have had a role to play. The information gleaned from individual and family interviews suggests that Mr. Cates is a somewhat passive individual who avoids confrontation with others and may deal with conflict by excessive ruminating and preoccupation. It is possible that this increased mental activity results in reduced attention to the external environment and may thus contribute to inefficient performance or minor incidents such as, for example, running a red light. While it cannot be confirmed whether or not such inattention contributed to his accident at work and thus to his current mental state, this history may have to be considered as a possible contributory factor.

I cannot say whether Mr. Cates will be "mentally" able to return to the type of work he performed in the past. Certainly, from the evidence, it appears that his nervous and distracted state has increased rather than decreased since the accident. I have recommended to Mr. Cates that he consider seeking professional help to counsel him through his current problems (specifically, his reaction to his father's death and to his injury). This type of therapeutic intervention may reduce his anxiety level.

Leslie Dean, Ph.D.

(b)   Discussion

This worker's compensation report attempted to evaluate whether Mr. Cates actually suffered "mental injury" and the extent to which it was the result of a work-related incident. Several aspects of the report should be noted.

First, the organization of the report tracked the legal analysis. After, as always, listing the sources of information, the examiner described the incident that allegedly precipitated the mental injury, then reported the evidence relevant to whether that injury existed, and finally tried to discern the extent to which the present clinical findings concerning Mr. Cates's mental problems related to the incident.

Second, the examiner attempted to seek corroboration of Mr. Cates's statements whenever possible. An MMPI was administered to seek verification of his present mental state. Mr. Cates's wife and fellow workers were consulted about both the present and past state of his mental health. Mr. Cates was interviewed on three separate occasions.

Third, an extensive historical review was conducted. Because the examiner took the time to develop Mr. Cates's work history, she became aware of the death of Mr. Cates's father. Through use of the Life Experiences Survey, she discovered the occurrence of other events that suggested an "accident-prone" person. Without these aids, the picture of Mr. Cates' mental injury and what "caused" it would have been incomplete.

Fourth, the examiner was extremely cautious in discussing the issue of causation. As discussed in § 10.04, she avoided labeling any one factor as the cause of Mr. Cates's current state and made it clear that his basic personality structure was a relevant consideration. Whether the work-related injury or some other phenomenon was the "proximate" cause of his current problems was left up to the factfinder. In this regard, however, it should be noted that, as pointed out in § 10.02(b)(2), the law generally holds that employers take employees as they find them. Thus, it is unlikely that compensation would be withheld merely upon proof that Mr. Cates's grief over his father's death or his "absent-mindedness" caused the physical injury. There is no defense in worker's compensation law of "contributory personality." It would have to be proven that the father's death, and not the work-related injury, was the proximate cause of Mr. Cates's mental state in order to deny compensation.

Finally, the report avoided the value judgment of whether the injury was "severe," and admitted the difficulty of predicting its future course. It did suggest, however, ways of remediating Mr. Cates' problem that might prove relevant, if compensation was to be awarded, to whether and how much money would be allocated to treatment.

15.09.   Transfer to Adult Court [Chapter 11]

(a)   Tom Young Report

This was a juvenile case, in which the referral source sought evaluation for the purpose of considering whether Tom Young should be transferred from juvenile to adult court See §§ 11.04(c)(1); 11.04(b). In the jurisdiction in which the referral occurred, the question of transfer turns upon a defendant's "amenability to treatment." In addition, transfer is prohibited if the client is "mentally retarded" or "criminally insane."

NAME: Tom Young
D.O.B.:   August 9, 1961

DATES OF INTERVIEWS:

1. Social history performed on October 13, 1978, by Theresa Rogers, M.S.W.
2. Psychological testing administered on October 13, 1978, and October 21, 1978, by Harvey A. Nicholson, Ph.D. Psychological tests included the Rorschach Inkblot Test, the Thematic Apperception Test (TAT), the Wechsler Adult Intelligence Scale (WAIS), the Stanford–Binet, the Bender–Gestalt, and the Competency Screening Test.
3. Psychiatric interviews conducted on October 21, 1978, by Patrick Roberts, M.D., and Harvey A. Nicholson, Ph.D., and on November 4, 1978, by Dr. Roberts.

CIRCUMSTANCES OF REFERRAL: Tom Young is a 17-year-old resident of Raleigh, who has been charged with breaking and entering and with rape. Tom was arrested on June 28, 1978, the day of the alleged rape, and has been held at the juvenile detention facility since his arrest.

Irving Jencks, Tom's attorney, referred Tom to the Clinic for an evaluation of his competency to stand trial, his level of mental functioning and mental status, and his amenability to treatment. A hearing to consider transfer of the case from juvenile to adult court will be held after the Clinic's evaluation is completed.

Information made available to the Clinic includes Tom's juvenile court record; the police report on the current offenses; a neurological evaluation dated July 3, 1978, by Dr. Dennis Evans of the Piedmont Hospital in Durham, conducted after Tom experienced a *grand mal* seizure on July 2, 1978; a court-ordered transfer report by the juvenile probation department, dated July 20, 1978; a psychiatric evaluation from Dr. James Farson of the Greensboro Psychiatric Center, dated August 13, 1978; medical records from several hospital admissions; and school records from the Raleigh city public schools, including disciplinary records and psychological reports from 1969, 1970, and 1973.

SOCIAL HISTORY:

Family Background: Mr. Harvey Young, the client's father, is 60 years old and is employed at the tobacco plant in Durham as a warehouse laborer. He often works 14 to 16 hours per day and earns about $250 per week. Because of the many hours he puts into work, Mr. Young has less contact with Tom than his wife does. He described himself in good health and denied that he drinks excessively. Mrs. Debbie Young, age 45, has been employed as a maid at the Holiday Inn for the past 13 years, and earns $80 per week. She has been in good health and has never experienced psychiatric problems or difficulties with substance abuse.

Mr. and Mrs. Young married soon after she became pregnant in ninth grade. They reported no marital problems. They have 11 children, ranging in age from 14 to 32. Tom is the fourth youngest child. It is interesting to note that a probation report indicates that Mr. and Mrs. Young told the probation officer about only five of their children. Among the children that they did not mention were two teenagers who have records with the Juvenile Court. Yet the Youngs

had stated that besides Tom, none of their children had ever been before the Juvenile Court.

Mr. Young explained that he and his wife do not have frequent contact with the older children, since "they are married, have their own lives, and live all over the United States." Tom described his relationships with his siblings, primarily the three who live at home, as "fine, we have no problems." He elaborated somewhat on his relationship with his youngest brother, George, age 14. Tom explained, "I like to be around him. I take him everywhere I go." Tom stated that he has always enjoyed living at home and that he is anxious to return. He stated that he "liked growing up" with his brothers and sisters and recalled enjoying playing in the woods with them.

Tom emphasized that he "likes" his parents equally, is close to both of them, and has "never had any problems" with them. He stated that when his parents disapprove of his behavior they "talk" to him. He insisted that he has never been disciplined in a harsh manner. However, a psychiatric report from Dr. Farson, dated September 1978, indicates that Tom described his family as very unstable. He apparently reported to Dr. Farson that his father used to be a severe alcoholic, who became violent at times and physically punished him.

Mr. and Mrs. Young reported to us that they never used physical punishment with any of their children. Mr. Young explained that they sometimes take away television viewing privileges as a form of discipline. It may be important to note that Mr. Young stated, "If you do anything else, they get you for child abuse."

Tom's father was quite dominant in the interview, making it difficult for Mrs. Young to talk. He sometimes smiled (almost as though he was proud) when discussing Tom's rape charge. Mrs. Young sat quietly, looked very depressed, and seemed to be daydreaming at times. Also, it appears that Tom's parents reinforce his avoidance and denial of certain issues. They denied that Tom has any history of behavioral problems, arrests, or serious alcohol problems. They supported Tom's claims of innocence on the present charges.

Education and Work History: Tom has been in special education classes throughout most of his schooling. He explained, "I have always had trouble learning. It's hard for me." His parents seemed to have little understanding of Tom's learning problems and claimed that they were never called in to the school by a teacher or counselor. According to a probation report, in 1970 the client was evaluated and determined to be educable mentally retarded. It is important to note that the school system has always believed Tom to be one year older than he really is. His parents enrolled him early and lied about his age because he was "a big boy."

Records of Tom's grades for his last three years of school show that his work was significantly below average. He was absent over 35 days every year. A school report in 1973 described the client as "immature but not a serious discipline problem" and commented on his short attention span in class. A probation report noted that later Tom was suspended eight times for truancy and showing disrespect to teachers. Tom's parents denied that the client had any behavioral problems in school and insisted, "He is a good, normal boy."

During tenth grade, Tom attended vocational–technical as well as special education academic classes. He learned bricklaying, and after he left school, he worked for short periods of time as a bricklayer. He has also worked in a saw mill, and at the time of the offense, he was employed by the rape victim's husband, Mr. Davis, as a farmworker. Tom has not had much experience in a structured work situation.

Social and Sexual Relationships: According to his parents, Tom has always been able to form and maintain friendships with peers. They explained that he has played on various sports teams even after leaving school; this gave the impression that he has been very socially active. In contrast, Tom explained that after he left school, he spent a great deal of time at home watching the "stories" on television by himself.

Tom claimed that he has had "ten girlfriends." He has had sexual intercourse with all of them, he said. The client had difficulty discussing sexual relationships openly. He did say that he broke up with one girlfriend after his arrest, but was too embarrassed to tell her that he was charged with rape.

Tom first engaged in sexual intercourse at age 16. He stated that he does not really enjoy sexual activity, despite the fact that he claims to have had frequent experience, but would not explain why it is not satisfying. He stated, "Girls just come over to the house while I watch the stories and they want to have sex." His father also mentioned that girls frequently call Tom at home.

The client explained that he "misses" girls very much, but since he has been in the dentention home, he has refused to participate in activities that include girls. For example, sometimes boys and girls are allowed to sit together in the evenings. Tom claimed that he goes to his room during these times. He explained that he does not want to be with girls since

his rape charge, and "they'll bust you even if you touch a girl."

Tom appeared to be very embarrassed, somewhat immature, and confused about sexual matters. It was very difficult for him to discuss the topic with women. Also, he stated that he could not look at the interviewer during the social history interview, regardless of the subject, because she was a "girl" and "I haven't talked to one for so long." Tom expressed difficulty in relating to girls at the detention facility. He seemed quite embarrassed about the charge of rape.

Tom was unable to describe relationships in detail and provided only brief answers to questions about interpersonal relationships. While he seems to be emotionally impoverished, or shallow, it should be noted that his vocabulary is probably limited, making it difficult for him to accurately describe his feelings.

Juvenile Record: Tom's previous juvenile record includes prior arrests for cruelty to animals, trespassing, and destruction of property (1972); five counts of destruction of property and trespassing (1974); and one runaway report (1977). None of these charges resulted in commitment to any juvenile detention program.

Health: Tom has suffered from head injuries and seizures. His first head injury occurred in 1974, when he was struck in the head by a swinging door while at school. He was knocked unconscious for three or four hours and was hospitalized. He was transferred to the Raleigh General Hospital for observation.

Last year Tom was hit in the head with a tree branch while cutting wood with his father. Mr. Young explained that for a period of ten minutes Tom was unconscious and "shaking hard all over." He was not taken to a physician at that time. In 1976, a local rescue squad was called to the Youngs' home when Tom arrived home from school in an "apparent deep sleep," and was confused and dazed. Tom was not hospitalized.

Last July, while in the detention facility, Tom experienced an episode that was diagnosed as a *grand mal* seizure (the most serious type of epileptic seizure). He was then evaluated by Dr. Evans, who reported that his electroencephalogram (EEG) was normal, meaning that no *sign* of brain lesions was evident. He prescribed Tegretol, an anticonvulsant, for Tom. The "cause" of the seizure has not been determined. The client has been taking the medication and having follow-up medical appointments.

Although all written reports indicate that Tom does not suffer from headaches or dizziness, he reported that he has headaches "every week or every month."

In fact, Mrs. Young stated that Tom complained of a headache the day before he was arrested. She stated that he came home early from work to lie down. According to the client's mother, aspirin relieved Tom's headache that day, as it generally does. Tom noted that besides headaches, he has frequent nosebleeds. He does not have a history of other health problems.

Psychiatric and Behavioral Information: Tom was evaluated by Dr. Farson of Greensboro Psychiatric Center in August 1978, in response to forensic questions asked by the Juvenile Court. Dr. Farson noted that Tom had been a bedwetter until age 8 and had a history of lying, breaking and entering, stealing, truancy, and running away from home. Tom was described as displaying anxiety, shallow affect, and emotional detachment. Although Tom was oriented to place and person, he was disoriented as to time. His memory of recent and remote events was poor. Tom's problems with concepts of time were apparent. It seemed that he often could not remember when a past event occurred (months ago? years ago?). Dr. Farson concluded that Tom had a serious personality disorder but that he was not psychotic. Recommendations for Tom included referral to the state hospital with behavioral therapy and chemotherapy, and the later possibility of transfer to the rehabilitation center for training in vocational skills.

In reference to his current situation, Tom explained that being "locked up" is becoming emotionally intolerable for him. He described feeling tense and frustrated and "when someone gets on my case, I blow, I act too fast." He has had disagreements with staff members in which he was physically restrained and was forced to remain in his room or in "solitary" as a result of his behavior. Tom claimed that recently when he was left alone in his room, he contemplated suicide and started to tie sheets together to hang himself. Tom's weekly visits from his mother are the only activities that help him "feel better."

Tom and his parents were reluctant to admit his past offenses. They explained Tom's charge of cruelty to an animal as his feeding a neighbor's hungry horse without first asking the owner. Also, his parents insisted that Tom had no other arrests, and never ran away from home, even though our records indicate otherwise. Tom denied use of drugs but stated that he sometimes drinks beer.

DESCRIPTION OF THE OFFENSE: During the interviews at the Clinic, Tom steadfastly denied any involvement in the break-in at the Davis home and the rape of Mrs. Davis, his employer's wife. Tom said that he rarely saw Mrs. Davis, although he and his

brothers had been employed by Mr. Davis for some time.

According to police reports, Mrs. Davis was attacked at about 6:45 A.M. on June 28, 1978, shortly after her husband left home to pick up the Young boys for work in his fields. After the rape, the attacker threatened Mrs. Davis and tied her up. He then fled, but she was able to escape in time to see him riding away from her house on a bicycle. Tom was arrested at his home a short time later.

PRESENT MENTAL STATUS AND PSYCHODYNAMIC FUNCTIONING:

Cognitive Functioning: Most noteworthy on both interviews and psychological testing were Tom's serious cognitive limitations. Tom scored in the moderately retarded range on standardized intelligence tests. His actual educational achievement is consistent with this finding: Tom is unable to read or to do simple arithmetic computations. He was able to remember only three digits at a time. He was also unable to perform simple abstractions, such as determining the item in a series that is different (e.g., shoes, shirt, car, and pants). Tom is able to tell time and to count at least through the teens.

There were indications that the intelligence tests may be an underestimate of Tom's adaptive behavior and that his "true" intelligence may be somewhat higher than his measured intelligence—perhaps in the mildly retarded range. First, Tom scored lower on the present test than on previous assessments (1969–73). Essentially, he has not made any academic progress since then; this may be due to lack of adequate stimulation at home, coupled with his social and emotional withdrawal. Thus, it is probable that Tom's potential for cognitive growth is somewhat higher than his current test scores indicate.

Second, Tom did show some ability suggestive of higher potential and motivation to master new learning. For example, on the WAIS Block Design, Tom had severe difficulty in putting the puzzles together. However, with help from the examiner, Tom was able to learn a trial-and-error strategy for assembling the puzzles—a feat in which he took considerable pride. Similarly, in the interview setting, Tom was able to make some use of cues provided by the interviewers and within the environment. For example, when asked to count, Tom looked at the clock for cues. He was able to reach 16 before he stopped, apparently from frustration. Tom also was able to use words that he did not know (e.g., "feelings") after they were defined for him by the interviewers.

Third, Tom's social competence within his own community was unclear from our assessment. It may or may not reflect adaptive behavior higher than measured intelligence.

Not surprisingly, Tom's understanding of the legal process is limited. As he put it, "I don't know about the words." Tom did not know the meaning of word "guilty," and he seemed to confuse being charged with a crime with being guilty of it. He appeared to have no comprehension of the possibility of being found innocent at a trial. Trials, in Tom's view, are simply to set one's punishment. There were also suggestions of very limited trust in his lawyer or lawyers generally, and of anticipation that a trial would, in some way, be stacked against him. At the same time, however, Tom also showed glimmers of sophistication about the process. He was aware of the purpose of a transfer hearing and of the distinction between juvenile and circuit court. He also knew that a lawyer's task is to "help you get out of trouble." Tom also understands the current charges against him.

Personality Functioning: On the bases of both projective testing and interviews, Tom appeared to have a limited capacity for relationships. He is somewhat negativistic, and he is unable to establish trust easily. He reported never having had a best friend. Tom withdraws, particularly in contexts in which he is frustrated or feels accused. Thus, Tom would turn away and become increasingly nonverbal if presented with questions to determine his knowledge or if questioned about topics related to his current charges (i.e., sexuality, relationships with his employer, etc.).

Tom recounted an incident exemplary of this style. He had a teacher who was "nice" and who he felt was trying to help him. However, the teacher mistakenly accused Tom of banging on the building one day. Tom decided on the basis of this incident alone that the teacher was "not on my side no more" and left school. Apparently, Tom has acquired what is sometimes called "learned helplessness." That is, he has come to expect failure, and when frustrated, he responds quickly and in a passive–aggressive manner. However, Tom did respond positively when the interview style was informal, "street-wise," and concrete. He may be able to make use of an empathic, nonthreatening relationship. In fact, with continued help and support, Tom was able to sustain attention through lengthy, frustrating testing sessions.

Tom's impulse control may often be tenuous, at least partially because of his poor verbal skills and resulting inability to label feelings. There may be a self-destructive element to his acting out. He noted that he seems to "hurt myself" by getting into trou-

ble. Tom expressed suicidal ideation several times, but it is our opinion that he is not an active suicidal risk. Rather, these threats seemed to be an attention-getting device reflective of his immaturity.

Tom clearly has limited skills in the expression of feelings. For example, he said that when he became angry one time recently (while in detention), he went into his room and started eating soap. Furthermore, he tends to lash out if he feels that someone cannot be trusted or may be taking advantage of him. This may involve difficulty in social perceptions (perceiving intentions and feelings of others). For example, Tom said that sometimes someone will play with him and that he will "accidentally" hit him. At the same time, Tom told of some fights with a degree of bravado, and some aggressive behavior appears congruent with his value system. As he put it, "I gotta do what I gotta do." Furthermore, in the present context, he claimed to be ready to "do my time and get out."

Tom steadfastly claimed innocence of the charges against him. Consequently, we were unable to construct a formulation of the dynamics underlying the offense, if it in fact occurred. He refused to discuss personal information that might have illuminated intrapsychic or interpersonal conflicts. As noted in the social history, Tom's discussion of sexuality seemed to have the primary purpose of presenting a "macho" image ("ten girlfriends"), which was not credible. His discussion of sexuality in the psychiatric interviews was even more limited and in the same vein. He presented himself as dropping girls at a whim or whenever they do not please him ("I'm famous for that"). Similarly, Tom would not go beyond a vague description in talking about his family.

CONCLUSIONS AND RECOMMENDATIONS:

Competency to Stand Trial: Tom clearly understands the nature of the charges against him, and he has a general understanding of the possible consequences of these charges. His understanding of the general nature of the proceedings against him and of his attorney's role is recounted above. Because of vocabulary deficits and difficulty in conceptualization, he will require careful, simple, and repeated explanations of procedure and strategy as they progress. Tom can be expected to give his attorney basic facts to aid in his defense, but (because of his general distrust of people) he will require patient, relaxed questioning by his attorney.

Transfer: The legal meaning of the terms "mental retardation" and "criminal insanity" in the context of transfer from juvenile court is not defined by statute. It is clear, however, that Tom is clinically mentally retarded, probably in the range of moderate to mild retardation.

On the "insanity" issue, while Tom's range of ideation is quite limited, the nature or quality of his ideation is generally reality-based and not psychotic (i.e., out of touch with reality) or bizarre.

Amenability to Treatment: We were unable to construct a formulation of the dynamics underlying the alleged offense with which we would feel comfortable. Thus, it is not possible to determine amenability to treatment in terms of the alleged rape. However, in terms of Tom's general personality and cognitive deficits, it is our impression that Tom would profit from a specialized treatment program. Specifically, without acquisition of more vocational and social skills, Tom cannot be expected to manage an independent or semi-independent, productive lifestyle. Tom has some mastery of simple skills and appears to be motivated to work within a prevocational training program. Within such a context, a counselor (preferably a black male) could informally assist him in labeling feelings, understanding intentions, and developing social skills. In short, there should be an educational focus rather than formal psychotherapy.

We would in fact recommend development of an educational plan for Tom, as required under P.L. 94-142 (the federal special education law), as a first step, regardless of the trial's outcome. Tom will require patience and informality initially, given his low frustration tolerance and limited capacity for relationships. It is important to note that a structured educational–treatment program would be included in our recommendation, whether or not Tom actually committed the rape. We do not feel there are sufficient general or actuarial data to predict the likelihood of recidivism in Tom's case. However, the plan described would most likely increase his impulse control, especially as he becomes more comfortable and has some successes.

Project Adventure in Asheville may be an appropriate treatment program for Tom. Besides providing individualized counseling, a recreation program based on skill building is offered, in which learning takes place in the community rather than in a traditional classroom. Funding could be made available through P.L. 94-142. However, if Tom is accepted, he may be placed on a waiting list. Also, an intake interview must first be arranged for Tom before a decision on admission would be made.

Patrick Roberts, M.D.
Harvey A. Nicholson, Ph.D.

(b) Discussion

Note first that the writers of this report discussed Tom's personality in considerable detail, including his family, education, and work history; his social and sexual relationships; his court record; and his health and psychiatric history. This is to be expected when the primary issue is the client's amenability to treatment. As noted throughout this chapter, the amount of historical material and discussion of personality and mental state will vary, depending upon the legal issue to be addressed.

Second, the writers discussed Tom's intellectual ability very carefully, concluding that estimates of intelligence derived from test results might have been too low. This was important, because part of the legal test for transfer in this jurisdiction involves the presence or absence of mental retardation; in addition, the level of Tom's intelligence was presumably relevant to the question of his amenability to treatment.

Third, the writers offered concrete suggestions for improving the attorney–client relationship, and thereby for enhancing the client's competency to stand trial.

Fourth, note that the writers took care to distinguish between the statutory terms "mental retardation" and "criminal insanity" in making clinical observations as to Young's mental state. They pointed out that the statutory terms are not defined, and then discussed "mental retardation" and "insanity" in the context of their clinical meaning. It was left to the legal system to determine whether the statutory definitions applied to Tom.

Fifth, since this case involved transfer [see § 11.03(c)], neither mental state at the time of the offense nor dangerousness was directly an issue. They would be relevant only insofar as the court would want information about "treatment to stop rape." Here, the writers specifically stated that they were unable to explain why the offense was committed or whether Tom would recidivate. If clinicians do not have sufficient data or a sufficiently solid opinion based on the data, they should not offer an opinion.

Finally, while avoiding opinion on the ultimate legal issue of Tom's amenability to treatment, the writers offered concrete treatment suggestions. Such recommendations are much more useful to the legal system than simple conclusory statements that an individual is or is not amenable to treatment.

15.10. Dispositional Review [Chapter 12]

(a) George and Gerald Jones Report

NAME: George and Gerald Jones
D.O.B.:   George—December 5, 1976
         Gerald—October 20, 1980
MOTHER: Suzanne Jones
FOSTER PARENTS: George—David and Jane Williams
                   Gerald—Molly Davidson

SOURCES OF INFORMATION:

1. Referral letter and notes from Sue Jacobson, Department of Social Services; predispositional report from Ms. Jacobson, dated August 1, 1982.
2. Records *in re* Ms. Jones from North State Hospital (NSH) (including admission and discharge summaries).
3. Report of evaluation of Ms. Jones by Jack Henderson, M.D., on August 30, 1982.
4. Report of evaluation of Ms. Jones by James Johnson, Ph.D., on October 31, 1982.
5. Letter *in re* Ms. Jones from Marian Disney, R.N., Community Mental Health Center (CMHC) of Johnstone County, dated May 1, 1983; phone conversation with Ms. Disney on May 15, 1983.
6. Intake evaluation report by Susan Hilton, M.S.W., CMHC of Johnstone County, dated January 10, 1978.
7. Phone conversation with Lynn Nelson, Broadview School (George's teacher), 1 March 1983, and face-to-face conversation, April 5, 1983.
8. Notes on visits between Ms. Jones and her children by Jeannette Sterling, December 30, 1982, through April 10, 1983; conversation with Ms. Sterling on March 15, 1983.
9. Interviews with Ms. Jones on March 1, May 1, and May 3, 1983, including administration of Shure–Spivack Problem-Solving Childrearing Style Interview on May 3.

10. Observation of Ms. Jones with George and Gerald on March 20, 1983.
11. Interview with Jane and David Williams on March 15, 1983.
12. Interview with George, including administration of the Vocabulary subtest of the Wechsler Intelligence Scale for Children—Revised (WISC-R), on March 15, 1983.
13. Classroom observation of George on May 5, 1983.
14. Interview with Molly Davidson on March 20, 1983.
15. Play interview with Gerald on March 20, 1983.

Records were requested from Stone Ridge Workshop at NSH, where Ms. Jones is now employed, but they have not been received.

REFERRAL: The Jones family was referred for evaluation by Sue Jacobson, Social Services caseworker. Suzanne Jones, age 26, has a history of hospitalization at NSH with a diagnosis of paranoid schizophrenia. At the time of the first hospitalization (1978), George was placed in foster care for about four months. He reentered foster care in August 1979, and he returned to his mother about two months later. After Ms. Jones became pregnant with Gerald in February 1980, she was unable to take her psychotropic medication, and her mental health deteriorated. After several instances of reported abuse, George was returned to foster care in June 1980. A few days later Ms. Jones was readmitted to NSH. The Williams home, where George has lived since July 1982, is his sixth foster home. Gerald was born in October 1980 while Ms. Jones was in NSH. He was immediately placed in foster care with Molly Davidson, with whom he has lived continuously.

Ms. Jones's visits with the children have been supervised under court order since an incident in spring 1982 when she experienced auditory hallucinations, lost control, and destroyed some property during a visit with George. She now has visits with George alone once a week and with George and Gerald together once a week. These visits are supervised by a Social Services worker.

The present evaluation is intended to assist Social Services in developing a permanent plan for the Jones children. The evaluation was ordered by Johnstone County Separate Juvenile Court in August 1982. According to Ms. Jacobson, the court sought assistance as to the probable effect of Ms. Jones's mental disorder on her ability to function as a parent and the effect of Ms. Jones herself on the mental health of the children. Ms. Jacobson also requested an opinion as to George's needs for treatment or preventive services. An opinion was also sought as to the Williamses' and Ms. Davidson's attachment to George and Gerald, respectively, and their ability to meet the children's special needs in the future.

EVALUATION OF MS. JONES:

History: Ms. Jones reported that her mother died when she was about two years old. She never knew her father. Following her mother's death, she went to live with her uncle and aunt and their four children (all four to ten years older than Ms. Jones). Ms. Jones's uncle worked in a factory, and her aunt, who died when Ms. Jones was 14, was a domestic worker. Ms. Jones reported that each of her cousins has made a satisfactory adjustment as an adult. She indicated that she sometimes thinks she is an embarrassment to the family because of her history of mental disorder. Sean, age 36, is married and owns a small business. Jennie, age 34, is married and living in Georgia. Kathryn, who is about age 32, is recently divorced and a secretary. Joan, age 30, is living with a dentist, and she owns a clothing shop. Ms. Jones has four older natural siblings, who live around the country, and one younger sister, who was adopted and whom she does not know. Ms. Jones was unable or unwilling to describe her childhood in much detail, but she said it was unremarkable.

Ms. Jones was married to John Morton in June 1982. The marriage was short-lived, however, and the divorce is currently being finalized. Ms. Jones had known Mr. Morton for about two years prior to their marriage. She said that they separated because of differences in religious beliefs and Mr. Morton's unreliability (drinking and unemployment). Mr. Morton has no contact with the children, and pays no child support.

Before dropping out of school, Ms. Jones obtained a tenth-grade education. She then went to live with a sister in Cleveland. She worked briefly as a secretary at a large company before becoming a dancer at about age 19. The latter occupation was apparently embarrassing to Ms. Jones, and she declined to discuss it except to say that the auditory hallucinations she experienced in the past sometimes consisted of voices making accusations about her conduct as a dancer. Apparently Ms. Jones began to become quite paranoid during her last months in Cleveland, and she obtained some mental health care there. She was hospitalized the day after returning to Mill Valley.

Ms. Jones was hospitalized at NSH from December 28, 1977, to January 5, 1978, and from June 5, 1980, to May 7, 1981. Since then she has been attending a vocational rehabilitation program at Stone Ridge and therapy at CMHC of Johnstone County. Ms. Jones sees Marian Disney, R.N., every other week for therapy. She is also involved in social activities at CMHC, and her medications (Prolixin, Artane, and Halcion) are monitored there.

Ms. Disney reported that Ms. Jones has been reliable in keeping appointments and cooperative. Since August 1982, Ms. Jones has reported no hallucinations, and Ms. Disney said that she has no reason to dispute that report. Ms. Disney has worked with Ms. Jones in maintaining cognitive control over her feelings and ideation. However, Ms. Disney is not sure that Ms. Jones would be able to apply these skills when under stress (e.g., to know what to say to herself if she began to hear voices). She sometimes does not remember things discussed and skills learned several sessions previously. Ms. Disney indicated that Ms. Jones has reported no episodes of aggression or inappropriate temper outbursts in recent months. However, she added that Ms. Jones has been under no particularly stressful situations, other than the current legal proceedings concerning her children. Ms. Jones gave a similar report of her recent mental status and stress level during her interviews with me.

Ms. Disney indicated that her current concern about Ms. Jones is "her tendency to withdraw and isolate herself." This impression was corroborated by history in the current evaluation. Ms. Jones said that there is no one inside or outside her family upon whom she can really depend. However, she is closest to her cousin Kathryn, and she is sometimes able to use her as a sounding board. According to Ms. Disney, Ms. Jones has not joined any activity or group on her own, although she does participate in social activities at CMHC.

Ms. Jones reported that she is now seeking employment through Vocational Rehabilitation. She is looking for a job as a custodian; in the meantime, she is considering doing volunteer work at the VA Hospital. At present, Ms. Jones is supported by Supplemental Security Income. She handles all of her own financial affairs and daily living skills.

Mental Status: Ms. Jones was cooperative for the evaluation and reliable in keeping appointments.

Ms. Jones's affect (expression of feelings) was generally flattened. Although she did show appropriate laughter at times, her access to affect appeared limited. Her demeanor was marked by a blank stare typical in chronic schizophrenia.

Ms. Jones's ideation was very concrete, although not bizarre. She was unable to solve common proverbs. She was not a very good historian, and she seemed to have some difficulty in remembering and describing her experiences. Some of her lack of verbal fluency was probably attributable to guardedness about the nature of the evaluation, however. Ms. Jones gave no sign of attending to hallucinations (which she denied having experienced in recent months), although she may have been somewhat distracted by inner experiences. Her performance on digit spans (five digits forward, three digits reversed) was about two standard deviations below the mean (i.e., a level surpassed by well over 95% of persons her age). Such deficits in short-term memory are sometimes associated with difficulties in attention. Reports from Ms. Disney of her having had difficulty in retaining directions and lessons are consistent with such a picture as well.

Ms. Jones's insight and judgment appeared somewhat improved over previous evaluations. For example, she described her medication as designed to "stop me from hearing voices and having temper tantrums, help me relax, and get a good night's sleep," and she recognized the need to take the medication on a regular basis. However, she seemed to have little insight about the origins of her disorder or patterns in her behavior, although she is aware that she has gotten out of control when she has experienced hallucinations. She recognizes that she has not really been tested with respect to her ability to maintain control during hallucinations, although she says that she knows what to do if they should recur (e.g., "hit a beanbag" if the voices make her angry; "tell myself they're not real—use rational thinking").

As already noted, Ms. Jones reported very sparse relationships. She said that there had been "loneliness" since her separation from her husband, but that she is "surviving." In view of her avoidant style, her capacity to form and maintain relationships may be limited.

Summary: Ms. Jones retains some of the symptomatology of schizophrenia (e.g., social isolation; flattened affect), but she does not appear to be actively paranoid at this point. She apparently has made slow but steady progress over the past few months in her general mental status. Her insight and judgment have improved, but her thinking remains very concrete.

EVALUATION OF GEORGE:

Interview: On interview, George related appropriately and cooperatively. He did show some signs of anxiety (e.g., nails bitten to the quick), and he was very aware of (although somewhat reluctant to talk about) the instability of home life he has experienced. George said that the reason that he had been placed in the foster care was that his mother had thrown him against the wall. Although he said that he enjoyed visiting his mother, he would prefer to live with someone else "just in case." As might be expected, given the proportion of his life spent in foster care, George's attachment to his mother is tenuous. When asked to draw a picture of his family, he drew the Williamses. Similarly, he drew a picture of a home (the one in which he currently lives) and pointed out where "Mommy" and "Daddy" (Rev. and Mrs. Williams) sleep. At the same time, though, he also does not seem very attached to the Williamses. He said that he would most like to live with Helen (a home from which George was removed because the foster father allegedly engaged in inappropriate sexual contact with a foster daughter), and Social Service notes indicate that he frequently telephones Helen during his visits to Ms. Jones.

Some of the content of George's interview material suggested that he may be preoccupied at times by concerns about aggression and his vulnerability. For example, when asked what animal he would most like to be, George replied that he would like to be an eagle, because "if somebody going around killing animals, I could be an eagle to fly so they couldn't get me." These suggestions are corroborated by home and school observations indicating significant emotional disturbance. Rev. and Mrs. Williams reported that George has a short attention span, often stares off into space, sleeps deeply and frequently (he actually fell asleep in the waiting room while I was interviewing the Williamses), and has difficulty in shifting moods (e.g., when he becomes angry, he stays angry for a prolonged period of time).

Lynne Nelson, George's teacher, also noted his difficulty in shifting moods and, in particular, marked responses to frustration. Ms. Nelson said that he is also very sensitive to discipline and becomes obstinate and pouting after being corrected. She noted that George easily becomes angry, and then he becomes quite aggressive at times and hits and pinches the other children and shows no remorse for having done so. He also has a tendency to disrupt the class by being noisy and silly and refusing to do his work. Ms. Nelson added that his misbehavior is especially marked after even a single day's absence from school; he seems to have difficulty when routines are disrupted. Ms. Nelson indicated that George seems to crave attention from adults and that he does best in one-to-one work, a tendency that was apparent during my classroom observation. Ms. Nelson is sufficiently concerned about George that she has made a referral for school psychological services.

Academic Achievement and Testing: George's academic progress is mildly delayed (around beginning first-grade level). He is in low groups in both math and reading, although he has begun making rapid progress in math, which he enjoys. A screening for intelligence was performed using the Vocabulary subtest of the WISC-R, the subtest that correlates most highly with Full-Scale IQ and school performance. It is noteworthy in that regard that George scored just above the mean for his age group; this suggests, in light of his poor schoolwork, that he is not working to his potential, perhaps because of interference by emotional factors. Care should be taken not to overinterpret this single subtest score, however.

Summary and Recommendations: Although George does not show signs of severe psychological disorder, he is clearly a troubled and perhaps somewhat troubling youngster. He appears to have substantial concern about the instability in his life, and he has difficulty in managing affect, especially anger. I strongly recommend his becoming involved in psychotherapy, both to help him to deal with the traumatic events he has experienced and to give him skills in controlling his feelings. Such treatment would preferably be long-term, in order to give him the possibility of exploring his feelings within a consistent relationship. My expectation is that it would take a number of sessions before he would begin to feel secure enough in the relationship to make good use of it therapeutically. Cognitive–behavioral work aimed at giving George skills in dealing with anger and increasing his attention span and tolerance for frustration would also be useful. In any case, some form of intervention would be especially important if there is a change of residence or custody.

EVALUATION OF GERALD:

Interview: Gerald appeared to be a remarkably bright, inquisitive 28-month-old boy. His play when with Molly Davidson (his foster mother) or me was structured and imaginative. He was highly verbal for a two-year-old. Gerald talked a great deal, and he did so in three-word sentences. With Ms. Davidson he was very polite (e.g., using "please" and "thank you" consistently), and his play was quite social for a child of his age. For example, he wanted to make sure that there were dolls to go with cars and other toys ("[Where are the] People, Mama?"). Ms. Davidson said that Gerald is close to his stepsister (an 8-year-old foster child whom Ms. Davidson is adopting). He

gets up to tell her good-bye every morning when she leaves for school, and he plays violin with her sometimes. (Ms. Davidson has involved both children in Suzuki violin lessons.)

Gerald's developmental milestones have generally been appropriate. He walked at 11 months. Toilet training is just beginning.

Summary: Gerald is a bright two-year-old who shows appropriate cognitive and social development.

NATURE OF THE FOSTER HOMES:

Williamses: Rev. and Mrs. Williams appear on first impression to be caring people. They have, for example, endeavored to involve Ms. Jones in some of the activities of their church, and they have kept communication open (e.g., permitting holiday visits and frequent phone calls). They also appear to have reasonable sensitivity to George's emotional needs. They are committed to long-term foster care, if necessary, for George. However, they have not really discussed the possibility of adoption at some point, and they perceive the best option as eventually returning George to his natural mother.

The Williamses are Pentacostalists, and they may have unnecessarily strict expectations. For example, they will not allow their children to play with other children in the neighborhood because of the "bad mouths" of the neighbor children. They also forbid dancing and rock music. No mention was made, however, of any conflicts with George concerning the household rules per se.

At the same time that I met with the Williamses, I was just beginning my evaluation of George. Consequently, I have not broached the possibility of his receiving psychological help with them. Assuming that long-term care by the Williamses continues, Social Services workers might explore their willingness to cooperate with a treatment program.

Ms. Davidson: Ms. Davidson is a single foster parent who apparently pays special attention to the intellectual stimulation of her children. As has already been noted, she has enrolled the children in Suzuki lessons. She encourages Gerald to watch *Sesame Street, Romper Room,* etc., but she denies access to TV cartoons because of the violence in them. She does permit "classical cartoons" (e.g., library showings of animated versions of *The Nutcracker*), however.

Ms. Davidson is a graduate of Peace College, and for several years she worked as a media specialist in Peace's laboratory school. She has recently been a substitute teacher, and she is working on setting up a preschool with some friends. She has obtained an elementary-school teaching job in St. Louis, and she will be moving there in July. She would like to take Gerald with her and indeed to adopt him.

Ms. Davidson's mother, a widow who lives in St. Louis, is also in the process of adopting three foster children, and she has taken care of foster children for some time. Ms. Davidson herself seemed to minimize the realistic problems of being a single parent. However, she apparently has substantial social support at present in church groups, and she will have the support of her family when she moves to Missouri.

RELATIONSHIP BETWEEN MS. JONES AND HER CHILDREN: On observation Ms. Jones seemed generally to be appropriately involved with the children, although Social Services notes suggest that she may be somewhat detached at times. During the play session, the children were, in her words, "hyperactive" and often somewhat out of control. She was generally slow to respond. When she did respond, she was not very effective. Gerald's behavior presented a particular contrast to his behavior with Ms. Davidson. Although he had frequently shown toys to his foster mother and talked with her, he seldom engaged in that behavior with Ms. Jones. He was also markedly less well behaved and polite, although the presence of a second child may have contributed to his misbehavior. (Gerald's identifying most of the toys as his own whenever George wanted to play with something was the instigation of much of the rowdiness.)

Ms. Jones appears to be trying to be a good parent (at least as good as one can be without custody). According to the Williamses, she calls George about every other day. During the interviews, she seemed at times to be asking for the "answers" about how to handle childrearing situations. At the same time, though, her skills in problem solving as a parent need more development. The structured interview on parental problem solving developed by Shure and Spivack* was administered. One aspect of the interview involves giving the respondent a series of vignettes about parent–child relations; the respondent is given the beginning of the story and the end (a positive outcome). The task then is to identify what the mother in the story might have said or done to achieve a positive result. Although Ms. Jones's answers were generally not bizarre or noticeably inappropriate, they were also sparse. That is, she sometimes seemed "stuck" in figuring out ways of getting from a prob-

lem to a successful resolution of the problem. It is likely that her concreteness of thought and limited relationships have adversely affected her ability to empathize with the children in a situation in which they are having difficulty.

Ms. Jones has made an effort to apply some of the childrearing concepts taught in the CARE program. For example, she describes "time out" as a primary disciplinary tool, and she apparently uses the technique on occasion during visits with the children (according to Social Services notes prepared by Ms. Sterling). However, there is an impression reported in the notes and in conversation with Ms. Sterling that she uses the technique somewhat arbitrarily without explanation to the children and without clear understanding of the concept. Ms. Sterling's impression that Ms. Jones may not fully understand the application of time out was corroborated during my own interviews with her. In response to one of the Shure–Spivack vignettes (about a child's shoplifting cookies from the grocery store), Ms. Jones initially talked only about how to get the cookies back to the grocery store. When pressed to identify the appropriate consequences for the child, she said, "The first time I'd just tell him. The second time he'd get a spanking. I don't think he should just go on time out for stealing. I don't think he'd learn from it." However, she had also said that time out *"always* works."

Ms. Jones said that she would prefer to regain custody of both children. However, she added that having only one would be "OK." If it came to that, she thinks that George would be the child for whom she could better care. Besides that Gerald has always lived in foster care, he requires more care because he is younger. Her first response was simply that George "helps me." There may be some role reversal with him, a tendency that has been commonly reported in clinical reports of abuse and neglect.

Ms. Jones denied that her hallucinations when they have occurred have contained content about the children. Although she was very reluctant to talk about the voices, she said that they made accusations about her having been a dancer (she refused to elaborate further) and her being unclean (e.g., "You smell"). Apparently, however, the hallucinations have often focused on the children, although without direct instructions of what to do to the children. The NSH records indicated that the hallucinations at the times of her hospitalizations often focused on accusations about her care of her children. More recently, Ms. Disney asked Ms. Jones to keep a log of hallucinations. Although, as already noted, she has not reported any for several months, prior to that time the

---

* *See* M. SHURE & G. SPIVACK, PROBLEM-SOLVING TECHNIQUES IN CHILDREARING (1978).

content often involved the children (e.g., "You should give your baby to someone who loves him"; "Does Mommy want this baby?"; 'You have to go back to the hospital so you can beat the boy"; "She's always hurting someone. Yaaa!"; "I can't wait until you lose the kid").

CONCLUSIONS: Although Ms. Jones's mental status appears to have improved in recent months, she continues to show residual signs of chronic schizophrenia (e.g., flattened affect, social isolation), which are likely to persist. A major concern is the question of recurrence of hallucinations and Ms. Jones's ability to keep control if and when they return. It is clear that the probability of florid paranoid symptoms is substantially decreased while Ms. Jones remains on medication. However, it is unclear what the probability is of her again experiencing hallucinations and losing control. Apparently she has not been under great stress in recent months. Accordingly, one cannot make very strong inferences from the recent lack of active hallucinatory behavior as to the probability of her losing control in the future. Based on previous behavior, it is at such times that the children would be at physical risk.

For the time being, the general treatment plan being used by CMHC seems appropriate for Ms. Jones. It might be useful to add work on empathy and problem solving with respect to the children themselves. Continuing work by Social Services on application of parental skills would also be appropriate. However, Ms. Jones's concrete thinking style and low relatedness make such work difficult.

On the basis of the one-time interviews with them, I do not feel confident in making strong statements about the adequacy of the Williams and Ms. Davidson as long-term foster parents or potential adoptive parents. Generally, however, the care given the children *sounds* appropriate. It is clear that Gerald is securely attached to Ms. Davidson (e.g., he uses her as "home base" for exploration of an unfamiliar setting). However, George appears not to be strongly attached to either Ms. Jones or any of the series of foster parents with whom he has lived.

George appears to have substantial concerns about his vulnerability and difficulty in managing affect, especially anger. He is also having both academic and social problems in school. I recommend his referral for psychotherapy, preferably long-term. A full psychoeducational evaluation would also be advisable. Gerald, on the other hand, appears well adjusted for a child of his age.

A final point that should be made is that Ms. Jones's

schizophrenia should not be viewed as an indicant per se of inability to function as an adequate parent. Recent research by Arnold Samaroff, Bertram Cohler, Norman Garmezy, and others indicates that, while children of schizophrenic mothers are at greater risk for developmental difficulties than children of normals, most of these differences are erased when comparisons are made with other diagnostic groups (e.g., mothers with affective disorders), and many of the differences, at least for young children, disappear when proper controls are added for social class and stress level. Moreover, many children of schizophrenic mothers appear to cope reasonably well. However, the risk level is related to the chronicity of the mother's condition. In general, the issue should be framed as to how Ms. Jones's specific difficulties affect her relationships with the children, given their specific needs.

David P. Rodriguez, Ph.D.

(b)   Discussion

The Jones report was prepared for a review of disposition in a child abuse case. It is important to note in that regard that the clinician took care to obtain records that might illuminate the degree of change that had occurred since the last review; he also interviewed the natural mother, both sets of foster parents, and the children themselves, both by themselves and with their mother. There were also conversations with Ms. Jones's therapist, the social worker, and the social service aide, and the clinician did a school visit. The checks with other sources (e.g., Ms. Jones's therapist) were helpful in that, besides giving a baseline against which to measure change, they indicated some relationships between Ms. Jones's mental disorder and her behavior with her children (e.g., child-related content of auditory hallucinations) that she had not disclosed. Exploration of diverse sources of information was also essential in reaching conclusions about specific issues related to the children's adjustment and the adequacy of the foster homes. Both types of issues are ancillary to questions of a parent's fitness, but both frequently arise in dispositional reviews.

Substantial attention was given to Ms. Jones's mental status, but it is important to note that it was not scrutinized for its own sake. Rather, the clinician was interested in changes in Ms. Jones's condition and the relationship between Ms. Jones's psychiatric problems and her care for her children. In fact, one interview was devoted largely to the Shure–Spivack vignettes on child-rearing situations.

Note also that in the conclusion to the report, the clinician informed the court and the social services department of the research showing little relationship between schizophrenia and parental incompetence [see § 12.05]. Elsewhere in the report, there were indirect references to research literature (e.g., a child's using an adult as "home base" for exploration as an indicator of attachment), which may have illuminated behavioral science information unlikely to be known to the court.

Finally, note the care with which conclusory statements, particularly predictive statements, were made. The clinician indicated that abusive incidents in the past all occurred in the context of Ms. Jones's hallucinations. He reported the apparent lack of hallucinations over the previous months, but he also noted that Ms. Jones had not been under much stress in that time. Therefore, he concluded that he was unable to draw a very firm conclusion as to the likelihood of Ms. Jones's experiencing hallucinations again or of being unable to control herself if they did recur. Similarly, the clinician emphasized the limited data base available to him for determining the suitability of the foster parents for long-term placement or adoption. In keeping with our usual injunction against ultimate-issue testimony, the clinician refrained from drawing conclusions as to whether Ms. Jones was an unfit parent and whether the children should be returned to her home.

15.11. Visitation Rights [Chapter 13]

(a) Jensen Report

NAMES: Franklin Jensen and children, Paula and
          Charles
D.O.B.:   Paula—January 5, 1976
          Charles—March 14, 1977

SOURCES OF INFORMATION:

1. Interviews with Mr. Jensen on November 14 and 21, 1981.
2. Interviews with Mrs. Sharon Simon (formerly Sharon Jensen) individually and with Mr. and Mrs. Simon together on November 16, 1981.
3. Separate interviews with Paula and Charles Jensen on November 16, 1981.
4. Brief interviews with State Penitentiary officials (Jason Tyler, Robert Walker, Dr. Herbert Wallen) and observation of visiting area on November 14, 1981; brief interview with Mr. Walker on November 21, 1981.
5. Review of the following records:
   a. Letter from Thomas A. Cass to Mr. Jensen's attorney, Michael Porter, concerning visitation record (dated November 14, 1981).
   b. State Penitentiary visiting regulations (dated December 26, 1981).
   c. Letter from Gregory N. Stroup to Mr. Jensen inviting him to be an interviewee in a television documentary on alcoholism (dated August 13, 1981).
   d. Letter from Mr. Jensen to Mr. Porter concerning history of visitation (dated May 21, 1981).
   e. Program from Alcoholics Anonymous (AA) banquet (dated March 7, 1978).
   f. Divorce decree (dated September 3, 1977).
   g. Letter from Murray Benson to Mr. Jensen concerning phone calls to school (dated August 2, 1981).
   h. Several letters from Mrs. Simon to Mr. Jensen; letter from Mr. Jensen to Mrs. Simon (dated October 13, 1981).
   i. Evaluation report by Dr. Carl L. Graham (dated October 6, 1981).
   j. Letter from Alan Gray to Mr. Jensen concerning travel policy (dated October 12, 1981).
   k. Depositions of Mr. Jensen, Daniel P. Downing, Thomas A. Cass, Bruce Michael Carroll, and Henry James Ramirez (all dated September 4, 1981).
6. Review of major criminal justice journals from 1977 to 1982.*

REFERRAL: Referral was made by Michael Porter of Brown, Brown, & Porter in Springfield, who is

---

* Journals included in this review were the JOURNAL OF CRIMINAL JUSTICE, the BRITISH JOURNAL OF CRIMINOLOGY, CRIME AND DELINQUENCY, CRIMINAL JUSTICE AND BEHAVIOR, and JOURNAL OF RESEARCH IN CRIME AND DELINQUENCY.

representing Franklin Jensen in a dispute with his former wife, Sharon Simon, over visitation of Mr. Jensen by their children, Paula (age six) and Charles (age nearly five). Mr. Jensen is incarcerated in the State Penitentiary as a result of concurrent life sentences that he received for the murder of Mrs. Simon's parents on October 8, 1976. The Jensens divorced on September 3, 1977. As a part of the settlement, Mr. Jensen was granted reasonable visitation. Between 1977 and January 1981, there were approximately 27 visits. In January 1981, Mrs. Simon discontinued these visits. She is contending that visits to the penitentiary are not in the best interests of the children, and she is requesting the court to terminate visitation there. She would permit visitation in Jefferson County. Mr. Porter has requested evaluation of whether continued visitation at the penitentiary would be in the best interests of Paula and Charles.

FACILITIES FOR VISITATION: Only the most recent (January 1981) visit by the children was at the new penitentiary facilities. All of the prison officials interviewed describe the visiting area in the current building as a marked improvement over the visiting room in the old penitentiary building. The old facility was described as uncomfortable in summer (it was not air-conditioned) and as having a gloomy, prison-like feel. Specifically, there were bars in the area and a glass wall separating the visitors from the captain's area, where any disturbance was visible to the visitors. The officers on duty were in the captain's area and accordingly not immediately available. The automatic doors closing also presented a hazard to children at times.

The visiting room at the new prison is a long, rectangular room (62 ½ × 34 feet), lined with comfortable chairs. The room is carpeted and there are no bars on the windows (although barbed wire is visible in the distance). Two female correctional officers are present at all times and supervise the inmates and visitors.

At present, one visit per week is allowed all offenders. All visitors are required to submit to a shakedown, which for children is limited to a "pat search." Children may bring a toy, and books are also available. Rest rooms are available inside the control doors, unlike the old facilities; the rest rooms are located across a corridor from the visiting area. Vending machines are also available in the corridor. Inmates are not allowed in the corridor.

At present, there is no orientation or preparation for children of offenders. There is also no special play

area. However, according to Dr. Herbert Wallen (associate warden), plans are under way for both programs, and they may be in place by spring.

The major problem with the visiting facilities at present is overcrowding. On Fridays, Mondays, and Tuesdays, adult visitors typically number 10 to 40. However, on Saturdays and Sundays, 60–70 adults commonly visit the penitentiary. On one Sunday in October, according to Dr. Wallen, 95 adults and 28 children visited.

Mr. Robert Walker, administrative assistant to the warden, indicated that the prison would make special arrangements for visits by children, if so ordered by the court. For example, visits might be arranged on Sunday mornings (before regular visiting hours) so that they might take place in a quiet atmosphere.

HISTORY OF VISITATION: As noted previously, there have been no visits by Mr. Jensen's children since last January. It was Mr. Jensen's perception that the visits became infrequent after his former wife married Charles Simon in July 1980. He claimed that Mrs. Simon gave no indication at the last visit that she was planning to seek termination of visitation rights. However, Mrs. Simon said that she had for some time (since the children passed the infancy stage) made known that she felt the penitentiary was not a good place for children to visit.

There are some points of agreement between Mr. Jensen and Mrs. Simon in their perceptions of the visits. Both believe that the visits were not traumatic for the children, and neither regards Mr. Jensen as a threat to the children. (Mrs. Simon qualified the latter belief as specific to "controlled settings," but she included therein any situation in which there would be supervision of the visitation, even if outside the penitentiary walls.)

However, there are obviously substantial differences in the parents' perception of the visits, too. Mr. Jensen described the visits as "super" and enjoyed by everyone concerned. He said that he read books to the children and that they seemed glad to see him. The visits also gave him a chance to get caught up on what the children had been doing.

Mrs. Simon said that she could not say that the children had been harmed by the visits, but that the children had not found them meaningful, either. She said that there was no more than 10 to 15 minutes of real interaction before the children tired. (Mr. Jensen indicated that the visits typically lasted two to three hours.) Mrs. Simon also said that there were frequently arguments between Mr. Jensen and her, and that these were sometimes somewhat upsetting to the children. However, Mr. Jensen claimed that discussions about property matters and so forth were always saved for the end of the visit so as not to be disruptive and that there was rarely arguing.

Mrs. Simon described the January 1981 visit as the "last straw," in that there had been a disruptive argument. (There had been a dispute between Mrs. Simon and Mr. Jensen about the place of burial of a hunting dog that belonged to Mr. Jensen and that the Simons had kept after Mr. Jensen's incarceration.) She had also gotten separated from the children in the control area at one point while being admitted. Mr. Jensen remembers Mrs. Simon and, to a lesser extent, Paula having been "cool" during the January visit. He also said that there were indeed some "sharp words, but no yelling, and that the visit was largely enjoyable.

Mrs. Simon objects primarily to the penitentiary as a place for children to visit. She indicated that she would not object to visits in Peoria. She also said that if, when the children get older, they ask to visit their father, she will not object. Mrs. Simon has also not objected to visits by Mr. Jensen's relatives. The penitentiary is unacceptable to her, however. As she put it, Mr. Jensen himself "would object violently to their [the children's] being among rapists and murderers." Mrs. Simon also said that the children had been exposed to profane language from inmates during the visits, although never from Mr. Jensen himself.

Mr. Simon indicated that he believed the visits to be disruptive. He said that Charles had once asked why his father was in a cage and, that after one visit, he had rebelled against doing something asked of him by pointing out that Mr. Simon is not his real father.

Mrs. Simon also said that the visits were disruptive of the family routine. Sunday is the only practical day for visits because of Mrs. Simon's work schedule. It is necessary to leave right after Sunday School to get to the penitentiary on time for visits, and the rest of Sunday is then gone.

Paula said that the visits were "kinda fun," although she did so without much apparent conviction. She said that the time was spent telling her father about what she had been doing. Charles talked about the drink machines in the visiting area and the opportunity for snacks. (Mrs. Simon said that she believed the most salient part of the visits for the children was the opportunity for treats, such as going to McDonald's.)

Mr. Jensen said that he believes that it is important for the children to continue visitation so that

they will come to know him. He pointed out that he had not been able to talk to his own father, who was an alcoholic, and that the topic of alcoholism had been taboo. As a result, he believes, he harbored resentment toward his father until rather recently (after "making amends" as part of his AA program). Mr. Jensen believes that the children will have less conflict about their family background if his history is open to discussion and he can explain his life to them. In his words, "alcoholism should not be buried" in a family.

THE CHILDREN'S RELATIONSHIP WITH MR. JENSEN: Both Paula and Charles described Mr. Jensen as their "other daddy" and Mr. Simon as their "real daddy." They also described Mr. Simon's natural children, all of whom are at least 15 and do not currently live with the Simons, as "brothers" and "sisters." Paula also included Mr. Simon, but not Mr. Jensen, in her family drawing. Charles refused to put either father in the drawing, although he described Mr. Simon as part of the family.

Both children described Mr. Jensen in positive terms and said that they wanted to visit him. However, the wish was mentioned only in response to a direct question and may have been the "nice" answer. All that Paula would say about Mr. Jensen, when asked to describe him, was that he was "neat" (an adjective delivered without affect, i.e., without emotion). She also gave an accurate physical description of Mr. Jensen but refused to talk about him as a person.

Both children gave a factual account in matter-of-fact terms about the nature and reasons for Mr. Jensen's confinement, although Paula seemed a bit reluctant to do so. Last summer (1981), Mrs. Simon explained to the children why Mr. Jensen is in prison, and they appear to have assimilated her explanation well and to have accepted the explanation to the degree that would be reasonable for children of their age. Mrs. Simon said that the children talked about the explanation frequently for about a week but have mentioned it seldom since then. She described Paula as having been a bit fearful; otherwise, the children's feelings toward their natural father did not appear to change. Mrs. Simon plans to continue to offer "objective, unemotional" responses to the children's questions. She said that she has tried to be careful not to speak negatively of Mr. Jensen in front of the children.

The Simons claimed that Mr. Jensen has not been active in attempting to maintain a relationship with the children. They noted that he is not paying child support and that he has not called the children. Letters and cards for the children have been addressed to Mrs. Simon at her place of employment.

Mr. Jensen stated that the desire for child support payments is unreasonable, in view of large lump-sum payments that he has made to Mrs. Simon. He also thought that Mrs. Simon would not permit phone calls and letters to the children, after the current action was filed. He seemed genuinely surprised—even shocked—to hear that Mrs. Simon said that she would allow such contact, although Mrs. Simon denied having given any indication that phone calls would not be permitted. Under former prison rules, inmates were allowed one call per month during daytime hours, and Mrs. Simon had told Mr. Jensen that she would prefer that he not call the children at the babysitter's. The school had also refused calls to the children. In about July, phones for inmates were installed, with a new limit of one ten-minute call per day. Phone visitation is now a possibility, therefore.

Mr. Jensen seems genuinely interested in the children. He was anxious, for example, to find out how they were doing when I interviewed them. On the other hand, he appeared not to know the children very well (perhaps unsurprisingly in view of the minimal contact), and he referred to them on occasion in somewhat impersonal terms ("the boy" and "the girl"). In fairness, though, it should be noted that Mr. Jensen referred to a number of people in his life in such terms; this may be a manner of speech for him.

EVALUATION OF MR. JENSEN: Mr. Jensen related appropriately. His reality testing (ability to discriminate reality from fantasy) appeared intact. He also appeared to have normal access to affect (emotion), and his range of affect was appropriate to the contact of our discussions. His speech did appear a bit pressured (e.g., hurried, lacking in coherence) at times, although not markedly so.

Mr. Jensen had a history of severe problems with alcohol abuse, which culminated in the murders for which he is now serving time. Before the murders, he had two drunk driving convictions, for which he received alcoholism treatment; he indicated that this was not very helpful at the time.

Mr. Jensen believes that he has changed substantially while in prison. He described himself as having been quite depressed during his first year in prison. His moods are now more even, and he believes that he has changed in his "ability to handle disappointments and resentments." Perhaps more significantly, Mr. Jensen appears to be more aware when he is in a

"blame cycle" and setting up a pattern of blaming others for his own difficulties. Mr. Jensen noted that it took him relatively long to pass the First Step of AA (admitting that one is an alcoholic) and that he has gone far in taking account of his strengths and weaknesses. Mr. Jensen has been an officer in the prison chapter of AA, and he has apparently taken advantage of other counseling programs in the institution. He is reported to have had no misconduct reports, and his work record is exemplary. He has apparently developed considerable skill as a paralegal; he has filed appellate briefs on behalf of other inmates, and has developed a sophisticated understanding of water-law problems related to some riverfront property that he owns.

CONCLUSIONS: I am aware of no research on the effect of prison visitation on families of inmates. A review of the major criminal justice journals for the past five years, while not exhaustive, corroborated this lack of research. Indeed, there were no publications in the journals reviewed on visitation generally or on programs for inmate families generally.

In the face of such a vacuum of systematic research, predictions of effects are necessarily somewhat speculative. In that connection, Dr. Graham's prediction that visits to the penitentiary will become the precipitants of conflict for the children as they grow older is plausible. On the other hand, it is at least as plausible that coming to know Mr. Jensen will reduce rather than exacerbate conflict. It is a truism of personality theory and research that ambiguity fosters anxiety; fantasies about the unknown frequently induce conflict and anxiety. The fact of their father's murder of their grandparents will doubtless be conflict-laden for the children as they grow older. It is not at all clear that visits to the penitentiary will add appreciably to those conflicts. Indeed, frank discussions and acknowledgments of the situation may help the children to master them. Although it would not be realistic to do so at this point (in view of the children's ages), the parties concerned may ultimately want to place visitation at the children's discretion (i.e., to the degree that they find comfortable and helpful).

For the short term, the best indicant of the effect of future visitation is the effect (or lack thereof) of previous visitation on the children. There appears to be no evidence that the visits have harmed the children. The children are apparently well adjusted. Their behavior on interview was well within normal limits, and they seem to have as much comprehension of the circumstances of Mr. Jensen's confinement as one might expect at their ages. On the other hand, as Mrs. Simon's remarks indicate, it is not clear that the visits have been very meaningful to the children, at least as they have been previously spaced. Visits would be more likely to have such an effect if there were more ongoing contact (e.g., letters, phone calls) than has previously been the case.

In that connection, it is clear that, for whatever reasons, the rules for contact between Mr. Jensen and the children have never been adequately clarified. Mrs. Simon appears to be willing to allow some forms of contact (e.g., phone visitation) that Mr. Jensen apparently believed were unacceptable to her. Perhaps the reason for the unclarity of rules is that this is the first time in which the children have been the focus of a dispute between Mr. Jensen and Mrs. Simon. According to Mrs. Simon, she and her lawyer had assumed that there would be no issue concerning the children (in the original divorce settlement). In view of Mr. Jensen's long sentence, they had expected (wrongly) that no right to visitation would be awarded. Accordingly, there was no negotiation on the bounds of reasonable visitation. Such discussions are clearly in order at this point.

Two additional points may be helpful. First, there has been no visitation since Mrs. Simon informed the children of the nature of Mr. Jensen's crime. If and when visitation (or indeed any form of contact) resumes, some empathic acknowledgment of the relevant facts (e.g., grownups sometimes do very bad things that are hard to understand) would be useful to reduce the children's discomfort. Second, although the visiting facilities at the new penitentiary are apparently markedly improved over the visiting room at the old prison, the situation is still not ideal. The room is reasonably comfortable; indeed, it looks like large waiting rooms in nonpenal settings. At the same time, though, there are not many special provisions for children (although some are planned), and overcrowding reduces privacy and increases noise during peak visiting hours. Therefore, if visitation at the penitentiary resumes, it would be best if it took place on a day other than Sunday or under special arrangements (e.g., Sunday morning). As noted previously, the prison administration may be amenable to making some special arrangements in order to decrease the probability of stress on the children. The visits have thus far apparently not been very stressful (thanks at least in part to Mrs. Simon's good-faith efforts to make visits reasonably pleasant when they have occurred). Further efforts to manage the environment by providing some private or quiet space are likely to

maximize the probability of enjoyable and meaningful visits.

Samantha Pauling, Ph.D.

(b) Discussion

The issue in the Jensen case was whether it would be harmful for two children to visit their father in prison. The father had been convicted of killing the children's grandparents. The parents had negotiated visitation rights as part of a divorce settlement subsequent to Mr. Jensen's conviction, but Mrs. Simon, Mr. Jensen's former spouse, had terminated the children's visits to the penitentiary. This report is noteworthy for several reasons.

First, as indicated by the enumeration of the sources of information, the evaluation was very comprehensive [see § 13.04]. Among other things, the clinician visited the penitentiary to observe the area where the visits were to occur, and talked to the parents, stepfather, children, and relevant therapists and prison authorities.

Second, the clinician's presentation of historical information was fairly detailed, particularly with reference to interfamily relationships and points of agreement and disagreement between the former spouses. In a case like this, where legal process will define the relationship between the parties, it is important for the report to provide data on how that relationship might work. The clinician's investigative role [see § 13.01(b)] is paramount here.

Third, the writer conducted a literature search in an attempt to establish the foundation for the conclusions she was going to draw. Since the literature revealed nothing about the effects of prison visitation on inmates' families, the writer properly labeled as "somewhat speculative" her conclusions on the issue. This cautious stance toward matters requiring a prediction is advocated throughout this book. It is particularly necessary here, where the adage that past behavior is the best predictor of future behavior was less likely to be true, given the emotional environment involved [see § 13.03(a)].

Fourth, the writer suggested very practical

steps for clarifying the relationship between the parties to the dispute. This approach, the mediator–consultant role discussed in § 13.01(a), is similar to that taken in the Mills case, discussed in § 15.02, where the examiner suggested that a conversation between the lawyer and his client could enhance the client's understanding of the lawyer's role and therefore could result in a more competent client.

Finally, the writer used virtually no jargon. Where clinical terms were used (e.g., "reality testing"), they were explained.

CHAPTER SIXTEEN

Glossary

The glossary is divided into two parts: legal terms and clinical and research terms.

16.01.   *Legal Terms*

No effort is made here to define specific crimes or torts, as their definition varies from jurisdiction to jurisdiction. For other definitions, see Black's Law Dictionary (5th ed. 1979).

A

ABSTRACT OF RECORD.   An abbreviated history of a legal case, from the initial filing to its resolution.

ACCESSORY.   A person who contributes to or aids in the commission of a crime, either before or after its commission.

ACCOMPLICE.   A person who knowingly aids the principal offender in the commission of a crime.

ACQUITTAL.   Used in criminal cases to designate a finding, after trial, that a defendant is not guilty of the crime charged.

ACTUS REUS.   The physical act or omission required for conviction of a particular crime; the act or omission must be one over which the person has conscious physical control.

ADJUDICATION.   The judgment rendered in a criminal or civil case.

ADJUDICATORY HEARING.   In juvenile court, the trial.

ADVERSARY SYSTEM.   A procedural system found in the United States and some other countries, in which each party has an opportunity to present opposing views in front of a tribunal that is not itself responsible for conducting an investigation into the facts. To be distinguished from an INQUISITORIAL SYSTEM (this glossary).

ADVERSE WITNESS.   A witness for the opposing party.

AGGRAVATING CIRCUMSTANCE.   In capital or determinate sentencing, a factor that, if proven, tends to enhance the sentence. To be distinguished from MITIGATING CIRCUMSTANCE (this glossary).

AMICUS CURIAE.   Literally, a "friend of the court"; a person or organization permitted by the court to provide information to the court relevant to the subject matter before it.

ANSWER.   A pleading in which the defendant in a civil case replies to the allegations made in the plaintiff's COMPLAINT (this glossary).

APPELLANT.   The party appealing a decision or judgment.

APPELLATE COURT.   A court that reviews the decision of a lower court, focusing on that court's rulings on the proper law to apply to the case and the proper interpretation of that law. To be distinguished from a trial court.

APPELLEE. The party against whom an appeal is taken.

APPREHENSION. In juvenile court, arrest.

ARRAIGNMENT. The stage of the criminal process at which a defendant is required to plead in court to a criminal charge.

ATTORNEY–CLIENT PRIVILEGE. A legal doctrine that permits a person to refuse to disclose, and to prevent others from disclosing, communications between the person and his or her lawyer (or the lawyer's agent) that are made during the course of their professional relationship. The privilege is deemed waived by the client under circumstances described in § 3.04(c).

AUTOMATISM. A defense to crime. Lack of conscious control of one's physical acts. See § 6.03(a).

B

BAIL. The release of an arrested person in exchange for security, usually money provided by a bail bondsperson who thereby becomes responsible for the released person's return; designed to ensure the person will appear in court on a specified date.

BAILIFF. A court official who keeps order in the courtroom and is "in custody" of the jury.

BENCH TRIAL. A nonjury trial.

BENCH WARRANT. A document issued by the court, or "bench," authorizing arrest of a person or seizure of property.

BEST INTERESTS. An amorphous term, used particularly in the juvenile and guardianship contexts, connoting the optimal arrangement or action under the totality of the circumstances. See § 9.02 and Chapter 13.

BEYOND A REASONABLE DOUBT. A STANDARD OF PROOF (this glossary) required to be met by the prosecution in criminal trials for each element of the crime charged; normally defined as a belief to a moral certainty that does not exclude all possible or imaginary doubt, but that is of such convincing character that a reasonable person would not hesitate to rely and act upon it in the most important of his or her own affairs.

BIFURCATED TRIAL. A two-phase trial in which guilt is determined in the first phase and sanity in the second phase. Another variant used, particularly in capital proceedings, is a first phase determining guilt and a second phase devoted to deciding what penalty should be imposed.

BIND OVER. To certify that there is probable cause for grand jury or trial proceedings.

BRANDEIS BRIEF. A brief using social science research to buttress its arguments. So called because the first Supreme Court case in which such a brief was submitted was drafted by Louis Brandeis, later a Supreme Court Justice.

BRIEF. A written argument filed with the court by counsel, always in appellate cases, occasionally at the trial level.

BURDEN OF PROOF. The necessity of proving a fact or facts in dispute. Technically, it consists of both the "burden of production" (the obligation of a party to provide sufficient evidence on a certain issue to avoid a directed verdict by the judge on that issue) and the "burden of persuasion" (the obligation of a party to persuade the factfinder of the truth of an issue, at least to the degree of certainty required by the STANDARD OF PROOF (this glossary).

C

CAPIAS. Literally, "that you take"; a blanket term referring to several types of writs that require a state official to take the person of the defendant into custody.

CAUSE OF ACTION. A legal claim.

CERTIORARI. A writ issued by a court to a lower court requiring it to produce a certified record of a case the superior court wishes to review. This is the primary method the United States Supreme Court uses to review cases.

CLEAR AND CONVINCING PROOF. A measure of persuasion greater than a mere PREPONDERANCE of evidence (this glossary) but less than BEYOND A REASONABLE DOUBT (this glossary); defined as proof that produces a firm belief or conviction as to the proposition sought to be established.

COMMON LAW. Judge-made law, as opposed to constitutional, statutory, or administrative law.

COMMUTATION. A reduction in punishment, as, for example, from a death sentence to life imprisonment.

COMPETENCY. The capacity to perform a given function with a degree of rationality, the requisite degree depending upon the function to be performed. Chapters 4, 5, and 9 all deal with various types of competency.

COMPLAINT. A pleading in which the plaintiff in a civil case asserts allegations against a named defendant.

CONCURRENT SENTENCE. A sentence served simultaneously with sentences for other crimes. To be distinguished from consecutive or CUMULATIVE SENTENCE (this glossary).

CONSERVATORSHIP. A guardianship (see GUARDIAN, this glossary) which in some states is limited to control over the ward's fiscal affairs and in others (e.g., California) permits control over the ward's physical person.

CONTEMPT. Willful disobedience to or disrespect of a court or legislative body, which may result in fines, incarceration, or other penalties designed to force the action desired by the condemning agency.

CONTINUANCE. A postponement, usually of trial.

CORAM NOBIS. A writ whose purpose is to correct a judgment made by the same court issuing the writ.

COUNT. A single allegation in a civil pleading, or a single charge in a criminal indictment or information.

COURT OF RECORD. A court whose proceedings are transcribed with a view toward appeal. To be distinguished from a court not of record, in which no transcription is taken.

CRIMINAL RESPONSIBILITY. One's accountability under the criminal law for one's acts; often equated with INSANITY (this glossary), but including notions underlying the AUTOMATISM doctrine (this glossary) and other legal doctrines as well.

CROSS-EXAMINATION. The questioning of a witness by an opposing party.

CUMULATIVE SENTENCE. A sentence consisting of several sentences imposed against one offender for separate crimes, to be served consecutively.

D

DECREE. A decision or order of the court.

DE FACTO. In fact; actually. To be distinguished from *DE JURE* (this glossary).

DEFAULT. When the defendant in a civil action fails to plead within the time allowed or fails to appear at trial.

DEFENDANT. The accused in a criminal case; the alleged tortfeasor (wrongdoer) in a TORT case (this glossary).

DE JURE. Legitimate; lawful, but not necessarily in fact. To be distinguished from *DE FACTO* (this glossary).

DEMURRER. In a civil action, a defense to the effect that the opposing party has failed to state a claim that is recognized by the law.

DEPOSITION. A proceeding in which a witness is questioned, or "deposed," out of court, usually by an opposing party. The deposition is transcribed for use both in preparation for trial and at the trial itself, where it may be entered in evidence in the witness's absence or used to impeach the witness if he or she testifies.

DETENTION HEARING. In juvenile court, the bail hearing.

DETERMINATE SENTENCE. A sentence whose length is established at the time of sentencing. To be distinguished from an INDETERMINATE SENTENCE (this glossary). See generally § 7.04.

DICTUM (pl. DICTA). A statement in a judicial decision that does not have the force of law or precedent because the court does not rely on it to decide the case.

DIMINISHED CAPACITY. A doctrine permitting clinical testimony relevant to *MENS REA* (this glossary). See § 6.03(b).

DIMINISHED RESPONSIBILITY. Although sometimes confused with DIMINISHED CAPACITY (this glossary), the term actually refers to a degree of mental impairment short of that necessary to meet the INSANITY test (this glossary). It does not negate *MENS REA* (this glossary), but it may be relevant at trial to reduce the grade of the offense, or, more likely, relevant at sentencing to mitigate the severity of punishment. Also known as "partial responsibility."

DIRECTED VERDICT. A verdict entered by the trial judge in a jury trial after a determination that the jury could not rationally decide the case any other way.

DIRECT EXAMINATION. Questioning of a witness at trial by the party calling the witness.

DISCOVERY. The process through which parties to an action find out, or "discover," facts known to each other or other relevant parties. Discovery devices include DEPOSITIONS (this glossary), INTERROGATORIES (this glossary), and physical and mental examinations.

DISPOSITIONAL HEARING. In juvenile court, the sentencing hearing.

DISSENT. An opinion in an appellate judicial decision that disagrees with the result in the court's, or majority, opinion.

DOUBLE JEOPARDY. The prohibition, found in common law and constitutional law, against multiple trials or punishments for the same offense.

DUE PROCESS. The constitutional guarantee found

in the Fifth and Fourteenth Amendments that the government will act fairly when it attempts to deprive a person of life, liberty, or property.

DURHAM RULE. A test for INSANITY (this glossary). See § 6.02(b).

E

EMANCIPATED MINOR. A minor who, as a result of exhibiting general control over his or her life, is found to be no longer in the care or custody of his or her parents or guardians and is thus accorded the rights of an adult.

ENJOIN. The act of requiring a person, by an injunction issued by a court, either to perform some act or to abstain or desist from some act.

EXCLUSIONARY RULE. A judicially created remedy designed to exclude illegally obtained evidence from a criminal trial.

EX PARTE. By or for one party; put another way, done in the absence of interested parties.

EXPERT WITNESS. A witness who, by virtue of specialized knowledge or skill, can provide the factfinder with facts and inferences drawn from those facts that will assist the factfinder in reaching a conclusion on the issue addressed by the witness. A lay witness is not generally permitted to offer opinions about the evidence; an expert witness is.

F

FELONY. An offense punishable by death or imprisonment in the penitentiary. To be distinguished from a MISDEMEANOR (this glossary).

FIDUCIARY. A person, such as a trustee or GUARDIAN (this glossary), whose duty is to act in the BEST INTERESTS (this glossary) of those whose property or person is held to be in his or her care.

FRYE TEST. A test governing the admissibility of scientific evidence announced in *Frye v. United States,* 293 F. 1013 (D.C. Cir. 1923), stating that such evidence must be derived from theories or procedures that are "generally accepted" by the relevant scientific community before it may be admitted into evidence.

G

GRAND JURY. See JURY (this glossary).

GUARDIAN. A person lawfully invested with the power to and charged with the duty of making personal and/or financial decisions for a person who, due to some deficiency, is considered incapable of doing so.

GUARDIAN AD LITEM. A person appointed by a court to represent the BEST INTERESTS (this glossary) of a minor or an incapacitated person who is involved in litigation.

GUILTY BUT MENTALLY ILL. A verdict in criminal cases that first enjoyed widespread popularity in the early 1980s, providing the jury with a compromise between a guilty verdict and a verdict of not guilty by reason of insanity. See § 6.03(d).

H

HABEAS CORPUS. Literally, "you have the body." Typically, a writ directing a state official in charge of detaining a person to produce that person in court so as to determine whether his or her liberty has been deprived in violation of due process.

HARMLESS ERROR. An error that does not require the reversal of judgment.

HEARSAY. Statements or acts described by a witness who did not directly perceive or hear them.

HOLOGRAPHIC WILL. A will written and signed by the testator, but unwitnessed. Admitted to PROBATE (this glossary) in approximately half the states.

HOSTILE WITNESS. A witness who is subject to cross-examination by the party who called him or her because he or she has evidenced antagonism toward that party during direct examination.

HYPOTHETICAL QUESTION. A question composed of proven or assumed facts designed to elicit an opinion from an expert witness.

I

IMPEACHMENT. An attack on the credibility of a witness.

IN CAMERA. Literally, "in chambers"; thus, out of the presence of the jury.

INCOMPETENCY. See COMPETENCY (this glossary).

INDETERMINATE SENTENCE. An indefinite sentence, with the minimum term usually set at the time of sentencing but the maximum term left up to parole authorities. To be distinguished from DETERMINATE SENTENCE (this glossary). See generally § 7.03.

INDICTMENT. A document issued by the grand

jury accusing the person named of a criminal act.

INFORMATION. A document issued in the absence of an indictment by a state official, usually the prosecutor, accusing the person named of a criminal act.

INFORMED CONSENT. Consent to a treatment that is based on adequate knowledge about the risks and benefits of the treatment, is not coerced, and is given while the individual is competent to do so.

INJUNCTION. An order from a court requiring a person to act or to abstain or desist from acting.

INQUISITORIAL SYSTEM. A procedural system in which the judge is the principal investigator as well as decisionmaker. To be distinguished from ADVERSARIAL SYSTEM (this glossary).

INSANITY. A lack of responsibility for one's acts due to mental dysfunction, or, in legal terms, MENTAL DISEASE OR DEFECT (this glossary). Incorrectly often used to designate INCOMPETENCY (this glossary). The various tests for insanity are discussed in § 6.02(b) and (c).

INSTRUCTION. An explanation of the law by the judge to the jury, designed to guide the jury in its deliberations.

INTAKE HEARING. In juvenile court, a preliminary hearing for the purpose of determining what disposition of a child charged with a delinquency or status offense is appropriate; dispositions range from diversion from the juvenile court system to adjudication (trial).

INTENT. Mental state ranging, in the law, from purpose to awareness of the consequences or risks of one's actions.

INTERROGATORIES. Written questions drafted by one party to a civil action and served on another party to the action, who then must answer the questions truthfully or state a valid reason why they cannot be answered.

INTESTATE. Without a will.

J

JUDICIAL NOTICE. Recognition by the court of a fact not proven by evidence.

JURY. A group of persons selected through *VOIR DIRE* (this glossary) to hear evidence. The "petit jury," composed of from 5 to 12 members, hears evidence at civil and criminal trials and returns a verdict. The "grand jury," composed of from 12 to 24 members in most states, investigates specific criminal charges brought to it by the prosecutor and issues an indictment if it finds probable cause

to believe that a crime was committed and a trial ought to be held.

JUVENILE. In most states, a person under the age of 18.

L

LEADING QUESTION. A question that suggests its answer; technically prohibited on direct examination.

LEAST RESTRICTIVE ALTERNATIVE. The concept that when the government is authorized to infringe upon individual liberty, it must do so in the least drastic manner possible. See § 8.03(h).

LEGAL FICTION. An assumption known to be false or of questionable validity, but adopted by courts to further legal analysis or promote certain policies, as in the assumption that a corporation is a "person" for purposes of criminal law, or the assumption that a family always acts in a child's BEST INTERESTS (this glossary).

LIABLE. In a civil case, a finding by the factfinder that the plaintiff has met the BURDEN OF PROOF (this glossary) on his or her claim.

LITIGATION. A lawsuit.

M

MANSLAUGHTER. The unlawful killing of another without "malice." Voluntary manslaughter is reckless or impulsive, but still intentional, homicide; involuntary manslaughter is negligent homicide.

MATERIAL. Relevant.

MENS REA. The specific state of mind (e.g., purposeful, knowing, reckless, or negligent) required for conviction of a crime; "guilty mind."

MENTAL DISEASE OR DEFECT. The threshold mental condition for the INSANITY defense (this glossary) and, in some states, for the DIMINISHED CAPACITY defense (this glossary). See § 6.02(c)(1); § 6.03(b).

MENTAL STATE (CONDITION) AT THE TIME OF THE OFFENSE. Those aspects of a criminal defendant's functioning that are relevant to INSANITY, *MENS REA*, AUTOMATISM, or DIMINISHED RESPONSIBILITY (this glossary).

MISDEMEANOR. A category of offense less serious than FELONY (this glossary); generally punishable by fine or imprisonment in jail, as opposed to the penitentiary, for a year or less.

MITIGATING CIRCUMSTANCE. In capital or determinate sentencing, a factor that, if proven, tends to reduce the sentence. More generally, any factor that tends to reduce culpability at trial or at sentencing.

MOOT. Undecided; in judicial decisions, a moot question is one that does not arise under the existing facts of the case.

MOTION. An application for a ruling or order from the court, either verbally or in writing.

MOTION IN LIMINE. A motion to limit or prohibit the introduction of certain evidence, usually triggering a pretrial hearing or removal of the jury to determine the admissibility issue.

MURDER. The unlawful killing of a human being with "malice."

N

NEGLIGENCE. An act or failure to act that the "reasonable man" would not have committed or have failed to commit.

NO BILL. A finding by the grand jury that no indictment should be issued; also known as "not a true bill."

NOLLE PROSEQUI. A formal entry upon the record by the plaintiff in a civil suit or the prosecutor in a criminal case declaring that he or she "will no[t] further prosecute" the case, but which, in criminal cases, does not amount to dropping the charge.

NOLO CONTENDERE. A pleading by a criminal defendant meaning "I will not contest" the charge.

NON COMPOS MENTIS. Not of sound mind.

O

OBJECTION. A formal exception to a statement made by a witness, lawyer, or judge, or a procedure followed by a lawyer or judge, designed to have the statement stricken from the record or the procedure aborted. If the objection is "overruled," as opposed to "sustained," it may be "preserved" by the objecting party in order to create a record for appellate review.

OPINION TESTIMONY. Testimony as to what the witness infers with respect to facts in dispute, as distinguished from personal knowledge of the facts themselves. Generally, only expert witnesses may offer opinions.

P

PARENS PATRIAE. The authority of the state to act as "parent"; traditionally exercised over children, the mentally ill, and the mentally retarded.

PAROLE. Conditional release of a convict before the expiration of his or her sentence; failure to abide by conditions of parole will result in the convict's serving the remainder of the sentence.

PARTIES. Those persons or entities involved in the litigation, as defined by the pleadings in civil cases and the INFORMATION or INDICTMENT (this glossary) in criminal cases.

PEREMPTORY CHALLENGE. The right, exercisable at *VOIR DIRE* (this glossary), to remove a person from participation on the jury for no stated reason; each side to a dispute is limited to a certain number of peremptory challenges. To be distinguished from "for-cause" challenges, which are unlimited in number but which require a legally recognized reason (such as evidence that the potential juror has a personal relationship with the defendant) before it can be exercised.

PETIT JURY. See JURY (this glossary).

PLAINTIFF. In civil cases, the person who initiates the litigation by filing a complaint.

PLEA BARGAINING. The process by which a criminal defendant seeks a reduced charge or recommended sentence from the prosecutor in exchange for a plea of guilty. See § 7.03(b)(2).

POLICE POWER. The authority of the state to act to protect the public welfare; punishing criminal offenders is the primary exercise of this authority.

POLLING THE JURY. Asking the individual members of the jury before it has been dismissed but after its verdict has been announced how they voted.

PRECEDENT. A judgment of a court that is viewed as authority for deciding similar cases similarly. See *STARE DECISIS* (this glossary).

PRELIMINARY HEARING. Any of a number of different pretrial hearings in the criminal process concerning issues such as probable cause to detain, bail, and whether a *PRIMA FACIE* case (this glossary) against the defendant exists. See § 2.04(a)(1).

PREPONDERANCE OF EVIDENCE. The standard of proof in civil cases, requiring sufficient evidence to show that a given proposition is more probable than not.

PRESUMPTION. An inference of fact or law that must be drawn by the factfinder upon proof of a predicate fact, unless other evidence rebuts the inference. An "irrebuttable presumption" is one that cannot be so rebutted, once the predicate fact is shown. For example, there is an irrebuttable presumption that children under the age of 7 cannot be criminally responsible, and a rebuttable presumption that children between the ages of 7 and 14 are not criminally responsible. In each case, age is the predicate fact that must be proven.

PRESUMPTION OF INNOCENCE. A presumption that a person charged with an offense is innocent, which can be rebutted through adequate proof of guilt. Not technically a PRESUMPTION (this glossary), since no predicate fact need be proven in order to benefit from the "presumption."

PRIMA FACIE. Sufficient proof to establish a claim before challenge by the opposing side.

PROBABLE CAUSE. A reasonable ground for belief in the truthfulness of a proposition. Most commonly used in the criminal law to refer to the degree of certainty required for issuing an arrest or search warrant, or for detaining an arrested person.

PROBATE. The process of certifying the validity of a will and distributing its bequests.

PROBATION. The suspension of a convicted offender's sentence on the condition that he or she abide by conditions set by the court. If these conditions are violated, the offender may be required to serve the remainder of the sentence.

PROSECUTOR. An official of the state responsible for charging persons with crime and representing the state against those so charged at pretrial and trial proceedings.

PROXIMATE CAUSE. Legal cause; generally refers to the event or occurrence closest in time to the injury without which the injury would not have occurred. See § 10.03(a)(3).

PSYCHOTHERAPIST (PSYCHOLOGIST)– PATIENT PRIVILEGE. A legal doctrine that permits, under limited circumstances, the patient to prevent disclosure of any communication between the patient and his or her treating clinician that was made during treatment. See § 3.04(c).

Q

QUASH. To annul.

R

RATIO DECIDENDI. The principal reason for a court's opinion.

REASONABLE DOUBT. See BEYOND A REASONABLE DOUBT (this glossary).

REBUTTAL. The introduction of evidence attempting to contradict evidence presented by the opposing side.

RECROSS-EXAMINATION. Questioning of a witness by the party that cross-examined the witness; follows REDIRECT EXAMINATION (this glossary).

REDIRECT EXAMINATION. Questioning of a witness by the party that questioned the witness on DIRECT EXAMINATION (this glossary); follows CROSS-EXAMINATION (this glossary). Often designed to "rehabilitate" the witness or to clarify his or her answers during cross-examination.

REGULATIONS. Rules of law promulgated by government agencies, as opposed to STATUTES (this glossary), passed by legislatures.

RESPONDENT. In appellate practice, the party responding to the appeal. In civil commitment and delinquency proceedings, the party subject to commitment. Analogous to DEFENDANT (this glossary).

S

SEARCH WARRANT. A written order issued by a magistrate or judge authorizing search of the named premises for the named items.

SELF-DEFENSE. A justification for a criminal act when it is based on a reasonable belief that one is in danger of immediate harm, and when it is in proportion to the perceived danger.

SEQUESTRATION. The act of barring from the courtroom a witness or the jury so as to prevent the witness or the jury from hearing evidence. Also, the act of prohibiting the jury from reading or observing media accounts of a trial.

SERVICE. The exhibition or delivery of a writ, notice, or injunction by an authorized individual to the person named in the document.

SINE QUA NON. An indispensable requirement.

STANDARD OF PROOF. The measure of proof that the party with the BURDEN OF PROOF (this glossary) must meet, as in proof by a PREPONDERANCE OF EVIDENCE, proof by CLEAR AND CONVINCING EVIDENCE, or proof BEYOND A REASONABLE DOUBT (this glossary).

STANDING. The right to litigate a given issue, usually dependent upon having a property interest or some other substantial interest that might be affected by legal resolution of the issue.

STARE DECISIS.   The legal principle stating that the legal rules expounded in decided cases govern subsequent cases; designed to ensure the consistency of legal rules.

STATUTE.   Law passed by a legislature and codified; to be distinguished from REGULATIONS or COMMON LAW (this glossary).

STAY.   A stopping of a judicial proceeding by order of the court.

STIPULATION.   An agreement by attorneys on opposing sides regarding a procedural or substantive matter involved in the litigation between the two sides. To be binding, it must be agreed to by the attorneys' clients.

SUBPOENA.   A process, or document, requiring a witness to appear and give testimony.

SUBPOENA *DUCES TECUM*.   A process, or document, requiring a witness or other person to produce named documents or records at trial or at another proceeding.

SUMMONS.   A writ directing the sheriff or other proper officer to notify the person named that an action has been commenced against him or her in the court that issued the writ, and that the person is required to appear there on the named day and answer the complaint made against him or her.

T

TESTAMENTARY CAPACITY.   Capacity to execute a will. See § 9.04.

TESTIMONY.   Evidence given by a witness under oath, as distinguished from written or other tangible evidence.

TORT.   An injury or wrong, committed intentionally or negligently, to the person or property of another. The act constituting a tort may also be a crime. See § 10.03.

TRANSFER HEARING.   In juvenile court, the hearing to determine whether a juvenile should be tried in adult court. Also called a "waiver hearing." See § 11.03(c).

TRANSCRIPT.   The official record of judicial proceedings.

TRIAL *DE NOVO*.   A separate, totally "new" trial; most commonly applied to the trial held in a court of record when a criminal defendant appeals the result in a court not of record.

TRUE BILL.   The finding by a grand jury that a criminal indictment is warranted.

U

UNDUE INFLUENCE.   Influence that causes a person not to act of his or her own free will.

UTTER.   To circulate (e.g., a forged check).

V

VENIRE.   The group of individuals from which jurors are selected.

VENUE.   The political division in which a court sits, and which thus determines which cases it may hear.

VERDICT.   The final judgment of the judge or jury in a criminal or civil case.

VOIR DIRE.   An examination of a prospective juror to determine whether he or she should serve. Also, a pretrial examination of a witness to determine whether he or she is competent or possesses the qualifications to testify, or whether the information the witness has to offer is admissible.

W

WAIVER.   The relinquishment of a right. If the right is of constitutional dimensions, it may be waived only under circumstances that are shown to lead to a knowing, intelligent, and voluntary decision.

WAIVER HEARING.   See TRANSFER HEARING (this glossary).

WARRANT.   A writ issued by a magistrate or judge in a criminal case authorizing an arrest or a search. See SEARCH WARRANT (this glossary).

WITNESS.   One who testifies as to what he or she has seen or heard.

WRIT.   An order issuing from a court requiring the performance of a specified act, or giving authority to have it done.

16.02.   *Clinical and Research Terms*

Many of the definitions in the following glossary are adapted from the AMERICAN PSYCHIATRIC ASSOCIATION, PSYCHIATRIC GLOSSARY (1984). Although some psychiatric diagnoses are defined, official definitions should be sought from the AMERICAN PSYCHIATRIC ASSOCIATION, DIAGNOSTIC AND STATISTICAL MANUAL OF MENTAL DIS-

ORDERS (3d ed. 1980), commonly called DSM-III. For more detailed description of statistical techniques relevant to the law, see D. W. BARNES, STATISTICS AS PROOF: FUNDAMENTALS OF QUANTITATIVE EVIDENCE (1983).

A

ABREACTION. Emotional release or discharge after recalling a painful experience that has been repressed because it was consciously intolerable.

ACTING OUT. Expressions of emotional conflicts or feelings in actions rather than words. The person is not aware of the meaning of such acts.

ADDICTION. Physiological dependence on a chemical substance, such as narcotics, alcohol, and most sedative drugs.

ADJUSTMENT DISORDER. A DSM-III category for maladaptive reactions to identifiable life events or circumstances. The symptoms generally lessen as the stress diminishes or as the person adapts to the stress.

AFFECT. The outward manifestation of a person's feelings, tone, or mood. "Affect" and "emotion" are commonly used interchangeably.

AKATHISIA. Motor restlessness ranging from a feeling of inner disquiet, often localized in the muscles, to inability to sit still or lie quietly; a side effect of some ANTIPSYCHOTIC DRUGS (this glossary).

AKINESIA. A state of motor inhibition; reduced voluntary movement.

ALIENATION. The estrangement felt in cultural settings one views as foreign, unpredictable, or unacceptable.

ALIENIST. Obsolete term of historical significance for a psychiatrist who testifies in court about a person's sanity or mental competence.

AMNESIA. Partial or total loss of memory. Some subcategories of amnesia refer to the etiology of the memory loss. "Psychogenic" amnesia refers to memory failure secondary to stressful emotional experiences that "cause" the person to be unable to remember certain events; other causes of amnesia include physical trauma (e.g., a blow to the head), chemical intoxication (e.g., alcohol blackouts), or disease processes (e.g., amnesia associated with epileptic seizures). Other subcategories refer to the period in time for which memory is impaired relative to the occurrence of a significant event (e.g., head trauma; see ANTEROGRADE,

this glossary). Still other subcategories refer to the type of cognitive function that accounts for the memory impairment. "Registration" amnesia refers to memories not available because, at the time the events occurred, the individual's mental state would not permit the permanent registration and storing of memory traces (e.g., severe intoxication); "recall" amnesia implies that the memory traces are intact, but that other factors interfere with their retrieval. Recall that is sketchy or patchy may be referred to as "partial" or "selective" amnesia.

AMPHETAMINES. A group of chemicals that stimulate the cerebral cortex of the brain; often misused by adults and adolescents to control normal fatigue and to induce euphoria.

ANALYSAND. A patient in psychoanalytic treatment.

ANTABUSE (DISULFIRAM). A drug used in treatment of alcoholism to create an aversive response to alcohol.

ANTEROGRADE. Amnesia for events occurring *after* a significant point in time. To be distinguished from RETROGRADE, which is defined as impairment in memory for events occurring *prior* to a significant point in time.

ANTIPSYCHOTIC DRUGS. Drugs used to control psychosis. See PHENOTHIAZINE DERIVATIVES (this glossary).

ANTISOCIAL PERSONALITY. See PERSONALITY DISORDERS (this glossary).

APPERCEPTION. Perception as modified and enhanced by one's own emotions, memories, and biases.

ATAXIA. Failure of muscle coordination; irregularity of muscle action.

AUTISM. A developmental disability caused by a physical disorder of the brain appearing during the first three years of life. Symptoms include disturbances in physical, social, and language skills; abnormal responses to sensations; and abnormal ways of relating to people, objects, and events.

AVERSION THERAPY. A therapy in which undesirable behavior is paired with a painful or unpleasant stimulus, resulting in the suppression of the undesirable behavior.

B

BARBITURATES. Drugs that depress the activities of the central nervous system; primarily used for sedation or treatment of EPILEPSY (this glossary).

BASE RATE. The frequency of occurrence of a particular phenomenon in a specified time frame. For example, the base rate for suicide in the general population is approximately 12 cases per 100,000 persons annually.

BAYESIAN EQUATION. In probability theory, a mathematical relationship that defines the probability of an event A occurring, given that event B did occur, as a function of the independent probabilities that A might (or might not) occur and the joint probabilities of B occurring with or without A occurring. For example, let A be the event that a person will attempt suicide, and let B be the event that the person scored above some cutoff score on a suicide prediction test. Assume that the initial probability of a suicide attempt $p(A) = .05$, and that the probability of no attempt $p(\text{not } A) = .95$. Assume also that of those who attempt suicide, 80% will have scored above the cutoff point on test B; thus, $p(B/A) = .80$. Finally, assume that of those who do not attempt suicide, 30% score above the cutoff point on B; $p(B/\text{not } A) = .30$. Given these figures, we can then compute the probability that a person will attempt suicide, given that he or she scored above the cutoff point, using the following equation:

$$p(A/B) = \frac{p(B/A) \times p(A)}{[p(B/A) \times p(A)] + [p(B/\text{not } A) \times p(\text{not } A)]}$$

$$= \frac{.80 \times .05}{(.80 \times .05) + (.30 \times .95)}$$

$$= \frac{.04}{.04 + .29}$$

$$= \frac{.04}{.33}$$

$$= .12$$

BEHAVIORISM. The school of psychological theory that holds that behavior is generally determined and explicable by principles of learning and conditioning.

BEHAVIOR THERAPY. A mode of treatment that focuses on modifying observable and, at least in principle, quantifiable behavior by means of systematic manipulation of the environmental and behavioral variables thought to be functionally related to the behavior. Some behavior therapy techniques include OPERANT CONDITIONING, TOKEN ECONOMY, AVERSION THERAPY, and BIOFEEDBACK (this glossary).

BEHAVIORAL SCIENCE(S). The study of human development, interpersonal relationships, values, experiences, activities, and institutions; fields within the behavioral sciences include psychiatry, psychology, cultural anthropology, sociology, political science, and ethology.

BENDER–GESTALT TEST. A psychological assessment technique in which the subject is required to accurately copy relatively simple stimulus figures that are presented to him or her. The organization and accuracy of the drawings can be scored by the examiner in light of developmental norms for different age groups, and may be useful in the gross screening for organic conditions that involve impairment in visual–motor areas.

BIOFEEDBACK. The use of instrumentation to provide information (feedback) about variations in one or more of the subject's own physiological processes not ordinarily perceived (e.g., brain wave activity, muscle tension, or blood pressure). Such feedback over a period of time can help the subject learn to control those processes, even though he or she is unable to articulate how the learning is achieved.

BIPOLAR DISORDER. A MAJOR AFFECTIVE DISORDER (this glossary) in which there are episodes of both MANIA and DEPRESSION (this glossary); formerly called "manic–depressive illness," circular or mixed type.

BOARD-CERTIFIED PSYCHIATRIST. A psychiatrist who has passed examinations administered by the American Board of Psychiatry and Neurology, and thus becomes certified as a medical specialist in psychiatry.

BOARD-ELIGIBLE PSYCHIATRIST. A psychiatrist who is eligible to take the examinations of the American Board of Psychiatry and Neurology; a psychiatrist who has completed an approved psychiatric residency training program.

BORDERLINE PERSONALITY. See PERSONALITY DISORDERS (this glossary).

C

CHARACTER DISORDER (CHARACTER NEUROSIS). A PERSONALITY DISORDER (this glossary) manifested by a chronic, habitual, maladaptive pattern of reaction that is relatively inflexible; that limits the optimal use of potential; and that often provokes the responses from the environment that the subject wants to avoid. In contrast to symptoms of NEUROSIS (this glossary), character traits are typically EGO-SYNTONIC (this glossary).

CIRCUMSTANTIALITY. Pattern of speech that is indirect and delayed in reaching its goal. Compare with TANGENTIALITY (this glossary).

CLANGING. A type of thinking in which the sound of a word, rather than its meaning, gives the direction to subsequent associations; punning and rhyming may substitute for logic, and speech may become increasingly a senseless association of sounds and decreasingly a vehicle for communication.

COGNITIVE. Refers to the mental process of comprehension, judgment, memory, and reasoning, as contrasted with emotional and volitional processes. Contrast with CONATIVE (this glossary).

COGNITIVE-BEHAVIOR MODIFICATION. Form of treatment that uses principles of learning to modify the cognitions of the individual as well as his or her behavior. The underlying theory of the interaction between cognitions and environmental contingencies is often called "social learning theory."

CONATIVE. Pertains to one's basic strivings as expressed in behavior and actions; volitional, as contrasted with COGNITIVE (this glossary).

CONFABULATION. Fabrication of stories in response to questions about situations or events that are not recalled.

CONFLICT. A mental struggle that arises from the simultaneous operation of opposing impulses, drives, external (environmental) demands, or internal demands; termed "intrapsychic" when the conflict is between forces within the personality, "extrapsychic" when it is between the self and the environment.

CONSCIOUS. The content of mind or mental functioning of which one is aware.

CONTROL. In research, the term is used in three contexts: (1) the process of keeping the relevant conditions of an experiment constant; (2) the process of causing an INDEPENDENT VARIABLE (this glossary) to vary in a specified and known manner; and (3) the use of a spontaneously occurring and discoverable fact as a check or standard of comparison to evaluate the facts obtained after the manipulation of the independent variable.

CONTROL GROUP. In the ideal case, a group of subjects matched as closely as possible to an experimental group of subjects on all relevant aspects and exposed to the same treatments or other phenomena except the independent variable under investigation.

CONVERSION. A DEFENSE MECHANISM (this glossary) by which intrapsychic conflicts that would otherwise give rise to anxiety are instead given symbolic external expression, including such symptoms as paralysis, pain, or loss of sensory function.

CORRELATION. The extent to which two measures vary together, or a measure of the strength of the relationship between two variables. It is usually expressed by r, a coefficient that varies between $+1.0$, perfect agreement, and -1.0, a perfect inverse relationship. A correlation coefficient of 0 would mean a perfectly random relationship. The correlation coefficient signifies the degree to which knowledge of one score or variable can predict the score on the other variable. A high correlation between two variables does not necessarily indicate a causal relationship between them: the correlation may follow because each of the variables is highly related to a third yet unmeasured factor.

COUNTERTRANSFERENCE. The clinician's partly unconscious or conscious emotional reactions to the patient. See also TRANSFERENCE (this glossary).

CRITERION VARIABLE. Something to be predicted.

D

DECOMPENSATION. The deterioration of existing defenses, leading to an increase in the behavior defended against.

DEFENSE MECHANISM. Unconscious intrapsychic processes serving to provide relief from emotional conflict and anxiety. Conscious efforts are frequently made for the same reasons, but true defense mechanisms are unconscious. Some of the common defense mechanisms defined in this glossary are CONVERSION, DENIAL, DISPLACEMENT, DISSOCIATION, IDENTIFICATION, INTROJECTION, PROJECTION, RATIONALIZATION, REACTION FORMATION, REGRESSION, and SUBSTITUTION.

DEINSTITUTIONALIZATION. Change in locus of mental health care from traditional, institutional settings to community-based services. Sometimes called "transinstitutionalization," which actually means moving from one facility to another.

DELIRIUM TREMENS. An acute and sometimes fatal brain disorder (in 10–15% of untreated cases) caused by total or partial withdrawal from excessive alcohol intake. Usually develops in 24–96 hours after cessation of drinking. Symptoms include fever, tremors, and ATAXIA (this glossary), and sometimes convulsions, frightening illusions, delusions, and HALLUCINATIONS (this glossary).

DEMENTIA. An ORGANIC MENTAL DISORDER (this glossary) in which there is a deterioration of previously acquired intellectual abilities of sufficient severity to interfere with social or occupational functioning. Memory disturbance is the most prominent symptom. In addition, there is impairment of abstract thinking, judgment, impulse control, and/or personality change. Dementia may be progressive, static, or reversible, depending on the pathology and the availability of effective treatment.

DENIAL. A DEFENSE MECHANISM (this glossary) used to resolve emotional conflict and allay anxiety by disavowing thoughts, feelings, wishes, needs, or external reality factors that are consciously intolerable.

DEPENDENT VARIABLE. The aspect of the subject that is measured after the manipulation of the INDEPENDENT VARIABLE (this glossary) and is assumed to vary as a function of the independent variable.

DEPERSONALIZATION. Feelings of unreality or strangeness concerning either the environment, the self, or both.

DEPRESSION. A condition marked by a disturbance in mood or emotion, often associated with feelings of helplessness, hopelessness, and low self-esteem.

DETERMINISM. The theory that one's emotional life and actions are determined by earlier events or physiological states.

DEVELOPMENTAL DISABILITY. A substantial handicap or impairment originating before the age of 18 that may be expected to continue indefinitely. The disability may be attributable to MENTAL RETARDATION (this glossary), cerebral palsy, EPILEPSY (this glossary), or other neurological conditions, and may include AUTISM (this glossary).

DIAGNOSTIC AND STATISTICAL MANUAL OF MENTAL DISORDERS (DSM)

  DSM-I. The first edition of the American Psychiatric Association's official classification of mental disorders, published in 1952.

  DSM-II. The second edition, published in 1968.

  DSM-III. The third and current edition, published in 1980.

DIATHESIS–STRESS HYPOTHESIS.. A theory that mental disorder is triggered by the interaction between environmental stressors and genetic predisposition.

DIPLOMATE. One who has been certified as having special competence in a particular professional specialty (e.g., see BOARD-CERTIFIED PSYCHIATRIST, this glossary). Diplomates in forensic mental health are recognized by the American Board of Forensic Psychiatry and the American Board of Forensic Psychology.

DISCRIMINANT ANALYSIS. A statistical classification procedure that selects from an initially large pool of predictor variables (e.g., test scores, demographic measures) a smaller number of measures, which, when mathematically combined, maximize the correct classification of individuals into nominal criterion groups (e.g., diagnoses).

DISORIENTATION. Loss of awareness of the relation of self to space, time or other persons; confusion.

DISPLACEMENT. A DEFENSE MECHANISM (this glossary) in which emotions, ideas, or wishes are transferred from their original object to a more acceptable substitute.

DISSOCIATION. A DEFENSE MECHANISM (this glossary) through which emotional significance and affect are separated and detached from an idea, situation, or object. Dissociation may defer or postpone experiencing some emotional impact, as, for example, in selective amnesia (see AMNESIA, this glossary).

DISSOCIATIVE DISORDER. Category of disorders in DSM-III in which there is a sudden, temporary alteration in normally integrated functions of consciousness, identity, or motor behavior, so that some part of one or more of these functions is lost. It includes psychogenic amnesia (see AMNESIA, this glossary), FUGUE, MULTIPLE PERSONALITY, and DEPERSONALIZATION (this glossary).

DOUBLE-BLIND. A study in which a number of treatments—for instance, one or more drugs and a placebo—are compared in such a way that neither the patient nor the persons directly involved in the treatment know which preparation is being administered.

DUALISM. The philosophical belief in the separation of mind and body.

DYSTONIA. Acute muscular spasms, often of the tongue, jaw, eyes, and neck, but sometimes of the whole body. Sometimes occurs during the first few days of antipsychotic drug administration.

E

ECOLOGICAL THEORY. Perspective in psychology, identified with Urie Bronfenbrenner and others, which emphasizes the interaction among the individual and the various systems affecting the individual in determining behavior.

ECOLOGICAL VALIDITY. The extent to which controlled experimental results can be generalized beyond the confines of the particular experimental context to contexts in the real world.

EGO. In psychoanalytic theory, one of the three major divisions in the model of the psychic apparatus, the others being the ID and the SUPEREGO (this glossary). The ego represents the sum of certain mental mechanisms, such as perception and memory, and specific defense mechanisms. It serves to mediate between the demands of primitive instinctual drives (the id), of internalized parental and social prohibitions (the superego), and of reality. The compromises between these forces achieved by the ego tend to resolve intrapsychic conflict and to serve an adaptive and executive function. Psychiatric usage of the term should not be confused with common usage, which connotes self-love or selfishness.

EGO-DYSTONIC. Aspects of a person's behavior, thoughts, and attitudes viewed as repugnant or inconsistent with the total personality. Contrast with EGO-SYNTONIC (this glossary).

EGO-SYNTONIC. Aspects of a person's behavior, thoughts, and attitudes viewed as acceptable and consistent with the total personality. Contrast with EGO-DYSTONIC (this glossary).

ELECTROENCEPHALOGRAM (EEG). A graphic (voltage vs. time) depiction of the brain's electrical potentials recorded by scalp electrodes. It is used for diagnosis in neurological and neuropsychiatric disorders and in neurophysiological research.

EMPIRICISM. A philosophical approach to knowledge maintaining that knowledge is acquired through observation and experience.

EPILEPSY. A disorder characterized by periodic motor or sensory seizures or their equivalents, and sometimes accompanied by a loss of consciousness or by certain equivalent manifestations. May be "idiopathic" (no known organic cause) or "symptomatic" (due to organic lesions). Accompanied by abnormal electrical discharges, which may be shown by EEG.

> **MAJOR EPILEPSY (GRAND MAL).** Gross convulsive seizures with loss of consciousness and of vegetative control.

> **MINOR EPILEPSY (PETIT MAL).** Nonconvulsive epileptic seizures or equivalents; may be limited only to momentary lapses of consciousness.

> **PSYCHOMOTOR EPILEPSY.** Recurrent periodic disturbances of behavior, usually originating in the temporal lobes, during which the patient carries out movements that are often repetitive and highly organized but semiautomatic in character.

ETIOLOGY. Causation, particularly with reference to disease.

EXPERIMENTAL RESEARCH. A research approach that tests causal linkages among variables. The experimenter manipulates the INDEPENDENT VARIABLE (this glossary), attempts to control extraneous conditions, and assesses the effect on a DEPENDENT VARIABLE (this glossary).

EXPLOSIVE PERSONALITY. A disorder of impulse control, in which several episodes of serious outbursts of relatively unprovoked aggression lead to assault on others or the destruction of property. There is no organic, epileptic, or any other personality disorder that might account for the behavior. Also called "intermittent explosive personality."

EXTERNAL VALIDITY. The degree to which results of a study can be generalized to the real world.

F

FALSE NEGATIVE. An erroneous opinion that something is not present or will not be present (e.g., an opinion of normal behavior when a mental disorder is actually present).

FALSE POSITIVE. An erroneous opinion that something is or will be present (e.g., an inaccurate diagnosis of mental illness or prediction of violent behavior.)

FIXATION. The arrest of psychosocial development at a particular stage.

FLIGHT OF IDEAS. Verbal skipping from one idea to another. The ideas appear to be continuous but are fragmentary and determined by chance or temporal associations.

FREE ASSOCIATION. In psychoanalytic therapy, spontaneous, uncensored verbalization by the patient of whatever comes to mind.

FREE-FLOATING ANXIETY. Severe, generalized, persistent anxiety not specifically ascribed to a particular object or event and often a precursor of panic.

FUGUE. A DISSOCIATIVE DISORDER (this glossary) characterized by AMNESIA (this glossary) and involving actual physical flight from the customary environment or field of conflict.

FUNCTIONAL DISORDER. A disorder in which the performance or operation of an organ or organ system is abnormal, but not as a result of known changes in structure.

G

GENERALIZABILITY. The degree to which conclusions of a study may be applied in situations beyond the conditions of the study itself. See also EXTERNAL VALIDITY (this glossary).

GRAND MAL. See EPILEPSY (this glossary).

H

HALLUCINATION. A sensory perception in the absence of an actual external stimulus. May occur in any of the senses.

HEURISTIC. Serving to encourage discovery of solutions to a problem.

HUMANISM. The school of psychological theory that holds that human behavior is ultimately purposeful. Humanists, such as Abraham Maslow and Carl Rogers, have stood as a "third force" opposing the deterministic underpinnings of behaviorist and psychoanalytic theories. Humanistic theories are also distinguished by their phenomenological approach; they generally emphasize the significance of understanding an individual's here-and-now experience (as opposed, for example, to the individual's childhood or history of reinforcement).

HYPERACTIVITY. Excessive motor activity, generally purposeful. It is frequently, but not necessarily, associated with internal tension or a neurological disorder. Usually the movements are more rapid than customary for a person.

HYPOGLYCEMIA. Abnormally low level of blood sugar.

HYSTERICAL PERSONALITY. See HISTRIONIC personality under PERSONALITY DISORDERS (this glossary).

I

ID. In Freudian theory, the part of the personality structure that harbors the unconscious and instinctual desires and strivings. See also EGO and SUPEREGO (this glossary).

IDEAS OF REFERENCE. Incorrect interpretation of casual incidents and external events as having direct reference to oneself. May reach sufficient intensity to constitute delusions.

IDENTIFICATION. A DEFENSE MECHANISM (this glossary) by which a person patterns himself or herself after some other person. Identification plays a major role in the development of one's personality and specifically of the superego. To be differentiated from "imitation" or "role modeling," which is a conscious process.

IDIOGRAPHIC. Referring to an individual case.

IDIOPATHIC. Of unknown cause.

ILLUSORY CORRELATION. An incorrect belief, often resulting from selective attention to unrepresentative occurrences, that two variables are correlated in a particular fashion when in fact they are not. See CORRELATION (this glossary).

IMPULSE DISORDERS. A varied group of nonpsychotic disorders in which impulse control is weak. The impulsive behavior is usually pleasurable, difficult to resist and EGO-SYNTONIC (this glossary).

INADEQUATE PERSONALITY. See PERSONALITY DISORDERS (this glossary).

INCIDENCE. The number of cases of a disease that come into being during a specific period of time.

INDEPENDENT VARIABLE. The variable under the experimenter's control.

INSANITY. A vague term for PSYCHOSIS (this glossary), now obsolete. Still used, however, in strictly legal contexts such as the insanity defense. See INSANITY (§ 16.01).

INTEGRATION. The organization and incorporation of both new and old data, experience, and emotional capacities into the personality.

INTELLIGENCE QUOTIENT (IQ). A numerical value, determined through psychological testing, that indicates a person's approximate level of intellectual functioning relative to either his chronological age or to other persons having similar demographic characteristics.

INTELLIGENCE TESTS. Any of several psychological techniques for systematically assessing the cognitive functioning and general problem solving ability of an individual relative to others of his or her own age or of similar demographic background. Intelligence tests typically result in an IQ score, which can be interpreted according to population norms to estimate a person's level of adaptive intelligence. Commonly used intelligence tests include the Wechsler Adult Intelligence Scale—Revised (WAIS-R), the Wechsler Intelligence Scale for Children (WISC), the Stanford–Binet, and the Peabody Picture Vocabulary Test.

INTERNAL VALIDITY. The degree to which any effects of an experimental intervention can be logically attributed to the intervention and to which rival hypotheses may be ruled out.

INTERVENING VARIABLE. Something intervening between a circumstance and its consequent, modifying the relation between the two. For example, appetite can be an intervening variable determining whether or not a given food will be eaten.

INTRAPSYCHIC. That which takes place within the psyche or mind.

INTROJECTION. A DEFENSE MECHANISM (this glossary) whereby loved or hated external objects are symbolically absorbed within oneself. The converse of projection. May serve as a defense against conscious recognition of intolerable hostile impulses.

K

KLEPTOMANIA. See MANIA (this glossary).

L

LABILE. Rapidly shifting, unstable (referring to emotions).

LEARNING DISABILITY. Difficulty experienced by school-age children of normal or above-normal intelligence in learning to read ("dyslexia"), write ("dysgraphia"), and/or calculate ("dyscalculia"). The disorder is believed to be related to slow developmental progression of perceptual–motor skills. See also MINIMAL BRAIN DYSFUNCTION (this glossary).

LIBIDO. The psychic drive or energy usually associated with the sexual instinct. ("Sexual" is used here in the broad sense to include pleasure- and love-object-seeking.)

LIMBIC SYSTEM. An area in the brain associated with the control of emotion, eating, drinking, and sexual activity.

LITHIUM CARBONATE. An alkali metal, the salt of which is used in the treatment of acute mania and as a maintenance medication to help reduce the duration, intensity, and frequency of recurrent affective episodes, especially in BIPOLAR DISORDER (this glossary).

LOOSENING OF ASSOCIATIONS. A disturbance of thinking in which ideas shift from one subject to another in an oblique or unrelated manner. When loosening of associations is severe, speech may be incoherent. Contrast with FLIGHT OF IDEAS (this glossary).

M

MAJOR AFFECTIVE DISORDERS. A group of disorders in which there is a prominent and persistent disturbance of mood (DEPRESSION or MANIA, this glossary). The disorder is usually episodic but may be chronic.

MALINGERING. Deliberate simulation or exaggeration of an illness or disability in order to avoid an unpleasant situation or to obtain some type of personal gain.

MANIA. A mood disorder characterized by excessive elation, hyperactivity, agitation, and accelerated thinking and speaking. Sometimes manifested as FLIGHT OF IDEAS (this glossary).

MANIC–DEPRESSIVE ILLNESS. See BIPOLAR DISORDER (this glossary).

MEAN. The arithmetic average of a set of observations; the sum of scores divided by the number of scores.

MEDIAN. The middle value in a set of values that have been arranged in order from highest to lowest.

MEDICAL MODEL. A perspective that views abnormal behavior as the product of an illness. The "illness" may be intrapsychic rather than organic.

MENTAL DISEASE. See MENTAL DISORDER (this glossary).

MENTAL DISORDER. Impairment in functioning due to a social, psychological, genetic, physical/chemical, or biological disturbance.

MENTAL RETARDATION. Significantly subaverage general intellectual functioning, existing concurrently with deficits in adaptive behavior and manifested during youth.

MENTAL STATUS EXAMINATION. The process of estimating psychological and behavioral function by observing the patient, eliciting his or her description of self, and formally questioning him or her. The mental status is reported in a series of narrative statements describing such things as AFFECT (this glossary), speech, thought content, perception, and COGNITIVE functions (this glossary).

MILIEU THERAPY. Socioenvironmental therapy in which the attitudes and behavior of the staff of a treatment service and the activities prescribed for the patient are determined by the patient's emotional and interpersonal needs.

MINIMAL BRAIN DYSFUNCTION (MBD). A disturbance of children, adolescents, and perhaps adults, without signs of major neurological or psychiatric disturbance. Characterized by decreased attention span, distractibility, increased activity, impulsivity, emotional lability, poor motor integration, disturbances in perception, and disorders of language development. See also LEARNING DISABILITY (this glossary).

MINNESOTA MULTIPHASIC PERSONALITY INVENTORY (MMPI). An OBJECTIVE PERSONALITY TEST (this glossary) composed of 566 items, which the subject scores as "true–false" as applied to himself or herself. The test contains ten scales for clinical assessment and three "validity" scales to assess the person's test-taking attitude or candor. Other popular tests of this type include the California Psychological Inventory and the Experiential World Inventory.

MODE. The most frequently occurring observation in a set of observations.

MULTIPLE PERSONALITY. A rare type of dissociative reaction in which the person adopts two or more personalities. In DSM-III, classified as a DISSOCIATIVE DISORDER (this glossary).

N

NARCISSISM (NARCISM). Self-love as opposed to object love (love of another person). To be distinguished from "egotism," which carries the connotation of self-centeredness, selfishness, and conceit. Egotism is but one expression of narcissism.

NARCOTIC. Any opiate derivative drug, natural or synthetic, that relieves pain or alters mood. May cause ADDICTION (this glossary).

NEUROLEPTIC. An antipsychotic drug.

NEUROLOGIST. A physician with postgraduate training and experience in the field of organic diseases of the nervous system, whose professional work focuses primarily on this area. Neurologists also receive training in psychiatry.

NEUROLOGY. The branch of medical science devoted to the study, diagnosis, and treatment of organic diseases of the nervous system.

NEUROSIS. In common usage, emotional disturbances of all kinds other than PSYCHOSIS (this glossary). It implies subjective psychological pain or discomfort beyond what is appropriate in the conditions of one's life. The meaning of the term has been changed since it was first introduced into standard nomenclatures. In DSM-III, the term

signifies a limited number of specific diagnostic categories, all of which are attributed to maladaptive ways of dealing with anxiety or internal conflict.

NOMOTHETIC. referring to comparisons between groups.

NOSOLOGY. The classification of diseases.

O

OBJECTIVE PERSONALITY TESTS. Psychological diagnostic tests that are highly structured and have a limited response format, usually one that can be reliably scored by a technician having little knowledge of the theoretical construction of the test or meaning of the responses obtained. Personality inventories consisting of "true–false" responses to series of descriptive statements are representative of this type of test. An example is the MINNESOTA MULTIPHASIC PERSONALITY INVENTORY (MMPI) (this glossary).

OCCUPATIONAL THERAPY. An adjunctive therapy that utilizes purposeful activities as a means of altering the course of illness. The patient's relationship to staff members and to other patients in the occupational therapy setting is often more therapeutic than the activity itself.

OPERANT CONDITIONING (INSTRUMENTAL CONDITIONING). A process by which, in theory, the results of the person's behavior determine whether the behavior is more or less likely to occur in the future.

ORGANIC BRAIN SYNDROME. See ORGANIC MENTAL DISORDER (this glossary).

ORGANIC MENTAL DISORDER. Transient or permanent dysfunction of the brain, caused by a disturbance of physiological functioning of brain tissue at any level of organization—structural, hormonal, biochemical, electrical, etc. Causes are associated with aging, toxic substances, or a variety of physical disorders.

ORIENTATION. Awareness of one's self in relation to time, place, and person.

ORTHOPSYCHIATRY. An approach that involves the collaborative effort of psychiatry, psychology, psychiatric social work, and other behavioral, medical, and social sciences in the study and treatment of human behavior in the clinical setting. Emphasis is placed on preventive techniques to promote healthy emotional growth and development, particularly of children.

OVERCOMPENSATION. A conscious or unconscious process in which a real or imagined physical or psychological deficit generates exaggerated correction.

P

PARADIGM. A way of looking at the world; the set of philosophical assumptions that underlies a discipline or school of thought.

PARANOIA. A condition characterized by the gradual development of an intricate, complex, and elaborate system of thinking based on (and often proceeding logically from) misinterpretation of an actual event. A person with paranoia often considers himself or herself endowed with unique and superior ability. Despite its chronic course, this condition does not seem to interfere with thinking and personality. To be distinguished from SCHIZOPHRENIA, paranoid type, and paranoid PERSONALITY DISORDER (this glossary), which are specific diagnoses of which paranoid ideation may be a part.

PARAPRAXIS. A faulty act, blunder, or lapse of memory, such as a slip of the tongue or misplacement of an article. According to Freud, these acts are caused by unconscious motives.

PASSIVE–AGGRESSIVE   PERSONALITY.   See PERSONALITY DISORDERS (this glossary).

PASSIVE–DEPENDENT PERSONALITY.   See DEPENDENT personality under PERSONALITY DISORDERS (this glossary).

PEDOPHILIA.   Sexual activity of adults with children as the objects.

PERSEVERATION.   Tendency to emit the same verbal or motor response again and again to varied stimuli.

PERSONALITY DISORDERS. Deeply ingrained, inflexible, maladaptive patterns of relating, perceiving, and thinking, of sufficient severity to cause either impairment in functioning or distress. Personality disorders are generally recognizable by adolescence or earlier, continue throughout adulthood, and become less obvious in middle or old age. Some personality disorders cited in DSM-III include the following:

ANTISOCIAL.   A lack of socialization along with behavior patterns that bring a person repeatedly into conflict with society; incapacity for significant loyalty to others or to social values; callousness; irresponsibility; impulsiveness; and inability to feel guilt or learn from experience or punishment. Frustration tolerance is low,

and antisocial people tend to blame others or give plausible rationalizations for their behavior. Characteristic behavior appears before age 15, although the diagnosis may not be apparent until adulthood.

BORDERLINE.   Instability in a variety of areas, including interpersonal relationships, behavior, mood, and self-image. Interpersonal relationships are often intense and unstable, with marked shifts of attitude. Frequently, there is impulsive and unpredictable behavior that is potentially physically self-damaging. There may be chronic feelings of emptiness and boredom, or brief episodes of PSYCHOSIS (this glossary).

COMPULSIVE.   Restricted ability to express warm and tender emotions; preoccupation with rules, order, organization, efficiency, and detail; excessive devotion to work and productivity to the exclusion of pleasure; indecisiveness.

DEPENDENT.   Inducing others to assume responsibility for major areas of one's life; subordinating one's own needs to those of others on whom one is dependent to avoid any possibility of independence; lack of self-confidence.

HISTRIONIC.   Excitability, emotional instability, overreactivity, and attention seeking, and often seductive self-dramatization, whether or not the person is aware of its purpose. People with this disorder are immature, self-centered, vain, and unusually dependent. Sometimes referred to as "hysterical personality."

NARCISSISTIC.   Grandiose sense of self-importance or uniqueness; preoccupation with fantasies of limitless success; need for constant attention and admiration; and disturbances in interpersonal relationships, such as lack of empathy, exploitativeness, and relationships that vacillate between the extremes of overidealization and devaluation.

PARANOID.   Pervasive and long-standing suspiciousness and mistrust of others; hypersensitivity and scanning of the environment for clues that selectively validate prejudices, attitudes, or biases. Stable psychotic features such as delusions and HALLUCINATIONS (this glossary) are absent.

PASSIVE–AGGRESSIVE.   Aggressive behavior manifested in passive ways, such as obstructionism, pouting, procrastination, intentional inefficiency, and obstinacy. The aggression often arises from resentment at failing to find gratification in a relationship with an individual or institution upon which the individual is over-dependent.

SCHIZOID.   Manifestations include shyness, oversensitivity, social withdrawal, frequent daydreaming, avoidance of close or competitive relationships, and eccentricity. Persons with this disorder often react to disturbing experiences with apparent detachment and are unable to express hostility and ordinary aggressive feelings.

SCHIZOTYPAL.   The essential features are various oddities of thinking, perception, communication, and behavior not severe enough to meet the criteria for SCHIZOPHRENIA (this glossary).

PERSONALITY TESTS.   See OBJECTIVE PERSONALITY TEST (this glossary).

PHENOTHIAZINE DERIVATIVES.   A group of psychotropic drugs that include Thorazine, Stelazine, Haldol, Mellaril, and Prolixin and can cause side effects such as AKATHISIA, DYSTONIA, and TARDIVE DYSKINESIA (this glossary). As a group of drugs, the phenothiazines are also known as ANTIPSYCHOTIC DRUGS.

PHOBIA.   An obsessive, persistent, unrealistic, intense fear of an object or situation. The fear is believed to arise through a process of displacing an internal (unconscious) conflict to an external object symbolically related to the conflict. See also DISPLACEMENT (this glossary).

PRECONSCIOUS.   Thoughts that are not in immediate awareness but can be recalled by conscious effort.

PREDICTOR VARIABLE.   The test or other form of performance that is used to predict the person's status on a criterion variable. For example, scores on the Scholastic Aptitude Test might be used to predict the criterion "finishing college within the top 33% of graduating class." Scores on the Scholastic Aptitude Test would be predictor variables.

PRESSURED SPEECH.   Rapid, accelerated, frenzied speech. Sometimes it exceeds the ability of the vocal musculature to articulate, leading to jumbled and cluttered speech; at other times it exceeds the ability of the listener to comprehend, as the speech expresses a FLIGHT OF IDEAS (as in MANIA, this glossary) or an unintelligible jargon.

PRIMACY EFFECT.   The tendency to have better recall of events that occur at the beginning of a sequence. To be distinguished from RECENCY EFFECT (this glossary).

PRIMARY PROCESS.   In psychoanalytic theory, the generally unorganized mental activity characteristic of the UNCONSCIOUS (this glossary). It is marked by the free discharge of energy and excitation without regard to the demands of environment, reality, or logic. See also SECONDARY PROCESS (this glossary).

PROGNOSIS.   The prediction of the future course of an illness.

PROJECTION.   A DEFENSE MECHANISM (this glossary) in which what is emotionally unacceptable in the self is unconsciously rejected and attributed (projected) to others.

PROJECTIVE DRAWINGS.   Any of several projective techniques requiring that the subject draw specific figures or objects. The clinician then draws inferences about the subject's personality, based on his or her interpretations of the style, manner, degree of detail, and other features of the drawings in light of the theoretical or empirically determined meaning of those features. Tests of this type include the Draw-a-Person test and the House–Tree–Person test.

PROJECTIVE TESTS.   Psychological diagnostic tests that utilize ambiguous stimulus material to elicit the subject's responses, usually in a relatively unstructured procedure. Because the subject must impose his or her own meanings and organization on the ambiguous material, the responses are viewed as projections of the subject's own personality. Scoring of projective tests is typically complex and may involve a significant amount of interpretation by the clinician. See, for example, RORSCHACH TEST (this glossary).

PSYCHIATRIC NURSE.   Any nurse employed in a psychiatric hospital or other psychiatric setting who has special training and experience in the management of psychiatric patients. Sometimes the term is used to denote only those nurses who have a master's degree in psychiatric nursing.

PSYCHIATRIC SOCIAL WORKER.   A social worker with specialized psychiatric training leading to a master's or doctoral degree.

PSYCHIATRIST.   A licensed physician who specializes in the diagnosis, treatment, and prevention of mental and emotional disorders. Training encompasses a medical degree and four years or more of approved residency training. For those who wish to enter a subspecialty, such as child psychiatry, psychoanalysis, administration, or the like, additional training is essential.

PSYCHOANALYST.   A person, usually but not always a psychiatrist, who has had training in psychoanalysis and who employs the techniques of psychoanalytic theory.

PSYCHODYNAMICS. The systematized knowledge and theory of human behavior and its motivation, the study of which depends largely upon the functional significance of emotion. Psychodynamics recognizes the role of unconscious motivation in human behavior. The theory of psychodynamics assumes that one's behavior is determined by past experience, genetic endowment, and current reality.

PSYCHOGENESIS. Production or causation of a symptom or illness by mental or psychic factors as opposed to organic ones.

PSYCHOLOGICAL TESTS. Any of a variety of systematic techniques for measuring human behavior. Personality tests are traditionally classified as either projective or objective measures. Other devices may be used to measure intelligence, attitudes, achievement, academic performance, or other aspects of behavior. See PROJECTIVE TESTS, OBJECTIVE PERSONALITY TESTS, and INTELLIGENCE TESTS (this glossary).

PSYCHOLOGIST. A person who holds a master's degree or doctorate from an accredited graduate training program in psychology. A psychologist may be involved in teaching, in research, or in an applied position. Those who apply psychological knowledge and techniques in the assessment and amelioration of abnormal or disturbed human behavior are usually "clinical psychologists" and, in most states, will require licensing or certification in order to practice. Other applied practitioners include "counseling psychologists," who typically work with less severely disturbed populations than do clinical psychologists (though many of the same assessment techniques and therapy principles may be utilized), and "school psychologists," who work with problems which arise in school settings.

PSYCHOLOGY. An academic discipline, a profession, and a science dealing with the study of mental processes and behavior of people and animals.

PSYCHOMOTOR EPILEPSY. See EPILEPSY (this glossary).

PSYCHOPATHIC PERSONALITY. An early term for ANTISOCIAL personality; see PERSONALITY DISORDERS (this glossary). Such persons are sometimes referred to as "psychopaths."

PSYCHOPATHOLOGY. The study of the significant causes and processes in the development of mental disorders. Also the manifestations of mental disorders.

PSYCHOSEXUAL DEVELOPMENT. A series of stages from infancy to adulthood, relatively fixed in time, determined by the interaction between a person's biological drives and the environment.

With resolution of this interaction, a balanced, reality-oriented development takes place; with disturbance, fixation and conflict ensue. This disturbance may remain latent or may give rise to characterological or behavioral disorders. The stages of development are (1) "oral," lasting from birth to 12 months or longer; (2) "anal," lasting usually from one to three years; (3) "phallic," occupying the period from about two and a half to six years; and (4) "Oedipal," overlapping somewhat with the phallic stage (ages four to six) and representing a time of inevitable conflict between the child and parents.

PSYCHOSIS. A major mental disorder of organic or emotional origin in which a person's ability to think, respond emotionally, remember, communicate, interpret reality, and behave appropriately is sufficiently impaired as to interfere grossly with the capacity to meet the ordinary demands of life. Often characterized by regressive behavior, inappropriate mood, diminished impulse control, and such abnormal mental content as delusions and HALLUCINATIONS (this glossary). The term is applicable to conditions having a wide range of severity and duration. See also SCHIZOPHRENIA, BIPOLAR DISORDER, DEPRESSION, ORGANIC MENTAL DISORDER, and REALITY TESTING, this glossary.

PSYCHOSURGERY. Surgical intervention to sever fibers connecting one part of the brain with another or to remove or destroy brain tissue, with the intent of modifying or altering severe disturbances of behavior, thought content, or mood. Such surgery may also be undertaken for the relief of intractable pain.

PSYCHOTHERAPY. A therapeutic procedure involving verbal interaction between a mental health professional and a client. Also, the interpersonal relationship that develops between them; the objective is to help alleviate the client's suffering and/or to increase his or her coping skills.

PSYCHOTROPIC. A term used to describe drugs that have a special action upon the psyche. See PHENOTHIAZINE DERIVATIVES (this glossary).

Q

QUANTITATIVE VARIABLE. An object of observation which varies in manner or degree in such a way that it may be measured.

Q-SORT. A personality assessment technique in which an individual "sorts" a series of descriptive statements into categories along some ordinal dimension, to reflect the degree to which each statement applies to a target person (either himself or herself, or someone else specified by the examiner).

R

RANDOM SAMPLE. A group of subjects selected in such a way that each member of the population from which the sample is derived has an equal or known chance (probability) of being chosen for the sample.

RATIONALIZATION. A DEFENSE MECHANISM (this glossary) in which the person attempts to justify or make consciously tolerable by plausible means, feelings, behavior, or motives that otherwise would be intolerable. Not to be confused with conscious evasion or dissimulation.

REACTION FORMATION. A DEFENSE MECHANISM (this glossary) in which a person adopts affects, ideas, attitudes, and behaviors that are the opposites of impulses he or she harbors either consciously or unconsciously (e.g., excessive moral zeal may be a reaction to strong but repressed asocial impulses).

REALITY TESTING. The ability to evaluate the external world objectively and to differentiate adequately between it and the internal world. Falsification of reality, as with massive denial or projection, indicates a severe disturbance of ego functioning and/or the perceptual and memory processes upon which it is partly based.

RECALL. The process of bringing a memory into consciousness. "Recall" is often used to refer to the recollection of facts, events, and feelings that occurred in the immediate past.

RECENCY EFFECT. The tendency to have better recall of events that occur at the end of a sequence. To be distinguished from PRIMACY EFFECT (this glossary).

REGRESSION. Partial or symbolic return to more infantile patterns of reacting or thinking. Manifested in a wide variety of circumstances, such as in patterns of sleep, play, and physical illness, and in many mental disorders.

RELIABILITY. The extent to which a test or procedure will yield the same result either over time or with different observers. The most commonly reported reliabilities are (1) "test–retest reliability," the correlation between the first and second test of a number of subjects; (2) "split-half reli-

ability," the correlation within a single test of two similar parts of the test; and (3) "interrater reliability," the agreement between different individuals scoring the same procedure or observations.

REMISSION. Abatement of an illness.

REPRESSION. A DEFENSE MECHANISM (this glossary) that banishes unacceptable ideas, fantasies, affects, or impulses from consciousness or that keeps out of consciousness what has never been conscious. Although not subject to voluntary recall, the repressed material may emerge in disguised form. Often confused with the conscious mechanism of SUPPRESSION (this glossary).

RETROGRADE AMNESIA. See AMNESIA, ANTEROGRADE, this glossary.

RORSCHACH TEST. A projective test requiring that the subject free-associate to ambiguous ink blots. The manner and content of the subject's perceptions and verbalizations are scored and interpreted by a trained clinician to reveal hypotheses and insights about the person's general psychological functioning. See PROJECTIVE TESTS (this glossary).

S

SCHIZOID. See PERSONALITY DISORDERS (this glossary).

SCHIZOPHRENIA. A large group of disorders, usually of psychotic proportion, manifested by characteristic disturbances of language and communication, thought, perception, affect, and behavior that last longer than six months. Thought disturbances are marked by alterations of concept formation that may lead to misinterpretation of reality, misperceptions, and sometimes delusions and HALLUCINATIONS (this glossary). Mood changes include ambivalence, blunting, inappropriateness, and loss of empathy with others. Behavior may be withdrawn, regressive, and bizarre. The clinical picture is not explainable by any of the ORGANIC MENTAL DISORDERS (this glossary).

SECONDARY GAIN. The external gain derived from any illness, such as personal attention and service, monetary gains, disability benefits, and release from unpleasant responsibility.

SECONDARY PROCESS. In psychoanalytic theory, mental activity and thinking characteristic of the EGO (this glossary) and influenced by the demands of the environment. Characterized by organization, systematization, intellectualization, and similar processes leading to logical thought and action in adult life. See also PRIMARY PROCESS (this glossary).

SELECTION BIAS. The inadvertent selection of a nonrepresentative sample of subjects or observations. A classic example is a 1936 *Literary Digest* poll that predicted a victory for Landon over Roosevelt in the presidential election because telephone directories were used as a basis for selecting respondents. In 1936 telephones were owned primarily by persons in higher socioeconomic brackets.

SENSORIUM. Synonymous with "consciousness." Includes the special sensory perceptive powers and their central correlation and integration in the brain. A clear sensorium conveys the presence of a reasonably accurate memory, together with orientation for time, place, and person.

SOCIAL WORK. The use of community resources and the conscious adaptive capacities of individuals and groups to better their adjustment to their environment.

SOCIOPATH. An unofficial term for ANTISOCIAL personality; see PERSONALITY DISORDERS (this glossary).

SOMATIC THERAPY. In psychiatry, the biological treatment of mental disorders (e.g., electroconvulsive therapy, psychopharmacological treatment). Contrast with PSYCHOTHERAPY (this glossary).

STANDARD DEVIATION (SD). A mathematical measure of the dispersion or spread of scores clustered about the MEAN (this glossary). In any distribution that approximates a normal curve in form, about 68% of the measurements will lie within one *SD* of the mean, and about 95% will lie within two *SD*s of the mean.

STATISTICAL SIGNIFICANCE. A finding that an observed phenomenon (e.g., a difference between two groups) is unlikely to have occurred by chance. Conventionally, in the social and behavioral sciences, findings are held to be statistically significant when $p < .05$; that is when a group difference of a given magnitude would be expected by chance fewer than 5 times in 100.

STRESS REACTION. An acute, maladaptive emotional response to industrial, domestic, civilian, or military disasters, and other calamitous life situations.

SUBCONSCIOUS. Obsolete term. Formerly used to include the PRECONSCIOUS and the UNCONSCIOUS (this glossary).

SUBSTITUTION. A DEFENSE MECHANISM (this glossary) by which an unattainable or unacceptable goal, emotion, or object is replaced by one that is more attainable or acceptable.

SUPEREGO. In psychoanalytic theory, that part of the personality structure associated with ethics, standards, and self-criticism. It is formed by identification with important and esteemed persons in early life, particularly parents. The supposed or actual wishes of these significant persons are taken over as part of the child's own standards to help form the conscience. See also EGO and ID (this glossary).

SUPPRESSION. The conscious effort to control and conceal unacceptable impulses, thoughts, feelings, or acts.

T

TANGENTIALITY. Replying to a question in an oblique or irrelevant way. Compare with CIRCUMSTANTIALITY (this glossary).

TARDIVE DYSKINESIA. Literally, "late-appearing abnormal movements"; a variable complex of movements developed in patients exposed to ANTIPSYCHOTIC DRUGS (this glossary). Typical movements include writhing or protrusion of the tongue, chewing, puckering of the lips, finger movements, toe and ankle movements, jiggling of the legs, or movements of neck, trunk, and pelvis.

TEMPORAL LOBE EPILEPSY. PSYCHOMOTOR EPILEPSY; see EPILEPSY (this glossary).

THEMATIC APPERCEPTION TEST (TAT). A PROJECTIVE TEST (this glossary) requiring that the subject create narrative stories in response to a series of pictured cards, usually portraying one or more persons. The subject's responses regarding the thoughts and feelings of the stimulus figures, the nature and quality of their relationship with each other, and techniques they employ in resolving personal or interpersonal problems are interpreted by the clinician to gain insight into the subject's own personality. For use with children, there is the Children's Apperception Test.

THOUGHT DISORDER. A disturbance of speech, communication, or content of thought, such as delusions, IDEAS OF REFERENCE, (this glossary), poverty of thought, FLIGHT OF IDEAS, PERSEVERATION, LOOSENING OF ASSOCIATIONS (all this glossary), etc. A formal thought disorder is a disturbance in the form of thought rather than the content of thought (e.g., loosening of associations).

TOKEN ECONOMY.   A system involving the application of the principles and procedures of OPERANT CONDITIONING (this glossary) to the management of a social setting such as a ward, classroom, or halfway house. Tokens are given contingent on completion of specified activities and are exchangeable for goods or privileges desired by the patient.

TRANSFERENCE.   The unconscious assignment to others of feelings and attitudes that were originally associated with important figures (parents, siblings, etc.) in one's early life. The clinician utilizes this phenomenon as a therapeutic tool to help the patient understand emotional problems and their origins. In the patient–clinician relationship, the transference may be negative (hostile) or positive (affectionate). See also COUNTERTRANSFERENCE (this glossary).

TRUE NEGATIVE.   An accurate opinion that something is not present or will not be present. (Compare FALSE NEGATIVE, this glossary.)

TRUE POSITIVE.   An accurate opinion that something is or will be present. (Compare FALSE POSITIVE, this glossary.)

U

UNCONSCIOUS.   That part of the mind or mental functioning of which the content is only rarely subject to awareness. It is a repository for data that have never been conscious (primary repression) or that may have become conscious briefly and later repressed (secondary repression). See REPRESSION (this glossary).

UNIPOLAR PSYCHOSES.   Recurrent major depressions. See MAJOR AFFECTIVE DISORDERS (this glossary).

V

VALIDITY.   Accuracy. The degree to which a type of measurement is related to a construct or criterion; for example, the level of CORRELATION (this glossary) between a test score and a criterion (e.g., school performance) which the test is designed to predict.

VARIABLE.   Any characteristic in any experiment that may assume different values. See INDEPENDENT VARIABLE and DEPENDENT VARIABLE (this glossary).

VARIANCE.   The square of the STANDARD DEVIATION (this glossary). Also used interchangeably with "variability."

W

WORD SALAD.   A rare form of speech disturbance, sometimes observed in persons suffering from schizophrenic disorders, marked by a mixture of words and phrases that lack comprehensive meaning or logical coherence.

Notes

In the following pages, references to materials are often made in abbreviated forms, some of which may not be familiar to the reader. To aid in using the notes, the most commonly abbreviated terms are listed below.

A.—Atlantic Reporter
A.L.R.—American Law Reports
C.F.R.—Code of Federal Regulations
F.—Federal Reporter
FED. R. CIV. P.—Federal Rules of Civil Procedure
FED. R. CRIM. P.—Federal Rules of Criminal Procedure
FED. R. EVID.—Federal Rules of Evidence
F.R.D.—Federal Rules Decisions
F. Supp.—Federal Supplement
L. REV.—Law Review

N.E.—Northeastern Reporter
N.W.—Northwestern Reporter
P.—Pacific Reporter
S.Ct.—Supreme Court Reporter
S.E.—Southeastern Reporter
So.—Southern Reporter
S.W.—Southwestern Reporter
U.S.—United States Supreme Court Reports
U.S.C.—United States Code
U.S. CONST.—United States Constitution

Chapter 1

1. *See* Grisso, Sales, & Bayless, *Law-Related Courses and Programs in Graduate Psychology Departments,* 37 AM. PSYCHOLOGIST 267 (1982).

2. *See* Monahan & Loftus, *The Psychology of Law,* 33 ANN. REV. PSYCHOLOGY 441 (1982).

3. CRIMINAL JUSTICE MENTAL HEALTH STANDARDS (1984).

4. Bazelon, *Veils, Values, and Social Responsibility,* 37 AM. PSYCHOLOGIST 115 (1982).

5. *Cf.* Bonnie & Slobogin, *The Role of Mental Health Professionals in the Criminal Process: The Case for Informed Speculation,* 66 VA. L. REV. 427 (1980), with Morse, *Crazy Behavior, Morals, and Science: An Analysis of Mental Health Law,* 51 S. CAL. L. REV. 527 (1978) [hereinafter cited as Morse, *Crazy Behavior*] and Morse, *Failed Explanations and Criminal Responsibility: Experts and the Unconscious,* 68 VA. L. REV. 971 (1982) [hereinafter cited as Morse, *Failed Explanations*].

6. *See, e.g.,* Loh, *Psycholegal Research: Past and Present,* 79 MICH. L. REV. 658 (1981).

7. The rule adopted in Durham v. United States, 214 F.2d 862 (1954), provided that a defendant is not criminally responsible if his or her unlawful act was the product of mental disease or defect. *See infra* § 6.02(b).

8. *See, e.g.,* T. SARBIN & J. MANCUSO, SCHIZOPHRENIA: MEDICAL DIAGNOSIS OR MORAL VERDICT? (1980); T. SZASZ, LAW, LIBERTY AND PSYCHIATRY (1963); T. SZASZ, THE MYTH OF MENTAL ILLNESS (rev. ed. 1974).

9. *Durham, supra* note 7, was finally overruled and replaced in the District of Columbia by the test found in the American Law Institute's (ALI's) MODEL PENAL CODE [see § 6.02(b)], United States v. Brawner, 471 F.2d 969 (1972). Along the way, the D. C. Circuit Court, led by then Chief Circuit Judge Bazelon, *see supra* note 4 and accompanying text, made several attempts to salvage

the *Durham* rule by limiting its terms. *See, e.g.,* Carter v. United States, 252 F.2d 608 (1957) (defining "product"); McDonald v. United States, 312 F.2d 847 (1962) (defining "mental illness").

10. Ideological conflicts may also be substantial within particular mental health professions, particularly when leaders of professional organizations attempt to shape mental health policy. *See, e.g.,* Kahle & Sales, *Comment on "Civil Commitment,"* 2 MENTAL DISABILITY L. REP. 677 (1978); Melton, *Organized Psychology and Legal Policymaking: Involvement in the Post-*Hinckley *Debate* 16 PROF. PSYCHOLOGY: RESEARCH PRAC. 810 (1985).

11. Such a division among the professions was observed, for example, in the amicus briefs submitted in Mills v. Rogers, 102 S.Ct. 2442 (1982) (regarding whether institutionalized patients have a constitutional right to refuse psychotropic medication), and Parham v. J.R., 442 U.S. 584 (1979) (regarding whether parents may admit their children to mental hospitals without a hearing).

12. *See* Poythress, *Psychiatric Expertise in Civil Commitment: Training Attorneys to Cope with Expert Testimony,* 2 LAW HUM. BEHAV. 1 (1978).

13. The most recent revision of the AMERICAN PSYCHIATRIC ASSOCIATION'S DIAGNOSTIC AND STATISTICAL MANUAL OF MENTAL DISORDERS (3d ed. 1980) (commonly described as DSM-III) features more precise diagnostic criteria than its predecessors. Consequently, diagnostic reliability appears improved. Rather than the interclinician agreement of less than 50% common even for gross diagnoses prior to DSM-III, *see* Spitzer & Fleiss, *A Re-Analysis of the Reliability of Psychiatric Diagnosis,* 125 BRIT. J. PSYCHIATRY 341 (1974), the field trials of DSM-III yielded kappa coefficients (a correlation) of about .80 for the most severe diagnoses, at least in broad categories. DSM-III at 470. However, there is reason to believe that the level of reliability of diagnoses during the field trials was spuriously inflated by artifacts in the research design. Morse, *A Preference for Liberty: The Case Against Involuntary Commitment of the Mentally Disordered.* 70 CALIF. L. REV. 54, 70 n.75 (1982).

14. Most correlation coefficients, when squared, indicate the proportion of variance in a given phenomenon (i.e., the proportion of individual or group differences) accounted for by a second variable.

15. The degree to which such control is achieved is called "internal validity." Generally, the highest level of internal validity is achieved in a true experiment, in which participants are randomly assigned to conditions that vary only with respect to one variable. Because of the appearance of unfairness attached to random assignment (e.g., it is difficult to imagine judges randomly assigning children to various custody arrangements), such a high level of control is rarely accomplished in research on problems of legal policy.

16. The real-world generalizability of a study is called its "external validity."

17. Mental health professionals often have persisted in particular forms of practice even in the face of unfavorable scientific evidence. *See, e.g.,* Morse, *Failed Explanations,*

supra note 5, at 991–1018 (noting lack of empirical support for psychoanalytic theory); Wade & Baker, *Opinions and Use of Psychological Tests: A Survey of Clinical Psychologists,* 32 AM. PSYCHOLOGIST 874 (1977) (noting persistent use of psychological tests, even when these are shown to be unreliable and invalid).

18. Although there are a number of kinds of reliability, in the present context "reliability" refers to the similarity of conclusion by two or more observers. Generally, it describes the degree of elimination of error in observation (i.e., the repeatability and stability of measurement).

19. *"Validity"* refers to the degree to which an observation actually measures something; commonly, it is established by the strength of correlation between one form of observation and a criterion (e.g., the validity of an instrument to measure disability in a guardianship proceeding may be established in part by a strong correlation with demonstrated performance on various tasks in the community).

20. Melton & Scott, *Evaluation of Mentally Retarded Persons for Sterilization: Contributions and Limits of Psychological Consultation,* 15 PROF. PSYCHOLOGY: RESEARCH PRAC. 34 (1984).

21. 93 WASH. 228, 608 P.2d 635 (1980).

22. *See* Moore, *Mental Illness and Responsibility,* 39 BULL. MENNINGER CLINIC 308 (1975). For some legal tests that are strictly "cognitive," there is no need to consider problems of volition. The historic *M'Naghten* test of insanity does not require examination of voluntariness of action, *see infra* § 6.02(a), although it is arguable that it is rooted in assumptions concerning the class of persons for whom choices to avoid criminal behavior are too hard. In general, the competencies also are theoretically cognitive, although in most instances (e.g., competency to confess), there is a prong of "voluntariness" in the test. *See infra* Chapter 5.

23. Grano, *Voluntariness, Free Will, and the Law of Confessions,* 65 VA. L. REV. 858, 886 (1979).

24. *See, e.g.,* B. SKINNER, SCIENCE AND HUMAN BEHAVIOR (1953); B. SKINNER, BEYOND FREEDOM AND DIGNITY (1971).

25. S. FREUD, *Psychopathology of Everyday Life,* in 6 THE STANDARD EDITION OF THE COMPLETE PSYCHOLOGICAL WORKS (J. Strachey ed. 1960) (orig. publ. 1901).

26. *E.g.,* H. HARTMANN, THE EGO AND THE PROBLEM OF ADAPTATION (1958) (orig. publ. 1939).

27. In Freud's initial theory, psychic structures developed through the process of interaction between (1) the infant and its collection of instinctual drives and (2) the demands and limits of reality. Later psychoanalytic theorists, *e.g.,* H. HARTMANN, *id.,* argued that some aspects of cognition were determined by innate, adaptive structures rather than a history of conflict. For a readable discussion of these and other basic developments in psychoanalytic theory, *see* P. HOLZMAN, PSYCHO-ANALYSIS AND PSYCHOPATHOLOGY (1970).

28. R. MAY, LOVE AND WILL 199 (1969).

29. There really is no single medical model—a point that is sometimes ignored, with resulting confusion. Psy-

chodynamic clinicians frequently assume, for example, intrapsychic "pathology." Hence, the disorder is believed to be an underlying disease that presents behavioral symptoms; however, the disease would not be viewed as a product of *organic* pathology. Regardless, the well-known criticisms of Szasz and others, *see supra* note 8, as to the social/moral observations required to determine that behavioral aberrations are the product of a disease apply to both organic and intrapsychic medical models.

30. An exception may lie where the epileptic man is aware of his condition and does not take proper percautions to ensure that no one is injured as a result of behavior caused by the illness. *See, e.g.,* People v. Decina, 2 N.Y.2d 133, 138 N.E.2d 799, 157 N.Y.S.2d 558 (1956); *see also infra* § 6.03(a).

31. *See* D. ROSENTHAL, GENETICS OF PSYCHOPATHOLOGY (1971).

32. Such a view is called a "diathesis–stress hypothesis." *See, e.g.,* Mednick, *A Learning-Theory Approach to Research in Schizophrenia,* 55 PSYCHOLOGICAL BULL. 315 (1958); Meehl, *Schizotaxia, Schizotypy, Schizophrenia,* 17 AM. PSYCHOLOGIST 827 (1962).

33. M. MOORE, LAW AND PSYCHIATRY: RETHINKING THE RELATIONSHIP (1984), has argued that there is no inherent conflict between psychiatry's view of personhood and the law's emphasis on "free will." Thus, Moore rejects what he calls the "hard determinist" position in favor of a "soft determinist" or "compatibilist" position. According to the latter view, a casual factor, whether it be physiological, environmental, or psychic, is not a compulsion unless it inteferes with one's reasoning process. Thus, for example, a poverty-striken childhood may lead a person to believe that crime is the best way to earn a living, which belief may in turn cause crime; however, to the extent that the person with such a history retains the ability to formulate desires and beliefs in an undisturbed fashion, he or she cannot be said to be compelled to commit crime.

While Moore's conceptualization of causation may be of some aid to clinicians and lawyers, *see, e.g., infra* § 6.02(c)(2), his approach does not eliminate the dilemma of determinism versus free will. He himself admits that a soft determinist must still "show that determinism is compatible with the principle that punishment is unjust unless the actor 'could have done other than he did,' " MOORE at 488 n.34, yet he makes no attempt to do so himself. For a more detailed treatment of his book, *see* Slobogin, *A Rational Approach to Responsibility,* 83 MICH. L. REV. 820 (1985).

34. There may be other ways of translating concepts of freedom into psychologically cogent constructs. For example, freedom may be discussed in terms of the breadth and efficacy of the range of behavioral alternatives available to an individual in a given situation. *See, e.g.,* M. MAHONEY & C. THORESEN, SELF-CONTROL: POWER TO THE PERSON (1974). Freedom might also be conceptualized in terms of *perceived* control. *See generally* CHOICE AND PERCEIVED CONTROL (L. Perlmuter & R. Monty eds. 1979). It is important to recognize, however, that these concepts still are incompatible with the theory of voluntary behavior on which the law is based.

35. Haney, *Psychology and Legal Change: On the Limits of a Factual Jurisprudence,* 4 LAW & HUM. BEHAV. 147, 165 (1980).

36. *See* American Psychological Association, *Ethical Principles of Psychologists,* 36 AM. PSYCHOLOGIST 633, principle 1 (1981).

37. An example of a bias against probabilistic, research-based evidence is reflected in the widely publicized "television intoxication" case, State v. Zamora, 361 So.2d 776 (2d D.C.A. 1978), *cert. denied,* 372 So.2d 472 (Fla. 1979). A researcher who intended to describe relevant research was excluded on the ground that her testimony was "speculative"; a psychiatrist who gave essentially the same testimony in terms of clinical conclusions was permitted to testify. The relevant portions of the trial transcript are included in J. MONAHAN & L. WALKER, SOCIAL SCIENCE IN LAW: CASES, MATERIALS AND PROBLEMS (1985).

Another example, mentioned in the text, of a bias against nonclinicians that is likely to result in less informed expert opinion comes when "nonmedical" psychologists are excluded from testifying as to the variables involved in eyewitness testimony, but clinical psychologists, who are likely to be much less knowledgeable about the research literature in cognitive psychology, are permitted to testify as experts. A survey of Michigan trial judges indicated that they would in fact prefer testimony by clinical psychologists in such an instance, and that they would undervalue testimony presented in nonconclusory, statistical terms. Poythress, *Psychological Issues in Criminal Proceedings: Judicial Preference Regarding Expert Testimony,* 10 CRIM. JUST. & BEHAV. 175 (1983); N. Poythress, Conflicting Postures for Mental Health Expert Witnesses: Prevailing Attitudes of Trial Court Judges (unpublished manuscript n.d.) (*see* § 14.05(a)).

38. Martin, *The Uncertain Rule of Certainty: An Analysis and Proposal for a Federal Evidence Rule,* 20 WAYNE L. REV. 781, 804–05 (1974).

39. An amusing account of one psychologist's attempt to describe to a jury his reservations about the term "reasonable psychological certainty" is found in Poythress, *Concerning Reform in Expert Testimony: An Open Letter from a Practicing Psychologist,* 6 LAW & HUM. BEHAV. 39 (1982); *see also* Morse, *Reforming Expert Testimony: An Open Response from the Tower (and Trenches),* 6 LAW & HUM. BEHAV. 45 (1982).

40. State v. Middleton, 668 P.2d 371 (Or. 1983).

41. State v. Loebach, 310 N.W.2d 58 (Minn. 1981).

42. *See* United States v. Mendenhall, 446 U.S. 544 (1980). In the actual surveillance of which this case was a part, the stops were not solely the result of correlation between those stopped and the profile. Tips from informants, information from ticket agents, and other sources all contributed.

43. Tribe, *Trial by Mathematics: Precision and Ritual in the Legal Process,* 84 HARV. L. REV. 1329 (1971).

44. Tribe would permit mathematical evidence to be presented to negate a misleading impression that might be left by expert opinion and perhaps to shift the burden of persuasion. *Id.* at 1377.

45. A Bayesian analysis provides a method for determining the probability that a certain event or events influenced another event. *See* Glossary.

46. Tribe, *supra* note 43, at 1368–72.

47. *Id.* at 1361–66.

48. *Id.* at 1372–75.

49. *Id.* at 1375–77.

50. Saks & Kidd, *Human Information Processing and Adjudication: Trial by Heuristics,* 15 LAW & SOC'Y. REV. 123 (1980–81).

51. *See id.* at 125 n.l. There is evidence that jurors believe "beyond a reasonable doubt" to be a *less* stringent test than other standards of proof. Kagehiro & Stanton, *The Effects of Standard of Proof and Quantification of Standard of Proof on Simulated Juror Decision Making,* 9 LAW & HUM. BEHAV. 159 (1985).

52. See Saks & Kidd, *supra* note 50.

53. Tribe, *supra* note 43, at 1330 n.2.

54. *See* Thibaut & Walker, *A Theory of Procedure,* 66 CALIF. L. REV. 541–45 (1978).

55. There is, of course, the possibility that the expert will be subtly swayed by the attorney's "preparation" of him or her for testimony and by the desire simply to be helpful. *See* M. SAKS & R. VAN DUIZEND, SCIENTIFIC AND TECHNOLOGICAL EVIDENCE IN LITIGATION (1983).

56. Freund, *Is the Law Ready for Human Experimentation?* 22 AM. PSYCHOLOGIST 393, 394 (1967).

57. *See, e.g.,* Melton, *Children's Competence to Consent: A Problem in Law and Social Science,* in CHILDREN'S COMPETENCE TO CONSENT (G. Melton, G. Koocher, & M. Saks eds. 1983); Melton, *Family and Mental Hospital as Myths: Civil Commitment of Minors,* in CHILDREN, MENTAL HEALTH, AND THE LAW (D. Reppucci, L. Weithorn, E. Mulvey, & J. Monahan eds. 1984).

58. *See* Melton, *Developmental Psychology and the Law: The State of the Art,* 22 J. FAM. L. 445 (1984) (empirical assumptions in family law are based on *a priori* social constructs); *see also* Perry & Melton, *Precedential Value of Judicial Notice of Social Facts: Parham as an Example,* 22 J. FAM. L. 633 (1984) (judicially noticed social facts sometimes take on precedential value of their own and obscure the meaning of case holdings).

59. "Legislative facts" refer to the rationales or social assumptions underlying policies. *See* Davis, *An Approach to Problems of Evidence in the Administrative Process,* 55 HARV. L. REV. 364, 404–07 (1942).

60. FED. R. EVID. 701.

61. *Id.* 702.

62. *See, e.g.,* Bazelon, *supra* note 4; Bonnie & Slobogin, *supra* note 5, at 456; Morse, *Crazy Behavior, supra* note 5, at 554–60; comment, *The Psychologist as Expert Witness: Science in the Courtroom,* 38 MD. L. REV. 539, 593–98 (1979). *See also Report of the Task Force on the Role of Psychology in the Criminal Justice System,* 33 AM. PSYCHOLOGIST 1099, 1105–06 (1978); AMERICAN PSYCHIATRIC ASSOCIATION,

STATEMENT ON THE INSANITY DEFENSE 13–14 (1982).

63. Rule 704 is designed to allow free introduction of expert testimony without quibbling about whether a specific opinion (e.g., conclusions that incorporate some of the test language) in fact reaches the ultimate issue. However, read together with Rule 702, it presumably would not permit testimony which is not based on specialized knowledge. It is our contention that, in the contexts at issue here, the ultimate issue is *not* within a mental health professional's field of special knowledge. *See* Bonnie & Slobogin, *supra* note 5, at 456.

64. *See* Morse, *Law and Mental Health Professionals: The Limits of Expertise,* 9 PROF. PSYCHOLOGY 389 (1978).

65. *Id.* at 392.

66. Diagnoses do not translate directly into "mental disease or defect," and certainly not into conclusions about the degree of impairment of certain functions. Diagnosis may relate to relevant research, however; regardless, it serves as a convenient shorthand. Thus, although we would prefer omission of diagnoses from forensic reports, we would not bar them. See § 6.06(a).

67. *See* Bonnie & Slobogin, *supra* note 5.

68. *See id.* It is important to note that a particular opinion, although equally relevant in two legal contexts, might be admissible in one context but not the other. Where the prejudicial import of evidence varies, so too would its admissibility. Hence, the standard of admissibility should be somewhat stricter in civil commitment proceedings, where experts' opinions typically go unchallenged, than in insanity cases, where jurors tend to be skeptical of experts' opinions. This point is developed further below.

69. Morse, *Failed Explanations, supra* note 5, at 978.

70. *Id.* at 979–80.

71. *See generally* Ennis & Litwack, *Psychiatry and the Presumption of Expertise: Flipping Coins in the Courtroom,* 62 CALIF. L. REV. 693 (1974); Morse, *Crazy Behavior, supra* note 5; Morse, *supra* note 64; comment, *supra* note 62.

72. *Cf.* Poythress, *Coping on the Witness Stand: Learned Responses to Learned Treatises,* 11 PROF. PSYCHOLOGY 139 (1980) (providing rebuttals to frequently cited assertions about the mental health professions).

73. J. PETERSON, E. FABRICANT, & K. FIELD, CRIME LABORATORY PROFICIENCY TESTING RESEARCH PROGRAM: FINAL REPORT (1978).

74. Falek & Moser, *Classification in Schizophrenia,* 26 ARCH. GEN. PSYCHIATRY 59 (1975); Koran, *The Reliability of Clinical Methods, Data and Judgments: Part 1,* 293 NEW ENG. J. MED. 642 (1975); Koran, *The Reliability of Clinical Methods, Data and Judgments: Part 2,* 293 NEW ENG. J. MED. 695 (1975).

75. G. MELTON, L. WEITHORN, & C. SLOBOGIN, COMMUNITY MENTAL HEALTH CENTERS AND THE COURTS: EVALUATION OF COMMUNITY-BASED FORENSIC SERVICES 43–55 (1985).

76. As already noted, experts should, of course, make clear the uncertainty attached to the opinions in such instances; they should also ask themselves whether the opinions they are about to give are in fact the products

of specialized knowledge, rather than purely common-sense judgments.

77. Morse, *Failed Explanations, supra* note 5.

78. *Id.* at 1016–18.

79. It should be noted that we are not arguing that psychodynamic opinions should be admissible simply because they have achieved widespread scientific acceptance. Such a standard is unlikely to correspond completely with usefulness to the trier of fact. *But see* Frye v. United States, 293 F. 1013 (D.C. Cir. 1923), briefly discussed in note 15, Chapter 14. Rather, we are convinced that opinions based on a coherent, if unproven, scientific theory may offer the factfinder some assistance in constructing the range of plausible explanations for particular behavior.

80. *See* Slobogin, *Dangerousness and Expertise,* 133 U. PA. L. REV. 97 (1984).

81. Although, as already noted, training will not eradicate the problems of interaction between law and mental health, training may inculcate a stance of appropriate caution. Our own experience suggests such an effect, although we do not have systematic data on the point. A parallel empirical question is whether legal decision-makers will accept such statements of caution, particularly when also faced with experts who clearly overstep the bounds of expertise. *See* § 14.05(a).

82. There have been several recent reviews of the state of the law with respect to qualifications for recognition as a mental health report. *See, e.g.,* Bonnie & Slobogin, *supra* note 5, at 457–61 and accompanying notes; Dix & Poythress, *Propriety of Medical Dominance of Forensic Mental Health Practice: The Empirical Evidence,* 23 ARIZ. L. REV. 961 (1981); Perlin, *The Legal Status of the Psychologist in the Courtroom,* 4 *Mental Disability L. Rep.* 194 (1980); Comment, *supra* note 62. Sales and his colleagues have reviewed the state of the law with respect to admissibility of psychologists' opinions on a number of legal issues. *See, e.g.,* Hafemeister & Sales, *Responsibilities of Psychologists under Guardianship and Conservatorship Laws,* 13 PROF. PSYCHOLOGY 354 (1982); Morris & Sales, *Psychological Testimony on the Insanity Defense,* AM. PSYCHOLOGIST (in press).

83. Tennessee allows social workers to testify on the former issue.

84. Schindler, Barren, & Beigel, *A Study of the Causes of Conflict between Psychiatrists and Psychologists,* 32 HOSP. COMMUNITY PSYCHIATRY 263 (1981).

85. *See also* Jenkins v. United States, 307 F.2d 637 (D.C. Cir. 1962) (en banc).

86. G. MELTON, L. WEITHORN, & C. SLOBOGIN, *supra* note 75, 52–53. Licensure, another easily determinable criterion, is also a poor measure of competence. *See* Koocher, *Credentialing in Psychology: Close Encounters with Competence?,* 34 AM. PSYCHOLOGIST 696 (1979).

87. Petrella & Poythress, *The Quality of Forensic Examinations: An Interdisciplinary Study,* 51 J. CONSULTING & CLINICAL PSYCHOLOGY 76 (1983).

88. The other major group of mental health professionals, psychiatric nurses, has been omitted from this brief discussion because they have not been included in the relevant research. However, at least for those nurses with substantial (master's-level) training in mental health, there is no reason to believe that they would be less competent experts. Also, where the opinions being offered concern research reports rather than clinical impressions, other professionals (e.g., sociologists, experimental psychologists) may offer the most extensive and up-to-date testimony.

89. G. MELTON, L. WEITHORN, & C. SLOBOGIN, *supra* note 75, 43–55. It is important to note that samples of forensic clinicians in this study were probably atypical. One group consisted of community mental health professionals who had participated in an extensive training program at the Institute of Law, Psychiatry, and Public Policy at the University of Virginia. The other group was composed of diplomates certified by the American Board of Forensic Psychology.

A showing of extensive forensic experience *alone,* however, is insufficient to indicate expertise in forensic mental health. Unfortunately, it is still common for forensic "experts" to render opinions obviously based on a misunderstanding of the legal question, or, perhaps even worse, to give reports that include nothing more than ultimate-issue conclusions without any foundation. Although judges who in effect defer mental health law decisions to experts may prefer such truncated, conclusory reports, the belief that the conclusory opinions offer any real assistance in legal decision-making should be recognized as an illusion. In short, experience alone is unlikely to be a valid measure of potential assistance to the factfinder. Demonstration of relevant knowledge, certification in forensic assessment, or a history of scholarship in the area is likely to be a more valid criterion.

90. Grisso, Sales, & Bayless, *supra* note 1.

91. Levine, Wilson, & Sales, *An Exploratory Assessment of APA Internships with Legal/Forensic Experiences,* 11 PROF. PSYCHOLOGY 64 (1980).

92. *See* Kurke, *Forensic Psychology: A Threat and a Response,* 11 PROF. PSYCHOLOGY 72 (1980).

Chapter 2

1. 42 U.S.C. § 1395aa–1395zz (1975).

2. 42 U.S.C. § 2689 (1975) (repealed by Mental Health Systems Act (1980)).

3. *See, e.g., id.* § 1396 (1983).

4. 42 C.F.R. § 27802 (1975). Federal law applies in all cases involving a "drug abuse prevention function conducted, regulated, or directly or indirectly assisted by any department or agency of the United States." *Id.*

5. *See, e.g.,* Marbury v. Madison, 5 U.S. (1 Cranch) 137 (1803).
6. *See, e.g.,* McCulloch v. Maryland, 17 U.S. (4 Wheat.) 317 (1819).
7. 28 U.S.C. § 1251. *See also* U.S. Const. art. III(d).
8. 28 U.S.C. §§ 1252, 1254.
9. 422 U.S. 563 (1975).
10. 441 U.S. 418 (1979).
11. 463 U.S. 354 (1983).
12. 457 U.S. 291 (1982).
13. *In re* Winship, 397 U.S. 358 (1970).
14. *See, e.g.,* United States v. Wade, 388 U.S. 218 (1967).
15. U.S. Const. amend. VI.
16. Gerstein v. Pugh, 420 U.S. 103 (1975).
17. C. Whitebread & C. Slobogin, Criminal Procedure: An Analysis of Cases and Concepts § 23.02(a) (1986).
18. McCarthy v. United States, 394 U.S. 459 (1969).
19. Project on Standards for Criminal Justice, Pleas of Guilty 1–2 (1968).

20. Apodaca v. Oregon, 406 U.S. 404 (1972); Johnson v. Louisiana, 406 U.S. 356 (1972).
21. Vitek v. Jones, 445 U.S. 488 (1980).
22. Neglect proceedings in which the *state* seeks custody over the child represent a unique category of case; *see generally* Chapter 12. They are not "civil" in the sense that term is used here, nor are they criminal, nor "quasi-criminal," as that term is used in this chapter. They are most closely analogous to administrative proceedings, described below, which involve an attempt by the state to deprive an individual of "property."
23. *See* Fed. R. Civ. P. 26.
24. *Id.* 48.
25. *See, e.g.,* Rennie v. Klein, 462 F. Supp. 1131 (D.N.J. 1978).
26. Addington v. Texas, 441 U.S. 418 (1979).
27. *See, e.g.,* Lessard v. Schmidt, 349 F. Supp. 1078 (1972).
28. McKeiver v. Pennsylvania, 403 U.S. 528 (1971).
29. *In re* Winship, 397 U.S. 358 (1970); *In re* Gault, 387 U.S. 1 (1967).

Chapter 3

1. Schmerber v. California, 384 U.S. 757, 761 (166). *See generally* C. Whitebread & C. Slobogin, Criminal Procedure: An Analysis of Constitutional Cases and Concepts ch. 15 (1986). For a full explication of the issues discussed in this and the following section, see Slobogin, Estelle v. Smith: *The Constitutional Contours of the Forensic Evaluation,* 31 Emory L.J. 71 (1982).
2. 218 U.S. 245 (1910).
3. Gilbert v. California, 388 U.S. 263, 266–67 (1967); United States v. Wade, 388 U.S. 218, 222–23 (1967); Schmerber v. California, 384 U.S. 757, 765 (1966).
4. Thornton v. Corcoran, 407 F.2d 695, 700 (D.C. Cir. 1969).
5. 451 U.S. 454 (1981).
6. *Id.* at 464 n.8.
7. Hoffman v. United States, 341 U.S. 479 (1951).
8. This ban applies in federal jurisdictions under 18 U.S.C. § 4244 (1976). The states that impose the ban by statute are Alabama, Arizona, Arkansas, Colorado, District of Columbia, Florida, Illinois, Massachusetts, Missouri, Montana, New York, Pennsylvania, South Carolina, Texas, Vermont, Virginia, and Washington.
9. Even if it can be assumed that the prosecutor acts in good faith, the prosecutor "cannot be certain that somewhere in the depths of his investigative apparatus, often including hundreds of employees, there was not some prohibited use of the compelled testimony." Kastigar v. United States, 406 U.S. 441, 469 (1971) (Marshall, J., dissenting). Discovering such abuse and proving it are extremely difficult, "for all proof lies in the hands of the government." Rief, *The Grand Jury Witness and Compulsory Testimony Legislation,* 10 Am. Crim. L. Rev. 829, 856–59 (1972).
10. Va. Code Ann. § 19.2-169.1(D) (1981).
11. *See* Slobogin, *supra* note 1, at 91–93 & n.87.

12. *See supra* note 8.
13. In practice, however, defendants, especially indigent defendants, are often evaluated by state-employed evaluators at the *state's* request well before formal notice is given. *See infra* text accompanying notes 26–30.
14. *See, e.g.,* United States v. Alright, 388 F.2d 719 (4th Cir. 1968); Alexander v. United States, 380 F.2d 33, 39 (8th Cir. 1967); State v. Swinburne, 324 S.W.2d 746 (Mo. 1959). *But see* Johnson v. People, 172 Colo. 72, 470 P.2d 37 (1970).
15. 451 U.S. at 465.
16. *See, e.g.,* State v. Huson, 73 Wash.2d 660, 440 P.2d 192 (1968), *cert. denied,* 393 U.S. 1096 (1968); Ala. Stat. § 12.34.083 (1980).
17. Lee v. County Court, 267 N.E.2d 452, 461–62; 318 N.Y.S.2d 705, 719 (1971).
18. Model Penal Code § 4.09 (1962). The states that have adopted this provision or one similar to it are Alabama, Alaska, Colorado, Illinois, Massachusetts, Missouri, Montana, New York, Texas, Vermont, and Virginia.
19. Fed. R. Crim. P. 12.2
20. *E.g.,* United States v. Leonard, 609 F.2d 1163 (5th Cir. 1980); Gibson v. Zahradnick, 581 F2d 75, 79 (4th Cir. 1978); United States v. Reifsteck, 535 F.2d 1030 (8th Cir. 1976). Presumably, the states governed by these circuit courts are constitutionally required to follow the dictates of these decisions. *See also* State v. Mulrine, 55 Del. 65, 183 A.2d 831 (1962); State v. Whitlow, 45 N.J. 3, 21, 210 A.2d 763, 772 (1965).
21. *See, e.g.,* United States v. Alvarez, 519 F.2d 1036 (3d Cir. 1975); Houston v. State, 602 P.2d 784 (Ala. 1979); Pratt v. State, 39 Md. App. 442, 448, 387 A.2d 779, 783 (1978); People v. Hilliker, 29 Mich. App. 543, 547, 185 N.W.2d 831, 833 (1971).
22. Va. Code Ann. § 19.2–169.5(E) (1982).

23. *Id.* §§ 19.2-169.5(E) & 19.2-168.1.

24. *See, e.g.,* CRIMINAL JUSTICE MENTAL HEALTH STAN-DARDS, standard 11-3.2 (1986) [hereinafter cited as STANDARDS].

25. *See generally* Louisell & Hazard, *Insanity as a Defense: The Bifurcated Trial,* 49 CALIF. L. REV. 805 (1961).

26. *See* State v. Shaw, 471 P.2d 715 (Ariz. 1970); State *ex rel.* Boyd v. Green, 355 So. 2d 789 (Fla. 1978); Sanchez v. State, 562 P. 2d 270 (Wyo. 1977).

27. California, Colorado, and Wisconsin still retain the procedure.

28. Alaska, Delaware, Illinois, Indiana, Massachusetts, Michigan, New Jersey, North Carolina, Pennsylvania, Vermont, Washington, and West Virginia permit the procedure on this basis.

29. *See, e.g.,* Gibson v. Zahradnick, 581 F.2d 75 (4th Cir. 1978).

30. Hollis v. Smith, 571 F.2d 685, 691 (2d Cir. 1978); Annot., 9 A.L.R. 3d 990, 999–1001 (1966).

31. 451 U.S. at 462–63.

32. *Id.* at 469 n.13.

33. 387 U.S. 1 (1967).

34. *See, e.g.,* Lessard v. Schmidt, 349 F. Supp. 1078 (1972).

35. *See, e.g.,* Suzuki v. Yuen, 617 F.2d 173, 177–78 (9th Cir. 1980); Cramer v. Tyars, 488 P.2d 793 (Cal. 1979); State *ex rel.* Kiritsis v. Marion Probate Court, 381 N.E.2d 1245 (Ind. 1978); People *ex rel.* Keith v. Keith, 38 Ill. 2d 405, 231 N.E.2d 387 (1967).

36. ____U.S.____, 106 S. Ct. 2988 (1986). *See also* French v. Blackburn, 428 F. Supp. 1351 (M.D.N.C. 1977), *aff'd,* 443 U.S. 901 (1979), which summarily affirmed a lower court holding that the Fifth Amendment does not apply to civil commitment.

37. Coleman v. Alabama, 399 U.S. 1 (1970); Wade v. United States, 388 U.S. 218 (1967); Hamilton v. Alabama, 368 U.S. 52 (1961).

38. *See, e.g.,* People v. Rosenthal, 617 P.2d 551 (Colo. 1980); Houston v. State, 602 P.2d 784 (Alaska 1979).

39. *E.g.,* Hollis v. Smith, 571 F.2d 685 (2d Cir. 1978); United States v. Cohen, 530 F.2d 43 (5th Cir.), *cert. denied,* 429 U.S. 855 (1976); United States v. Greene, 497 F.2d 1068 (7th Cir. 1974), *cert. denied,* 420 U.S. 909 (1975); United States v. Mattson, 469 F.2d 1234 (9th Cir. 1972), *cert. denied,* 410 U.S. 986 (1973); United States *ex rel.* Stukes v. Shovlin, 464 F.2d 1211 (3d Cir. 1972); Thornton v. Corcoran, 407 F.2d 695 (D.C. Cir. 1969); United States v. Albright, 388 F.2d 719 (4th Cir. 1968); Houston v. State, 602 P.2d 784 (Alaska 1979); Presnell v. State, 241 Ga. 49, 243 S.E.2d 496 (1978); People v. Larsen, 74 Ill. 2d 348, 385 N.E.2d 679 (1979); People v. Martin, 386 Mich. 407, 192 N.W.2d 215 (1971), *cert denied,* 408 U.S. 929 (1972); State v. Whitlow, 45 N.J. 3, 210 A.2d 763 (1965); State v. Wilson, 26 Ohio App. 2d 23, 268 N.E. 2d 814 (1971); Shepard v. Bowe, 250 Or. 288, 442 P.2d 238 (1968); Commonwealth v. Stukes, 435 Pa. 535, 257 A.2d 828 (1969).

40. 451 U.S. at 470 & n.14.

41. 388 U.S. 218 (1967).

42. *Id.* at 230–31.

43. *Id.* at 231.

44. No. 78-1451 (D.C. Cir. Dec. 24, 1980).

45. *Id.* at 24.

46. *Id.* at 27.

47. Thornton v. Corcoran, 407 F.2d 695 (D.C. Cir. 1969); STANDARDS, *supra* note 24, standard 7-3.6(c)(ii), 7-3.6(d), and accompanying commentary.

48. 388 U.S. at 237–38.

49. *See* STANDARDS, *supra* note 24, standard 7-3(c)(i) and accompanying commentary.

50. *See, e.g.,* Lewin, *Indigency—Informal and Formal Procedures to Provide Partisan Psychiatric Assistance to the Poor,* 52 IOWA L. REV. 453, 487 (1966); Note, *The Indigent's Right to an Adequate Defense: Expert and Investigational Assistance in Criminal Proceedings,* 44 CORNELL L. REV. 632, 639–41 (1970).

51. 105 S.Ct. 1087 (1985); (1985); *see also* Satterfield v. Mitchell, 572 F.2d 443 (4th Cir. 1978); Thigpen v. State, 372 So.2d 385 (Ala. 1979); McGarty v. O'Brien, 188 F.2d 141, 144 (1st Cir.), *cert. denied,* 339 U.S. 966 (1950). *But see* Hammett v. State, 578 S.W.2d 699, 720–21 (Tex. Crim. App. 1979) (Odum, Roberts, & Phillips, JJ., concurring); ALA. CODE § 15-12-21(d) (1975) (allowing $500 for expert assistance).

52. For a description of such a program in Virginia, see G. MELTON, L. WEITHORN, & C. SLOBOGIN, COMMUNITY MENTAL HEALTH CENTERS AND THE COURTS: AN EVALUATION OF COMMUNITY-BASED FORENSIC SERVICES (1985).

53. 425 F. Supp. 1038 (E.D.N.Y. 1976), *aff'd,* 556 F.2d 556 (2d Cir. 1977).

54. 425 F. Supp. at 1025.

55. 519 F.2d 1036 (3d Cir. 1975). *See also* Houston v. State, 602 P.2d 784 (Ala. 1979); Pratt v. State, 39 Md. App. 442, 387 A.2d 779 (1978), *aff'd,* 284 Md. 516, 398 A.2d 421 (1979).

56. 519 F.2d at 1047.

57. Carr v. Watkins, 227 Md. 578, 177 A.2d 841 (1962); Berry V. Moench, 8 Utah 2d 191, 331 P.2d 814 (1958). *Cf.* Roe v. Ingraham, 480 F.2d 102 (2d Cir. 1973); Hammond v. Setna Ins., Ohio, 243 F. Supp. 793 (1965).

58. The most significant limitation in the present context is the traditional rule that the privilege may not be asserted at any civil or criminal trial by an individual whose mental state is at issue in that trial. *See infra* § 3.04(c).

59. Those states that recognize both a psychologist–patient and a social worker–patient privilege are Colorado, Kentucky, Louisiana, Michigan, Oregon, South Dakota, Utah, and Virginia. Those that recognize only a psychologist–patient privilege are Alaska, Arizona, Arkansas, California, Connecticut, Georgia, Idaho, Illinois, Indiana, Kansas, Maryland, Massachusetts, Michigan, Minnesota, Mississippi, Missouri, New Hampshire, New Jersey, New Mexico, New York, Ohio, Oklahoma, Pennsylvania, Tennessee, Texas, Vermont, Washington, Wisconsin, and Wyoming.

60. *See generally* Roche, *The Position for Confidentiality of the Presentence Investigation Report,* 29 ALBANY L. REV. 206 (1965).

61. Chandler v. Florida, 449 U.S. 560 (1981); Richmond Newpapers, Inc. v. Virginia, 448 U.S. 555 (1980).

62. Block v. Sacramento Clinical Labs, 131 Cal. App. 3d 306, 182 Cal. Rptr. 438 (1982).

63. The following states require child abuse to be reported: Alabama, Alaska, Arizona, Arkansas, California, Colorado, Connecticut, Delaware, Florida, Georgia, Hawaii, Idaho, Illinois, Iowa, Kentucky, Louisiana, Maine, Maryland, Massachusetts, Michigan, Minnesota, Missouri, Nebraska, Nevada, New Hampshire, New Jersey, New Mexico, New York, North Carolina, North Dakota, Ohio, Oklahoma, Oregon, Pennsylvania, Rhode Island, South Carolina, Tennessee, Virginia, Washington, West Virginia, Wisconsin, and Wyoming.

64. *See, e.g.,* CAL. EVID. CODE § 1024 (West 1980); CONN. GEN. STAT. ANN. § 52-146(f) (West Supp. 1983); KY. REV. STAT. ANN. § 335.170 (Bobbs-Merrill 1980); LA. REV. STAT. ANN. § 37:2714 (West 1974 & Supp. 1983); MASS. ANN. LAWS Ch. 233, § 20B(A) (Michie/Law. Co-op. 1975); N.M. STAT. ANN. § 43-1-19 (1978 & Supp. 1979); N.Y. CIV. PRAC. LAW § 4508 (McKinney 1976); OKLA. STAT. ANN. tit. 59, § 261.6 (West Supp. 1982–83); OR. REV. STAT. § 675.580 (1979); S.D. COMP. LAWS ANN. § 36-26-30 (1977); TEX. REV. CIV. STAT. ANN. art. 5561 (H) (Vernon Supp. 1982); UTAH CODE ANN. § 58-35-10 (Supp. 1981).

65. Tarasoff v. Regents, Univ. of Cal., 551 P.2d 334 (Cal. 1976).

66. *See* Lipari v. Sears, Roebuck, 497 F. Supp. 185 (1980) (Nebraska); Bradley Center, Inc. v. Wessner, 161 Ga. App. 262, 287 S.E. 2d 716 (1982); Estate of Mathes v. Ireland, 419 N.E.2d 782 (Ind. 1981); Cairl v. State, 323 N.W.2d 20 (Minn. 1982); McIntosh v. Milano, 168 N.J. Super. 459, 403 A.2d 500 (1979).

67. Hicks v. United States, 511 F.2d 407, 415–16 (D.C. Cir. 1975). Hawaii has granted court-ordered psychiatrists immunity from *Tarasoff*-type claims. Seibel v. Kemble, 631 P.2d 173 (Haw. 1981).

68. A number of courts have refused to recognize a duty-to-warn claim under the particular circumstances of the case, but have otherwise left the question open: Matter of Estate of Votteller, 327 N.W.2d 759 (Iowa 1982) (no duty to warn where victim knows of danger); Ross v. Central Louisana State Hospital, 392 So.2d 698 (La. App. 1980) (no duty to warn of need for medications where evidence shows schizophrenia does not increase patient's dangerousness, and medication does not reduce it); Furr v. Spring Grove State Hospital, 53 Md. App. 474, 454 A.2d 414 (1983) (no duty to warn where victim not identifiable); Show v. Glickman, 45 Md. App. 718, 415 A.2d 625 (1980) (no duty to warn where patient does not divulge intent to injure third party); Cairl v. State, 323 N.W.2d 20 (Minn. 1982) (no duty to warn in the absence of specific threat to specific person); Sherrill v. Wilson, 653 S.W.2d 661 (Mo. enbanc 1983) (no duty to control where danger directed at the general public); Leedy v. Harnett, 510 F. Supp. 1125 (M.D. Pa. 1981) (no duty to warn where

danger posed to plaintiffs does not differ from that posed to anyone else patient may have contact with).

69. Thompson v. County of Alameda, 27 Cal. 3d 741, 614 P.2d 728, 167 Cal. Rptr. 70 (1980). However, it should be noted that the same court found a clinician liable for harm to the threatened victim's son, as well as the victim herself, on the grounds that the former harm was "foreseeable." Hedlund v. Superior Court, 34 Cal. 3d 695, 669 P.2d 41, 194 Cal. Rptr. 805 (1983).

70. *See* Note, *Where the Public Peril Begins: A Survey of Psycho-Therapists to Determine the Effects of* Tarasoff, 31 STAN L. REV. 165 (1978).

71. *Official Actions, Council on Psychiatry and Law,* 141 AM. J. PSYCHIATRY 487 (1984).

72. For states that apply the balancing approach, see CAL. EVID. CODE § 1010-28(f) (West 1967); CONN. GEN. STAT. ANN. § 52-146(c) (West Supp. 1983); ILL. ANN. STAT. ch. 91½, § 810(a)(1) (Smith–Hurd Supp. 1983–84); ME. REV. STAT. ANN. tit. 32, § 7005 (Supp. 1982–83); MASS. ANN. LAWS ch. 233, § 20B(c) (Michie/Law. Co-op 1975); *Tenn. Code Ann.* § 24-1-207 (1980); VA. CODE ANN. § 8.01-400.2 (Supp. 1983).

73. For a general treatment of the informed consent doctrine, see Meisel, Ross, & Appelbaum, *Toward a Model of the Legal Doctrine of Informed Consent,* 134 AM. J. PSYCHIATRY 285 (1977).

74. For a discussion of malpractice and negligent misdiagnosis actions, see R. SLOVENKO, PSYCHIATRY AND LAW 399–400 (1973).

75. These are California, Massachusetts, Michigan, Missouri, Nevada, New York, Ohio, Oregon, and Pennsylvania.

76. American Psychological Association, *Ethical Principles of Psychologists,* 36 AM. PSYCHOLOGIST 633 (1981) [hereinafter cited as *APA Principles*].

77. AMERICAN PSYCHOLOGICAL ASSOCIATION, STANDARDS FOR PROVIDERS OF PSYCHOLOGICAL SERVICES (1977) [hereinafter cited as APA STANDARDS].

78. "[Psychologists] only provide services and only use techniques for which they are qualified by training and experience." *APA Principles, supra* note 76, principle 2.

79. Diamond & Louisell, *The Psychiatrist as an Expert Witness: Some Ruminations and Speculations,* 63 MICH. L. REV. 1335 (1965).

80. Shah, *Editorial,* APA Monitor, Feb. 1977, at 2.

81. WHO IS THE CLIENT? (J. Monahan ed. 1980).

82. *APA Principles, supra* note 76, principle 3c.

83. "When a psychologist agrees to provide services to a client at the request of a third party, the psychologist assumes the responsibility of clarifying the nature of the relationships to all parties concerned." *APA Principles, supra* note 76, principle 6.6.

84. Psychologists have the responsibility to "fully inform consumers as to the purpose and nature of an evaluative . . . procedure." *APA Principles, supra* note 76, principle 6.

85. Clingempeel, Mulvey, & Repucci, *A National Study of Ethical Dilemmas of Psychologists in the Criminal Justice Sys-*

tem, in WHO IS THE CLIENT?, *supra* note 81 at 126. (Three-fourths of the survey respondents identified confidentiality issues as among the three major ethical dilemmas.) *See also* Siegel, *Privacy, Ethics, and Confidentiality,* 10 PROF. PSYCHOLOGY 249, 352 (1979) (referring to "evidence of the mounting concern across the country about the apparent collision course being travelled by those helping professionals who adhere to the concept of the Hippocratic Oath . . . and those who are caught up in the public's need, and perhaps right, to know").

86. Statutes may identify explicit exceptions to ordinary confidentiality practices—for example, the requirement to notify authorities upon learning of the abuse of children. *See infra* § 3.04(a).

87. The concern for public safety underlying the *Tarasoff* ruling, *see supra* § 3.04(b), is paralleled by the clinician's ethical obligation to breach confidence if there is a "clear danger to the person or to others." *APA Principles, supra* note 76, principle 5.

88. *See* Siegel, *supra* note 85, at 249–50.

89. There has been limited empirical research on the relationship between levels of confidentiality and degree of self-disclosure in either therapy or in forensic situations. A recent analogue study involving college student subjects demonstrated a direct relationship between level of confidentiality and level of self-disclosure.

Woods & McNemara, *Confidentiality: Its Effect on Interview Behavior,* 11 PROF. PSYCHOLOGY 714 (1980).

90. *APA Principles, supra* note 76, principle 6.

91. *Id.* principle 5.

92. APA STANDARDS, *supra* note 77, at 9 (standard 2.3.5 requires the clinician to "assist the user in limiting disclosure only to information required by the present circumstance").

93. In this case, the clinical staff agreed to release a post hoc opinion regarding mental state at the time of the offense *only* if the defendant's attorney provided a written authorization for the amended report. The attorney refused to provide such a release, and no report was sent.

94. *APA Principles, supra* note 76, principle 3c. *See also* APA STANDARDS, *supra* note 77, standard 2.2.2 (requires psychologists to "safeguard the interests of the user with regard to personal, legal, and civil rights").

95. Given the Supreme Court's recent decision in Hudson v. Palmer, 468 U.S. 517 (1984), in which the Court held that a prisoner has no "reasonable expectation of privacy" even as to personal effects located in his or her cell, this may no longer be a colorable argument. However, the general issue raised by this example remains: When, if ever, may a clinical opinion rely on illegally obtained evidence?

96. *See supra* note 87.

Chapter 4

1. Winick, *Incompetency to Stand Trial: Developments in the Law,* in MENTALLY DISORDERED OFFENDERS: PERSPECTIVES FROM LAW AND SOCIAL SCIENCE 3 (J. Monahan & H. Steadman eds. 1983).

2. *Id.* at 3–4. *See also* GROUP FOR THE ADVANCEMENT OF PSYCHIATRY, MISUSE OF PSYCHIATRY IN THE CRIMINAL COURTS: COMPETENCY TO STAND TRIAL (1974).

3. 2 W. BLACKSTONE, COMMENTARIES ON THE LAW OF ENGLAND 2181 (W. Jones ed. 1916). Blackstone also notes the requirement that the defendant be competent throughout all phases of the criminal process, going on to state that if the defendant "loses his senses" after conviction but prior to judgment, judgment shall not be pronounced, and if the defendant "becomes of nonsane memory" after judgment, execution shall be stayed. *Id.* at 2182.

4. Frith's Case, 22 How. St. Tr. 307 (1790).

5. J. MILLER, HANDBOOK ON CRIMINAL LAW 28–32 (1934). While the substantive criminal law is found in statute in this country, its original source was the English common law.

6. United States v. Lawrence, 26 F. Cas. 887 (D.C. Cir. 1835).

7. Youtsey v. United States, 97 F. 937, 940–41 (6th Cir. 1899).

8. Drope v. Missouri, 420 U.S. 162, 172 (1975).

9. *Incompetency to Stand Trial,* 81 HARV. L. REV. 454, 457–58 (1967).

10. Dusky v. United States, 362 U.S. 402 (1960).

11. *Id.*

12. As is true in other areas (e.g., civil commitment; *see infra* Chapter 8), statutory definitions vary among the states. The statutory definitions are collected in Favole, *Mental Disability in the American Criminal Process: A Four-Issue Survey,* in MENTALLY DISORDERED OFFENDERS: PERSPECTIVES FROM LAW AND SOCIAL SCIENCE 247 (J. Monahan & H. Steadman eds. 1983).

13. One commentary has observed that despite the fact that concerns for fairness underlie the competency doctrine, "as a practical matter . . . these considerations cannot require that every defendant have 'a high degree of performance capacity' . . . Many defendants lack the intelligence or the legal sophistication to participate actively in the conduct of their defense. But enlarging the class of persons considered incompetent to stand trial to include all such defendants would fundamentally alter the administration of the criminal law." *Incompetency to Stand Trial, supra* note 9, at 459.

14. Wieter v. Settle, 193 F. Supp. 318, 321–22 (W.D. Mo. 1961).

15. Favole, *supra* note 12, at Table 1, 248–57.

16. MICH. STAT. ANN. § 800 (1020) (1) (1985).

17. N.J. STAT. ANN. § 2C:4-4 (1985).

18. CRIMINAL JUSTICE MENTAL HEALTH STANDARDS, standard 7-4.1 (1984) [hereinafter cited as STANDARDS].

19. The commentary urges that the evaluation of competency consider (1) whether the defendant has a perception of the process not distorted by mental illness or disability; (2) whether the defendant has the capacity to maintain the attorney–client relationship, including the ability to discuss the facts with counsel without "paranoid distrust," and to discuss strategy; (3) whether the defendant can recall and relate factual information; (4) whether, if necessary, the defendant has the ability to testify in his or her own defense; and (5) whether these skills are proportional to the relative complexity and severity of the case. *Id.* at 7-152–7-154.

20. GROUP FOR THE ADVANCEMENT OF PSYCHIATRY, *supra* note 2, at 896–97.

21. Winick, *supra* note 1, at 9.

22. AMERICAN PSYCHIATRIC ASSOCIATION, THE PRINCIPLES OF MEDICAL ETHICS, WITH ANNOTATIONS ESPECIALLY APPLICABLE TO PSYCHIATRY, § 4, anno. 13, at 7 (1981). *See also supra* Chapter 3, for more detailed discussion of the ethical contours of the forensic evaluation.

23. STANDARDS, *supra* note 18, standard 7-3.2(d).

24. Pate v. Robinson, 383 U.S. 375 (1966); Drope v. Missouri, 420 U.S. 162 (1975).

25. Drope v. Missouri, 420 U.S. at 180.

26. STANDARDS, *supra* note 18, standard 7-4.2(c).

27. *Id.* commentary at 7-160–7-161.

28. Rosenberg & McGarry, *Competency for Trial: The Making of an Expert,* 128 AM. J. PSYCHIATRY 82 (1972).

29. R. ROESCH & S. GOLDING, COMPETENCY TO STAND TRIAL 50–52 (1980).

30. *Id.* at 193–97; Roesch & Golding, *Legal and Judicial Interpretation of Competency to Stand Trial,* 16 CRIMINOLOGY 420 (1978).

31. Geller & Lister, *The Process of Criminal Commitment for Pretrial Psychiatric Examination: An Evaluation,* 135 AM. J. PSYCHIATRY 53 (1978).

32. A. STONE, MENTAL HEALTH AND THE LAW: A SYSTEM IN TRANSITION 63 (1976).

33. Even for prisoners, there is a residual liberty interest in avoiding forced psychiatric treatment. *See* Vitek v. Jones, 445 U.S. 480 (1980).

34. Typically, statutes providing for the hospitalization of defendants for evaluation of competency to stand trial fail to provide explicit authority for involuntary treatment of those defendants.

35. R. ROESCH & S. GOLDING, *supra* note 29, at 191–93; Roesch & Golding, *supra* note 30.

36. Burt & Morris, *A Proposal for the Abolition of the Incompetency Plea,* 40 U. CHI. L. REV. 66, 88 (1972).

37. *Id.*

38. Roesch & Golding, *Treatment and Disposition of Defendants to Stand Trial: A Review and Proposal,* 2 INT'L J. L. PSYCHIATRY 349, 365 (1979). *See also* LABORATORY OF COMMUNITY PSYCHIATRY, COMPETENCY TO STAND TRIAL AND MENTAL ILLNESS (1974).

39. Laben, Kashgarian, Nessa, & Spencer, *Reform from the Inside: Mental Health Center Evaluations of Competency to Stand Trial,* 5 J. COMM. PSYCHOL. 52 (1977). One of us (Petrila) began the decentralization of the Missouri forensic system when he was Director of Forensic Services from 1979 to 1981. Two of us (Melton and Slobogin) were involved in decentralizing the Virginia forensic system; our experiences are recounted in G. MELTON, L. WEITHORN, & C. SLOBOGIN, COMMUNITY MENTAL HEALTH CENTERS AND THE COURTS: AN EVALUATION OF COMMUNITY-BASED FORENSIC SERVICES (1985).

40. In 1979, at least 4 of the 11 federal circuits and 17 states allowed psychologists to testify on essentially the same footing as psychiatrists. These included California, Colorado, Georgia, Indiana, Kentucky, Maryland, Michigan, New Mexico, Oklahoma, Oregon, Pennsylvania, Rhode Island, South Dakota, Tennessee, Texas, Virginia, and Wisconsin. Comment, *The Psychologist as Expert Witness: Science in the Courtroom?,* 38 MD. L. REV. 539, n.21, n.22, p. 546, and Appendix (1979).

41. U.S. CONST. amend. VI.

42. U.S. CONST. amend. VIII.

43. *Incompetency to Stand Trial, supra* note 9, at 470.

44. Carter v. United States, 252 F.2d 608, 617–18 (D.C. Cir. 1957).

45. R. ROESCH & S. GOLDING, *supra* note 29, at 193.

46. *Id.*

47. *See, e.g.,* LABORATORY OF COMMUNITY PSYCHIATRY, *supra* note 38 (Massachusetts); H. STEADMAN, BEATING A RAP?: DEFENDANTS FOUND INCOMPETENT TO STAND TRIAL (1979) (New York); R. ROESCH & S. GOLDING, *supra* note 29 (North Carolina); Hess & Thomas, *Incompetency to Stand Trial: Procedures, Results and Problems,* 119 AM. J. PSYCHIATRY 713 (1963) (Michigan); Petrila, *The Insanity Defense and Other Mental Health Dispositions in Missouri,* 5 INT'L J. L. PSYCHIATRY 81 (1982); Pfeiffer, Eisenstein, & Dabbs, *Mental Competency Evaluations for the Federal Courts,* 144 J. NERVOUS MENTAL DISEASE 320 (1967); Vann, *Pretrial Determination and Judicial Decisionmaking: An Analysis of the Use of Psychiatric Information in the Administration of Criminal Justice,* 43 U. DET. L.J. 13 (1965); Williams & Miller, *The Processing and Disposition of Incompetent Mentally Ill Offenders,* 5 LAW & HUM. BEHAV. 245 (1981) (Florida).

48. Roesch & Golding, *supra* note 38, at 349–50.

49. 406 U.S. 715 (1972).

50. *Id.* at 737–38.

51. A. STONE, *supra* note 32, at 212.

52. Roesch & Golding, *supra* note 38, have summarized a dozen proposals that deal with limitations on treatment and/or disposition of criminal charges. They note that most of the proposals advocate a six-month limit on treatment, with an additional six months available if needed—an addendum that Stone has also suggested, *supra* note 32, at 212. Other suggested time limits on commitment have ranged from 90 days, with a possible 90-day extension (the ABA) to six months, with indef-

inite extensions of one year available (Law Reform Commission of Canada).

53. Roesch & Golding, *supra* note 38, at 355.

54. *Id.* at 357. Those states allowing automatic commitment were Alabama, Colorado, Connecticut, District of Columbia, Georgia, Idaho, Indiana, Louisiana, Missouri, Montana, Nebraska, Nevada, New York, North Dakota, Ohio, South Dakota, Utah, Virginia, Wisconsin and Wyoming. Those states that did not limit the length of commitment included Alaska, Arkansas, Colorado, Delaware, the District of Columbia, Hawaii, Idaho, Illinois, Kentucky, Maryland, Massachusetts, Mississippi, Missouri, Montana, Nebraska, New Hampshire, Nevada, New jersey, New Mexico, Oklahoma, Tennessee, Utah, Vermont, Virginia and Wyoming. *See id.* Table 2.

55. H. STEADMAN, *supra* note 47, at 103–04.

56. STANDARDS, *supra* note 18, standard 7-4.9.

57. *Id.* standard 7-4.11.

58. 406 U.S. 715 at 738.

59. New York's experience is illustrative of this point. For example, an individual committed as incompetent to stand trial may receive no passes or furloughs unless an internal review by a forensic committee occurs. This practice is not required when a civilly committed patient is involved. The regulations governing this practice focus on the patient's supposed dangerousness. Anecdotal evidence suggests that the issue of the individual's restoration to competency over time may assume secondary importance because of staff preoccupation with dangerousness. In turn, this may result in increased reluctance on the part of staff to move for dismissal of charges, in part because facility control over the individual would be loosened.

60. Roesch & Golding, *supra* note 38, at 364. In 1979, 27 states and the District of Columbia had no guidelines for dismissing charges. These states included Alabama, Alaska, Arkansas, California, Colorado, Delaware, the District of Columbia, Georgia, Hawaii, Indiana, Iowa, Kentucky, Louisiana, Mississippi, Missouri, Nebraska, Nevada, New Hampshire, New Jersey, New Mexico, Ohio, Oklahoma, South Dakota, Tennessee, Texas, Utah, Vermont and Virginia. Roesch & Golding, *supra* note 38.

61. Gobert, *Competency to Stand Trial: A Pre- and Post-*Jackson *Analysis,* 40 TENN. L. REV. 659–60 (1973).

62. Burt & Morris, *supra* note 36.

63. *Id.* at 76.

64. FIRST TENTATIVE DRAFT: CRIMINAL JUSTICE MENTAL HEALTH STANDARDS, standard 7-4.13 (1983).

65. *Id.* alternative A.

66. *Id.* alternative B.

67. Both times are given, apparently reflecting ambivalence on the part of the drafters.

68. *Id.* Alternative B.

69. *Id.* commentary at 7-239.

70. *Id.* alternative C.

71. *Id.* commentary at 7-240.

72. *See generally id.* standards 7-7.3–7-7.11.

73. 46 A.L.R. 3d 544 (1972).

74. *See, e.g.,* Commonwealth *ex rel.* Cummins v. Price, 421 Pa. 396, 218 A.2d 758 (1966), *cert. denied,* 385 U.S. 869. The court in *Cummins* noted that "for over 100 years, lack of memory in murder cases has been a common and frequent defense." 218 A.2d at 760. However, to recognize amnesia as a bar to trial would "turn over the determination of crime and criminal liability to psychiatrists, whose opinions are usually based in large part upon defendant's self-serving statements, instead of to Courts and juries." *Id.* at 763.

75. State v. McClendon, 103 Ariz. 103, 437 P.2d 421, 424, 425 (1968).

76. 129 App. D.C. 107, 391 F.2d 460 (1968).

77. 391 F.2d at 463–64.

78. 325 F. Supp. 485 (D.C. Tenn. 1971).

79. Winick, *Psychotropic Medication and Competence to Stand Trial,* 1977 AM. BAR FOUND. RESEARCH J. 769 (1977).

80. *See supra* note 13.

81. *See* those studies cited *supra* note 47.

82. Winick, *supra* note 79.

83. STANDARDS, *supra* note 18, commentary at 7-245.

84. *Id.* standard 7-4.14. *See also* GROUP FOR THE ADVANCEMENT OF PSYCHIATRY, *supra* note 2, at 904.

85. 389 A.2d 1379 (1978).

86. *Cf., e.g.,* the case of Project Release v. Cuomo, 722 F.2d (2d Cir. 1983), in which the court of appeals upheld administrative procedures for determining a nonconsenting patient's competency to refuse treatment and need for treatment, *with* Rogers v. Comm'r Dep't of Mental Health, 390 Mass. 489, 458 N.E.2d 308 (1983), in which the Supreme Judicial Court of Massachusetts ruled that *judicial* determinations of these issues were a prerequisite to treating a nonconsenting patient.

87. LABORATORY OF COMMUNITY PSYCHIATRY, *supra* note 38; R. ROESCH & S. GOLDING, *supra* note 29; H. STEADMAN, *supra* note 47.

88. Steadman, Monahan, Hartshorne, Davis, & Robbins, *Mentally Disordered Offenders: A National Survey of Patients and Facilities,* 6 LAW & HUM. BEHAV. 31 (1982).

89. *Id.* at 33.

90. R. ROESCH & S. GOLDING, *supra* note 29, at 47–49.

91. H. STEADMAN, *supra* note 47.

92. *Id.* at 30.

93. *Id.* at 30–31.

94. *Id.* at 30–33.

95. *Id.* at 33–37.

96. For a review, *see* R. ROESCH & S. GOLDING, *supra* note 29, at 52–54.

97. *Id.* at 151.

98. *Id.* at 148–49.

99. Poythress & Stock, *Competency to Stand Trial: A Historical Review and Some New Data,* 8 J. PSYCHIATRY L. 131 (1980).

100. LABORATORY OF COMMUNITY PSYCHIATRY, *supra* note 38; Golding, Roesch, & Schreiber, *Assessment and Conceptualization of Competency to Stand Trial: Preliminary Data*

on the Interdisciplinary Fitness Interview, 8 LAW & HUM. BEHAV. 321 (1984); Roesch, Determining Competency to Stand Trial: An Examination of Evaluation Procedures in an Institutional Setting & 47 J. CONSULTING CLINICAL PSYCHOLOGY 542 (1979).

101. Golding, Roesch, & Schreiber, supra note 100.

102. R. ROESCH & S. GOLDING, supra note 29, at 188–91; Roesch, A Brief, Immediate Screening Interview to Determine Competency to Stand Trial: A Feasibility Study, 5 CRIM. JUST. BEHAV. 241 (1978).

103. R. ROESCH & S. GOLDING, supra note 29, at 188–91.

104. Golding, Roesch, & Schreiber, supra note 100.

105. Poythress & Stock, supra note 99.

106. See, e.g., R. ROESCH & S. GOLDING, supra note 29, at 188–91; Roesch, supra note 102.

107. See Golding, Roesch, & Schreiber, supra note 100.

108. See G. MELTON, L. WEITHORN, & C. SLOBOGIN, supra note 39; PETRELLA & POYTHRESS, The Quality of Forensic Examinations: An Interdisciplinary Study, 51 J. CONSULTING CLINICAL PSYCHOLOGY 76 (1983).

109. R. ROESCH & S. GOLDING, supra note 29, at 50–52; Roesch, supra note 102.

110. See, e.g., Roesch, Eaves, Sollner, Normandin, & Glackman, Evaluating Fitness to Stand Trial: A Comparative Analysis of Fit and Unfit Defendants, 4 INT'L J.L. PSYCHIATRY 145 (1981).

111. See, e.g., G. MELTON, L. WEITHORN, & C. SLOBOGIN, supra note 39.

112. See AMERICAN PSYCHIATRIC ASSOCIATION, DIAGNOSTIC AND STATISTICAL MANUAL OF MENTAL DISORDERS 470 (3d ed. 1980).

113. See, e.g., LABORATORY OF COMMUNITY PSYCHIATRY, supra note 38, at 100; R. ROESCH & S. GOLDING, supra note 29, at 188–91; Golding, Roesch, & Schreiber, supra note 100; Poythress & Stock, supra note 99; Roesch, supra note 102.

114. See generally G. MELTON, L. WEITHORN, & C. SLOBOGIN, supra note 39.

115. See Torrey & Taylor, Cheap Labor from Foreign Nations, 130 AM. J. PSYCHIATRY 428 (1973).

116. Cf. LABORATORY OF COMMUNITY PSYCHIATRY, supra note 38, at 67 (Competency Screening Test intended for administration by laypersons).

117. For a report of the complete project, see id.

118. Lipsitt, Lelos, & McGarry, Competency for Trial: A Screening Instrument, 128 AM. J. PSYCHIATRY 105 (1971).

119. LABORATORY OF COMMUNITY PSYCHIATRY, supra note 38, at 98.

120. See, e.g., R. ROESCH & S. GOLDING, supra note 29, at 60–61.

121. Id. at 63, 181–83.

122. Id. at 148–49; Roesch, supra note 102.

123. LABORATORY OF COMMUNITY PSYCHIATRY, supra note 38, at 69.

124. R. ROESCH & S. GOLDING, supra note 29, at 60.

125. Randolph, Hicks, & Mason, The Competency Screening Test: A Replication and Extension, 8 CRIM. JUST. BEHAV. 471 (1981).

126. LABORATORY OF COMMUNITY PSYCHIATRY, supra note 38, at 98–125.

127. Id. at 100.

128. Id. at 41.

129. Reliability varied with both the degree of incompetence of the defendant and the experience of the rater. Id. at 120.

130. Schreiber, Assessing Competency to Stand Trial: A Case Study of Technology Diffusion in Four States, 6 BULL. AM. ACAD. PSYCHIATRY L. 439 (1978).

131. LABORATORY OF COMMUNITY PSYCHIATRY, supra note 38, at 98–125.

132. S. Golding & R. Roesch, Interdisciplinary Fitness Interview Training Manual (unpublished manuscript n.d.).

133. Golding, Roesch, & Schreiber, supra note 100.

134. Id.

135. Id.

136. Cf. Davidson & Saul, Youth Advocacy in the Juvenile Court: A Clash of Paradigms, in LEGAL REFORMS AFFECTING CHILD AND YOUTH SERVICES (G. Melton ed. 1982) (juvenile courts are wedded to case-by-case analyses of juvenile delinquency).

137. S. Golding & R. Roesch, supra note 132, at 8.

138. G. MELTON, L. WEITHORN, & C. SLOBOGIN, supra note 39, at 104–06, 109–10.

139. Id.

Chapter 5

1. Such a logic underlies the principle of least restrictive alternative in civil contexts. See, e.g., Shelton v. Tucker, 364 U.S. 479 (1960); Lake v. Cameron, 364 F.2d 657 (D.C. Cir. 1966).

2. Literally "the sovereign as parent," "parens patriae" refers to the state's power and duty to care for dependent persons.

3. There are a few legal questions that do require findings akin to general incompetency (e.g., civil commitment based on inability to care for oneself; guardianship, when not limited to specific purposes). However, even when civil commitment is based on inability to care for oneself, it cannot be assumed that the patient is incompetent to make all important decisions or that his or her liberty and privacy interests are extinguished by the fact of commitment or the mental disorder leading to it. See, e.g., Youngberg v. Romeo, 457 U.S. 307 (1982); Rogers v. Okin, 634 F.2d 650 (1st Cir. 1980), remanded on other grounds sub nom. Mills v. Rogers, 457 U.S. 291 (1982).

4. Strictly speaking, competency to testify is not a "criminal" issue, in that the question can also be raised in

civil trials when a prospective witness's competency is in question. Consider, for example, the case in which a five-year-old child is the primary witness to an accident alleged to result from a civil respondent's negligence. However, we are considering the issue in this chapter because it arises most commonly when a questionably competent person is the victim of a criminal offense.

5. Portions of this section previously appeared in Melton, *Making Room for Psychology in* Miranda *Doctrine: Juveniles' Waiver of Rights,* 7 LAW & HUM. BEHAV. 67, 77–80 (1983).

6. As Kamisar has argued, "necessity" may have colored some concepts of what was "fair." That is, police practices may have sometimes been upheld because of a desire not to "hamstring" the police more than an honest appraisal of the coerciveness of the practice. *See* Kamisar, *A Dissent from the* Miranda *Dissents: Some Comments on the "New" Fifth Amendment and the "Old" Voluntariness Test,* 65 MICH. L. REV. 59, 82–89 (1966).

7. For a more comprehensive review of the law of confessions, *see generally* C. WHITEBREAD & C. SLOBOGIN, CRIMINAL PROCEDURE: AN ANALYSIS OF CASES AND CONCEPTS ch. 16 (1986).

8. 297 U.S. 278.

9. For a listing of these cases through the late 1950s, see Spano v. New York, 360 U.S. 315 n. 2 (1959).

10. *See* Fikes v. Alabama, 352 U.S. 191, 197. *But cf.* Kamisar, *What Is an "Involuntary" Confession? Some Comments on Inbau and Reid's Criminal Interrogation and Confessions,* 17 RUTGERS L. REV. 728, at 755–59 (1963) (Supreme Court rarely directly analyzed the willfulness of the defendant's confession).

11. *See* Escobedo v. Illinois, 378 U.S. 478 (1964); Massiah v. United States, 377 U.S. 201 (1964). The Supreme Court resurrected *Massiah* Sixth Amendment analysis in Brewer v. Williams, 430 U.S. 387 (1977); *see* Kamisar, Brewer v. Williams, Massiah, *and* Miranda: *What Is Interrogation? When Does It Matter?,* 67 GEO. L. REV. 1 (1978).

12. 384 U.S. 436 (1965).

13. *Id.* at 444. Voluntary confessions taken in violation of this rule may still be admissible for purposes other than establishing the guilt of the defendant. *See* Oregon v. Hass, 420 U.S. 714 (1975) (statements obtained in violation of *Miranda* may be used to impeach defendant's testimony); Michigan v. Tucker, 417 U.S. 433 (1974) (evidence derived from leads in statement taken in violation of *Miranda* held admissible); Milton v. Wainwright, 407 U.S. 371 (1972) (admission of confession taken in violation of defendant's right to counsel held to be harmless error); Harris v. New York, 401 U.S. 222 (1971) (statement obtained in violation of *Miranda* may be used to impeach defendant's testimony but not as part of prosecution's case-in-chief).

14. 384 U.S. at 444.

15. *Id.* at 444–45.

16. *See id.* at 455–57. *See also* Rhode Island v. Innis, 446 U.S. 291, 301 (1980).

17. *See* Spano v. New York, 360 U.S. 315, 326 (1959) (Douglas, J., concurring).

18. For an eloquent critique of this body of law, see Kamisar, *supra* note 6.

19. *See supra* note 13.

20. *Cf.* Rhode Island v. Innis, 446 U.S. at 298–302 (*Miranda* involved more than express questioning of a defendant while in custody; it was intended to support the will of the defendant in the "interrogation environment," regardless of police intent). Chief Justice Burger's opinion concurring in the judgment is a particularly clear statement that *Miranda* is not likely to be overruled: "The meaning of *Miranda* has become reasonably clear and law enforcement practices have adjusted to its strictures; I would neither overrule *Miranda,* disparage it, nor extend it at this late date." *Id.* at 304.

21. For a recent Supreme Court case decided according to an analysis of due process, see Mincey v. Arizona, 437 U.S. 385 (1978) (statements taken from wounded suspect while in intensive care in helpless, debilitated condition inadmissible).

22. Oregon v. Hass, 420 U.S. 714 (1975); Harris v. New York, 401 U.S. 222 (1971).

23. Milton v. Wainwright, 407 U.S. 317 (1972).

24. Beckwith v. United States, 425 U.S. 341 (1976).

25. *Miranda* itself was of course concerned with psychological coercion. After reviewing the cases involving physical brutality that the Court had previously decided, 384 U.S. at 445–48, Chief Justice Warren stressed that "the modern practice of in-custody interrogation is psychologically rather than physically oriented." *Id.* at 448. The opinion then went on to describe psychological ploys prescribed by police interrogation manuals and designed to "persuade, trick, or cajole" the defendant "out of exercising his constitutional rights." *Id.* at 448–55.

26. The consensus may not be as universal as one would expect, however. A case decided shortly after *Miranda* is illustrative. In Davis v. North Carolina, 384 U.S. 737 (1966), Davis, accused of rape and murder, confessed after being held incommunicado for 16 days and being fed a diet of two sandwiches and peanuts daily (he lost 15 pounds during this period). At one point, he was required to walk 14 miles in order to disprove an alibi. Each of the lower courts through the Fourt Circuit held Davis's confession to be voluntary, as did two Supreme Court Justices (Clark and Harlan).

27. *See* Miranda v. Arizona, 384 U.S. at 515 (Harlan, J., dissenting).

28. *See* Brewer v. Williams, 430 U.S. 387 (1977). *Brewer* was actually a Sixth Amendment case dealing with police behavior in the absence of counsel. The issue of coercion was thus not directly addressed, although the Court suggested that the defendant was pressured into leading the police to incriminating evidence.

29. 446 U.S. 291 (1980).

30. In a proposal for a substantially modified test of due process voluntariness, Grano has suggested that this

problem might be alleviated by clearly separating the three doctrines included within voluntariness doctrine: prohibition of undue impairment of mental freedom; prohibition of police taking undue advantage of the accused; prohibition of police creating an unnecessary risk of a false confession. Grano, *Voluntariness, Free Will, and the Law of Confessions,* 65 VA. L. REV. 859 (1979).

31. White, *Police Trickery in Inducing Confessions,* 127 U. PA. L. REV. 581 (1979). While the ultimate determination of the fairness of these and other police tactics is a moral or legal one, behavioral scientists might provide legal policymakers with information both about the effectiveness of such tactics in evoking confessions and about defendants' subjective experience of these tactics. One means of gathering such data would be to present participants with hypothetical situations involving interrogation, as Grisso did with juveniles. *See* T. GRISSO, JUVENILES' WAIVER OF RIGHTS: LEGAL AND PSYCHOLOGICAL COMPETENCE (1981). Such research might also be of help to police and judges in terms of implementing existing law. For instance, "interrogation" under *Miranda* is defined as "any word or actions on the part of the police . . . that the police should know are reasonably likely to elicit an incriminating response from the subject." Rhode Island v. Innis, 446 U.S. 291, 301 (1980). Behavioral research may assist police in judging the likely responses of certain types of individuals to particular police conduct.

32. *Slip op.,* December 10, 1986.

33. Typically, the reliability of a confession is left up to the trier of fact. *See* Crane v. Kentucky, __U.S.__, 106 S.Ct. 2142 (1986).

34. We do not mean to suggest that this lack of attention to clinical opinion is really a problem for the mental health professional. We believe strongly that clinicians should limit their evaluations to the questions asked and that they should neither usurp the role of legal decisionmaker nor allow it to be thrust upon them.

   However, we do wish to make clear both to mental health professionals and to attorneys who might employ them that clinical evaluation of competency to confess is likely to be neither as valuable nor as simple as might appear on first glance.

35. *See* T. GRISSO, *supra* note 31; Leiken, *Police Interrogation in Colorado: The Implementation of* Miranda. 47 DEN. L.J. 1; Seeburger & Wettick, Miranda *in Pittsburgh: A Statistical Study,* 29 PITT. L. REV. 1 (1967); Younger, *Results of a Survey Conducted in the District Attorney's Office of Los Angeles County Regarding the Effect of the* Miranda *Decision upon the Prosecution of Felony Cases,* 5 AM. CRIM. L.Q. 32 (1966); Project, *Interrogations in New Haven: The Impact of* Miranda. 76 YALE L.J. 1521 (1967).

36. It was acknowledged in *Miranda* that once-stated warnings would not buttress the rights consciousness of many defendants in resisting the police. The Fifth Amendment-based right to counsel during interrogation developed from this acknowledgment. 384 U.S. at 469–71.

37. T. GRISSO, *supra* note 31.

38. More generally, opinions on any ultimate legal issue

should be avoided by mental health experts. *See infra* §§ 1.04, 14.05.

39. *Cf.* Morse, *Crazy Behavior, Morals, and Science: An Analysis of Mental Health Law,* 51 S. CAL. L. REV. 527 (1978) (advocating similar use of data in mental health cases generally).

40. Boykin v. Alabama, 395 U.S. 238 (1969).

41. Henderson v. Morgan, 426 U.S. 637 (1976).

42. Boykin v. Alabama, 395 U.S. 238 (1969).

43. Annot., *Compliance with Federal Constitutional Requirement that Guilty Pleas Be Made Voluntarily and with Understanding, in Federal Cases Involving Allegedly Incompetent State Convicts,* 38 A.L.R. Fed. 238 § 5(a) (1978); Annot., *Degree of Mental Competency, Required of Accused Who Pleads Guilty, Sufficient to Satisfy Requirement, of Rule 11 of Federal Rules of Criminal Procedure that Guilty Pleas Be Made Voluntarily and with Understanding,* 31 A.L.R. Fed. 375 § 3 (1977).

44. 423 F.2d 113 (9th Cir. 1970).

45. DeKaplany v. Enomoto, 540 F.2d 975, 985–86 (9th Cir. 1976); Sieling v. Dunbar, 423 F.2d 211 (9th Cir. 1973).

46. United States v. Masthers, 539 F.2d 721, 726 n.30 (D.C. Cir. 1976), *rehearing* en banc *denied,* 539 F.2d 732 (1976).

47. 423 F.2d at 1194 (citations omitted).

48. *See generally* 13 LAW SOC'Y REV. (1979) (special issue on plea bargaining).

49. McLaughlin v. Royster, 346 F. Supp. 297 (E. D. Va. 1972). The Supreme Court has held valid a guilty plea made under circumstances similar to those in *McLaughlin. See* North Carolina v. Alford, 400 U.S. 25 (1970).

50. *"Sua sponte"* refers to a judge's raising an issue spontaneously (without a motion by the relevant party or parties).

51. For a list of relevant cases, see Frendak v. United States, 408 A.2d 364, at 373 nn. 13–14 (D.C. 1979).

52. 346 F.2d 812 (1965).

53. *Id.* at 818–19.

54. *See, e.g.,* United States v. Robertson, 507 F.2d 1148, 1161 (D.C. Cir. 1974) (separate opinion of Bazelon, C.J.). On the other hand, courts in some jurisdictions have appeared to rely exclusively on a test of whether the evidence points toward an insanity defense, lest a defendant innocent by reason of insanity be erroneously convicted. *See, e.g.,* State v. Smith, 88 Wash.2d 639, 642–43; 564 P.2d 1154, 1156 (1977) *(en banc).*

55. 408 A.2d 364 (1979).

56. 400 U.S. 25 (1970) (defendant protesting innocence may still enter a guilty plea).

57. 422 U.S. 806 (1975) (defendant has right to self-representation).

58. 408 A.2d at 376.

59. *Id.* at 376–78.

60. *Id.* at 378.

61. *Id.* at 378.

62. *Id.* at 380 n.29. *See* Roth, Appelbaum, Sallee, Reynolds, & Huber, *The Dilemma of Denial in the Assessment of Competency to Refuse Treatment,* 139 AM. J. PSYCHIATRY 910 (1982).

63. 422 U.S. 806 (1975).

64. *Id.* at 820.

65. *Id.* at 834.

66. *Id.* at 834–35, n.46.

67. *Id.* at 835.

68. *Id.* at 835.

69. *Id.* at 836. For cases developing this point, see Annot., *Accused's Right to Represent Himself in State Criminal Proceedings—Modern State Cases,* 98 A.L.R. 3d 13 § 12.

70. 422 U.S. at 836.

71. *Id.* at 835.

72. A striking example of this principle is found in Hsu v. United States, 392 A.2d 972 (D.C. 1978). The defendant in a perjury trial had a Ph.D. in engineering and had extensive experience as a *pro se* litigant in civil landlord–tenant cases. The trial judge inquired of the defendant simply whether he was familiar with jury trials. The appellate court held that Hsu had not made a knowing and intelligent waiver of his right to counsel. Indeed, the experience in minor legal matters may have misled him with respect to the seriousness and complexity of his situation in the instant case.

73. *See, e.g.,* Cordoba v. Harris, 473 F. Supp. 632 (S.D.N.Y. 1979).

74. Portions of this section previously appeared in Melton, *Children's Competency to Testify,* 5 LAW & HUM. BEHAV. 73 (1981).

75. The witness could, of course, actually be the defendant, although the issue of competency to testify is more likely to arise with prosecution witnesses.

76. *See generally* E. LOFTUS, EYEWITNESS TESTIMONY (1979).

77. In the majority of states, the rule for assessing competency of a child witness is established by case law alone. In those states where there is a statutory guideline, children under age ten are presumed incompetent, and children above age ten are presumed competent. Even in these states, however, with the exception of Arkansas, these presumptions are reputtable. Siegel & Hurley, *The Role of the Child's Preference in Custody Proceedings,* 11 FAM. L.Q. 1, 33–35 (1977). Courts have held children competent as young as four years old. Stafford, *The Child as a Witness,* 37 WASH. L. REV. 303, 305 (1962).

78. This principle is well established in case law. For reviews of the scores of supporting cases, see Collins & Bond, *Youth as a Bar to Testimonial Competence,* 8 ARK. L. REV. 100 (1954); Siegel & Hurley, *supra* note 77; Stafford, *supra* note 77; Thomas, *The Problem of the Child Witness,* 10 WYO. L.J. 214 (1956); Note, *The Competency of Children as Witnesses,* 39 VA. L. REV. 358 (1953). *See, e.g.,* United States v. Perez, 526 F.2d 859 (5th Cir. 1976); United States v. Schoefield, 465 F.2d 560 (D.C. Cir. 1975), *cert. denied,* 409 U.S. 881 (1972).

79. Rex v. Brasier, 1 Leach 199, 168 Eng. Rep. 202 (1770). "[T]hat an infant, though under age of seven years, may be sworn in a criminal prosecution, provided such infant appears, on strict examination by the Court, to possess a sufficient knowledge of the nature and consequences of an oath . . . for there is no precise or fixed rule as to the time within which infants are ex-

cluded from giving evidence; but their admissibility depends upon the sense and reason they entertain of the danger and impropriety of falsehood, which is to be collected from their answers to questions propounded to them by the court; but if they are found incompetent to take an oath, their testimony cannot be received." 1 Leach 199, 200, 168 Eng. Rep. 202, 203.

80. 159 U.S. 523 (1895).

81. *Id.* at 524–25.

82. The *voir dire* in *Wheeler* was exemplary: "The boy . . . said among other things that he knew the difference between the truth and a lie; that if he told a lie the bad man would get him, and that he was going to tell the truth. When further asked what they would do to him in court if he told a lie, he replied they would put him in jail. He also said that his mother had told him that morning to 'tell no lie,' and in response to a question as to what the clerk said to him, when he held up his hand, he answered, 'don't you tell no story.' " *Id.* at 524.

83. One commentator suggested a "typical group of questions": "What is your name? How old are you? Where do you live? Do you go to School? Do you go to Sunday School? Do you know what happens to anyone telling a lie? Do you know why you are here today? Would you tell a true story or a wrong story today? Suppose you told a wrong story, do you know what would happen? Do you know what an oath is? Did you ever hear of God?" Note, *supra* note 78, at 362. A somewhat more recent commentator, Stafford, *supra* note 77, at 316, also suggested that an assessment of a child's competency should include "questions about his attendance at church or Sunday School, including his frequency of attendance, names of his teachers, pastor and location of his church." Besides raising a constitutional issue, these questions are probably of little probative value today in view of changing norms of church attendance. Regardless, from a cognitive–developmental perspective, such questions would shed little light on the child's ability to apply moral principles. Questions about church attendance are nonetheless still commonly used. Siegel & Hurley, *supra* note 77, at 36. *See, e.g.,* Brown v. United States, 388 A.2d 451, 458 (D.C. Mun. Ct. App. 1978).

84. *See, e.g.,* State in Interest of R.R., 79 N.J. 97, 398 A.2d 76 (1979); State v. Manlove, 441 P.2d 229 (N.M., 1968); Posey v. United States, 41 A.2d 300 (D.C. Mun. Ct. App. 1945); State v. Collier, 23 Wa. 2d 678, 162 P.2d 267 (1945); People v. Delaney, 52 Cal. App. 765, 199 Pac.896 (1921). Given that part of the reason an oath is administered is to subject the witness to penalties of perjury if he or she lies, there has been some question whether young children (usually under age seven) could ever be competent because of their lack of potential criminal liability under common law and, in some states, by statute. Such a view seems overly narrow, particularly given that the oath itself (and the threat of punishment, whether divine or secular, for lack of adherence to it) probably has little effect on behavior. In fact,

the argument of a necessity of potential liability for perjury has generally not been sustained. Stafford, *supra* note 77, at 317–18.

85. "A child is competent to testify if it possesses the capacity to observe events, to recollect and communicate them, and has the ability to understand questions and to frame and make intelligent answers, with a consciousness of the duty to speak the truth." Cross v. Commonwealth, 195 Va. 62, 64, 77, S.E.2d 447, 449 (1953).

86. The standard for competency as a witness at the event itself may be lower than the standard for competency to testify. Courts have occasionally ruled children competent who were found to be incompetent at earlier trials. Apparently the courts assumed that the earlier deficit was in their capacity to observe, encode, and conceptualize their experiences. Cross v. Commonwealth, *id.*; Burnham v. Chicago G.W.R.R., 340 Mo. 25, 100 S.W.2d 858 (1937) (child found incompetent in prior trial allowed to testify after dream supposedly refreshed memory). It is noteworthy that these courts apparently assumed a sequence of psychological development that is reversed in reality. *See infra* discussions of memory and cognitive development.

87. The child must have been able to form a "just impression of the facts." There is the "danger that a child will intermingle imagination with memory and thus have incorrect statements irretrievably engraved on the record by a guileless witness with no conception that they are incorrect or that the words should not have been spoken." Stafford, *supra* note 77, at 309.

88. People v. Delaney, 52 Cal. App. 765, 199 Pac. 896 (1921); Macale v. Lynch, 110 Wash. 444, 188 Pac. 517 (1920). Suggestibility is a particularly important issue when the defendant is a parent or other significant adult in the child's life. *See* Gelhaar v. State, 41 Wisc. 2d 230, 163 N.W. 2d 609 (1969); State v. Hunt, 2 Ariz. App. 6, 406 P.2d 208 (1965); Benedek & Benedek, *The Child's Preference in Michigan Custody Disputes,* AM. J. FAM. THERAPY 37, 40 (1979); Siegel & Hurley, *supra* note 77, at 13–16.

89. Riggs v. State, 235 Ind. 499, 135 N.E.2d 247 (1956). In that case, the trial court erred in not seeking such validation of testimony of a 12-year-old girl who was asked simply, "Did you have sexual intercourse with Hiram Riggs?" She answered affirmatively without any additional details. No evidence was presented of the girl's understanding of "sexual intercourse." *See also* Fitzgerald v. United States, 412 A.2d 1 (D.C. 1980) (jury instruction on corroboration of minors' allegations required in sex-offense cases).

90. J. WIGMORE, WIGMORE ON EVIDENCE § 509 (3d ed. 1940).

91. *Id.* at 601.

92. Marin, Holmes, Guth, & Kovac, *The Potential of Children as Eyewitnesses: A Comparison of Children and Adults on Eyewitness Tasks,* 3 LAW & HUM. BEHAV. 295 (1979).

93. *Id.* at 304.

94. Brown, *Judgments of Recency for Long Sequences of Pictures: The Absence of a Developmental Trend,* 15 J. EXPERIMENTAL CHILD PSYCHOLOGY 473 (1973); Brown & Campione, *Recognition Memory for Perceptually Similar Pictures in Preschool Children,* 15 J. EXPERIMENTAL CHILD PSYCHOLOGY 356 (1972); Brown & Scott, *Recognition Memory for Pictures in Preschool Children,* 11 J. EXPERIMENTAL CHILD PSYCHOLOGY 401 (1971); Corsini, Jacobers, & Leonard, *Recognition Memory of Preschool Children for Pictures and Words,* 16 PSYCHONOMIC SCI. 192 (1969); Nelson, *Memory Development in Children: Evidence from Nonverbal Tasks,* 25 PSYCHONOMIC SCI. 346 (1971); Perlmutter & Myers, *Recognition Memory Development in 2- to 4-year-olds,* 10 DEV. PSYCHOLOGY 447 (1974); Perlmutter & Myers, *Young Children's Coding and Storage of Visual and Verbal Material,* 46 CHILD DEV. 215 (1975); Perlmutter & Myers, *Recognition Memory in Preschool Children,* 12 DEV. PSYCHOLOGY 271 (1976); Standing, Conezio, & Haber, *Perception and Memory for Pictures: Single-Trial Learning of 2500 Visual Stimuli,* 19 PSYCHONOMIC SCI. 73 (1970).

95. Emmerich & Ackerman, *Developmental Differences in Recall: Encoding or Retrieval?,* 25 J. EXPERIMENTAL CHILD PSYCHOLOGY 514 (1978); Kobasigawa, *Utilization of Retrieval Cues by Children in Recall,* 45 CHILD DEV. 127 (1974); Perlmutter & Ricks, *Recall in Preschool Children,* 27 J. EXPERIMENTAL CHILD PSYCHOLOGY 423 (1979); Ritter, Kaprive, Fitch, & Flavell, *The Development of Retrieval Strategies in Young Children,* 5 COGNITIVE PSYCHOLOGY 310 (1973).

96. *See, e.g.,* Brown & Scott, *supra* note 94 (28-day testing intervals).

97. *See* J. FLAVELL, THE DEVELOPMENTAL PSYCHOLOGY OF JEAN PIAGET (1963), for a comprehensive review of Piagetian terminology, theory, and research.

98. J. PIAGET, THE CHILD'S CONCEPTION OF TIME (1969) (orig. publ. 1927).

99. Berndt & Wood, *The Development of Time Concepts through Conflict Based on a Primitive Duration Capacity,* 45 CHILD DEV. 825 (1974); Levin, *The Development of Time Concepts in Young Children: Reasoning about Duration,* 48 CHILD DEV. 435 (1977); Siegler & Richards, *Development of Time, Speed, and Distance Concepts,* 15 DEV. PSYCHOLOGY 288 (1979); Weinreb & Brainerd, *A Developmental Study of Piaget's Groupement Model of Speed and Time Concepts,* 46 CHILD DEV. 176 (1975).

100. *See, e.g.,* ALTERNATIVES TO PIAGET: CRITICAL ESSAYS ON THE THEORY (L. Siegel & C. Brainerd eds. 1978) [hereinafter cited as ALTERNATIVES].

101. Borke, *Interpersonal Perception of Young Children: Egocentism or Empathy?,* 5 DEV. PSYCHOLOGY 263 (1971); Borke, *The Development of Empathy in Chinese and American Children between 3 and 6 Years of Age: A Cross-Cultural Study,* 9 DEV. PSYCHOLOGY 102 (1973); Borke, *Piaget's Mountains Revisited: Changes in the Egocentric Landscapes,* 11 DEV. PSYCHOLOGY 240 (1975); Borke, *Piaget's View of Social Interaction and the Theoretical Construct of Empathy,* in ALTERNATIVES, *supra* note 100 [hereinafter cited as *Piaget's View*].

102. The classical Piagetian assessment of this ability invokes a task of reproducing the view of a particular scene (i.e., a model of three mountains) from different vantage points. *See* J. PIAGET & B. INHELDER, THE CHILD'S CONCEPTION OF SPACE (1956).

103. *But see* Chandler & Greenspan, *Ersatz Egocentrism: A Reply to H. Borke,* 7 DEV. PSYCHOLOGY 104 (1972) (Borke's tasks actually involved taking perspective of oneself rather than of others). For a reply, see Borke, *Chandler and Greenspan's "Ersatz Egocentrism": A Rejoinder,* 7 DEV. PSYCHOLOGY 107 (1972).

104. Siegel, *The Relationship of Language and Thought in the Preoperational Child: A Reconsideration of Nonverbal Alternatives to Piagetian Tasks,* in ALTERNATIVES, *supra* note 100.

105. *See* Brainerd, *Learning Research and Piagetian Theory,* in ALTERNATIVES, *supra* note 100.

106. Of course, this effect may mean a child's description of an event may be weighted toward the latest-occurring aspect of that event.

107. *See* Austin, Ruble, & Trabasso, *Recall and Order Effects as Factors in Children's Moral Judgments,* 48 CHILD DEV. 470 (1977); Bryant & Trabasso, *Transitive Inferences and Memory in Young Children,* 232 NATURE 456 (1971).

108. There are other criticisms of Piagetian theory. Information-processing theorists, *e.g.,* H. KLAUSMEIER, and ASSOCIATES COGNITIVE LEARNING AND DEVELOPMENT: INFORMATION-PROCESSING AND PIAGETIAN PERSPECTIVES (1979), and learning theorists, *e.g.,* Brainerd, *supra* note 105; Cornell, *Learning to Find Things: A Reinterpretation of Object Permanence Studies,* in ALTERNATIVES, *supra* note 100; *and* Overton & Reese, *Models of Development: Methodological Implications,* in LIFE-SPAN DEVELOPMENTAL PSYCHOLOGY: METHODOLOGICAL ISSUES (1973), have argued that mentalistic explanation of broad cognitive structures are unnecessary and less parsimonious than traditional learning principles. The assumption of universal developmental process has also been brought into question by cross-cultural research on Piagetian tasks. *See, e.g.,* Ashton, *Cross-Cultural Piagetian Research: An Experimental Procedure,* 45 HARV. EDUC. REV. 475 (1975); Hollos, *Cross-Cultural Research in Psychological Development in Rural Communities,* in RURAL PSYCHOLOGY (A. Childs & G. Melton eds. 1983). However, as noted in the accompanying text, while these criticisms have considerable import for theory development, they do not moot the basic point presented here that young children tend to have difficulty in conceptualizing complex events. For the purposes of formulating policy on children's competency to testify, reasons why there are developmental factors in conceptual skills are less important than descriptions of their existence.

109. Borke, *Piaget's View, supra* note 101, at 38.

110. *See supra* notes 100–102 and accompanying text.

111. In a largely critical essay on the philosophical assumptions of Piagetian theory, Hall and Kaye made a similar point: "If psychologists are interested in describing the normal course of cognitive development, much of Piaget's theory may be of use. If, on the other hand, the theorist is interested in determining the child's ultimate capacity at any given time, he would use the approach exemplified by Trabasso." Hall & Kaye, *The Necessity of Logical Necessity in Piaget's Theory,* in ALTERNATIVES, *supra* note 100, at 165–66.

112. Bernstein & Cowan, *Children's Concepts of How People Get Babies,* 46 CHILD DEV. 77 (1975).

113. Kreitler & Kreitler, *Children's Concepts of Sexuality and Birth,* 37 CHILD DEV. 363 (1966).

114. Monge, Dusek, & Lawless, *An Evaluation of the Acquisition of Sexual Information through a Sex Education Class,* 13 J. SEX RESEARCH 170 (1977).

115. *Id.* at 179.

116. Burton, *Honesty and Dishonesty,* in MORAL DEVELOPMENT AND BEHAVIOR: THEORY, RESEARCH, AND SOCIAL ISSUES (T. Lickona ed. 1976) [volume hereinafter cited as MORAL DEVELOPMENT].

117. N. Groth, The Psychology of the Sexual Offender: Rape, Incest, and Child Molestation (workshop presented by Psychological Associates of the Albemarle in Charlotte, N.C., March 1980).

118. *See generally* MORAL DEVELOPMENT, *supra* note 116.

119. The correlation between moral judgments and moral behavior is in fact rather modest. *See* Mischel & Mischel, *A Cognitive Social-Learning Approach to Morality and Self-Regulation,* in MORAL DEVELOPMENT, *supra* note 116.

120. Kohlberg, *Stage and Sequence: The Cognitive–Developmental Approach to Socialization,* in HANDBOOK OF SOCIALIZATION THEORY AND RESEARCH (D. Goslin ed. 1969); Kohlberg, *From Is to Ought: How to Commit the Naturalistic Fallacy and Get Away with It,* in COGNITIVE DEVELOPMENT AND EPISTEMOLOGY (T. Mischel ed. 1971); Kohlberg, *Moral Stages and Socialization: The Cognitive–Developmental Approach,* in MORAL DEVELOPMENT, *supra* note 116. For critiques of Kohlberg's theory, see Kurtines & Greif, *The Development of Moral Thought: Review and Evaluation of Kohlberg's Approach,* 31 PSYCHOLOGICAL BULL. 453 (1974); Mischel & Mischel, *supra* note 119; Simpson, *Moral Development Research: A Case of Scientific Cultural Bias,* 17(2) HUM. DEV. 81.

121. Adherents to social learning theory, the major competing theory of moral development, would agree; *see* Mischel & Mischel, *supra* note 119. From their point of view, children's behavior would be influenced primarily by the rewards, punishments, and models available in a given situation (in interaction with a child's cognitive competencies).

122. J. PIAGET, THE MORAL JUDGMENT OF THE CHILD (1965) (orig. publ. 1932).

123. *See* Kohlberg, *Stage and Sequence* and *From Is to Ought, supra* note 120.

124. *See* J. PIAGET, *supra* note 122.

125. *See generally* E. LOFTUS, *supra* note 76.

126. 159 U.S. at 524–25.

127. Marin, Holmes, Guth, & Kovac, *supra* note 92.

128. Hoving, Hamm, & Galvin, *Social Influence as a Function*

of Stimulus Ambiguity at Three Age Levels, 1 Dev. Psy-CHOLOGY 631 (1969).

129. Marin, Holmes, Guth, & Kovac, *supra* note 92.

130. Allen & Newston, *Development of Conformity and Independency* 22 J. PERSONALITY SOC. PSYCHOLOGY 18 (1972).

131. Developmental change in perceived authority of court officials is an empirical assumption that is still largely untested, however.

132. Fodor, *Resistance to Social Influence among Adolescents as a Function of Moral Development,* 85 J. SOC. PSYCHOLOGY 121 (1971).

133. *See supra* notes 118–124 and accompanying text; *see also* Melton, *Children's Concepts of Their Rights,* 9 J. CLINICAL CHILD PSYCHOLOGY 186 (1980).

134. There is some evidence that young children may be able to consider intention and other social and ethical factors better than Piaget argued that they could. Austin, Ruble, & Trabasso, *supra* note 107; Darley, Klosson, & Zanna, *Intuitions and their Contexts in the Moral Judgments of Children and Adults,* 49 CHILD DEV. 66 (1978). However, the weight of empirical evidence nonetheless clearly indicates that moral judgment is "indisputably developmental," Lickona, *Research on Piaget's Theory of Moral Development,* in MORAL DEVEL-OPMENT, *supra* note 116, at 239. Young children's moral judgments, while subject to social influence, are strongly affected by their cognitive limitations.

135. Courts do in fact often allow attorneys great freedom in posing leading questions to children so that they might give more complete answers. Stafford, *supra* note 77, at 320.

136. There are concerns about whether testimony is unduly stressful for children, particularly when they have to confront defendants who have assaulted or sexually abused them. *See* Melton, *Psycholegal Issues in Child Victims' Interaction with the Legal System,* 5 VICTIMOLOGY 274 (1980–81). To the extent to which these concerns are well founded, the state's *parens patriae* interest in protecting children may conflict with its interest in punishing and incapacitating child molesters.

137. *See* Marin, Holmes, Guth, & Kovac, *supra* note 92.

138. Grisso & Lovinguth, *Lawyers and Child Clients: A Call for Research,* in THE RIGHTS OF CHILDREN: LEGAL AND PSYCHOLOGICAL PERSPECTIVES (J. Henning ed. 1982); Wald, *Legal Policies Affecting Children: A Lawyer's Request for Aid,* 47 CHILD DEV. 1 (1976).

139. *See* Loftus & Monahan, *Trial by Data: Psychological Research as Legal Evidence,* 35 AM. PSYCHOLOGIST 270 (1980).

140. *See* Goodman & Michelli, *Would You Believe a Child Witness?,* 19(11) PSYCHOLOGY TODAY 80 (1981).

141. 4 W. BLACKSTONE, COMMENTARIES 24 (9th ed. 1978).

142. *See* Note, *The Eighth Amendment and the Execution of the Presently Incompetent,* 32 STAN. L. REV. 765 (1980); Note, *Mental Aberration and Post-Conviction Sanctions,* 15 SUF-FOLK U. L. REV. 1219 (1981); Cameron v. Fisher, 320 F.2d 731 (D.C. Cir. 1976); State v. Hehman, 520 P.2d 507 (Ariz. 1974); Commonwealth v. Robinson, 431 A.2d 901 (Penn. 1981).

143. 531 F.2d 83 (2d Cir. 1976).

144. The right comes in many forms. Some jurisdictions require that the court address the defendant personally, United States v. Byars, 290 F.2d 515 (6th Cir. 1961), while others hold that inquiry by the defense attorney is sufficient, Cummingham v. State, 575 P.2d 936 (Nev. 1978). Some limit the right to certain crimes, Brogan v. Banmiller, 136 A.2d 141 (Pa. App. 1957) (allocution applicable only to murder), and some do not permit its exercise when conviction is by plea, Goodloe v. State, 486 S.W.2d 430 (Mo. 1972).

145. 656 F.2d 512 (9th Cir. 1981).

146. Mempa v. Rhay, 389 U.S. 128 (1967).

147. For instance, many states require a showing of prejudice before a violation of the right is found and re-sentencing ordered. *See* Annot., 96 A.L.R.2d 1292, 1296.

148. Chavez v. United States, *supra* note 145.

149. *See, e.g.,* Fla.R.Crim.Pro. 3.720(a).

150. See commentary to CRIMINAL JUSTICE MENTAL HEALTH STANDARDS, standard 7-5.2 (1984) [hereinafter cited as STANDARDS].

151. STANDARDS, *supra* note 150, standard 7-5.2(a).

152. The precise test is "whether the defendant has the sufficient present ability to consult with the defendant's attorney with a reasonable degree of rational understanding and whether the defendant has a rational as well as factual understanding of the sentence proceedings." STANDARDS, *supra* note 150, standard 7-5.2(a)(i).

153. STANDARDS, *supra* note 150, standard 7-5.2(b).

154. Fla.Stats. 922.07 (1986).

155. STANDARDS, *supra* note 150, standard 7-5.7(b).

156. _____U.S._____, 106 S.Ct. 2595 (1986).

157. STANDARDS, *supra* note 150, standard 7-5.8(d)(f).

158. 429 U.S. 1012 (1976).

159. *See generally* Strafer, *Volunteering for Execution,* 74 J. CRIM. L. & CRIM. 860 (1983); Note, *Insanity of the Condemned,* 88 YALE L. J. 533 (1979).

160. 663 F.2d 1004 (10th Cir. 1981).

Chapter 6

1. These doctrines include the concepts of "provocation," "self-defense," and "duress." The provocation doctrine, which is relevant only in homicide cases, might call for clinical testimony on the issue of whether the homicide was "committed under the influence of extreme mental or emotional disturbance for which there is a reasonable explanation or excuse," reasonableness to be determined "from the viewpoint of a person in the actor's situation under the circumstances as he believes them to be." MODEL PENAL CODE § 1962 210.3(1). Many states reject this subjective approach to provocation, however, and adhere to the common-law ap-

proach permitting evidence of provocation only in certain specified circumstances (e.g., discovery of victim with spouse). In these states, clinical testimony would be irrelevant.

Self-defense is a defense to crime if the person (1) cannot avoid the threatened harm without using force or giving up some right (such as the right to remain in one's home); and (2) the force used is not unreasonable in view of the threat. Again, these criteria have traditionally been defined objectively, but modern relaxation of the rules might permit a clinician to testify about a defendant's perception of the threat and the degree of force needed to protect himself or herself.

Duress is a defense when the defendant is forced by a third agent to commit the criminal act (e.g., because someone is holding a gun to his or her head). Although the degree of force required to permit the defense is usually objectively defined, some states may allow testimony as to the subjective beliefs of the defendant claiming duress. A variant of duress is the so-called "brainwashing defense," raised (unsuccessfully) in the Patty Hearst case. One could argue that a "brainwashed" individual is in thrall to his or her brainwashers and therefore acts under duress. Comment, *Brainwashing: Fact, Fiction and Criminal Defense,* 44 UMKC L. REV. 438, 473–74 (1976).

Since, to date, mental health professionals are seldom called upon to address these issues even in those states that permit individualized assessment of provocation, self-defense, or duress, they are not discussed further in this book. A discussion of these doctrines may be found in W. LaFave & A. SCOTT, THE CRIMINAL LAW 572–86, 391–97, and 374–81, respectively (1972).

2. D. ABRAHAMSEN, THE PSYCHOLOGY OF CRIME 106 (1967); Morse, *Crazy Behavior, Morals, and Science: An Analysis of Mental Health Law,* 51 S. CAL. L. REV. 527 (1978); Weintraub, *Insanity as a Defense: A Panel Discussion,* 37 F.R.D. 365, 372 (1964).

3. N. MORRIS, MADNESS AND THE CRIMINAL LAW (1982).

4. 1 NAT'L COMM'N ON REFORM OF FED. CRIM. LAWS, WORKING PAPERS 248–51 (1970).

5. Guttmacher, *Principal Difficulties with the Present Criteria of Responsibility and Possible Alternatives,* in commentary to MODEL PENAL CODE § 171 (Tent. Draft No. 4 1955).

6. A. GOLDSTEIN, THE INSANITY DEFENSE 223 (1967); Bonnie, *The Moral Basis of the Insanity Defense,* 69 A.B.A. J. 194–97 (1983); Diamond, *With Malice Aforethought,* 2 ARCH. CRIM. PSYCHIATRY 1 (1957); Hart, *The Aims of the Criminal Law,* 23 LAW & CONTEMP. PROBS. 401 (1958); PACKER, MENS REA AND THE SUPREME COURT, 1962 SUP. CT. REV. 107.

7. After the *Hinckley* verdict in 1982, over 40 bills proposing the abolition or modification of the defense were introduced in the United States Congress, and similar bills were proposed in several state legislatures.

8. Pasewark, Seidenzahl, & Pantle, *Opinions about the Insanity Plea,* 8 J. FORENSIC PSYCHIATRY 8 (1981).

9. *Id.*

10. Cooke & Sikorski, *Factors Affecting Length of Hospitaliza-*

tion of Persons Adjudicated Not Guilty by Reason of Insanity, 2 BULL. AM. ACAD. PSYCHIATRY L. 251 (1974).

11. Petrila, *The Insanity Defense and Other Mental Health Dispositions in Missouri,* 5 INT'L J.L. PSYCHIATRY 81 (1982).

12. *Hearing before Subcomm. on Crim. Justice, House Comm. on the Judiciary,* Cong. (Sess. July 22, 1982) (statement of Steadman).

13. Hastings & Bonnie, *A Survey of Pretrial Psychiatric Evaluations in Richmond, Virginia,* 1 DEV. MENTAL HEALTH L. 9 (1981).

14. *Hearing before Subcomm. on Crim. Justice, House Comm. on the Judiciary,* Cong. (Sess. Sept. 9, 1982) (statement of Rodriguez) [hereinafter cited as Rodriguez Statement].

15. A. MATTHEWS, *Mental Disability and the Criminal Law* (1970); N. WALKER & S. MCCABE, CRIME AND INSANITY IN ENGLAND (1973).

16. Pasewark, Seidenzahl, & Pantle, *supra* note 8.

17. H. Steadman & J. Braff, *Defendants Not Guilty by Reason of Insanity,* in MENTALLY DISORDERED OFFENDERS: PERSPECTIVES FROM LAW AND SOCIAL SCIENCE 118 (J. Monahan & H. Steadman eds. 1983) (citing K. FUKUNAGA, THE CRIMINALLY INSANE (1977)).

18. Steadman, Monahan, Hartstone, Davis, & Robbins, *Mentally Disordered Offenders: A National Survey of Patients and Facilities,* 6 LAW & HUM. BEHAV. 31, 36 (1982).

19. Rodriguez Statement, *supra* note 14.

20. Steadman, Pantle, & Pasewark, *Factors Associated with a Successful Insanity Defense,* 140 AM. J. PSYCHIATRY 401 (1983).

21. The states, number of NGRI verdicts, ratio of verdicts to felony arrests, and sources for the data are as follows:

   • Wyoming—1 between 1970 and 1972, .005% estimated. Pasewark & Lanthorn, *Disposition of Persons Utilizing the Insanity Defense,* 5 J. HUMANICS 87 (1977)

   • Illinois—50 in 1979, .23%. REP. OF THE (ILLINOIS) DEP'T OF MENTAL HEALTH COMM. ON CRIM. JUSTICE & MENTAL HEALTH SYS. (1982) [hereinafter cited as ILLINOIS REPORT].

   • Florida—119 in 1981, .34%. CENTER FOR GOVERNMENTAL RESPONSIBILITY, THE INSANITY DEFENSE IN FLORIDA (1983).

   • California—259 in 1980, .6%. Turner & Ornstein, *Distinguishing the Wicked from the Mentally Ill,* 3 CAL. LAW. 42 (1983).

   • New York—55 per year between 1976 and 1978, .65%. Steadman, *Insanity Acquittals in New York State, 1965–1978,* 137 AM. J. PSYCHIATRY 321 (1980).

22. Steadman, Monahan, Hartstone, Davis, & Robbins, *supra* note 18, at 33.

23. In 1978, there were approximately 2,284,495 felony arrests. FBI UNIFORM CRIME REPORTS, CRIME IN THE UNITED STATES 185 (1979).

24. In Oregon, between 1978 and 1980, 80% of NGRI verdicts were the result of agreements between prosecution and defense and did not go to trial; 17% were the result of bench trials; and only 3% had gone through a jury trial. J. Rogers & J. Bloom, Characteristics of Persons Committed to Oregon's Psychiatric Security

Review Board (paper presented to AAPL in San Diego, California, Oct. 1981). See also, Rogers, Bloom, & Manson, *Insanity Defenses: Contested or Conceded?* 141 Am. J. Psychiatry 885 (1984). A Michigan study found that 90% of those defendants found NGRI were adjudicated in nonjury trials, often through a quasi-plea-bargaining process. Smith & Hall, *Evaluating Michigan's Guilty But Mentally Ill Verdict,* 16 U. Mich. J.L. Ref. 77, 94 (1982).

25. Hastings & Bonnie, *supra* note 13 (100% in Richmond, Virginia, in 1976); Pasewark, Pantle, & Steadman, *Characteristics and Disposition of Persons Found Not Guilty by Reason of Insanity in New York State, 1971–1976,* 136 Am. J. Psychiatry 655, 658 (1979) (68.9% in New York in 1971–76); Petrila, *The Pre-Trial Examination Process in Missouri: A Descriptive Study,* 9 Bull. Am. Acad. Psychiatry L. 60 (1981) (65% in Missouri in 1978); Rodriguez Statement, *supra* note 14 (81% in New Jersey in 1982).

26. Note, *Commitment Following an Insanity Acquittal,* 94 Harv. L. Rev. 605 (1981).

27. Morris, *Acquittal by Reason of Insanity,* in Mentally Disordered Offenders: Perspectives From Law and Social Science 70–72 (J. Monahan & H. Steadman eds. 1983); Note, *supra* note 26, at 605–06.

28. Morris, *supra* note 27, at 67–68.

29. Goldstein & Katz, *Abolish the "Insanity Defense"—Why Not?,* 72 Yale L.J. 853 (1963).

30. Pasewark, Pantle, & Steadman, *supra* note 25.

31. Criss & Racine, *Impact of Change in Legal Standard for Those Adjudicated Not Guilty by Reason of Insanity 1975–1979 in Michigan,* 8 Bull. Am. Acad. Psychiatry L. 261, 266–67 (1981).

32. Illinois Report, *supra* note 21.

33. Pantle, Pasewark, & Steadman, *Comparing Institutionalization Periods and Subsequent Arrests of Insanity Acquittees and Convicted Felons,* 8 J. Psychiatry L. 305 (1980); Pasewark, Pantle, & Steadman, *Detention and Rearrest Rates of Persons Found Not Guilty by Reason of Insanity and Convicted Felons,* 139 Am. J. Psychiatry 892 (1982).

34. Phillips & Pasewark, *Insanity Pleas in Connecticut,* 8 Bull. Am. Acad. Psychiatry L. 325 (1980).

35. Rodriguez Statement, *supra* note 14.

36. Steadman & Cocozza, *Selective Reporting and the Public's Misconceptions of the Criminally Insane,* 41 Pub. Opinion Q. 523 (1978).

37. Pantle, Pasewark, & Steadman, *supra* note 33; Pasewark, Pantle, & Steadman, *supra* note 33.

38. Phillips & Pasewark, *supra* note 34.

39. Cocozza, Melick, & Steadman, *Trends in Violent Crime among Ex-Mental Patients,* 16 Criminology 317 (1978).

40. 18 Idaho Code § 107 (1982); Mont. Laws ch. 713 (1979); Utah Code § 76-2-304.5 (1983).

41. Jones, The Law and Legal Theory of the Greeks 264 (1965); Platt & Diamond, *The Origins and Development of the "Wild Beast" Concept of Mental Illness and Its Relation to Theories of Criminal Responsibility,* 1 J. Hist. Behavioral Sci. 355 (1965).

42. Becker, *Durham Revisited: Psychiatry and the Problem of Crime,* in Diagnosis and Debate 43 (R. Bonnie ed. 1977).

43. *Id.* at 44.

44. 1 Hale, Pleas of the Crown 14 (1847 edition).

45. Rex v. Arnold, 16 How. St. Tr. 695 (1724).

46. Platt & Diamond, *The Origins of the "Right and Wrong" Test of Criminal Responsibility,* 54 Calif. L. Rev. 1227 (1966).

47. 10 Cl. & F. 200, 8 Eng. Rep. 718 (H.L. 1843).

48. I. Ray, A Treatise on the Medical Jurisprudence of Insanity (1833) (cited in Becker, *supra* note 42, at 50).

49. *See id.* at 34.

50. A. Zilboorg, Mind, Medicine and Man 273 (1943).

51. Parsons v. State, 81 Ala. 577, 596, 2 So. 854 (1886).

52. *See* A. Goldstein, *supra* note 6, at 13; 2 Stephen, A History of the Criminal Law of England 168 (1883).

53. *See, e.g.,* Commonwealth v. Woodhouse, 164 A.2d 98, 106 (Pa. 1960); Sollars v. State, 316 P.2d 917, 920 (Nev. 1957); Waelder, *Psychiatry and the Problems of Criminal Responsibility,* 101 U. Pa. L. Rev. 378, 383 (1952); Wootten, Book Review, 77 Yale L.J. 1019, 1026–27 (1968) (reviewing A. Goldstein, The Insanity Defense (1967)).

54. S. Glueck, Law and Psychiatry 54, 57–58 (1962); H. Weihofen, Mental Disorder as a Criminal Defense 85 (1954).

55. Durham v. United States, 214 F.2d 862, 873–74 (D.C. Cir. 1954); Wechsler, *The Criteria of Criminal Responsibility,* 22 U. Chi. L. Rev. 367, 375 (1954).

56. State v. Jones, 50 N.J. 369 (1871).

57. 214 F.2d 862 (D.C. Cir. 1954).

58. *See, e.g.,* Blocker v. United States, 288 F.2d 853 (D.C. Cir. 1961).

59. See Becker, *supra* note 42, at 57, for a description of this event.

60. *Id.*

61. 312 F.2d 847 (D.C. Cir. 1962).

62. *Id.* at 850–51.

63. United States v. Brawner, 471 F.2d 969 (D.C. Cir. 1972).

64. Maine adopted the "product" test in 1964, Me. Rev. Stat. Ann. tit. 15, § 102 (1964), but repealed its statute and adopted a modified version of the ALI test in 1975, *id.* tit. 17A, § 58 (1975).

65. Model Penal Code § 4.01(1) (Tent Draft No. 4 1955).

66. *Id.* § 4.01 comment.

67. *Id.* § 4.0(2).

68. For instance, in United States v. Brawner, 471 F.2d 969, 1029 (D.C. Cir. 1972), Judge Bazelon concurred in the majority's decision to reject the product test and adopt the ALI test, but also cautioned: "At no point in its opinion does the court explain why the boundary of a legal concept—criminal responsibility—should be marked by medical concepts, especially when the validity of the 'medical model' is seriously questioned by some eminent psychiatrists."

69. State v. Johnson, 399 A.2d 469, 476 (R.I. 1979).

70. Criminal Justice Mental Health Standards, standard 7-6.1 (1984) [hereinafter cited as Standards]; American Psychiatric Association, Statement on the Insanity Defense 12 (1982) [hereinafter cited as APA Statement].

71. STANDARDS, *supra* note 70, at 329–32; APA STATEMENT, *supra* note 70, at 11. A different conceptual approach that produces the same result is one proposed by Michael Moore. He suggests that the test for insanity should be whether the person "is so irrational as to be non-responsible." M. MOORE, LAW AND PSYCHIATRY: RE-THINKING THE RELATIONSHIP 245 (1984). By shifting the focus in the insanity inquiry to the rationality of one's reasons for acting, the degree to which one is "compelled" becomes irrelevant. *See* Slobogin, *A Rational Approach to Responsibility,* 83 MICH. L. REV. 820 (1985).

72. STANDARDS, *supra* note 70, at 331.

73. 18 U.S.C. § 402 (1984).

74. For a complete, but somewhat outdated, list of state and federal rules as of 1981, see Favole, *Mental Disability in the American Criminal Process: A Four-Issue Survey,* in MENTALLY DISORDERED OFFENDERS: PERSPECTIVES FROM LAW AND SOCIAL SCIENCE 257–69 (J. Monahan & H. Steadman eds. 1983).

75. *See, e.g.,* United States v. Brawner, 471 F.2d 969, 994 (D.C. Cir. 1972) (Bazelon, J., concurring); S. HALLECK, PSYCHIATRY AND THE DILEMMAS OF CRIME 341–42 (1967). Professor Norval Morris makes much the same point, but argues from this premise that rather than expanding the insanity defense, it should be eliminated: "It is hard to see why a special rule . . . should be made for the mentally ill." N. MORRIS, *supra* note 3, at 61.

76. M. MOORE, *supra* note 71, chs. 2 & 6, argues that one's environment is usually irrelevant to responsibility determinations because it does not normally disturb our capacity for rational action, which, he argues, is the only criterion by which we can assess illness and criminal culpability.

77. Durham v. United States, 214 F.2d 862 (1954).

78. W. LaFAVE & A. SCOTT, *supra* note 1, at 275.

79. A. GOLDSTEIN, *supra* note 6, at 33.

80. *See supra* note 25.

81. *See, e.g.,* McDonald v. United States, 312 F.2d 847, 851 (D.C. Cir. 1962) ("any abnormal condition of the mind which *substantially* affects mental or emotional processes and *substantially* impairs behavior controls") (emphasis added); Snider v. Smith, 187 F. Supp. 299 (1960); A. GOLDSTEIN, *supra* note 6, at 48.

82. Pollard v. United States, 282 F.2d 450 (6th Cir. 1960); Lee v. Thompson, 452 F. Supp. 165, 167–68 (1977); Government of the Virgin Islands v. Downey, 396 F. Supp. 349 (D.C.V.I. 1975).

83. Kane v. United States, 399 F.2d 730, 733-36 (9th Cir. 1969); State v. Hall, 214 N.W.2d 205 (Iowa 1974); People v. Kelly, 10 Cal. 3d 565, 517 P.2d 875, 111 Cal. Rptr. 171 (1973); Beasley v. State, 50 Ala. 149 (1874).

84. The ABA version is found in STANDARDS, *supra* note 70, standard 7-6.1, which defines "mental disease or defect" as: "(i) impairments of mind, whether enduring or transitory; or, (ii) mental retardation, which substantially affected the mental or emotional processes of the defendant at the time of the alleged offense." The American Psychiatric Association's version is found in the next sentence of the text.

85. APA STATEMENT, *supra* note 70, at 12.

86. Phillips & Pasewark, *supra* note 34.

87. Carter v. United States, 252 F.2d 608, 616 (D.C. Cir. 1957).

88. M. MOORE, *supra* note 71, chs. 1, 2, 6, 9, 10.

89. For further explication of Moore's thesis, see Slobogin, *supra* note 71.

90. A. GOLDSTEIN, *supra* note 6, at 49–53.

91. *Id.* at 50.

92. *Id.* at 51–53.

93. Becker, *supra* note 42, at 46–48.

94. *Id.* at 48–49. *See* United States v. Freeman, 357 F.2d 606, 615–18 (2d Cir. 1966), for a slightly different view of the *M'Naghten* case.

95. For instance, the acquittal rates expressed as a percentage of felony prosecutions for the five states listed earlier, *supra* note 21, would produce the following order, proceeding from the state with the lowest percentage to the state with the highest: Wyoming, Illinois, Florida, California, New York. Yet Wyoming, Illinois, and California used the ALI test, Florida used *M'Naghten,* and New York used a liberalized version of *M'Naghten* during the period in which the relevant data were collected.

California has since reverted to a version of *M'Naghten.* Preliminary reports suggest that this change has cut acquittals in half. Mathews, *California Insanity Pleas Drop by Half after Voters' Crackdown,* Washington Post, Feb. 5, 1984, at A, col. 1. Similarly, in Alaska, between October 1982, when Alaska replaced the ALI test with *M'Naghten,* and July 1984, the number of insanity acquittals dropped to *zero.* Personal communication with James Scoles, Alternative Care Coordinator, Department of Health and Social Services, July 13, 1984. At present, it is difficult to ascertain the extent to which the change in acquittals is due to the change in test language. For instance, in Alaska, the same act that changed the insanity test also adopted a "guilty but mentally ill" verdict. ALASKA STAT. § 12.47.050 (1982). In California, public outrage at the *Hinckley* verdict coincided with the passage of the new test.

96. MODEL PENAL CODE § 4.01 comment (Tent. Draft No. 4 1955).

97. Allen, *The Rule of the American Law Institute's Model Penal Code,* 45 MARQ. L. REV. 494, 501 (1972).

98. MODEL PENAL CODE § 4.01 comment (Tent. Draft No. 4 1955).

99. A. GOLDSTEIN, *supra* note 6, at 70–75.

100. *See, e.g.,* United States v. Kunak, 17 C.M.R. 346, 357–58 (1954).

101. *See* Favole, *supra* note 74.

102. *See, e.g.,* State v. Levier, 601 P.2d 1116 (Kan. 1979); State v. Law, 244 S.E.2d 302 (S.C. 1978); Hill v. State, 339 So. 2d 1382 (Miss. 1976); State v. Jacobs, 205 N.W.2d 662 (Neb. 1973); Commonwealth v. Woodhouse, 164 A.2d 98, 106 (Pa. 1960); Sollars v. State,

316 P.2d 917; 920 (Nev. 1957); Hechtman, Practice Commentaries following N.Y. Penal Law § 30.05, at 69.

103. Thompson v. Commonwealth, 193 Va. 704, 717, 70 S.E.2d 284, 291–92 (1952).

104. STANDARDS, *supra* note 70, standard 7-6.1 & commentary; APA STATEMENT, *supra* note 70, at 10–12. Moore's formulation would accomplish the same result by focusing on rationality as the sole criterion of responsibility. *See* Moore, *supra* note 71, ch. 6.

105. As of 1983, 32 states place the burden on the defendant: Alabama, Alaska, Arizona, Arkansas, California, Connecticut, Delaware, District of Columbia, Georgia, Hawaii, Indiana, Kentucky, Louisiana, Maine, Minnesota, Missouri, Nevada, New Hampshire, New Jersey, North Carolina, Ohio, Oregon, Pennsylvania, Rhode Island, South Carolina, Texas, Vermont, Virginia, Washington, West Virginia, Wisconsin, and Wyoming. Sixteen states put the burden on the prosecution: Colorado, Florida, Illinois, Iowa, Kansas, Maryland, Massachusetts, Michigan, Mississippi, Nebraska, New Mexico, New York, North Dakota, Oklahoma, South Dakota, and Tennessee.

106. 18 U.S.C. § 402(b) (1984).

107. *See, e.g.,* Commonwealth v. Vogel, 440 Pa. 1, 2, 268 A.2d 89, 90 (1970).

108. *See generally* Addington v. Texas, 441 U.S. 418 (1979); APA STATEMENT, *supra* note 70, at 12–13.

109. Again using the five-state acquittal rates described, *supra* note 95, the three states with the lowest acquittal rates (Wyoming, Illinois, and Florida) place the burden on the prosecution, as does the state with the highest acquittal rate (New York), while the state with the second highest acquittal rate (California) places the burden on the defendant.

110. STANDARDS, *supra* note 70, standard 7-6.9.

111. A GOLDSTEIN, *supra* note 6, at 113.

112. Fain v. Commonwealth, 78 Ky. 183 (1879); H.M. Advocate v. Fraser, 4 Couper 70 (1878).

113. *See generally* P. LOW, J. JEFFRIES, & R. BONNIE, CRIMINAL LAW: CASES AND MATERIALS 152–54 (1982). Most of the decisions finding automatism in such cases are British or Canadian. *But see* Featherstone v. Clark, 293 F. Supp. 508 (W.D. ex. 1978); Sprague v. State, 52 Wis. 2d 89, 187 N.W.2d 784 (1971).

114. Tift v. State, 17 Ga. App. 663, 88 S.E. 41 (1916). *Cf.* State v. Gooze, 14 N.J. Super. 277, 81 A.2d 811 (1951); People v. Decina, 2 N.Y. 2d 133 157 N.Y.S. 2d 558, 138 N.E.2d 799 (1956).

115. *See, e.g.,* P. LOW, J. JEFFRIES, & R. BONNIE, *supra* note 113, at 152; Rose, *Criminal Responsibility and Competency as Influenced by Organic Disease,* 35 MO. L. REV. 326 (1970).

116. Bratty v. Attorney-General for Northern Ireland, 3 All E.R. 535 (1961); Regina v. Kemp, 3 All E.R. 249 (1956).

117. Gifford, Murawski, Kline, & Sachar, *An Unusual Adverse Reaction to Self-Medication with Prednisone: An Irrational Crime during a Fugue State,* 7 INT'L J. PSYCHIATRIC MED.

97 (1976). *See also* Luparello, *Features of Fugue: A Unified Hypothesis of Regression,* 18 J. AM. PSYCHOANALYTIC ASS'N 379, 380 (1970).

118. *See supra* cases cited note 82.

119. MODEL PENAL CODE § 2.02 (Official Draft 1962).

120. The ABA has criticized use of this term because it suggests that clinical testimony on the issue of *mens rea* is a "doctrine" like the insanity defense, when in fact it is merely an evidentiary rule that permits relevant testimony on an issue pertinent to most criminal trials. STANDARDS, *supra* note 70, standard 7-6.2 and commentary. Though we agree with the ABA's position, many jurisdictions do not (see below). As a result, it is more accurate to refer to the general concept of clinical testimony on *mens rea* as a doctrine, and we continue to use the term "diminished capacity" as a shorthand designation for the various exceptions to the evidentiary principle noted below.

121. Over two-thirds of the states that have the death penalty follow the Model Penal Code's formulation in requiring the capital sentencing authority to consider as possible "mitigating" factors: (1) whether the capital offense "was committed while the defendant was under the influence of extreme mental or emotional disturbance," and (2) whether, at the time of the offense, "the capacity of the defendant to appreciate the criminality [wrongfulness] of his conduct or to conform his conduct to the requirements of the law was impaired as a result of mental disease or defect or intoxication." P. LOW, J. JEFFRIES, & R. BONNIE, *supra* note 113, at 811.

122. Because of this difficulty, Morse has proposed that a person who can show diminished responsibility arbitrarily receive half the punishment normally received for the crime. Morse, *Diminished Capacity: A Moral and Legal Conundrum,* 2 INT'L J. PSYCHIATRY, 271 (1979).

123. Arizona, Delaware, Florida, Georgia, Louisiana, Maryland, Minnesota, North Carolina, Ohio, Oklahoma, Tennessee, West Virginia, Wisconsin, and Wyoming.

124. The following states have indicated, either by statute or judicial decision, that expert testimony on *mens rea* is admissible, at least under certain circumstances: Alaska, Arkansas, California, Connecticut, Colorado, Hawaii, Idaho, Iowa, Kansas, Kentucky, Maine, Massachusetts, Michigan, Missouri, Montana, Nevada, New Jersey, New Mexico, New York, Oregon, Pennsylvania, Rhode Island, Texas, Utah, Vermont, and Washington. *See also infra* notes 125–31. The ABA has also recommended that such testimony be admitted. STANDARDS, *supra* note 70, standard 7-6.2.

125. State v. Hines, 445 A.2d 314 (Conn. 1982); Commonwealth v. Walzack, 360 A.2d 914 (Pa. 1976); People v. Wetmore, 22 Cal. 3d 318, 583 P.2d 1308, 149 Cal. Rptr. 265 (1978).

126. *See* Hughes v. Mathews, 576 F.2d 1250 (7th Cir.), *cert. dismissed sub nom.,* Israel v. Hughes, 439 U.S. 801 (1978).

127. *See, e.g.,* Simpson v. State, 381 N.E.2d 122 (Ind. 1978); People v. Loving, 258 Cal. App. 2d 84, 65 Cal. Rptr. 425 (1968); Bradshaw v. State, 353 So. 2d 188 (Fla.

1st D.C.A. 1978); Waye v. Commonwealth, 219 Va. 683, 251 S.E.2d 202 (1979).

128. *See, e.g.,* United States v. Bright, 517 F.2d 584 (2d Cir. 1975).

129. Massachusetts and Texas clearly impose this limitation. The cases permitting expert testimony on *mens rea* in Pennsylvania, Nevada, New Mexico, Rhode Island, and Washington were homicide cases, leaving it unclear whether they would restrict the use of such testimony to homicide charges only.

130. Only Colorado, New Jersey, and Oregon have specifically held that evidence of diminished capacity is admissible to negate general intent.

131. *See, e.g.,* Ohio v. Wilcox, 436 N.E.2d 523 (Ohio 1982); State v. Schantz, 403 P.2d 521 (Ariz. 1965).

132. *See* Bonnie & Slobogin, *The Role of Mental Health Professionals in the Criminal Process: The Case for Informed Speculation,* 66 VA. L. REV. 427, 473–77 (1980).

133. 517 F.2d 584 (2d Cir. 1975).

134. *See* FED. R. EVID. 404, 405.

135. 247 F. Supp. 743 (S.D.N.Y.) 1965).

136. *See* W. LAFAVE & A. SCOTT, *supra* note 1, at 341–47.

137. People v. Kelly, 10 Cal. 3d 565, 516 P.2d 875, 111 Cal. Rptr. 171 (1973); Chittum v. Commonwealth, 211 Va. 12, 174 S.E.2d 779 (1970).

138. W. LAFAVE & A. SCOTT, *supra* note 1, at 348.

139. *Id. See also* Minneapolis v. Altimus, 306 Minn. 462, 238 N.W.2d 851 (1976); MODEL PENAL CODE §§ 2.08(4), 5(c) (1962).

140. W. LAFAVE & A. SCOTT, *supra* note 1, at 342–43.

141. *See, e.g.,* Driver v. Hinnant, 346 F.2d 761 (4th Cir. 1966). *Cf.* Robinson v. California, 370 U.S. 660 (1962).

142. United States v. Moore, 486 F.2d 1139 (D.C. Cir. 1973); United States v. Sullivan, 406 F.2d 180 (2d Cir. 1969); People v. Vorrero, 227 N.E.2d 18 (N.Y. 1967); Roberts v. State, 41 Wis. 2d 537, 164 N.W.2d 525 (1969).

143. Beasley v. State, 50 Ala. 149 (1874); People v. Kelly, 10 Cal. 3d 565, 516 P.2d 875, 111 Cal. Rptr. 171 (1973); W. LAFAVE & A. SCOTT, *supra* note 1, at 348 n.52.

144. Alaska, Delaware, Georgia, Illinois, Indiana, Kentucky, Maryland, Michigan, New Mexico, South Carolina, South Dakota, and Utah.

145. *See* MICH. COMP. LAWS ANN. §§ 768.29a(2) & 768.36 (1982).

146. According to Smith & Hall, *supra* note 24, at 101, the percentage of acquittals since passage of Michigan's GBMI law has actually increased slightly. *See also* Slobogin, *The GBMI Verdict: An Idea Whose Time Should Not Have Come,* 53 GEO WASH. L. REV. 494, 506–10 (1985).

147. *See* Favole, *supra* note 74, at 283–95. For further discussion of the verdict, *see* Slobogin, *supra* note 146.

148. Florida, Hawaii, Maryland, New Hampshire, New York, Ohio, Pennsylvania, and Virginia.

149. Smith & Hall, *supra* note 24, at 95–100.

150. Pasework, *Insanity Plea: A Review of the Research Literature,* 9 J. PSYCHIATRY L. 357 (1981).

151. The four studies, in the order in which they appear in the table, are as follows: Cooke & Sikorski, *Factors Affecting Length of Hospitalization in Persons Adjudicated Not Guilty By Reason of Insanity,* 2 BULL. AM. ACAD. PSYCHIATRY & L. 251 (1975); Criss & Racine, *supra* note 31; Pasework, Pantle, & Steadman, *supra* note 25; Steadman, *supra* note 21. *See also* Kaplan, *The Mad and the Bad: An Inquiry into the Disposition of the Criminally Insane,* 2 J. MED. PHIL. 244 (1977); Singer, *Insanity Acquittal in the Seventies: Observations and Empirical Analysis of One Jurisdiction,* 2 MENTAL DISABILITY L. REP. 405 (1978).

152. Some condensing of the original data was necessary to make the studies more nearly comparable. For example, in the category "Type of offense," the subcategory "Murder" includes murder, manslaughter, and attempted murder; the subcategory "Other assault" includes other types of assault (e.g., felonious assault), criminal sexual conduct (e.g., rape, forced sodomy), and armed robbery. The data are not directly comparable in all categories; for example, "Prior criminal record" was recorded by Cooke and Sikorski as prior conviction, while the other studies used prior arrest as the measure. The percentages in Table 6-1 are rounded to the nearest whole percent; in some instances the figures are extracted directly from the studies cited, while in other instances they are based on our calculations of data presented. Where calculations were made by us, only the *n* for which data were available was used in determining percentages.

153. Gleick, *Getting Away with Murder,* NEW TIMES 21 (Aug. 1978).

154. Robey commented that his review of 203 NGRI patients committed to Michigan's Center for Forensic Psychiatry by mid 1973 "showed less than half of them to be both medically and legally appropriate." The basis for his "second-guessing" of the NGRI adjudications was not indicated. Robey, *Guilty But Mentally Ill,* 6 BULL. AM. ACAD. PSYCHIATRY L. 374, 375 (1978).

155. *See* Petrila, Selle, Rouse, Evans, & Moore, *The Pre-Trial Examination Process in Missouri: A Descriptive Process,* 9 BULL. AM. ACAD. PSYCHIATRY & L. 60 (1981) (reporting that a study of pretrial evaluations in Missouri in 1978 revealed that only 1 of 127 defendants recommended as NGRI was diagnosed as having a personality disorder).

156. Howard & Clark, *When Courts and Experts Disagree: Discordance Between Insanity Recommendations and Adjudications,* 9 LAW & HUM. BEHAV. 385 (1985).

157. Criss & Racine, *supra* note 31.

158. Pasework, Pantle, & Steadman, *supra* note 25.

159. This account is taken from Gleick, *supra* note 153, and Bedau, *Rough Justice: The Limits of Novel Defenses,* 8 HASTINGS CENTER REP. 8 (1978).

160. Bedau, *supra* note 159; Berkman, *The State of Michigan versus a Battered Wife: A Case Study,* 44 BULL. MENNINGER CLINIC 603 (1980).

161. "[A]ggressive behavior has been extensively reported in association with temporal lobe epilepsy. . . . it would be difficult to cite . . . another medical or neurologic

illness in which aggressive behavior is described so regularly." Devinsky & Bear, *Varieties of Aggressive Behavior in Temporal Lobe Epilepsy,* 141 AM. J. PSYCHIATRY 651, 653 (1984).

162. V. MARK & E. ERVIN, VIOLENCE AND THE BRAIN (1970). Ratner and Shapiro have stated, "It is our belief that the presence of a documented neurological deficit in an individual suffering from episodic dyscontrol syndrome should be considered strong evidence, *under certain circumstances,* for inability of the individual to conform his conduct to the requirements of the law by virtue of a mental defect' (emphasis added). Ratner & Shapiro, *The Episodic Dyscontrol Syndrome and Criminal Responsibility,* 7 BULL. AM. ACAD. PSYCHIATRY & L. 422 (1979). The authors do not indicate what those requisite circumstances would be.

163. See J. DELGADO, PHYSICAL CONTROL OF THE MIND (1969). (One of the more dramatic and, on the surface, compelling demonstrations by Delgado was that "cerebral stimulation produced inhibition of aggressive behavior, and a bull in full charge could be abruptly stopped . . ." *Id.* at 168. *But see infra* note 165.

164. E. VALENSTEIN, BRAIN CONTROL (1973).

165. Regarding Delgado's demonstration with the bull (*see supra* note 163) Valenstein commented : "[A]ctually there is no good reason for believing that the stimulation had any direct effect on the bull's aggressive tendencies. An examination of the film record makes it apparent that the charging bull was stopped because as long as the stimulation was on it was forced to turn around in the same direction continuously. . . . any scientist with knowledge in this field could conclude only that the stimulation had been activating a neural pathway controlling movement. . . . Most writers have simply overlooked the major effect on the motor system, preferring the more dramatic interpretation of the stimulation as a pure pacifier, and no one has taken the trouble to correct this impression." *Id.* at 98–99. Other studies reviewed by Valenstein revealed that "stimulation at a number of places in the amygdala may produce aggressive responses but only in violent patients, not in patients who have no aggressive tendencies. The possibility that the response produced by the stimulation, therefore, may reflect the patient's personality rather than the specific function of the area stimulated may produce misleading conclusions concerning the brain area responsible for the behavior. Animal studies have also indicated that the temperament of the subject may contribute significantly to the response evoked by brain stimulation, and in some instances it may be a better predictor than the anatomical site of the electrode." *Id.* at 244. Valenstein further noted: "It should be apparent that the changes that follow amygdalectomy can be very unpredictable and far reaching. Characterizing the total effects of these operations by such phrases as 'taming' and 'hypersexuality' can be very misleading. Often the observations that have led to

the use of such labels were limited to the restricted conditions of the laboratory or hospital. . . . The primary changes produced by these temporal lobe operations in animals may have little to do with the regulation of aggression and sexuality. . . . It would be very surprising indeed if the brain were organized into spatially discrete units that conform to our abstract categorizations of behavior." *Id.* at 142.

166. Valenstein, *id.* at 244, quoted from an earlier study by Chapman: "Some of the clinical features of temporal lobe epilepsy may be reproduced by electrical stimulation of the amygdaloid nuclear region. This was true in five out of six of our patients. The one major feature of their illness that could not be reproduced was assaultive behavior. In no instance was any subjective or behavioral response evoked that remotely resembled aggressiveness. This finding was disconcerting as the major reason for selecting these patients for the electrical coagulation was intractable assaultiveness."

167. Blumer, *Temporal Lobe Epilepsy and Its Psychiatric Significance,* in PSYCHIATRIC ASPECTS OF NEUROLOGIC DISEASE (D. F. Benson & D. Blumer eds. 1975); Blumer, *Epilepsy and Violence,* in RAGE/HATE/ASSAULT AND OTHER FORMS OF VIOLENCE (Madden & J. Lion eds. 1976).

168. Devinsky & Bear, *supra* note 161, at 654.

169. Delgado-Escueta, Mattson, Goldensohn, Speigel, Madsen, Crandall, Dreifuss, & Porter, *The Nature of Aggression during Epileptic Seizures,* 305 NEW ENG. J. MED. 711, 715 (1981). (In this study, the expert panel carefully reviewed 33 epileptic attacks by 19 patients, all of which had been fully documented on videotape. The attacks all "appeared suddenly, without evidence of planning, and lasted an average of 29 seconds . . . Aggressive acts were stereotyped, simple, unsustained, and never supported by consecutive series of purposeful movements." *Id.*)

170. Devinsky & Bear, *supra* note 161, at 654.

171. "It is further remarkable how even during extreme outbursts a measure of control seems to be present: the rage is frightening, furniture is destroyed, a family member is struck, but rarely is someone injured." Blumer, *Epilepsy and Violence, supra* note 167, at 210.

172. Blumer, *Temporal Lobe Epilepsy and Its Psychiatric Significance, supra* note 168 at 187.

173. Walker, *Murder or Epilepsy?,* 133 J. NERVOUS MENTAL DISEASE 430 (1961).

174. Blumer & Benson, *Personality Changes with Frontal and Temporal Lobe Lesions,* in PSYCHIATRIC ASPECTS OF NEUROLOGIC DISEASE (D. F. Benson & D. Blumer eds. 1975).

175. See supra notes 170–72 and accompanying text.

176. Himwich, Bowman, Daly, Fazekas, Wortis, & Goldfarb, *Changes in Cerebral Bloodflow and Arteriovenous Oxygen Difference during Insulin Hypoglycemia,* 93 J. NERVOUS MENTAL DISEASE 362, 364 (1941).

177. Himwich, *A Review of Hypoglycemia, Its Physiology and Pathology, Symptomatology and Treatment,* 11 AM. J. DIGESTIVE DISEASES 1, 4–5 (1944).

178. Lyle, *Temporary Insanity: Some Practical Considerations in a Legal Defense*, 8 J. ORTHOMOLECULAR PSYCHIATRY (1979).

179. Gittler, *Spontaneous Hypoglycemia*, 62 N.Y. STATE J. MED. 235, 239 (1962).

180. The transitory nature of the episode is also of diagnostic importance and has been dramatically demonstrated in the treatment of individual cases. Wilder wrote: "As a rule (hypoglycemic states) are promptly reversible by an intravenous injection of glucose . . . The effect is so miraculous that the needle is still in the patient's vein and a severe coma or psychosis has already been transformed into complete normalcy." Wilder, *Sugar Metabolism and Its Relation to Criminology*, in HANDBOOK OF CORRECTIONAL PSYCHOLOGY 101 (R. Lindner & Seliger eds. 1947).

181. AMERICAN PSYCHIATRIC ASSOCIATION, DIAGNOSTIC AND STATISTICAL MANUAL OF MENTAL DISORDERS (3d ed. 1980).

182. Data have been presented showing that dissociative disorder as a primary diagnosis in psychiatric populations is "much less than one-tenth of one percent (0.1%)." Cleary, *Dissociative States—Disproportionate Use as a Defense in Criminal Proceedings*, AM. J. FORENSIC PSYCHOLOGY 157, 159 (1983).

183. "The premorbid personality of a person who experiences dissociative states usually reveals emotional immaturity, self-centeredness and episodic emotional disturbances in childhood and adolescence." Showalter, Bonnie, & Roddy, *The Spousal-Homicide Syndrome*, 3 INT'L. J.L. PSYCHIATRY 117, 133 (1980).

184. Akhtar & Brenner, *Differential Diagnosis of Fugue-Like States*, 40 J. CLINICAL PSYCHIATRY 381 (1979).

185. Sandberg, Koeph, Ishihara, & Hauschka, *An XYY Male*, 2 LANCET 488 (1961).

186. Craft, *The Current Status of XYY and XXY Syndromes: A Review of Treatment Implications*, 1 INT'L J.L. PSYCHIATRY 319, 319–320 (1978).

187. Jarvik, Klodin, & Matsuyama, *Human Aggression and the Extra Y Chromosome: Fact or Fantasy*, 28 AM. PSYCHOLOGIST 674 (1973).

188. Walzer, Gerald, & Shah, *The XYY Genotype*, 29 ANN. REV. MED. 563 (1978).

189. Craft, *supra* note 186.

190. Walzer, Gerald, & Shah, *supra* note 188.

191. Jarvik, Klodin, & Matsuyama, *supra* note 187, at 679–80.

192. Craft, *supra* note 186, at 321.

193. "Since it is probable that there is considerable variability in the phenotypic development of XYY males, it is inappropriate to allude to an XYY syndrome. The term syndrome implies a degree of symptom consistency that is not supported by the data available at this time." Walzer, Gerald, & Shah, *supra* note 188, at 568.

194. H. FINGARETTE & A. HASSE, MENTAL DISABILITIES AND CRIMINAL RESPONSIBILITY ch. 11 (1979). Some studies they cite include WALLGREEN & BARRY, ACTIONS OF ALCOHOL 806 (1970); Merry, *The Loss of Control Myth*, 1 LANCET 1257 (1966).

195. H. FINGARETTE & A. HASSE, *supra* note 194, at 184–85.

196. *Id.* at 178.

197. *Id.* at 182.

198. *See e.g.*, LINDESMITH, ADDICTION AND OPIATES (1968); O'Donnell, *A Follow-up of Narcotic Addicts*, 34 J. ORTHOPSYCHIATRY 948 (1964); R. ROBBINS, A FOLLOW-UP OF VIETNAM DRUG USERS, SPECIAL ACTIONS OFFICE FOR DRUG ABUSE PREVENTION, EXECUTIVE OFFICE OF THE PRESIDENT (1973).

199. H. FINGARETTE & A. HASSE, *supra* note 194, at 165.

200. R. ROBBINS, *supra* note 198.

201. H. FINGARETTE & A. HASSE, *supra* note 194, at 165.

202. *See* Florida v. Zamora, 361 So.2d 776 (Fla.App. 1978).

203. *See* State v. Felde, 422 So.2d 370 (La. 1982); POST-TRAUMATIC STRESS DISORDER AND THE WAR VETERAN (W. Kelly) ed. 1985); Apostle, *The Unconsciousness Defense as Applied to Post-Traumatic Stress Disorder in a Vietnam Veteran*, 8 BULL. AM. ACAD. PSYCHIATRY L. 426 (1980).

204. *See* United States v. Hearst, 412 F. Supp. 889 (N.D.Cal. 1976).

205. Horney, Menstrual Cycles and Criminal Responsibility, 2 LAW & HUM. BEHAV. 25 (1978).

206. Rada, *Plasma Androgens and the Sex Offender*, 8 BULL. AM. ACAD. PSYCHIATRY L. 456 (1980).

207. Conn, *The Myth of Coercion through Hypnosis: A Brief Communication*, 19 INT'L J. CLINICAL EXPERIMENTAL HYPNOSIS 95 (1981).

208. P. DIXON, THE OFFICIAL RULES (1978).

209. H. Stock & N. Poythress, Psychologists' Opinions on Competency and Sanity: How Reliable? (paper presented at the American Psychological Association Annual Convention, New York, August 1979).

210. Fukunaga, Pasewark, Hawkins, & Gudeman, *Insanity Plea: Inter-examiner Agreement and Concordance of Psychiatric Opinion and Court Verdict*, 5 LAW & HUM. BEHAV. 325 (1981).

211. L. Raifman, Interjudge Reliability of Psychiatrists' Evaluations of Criminal Defendants' Competency to Stand Trial and Legal Sanity (paper presented at the American Psychology–Law Society Convention, Baltimore, October 1979).

212. Rogers Criminal Responsibility Assessment Scales (available from Psychological Assessment Resources, Inc., Odessa, Fla.). *See also* Rogers & Cavanaugh, *The Rogers Criminal Responsibility Assessment Scales*, 160 ILL. MED. J. 164 (1981).

213. Rogers, Dolmetsch, & Cavanaugh, *An Empirical Approach to Insanity Evaluations*, 37 J. CLINICAL PSYCHOLOGY 683 (1981).

214. A correlation coefficient is a measure of linear association between two sets of scores, or, in the present case, two sets of judgments by different examiners. A correlation coefficient may take any value between + 1.00, which indicates a perfect positive correlation

(or perfect agreement), and −1.00, which would indicate a perfect negative correlation (total disagreement). A correlation coefficient of .00 indicates that the two sets of scores (or judgments) are not linearly related, that the scores (or judgments) are determined by different factors, and that prediction of one set of scores from the other is poor. In the study cited, the correlation of +.82 indicates fairly high agreement between the clinicians. *See* F. GHISELLI, THEORY OF PSYCHOLOGICAL MEASUREMENT chs. 5 & 6 (1964).

215. Rogers, Wasyliw, & Cavanaugh, *Evaluating Insanity: A Study of Construct Validity,* 8 LAW & HUM. BEHAV. 293 (1984).

216. Kappa is a statistic for measuring agreement between examiners on nominal categories, such as diagnosis or, in the present context, legal sanity–insanity. It is considered to be a conservative statistic because agreement between examiners is corrected to eliminate the effects of chance agreement. A kappa of +1.00 reflects perfect interrater agreement, while a kappa of .00 indicates that examiners agree at the level obtainable by chance alone (negative values indicate less than chance agreement). *See* Cohen, *A Coefficient of Agreement for Nominal Scales,* 20 EDUC. PSYCHOLOGICAL MEASUREMENT 37 (1960).

217. Rogers, Seman, & Wasyliw, *The RCRAS and Legal Insanity: A Cross-Validation Study,* 39 J. CLINICAL PSYCHOLOGY 544 (1983).

218. *See* G. MELTON, L. WEITHORN, & C. SLOBOGIN, COMMUNITY MENTAL HEALTH CENTERS AND THE COURTS: AN EVALUATION OF COMMUNITY-BASED FORENSIC SERVICES (1985).

219. Staller & Geertsma, *The Consistency of Psychiatrists' Clinical Judgments,* 137 J. NERVOUS & MENTAL DISEASE 58 (1963).

220. *Id.*

221. Morse, *Failed Explanations and Criminal Responsibility: Experts and the Unconscious,* 68 VA. L. REV. 971, 1022 (1982).

222. *See supra* note 24 and accompanying text.

223. Bonnie & Slobogin, *supra* note 132.

224. *See* Bridgeman & Marlowe, *Jury Decision-Making: An Empirical Study Based on Actual Felony Trials,* 64 J. APPLIED PSYCHOLOGY 91 (1979); Read, Rusk, Morris, & Bozzetti, *Psychiatrists and the Jurors' Dilemma,* 6 BULL. AM. ACAD. PSYCHIATRY & L. 1 (1978); Simon, *The Dynamics of Jury Behavior,* in THE ROLE OF THE FORENSIC PSYCHOLOGIST (G. Cooke ed. 1980).

225. Daniel & Harris, *Female Offenders Referred for Pre-Trial Psychiatric Evaluation,* 9 BULL. AM. ACAD. PSYCHIATRY & L. 40 (1981).

226. Fukunaga, Pasewark, Hawkins, & Gudeman, *supra* note 210.

227. Poythress, unpublished data (1982).

228. Rogers, Cavanaugh, Seman, & Harris, *Legal Outcome and Clinical Findings: A Study of Insanity Evaluations,* 14 BULL. AM. ACAD. PSYCHIATRY & L. 219 (1986).

229. Trust, more than expertise, may influence a listener

to adopt a speaker's position. *See infra* § 14.04(b).

230. "This hypothesis lends itself to empirical validation. Groups of experts in psychology could be examined to determine if they uniquely possess the wisdom required to evaluate whether the applicable legal standard has been met." Comment, *The Psychologist as Expert Witness: Science in the Courtroom,* 38 MD. L. REV. 539, 596 n. 274 (1979) (citing Veatch, *Generalization of Expertise,* 1 HASTINGS CENTER REP. No. 2 (1973)).

231. Rogers Criminal Responsibility Assessment Scales, *supra* note 212.

232. *Id.* at 1.

233. *Id.* at 10–11.

234. A fourth hypothesis, that the use of the scales would result in acceptable levels of interrater reliability, has also been tested. *See supra* notes 212–215 and accompanying text.

235. *See supra* notes 213–217.

236. Rogers Criminal Responsibility Assessment Scales, *supra* note 212, at 33.

237. *See supra* note 232 and accompanying text.

238. *See supra* note 233 and accompanying text.

239. Morse, *Crazy Behavior, Morals and Science: An Analysis of Mental Health Law,* 51 S. CAL. L. REV. 527 (1978); Comment, *supra* note 230.

240. *See supra* notes 213–217.

241. For a discussion of investigative reporting as a possible clinical procedure, *see* Levine, *Investigative Reporting as a Research Method: An Analysis of Bernstein and Woodward's ALL THE PRESIDENT'S MEN,* 35 AM. PSYCHOLOGIST 626 (1980).

242. Bonnie & Slobogin, *supra* note 132, at 504.

243. In Missouri in 1978, of 480 referrals for pretrial examination, only 37.3% were assigned diagnoses of psychoses, mental retardation, or organic brain syndrome. Petrila, Selle, Rouse, Evans, & Moore, *supra* note 155, at Table 11.

244. *See supra* notes 9–15 and accompanying text.

245. *See supra* note 24 and accompanying text.

246. Slobogin, Melton, & Showalter, *The Feasibility of a Brief Evaluation of Mental State at the Time of the Offense,* 8 LAW & HUM. BEHAV. 305 (1984).

247. Morse, *supra* note 221, at 1049.

248. Sigelman, Budd, Spanhel, & Schoenrock, *When in Doubt, Say Yes: Acquiescence in Interviews with Mentally Retarded Persons,* 19 MENTAL RETARDATION 53 (1981).

249. Rogers, *Toward an Empirical Model of Malingering and Deception,* 2 BEHAV. SCI. L. 93 (1984).

250. The classic study on response set validity is Gough, *The F Minus K Dissimulation Index for the MMPI,* 14 J. CONSULTING CLIN. PSYCHOLOGY 408 (1950). Experienced forensic psychologists indicate that a "fake bad" MMPI and a benign Rorschach together suggest malingering. Cooke & Jackson, *Competence to Stand Trial: Role of the Psychologist,* 2 PROF. PSYCHOLOGY 373 (1971). Recent studies of offender populations, however, suggest that conventional MMPI indices for detecting "fake bad" response sets may be invalid with these subjects (e.g., high F score may be valid with many offenders).

See E. MEGARGEE & M. BOHN, CLASSIFYING CRIMINAL OFFENDERS (1979).

251. See, e.g., Bradford & Smith, Amnesia and Homicide: The Padola Case and a Study of Thirty Cases, 7 BULL. AM. ACAD. PSYCHIATRY L. 219 (1979); Taylor & Kopelman, Amnesia for Criminal Offenses, 14 PSYCHOLOGICAL MED. 581 (1984) (23% of those studied claimed amnesia).

252. Schacter, Amnesia and Crime: How Much Do We Really Know? 41 AM PSYCHOLOGIST 286, 290–91 (1986). This article is an excellent review of the literature on amnesia.

253. Schacter, supra note 252, at 291–94.

254. R. JULIEN, A PRIMER OF DRUG ACTION 43 (1975).

255. Id. at 147.

256. For a concise discussion of different types of amnesia and clinical conditions associated with them, see Koson & Robey, Amnesia and Competency to Stand Trial, 130 AM. J. PSYCHIATRY 588 (1973).

257. Redlich, Ravitz, & Dession, Narcoanalysis and Truth, 107 AM. J. PSYCHIATRY 586 (1951).

258. Gerson & Victoroff, Experimental Investigation into the Validity of Confessions Obtained under Sodium Amytal Narcosis, 9 J. CLINICAL PSYCHOPATHOLOGY 359 (1948).

259. Spector & Foster, Admissibility of Hypnotic Statements: Is the Law of Evidence Susceptible?, 38 OHIO ST. L. J. 567 (1977); Ruffa, Hypnotically Induced Testimony: Should It Be Admitted?, 19 CRIM. L. BULL. 293 (1983).

260. Packer, The Use of Hypnotic Techniques in the Evaluation of Criminal Defendants, 9 J. PSYCHIATRY L. 313 (1981).

261. Frye v. United States, 293 F. 1013, 1014 (1923).

262. Cameron, The Mental Health Expert: A Guide to Direct and Cross-Examination, 2 CRIM. JUST. J. 299, 309 (1979).

263. N. Poythress, Is There a Baby in the Bath Water?: Psychological Tests and Expert Testimony (paper presented at the American Psychology–Law Society Convention, Boston, 1981).

264. Kubie, The Ruby Case: Who or What Was on Trial?, 1 J. PSYCHIATRY L. 475 (1973).

265. See supra note 250 and accompanying text.

266. In a study of 107 pretrial examinations at a Massachusets, diagnosis perfectly predicted insanity opinion. Each of 31 cases diagnosed as psychotic was recommended as not criminally responsible; none of the nonpsychotic defendants received such a recommendation. McGarry, Competency for Trial and Due Process via the State Hospital, 122 AM. J. PSYCHIATRY 623 (1965).

267. Morse, supra note 239.

268. The term "chemically induced" is somewhat of an overstatement. The behavioral symptoms of some disorders can be induced by the administration of certain drugs, though the long-term impact is not to induce the long-range (prognostic) features. See Julien, supra note 254; Stone, Drug-Related Schizophrenic Syndromes, 11 INT'L J. PSYCHIATRY 391 (1973).

269. See, e.g., Hafner & Boker, Mentally Disordered Violent Offenders, 8 SOC. PSYCHIATRY 220 (1973).

270. Two kinds of prognostic statements may be of interest to the factfinder—those having to do with the progression of the disorder itself, and those having to do with how the defendant might be managed by the mental health system if he or she is acquitted and subsequently committed. The examiner's statements regarding diagnosis and the relative severity of the disorder as perceived for mental health purposes may suggest to the judge or jury whether or not the defendant's commitment would be supported.

271. For an excellent analysis of the limits of clinical inquiry into such legally defined mental elements as "intent," see Clark, Clinical Limits of Expert Testimony on Diminished Capacity, 5 INT'L J.L. PSYCHIATRY 155 (1982).

272. Morse, supra note 239.

273. Though there is one psychodynamic model, there are several schools of thought invoking psychodynamic concepts—Freudian, Jungian, Adlerian, and so forth. For our purposes, their similarities—especially the focus on unconscious determinants of behavior—are more important than their differences.

274. In California, which until recently required that the defendant "meaningfully' and "maturely" consider his or her actions, see, e.g., People v. Wolff, 61 Cal. 2d 795, 394 P.2d 959, 40 Cal Rptr. 271 (1964), such formulations were also offered in support of a diminished capacity defense. See, e.g., People v. Gorshen, 51 Cal. 2d 716, 336 P.2d 492 (1959). Since 1981, when California's legislature reinstated the traditional, consciousness-oriented notion of intent, CAL. PENAL CODE § 1026.5 (1985), this kind of testimony should no longer be relevant.

275. Revitch, Sexually Motivated Burglaries, 6 BULL. AM. ACAD. PSYCHIATRY L. 277 (1978).

276. For a comprehensive critique of psychodynamic explanations of criminal behavior, see Morse, supra note 221.

277. In one study of the consistency of psychiatric judgments, psychiatrists were asked to rate the applicability of 565 descriptive statements to the clinical data from a videotaped patient interview. Ratings ranged from 5 (totally applicable) to 0 (does not apply). Nested in the 565 items were 8 "nonsense" items that were deemed by the investigators to be fanciful, extremely esoteric, and completely beyond the data demonstrated in the interview. Several of these items involved psychodynamic symbolism—for example, "At this point, the patient's depreciation of the introjected father's penis is revealed," or "The loss of a boy friend is painful for the patient because it reawakens her secondary envy of mother's breast." Though the psychiatrists had been instructed to give inapplicable items a rating of 0, three of the nonsense items were scored across six categories of applicability; four others were scored in five of the possible six categories. Staller & Geertsma, supra note 216.

278. Ayllon, Haughton, & Hughes, Interpretation of Symptoms: Fact or Fiction?, 3 BEHAV. RESEARCH & THERAPY 1 (1965).

279. *Id.* at 3.

280. And the theory used to explain behavior may significantly influence third-party judgments about the responsibility of the actor. *See* Farina, Fisher, & Getter, *Some Consequences of Changing People's Views Regarding the Nature of Mental Illness,* 87 J. ABNORMAL PSYCHOLOGY 272 (1978).

Chapter 7

1. A. CAMPBELL, THE LAW OF SENTENCING 21 (1978).

2. The following discussion is taken generally from *id.* at 24–41.

3. Dershowitz has noted that psychiatry has traditionally served three major functions in the criminal process: participating in the determination of past culpability (the insanity defense); present capacity (competency to stand trial); and the prediction of future dangerousness (sentencing, the need for commitment). Dershowitz, *The Role of Psychiatry in the Sentencing Process,* 1 INT'L J.L. PSYCHIATRY 63, 76 (1978).

4. Psychiatrists seem to be of most use at disposition, both because their expertise is used most appropriately in responding to the questions of rehabilitation and prediction posed at sentencing, and because they are removed at sentencing from the kind of value judgments inherent in a determination of criminal responsibility. *See, e.g.,* R. Campbell, *Sentencing: The Use of Psychiatric Information and Presentence Reports,* 60 KY. L. J. 285, 286–87 (1972).

5. In the 1970s, several courts suggested that clinical predictions were too suspect for use in civil commitment. *See generally infra* § 8.02(c) for a more detailed discussion. In the early 1980s, however, the United States Supreme Court held that clinical predictions were reliable enough for use even in capital sentencing. *See infra* note 136 and accompanying text. But its conclusion that clinical practices have sufficient reliability to be used in legal process is based on an assessment of the needs of the legal system, not on an empirical inquiry into the reliability of those predictions from a scientific point of view.

6. Jurek v. Texas, 428 U.S. 262 (1976).

7. Dershowitz, *supra* note 3, has concluded that the continued role of psychiatry in the sentencing process is uncertain, because the objectives of most sentencing reform efforts are the reduction of discretion in sentencing, and renewed emphasis on the *crime* that has been committed rather than the *criminal* who has committed it.

8. N. KITTRIE & E. ZENOFF, SANCTIONS, SENTENCING AND CORRECTIONS 362 (1981).

9. *Id.* at 363.

10. *Id.* at 367.

11. *Id.* at 363, 367.

12. *Id.* at 368.

13. R. Campbell, *supra* note 4, at 288.

14. *Id.* at 288 n. 21, and sources cited there.

15. Cavender & Mushenko, *The Adoption and Implementation of Determinate-Based Sanctioning Policies: A Critical Perspective,* 17 GEO. L.R. 425, 430 (1983).

16. *Id.*

17. Dershowitz, *supra* note 3, at 63–64.

18. *Id.*

19. *Id.*

20. Cavender & Meshenko, *supra* note 15, at 434.

21. *Id.*

22. TRANSACTIONS OF THE NATIONAL CONGRESS ON PRISONS AND REFORMATORY DISCIPLINE (ALBANY 1871) (Weeds & Parsons eds. 1970) (quoted by Dershowitz, *supra* note 3, at 65).

23. Dershowitz, *supra* note 3, at 66.

24. *Id.*

25. Fennell & Hall, *Due Process at Sentencing: An Empirical and Legal Analysis of the Disclosure of Presentence Reports in Federal Courts,* 93 HARV. L. REV. 1613, 1621–22 (1980).

26. Williams v. New York, 337 U.S. 241 (1948).

27. Von Hirsch & Hanrahan, Determinate Penalty Systems in America: An Overview, 27 CRIME DELINQ. 289, 294 (1981).

28. Several states and the United States Congress, in moving to determinate sentencing, have established a sentencing commission to fix penalties. *See infra* § 7.04(b).

29. The United States Supreme Court observed in 1980 that "one could argue without fear of contradiction by any decision of this Court that for crimes concededly classified and classifiable as felonies, that is, as punishable by significant terms of imprisonment in a state penitentiary, the length of the sentence actually imposed is purely a matter of legislative prerogative." Rummel v. Estelle, 445 U.S. 263, 274 (1980) (upholding a mandatory life sentence for a third felony offense, the three offenses in total involving less than $300).

30. It is estimated that 85% of federal criminal cases are disposed of through guilty pleas. Clearly, *Plea Negotiation and Its Effects on Sentencing,* 37 FED. BAR J. 62 (1978).

31. N. KITTRIE & E. ZENOFF, *supra* note 8, at 166–67.

32. Approximately a dozen states have provisions for jury sentencing. A CAMPBELL, *supra* note 1 at 227 n. 24 and accompanying text.

33. The United States Supreme Court has noted that "we begin with the general proposition that once it is determined that a sentence is within the limitations set forth in the statute under which it is imposed, appellate review is at an end." Dorszynski v. United States, 418 U.S. 424, 431 (1974).

34. A. CAMPBELL, *supra* note 1, at 52.

35. Morrissey v. Brewer, 408 U.S. 471, 477 (1972).

36. A. CAMPBELL *supra* note 1, at 416. For a discussion of the bases for parole board action, *see* Dawson, *The Decision to Grant or Deny Parole: A Study of Parole Criteria in Law and Practice,* 1966 WASH. U.L.Q. 23 (1966).

37. 408 U.S. at 484–488.

38. Dix, *Expert Prediction Testimony in Capital Sentencing: Evidentiary and Constitutional Considerations,* 19 AMER. CRIM. L. REV. 1, 15 (1981).

39. Weismann, *Sentencing Due Process: Evolving Constitutional Principles,* 18 WAKE FOREST L. REV. 523 (1982), argues that the Constitution requires a more formalized process when determinate sentencing is adopted. This argument has not yet been accepted by the courts.

40. Williams v. New York, 337 U.S. 241, 247 (1948).

41. *Id.; see also* Roberts v. United States, 445 U.S. 552 (1980)

42. FED. R. CRIM. P. 32(c)(1).

43. This description of the preparation of the presentence report and its contents is taken primarily from Fennell & Hall, *supra* note 25, at 1623–1628.

44. Schmolesky & Thorson, *The Importance of the Presentence Investigation Report after Sentencing,* 18 CRIM. L. BULL. 406, 408 (1982).

45. Fennell & Hall, *supra* note 25, at 1626.

46. Mempa v. Rhay, 389 U.S. 128 (1967); Townsend v. Burke, 334 U.S. 736 (1948).

47. United States v. Tucker, 404 U.S. 443 (1972).

48. Roberts v. United States, 445 U.S. 552 (1980).

49. United States v. Grayson, 438 U.S. 41 (1978).

50. VonHirsch & Hanrahan, *supra* note 27, at 291.

51. VonHirsch, *Recent Trends in American Criminal Sentencing Theory,* 42 MD. L. REV. 6 (1983). Von Hirsch points out that incapacitation and deterrence also play roles in a determinate sentence scheme. However, the notion of "commensurate" punishment or "just deserts" (i.e., the idea that the offender is punished in proportion to the severity of the offense) seems to have had the most impact as a conceptual underpinning for statutory revision. In large part, this is probably because of the overarching influence that Von Hirsch has had on this movement; he favors this particular variation on determinate sentencing, and his book, DOING JUSTICE (1976), has become the basic text of the determinate sentence advocates.

52. VonHirsch, *Recent Trends, supra* note 51, at 29.

53. One of the most influential articles in this regard was Martinson, *What Works?: Questions and Answers about Prison Reform,* 1974 THE PUBLIC INTEREST 22 (1974), which concluded that "with few and isolated exceptions, the rehabilitative efforts that have been reported so far had no appreciable effect on recidivism." *But see supra* notes 183–186 and accompanying text.

54. Monahan & Ruggiero, *Psychological and Psychiatric Aspects of Determinate Criminal Sentencing,* 3 INT'L J.L. PSYCHIATRY 143 (1980).

55. Hogarth, *Can Psychiatry Aid Sentencing?,* 2 INT'L J.L. PSYCHIATRY 499, 501 (1979). He concludes that psychiatry has a role, but only if as an initial step coerced treatment in the name of rehabilitation is ended, thereby rendering the therapist–offender relationship benign.

56. Greenberg & Humphries, *The Cooptation of Fixed Sentencing Reform,* 26 CRIME DELINQ. 206, 208, (1980).

57. Alschuler, *Sentencing Reform and Prosecutorial Power: A Critique of Recent Proposals for "Fixed" and "Presumptive" Sentencing,* 126 U. PA. L. REV. 550, 552–53 (1978).

58. Tonry, *Real Offense Sentencing: The Model Sentencing and Correction Act,* 72 J. CRIM. L. CRIMINOLOGY 1550, 1551 (1981).

59. Von Hirsch, *Constructing Guidelines for Sentencing: The Critical Choices for the Minnesota Sentencing Guidelines Commission,* 5 HAMLINE L. REV. at 164, 169–70 (1982). This and other articles on determinate sentencing are collected in a *Symposium on Determinate Sentencing,* 5 HAMLINE L. REV. 161 (1982). For a generally favorable critique of sentencing commission proposals *see* Feinberg, *Sentencing Reform and the Proposed Federal Criminal Code,* 5 HAMLINE L. REV. 217 (1982).

60. Cavender & Mushenko, *supra* note 15, at 448.

61. Cavender & Mushenko, *supra* note 15, reported that at of the time of their article (1983), Alaska, Arizona, California, New Jersey, New Mexico, and North Carolina had adopted presumptive sentencing. *Id.* at 447, n. 81.

62. As of 1983, Colorado, Illinois, Indiana, Missouri, and Tennessee used a definite sentencing scheme. *Id.* at 447, n. 82. Maine has a variety of this type of sentencing. *Id.* at Table 2, 462.

63. These factors are listed in *Research Project: Minnesota Sentencing Guidelines,* 5 HAMLINE L. REV. 273, 412–15.

64. Efforts at banning or sharply curtailing plea bargaining have been made in Alaska, Wayne County (Michigan), and "Hampton" County (a pseudonym for another Michigan county). Studies into the impact of such efforts are summarized in 1 RESEARCH ON SENTENCING: THE SEARCH FOR REFORM (Blumstein, Cohen, Martin, & Tonry eds.) ch. 4. The reviewers conclude that plea bargaining bans and mandatory and determinate sentencing laws have produced "modest changes" in sentencing outcome, primarily in the direction of some increases of prison use for marginal offenders who might not previously have received a prison sentence. *Id.* at 185–86. They also found that partial bans on plea bargaining were readily circumvented, (e.g., a ban on sentence bargaining produced an increase in charge bargaining). *Id.* at 185, 196–98.

65. Alschuler, *supra* note 57, at 551.

66. *E.g.,* Maine and Minnesota.

67. *See generally* Lagoy, Hussey, & Kramer, *A Comparative Assessment of Determinate Sentencing in the Four Pioneer States,* 24 CRIME DELINQ. 385 (1978).

68. Weismann, *supra* note 39, at 524.

69. Weismann, *Determinate Sentencing and Psychiatric Evidence: A Due Process Examination,* 27 ST. LOUIS U.L.J. 343 (1983).

70. Knapp, *Impact of the Minnesota Sentencing Guidelines on Sentencing Practices,* 5 HAMLINE L. REV. 237 (1982).

71. *Id.* at 240.

72. *Id.* at 247.

73. *Id.* at 242.

74. *Id.* at 252.

75. *Id.* at 253.

76. *Id.* at 255.

77. Clear, Hewitt, & Regoli, *Discretion and the Determinate*

Sentence: Its Distribution, Control, and Effect on Time Served, 24 CRIME DELINQ. 428 (1978).

78. *Id.* at 443–44.

79. *Id.* at 443.

80. Lagoy, Hussey, & Kramer, *supra* note 67, at 385.

81. *Id.*

82. Monahan & Ruggiero, *supra* note 54, at 143. It is also difficult to overestimate the desire of defense counsel to bring to the attention of the court any factor in mitigation of the defendant's actions. For example, in 1981, when nearly everyone was predicting the demise of the rehabilitative model, an article by a defense attorney appeared predicting the increased use of social and behavioral scientists on behalf of the defense. Gitchoff, *Expert Testimony at Sentencing,* NAT'L J. CRIM. DEF. 101, 107 (1981).

83. *See supra* note 63.

84. In 1980, 45 states had habitual offender statutes. *See* Comment, *The Constitutional Infirmities of Indiana's Habitual Offender Statute,* 13 IND. L. REV. 597 n.i. (1980).

85. IND. CODE, § 35-50-2-8(d) (Supp. 1983).

86. *Id.* at § 35-50-2-8(e).

87. Comment, *Selective Incapacitation: Reducing Crime through Predictions of Recidivism,* 96 HARV. L. REV. 512 511, (1983).

88. *Id.* at 513.

89. 445 U.S. 263 (1980).

90. Note, Rummel v. Estelle: *Sentencing Without a Rational Basis,* 32 SYRACUSE L. REV. 803 (1981); Comment, *Salvaging Proportionate Prison Sentencing: A Reply to* Rummel v. Estelle, 15 U. MICH. J.L. REFORM 285 (1982).

91. 463 U.S. 277 (1983).

92. In 1977, one report said that 28 states had such statutes. GROUP FOR THE ADVANCEMENT OF PSYCHIATRY, PSYCHIATRY AND SEX PSYCHOPATH LEGISLATION: THE 30S TO THE 80S 950, n. 15 (1977). However, since publication of the report commending abolition of such statutes, at least 13 states have repealed their statutes, including Alabama, Florida, Indiana, Iowa, Michigan, Minnesota, Missouri, Ohio, Pennsylvania, Rhode Island, Vermont, Virginia, and Wisconsin. At the time of this writing, only five jurisdictions allowed for the *indefinite* confinement of sexual psychopaths (Colorado, Illinois, Manhattan, Minnesota, and the District of Columbia). CRIMINAL JUSTICE MENTAL HEALTH STANDARDS, standard 7-347, 7-348 n. 17 (1984).

93. Annot., 96 A.L.R. 3d 840, 842 (1979).

94. GROUP FOR THE ADVANCEMENT OF PSYCHIATRY, *supra* note 92, at 842.

95. Comment, *Commitment of Sexual Psychopaths and the Requirements of Procedural Due Process,* 44 FORDHAM L. REV. 923, 927 (1976).

96. 386 U.S. 605 (1967).

97. Comment, *supra* note 96, at 933 nn. 68–69.

98. *Minnesota ex rel.* Pearson v. Probate Court, 309 U.S. 270 (1940).

99. *See* Allen v. Illinois, discussed in § 3.02(d).

100. *Taken from* GROUP FOR THE ADVANCEMENT OF PSYCHIATRY, *supra* note 92, at 861–67.

101. *Id.* at 935.

102. CRIMINAL JUSTICE MENTAL HEALTH STANDARDS, *supra* note 92, standard 7-8.1.

103. GROUP FOR THE ADVANCEMENT OF PSYCHIATRY, *supra* note 92, at 935.

104. *Id.* at 936.

105. *Id.* at 937.

106. *Id.*

107. *See supra* note 92.

108. 18 U.S.C. § 5005–5026.

109. *Sentencing of Youthful Misdemeanants under the Youth Corrections Act: Eliminating Disparities Created by the Federal Magistrate Act of 1979,* 51 FORDHAM L. REV. 1254, 1254 and notes (1983).

110. Ritz, *Federal Youths Corrections Act: The Continuing Charade,* 13 U. RICH. L. REV. 743 (1979)

111. 18 U.S.C. § 5006 (d).

112. *Id.* § 4216.

113. *Id.* § 5010 (d), as interpreted by the United States Supreme Court in Doreszynski v. United States, 418 U.S. 424 (1974).

114. 18 U.S.C. § 5010 (b).

115. *Id.* § 5006 (f).

116. *Id.* § 5017.

117. *Id.* § 5021.

118. Ritz, *supra* note 110, at 743–958.

119. *Id.* at 759.

120. *Id.* at 764.

121. A. CAMPBELL, *supra* note 1, at 131.

122. 18 U.S.C. § 4251–4255.

123. *Id.* § 4252.

124. *Id.* § 4251 (a).

125. Furman v. Georgia, 408 U.S. 238 (1972).

126. *Id.* at 293 (Brennan, J.).

127. *Id.* at 251 (Douglas, J.).

128. Woodson v. North Carolina, 428 U.S. 280, 305 (1976).

129. *Id.* (striking down the mandatory imposition of the death sentence upon conviction of first-degree murder).

130. Proffitt v. Florida, 428 U.S. 242 (1976).

131. Lockett v. Ohio, 438 U.S. 586, 597 (1978).

132. *Id.* (quoting Woodson v. North Carolina, 428 U.S. at 304).

133. *See generally* Dix, *Appellate Review of the Decision to Impose Death,* 68 GEO. L. REV. 97 (1979), for a description of typical statutes in this regard.

134. About 24 states have such provisions. *See* Bonnie, *Psychiatry and the Death Penalty: Emerging Problems in Virginia,* 66 VA. L. REV. 167, 184 (1980).

135. *Id.* Eight states (Colorado, Idaho, Maryland, New Mexico, Oklahoma, Oregon, Virginia, and Washington) make dangerousness a consideration at capital sentencing. Dix, *Expert Prediction Testimony in Capital Sentencing: Evidentiary and Constitutional Considerations,* 19 AM. CRIM. L. REV. 1, 4, n. 20 (1981).

136. Jurek v. Texas, 428 U.S. 262 (1976); Barefoot v. Estelle, 463 U.S. 880 (1983).

137. 463 U.S. 880, 896

138. *Id.* at 937, n. 15 (Blackmun, J., dissenting), n. 15.

139. *See generally* Dix, *supra* note 133; Bonnie, *supra* note 134.

140. Gardner v. Florida, 430 U.S. 349 (1977).

141. In 1981, three states (Idaho, Louisiana, and Virginia) specified that the rules of evidence did apply and six states (Alabama, Florida, Montana, Nevada, Tennessee, and Washington) specified that rules of evidence did not apply. Dix, *supra* note 135, at 9 nn. 39, 40.

142. 105 St.Ct. 1087 (1985).

143. *See, e.g.,* Bohmer, *Bad or Mad: The Psychiatrist in the Sentencing Process,* 4 J. PSYCHIATRY & L. 23 (1976).

144. Schmolesky & Thorson, *supra* note 44, at 407–11.

145. *Id.* at 423. *See also* the articles and cases cited by these authors at nn. 91–95 and accompanying text. *See particularly* Coffee, *The Future of Sentencing Reform: Emerging Legal Issues in the Individualization of Justice,* 73 MICH. L. REV. 1361 (1975), *cited at* 422 n. 92.

146. FED. R. CRIM. P. 32(3)(A).

147. *Id.*

148. *Id.*

149. Fennell & Hall, *supra* note 25.

150. *Id.* at 1652.

151. Clancy, Bartolomeo, Richardson, & Wellford, *Sentence Decisionmaking: The Logic of Sentence Decisions and the Extent and Sources of Sentence Disparity,* 72 J. CRIM. L. & CRIMINOLOGY 524, 535 (1981). Factors that influenced sentence disparity included (1) the judges' overall value orientations about the functions of the criminal sanction; (2) judgments about the appropriate goal of case-specific sentences; (3) perceptions about the severity of the sentences themselves; (4) a predisposition to impose relatively harsh or lenient sanctions; and (5) the manner in which each judge perceived the seriousness of the particular attributes of a given case. *Id.* at 553–54. *See also* Forst & Wellford, *Punishment and Sentencing: Developing Sentencing Guidelines Empirically from Principles of Punishment,* 33 RUTGERS L. REV. 799 (1981).

152. Diamond, *Order in the Court: Consistency in Criminal Court Decisions,* in PSYCHOLOGY AND THE LAW (Volume 2 of the American Psychological Association's Master Lecture Series, J. Scheirer & B. Hammonds eds. 1983).

153. *See generally* W. Austin & M.K. Utne, *Sentencing: Discretion and Justice in Judicial Decision-Making,* in PSYCHOLOGY IN THE LEGAL PROCESS (B. Sales ed. 1977).

154. Uhlman & Walker, *"He Takes Some of My Time; I Take Some of His": An Analysis of Judicial Sentencing Patterns in Jury Cases,* 14 LAW & SOC'Y 323 (1980).

155. Baab & Furgeson, *Comment: Texas Sentencing Practices: A Statistical Study,* 45 TEX. L. REV. 471 (1967).

156. *Id.* at 485–86.

157. Campbell, *The Influence of Psychiatric Pre-Sentence Reports,* 4 INT'L J.L. & PSYCHIATRY 89 (1981).

158. *Id.* at 104.

159. Smith, *A Review of the Presentence Diagnostic Procedure Study in North Carolina,* 8 N.C. CENTRAL L.J. 17, 31 n. 27 (1976).

160. Campbell, *supra* note 157.

161. Dershowitz, *supra* note 3, at 68.

162. In Bohmer's study, courts' agreement with psychiatric recommendations was 42% when incarceration was advised, and only 37% when probation was advised. Bohmer, *supra* note 143, at 34–35.

163. *Id.* at 36.

164. Sidley, *The Evaluation of Prison Treatment and Preventive Detention Programs: Some Problems Faced by the Patuxent Institution,* 2 BULL. AM. ACAD. PSYCHIATRY & L. 73 (1974).

165. Konecni, Mulcahy, & Ebbesen, *Prison or Mental Hospital: Factors Affecting the Processing of Persons Suspected of Being "Mentally Disordered Sex Offenders,"* in NEW DIRECTIONS IN PSYCHOLEGAL RESEARCH (P. Lipsitt & B. Sales eds. 1980). (If 9 cases in which the court ordered a continuance for further psychiatric studies are discounted, the concordance rate for the remaining 104 cases is 99%.)

166. *Id.*

167. The prominence of social control over humanistic motivations in the incarceration of these special-track offenders may also be reflected in the relative lack of treatment provided. One study of treatment at the Center for the Diagnosis and Treatment of Dangerous Persons, in Massachusetts, revealed that patients received an average of 2.41 hours of treatment per *month.* Schwitzgebel, *Professional Accountability in the Treatment and Release of Dangerous Persons,* in PERSPECTIVES IN LAW AND PSYCHOLOGY (B. Sales ed. 1977).

168. NATIONAL INSTITUTE OF CORRECTIONS, OFFENDER NEEDS ASSESSMENT: MODELS AND APPROACHES (1984).

169. Bartholomew, *Some Problems of the Psychiatrist in Relation to Sentencing,* 15 CRIM. L.Q. 325, 329–34, 339 (1973).

170. Dix, *Clinical Evaluation of the "Dangerousness" of "Normal" Criminal Defendants,* 66 U. VA. L. REV. 523 (1981).

171. Caravello, Ginnetti, Ford, & Lawall, *An Investigation of Treatment Recommendations Made by a Court Clinic,* 9 BULL. AM. ACAD. PSYCHIATRY & L. 224 (1981). Selective referrals alone do not account for the high frequency of treatment oriented recommendations. Psychiatrists' commitment to the medical model may bias them toward dispositional attributions of the offenders' social problems. One author has noted that "Prominent forensic psychiatrists almost uniformly express the view that pre-sentence reports ought to advocate lenient, individualized treatment." Campbell, *supra* note 157, at 95.

172. NATIONAL INSTITUTE OF CORRECTIONS, *supra* note 168, at 18.

173. *Id.*

174. E. MEGARGEE & M.J. BOHN, CLASSIFYING CRIMINAL OFFENDERS (1979). For a conceptual and theoretical discussion of offender classification systems, *see* Clements, *The Future of Offender Classification,* 8 CRIM. JUST. & BEHAV. 15 (1981).

175. Campbell, *supra* note 157, at 95.

176. This bias may be particularly hard to resist for the

clinician who is familiar with the appalling conditions in many prison settings.

177. Bohmer, *The Court Psychiatrist: Between Two Worlds,* 16 DUQ. L. REV. 601 (1977–1978).

178. Bartholomew, *supra* note 169.

179. *Supra* note 53.

180. *See, e.g.,* VonHirsch, *supra* note 51, at 9.

181. *See* Quay, *The Three Faces of Evaluation: What Can Be Expected to Work?,* 4 CRIM. J. & BEHAV. 341 (1977); Palmer, *Martinson Revisited,* 1975 J. RES. CRIME & DE-LINQ. 133 (1975).

182. For some hopeful signs, *see* Jeffrey & Woolpert, *Work Furlough as an Alternative to Incarceration,* 60 J. CRIM. L. & CRIMINOL. 405 (1974); Craft, Stephenson, & Granger, *A Controlled Trial of Authoritarian and Self-Governing Regimes with Adolescent Psychopaths,* 34 AM. J. ORTHO-PSYCH. 543 (1964); *see generally* Palmer, *supra* note 185, at 134–37.

183. "In practice, students of the indeterminate sentence have repeatedly observed that patients and inmates are drawn to game-playing—known colloquially as 'shamming,' 'conning,' or, in the parole release context, 'programming'—in order to convince their keepers that rehabilitative efforts have been successful and that release is in order." D. WEXLER, CRIMINAL COMMITMENTS AND DANGEROUS MENTAL PATIENTS: LEGAL ISSUES OF CONFINEMENT, TREATMENT, AND RE-LEASE 22 (1976).

184. Podgers, *The Psychiatrist's Role in Death Sentence Debated,* 66 A.B.A. J. 1509 (1980) (quoting Ohio State University law professor David Goldberger).

185. Walker, *Measuring the Seriousness of Crimes,* 18 BR. J. CRIM. 348 (1978); Monahan & Ruggiero, *supra* note 54, at 146.

186. Bonnie, *supra* note 134, at 185.

187. Bonnie has noted that this is particularly relevant in capital cases: "The substantive inquiry in a capital sentencing proceeding . . . is not restricted to behavioral impairments arising out of mental disease or defect. The door in this sense is open to the full spectrum of explanations that may be offered . . . ." *Id.* at 184–85. This leaves the clinician free to explore unconventional (i.e., non-DSM-III) syndromes or levels of emotional or psychological impairment that fall short of diagnostic significance. *See, e.g.,* Showalter, Bonnie, & Roddy, *The Spousal-Homicide Syndrome,* 3 INT'L J.L. & PSYCHIATRY 117 (1980); Ciccone & Kaskey, *Life Events and Antisocial Behavior,* 7 BULL. AM. ACAD. PSYCHIATRY & L. 63 (1979). *See also* Bonnie & Slobogin, *The Role of Mental Health Professionals in the Criminal Process: The Case for Informed Speculation,* 66 VA. L. REV. 427 (1980).

188. H. KALVEN & H. ZEISEL, THE AMERICAN JURY 301–05 (1971).

189. Cooke & Pogany, *The Influence on Judges' Sentencing Practices of a Mental Evaluation,* 3 BULL. AM. ACAD. PSY-CHIATRY & L. 245 (1975).

190. Austin, *The Concept of Desert and Its Influence on Simulated Decision Makers' Sentencing Decisions,* 3 LAW & HUM. BEHAV. 163 (1979).

191. *Id.* at 179–80.

192. Dix, *Participation by Mental Health Professionals in Capital Murder Sentencing,* 1 INT'. J.L. & PSYCHIATRY 283 (1978).

193. *Id.* at 292.

194. Henderson & Gitchoff, *Using Experts and Victims in the Sentencing Process,* 17 CRIM. L. BULL. 226 (1981).

195. A clear example of the importance of methodology in questionnaire research is found in the critique by Dohrenwend, Egri, & Mendelsohn, *Psychiatric Disorder in the General Population: A Study of the Problem of Clinical Judgment,* 127 AM. J. PSYCHIATRY 1304 (1971), of an earlier study by L. SROLE, T. LANGNER, S. MICHAEL, M. OPLER, & T. RENNIE, MENTAL HEALTH IN THE ME-TROPOLIS (1962), showing that many of the significant results of the earlier study were methodological artifacts.

196. ALA. CODE § 13A-5-51(5) (1975). *See also supra* note 134.

197. Clanon, *Public Protection and the Trend to Determinate Sentence Structure,* 7 BULL. AM. ACAD. PSYCHIATRY & L. 179, 181 (1979).

198. Monahan, *The Case for Prediction in the Modified Desert Model of Criminal Sentencing,* 5 INT'L J.L. PSYCHIATRY 103 (1982).

199. *See supra* notes 135–137 and accompanying text.

200. Rubin, *Prediction of Dangerousness in Mentally Ill Criminals,* 27 ARCH. GEN. PSYCHIATRY 397, 397–98 (1972).

201. The most comprehensive study is J. MONAHAN, PRE-DICTING VIOLENT BEHAVIOR: AN ASSESSMENT OF CLIN-ICAL TECHNIQUES (1981) [hereinafter cited as J. MON-AHAN, PREDICTING VIOLENT BEHAVIOR]. *See also* D. Levine, *The Concept of Dangerousness: Criticism and Compromise,* in PSYCHOLOGY IN THE LEGAL PROCESS (B. Sales ed. 1977); Levinson & Ramsay, *Dangerousness, Stress, and Mental Health Evaluations,* 20 J. HEALTH SOC. BE-HAV. 178 (1979); Monahan, *The Prediction of Violence,* in COMMUNITY MENTAL HEALTH AND THE CRIMINAL JUS-TICE SYSTEM (J. Monahan ed. 1976).

202. Cockroft, *Government Liability for Mistakes in the Parole and Probation of Dangerous Convicts,* 2 CRIM. JUST. J. 117 (1978).

203. This has been observed in studies from a variety of legal contexts. *See* Poythress, *Mental Health Expert Testimony: Current Problems,* 5 J. PSYCHIATRY & L. 201 (1977) (*see* in particular Table 2, showing several studies of high concordance rates between psychiatrists' predictions of dangerousness and judges' decisions to civilly commit); Cocozza & Steadman, *Prediction in Psychiatry: An Example of Misplaced Confidence in Experts,* 25 SOC. PROBS. 266 (1978) (reporting 86.7% concordance rate between psychiatrists' predictions of dangerousness and judges' decisions to commit individuals determined incompetent for trial).

204. J. Monahan & H. Steadman, *Crime and Mental Disorder: An Epidemiological Approach,* in CRIME AND JUSTICE: AN ANNUAL REVIEW OF RESEARCH (N. Morris & M. Tonry eds. 1983).

205. Levinson & Ramsay, *supra* note 201.

206. J. MONAHAN, PREDICTING VIOLENT BEHAVIOR, *supra* note

201. *See also* Megargee, *The Prediction of Dangerous Behavior,* in THE ROLE OF THE FORENSIC PSYCHOLOGIST (G. Cooke ed. 1980); Shah, *Dangerousness: Some Definitional, Conceptual, and Public Policy Issues,* in PERSPECTIVES IN LAW AND PSYCHOLOGY (B. Sales ed. 1977).

207. *Cf.* Holland, *Diagnostic Labelling: Individual Differences in the Behavior of Clinicians Conducting Presentence Evaluations,* 6 CRIM. JUST. BEHAV. 187 (1979); Garvey, *The Criminal: A Psychiatric Viewpoint,* 8 J. PSYCHIATRY & L. 457 (1980).

208. Megargee concluded that no psychological test has been developed "which will adequately *post*dict, let alone *predict,* violent behavior." E. Megargee, *The Prediction of Violence with Psychological Tests,* in CURRENT TOPICS IN CLINICAL AND COMMUNITY PSYCHOLOGY 145 (C. Spielberger ed. 1970). Monahan noted Megargee's earlier conclusion and found that the subsequent decade of research on psychological tests "would do little to modify his conclusion." J. MONAHAN, PREDICTING VIOLENT BEHAVIOR, *supra* note 201, at 80.

209. Pfohl, *From Whom Will We Be Protected?: Comparative Approaches to the Assessment of Dangerousness,* 2 INT'L. J.L. PSYCHIATRY 55 (1979).

210. *Id.* at 60.

211. Steadman, *Some Evidence on the Inadequacy of the Concept and Determination of Dangerousness in Law and Psychiatry,* 1 J. PSYCHIATRY & L. 409 (1973); Cocozza & Steadman, *supra* note 203; Steadman & Cocozza, *Psychiatry, Dangerousness and the Repetitively Violent Offender,* 69 J. CRIM. L. & CRIMINOLOGY 226 (1978).

212. Steadman, *supra* note 211 at 419, described over 18 criteria of dangerousness cited in court psychiatric reports.

213. *Id.* at 421.

214. Cocozza & Steadman, *supra* note 203.

215. *See supra* notes 166–167 and accompanying text.

216. Dix, *The Death Penalty, "Dangerousness," Psychiatric Testimony, and Professional Ethics,* 5 AM. J. CRIM. L. 151 (1977).

217. *Id.* at 158.

218. *Id.*

219. *Id.* at 172.

220. The Texas Court of Criminal Appeals affirmed the jury's imposition of the death penalty, though not without scathing dissent from Judge Odom, who commented: "I am unable to find that much of the testimony offered was from this side of the twilight zone" (quoted by Dix, *id.* at 165).

221. *See, e.g.,* Bonnie, *supra* note 134; Dix, *supra* note 216; Slobogin, *Dangerousness and Expertise,* U. PA. L. REV (1984).

222. Wenk, Robison, & Smith, *Can Violence Be Predicted?* 18 CRIME DELINQ. 393 (1972).

223. Baxstrom v. Herold, 383 U.S. 107 (1966).

224. Steadman & Cocozza, *The Prediction of Dangerousness—Baxstrom: A Case Study,* in THE ROLE OF THE FORENSIC PSYCHOLOGIST (G. Cooke ed. 1980).

225. Dixon et al. v. Attorney General of the Commonwealth of Pennsylvania, 325 F. Supp. 966 (1971).

226. T. THORNBERRY & J. JACOBY, THE CRIMINALLY INSANE: A FOLLOW-UP OF MENTALLY ILL OFFENDERS (1979).

227. Mullen & Reinehr, *Predicting Dangerousness of Maximum Security Forensic Patients,* 10 J. PSYCHIATRY & L. 223 (1982).

228. Kozol, Boucher, & Garofalo, *The Diagnosis and Treatment of Dangerousness,* 18 CRIME DELINQ. 371 (1972).

229. Rappeport, *Enforced Treatment: Is It Treatment?,* 2 BULL. AM. ACAD. PSYCHIATRY & L. 148 (1974).

230. Sidley, *supra* note 164.

231. Steadman & Cocozza, *supra* note 211.

232. Cocozza & Steadman, *supra* note 203.

233. Sepejak, Menzies, Webster, & Jensen, *Clinical Prediction of Dangerousness: Two-Year Follow-Up of 408 Pre-Trial Forensic Cases,* 11 BULL. AM. ACAD. PSYCHIATRY & L. 171 (1983).

234. Levinson & Ramsay, *supra* note 201.

235. Monahan, *The Prediction of Violent Behavior: Developments in Psychology and Law,* in PSYCHOLOGY AND THE LAW (Volume 2 of the American Psychological Association's Master Lecture Series, J. Schreirer and B. Hammonds eds. 1983).

236. *Id.* at 159.

237. *See* Allen, Book Review, 73 MICH. L. REV. 1517, 1526 (1975).

238. Dix, *supra* note 170, at 544.

239. Monahan, *The Prediction of Violent Criminal Behavior: A Methodological Critique and Prospectus,* in DETERRENCE AND INCAPACITATION: ESTIMATING THE EFFECTS OF CRIMINAL SANCTIONS ON CRIME RATES 244 (A. Blumstein, J. Cohen, & D. Nagin eds. 1978).

240. Monahan, *The Prediction of Violent Behavior: Toward a Second Generation of Theory and Policy,* 141 AM. J. PSYCHIATRY 10, 11 (1984).

241. Mullen & Reinehr, *supra* note 227.

242. Kozol, Boucher, & Garofalo, *supra* note 228.

243. P. MEEHL, CLINICAL VERSUS STATISTICAL PREDICTION: A THEORETICAL ANALYSIS AND A REVIEW OF THE EVIDENCE (1954).

244. It is not necessary that predictions be purely clinical or purely statistical. A clinician might yield a prediction after reviewing, among other things, data of a statistical nature (e.g., number of prior arrests); similarly, clinical judgments may be coded in some quantitative fashion (e.g., schizophrenic = 1, other diagnoses = 0) for inclusion in an actuarial procedure. *See* J. MONAHAN, PREDICTING VIOLENT BEHAVIOR, *supra* note 201, at 97.

245. Classification accuracy is inflated when the equation is applied to the derivation sample because the development of the equation capitalized on the characteristics of the particular sample. Thus, cross-validation is needed.

246. For this reason, one legal critic has argued that testimony about dangerousness should be limited to actuarial type information in certain circumstances (primarily, when the defendant chooses not to use clinical prediction testimony); though there may be no substantial gain in predictive precision, the fact finder

will stand a better chance of finding out the basis for the prediction. Slobogin, *supra* note 221.

247. *See, e.g.,* Carroll, *Judgments of Recidivism Risk: The Use of Base-Rate Information in Parole Decisions,* in NEW DIRECTIONS IN PSYCHOLEGAL RESEARCH (P. Lipsitt & B. Sales eds. 1980).

248. Tawshunski, *Note: Admissibility of Mathematical Evidence in Criminal Trials,* 21 AM. CRIM. L. REV. 55 (1983).

249. Cocozza & Steadman, *Some Refinements in the Measurement and Prediction of Dangerous Behavior,* 131 AM. J. PSYCHIATRY 1012 (1974).

250. T. THORNBERRY & J. JACOBY, *supra* note 226.

251. Steadman & Cocozza, *The Dangerousness Standard and Psychiatry: A Cross National Issue in the Social Control of the Mentally Ill,* 63 SOCIOLOGY & SOC. RESEARCH 649 (1979).

252. *Id.*

253. *Id.*

254. *See supra* note 245.

255. "A witness is an expert and is qualified to give expert testimony if the judge finds that to perceive, know, or understand the matter concerning which the witness is to testify requires special knowledge, skill, expertise or training . . . ." MODEL CODE OF EVIDENCE rule 402 (1942).

256. FED. R. EVID. 702 (requiring that the witness's "specialized knowledge will assist the trier of fact"). *See* Bonnie & Slobogin, *supra* note 187, at 461–66.

257. Levinson & Ramsay, *supra* note 201.

258. *Cf.* Poythress, *Psychological Issues in Criminal Proceedings:*

Judicial Preference Regarding Expert Testimony, 10 CRIM. JUST. & BEHAV. 175 (1983).

259. Slobogin, *supra* note 221.

260. *See supra* note 221.

261. Black, *Due Process for Death: Jurek v. Texas and Companion Cases,* 26 CATH. U.L. REV. 1, 5 (1977).

262. Barefoot v. Estelle, 463 U.S. 880, 896 (1983)

263. Dix, *supra* note 216, at 167.

264. The information in this table is based on the relationships discussed by J. MONAHAN, PREDICTING VIOLENT BEHAVIOR, *supra* note 201. *See also* Table 8-1.

265. J. MONAHAN, PREDICTING VIOLENT BEHAVIOR, *supra* note 201.

266. *See supra* note 203 and accompanying text.

267. *See supra* notes 216–219 and accompanying text.

268. Guze, in his study of the relationship between criminality and mental disorder, used an abbreviated criterion for the diagnosis of sociopathy—one that would not satisfy contemporary (i.e., DSM-III) standards for antosocial personality. S. GUZE, CRIMINALITY AND PSYCHIATRIC DISORDERS (1976). *See also* Dix, *supra* note 216, at 177–88; Walshe-Brennan, *Classification Inconsistencies in Defining the Criminally Mentally Abnormal,* 18 MED. SCI. & L. 283 (1978) (discussing the vagaries of the term "psychopath").

269. *See supra* note 208 and accompanying text.

270. Steadman & Cocozza, *supra* note 211.

271. Dix, *supra* note 216, at 169.

272. *See* CRIMINAL JUSTICE MENTAL HEALTH STANDARDS, standard 7-3.9(b) (1984).

Chapter 8

1. *See infra* text accompanying notes 31–33 for a definition of the state's police power.

2. Hawaii v. Standard Oil Co., 405 U.S. 251, 257 (1972) (quoting W. BLACKSTONE, COMMENTARIES 47).

3. The notion that criminal offenses must be explicitly defined is a principle of constitutional dimension. *See generally* Lanzetta v. New Jersey, 306 U.S. 451, 453 (1939); H. PACKER, THE LIMITS OF THE CRIMINAL SANCTION 88–91 (1968).

4. Addington v. Texas, 441 U.S. 418, 428 (1978).

5. *Id.; see infra* § 8.02(e).

6. The exception to this rule is the open-ended sentence available under some special sentencing schemes. *See supra* § 7.05.

7. R. BONNIE, PSYCHIATRISTS AND THE LEGAL PROCESS: DIAGNOSIS AND DEBATE 24–26 (1977).

8. A. STONE, MENTAL HEALTH AND THE LAW: A SYSTEM IN TRANSITION 45 (1975).

9. T. SZASZ, LAW, LIBERTY, AND PSYCHIATRY 240 (1963).

10. *See generally* Morse, *Crazy Behavior, Morals and Science: An Analysis of Mental Health Law,* 51 S. CAL. L. REV. 527 (1978).

11. The first, and most important, of these lawsuits in terms of influence was Lessard v. Schmidt, 349 F. Supp. 1078

(E.D. Wis. 1972). It is discussed in more detail throughout this chapter.

12. The seminal right to treatment case is Wyatt v. Stickney, 325 F. Supp. 781 (M.D. Ala. 1971), *aff'd. sub nom.* Wyatt v. Aderholdt, 503 F.2d 1305 (5th Cir. 1974). These cases had enormous influence upon subsequent litigation in this area. In NYSARC v. Rockefeller, 357 F. Supp. (E.D.N.Y. 1973) (the Willowbrook litigation), the court adopted a "right to habilitation" theory, which, in practice, resulted in the same types of relief afforded the plaintiffs in *Wyatt.*

13. *See, e.g.,* Mills v. Rogers, 457 U.S. 291 (1982); *infra* § 9.03(b). No court has rejected the argument that patients retain residual liberty interests in preventing unwanted treatment. The litigation on this issue tends to be over the scope of the right (does it extend only to voluntary patients? to some involuntary patients? to all involuntary patients?) and whether the process by which the relative strength of the state's interest in providing treatment and the individual interest in liberty and privacy were balanced is legal/judicial or medical/administrative in nature. *Compare, e.g.,* Project Release v. Cuomo, 722 F.2d 960 (2d Cir. 1983), endorsing administrative proceedings for determining patient ca-

pacity and need for treatment, *with* Rogers v. Comm'r Dept. of Mental Health, 390 Mass. 489, 458 N.E.2d 308 (1983), which requires judicial proceedings.

14. S. J. BRAKEL & R. S. ROCK, THE MENTALLY DISABLED AND THE LAW 1 (1971).

15. *Id.* at 1–2.

16. *Id.* at 2.

17. *Id.*

18. *Id.*

19. *Id.* For further discussion of the development of English law, see Dershowitz, *The Origins of Preventive Confinement in Anglo-American Law, Part I: The English Experience,* 43 U. CIN. L. REV. 1 (1974).

20. S. J. BRAKEL & R. S. ROCK, *supra* note 14, at 3.

21. *Id.* at 4.

22. *Id.* For further discussion of the development of American law, see Dershowitz, *The Origin of Preventive Confinement in Anglo-American Law, Part II: The American Experience,* 43 U. CIN. L. REV. 781 (1974).

23. S.J. BRAKEL & R.S. ROCK, 14, at 6.

24. *Id.*

25. *Id.* at 34.

26. For example, a Mrs. E.P. Packard, committed for three years solely on the word of her husband and because she expressed opinions he did not like, campaigned for increased safeguards at the time of commitment. *Id.* at 7–8.

27. The person primarily responsible for public concern with the problems of the mentally disabled and the dramatic increase in the creation of institutions for the disabled was Dorothea Dix, whose efforts resulted in federal grants of land to the states for the establishment of hospitals and the building of at least 32 hospitals in this country and abroad. *Id.* at 8 n. 39 and text.

28. N. COLEMAN & L. GILBERT, STALKING THE LEAST RESTRICTIVE ALTERNATIVE: LITIGATIVE AND NON-LITIGATIVE STRATEGIES FOR THE INDIGENT MENTALLY DISABLED 12 (and sources cited there) (1979).

29. For a discussion of psychotropic medications and their impact, *see* 2 THE PRESIDENT'S COMMISSION ON MENTAL HEALTH, TASK FORCE REPORT: NATURE AND SCOPE OF THE PROBLEM 55–56 (and sources cited there) (1978).

30. Mental Retardation Facilities and Community Mental Health Centers Construction Act (P.L. 88-164, 1963).

31. *Developments in the Law: Civil Commitment of the Mentally Ill,* 87 HARV. L. REV. 1190, 1207–08 (1974). This article is an exhaustive discussion of civil commitment law, including a description of case law, statutory law, and commentary up to the time of its publication. It is recommended to those interested in delving more deeply into the jurisprudential bases for civil commitment.

32. *Id.* at 1209–10.

33. *Id.* at 1222.

34. Proschaska v. Brinegar, 251 Iowa 834, 102 N.W.2d 870, 872 (1960).

35. *Id.*

36. D. WEXLER, MENTAL HEALTH LAW: MAJOR ISSUES 23 (1981).

37. S.J. BRAKEL & R.S. ROCK, *supra* note 14, at 60.

38. *Id.*

39. *Id.* at 59–60.

40. See, e.g., T. SZASZ, *supra* note 9; T. SZASZ, PSYCHIATRIC JUSTICE 269 (1965).

41. One of the best known is Rosenhan, *On Being Sane in Insane Places,* 179 SCIENCE 150 (1973). In this study, eight individuals, feigning mental illness, were admitted to a number of mental health facilities. Staff members reportedly never detected the deception.

42. The most influential article arguing this position is probably Ennis & Litwack, *Psychiatry and the Presumption of Expertise: Flipping Coins in the Courtroom,* 62 CALIF. L. REV. 693 (1974).

43. Humphrey v. Cady, 405 U.S. 504, 509 (1972).

44. 406 U.S. 715 (1972); *see supra* § 4.04 for a discussion of the *Jackson* decision.

45. 406 U.S. at 737. Wexler observes that this invitation was "rather rudely retracted in some later cases," noting the Court's increased tendency to decide cases on narrow grounds—a tendency Wexler attributes tentatively to the difficulty of the issues the cases raised. D. WEXLER, *supra* note 36, at 52 n. 13.

46. Lessard v. Schmidt, 349 F. Supp. 1078, 1094 (E.D. Wis. 1972) (quoting Livermore Malmquist and Meehl, *On the Justifications for Civil Commitment,* 117 U. PA. L. REV. 75, 80 (1968)).

47. Commonwealth ex. rel. Finken v. Roop, 339 A.2d 764, 778 (1978).

48. *Id.*

49. 1 MENTAL HEALTH LAW PROJECT, LEGAL RIGHTS OF THE MENTALLY DISABLED 37 (1975).

50. A. STONE, *supra* note 8, at 1.

51. Wyatt v. Stickney, 325 F. Supp. 781 (M.D. Ala. 1971), *aff'd sub nom.* Wyatt v. Aderholdt, 503 F. 2d 1305 (5th Cir. 1974). For the impact of the *Wyatt* litigation, *see* Special Project, *The Remedial Process in Institution Reform Litigation,* 78 COLUM. L. REV. 784 (1978).

52. Scott, *The Treatment Barrier,* 46 BRIT. J. MED. PSYCHIATRY 45, 46 (1973).

53. *See, e.g.,* Farina, Thaw, Laverne, & Mangone, *People's Reactions to a Former Mental Patient Moving to Their Neighborhood,* 2 J. COMMUNITY PSYCHOLOGY 108 (1974).

54. Kiesler, *Mental Hospitals and Alternative Care: Noninstitutionalization as Potential Public Policy for Mental Patients,* 37 AM. PSYCHOLOGIST 349, 350–51 (1982).

55. State ex rel. Hawks v. Lazaro, 202 S.E.2d 109, 120 (1974).

56. Lessard v. Schmidt, 349 F. Supp. 1078 (E.D. Wis. 1973), *vacated on other grounds,* 414 U.S. 473 (1973), *on remand,* 379 F. Supp. 1376 (E.D. Wis. 1974), *vacated on other grounds,* 421 U.S. 957 (1975) *on remand,* 413 F. Supp. 1318 (E.D. Wis. 1976).

57. *Id.* at 1089.

58. *Id.*

59. *In re* Ballay, 482 F.2d 648, 659 (D.C. Cir. 1973).

60. State *ex rel.* Hawks v. Lazaro, 202 S.E.2d at 121.

61. Other patient advocates sought to limit the use of commitment by making provision of institutional care by the states prohibitively expensive. This strategy formed

the underpinning of at least some of the lawsuits filed challenging institutional conditions. MENTAL HEALTH LAW PROJECT, *supra* note 49, at 40.

62. 387 U.S. 1 (1967).

63. Dershowitz, *Psychiatry in the Legal Process, A Knife That Cuts Both Ways,* in THE PATH OF THE LAW FROM 1967 71–83 (A. Sutherland ed. 1968).

64. For a general discussion, see Note, *Overt Dangerous Behavior as a Constitutional Requirement for Civil Commitment of the Mentally Ill,* 44 U. CHI. L. REV. 562 (1977). The courts split on whether an overt act is constitutionally required as part of the proof of dangerousness. *Compare* Project Release v. Prevost, 722 F.2d 960 (2d Cir. 1983) (overt act not required) *with* Goldy v. Beal, 429 F. Supp. 640 (M.D. Pa. 1976) (overt act required).

65. *See, e.g.,* Dixon v. Attorney General, 325 F. Supp. 966 (N.D. Pa. 1971); Wessel v. Pryor, 461 F. Supp. 1144 (E.D. Ark. 1978); State *ex rel.* Hawks v. Lazaro, 202 S.E.2d 109 (W. Va. Sup. Ct. App. 1974).

66. 422 U.S. 563 (1975).

67. *Id.* at 573.

68. *Id.* at 576.

69. Some, for example, have argued that the Supreme Court declared the existence of a constitutional right to treatment—an argument belied by later statements by the Court. For instance, in Pennhurst State School and Hosp. v. Halderman, 451 U.S. 1 (1981), the Court stated that it had "never found that the involuntarily committed have a constitutional 'right to treatment,' much less the voluntarily committed." Others have criticized the holding, primarily for its caution. *See, e.g., The Right to Treatment Case—That Wasn't,* 30 U. MIAMI L. REV 486 (1976). Still others have acknowledged the limited nature of the holding, but have argued that the Court's focus on the liberty interest of patients was a necessary step toward a broader affirmation of rights. *See, e.g.,* O'Connor v. Donaldson: *The Supreme Court Sidesteps the Right to Treatment,* 13 CAL. W.L. REV. 168 (1976). For a critique of various right-to-treatment theories, *see* Spece, *Preserving the Right to Treatment: A Critical Assessment and Constructive Development of Constitutional Right to Treatment Theories,* 20 ARIZ. L. REV. 1 (1978).

70. 422 U.S. at 580 (Burger, C.J., concurring).

71. Donaldson v. O'Connor, 493 F.2d 507, 520 (5th Cir. 1974).

72. 422 U.S. at 582.

73. *Id.* at 582–83.

74. 441 U.S. 418 (1978).

75. *In re* Winship, 397 U.S. 358 (1970).

76. 441 U.S. at 426.

77. *Id.* at 428.

78. *Id.* at 429.

79. *Id.*

80. 442 U.S. 584 (1979).

81. *Id.* at 591.

82. *Id.*

83. J.R. v. Parham, 413 F. Supp. 112, 139 (1976).

84. 442 U.S. at 600.

85. *Id.* at 600–01.

86. *Id.* at 602.

87. *Id.*

88. *Id.* at 604.

89. *Id.* at 603.

90. *Id.* at 605.

91. *Id.* at 606–07.

92. *Id.* at 607.

93. *Id.* at 609.

94. *Id.*

95. *See, e.g.,* Youngberg v. Romeo, 102 S.Ct. 2452 (1982), where the Supreme Court directed the federal judiciary to defer more readily to the judgment exercised by professionals charged with administration and treatment decisions.

96. *See, e.g.,* Project Release v. Prevost, 722 F.2d 960 (2d Cir. 1983), in which the court upheld the New York commitment law, which relies heavily on medical judgment and administrative processes for determining a patient's capacity to consent to treatment. *See also* NYSARC v. Carey, 706 F.2d 956 (2d Cir. 1983), in which the Court of Appeals remanded for rehearing in light of the *Youngberg* holding a decision by the lower court that it would not modify the Willowbrook consent judgment, despite expert testimony on behalf of the state that the proposed modifications (having to do with the size of the community placements in which the institutionalized patients were being placed) comported with acceptable professional judgment.

97. *See, e.g.,* the dissent of Justice Brennan in the *Parham* case, 442 U.S. at 625, in which he criticized the majority opinion; in large measure his remarks were based upon the criticisms of clinical expertise noted earlier in this chapter.

98. *See, e.g.,* Melton, *Family and Mental Hospital as Myths: Civil Commitment of Minor,* in CHILDREN, MENTAL HEALTH, AND THE LAW (N. Reppucci, L. Weithorn, E. Mulvey, & J. Monahan eds. 1984).

99. VT. STAT. ANN. tit. 18, § 7101 (17) (Supp. 1984).

100. TEX. REV. CIVIL STAT. art 5547-4(k) (Supp. 1982–83).

101. Roth, *A Commitment Law for Patients, Doctors, and Lawyers,* 136 AM. J. PSYCHIATRY 1121 (1979).

102. A. STONE, *supra* note 8.

103. These states and their statutes are as follows: Alaska, ALASKA STAT. § 47.30.700 (1984); Delaware, DEL. CODE ANN. tit. 16 § 5001 (i) (1983) (the criterion is contained within the definition of mental illness); Florida, FLA. STAT. ANN. § 394-467 (Supp. 1985); Hawaii, HAWAII REV. STAT. § 334-1 (Supp. 1984) (the criterion is contained within the definition of dangerousness to others); Iowa, IOWA CODE ANN. § 299.1.1 (Supp. 1983–84) (the criterion is contained within the definition of mental illness); Kansas, KAN. STAT. ANN. § 59-2902(a) (Cum. Supp. 1982) (the criterion is included as an alternative basis for commitment when coupled with dangerousness); Michigan, MICH. STAT. ANN. § 14.800(401)(c) (1980) (the criterion is included as one criterion for commitment when combined with dangerousness); New York, N.Y. Mental Hygiene Law §

9.01 (McKinney 1978) (the criterion is included in the definition of "need of involuntary care and treatment," which is required for nonemergency involuntary commitment); South Carolina, S.C. CODE ANN. § 44-17-580(1) (1976) (the criterion is included as an alternative criterion for commitment when combined with a need for treatment); Utah, UTAH CODE ANN. § 64-7-36(10)(c) (Supp. 1983) (the criterion is included as one of the criteria for involuntary commitment); and Wyoming, WYO. STAT. ANN. 25-10-101(viii) (Supp. 1983) (the criterion is included within the definition of mentally ill person).

104. See supra note 13.

105. For a good discussion and critique of proposals that voluntary admissions be encouraged through use of a "voluntary commitment contract" (an agreement signed by a competent individual authorizing mental health treatment during future periods of illness), see Dresser, *Ulysses and the Psychiatrists: A Legal and Policy Analysis of the Voluntary Commitment Contract,* 16 HARV. C.R.-C.L. L. REV. 777. Dresser concludes that such a contract may well be another coercive treatment mode.

106. A number of courts have found that the statutory distinction between voluntary and involuntary status is irrelevant in determining the rights of individuals confined under those labels. See, e.g., Society for Good Will to Retarded Children, Inc. v. Cuomo, 737 F.2d 1253 (2d Cir. 1984), in which the Court of Appeals rejected as "irrelevant" the distinction between a voluntary and involuntary patient for the purpose of determining the rights of an institutionalized individual. The court found that those held in state institutions for the retarded have rights at least equal to those of prison inmates, and since the latter are entitled to safe and humane conditions, so are the former.

107. Schwitzgebel, *Survey of State Civil Commitment Statutes,* in CIVIL COMMITMENT AND SOCIAL POLICY: AN EVALUATION OF THE MASSACHUSETTS MENTAL HEALTH REFORM ACT OF 1970 50–51, 53 (1981).

108. ALASKA STAT. § 47.30.070(i) (1984).

109. PA STATE. ANN. tit. 50, § 7301(a) (Supp. 1983–84).

110. ARK. STAT. ANN. §§ 59-1410, 59-1401(a) Supp. 1983.

111. IND. CODE ANN. § 16-14-9.1-1(c) Supp. (1985).

112. Suzuki v. Yuen, 7617 F.2d 173, 176 (9th Cir. 1980).

113. See, e.g., HAWAII REV. STAT. § 334-1 (Supp. 1984); KY. REV. STAT. ANN. § 202A.030 (Baldwin 1980); N.M. STAT. ANN. § 43-1-3(E) (1978).

114. Brooks, *Defining the Dangerousness of the Mentally Ill: Involuntary Civil Commitment,* in MENTALLY ABNORMAL OFFENDERS (M. & A. Craft eds. 1984).

115. ALASKA STAT. § 47.30.070(i) (1984).

116. PA. STAT. ANN. tit. 50, § 7301(a) (1983–84 Supp.).

117. 422 U.S. 563 (1975).

118. *Id.* at 575.

119. *Id.*

120. These states include Arizona, Arkansas, California, Colorado, Connecticut, Florida, Georgia, Hawaii, Idaho, Illinois, Indiana, Kansas, Kentucky, Maine, Massachusetts, Michigan, Minnesota, Mississippi, Montana, Nebraska, Nevada, New Mexico, North Carolina, North Dakota, Ohio, Oklahoma, Oregon, Pennsylvania, South Dakota, Tennessee, Utah, Vermont, Virginia, Washington, West Virginia, and Wisconsin. See Beis, *State Involuntary Commitment Statutes,* 7 MENTAL DISABILITY L. REP. 358–69, *reprinted from* E. BEIS, MENTAL HEALTH AND THE LAW (1983). New York's statute permits commitment of the gravely disabled by virtue of judicial interpretation. Project Release v. Prevost, 722 F.2d 960 (2d Cir. 1983).

121. NEV. REV. STAT. § 433A.310(1).

122. *Id.* § 433.194.

123. See Beis, *supra* note 120.

124. See Stromberg & Stone, *A Model State Law on Civil Commitment of the Mentally Ill,* 20 HARV. J. LEGIS. 275, 302–03 (1983).

125. See, e.g., the September 1983 issue of HOSP. & COMMUNITY PSYCHIATRY, much of which is devoted to this subject.

126. When the Coalition for the Homeless brought suit to compel New York State to provide housing for the homeless mentally ill, Mayor Koch of New York was quoted as saying, "I hope [the plaintiffs have] success in [the] suit in getting the state to reinstitutionalize those who need it . . . ." N.Y. Times, May 21, 1982, section A, at 1, col. 1.

127. These states include Colorado, Connecticut, Delaware, Florida, Hawaii, Indiana, Iowa, Kansas, Kentucky, Louisiana, Maine, Maryland, Michigan, New Jersey, New Mexico, New York, South Carolina, Tennessee, Wisconsin, and Wyoming. Beis, *supra* note 120. In addition, Schwitzgebel includes Alaska, Arizona, Mississippi, Missouri, North Dakota, Oklahoma, Rhode Island, South Dakota, Texas, Utah, and Vermont among the states using this criteria. Schwitzgebel, *supra* note 107.

128. COLO. REV. STAT. ANN. § 27-10-102(7) (Supp. 1984).

129. Schwitzgebel, *supra* note 107, at 54.

130. Shelton v. Tucker, 364 U.S. 479 (1960). The Court struck down an Arkansas law requiring teachers to list affiliations with organizations. The Court announced that even a legitimate governmental purpose "cannot be pursued by means that broadly stifle fundamental personal liberties when the end can be more narrowly achieved. The breadth of legislative abridgment must be viewed in the light of less drastic means for achieving the same basic purpose." 364 U.S. at 488.

131. 364 F.2d 657 (D.C. Cir. 1966).

132. This decision, and the same court's decision in Rouse v. Cameron, 373 F.2d 451 (D.C. Cir. 1966) in which a statutorily based right to treatment was announced, are prototypical examples of how doctrines announced in response to perceived statutory mandate may develop—given the right climate and a persuasive analysis—into constitutional doctrine in decisions by other courts wishing to reach the same result but lacking a similar statutory predicate.

133. 364 F.2d at 660.

134. *See, e.g.,* Welsch v. Likens, 373 F. Supp. 487 (D. Minn. 1974). The judicial and legislative development of the doctrine is described in Hoffman & Foust, *Least Restrictive Treatment of the Mentally Ill: A Doctrine in Search of Its Senses,* 14 SAN DIEGO L. REV. 1100 (1977).

135. Hoffman & Foust, *supra* note 134, at 1112–15. At the time of their article, the authors counted 20 states that referred explicitly to the doctrine in their commitment laws, including Colorado, Connecticut, Delaware, Indiana, Minnesota, Mississippi, Montana, Nebraska, Nevada, New Hampshire, New Jersey, North Carolina, Rhode Island, South Dakota, Tennessee, Utah, Virginia, Washington, West Virginia, and Wisconsin. *Id.* at n. 48. They found that 15 jurisdictions referred to it implicitly: Arizona, the District of Columbia, Florida, Illinois, Iowa, Kansas, Maine, Massachusetts, Michigan, New Mexico, North Dakota, Ohio, and Pennsylvania. *Id.* at n. 49.

136. Hoffman & Foust, *supra* note 134.

137. Chambers, *Alternatives to Civil Commitment of the Mentally Ill,* 70 MICH. L. REV. 1107, 1168 (1972).

138. *See, e.g.,* Dixon v. Weinberger, 405 F. Supp. 974 (D.D.C. 1975), ordering creation of suitable residential facilities that would allow the implementation of patients' rights to be treated in the least restrictive environment.

139. Pennhurst State School and Hosp. v. Haldemann, 451 U.S. 1, 29 (1981). The court noted that it had never imposed on the states "such open-ended and *potentially* burdensome obligations as providing 'appropriate' treatment in the 'least restrictive environment.' "

140. *See, e.g.,* Garrity v. Gallen, 522 F. Supp. 171 (D.N.H. 1981), in which the court held that there was no constitutional or federal statutory right held by patients entitling them to the development of community-based treatment programs and facilities.

141. *See, e.g.,* Stromberg & Stone, *A Model State Law on Civil Commitment of the Mentally Ill,* 20 HARV. J. LEG. 275 (1983); Hoffman & Dunn, *Beyond* Rouse *and* Wyatt: *An Administrative Law Model for Expanding and Implementing the Mental Patient's Right to Treatment,* 61 VA. L. REV. 297 (1975); sources cited *supra* notes 142–143.

142. A. STONE, *supra* note 8, at 66–71.

143. Roth *supra* note 101.

144. *Id.* at 1121.

145. A. STONE, *supra* note 8, at 66–67.

146. Roth, *supra* note 101, at 1122.

147. *Id.;* A. STONE, *supra* note 8, at 67.

148. Roth, *supra* note 101, at 1123.

149. *Id.*

150. *Id.* at 1124–25.

151. A. STONE, *supra* note 8, at 70.

152. *Id.*

153. Morse, *A Preference for Liberty: The Case against Involuntary Commitment of the Mentally Disordered,* 70 CALIF. L. REV. 54, 87–93 (1982).

154. In California, the decision is made by attending staff, or mental health professional designated by the county, or a police officer, who has the authority to have an individual admitted on an emergency basis. CAL WELF. INST. CODE § 5150 (Supp. 1984).

155. Emergency admissions in Washington are effected either by a mental health professional designated by the county, or by a police officer. WASH. REV. CODE. ANN. tit. 71.05.150 (Supp. 1985).

156. N.Y. Mental Hygiene Law §§ 9.37, 9.39 (McKinney 1978).

157. VA. CODE ANN. § 37.1-67.1 (Supp. 1983).

158. For example, in New York, the statute speaks only of the "opinion" of the director of county mental health services that the individual is mentally ill, needs immediate care and treatment, and presents a likelihood of serious harm to self or others. N.Y. Mental Hygiene Law § 9.37 (McKinney 1978). In Washington, the mental health professional is required to conduct an investigation of allegations that the person is mentally disordered and, as a result, presents a likelihood of serious harm to self or others or is gravely disabled, but no standard governs its determination that emergency care is needed. WASH REV. CODE ANN. tit. 71.05.150 (Supp. 1985). In Virginia, the judge or magistrate needs only to rely upon a sworn petition of the applicant, or act upon his or her own motion, in which case "probable cause" is required—the pertinent issue in any case is whether the person is mentally ill and in need of hospitalization. VA. CODE ANN. § 37.1-67.1 (Supp. 1983).

159. CAL. WELF. INST. CODE § 5150 (Supp. 1984).

160. VA. CODE ANN. § 37.1-67.1 (Supp. 1983).

161. CAL. WELF. INST. CODE § 5150 (Supp. 1984).

162. WASH. REV. CODE ANN. tit. 71.05.150 (Supp. 1985).

163. N.Y. Mental Hygiene Law § 9.39(a) (McKinney 1978).

164. *Id.*

165. VA. CODE ANN. § 37.1-67.3 (Supp. 1983).

166. WASH. REV. CODE ANN. tit. 71.05.200 (1975).

167. N.Y. Mental Hygiene Law § 9.39 (McKinney 1978).

168. CAL. WELF. INST. CODE § 5157 (Supp. 1984).

169. *Id.*

170. New York law provides only for the giving of "notice" to the patient. N.Y. Mental Hygiene Law § 9.39 (McKinney 1978). This provision was challenged as being constitutionally defective, but was upheld on the ground that no evidence demonstrated that patients were in fact not receiving the "notice" that was "due." Project Release v. Prevost, 722 F.2d 960 (2d Cir. 1983). The court's reasoning on this issue is more a model of circularity than of clarity.

171. WASH. REV. CODE ANN. tit. 71.05.460 (1975); VA. CODE ANN. § 37.1-67.3 (Supp. 1983); CAL. WELF. INST. CODE § 5157 (Supp. 1984). As noted, all patients in New York are entitled to the services of the Mental Health Information Service.

172. In New York, the patient (or any relative or friend on his or her behalf) may file within 30 days for review of a judicial decision authorizing detention, in which

case a jury is summoned to hear the case. N.Y. Mental Hygiene Law § 9.35 (McKinney 1978). In Virginia, the person has the right to appeal within 30 days for *de novo* hearing in front of a jury. VA. CODE ANN. § 37.1-67.6 (Supp. 1983).

173. The United States Supreme Court, in Addington v. Texas, 441 U.S. 418 (1978), held that the Constitution requires that, *at a minimum*, the state prove its case in a commitment hearing by "clear and convincing evidence." The states are free to impose the stricter burden of "beyond a reasonable doubt" if they so choose.

174. Virginia, for example, does not exclude hearsay evidence at the commitment proceeding. The court may accept written certification of the examining physician's findings. VA. CODE ANN. § 37.1-67.3 (Supp. 1983).

175. In Washington, the individual has the right to remain silent, though in certain circumstances the physician–patient privilege may be deemed waived by the court. WASH. REV. CODE ANN. tit. 71.05.200, 71.05.250 (1975). The privilege against self-incrimination does not apply to a physician's evaluation conducted for the purpose of determining the appropriateness of continued detention in the other jurisdictions under discussion. *See, e.g.,* Conservatorship of Mitchell (1981), 114 Cal.3d 606, 170 Cal. Rptr. 759.

176. An independent clinician is available to the patient in Washington. WASH. REV. CODE ANN. tit. 71.05.470 (1975). California provides an interpreter if necessary. CAL. WELF. INST. CODE. § 5157 (Supp. 1984).

177. VA. CODE ANN. § 37.1-67.3 (Supp. 1983).

178. *Id.*

179. WASH. REV. CODE ANN. tit. 71.05.240 (Supp. 1985).

180. *Id.*

181. WASH. REV. CODE ANN. tit. 71.05.280–320 (Supp. 1985).

182. CAL. WELF. INST. CODE § 5250 (Supp. 1984).

183. *Id.* §§ 5251, 5252 (Supp. 1984).

184. *Id.* § 5256.4 (Supp. 1984).

185. *Id.* § 5257 (Supp. 1984).

186. *Id.* §§ 5350–5371 (Supp. 1984).

187. N.Y. Mental Hygiene Law, §§ 9.27, 9/31 (McKinney 1978).

188. *Id.* § 9.27 (McKinney 1978).

189. *Id.* § 9.31 (McKinney 1978).

190. In *Parham,* Justice Brennan, while vigorously criticizing Chief Justice Burger's analysis, read the Constitution to permit nonjudicial forms of admission for children to mental health facilities, if followed within a reasonable time by judicial hearing with procedural protection for the patient. He found such proceedings acceptable because of the "special considerations" presented by the parent–child relationship. He also noted his belief that preadmission *judicial* determinations were required for adults. 442 U.S. at 632–33 (Brennan, J., concurring and dissenting).

191. *See supra* notes 29, 30. *See also* Kiesler, *Public and Profes-*

sional Myths about Mental Hospitalization: An Empirical Reassessment of Policy Related Beliefs, 37 AM. PSYCHOLOGIST 1323 (1982); Kiesler & Sibulkin, *Episodic Rate of Mental Hospitalization,* 141 AM. J. PSYCHIATRY 44 (1984).

192. In general, law effects have been assessed through time-series designs. *See, eg.,* Felix v. Milliken, 463 F. Supp. 1360 (E.D. Mich. 1978). For discussion of the strengths and weaknesses of such "quasi-experimental" research designs, *see generally* D. CAMPBELL & J. STANLEY, EXPERIMENTAL AND QUASI-EXPERIMENTAL DESIGNS FOR RESEARCH (1966); EXPERIMENTATION IN THE LAW: REPORT OF THE FEDERAL JUDICIAL CENTER ADVISORY COMMITTEE ON EXPERIMENTATION IN THE LAW 107–12 (1981). *See also* 33 NEB. SYMP. ON MOTIVATION (G. Melton ed. 1985) (examining the circumstances under which law affects behavior).

193. Luckey & Berman, *Effects of a New Commitment Law on Involuntary Admissions and Service Utilization Patterns,* 3 LAW & HUM. BEHAV. 149 (1979).

194. NEB. REV. STAT. §§ 83-1001 to 83-1081 (Reissue 1981 and Cum. Supp. 1982).

195. Nebraska uses an interdisciplinary quasi-judicial board for civil commitment. *Id.* §§ 83-1017, 83-1018, and 83-1035 through 83-1081. This administrative mechanism has been held to provide sufficient protection of the respondent's right to due process. Doremus v. Farrell, 407 F. Supp. 509 (D. Neb. 1975). Nebraska's procedures are also unusual in that the county attorney, who is also the criminal prosecutor, functions as both gatekeeper (e.g., in determining whether there is cause to hospitalize someone involuntarily) and prosecutor in commitment proceedings. NEB. REV. STAT. §§ 83-1024 and 83-1053 (Reissue 1981 and Cum. Supp. 1982). Although there is considerable potential for abuse in such a situation (e.g., the county attorney can move to civilly commit an individual when evidence is too weak for him or her to pursue criminal prosecution), the procedure is a particularly close analogue to prosecutorial gatekeeping in the criminal process. *See supra* § 2.04(a).

196. The methodological problems of pre–post designs can be greatly attenuated if there are *repeated* prechange and postchange observations. The research then compares the slope of curves prior to and following the "interruption" by a change in the law. *See* Campbell, *Reforms as Experiments,* 24 AM. PSYCHOLOGIST 409 (1969).

197. Kiesler, *supra* note 54. Kiesler has reported that while the number of inpatient episodes in state and county mental health facilities fell from 819,000 in 1955 to 599,000 in 1975, they increased in general hospital psychiatric units, community mental health centers, Veterans Administration psychiatric units, and private facilities from 477,000 to 1.2 million in the same time period. *Id.* at 350.

198. *See* Morse, *supra* note 153, at 67–79.

199. The often flagrant failure to apply the legal standards for civil commitment has been documented in nu-

merous jurisdictions. *See, e.g.,* Hiday, *Reformed Commitment Procedures: An Empirical Study in the Courtroom,* 11 LAW SOC'Y REV. 651 (1977); Hiday, *The Role of Counsel in Civil Commitment: Changes, Effects, Determinants,* 5 J. PSYCHIATRY & L. 551 (1977); Hiday, *Court Discretion: Application of the Dangerousness Standard in Civil Commitment,* 5 LAW & HUM. BEHAV. 275 (1981); Hiday & Markell, *Components of Dangerousness: Legal Standards in Civil Commitment,* 3 INT'L J.L. PSYCHIATRY 405 (1980); Lipsitt & Lelos, *Decision Makers in Law and Psychiatry and the Involuntary Commitment Process,* 17 COMMUNITY MENTAL HEALTH J. 114 (1981); Stier & Stoebe, *Involuntary Hospitalization of the Mentally Ill in Iowa: The Failure of the 1975 Legislation,* 64 IOWA L. REV. 1284 (1979); Warren, *Involuntary Commitment for Mental Disorder: The Application of California's Lanterman–Petris–Short Act,* 11 LAW SOC'Y REV. 629 (1977); Wexler & Scoville, *The Administration of Psychiatric Justice: Theory and Practice in Arizona,* 13 ARIZ. L. REV. 1 (1971); Wickham, HOSPITALIZATION OF THE MENTALLY ILL IN IDAHO AND THE NEED FOR REFORM, IDAHO L. REV. 211 (1980); Yesavage, *A Study of Mandatory Review of Civil Commitment,* 41 ARCH. GEN. PSYCHIATRY 229 (1984); Zander, *Civil Commitment in Wisconsin: The Impact of* Lessard v. Schmidt, 1976 WIS. L. REV. 503.

200. Stier & Stoebe, *supra* note 199, at 1386–87.

201. *Id.* at 1386.

202. Hoffman & Foust, *supra* note 134.

203. Monahan, Ruggiero, & Friedlander, *The Stone–Roth Model of Civil Commitment and the California Dangerousness Standard: An Operational Comparison,* 39 ARCH. GEN. PSYCHIATRY 1267 (1982).

204. *See, e.g.,* Stone, *Psychiatric Abuse and Legal Reform: Two Ways to Make a Bad Situation Worse,* 5 INT'L J.L. PSYCHIATRY 9, 10–16 (1982).

205. The Supreme Court itself has unfortunately fallen prey to this misconceptualization. *See, e.g.,* Parham v. J.R., 442 U.S. 584, 604–05 (1979); Addington v. Texas, 441 U.S. 418, 429 (1979). The fundamentally moral–legal nature of the civil commitment process has been articulately discussed by Morse, *supra* note 10.

206. *See generally* Thibaut & Walker, *A Theory of Procedure,* 66 CALIF. L. REV. 541 (1978).

207. *See generally* the studies cited *supra* note 199.

The Supreme Court acknowledged the research on the sloppiness of commitment procedures in Parham v. J.R., 442 U.S. 584, 609 (1979), but curiously used the literature to support *loosening* of procedural rigor. The Court suggested that the "illusory" nature of civil commitment made the hearing nothing more than "time-consuming procedural minuets" unworthy of judges' and clinicians' time. *Id.* at 605.

Professor Morse has also concluded that legalization of civil commitment has not, and will not, result in formal, adversary procedures and adequate rigor of legal decisionmaking. However, he reaches a policy conclusion opposite to that of the Supreme Court. Rather than accept an inherent, intolerably high number of erroneous commitments, he argues that civil commitment should simply be abolished. Morse, *supra* note 153, at 67–79.

208. Stier & Stoebe, *supra* note 199.

209. *See, e.g.,* the articles by Hiday, *supra* note 199; Wexler & Scoville, *supra* note 199; Andalman & Chambers, *Effective Counsel for Persons Facing Civil Commitment: A Survey, a Polemic, and a Proposal,* 45 MISS. L.J. 43 (1974); Cohen, *The Function of the Attorney and the Commitment of the Mentally Ill,* 44 TEX. L. REV. 424 (1966); State ex. rel. Memmel v. Mundy, 75 Wis. 2d 276, 249 N.W. 2d 573 (1977).

210. Poythress, *Psychiatric Expertise in Civil Commitment: Training Attorneys to Cope with Expert Testimony,* 2 LAW & HUM. BEHAV. 1 (1978).

211. Zwerling, Conte, Plutchik, & Karasu, *"No-Commitment Week": A Feasibility Study,* 135 AM. J. PSYCHIATRY 1198 (1978).

212. *See, e.g.,* Stone, *supra* note 204, at 19. In extemporaneous remarks at the Sixth International Symposium on Law and Psychiatry, University of Virginia, June 13, 1981, Seymour Halleck, a well-known scholar in forensic psychiatry at the University of North Carolina, argued that psychiatric residents should not be permitted to commit patients. Dr. Halleck's reasoning was that the experience is corrupting, in that it teaches psychiatry as social control rather than as healing, and in that it may predispose some psychiatrists to the expression of power for its own sake.

213. Kiesler, *supra* note 54, at 359.

214. We do not argue that civil commitment should be abolished. Although a strong case can be made for abolition, *see* Morse, *supra* note 153, it is clear that such a position is politically untenable and will continue to be so for the foreseeable future. We note here the literature on efficacy of alternative care as a prelude to our discussion of the proper role of clinicians in civil commitment. *See infra* § 8.07.

215. *See* Morse, *supra* note 153, at 77–79.

216. *See generally* E. GOFFMAN, ESSAYS ON THE SOCIAL SITUATION OF MENTAL PATIENTS AND OTHER INMATES (1961); Goldstein, *The Sociology of Mental Health and Illness,* 5 ANN. REV. SOC. 381 (1979).

Civil commitment frequently brings with it a multiplicity of legal as well as social disabilities. *See generally* D. WEXLER, *supra* note 36; text, *supra* § 8.02(c).

217. Kiesler, *supra* note 54.

218. *Id.* at 357–58.

219. *Id.* at 357.

220. *Id.* at 358–59.

221. *See* Morse, *supra* note 153, at 79–84.

222. *Id.; see also* Johnson, *The Constitution and the Federal District Judge,* 54 TEX. L. REV. 903, 909 (1976) (discussing the recalcitrance of Alabama authorities in implementing a court order to provide humane care and treatment).

223. State hospitals are generally perceived as undesirable places in which to work, and financial inducements alone have often failed to facilitate recruitment and retention of professional staff for state hospitals.

Stickney, Wyatt v. Stickney: *Background and Postcript,* in THE RIGHT TO TREATMENT FOR MENTAL PATIENTS 29, 39–41 (S. Golann & W. Fremouw eds. 1976); Stone, *supra* note 204, at 20–21.

224. Torrey & Taylor, *Cheap Labor from Poor Nations,* 130 AM. J. PSYCHIATRY 428 (1973).

225. J. MONAHAN, THE CLINICAL PREDICTION OF VIOLENT BEHAVIOR 77–82 (1981).

226. Morse, *supra* note 153, at 98–103.

227. In civil commitment, there is unfortunately a high probability that a respondent may be placed in unnecessarily restrictive and even harmful conditions on the basis of an opinion of low reliability and validity. In view of the weight placed on these opinions, clinicians must be ever mindful of their responsibilities and exercise great caution. *See* American Psychological Association, *Ethical Principles of Psychologists,* 36 AM. PSYCHOLOGIST 633 (1981), Principles 1f, 3c, and 8c. These issues are discussed generally in § 3.05.

228. *See generally* ALTERNATIVES TO MENTAL HOSPITAL TREATMENT (L. Stein & M. Test eds. 1978); Kiesler, *supra* note 54; Morse, *supra* note 153, at 84–87 and accompanying citations.

229. *See* Kiesler, *supra* note 191, at 1331.

230. *See* Kahle & Sales, *Due Process of Law and the Attitudes of Professionals toward Civil Commitment,* in NEW DIRECTIONS IN PSYCHOLOGICAL RESEARCH 265 (P. Lipsitt & B. Sales eds. 1979).

231. Kiesler, *Mental Health Policy as a Field of Inquiry for Psychology,* 35 AM. PSYCHOLOGIST 1066, 1073–74 (1980).

232. *See, e.g.,* Zander, *supra* note 199, at 523, 524–26, 530–31, 539–42, 549–51, 552–54 (describing civil commitment hearings in Dane County, Wisconsin).

233. *See* Wexler, *The Structure of Civil Commitment: Patterns, Pressures, and Interactions in Mental Health Legislation,* 7 LAW & HUM. BEHAV. 1 (1983).

234. *See* Addington v. Texas, 441 U.S. 418 (1979).

235. *See supra* note 209.

236. MODEL CODE OF PROFESSIONAL RESPONSIBILITY, canon 7 (1979).

237. In their role as "counselors," attorneys often themselves define the course that clients should follow. *See generally* D. ROSENTHAL, LAWYER AND CLIENT: WHO'S IN CHARGE? (1974).

238. MODEL CODE OF PROFESSIONAL RESPONSIBILITY EC 7–11 (1979).

239. *Id.* EC 7–12.

240. *See, e.g.,* Brakel, *Legal Aid In Mental Hospitals,* 1981 A.B.F. RESEARCH J. 21 (1981); Woody, *Public Policy and Legal Aid in Mental Hospitals: The Dimension of the Problem and Their Implications for Legal Education and Practice,* 1982 A.B.F. RES. J. 237 (1982).

241. Without an advocate, the rights to cross-examination, presentation of evidence, independent evaluation, and so forth are essentially illusory.

242. *See* M. SAKS & R. HASTIE, SOCIAL PSYCHOLOGY IN COURT 119–33 (1978).

243. D. WEXLER, *supra* note 36, at 99.

244. Slobogin, *The Attorney's Role in Civil Commitment,* 1 MENTAL HEALTH LEGAL STUDIES CENTER NEWSLETTER 1, 2 (1979).

245. *See, e.g., Preparation and Trial of a Civil Commitment Case,* 5 MENTAL DISABILITY L. REP. 201, 281 (1981); Slobogin, *supra* note 244.

246. ARIZ. REV. STAT. ANN. § 36-537 (Supp. 1983).

247. The Division of Mental Health Advocacy in the Department of the Public Advocate in New Jersey is exemplary of the utility of integration of mental health professionals into legal aid for the mentally disabled. *See* Perlin, *An Invitation to the Dance: An Empirical Response to Chief Justice Warren Burger's "Time-Consuming Procedural Minuets" Theory in* Parham v. J.R., 9 BULL. AM. ACAD. PSYCHIATRY L. 149 (1981).

248. *See* Farrell, *The Right of an Indigent Civil Commitment Defendant to Psychiatric Assistance of His Choice at State Expense,* 11 IDAHO L. REV. 141 (1975); *but see In re* Gannon, 123 N.J. Super. 104, 301 A.2d 493 (Somerset Co. Ct. 1973).

249. Pokorny, *Prediction of Suicide in Psychiatric Patients: A Prospective Study,* 40 ARCH. GEN. PSYCHIATRY 249, 257 (1983).

250. *Id.* at 255.

251. *Id.*

252. *Id.* at 257.

253. *See, e.g.,* NEB. REV. STAT. § 83-1009 (Reissue 1981).

254. *See, e.g.,* CAL. WELF. INST. CODE §§ 5350 Para. 5371 (Deering 1979 and Supp. 1983).

255. *See* Searight, Oliver, & Grisso, *The Community Competence Scale: Preliminary Reliability and Validity,* 11 AM. J. COMMUNITY PSYCHOLOGY 609 (1983); P. Anderton, The Elderly, Incompetency, and Guardianship (1979) (unpublished M.S. thesis, St. Louis University).

256. Issues in the use of guardianship are discussed in Massad & Sales, *Guardianship: An Alternative to Institutionalization?,* 24 AM. BEHAV. SCIENTIST 755 (1981).

257. *See* J. MONAHAN, *supra* note 225, at 6–7 and sources cited there.

258. *See* J. MONAHAN, *supra* note 225, at 56–60; Monahan, *The Prediction of Violent Behavior: Toward a Second Generation of Theory and Policy,* 141 AM. J. PSYCHIATRY 10, 11 (1984).

259. Monahan, *supra* note 258, at 13.

260. Rofman, Askinazi, & Fant, *The Prediction of Dangerous Behavior in Emergency Civil Commitment,* 137 AM. J. PSYCHIATRY 1061 (1980).

261. *See* Roth, *Dangerousness: In the Eye of the Beholder?,* 138 AM. J. PSYCHIATRY 995 (1981).

262. Werner, Rose, Yesavage, & Seeman, *Psychiatrists' Judgments of Dangerousness in Patients on an Acute Care Unit,* 141 AM. J. PSYCHIATRY 263 (1984).

263. *See* Chapman & Chapman, *Illusory Correlations as an Obstacle to the Use of Valid Psychodiagnostic Signs,* 74 J. ABNORMAL PSYCHOLOGY 271 (1969).

264. Werner, Rose, Yesavage, & Seeman, *supra* note 262, at 64–66. *See also* J. MONAHAN, *supra* note 225, at 36–37.

265. Werner, Rose, Yesavage, & Seeman, *supra* note 262, at 264–65.

266. *See generally* J. MONAHAN, *supra* note 225, at 28–38. Clinicians' reliance on intuition, even when contrary to empirical evidence, is not unique to prediction of violent behavior. *See* Morse, *Failed Explanations and Criminal Responsibility: Experts and the Unconscious,* 68 VA. L. REV. 971 (1982); Wade & Baker, *Opinions and Use of Psychological Tests: A Survey of Clinical Psychologists,* 32 AM. PSYCHOLOGIST 874 (1977).

267. Beigel, Berren, & Harding, *The Paradoxical Impact of a Commitment Statute on Prediction of Dangerousness,* 141 Am. J. Psychiatry 373 (1984).

268. J. MONAHAN, *supra* note 225, especially ch. 6.

269. *Id.* at 109–12; *see* R. NOVACO, ANGER CONTROL: THE DEVELOPMENT AND EVALUATION OF AN EXPERIMENTAL TREATMENT (1975).

270. *See, e.g.,* People v. Keith, 38 Ill. 2d 405, 410–11, 231 N.E.2d 387, 390 (1967).

271. The Supreme Court rejected a definitive link between the Fifth Amendment and criminal proceedings in *In re Gault,* 387 U.S. 1, 49 (1967): "[T]he availability of the privilege does not turn upon the type of proceeding in which its protection is invoked, but upon the nature of the statement or admission and the exposure which it invites. The privilege may, for example, be claimed in a civil or administrative proceeding, if the statement is or may be inculpatory."

272. Andersen v. Maryland, 427 U.S. 463, 475 (1976); Bellis v. United States, 417 U.S. 85, 88 (1974); United States v. White, 322 U.S. 694, 698 (1944).

273. The imposition of sanctions for refusing to talk in civil commitment hearings is problematic. For example, should a mute catatonic person be held in contempt of court? *Cf.* Slobogin, Estelle v. Smith: *The Constitutional Contours of the Forensic Evaluation,* 32 EMORY L.J. 71, 103–06 (1982).

274. Once the possibility of mental disorder is raised, mental health professionals often tend to perceive behavior as a function of the mental disorder. *See, e.g.,* Langer & Abelson, *A Patient by Any Other Name . . . : Clinician Group Difference in Labeling Bias,* 42 J. CONSULTING CLINICAL PSYCHOLOGY 4 (1974); Rosenhan, *supra* note 41; Rosenhan, *The Contextual Nature of Psychiatric Diagnosis,* 84 J. ABNORMAL PSYCHOLOGY 462 (1975).

275. *See Preparation and Trial of a Civil Commitment Case,* 5 MENTAL DISABILITY L. REP. 201, 205–06 (1981), and cases cited there.

276. Even under relatively legalistic statutes, there may be no right to counsel at the temporary detention hearing; *see, e.g.,* VA. CODE ANN. § 37.1-67.3 (Cum. Supp. 1983). Under "medical" statutes, there may be a right to consult counsel after admission but no automatic appointment of counsel; *see, e.g.,* N.Y. Mental Hygiene Law § 9.07 (McKinney 1978).

277. State statutes may require the presentation of information about the process and rights within it. Regardless, though, such "warnings" are ethically required. *See* American Psychological Association, *supra* note 227, Principles 6 and 8a. In presenting the rele-

vant information, clinicians should try to ensure that, insofar as possible, respondents actually understand the rights and their applicability in their own cases. Too frequently, clinicians obey the letter but not the spirit of the law through rote recitation of rights and subtle coercion to cooperate. *See generally* C. LIDZ, A. MEISEL, E. ZERUBAVEL, M. CARTER, R. SESTAK, & L. ROTH, INFORMED CONSENT: A STUDY OF DECISION-MAKING IN PSYCHIATRY (1984).

278. *See In re* Scott L., 469 A.2d 1336 (N.H. 1983).

279. *See, e.g.,* VA. CODE ANN. §§ 37.1-65 and 37.1067.3 (Cum. Supp. 1983).

280. *Cf.* Stone, *supra* note 8, at 19–20. Because the "prescreener" is based in a community mental health center, he or she can be especially important in making the proper links among prehospital community-based care, the hospital, and community-based aftercare.

281. *See* Wexler, *supra* note 233.

282. 442 U.S. 584 (1979).

283. *See* J. KNITZER, UNCLAIMED CHILDREN: THE FAILURE OF PUBLIC RESPONSIBILITY TO CHILDREN AND ADOLESCENTS IN NEED OF MENTAL HEALTH SERVICES 54–57 and 113–29 (1982); Perlin, *supra* note 247, at 150.

284. *See generally* Melton, *supra* note 98.

285. *Id. See also* Perry & Melton, *Precedential Value of Judicial Notice of Social Facts:* Parham *as an Example,* 22 J. FAM. L. (1984).

286. *See, e.g.,* J.L. v. Parham, 412 F. Supp. 112, 124 (M.D. Ga. 1976); J. KNITZER, *supra* note 283, at 11–12 h.n. 23 and 46.

287. *See, e.g.,* J. KNITZER, *supra* note 283, at 11 n. 21.

288. *See, e.g.,* 412 F. Supp. at 112, 124; L. OLSON, A POINT IN TIME STUDY OF CHILDREN AND ADOLESCENTS IN STATE HOSPITALS 5 (1981).

289. *See generally* J. KNITZER, *supra* note 283, at 67–78; *see also infra* note 293.

290. Quay, *Residential Treatment,* in PSYCHOPATHOLOGICAL DISORDERS OF CHILDHOOD 387, 390 (H. Quay & J. Werry eds. 2d ed. 1979); Winsberg, Bialer, Kupietz, Botti, & Balka, *Home vs. Hospital Care of Children with Behavior Disorders: A Controlled Investigation,* 37 ARCH. GEN. PSYCHIATRY 413 (1980).

291. *See* Miller & Kenney, *Adolescent Delinquency and the Myth of Hospital Treatment,* 12 CRIME DELINQ. 38 (1966).

292. Highly intrusive treatments are common in some residential schools and group homes. *See, e.g.,* Milonas v. Williams, 691 F.2d 931 (10th Cir. 1982).

293. There is evidence that, as juvenile justice standards tighten, juvenile mental health admissions increase. *See* Warren, *New Forms of Social Control: The Myth of Deinstitutionalization,* 24 AM. BEHAV. SCIENTIST 724 (1981).

294. Many hospitalized youth are wards of the state. The lack of accountability of their guardians is well documented. *See, e.g.,* Bush & Gordon, *Client Choice and Bureaucratic Accountability: Possibilities for Responsiveness in a Social Welfare Bureaucracy,* 34(4) J. SOC. ISSUES 22 (1978).

295. *See* Perlin, *supra* note 247, at 156–60.

296. 445 U.S. 480 (1980).

297. *id.* at 568–70.

298. *id.* at 567–70.

299. *See, e.g.,* Churgin, *The Transfer of Inmates to Mental Health Facilities: Developments in the Law,* in MENTALLY DISORDERED OFFENDERS: PERSPECTIVES FROM LAW AND SOCIAL SCIENCE 207, 219–23 (J. Monahan & H. Steadman eds. 1983).

300. CRIMINAL JUSTICE MENTAL HEALTH STANDARDS, standard 7-10.5 (1984) [hereinafter cited as STANDARDS].

301. *Id.*

302. *Id.,* standard 7-10.4.

303. *See* Estelle v. Gamble, 429 U.S. 97 (1976).

304. STANDARDS, *supra* note 300, standards through 7-10.5.

305. There are no formal studies of the content of services in transfer facilities. However, Monahan and colleagues reported that their "impression from visiting several transfer facilities is that they are 'hospitals' in name only." Monahan, Davis, Hartstone, & Steadman, *Prisoners Transferred to Mental Hospitals,* in MENTALLY DISORDERED OFFENDERS: PERSPECTIVES FROM LAW AND SOCIAL SCIENCE 233, 243 (J. Monahan & H. Steadman eds. 1983).

   The norm within prisons themselves is that treatment is virtually nonexistent. New York, for example, has 25,000 inmates served by 120 mental health workers, including only 30 psychologists and 1 psychiatrist. Reveron, *Mentally Ill—And Behind Bars,* 13(3) A.P.A. MONITOR 10 (1982).

306. *See* Roth, *Correctional Psychiatry,* in MODERN LEGAL PSYCHIATRY AND FORENSIC SCIENCE 677, 684–87 (W. Curran, A. McGarry, & C. Petty eds. 1980).

307. *See supra* note 305.

308. *See* Churgin, *supra* note 299, at 226–27.

309. G. MELTON, L. WEITHORN, & C. SLOBOGIN, COMMUNITY MENTAL HEALTH CENTERS AND THE COURTS: AN EVALUATION OF COMMUNITY-BASED FORENSIC SERVICES (1985); Favole, *Mental Disability in the American Criminal Process: A Four Issue Survey,* in MENTALLY DISORDERED OFFENDERS: PERSPECTIVES FROM LAW AND SOCIAL SCIENCE 247, 283 (J. Monahan & H. Steadman eds. 1983) ("Only West Virginia and Indiana have statutes that seem sure to withstand a *Vitek*-type challenge"); Hartstone, Steadman, & Monahan, *Vitek and Beyond: The Empirical Context of Prison-to-Hospital Transfers,* 45 LAW CONTEMP. PROBS. 125 (1982) (*Vitek* will have an impact only if Department of Corrections hospitals are included); Monahan, Davis, Hartstone, & Steadman, *supra* note 305, at 241.

310. Monahan, Davis, Hartstone, & Steadman, *supra* note 305.

311. Runck, *NIMH Report: Study of 43 Jails Shows Mental Health Services and Inmate Safety Are Compatible,* 34 HOSP. & COMMUNITY PSYCHIATRY 1007 (1983).

312. For reviews, see Hermann, *Assault on the Insanity Defense: Limitations on the Effectiveness and Effect of the Defense of Insanity,* 14 RUTGERS L.J. 241, 312–59 (1983);

Morris, *Acquittal by Reason of Insanity: Developments in the Law,* in MENTALLY DISORDERED OFFENDERS: PERSPECTIVES FROM LAW AND SOCIAL SCIENCE 65, 70–72 (J. Monahan & H. Steadman eds. 1983).

313. Hermann, *supra* note 312, at 329–59; Note, *Commitment Following an Insanity Acquittal,* 94 HARV. L. REV. 605 (1981).

314. Addington v. Texas, 441 U.S. 418 (1979).

315. *See* Hermann, *supra* note 312, at 337–38. This can be a significant difference when amorphous issues such as mental illness and dangerousness are involved. The ABA would place the burden on the state by clear and convincing evidence, as in civil commitment. *See infra* note 324.

316. Note, *supra* note 313, at 605-07.

317. *Id.* at 339–42.

318. *In re* Franklin, 496 P.2d 465, 471 & n.6 Cal. (1972); Chase v. Kearns, 278 A.2d 132, 134 (Me. 1971); *In re* Lewis, 403 A.2d 1115, 1117 (Del. 1979).

319. In some jurisdictions, insanity acquittals occur most frequently in cases involving property crimes. *See, e.g.,* Petrila, *The Insanity Defense and Other Mental Health Dispositions in Missouri,* 5 INT'L J.L. PSYCHIATRY 81 (1982); Rogers & Bloom, *Characteristics of Persons Committed to Oregon's Psychiatric Security Review Board,* 10 BULL. AM. ACAD. PSYCHIATRY & LAW 155 (1982).

320. Such a standard prevails in federal courts and one-third of the states. Hermann, *supra* note 312, at 270–71. In such jurisdictions, a reasonable doubt as to sanity cannot be said to imply clear and convincing evidence of mental illness, even at the time of the offense.

321. 103 S.Ct. 3043 (1983). For a critique of *Jones,* see Hermann, *Automatic Commitment and Release of Insanity Acquittees: Constitutional Dimensions,* 14 RUTGERS L.J. 667 (1983).

322. 103 S.Ct. at 3049.

323. *Id.* at 3050.

324. *Id.* at 3051–53. The ABA would limit the length of criminal commitment to the maximum term the individual would have received had he or she been convicted. STANDARDS, *supra* note 300, standard 7-7.7. The acquittee may petition for release periodically; at these hearings, the *state* would bear the burden of proof. *Id.,* Standard 7-7.8.

325. Steadman & Braff, *Defendants Not Guilty by Reason of Insanity,* in MENTALLY DISORDERED OFFENDERS: PERSPECTIVES FROM LAW AND SOCIAL SCIENCE 109, 118–119 (J. Monahan & H. Steadman eds. 1983).

326. *See* J. BRAKEL, J. PARRY, & B. WEINER, THE MENTALLY DISABLED AND THE LAW, Table 2-5 (1986).

327. *See generally* Dybwad & Herr, *Unnecessary Coercion: An End to Involuntary Civil Commitment of Retarded Persons,* 31 STAN. L. REV. 753 (1979).

328. Fla.Stats. § 393.063(23) (1986).

329. *Id.* § 393.11(1)(c).

330. *Id.* § 393.11(1)(b).

331. *Id.* § 393.11(2)(c).

332. *Id.* § 394.467(1)(a)2.

333. *Id.* § 393.115(1).

334. *See, e.g.,* United States v. Shorter, 343 A.2d 569, 571–72 (D.C. 1975).

335. Ellis & Luckasson, *Mentally Retarded Criminal Defendants,* 53 GEO. WASH. L. REV. 414, 466–70 (1985).

336. STANDARDS, *supra* note 300, standards 7-7.4(b), 7-7.8 (1984).

Chapter 9

1. Section 504 of the Rehabilitation Act of 1973, 29 U.S.C. § 794 (1976), requires recipients of federal funds to refrain from discrimination against handicapped persons. Similarly, the Education for All Handicapped Children Act of 1975, P.L. 94-142, 20 U.S.C. §§ 1412(1) and 1414(a)(1)(c)(ii) (1976), threatens loss of federal special education grants if a school system fails to make an affirmative effort to provide a free appropriate public education to all handicapped children.

2. Disabled persons are entitled to support under the Social Security Administration's programs of Disability Insurance and Supplemental Security Income. *See infra* § 9.06.

3. For example, mental health professionals might be asked to evaluate whether a child has special educational needs, as defined by the Education for All Handicapped Children Act, *supra* note 1.

4. The history of guardianship law is reviewed in Regan, *Protective Services for the Elderly: Commitment, Guardianship, and Alternatives,* 13 WM. MARY L. REV. 569, 570–73 (1972).

5. *See In re* Gault, 387 U.S. 1, 16–17 (1967).

6. All but seven states and the District of Columbia distinguish between guardianship (conservatorship) of the estate and guardianship of the person. B. SALES, D.M. POWELL, & R. VAN DUIZEND, DISABLED PERSONS AND THE LAW: STATE LEGISLATIVE ISSUES 461 (1982).

7. California uses the term "conservatorship" for its scheme for civil commitment of gravely disabled persons. CAL. WELF. INST. CODE §§ 5350 through 5371 (Deeling 1979 and Cum. Supp. 1983).

8. Seventeen states expressly distinguish between general and limited guardianship. B. SALES, D.M. POWELL, & R. VAN DUIZEND, *supra note* 6, at 462.

9. *Id.* at 461–62.

10. *See generally* CHILDREN'S COMPETENCE TO CONSENT (G. Melton, M. Saks, & G. Koocher eds. 1983) [hereinafter cited as CHILDREN'S COMPETENCE]; Melton, *Toward "Personhood" for Adolescents: Autonomy and Privacy as Values in Public Policy,* 38 AM. PSYCHOLOGIST 99 (1983).

11. For example, minors generally are unable to enter contracts, except for "necessaries." *See, e.g.,* Halbman v. Lemke, 99 Wis. 2d 241, 298 N.W.2d 562 (1980).

12. Some states have enacted provisions providing for minors' independent consent to treatment. *See generally* Wadlington, *Consent to Medical Care for Minors: The Legal Framework,* in CHILDREN'S COMPETENCE, *supra* note 10.

13. A special showing that the minor is "mature" will often be required before he or she is permitted to exercise self-determination. *See* Wadlington, *Minors and Health*

Care: The Age of Consent, 73 OSGOODE HALL L.J. 115 (1973). The mature minor rule has had its most controversial application in abortion law. *See* Melton, *Minors and Privacy: Are Legal and Psychological Concepts Compatible?,* 62 NEB. L. REV. 455, 463–72 (1983).

14. B. SALES, D.M. POWELL, & R. VAN DUIZEND, *supra* note 6, at 464.

15. *See, e.g.,* Parham v. J.R., 442 U.S. 182 (1979); *but see* W. WADLINGTON, C. WHITEBREAD, & S. DAVIS, CHILDREN IN THE LEGAL SYSTEM 182 (1983) (noting that assumptions about the "natural bonds of affection" in Blackstone and Kent refer to the treatment of bastards).

16. *See* B. SALES, D. M. POWELL, & R. VAN DUIZEND, *supra* note 6, at 13–14.

17. *See id.* at 114.

18. *See infra* § 9.02(b).

19. *See* B. ENNIS & L. SIEGEL, THE RIGHTS OF MENTAL PATIENTS: THE BASIC ACLU GUIDE TO A MENTAL PATIENT'S RIGHTS 74–77 (1973).

20. *See* B. SALES, D. M. POWELL, & R. VAN DUIZEND, *supra* note 6, at 462.

21. *See supra* note 7.

22. Regan, *supra* note 4, at 605.

23. B. SALES, D. M. POWELL, & R. VAN DUIZEND, *supra* note 6, at 463.

24. Regan, *supra* note 4, at 605–06.

25. Ten states provide no statutory right to counsel. B. SALES, D. H. POWELL, & R. VAN DUIZEND, *supra* note 6, at 463.

26. Twenty-two states provide the respondent with a right to a jury. *Id.*

27. The right to be present is guaranteed in only 38 states, *id.,* and that right is often waivable with only a doctor's certificate that the respondent is unable to attend.

28. B. SALES, D. M. POWELL, & R. VAN DUIZEND, *supra* note 6, at 463.

29. *Id.* at 464.

30. A state-by-state review of standards is included in *id.* at 469–75.

31. Alexander, *Premature Probate: A Different Perspective on Guardianship for the Elderly,* 31 STAN. L. REV. 1003, 1015–16 (1979).

32. *In re* Oltmer, 336 N.W.2d 560 (Neb. 1983).

33. *Id.* at 562 (Krivosha, C.J., and Caporale, J., dissenting).

34. Estate of Galvin v. Galvin, 112 Ill. App. 3d 677, 445 N.E.2d 1223 (1st Dist. Ct. App. 1983).

35. Plumer v. Early, 190 Cal. Rptr. 578 (3d Dist. Ct. App. 1983).

36. Searight, Oliver, & Grisso, *The Community Competence*

Scale: Preliminary Reliability and Validity, 11 AM. J. COM-
MUNITY PSYCHOLOGY 609 (1983); T. Anderton, The Elderly, Incompetency, and Guardianship (1979) (unpublished M.S. thesis, St. Louis University); P. Loeb, Validity
of the Community Competence Scale with the Elderly
(1983) (unpublished Ph.D. dissertation, St. Louis University).

37. The primary validity studies have compared small
numbers of elderly persons (12 per group) living in the
community with different levels of nursing care in a
home for the elderly, P. Loeb, *supra* note 36, and dein-
stitutionalized residents of a boarding home with residents of cooperative apartments, Searight, Oliver, &
Grisso, *supra* note 36. No studies of the validity of the
CCS in making assessments for guardianship or commitment have yet been undertaken.

38. The instrument was derived from surveys of professionals and elderly nonprofessionals as to the components of competency for an elderly person. P. Anderton, *supra* note 36.

39. The concept of competency to live in the community
was found to be unitary, without differentiation of
management of property nd person. *Id.*

40. For a discussion of the alternatives, see Hodgson,
*Guardianship of Mentally Retarded Persons: Three Approaches
to a Long Neglected Problem.* 37 ALB. L. REV. 407 (1973).

41. Consider, for example, the circumstance in which a
wealthy elderly man takes a young woman as his paramour and wills most of his estate to her.

42. Most states provide for examination of the respondent,
usually by a physician, but in some states by a psychologist or a multidisciplinary team. B. SALES, D. M. POW-
ELL, R. Van Duizend, *supra* note 6, at 463.

43. *See, e.g.,* Rogers v. Commissioner of the Department of
Mental Health, 390 Mass. 489 (1983); *In re* Roe, 421
N.E.2d 40 (Mass. 1981); Saikewicz v. Superintendent
of Belchertown State School, 370 N.E.2d 417 (Mass.
1977); *In re* Grady, 426 A.2d 467 (N.J. 1981); *In re*
Quinlan, 335 A.2d 647 (N.J. 1976), *cert. denied,* 429
U.S. 922 (1976).

44. For example, an individual may have a personal preference to avoid particular kinds of side effects (e.g.,
loss of hair), even if it means consequences that most
people would find more noxious.

45. *See* Melton & Scott, *Evaluation of Mentally Retarded Persons
for Sterilization: Contributions and Limits of Psychological
Consultation,* 15 PROF. PSYCHOLOGY: RESEARCH PRAC.
34, 35–36 (1984); *cf. In re* Hayes, 93 Wash. 228, 608
P.2d 635 (1980), and *In re* Grady, 85 N.J. 235, 426
A.2d 467 (1981).

46. For an example of the difficulties in applying a subjective substituted judgment standard, *see* Saikewicz v. Superintendent of Belchertown State Hospital, 370 N.E.2d
417 (1977), in which the court attempted to discern
what the subjective wishes of a profoundly retarded
man would have been.

47. Although the doctrine of informed consent has deep
roots in Anglo-American reverence for individual lib-

erty, the doctrine really did not develop until the 1960s.
J. KATZ, THE SILENT WORLD OF DOCTOR AND PATIENT
59–80 (1984); C. LIDZ, A. MEISEL, E. ZERUBAVEL, M.
CARTER, R. SESTAK, & L. ROTH, INFORMED CONSENT:
A STUDY OF DECISIONMAKING IN PSYCHIATRY 11–12
(1984) [hereinafter cited as INFORMED CONSENT]. The
first informed consent case is usually considered to have
been Salgo v. Leland Stanford Jr. Univ. Bd. of Trustees,
317 P.2d 170 (Cal. Dist. Ct. App. 1957).

48. *See* J. KATZ, *supra* note 47, at 49; Wadlington, *supra*
note 12, at 59.

49. *See* J. KATZ, *supra* note 47, at 69–71; Wadlington, *supra*
note 12, at 64–65.

50. INFORMED CONSENT, *supra* note 47, at 4.

51. *See* J. KATZ, *supra* note 47.

52. *Id.* at °6–87.

53. *See generally* INFORMED CONSENT, *supra* note 47, at 5,
22–23.

54. The challenge came in Canterbury v. Spence, 464 F.2d
772 (D.C. Cir. 1972), *cert. denied,* 409 U.S. 1064 (1972).

55. *See, e.g.,* Natanson v. Kline, 350 P.2d 1093, *reh'g denied,*
354 P.2d 670 (Kan. 1960). A number of states still rely
upon this standard, which is akin to the standard used
in malpractice torts. J. KATZ, *supra* note 47, at 80–82.

56. *See supra* note 54.

57. *See, e.g.,* Canterbury v. Spence, 464 F.2d 772 (D.C. Cir.
1972).

58. The subjective test has been rarely adopted. INFORMED
CONSENT, *supra* note 47, at 343 nn. 35–36 and accompanying text.

59. *Id.* at 12.

60. *See* J. KATZ, *supra* note 47, at 80–84.

61. *Id.* at 83.

62. In *Canterbury* itself, the court was concerned "that patients occasionally become so ill or emotionally distraught on disclosure as to foreclose a rational decision,
or complicate or hinder the treatment, or perhaps even
pose psychological damage to the patient." 464 F.2d at
789. The doctrine permitting lack of disclosure, allegedly in order to protect the patient from harm, is called
"therapeutic privilege." *See* INFORMED CONSENT, *supra*
note 47, at 18–19.

63. J. KATZ, *supra* note 47, at 83.

64. *See supra* note 13.

65. A physician might seek much consultation, for example, before performing an abortion on a minor. *See*
Melton, *supra* note 13, at 468 n. 68 and accompanying
text.

66. *See, e.g.,* VA. CODE ANN. § 54-325.12(B) (Reissue 1981),
which provides sterilization procedure.

67. *See* Melton, *supra* note 13.

68. Roth, Meisel, & Lidz, *Tests of Competency to Consent to
Treatment,* 134 AM. J. PSYCHIATRY 279 (1977).

69. CRIMINAL JUSTICE MENTAL HEALTH STANDARDS commentary at 333 (1984).

70. *See* Roth, Appelbaum, Sallee, Reynolds, & Huber, *The
Dilemma of Denial in the Assessment of Competency to Refuse
Treatment,* 139 AM. J. PSYCHIATRY 910 (1982).

71. Thompson, *Psychological Issues in Informed Consent,* in 3 MAKING HEALTH CARE DECISIONS 83, 86–103 (The President's Commission for the Study of Ethical Problems in Medicine and Biomedical and Behavioral Research ed. 1983).

72. A. STONE, MENTAL HEALTH AND LAW: A SYSTEM IN TRANSITION 65–70 (1975).

73. *Id.* at 68–69.

74. Often used in the treatment of schizophrenia, the phenothiazines, also called "antipsychotic medications," "neuroleptics," or "major tranquilizers," are controversial in part because of their side effects. These may include extrapyramidal symptoms such as "muscle spasms, irregular flexing, writhing or grimacing movements, and protrusion of the tongue (dystonic reactions); motor restlessness, and inability to stay still (akathesia); and mask-like face, drooping, stiffness and rigidity, shuffling gait, and tremors (pseudo-parkinsonian syndrome). . . . Nonmuscular physical side effects that regularly result from antipsychotic drugs include drowsiness, dizziness, blurred vision, dry mouth, 'torn-up' stomach, low blood pressure, palpitations, skin rashes, and constipation." Brief of *amici curiae* American Psychological Association, American Orthopsychiatric Association, and National Mental Health Association at 4–5 (citations omitted), Mills v. Rogers, 457 U.S. 291 (1982). Of particular concern is the possibility of developing "tardive dyskinesia," a generally irreversible neurological syndrome that occurs among about 10–20% of patients on maintenance doses of phenothiazines. *See* Munetz, Roth, & Cornes, *Tardive Dyskinesia and Informed Consent: Myths and Realities,* 10 BULL. AM. ACAD. PSYCHIATRY L. 77 (1982). Phenothiazines also have adverse psychological side effects. They sometimes impair concentration or create agitation or depression, and the physical side effects may induce stigma or shame. Brief of amicus curiae at 6–8, Mills v. Rogers. Although the phenothiazines doubtless help some patients, there are also equally effective psychological therapies in many cases. B. KARON & G. VANDENBOS, PSYCHOTHERAPY OF SCHIZOPHRENIA: THE TREATMENT OF CHOICE (1981).

75. Monahan, Ruggiero, & Friedlander, *The Stone–Roth Model of Civil Commitment and the California Dangerousness Standard: An Operational Comparison,* 39 ARCH. GEN. PSYCHIATRY 1267 (1982).

76. *See, e.g.,* Kaimowitz v. Department of Mental Health, No. 73-19434-AW (Cir. Ct. Wayne County, Mich., July 10, 1973) (institutionalized patients unable to give voluntary consent to psychosurgery), *abstracted in* 13 CRIM. L. REP. 2452 (1973), *reprinted in* A. BROOKS, LAW, PSYCHIATRY, AND THE MENTAL HEALTH SYSTEM 902 (974); *see* D. WEXLER, MENTAL HEALTH LAW: MAJOR ISSUES 193–212 (1981).

77. *See generally* E. GOFFMAN, ASYLUMS (1971).

78. The management of patients' consent to various forms of treatment and hospitalization itself is vividly described in J. KATZ, *supra* note 47, and INFORMED CONSENT, *supra* note 47.

79. Grisso & Vierling, *Minors' Consent to Treatment,* 9 PROF. PSYCHOLOGY 412, 421–23 (1978); Melton, *Decision Making by Children: Psychological Risks and Benefits,* in CHILDREN'S COMPETENCE, *supra* note 10, at 21, 24–26.

80. Melton, *Sexually Abused Children and the Legal System: Some Policy Recommendations,* 13 AM. J. FAM. THERAPY 61 (1985).

81. For a brief review of recent cases, *see* Parry, *Right to Refuse Psychotropic Medication,* 8 MENTAL PHYSICAL DISABILITY L. REP. 83 (1984).

82. As discussed *infra* in the text accompanying notes 88–104, the courts have seemed to be particularly concerned about the side effects of the phenothiazines and the drugs' allegedly "mind-altering" qualities. The cases have explicitly excluded consideration even of other powerful psychotropic medication, such as lithium and the antidepressants. *See, e.g.,* Rogers v. Okin, 634 F.2d 650, 650 n. 1 (1st Cir. 1980).

83. Parry, *supra* note 81, at 85.

84. Callahan & Longmire, *Psychiatric Patients' Right to Refuse Psychotropic Medication: A National Survey,* 7 MENTAL PHYSICAL DISABILITY L. REP. 494 (1983).

85. In reviewing recent cases, Parry, *supra* note 81, noted that "[a]reas of serious judicial disagreement concern the definition of emergency, the status of dangerous or incompetent patients, and the method of substitute decisionmaking that should be used following an incompetency adjudication." The Supreme Court has twice remanded the question. Rennie v. Klein, 458 U.S. 1119 (1982); Mills v. Rogers, 457 U.S. 291 (1982).

86. The major mental health organizations have entered amicus briefs urging divergent points of view in several right-to-refuse cases. *E.g.,* Mills v. Rogers, 457 U.S. 291 (1982); United States v. Leatherman, No. 82-0091 (D.D.C. Oct. 5, 1983), *abstracted in* 8 MENTAL PHYSICAL DISABILITY L. REP. 104 (1984); Rogers v. Commissioner of Department of Mental Health, 390 Mass. 489 (1983).

87. *See, e.g.,* Applebaum & Gutheil, *Rotting with Their Rights On: Constitutional Theory and Clinical Reality in Drug Refusal by Psychiatric Patients,* 7 BULL. AM. ACAD. PSYCHIATRY L. 306 (1979).

88. 478 F. Supp. 1342 (1979).

89. *Aff'd in part, rev'd in part,* 634 F.2d 650 (1st Cir. 1980) *(Rogers II), vacated and remanded sub nom.* Mills v. Rogers, 457 U.S. 291 (1982) *(Rogers III), considered in the light of state law,* Rogers v. Commissioner of Department of Mental Health, 390 Mass. 489 (1983) *(Rogers IV).*

90. 478 F. Supp. at 1365–66.

91. 634 F.2d at 650–51.

92. The right to privacy has been developed primarily in cases involving matters of contraception, abortion, and the family. *See, e.g.,* Roe v. Wade, 410 U.S. 113, 152–53 (1973); Eisenstadt v. Baird, 405 U.S. 438, 453 (1972); Griswold v. Connecticut, 381 U.S. 479, 484 (1965).

93. 478 F. Supp. at 1366.

94. *See supra* note 74.

95. 634 F.2d at 650 n. 1 and accompanying text.

96. *Id.* at 651 n.2.

97. 478 F. Supp. at 1366–67.

98. *Id.* at 1367. The First Circuit Court also adopted this terminology. *Rogers II,* 634 F.2d at 655.

99. 478 F. Supp. at 1367.

100. Lithium is a commonly used treatment for mania and sometimes other affective disorders. *See* J. SCHILD-KRAUT, NEUROPSYCHOPHARMACOLOGY AND THE AF-FECTIVE DISORDERS (1970).

101. *See supra* note 82.

102. 478 F. Supp. at 1367.

103. *See supra* note 92.

104. *See supra* note 74.

105. *See, e.g., Rogers II,* 634 F.2d at 651 (noting lack of contest over existence of some right to refuse).

106. 720 F.2d 266 (1983). Like *Rogers, Rennie* has had a rather extensive history. The federal district court had established procedures to protect the right to refuse, 462 F. Supp. 1131 (D.N.J. 1978) *and* 476 F. Supp. 1294 (D.N.J. 1979). Both parties appealed to the Third Circuit Court of Appeals, which agreed that a constitutional right to treatment exists but which upheld the constitutionality of New Jersey's procedures. Rennie v. Klein, 653 F.2d 836 (1981). The decision was appealed to the Supreme Court, 458 U.S. 1119 (1982), which remanded the case for reconsideration in light of Youngberg v. Romeo, 457 U.S. 307 (1982).

107. 720 F.2d at 269.

108. N.J. Administrative Bulletin 78-3.

109. S. Morse, Cases and Materials on Mental Health Law 886 (1982) (unpublished manuscript).

110. 458 N.E.2d 308 (Mass. 1983).

111. "Emergency" was defined to include only those instances in which "a patient poses an imminent threat of harm to himself or others, and . . . there is no less intrusive alternative to antipsychotic drugs." *Id.* at 321.

112. *Id.* at 318.

113. *Id.* at 318.

114. *Id.* at 317.

115. *Id.* at 314, 317.

116. *See supra* note 109. A position midway between those of the Third Circuit and the Massachusetts Supreme Judicial Court was adopted by the First Circuit in *Rogers II,* 634 F.2d 650.

117. *See generally* J. KATZ, *supra* note 47.

118. Epstein & Lasagna, *Obtaining Informed Consent: Form or Substance?,* 123 ARCH. INTERNAL MED. 682 (1969).

119. Grunder, *On the Readability of Surgical Consent Forms,* 302 NEW ENG. J. MED. 900 (1980); Morrow, *How Readable Are Subject Consent Forms?,* 244 J.A.M.A. 56 (1980).

120. INFORMED CONSENT, *supra* note 47, at 93–94.

121. *See, e.g., id.* at 86–88.

122. *See, e.g., id.* at 187–88.

123. A very sensitive discussion of these issues is presented in J. KATZ, *supra* note 47, at 165 *et seq.*

124. *See supra* note 62.

125. INFORMED CONSENT, *supra* note 47, at 25.

126. *Id.* at 24.

127. *Id.* at 26–28.

128. Roth, Lidz, Meisel, Soloff, Kaufman, Spiker, & Foster,

Competency to Decide about Treatment or Research: An Overview of Some Empirical Data, 5 INT'L J.L. PSYCHIATRY 29 (1982).

129. Soskis, *Schizophrenic and Medical Inpatients as Informed Drug Consumers,* 35 ARCH. GEN. PSYCHIATRY 645 (1978).

130. Munetz, Roth & Cornes, *supra* note 74, at 85.

131. *See* Melton, *Developmental Psychology and the Law: The State of the Art,* 22 J. FAM. L. 445, 463–65 (1984), and the studies cited there. *See generally* CHILDREN'S COMPETENCE, *supra* note 10.

132. *See, e.g.,* Weithorn & Campbell, *The Competency of Children and Adolescents to Make Informed Treatment Decisions,* 53 CHILD DEV. 1589 (1982).

133. *Id.; see also* Lewis, *Decision Making Related to Health: When Could/Should Children Behave Responsibly?,* in CHILDREN'S COMPETENCE, *supra* note 10.

134. *See generally* J. KATZ, *supra* note 47; INFORMED CONSENT, *supra* note 47.

135. Roth & Applebaum, *Involuntary Treatment in Medicine and Psychiatry,* 141 AM. J. PSYCHIATRY 202 (1984).

136. *See generally* Interpersonal Relations in Health Care, 35(1) J. SOC. ISSUES (winter issue 1979).

137. *Cf.* J. BREHM, A THEORY OF PSYCHOLOGICAL REACTANCE (1966).

138. Saks, *Social Psychological Contributions to a Legislative Subcommittee on Organ and Tissue Transplants,* 33 AM. PSYCHOLOGIST 680 (1978).

139. *Cf.* Schwartz, *Elicitation of Moral Obligation and Self-Sacrificing Behavior: An Experimental Study of Volunteering to Be a Bone Marrow Donor,* 15 J. PERSONALITY SOC. PSYCHOLOGY 283 (1970).

140. *See, e.g.,* Weithorn & Campbell, *supra* note 132.

141. 634 F.2d at 654.

142. Stone, *Psychiatric Abuse and Legal Reform: Two Ways to Make a Bad Situation Worse,* 5 INT'L J.L. PSYCHIATRY 9, 20–22 (1982).

143. *See* J. KATZ, *supra* note 47.

144. Weithorn, *Involving Children in Decisions Affecting Their Own Welfare: Guidelines for Professionals,* in CHILDREN'S COMPETENCE, *supra* note 10.

145. *See* J. KATZ, *supra* note 47, especially ch. 6.

146. STANDARDS REGARDING CONSENT FOR TREATMENT AND RESEARCH INVOLVING CHILDREN (Division of Child, Youth & Family Services, American Psychological Association 1982).

147. Melton, *supra* note 79, at 30–31, and citations there.

148. 45 C.F.R. part 46 (1983).

149. *See, e.g.,* 10 C.F.R. part 745 (1984) (Dept. of Energy); 16 C.F.R. part 1028 (1984) (Consumer Product Safety Commission); 21 C.F.R. parts 50 and 56 (1983) (Food & Drug Administration).

150. Keith-Spiegel, *Children and Consent to Participate in Research,* in CHILDREN'S COMPETENCE, *supra* note 10, at 179, 180–81.

151. 132 J.A.M.A. 1090 (1946).

152. A notable and relatively common example would be drug research, in which the effect on humans and particular groups (e.g., children) is not completely predictable from animal studies.

153. NATIONAL COMMISSION FOR THE PROTECTION OF HUMAN SUBJECTS OF BIOMEDICAL AND BEHAVIORAL RESEARCH, THE BELMONT REPORT: ETHICAL PRINCIPLES AND GUIDELINES FOR THE PROTECTION OF HUMAN SUBJECTS OF RESEARCH, (1979).

154. In addition, there are special regulations for research on fetuses, pregnant women, and *in vitro* fertilization. 45 C.F.R. part 46(B) (1983).

155. *Id.* at § 46.102(g).

156. Confidentiality may be substantially more limited than most researchers and participants imagine. *See* D. NELKIN, SCIENCE AS INTELLECTUAL PROPERTY: WHO CONTROLS SCIENTIFIC RESEARCH? chs. 3 and 4 (1983); Morris, Sales, & Berman, *Research and the Freedom of Information Act,* 36 AM. PSYCHOLOGIST 819 (1981).

157. 45 C.F.R. §§ 45.116(a) and (b) (1983).

158. A common issue in social-psychological research is the use of deception so as to minimize the effects of participants' knowledge of the purpose of the experiment. *See* Geller, *Alternatives to Deception: Why, What, and How?,* in THE ETHICS OF SOCIAL RESEARCH: SURVEYS AND EXPERIMENTS (J. Sieber ed. 1982).

159. 45 C.F.R. § 46.116(c) (1983).

160. *Id.* at § 46.306.

161. *Id.* at § 46.305(a)(2).

162. *Id.* at §§ 46.402(b), 46.402(c), and 46.408.

163. *Id.* at §§ 46.405, 46.406, and 46.407.

164. *Id.* at § 46.409.

165. *Id.* at § 46.408(c).

166. Proposed regulations were published at 43 Fed. Reg. 53,590 (1978).

167. *See, e.g.,* Stanley & Stanley, *Psychiatric Patients in Research: Protecting Their Autonomy,* 22 COMPREHENSIVE PSYCHIATRY 420 (1981).

168. For such an integration, *see* B. Stanley, Informed Consent and Competence: A Review of Empirical Research (January 12, 1981) (paper presented at workshop of the National Institute of Mental Health on "Empirical Research on Informed Consent with Subjects of Uncertain Competence").

169. *See, e.g.,* McCollum & Schwartz, *Pediatric Research Hospitalization: Its Meaning to Parents,* 3 PEDIATRIC RESEARCH 199 (1969).

170. Thompson, *supra* note 71, at 89–91.

171. *See generally* Weithorn, *Children's Capacities to Decide about Participation in Research,* 5(2) IRB: A REVIEW OF HUMAN SUBJECTS RESEARCH 1 (1983), and studies cited therein.

172. *See* Stanley, *supra* note 168, and studies cited therein.

173. *See, e.g.,* P. Keith-Spiegel & T. Maas, Consent to Research: Are There Developmental Differences? (August 1981) (paper presented at the meeting of the American Psychological Association, Los Angeles).

174. Most state statutes simply use this phrase or some variation on it and provide no further definition. 11 AM. JUR. *Testamentary Capacity* §§ 159, 161 (1985).

175. This test was first established in the case of Banks v. Goodfellow, 1870 5 Q.B. 549. For a discussion of this case, the evolution of the doctrine of testamentary capacity, and some reflections on the role of the expert witness in assisting the courts in determining whether capacity exists, *see* Spaulding, *Testamentary Competency: Reconciling Doctrine with the Role of the Expert Witness,* 9 LAW & HUM. BEHAV. 113 (1985).

176. 79 Am. Jur. 2d *Wills,* § 71 at 329 (1975) [hereinafter cited as Wills].

177. *See generally id.* §§ 77–101.

178. For a discussion, *see* 18 AM. JUR. POF 2d *Mentally Disordered Testator's Execution of Will during Lucid Interval* § 1 (1979).

179. *Wills, supra* note 176, § 87 at 341.

180. T. SZASZ, LAW, LIBERTY AND PSYCHIATRY 75–76 (1963). A similar view is expressed in Note, *Testamentary Capacity in a Nutshell: A Psychiatric Reevaluation,* 18 STAN. L. REV. 1119 (1966). *But see* Slough, *Testamentary Capacity: Evidentiary Aspects,* in 2 LANDMARK PAPERS ON ESTATE PLANNING: WILLS, ESTATES, AND TRUSTS 594, 610–11 (A. Winard ed. 1968).

181. Langbein, *Living Probate: The Conservatorship Model,* 77 MICH. L. REV. 63, 67 (1978).

182. *Contemporary Ante-Mortem Statutory Formulations: Observations and Alternatives,* 32 CASE W. REV. L. REV. 823 (1982).

183. *See generally* Perr, *Wills, Testamentary Capacity and Undue Influence,* 9 BULL. AM. ACAD. PSYCHIATRY & L. 15 (1981); Hogan, *When Does Influence Become Undue?,* 7 LOYOLA U.L.J. 629 (1976).

184. Spaulding, *supra* note 175, at 138.

185. *Id.* at 133–38.

186. Note, *supra* note 180, at 1139.

187. W. BROMBERG, THE USES OF PSYCHIATRY IN THE LAW: A CLINICAL VIEW OF FORENSIC PSYCHIATRY 254 (1979).

188. 42 U.S.C. § 401 *et seq.* (1983 and Cum. Supp. 1985).

189. *Id.* § 1381 *et seq.* (1983 and Cum. Supp. 1985).

190. 42 U.S.C. § 421; 20 C.F.R. § 404. 1503 (1983).

191. *Id.*

192. 20 C.F.R. § 404.1503(d) (1983).

193. *See generally* Gilbert & Peters, *The Social Security Disability Claim,* 24 PRAC. LAW. 47, 53 (1979).

194. *See generally* 20 C.F.R. § 404.929 *et seq.* (1983).

195. *Id.* § 404.1517.

196. *Id.* § 404.953.

197. 42 U.S.C. § 423(d)(1)(A) (1983 and Cum. Supp. 1985).

198. *Id.* § 423(d)(2)(A). The standards for determining eligibility for SSI benefits are identical. *See, e.g., id.* § 1382 (a)(3)(A).

199. *See generally* 20 C.F.R. § 404.1520 through 404.1574 (1983).

200. *Id.* § 404.1508.

201. *Id.* § 404.1566.

202. *Id.* § 404.1566(c).

203. The full history of the case is as follows: Mental Health Association of Minnesota v. Schweiker, 554 F. Supp. 157 (D. Minn. 1982), *modified and affirmed,* Mental Health Association of Minnesota v. Heckler, 720 F.2d 965 (8th Cir. 1983).

204. *Statement of Peter J. McGough, Associate Director, Human Resources Division, General Accounting Office, before the Senate*

Special Comm. on Aging, 98th Cong., First Sess. 6 (1983) [hereinafter cited as GAO Testimony].

205. *Id.*

206. 20 C.F.R. § 404.1521(b)(1983).

207. The PRTF and related forms can be obtained by writing to Social Security Administration, Office of Disability, Division of Medical and Vocational Policy, 3-A-10 Operations Building, 6401 Security Bld., Baltimore, Maryland 21235.

208. GAO Testimony, *supra* note 204, at 16.

209. 20 C.F.R. § 404, App. 1, 12.00(A) (1985).

210. *Id.* § 404.1545(a)(c).

211. Form SSA-4734-F4(3-82). *See supra* note 207.

212. 20 C.F.R. § 404.1520(f) (1983).

213. *Id.* § 404, App. 2,200.00 (Table 1). *See supra* note 207.

214. SSA Program Circular, Office of the New York Regional Commissioners, No. 6-79, August 22, 1979.

215. 20 C.F.R. App. 1, 12.00(A) (1983).

216. SSA Program Circular, *supra* note 214, at 3.

217. 20 C.F.R. § 404.1530(a) (1983).

Chapter 10

1. J. O'CONNELL & R. HENDERSON, TORT LAW: NO-FAULT AND BEYOND 1–2 (1975). The authors provide an excellent summary of the development of the principle of "fault" as a determinant in adjudicating the compensability of injuries.

2. *Id.*

3. *Id.*

4. *Id.* at 3.

5. *Id.* at 6.

6. RESTATEMENT (SECOND) OF THE LAW OF TORTS § 6 Comment (1965).

7. J. DOOLEY, MODERN TORT LAW: LIABILITY AND LITIGATION (rev. ed. by Lindahl 1982).

8. *Id.* at 8.

9. *Id.*

10. *Id.*

11. 81 AM. JUR. 2d *Workmen's Compensation* §§ 1–239 at 698 (1976) [hereinafter cited as 81 *Workmen's Compensation*].

12. See generally LARSON'S WORKMEN'S COMPENSATION LAW §§ 4.20–5.30 (rev. ed. by M. Bender 1982) [hereinafter cited as LARSON'S]. This multivolume work, updated periodically, is the most comprehensive description of the worker's compensation system available. It is an excellent and exhaustive compendium of information on every facet and phase of this system. Most law libraries will have a copy, and worker's compensation boards should as well.

13. We have chosen to use the term "mental injury" rather than "psychiatric injury," because use of the latter term appears to inherently limit participation in these proceedings to psychiatrists. However, nearly any clinical profession may find itself involved in evaluating mental injury in a worker's compensation or tort context; indeed, Bromberg has noted that "every type of medical specialist is currently utilized in studying industrial, automobile, and household injuries. The list extends from surgeons to neurologists, neurosurgeons, orthopedic specialists, psychiatrists, electromyographers, electroencephalographers, nuclear medicine specialists (brain scan and tomography), plastic surgeons, otolaryngologists, opthalmologists, radiologists, dermatologists, internists, psychiatric and clinical psychologists." W. BROMBERG, THE USES OF PSYCHIATRY IN THE LAW: A CLINICAL VIEW OF FORENSIC PSYCHIATRY 311 (1979).

14. *Determining the Compensability of Mental Disabilities,* 55 U.S.C. L. REV. 193, 195 (1981).

15. LARSON'S, *supra* 12, § 4.50.

16. *Id.*

17. Joseph, *The Causation Issue in Worker's Compensation Mental Disability Cases: An Analysis, Solutions, and a Perspective,* 36 VAND. L. REV. 263 (1983). Joseph also provides an excellent bibliography of the literature on the issue of causation in mental injury cases, *id.* at 264 n. 2, as well as readings on general problems raised in mental injury cases, *id.* at 267 n. 8. The reader interested in exploring these matters in more detail is urged to begin with these references.

18. 81 *Workmen's Compensation, supra* note 11, at 699.

19. *Id.*

20. J. O'CONNELL & R. HENDERSON, *supra* note 1, at 74.

21. "The purpose of workmen's compensation acts is not limited to the payment of compensation to injured employees during the period of their incapacity; it extends as well to persons who are dependent upon such an employee for support, and who are deprived of such support by reason of his death . . . it may be said that a dependent is one who looked to or relied on the decedent for support and maintenance, in whole or in part." 81 *Workmen's Compensation, supra* note 11, at 851–52.

22. *Id.* at 702; J. O'CONNELL & R. HENDERSON, *supra* note 1, at 74.

23. LARSON'S, *supra* note 12, § 2.40.

24. *Id.*

25. Compensable diseases and injuries include the following: anthrax, apoplexy, cerebral hemorrhage, stroke, paralysis, heart attack, and other ailments; injuries by animals or insects; arm and wrist injuries; assaults, attacks, and shootings; damage to or loss of artificial limbs or members; injuries while indulging in recreation, amusements, athletic contests, entertainments, and employer-sponsored social affairs, such as outings, picnics, parties, etc.; back injuries; burns from fires, caustics, electricity, acids, or boiling water, and blisters; cancer; compressed air illness; drowning; Dupuytreau's contracture; electric shock; emphysema; fright, shock, or excitement; explosions; injuries from heat, cold, storm, lightning, and diseases resulting from exposure; eye in-

jury, face injuries, and, occasionally, disfigurement; injuries from falling, thrown, or flying objects; injuries from falling, slipping, or tripping; foot injuries and infections or diseases due thereto; hand injuries and infections and diseases; head injuries; hearing loss or interference; hernia; infection; inhalation of gases, fumes, dust, etc.; leg or hip injuries; injuries from machinery, equipment, and vehicles; mental, emotional, or nervous disorders; muscle injuries; nerve injuries; occupational diseases; overwork or exhaustion; pneumonia; poisoning; radiation injuries or diseases; sexual organ injuries; silicosis and other dust diseases; skin diseases; tuberculosis; typhoid fever contracted from drinking contaminated water furnished by an employer; and ulcers. 82 AM. JUR. 2d *Workmen's Compensation* §§ 240–690 at 72–75 (1976) [hereinafter cited as 82 *Workmen's Compensation*].

26. *Id.* at 28.
27. LARSON'S *supra* note 12, § 6.00.
28. *Id.*
29. *Id.*
30. *Id.* § 6.50.
31. 82 *Workmen's Compensation, supra* note 25, at 28; LARSON'S *supra* note 12 § 14.00 *et seq.*
32. *Determining the Compensability of Mental Disabilities, supra* note 14, at 210–11.
33. 82 *Workmen's Compensation, supra* note 25, at 254.
34. *Id.* at 235.
35. *Id.* at 270.
36. LARSON'S, *supra* note 12, § 38.00 *et seq.*
37. *Id.* §§ 38.80, 38.81.
38. *Id.*
39. 82 *Workmen's Compensation, supra* note 25, at 208.
40. *Id.*
41. *Id.* at 221.
42. *Id.*
43. *Id.* at 254.
44. *Id.* at 235.
45. *Id.* at 270.
46. Joseph, *supra* note 17, at 286.
47. 82 *Workmen's Compensation, supra* note 25, at 270.
48. LARSON'S *supra* note 12, § 42.22.
49. While hearing officers render initial determinations concerning the compensability of a particular claim, judicial review is available. One of the primary functions of judicial review is to determine whether the law was properly applied. This determination requires the court to interpret the law as established by statute, and, specifically, to determine whether certain disabilities are compensable within the meaning of the statute. Hence the references in this section to the courts, which have "made" most of the law in this area through their appellate oversight of the administrative hearing process.
50. Annot. 97 A.L.R. 3d 161, 168 (1980).
51. *Id.*
52. LARSON'S, *supra* note 12, § 42.20.
53. Annot., *supra* note 50, at 16.
54. Joseph, *supra* note 17, at 288.

55. *Id.* at n. 104. The case citations from which these examples derive are omitted here, but are supplied in the source.
56. LARSON'S, *supra* note 12, § 42.21.
57. *Id.*
58. Joseph, *supra* note 17 at 291.
59. LARSON'S *supra* note 12, § 42.23.
60. Annot., at 173 *supra* note 50, 1–86.
61. *Id.* at 173.
62. Jose v. Equifax, Inc., 556 S.W.2d 82, 84 (Tenn. 1977).
63. *Determining the Compensability of Mental Disabilities, supra* note 14, at 211.
64. *See generally* W. PROSSER, LAW OF TORTS (4th ed. 1971).
65. *Id.* at 324.
66. *Id* at 324–25.
67. 17 Cal. 3d 425, 557 P.2d 334, 131 Cal. Rptr. 14 (1976).
68. R. SLOVENKO, PSYCHIATRY AND LAW 278 (1973).
69. RESTATEMENT (SECOND) OF THE LAW OF TORTS § 282 (1965).
70. H. OLECK, OLECK'S TORT LAW PRACTICE MANUAL 127 (1982).
71. *Id.* (quoting BLACK'S LAW DICTIONARY 1103 (5th ed. 1979)).
72. R. SLOVENKO, *supra* note 68, at 278.
73. *Id.* at 296 (quoting Lord Chancellor Francis Bacon).
74. *Id.* at 297.
75. *Id.* at 298.
76. Roberts & Wilkinson, *Developing a Positive Picture at Trial,* 19 TRIAL 56 (1983).
77. Theis, *The Intentional Infliction of Emotional Distress: A Need for Limits on Liability,* 27 DEPAUL L. REV. 275 (1977).
78. *Intentional Infliction of Emotional Distress—Escaping the Impact Rule in Arkansas,* 35 ARK. L. REV. 533, 536–37 (1980).
79. *Id.* at 535–36.
80. Lambert, *Tort Liability for Psychic Injuries: Overview and Update,* 37 ATLA. L.J. 1 (1978).
81. M. MINZER J. NATES, C. KIMBALL, D. AXELROD, & R. GOLDSTEIN, 1 DAMAGES IN TORT ACTIONS 6-4–6-5 (1983).
82. Millard, *Intentionally and Negligently Inflicted Emotional Distress: Toward a Coherent Reconciliation,* 15 IND. L. REV. 617 (1982). Millard says the following jurisdictions recognize the tort: Alabama, Arizona, Arkansas, California, Colorado, Connecticut, District of Columbia, Florida, Georgia, Hawaii, Idaho, Illinois, Iowa, Kansas, Louisiana, Maine, Massachusetts, Michigan, Missouri, Nebraska, Nevada, New Jersey, New York, North Carolina, Oklahoma, Oregon, Pennsylvania, South Carolina, South Dakota, Tennessee, Utah, Vermont, Virginia, Washington, West Virginia, and Wisconsin. *Id.* at 631 n. 94.
83. M. MINZER, J. NATES, C. KIMBALL, D. AXELROD, & R. GOLDSTEIN, *supra* note 81, at 6-22–6-23.
84. *Id.* at 6-27.
85. *Id.* (citing RESTATEMENT (SECOND) OF THE LAW OF TORTS (1965)).
86. *Id.* at 6-32–6-33.
87. H. OLECK, *supra* note 70, at 77.
88. Such conduct has included the following: assaults; in-

terference with the enjoyment of property; threats; discrimination; defamation; false imprisonment; malicious prosecution; interference with business relationships; wrongful eviction; unlawful suspension from a labor union; detention by an undertaker of the dead body of the plaintiff's son for the purpose of collecting an account; fraudulent inducement to enter a bigamous marriage; and sending a package containing a dead rat instead of an expected loaf of bread. M. MINZER, J. NATES, C. KIMBALL, D. AXELROD & R. GOLDSTEIN, *supra* note 81 at 6-38–6-41.

89. *Id.* at 6-77–6-78.

90. Annot., 20 A.L.R. 4th 773 (1983).

91. Annot., 40 A.L.R. 3d 1290. (1971).

92. M. MINZER, J. NATES, C. KIMBALL, D. AXELROD, & R. GOLDSTEIN, *supra* note 81, at 6-77–6-78.

93. RESTATEMENT (SECOND) OF THE LAW OF TORTS § 46 comment j (1965).

94. M. MINZER, J. NATES, C. KIMBALL, D. AXELROD, & R. GOLDSTEIN, *supra* note 81 at 6-52.

95. These states are Alabama, California, Connecticut, Hawaii, Louisiana, Maine, Missouri, and Washington. *Administering the Tort of Negligent Infliction of Mental Distress: A Synthesis,* 4 CARDOZO L. REV. 487, 488 n. 7 (1983).

96. *Id.* at 488–89 and n. 9.

97. Dillon v. Legg, 441 p.2d 912 (1968).

98. M. MINZER, J. NATES, C. KIMBALL, D. AXELROD, & R. GOLDSTEIN, *supra* note 81, at 5-14–5-19.

99. These different policy limitations on recovery are discussed clearly by Lambert, *supra* note 80; *see also Negligent Infliction of Emotional Distress—Bystander Recovery,* 21 DUQ. L.R. 797 (1983); Leibson, *Recovery of Damages for Emotional Distress Caused by Physical Injury to Another,* 15 J. FAM. L. 163 (1976–77).

100. *Culbert* v. *Sampson's Supermarkets, Inc.,* 444 A.2d 433 (Me. 1982) (discussed in *Negligent Infliction of Emotional Distress—Bystander Recovery, supra* note 99).

101. Shepard v. Superior Court, 76 Cal. App. 3d 16, 142 Cal. Rptr. 612 (1977).

102. This case is discussed in detail in *Strict Product Liability—Recovery for Emotional Distress,* 17 DUQ. L. REV. 535 (1978).

103. M. MINZER, J. NATES, C. KIMBALL, D. AXELROD, & R. GOLDSTEIN, *supra* note 81, at 6-47.

104. Blinder, *The Abuse of Psychiatric Disability Determinations,* 1979 MED. TRIAL TECH. Q. 84, 86 (1979).

105. Sheeley, CLINICAL PSYCHIATRY NEWS (June 1980), *quoted in* Marcus, *Compensation Payments—Blessing or Curse,* 1983 MED. TRIAL TECH Q. 319, 321 (1983).

106. Marcus, *Causation in Psychiatry: Realities and Speculations,* 1983 MED. TRIAL TECH. Q. 424 (1983).

107. *Id.* at 430.

108. *Id.* at 431–32.

109. H. DAVIDSON, FORENSIC PSYCHIATRY 92 (2a ed. 1965).

110. *Id.* at 65.

111. W. BROMBERG, *supra* note 13, at 322.

112. *Determining the Compensability of Mental Disabilities, supra* note 14, at 213.

113. Roberts & Wilkinson, *supra* note 76, at 58–59.

114. R. SLOVENKO, *supra* note 68, at 294.

115. *Id.* at 300.

116. Kinzie, Fredrickson, Ben, Fleck, & Kauls, *Posttraumatic Stress Disorder among Survivors of Cambodian Concentration Camps,* 141 AM. J. PSYCHIATRY 645 (1984).

117. Eaton, Sigal, & Weinfeld, *Impairment in Holocaust Survivors after 33 years: Data from an Unbiased Community Sample,* 139 AM. J. PSYCHIATRY 773 (1982).

118. Terr, *Psychic Trauma in Children: Observations following the Chowchilla School Bus Kidnapping,* 138 AM. J. PSYCHIATRY 14 (1981).

119. Titchener & Kapp, *Family and Character Change at Buffalo Creek,* 133 AM. J. PSYCHIATRY 295 (1976); Erikson, *Loss of Communality at Buffalo Creek,* 133 AM. J. PSYCHIATRY 302 (1976); Wilkinson, *Aftermath of a Disaster: The Collapse of the Hyatt Regency Hotel Skywalks,* 140 AM. J. PSYCHIATRY 1134 (1983).

120. *See generally* L. KEISER, THE TRAUMATIC NEUROSES (1968); M. TRIMBLE, POST-TRAUMATIC NEUROSIS: FROM RAILWAY SPINE TO THE WHIPLASH (1981).

121. L. KEISER, *supra* note 120, at 41.

122. AMERICAN PSYCHIATRIC ASSOCIATION, DIAGNOSTIC AND STATISTICAL MANUAL OF MENTAL DISORDERS 238 (3d ed. 1980).

123. Alexander, *"Burning Out" versus "Punching Out,"* 6 J. HUM. STRESS 37 (1980) (describing the gradual "burning out" of air traffic controllers).

124. Wilkinson, *supra* note 119, at 1136.

125. R. SLOVENKO, *supra* note 68, at 300.

126. Roberts & Wilkinson, *supra* note 76, at 58.

127. *Id.*

128. *Id.*

129. Smith, *The Expert Witness: Maximizing Damages for Psychic Injuries,* 18 TRIAL (4) 51 (1982). Smith summarizes some of the literature concerning psychological impact upon individuals who have undergone stressful events, as well as the grieving process and the characteristics of pathological grief.

130. *Id.* at 51.

131. W. BROMBERG, *supra* note 13, at 318–22.

132. *Id.* at 332–33.

133. *Id.* at 334–35.

134. *Id.*

135. Woody, *The Pain/Intelligence Nexus in Personal Injury Litigation,* 1979 MED. TRIAL TECH. Q. 249 (1979).

136. W. BROMBERG, *supra* note 13, at 331. For a detailed discussion of malingering, *see* H. DAVIDSON, *supra* note 109. Ch. 12.

137. W. BROMBERG, *supra* note 13, at 331.

138. *Id.*

139. *See, e.g.,* Horowitz, Schafer, Hiroto, Wilner, & Levin, *Life Event Questionnaires for Measuring Presumptive Stress,* 39 PSYCHOSOMATIC MED. 413 (1977); Fairbank & Hough, *Life Event Classifications and the Event—Illness Relationship,* 5 J. HUM. STRESS 41 (1979); Andrews, *Life Event Stress and Psychiatric Illness,* 8 PSYCHOLOGICAL MED. 545 (1978); Zautra & Beier, *The Effects of Life Crisis on Psychological Adjustment,* 6 AM. J. COMMUNITY PSY-

CHOLOGY 125 (1978). *But see* Thoits, *Undesirable Life Events and Psychophysiological Distress: A Problem of Operational Confounding,* 46 AM. SOC. REV. 97 (1981).

140. Dohrenwend, Krasnoff, Askenasy, & Dohrenwend, *Exemplification of a Method for Scaling Life Events: The PERI Life Events Scale,* 19 J. HEALTH SOC. BEHAV. 205 (1978). Other available scales include the Social Readjustment Rating Scale, Holmes & Rahe, *The Social Readjustment Rating Scale,* 11 J. PSYCHOSOMATIC RESEARCH 213 (1967), and the Life Experiences Survey, Sarason, Johnson, & Siegel, *Assessing the Impact of Life Changes: Development of the Life Experiences Survey,* 46 J. CONSULTING CLINICAL PSYCHOLOGY 932 (1978); both of these are considerably briefer (43 and 47 items, respectively) than the PERI Life Events Scale. Different scales have been designed to assess different aspects of the life change experience: Fairbank and Hough, *supra* note 139, focus on the individual's perceived sense of control over the events; Sarason, Johnson, & Siegel focus on the subject's perception of the impact of the change event (positive or negative impact). Both of these are variations on the original Holmes & Rahe assessment, which focuses on the number of life change events in a given time frame. A recent review by Rahe concludes that most studies have found a low, positive correlation (.16–.36) between recent life change events and psychological distress, and that the literature to date fails to compellingly demonstrate the superiority of any aspect of life event assessment over a simple counting of the number of life change events. Rahe, *Life Change Events and Mental Illness: An Overview,* 5 J. HUM. STRESS 2 (1979).

141. As noted elsewhere in the text, the individual's prior adjustment is a significant issue in considering compensation for accidental injury. Several studies have shown an increase in the number of stressful life events *prior* to many "accidents"; *see* review by Levinson, Hirschfield, Hirschfield, & Dzubay, *Recent Life Events and Accidents: The Role of Sex Differences,* 9 J. HUM. STRESS 4 (1983). Another study concluded, "A person who has developed a psychiatric disability after a compensable accident was under great psychological stress before the accident. He sent out signals of being accident prone and that 'an accident was waiting to happen.' . . . The accident did not cause the disability, for it was 'subconsciously' caused by the patient himself. Therefore, the nature of the accident is unimportant in understanding the disability." Hirschfield & Behan, *The Accident Process: I. Etiological Considerations of Industrial Injuries,* 186 J.A.M.A. 193 (1963). *But see* Modlin, *The Post Accident Anxiety Syndrome: Psychosocial Aspects,* 123 AM. J. PSYCHIATRY 1008 (1967) (finding no increase in stressful life events prior to the accident). *See generally* Heiman & Shanfield, *Psychiatric Disability Assessment: Clarification of Problems,* 19 COMPREHENSIVE PSYCHIATRY 449 (1978).

142. Ebaugh & Benjamin, *Trauma and Mental Disorder,* in TRAUMA AND DISEASE (Bradhy & Kahn eds. 1937)

143. Blinder, *supra* note 104, at 88.

144. Shands, *Comments on "Causal Relation" in Workmen's Compensation Proceedings,"* PSYCHIATRY L. 245–46, 253 (1974).

145. *See* the cases summarized in Lasky, *Psychiatry and California Worker's Compensation Laws: A Threat and a Challenge,* 17 CAL. WEST L. REV. 1 (1980).

146. Blinder, *supra* note 104, at 84–85.

147. *See, e.g.,* Roberts & Wilkinson, *supra* note 76.

Chapter 11

1. *See generally* M. LEVINE & A. LEVINE, A SOCIAL HISTORY OF HELPING SERVICES: COURT, CLINIC, SCHOOL, AND COMMUNITY (1970).

2. Many state statutes still expressly describe the purpose of the juvenile justice system to be rehabilitative. Even the proposals most oriented toward a "just deserts" model still place substantial emphasis upon clinicians' input. *See* Morse & Whitebread, *Mental Health Implications of the Juvenile Justice Standards,* in LEGAL REFORMS AFFECTING CHILD AND YOUTH SERVICES (G. Melton ed. 1982).

3. Although the term "infant" has come to have a colloquial meaning referring to very young children, in law the use is broader—for example, it is synonymous in some contexts with "minor"—and suggests both the continual raising of the threshold age for special status and the law's lack of recognition of the differences among children of various ages. The virtual absence of the term "adolescence" from legal commentary is illustrative. *See* F. ZIMRING, THE CHANGING LEGAL WORLD OF ADOLESCENCE xi–xii (1982).

4. W. LaFAVE & A. SCOTT, CRIMINAL LAW 351–52 (1972).

5. *See generally* J. KETT, RITES OF PASSAGES (1977); Bakan, *Adolescence in America: From Idea to Social Fact,* in TWELVE TO SIXTEEN: EARLY ADOLESCENCE (J. Kagan & R. Coles eds. 1971); Kett, *The History of Age Grouping in America,* in YOUTH: TRANSITION TO ADULTHOOD (J. Coleman, ed. 1974).

6. *See* Bakan, *supra* note 5; A. PLATT, THE CHILD SAVERS: THE INVENTION OF DELINQUENCY (2d ed. 1977).

7. G. S. HALL, ADOLESCENCE: ITS PSYCHOLOGY AND ITS RELATIONS TO PHYSIOLOGY, ANTHROPOLOGY, SOCIOLOGY, SEX, CRIME, RELIGION, AND EDUCATION (1904).

8. *See generally* J. KETT, *supra* note 5.

9. The first juvenile code (in Illinois) was not enacted until 1899. The development of the juvenile court was coincident with the adoption of compulsory education and child labor laws. *See* Bakan, *supra* note 5.

10. The *parens patriae* power is based on the state's duty to protect dependent persons and their property. The application of this power to quasi-criminal jurisprudence is dubious; it is certainly outside the scope of the meaning

of the term in common law for centuries. *In re* Gault, 387 U.S. 1, 16–17 (1967).

11. This practice of using civil terms (e.g., "respondent" instead of "defendant") persists in most jurisdictions, despite the repudiation of the concept that the juvenile court is *really* civil.

12. *In re* Gault, 387 U.S. 1, 14 n.14.

13. The "legal realism" school of jurisprudence, which was especially influential in the first half of this century, is based on a belief that the law is not a static, "natural" whole, but that it should respond to social realities and needs. *See generally* P. ROSEN, THE SUPREME COURT AND SOCIAL SCIENCE (1972); Woodard, *The Limits of Legal Realism: An Historical Perspective,* 54 VA. L. REV. 689 (1968).

14. The use of the term "science" is arguably a misnomer, in that the reformers were actually interested in the application of *social welfare* principles to the law. The "science" involved was to be experts' judgments of the best interests of the child, as derived from new penological principles. *See generally* A. PLATT, *supra* note 6.

15. *See* W. MURPHY & C. PRITCHETT, COURTS, JUDGES, AND POLITICS: AN INTRODUCTION TO THE JUDICIAL PROCESS 5 (3d ed. 1979).

16. Address to the National Council of Juvenile Court Judges (1950), *cited in* Empey, *Introduction: The Social Construction of Childhood and Juvenile Justice,* in THE FUTURE OF CHILDHOOD AND JUVENILE JUSTICE 1, 25 (L. Empey ed. 1979).

17. *Social facts* are the "recurrent patterns of behavior on which policy must be based." D. HOROWITZ, THE COURTS AND SOCIAL POLICY 45 (1977).

18. Kent v. United States, 383 U.S. 541, 556 (1966).

19. 387 U.S. 1 (1967).

20. *Id.* at 28.

21. *Id.* at 19.

22. *Id.* at 18.

23. *Id.* at 26.

24. *Id.* at 13.

25. *See generally* Melton, *Children's Competence to Consent: A Problem in Law and Social Science,* in CHILDREN'S COMPETENCE TO CONSENT (G. Melton, G. Koocher, & M. Saks eds. 1983).

26. 387 U.S. at 31–57.

27. *Id.* at 17. The notion that juveniles are primarily owed custody was recently revived by the Supreme Court in a decision upholding preventive detention of juveniles awaiting adjudication. Schall v. Martin, 467 U.S. 253 (1984).

28. 387 U.S. at 19.

29. McKeiver v. Pennsylvania, 403 U.S. 528, 547 and 551 (1971).

30. *See, e.g.,* V. STAPLETON & L. TEITELBAUM, IN DEFENSE OF YOUTH: A STUDY OF THE ROLE OF COUNSEL IN AMERICAN JUVENILE COURTS (1972); Platt & Friedman, *The Limits of Advocacy: Occupational Hazards in Juvenile Court,* 116 U. PA. L. REV. 1156 (1968). Preliminary data from a national study by Patricia J. Falk and Gail S. Perry at the University of Nebraska–Lincoln suggests that ju-

venile court judges are still reluctant to permit full adversariness. They were more likely than juvenile attorneys themselves to favor attorneys' adoption of a guardian's role.

31. *See, e.g.,* JUVENILE JUSTICE STANDARDS RELATING TO COUNSEL FOR PRIVATE PARTIES (1980); V. STAPLETON & L. TEITELBAUM, *supra* note 30; Ferster, Courtless, & Snethen, *The Juvenile Justice System: In Search of the Role of Counsel,* 39 FORDHAM L. REV. 375 (1971); Kay & Segal, *The Role of the Attorney in Juvenile Court Proceedings: A Non-Polar Approach,* 61 GEO. L.J. 1401 (1973); McAnany, *Gault Attorneys in the Second Decade: Some Normative Reflections,* 29 JUV. FAM. CT. J. 37 (1978); McMillan & McMurtry, *The Role of the Defense Lawyer in Juvenile Court: Advocate or Social Worker?* 14 ST. LOUIS U.L.J. 561 (1970); G. Perry, Attorney Representational Styles in Juvenile Court: Eenie, Meenie, Miney, Moe (1983) (unpublished M.A. thesis, University of Nebraska–Lincoln).

32. Exceptions are the volumes on Abuse and Neglect, Noncriminal Misbehavior, and Schools and Education.

33. *See* JUVENILE JUSTICE STANDARDS: SUMMARY AND ANALYSIS (1982).

34. For such a summary with special emphasis on forensic mental health, see Morse & Whitebread, *supra* note ∟.

35. The decriminalization of status offenses has yet to be endorsed by the ABA. *See supra* note 32.

36. W. WADLINGTON, C. WHITEBREAD, & S. DAVIS, CHILDREN IN THE LEGAL SYSTEM 198–99 (1983).

37. Juvenile Justice and Delinquency Prevention Act, 42 U.S.C. § 5633(c) (1982).

38. Consistent with this perspective, the Reagan administration has placed the emphasis of its juvenile justice programs on serious juvenile crime. Cunningham, *Discretionary Justice: The Furor over Juvenile Research Funds,* 15(7) A.P.A. MONITOR 1, 21 (1984); *OJJDP Targets Juvenile Gangs, Chronic Offenders,* 4(9) JUST. ASSISTANCE NEWS 3 (1983).

39. *See* Miller, *Juvenile Justice From Rhetoric to Rhetoric,* in THE FUTURE OF CHILDHOOD AND JUVENILE JUSTICE 66, 70–71 (L. Empey ed. 1979).

40. Strictly speaking, even the most serious offenses by the oldest juveniles result in offender-based dispositions in *juvenile* court. However, these juvenile offenders are often liable to transfer to *criminal* court, where they may face offense-based sentences. *See* § 11.03(c)(2).

41. The question of whether juvenile and adult defendants are sufficiently different to warrant separate systems is considered in a single footnote, JUVENILE JUSTICE STANDARDS RELATING TO DISPOSITIONS commentary at 19 n. 5 (1980).

42. The right to treatment in juvenile justice has been based on a theory that, if liberty is deprived for the purpose of treatment (as the juvenile justice system has purported to do), it is a denial of due process to deny such treatment. *See, e.g.,* Nelson v. Heyne, 491 F.2d 352 (7th Cir. 1974); Morgan v. Sproat, 432 F. Supp. 1130 (S.D. Miss. 1977); Pena v. N.Y. State Div. for Youth, 419 F. Supp. 203 (S.D.N.Y. 1976); Morales v. Turman, 364 F.

Supp. 166 (E.D. Tex. 1973); Inmates of Boys Training School v. Affleck, 346 F. Supp. 1354 (D.R.I. 1973).

43. JUVENILE JUSTICE STANDARDS RELATING TO DISPOSITIONS § 4.1(D)(1) (1980).

44. Although the JUVENILE JUSTICE STANDARDS RELATING TO DISPOSITIONS (1980) provide for offender-related dispositions, the JUVENILE JUSTICE STANDARDS RELATING TO COURT ORGANIZATION AND ADMINISTRATION (1980) provide for a family court, with the interest in part of centralizing services to the family. Hence, it appears that family dispositions are envisioned for probationers.

45. JUVENILE JUSTICE STANDARDS RELATING TO COURT ORGANIZATION AND ADMINISTRATION § 1.1(A) (1980).

46. For statements by juvenile court judges in opposition to removal of status offense jurisdiction, see Arthur, Status Offenders Need a Court of Last Resort, 57 B.U.L. Rev. 631 (1977); Polier, Myths and Realities in the Search for Juvenile Justice, 1(2) RESOLUTIONS OF CORRECTIONAL PROBS. ISSUES 9 (1975).

47. See supra note 30.

48. See VA. CODE ANN. § 16.1-241; § 16.1-246; through 280 (1982).

49. See, e.g., ME. REV. STAT. ANN. tit. 15, § 3318 (1980); NEB. REV. STAT. § 43-258(1) (Cum. Supp. 1982).

50. See, e.g., State ex rel. Causey, 363 So.2d 472 (La. 1978); In re S.W.T., 277 N.W.2d 507 (Minn. 1979). See generally Grisso, Miller, & Sales, Competence to Stand Trial in Juvenile Court (submitted for publication).

51. See Grisso, Miller, & Sales, supra note 50.

52. See, e.g., In re C.W.M., 407 A.2d 617 (D.C. App. 1979).

53. 421 U.S. 519, 529 (1975).

54. See, e.g., JUVENILE JUSTICE STANDARDS RELATING TO TRANSFER BETWEEN COURTS § 2.2(C) (3) (1980).

55. See, e.g., Blomberg, Widening the Net: An Anomaly in the Evaluation of Diversion Programs, in HANDBOOK OF CRIMINAL JUSTICE EVALUATION (M. Klein & K. Teilmann eds. 1980); Mulvey & Hicks, The Paradoxical Effect of a Juvenile Code Change in Virginia, 10 AM. J. COMMUNITY PSYCHOLOGY 705 (1982); Nejelski, Diversion: Unleashing the Hounds of Heaven?, in PURSUING JUSTICE FOR THE CHILD (M. Rosenheim ed. 1976).

56. W. WADLINGTON, C. WHITEBREAD, & S. DAVIS, supra note 36, at 550.

57. It has been our experience that clinical reports are often used for evidence of mitigation, preparatory to striking a bargain (1) to reduce the charges in exchange for a guilty plea, (2) to drop the charges, or (3) to recommend probation in exchange for a guarantee of participation in a treatment program. In some jurisdictions, even most insanity defenses are the result of prosecution stipulation. See, e.g., Petrila, The Insanity Defense and Other Mental Health Dispositions in Missouri, 5 INT'L J.L. PSYCHIATRY 81 (1982).

58. JUVENILE JUSTICE STANDARDS RELATING TO TRANSFER BETWEEN COURTS § 2.2 (1980).

59. W. WADLINGTON, C. WHITEBREAD, S. DAVIS, supra note 36, at 516; see generally Mulvey, Judging Amenability to Treatment in Juvenile Offenders, in CHILDREN, MENTAL

HEALTH, AND THE LAW (N.D. Reppucci, L. Weithorn, E. Mulvey, & J. Monahan eds. 1984).

60. Whether a respondent is found to be not innocent should, of course, turn on whether the state can prove its charges beyond a reasonable doubt—not whether the defense attorney or the judge thinks that the respondent is in need of, or amenable to, treatment.

61. See supra notes 30–31.

62. The ABA's MODEL CODE OF PROFESSIONAL RESPONSIBILITY, EC 7-11 and 7-12, gives ambiguous guidance as to the proper style of representation of a questionably competent client.

63. Grisso, Juveniles' Consent in Delinquency Proceedings, in CHILDREN'S COMPETENCE TO CONSENT 131, 144–45 (G. Melton, G. Koocher, & M. Saks eds. 1983); see generally Grisso & Lovinguth, Lawyers and Child Clients: A Call for Research, in THE RIGHTS OF CHILDREN: LEGAL AND PSYCHOLOGICAL PERSPECTIVES (J. Henning ed. 1982).

64. T. GRISSO, JUVENILES' WAIVER OF RIGHTS: LEGAL AND PSYCHOLOGICAL COMPETENCE (1981).

65. Id.; Melton, Children's Concepts of Their Rights, 9 J. CLINICAL CHILD PSYCHOLOGY 186 (1980).

66. T. GRISSO, supra note 64, at 118–20.

67. Id.

68. Id. at 59–93.

69. Id. at 83–84.

70. See id. at 64 nn. 6–7, and cases cited there.

71. See Resolution of the ABA on Learning Disabilities and the Juvenile Justice System (adopted by the House of Delegates, Aug. 1983).

72. N. DUNIVANT, A CAUSAL ANALYSIS OF THE RELATIONSHIP BETWEEN LEARNING DISABILITIES AND JUVENILE DELINQUENCY (1984); N. DUNIVANT, IMPROVING ACADEMIC SKILLS AND PREVENTING DELINQUENCY OF LEARNING-DISABLED JUVENILE DELINQUENTS: EVALUATION OF THE ACLD REMEDIAL PROGRAM (1984).

73. We do not mean to imply that adult defendants do not sometimes have similar views. Nonetheless, it has been our experience that adults much more frequently perceive forensic evaluations as a possible opportunity to "beat the rap." On the other hand, juveniles more often are anxious or resistant about the evaluation, presumably because of the developmentally appropriate concern with fashioning an identity; see E. ERIKSON, IDENTITY: YOUTH AND CRISIS (1968). In that connection, it is threatening to perceive an identity fragile because of immaturity as even more tenuous because of mental disorder. Also, for some youths, delinquent values and identification may solidify connection with a delinquent peer culture. See Quay, Classification, in PSYCHOPATHOLOGICAL DISORDERS OF CHILDHOOD 1, 19–21 (H. Quay & J. Werry eds. 2d ed. 1979).

74. Aggressive behavior is common in depressed adolescents. See, e.g., Chiles, Miller, & Cox, Depression in an Adolescent Delinquent Population, 37 ARCH. GEN. PSYCHIATRY 1179 (1980).

75. There is a question of whether juveniles may be constitutionally transferred to criminal courts if they are treatable, but the state has failed to develop the nec-

essary programs. Haziel v. United States, 404 F.2d 1275, 1280 (D.C. Cir. 1968).

76. Mulvey, *supra* note 59, at 201.

77. *See, e.g.,* VA. CODE ANN. § 16.1-278 (1982).

78. VA. CODE ANN. § 16.1-279(E) (Cum. Supp. 1984).

79. *E.g.,* ALASKA STAT. § 47.10.080(b)(4) (1979); ARK. STAT. ANN. § 45-436(3)(b)(vii) (Cum. Supp. 1983); COLO. REV. STAT. § 19-3-113(4) (Cum. Supp. 1983); CONN. GEN. STAT. § 46b-140(a) (Cum. Supp. 1984); FLA. STAT. § 39.11(1)(a)(1) (1984); IDAHO CODE § 16-1814(4) (1984) (effective July 1, 1985); IND. CODE ANN. § 31-6-4-15.5(b)(4) (Burns Cum. Supp. 1984); IOWA CODE ANN. § 232.52(2)(a) (West Cum. Supp. 1984); ME. REV. STAT. ANN. tit. 15, § 3314(1)(B) (1980); MASS. GEN. LAWS ANN. ch. 119, § 62 (1969); MISS. CODE ANN. § 43-21-605(1)(c) (1981); NEV. REV. STAT. § 62.211(1)(g) (1981); N.C. GEN. STAT. § 7A-649(2) (1981); R.I. GEN. LAWS § 14-1-32 (1983); UTAH CODE ANN. § 78-3a-39(7) (1983); WIS. STAT. § 48.34(5) (West 1983); WYO STAT. § 14-6-229(f)(i) (1984).

80. *E.g.,* FLA. STAT. § 39.11(1)(f) (West Cum. Supp. 1984); MISS. CODE ANN. 43-21-605(1)(e) (1981); N.C. GEN. STAT. § 7A-649(4) (1981).

81. *E.g.,* CONN. GEN. STAT § 46b-140(c) (Cum. Supp. 1984); NEV. REV. STAT. § 62.211(1)(f) (1981).

82. *E.g.,* IOWA CODE ANN. § 232.52(2)(f) (West Cum. Supp. 1984); MD. CTS. JUD. PROC. CODE ANN. § 3-820(h) (1984); MICH. STAT. ANN. § 27.3178(598.18) (1984); N.J. REV. STAT. § 2A:4-61(b)(7) (West Cum. Supp. 1984); S.D. CODIFIED LAWS ANN. § 26-8-39 (Supp. 1983); UTAH CODE ANN. § 79-3a-39(10) (Supp. 1983); WYO. STAT. § 14-6-229(f)(iv) (1984).

83. There is an argument to be made, however, that conditions of probation must be "fair and rationally related to a sensible plan for rehabilitation." C. WHITEBREAD & M. PAULSEN, JUVENILE LAW AND PROCEDURE 176 (1974).

84. VA. CODE ANN. § 16.1-278 (1982).

85. *See supra* note 75.

86. *See supra* note 42.

87. THE REHABILITATION OF CRIMINAL OFFENDERS: PROBLEMS AND PROSPECTS (L. Sechrest, S. White, & E. Brown eds. 1979).

88. *Id.* at 37–42.

89. G. MELTON, CHILD ADVOCACY: PSYCHOLOGICAL ISSUES AND INTERVENTIONS 66–68 (1983); Barrett, Hampe, & Miller, *Research on Child Psychotherapy,* in HANDBOOK OF PSYCHOTHERAPY AND BEHAVIOR CHANGE (S. Garfield & A. Bergin eds. 2d ed. 1978); Levitt, *The Results of Psychotherapy with Children: An Evaluation,* 21 J. CONSULTING PSYCHOTHERAPY 186 (1957); Levitt, *Research on Psychotherapy with Children,* in HANDBOOK OF PSYCHOTHERAPY AND BEHAVIOR CHANGE: AN EMPIRICAL ANALYSIS (A. Bergin & S. Garfield eds. 1st ed. 1971).

90. *See* Bergin & Suinn, *Individual Psychotherapy and Behavior Therapy,* 24 ANN. REV. PSYCHOLOGY 509 (1973); Gomes-Schwartz, Hadley, & Strupp, *Individual Psychotherapy and Behavior Therapy,* 29 ANN. REV. PSYCHOLOGY 435 (1978).

91. H. COHEN & J. FILIPCZAK, A NEW LEARNING ENVIRONMENT (1971); Johnson, *An Environment for Treating Youthful Offenders: The Robert F. Kennedy Youth Center,* 2 OFFENDER REHAB. 159 (1977); Kifer, Lewis, Green, & Phillips, *Training Predelinquent Youths and Their Parents to Negotiate Conflict Situations,* 7 J. APPLIED BEHAV. ANALYSIS 357 (1974); Minkin, Braukman, Minkin, Timbers, Timbers, Fixsen, Phillips, & Wolf, *The Social Validation and Training of Conversation Skills,* 9 J. APPLIED BEHAV. ANALYSIS 127 (1976); Phillips, *Achievement Place: Token Reinforcement Procedures in a Home-Style Rehabilitation Setting for "Pre-Delinquent" Boys,* 1 J. APPLIED BEHAV. ANALYSIS 213 (1968); Phillips, Phillips, Fixsen, & Wolf, *Achievement Place: Modification of the Behaviors of Predelinquent Boys within a Token Economy,* 4 J. APPLIED BEHAV. ANALYSIS 45 (1971).

92. Cavior & Schmidt, *Test of the Effectiveness of a Differential Treatment Strategy at the Robert F. Kennedy Center,* 5 CRIM. JUST. BEHAV. 131 (1978); Johnson, *Behavior Modification in the Correctional Setting,* 4 CRIM. JUST. BEHAV. 397 (1971).

93. The initial report of vocationally oriented psychotherapy was in Massimo & Shore, *The Effectiveness of a Vocationally Oriented Psychotherapy,* 33 AM. J. ORTHOPSYCHIATRY 634 (1963).

94. B. GOLDENBERG, BUILD ME A MOUNTAIN: YOUTH, POVERTY, AND THE CREATION OF NEW SETTINGS (1971).

95. Massimo & Shore, *supra* note 93; Ricks, Umbarger, & Mack, *A Measure of Increased Temporal Perspective in Successfully Treated Adolescent Boys,* 69 J. ABNORMAL SOC. PSYCHOLOGY 685 (1964); Shore & Massimo, *Comprehensive Vocationally Oriented Psychotherapy for Adolescent Delinquent Boys: A Follow-up Study,* 36 AM. J. ORTHOPSYCHIATRY 609 (1966); Shore & Massimo, *Five Years Later: A Follow-Up Study of Comprehensive Vocationally Oriented Psychotherapy,* 39 AM. J. ORTHOPSYCHIATRY 769 (1969); Shore & Massimo, *After Ten Years: A Follow-Up Study of Comprehensive Vocationally Oriented Psychotherapy,* 43 AM. J. ORTHOPSYCHIATRY 128 (1973); Shore & Massimo, *Fifteen Years after Treatment: A Follow-Up Study of Comprehensive Vocationally Oriented Psychotherapy,* 49 AM. J. PSYCHOTHERAPY 240 (1979) [hereinafter cited as *Fifteen Years*]; Shore, Massimo, Kisielawski, & Moran, *Object Relations Changes Resulting from Successful Psychotherapy with Adolescent Delinquents and their Relationship to Academic Performance,* 5 J. AM. ACAD. CHILD PSYCHIATRY 93 (1966).

96. For further discussion of the program content, see G. MELTON, *supra* note 89, at 68–72.

97. Massimo & Shore, *supra* note 93, at 636.

98. Some have suggested that large residential programs are inherently destined to fail. *See, e.g.,* W. WOLFENSBERGER, THE ORIGIN AND NATURE OF OUR INSTITUTIONAL MODELS (1975).

99. G. MELTON, *supra* note 89, at 84–87.

100. Shore & Massimo, *Fifteen Years, supra* note 95, at 245.

101. The problem of juveniles' violence against other family members is most often a reflection of violence as a pattern of interaction in the family. *See* Patterson, *The Aggressive Child: Victim and Architect of a Coercive System,*

in Behavior Modification and Families: I. Theory and Research (E. Mash, L. Hamerlynck, & L. Handy eds. 1976); Post, *Adolescent Parricide in Abusive Families,* 61 Child Welfare 445 (1982).

102. Especially in status offense cases, parents are often complainants because of their children's "uncontrollability," promiscuity, or running away. *See* J. Murray, Status Offenders: A Sourcebook 6 (1983).

103. *See generally* Hetherington & Martin, *Family Interaction,* in Psychopathological Disorders of Childhood (H. Quay & J. Werry eds. 2d ed. 1979).

104. *Id.* at 260, 263–64, and studies cited there; Patterson, *supra* note 101.

105. Hetherington & Martin, *supra* note 103, at 261–63, and studies cited there.

106. L. Eron, L. Walder, & M. Lefkowitz, Learning of Aggression in Children 75–78 (1971).

107. Hetherington & Martin, *supra* note 103, at 266.

108. S. Minuchin, Families of the Slums: An Exploration of Their Structure and Treatment (1967).

109. Herbert & Baer, *Training Parents as Behavior Modifiers: Self-Recording of Contingent Attention,* 5 J. Applied Behav. Analysis 139 (1972); Lobitz & Johnson, *Normal versus Deviant Children: A Multimethod Comparison,* 3 J. Abnormal Child Psychology 353 (1975); Wahler, *Oppositional Children: A Quest for Parental Reinforcement Control,* 3 J. Applied Behav. Analysis 159 (1968).

110. Hetherington & Martin, *supra* note 103, at 268–76, and studies cited there.

111. *Id.* at 271 and studies cited there.

112. *E.g.,* Patterson, *Interventions for Boys with Conduct Problems: Multiple Settings, Treatments, and Criteria,* 42 J. Consulting Clinical Psychology 471 (1974).

113. Such a focus is unsurprising, in that many behaviorally oriented family treatment programs have emphasized efforts to increase parental control. *See, e.g.,* Whaler, *Deviant Child Behavior within the Family: Developmental Speculations and Behavior Change Strategies,* in Handbook of Behavior Modification and Behavior Therapy (H. Leitenberg ed. 1976). Programs of this sort are ideally suited to the alleviation of "incorrigibility."

114. Post, *supra* note 101, at 454.

115. *See supra* note 92 and accompanying text.

116. *See supra* note 77 and accompanying text.

117. J. Garbarino, Children and Families in the Social Environment 167–68 (1982); Maccoby, Johnson, & Church, *Community Integration and the Social Control of Juvenile Delinquency,* 14 J. Soc. Issues 38 (1958).

118. *See* Davidson & Saul, *Youth Advocacy in the Juvenile Court: A Clash of Paradigms,* in Legal Reforms Affecting Child and Youth Services (G. Melton ed. 1982).

119. Davidson, Seidman, Rappaport, Berck, Rapp, Rhodes, & Herring, *Diversion Program for Juvenile Offenders,* 13(2) Soc. Work 40 (1977).

120. Davidson & Rapp, *A Multiple Strategy Model of Child Advocacy,* 21 Soc. Work 225 (1976); G. Melton, *supra* note 89, at 54–64.

121. Edwards, Greene, Abramowitz, & Davidson, *National*

Health Insurance, Psychotherapy, and the Poor, 34 Am. Psychologist 411 (1979); Lorion, *Socioeconomic Status and Traditional Treatment Approaches Reconsidered,* 79 Psychological Bull. 263 (1973); Lorion, *Patient and Therapist Variables in the Treatment of Low-Income Patients,* 81 Psychological Bull. 344 (1974).

122. A significant issue of equal protection exists when one of two juveniles equally amenable to treatment (given unlimited resources) is transferred and the other is not, because the latter youth's family has more resources available or simply is more willing to cooperate.

123. Weinstein, *Project Re-Ed Schools for Emotionally Disturbed Children: Effectiveness as Viewed by Referring Agencies, Parents, and Teachers,* 35 Exceptional Children 703 (1969).

124. The Rehabilitation of Criminal Offenders, *supra* note 87, at 88–89.

125. G. Melton, *supra* note 89, at 68–69.

126. *See* King, *The Ego and the Integration of Violence in Homicidal Youth,* 45 Am. J. Orthopsychiatry 134 (1975).

127. For a discussion of the relationship between cognitive and affective development, *see* Brooks, *Psychoeducational Assessment: A Broader Perspective,* 10 Prof. Psychology 708 (1979). *See also* G. Melton, *supra* note 89, at 73–81; Dishion, Loeber, Stouthmer-Loeber, & Patterson, *Skill Deficits and Male Adolescent Delinquency,* 12 J. Abnormal Child Psychology 37 (1984).

128. *See* G. Spivack, J. Platt, & M. Shure, The Problem-Solving Approach to Adjustment (1976).

129. *See supra* notes 71 and 72 and accompanying text.

130. Brooks, *supra* note 127.

131. 20 U.S.C. §§ 1401 *et seq.* (1982) (as amended).

132. The Education for All Handicapped Children Act has a "zero-reject" policy. No matter how disturbed a youngster is or where he or she lives, the youngster is owed a free appropriate public education, *Id.* at § 1412.

133. When a behavior problem is related to a special educational need, the procedural protections of the Education for All Handicapped Children Act and its guarantee of a free appropriate public education apply. S-1 v. Turlington, 635 F.2d 342 (5th Cir. 1981); Doe v. Koger, 480 F. Supp. 225 (N.D.Ind. 1979); Howard S. v. Friendswood Indep. School Dist., 454 F. Supp. 634 (S.D.Tex. 1978); Stuart v. Nappi, 443 F. Supp. 1234 (D. Conn. 1978).

134. Group for the Advancement of Psychiatry, Psychopathological Disorders in Childhood: Theoretical Considerations and a Proposed Classification 249–50 (1966).

135. American Psychiatric Association, Diagnostic and Statistical Manual of Mental Disorders 45, 49 (3d ed. 1980).

136. *See supra* note 74.

137. Quay, *A Critical Analysis of DSM-III as a Taxonomy of Psychopathology in Childhood and Adolescence,* in Contemporary Issues in Psychopathology (T. Milon & G. Klerman eds. 1986.)

138. Offer, Ostrov, & Howard, *The Mental Health Profession-*

al's Concept of the Normal Adolescent, 38 ARCH. GEN. PSYCHIATRY 149 (1981).

139. *Compare* R. HOLT, METHODS IN CLINICAL RESEARCH: VOL. 2 PREDICTION AND RESEARCH (1978) *and* P. MEEHL, CLINICAL VERSUS STATISTICAL PREDICTION: A THEORETICAL ANALYSIS AND A REVIEW OF THE EVIDENCE (1954).

140. Monahan, *Childhood Predictors of Adult Criminal Behavior,* in EARLY CHILDHOOD INTERVENTION AND JUVENILE DELINQUENCY (F. Dutile, C. Fost, & D. Webster eds. 1982).

141. J. MONAHAN, THE CLINICAL PREDICTION OF VIOLENT BEHAVIOR 72–73 (1981).

142. J. KNITZER, UNCLAIMED CHILDREN: THE FAILURE OF PUBLIC RESPONSIBILITY TO CHILDREN AND ADOLESCENTS IN NEED OF MENTAL HEALTH SERVICES 11–12 n. 24 (1982). Consistent with the referral route from juvenile courts, the most common diagnoses in children's inpatient facilities are conduct disorders. *See, e.g.,* Kashani & Cantwell, *Characteristics of Children Admitted to Inpatient Community Mental Health Center,* 40 ARCH. GEN. PSYCHIATRY 397 (1983).

143. *See* Warren, *New Forms of Social Control: The Myth of Deinstitutionalization,* 24 AM. BEHAV. SCIENTIST 724 (1981). *See also* Krisberg & Schwarts, *Rethinking Juvenile Justice,* 29. CRIME DELINQ. 333, 360 (1983)

144. Remarkably, about 40% of administrators of residential treatment facilities admit that their treatment decisions are often the product of agency policies that may conflict with the needs of the child. H. Quay, Mental Health Administrators' Attitudes toward "Children's Rights": A National Survey (August 1983) (paper presented at the meeting of the American Psychological Association, Anaheim, California). *See also*

Billingsley, *Bureaucratic and Professional Orientation Patterns in Casework,* 38 SOC. SERV. REV. 400 (1964).

145. Lewis & Shanok, *The Use of a Correctional Setting for the Follow-Up Care of Psychiatrically Disturbed Adolescents,* 137 AM. J. PSYCHIATRY 953 (1980).

146. Linney, *Deinstitutionalization in the Juvenile Justice System,* in CHILDREN, MENTAL HEALTH, AND THE LAW 211, 224 (N.D. Reppucci, L. Weithorn, E. Mulvey, & J. Monahan eds. 1984).

147. *See supra* note 144.

148. In keeping with this theory, some have argued that all juvenile and domestic relations matters should be joined in a single family court. *See, e.g.,* JUVENILE JUSTICE STANDARDS RELATING TO COURT ORGANIZATION AND ADMINISTRATION (1980).

149. Mulvey, *Family Courts: The Issue of Reasonable Goals,* 6 LAW HUM. BEHAV. 49 (1982).

150. *Cf.* Melton & Lind, *Procedural Justice in Family Court: Does the Adversary System Make Sense?,* in LEGAL REFORMS AFFECTING CHILD AND YOUTH SERVICES (G. Melton ed. 1982).

151. In general, voluntary consent is likely to enhance the efficacy of services. *See* Melton, *Decision Making by Children: Psychological Risks and Benefits,* in CHILDREN'S COMPETENCE TO CONSENT 21, 30–31 (G. Melton, G. Koocher, & M. Saks eds. 1983).

152. *See* Carroll & Reppucci, *Meanings That Professionals Attach to Labels for Children,* 46 J. CONSULTING CLINICAL PSYCHOLOGY 372 (1978).

153. *See* Melton, *Toward "Personhood" for Adolescents: Autonomy and Privacy as Values in Public Policy,* 38 AM. PSYCHOLOGIST 99 (1983).

154. Morse & Whitebread, *supra* note 2, at 23–24.

Chapter 12

1. It is often difficult to separate the interests of child, parent, and state. For example, the state has an interest in the socialization of the child to be a productive citizen, but it also has an interest in the preservation of the family as a basic social institution and a buffer between the state and the individual. Similarly, parents are usually assumed to act on behalf of the child, but their interests may be demonstrably in conflict with, or at least different from, the child's. The child has an interest in preserving his or her care (and, therefore, in parental autonomy), but may also have independent interests in liberty and privacy. *See* G. MELTON, CHILD ADVOCACY: PSYCHOLOGICAL ISSUES AND INTERVENTIONS 3–9 (1983); Melton, *Children's Rights: Where Are the Children?,* 52 AM. J. ORTHOPSYCHIATRY 530 (1982).

2. *See generally* J. GIOVANNONI & R. BECERRA, DEFINING CHILD ABUSE (1979). Statutes violate the due process clause of the Fourteenth Amendment if they are so vague as to permit unbridled discretion or to fail to give adequate warning of the conduct that may result in sanctions.

3. The harms embedded in the foster care system have been well documented. *See, e.g.,* Bush & Gordon, *Client Choice and Bureaucratic Accountability: Possibilities for Responsiveness in a Social Welfare Bureaucracy,* 34(2) J. SOC. ISSUES 22 (1978); Mnookin, *Foster Care: In Whose Best Interest?,* 43 HARV. EDUC. REV. 599 (1973). Of course, state intervention need not take the form of removal from the home.

4. W. WADLINGTON, C. WHITEBREAD, & S. DAVIS, CHILDREN IN THE LEGAL SYSTEM 789 (1983).

5. *See, e.g.,* J. GOLDSTEIN, A. FREUD, & A. SOLNIT, BEFORE THE BEST INTERESTS OF THE CHILD 71 (1979).

6. *See infra* note 53 and accompanying text.

7. Swoboda, Elwork, Sales, & Levine, *Knowledge of and Compliance with Privileged Communication and Child-Abuse-Reporting Laws,* 9 PROF. PSYCHOLOGY 448 (1978).

8. *But see* Pelton, *Child Abuse and Neglect: The Myth of Classlessness,* 48 AM. J. ORTHOPSYCHIATRY 608 (1978).

9. There is often an additional discretionary judgment, shared with the prosecuting attorney, as to whether criminal child abuse charges will be brought.

10. *See generally* A. PLATT, THE CHILD SAVERS: THE INVENTION OF DELINQUENCY (2d ed. 1977); Mnookin, *Children's Rights: Beyond Kiddie Libbers and Child Savers,* 7 J. CLINICAL CHILD PSYCHOLOGY 163 (1978).

11. *See, e.g.,* Feshbach & Feshbach, *Child Advocacy and Family Privacy,* 34(2) J. SOC. ISSUES 168 (1978); Garbarino, *The Price of Privacy in the Social Dynamics of Child Abuse,* 56 CHILD WELFARE 565 (1977); Garbarino, Gaboury, Long, Grandjean, & Asp, *Who Owns the Children? An Ecological Perspective on Public Policy,* in LEGAL REFORMS AFFECTING CHILD AND YOUTH SERVICES (G. Melton ed. 1982).

12. *See, e.g.,* Gray, Culter, Dean, & Kempe, *Prediction and Prevention of Child Abuse and Neglect,* 35(2) J. SOC. ISSUES 127 (1978).

13. Advocates of this position would enlist neighbors in the intervention, as well as formal services. *See generally* PROTECTING CHILDREN FROM ABUSE AND NEGLECT: DEVELOPING AND MAINTAINING EFFECTIVE SUPPORT SYSTEMS FOR FAMILIES (J. Garbarino & H. Stocking eds. 1980).

14. *See, e.g.,* Wald, *State Intervention on Behalf of "Neglected" Children: A Search for Realistic Standards,* 27 STAN. L. REV. 985 (1975).

15. Professor Wald was the reporter for the volume on JUVENILE JUSTICE STANDARDS RELATING TO ABUSE AND NEGLECT (tentative draft 1977) [hereinafter cited as STANDARDS].

16. J. GOLDSTEIN, A. FREUD, & A. SOLNIT, BEYOND THE BEST INTERESTS OF THE CHILD (1973); J. GOLDSTEIN, A. FREUD, & A. SOLNIT, *supra* note 5.

17. J. GOLDSTEIN, A. FREUD, & A. SOLNIT, *supra* note 5, at 194 (Child Placement Code of Hampstead-Haven).

18. *Id.* at Para. 10.5.

19. *Id.* at Para. 30.9.

20. *See infra* notes 75–83.

21. Gelles & Straus, *Violence in the American Family,* 35(2) J. SOC. ISSUES 15, 30 (1979).

22. STANDARDS, *supra* note 15, § 2.1(A).

23. *Id.* commentary at 63.

24. *Id.* commentary at 63–64.

25. FLA. STAT. ANN. § 827.07(2)(f) (1976).

26. *Id.* § 827.07(2)(b) and (c).

27. WYO. STAT. ANN. § 14-3-202(B) (1977).

28. *E.g.,* FLA. STAT. ANN. § 827.07(2)(d)(1) (1976); ILL. ANN. STAT. ch. 23 § 2053(e) (Cum. Supp. 1984).

29. N.Y. Family Court Act § 1012(i) (McKinney 1983).

30. *E.g.,* MD. ANN. CODE art. 27 § 35A(b)(7)(a) (Cum. Supp. 1983).

31. *Compare* Bowers v. State, 283 Md. 115, 389 A.2d 341 (1978) *and* State v. Meinert, 225 Kan. 816, 594 P.2d 232 (1979).

32. *See generally* Maurer, *Corporal Punishment,* 29 AM. PSYCHOLOGIST 614 (1974); Melton, *Legal Policy and Child Development Research: A Selective Review,* 3(3–4) CHILD YOUTH SERVICES 1, 16–17 (1980–81); *cf.* Bersoff & Prasse, *Applied Psychology and Judicial Decisionmaking: Corporal Punishment as a Case in Point,* 9 PROF. PSYCHOLOGY 400 (1978).

33. STANDARDS, *supra* note 15, § 2.1(B).

34. *Id.* commentary at 65–66.

35. *See* Bulkley, *Analysis of Civil Child Protection Statutes Dealing with Sexual Abuse,* in CHILD SEXUAL ABUSE AND THE LAW 81, 82 n. 6 (National Legal Resource Center for Child Advocacy & Protection ed. 1981).

36. *Id.* at 82 n. 7.

37. STANDARDS, *supra* note 15, § 2.1(D) and commentary.

38. *Id.* commentary at 70–71.

39. *Id.* commentary at 72.

40. *See* Bulkley, *supra* note 35, at 82 n. 10.

41. At least 21 states and the District of Columbia have a special provision for sexual abuse in the civil child abuse statute. *Id.* at 82.

42. *Id.* at 82.

43. *See generally* Hetherington & Martin, *Family Interaction,* in PSYCHOPATHOLOGICAL DISORDERS OF CHILDHOOD (H. Quay & J. Werry eds. 2d ed. 1979).

44. STANDARDS, *supra* note 15, § 2.1(C).

45. WYO. STAT. ANN. § 14-3-202(ii)(A) (1977).

46. *See supra* notes 2 and 31 and accompanying text.

47. J. GIOVANNONI & R. BECERRA, *supra* note 2.

48. *Id.*

49. *Id.* at 48–56.

50. Kempe, Silverman, Steele, Droegemuller, & Silver, *The Battered-Child Syndrome,* 181 J.A.M.A. 17 (1962).

51. W. WADLINGTON, C. WHITEBREAD, & S. DAVIS, *supra* note 4, at 789.

52. 42 U.S.C. §§ 5101–5106 *et seq.* (1982) (as amended). *See also The Child Abuse Prevention and Treatment Act of 1983,* 1 WASH. REP. 1 (1984) [hereinafter cited as *Child Abuse*].

53. *Child Abuse, supra* note 52, at 3 (citing NCCAN statistics).

54. *See generally* P. ARIES, CENTURIES OF CHILDHOOD: A SOCIAL HISTORY OF FAMILY LIFE (1962).

55. Parke & Collmer, *Child Abuse: An Interdisciplinary Analysis,* in 5 CHILD DEVELOPMENT RESEARCH 513 (E. M. Hetherington ed. 1975).

56. J. GARBARINO & G. GILLIAM, UNDERSTANDING ABUSIVE FAMILIES (1980), *cited in* J. GARBARINO & A. GARBARINO, EMOTIONAL MALTREATMENT OF CHILDREN 8 (1980).

57. J. GARBARINO & A. GARBARINO, *supra* note 56, at 18–20.

58. D. GIL, VIOLENCE AGAINST CHILDREN: PHYSICAL ABUSE IN THE UNITED STATES 6 (1970).

59. Gelles, *Child Abuse as Psychopathology: A Sociological Critique and Reformulation,* 43 AM. J. ORTHOPSYCHIATRY 611 (1973).

60. Spinetta & Rigler, *The Child Abusing Parent: A Psychological Review,* 77 PSYCHOLOGICAL BULL. 296, 299 (1972) (citations omitted).

61. *Id.* at 299.

62. *Id.* at 299–300.

63. Wright, *The "Sick but Slick" Syndrome as a Personality Component of Parents of Battered Children,* 32 J. CLINICAL PSYCHOLOGY 41 (1976).

64. The battering parents scored lower than nonbattering parents on the Rorschach Bizarre Content score and higher on the Rosenzweig Group Conformity rating,

the Rosenzweig Intropunitiveness scale, the MMPI *L* scale, and the MMPI *K* scale. There was a marginally significant tendency for the battering parents to score higher on the MMPI *Pd* scale.

65. *See, e.g.,* Spinetta & Rigler, *supra* note 60, at 299–300.

66. *See, e.g., id.* at 298; Williams, *Child Abuse,* in HANDBOOK OF CLINICAL CHILD PSYCHOLOGY 1219, 1224 (C. E. Walker & M. Roberts eds. 1983).

67. D. GIL, *supra* note 58, at 114; *see also* Jayaratne, *Child Abusers as Parents and Children: A Review,* 22 SOC. WORK 5 (1977). One study that included a comparison group did find substantial differences in the childhoods of abusers and nonabusers, with the abusers much more likely to have had a disrupted childhood in general and to have been significantly more likely to have been abused by their fathers (there was no difference in history of abuse by the women's mothers). Scott, *Attachment and Child Abuse: A Study of Social History Indicators among Mothers of Abused Children,* in TRAUMATIC ABUSE AND NEGLECT AT HOME (G. Williams & J. Money eds. 1980). Unfortunately, however, Scott did not use an appropriate comparison group, and the conclusions that can be drawn from the study are limited. The comparison group was from a general medical clinic without appropriate matching for social class and other variables.

68. There is a need to teach parents to reward good behavior and ignore or extinguish bad behavior. *See generally* W. MIKULAS, BEHAVIOR MODIFICATION: AN OVERVIEW (1972).

69. *See* Patterson, *The Aggressive Child: Victim and Architect of a Coercive System,* in 1 BEHAVIOR MODIFICATION AND FAMILIES (E. Mash, L. Hamerlynck, & L. Handy eds. 1976).

70. *See generally* M. SHURE & G. SPIVACK, PROBLEM-SOLVING TECHNIQUES IN CHILD-REARING (1978).

71. *See generally* D. MEICHENBAUM, COGNITIVE-BEHAVIOR MODIFICATION: AN INTEGRATIVE APPROACH (1977); R. NOVACO, ANGER CONTROL: THE DEVELOPMENT AND EVALUATION OF AN EXPERIMENTAL TREATMENT (1975).

72. Rosenberg & Reppucci, *Abusive Mothers: Perceptions of their Own and their Children's Behavior,* 51 J. CONSULTING CLINICAL PSYCHOLOGY 674 (1983).

73. *See, e.g.,* Gil, *The United States versus Child Abuse,* in THE SOCIAL CONTEXT OF CHILD ABUSE AND NEGLECT (L. Pelton ed. 1981).

74. *See* W. RYAN, BLAMING THE VICTIM (2d ed. 1976).

75. Erlanger, *Social Class and Corporal Punishment in Childrearing: A Reassessment,* 39 AM. SOC. REV. 68 (1974); Stark & McEvoy, *Middle Class Violence,* 4 PSYCHOLOGY TODAY 52 (1970); *see also* Korsch, Christian, Gozzi, & Carlson, *Infant Care and Punishment: A Pilot Study,* 55 AM. J. PUB. HEALTH 1880 (1965).

76. Anderson & Anderson, *Psychologists and Spanking,* 5(2) J. CLINICAL CHILD PSYCHOLOGY 46 (1976).

77. American Psychological Association, Resolution on Corporal Punishment (adopted by the Council of Representatives, January 1975).

78. *See, e.g.,* NATIONAL EDUCATION ASSOCIATION, REPORT OF THE TASK FORCE ON CORPORAL PUNISHMENT (1972).

79. Gelles & Straus, *supra* note 21.

80. *Id.* at 22–23.

81. *Id.* at 23.

82. *Id.* at 23.

83. *Id.* at 23.

84. Pelton, *supra* note 8.

85. Garbarino & Crouter, *Defining the Community Context for Parent–Child Relations: The Correlates of Child Maltreatment,* 49 CHILD DEV. 604 (1978).

86. *See* Rosenberg & Reppucci, *Child Abuse: A Review with Special Focus on an Ecological Approach in Rural Communities,* in RURAL PSYCHOLOGY 305, 315–16, and 322–24 (A. Childs & G. Melton eds. 1983).

87. *See, e.g.,* U. BRONFENBRENNER, THE ECOLOGY OF HUMAN DEVELOPMENT: EXPERIMENTS BY NATURE AND DESIGN (1979); J. GARBARINO, CHILDREN AND FAMILIES IN THE SOCIAL ENVIRONMENT (1982).

88. *See, e.g.,* Justice & Duncan, *Child Abuse as a Work-Related Problem,* 23 CORRECTIVE SOC. PSYCHIATRY JUV. BEHAV. TECHNOLOGY, METHODS, THERAPY 53 (1977).

89. "Behavioral repertoire" refers to the range of behaviors available to an individiual in a particular situation.

90. Infants are more vulnerable, hence more easily injured, and therefore more likely to be reported as abused. Also, older children can often escape the abuser for periods of time.

91. Gelles & Straus, *supra* note 21, at 25.

92. *See* Friedrich & Boriskin, *The Role of the Child in Abuse: A Review of the Literature,* 46 AM. J. ORTHOPSYCHIATRY 580 (1976).

93. *See* R. BELL & L. HARPER, CHILD EFFECTS ON ADULTS 56–57 (1977); Patterson, *supra* note 69.

94. There is a substantial literature on differences in temperament among infants. *See generally* A. THOMAS, S. CHESS, & H. BIRCH, TEMPERAMENT AND BEHAVIOR DISORDERS IN CHILDREN (1968).

95. *See* G. MELTON, *supra* note 1, at 48–52.

96. Cochran & Brassard, *Child Development and Personal Social Networks,* 50 CHILD DEV. 601 (1979).

97. *See, e.g.,* Gelles & Straus, *supra* note 21, at 33.

98. Garbarino & Crouter, *supra* note 85.

99. Garbarino & Sherman, *High-Risk Neighborhoods and High-Risk Families: The Human Ecology of Child Maltreatment,* 51 CHILD DEV. 188 (1980).

100. Sudia, *What Services Do Abusive and Neglecting Families Need?,* in THE SOCIAL CONTEXT OF CHILD ABUSE AND NEGLECT 268, 274 (L. Pelton ed. 1981).

101. Cohn, *Essential Elements of Successful Child Abuse and Neglect Treatment,* 3 CHILD ABUSE NEGLECT 491 (1979).

102. Rosenberg & Hunt, *Child Maltreatment: Legal and Mental Health Issues,* in CHILDREN, MENTAL HEALTH, AND THE LAW 79, 92 (N. D. Reppucci, L. Weithorn, E. Mulvey, & J. Monahan eds. 1984).

103. Zigler, *Controlling Child Abuse in America: An Effort Doomed to Failure?,* in CRITICAL PERSPECTIVES ON CHILD ABUSE (R. Bourne & E. Newberger eds. 1979).

104. *Child Abuse, supra* note 52, at 3.

105. Rosenberg & Hunt, *supra* note 102, at 92.

106. For a contrary view, *see* Wolfe, *Treatment of Abusive*

Parents: A Reply to the Special Issue, 13 J. CLINICAL CHILD PSYCHOLOGY 192 (1984).

107. *See supra* note 3. Michael Wald and his colleagues at Stanford University are currently conducting a study comparing maltreated children left in the home with those in foster care.

108. 310 N.W.2d 58 (Minn. 1981).

109. *See* FED. R. EVID. 404.

110. 310 N.W.2d at 64.

111. *See* FED R. EVID. 403.

112. When character evidence has been admitted, it has typically been in the form of evidence as to prior abusive acts in order to show motive, intent, and so forth. Grabill v. State, 621 P.2d 802 (Wyo. 1980). *But see* Harvey v. State, 604 P.2d 586 (Alaska 1979).

113. The burden is in effect shifted to the defendant, who must convince the jury that he or she is one of the *X%* of persons with his or her characteristics who is not a battering parent.

114. *See* American Psychological Association, *Ethical Principles of Psychologists,* 36 AM. PSYCHOLOGIST 633 (1981), principles 1a, 8, and 8c.

115. *See, e.g.,* Iowa v. Mueller, 344 N.W.2d 262 (Iowa Ct. App. 1983).

116. *See, e.g.,* State v. Wilkerson, 295 N.C. 559, 247 S.E.2d 905 (1978) (upholding admissibility of testimony by pediatrician and pathologist as to nonaccidental nature of injuries sustained by child).

117. *See* Williams, *supra* note 66, at 1228–29.

118. It is questionable whether the inferences drawn would be based on more than commonsense. Conclusions as to the meaning of the behavior may also invade the province of the factfinder in determining whether abuse has occurred.

119. There has been an attempt in many states to reduce the number of children "lost" in foster care by requiring periodic reviews. *See, e.g.,* NEB. REV. STAT. §§ 43-1301 *et seq.* (Cum. Supp. 1982). *See generally* Musewicz, *The Failure of Foster Care: Federal Statutory Reform and the Child's Right to Permanence,* 54 S. CAL. L. REV. 633 (1981).

120. *See, e.g.,* STANDARDS, *supra* note 15, § 6.4(C).

121. Such review is necessary to determine whether the child may be returned to his or her home, or, if already in the custody of the parents, whether dispositional conditions should be removed. *See, e.g.,* NEB. REV. STAT. § 43-288 (Cum. Supp. 1982).

122. States increasingly have special reviews of state efforts to maintain stability for children in foster care. *See supra* note 119. They also usually must document their services to the family if there is ever consideration of termination of parental rights. *See infra* notes 136–37 and accompanying text.

123. *See, e.g.,* NEB. REV. STAT. § 43-1316 (Cum. Supp. 1982).

124. *Cf.* Bonnie & Slobogin, *The Role of Mental Health Professionals in the Criminal Process: The Case for Informed Speculation,* 66 VA. L. REV. 427 (1980); Morse, *Law and Mental Health Professionals: The Limits of Expertise,* 9 PROF. PSYCHOLOGY 389 (1978).

125. *See, e.g.,* STANDARDS, *supra* note 15, § 8.2; MODEL STATUTE FOR TERMINATION OF PARENTAL RIGHTS § 12(1) (National Council of Juvenile Court Judges) [hereinafter cited as MODEL STATUTE]. Reprinted in C. Wadlington, C. Whitebread, & S. Davis, *supra* note 4, at 882.

126. CAL. CIV. CODE § 232(a)(7) (West Supp. 1984).

127. *E.g.,* N.Y. Family Court Act §§ 622, 623 (McKinney 1983).

128. The difficulty of the issue is reflected in the Supreme Court's seemingly conflicting 5–4 decisions in Santosky v. Kramer, 102 S.Ct. 1388 (1982) (termination of parental rights requires clear and convincing evidence), and Lassiter v. Dep't of Social Services, 452 U.S. 18 (1981) (there is no constitutional right to counsel for respondents in all termination cases). *See* Besharov, *Terminating Parental Rights: The Indigent Parent's Right to Counsel after* Lassiter v. North Carolina, 15 FAM. L.Q. 205 (1981); Note, *Why Not Beyond a Reasonable Doubt?,* 62 NEB. L. REV. 602 (1983).

129. State v. Robert H., 118 N.H. 713, 716, 393 A.2d 1387, 1389 (1978).

130. Santosky v. Kramer, 102 S.Ct. 1388, 1399.

131. NEB. REV. STAT. § 43-292(4) (Cum. Supp. 1982).

132. *Id.* at § 43-292(5).

133. MODEL STATUTE, *supra* note 127, § 12(1).

134. *Id.* at §§ 12(1) and 12(2).

135. *Id.* at § 12(3).

136. *E.g.,* VA. CODE ANN. § 16.1-283(C) (1982).

137. *E.g.,* N.Y. Family Court Act § 1026 (McKinney 1983).

138. STANDARDS, *supra* note 15, § 8.2(B)(1).

139. *Id.* §§ 8.2(B)(2) and 8.2(B)(3).

140. *Id.* § 8.3.

141. *Id.* § 8.4.

142. *Id.* § 8.5(A).

143. *See, e.g.,* Colo. in re L.D., 671 P.2d 940 (Colo. 1983); Custody of Minor (No. 3), 454 N.E.2d 924 (Mass. Ct. App. 1983), In re R.D.J., 340 N.W.2d 415 (Neb. 1983); In re Fant, 335 N.W.2d 314 (Neb. 1983); In re Spradlin, 214 Neb. 834 (1983); In re Doe, 465 A.2d 924 (N.H. 1983); In re Guardianship of D.N., 464 A.2d 1221 (N.J. Juv. & Dom. Rel. Ct., Monmouth County, 1983); In re Melissa, 459 N.Y.S.2d 10 (N.Y. App. Div. 1983); In re Candie Lee "W.," 458 N.Y.S.2d 347 (N.Y. App. Div. 1983); In re Tonya Louise M., 458 N.Y.S.2d 370 (N.Y. App. Div. 1982); In re Jason B., 458 N.Y.S.2d 180 (N.Y. Fam. Ct. 1983); In re Gabriel G., 460 A.2d 441 (R.I. 1983); In re Stephanie, 456 A.2d 268 (R.I. 1983); S.C. Department of Soc. Services v. Martell, 307 S.E.2d 601 (S.C. 1983).

144. *See* Alsager v. District Court of Polk County, Iowa, 406 F. Supp. 10 (S.D. Iowa 1975), *aff'd,* 545 F.2d 1137 (8th Cir. 1976) (statute permitting termination on ground of "unfitness" is unconstitutionally vague). There is a plausible argument that statutes that provide for termination on the ground of unfitness resulting from "mental illness" are void for vagueness unless there is further definition. *Cf. Developments in the Law—Civil Commitment of the Mentally Ill,* 87 HARV.

L. REV. 1190, 1253–58 (1974) (analyzing use of "mental illness" as threshold in civil commitment statutes).

145. *See supra* note 143.

146. *See, e.g.,* H. GRUNEBAUM, J. WEISS, B. COHLER, C. HARTMAN, & D. GALLANT, MENTALLY ILL MOTHERS AND THEIR CHILDREN (1975); Cohler, Grunebaum, Weiss, *et al., Disturbance of Attention among Schizophrenic, Depressed and Well Mothers and Their Children,* 18 J. CHILD PSYCHOLOGY PSYCHIATRY 115 (1977); Kauffman, Grunebaum, Cohler, & Gamer, *Superkids: Competent Children of Psychotic Parents,* 136 AM. J. PSYCHIATRY 11 (1979); Sameroff, Barocas, & Seifer, *Rochester Longitudinal Study Progress Report,* in CHILDREN AT RISK FOR SCHIZOPHRENIA (W. Watt, J. Rolf, & E. Anthony eds. 1983).

147. The increased level of disorders might be the result of inheritance rather than poor parenting per se. *See generally* D. ROSENTHAL, GENETICS OF PSYCHOPATHOLOGY (1971).

148. *See supra* note 146.

149. *Id.*

150. *See* Reiss, *Families and the Etiology of Schizophrenia,* 14 SCHIZOPHRENIA BULL. 9 (1975).

151. *See* Cytryn, McKnew, Zahn-Waxler, Radke-Yarrow, Gaensbauer, Harmon, & Lamour, *A Developmental View of Affective Disturbances in the Children of Affectively Ill Parents,* 141 AM. J. PSYCHIATRY 219 (1984); Gaensbauer, Harmon, Cytryn, & McKnew, *Social and Affective Development in Infants with a Manic–Depressive Parent,* 141 AM. J. PSYCHIATRY 223 (1984).

152. *See supra* note 61.

153. Mild mental retardation tends to be identified primarily by the schools. After completion of schooling, most mildly retarded persons are no longer labeled retarded. *See generally* J. MERCER, LABELING THE MENTALLY RETARDED: CLINICAL AND SOCIAL SYSTEM PERSPECTIVES ON MENTAL RETARDATION (1973).

154. *Id.*

155. Lubs & Maes, *Recurrence Risk in Mental Retardation,* in 3 RESEARCH TO PRACTICE IN MENTAL RETARDATION (P. Mittler ed. 1977).

156. E. REED & S. REED, MENTAL RETARDATION: A FAMILY STUDY (1965).

157. Jacob, Favorini, Meisel, & Anderson, *The Alcoholic's Spouse, Children and Family Interactions: Substantive Findings and Methodological Issues,* 39 J. STUD. ALCOHOL 1231 (1978).

158. Pytkowicz, *Introduction: Female Alcoholism: Impacts on Women and Children,* in 7 CURRENTS IN ALCOHOLISM 429, 430–31 (M. Galanter ed. 1979).

159. G. VAILLANT, THE NATURAL HISTORY OF ALCOHOLISM 65 (1983).

160. *E.g.,* M. SHURE & G. SPIVACK, *supra* note 70; A. Stolberg & A. Ullman, Single Parenting Questionnaire: Development, Validation, and Applications Manual (1983) (unpublished manuscript, Virginia Commonwealth University Department of Psychology).

161. *E.g.,* Schaefer, *Children's Reports of Parental Behavior: An Inventory,* 36 CHILD DEV. 417; Shaefer & Bell, *Development of a Parental Attitude Research Instrument,* 29 CHILD DEV. 339 (1958).

162. *E.g.,* Jones, Reid, & Patterson, *Naturalistic Observation in Clinical Assessment,* in 3 ADVANCES IN PSYCHOLOGICAL ASSESSMENTS (P. McReynolds ed. 1976); Kracke, *A Survey of Procedures for Assessing Family Conflict and Dysfunction,* 8 FAM. THERAPY 241 (1981); Moos & Moos, *A Typology of Family Social Environments,* 15 FAM. PROCESS 357 (1976); F. van der Veen, Family Concept Q-Sort (1960) (unpublished manuscript, Dane County Guidance Center, Madison, Wis.).

163. *E.g.,* R. HELFER, J. HOFFMEISTER, & C. SCHNEIDER, A MANUAL FOR USE OF THE MICHIGAN SCREENING PROFILE OF PARENTING (1978); J. MILNER, THE CHILD ABUSE POTENTIAL INVENTORY (1980); S. Bavolek, Primary Prevention of Child Abuse (1980) (unpublished manuscript, University of Wisconsin, Department of Special Education).

164. T. Grisso, Forensic Assessment in Juvenile and Family Cases: The State of the Art 8–9 (June 1, 1984) (keynote address, Summer Institute on Mental Health Law, University of Nebraska–Lincoln).

Chapter 13

1. *See* Glick, *Children of Divorced Parents in Demographic Perspective,* 35(4) J. SOC. ISSUES 170 (1979).

2. There has been, of course, increasing attention to the role of family systems in causing mental disorders. *See, e.g.,* S. MINUCHIN, FAMILIES AND FAMILY THERAPY (1974).

3. Divorce cases might be best conceptualized as a system of private bargaining. *See* Mnookin & Kornhauser, *Bargaining in the Shadow of the Law: The Case of Divorce,* 88 YALE L.J. 950 (1979).

4. G. MELTON, L. WEITHORN, & C. SLOBOGIN, COMMUNITY MENTAL HEALTH CENTERS AND THE LAW: AN EVALUATION OF COMMUNITY-BASED FORENSIC SERVICES (1985), at 71–72.

5. *Id.* 70–73.

6. Although the Juvenile Justice Standards would establish a family court with jurisdiction over both delinquency and divorce, JUVENILE JUSTICE STANDARDS RELATING TO COURT ORGANIZATION AND ADMINISTRATION (1980), few states have adopted such a model. *But see* DEL. CODE ANN. tit. 10 § 921 (Cum. Supp. 1982); HAWAII REV. STAT. §§ 571-11 to 571-14, and 580-11 (Supp. 1983); R.I. GEN. LAWS § 8-10-3 (Cum. Supp. 1983); VA. CODE ANN. § 16.1-241 (Cum. Supp. 1983) (juvenile and domestic relations court has concurrent jurisdiction over child custody in divorce).

7. G. MELTON, L. WEITHORN, & C. SLOBOGIN, *supra* note 4, at 74.

8. Judges tend to weigh "responsibility" issues more heavily

than do clinicians. Lowery, *Child Custody Decisions in Divorce Proceedings: A Survey of Judges,* 12 PROF. PSYCHOLOGY 492 (1981). Conceivably, however, the moral development literature might give some clues as to the parent more likely to socialize moral values. T. Grisso, Forensic Assessment in Juvenile and Family Cases: The State of the Art 16 (June 1, 1984) (keynote address to the Summer Institute on Mental Health Law, University of Nebraska–Lincoln).

9. Our usual injunction against ultimate-issue testimony is, of course, relevant, even if the scientific basis were more extensive.

10. T. Grisso, *supra* note 8, at 8–9.

11. Hall & Hare-Mustin, *Sanctions and the Diversity of Ethical Complaints against Psychologists,* 38 AM. PSYCHOLOGIST 714, 726–27 (1983).

12. American Psychological Association, *Ethical Principles of Psychologists,* 36 AM. PSYCHOLOGIST 633 (1981).

13. *See generally* Morse, *Crazy Behavior, Morals, and Science: An Analysis of Mental Health Law,* 51 S. CAL. L. REV. 527 (1978).

14. Morse, *Law and Mental Health Professionals: The Limits of Expertise,* 9 PROF. PSYCHOLOGY 389, 395 (1978).

15. *See* Derdeyn, *Child Custody Consultation,* 45 AM. J. ORTHOPSYCHIATRY 791, 795 (1975). The child's lack of standing may frustrate his or her sense of fairness. Melton & Lind, *Procedural Justice in Family Court: Does the Adversary Model Make Sense?,* in LEGAL REFORMS AFFECTING CHILD AND YOUTH SERVICES (G. Melton ed. 1982). The inadequacy of advocacy of children's wishes by guardians *ad litem* is explored in note, *Lawyering for the Child: Principles of Representation in Custody and Visitation Disputes Arising from Divorce,* 87 YALE L.J. 1126 (1978).

16. 466 U.S. 429 (1984).

17. *Id.* at 431.

18. *Id.* at 434.

19. Rubin, *Experimental Research on Third-Party Intervention in Conflict: Toward Some Generalizations,* 87 PSYCHOLOGICAL BULL. 379 (1980).

20. *See* Crouch, *Divorce Mediation and Legal Ethics,* 16 FAM. L.Q. 219 (1982).

21. "Arbitration" is distinguished from "mediation" by the binding nature of the arbitrator's decision. Among the proposals for arbitration of custody disputes by mental health professionals are Kubie, *Provisions for the Care of Children of Divorced Parents: A New Legal Instrument,* 73 YALE L.J. 1197 (1964); Moskowitz, *Divorce–Custody Dispositions: The Child's Wishes in Perspective,* 18 SANTA CLARA L. REV. 427 (1978); Spencer & Zammit, *Mediation–Arbitration: A Proposal for Private Resolution of Disputes between Divorced or Separated Parents,* 1976 DUKE L.J. 911. These proposals are criticized in Melton & Lind, *supra* note 15.

22. *See, e.g.,* CAL. CIV. CODE § 4600 (West 1983); DEL. CODE ANN. tit. 13 § 725.

23. *Cf.* Bazelon, *Psychiatrists and the Adversary Process,* 230 SCI. AM. 18 (1974).

24. Spanier & Anderson, *The Impact of the Legal System on Adjustment to Marital Separation,* 41 J. MARRIAGE FAM.

605 (1979). *Cf.* Frank, Berman, & Mazur-Hart, *No Fault Divorce and the Divorce Rate: The Nebraska Experience—An Interrupted Time Series Analysis and Commentary,* 58 NEB. L. REV. 1 (1978).

25. *Survey of American Family Law,* 10 FAM. L. REP. 3017 (1984).

26. The much-discussed standard suggested by J. GOLDSTEIN, A. FREUD, & A. SOLNIT, BEYOND THE BEST INTERESTS OF THE CHILD (1973), would have such an effect by vesting control over visitation in the custodial parent.

27. Mnookin & Kornhauser, *supra* note 3, at 981–83. "Intangible" factors, such as the desire to save face, become especially important in the context of a "zero-sum" game in which there is a winner-take-all situation. *See generally* J. RUBIN & B. BROWN, THE SOCIAL PSYCHOLOGY OF BARGAINING AND NEGOTIATION (1975).

28. *See generally* J. THIBAUT & L. WALKER, PROCEDURAL JUSTICE: A PSYCHOLOGICAL ANALYSIS (1975); Melton & Lind, *supra* note 15; Thibaut & Walker, *A Theory of Procedure,* 66 CALIF. L. REV. 541 (1978).

29. Pruitt & Johnson, *Mediation as an Aid to Face Saving in Negotiation,* 14 J. PERSONALITY SOC. PSYCHOLOGY 239 (1970).

30. Erickson, Holmes, Frey, Walker, & Thibaut, *Functions of a Third Party in the Resolution of Conflicts: The Role of a Judge in Pretrial Conferences,* 30 J. PERSONALITY SOC. PSYCHOLOGY 293 (1974).

31. *See generally* Bahr, *An Evaluation of Court Mediation for Divorce Cases with Children,* 2 J. FAM. ISSUES 39 (1981); Koch & Lowery, *Evaluation of Mediation as an Alternative to Divorce Litigation,* 15 PROF. PSYCHOLOGY: RESEARCH PRAC. 109 (1984).

32. Koch & Lowery, *supra* note 31, at 113.

33. *See, e.g.,* Pearson, *Child Custody: Why Not Let the Parents Decide?,* 20 JUDGES' J. 4 (1981).

34. *Id.* at 7.

35. *Id.* at 7.

36. *Id.* at 7.

37. Pearson, Thoennis, & VanderKooi, *The Decision to Mediate: Profiles of Individuals Who Accept and Reject the Opportunity to Mediate Contested Child Custody and Visitation Issues,* 6 J. DIVORCE 17 (1982); J. Pearson, The Denver Custody Mediation Project: Progress Report No. 4 (March 15, 1981) (unpublished manuscript), at 9.

38. J. Pearson, *supra* note 37, at 10.

39. *Id.* at 11.

40. *Id.* at 11–12.

41. Scott & Derdeyn, *Rethinking Joint Custody,* 45 OHIO ST. L.J. 455, 464–65 nn. 41–42 (1984).

42. *Id.; see* Chapsky v. Wood, 26 Kan. 650 (1881).

43. *See, e.g.,* Hines v. Hines, 192 Iowa 569, 185 N.W. 9 (1921).

44. *See* Mnookin, *Child-Custody Adjudication: Judicial Functions in the Face of Indeterminancy,* 39 LAW CONTEMP. PROBS. 226 (1975).

45. Derdeyn, *Child Custody in Historical Perspective,* 133 AM. J. PSYCHIATRY 1369 (1976).

46. *See, e.g.,* State *ex rel.* Watts v. Watts, 77 Misc. 2d 178; 350 N.Y.S.2d 285 (N.Y. Fam. Ct. 1973).

47. *See, e.g.,* CAL. CIV. CODE § 4600 (West 1983); OR. REV. STAT. § 107.105(1)(a) (1982).

48. *See, e.g.,* McCreery v. McCreery, 218 Va. 352, 237 S.E.2d 167 (1977).

49. Saviers v. Saviers, 92 Idaho 117, 438 P.2d 268 (1968); State by St. Louis County Welfare Department v. Niemi, 284 Minn. 225, 169 N.W.2d 758 (1969).

50. Race of a parent's new spouse is one such factor. *See supra* notes 16–18 and accompanying text.

51. *See* Whobrey, Sales, & Lou, *Social Science and the Best Interests Standard: Another Case for Informed Speculation,* in THE PSYCHOLOGIST AND CHILD CUSTODY DETERMINATIONS: ROLES, KNOWLEDGE AND EXPERTISE (L. Weithorn ed. in press).

52. Uniform Marriage and Divorce Act § 402 (1970, as amended 1971, 1973).

53. 140 N.W.2d 152 (1966).

54. *Id.* at 155.

55. *Id.* at 156.

56. *Id.* at 154.

57. *Id.* at 156.

58. Mnookin, *supra* note 44, at 262.

59. *See, e.g.,* Bezio v. Patenaude, 381 Mass. 563 (1980).

60. Complainant v. Defendant, 10 FAM. L. REP. 1097 (Fairfax County Circ. Ct., Sept. 23, 1983).

61. "Joint custody" refers to divorced parents' joint legal authority over a child. *See infra* notes 69–80 and accompanying text.

62. J.L.P. v. D.J.P., 643 S.W.2d 865 (Mo. Ct. App. W. Dist. 1982).

63. *Survey of American Family Law, supra* note 25, at 3026–27.

64. *Id.*

65. *See, e.g., In re* Ditter, 326 N.W.2d 675, 212 Neb. 855 (1982) *(per curiam).*

66. *In re* Desjardins, 10 FAM. L. REP. 1229 (Calif. Ct. App. 4th Dist. Jan. 25, 1984). *But see* Herron v. Seizak, 10 FAM. L. REP. 1133 (Pa. Super. Ct. Dec. 2, 1983).

67. Melton, *Developmental Psychology and the Law: The State of the Art,* 22 J. FAM. L. 445, 453–55 (1984); Wadlington, *Portrait of the Judge as Popular Author: An Appeal for Anonymity and Restraint in Domestic Relations Opinions,* 1 FAM. L.Q. 77 (1967).

68. *In re* Desjardins, 10 FAM. L. REP. at 1230.

69. *See* Scott & Derdeyn, *supra* note 41, at 469–70. The movement has also been spurred by·fathers' groups. *Id.* at 462 nn. 30–31, and accompanying text.

70. CAL. CIV. CODE § 4600.5 (West. Supp. 1983). *See* Scott & Derdeyn, *supra* note 41, at 456 n. 3.

71. Scott & Derdeyn, *supra* note 41, at 456 n. 3.

72. *Id.* at 472.

73. Clingempeel & Reppucci, *Joint Custody after Divorce: Major Issues and Goals for Research,* 91 PSYCHOLOGICAL BULL. 102, 103 (1982).

74. Cal. Assembly Bill 238, ch. 304, *reported in* 9 FAM. L. REP. 26400 (1983).

75. Scott & Derdeyn, *supra* note 41.

76. *E.g.,* FLA. STAT. ANN. § 61.13(2)(b) (West Supp. 1983); LA. CIV. CODE ANN. art. 146(C) (West Supp. 1983).

77. Scott & Derdeyn, *supra* note 41, at 475–77.

78. *Id.* at 472–73 and sources cited there.

79. *Id.* at 475–77.

80. *Id.* at 476–77.

81. J. GOLDSTEIN, A. FREUD, & A. SOLNIT, *supra* note 26.

82. Crouch, *An Essay on the Critical and Judicial Reception of* BEYOND THE BEST INTERESTS OF THE CHILD, 13 FAM. L.Q. 49 (1979).

83. Katkin, Bullington, & Levine, *Above and Beyond the Best Interests of the Child: An Inquiry into the Relationship between Law and Social Action,* 8 LAW SOC'Y REV. 669 (1974); Melton, *The Psychologist's Role in Juvenile and Family Law,* 7 J. CLINICAL CHILD PSYCHOLOGY 189, 190 (1978).

84. J. GOLDSTEIN, A. FREUD, & A. SOLNIT, *supra* note 26. This view has been criticized by Wald, *Thinking about Public Policy toward Abuse and Neglect of Children: A Review of* BEYOND THE BEST INTERESTS OF THE CHILD, 78 MICH. L. REV. 645, 655–70 (1980); *see also* Melton, *Children's Rights: Where Are the Children?,* 52 AM. J. ORTHOPSYCHIATRY 530 (1982).

85. J. GOLDSTEIN, A. FREUD, A. SOLNIT, *supra* note 26, Child Placement Code of Hampstead-Haven, Para. 30.5.

86. *Id.* at 101.

87. There is increasing evidence that infants form multiple attachments, although they tend to prefer the primary caretaker in times of stress. These studiess are reviewed with attention to their implication for policy in Clingempeel & Reppucci, *supra* note 73, at 112–13. *See also* Thompson, *The Father's Case in Child Custody Disputes: The Contributions of Psychological Research,* in FATHERHOOD AND FAMILY POLICY 53, 90–94 (M. Lamb & A. Sagi eds. 1983).

88. J. GOLDSTEIN, A. FREUD, & A. SOLNIT, *supra* note 26, at 153.

89. *Id.* at 54 and 62–63.

90. Mnookin & Kornhauser, *supra* note 3, at 981–83.

91. Reppucci, *The Wisdom of Solomon: Issues in Child Custody Determination,* in CHILDREN, MENTAL HEALTH, AND THE LAW (N. D. Reppucci, L. Weithorn, E. Mulvey, & J. Monahan eds. 1984).

92. J. GOLDSTEIN, A. FREUD, & A. SOLNIT, *supra* note 26, Child Placement Code of Hampstead-Haven, Para. 10.5.

93. *Cf.* Agopian, *Parental Child Stealing: Participants and the Victimization Process,* 5 VICTIMOLOGY 263 (1980).

94. Mnookin & Kornhauser, *supra* note 3.

95. A "longitudinal study" is one in which the participants are observed at various points across time.

96. Hetherington, *Divorce: A Child's Perspective,* 34 AM. PSYCHOLOGIST 851 (1979); Hetherington, Cox, & Cox, *Divorced Fathers,* 25 FAM. COORDINATOR 417 (1976); Hetherington, Cox, & Cox, *The Aftermath of Divorce,* in MOTHER/CHILD FATHER/CHILD RELATIONSHIPS (J. Stevens & M. Mathews eds. 1978); Hetherington, Cox, & Cox, *The Development of Children in Mother-Headed Families,* in THE AMERICAN FAMILY: DYING OR DEVELOPING (D. Reiss & H. Hoffman eds. 1979); Hetherington, Cox, & Cox, *Family Interaction and the Social, Emotional, and*

Cognitive Development of Children Following Divorce, in THE
FAMILY: SETTING PRIORITIES (V. Vaughn & T. Brazel-
ton eds. 1979); Hetherington, Cox, & Cox, *Play and
Social Interaction in Children Following Divorce,* 35(4) J.
SOC. ISSUES 26 (1979); Hetherington, Cox, & Cox,
Effects of Divorce on Parents and Children, in NONTRADI-
TIONAL FAMILIES (M. Lamb ed. 1982).

97. J. WALLERSTEIN & J. KELLY, SURVIVING THE BREAKUP:
HOW CHILDREN AND PARENTS COPE WITH DIVORCE
(1980); Kelly & Wallerstein, *The Effects of Parental Di-
vorce: Experiences of the Child in Early Latency,* 46 AM. J.
ORTHOPSYCHIATRY 20 (1976); Kelly & Wallerstein, *Part-
Time Parent, Part-Time Child: Visiting after Divorces,* 6 J.
CLINICAL CHILD PSYCHOLOGY 51 (1977); Wallerstein,
*Children of Divorce: Preliminary Report of a Ten-Year Fol-
low-Up of Young Children,* 54 AM. J. ORTHOPSYCHIATRY
444 (1984); Wallerstein & Kelly, *The Effects of Parental
Divorce: The Adolescent Experience,* in CHILDREN AT PSY-
CHIATRIC RISK (E. J. Anthony & C. Koupernik eds.
1974); Wallerstein & Kelly, *The Effects of Parental Di-
vorce: The Experiences of the Preschool Child,* 14 J. AM.
ACAD. CHILD PSYCHIATRY 600 (1975); Wallerstein &
Kelly, *The Effects of Parental Divorce: Experiences of the
Child in Later Latency,* 46 AM. J. ORTHOPSYCHIATRY 256
(1976).

98. A "quasi-experimental" study is one in which there
is an attempt to minimize uncontrolled variables, but
there is no random assignment of participants to experimental conditions, as in a true experiment. In
particular, the Hetherington, Cox, & Cox study, *supra*
note 96, permitted comparisons with children in intact families at various points across time.

99. Thompson, *supra* note 87, at 83. For other summaries
of research on the effects of divorce on children, see
Hetherington, *supra* note 96; King & Kleemeier, *The
Effect of Divorce on Parents and Children,* in HANDBOOK
OF CLINICAL CHILD PSYCHOLOGY (C. E. Walker & M.
Roberts eds. 1983). *See generally Children of Divorce,* 35(4)
J. SOC. ISSUES (T. Leviton ed. 1979) (symposium is-
sue). The discussion *infra* in the text accompanying
notes 100–09 is drawn primarily from the authorities
cited in notes 96 and 97 *supra.*

100. Studies on this point are reviewed in Emery, *Interparental Conflict and the Children of Discord and Divorce,* 92
PSYCHOLOGICAL BULL. 310 (1982); Scott & Derdeyn,
supra note 41, at 490–92.

101. Hetherington, *supra* note 96, at 855.

102. *See supra* note 100.

103. Scott & Derdeyn, *supra* note 41, at 488–90.

104. Hetherington, *supra* note 96, at 856. *Cf.* Turner, *Divorced Fathers Who Win Contested Custody of their Children:
An Exploratory Study,* 54 AM. J. ORTHOPSYCHIATRY 498
(1984) (some fathers who sought and won custody
had not been very involved with their children prior
to the divorce; others had been intensely involved).

105. Wallerstein, *supra* note 97.

106. Clingempeel & Reppucci, *supra* note 73, at 117, and
studies cited there.

107. *Id.* at 115, and studies cited there.

108. *See id.* at 117; Steinman, *The Experience of Children in a
Joint-Custody Arrangement: A Report of a Study,* 51 AM. J.
ORTHOPSYCHIATRY 403, 411–12 (1981).

109. *See* Hetherington, *supra* note 96, at 852 and 854.

110. Thompson, *supra* note 87, at 83–84 (citations omitted).

111. *See supra* note 45 and accompanying text.

112. K. Gersick, Fathers by Choice: Characteristics of Men
Who Do and Do Not Seek Custody of Their Children
Following Divorce (1975) (unpublished doctoral dissertation, Harvard University), cited in Thompson, *supra*
note 87, at 84–85.

113. A possible exception is for very young children, where
there may be a preference for the primary caretaker,
who typically is the mother. *See* Thompson, *supra* note
87, at 66 and 92–93.

114. *Id.* at 74–77.

115. Santrock & Warshak, *Father Custody and Social Development in Boys and Girls,* 35(4) J. SOC. ISSUES 112 (1979).

116. *Id.*

117. *See* Clingempeel & Reppucci, *supra* note 73, at 119–
23.

118. Mothers' availability is related to sons' academic
achievement. Hoffman, *Maternal Employment: 1979,* 34
AM. PSYCHOLOGIST 859, 863 (1979). Father absence
adversely affects adolescent girls' ability to relate easily to boys. Hetherington, *Effects of Father Absence on
Personality Development in Adolescent Daughters,* 7 DEV.
PSYCHOLOGY 313 (1972).

119. Clingempeel & Reppucci, *supra* note 73; Scott & Derdeyn, *supra* note 41.

120. Clingempeel & Reppucci, *supra* note 73, at 124.

121. Scott & Derdeyn, *supra* note 41, at 494.

122. *Id.* at 488.

123. *Id.* at 495.

124. *Id.* at 495.

125. *See, e.g., supra* note 30.

126. Steinman, *supra* note 108.

127. *Id.* at 414.

128. Clingempeel & Reppucci, *supra* note 73.

129. The one exception is a study that was not focused
specifically on child care arrangements following divorce: C. STACK, ALL OUR KIN: STRATEGIES FOR SUR-
VIVAL IN A BLACK COMMUNITY (1974). *See* Clingempeel & Reppucci, *supra* note 73, at 116.

130. Melton, *supra* note 67, at 472 n. 119, and accompanying text.

131. *E.g.,* Kirkpatrick & Smith, *Lesbian Mothers and Their
Children,* 51 AM. J. ORTHOPSYCHIATRY 545 (1981).

132. *Id.;* Hoeffer, *Children's Acquisition or Sex-Role Behavior in
Lesbian-Mother Families,* 51 AM. J. ORTHOPSYCHIATRY
536 (1981).

133. *See* Siegel & Hurley, *The Role of the Child's Preference in
Custody Proceedings,* 11 FAM. L.Q. 1 (1977); E. Greenberg, An Empirical Determination of the Competence
of Children to Participate in Child Custody Decision-
Making 11–19 (1983) (unpublished doctoral disser-

tation, University of Illinois at Urbana–Champaign); *see also* Benedek & Benedek, *The Child's Preference in Michigan Custody Disputes,* 7 AM. J. FAM. THERAPY 37 (1979); Bersoff, *Representation for Children in Custody Decisions: All That Glitters Is not* Gault, 15 J. FAM. L. 27 (1976–77).

134. NEB. REV. STAT. § 42-364(1)(b) (Cum. Supp. 1982).

135. E. Greenberg, *supra* note 133.

136. *See id.* at 152.

137. *See generally* CHOICE AND PERCEIVED CONTROL (L. Perlmuter & R. Monty eds. 1979); Melton, *Decision Making by Children: Psychological Risks and Benefits,* in CHILDREN'S COMPETENCE TO CONSENT (G. Melton, G. Koocher, & M. Saks eds. 1983).

138. Melton, *supra* note 67, at 468; Melton, *Sexually Abused Children and the Legal System: Some Policy Recommendations,* 13 AM. J. FAM. THERAPY 61 (1985) (elaboration of testimony before the U.S. Senate Subcommittee on Juvenile Justice, May 22, 1984).

139. This position is also recommended by Derdeyn, *supra* note 15, at 795.

140. One instance in which access to one parent (and the child) might be sufficient is if that parent's competence is in question and he or she seeks only to rebut that argument. Even in that example, though, it would be very helpful to have the other parent's perspective available so as to focus the evaluation appropriately.

141. A stark example of treating clinicians' tendency to take sides in custody disputes is presented in Derdeyn, *supra* note 14, at 798–99.

142. "Psychotherapist privilege" is the privilege to keep information from therapy from being admitted into evidence in a legal proceeding.

143. Psychotherapist privilege is not available at all in about one-third of the states, and it is often not available to clients of social workers and sometimes psychologists. Ehrenreich & Melton, *Ethical and Legal Issues in the Treatment of Children,* in HANDBOOK OF CLINICAL CHILD PSYCHOLOGY 1285, 1298 (C. Walker & M. Roberts eds. 1983).

144. It is at least arguable that, when a client divulges information in the presence of another client (especially a spouse with whom he or she may become involved in litigation), he or she has waived any expectation of privacy. On the other hand, such a rule would frustrate the purposes of psychotherapist privilege, and it might deter spouses from seeking counseling in an attempt to save their marriage or to resolve issues outside court. *Cf.* Minn. v. Andring, C2-82-294 (Minn. Sup. Ct. Jan. 13, 1984), *abstracted in* 8 MENTAL PHYSICAL DISABILITY L. REP. 121 (1984) (privilege applicable in group therapy).

145. The question of who owns the privilege (child or parent) in child therapy is unclear. Ehrenreich & Melton, *supra* note 143, at 1298–99. The issue is still more muddled in exercise of the privilege in custody disputes. Because of the potential conflict of interest, at least one court has required appointment of a guardian *ad litem* to decide whether to exercise privilege on behalf of a child when the child was too young to exercise it competently. Nagle v. Hooks, 9 FAM. L. REP. 2529 (Md. Ct. App. May 31, 1983).

146. It has been argued that marriage counselor privilege cannot be invoked in a custody dispute, because the exclusion of evidence as to the parents' fitness interferes with the child's constitutional right to due process. M. v. K., 9 FAM. L. REP. 2006 (N.J. Super. Ct. Chancery Div. Bergen County Aug. 24, 1982).

Chapter 14

1. Ennis & Litwack, *Psychiatry and the Presumption of Expertise: Flipping Coins in the Courtroom,* 62 CAL. L. REV. 693 (1974).

2. Bazelon, *Psychiatrists and the Adversary Process,* 230(16) SCI. AM. 18 (1974).

3. Strauss, *Psychiatric Testimony, with Special Reference to Cases of Post-Traumatic Neurosis,* 1 FORENSIC SCI. 77 (1972).

4. "One New Jersey psychiatrist reportedly received $10,000 for a single psychiatric consultation. Such large fees lead some observers to question how well the neutrality of the witness holds up under the presssure of pleasing a client who is paying high prices for a particular verdict." Shell, *Psychiatric Testimony: Science or Fortune Telling,* 7 BARRISTER 6 (1980).

5. Morse, *Crazy Behavior, Morals, and Science: An Analysis of Mental Health Law,* 51 S. CAL. L. REV. 527 (1978); Comment, *The Psychologist as Expert Witness: Science in the Courtroom,* 38 MD. L. REV. 539 (1979).

6. Brodsky & Poythress, *Expertise on the Witness Stand: A Practitioner's Guide,* in PSYCHOLOGY, PSYCHIATRY AND THE LAW: A CLINICAL AND FORENSIC HANDBOOK (C. P. Ewing ed. 1985), 391.

7. Bluglass, *The Psychiatric Court Report,* 19 MED. SCI. L. 121 (1979).

8. McGarry, *Competency for Trial and Due Process Via the State Hospital,* 122 AM. J. PSYCHIATRY 623 (1965).

9. In the *Hinckley* case, one psychiatrist submitted his findings in a 900-page report. The sheer volume, we suspect, might have ensured that the jurors would be unlikely to read or understand everything included.

10. Petrella & N. Poythress, Forensic Evaluations for Criminal Courts—An Interdisciplinary Study (1979) (unpublished manuscript on file with the Department of Training and Research, Center for Forensic Psychiatry, P.O. Box 2060, Ann Arbor, Mich. 48106).

11. Hallerstein, *Ethical Problems of Psychological Jargon,* 9 PROF. PSYCHOLOGY 111 (1978).

12. *See generally* Brodsky & Robey, *On Becoming an Expert*

Witness: Issues of Orientation and Effectiveness, 3 PROF. PSY-CHOLOGY 173 (1972); Keller, *Pretrial and Trial Preparations and Strategies for Psychologist Expert Witness in Michigan,* 3 ACADEMIC PSYCHOLOGY BULL. 333 (1981); Watson, *On the Preparation and Use of Psychiatric Expert Testimony: Some Suggestions in an Ongoing Controversy,* 6 BULL. AM. ACAD. PSYCHIATRY L. 226 (1978).

13. Banks & Poythress, *The Elements of Persuasion In Expert Testimony,* 10 J. PSYCHIATRY L. 173 (1982).

14. Brodsky & Poythress, *supra* note 6.

15. In Frye v. United States, 293 F. 1013 (D.C. Cir. 1923), the court so held in excluding polygraph evidence. *Frye* has seldom been applied to psychological testimony, although some have argued it should be. *See, e.g.,* Comment, People v. Murtishaw: *Applying the* Frye *Test to Psychiatric Predictions of Dangerousness in Capital Cases,* 70 CAL. L. REV. 1069 (1982). There are considerable practical problems with the *Frye* rule (e.g., what is "general acceptance?"). Moreover, it can be argued that normal evidentiary rules deal sufficiently with validity concerns about expert testimony. For a discussion of these issues, see Slobogin, *Dangerousness and Expertise,* 133 U. PA. L. REV. 97, 137–48 (1984).

16. FED. R. EVID. 703. *See infra* § 14.04(d) for a discussion of the issue of "reasonable reliance."

17. Petrella & Poythress, *The Quality of Forensic Evaluations: An Interdisciplinary Study,* 51 J. CONSULTING CLINICAL PSYCHOLOGY 76 (1983); Dix & Poythress, *Propriety of Medical Dominance of Forensic Mental Health Practice,* 23 ARIZ. L. REV. 961 (1981).

18. The most widely cited cases are Jenkins v. United States, 307 F. 2d 637 (D.C. Cir. 1962), People v. Hawthorne, 293 Mich. 15, 291 N.W. 205 (1940), and Watson v. State, 273 S.W.2d 879 (1955). More extensive reviews of case law applicable in various states are found in Miller, Lower, & Bleechmore, *The Clinical Psychologist as an Expert Witness on Questions of Mental Illness and Competency,* 4 LAW PSYCHOLOGY REV. 115 (1978); Comment, *supra* note 5 (Appendix of Cases).

19. *See* Poythress, *Psychological Issues in Criminal Proceedings: Judicial Preference Regarding Expert Testimony,* 10 CRIM. JUST. BEHAV. 1975 (1983).

20. American Psychological Association, *Ethical Principles of Psychologists,* 36 AM. PSYCHOLOGIST 633 (1981). Principle 4 states, "Psychologists present the science of psychology and offer their services, products, and publications fairly and accurately, avoiding misrepresentation through sensationalism, exaggeration, or superficiality." While this principle deals primarily with public announcements of services, it applies equally well to representation in court.

21. For a sampling of empirical studies on the relative importance of credentials versus trustworthiness, *see* Birnbaum & Stegner, *Source Credibility in Social Judgment: Bias, Expertise and the Judge's Point of View,* 37 J. PERS. SOC. PSYCHOLOGY 48 (1979); McGinnies & Ward, *Better Liked Than Right: Trustworthiness and Expertise as Factors in Credibility,* 6 PERS. SOC. PSYCHOLOGY BULL. 467 (1980).

For a general review of social sciences literature on expertise and persuasion, *see* R. APPELBAUM & K. ANATOL, STRATEGIES FOR PERSUASIVE COMMUNICATION (1974).

22. Hesitations ("uh, er,"), qualifiers ("probably," "maybe," "perhaps") and intensifiers ("most certainly") are among the features of witness speech identified by researchers as "powerless" speech (i.e., less persuasive). *See* Erickson, Lind, Johnson, & O'Barr, *Speech Style and Impression Formation in a Court Setting: The Effects of "Powerful" and "Powerless" Speech.* 14 J. EXPERIMENTAL SOC. PSYCHOLOGY 266 (1978); W. O'BARR, LINGUISTIC EVIDENCE: LANGUAGE, POWER, AND STRATEGY IN THE COURTROOM (1982).

23. Dixon & Blondis, *Cross-Examination of Psychiatric Witnesses in Civil Commitment Proceedings,* 1 MENTAL DISABILITY L. REP. 164 (1976); Twardy & Siomopoulos, *Medical Testimony—Mental Health Proceeding—Direct and Cross-Examination of a Defendant's Clinical Psychologist—Part I,* 23 MED. TRIAL TECH. Q. 66 (1976); Twardy & Siomopoulos, *Medical Testimony—Mental Health Proceeding—Direct and Cross-Examination of a Defendant's Clinical Psychiatrist—Part II,* 23 MED. TRIAL TECH. Q. 187 (1976); Cameron, *The Mental Health Expert: A Guide to Direct and Cross-Examination,* 2 CRIM. JUST. J. 299 (1979); J. ZISKIN, COPING WITH PSYCHIATRIC AND PSYCHOLOGICAL TESTIMONY (3d ed. 1980).

24. Brodsky, *The Mental Health Professional on the Witness Stand: A Survival Guide,* in PSYCHOLOGY IN THE LEGAL PROCESS (B. Sales ed. 1977). *See also* Brodsky & Poythress, *supra* note 6.

25. Perr, *Cross-Examination of the Psychiatrist, Using Publications,* 5 BULL. AM. ACAD. PSYCHIATRY L. 327 (1977); Pollack, *Cross-Examination of the Psychiatrist Using Publications: Point–Counter Point,* 5 BULL. AM. ACAD. PSYCHIATRY L. 332 (1977).

26. Diem, *Evidence—The Use of Learned Treatises on Cross-Examination of a Medical Expert—Treatises Which an Expert Has Used in His Studies Are Acceptable for the Sole Purpose of Impeaching His Testimony,* 6 TEX. TECH. L. REV. 237 (1974).

27. Poythress, *Coping on the Witness Stand: Learned Responses to "Learned Treatises,"* 11 PROF. PSYCHOLOGY 139 (1980).

28. *See* FED. R. EVID. 703.

29. Note, *Hearsay Bases of Psychiatric Opinion Testimony: A Critique of Federal Rules of Evidence 703,* 51 S. CAL. L. REV. 129 (1977).

30. Morse, *supra* note 5.

31. Bonnie & Slobogin, *The Role of Mental Health Professionals in the Criminal Process: The Case for Informed Speculation,* 66 VA. L. REV. 427 (1980).

32. N. Poythress, Conflicting Postures for Mental Health Expert Witnesses: Prevailing Attitudes of Trial Court Judges (1981) (unpublished manuscript on file with the Department of Training & Research, Center for Forensic Psychiatry, P.O. Box 2060, Ann Arbor, Mich. 48106). *See also* G. MELTON, L. WEITHORN, & C. SLOBOGIN, COMMUNITY MENTAL HEALTH CENTERS AND THE COURTS:

AN EVALUATION OF COMMUNITY-BASED FORENSIC SERVICES (1985).

33. The "irony" is debatable. On the one hand, statistical and actuarial data from well-designed research may be the most solid scientific data that clinicians could produce. However, the rejection of such data is understandable in light of the courts' concern for the disposition of an individual case, *see infra* § 1.03(b), and the well-documented difficulty that decisionmakers have in bringing statistical information describing group behavior to bear on decisions about individuals. *See, e.g.,* Carroll, *Judgments of Recidivism Risk: The Use of Base-Rate Information in Parole Decisions,* in NEW DIRECTIONS IN PSYCHOLEGAL RESEARCH (P. Lipsitt & B. Sales ed. 1980).

34. Meerloo, *Emotionalism in the Jury and the Court of Justice: The Hazards of Psychiatric Testimony,* 139 J. NERVOUS MENTAL DISEASE 294 (1964).

35. Morse, *Reforming Expert Testimony: A Response from the Tower (and the Trenches),* 6 LAW & HUM. BEHAV. 45 (1982). Morse notes that attorneys often take their business elsewhere when he informs them that he will not testify to ultimate issues. Anecdotally, a colleague recalled his experience setting up private practice in New York: One attorney told him candidly, "This is how forensic psychology works—I send you money, and you send me an opinion I can use in court" (Revland, personal communication).

36. Brodsky & Poythress, *supra* note 6, 407–08.

37. Bradley, *Overconfidence in Ignorant Experts,* 17 BULL. PSYCHONOMIC SOC'Y 82 (1981).

38. However, there is some evidence to suggest that mental health professionals would welcome evidentiary restraints that would prohibit ultimate-issue testimony. *See* Melton, *Organized Psychology and Legal Policymaking: Involvement in the Post-*Hinckley *Debate,* 16 PROF. PSYCHOLOGY: RESEARCH PRAC. 810 (1985).

39. Recommendation 5 from the Report of the Task Force on the Role of Psychology in the Criminal Justice System, in WHO IS THE CLIENT? (J. Monahan, ed. 1980).

40. The clinical staff at one state forensic hospital routinely includes the following statement in reports to the court: "The staff at _____ hospital recognize and respect that judgments regarding a criminal defendant's competency to stand trial and criminal responsibility are to be made by a judge or jury, not by mental health professionals. As such, our opinions should be regarded as only advisory."

41. *See* Poythress, *Concerning Reform in Expert Testimony: An Open Letter from a Practicing Psychologist,* 6 LAW & HUMAN BEHAV. 39 (1982).

Index

Mitigating circumstances, 191–193
  in capital sentencing, 182
  in determinate sentencing, 175, 177
Moral development, 103, 104

N

Narcoanalysis, 153, 154
National Center on Child Abuse and Neglect,
  314
Neglect, child, 309–327
Negligence, 127, 250, 271, 272, 278
Negligent misdiagnosis, 36, 48, 49
North Carolina v. Alford, 98

O

O'Connor v. Donaldson, 218, 223, 224
O'Kon v. Roland, 130
Overt act, 217, 222

P

Painter v. Bannister, 334
Palmore v. Sidoti, 331
Parens patriae, 211, 214–220, 225, 226, 246, 292,
  309
Parham v. J.R., 219, 240
Parole board, 29, 170, 171, 175, 180, 181
Paternalism, 5, 292
Pathological intoxication, 131
PERI Life Events Scale, 285
Personality theories, 7, 8
Piagetian theory, 102, 103
Plea bargaining, 28, 298
Police power, 211, 214, 218
Positional risk, 274
Posttraumatic stress disorder, 284
Presentence report, 172, 183, 184
Product liability, 278, 281
Proximate cause, 278, 279, 281, 282
Psychic trauma (*see* Mental injury)
Psychodynamic theory, 7, 122, 143, 159–163,
  311
Psychological parent, 311, 336
Psychological testing

child custody evaluations, 330
competency to stand trial evaluations, 90
juvenile evaluations, 306
mental state defense cases, 155, 156
personal injury cases, 283
presentence evaluations, 188
violence prediction, 196, 206

Q

Quasi-criminal proceedings, 32, 33

R

Reasonable Man test, 278
Recidivism, 114, 115, 197–203, 303, 319
Rehabilitation, 165, 166, 168–172, 180, 181
Rennie v. Klein, 254
Report writing, 350–354, 373–416
Residual functional capacity, 265
Retribution, 165–168, 172
Revocation of parole, 170, 171
Rhode Island v. Innis, 95
Right to counsel (*see* Sixth Amendment)
Right to refuse treatment, 222, 250–256
Right to treatment, 216
Rogers Criminal Responsibility Assessment Scales,
  142, 144–147
Rogers v. Okin, 253, 254
Rummel v. Estelle, 178

S

Saddler v. United States, 107
Scientific data, 8–12
Scientific method, 5, 6
Sentencing, 28, 165–207
  clinician's impact on, 185, 186
  sample report, 386
  treatment considerations, 188, 189
Sentencing commissions, 174
Sex offenders, 41, 178, 179, 185, 186
Sixth Amendment, 35, 43–46
Social Security Disability, 261–268
Solem v. Helm, 178
Specht v. Patterson, 179